BASIC FINANCIAL MANAGEMENT
Frequently Used Symbols

	Certainty equivalent coefficient in period t
CF_t	Annual after-tax expected cash flow in time period t
ROR	Accounting rate of return
	Beta of an asset, the slope of the regression or characteristic line
CL	Degree of combined leverage
FL	Degree of financial leverage
OL	Degree of operating leverage
AA	Equivalent annual annuity
BIT	Earnings before interest and taxes
OQ	Economic order quantity
PS	Earnings per share
V	Future value
VIF	Future value interest factor
VIFA	Future value interest factor for an annuity
	Annual growth rate
)	the initial cash outlay
RR	Internal rate of return
c	Cost of internal common equity (also Kc)
d	After-tax cost of debt
o	Weighted cost of capital
p	Cost of preferred stock
/B	Market-to-book ratio

MCC	Marginal cost of capital
MIRR	Modified internal rate of return
NPV	Net present value
PMT	Periodic level payment of an annuity
P/E	Price/earnings ratio
PV	Present value
PVIF	Present value interest factor
PVIFA	Present value interest factor for an annuity
R	Investor's required and/or expected rate of return
R_f	Risk free rate of return
ROA	Return on assets
ROE	Return on common equity
RP	Risk premium
SML	Security market line
σ	Standard deviation (lowercase sigma)
σ^2	Variance (standard deviation squared)
TIE	Times interest earned
T	Tax rate
WCC	Weighted cost of capital
W_d, W_c	Percentage (weights) of funds provided by debt and common equity respectively
YTM	Yield to maturity

Canadian Edition

BASIC FINANCIAL MANAGEMENT

To our families…

Canadian Edition

BASIC FINANCIAL MANAGEMENT

J. WILLIAM PETTY
Baylor University

ARTHUR J. KEOWN
Virginia Polytechnic Institute

DAVID F. SCOTT, JR
University of Central Florida

JOHN D. MARTIN
University of Texas at Austin

DAVID W. McPEAK
University of Ottawa

PRENTICE HALL CANADA INC.

Canadian Cataloguing in Publication Data

Main entry under title:

Basic Financial Management

Canadian ed.
ISBN: 0-13-287566-7

1. Business enterprises – Finance. 2. Corporations
– Finance. I. Petty, J. William, 1942–

HG4026.B3 1994   658.15   C93-094552-2

© 1994
   Prentice-Hall Canada Inc., Scarborough, Ontario

Prentice-Hall, Inc., Englewood Cliffs, New Jersey
Prentice-Hall International (UK) Limited, London
Prentice-Hall of Australia, Pty. Limited, Sydney
Prentice-Hall Hispanoamericana, S.A., Mexico City
Prentice-Hall of India Private Limited, New Delhi
Prentice-Hall of Japan, Inc., Tokyo
Simon & Schuster Asia Private Limited, Singapore
Editora Prentice-Hall do Brasil, Ltda., Rio de Janeiro

ISBN: 0-13-287566-7

Acquisitions Editor: Suzanne Tyson
Developmental Editor: Maurice Esses
Production Editor: Valerie Adams
Production Coordinator: Deborah Starks
Permissions: Robyn Craig
Design: Carole Giguère
Cover Image: Doug Plummer
Page Layout: Steve Lewis

Original U.S. edition published by Prentice-Hall, Inc.
A division of Simon & Schuster
Englewood Cliffs, N.J.
© 1993, Prentice-Hall Inc.

1 2 3 4 5 RRD 98 97 96 95 94

Printed and bound in the U.S.A.

CONTENTS IN BRIEF

CONTENTS

PART III

FINANCIAL STRUCTURE AND DIVIDEND POLICY DECISIONS

8

9

Planning the Firm's Financing Mix   *403*

10

Dividend Policy and Internal Financing   *461*

PART IV

FINANCIAL ANALYSIS, PLANNING, AND CONTROL

11

Evaluating Financial Performance   *500*

12

Financial Forecasting, Planning, and Budgeting   *549*

APPENDIX 12A: Microcomputers and Spreadsheet Software in Financial Planning   *583*

24
Financial Management: Small and Mid-Sized Business Perspective *971*

Appendices

Glossary *1025*

Index *1039*

PREFACE

Historical circumstances are a driving force underlying the development and practice of financial management. For example, in the 1970s volatile energy prices, interest rates, and exchange rates dominated both the financial press and the economic environment within which financial decisions were made. These factors led to the development of new commodity and financial futures markets in which firms could hedge their risk exposure and speculate on the directions of anticipated price movements. Similarly, in the 1980s corporate control contests have resulted in the restructuring of corporate Canada. This unprecedented wave of transactions has included corporate divestitures, leveraged buyouts, joint ventures, spin-offs, split-ups, employee stock option plans (ESOPs), partial public offerings, project financings, and a host of other types of transactions which have filled the financial press during the 1980s and early nineties.

Some have characterized this latest wave of corporate control contests simply as evidence of the continual tug-of-war between the capital market and corporate managements for control over financial resources. If this is true, then it would appear that the 1980s were a time of unprecedented victory for the capital markets. Many of the largest corporations have fallen victim to the "bust-up merger" as they have been bought up and their assets sold to the highest bidder. This, in turn, means that the investment and financing decisions of even the very largest firms are subject to an unprecedented level of scrutiny by the capital markets.

Some practicing financial managers have cried foul, saying that investors in the capital markets are too short-term oriented or myopic. This, they argue, has placed undue pressure on the corporate manager to produce short-term profits to the exclusion of making long-term commitments. The evidence from the academic community, however, has not supported this contention. Furthermore, as the pressures of international competition continue unabated, serious consideration must be given to the impact the capital markets have on the firm's competitiveness in world markets through its influence on the firm's investment and financing choices. Consequently, it is our belief that the events of the 1980s and early 1990s have heightened the importance of corporate finance in the overall formula for corporate competitiveness and success.

In this text we have endeavoured to provide the introduction to financial decision making, which is rooted in both the current state of our understanding of financial theory and in current world economic conditions. This focus is evident in a number of ways, perhaps the most obvious being the attention to the concepts of risk and return, the related notion of opportunity costs, capital markets and their influence on corporate financial decisions. We believe the increased emphasis on capital markets is consistent with their influence on corporate financial decisions.

Pedagogy and Target Audience

Basic Financial Management provides the reader with an overview of financial management as intended for an introductory course in the subject. Such a course might be taught over one academic year or two semesters. The orientation continues to be managerial with an emphasis on the identification and solution of the financial problems confronting the business enterprise.

Decision making within an enterprise valuation framework is stressed throughout the text, and thereby, provides a unifying theme across all discussions. In the preparation of the manuscript, three primary standards were used. First, we have made a strong effort to offer completeness in the treatment of each topic. Second, we have given readability a high priority. We have taken extra care to use a clear and concise writing style, especially in the treatment of concepts requiring the use of mathematics. Third, complete, step-by-step examples are frequently used to increase clarity and to crystallize the critical issues in the student's mind. In summary, the pedagogical approach taken, particularly for the more difficult topics, progresses from an intuitive presentation of the problem to the introduction and illustration of the appropriate decision-making framework.

The First Canadian Edition

Besides the expanded emphasis on the role of the capital markets in corporate financial decision making, there are a number of important features in this text that may not be so obvious.

1. We have worked to add life to the chapter presentations by adding a number of readings on Canadian business practice, called "Basic Financial Management in Practice."

2. Also, given the continued ethical questions being addressed in the press, we have, on several occasions, offered the student value orientations we believe will be helpful. The basic notion of what constitutes ethical behaviour is not clear-cut. However, we have tried to provide some definitions, which will provide a fundamental starting point for considering the issues as they relate to financial decision making.

3. In view of the continued globalization of world markets, we have included "International Financial Management" sections throughout the text.

4. A separate appendix has been added that demonstrates the use of a calculator (the Texas Instruments BA II Plus). We have also designed an insert card to the text that shows how to find the compound value interest factors and the present value interest factors without use of the table values. (In the student guide, we provide a complete article on the use of all the popular financial calculators.)

5. Chapters include self-test questions and study problems for quantitative analyses of topics covered.

In addition to these features just mentioned, we also would like to emphasize the following examples of financial topics found in the first Canadian edition of *Basic Financial Management*:

1. In our introduction to the financial environment, we have examined the financial structure of financial markets, the term structure of interest rates, and the Canadian income tax system. We have also featured one of the major players in this environment, the Canadian banks.

2. We have emphasized the influence of capital markets by examining the risk and return framework by which financial decisions are made. This presentation includes a discussion on the capital asset pricing model and the importance of systematic risk. The arbitrage pricing model is examined in the appendix of Chapter 3 to give the instructor added flexibility.

3. Chapter 4 has integrated the principles of financial valuation in order for the student to appreciate how we can value financial assets such as single period payments, annuities, mortgage loans, bonds, preferred shares, and common shares.

4. Chapter 5 includes material on determining the weighted marginal cost of capital and the required rate of return of individual projects.

5. In Chapter 6, we examine capital budgeting decisions by emphasizing how to measure a project's benefits and costs. Consequently, the student will find the concept of "relevant cash flows" easier to understand.

6. Chapter 7 examines the application of capital budgeting techniques to expansion and replacement projects. We also discuss the importance of incorporating risk techniques into capital budgeting decisions.

7. In the Chapters 8, 9 and 10 we discuss leverage, capital structure theory, and the relevance of dividend policy. Furthermore, we examine empirical evidence from surveys of management opinions on capital structure and dividend policy. We also discuss business cycles and financing behaviour.

8. Chapter 11 and 12 examine the topics of financial performance and financial forecasting. The appendix of Chapter 12 includes a discussion on how to use a spreadsheet to develop a cash budget.

9. Chapters 13, 14, 15, and 16 discuss the major topics of working capital management. The emphasis of these chapters is to introduce the business practices used in managing cash, accounts receivable, inventory and accounts payable. We also examine how to determine the cost of using short-term financing.

10. Chapters 17, 18, 19, and 20 examine how funds are raised in capital markets in Canada and some of the financial instruments used to raise funds. This discussion has incorporated Canadian business practice and regulations. We also discuss some of the financial instruments used in hedging risk of a portfolio.

11. Chapters 21, 22, 23 and 24 include special topics in financial management. In Chapter 21 we look at the restructuring of firms, which has become a predominant issue in the media. To bring the chapter up to date, we have added a section on why mergers and acquisitions might create value, an important question with no easy answer for those managers contemplating such a decision. We also look at the more recent approaches used in valuing a firm, which include what we refer to as the chop-shop approach and the free-cash flow valuation model. Chapter 22 has included Canadian business practices used in the financial reorganization of a firm. Changes to the Insolvency and Bankruptcy Act in 1992 have changed the business practices of Canadian firms in financial distress. Chapter 23 examines the impact of international business finance on financial management in the Canada. Finally, Chapter 24 examines the relevance of capital budgeting techniques for the owner-manager of the small firm. Small firms have been criticized for not joining the bandwagon of the discounted cash flow models. Maybe there is a rationale for such actions on the part of the small-firm managements. This issue is now addressed in the chapter.

This list does not completely describe all the major changes made to the first Canadian edition. However, it highlights the types of changes we have committed ourselves to making in order that *Basic Financial Management* will reflect the very best thinking that financial scholars have to offer.

Acknowledgments

We gratefully acknowledge the assistance, support, and encouragement of those individuals who have contributed to the successful completion and of the first Canadian edition of Basic Financial Management. Specifically, we wish to recognize the following reviewers:

- Elizabeth Maynes
  York University

- G. Srinivasan
  University of New Brunswick

- Michael Robinson
  University of Calgary

- Carmine Fabiilli
  Algonquin College

- Pradeep Jalan
  University of Regina

- Keith J. Barrett
  Humber College

In addition, we'd like to express our appreciation to Keith J. Barret for his assistance in preparing the *Instructor's Manual with Solutions* and the second set of problems.

Readers wishing further information on excerpts provided through the cooperation of Statistics Canada may obtain copies of related publications by mail from: Publications Sales, Statistics Canada, Ottawa, Ontario, K1A 0T6.

Finally, we thank the Prentice Hall staff who were a treat to work with, including Suzanne Tyson, Jacqueline Wood, Maurice Esses, Judith Dawson, Valerie Adams, and Maryrose O'Neill. Their extraordinary patience and fine support throughout the writing, production, and marketing of the text were extremely valuable. Their guidance and help has had a significant and positive impact on the quality of the text.

Even with the very fine efforts of all involved in preparing the first Canadian edition of *Basic Financial Management*, some errors inevitably will exist. For these, the authors must accept final responsibility.

J.D.M
J.W.P
A.J.K.
D.F.S.
D.W.M

PART ONE

The Scope and Environment of Financial Management

CHAPTER *1*   *The Role of Financial Management*

Financial management during this century has undergone dramatic changes. Whereas financial managers were once limited to some bookkeeping, cash management, and the acquisition of funds, they now have a major voice in all aspects of raising and allocating financial capital. This book will introduce you to specific problems and areas that concern the financial manager. First, we explain the environment surrounding the problem, then we propose a method of dealing with the problem. We will also stress the interrelationships among the financial manager's various concerns and decisions. To develop a proper perspective on the role of the financial manager and the financial decision-making process, we will look first at the development of financial thought. Finally, we provide a brief overview of the firm's basic financial statements as a review in the appendices to this chapter.

DEVELOPMENT OF FINANCIAL THOUGHT

At the turn of the century, financial thought focused on the legal environment within which the firm operated. The topics receiving most attention were mergers, formation of new companies, investment banking, public regulation, and the process of raising funds in the capital markets. The economic and business activity of the time determined what was of primary importance in the finance field.

In the 1920s the economy began to expand, and raising new funds in the capital markets became more important. As a result, the emphasis shifted from mergers and regulation to methods and procedures for acquiring funds.

Business failures during the Great Depression of the 1930s helped change the focus of finance. While finance continued to be taught as a descriptive, or "how to" discipline, increased emphasis was placed on bankruptcy, liquidity management, and avoidance of financial problems. The political changes that dominated the 1930s also influenced the field of finance, bringing increased government regulation and control of both business and the securities market, and increased requirements to disclose large volumes of corporate financial data. These data allowed analysts to assess potential corporate performance more effectively, thus stirring new interest in financial analysis.

During the 1940s and early 1950s financial theory continued to be taught as a descriptive discipline. The major financial texts of the day continued to emphasize methods and instruments for fund-raising, corporate bankruptcy and reorganization, and mergers and consolidations. Increased emphasis was given, however, to liquidity management, financial planning, and cash budgeting.[1]

During the mid-1950s the field of finance underwent drastic changes. First, the point of view shifted from that of an outsider assessing the condition and performance of a firm to that of an insider charged with the management and control of the firm's financial operations. The work of Joel Dean promoted the area of capital budgeting as a major topic in finance. This led to an increased interest in related topics, most notably firm valuation. Interest in these topics grew and in turn spurred interest in security analysis, portfolio theory, and capital structure theory. In effect the field of finance evolved from a descriptive discipline dealing primarily with mergers, regulation, and the raising of capital funds to a more quantitative discipline with significant developments in areas such as portfolio diversification and construction, the relationship between risk and return as described by Capital Asset Pricing Model (CAPM) and the Arbitrage Pricing Model (APM), the valuation of options as described by the Black and Scholes model, and the valuation of derivative securities.

The evolution of the field of finance continues at a lively pace. Economic activity, financing innovations, and new theoretical developments are constantly reshaping financial thought. For example, the October 1987 stock market crash forced a rethinking of how stocks are priced. In addition, the opening of markets abroad has created new and exciting opportunities for internationalizing the firm's operations. This has, in turn, created a need for financial managers to better understand the financial systems of other countries and the role of the financial manager in the multinational corporation. Finally, the occurrence of economic recessions like the one in the early 1990s has created new challenges for the financial manager. With increasing frequency, financial managers are faced with the task of cutting costs and turning around earnings.

Before discussing the financial decision-making process, we will examine the appropriate goal of the firm; we can then better understand the role and significance of financial decision making.

---

[1]Among the major financial texts of this period were Arthur S. Dewing's *Financial Policy of Corporations*, which went through five revisions between 1920 and 1953, and Charles W. Gerstenberg's *Financial Organization and Management of Business*, first published in 1939.

GOAL OF THE FIRM

In finance, the goal of the firm is to maximize shareholder wealth, or to maximize the total market value of shareholder's common shares. As we will see, this is an extremely inclusive goal, since it is affected by all financial decisions. To better understand it, we discuss profit maximization as a possible goal of the firm. Then we will compare it to the goal of maximizing shareholder wealth to see why, in finance, the latter is the more appropriate goal for the firm.

Profit Maximization

While profit maximization is frequently used as the goal of the firm in microeconomics courses, the goal of profit maximization stresses the efficient use of capital resources. This goal may, however, fail to consider many of the complexities of the real world that financial managers try to address in their decisions. Profit maximization functions largely as a theoretical goal; economists use it to prove how firms behave rationally to increase profit. In the more applied discipline of financial management, however, firms must deal every day with two major factors: uncertainty and time.[2]

Uncertainty of Returns

Microeconomics courses ignore uncertainty and risk in order to present theory. Projects and investment alternatives are compared by examining their expected values or weighted average profits. Whether or not one project is riskier than another does not enter these calculations; economists do discuss risk, but only tangentially.[3] In reality, projects do differ with respect to risk characteristics, and failing to recognize these differences can result in incorrect decisions in the practice of financial management. To better understand the implications of ignoring risk, let us look at two mutually exclusive investment alternatives (that is, only one can be accepted). The first project involves the use of existing plant to produce plastic combs, a product with an extremely stable demand. The second project uses existing plant to produce electric vibrating combs. This latter product may catch on and do well, but it could also fail. The possible outcomes (optimistic prediction, pessimistic prediction, and expected outcome) are given in Table 1-1.

No variability is associated with the possible outcomes for the plastic comb project. If things go well, poorly, or as expected, the outcome will still

TABLE 1-1
Possible Project Outcomes

	Profit	
	Plastic Comb	*Electric Comb*
Optimistic prediction	$10,000	$20,000
Expected outcome	10,000	10,000
Pessimistic prediction	10,000	0

[2]Profit maximization focuses only on the amount and not on the risk assumed in obtaining the expected profits.

[3]For example, see Robert S. Pindyck and Daniel L. Rubenfeld, *Microeconomics*, 2nd ed. New York: Macmillan, 1992, pp. 244–46.

be $10,000. With the electric comb, however, the range of possible outcomes goes from $20,000 if things go well, to $10,000 if they go as expected, to zero if they go poorly. If we look just at the expected outcomes, the two projects appear equivalent. They are not. The returns associated with the electric comb involve a much greater degree of uncertainty or risk.

An evaluation of these two projects in terms of maximizing profits ignores uncertainty and considers these projects equivalent in terms of desirability. Therefore we must look to a more viable goal. Later in this text we will examine the relationship between risk and expected return. In fact, the risk component has everything to do with determining expected returns and correctly making investment decisions.

Timing of Returns

Another problem with using the goal of profit maximization is that it ignores the timing of the project's returns. To illustrate, let us re-examine our plastic comb versus electric comb investment decision. This time let us ignore risk and say that each of these projects is going to return a profit of $10,000 for one year; however, it will be one year before the electric comb can go into production, while the plastic comb can begin production immediately. The timing of the profits from these projects is illustrated in Table 1-2.

In this case the total profits from each project are the same, but the timing of the returns differs. As we will see later, money has a definite time value. Thus, the plastic comb project is the better of the two. After one year the $10,000 profit from the plastic combs could be invested in a savings account earning 5 percent interest. At the end of the second year it would have grown to $10,500. Since investment opportunities are available for money in hand, we are not indifferent to the timing of the returns. Given equivalent cash flows from profits, we want those cash flows sooner rather than later.[4] Therefore, the financial manager must always consider the possible timing of cash flows in financial decision making.

Overall, the real-world factors of risk and timing force us to look beyond a simple goal of profit maximization as a decision criterion. We will turn now to an examination of a more viable goal for the firm: maximization of shareholder wealth.

Maximization of Shareholder Wealth

In formulating our goal of maximization of shareholder wealth we are doing nothing more than modifying the goal of profit maximization to deal with the complexities of the operating environment. We have chosen maximization of shareholder wealth—that is, maximization of the market value of the

| | Profit | | TABLE 1-2 |
	Plastic Comb	Electric Comb	Timing of Profits
Year 1	$10,000	$ 0	
Year 2	0	10,000	

---

[4]The goal of profit maximization also ignores the dividend decision. In fact, if the goal of the firm was solely profit maximization, it would not pay any dividends at all and thereby maximize profits.

firm's common shares—because the effects of all financial decisions are thereby included. The shareholders react to poor investment or dividend decisions by causing the total value of the firm's common shares to fall and they react to good decisions by pushing the price of the shares up.

BASIC FINANCIAL MANAGEMENT IN PRACTICE

The following excerpt from the article "What Should Corporations Maximize?" by Chamberlain and Gordon examines the traditional assumption that a firm's investment and financing decisions should maximize the current market value of its shares.

When Are Managements Servants of Shareholders?

When the ownership of shares in public corporations is widely distributed among portfolio investors, their interest is served by investment and financing policies that maximize current share price. But in this case, immediate control of the corporation is in the hands of management and its interest may be served by different policies. What are these policies? To get at them, we must first establish the conditions under which management will follow policies which maximize current share price.

It requires a view of the corporation that it is engaged solely in production. Opportunities to earn an abnormal return on capital are random accidents of nature. They are independent of management's performance, and the positive or negative windfalls that results accrue to the residual shareholders' equity in the firm. Furthermore, shareholders are completely informed on a manager's performance exactly and managers who are dismissed due to bankruptcy or contraction of the firm move to another job without loss of human capital.

A More Realistic View

A more realistic view of the firm is that it engages in two classes of activities. One is production and the other is a range of activities intended to make the production profitable. The development of new products and methods of production, marketing, advertising, employee relations and organizational innovations are among the non-production activities undertaken to maintain and increase the spread between price and production cost and to expand sales at these favourable margins. Success in these activities generates incremental cashflow, and shareholders benefit through increases in the market value of the firm's shares.

Management participates too through higher base compensation, bonuses and stock options

plans. However, total compensation for a given managerial position varies little among firms. Even bonuses and stock options plans, though sometimes large in comparison with a manager's salary, capture relatively little of the differential performance among individuals and firms. The other way in which management can share in the rents generated by successful performance is through promotions or more attractive jobs elsewhere which are made possible by the firm's growth. In contrast, dismissal due to bankruptcy or contraction of the firm seriously impairs the manager's human capital due to some period of unemployment followed by a possible inferior new position.

Conclusion: Manager and Shareholder Goals May Clash

The managements of corporations owned by portfolio investors thus have a particular interest in the firm's long-run growth and survival. A high rate of growth in compensation and indirectly through a reduction in the probability of bankruptcy. This objective is ordinarily served by a lower debt-equity ratio than that which maximizes current share price. A higher ratio creates a higher probability of bankruptcy in the near future. Indifference to short term share price maximization would also result in a policy of paying no dividends and using earnings to maximize the firm's growth rate.

However, the larger the spread between actual dividend and debt policies and those that maximize share price, the greater the threat of a hostile takeover. Hence, management will set the dividend rate and the debt-equity ratio to achieve a balance between the desire for growth and survival in the long run and the avoidance of a hostile takeover in the short run. The likely result still is a lower dividend rate and a higher rate of growth in capital than under a policy of maximizing share price. Also, expenditures to facilitate growth, such as marketing, research and development, are also likely at a higher rate.

Source: Adapted from: Trevor W. Chamberlain and Myron J. Gordon, "What Should Corporations Maximize?" *Canadian Investment Review* (Fall 1991), pp. 41–45.

In order to employ this goal, we need not consider every share price change to be a market interpretation of the worth of our decisions. Other factors, such as economic expectations, also affect share price movements. What we do focus on is the effect that our decision should have on share price if everything were held constant. The market price of the firm's shares reflects the value of the firm as seen by its owners. It takes into account uncertainty or risk, time, and any other factors that are important to the owners. Thus, the framework of maximization of shareholder wealth allows for a decision environment that includes the complexities and complications of the real world. As we follow this goal throughout our discussions, we have to keep in mind one more question: who exactly are the shareholders? Shareholders are the legal owners of the firm.

The Agency Problem

While our goal for the firm will be maximization of shareholder wealth, in reality the agency problem may interfere with the implementation of this goal. One form of the agency problem occurs because of the separation of management and the ownership of the firm. The firm's managers can be properly thought of as agents for the firm's shareholders. To ensure that agent-managers act in the shareholders' best interests requires that they have (1) proper incentives to do so and (2) that their decisions are monitored. The incentives usually take the form of executive compensation plans and managerial "perks." For example, perks may take the form of a bloated support staff, country club memberships, luxurious corporate planes, or other amenities of a similar nature. Monitoring requires that certain costs be borne by the shareholders, such as (1) bonding the managers, (2) auditing financial statements, (3) structuring the organization in unique ways that limit useful managerial decisions, and (4) reviewing the costs and benefits of managerial perks. The main point is that these costs are ultimately covered by the owners of the company—its common shareholders. It is difficult to measure exactly how significant a problem this is. However, while this problem may interfere with the implementation of the goal of maximization of shareholder wealth in some firms, it does not affect the goal's validity.

Another form of the agency problem stems from the conflict of interest between shareholders and bondholders. Acting in the shareholders' best interests might cause management to invest in extremely risky projects. Existing investors in the firm's bonds could logically take a dim view of such an investment policy. In fact, this type of investment policy could lead to a downward revision of the bond rating the firm currently enjoys. A lowered bond rating in turn would lower the current market value of the firm's bonds. To reduce this conflict of interest, the creditors (bond investors) and shareholders may agree to include several protective covenants in the bond contract. These bond covenants are discussed in more detail in Chapter 19, but essentially they may be thought of as restrictions on managerial decision making. Typical covenants restrict payment of cash dividends on common shares, limit the acquisition or sale of assets, or limit further debt financing. To make sure that the protective covenants are complied with by management means that monitoring costs are incurred. Like all monitoring costs,[5] they are borne by common shareholders.

---

[5]For a more detailed discussion of monitoring costs with respect to the use of leverage, see Chapter 8.

The costs associated with the agency problem are also difficult to measure, but occasionally we can see the effect of this problem in the marketplace. For example, if the market feels that the management of a firm is damaging shareholder wealth, we might see a positive reaction in the share price to the removal of that management. On the day following the death of John Dorrance, Jr., chairman of Campbell Soup, in 1989, Campbell's share

---

BASIC FINANCIAL MANAGEMENT IN PRACTICE

Bradford Cornell and Alan C. Shapiro on Stockholder-Manager Agency Conflicts

Managers, like all other economic agents, are ultimately concerned with maximizing their own utility, subject to the constraints they face. Although management is legally mandated to act as the agent of shareholders, the laws are sufficiently vague that management has a good deal of latitude to act in its own behalf. This problem, together with the separation of ownership and control in the modern corporation, results in potential conflicts between the two parties. The agency conflict between managers and outside shareholders derives from three principal sources.[6]

The first conflict arises from management's tendency to consume some of the firm's resources in the form of various perquisites. But the problem of overconsumption of "perks" is not limited to corporate jets, fancy offices, and chauffeur-driven limousines. It also extends, with far greater consequences for shareholders, into corporate strategic decision-making. As Michael Jensen points out, managers have an incentive to expand the size of their firms beyond the point at which shareholder wealth is maximized.[7] Growth increases managers' power and perquisites by increasing the resources at their command. Because changes in compensation are positively related to sales growth, growth also tends to increase managerial compensation.[8]

As Jensen has argued persuasively, the problem of overexpansion is particularly severe in companies that generate substantial amounts of "free

cash flow"—that is, cash flow in excess of that required to undertake all economically sound investments (those with positive net present values).[9] Maximizing shareholder wealth dictates that free cash flow be paid out to shareholders. The problem is how to get managers to return excess cash to the shareholders instead of investing it in projects with negative net present values or wasting it through organizational inefficiencies.

A second conflict arises from the fact that managers have a greater incentive to shirk their responsibilities as their equity interest falls. They will trade off the costs of putting in additional effort against the marginal benefits. With a fixed salary and a small equity claim, professional managers are unlikely to devote energy to the company equivalent to that put forth by an entrepreneur.

Finally, their own risk aversion can cause managers to forgo profitable investment opportunities. Although the risk of potential loss from an investment may be diversified in the capital markets, it is more difficult for managers to diversify the risks associated with losing one's salary and reputation. Forgoing profitable, but risky, projects amounts to the purchase by management of career insurance at shareholder expense.

Source: Bradford Cornell and Alan C. Shapiro, "Financing Corporate Growth," *Journal of Applied Corporate Finance*, 1 (Summer 1988), pp. 6–22.

---

[6]The agency conflict is discussed in Michael C. Jensen and William H. Meckling, "Theory of the Firm: Managerial Behavior, Agency Costs and Ownership Structure," *Journal of Financial Economics*, October 1976, pp. 305–360.

[7]Michael C. Jensen, "Agency Costs of Free Cash Flow, Corporate Finance, and Takeovers," *American Economic Review*, May 1986, pp. 323–329.

[8]Evidence on this point is supplied by Kevin J. Murphy, "Corporate Performance and Managerial Remuneration: An Empirical Analysis," Journal of Accounting and Economics, April 1985, pp. 11–42.

[9]We define the net present value concept in Chapter 6. Very briefly, an investment's present value represents its expected contribution to the value of the firm's common stock and, consequently, shareholder wealth.

price rose about 15 percent. Some investors felt that Campbell's relatively small growth in earnings might be improved with the departure of Dorrance. There was also speculation that Dorrance was the major obstacle to a possible positive reorganization.

FINANCIAL DECISIONS AND RISK-RETURN RELATIONSHIPS

Much of our future discussion will centre on evaluation of risk-return tradeoffs available to the financial manager. We will, in fact, find that almost all financial decisions involve some sort of risk-return tradeoff. The more risk the firm is willing to assume, the higher the expected return from the given course of action. For example, a firm may decide to hold less inventory on hand, in order to obtain a higher than expected return. However, the firm will also incur a greater risk of running out of inventory and alienating customers. As we will see, similar examples will turn up in the areas of financial structure and management of long-term assets.

Figure 1-1 is a graphic presentation of the financial decision-making process. The managers who make financial decisions on behalf of the firm are required to make tradeoffs between risk and return, given the firm's goal of maximizing shareholder wealth. The effectiveness of the manager's financial decisions is reflected in any changes occurring in the firm's share price.

WHY PRICES REFLECT VALUE

Throughout this text we have adopted shareholder wealth maximization as our goal. Let's take a closer look at this goal. First, let's define what we mean by shareholder wealth with respect to a business. For a corporation, the wealth of the shareholders at any point in time is simply the market value of the common shares. Thus, decisions that maximize shareholder wealth are those that lead to an increase in the market share price. To understand why good financial decisions are reflected in positive share price adjustments, as well as how securities are valued or priced by the financial markets, it is necessary to have an understanding of the concept of efficient markets.

Efficient Markets

The **efficient market hypothesis** actually deals with the speed with which information is impounded into security prices.[10] Under the efficient market hypothesis, information is reflected in security prices with such speed that

---

[10]The efficient market hypothesis has been divided into three forms according to information type: weak, semi-strong, and strong. The weak form evaluates whether all historical pricing information has been incorporated into current share prices. The semi-strong form evaluates whether both historical pricing information and public information have been incorporated into current share prices. Finally, the strong form evaluates whether all information, public and nonpublic, is incorporated into current share prices and whether any type of investor can make an excess profit. For a more detailed discussion, see Edwin J. Elton and Martin J. Gruber, *Modern Portfolio Theory And Investment Analysis* (John Wiley & Sons, Inc., 4th ed., New York, 1991).

FIGURE 1-1
Financial Decision-Making
Process

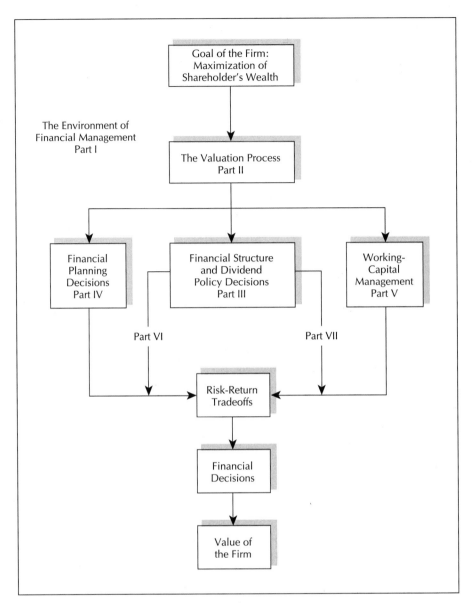

there are no opportunities for investors to profit from publicly available information. In effect, an efficient market is one characterized by a large number of profit-driven individuals who act independently of one another. In addition, new information regarding securities arrives in the market in a random manner. Given this setting, investors adjust to this new information immediately and buy and sell the security until they feel that the market price correctly reflects the new information. Whether or not the price adjustment turns out to be correct is not important, but it is important that the price adjustment not be biased—that is, investors cannot predict whether or not it is an over- or under-adjustment.

Just how quickly and what types of information are immediately reflected in security prices determine how efficient the market actually is.

BASIC FINANCIAL MANAGEMENT IN PRACTICE

Milton Friedman on Ethics

In a free-enterprise, private-property system, a corporate executive is an employee of the owners of the business. He has direct responsibility to his employers. That responsibility is to conduct the business in accordance with their desires, which generally will be to make as much money as possible while conforming to the basic rules of the society, both those embodied in law and those embodied in ethical custom. Of course, in some cases his employers may have a different objective. A group of persons might establish a corporation for an eleemosynary purpose—for example, a hospital or a school. The manager of such a corporation will not have money profit as his objective but the rendering of certain services.

In either case, the key point is that, in his capacity as a corporate executive, the manager is the agent of the individuals who own the corporation or establish the eleemosynary instruction, and his primary responsibility is to them.

Needless to say, this does not mean that it is easy to judge how well he is performing his task. But at least the criterion of performance is straightforward, and the persons among whom a voluntary contractual arrangement exists are clearly defined.

Of course, the corporate executive is also a person in his own right. As a person, he may have many other responsibilities that he recognizes or assumes voluntarily—to his family, his conscience, his feelings of charity, his church, his clubs, his city, his country. He may feel impelled by these responsibilities to devote part of his income to causes he regards as worthy, to refuse to work for particular corporations, even to leave his job, for example, to join his country's armed forces. If we wish, we may refer to some of these responsibilities as "social responsibilities." But in these respects he is acting as a principal, not an agent; he is spending his own money or time or energy, not the money of his employers or the time or energy he has contracted to devote to their purposes. If these are "social responsibilities," they are the social responsibilities of individuals, not of business.

What does it mean to say that the corporate executive has a "social responsibility" in his capacity as a businessman? If this statement is not pure rhetoric, it must mean that he is to act in some way that is not in the interest of his employers. For example, that he is to refrain from increasing the price of the product in order to contribute to the social objective of preventing inflation, even though a price increase would be in the best interests of the corporation. Or that he is to make expenditures on reducing pollution beyond the amount that is in the best interests of the corporation or that is required by law in order to contribute to the social objective of improving the environment. Or that, at the expense of corporate profits, he is to hire "hard-core" unemployed instead of better-qualified available workmen to contribute to the social objective of reducing poverty.

In each of these cases, the corporate executive would be spending someone else's money for a general social interest. Insofar as his actions with his "social responsibility" reduce returns to stockholders, he is spending their money. Insofar as his actions raise the price to customers, he is spending the customers' money. Insofar as his actions lower the wages of some employees, he is spending their money.

The stockholders or the customers or the employees could separately spend their own money on the particular actions if they wished to do so. The executive is exercising a distinct "social responsibility," rather than serving as an agent of the stockholders or the customers or the employees, only if he spends the money in a different way than they would have spent it.

But if he does this, he is in effect imposing taxes, on the one hand, and deciding how the tax proceeds shall be spent, on the other.

Source: Milton Friedman, "The Social Responsibility of Business Is to Increase Its Profits," *The New York Times Magazine* (September 13, 1970), 33, pp. 122–126.

For our purposes, the point is that it is investors competing for profits that ensures that security prices will appropriately reflect the expected earnings and risks involved, and thus the true value of the firm.

ETHICS AND ETHICAL BEHAVIOUR IN FINANCIAL MANAGEMENT

Defining ethics and ethical behaviour is simple. Ethical behaviour means doing the right thing. A difficulty arises, however, in attempting to define what we mean by doing the right thing. The source of the problem lies in the fact that each of us has his or her own unique set of values. These values, in turn, form the basis for our personal judgments as to what is the right thing to do. After all, the very essence of personal freedom lies in each individual's right to make choices. However, individuals in a society are not completely free. Every society adopts a set of rules or laws that prescribe what it believes to be doing the right thing. In a sense, we can think of laws as a set of rules that reflect the values of the society as a whole, as they have evolved up to the present time. There are some who would argue that ethical behaviour is more than simply obeying the law. However, for the purposes of this text, we recognize that individuals in a free society have a right to disagree about what constitutes doing the right thing. For this reason, we will seldom venture beyond the basic notion that ethical conduct involves abiding by society's rules. However, we will endeavour to make you aware of some of the ethical dilemmas, which have arisen in recent years, with regard to the practice of financial management. These dilemmas generally arise where some form of individual behaviour is found to be at odds with the wishes of a large portion of the population, even though that behaviour is not prohibited by law. Ethical dilemmas can therefore provide a catalyst for debate and discussion, which may eventually lead to a revision in the body of law. So, as we embark on our study of finance and encounter ethical dilemmas, we encourage you to think through the issue and form your own opinion.

OVERVIEW OF THE TEXT

This text is divided into seven parts, each dealing with one major area of financial concern:

- The Scope and Environment of Financial Management
- Valuation and the Management of Long-Term Investments
- Financial Structure and Dividend Policy
- Financial Analysis, Planning, and Control
- Working Capital Management
- Long-Term Financing
- Special Topics in Financial Management

Figure 1-1 relates these sections to the financial decision-making process, indicating where each decision is discussed in the text. We describe these sections briefly below.

Part I: The Scope and Environment of Financial Management

Part I begins by discussing the history and role of financial management and develops the goal of the firm to be used in financial decision making.

Chapter 2 presents the financial environment in which these decisions are to be made. Since this environment sets the ground rules, we must understand both legal and tax regulations before decision principles can be formulated.

Part II: Valuation and the Management of Long-Term Investments

Part II examines the mathematics of finance and the concept of the time value of money. An understanding of this topic allows us to compare benefits and costs that occur in different time periods. We also examine a risk-return framework that enables us to determine how the firm and its assets are valued. It looks at valuation models that attempt to explain how different financial decisions affect the price of the firm's shares. After the valuation principles are established we discuss the capital budgeting decision which involves the financial evaluation of investment proposals in fixed assets. We then introduce methods to incorporate risk into the analysis. Finally, we examine the financing of a firm's projects, looking at what costs are associated with alternative ways for raising new funds.

Part III: Financial Structure and Dividend Policy

Part III examines the firm's capital structure along with the impact of leverage on returns to the enterprise. Once these relationships between leverage and valuation are presented, we examine the process of planning the firm's financing mix. This part closes with a discussion of the determination of the dividend–retained earnings decision.

Part IV: Financial Analysis, Planning, and Control

Part IV introduces the basic financial tools which a financial manager uses to maintain control over the firm and its operations. These tools enable the financial manager to locate potential problem areas and to plan for the future. Also introduced are the preparation of the cash flow statement and ratio analysis, which allow the financial manager to achieve greater control over ongoing operations.

Part V: Working Capital Management

The fifth part of the book deals with working-capital management, the management of current assets. We discuss the methods for determining the appropriate investment in cash, marketable securities, inventory, and accounts receivable. The risks associated with these investments, and the control of these risks, also are examined.

Part VI: Long-Term Financing

Part VI describes and analyzes the various sources of long-term funding available to the firm, examining both the pros and cons of these sources and their particular characteristics.

Part VII: Special Topics in Financial Management

The final part of the book begins with a discussion of corporate restructuring including mergers, spinoffs, and leveraged buyouts. We also discuss how financial decisions are affected by the international environment. Finally, the last chapter examines financial management from the perspective of the owner-manager of a small firm.

SUMMARY

This chapter outlines the framework for this book by first tracing the development of financial thought from the turn of the century to the present. During the early part of this century, the field of finance reacted and changed with the prevailing economic environment. Business failures and the Depression of the thirties created concern and interest in working-capital management and bankruptcy. More recently, increased inflation and new theoretical developments have continued to reshape financial thought.

In financial management, the goal of the firm is to maximize shareholders' wealth. This goal was preferred to the idea of profit maximization because both uncertainty and time were accounted for in the process of making financial decisions in a real-world environment.

Finally, the financial decision-making framework is presented and the format of the book is related to this process. The seven parts of the book are briefly previewed.

STUDY QUESTIONS

1-1. How has financial thought developed over the past century? What factors have affected it?

1-2. What are some of the problems involved in the use of profit maximization as the goal of the firm? How does the goal of shareholder wealth maximization deal with those problems?

1-3. Compare and contrast the goals of profit maximization and maximization of shareholder wealth.

1-4. Firms often involve themselves in projects that do not result directly in profits; for example, IBM and Mobil Oil frequently support public television broadcasts. Do these projects contradict the goal of maximization of shareholder wealth? Why or why not?

1-5. What is the relationship between financial decision making and risk and return? Would all financial managers view risk-return tradeoffs similarly?

APPENDIX 1A: The Language of Finance: The Accounting Statements

As we set the stage for gaining a better understanding of financial management, it is imperative that we know the "language" of finance in describing a company's financial position. To a large extent, the language of finance is contained in the firm's financial or accounting statements. Most of us have been exposed to a basic financial accounting course, in which this information is presented; however, we refresh our memory of these basic statements.

In this appendix, we will:

1. Look at the format of basic financial statements;

2. Review some of the more important accounting principles used in reporting a firm's financial activities;

3. Describe briefly some of the significant relationships in the accounting data from the perspective of a financial manager;

4. Offer a brief caveat about the appropriate use of accounting information, and introduce the Free Cash Flow concept.

BASIC FINANCIAL STATEMENTS

Three financial statements generally serve to depict the financial status of a firm: the balance sheet, the income statement, and the statement of changes in financial position. The first two statements are described in this appendix, and the last one, the statement of changes in financial position, is presented in Chapter 11, where we develop in detail a framework for analyzing a company's financial strengths and weaknesses.

Balance Sheet

The **balance sheet** represents a statement of the financial position of the firm on a given date, including its asset holdings, liabilities, and owner-supplied capital. Assets represent the resources owned by the firm, whereas liabilities and owner's equity indicate how those resources were financed. Table 1A-1 gives an example balance sheet for Jimco, Inc., as of December 31, 1993. Jimco had $31 million in assets, which it financed with $10 million in current (short-term) liabilities that must be repaid within the current year, $10,700,000 in noncurrent (long-term) liabilities, and $10,300,000 in owner-supplied funds. (Each term used in the balance sheet is defined in Appendix 1B.)

Limitations of the Balance Sheet

A firm's balance sheet is typically prepared within the guidelines of "generally accepted accounting practice."[11] However, we must be aware of the following limitations of the statement:

1. The balance sheet does not reflect current value, because accountants have adopted historical cost as the basis for valuing and reporting assets and liabilities.

2. Estimates must be used to determine the level of several accounts according to different criteria. Examples include accounts receivable estimated in terms of collectibility, inventories based on saleability, and fixed (noncurrent) assets based on useful life.[12]

3. The depreciation of long-term assets is accepted practice; however, appreciation or enhancement in asset values is generally ignored.[13] This is par-

---

[11]The sources of accounting principles are many; however, the main contributors include: The Accounting Standards Committee, The Auditing Standards Committee, and The Accounting and Auditing Guidelines from the Canadian Institute of Chartered Accountants.

[12]In the opinion of the Accounting Standards Committee of the CICA, the preparation of financial statements requires estimating the effects of subsequent events (CICA Handbook 3820.01–.13 and 1506.21–.23). Examples of items for which estimates are necessary include doubtful accounts receivables, inventory obsolescence, the service lives and salvage values of depreciable assets, the periods expected to derive benefit from a deferred cost, liabilities under warranties, and the size and value of mineral reserves. Since subsequent events cannot be perceived with certainty, estimating requires the exercise of judgment. The implication here is that no reference guidelines can be constructed regarding these estimates; thus subjectivity enters in determining the affected accounts.

[13]*CICA Handbook*, 3060.01–3060.06

Assets

Current assets

Cash	$ 1,400	
Marketable securities—at cost (market value, $320)	300	
Accounts receivable	10,000	
Inventories	12,000	
Prepaid expenses	300	
Total current assets		$24,000

Fixed assets

Land		2,000	
Plant and equipment	$12,300		
Less: Accumulated depreciation	7,300		
Net plant and equipment		5,000	
Total fixed assets			7,000
Total assets			$31,000

Liabilities and Owners' Equity

Current liabilities

Accounts payable	$ 3,000	
Notes payable, 9%, due March 1, 1994	3,400	
Accrued salaries, wages, and other expenses	3,100	
Current portion of long-term debt	500	
Total current liabilities		$10,000

Long-term liabilities

Deferred income taxes	1,500	
First mortgage bonds, 7%, due January 1, 1999	6,300	
Debentures, 8%, due June 30, 1999	2,900	
Total long-term liabilities		10,700

Owners' equity

Common shares (100,000 Shares Outstanding)	100	
Contributed Surplus	2,000	
Retained earnings	8,200	
Total owners' equity		10,300
Total liabilities and owners' equity		$31,000

ticularly crucial to firms holding large investments in appreciable assets such as land, timberlands, and mining properties.

4. Many items that have financial value are omitted from the balance sheet because they involve extreme problems of objective evaluation. The most obvious example consists of the human resources of the firm.[14]

In most cases little can be done to alleviate these shortcomings; however, we should at least be aware of their existence in order to temper the analysis accordingly.

---

[14]The subject of human resource accounting has received increased attention in recent years. For an overview of the subject, see Edwin H. Caplan and Stephen Landeckich, *Human Resource Accounting: Past, Present, and Future* (National Association of Accountants, 1974); and Eric Flamholtz, *Human Resource Accounting* (Encino, CA: Dickinson Publishing Company, 1974).

Income Statement

The **income statement** represents an attempt to measure the net results of the firm's operations over a specified interval, such as one quarter or one year. The income statement (sometimes referred to as a **profit and loss statement**) is compiled on an accrual basis rather than a cash basis. This means that an attempt is made to match the firm's revenues from the period's operations with the expenses incurred in generating those revenues. A condensed income statement for the year ended December 31, 1993, is provided in Table 1A-2 for Jimco, Inc. (The terms used in the income statement are defined in Appendix 1B.)

In looking at the income statement, it is helpful to think of it as comprising three types of activities: (1) the cost of producing or acquiring the goods or services sold; (2) the expenses incurred in marketing and distributing the product or service to the customer, along with administrative operating expenses; and (3) the financing costs of doing business, for example, interest expense and dividend payments to the preferred stockholders. Figure 1A-1 shows these three "income-statement activities."

Net Income and Cash Flow

As already suggested, the reported revenues and expenses need not represent actual cash flows for the period, so that the computed net earnings for the period do not equal the actual cash provided by the firm's operations. There are two basic reasons why the firm's net income does not equal net cash flow for the period. First, revenues and expenses are included in the income statement even though no cash flow might have occurred. For example, sales revenues consist of credit as well as cash sales. Furthermore, cash collections from prior period credit sales are not reflected in the current period's sales revenues. In addition, the expenses for the period represent all those expenditures made in the process of generating the period's revenues. Thus, wages, salaries, utilities, and other expenses may not be paid during the period in which they are recognized in the income statement. Second, certain expenses included within the income statement are not cash expenses at all. For example, depreciation expense does

TABLE 1A-2
Jimco, Inc. Statement of Income for the Year Ended December 31, 1993 ($000 except per share data)

Net sales		$51,000
Cost of goods sold		(38,000)
Gross profit		$13,000
Operating expenses		
Selling expenses	$ 3,100	
Depreciation expense	500	
General and administrative expense	5,400	(9,000)
Net operating income (NOI) or Earnings before interest and taxes (EBIT)		$ 4,000
Interest expense		(1,000)
Earnings before taxes (EBT)		$ 3,000
Income tax provision[a]		(1,200)
Net income (NI)		$ 1,800
Disposition of net income		
Dividends of common shares		$ 300
Change in retained earnings		1,500
Per share data (dollars)		
Number of common shares	100,000 shares	
Earnings per common share ($1,800,000 / 100,000 shares)		$ 18
Dividends per common share ($300,000 / 100,000 shares)		$ 3

[a]A tax rate of 40% on all income is assumed here for simplicity.

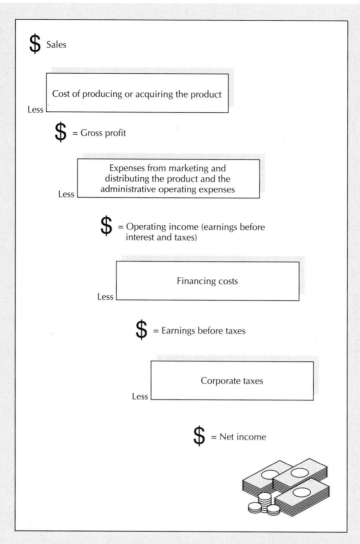

not involve a cash outflow to the firm, yet it is deducted from revenues for the period in computing net income. Other examples of noncash expenses include the amortization of goodwill, patent rights, and bond discounts. Finally, some cash outflows will not be shown as "expenses" in the income statement, but will be recorded on the balance sheet as investments, such as plant and equipment. We will elaborate often on the difference between cash flow and net income, not just when we prepare the cash budget in Chapter 12 or when we prepare a statement of changes in financial position in Chapter 11, but also when we analyze investment and financing decisions.

BASIC ACCOUNTING PRINCIPLES

There are a vast number of "generally acceptable accounting principles" (GAAP) that have been developed over the years. These guidelines cover almost every imaginable situation for reporting financially related transactions of the firm. Some of the more important ones for the study of finance include: (1) the historical cost principle; (2) the accrual or matching principle; (3) inventory valuation guidelines; and (4) methods for reporting the depreciation of long-term (fixed) assets, such as plant and equipment.

Historical Cost Principle

The historical cost principle provides the basis for determining the book values of the firm's balance sheet accounts. The primary advantage of historical cost is its objectivity. Its primary disadvantage relates to the fact that the asset balances do not correspond to market values or replacement costs. Furthermore, since asset book values are not equal to market values, the book value of owners' equity does not equal its market value. In analyzing the firm's financial statements, the analyst must keep in mind that asset balances reflect historical costs of the related assets and not current market values.

Matching Principle

To compute net income for a given year's operations, accountants must identify all revenue and expense items that belong within that year. The **accrual basis of accounting** attempts to allocate revenue and expense properly among the years that an enterprise is in operation. This method utilizes the **revenue realization principle** to assure that revenue is recognized in the period in which it is earned, and it uses the **matching principle** to determine the expenses necessary during the period for the revenue to be generated. These expenses are thus matched against revenue for the period. The basic principle, therefore, involves matching expenses with the revenues, or "Let the expense follow the revenue." Thus, wage expense is not recognized when it is paid nor necessarily when work is performed, but when the work performed actually contributes to revenues.

An example of the potential difficulties posed for the analyst in implementation of the matching principle can be found in the depreciation policies followed by different firms for like assets. For example, one major food processor, referred to here as food processor A, depreciates its machines over 10 years. Another major food processor, food processor B, depreciates its machines over 16 years. Other things being equal, food processor A would report higher expenses and lower profits from its operations than would food processor B. The difficulties encountered with the different depreciation methods used for accounting purposes do not occur for tax purposes since the majority of assets are required to be depreciated by the declining balance method.

ACCOUNTING FOR INVENTORIES AND COST OF GOODS SOLD

Several methods can be used to determine a firm's cost of goods sold. Each relates to the basis used in valuing the firm's inventory, since the firm's purchases that are not passed through the income statement as cost of goods sold remain in the firm's inventory account. We will discuss two common methods for determining the cost of goods sold and consequently the value of the inventory account. The first involves assigning to the period's cost of goods sold the prices paid for the oldest items of inventory held by the firm at the beginning of the period. This is commonly referred to as the **first-in, first-out** or **FIFO** method. The second assigns the cost of the most recently purchased inventory items to the period's cost of goods sold. This is called the **last-in, first-out** or **LIFO** method. The method selected can have a material effect on the firm's computed net earnings during a period where the prices of its purchases consistently rose or fell. For example, in a period when prices have been increasing, the use of the FIFO method results in a lower cost of goods sold, a larger gross profit, a higher tax liability, a higher inventory amount, and a higher net earnings figure than LIFO; LIFO (which costs the firm's sale items using the most recent prices paid by the firm) will result in a lower inventory amount, a higher cost of goods sold figure, and, consequently, lower gross profits, lower taxes, and lower net earnings. The opposite result would follow should prices have fallen during the period.

What importance should be attached to the choice of methods for determining cost of goods sold? Under either method the cash flows that result from sales will be the same, for the actual cost of the items sold does not vary with the method chosen for computing cost of goods sold. However, a very real cash flow effect can result in terms of the amount of taxes that the firm must pay. During a period of rising prices LIFO results in lower taxes being paid than FIFO, while during a period of falling prices the opposite is true.[15] Furthermore, it should be noted that the reported inventory amounts may vary considerably with the application of one method as compared with the other—but the physical quantity and composition of the goods are not affected.

DEPRECIATION OF FIXED ASSETS

Depreciation expense represents an allocation of the cost of a fixed asset over its useful life. The objective is to match such costs with the revenues that result from their utilization in the enterprise. Furthermore, depreciation expense is used to reduce the balance sheet book value of the firm's fixed assets. Thus, the method used to determine depreciation expense also serves as the basis for determining the book value of fixed assets. The two methods that are commonly used for computing depreciation for accounting purposes are the straight line and the double-declining balance methods. However, for tax purposes, the depreciation methods for writing off the investment value of an asset are different from those methods used for accounting purposes. Depreciation for tax purposes will be discussed in Chapter 2.

IMPORTANT RELATIONSHIPS IN ACCOUNTING DATA

Financial managers make extensive use of the firm's accounting information. Chapter 11 outlines in detail how the firm uses such information. However, it will be helpful to look briefly at some of the more important accounting relationships as a basis for our understanding of capital budgeting, working capital management and other key areas.

There are an almost unlimited number of relationships we could consider. However, there are at least three relationships that have an important effect on the firm and the shareholder's value.

1. **The amount of operating profits per dollar of sales.** This relationship indicates management's ability to control both cost of goods sold and operating expense (such as selling and administrative expenses) relative to sales. This relationship is important to a firm's financial well-being and bears upon the value investors are willing to pay for the company.[16]

---

[15]Revenue Canada has indicated through its Interpretation Bulletin (IT473) that the use of the LIFO assumption is not recommended for determining the cost of inventory for tax purposes. Moreover, the CICA recommends that, "the method selected for determining cost should be the one which results in the fairest matching of costs against revenues regardless of whether or not the method corresponds to the physical flow of goods" (*CICA Handbook*, 3030.09).

[16]The term "profits" is used interchangeably with "earnings" or "income."

2. **The amount of the firm's assets compared to its sales.** This relationship tells us how efficiently management is using the firm's assets to create sales. All companies must make an investment in assets in order to generate sales. You cannot have any significant amount of sales without investing in assets, such as accounts receivable, inventories, equipment, and possibly real estate. However, you would prefer to invest less rather than more.

3. **Debt to equity.** We shall see later that the use of debt increases the firm's risk and, in turn, the risk exposure for the company's investors. The increased risk would then affect the investor's required rate of return on their investments, and thereby may alter the firm's value.[17] Thus, the ratio of debt to equity is an important relationship for the financial manager.

A Word of Caution

Although accounting information is vital in our study of a company's finances, a large body of evidence suggests that investors (shareholders) look behind accounting numbers to discover the underlying economic reality of a firm's performance. Thus, the economic reality of a firm's operations is ultimately reflected in the cash flow it provides to its investors, not its reported earnings. Specifically, we will identify the firm's free cash flow to be the amount of cash that is available for distributing to its investors not only after operating expenses have been paid, but after any investments have been made that will generate future cash flows. Free cash flow is defined as follows:

$$\begin{matrix} \text{Free cash} \\ \text{flow} \end{matrix} = \begin{matrix} \text{Operating} \\ \text{profits} \end{matrix} - \begin{matrix} \text{Income} \\ \text{taxes} \end{matrix} - \begin{matrix} \text{Additional investment} \\ \text{in assets} \end{matrix}$$

Throughout our study, we will refer to the firm's free cash flow. It is a basic concept in financial management.

APPENDIX 1B: Glossary of Accounting Terms

accelerated depreciation A term encompassing any method for computing depreciation expense wherein the charges decrease with time. Examples of accelerated methods include sum-of-the-years' digits and double-declining balance as contrasted with straight-line.

accounts payable A current liability representing the total amount owed by a firm from its past (unpaid) credit purchases.

accounts receivable A current asset including all monies owed to a firm from past (uncollected) credit sales.

accrual basis of accounting The method of recognizing revenues when the earning process is virtually complete and when an exchange transaction has occurred, and recognizing expenses as they are incurred in generating those revenues. Thus, revenues and expenses recognized under the accrual basis of accounting are independent of the time when cash is received or expenditures are made. This contrasts with the cash basis of accounting.

accrued salaries and wages Salary and wage expense the firm owes but has not yet paid (a current liability).

accumulated depreciation The sum of depreciation charges on an asset since its acquisition. This total is deducted from gross fixed assets to compute net fixed assets. This balance sheet entry is sometimes referred to as the reserve for depreciation, accrued depreciation, or the allowance for depreciation.

administrative expense An expense category used to report expenses incurred by the firm but not reflected in specific activities such as manufacturing or selling.

amortizing The procedure followed in allocating the cost of long-lived assets to the periods in which their benefits are derived. For capital (fixed) assets, amortization is

---

[17]The relationship between a firm's use of debt and the value of the firm is a complex one, which will be studied in depth in later chapters.

called depreciation expense, whereas for wasting assets (natural resources), it is called depletion expense.

asset Anything owned by a firm or individual that has commercial value.

authorized share capital A term used to indicate the total number of shares of stock the firm can issue and is specified in the articles of incorporation.

bad debt expense An adjustment to income and accounts receivable reflecting the value of uncollectible accounts.

balance sheet A statement of financial position on a particular date. The balance sheet equation is as follows: total assets = total liabilities + owners' equity.

bond Long-term debt instrument carried on the balance sheet at its face amount or par value (usually $1000 per bond), which is payable at maturity. The coupon rate on the bond is the percentage of the bond's face value payable in interest each year. Bonds usually pay interest semiannually.

book value The net amount of an asset shown in the accounts of a firm. When referring to an entire firm, it relates the excess of total assets over total liabilities (also referred to as owners' equity and net worth).

capital Sometimes, the total assets of a firm; at other times, the owners' equity alone.

capital assets Identifiable assets that: (a) are held for use in the production or supply of goods and services for rental to others, for administrative purposes or for the development, construction, maintenance, or repair of other capital aasets; (b) have been acquired, constructed or developed with the intention of being used on a continuing basis; and (c) are not intended for sale in the ordinary course of business (*CICA Handbook*, 3060.04).

capital cost allowance system A system that permits a taxpayer to deduct a portion of the depreciable property's capital cost as an expense. (See Chapter 2, Appendix 2A.)

capitalization Shareholders' equity plus the par value of outstanding bonds.

cash flow The excess (deficiency) of cash receipts over cash disbursements for a given period.

common share A term used to represent the claim of residual owners of the firm. These owners have claim to earnings and asset values remaining after the claims of all creditors and preferred shareholders are satisfied.

contributed surplus A surplus paid-in by shareholders which includes premiums on shares issued, any portion of the proceeds of issue of shares without par value not allocated to share capital, gain on forfeited shares, proceeds arising from donated shares, credits resulting from redemption or conversion of shares at less than the amount set up as share capital, and any other contribution by shareholders in excess of amounts allocated to share capital. (*CICA Handbook*, 3250.05)

cost of goods sold The total cost allocated to the production of a completed product for the period.

current assets Assets that are normally converted into cash within the operating cycle of the firm (normally a period of one year or less). Such items as cash, accounts receivable, marketable securities, prepaid expenses, and inventories are frequently found among a firm's current assets.

current liabilities Liabilities or debts of the firm that must be paid within the firm's normal operating cycle (usually one year or less), such as accounts and notes payable, income taxes payable, and wages and salaries payable.

debentures Long-term debt (bonds) that are secured only by the integrity of the issuer (that is, no specific assets are pledged as collateral).

deferred income taxes Income taxes that a firm recognizes as being owed based upon its earnings but that are not payable until a later date.

depreciable life The period over which an asset is depreciated.

depreciation expense Amortization of plant, property, and equipment cost during an accounting period.

dividend A distribution of earnings to the owners of a corporation in the form of cash (cash dividend) or shares (stock dividend).

double-declining balance depreciation A method for computing declining balance depreciation expense in which the constant percentage is equal to $2/N$, where N represents the depreciable life of the asset.

earnings A synonym for net income or net profit after taxes. Owing to the ambiguity that arises in using the general term earnings, it is usually avoided in favour of more specific terms such as net operating earnings or earnings after taxes.

earnings after taxes (EAT) Other terms often used synonymously are net income and net profit after taxes.

earnings before interest and taxes (EBIT) A commonly used synonym for net operating income. Note that where other income exists, EBIT equals net operating income plus other income.

earnings before taxes (EBT) Total net earnings after the deduction of all tax-deductible expenses.

earnings per share (EPS) Net income after taxes available to the common shareholders (after preferred dividends) divided by the number of outstanding common shares.

equity financing The raising of funds through the sale of common or preferred shares.

extraordinary item A revenue or expense that is both unusual in nature and infrequent in occurrence. Such items and their tax effects are separated from ordinary income in the income statement.

FIFO A method for determining the inventory cost assigned to cost of goods sold wherein the cost of the oldest items in inventory is charged to the period's cost of goods sold (first in, first out). Ending inventories therefore will reflect the prices paid for the most recent purchases. See also the discussion in Appendix 1A.

fixed assets See **capital assets**.

general and administrative expense Expenses associated with the managerial and policy-making aspects of a business.

goodwill Included as an asset entry in the balance sheet to reflect the excess over fair market value paid for the assets of an acquired firm.

gross profit The excess of net sales over cost of goods sold.

income statement The statement of profit or loss for the period comprised of net revenues less expenses for the period. (See **accrual basis of accounting**.)

income tax An annual expense incurred by the firm based upon income and paid to a governmental entity.

intangible asset An asset that lacks physical substance, such as goodwill or a patent.

interest expense The price paid for borrowed money over some specified period of time.

inventory The balance in an asset account such as raw materials, work in process, or finished goods. (See **LIFO** and **FIFO**.)

lease A contract requiring payments by the user (lessee) to its owner (lessor) for the use of an asset. In accordance with disclosure requirements of the *CICA Handbook* (3065.21), the gross amount of assets under capital leases and related accumulated amortization should be disclosed. However for operating leases, only the future minimum lease payments, in the aggregate and for each of the five succeeding years, is required for disclosure purposes.

liability An obligation to pay a specified amount to a creditor in return for some current benefit.

LIFO A method for determining the inventory cost assigned to cost of goods sold whereby the cost of the most recent purchases of inventory is assigned to the period's cost of goods sold (last-in, first-out). Ending inventories thus contain the cost of the oldest items of inventory.

liquid assets Those assets of the firm that can easily be converted into cash with little or no loss in value. Generally included are cash, marketable securities, and sometimes accounts receivable.

long-term debt All liabilities of the firm that are not due and payable within one year. Examples include installment notes, equipment loans, and bonds payable.

marketable securities The securities (bonds and shares) of other firms and governments held by a firm.

net income See **earnings after taxes (EAT)**.

net operating income (NOI) Income earned by a firm in the course of its normal operations. Calculated as net sales less the sum of cost of goods sold and operating expenses.

net plant and equipment Gross plant and equipment less accumulated depreciation.

net sales Gross sales less returns, allowances, and cash discounts taken by customers.

notes payable A liability (normally short-term) of the firm representing a monetary indebtedness.

operating expense Any expense incurred in the normal operation of a firm.

owners' equity Total assets minus total liabilities, sometimes referred to as net worth.

par value The face value of a security.

patent The rights to the benefits of one's invention granted to the inventor by the government.

preferred share The capital share of the owners of the firm whose claim on assets and income is secondary to that of bondholders but preferred as to that of the common shareholders.

profit and loss statement Another name for the income statement.

retained earnings The sum of a firm's net income over its life less all dividends paid.

selling expense An expense incurred in the selling of a firm's product. Examples would include salespeople's commissions and advertising expenditures.

sinking fund Assets and their earnings set aside to retire long-term debt obligations of the firm. Payments into sinking funds are made after taxes and are usually described in the bond indenture (contract between the borrowing firm and the bondholders).

share capital All outstanding common and preferred shares.

stock dividend A dividend that results in a transfer of retained earnings to the capital shares and contributed surplus accounts. This contrasts with a cash dividend. (See **dividend**.)

SELECTED REFERENCES

Anthony, Robert N. "The Trouble with Profit Maximization," *Harvard Business Review*, 38 (November–December 1960), 126–134.

Barnea, Amir, Robert A. Haugen, and Lemma W. Senbet. "Market Imperfections, Agency Problems, and Capital Structure: A Review," *Financial Management*, 10 (Summer 1981), 7–22.

Beranek, William. "Research Directions in Finance," *Quarterly Review of Economics and Business*, 21 (Spring 1981), 6–24.

Bowle, Norman E., and Ronald F. Duska. *Business Ethics*. Second Edition. Englewood Cliffs, NJ: Prentice-Hall, Inc., 1990.

Branch, Ben. "Corporate Objectives and Market Performance," *Financial Management*, 2 (Summer 1973), 24–29.

Buhholz, Rogene A. *Fundamental Concepts and Problems in Business Ethics*. Englewood Cliffs, NJ: Prentice-Hall, Inc., 1989.

Cisel, David H., and Thomas M. Carroll. "The Determinants of Executive Salaries: An Econometric Survey," *Review of Economics and Statistics*, 62 (February 1980), 7–13.

Cooley, Phillip L. "Managerial Pay and Financial Performances of Small Business," *Journal of Business* (September 1979), 267–276.

Donaldson, Gordon. "Financial Goals: Management vs. Stockholders," *Harvard Business Review*, 41 (May–June 1963), 116–129.

Findlay, M. Chapman, III, and G. A. Whitmore. "Beyond Shareholder Wealth Maximization," *Financial Management*, 3 (Winter 1974), 25–35.

Findlay, M. Chapman, III, and E. E. Williams. "A Positivist's Evaluation of the New Finance," *Financial Management*, 9 (Summer 1980), 7–17.

Friedman, Milton. "The Social Responsibility of Business Is to Increase Its Profits," *The New York Times Magazine* (September 13, 1970), 33, 122–126.

Hand, John H., William P. Lloyd, and Robert B. Rogow. "Agency Relationships in the Close Corporation," *Financial Management*, 11 (Spring 1982), 25–30.

Jensen, Michael, and William H. Meckling. "Theory of the Firm: Managerial Behavior, Agency Costs, and Ownership Structure," *Journal of Financial Economics*, 2 (October 1976), 305–360.

Pindyck, Robert S. and Daniel L. Rubenfeld. *Microeconomics*. 2nd Edition. New York: Macmillian, 1992.

Simkowitz, Michael A., and Charles P. Jones. "A Note on the Simultaneous Nature of Finance Methodology," *Journal of Finance*, 27 (March 1972), 103.

Solomon, Ezra. *The Theory of Financial Management*. Chaps. 1 and 2. New York: Columbia University Press, 1963.

Weston, J. Fred. "Developments in Finance Theory," *Financial Management*, 10 (1981), 5–22.

CHAPTER *2* — *The Financial Environment*

- The Structure of the Financial Market

- Legal Forms of Business Organization

- The Canadian Income Tax System

During the 1980s and the early 1990s the financial environment changed dramatically. Perhaps at no time since the Great Depression of the 1930s have the corporations of North America undergone such a restructuring. Continuous and rapid change is the norm as worldwide competition develops rapidly in the product markets as well as in the financial markets. It is essential that in this setting that the financial manager have a good grasp of the basic elements of the financial environment. In this chapter, we examine three such elements:

1. This chapter surveys the **financial markets**, in which firms seek financing for their investments. We review four basic concepts: the structure of the financial market; the role of opportunity costs in determining interest rates; the impact of inflation on rates of interest; and the relationship between interest rates and the length of time until a security matures, which we call the term-to-maturity. In Chapter 3, we will examine the relationship between risk and rates of return, and in Chapter 17 we examine the institutional setting in which firms buy and sell securities.

2. Next we will identify the basic legal forms of **business organization** that are used to shape and support their activities. We focus our attention on the sole proprietorship, the partnership and the corporation.

3. This chapter also reviews some key elements of the corporate tax environment, or the Income Tax Act, which are important influences on business behaviour.

Perspective in Finance

When you borrow money from a commercial bank to finance a purchase of stereo equipment or take out a mortgage to pay for a new home, you have used this country's financial market system. The average individual (and you are not that because of your study of financial management) tends to take the reality of the financial markets for granted. But they were not always there, and they have evolved amidst much controversy over a long period of time.

Recent years have produced heated debates over alterations in our financial system—this just illustrates the dynamic nature of these markets. Much of that debate followed the collapse of the equity markets on Monday, October 19, 1987, when both the Toronto Stock Exchange 300 Index and the Dow Jones Industrial Average fell by an unprecedented 407 and 508 points, respectively. Like banks, the equity markets are another piece of our complex financial market system. The financial market system must have the confidence of those who must use it. If the financial market system did not exist, real assets (like your home) do not get produced at an adequate rate and the populace suffers. We now examine the structure of the financial market.

THE STRUCTURE OF THE FINANCIAL MARKET

Financial markets are institutions and procedures that facilitate transactions in all types of financial claims. The purchase of your home, the common shares you may own, and your life insurance policy all took place in some type of financial market. Why do financial markets exist? What would the economy lose if our complex system of financial markets were not developed? We will address these questions here.

Some economic units, such as governments and business enterprises, spend more during a given period of time than they earn. Other economic units, such as persons and unincorporated businesses, spend less on current consumption than they earn. For example, business firms in the aggregate usually spend more during a specific time period than they earn. Households in the aggregate spend less on current consumption than they earn. As a result, some mechanism is needed to facilitate the transfer of savings from those economic units with a surplus to those with a deficit. That is precisely the function of financial markets. Financial markets exist in order to allocate the supply of savings in the economy to the demanders of those savings. The central characteristic of a financial market is that it acts as the vehicle through which the forces of demand and supply for a specific type of financial claim (such as a corporate bond) are brought together.

Now, why would the economy suffer without a developed financial market system? The answer is simple. The wealth of the economy would be less without the financial markets. The rate of capital formation would not be as high if financial markets did not exist.[1] This means that the net additions during a specific period to the stocks of (1) dwellings, (2) productive plant and equipment, (3) inventory, and (4) consumer durables would occur at lower rates.[2] Figure 2-1 clarifies the rationale behind this assertion. The

[1] The rate of capital formation in Canada is dependent on the efficiency of its financial markets to provide a mechanism that facilitates the process of borrowing and lending.

[2] Canada is considered a capital-scarce country, having to offer a premium on interest rates to attract investors. Consequently, the capital investments of firms which desire to modernize, become more expensive as compared to firms located in capital-rich countries.

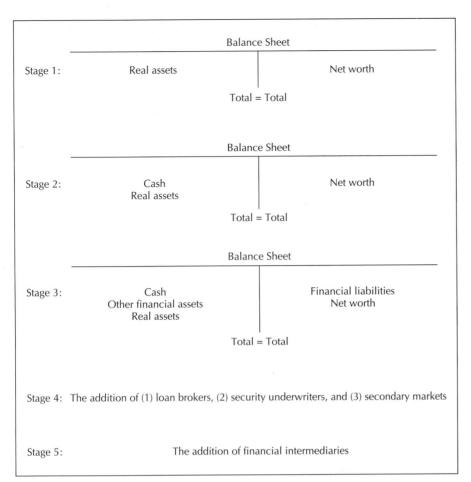

FIGURE 2-1
The Development of a
Financial Market System

abbreviated balance sheets in the figure refer to firms or any other type of economic units that operate in the private as opposed to governmental sectors of the economy. This means that such units cannot issue money to finance their own activities.

At stage 1 in Figure 2-1 only real assets exist in the hypothetical economy. Real assets are tangible assets like houses, equipment, and inventories. They are distinguished from financial assets, which represent claims for future payment on other economic units. Common and preferred shares, bonds, bills, and notes all are types of financial assets. If only real assets exist, then savings for a given economic unit, such as a firm, must be accumulated in the form of real assets. If the firm has a great idea for a new product, that new product can be developed, produced, and distributed only out of company savings (retained earnings). Furthermore, all investment in the new product must occur simultaneously as the savings are generated. If you have the idea, and we have the savings, there is no mechanism to transfer our savings to you. This is not a good situation.

At stage 2 paper money comes into existence in the economy. Here, at least, you can store your own savings in the form of money. Thus, you can finance your great idea by drawing down your cash balances. This is an improvement over stage 1, but there is still no effective mechanism to transfer our savings to you. You see, we will not just hand you our dollar bills. We will want a receipt.

The concept of a receipt which represents the transfer of savings from one economic unit to another is a monumental advancement. The economic unit with excess savings can lend the savings to an economic unit that needs them. To the lending unit these receipts are identified as "other financial assets" in stage 3 of Figure 2-1. To the borrowing unit, the issuance of financial claims (receipts) shows up as "financial liabilities" on the stage 3 balance sheet. The economic unit with surplus savings will earn a rate of return on those funds. The borrowing unit will pay that rate of return, but it has been able to finance its great idea.

In stage 4 the financial market system becomes more sophisticated because loan brokers help locate pockets of excess savings and channel such savings to economic units needing the funds. Some economic units will actually purchase the financial claims of borrowing units and sell them at a higher price to other investors; this process is called **underwriting**.[3] Further evidence for the sophistication of the financial markets is the development of a secondary market which enables trading in already-existing financial claims. For example, the sale of Northern Telecom common shares between a friend and yourself represents a secondary market transaction. Secondary markets reduce the risk of investing in financial claims. Should you need cash, you can liquidate your claims in the secondary market. This induces savers to invest in securities.

Stage 5 represents the progression of the financial markets toward specialization as seen by the different functions of financial intermediaries. You can think of financial intermediaries as the major financial institutions with which you are used to dealing. These include commercial banks, trusts and mortgage and loan companies, credit unions, life insurance companies, and mutual funds. Financial intermediaries share a common characteristic: they offer their own financial claims, called indirect securities, to economic units with excess savings. The proceeds from selling their indirect securities are then used to purchase the financial claims of other economic units. These latter claims can be called direct securities. Thus, a mutual fund might sell mutual fund shares (their indirect security) and purchase the common shares (direct securities) of some major corporations. A life insurance company sells life insurance policies and purchases huge quantities of corporate bonds. Financial intermediaries thereby involve many small savers in the process of capital formation. This means there are more "good things" for everybody to buy.

A developed financial market system provides for a greater level of wealth in the economy. In the absence of financial markets, savings are not transferred to the economic units most in need of those funds. Financial markets bring together net savers and net users of funds. For example, banks accumulate the savings of individual investors and in return pay interest to these investors for use of these funds. On the other hand, growing companies are frequently net users of funds because their expenditures often exceed their income. A growth company might borrow funds (i.e., sell debt securities) from the insurance company. This act is a typical financial market transaction.

In the following article, we profile one of the more important financial institutions in Canada, the banking industry.[4]

[3]Underwriting will be discussed in more detail in Chapter 17.

[4]Other profiles of Canadian financial institutions are presented in Chapters 17 and 24.

BASIC FINANCIAL MANAGEMENT IN PRACTICE

Banking

Banks are the main sources of financial services in Canada and provide over 100 retail financial services. These services normally include savings and checking accounts, loans with or without security, lines of credit, credit cards, financial leasing and banking-related data processing services. Banks also handle foreign trade-related transactions, maintain safe-deposit facilities and accept deposits.

Canadian banks are chartered under the Bank Act, which is subject to regular parliamentary review. Banking is one of the most heavily regulated industries in Canada: the goals of such legislation are to ensure bank solvency, to help banks remain effective, efficient and competitive and to maintain public confidence in the banking system. While the federal government has sole jurisdiction over banks and the banking system, provincial governments can influence banking activities through their securities laws, contract law and consumer protection legislation.

The Bank Act lists banks under its Schedule I or Schedule II, according to the diversity of the public distribution of their shares. Schedule I banks are widely held; no individual investor can own more than 10 percent. Moreover, no group of non-residents, except U.S. investors, can own more than 25 percent of any class of shares. Therefore, the Schedule I banks are Canadian-owned. Most Schedule II banks are closely held subsidiaries of foreign banks.

Retail banking traditionally requires a local presence. Schedule I banks operate nation-wide branch systems in a diverse range of markets, from very small villages to large metropolitan areas. These branches represent over 60 percent of the retail outlets provided by all financial institutions.

Chartered banks are the major suppliers of consumer and commercial credit in Canada. Business loans constitute the largest element of their asset holdings, followed by mortgage loans and consumer loans. The banks' domestic commercial credit operations encompass a wide range of borrowers, including small businesses, large firms operating across Canada and different levels of government. Banks are the primary source of financing to small businesses and provide a range of support services. Larger Canadian companies rely on banks from short-term working capital and a number of other services such as treasury, cash management, trade finance services and the underwriting and distribution of corporate securities. Banks also underwrite and distribute the debt issues of Canadian Governments and Crown corporations and invest their surplus funds in government and corporate securities.

Banks face intense competition in commercial markets, as trust companies, life insurance companies and securities dealers also seek to expand their share of commercial financing. With the slower growth in commercial lending, Schedule I banks have focused their efforts further on the small business market. While the intense competition is beneficial for corporations seeking funds, it has put pressure on the earnings of several Schedule II banks. Schedule I banks also have an advantage in that their retail deposit bases often provide funds at lower costs than the wholesale money markets upon which the Schedule II banks rely.

While Schedule I banks are the main suppliers of commercial credit, foreign banks have had a presence in this market in Canada for many years. The 1980 Bank Act acknowledged their influence and the increased influence and the increased competition that their operations have provided in the Commercial credit markets. In allowing them to operate in Canada, the Bank Act requires the foreign banks to establish subsidiaries (Schedule II banks) or representative offices. Foreign bank subsidiaries can be closely held indefinitely, but their combined Canadian dollar assets, excluding those held by U.S.-controlled Schedule II banks, cannot exceed 12 percent of the domestic assets of the Canadian banking system. The size of individual banks is controlled through regulatory approval of their capital bases. Schedule II banks are small relative to domestic banks because of the competition from Schedule I banks and other sources of commercial financing.

To compete with Schedule I banks, Schedule II banks tend to seek niche markets. Many focus on wholesale banking operations and try to attract Canadian customers by providing services that are not generally available at local banks. Schedule II banks are also oriented towards commercial banking services because of the practical difficulties in establishing large retail branch networks. Some Schedule II banks are in the Canadian market to better serve their international clients rather than to seek a share of the Canadian market.

Continued on page 30

Continued from page 29

Canadian-owned banks are very active abroad. They operate through foreign branches and many subsidiary and agency offices. They also have correspondent relationships with financial institutions worldwide. They accept deposits, extend loans, participate in underwriting of corporate securities and loan syndications, and provide new products such as interest rate and foreign exchange swaps.

Source: Adapted from: "Industry Profile, 1990–1991, Banking" (Communications Branch, Industry, Science and Technology Canada, 1991).

Interest Rates

Net users of funds must compete with one another for the funds supplied by net savers. Consequently, to obtain financing a firm must offer the supplier a rate of return competitive with the next best investment alternative.[5] We refer to the rate of return on this next best investment alternative as the supplier's opportunity cost of capital. The opportunity cost concept is crucial in financial management and we will refer to it often.

The price of using someone else's savings is expressed in terms of interest rates. The financial market system helps to move funds to the most-productive end use. Those economic units with the most-promising projects should be willing to bid the highest (in terms of rates) to obtain the savings. When a rate of interest is quoted, it is generally the nominal, or observed rate. On the other hand, the real rate of interest, represents the rate of increase in actual purchasing power after adjusting for the inflation rate. For example, if you have $100 today and loan it to someone for a year at a nominal rate of interest of 11.3 percent, you will get back $111.30 in one year. But, if during the year prices of goods and services increase by 5 percent, it will take $105 at year end to purchase the same goods and services that $100 purchased at the beginning of the year. What was your increase in purchasing power over the year? The quick and dirty answer is found by subtracting the inflation rate from the nominal rate, $11.3\% - 5\% = 6.3\%$, but this is not exactly correct. To be more precise, let the nominal rate of interest be represented by r, the anticipated rate of inflation by i, and the real rate of interest by R. Using these notations, we can express the relationship between the nominal interest rate, the rate of inflation and the real rate of interest as follows:

$$1 + r = (1 + R)(1 + i) \qquad (2\text{-}1)$$

or

$$r = R + i + iR$$

Consequently, the nominal rate of interest (r) is equal to the sum of the real rate of interest (R), the inflation rate (i), and the product of the real rate and the inflation premium.[6] This relationship between nominal rates, real rates, and the rate of inflation has come to be called the **Fisher effect**.[7] Equation (2-1) describes how the observed nominal rate of interest includes both the real rate of interest and the inflation rate.

---

[5]Financial managers should make investment and financing decisions on current or marginal information and not on historical or average costs.

[6]The inflation premium is not tied to the actual inflation rate at a given time, but rather to the expected inflation for the duration of the security's life.

[7]This relationship was analyzed many years ago by Irving Fisher.

Substituting into equation (2-1) using a nominal rate of 11.3 percent and an inflation rate of five percent, we calculate the real rate of interest, R, as follows:

$$r = R + i + (i)(R)$$

$$.113 = R + .05 + (.05)(R)$$

$$R = 6\%$$

Thus, at new higher prices, your purchasing power will have increased by only six percent although have $11.30 more than you had at the start of the year. To see why, let's assume that at the outset of the year one unit of the market basket of goods and services costs $1, so you could purchase 100 units with your $100. Now, at the end of the year you have $11.30 more, but each unit now costs $1.05 (remember the five percent rate of inflation). How many units can you buy at the end of the year? The answer is 106 units ($111.30/$1.05), which represents a six percent increase in real purchasing power.[8]

The Term Structure of Interest Rates

The relationship between a debt security's rate of return and the length of time until the debt matures is known as the **term structure of interest rates**. For the relationship to be meaningful to us, all the factors other than maturity, such as the chance of the bond defaulting, must be held constant. Thus, the term structure reflects observed rates or yields on similar securities, except for the length of time until maturity, at a particular moment in time. Figure 2-2 shows an example of the term structure of interest rates. The curve is upward sloping, indicating that longer terms to maturity command higher returns, or yields. In this hypothetical term structure, the rate of interest on a five-year note or bond is 11.5 percent, whereas the comparable rate on a twenty-year bond is 13 percent.

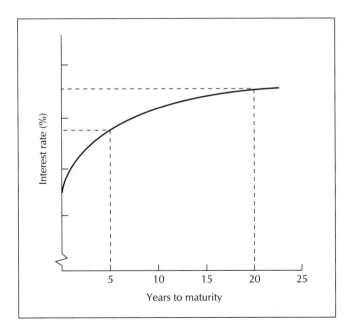

FIGURE 2-2
The Term Structure of Interest Rates

[8]The time value of money will be discussed in greater detail in Chapter 4.

Observing Historical Term Structures of Interest Rates

The term structure of interest rates is dependent on the financial environment and as a result will change over time. The particular term structure observed today may be quite different from either the term structure of a month ago or the term structure of a month from now.[9] A perfect example of the changing term structure, or the yield curve, was witnessed during the early days of the Persian Gulf crisis in August 1990. Figure 2-3 shows the yield curves one day prior to the Iraqi invasion of Kuwait and then again just three weeks later. The change is noticeable, particularly for long-term interest rates. Investors quickly developed new fears about the prospect of increased inflation to be caused by the crisis and consequently increased their required rates of return.

Although the upward-sloping curve in Figure 2-2 is the one most commonly observed, yield curves can assume several shapes. Sometimes the term structure is downward-sloping; at other times it rises and then falls (hump-backed); and at still other times it may be relatively flat. Figure 2-4 shows some yield curves at different points in time.

FIGURE 2-3
Changes in the Term Structure of Interest Rates at the Outbreak of the Persian Gulf Crisis

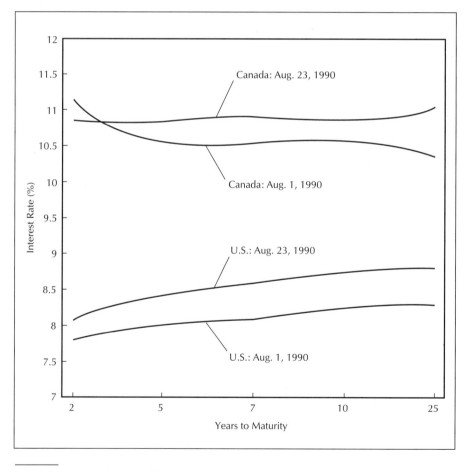

[9]For a discussion of the problems involved in actually estimating the term structure at any point in time, see Willard T. Carleton and Ian A. Cooper, "Estimation and Uses of the Term Structure of Interest Rates," *Journal of Finance*, 31 (September 1976), 1067–1084.

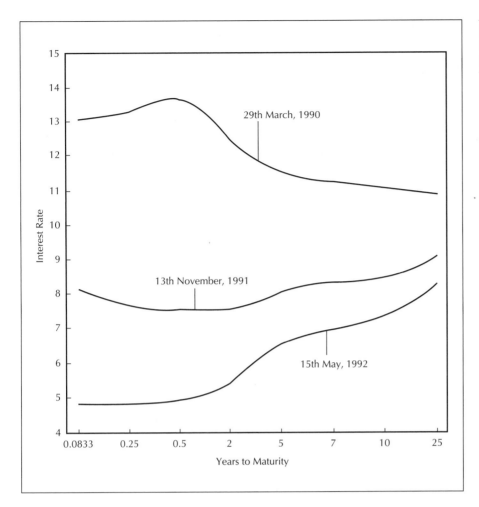

FIGURE 2-4
Historical Term Structure of
Interest Rates

Trying to Explain the Shape of the Term Structure

A number of theories may explain the shape of the term structure of interest rates at any point in time. Three possible explanations are presented: (1) the unbiased expectations theory, (2) the liquidity preference theory, and (3) the market segmentation theory.[10] We now examine each of these theories in greater detail.

The Unbiased Expectations Theory

The **unbiased expectations theory** says that the term structure is determined by an investor's expectations about future interest rates.[11] To see how this works, consider the following investment problem faced by Mary Maxell. Mary has $10,000 that she wants to invest for two years, at which time she plans to use her savings to make a down payment on a new home. Wanting not to take any risk of losing her savings, she decides to invest in

---

[10]See Richard Roll, *The Behavior of Interest Rates: An Application of the Efficient Market Model to U.S. Treasury Bills* (Basic Books, Inc., New York, 1970).

[11]Irving Fisher thought of this idea in 1896. The theory was later refined by J. R. Hicks in: *Value and Capital* (London: Oxford University Press, 1946) and F. A. Lutz and V. C. Lutz, *The Theory of Investment in the Firm* (Princeton University Press, Princeton, N.J., 1951).

Government of Canada securities. She has two choices. First, she can purchase a government security that matures in two years, which offers her an interest rate of nine percent per year.[12] If she does this, she will have $11,881 in two years, calculated as follows:[13]

Principal amount	$10,000
Plus: year 1 interest (.09 × $10,000)	900
Principal plus interest at the end of year 1	$10,900
Plus: year 2 interest (.09 × $10,900)	981
Principal plus interest at the end of year 2	$11,881

Alternatively, Mary could buy a government security maturing in one year that pays an eight-percent rate of interest. She would then need to purchase another one-year security at the end of the first year. Which alternative Mary will prefer obviously depends in part upon the rate of interest she expects to receive on the government security she will purchase a year from now. We cannot tell Mary what the interest rate will be in a year; however, we can at least calculate the rate that will give her the same two-year total savings she would get from her first choice, or $11,881. The interest rate can be calculated as follows:

Savings needed in two years:	$11,881
Savings at the end of the year 1: $10,800 × (1 + .08)	$10,800
Interest needed in year 2:	$ 1,081

For Mary to receive $1,081 in the second year, she would have to earn about ten percent on her second-year investment, computed as follows:

$$\frac{\text{Interest received for year 2}}{\text{Investment made at beginning of year 2}} = \frac{\$1,081}{\$10,800} = 10.8\%$$

So the term structure of interest rates for our example consists of the one-year interest rate of eight percent and the two-year rate of nine percent which is shown in Figure 2-5. This Figure also provides information about the expected one-year rate for investments made one year hence. In a sense, the term structure contains implications about investor expectations of future interest rates and is called the unbiased expectations theory of the term structure of interest rates.

Although we can see a relationship between current interest rates with different maturities and the investor's expectations about future interest rates, is this the whole story? Are there influences other than the investor's expectations about future interest rates? Probably, so let's continue to think about Mary's dilemma.

---

[12]When the Government of Canada and other governments issue securities to help finance government expenses, they issue these securities with different times to maturity, depending on the government's funding needs.

[13]We could also calculate the principal plus interest for Mary's investment using the following compound interest equation: $\$10,000(1 + .09)^2 = \$11,881$. The mathematics will be examined in greater detail in Chapter 4.

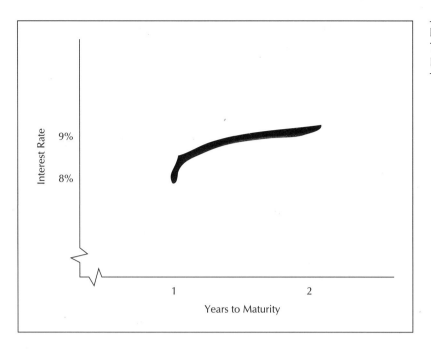

FIGURE 2-5
Term Structure of Interest
Rates

Liquidity Preference Theory

In presenting Mary's choices, we have suggested that she would be indifferent between buying the two-year government security offering a nine-percent return and two consecutive one-year investments, offering eight and ten percent, respectively. However, that would be so only if she is unconcerned about the risk associated with not knowing the rate of interest on the second security at the time she chooses it. If Mary is risk-averse (that is, she dislikes risk), she might not be satisfied with a ten-percent return on the second one-year government security. She might require some additional expected return to be truly indifferent. Mary may in fact decide that she will expose herself to the uncertainty of future interest rates only if she can reasonably expect to earn an added one-half percent in interest (0.5%), or 10.5 percent on the second one-year investment. This risk premium (additional required interest rate) to compensate Mary for the risk of changing future interest rates is known as the **liquidity premium**; and it is this idea that underlies the **liquidity preference theory** of the term structure. In the liquidity preference theory, investors require liquidity premiums to compensate them for buying securities that expose them to the risks of fluctuating interest rates.

Market Segmentation Theory

The **market segmentation theory** explains the term structure of interest rates by building on the idea that legal restrictions and personal preferences limit choices for investors to certain ranges of maturities.[14] For example, commercial banks prefer short- to medium-term maturities because of the short-term nature of their deposit liabilities. Investors prefer not to invest in long-term securities. Life insurance companies, on the other hand, have longer term liabilities, so this type of investor prefers longer maturities in

---

[14]An early advocate of this theory was J. M. Culbertson, "The Term Structure of Interest Rates," *Quarterly Journal of Economics*, 71 (November 1957), pp. 489–505.

investments. At the extreme, the market segmentation theory implies that the rate of interest for a particular security is determined solely by demand and supply for a given maturity, and that it is independent of the demand and supply for securities having different maturities. A more moderate version of the theory allows investors strong maturity preferences, but it also allows them to modify their feelings and preferences if significant yield inducements occur.[15]

In Chapter 17 we will examine more closely the process of issuing shares and bonds in the financial markets. For now we have introduced the importance of the financial markets and the role of interest rates in the marketplace.

Perspective in Finance

The yield curve provides an investor with the following financial information.[16] (1) The shape of the yield curve provides a prediction of future interest rates—for example, an upward-sloping yield curve implies a forecast of higher interest rate levels. (2) The yield curve provides lenders and borrowers with a method to estimate the levels of risk and return when choosing the terms of maturity for debt transactions—for example, a lender can evaluate the additional risk incurred by estimating the incremental yield that occurs with a longer term of maturity for the loan. (3) The yield curve can be used as an instrument to select individual securities—for example, securities that are priced too low (i.e., yield-to-maturity too high) lie above the yield curve. (4) The yield curve provides assistance in the pricing of new securities—for example, the issuer of new debt will set the coupon rate slightly above the yield of a comparable instrument that is located on the yield curve so as to make it attractive to the market. (5) The yield curve provides information to participants which "ride the yield curve" in the money market—for example, an upward-sloping yield curve would provide an investor with the opportunity to invest in a security whose maturity is longer than the investor's holding period, and then to sell the security prior to maturity in order to obtain a greater return.

LEGAL FORMS OF BUSINESS ORGANIZATION

The legal forms of business organization are quite diverse and numerous. However, there are three basic categories: the sole proprietorship, the partnership, and the corporation. We will first examine the nature of these forms and how to judge the best form for a particular company.

The Nature of the Organizational Forms

In coming to understand the basic differences between each legal organizational form, we ought to know the definition of each form, the procedures necessary for originating the form, and the advantages and disadvantages of each. The following article examines each of the organizational forms and describes their differences.

---

[15]See for example Franco Modigliani and Richard Sutch, "Innovations in Interest Rate Policy," *American Economic Review* (May 1966), pp. 178–197.

[16]S. Kerry Cooper and Donald R. Fraser, "The Term Structure of Interest Rates"; In: *The Financial Marketplace* (Don Mills, Ontario: Addison-Wesley Publishing Company, 3rd edition, 1990) p. 172.

BASIC FINANCIAL MANAGEMENT IN PRACTICE

Carefully Evaluate Your Firm's Ownership Structure

One of the questions most frequently asked by those starting a business is: "Which type of ownership structure should I use?" This important choice should be carefully evaluated, not only by those wishing to go into business, but also by those who are already in business. What follows is a general overview of the advantages and disadvantages of the three basic types of business ownership: The sole proprietorship, the partnership and the corporation.

The Sole Proprietorship

The simplest and the most common form of business ownership is the sole proprietorship. Sole proprietorship means that the business is owned and operated by one individual. This individual has complete freedom of operation: when an action must be taken or when a business decision is required, it is not necessary to obtain the consent of another person. Also, the proprietor receives all the profits generated by the business. Initial start-up costs are minimal, and the payment of fees for registration and verification of the company name is usually all that is required to create the business. The proprietor can sell the business or cease operating whenever he wishes to do so.

However, there are certain disadvantages to this form of business ownership, the greatest of which is the owner's unlimited liability. This means that the owner is responsible for all of his company's debts. If the business fails, therefore, creditors may seize his personal assets in order to satisfy these debts. Another disadvantage is limited capital-raising ability. The personal assets of the average individual do not predispose lenders to take risks, and may not by themselves provide the capital required to finance the business. Also, one person may not have the skills adequate to cope with all the potential situations the company may encounter. Finally, the owner is personally responsible for all losses. Gains and losses are included on the individual's personal income tax return and are subject to personal tax rates.

The Partnership

A partnership is formed when two or more individuals share in the ownership of a business. When the same individuals share in the management or control of the business, the organization is legally referred to as a general partnership. Shared control allows partners' abilities to complement each other (two heads are better than one). Start-up costs for a general partnership are the same as those of a sole proprietorship, however it is advisable that a partnership agreement be drawn up, even among relatives and friends. This agreement should clearly spell out all of the responsibilities, rights and duties of the parties involved and should include the following: duration of the partnership, salaries and withdrawals of each partner; amount of capital invested by each partner, settlement in the event of disability or death; distribution of assets in the event of dissolution; division of profits and losses; provision for settlement of disputes among partners; and, provision for the addition and withdrawal of partners.

This agreement should be drawn up by a legal representative and reviewed by each partner's own counsel in order to ensure that the partners' best interests have been taken into consideration. (This will, of course, add to the cost of forming a partnership.) In a partnership, the assets of all the partners are combined, thus making it easier to acquire capital to finance operations. Financial institutions will be more willing to lend money to partnerships because the partners share the debt. Any partner can bind the entire partnership in a business arrangement even though the remaining partners are not aware of, or in agreement with, the decision. Partners are liable for all business debts. Creditors can pursue all of the general partners for these debts, regardless of stipulations in a partnership agreement. It is up to the partners to settle any differences among themselves.

The disadvantages of the unlimited personal liability imposed by a general partnership arrangement can be avoided by forming a limited partnership.[17] A limited partnership has one or more partners whose losses are limited to their initial investment. Creditors cannot pursue a limited partner, and such a partner can have no say in the management of the business. However, a limited partnership must have at least one general partner with unlimited liability. Transfer of ownership in the case of a partnership is more complicated than a sole proprietorship. A limited partner can sell his or

Continued on page 38

---

[17]The limited partnership has been a major vehicle for financing ventures with limited lives, such as real estate developments or oil and gas exploration in Canada.

Continued from page 37

her interest at any time, however for a general partner this may be more difficult. Depending on the provisions of the partnership agreement, transfer of a general partner's interest to another party may be subject to the approval of the other general partners. Profits and losses are distributed among the partners in the fashion agreed upon and are included in their personal income tax returns, and are thus subject to personal tax rates.

The Corporation

A corporation is an association of shareholders created under law, and is regarded as a legal entity, separate and distinct from its owners and directors. This separation creates limited liability for the owners. Any legal liability as a result of business activities is limited to the amount of their investment in the company. A corporation is the most attractive form of business for raising capital because of the limited liability of the owners and because it provides access to alternative methods of raising funds. These methods include borrowing money, selling bonds, and issuing preferred or common stock. It is, in fact, the shareholders that own the company. Ownership of common stock generally carries with it the right to vote at the annual shareholders' meeting. It is the common shareholders who elect the board of directors, who in turn appoint the officers of the corporation. Furthermore, publicly traded shares are easily transferred whenever the shareholder wishes to do so. The corporation is therefore long-lived and able to continue in existence indefinitely, unless restricted by its charter. Thus the business would not cease to exist abruptly, as may be the case with the death of a partner or proprietor. Finally, corporations generally pay a lower tax rate than individuals.

Incorporation is not without its share of disadvantages, however. Federal or provincial law governs the provisions under which the company's charter (raison d'être) is granted. Provincial registration restricts the company to within a particular province. Another disadvantage is that corporate activities are limited to those specifically granted by its charter. The costs associated with incorporation are generally higher than for other types of business ownership due to the amount of paperwork required by governments and legal implications associated with share offerings. Finally, the major disadvantage of incorporation is the non-deductibility of dividends in determining the company's net income. Shareholders must pay taxes on the dividends they receive which are paid from after-tax earnings. Dividends are thus subject to double taxation.

Keep in mind that there is no one type of ownership structure that is best. Each situation must be looked at individually to determine the most advantageous choice, and once this choice has been made, it is not irrevocable. The type of structure can be changed as circumstances dictate. It is often a good idea to obtain professional advice before making such an important decision.

Source: Concordia University Business Consultants, "Carefully Evaluate Your Firm's Ownership Structure," In: *Profits*, by Federal Business Development Bank, 11 (Autumn 1991), p. 4.

Comparison of Organization Forms

Owners of new businesses have some important decisions to make in choosing an organizational form. Not only must they consider a number of different factors, new owners might find that the variables they examine to make their decision may be in conflict. One consideration might suggest that a partnership is the best route, while another might indicate that a corporation is best. Table 2-1 provides an overview of the most important criteria. The bottom line in the table suggests a favoured form of business organization given the particular list of factors above.

Perspective in Finance

The decision as to which organizational form is most suitable should include an evaluation of the relative costs involved in carrying out the firm's business affairs. The decision to minimize organizational costs complies with the firm's goal of maximizing the shareholder's wealth.

Management Control and Regulations

The sole proprietor has absolute control of the firm and is not restrained by government regulation. With the few exceptions relating to assumed or fictitious names and special licensing, the sole proprietorship may operate in any province without complying with registration and qualification requirements. The general partnership is likewise not impeded by any significant government regulations. However, since control within this legal form of business is normally based upon the majority vote, an increase in the number of partners reduces each partner's voice in management. The limited partnership is characterized by a restricted separation of ownership from control: there is no such separation in the sole proprietorship and the general partnership. As to government regulation, the limited partnership requires detailed registration to inform the public of the authority of the individual partners. Within the corporation, the control factor has two dimensions: (1) the formal control vested in the shareholders having the majority of the voting common shares and (2) the functional control exercised by the corporate officers in conducting the daily operations. For the small corporation, these two controls usually rest in the same individuals. However, as the size of the corporation increases, the two facets become distinctly separate.[18] Finally, the corporation is encumbered with substantial government regulation in terms of registrations as well as compliance with statutory requirements. For businesses wanting to operate in different provinces of Canada, the provisions governing incorporation are found in the Canada Business Corporation Act (CBCA). Under this act, the corporation is treated as a natural person, which has rights, powers and privileges of a natural person. Furthermore, the CBCA vests the corporate director with managing the business and affairs of the corporation. However, the Act recognizes that the power of the director's management is subject to the corporation's bylaws or unanimous shareholder agreement.[19]

Organization Requirements and Costs

In every instance, the sole proprietorship is the "cheapest" organization to organize. Generally, no legal requirement must be satisfied; the owner simply begins operating. (Exceptions do exist, depending upon the nature of the product or service.) The general partnership may possibly be as inexpensive to create as the proprietorship, in that no legal criterion must be met. However, if a partnership is to be functional in the long term, a written agreement is usually advisable. The importance of this contract cannot be overemphasized. This document, if properly prepared, may serve to avoid personal misunderstandings and may even minimize several disadvantages usually associated with the partnership form of organization. The limited partnership is more expensive, owing to statutory requirements. The partners must provide a certification of the general partners and the limited partners and indicate the rights and responsibilities of each. Also, a written

---

[18]Considerable attention has been given to the potential conflict between management and shareholders. Approaches which can be used to obtain more homogeneous expectations between investors and managers include encouraging managers to adopt more of a private owner's perspective by relating their compensation more closely to share-price performance and increasing the use of debt to buy back the firm's common shares.

[19]CCH Editorial Staff. *Canada Business Corporations Act with Regulations 1991*, 8th ed. (Don Mills, Ont: CCH Canadian Limited, 1991).

TABLE 2-1 Selection of Legal Form of Organization

Form of Organization	Organizational Requirements and Costs	Liability of the Owners	Continuity of the Business
Sole proprietorship	Minimum requirements: Generally no registration or filing fee.	Unlimited liability.	Dissolved upon proprietor's death.
General partnership	Minimum requirements: Generally no registration or filing fee. Partnership agreement not legally required but is strongly suggested.	Unlimited liability.	Unless partnership agreement specifies differently, dissolved upon withdrawal or death of partner.
Limited partnership	Moderate requirements: Written agreement often required, including identification of general and limited partners.	General partners: Unlimited liability. Limited partners: Liability limited to investment in company.	General partners: Same as general partnership. Limited partners: Withdrawal or death does not affect continuity of business.
Corporation	Most expensive and greatest requirements: Filing fees; compliance with federal and provincial regulations for corporations.	Liability limited to investment in company.	Continuity of business unaffected by shareholder withdrawal or death.
Form of organization normally favoured	Proprietorship or general partnership	Limited partnership or corporation	Corporation

agreement is compulsory. The corporation is typically the most expensive form of business. As stated earlier, compliance with numerous statutory provisions is required. The legal costs and the time involved in creating a corporation exceed those for the other legal types of organization. In short, the organizational requirements increase as the formality of the organization increases. However, this consideration is of minimum importance, and to forgo a choice because of its initial cost may prove to be expensive in the long run.

Liability of the Owners

The sole proprietorship and the general partnership have an inherent disadvantage: the feature of unlimited liability. For these organizations, there is no distinction between business assets and personal assets. The creditors lending money to the business can require the owners to sell personal assets if the firm is financially unable to repay its loans. The limited partnership alleviates this problem for the limited partner. However, a limited partner must be careful to maintain this protection. Failure to give due notice or to refrain from actively participating in management may result in the loss of this privilege. The corporation has a definite advantage in terms of limited liability, since creditors are able only to look at corporate assets in resolving claims. However, this advantage for the corporation may not always be realized. If a firm is small, its president may be required to guarantee a loan personally. Also, if the corporate form is being used to defraud creditors, the courts may "pierce the corporate veil" and hold the owners personally liable. In fact, the CBCA has extended the principle of statutory liability to cover a greater range of actions concerning the payment of corporate funds by cor-

Transferability of Ownership	Management Control and Regulations	Attractiveness for Raising Capital	Income Taxes
May transfer ownership in company name and assets.	Absolute management freedom, negligible formal requirements.	Limited to proprietor's personal capital.	Income from the business is taxed as personal income to the proprietor.
Requires the consent of all partners.	Majority vote of partners required for control; negligible formal requirements.	Limited to partners' ability and desire to contribute capital.	Income from the business is taxed as personal income to the partners.
General partners: Same as general partnership.	General partners: Same as general partnership.	General partners: Same as general partnership.	General partners: Same as general partnership.
Limited partners: May sell interest in the company.	Limited partners: Not permitted any involvement in management.	Limited partners: Limited liability provides a stronger inducement in raising capital	Limited partners: Same as general partnership.
Easily transferred by transferring shares.	Shareholders have final control, but usually board of directors controls company policies.	Usually the most attractive form for raising capital.	The corporation is taxed on its income and the shareholder is taxed when dividends are paid.
Depends upon the circumstances.	Control: Depends upon the circumstances. Regulation: Proprietorship and general partnership.	Corporation	Depends upon the circumstances.

porate directors.[20] Nevertheless, the limitation of liability is usually an important concern in the selection of the legal organization.

Continuity of Business

The continuity of the business is largely a function of the legal form of organization. The sole proprietorship is immediately dissolved upon the owner's death. Likewise, the general partnership is terminated upon the death or withdrawal of a partner. This weakness can be minimized in the partnership through a written agreement which specifies what is to occur if a partner dies or desires to withdraw. Failure to incorporate such a provision into the agreement may result in a forced liquidation of the firm, possibly at an inopportune time. Finally, the corporation offers the greatest degree of continuity. The status of the investor simply does not affect the corporation's existence. The corporate business organization has a distinct advantage in its perpetual nature.

Transferability of Ownership

Transferability of ownership is intrinsically neither good nor bad; its desirability depends largely upon the owners' preferences. In certain businesses the owners may want the option to evaluate any prospective new investors.

[20]The CBCA specifies situations in which a director is severally liable because of a vote on a corporate resolution that has led to a corporate loss. These situations include: the consideration received for the issue of shares is less than fair market value; payments of commissions which are not reasonable to any person who is involved with the repurchase of shares; payments of indemnity to corporate directors or officers, which are inappropriate to those specified in the act; and payments (e.g., financial assistance) to shareholders, which are inappropriate to those specified in the act.

In other circumstances, unrestricted transferability may be preferred. The sole proprietor has complete freedom to sell any interest in the business. At the other extreme, members of a general partnership may not sell or assign their interest without the prior consent of the remaining partners. However, this limitation may be removed by providing otherwise in the partnership agreement. The limited partnership has a twofold nature: the assignment of interest by general partners requires the prior consent of the other partners, while the limited partners have unrestricted transferability. The corporation affords the investors complete flexibility in transferring their interest.

Income Taxes

Income taxes frequently have a major impact upon the owner's selection of the legal form of business. The sole proprietorship and the partnership organization are not taxed as separate entities; the owners report business profits on their personal tax returns. The earnings from the company are taxable to the owner, regardless of whether these profits have been distributed to the investors. This feature may place the owner in a cash squeeze if taxes are due but income has been retained within the company. On the other hand, the corporation is taxed as a separate and distinct entity. This same income is taxed again when distributed to the shareholder in the form of dividends. Determination of the best form of legal entity with respect to taxes should be based upon the objective of maximizing the after-tax profits to the owners.[21] This decision depends partly upon the tax rates for individuals relative to rates for the corporation. Also, whether or not the profits are to be retained in the business or paid as dividends to the common shareholders also is important.

Attractiveness for Raising Capital

As a result of the limited liability, the ease of transferring ownership through the sale of common shares, and the flexibility in dividing the shares, the corporation is the most effective business entity in terms of attracting new capital. In contrast, the unlimited liability of the sole proprietorship and the general partnership are deterrents to raising equity capital. Between these extremes, the limited partnership does provide limited liability for the limited partners, which has a tendency to attract wealthy investors. However, the impracticality of having a large number of partners and the restricted marketability of an interest in a partnership prevent this form of organization from competing effectively with the corporation. The article on page 43 examines some of the problems that can occur in a limited partnership.

THE CANADIAN INCOME TAX SYSTEM

Objectives of Income Tax System

The major objective of the tax reform measures of 1987 was to generate revenues in order to finance the federal Government's expenditures. Tax reform was also implemented to achieve social and economic objectives such as (1)

[21]The firm's objective is to maximize the shareholder wealth. However, since no risk is involved in selecting the form of business, maximizing profits will also maximize wealth.

BASIC FINANCIAL MANAGEMENT IN PRACTICE

Agency Problems in Canadian Oil and Gas Limited Partnerships

An agency problem exists if the principal finds it too expensive to monitor all of the agent's actions and to specify exactly what the agent should do in every conceivable situation, in order to preclude the agent from enhancing his well-being at the expense of the principal. Principals delegate decision-making authority to agents due to lack of time and expertise. Because agents typically know more about their tasks than their principals, any business enterprise involving an agency relationship is not expected to function as well as it would if all information were costlessly shared or if the incentives of principal and agent were aligned. Lack of alignment leads to agency costs, and much research has been devoted to determining arrangements which will minimize these costs.

Agency theory also applies to one segment of the Canadian oil and gas industry, the limited partnership—a popular organizational arrangement employed to finance exploration and development activities.

In this arrangement, the liability of the limited partners is limited to the money they are required to contribute to the partnership as specified by the cost-sharing arrangement. Such is not the case for the general partner, who has unlimited liability. For this reason, the general partner has exclusive control over the activities of the partnership. Thus, the limited partners are the principals and the general partner, the agent.

Tax Considerations

Since oil and gas drilling programs are characterized by large losses in the first year of operation, a partnership is attractive, as it allows these losses to flow to the individual tax returns of the limited partners, an arrangement usually not possible if the venture is organized as a corporation. Although the partnership has considerable freedom in allocating the costs or losses incurred among the partners, the Income Tax Act requires that the partner to whom the cost component accrues must literally bear the cost. The person's capital account must be directly affected (that is, his investment must be "at risk").

Agency Problems

Although there are different types of arrangements for sharing the partnership revenues and costs, certain agency problems are common to all. For example, because the general partner or its affiliate act as operator of the drilling program, it provides goods and services to the partnership for a fee. Since the general partner incurs only a fraction of the fee as a member of the partnership but receives all of the fee as provider of the good or service, the temptation to artificially inflate the fee is present. It is often difficult to establish whether and to what extent costs have been inflated, as the limited partners lack the necessary information, expertise and time.

The general partner is usually involved in several drilling prospects, giving rise to another agency problem—divergence of his interests from those of the limited partners. For example, the general partner may direct one partnership's drilling activities to acquire geological data relevant to the general partner's other drilling prospects in the area. In the industry, this practice is referred to as "proving up the general partner's prospects with the limited partner's funds."

One of the major types of cost and revenue sharing arrangements between general and limited partners is the functional allocation sharing arrangement. In this type of arrangement, the limited partner bears all of the costs which are immediately deductible for tax purposes (intangible costs), while the general partner bears all of the costs that must be capitalized and then depreciated for tax purposes (tangible costs). The general partner receives a certain percentage of all revenues. This arrangement is designed to maximize the limited partner's tax deductions early in the life of the partnership. Usually, a large percentage of the limited partners' investments in the first year is tax deductible.

Although this arrangement creates a very favourable tax situation, agency problems can result. Because most of the drilling costs are expensed while most of the well completion costs must be capitalized and depreciated, the general partner bears almost none of the initial costs of drilling and almost all of the final costs of well completion. This creates a tendency for the general partner to under-complete wells, that is, abandon wells which should be completed. The undercompletion problem is especially acute when wells of marginal profitability are considered. The problem disappears when the well is very profitable.

Other forces can act to reduce exploitation of the limited partnerships. If the general partner builds

Continued on page 44

Continued from page 43

a reputation for high payouts to limited partners, he will be able to obtain financing in future limited partnerships on more favourable terms. On the other hand, a general partner with a history of low payouts to limited partners would have a difficult time obtaining financing.

Clearly, such considerations are more important to a general partner expecting to be in the oil and gas business for many years. Developing a favourable reputation is not important to a fly-by-night operator.

Source: Jacques A. Schnabel and Philip C. Chang, "Agency Problems in Canadian Oil and Gas Limited Partnerships," CGA Magazine (November, 1989), pp. 45–49.

to stimulate the economy, (2) to encourage investment in certain regions or economic sectors, and (3) to encourage particular economically disadvantaged groups within our society. For example, the federal Government can use tax legislation to stimulate the economy by reducing the taxes payable of an individual. The underlying assumption of this type of economic stimulation is that an increase in discretionary income would increase the demand for products and thereby generate new jobs. Tax reform provided an opportunity for Revenue Canada to replace many of the existing deductions with a tax credit system for individuals. For example, tax credits have been created for individuals who are dependents or individuals who attend university and pay university tuition. In summary, the federal Government introduced the Tax Reform Bill to create a taxation system which fulfilled the following goals: stability and dependability of revenues, fairness, progressiveness, simplicity and ease of compliance, social and economic goals, balance between sectors, and international competitiveness.[22]

Types of Taxpayers

In order to understand the tax system, we must first ask what constitutes a "taxpayer." The Canadian Income Tax Act includes within the definition of a taxpayer, any person whether or not liable to pay tax.[23] The concept of a person includes an individual, a corporate or political body, heirs, executors, administrators, or other legal representatives of such a person.[24] The definition of an individual applies not only to the employees of a company and self-employed persons owning their own business, but also to the members of a partnership.[25]

These individuals report their income to Revenue Canada by filing personal tax returns. In a similar manner, a corporation reports its income by filing a corporate tax return as a separate legal entity with Revenue Canada. The owners (shareholders) of a corporation need not report corporate earnings in their personal tax returns, except when all or part of the profits are distributed in the form of dividends. Finally, estates and trusts must also file

[22]The Honourable Michael H. Wilson "Income Tax Reform. Tax Reform 1987." (Department of Finance, Canada, 1987).

[23]CCH Canadian Limited, "Interpretation," *Canadian Income Tax Act With Regulations 1991*. Part XVII Section 248(1): 61st edition, (Don Mills, Ontario, 1991).

[24]Ibid.

[25]Each partner reports their individual share of the partnership's income and pays taxes on this share of the income.

a tax return with Revenue Canada but these entities pay taxes on any income generated using the same rules as an individual.[26]

Although the taxes levied on income earned by an estate or a trust represent an important source of income to the federal Government, neither is especially relevant to the financial manager. Since most firms of any size are corporations, we will restrict our interest to the corporation. In doing so, a caveat is necessary. Tax legislation can be quite complex, with numerous exceptions to most general rules. The laws can also change quickly, and certain details discussed here may no longer apply. It could be said appropriately that "a little knowledge is a dangerous thing."

Tax Considerations

There are several aspects of existing tax legislation that have relevance for the financial manager, these being (1) the effects of depreciation on the taxpayer's taxes, (2) the tax treatment of non-capital losses, (3) the recognition of net capital gains and losses, and (4) the deductions and credits for dividends. Let us look at each of these tax provisions in turn.[27]

Depreciation

The Canadian Government encourages taxpayers to invest in fixed assets for business use by permitting them to write off (depreciate) the investment value of an asset through the use of the capital cost allowance system. The amount of depreciation (write-off) claimed by a taxpayer for tax purposes on an asset is called a **capital cost allowance (CCA)**.

Revenue Canada uses the term, **capital cost (C_0)**, to describe the concept of investment value for an asset. Hence, the capital cost of an asset is the sum of the purchase cost of the asset and any incremental cost associated with the installation, engineering, training or administration of the purchase. In addition, Revenue Canada defines **Undepreciated Capital Cost (UCC)** of an asset as the capital cost of the asset net of any capital cost allowances claimed by the firm.

The capital cost allowance system classifies all depreciable assets into groups, called assets classes, which specify both the method of depreciation and the capital cost allowance rate.[28] Revenue Canada administers the capital cost allowance system on the basis of asset classes and not on the basis of an individual depreciable asset. As a result, we define the UCC of an asset class as the sum of UCCs for each depreciable asset in the class.

When a taxpayer depreciates or writes off a portion of the undepreciated capital cost of an asset class each year, the taxpayer is reporting the sum of capital cost allowances from the depreciation of assets in an asset class. Each taxpayer is entitled to claim any amount of capital cost allowances up to a maximum which is limited by the CCA rate of the asset class. The capital cost allowance is determined as follows:

$$CCA = (UCC_n)(d)$$

where   CCA = the capital cost allowance in year n

---

[26]CCH Canadian Limited, "Trusts And Their Beneficiaries," *Canadian Income Tax Act, With Regulations 1991.* Part I Section 104(2): 61st edition, (Don Mills, Ontario, 1991).

[27]The effect of each of these considerations on taxes payable is examined in Appendix 2A.

[28]For a more detailed discussion of asset classes, see Chapter 7.

$$UCC_n = \text{the undepreciated capital cost of the asset class after}$$
$$\text{adjustments for dispositions or purchases made during}$$
$$\text{year } n$$

$$d = \text{the capital cost allowance rate}$$

The majority of depreciable assets belong to asset classes which require the declining balance method to write off the asset's value. As long as a depreciable asset is being employed for business use, a taxpayer is entitled to claim the capital cost allowances from the depreciation of the asset. By reporting the capital cost allowances from each asset class, the taxpayer reduces the taxable income of the business, and in turn, the taxpayer pays less in taxes.

The sale of a depreciable asset causes the taxpayer to lose its claim to any future capital cost allowances from this asset. In addition, Revenue Canada requires the taxpayer to adjust the undepreciated capital cost of the asset class by subtracting the undepreciated capital cost of the asset from the undepreciated capital cost of the asset class.

The sale of an asset may also cause the termination of both the project and the asset class. For tax purposes, Revenue Canada requires that the firm adjust for capital cost allowance deductions which are lost because the asset is sold and the asset class is terminated. If the proceeds from the sale of the asset or salvage value is greater than the undepreciated capital cost of the asset class, the taxpayer has written off the asset too rapidly. In this situation, Revenue Canada requires the taxpayer to report recaptured depreciation because the asset class is being terminated. The amount of recaptured depreciation to be reported is determined from the difference between the undepreciated capital cost (UCC_n) of the asset class and the lessor of either the salvage value (SV_n) or the original capital cost (C_0) of the asset to be salvaged.

$$\frac{\text{recaptured}}{\text{depreciation}} = UCC_n - \text{lesser of: } \begin{cases} SV_n \\ \text{or} \\ C_0 \end{cases}$$

Since both the salvage value and the original capital cost are greater than the UCC_n of the asset class in this situation, the recaptured depreciation is added to the taxpayer's taxable income.

If the salvage value is less than the undepreciated capital cost of the asset class, the taxpayer has written off the asset too slowly. In this situation, Revenue Canada requires the taxpayer to report a terminal loss because the asset class is being terminated. The amount of terminal loss to be reclaimed is determined from the difference between the undepreciated capital cost of the asset class and the salvage value of the asset to be salvaged.

$$\text{terminal loss} = UCC_n - SV_n$$

The terminal loss is subtracted from the taxpayer's taxable income since the salvage value (SV_n) is less than the UCC_n of the asset class.

Non-Capital Loss Deduction

If a corporation incurs an operating loss in a given fiscal year, this corporation is permitted to apply this type of non-capital loss as a deduction against income earned in other years.[29] In other words, Revenue Canada permits a

[29]A non-capital loss is defined in section 118(8)(b) of the Income Tax Act. Eligible losses include losses from business, losses from property, and allowable business investment losses.

carryback or a carryforward of a non-capital loss. The taxpayer must first apply the loss against income in three prior years (carryback). If this loss has not been completely absorbed by the income in these three years, then the loss may be carried forward to each of the seven following years (carryforward). At that time, any loss still remaining may no longer be used as a tax deduction. To illustrate, a 1994 operating loss may be used as a deduction against income earned in 1991, 1992 and 1993. As a result, this deduction lowers taxable income which in turn can be used to reclaim taxes paid, in whole or in part, during 1991, 1992, and 1993. If any part of the loss still remains, this amount may be used to reduce taxable income, if any, during the seven-year period of 1995 through 2001. It should be noted that the income or losses from business operations for both the partnership and the proprietorship flow through to the individual and are taxed at this level. In other words, non-capital losses of the partnership or the proprietorship are combined with the individual's other non-capital losses and are eligible for the carryback or the carryforward provisions.[30]

Net Capital Gains and Losses

A corporation incurs a capital gain if the selling price is greater than the purchase cost for both depreciable and capital assets; conversely, a capital loss occurs if the selling price is less than the purchase cost of a capital asset. As a result of 1987 tax reform measures, both capital gains and capital losses continue to be given preferential tax treatment. Revenue Canada levies a tax on the following portions of both capital gains and capital losses: one-half for years prior to 1987, two-thirds for 1988 and 1989, and three-quarters for years after 1989. A corporation that has capital losses which exceed capital gains in any year may not deduct these net capital losses from ordinary income. Revenue Canada requires that net capital losses be first carried back and applied against net capital gains in each of the three years before the current year.[31] If the loss is not completely used in the three prior years, any remaining loss may be carried forward and applied against any net capital gains indefinitely. For example, if a corporation has an $80,000 net capital loss in 1993, it may apply this loss against any net capital gains in 1990, 1991, and 1992. If any net capital loss remains, it may be carried forward indefinitely.

Net capital gains or losses which are incurred by either the partnership or proprietorship flow through to the individual and are taxed at this level. As a result, the net capital gains or losses which are incurred by either the partnership or the proprietorship are combined with the individual's other net capital gains or losses. Furthermore, Revenue Canada now permits the individual to benefit from a lifetime capital gains deduction of $100,000 or a lifetime taxable capital gains deduction of (3/4)($100,000) or $75,000. For example, suppose each individual of a partnership receives $10,000 in net capital gains or (3/4)($10,000) = $7,500 in net taxable capital gains from the sale of marketable securities in 1991. Each individual would be eligible to use $7,500 of the lifetime taxable capital gains deduction of $75,000 to effec-

---

[30]During the early years of a small business, it is highly likely that the business may incur non-capital losses. This flow-through provision in the Income Tax Act becomes an important consideration when choosing whether to incorporate or to remain either as a proprietorship or partnership.

[31]A net capital loss is defined in section 111(8)(a) of the Income Tax Act. Capital losses exclude losses on listed property and allowable business investment losses.

tively reduce the taxes payable on this type of income to zero. Thus, Revenue Canada provides preferential tax treatment for individuals receiving this type of income and who have not exhausted their $75,000 lifetime taxable capital gains deduction.

Deductions and Credits for Dividends

The earnings generated by a corporation are potentially subject to "double taxation," first at the corporate level and then at the shareholder level as the firm's profits are distributed in the form of dividends. However, Revenue Canada permits corporations to deduct from their taxable income all dividends received from a taxable Canadian corporation or a subsidiary corporation that is a Canadian resident. For instance, if corporation A receives dividends of $1,000 in its fiscal year from ownership of common shares in a taxable Canadian corporation B, the $1,000 in dividends received will be deducted from taxable income of corporation A and result in no corporate taxes payable on intercorporate dividends received. It should be noted that dividends received by either the partnership or the proprietorship from other Canadian corporations are taxed at the individual's level and not at the level of the business. However, individuals are able to deduct a dividend tax credit from their taxes payable. The dividend tax credit is determined as follows:

$$\text{Dividend Tax Credit} = 13.33\% \text{ of Grossed-up Amount of Dividends}$$

where, Grossed-up Amount = (Dividend Amount) + (25% of Dividend Amount)

As a result, Revenue Canada enables individuals to diminish the effect of "double taxation" on their dividend income by deducting the dividend tax credit from their taxable income.

Other Tax Considerations

Revenue Canada classifies corporations for tax purposes as either a public corporation, a private corporation, a Canadian-controlled private corporation or other corporations. In effect, the "public corporation" is differentiated from the "private corporation" on the basis of whether any of the corporation's shares are listed on a Canadian stock exchange. Furthermore, the "Canadian-controlled private corporation" is differentiated from a "private corporation" on the basis of control.[32]

Canadian-Controlled Private Corporations (CCPCs) enjoy a lower basic corporate tax rate on active business income as compared to public corporations.[33] The lower basic corporate tax rate for CCPCs occurs because of the Small Business Deduction (SBD). The SBD reduces the net federal tax rate to 12.84 percent on active business income for CCPCs. However, Revenue Canada does place a limit of $200,000 on the amount of income that the CCPC can use to determine the amount of the deduction. Furthermore, if the shares of a CCPC meet the requirements of a qualified small business corpo-

---

[32]Robert E. Beam and Stanley N. Laiken, "Integration for Business and Investment Income of the Private Corporation"; In: *Introduction To Federal Income Taxation In Canada*, 11th edition, (CCH Canadian Limited, Don Mills, Ontario: 1990–91).

[33]The term "active business" is defined in section 125(7)(a) of the Income Tax Act. The term includes any business of a corporation other than that of a specified investment business or a personal services business.

ration share, they are eligible for an additional capital gains exemption of $400,000 or a taxable capital gains exemption of $300,000. Thus, the owners of CCPC shares may be eligible for a total capital gains exemption of $500,000 or a taxable capital gains exemption of $375,000.

Given the globalization of the economy, income may originate in a foreign country. As a financial manager, you would obviously consider the firm's place of residence for tax purposes when deciding where to locate your business, since a firm can minimize its taxes by reporting as much income in the low-tax-rate countries and as little as possible in the high-tax-rate countries. Of course, other factors, such as political risk, may discourage your efforts to minimize taxes across national borders. Most Canadian tax treaties with foreign countries require that income be taxed first in the country where it was earned. If income originates in a foreign country, the tax rates and the method of taxing the firm frequently vary. Table 2-2 sheds some light as to basic differences in tax rates in several industrialized countries. In some cases, Canada levies a higher tax rate than that of the country where it was earned. If under these circumstances the firm is a resident of Canada, it will pay taxes to Revenue Canada at the higher tax rate. However, Revenue Canada provides tax relief on the portion of taxes owed to the country where the income is earned through the use of the foreign tax credit.

In addition to this type of tax credit, the federal government provides an investment tax credit to corporations in order to stimulate new investment in Canada in areas of scientific research and experimental development. Again, the investment tax credit reduces federal taxes payable and is determined as a percentage of qualifying expenditures net of government grants or other forms of related government or non-government assistance.[34]

Perspective in Finance

Few financial managers know and understand complex tax law. The fact is you need not be a tax wizard to be a good financial manager. However, you do need to know how taxes relate to investment decisions, financing decisions, and dividend policies of the firm.

Country	Income Tax Rate[1]	Value Added Tax
France	34–42%	5.5–22%
Japan	28–37.5%	3% Consumption Tax
Korea	20–34%	10%
United Kingdom	25–33%	17.5%
United States	15-34%	none; State and Local taxes vary up to 8%

[1] Range includes preferential tax treatment for small business
Source: *International Tax Summaries*, Cooper & Lybrand International Tax Network (New York: John Wiley, 1992).

TABLE 2-2
Comparison of Foreign Corporate Taxes

---

[34]Generally, the Government of Canada enacts legislation on tax investment tax credits when capital investment needs to be accelerated. The investment tax credit allows for a tax credit on net qualifying expenditures of up to 20%–35% depending on the type of corporation and the location within Canada. This is a direct tax credit; that is, it can be used to offset taxes that are due. If the firm has no current taxes, the firm has been able to carry it back for up to three years or forward for up to ten years.

Implications of Taxes in Financial Decision Making

Taxes play an important role in financial decision making. Hardly a decision is made by the financial manager without considering the impact of taxes. Although a complete understanding of these tax consequences is not feasible until the underlying financial principles have been presented, a brief integration of taxes into the three primary decision areas of the financial manager is helpful.

Taxes and Capital Investment Decisions

As will be explained in more depth later, income taxes are a significant element in evaluating the firm's investment decisions. When the company is analyzing the possible acquisition of a plant or equipment, the returns from the investment should be measured on an after-tax basis. Otherwise the company will be omitting an important variable. For example, suppose management is considering the purchase of production equipment costing $1,000. If the $1,000 is spent, the financing of the expenditure must come from after-tax dollars. Stated differently, the firm may keep this $1,000 without having to be concerned about any tax consequences. However, if the capital is expended on a capital project (plant or equipment), a portion of the cash inflows to be received from the investment will be taxed. Ignoring the time value of money, assume the project, if accepted, is expected to generate $1,200 in cash inflows before taxes, which at first might appear to be satisfactory. However, this $1,200 is before-tax dollars, which simply means that the firm has not paid the taxes that will be owed as a result of receiving these funds. If the company eventually has to pay $300 in taxes, only $900 will be received in cash flows after-tax, which is the amount directly comparable with the $1,000 investment cost. Clearly, the project is undesirable, but the taxes had to be included in the analysis before this fact could be determined.

In computing the after-tax cash flows which result from an investment decision, we should note that the method of depreciation affects both the amount of capital cost allowance to be declared and the timing of the capital cost allowance to be declared. Capital cost allowances reduce taxable income which in turn reduces taxes payable and increases the amount of cash flow after taxes. A tax depreciation method, such as the declining balance method, will have an impact upon the timing of cash flows since there is a greater amount of capital cost allowances available to reduce taxable income during the earlier years of the project's life as compared to the smaller amounts of capital cost allowances available in later years. In this manner, lower taxes are paid in the initial years with counterbalancing higher taxes in later years. If the time value of money is recognized, this shift in taxes to later time periods is beneficial.

Taxes and the Firm's Capital Structure

The second major policy variable for the financial manager is to determine the appropriate mix between debt and equity financing. Extensive controversy on this issue has continued for well over three decades. However, regardless of the different views maintained, the tax laws do give debt financing a definite cost advantage over preferred shares and common shares.[35] As

[35]The tax advantage of debt for the corporation is a tax disadvantage to the investor holding the firm's debt. This issue is addressed more fully in Chapter 9.

already noted, interest payments are a tax-deductible expense, while dividend payments to preferred shareholders and to common shareholders may not be used as deductions in computing a corporation's taxable profits.

Taxes and Corporate Dividend Policies

The importance of taxes with respect to the firm's dividend policy is recognized primarily at the common shareholder level rather than at the corporate level. However, since the financial manager's objective is to maximize the common shareholder's wealth, the impact of taxes upon the shareholder is important. Remember that corporate earnings are taxed, whether or not the earnings are paid out in dividends or retained to be reinvested. Yet if the dividends are paid, the investor will be required to report this income. On the other hand, if the profits are retained and reinvested, the price of the company's share should increase. However, until the share is actually sold at a gain, the shareholder is not required to recognize the income. Hence, the opportunity for the firm's common investors to delay the tax payment might influence their preference between capital gains and dividend income. In turn, this preference may affect the corporation's dividend policy.

SUMMARY

Financial managers should be aware of the external influences affecting the company. This chapter has examined three key elements: the financial markets, the legal forms of business organization and the tax structure.

The Financial Markets

The financial markets provide the avenue for bringing together savers and borrowers. Equally important, the markets provide management an indication of the investor's opportunity costs, which suggest the rates of return being required by the investors.

The rates in the financial markets are based on the demand and supply of money in the economy, as reflected in the risk-free rate of return. Also, the investor is rewarded for the potential loss of purchasing power resulting from inflation. The rates are further influenced by the risk level of the investment and the length of time until the security matures.

Legal Forms of Organization

The sole proprietorship is a business operation owned and managed by a single individual. The initiation of this form of business is extremely simple and generally does not involve any substantial organizational costs. The proprietor has complete control of the firm but must be willing to assume full responsibility for the outcome.

The general partnership, which is simply a coming together of two or more individuals, is quite similar to the sole proprietorship. The limited partnership has been created to permit all but one of the partners to have limited liability if this is agreeable to all partners.

The corporation has served to increase the flow of capital from the investment public to the business community. Although larger organizational costs and regulations are imposed upon this legal entity, the corporation is more conducive to raising large amounts of capital. Limited liability, continuity of life, and ease of transfer in ownership, which increases the marketability of the investment, have contributed greatly in attracting large numbers of investors into the business. The formal control of the corporation is vested in the parties having the greatest number of shares. However, day-to-day operations are determined by the corporate officers, who theoretically serve on behalf of the common shareholders.

Taxes

Several forms of taxation exist; however, the primary tax concern in a business relates to income taxation. The Canadian Income Tax System has the following objectives: (1) to provide a revenue source for the federal Government, (2) to stimulate the economy, (3) to encourage particular economically disadvantaged groups within our society and (4) to encourage investment in certain regions or economic sectors. The Canadian Income Tax Act includes within the definition of a taxpayer the following entities: individuals, corporate and political bodies, heirs, executors, administrators, or other legal representatives of such a person. Only information on the corporate entity has been given here.

A corporation's net income for accounting purposes must be adjusted to obtain a corporation's taxable income. The adjustments to net income account for the preferential tax treatment of capital gains and capital losses, the difference between depreciation for accounting purposes and depreciation for tax purposes, and the treatment of dividends received from other Canadian corporations. The taxation system influences the investment decision through both the method and rate of depreciation. The decision of choosing the appropriate mix of financing for a firm is influenced by the cost advantage of debt over the costs of preferred and common share financing. Finally, the decision of choosing whether the firm should distribute dividends or retain earnings is influenced by the tax status of the firm's shareholders.

STUDY QUESTIONS

2-1. Explain the term "opportunity cost" with respect to the cost of funds to the firm.

2-2. Explain the Fisher effect in terms of the impact of inflation on nominal rates of returns.

2-3. Define the "term structure of interest rates."

2-4. Define (a) sole proprietorship, (b) partnership, and (c) corporation.

2-5. Identify the primary characteristics of each form of legal organization.

2-6. Using the following criteria, specify the legal form of business that is favoured: (a) organizational requirements and costs, (b) liability of the owners, (c) continuity of business, (d) transferability of ownership, (e) management control and regulations, (f) capability to raise capital, and (g) income taxes.

2-7. Does a partnership pay taxes on its income? Explain.

2-8. When a corporation receives a dividend from another corporation, how is it taxed?

2-9. What is the difference between a non-capital loss and a net capital loss?

2-1A. (*Inflation and Interest Rates*) What would you expect the nominal rate of interest to be if the real rate is 4 percent and the expected inflation rate is 7 percent? What would the "inflation premium" be?

2-2A. (*Inflation and Interest Rates*) Assume the expected inflation rate to be 4 percent. If the current real rate of interest is 6 percent, what ought the nominal rate of interest be? What about the "inflation premium"?

2-3A. (*Inflation and Interest Rates*) What would you expect the nominal rate of interest to be if the real rate is 5 percent and the expected inflation rate is 3 percent? What would the "inflation premium" be?

2-4A. (*Inflation and Interest Rates*) Assume the expected inflation rate to be 4 percent. If the current real rate of interest is 6 percent, what ought the nominal rate of interest be? What about the "inflation premium"?

APPENDIX 2A: The Corporate Taxation System

In finance, the concept of "free cash flows" is important because of its use in establishing the financial position of the firm. As we have indicated in the Appendix of Chapter 1, one of the components required in determining free cash flows is the amount of taxes payable by the firm. The amount of taxes payable by the firm is dependent on the firm's taxable income. A financial manager must realize that accounting income cannot be used as a substitute for taxable income because of the following differences: the depreciation methods used to determine the capital cost allowances; the tax treatment of capital gains or losses; and the treatment of incorporate dividends. As a result, in the next section we outline the major adjustments used to convert accounting income into taxable income.

COMPUTING TAXABLE INCOME

The accounting income of a corporation, as derived from the Net Income Statement, must be adjusted to obtain taxable income for tax purposes. A corporation's net income, for accounting purposes, is based upon the gross income from all sources, except for allowable exclusions, less any tax-deductible expenses. Gross income equals the firm's dollar sales from its product less the cost of producing or acquiring the product. Tax-deductible expenses include any operating expenses, such as marketing expenses and administrative expenses. Also, the interest expense paid on the firm's outstanding debt is a tax-deductible expense. However, dividends paid to the firm's shareholders, either preferred or common shareholders, are not deductible expenses. Other taxable income includes interest income and dividend income.

To demonstrate how to compute a corporation's net income for accounting purposes, consider the J and S Corporation, a manufacturer of home accessories. The firm, originally established by Kelly Stites, has sales of $5,000,000 for the year. The cost of producing the accessories totalled $2,300,000. Operating expenses were $1,000,000. The firm sold marketable securities for $1,550,000 that originally cost $750,000, but incurred a capital loss of $500,000 on the sale of shares. In addition, this firm received $200,000 in dividends from shares owned in another Canadian corporation. This firm has $1,250,000 in debt outstanding, with a 16 percent interest rate, which resulted in an interest expense of ($1,250,000)(.16) or $200,000. Management paid $100,000 in dividends to the firm's common shareholders. The firm's combined tax rate is

45 percent. The J and S Corporation reported net income of $1,100,000 for accounting purposes as shown in Table 2A-1.

Revenue Canada requires the corporation to report taxable income in order to calculate taxes payable. Table 2A-2 shows the procedure that enables the corporation to adjust the net income for accounting purposes to obtain taxable income.

In extending our example of J and S Corporation, this corporation will claim depreciation for tax purposes as a capital cost allowance of $250,000. The corporation also incurred a recaptured capital cost allowance of $250,000 on the sale of its only fixed asset. The taxable income for J and S would be $1,875,000 as shown in Table 2A-3.

Once we know J and S Corporation's taxable income, we can next determine the amounts of taxes payable by the firm.

Financial Perspective

Returns from a capital investment must be examined on an after-tax basis in order to improve the estimation of the investment's cash flows. As we examine various issues in financial management, the appropriate tax rate to be used will

TABLE 2A-1
Net Income Statement of
J and S Corporation

Sales		$5,000,000
Cost of Goods Sold		$2,300,000
Gross Profit		$2,700,000
Operating Expenses:		
Administrative Expenses	$400,000	
Depreciation Expenses	$150,000	
Marketing Expenses	$450,000	$1,000,000
Operating Income		$1,700,000
Other Income:		
Dividends from other Corporations		$ 200,000
Gain on Investment		$ 800,000
Loss on Shares		$ 500,000
Earnings before Interest and Taxes		$2,200,000
Interest Expense		$ 200,000
Earnings before Taxes		$2,000,000
Tax Provision (@45%)		$ 900,000
Net Income		$1,100,000

Note: Dividends paid to common shareholders ($100,000) are not tax deductible expenses.

TABLE 2A-2
Corporation's Taxable
Income

	Net Income (Accounting purposes)
Add:	Tax Provision
	Taxable Capital Gain
	Accounting Depreciation Expense
	Recaptured Depreciation
	Loss on Investment
Deduct:	Gain from Investment
	Capital Cost Allowance
	Terminal Loss
	Taxable Capital Losses
	Net Income for Tax Purposes
Deduct:	Dividends from other Canadian Corporations
	Taxable Income

	Net Income (Accounting purposes)	$1,100,000
Add:	Tax Provision	900,000
	Taxable Capital Gain (.75)($800,000)	600,000
	Accounting Depreciation Expense	150,000
	Loss on Sale of Shares	500,000
	Recaptured Capital Cost Allowance	250,000
Deduct:	Gain from Sale of Marketable Shares	−800,000
	Capital Cost Allowance	−250,000
	Taxable Capital Losses (.75)($50,000)	−375,000
	Net Income for Tax Purposes	$2,075,000
Deduct:	Dividends from other Canadian Corporations	−200,000
	Taxable Income	$1,875,000

be a tax rate that combines both federal and provincial corporate tax rates. To understand the use of the combined corporate tax rate, we must examine the computation required to determine the total taxes payable by a corporation. Furthermore, we should note the importance of how both revenue size and type of corporation affects the taxes payable by a corporation.

COMPUTING THE TAXES OWED

The calculation which determines federal tax payable for a corporation requires the use of the basic corporate tax rate of 38 percent. However, Revenue Canada allows the basic corporate tax rate to be reduced through various deductions. An example of this type of deduction is the provincial abatement which enables corporations residing in one of the Canadian provinces or territories to reduce the basic corporate tax rate of 38 percent by 10 percent to 28 percent.

Another important deduction that is used to reduce the basic corporate tax rate is the Small Business Deduction (SBD) which can be claimed by Canadian-Controlled Private Corporations (CCPCs). The SBD reduces the net federal tax rate to 12.84 percent on active business income for CCPCs. For example, the net federal tax rate of a CCPC is determined as follows:

	Basic corporate tax rate	38.00%
Deduct:	Provincial abatement	−10.00%
	Federal tax rate	28.00%
Deduct:	Small business deduction	−16.00%
Add:	Federal surtax (3% of 28%)	0.84%
	Net federal tax rate	12.84%

In an attempt to improve on productivity and to facilitate the restructuring of operations, Revenue Canada requires manufacturing and processing profits to be taxed the net federal tax rate of 23.84 percent in 1992, 22.84 percent in 1993 and 21.84 percent in 1994. The corporate tax rate is levied on manufacturing and processing profits other than profits eligible for the small business deduction.

The Government of Canada also levies a corporate surtax of 3 percent on federal taxable income. This corporate surtax is determined as follows:

$$\text{Corporate surtax} = .03 \times (\text{basic corporate tax rate} - \text{provincial abatement}) \times \text{taxable income}$$

$$= .03 \times (.38 - .10) \times \text{taxable income}$$

$$= .0084 \times \text{taxable income}$$

TABLE 2A-4 Total Tax Payable for Corporations		
	Taxable Income (A)	
	Tax at 38 percent on the amount A	
Deduct:	Provincial Abatement (10 percent of A)	
	Small Business Deduction (16 percent of A)	
	Manufacturing & Processing Profit Deduction (5 percent of A)	
Add:	Corporate Surtax $[(0.03)(.38A - .10A)]$	
Deduct:	Foreign Business Income Tax Credit	
	Investment Tax Credit	
	Federal Tax Payable (Part I Tax)	
Add:	Provincial Tax Payable (17 percent of A)	
	Total Tax Payable	

NOTE: The 17 percent tax rate represents an example of a provincial tax rate.

TABLE 2A-5 Provincial Corporate Tax Rates for 1992

Province	*Corporate Tax Rate*
Newfoundland	10–17 percent
Nova Scotia	5–16 percent
Prince Edward Island	10–15 percent
New Brunswick	9–17 percent
Quebec	3.75–6.9 percent
Ontario	10–15.5 percent
Manitoba	10–17 percent
Saskatchewan	10–17 percent
Alberta	6.0–15.5 percent
British Columbia	10–16 percent
Yukon Territory	2.5–10 percent
Northwest Territories	5–12 percent

TABLE 2A-6 Total Taxes for J and S Corporation

	Taxable Income	$1,875,000 (A)
	Tax at 38 percent on the amount A	712,500
Deduct:	Provincial Abatement (10% of A)	− 187,500
Add:	Corporate Surtax $[(0.03)(.38A - .10A)]$	15,750
	Federal Tax Payable (Part I Tax)	$ 540,750
Add:	Provincial Tax Payable (16% of A)	$ 300,000
	Total Tax Payable	$ 840,750

A summary of the calculation used to determine the total taxes payable by a corporation is shown in Table 2A-4.

The Provincial Abatement enables the provinces to impose their own tax rate as shown in Table 2A-5.

The federal Government allows all taxpayers, including corporations, certain tax credits such as the foreign business income tax credit and the investment tax credit. The purpose of each of these tax credits is to reduce federal taxes payable.

Most provinces depend on Revenue Canada to collect their corporate taxes. However three provinces, Quebec, Ontario, and Alberta, collect their own corporate taxes. Provinces which permit the Canadian Government to collect their corporate taxes will apply their own corporate tax rate to taxable income to obtain provincial taxes payable as shown in Table 2A-5. Both federal tax payable and provincial tax payable are then added together to obtain the total tax payable by the firm.

For example, suppose that the headquarters for J and S Corporation were situated in Nova Scotia where the provincial corporate tax rate is 16 percent, the total tax payable for this corporation is shown in Table 2A-6.

	Net Income (Accounting purposes)	$1,200,000
Add:	Tax Provision	800,000
	Taxable Capital Gain (.75)($100,000)	75,000
	Accounting Depreciation Expense	100,000
	Loss on Sale of Land	50,000
	Recaptured Depreciation	150,000
Deduct:	Gain from Sale of Old Machine	−100,000
	Capital Cost Allowance	−110,000
	Taxable Capital Losses (.75)($50,000)	− 37,500
	Net Income for Tax Purposes	$2,127,500
Less:	Dividends from other Canadian Corporations	−100,000
	Taxable Income	$2,027,500
	Taxable Income	$2,027,500 (A)
	Tax at 38 percent on the amount A	770,450
Deduct:	Provincial Abatement (10 percent of A)	−202,750
Add:	Corporate Surtax [(0.03)(.38A − .10A)]	17,031
	Federal Tax Payable (Part I Tax)	$ 584,731
Add:	Provincial Tax Payable (15 percent of A)	$ 304,125
	Total Tax Payable	$ 888,856

NOTE: The $75,000 Griggs paid in dividends is not tax deductible.

Corporate Taxes: An Example

To illustrate certain portions of the tax laws for a corporation, assume that the Griggs Corporation is a public corporation with a net income of $1,200,000 for accounting purposes. The firm reported in its Net Income Statement a tax provision of $800,000 and included in other income $100,000 in dividends received from another Canadian corporation. In turn, it paid $40,000 in interest and $75,000 in dividends. Also included in other income is an accounting gain of $100,000 for the sale of an old machine. For tax purposes, this old machine had originally cost $200,000 and is now sold for $300,000. The undepreciated capital cost of the asset class in which the old machine belongs is $50,000. Since this asset class is being closed upon the sale of this old machine, the firm is required to declare a recaptured depreciation of $150,000 in the fiscal year. The firm reported $100,000 in depreciation expenses for accounting purposes but incurred capital cost allowances of $110,000. Finally, the company sold a piece of land for $50,000 that had cost $100,000 six years ago.

Based upon a federal corporate tax rate of 38 percent and a provincial tax rate of 15 percent, Griggs's tax liability is $888,856, as shown in Table 2A-7.

As mentioned earlier, the appropriate rate to be used in financial analyses is the combined corporate tax rate, the tax rate that combines federal and provincial corporate tax rates. Thus, when making financial decisions involving taxes, always use the combined corporate tax rate in your calculations.

STUDY PROBLEMS (SET A)

2A-1A. (*Taxable Income*) The William B. Waugh Corporation is a large clothing retailer. During the most recent year the company generated sales of $3 million. The combined cost of goods sold and the operating expenses were $2.1 million. The firm reported neither depreciation expenses nor capital cost allowances for the fiscal year. Also, $400,000 in interest expense was paid during the year. The firm received $6,000 during the year in dividend income from 1,000 common shares of a Canadian corporation that had been purchased three years previously. However, these common shares were sold toward the end of the year for $100 per share; its initial cost was $80 per share. The company also sold land that had been recently purchased and had been held for only four months. The selling price was $50,000; the cost was $45,000.

a. Given that William B. Waugh's combined corporate tax rate is 45 percent, determine the corporation's net income by illustrating the Net Income Statement.

b. Determine the corporation's taxable income for tax purposes.

2A-2A. (*Taxable Income*) Sales for L. B. Menielle, Inc., during the past year amounted to $5 million. Gross profits for the year were $3 million. Operating expenses totalled $1 million. The firm reported neither depreciation expenses nor capital cost allowances for the fiscal year. The interest and dividend income from securities owned of a Canadian corporation were $20,000 and $25,000, respectively. The firm's interest expense was $100,000. The firm sold securities on two occasions during the year, receiving a gain of $40,000 on the first sale but losing $50,000 on the second.

a. Given that L. B. Menielle's combined corporate tax rate is 45 percent, determine the corporation's net income by illustrating the Net Income Statement.

b. Determine the corporation's taxable income for tax purposes.

2A-3A. (*Corporate Income Tax*) Sandersen, Inc., sells minicomputers. During the past year the company's sales were $3 million. The cost of its merchandise sold came to $2 million, and cash operating expenses were $400,000. The firm reported a depreciation expense of $100,000, but had capital cost allowances of $100,000 for the fiscal year. Sandersen, Inc., paid $150,000 in interest on bank loans. Also, the corporation received $50,000 in dividend income from another Canadian corporation but paid $25,000 in the form of dividends to its own common shareholders.

a. Given that Sandersen's combined corporate tax rate is 45 percent, determine the corporation's net income by illustrating the Net Income Statement.

b. Determine the corporation's taxable income for tax purposes.

c. Determine the corporation's total taxes payable assuming the federal tax rate is 38 percent, the corporate surtax is 3 percent, the provincial abatement is 10 percent and the provincial tax rate is 16 percent.

2A-4A. (*Corporate Income Tax*) A. Don Drennan, Inc., had sales of $6 million during the past year. The company's cost of goods sold was 70 percent of sales, cash operating expenses were $750,000, and depreciation expenses were $50,000. The firm claimed capital cost allowances of $75,000 for tax purposes. In addition, the firm sold a capital asset (stock) for $75,000, which had been purchased five months earlier at a cost of $80,000.

a. Given that A. Don Drennan's combined corporate tax rate is 45 percent, determine the corporation's net income by illustrating the Net Income Statement.

b. Determine the corporation's taxable income for tax purposes.

c. Determine the corporation's total taxes payable assuming the federal tax rate is 38 percent, the corporate surtax is 3 percent, the provincial abatement is 10 percent and the provincial tax rate is 15 percent.

2A-5A. (*Taxable Income*) The Robbins Corporation is an oil wholesaler. The company's sales last year were $1 million, with the cost of goods sold equal to $600,000. The firm paid interest of $200,000, and its cash operating expenses were $100,000. Depreciation expenses were reported at $150,000, but the firm claimed $125,000 in capital cost allowances during the fiscal year. Furthermore, the firm received $40,000 in dividend income while paying only $10,000 in dividends to its preferred shareholders.

    a. Given that Robbins' combined corporate tax rate is 45 percent, determine the corporation's net income by illustrating the Net Income Statement.

    b. Determine the corporation's taxable income for tax purposes.

2A-6A. (*Corporate Income Tax*) The Fair Corporation had sales of $5 million this past year. The cost of goods sold was $4.3 million and cash operating expenses were $100,000. Depreciation expenses were reported at $100,000, but the firm claimed $125,000 in capital cost allowances. Dividend income totalled $50,000. The firm sold an old machine to terminate the asset class and incurred a recaptured capital cost allowance of $120,000. This sale of the old machine also created a capital gain of $50,000 and an accounting gain of $70,000. The firm received $150 per share from the sale of 1,000 shares of stock. The stock was purchased for $100 per share three years ago.

    a. Given that Fair's combined corporate tax rate is 45 percent, determine the corporation's net income by illustrating the Net Income Statement.

    b. Determine the corporation's taxable income for tax purposes.

    c. Determine the corporation's total taxes payable assuming the federal tax rate is 38 percent, the corporate surtax is 3 percent, the provincial abatement is 10 percent, and the provincial tax rate is 15 percent.

2A-7A. (*Taxable Income*) Sales for J. P. Hulett, Inc., during the past year amounted to $4 million. The firm supplies statistical information to engineering companies. Gross profits totalled $1 million while cash operating and depreciation expenses were $500,000 and $350,000, respectively. The firm reported $340,000 in capital cost allowances for tax purposes. Dividend income for the year was $12,000.

    a. Given that J. P. Hulett's combined corporate tax rate is 45 percent, determine the corporation's net income by illustrating the Net Income Statement.

    b. Determine the corporation's taxable income for tax purposes.

2A-8A. (*Corporate Income Tax*) Anderson, Inc., sells computer software. The company's past year's sales were $5 million. The cost of its merchandise sold came to $3 million. Cash operating expenses were $175,000, plus depreciation expenses totaling $125,000. The firm reported $135,000 in capital cost allowances for tax purposes. An old machine was sold which created a terminal loss of $25,000 and an accounting loss of $30,000. Furthermore, the firm paid $200,000 interest on loans. The firm sold stock during the year, receiving a $40,000 gain on a stock owned for six months but losing $60,000 on stock held four months.

    a. Given that Anderson's combined corporate tax rate is 45 percent, determine the corporation's net income by illustrating the Net Income Statement.

    b. Determine the corporation's taxable income for tax purposes.

    c. Determine the corporation's total taxes payable assuming the federal tax rate is 38 percent, the corporate surtax is 3 percent, the provincial abatement is 10 percent, and the provincial tax rate is 15 percent.

2A-9A. (*Corporate Income Tax*) G. R. Edwin, Inc., reported both a net income of $203,500 and a tax provision of $166,500 for accounting purposes. The firm reported neither depreciation expenses nor capital cost allowances.

a. Determine the corporation's total taxes payable assuming the federal tax rate is 38 percent, the corporate surtax is 3 percent, the provincial abatement is 10 percent and the provincial tax rate is 15 percent.

b. Given the information in Part (a) of this problem, determine the firm's combined corporate tax rate.

STUDY PROBLEMS (SET B)

2A-1B. (*Taxable Income*) The M. M. Roscoe Corporation is a large clothing retailer. During the most recent year the company generated sales of $4 million. The combined cost of goods sold and the operating expenses were $3.2 million. The firm reported neither depreciation expenses nor capital cost allowances for the fiscal year. Also, $300,000 in interest expense was paid during the year. The firm received $5,000 during the year in dividend income from 1,000 common shares of a Canadian corporation that had been purchased three years previously. However, these common shares were sold toward the end of the year for $100 per share; its initial cost was $80 per share. The company also sold land that had been recently purchased and had been held for only four months. The selling price was $55,000; the cost was $45,000.

a. Given that M. M. Roscoe's combined corporate tax rate is 45 percent, determine the corporation's net income by illustrating the Net Income Statement.

b. Determine the corporation's taxable income for tax purposes.

2A-2B. (*Taxable Income*) Sales for J. P. Enterprises during the past year amounted to $5 million. Gross profits for the year were $2.5 million. Operating expenses totalled $900,000. The firm reported neither depreciation expenses nor capital cost allowances for the fiscal year. The interest and dividend income from securities owned of a Canadian corporation were $15,000 and $20,000, respectively. The firm's interest expense was $100,000. The firm sold securities on two occasions during the year, receiving a gain of $45,000 on the first sale but losing $60,000 on the second.

a. Given that J. P. Enterprises' combined corporate tax rate is 45 percent, determine the corporation's net income by illustrating the Net Income Statement.

b. Determine the corporation's taxable income for tax purposes.

2A-3B. (*Corporate Income Tax*) Carter B. Daltan, Inc., sells minicomputers. During the past year the company's sales were $3.5 million. The cost of its merchandise sold came to $2 million, and cash operating expenses were $500,000. The firm reported depreciation expense was $150,000, but had capital cost allowances of $150,000 for the fiscal year. Carter B. Daltan, Inc., paid $165,000 in interest on bank loans. Also, the corporation received $55,000 in dividend income from another Canadian corporation but paid $25,000 in the form of dividends to its own common shareholders.

a. Given that Carter B. Daltan's combined corporate tax rate is 45 percent, determine the corporation's net income by illustrating the Net Income Statement.

b. Determine the corporation's taxable income for tax purposes.

    c. Determine the corporation's total taxes payable assuming the federal tax rate is 38 percent, the corporate surtax is 3 percent, the provincial abatement is 10 percent, and the provincial tax rate is 16 percent.

2A-4B. (*Corporate Income Tax*) Kate Menielle, Inc., had sales of $8 million during the past year. The company's cost of goods sold was 60 percent of sales; cash operating expenses of $750,000; and depreciation expenses of $150,000. The firm claimed capital cost allowances of $275,000 for tax purposes. In addition, the firm sold a capital asset (stock) for $75,000, which had been purchased five months earlier at a cost of $80,000.

    a. Given that Kate Menielle's combined corporate tax rate is 45 percent, determine the corporation's net income by illustrating the Net Income Statement.

    b. Determine the corporation's taxable income for tax purposes.

    c. Determine the corporation's total taxes payable assuming the federal tax rate is 38 percent, the corporate surtax is 3 percent, the provincial abatement is 10 percent, and the provincial tax rate is 15 percent.

2A-5B. (*Taxable Income*) The Burgess Corporation is an oil wholesaler. The company's sales last year were $2.5 million, with the cost of goods sold equal to $700,000. The firm paid interest of $200,000, and its cash operating expenses were $150,000. Depreciation expenses were reported at $50,000, but the firm claimed $25,000 in capital cost allowances during the fiscal year. Furthermore, the firm received $50,000 in dividend income while paying only $15,000 in dividends to its preferred shareholders.

    a. Given that Burgess's combined corporate tax rate is 45 percent, determine the corporation's net income by illustrating the Net Income Statement.

    b. Determine the corporation's taxable income for tax purposes.

2A-6B. (*Corporate Income Tax*) The Aka Corporation had sales of $5.5 million this past year. The cost of goods sold was $4.6 million and cash operating expenses were $125,000. Depreciation expenses were reported at $75,000, but the firm claimed $100,000 in capital cost allowances. Dividend income totalled $50,000. The firm sold an old machine to terminate the asset class and incur a recaptured capital cost allowance of $140,000. This sale of the old machine also created a capital gain of $50,000 and an accounting gain of $70,000. The firm received $125 per share from the sale of 1,000 shares of stock. The stock was purchased for $100 per share three years ago.

    a. Given that Aka's combined corporate tax rate is 45 percent, determine the corporation's net income by illustrating the Net Income Statement.

    b. Determine the corporation's taxable income for tax purposes.

    c. Determine the corporation's total taxes payable assuming the federal tax rate is 38 percent, the corporate surtax is 3 percent, the provincial abatement is 10 percent, and the provincial tax rate is 15 percent.

2A-7B. (*Taxable Income*) Sales for Diana Schubert, Inc., during the past year amounted to $5 million. The firm supplies statistical information to engineering companies. Gross profits totalled $1.2 million while cash operating and depreciation expenses were $500,000 and $400,000, respectively. The firm reported $300,000 in capital cost allowances for tax purposes. Dividend income for the year was $15,000.

    a. Given that Diana Schubert's combined corporate tax rate is 45 percent, determine the corporation's net income by illustrating the Net Income Statement.

    b. Determine the corporation's taxable income for tax purposes.

2A-8B. (*Corporate Income Tax*) Williams, Inc., sells computer software. The company's past year's sales were $4.5 million. The cost of its merchandise sold came to $2.2 million. Cash operating expenses were $175,000, plus depreciation expenses totaling $130,000. The firm reported $135,000 in capital cost allowances for tax purposes. An old machine was sold which created a terminal loss of $25,000 and an accounting loss of $30,000. Furthermore, the firm paid $200,000 interest on loans. The firm sold stock during the year, receiving a $40,000 gain on a stock owned for six months but losing $60,000 on stock held four months.

  a. Given that Williams' combined corporate tax rate is 45 percent, determine the corporation's net income by illustrating the Net Income Statement.

  b. Determine the corporation's taxable income for tax purposes.

  c. Determine the corporation's total taxes payable assuming the federal tax rate is 38 percent, the corporate surtax is 3 percent, the provincial abatement is 10 percent, and the provincial tax rate is 15 percent.

2A-9B. (*Corporate Income Tax*) J. Johnson, Inc., reported both a net income of $198,000 and a tax provision of $162,000 for accounting purposes. The firm reported neither depreciation expenses nor capital cost allowances.

  a. Determine the corporation's total taxes payable assuming the federal tax rate is 38 percent, the corporate surtax is 3 percent, the provincial abatement is 10 percent, and the provincial tax rate is 15 percent.

  b. Given the information in Part (a) of this problem, determine the firm's combined corporate tax rate.

SELECTED REFERENCES

Amihud, Yakov and Haim Mendelson. "Liquidity, Maturity, and the Yields on U.S. Treasury Securities," *The Journal of Finance*, 46 (September 1991), 1411–1426.

Beam, Robert E., and Stanley N. Laiken. *Introduction To Federal Income Taxation In Canada*. 11th ed. Don Mills, Ontario: CCH Canadian Limited, 1990-1991.

Carleton, Willard T., and Ian A. Cooper. "Estimation and Uses of the Term Structure of Interest Rates," *Journal of Finance*, 31 (September 1976), 1067–1084.

Carlton, Colin. "Risk and Return in Canada's Capital Markets: A Historical Perspective," *Canadian Investment Review*, 2 (Spring 1989), 9–15.

CCH Canadian Limited. *Canadian Income Tax Act With Regulations 1991*. 61st ed. Don Mills, Ontario: CCH Canadian Limited, 1991.

Cooper, S. Kerry and Donald R. Fraser. *The Financial Marketplace*. 3rd ed. Don Mills, Ontario: Addison-Wesley Publishing Company, 1990.

Collins, J. Markham and Roger P. Bey. "The Master Limited Partnership: An Alternative to the Corporation," *Financial Management*, 15 (Winter 1986), 5–14.

Culbertson, John M. "The Term Structure of Interest Rates," *Quarterly Journal of Economics*, LXXI, (November 1957), 499–502, 507–509.

Echols, Michael E., and Jan Walter Elliott. "A Quantitative Yield Curve Model for Estimating the Term Structure of Interest Rates," *Journal of Financial and Quantitative Analysis*, 11 (March 1976), 87–114.

Estrella, Arturo and Gikas A. Hardouvelis. "The Term Structure as a Predictor of Real Economic Activity," *The Journal of Finance*, 46 (June 1991), 555–576.

Fama, Eugene F. and Michael C. Jensen. "Separation of Ownership and Control," *The Journal of Law and Economics*, XXVI (June 1983), 301–325.

Fisher, Irving. "Appreciation and Interest," *Publications of the American Economic Association*, XI (August 1986), 23–29.

Ibbotson Roger G. and Rex A. Sinquefield. *Stocks, Bonds, Bills, and Inflation: Historical Returns* (Chicago: Dow Jones-Irwin, 1989).

Jensen, Michael C. "Eclipse of the Public Corporation," *Harvard Business Review* (September–October 1989), 61–75.

Martin, John, Samuel Cox and Richard MacMinn. *The Theory of Finance: Evidence and Applications* Hinsdale, Ill.: Dryden Press, 1988.

McCulloch, J. Huston. "Measuring the Term Structure of Interest Rates," *Journal of Business*, 44 (January 1971), 19–31.

Rose, Andrew K. "Is the Real Interest Rate Stable?" *The Journal of Finance*, 43 (December 1988), 1095–1112.

Van Horne, James C. *Financial Market Rates and Flows*. 2nd ed. Englewood Cliffs, N.J.: Prentice-Hall Publishing Co., 1984.

PART TWO

Valuation and the Management of Long-Term Investments

CHAPTER 3   *Risk and Rates of Return*

- Expected Return

- Risk

- Risk and Expected Return of a Portfolio

- The Investor's Required Rate of Return

- Rates of Return: The Investor's Experience

Since we live in a world of uncertainty, how we see risk is vitally important in almost all dimensions of our life; certainly risk must be considered in our financial decision making. The Greek poet and statesman Solon, writing in the six century B.C. stated:

> There is risk in everything that one does, and no one knows where he will make his landfall when his enterprise is at its beginning. One man, trying to act effectively, fails to foresee something and falls into great and grim ruination, but to another man, one who is acting ineffectively, a god gives good fortune in everything and escape from his folly.[1]

While Solon would have given more credit to Zeus than we might for the outcomes of our ventures, his insight reminds us that little is new in this world, including the need to acknowledge and compensate as best we can for the risks we encounter.

Without intending to be trite, risk means different things to different people, depending upon the context and upon how they feel about chances. For the student, risk is the possibility of failing an exam, or the chance of making his or her best grades. For the coal miner or the oil-field worker, risk is the chance of an explosion in the mine or at the well site. For the retired person, risk means perhaps not being able to live comfortably on a fixed income. For the entrepreneur, risk is the chance that a new venture will fail. In the financial context, we want to understand risk so we can assess the level of risk inherent in an investment.

---

[1]Translated by Arthur W. H. Adkins from the Greek text of Solon's poem "Prosperity, Justice and the Hazards of Life," in M. L. West, *Iambi et Elegi Gracci ante Alexandrum Canttati.* Vol. 2, Oxford, Clarendon Press, 1972.

In addition to an understanding of risk, we want a grasp of the relationship between risk and the rates of return that we might expect to earn on an investment. In the previous chapter, we referred to the discount rate or interest rate as the opportunity cost of funds, but we did not look at the causes for why that rate may be high or low. For example, in 1992, you could buy bonds issued by Dupont that promised to pay an 8.4 percent rate of return. You could, on the other hand, buy bonds issued by Chrysler that would give you a 16 percent rate of return, provided that Chrysler makes the payments to the investors as promised. Why the difference?

In this chapter, we will examine the factors that determine rates of return (discount rates) in the capital markets. We will show how risk is an integral force underlying these returns. We will be answering some important questions about risk and rates of return, including the following:

- What do we mean by expected rates of return? How do we measure the expected return on an investment?

- What is risk? How can it be measured?

- How does diversification of investments affect the risk and expected returns of a portfolio of assets?

- What determines the investor's required rates of return for securities with different levels of risk?

- What can we learn from history about the relationship between risk and investor returns?

EXPECTED RETURN

The expected benefits or returns that an investment generates come in the form of cash flows. Cash flows, not accounting profits, are the relevant variable that the financial manager uses to measure returns. Although accounting information is vital in our study of a company's finances, a large body of evidence suggests that investors or shareholders look behind accounting numbers to discover the underlying economic reality of an investment's or a firm's performance. For example, the economic reality of a firm's operations is ultimately reflected in the cash flow it provides to its investors, not its reported earnings. Specifically, we will identify the firm's free cash flow to be the amount of cash that is available for distributing to its investors not only after operating expenses have been paid, but after any investments have been made that will generate future cash flows. Free cash flow is defined as follows:

$$\text{Free cash flow} = \text{Operating profit} - \text{Income taxes} - \text{Additional investment in assets}$$

This principle of using cash flows to measure returns holds true regardless of the type of investment, whether it is an investment into the firm's operations or an investment into a debt instrument, preferred share, or common share.

Perspective in Finance

Continue to remember that future cash flows, not the reported earnings figure, determine the investor's rate of return.

TABLE 3-1

Measuring the Expected
Return

State of the Economy	Probability of the States[a]	Cash Flows from the Investment	Percentage Returns (Cash Flow/ Investment Cost)
Economic recession	20%	$1000	10% ($1000/$10,000)
Moderate economic growth	30%	1200	12% ($1200/$10,000)
Strong economic growth	50%	1400	14% ($1400/$10,000)

[a]The probabilities assigned to the three possible economic conditions have to be determined subjectively, which requires management to have a thorough understanding of both the investment cash flows and the general economy.

In an uncertain world, an accurate measurement of expected future cash flows is frequently not easy to ascertain for an investor. To illustrate: Assume you are considering an investment costing $10,000, where the future cash flows from owning the security depend upon the state of the economy, and these cash flows have been estimated in Table 3-1.

Thus, in any given year, the investment could produce any one of three possible cash flows depending upon the particular state of the economy. With this information, how should we select the cash flow estimate that means the most in measuring the investment's expected rate of return? Our approach to answering this question relies on descriptive statistics. (A brief review of probability distributions and descriptive statistics is presented in Appendix 3A.) This approach provides an objective method of calculating the expected cash flow.[2] The expected cash flow is simply the weighted average of the possible cash flow outcomes where the weights are the probabilities of the occurrence of the various states of the economy. Let X_i designate the ith possible cash flow; N reflects the number of possible states of the economy, and $P(X_i)$ indicates the probability that the ith cash flow or state of economy will occur. The expected cash flow, $\overline{X}$, may then be calculated as follows:

$$\overline{X} = X_1 P(X_1) + X_2 P(X_2) + ... + X_N P(X_N) \tag{3-1}$$

or

$$\overline{X} = \sum_{i=1}^{N} X_i P(X_i)$$

For the present illustration

$$\overline{X} = (.5)(\$1400) + (.3)(\$1200) + (.2)(\$1000) = \$1260$$

In addition to computing an expected dollar return from an investment, we can also calculate an expected percentage rate of return earned on the $10,000 investment on the security. The last column in Table 3-1 shows that the $1,400 cash inflow, assuming strong economic growth, represents a 14 percent return ($1,400 ÷ $10,000). Similarly, the $1,200 and $1,000 cash flows result in 12 percent and 10 percent returns, respectively. Using these percentage returns in place of the dollar amounts, the expected rate of return, $\overline{R}$, is expressed as follows:

$$\overline{R} = R_1 P(R_1) + R_2 P(R_2) + ... + R_N P(R_N) \tag{3-2}$$

[2]The expected value of cash flows is dependent on the different possible cash flows that occur because of an event and the likelihood or probability of the event occurring.

or

$$\overline{R} = \sum_{i=1}^{N} R_i P(R_i)$$

In our example:

$$\overline{R} = (.5)(14\%) + (.3)(12\%) + (.2)(10\%) = 12.6\%$$

With our concept and measurement of expected returns, let's consider the other side of the investment coin: risk.

RISK

To gain a basic understanding of investment risk, there are at least three fundamental questions that we must ask:

1. What is risk?

2. How do we know the amount of risk associated with a given investment. That is, how do we measure risk?

3. If we choose to diversify our investments by owning more than one asset, as most of us do, will such diversification impact the riskiness of our combined portfolio of investments?[3]

What Is Risk?

Perspective in Finance

Risk is the potential variability in future cash flows. That variability reflects risk can easily be shown by examining a coin toss game. Consider the possibility of flipping a coin—heads you win, tails you lose—for 25 cents with your finance professor. Most likely you would be willing to take on this game, indicating that the utility gained from winning 25 cents is about equal to the utility lost if you lose 25 cents. On the other hand, if the flip is for $1,000 you may be willing to play only if you are offered more than $1,000 if you win, say $1,500 if it turns out heads and lose $1,000 if it turns out tails. In each case the probability of winning and losing is the same; that is, there is an equal chance that the coin will land heads or tails; but the width of the dispersion changes, and that is why the second coin toss is more risky and why it will not be taken unless the payoffs are altered. The key here is the fact that only the dispersion changes; the probability of winning or losing is the same in each case. The wider the range of possible events that can occur, the greater the risk.

To help us grasp the fundamental meaning of risk, consider two possible investments:

1. The first investment is a Government of Canada Treasury bill, a government security that matures in 3 months and promises to pay an annualized return of 8 percent. If we purchase and hold this security for 3 months, we are virtually assured of receiving no more and no less

---

[3]The logic in this section is the same as that used in Chapter 7 for capital budgeting under uncertainty.

than an annualized return of 8 percent. For all practical purposes, the risk of loss is nonexistent.[4]

2. The second investment involves the purchase of common shares of a local publishing company. Looking at the past returns of this firm's common shares, we have made the following estimate of the annual returns from the investment:

Chance of Occurrence	Rate of Return on Investment
1 chance in 10 (10%)	0%
2 chances in 10 (20%)	5%
4 chances in 10 (40%)	15%
2 chances in 10 (20%)	25%
1 chance in 10 (10%)	30%

Investing in the publishing company could conceivably provide a return as high as 30 percent if all goes well or no return (zero percent) if everything goes against the firm. However, in future years, both good and bad, we could expect a 15 percent return on average.[5]

$$\overline{R} = (.10)(0\%) + (.20)(5\%) + (.40)(15\%) + (.20)(25\%) + (.10)(30\%) = 15\%$$

Comparing the Treasury bill investment with the publishing company investment, we see that the Treasury bills offer an expected 8 percent rate of return, while the publishing company has an expected rate of return of 15 percent. However, our investment in the publishing firm is clearly more "risky"—that is, it has greater uncertainty as to the final outcome. Stated somewhat differently, there is a greater variation or dispersion of possible returns, which in turn implies greater risk.[6] Figure 3-1 shows these differences in the form of discrete probability distributions.

Although the return from investing in the publishing firm is clearly less certain than for Treasury bills, quantitative measures of risk are useful when the difference between two investments is not so evident. Examples of such measures are the **standard deviation** (σ) and the **coefficient of variation** (γ) (see Appendix 3A for a review of these descriptive statistics). The standard deviation is simply the square root of the "average squared deviation of each possible return from the expected return."

That is

$$\sigma = \sqrt{\sum_{i=1}^{N} (R_i - \overline{R})^2 \, P(R_j)} \tag{3-3}$$

---

[4]A 3-month Treasury bill is essentially riskless in terms of any chance of default by the government of Canada, but the presence of inflation places the investor at some risk in knowing with certainty the eventual real return, that is, the return after adjusting for loss of purchasing power.

[5]We assume that the particular outcome or return earned in one year does not affect the return earned in the subsequent year. Technically speaking, the distribution of returns in any year is assumed to be independent of the outcome in any prior year.

[6]How can we possibly view variations above the expected return as risk? Should we not be concerned only with the negative deviations? Some would agree and view risk as only the negative variability in returns from a predetermined minimum acceptable rate of return. However, as long as the distribution of returns is symmetrical, the same conclusions will be reached.

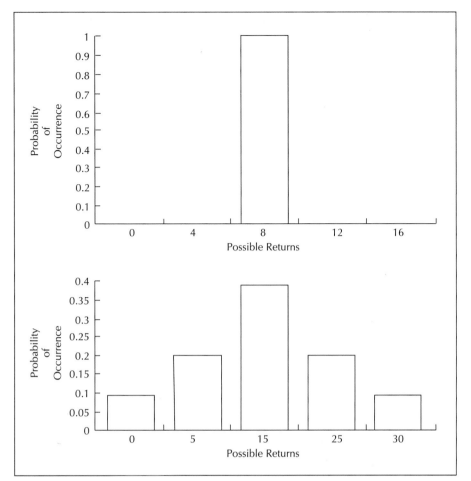

FIGURE 3-1
Probability Distributions of
Returns for a Treasury Bill
and a Publishing Company

where N = the number of possible outcomes or different rates of
return on the investment

R_i = the value of the ith possible rate of return

$\overline{R}$ = the expected value of the rates of return

$P(R_i)$ = the chance or probability that the ith outcome or return
will occur.

For the publishing company, the standard deviation would be 9.22 percent,
determined as follows:

$$\sigma = [(0\% - 15\%)^2(.10) + (5\% - 15\%)^2(.20) + (15\% - 15\%)^2(.40)$$

$$+ (25\% - 15\%)^2(.20) + (30\% - 15\%)^2(.10)]^{(1/2)}$$

$$= \sqrt{85\%} = 9.22\%$$

Although the standard deviation of returns provides us with a quantitative
measure of an asset's riskiness, how should we interpret the results? What
does it mean? Is the 9.22 percent standard deviation for the publishing company investment good or bad? We can answer this question only by comparing the investment in the publishing firm against other investments. The
attractiveness of a security with respect to its return and risk cannot be
determined in isolation. Only by examining other available alternatives can

we reach a conclusion about a particular investment's risk. For example, if another investment, say an investment in a firm that owns a local radio station, has the same expected return as the publishing company (15 percent) but with a standard deviation of 7 percent, we would consider the risk associated with the publishing firm (9.22 percent) to be excessive. We could verify this decision quantitatively by determining the coefficient of variation which provides us with a measure of the relative dispersion of a probability distribution—that is, the risk per unit of return. Mathematically, it is defined as the standard deviation divided by the expected value, or

$$\gamma = \frac{\sigma}{\overline{R}} \qquad (3\text{-}4)$$

In our example for the publishing firm,

$$\gamma = \frac{9.22}{15} = .61$$

In our example for the firm which owns the local radio station,

$$\gamma = \frac{7}{15} = .47$$

As a result, the investment into the publishing firm has a greater risk per unit return than that of the investment into the firm which owns the local radio station. In the technical jargon of modern portfolio theory, the radio company investment is said to "dominate" the publishing firm investment. In common sense terms, this condition is due to the fact that the radio company investment has the same expected return as the publishing company investment but is less risky.

The attractiveness of the radio company investment over the publishing company investment, which has the same expected return but greater risk, is readily apparent. The real difficulty in selecting the "better" investment comes when one investment has a higher expected return but also exhibits greater risk. The coefficient of variation is especially attractive if the projects have unequal returns and standard deviations. This quantitative measure uses the ratio of standard deviation to expected return to compare the relative riskiness of two projects. Thus, the use of the coefficient of variation along with the standard deviation is especially important when two projects of unequal returns are being compared. To ignore the coefficient of variation in this case could lead to misconceptions as to the relative level of uncertainty contained in each project.

Perspective in Finance

The first Chinese symbol represents danger, the second stands for opportunity. The Chinese define risk as the combination of danger and opportunity. Greater risk, according to the Chinese, means we have greater opportunity to do well, but also greater danger to do badly.

RISK AND EXPECTED RETURN OF A PORTFOLIO

Our analysis has focused on the risk and return associated with each individual investment or project under consideration. However, firms do not just invest in a single investment but are generally involved in a number of investments at any one time. As a result, we examine how the expected return and the risk of a portfolio of investments can be quantified.

Expected Return of a Portfolio

Suppose we are considering combining two assets, putting two-thirds of our money in investment A which has an expected return of 12 percent and the remaining third in investment B which has an expected return of 18 percent. The expected return of this 2-asset portfolio is the weighted average of the expected returns from each investment. In this case of portfolios the weighting is defined in terms of the percentages of money invested in each investment: two-thirds of our money in investment A and one-third in investment B. The equation for the expected return of a portfolio is defined as follows:

$$\overline{R}_p = (W_A)(\overline{R}_A) + (W_B)(\overline{R}_B) \tag{3-5}$$

where

$\overline{R}_p$ = the expected return of portfolio

W_A = the weight or fraction of total funds invested in asset A

$\overline{R}_A$ = the expected return of investment A

W_B = the weight or fraction of total funds invested in asset B

$\overline{R}_B$ = the expected return of investment B

For our example,

$$\overline{R}_p = (.67)(12\%) + (.33)(18\%)$$
$$\overline{R}_p = 14\%$$

Thus, our portfolio of two assets has an expected return of 14 percent.

Risk of a Portfolio

Risk has been defined as the variability of future returns and can be measured by the standard deviation. Let's consider for the moment how risk is affected if we diversify our investment by holding a variety of investments. The degree to which the diversification affects a portfolio is a function of the relationship between the pattern of cash flows from the new investment and the existing investment. For example, let us look at a company that doubles its size by adding a new division. First, assume that the cash flows from both the original company and the new division move directly with the business cycle. Time Chart A of Figure 3-2 illustrates that the cash flows of the firm and the division move together and there is no diversification effect. In other words, the effect of cash flows moving together causes their percentage variability to remain the same. In this case, diversification has no effect on the portfolio. If, on the other hand, the new division produced cash flows that were countercyclical, the two series of cash flows would move in opposite

FIGURE 3-2
Diversification Effects on
Cash Flow

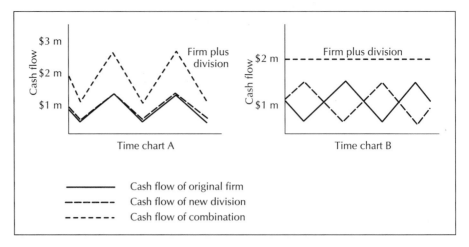

- Cash flow of original firm
- Cash flow of new division
- Cash flow of combination

directions, and diversification would affect the portfolio. Time Chart B of Figure 3-2 illustrates the diversification effects on the cash flows of the firm and the division. In this case, because the variability of the cash flows of the original firm and the new division move in opposite directions, the variability of their combination is totally eliminated.

Obviously, the degree to which the total risk is reduced becomes a function of how the two sets of cash flows or returns move together. In order to measure this relationship, we use the concept of correlation. Correlation measures the linear relationship between any two sets of values. The correlation coefficient, a statistical measure, tells us two things about this relationship. First, it can take on either a positive or a negative sign. A positive sign indicates that the variables tend to move in the same direction; a negative sign, that they move in opposite directions. Also, the value that the correlation coefficient takes on, ranging from +1.0 down to –1.0, provides us with information about the degree or strength of this relationship. If its value is near zero, the linear relationship is weak; however, if the relationship is close to either +1.0 or –1.0, there is a strong linear relationship between the two variables. Letting ρ denote the correlation coefficient, R_p the return on the new investment, and R_{Firm} the return on the firm, Figure 3-3 graphically illustrates several possible situations.

The degree of correlation between investments takes on importance because it determines the extent to which the diversification portfolio effect will reduce the risk level of the combination. Negatively correlated combinations will provide the greatest level of risk reduction, whereas perfectly positively correlated investments, those with correlation coefficients of +1.0, will not provide any diversification effect. If one thinks about it, it makes sense. Any impact from diversification results from combining investments with divergent return or cash flow patterns. If the correlation coefficient is 1.0, these patterns are identical; hence, there is no diversification value present. If, on the other hand, the correlation coefficient is –1.0, then the patterns move in opposite directions; hence, the diversification value is maximum.

Portfolio Risk: A Mathematical Illustration

To illustrate mathematically, suppose we are considering combining two assets, putting two-thirds of our money in investment A and the remaining third in investment B, and we want to determine the risk or standard devia-

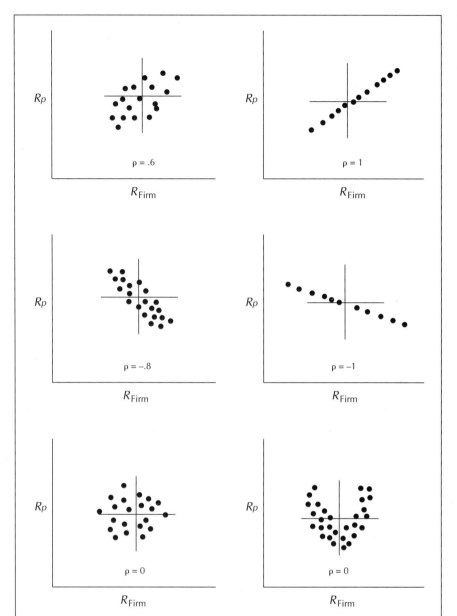

FIGURE 3-3
Illustrations of Various
Degrees of Correlation

tion of this combination. The mathematical formula for the standard deviation of this two-asset combination is given in Equations (3-6) and (3-7).

$$\sigma_{A+B} = \sqrt{\text{Variance } (A + B)} \qquad (3\text{-}6)$$

$$\sigma_{A+B} = \sqrt{W^2_A\sigma^2_A + W^2_B\sigma^2_B + 2W_AW_B\rho_{AB}\sigma_A\sigma_B} \qquad (3\text{-}7)$$

where σ_{A+B} = the standard deviation of the combination of asset A and asset B

           W_A = the weight or fraction of total funds invested in asset A

           W_B = the weight or fraction of total funds invested in asset B

$$\sigma_A = \text{the standard deviation of asset A}$$

$$\sigma_B = \text{the standard deviation of asset B}$$

$$\rho_{AB} = \text{the correlation coefficient between assets A and B}$$

Now let us assume that Table 3-2 provides the relevant information about each of these investments. If there is no diversification effect at all—that is, $\rho_{AB} = 1.0$—the standard deviation of this combination should be equal to its weighted average, 26.66 percent. That is to say that 26.66 percent is the weighted average standard deviation of this portfolio. If we had not discussed portfolio risk, we would expect the risk or standard deviation of this combination to be equal to its weighted average. However, there is a diversification portfolio effect, and its degree depends upon the correlation between the assets being combined. This can be shown mathematically by substituting the values provided in Table 3-2 into Equation (3-7). This results in the following reduction in Equation (3-7):

$$\sigma_{A+B} = \sqrt{\left(\frac{2}{3}\right)^2(.2)^2 + \left(\frac{1}{3}\right)^2(.4)^2 + 2\rho_{AB}\left(\frac{2}{3}\right)\left(\frac{1}{3}\right)(.2)(.4)}$$

$$\sigma_{A+B} = \sqrt{.0356 + .0356\rho_{AB}}$$

TABLE 3-2
Two-Asset Example of Diversification

Asset	σ	Weights (W)	$\sigma \times$ Weights
A	20%	2/3	13.33%
B	40	1/3	13.33%
		Weighted average $\sigma_{A+B} =$	26.66%

The only variable we now need in order to determine the standard deviation for the combination of assets is their correlation coefficient. Letting the correlation coefficient between assets A and B (ρ_{AB}) vary between +1.0 and –1.0 results in the following standard deviation for the combination:

	If $\rho_{AB} = 1.0$	If $\rho_{AB} = 0.0$	If $\rho_{AB} = -1.0$
$\sigma_{A+B} =$	$\sqrt{.0712} = 26.68\%$	$\sqrt{.0356} = 18.9\%$	$\sqrt{0} = 0\%$

Thus, the degree of correlation between investments determines to what extent risk can be eliminated when they are combined. It should be noted that the difference between the weighted average standard deviation (26.66%) and the one calculated using Equation (3-7) and assuming ρ_{AB} equals 1.0 (26.68%) is merely the result of rounding error.

Unfortunately, in the real world perfectly negatively correlated investments are almost never found. In fact, most investments tend to be positively correlated with each other. Still, as long as positive correlations are not perfect, there will be a reduction in overall risk from these combinations. Historically, this desire to reduce the overall risk of the firm through diversification has led to much of the merger activity of the past.

Risk and Diversification

You may recall the disaster at the Union Carbide plant in Bhopal, India, that occurred in the summer of 1984. Thousands of individuals were killed or injured. While the financial considerations cannot compare to the loss of life, if you had invested your life savings of $400,000 in Union Carbide shortly before the Bhopal tragedy, the value of your savings would have declined by 40 percent to $240,000 almost overnight.[7] Or what if you had been fortunate enough to buy some Pennzoil stock in November 1985 immediately before Pennzoil was awarded $10.5 billion by the courts against Texaco for alleged misconduct in "tortuously" outbidding Pennzoil in Texaco's acquisition of Getty Oil Company? Based upon this single event, Pennzoil stock almost doubled from $46 per share to $90 per share in a matter of days. Texaco stock, on the other hand, declined from $38 to $25.[8]

The events affecting Union Carbide, Texaco, and Pennzoil were unique to those firms; they had little, if any, impact on other companies. Other examples of events that are unique to a single company include labour strikes, the discovery of a new product or the sudden obsolescence of an old one, errors in judgment by a firm's management regarding a large capital investment, and the resignation or death of a key executive.

How do you feel about these unique events? Obviously, if you had been a shareholder in Pennzoil you would have felt great, but you might have decided to invest in Texaco (not a bad company), or even worse, Union Carbide. Most of us would like to avoid such fluctuations; that is, we are risk-averse. Wouldn't it be great if we could reduce the risk associated with our portfolio, without having to accept a lower expected return? Good news: it is possible!

Partitioning the Risk

If we diversify our investments across different securities, rather than investing in only one security, the variability in the returns of our portfolio should decline. The reduction in risk will occur if the security returns within our portfolio do not move precisely together over time—that is, if they are not perfectly correlated. Figure 3-4 shows graphically what we might expect to happen to the variability of returns as we add additional securities to the portfolio.[9] The reduction occurs because some of the volatility in returns of a security are unique to that security. The unique variability of a single security tends to be countered by the uniqueness of another security.[10] However, we should not expect to eliminate all risk from our portfolio. In practice, it would be rather difficult to cancel all the variations in returns of a portfolio because share prices have some tendency to move together. Thus, we can divide the total risk (total variability) of our portfolio into two types of risk: (1) **firm-specific** or **company-unique risk** and (2) **market-related risk**. Company unique risk might also be called **diversifiable risk**, since it can be diversified away. Market risk is **nondiversifiable risk**; it cannot be eliminated, no matter how much we diversify. Figure 3-4 illustrates these two types

---

[7]See "Union Carbide Shares Acquired by Bass Group," *Wall Street Journal,* January 21, 1985, pp. 2–3. We must add that the price of the stock recovered in about six months.

[8]See "Pennzoil Rejects Texaco Offer," *Wall Street Journal,* January 8, 1986, p. 3. The final settlement after Texaco filed for bankruptcy was $3 billion.

[9]The desire to reduce risk through diversification is the underlying motivation for the creation of mutual funds.

[10]This concept will also be presented in Chapter 7 with respect to the risk of capital investments.

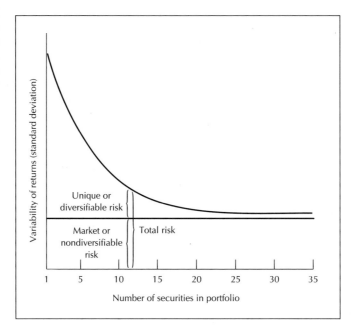

FIGURE 3-4
Variability of Returns Compared with Size of Portfolio

of risk. Total risk decreases until we have approximately 20 securities, and then the decline becomes very slight.[11] The remaining risk is the portfolio's market risk. At this point, our portfolio is highly correlated with all securities in the marketplace. Events that affect our portfolio now are not so much unique events, but changes in the general economy, major political events, and sociological changes. Examples would include changes in general interest rates, or changes in tax legislation that affect companies, or increasing concerns by the public about business practices on the environment.

Since we can remove the unique, or unsystematic risk, there is no reason to believe that the market will reward us with additional returns for assuming risk that could be avoided by simply diversifying. Our new measure of risk should therefore measure how responsive a security or portfolio is to changes in a "market portfolio," such as the TSE 300 Index.[12] This relationship could be determined by plotting past returns, say on a monthly basis, of a particular security or a portfolio of shares against the returns of the "market portfolio" for the same period.

Measuring Market Risk: an Example

To help clarify the idea of systematic risk, let us examine the relationship between the common stock returns of Spar Aerospace and the returns of the TSE 300 Index. Table 3B-1 of Appendix B presents the monthly returns for Spar Aerospace and for the TSE 300 Index for 60 months ending December

---

[11]A number of studies have noted that portfolios consisting of approximately 20 randomly selected common securities have virtually no unique or diversifiable risk. See Robert C. Klemkosky and John D. Martin, "The Effect of Market Risk on Portfolio Diversification," *The Journal of Finance*, March 1975, pp. 147–154.

[12]The Toronto Stock Exchange (TSE 300) Composite Index is a stock index that measures the combined performance of 300 companies in Canada. The Toronto Stock Exchange sets the criteria for inclusion in the TSE 300 Composite Index. In contrast, the New York Stock Exchange Index is an index that reflects the performance of all stocks listed on the New York Stock Exchange.

1992. These monthly returns, or "holding-period returns," as we oftentimes call them, are calculated as follows:[13]

$$R_t = \left(\frac{P_t}{P_{t-1}}\right) - 1 \qquad (3\text{-}8)$$

where, R_t = the holding-period return in month t for Spar Aerospace (or for the TSE 300 Index) and

P_t = the price of Spar Aerospace's share (or the TSE 300 Index) at the end of month t.

For instance, the holding-period return for Spar Aerospace and the TSE 300 Index for February 1989 is computed as follows:

$$\frac{\text{Spar Aerospace}}{\text{return for February 1989}} = \frac{\text{Share price end of February 89}}{\text{Share price end of January 89}} - 1$$

$$= \left(\frac{14.88}{15.25}\right) - 1 = -2.43\%$$

$$\frac{\text{TSE 300 Index}}{\text{return for February 1989}} = \frac{\text{Index value end of February 89}}{\text{Index value end of January 89}} - 1$$

$$= \left(\frac{3572.1}{3616.6}\right) - 1 = -1.25\%$$

Table 3-3 shows the computed averages of the returns and the standard deviation of these returns for both Spar Aerospace and the TSE 300 Index. Since we are using historical data for returns, we assume that each observation has an equal probability of occurrence. Thus, the average return is found by summing the returns and dividing by the number of months,

$$\text{Average return} = \frac{\sum\limits_{t=1}^{n} \text{returns in month } t}{\text{number of months}}$$

and the standard deviation is computed as:

$$\text{Standard deviation} = \sqrt{\frac{\sum\limits_{t=1}^{n} (\text{return in month } t - \text{average return})^2}{\text{number of months} - 1}}$$

The average monthly return for Spar Aerospace and the TSE 300 Index are found to be –0.015 percent and 0.345 percent, respectively. We also see that

	TSE 300 Index	Spar Aerospace
Average Monthly Holding-Return	0.345%	–0.015%
Standard Deviation	3.21%	8.73%
Correlation Coefficient		0.23

TABLE 3-3
Statistics for Monthly Holding-Returns for TSE 300 Index and Spar Aerospace, January 1988 to December 1992

---

[13]For simplicity's sake, we are ignoring the dividend that the investor receives from the share as part of the total return. That is, letting D_t equal the dividend received by the investor in month t, the holding-period return would more accurately be measured as:

$$R_t = \frac{P_t + D_t}{P_{t-1}} - 1 \qquad (3\text{-}8A)$$

Spar Aerospace has experienced greater volatility of returns over the five years, or a standard deviation of 8.73 percent compared to 3.21 percent for the TSE 300 Index. As explained earlier, we could avoid some of this risk (reduce the standard deviation) by diversifying our portfolio and owning common shares other than Spar Aerospace.

Figure 3-5 illustrates the relation between Spar Aerospace's returns and the TSE 300 Index returns. If we draw a line of "best fit" through these returns, the slope of the line is 0.63. The slope of this line of best fit, which we call the "characteristic line," indicates the average movement in the share price of Spar Aerospace in response to a movement in the general market portfolio (TSE 300 Index). The slope of the characteristic line, the ratio of the rise of the line relative to the run of the line, is called "**beta**" in finance.[14]

Perspective in Finance

The slope of the characteristic line is called "beta" and it is a measure of a systematic or market risk.

Measuring a Portfolio's Beta

Figure 3-5 shows that on average a 1.0 percent change in the return of the TSE 300 Index causes a change of 0.63 percent in the return of Spar Aerospace. Yet, we also see a lot of fluctuation around the characteristic line.[15]

FIGURE 3-5
Monthly Holding-Period Returns, Spar Aerospace and the TSE 300 Index (January 1988–December 1992)

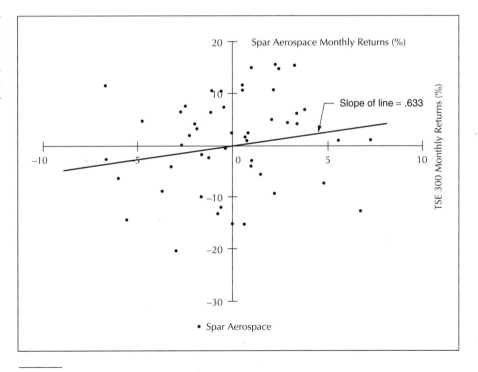

[14]For our purposes, we are primarily interested in understanding the concept of beta. Appendix 3B demonstrates how to calculate the beta of Spar Aerospace. Betas are also reported by investment services, for example: the Polymetric Report lists betas for Canadian companies and Merril Lynch, Pierce, Fenner & Smith Investment Survey lists betas for companies in the United States.

[15]A security with a zero beta has no systematic risk, while a security with a beta of one has systematic or market risk equivalent with the "typical" security in the marketplace. Most securities have betas between 0.60 and 1.60.

However by diversifying our holdings to own shares of 20 companies with betas of about 0.63, we could essentially eliminate the variation of the line. We would remove almost all the volatility in returns, except for what is caused by the general market, which is represented by the slope of the line. If we plotted the returns of our 20-stock portfolio against the TSE 300 Index, the points of our new graph would fit nicely along a straight line with a slope of 0.63. The new graph would look something like the one shown in Figure 3-6.

One remaining question needs to be addressed. Assume we want to diversify our portfolio, as we have just suggested, but instead of acquiring securities with the same beta as Spar Aerospace (0.63), we buy shares of 8 companies with betas of 0.63 and share of 12 companies with betas of 1.5. What would the beta of our portfolio become? As it works out, the "beta portfolio" is simply the average of the individual betas of the companies' shares. Actually, the portfolio beta is a weighted average of the individual security's betas, whereby the weights are equal to the proportion of the portfolio invested in each security. Thus, the beta (β) of a portfolio consisting of N securities is equal to:

$$\beta_{\text{Portfolio}} = \sum_{j=1}^{N} (\text{percentage invested security } j) \times (\text{security } j\text{'s } \beta)$$

So for our new portfolio, the beta would simply be 1.15, calculated as follows:

$$\beta_{\text{Portfolio}} = \left(\frac{8}{20} \times .63\right) + \left(\frac{12}{20} \times 1.50\right)$$

$$= 1.15$$

An increase or decrease of one percent in the returns of the general market portfolio (TSE 300 Index) would on average change 1.15 percent, meaning that our new portfolio has more systematic or market risk than has the market portfolio.

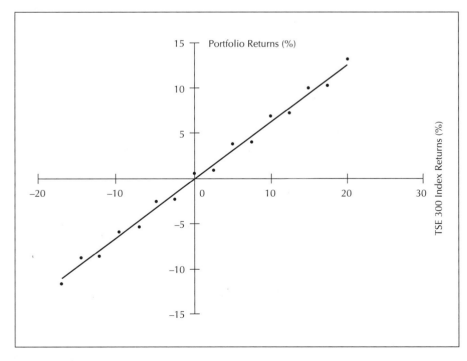

FIGURE 3-6
Holding Period Returns: Hypothetical Portfolio and TSE 300 Index

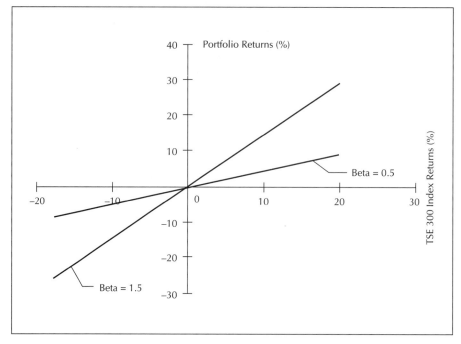

So we can conclude that the beta of a portfolio is determined by the betas of the individual security betas. If we have a portfolio consisting of securities with low betas, then our portfolio will have a low beta. The reverse of this observation also holds true. Figure 3-7 illustrates these situations.

The concept of beta is an underlying concept used in measuring a security's risk. It also proves useful when we attempt to specify what the relationship should be between an investor's required rate of return and the security's market risk.

Perspective in Finance

We may reduce risk by diversifying our portfolio, but only to a point. What we remove is company-unique risk of specific risk (also known as diversifiable or unsystematic risk). Systematic risk or market risk (also termed nondiversifiable risk) cannot be eliminated.

THE INVESTOR'S REQUIRED RATE OF RETURN

In this section we examine the concept of the investor's required rate of return, especially as it relates to the riskiness of the asset, and then we see how the required rate of return is measured.

The Required Rate of Return Concept

The investor's required rate of return may be defined as the minimum rate of return necessary to attract an investor to purchase or hold a security. This definition considers the investor's opportunity cost of making an investment;

that is, if an investment is made, the investor must forgo the return available from the next best investment. This "forgone return" is an opportunity cost of undertaking the investment and consequently is the investor's required rate of return. In other words, we invest with the intention of achieving a rate of return sufficient to warrant making the investment. The investment will be made only if the purchase price is low enough relative to the expected future cash flows to provide a rate of return greater than or equal to our required rate of return.

To help us better understand the nature of an investor's required rate of return, we may separate the return into its basic components: the risk-free rate of return plus a risk premium. The investor's required rate of return is expressed as follows:

$$R = R_f + RP \qquad\qquad (3\text{-}10)$$

where, R = the investor's required rate of return

          R_f = the risk-free return

          RP = the risk premium

The risk-free rate of return rewards us for deferring consumption, and not for assuming risk; that is, the risk-free return reflects the basic fact that we invest today so that we can consume more later. By itself, the riskless or risk-free rate should be used only as the required rate of return, or discount rate, for riskless investments. Typically, our measure for the risk-free rate of return is the Government of Canada Treasury bill rate.

The risk premium, RP, is the additional return we must expect to receive for assuming risk. As the level of risk increases, we will demand additional expected returns. Even though we may or may not actually receive this incremental return, we must have reason to expect it; otherwise, why should we expose ourselves to the chance of losing all or part of our money?

EXAMPLE

To demonstrate the concept of required rate of return, let us take Bell Canada, which has bonds that mature on April 15th, 2010. Based upon the market price of these bonds in April of 1992, we can determine that investors are expecting a 10 percent return. The 3-month Treasury bill rate at that time was about 7 percent, which means that Bell Canada bondholders were requiring a risk premium of 3 percent.[16] Stated as an equation, we have

$$\begin{aligned}
\text{required rate} &= \text{risk-free rate } (R_f) + \text{risk premium } (RP) \\
&= 7\% + 3\% \\
&= 10\% \ \blacksquare
\end{aligned}$$

---

[16] The risk premium here can be thought of as a composite of a "default risk premium" (reflected in the difference in the bond's rate of return and the rate on a similar maturity government bond) and "term structure" premium (reflected in the difference in the 3-month Treasury bill rate and the long-term government bond rate).

Measuring the Required Rate of Return

The investor's required rate of return has been described in Equation (3-10) by the following terms: (1) systematic risk is the relevant source of risk and (2) the required rate of return, R, equals the risk-free rate, R_f, plus a risk premium, RP. However, we have difficulty in applying this equation to real-world examples because of the problems in estimating the risk premium. In an attempt to overcome these difficulties, the **Capital Asset Pricing Model (CAPM)** offers an intuitive approach for thinking about the return that an investor requires on an investment, given the asset's systematic or market risk.

Equation (3-10) provides the natural starting point for measuring the investors' required rate of return. Rearranging this equation to solve for the risk premium (RP), we have

$$RP = R - R_f \qquad (3\text{-}11)$$

which simply says that the risk premium for a security, RP, equals the security's expected return, R, less the risk-free rate existing in the market, R_f. For example, if the expected return for a security is 15 percent and the risk-free rate is 7 percent, the risk premium is 8 percent. Also, if the expected return for the market, R_m, is 12 percent, and the risk-free rate, R_f, is 7 percent, the risk premium, RP, for the general market would be 5 percent. This 5 percent risk premium would apply to any security having systematic (nondiversifiable) risk equivalent to the general market, or a beta of 1.

In this same market, a security with a beta of 2 should provide a risk premium of 10 percent, or twice the 5 percent risk premium existing for the market as a whole.[17] Hence, in general, the appropriate required rate of return for the jth security, R_j, should be determined by

$$R_j = R_f + \beta_j(R_m - R_f) \qquad (3\text{-}12)$$

Equation (3-12) is the capital asset pricing model (CAPM). This equation designates the risk-return tradeoff existing in the market, where risk is defined in terms of beta. Figure 3-8 illustrates the CAPM as the security market line.[18] As presented in this figure, securities with betas equal to 0, 1, and 2 should have required rates of return as follows:

If $\beta_j = 0.0$: $R_j = 7\% + 0.0(12\% - 7\%) = 7$ percent

---

[17]Empirical evidence suggests that betas for individual securities are highly unstable over time. Thus, when you calculate a beta for a firm based on historical data, you have no assurance that the beta will remain the same in the next period.

[18]Two key assumptions are made in using the security market line. First, we assume that the marketplace where securities are bought and sold is highly efficient. Market efficiency indicates that the price of an asset responds quickly to new information, thereby suggesting that the price of a security reflects all available information. As a result, the current price of a security is considered to represent the best estimate of its future price. Second, the model assumes that a perfect market exists. A perfect market is one in which information is readily available to all investors at a nominal cost. Also, securities are assumed to be infinitely divisible, with any transaction costs incurred in purchasing or selling a security being negligible. Furthermore, investors are assumed to be single-period wealth maximizers who agree as to the meaning and the significance of the available information. Finally, within the perfect market, all investors are "price takers," which simply means that a single investor's actions cannot affect the price of a security. These assumptions are obviously not descriptive of reality. However, from the perspective of positive economics, the mark of a good theory is the accuracy of its predictions and not the validity of the simplifying assumptions that underlie its development.

FIGURE 3-8
Security Market Line

If $\beta_j = 1.0$: $R_j = 7\% + 1.0(12\% - 7\%) = 12$ percent

If $\beta_j = 2.0$: $R_j = 7\% + 2.0(12\% - 7\%) = 17$ percent

where the risk-free rate, R_f, is 7 percent and the expected market return, R_m, is 12 percent.[19]

Criticisms of CAPM

For several years, CAPM was touted as the "new investment technology" and received the blessings of the vast majority of professional investors and finance professors. The CAPM is largely attractive because of its ability to present important theoretical insights in simple and practical terms that could be applied in practice. In more recent years, however, researchers have questioned whether the model really works.[20]

The CAPM, like any abstract theory, has weaknesses. For example, we might question whether the risk of an asset can be totally captured in a single dimension of sensitivity to the market, as CAPM proposes. There is some evidence that such things as the firm's size and even the time of year may affect risk-return relationships.[21] Also, we could become discouraged in our efforts to measure a security's beta if we find that different computation methods and different periods of measurement (e.g., using three years of data versus

[19]For more detailed treatment of this model, see B. Rosenberg, "The Capital Asset Pricing Model and the Market Model," *Journal of Portfolio Management*, Winter 1981, pp. 5–16.

[20]See Anise Wallace, "Is Beta Dead?" *Institutional Investor*, July 1980, pp. 23–30.

[21]See C. Barry and S. Brown, "Differential Information and the Small Firm Effect," *Journal of Financial Economics*, June 1984, pp. 283–294; N. Chen and D. Hsieh, "An Exploratory Investigation of the Firm Size Effect," *Journal of Financial Economics*, September 1985, pp. 451–471; and J. Jaffe and R. Westerfield, "The Week-End Effect in Common Stock Returns: The International Evidence," *Journal of Finance*, June 1985, 433–454.

five years) give noticeably different results. An even more basic issue is our ability to test the model empirically. Some would argue that we cannot verify the accuracy of the model because we cannot know with certainty that we are using the "true market portfolio" in comparing returns and systematic risk.[22]

While the critics of CAPM have been vocal, the model is still widely used. An alternative theory for the explanation of an investor's required rate of return on an asset is the **arbitrage pricing model (APM)**. This newer model considers multiple economic factors in explaining the required rate of return, rather than looking at systematic risk or general market returns as the single determinant of an investor's required rate of return. Despite the APM having some desirable features and potential for the future, it has yet to be of much practical use. Nevertheless, we have provided a brief treatment of the model in Appendix C at the end of this chapter.

Whichever model is used, one key point remains. In order to formulate a complete concept or understanding of security valuation, a topic of the next chapter, we must understand the nature of the investor's required rate of return. The required rate of return which serves as the discount rate in the valuation process is the investor's minimum acceptable return that would induce an investor to purchase or hold a security.

RATES OF RETURN: THE INVESTOR'S EXPERIENCE

In speaking of expected rates of return, we have used a number of hypothetical examples; however, it is also interesting to look at returns that investors have actually received. Hatch and White have provided average monthly rates of return for the period between 1950 and 1986.[23] In their results, they summarize, among other things, the monthly returns for four portfolios of securities which contain:

1. Government of Canada Treasury bills
2. Long-term government of Canada bonds
3. Long-term industrial bonds
4. Equities

Before comparing these returns, we should first think about what to expect. First, we would intuitively expect a Treasury bill to be the least risky of the four portfolios. Since a Treasury bill has a short-term maturity date, the price is less volatile (less risky) than the price of an intermediate- or a long-term government security.[24] In turn, since there is a chance of default on an industrial bond, which is essentially nonexistent for government securities, a long-term government bond is less risky than a long-term industrial bond. Finally, common stock of companies is more risky than an industrial bond.

---

[22]See, for example, Richard Roll, "A Critique of the Asset Pricing Theory's Tests," *Journal of Financial Economics*, March 1977, 129–176.

[23]James E. Hatch and Robert W. White, *Canadian Stocks, Bonds, Bills, and Inflation: 1950–1987.* Charlottesville, Virginia: The Research Foundation of the Institute of Chartered Financial Analysts, 1988, pp. 161–166.

[24]The greater volatility for long-term bonds relative to short-term bonds will be discussed in detail in Appendix 4A of Chapter 4.

With this in mind, we could reasonably expect different rates of return to the holders of these varied securities. If the market rewards an investor for assuming risk, the average annual rates of return should increase as risk increases.

A comparison of the annual rates of return for the four Canadian portfolios for the years 1950–1986 is provided in Table 3-4. Four aspects of these returns are included: (1) the average nominal annual rate of return; (2) the standard deviation of the returns, which measures the volatility or riskiness of the portfolios; (3) the average real annual rate of return, which is the nominal return less the inflation rate; and (4) the risk premium, which represents the additional return received beyond the risk-free rate (Treasury bill rate) for assuming risk. Looking first at the two columns of average monthly returns and standard deviations, we gain a good overview of the risk-return relationships that have existed over the 37 years ending in 1986. For the most part, there has been a positive relationship between risk and return, with Treasury bills being least risky and common shares being most risky. However, long-term government bonds have been riskier than industrial bonds. This aberration has largely been the result of the five years from 1978 through 1982, a period when interest rates rose to all-time highs, which had a significantly negative impact on bond prices.

Ibbotson and Sinquefield examined the monthly returns of portfolios containing the same type of American securities over the years 1950 to 1986.[25] The authors also indicated that U.S. treasury bills are the least risky and common shares are most risky of the four portfolios. Again, long-term government bonds are riskier than corporate bonds because of the very high interest rates that were experienced in the American economy.

International Financial Management

An investment in government bonds in the early nineties would have done quite well, whether you lived in Canada and invested Government of Canada

Securities	Average Monthly Returns		Standard Deviation of Returns		Real Average Monthly Returns[a]		Risk Premiums[b] of Returns	
	CAN	USA	CAN	USA	CAN	USA	CAN	USA
Equities	10.1	10.9	43.6	39.9	6.3	6.9	5.4	6.2
Long-Term Industrial Bonds	5.3	5.0	22.9	25.7	1.5	1.0	0.6	0.3
Long-Term Government Bonds	4.6	4.5	23.5	27.2	0.8	0.5	–0.1	–0.2
Government of Canada Treasury Bills	4.7	4.7	3.4	8.7	0.9	0.7	0	0

TABLE 3-4
A Comparison of Monthly Rates of Return 1950–1986

[a]Real return equals the nominal return less the average inflation rate from 1950 through 1986 of 3.8 and 4.0 percent for Canada and the United States, respectively.

[b]Risk premium equals the security return less the average risk-free rate (Treasury bills) of 4.7 percent for both Canada and the United States.

Sources: (1) James E. Hatch and Robert W. White, *Canadian Stocks, Bonds, Bills, and Inflation: 1950–1987* (Charlottesville, Virginia: The Research Foundation of the Institute of Chartered Financial Analysts, 1988), pp. 161-166; and (2) Roger G. Ibbotson and Rex A. Sinquefield, *Stocks, Bonds, Bills, and Inflation: Historical Returns*. (Chicago, IL. Dow Jones-Irwin, 1989), p. 14.

---

[25]Roger G. Ibbotson and Rex A. Sinquefield, *Stocks, Bonds, Bills, and Inflation: Historical Returns (1926–1987)*, Chicago, IL: Dow Jones-Irwin, 1989.

FIGURE 3-9
Returns on Government
Bonds in Different Countries

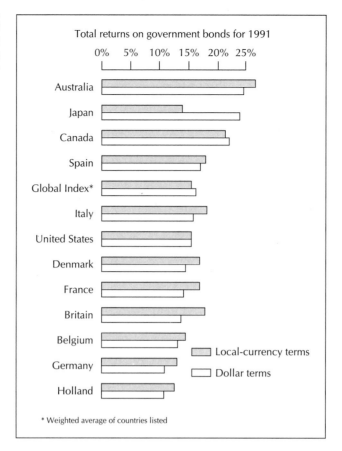

bonds or invested abroad. Figure 3-9 shows the rates of return an investor would have earned buying government bonds in different countries and the average return, as estimated by J.P. Morgan's Global Index of government bonds. (Note: U.S.-Dollar term returns are affected by currency rates at the time of conversion.)

The high returns, which consisted of the interest received and the price increases in the bonds during the year, were attributable to decreasing interest rates and declining inflation rates. Australia, Japan and Canada clearly had the highest returns, while European countries, with the exception of Spain, produced lower returns.

SUMMARY

Chapter 3 has examined the relationship between risk and rates of return. The variability of returns is the factor that defines risk for investors and financial managers. There is no simple way to measure risk, and individuals take diverse attitudes toward risk taking. There is an important distinction between nondiversifiable risk and diversifiable risk. The only relevant risk, given an investor's opportunity to diversify a portfolio, is a security's nondiversifiable risk, which is also referred to as systematic risk or market risk.

The Capital Asset Pricing Model (CAPM) is useful in determining an appropriate required rate of return given an asset's systematic risk, as measured by its beta, or the way a share responds to changes in the market returns. The model offers the advantage of being relatively intuitive, but it is not definitive. CAPM's assumptions and limitations suggest that critics will continue to look carefully for a more complete explanation for how rates are determined in the capital markets. Nevertheless, our observations do suggest that in general there is a relationship between risk and return in the capital markets. Thus, we may confidently say that as a general rule, investors determine an appropriate required rate of return, depending upon the amount of risk inherent in the security. This minimum acceptable rate of return is equal to the risk-free rate plus a return premium for assuming the risk associated with the investment. In addition, the amount of the return premium, given a particular degree of risk, is dependent upon the investor's attitude toward the risk-return tradeoff. Simply stated, individual investors perceive risk differently and have different propensities for assuming risk.

STUDY QUESTIONS

3-1. **a.** What is meant by "the investor's required rate of return"?

   b. How have we measured the riskiness of an asset?

   c. How should the proposed measurement of risk be interpreted?

3-2. What is (a) unique risk and (b) systematic risk (market or nondiversifiable risk)?

3-3. What is the meaning of beta? How is it used to calculate R, the investor's required rate of return?

3-4. Define the security market line. What does it represent?

3-5. How do we measure the beta for a portfolio?

3-6. If we were to graph the returns of a share against the returns of the TSE 300 Index, and the points did not follow a very neat pattern, what could we say about that share? If the share's returns tracked the TSE 300 returns very closely, then what could we say?

3-7. Over the past six decades, we have had the opportunity to observe the rates of return and variability of these returns for different types of securities. Summarize these observations.

SELF-TEST PROBLEMS

ST-1. (*Expected Return and Risk*) Universal Corporation is planning to invest in a security that has several possible rates of return. Given the following probability distribution of returns, what is the expected rate of return on the investment? Also compute the standard deviation of the returns. What do the resulting numbers represent?

Probability	Return
.10	−10%
.20	5%
.30	10%
.40	25%

ST-2. (*Capital Asset Pricing Model*) Using the CAPM, estimate the appropriate required rate of return for the three securities listed in the following table, given that the risk-free rate is 5 percent, and the expected return for the market is 17 percent.

Security	Beta
A	.75
B	.90
C	1.40

ST-3. (*Expected Return and Risk*) Given the holding period returns shown below, calculate the average returns and the standard deviations for the Kaifu Corporation and for the market.

Month	Market	Kaifu Corp.
1	2%	4%
2	3%	6%
3	1%	0%
4	−1%	2%

ST-4. (*Holding-Period Returns*) From the price data below, compute the holding period returns.

Time	Share Price
1	$10
2	13
3	11
4	15

ST-5. (*Security Market Line*) Determine the expected return and the beta for the following portfolio.

Security	Percentage of Portfolio	Beta	Expected Return
1	40%	1.00	12%
2	25%	0.75	11%
3	35%	1.30	15%

The risk-free rate is 8 percent. Also, the expected return on the market portfolio is 12 percent.

Given the information above, draw the security market line and show where your securities fit on the graph. How would you interpret your findings?

STUDY PROBLEMS (SET A)

3-1A. (*Expected Rate of Return and Risk*) Pritchard Press, Inc., is evaluating a security. One-year Treasury bills are currently paying 9.1 percent. Calculate the investment's expected return and its standard deviation. Should Pritchard invest in this security?

Probability	Return
.15	5%
.30	7%
.40	10%
.15	15%

3-2A. (*Expected Rate of Return and Risk*) Syntex, Inc., is considering an investment in one of two common shares. Given the information below, which investment is better, based upon risk (as measured by the standard deviation) and return?

Common Share A		Common Share B	
Probability	Return	Probability	Return
		.20	−5%
.30	11%	.30	6%
.40	15%	.30	14%
.30	19%	.20	22%

3-3A. (*Expected Rate of Return and Risk*) Friedman Manufacturing, Inc., has prepared the following information regarding two investments under consideration. Which investment should be accepted?

Common Share A		Common Share B	
Probability	Return	Probability	Return
.20	−2%	.10	4%
.50	18%	.30	6%
.30	27%	.40	10%
		.20	15%

3-4A. **a.** (*Required Rate of Return Using CAPM*) Compute a "fair" rate of return for the common shares of IBM given a Beta of 1.2. The risk-free rate is 6 percent and the market portfolio (Toronto Stock Exchange 300 Index) has an expected return of 16 percent.

b. Why is the rate you have computed a "fair" rate?

3-5A. (*Estimating Beta*) The figure below illustrates the relationship between the holding-period returns for Aram, Inc., and the TSE 300 Index. Estimate the firm's beta.

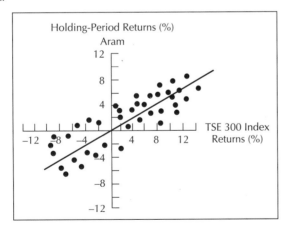

3-6A. (*Capital Asset Pricing Model*) Johnson Manufacturing, Inc., is considering several investments. The rate on Treasury bills is currently 6.75 percent, and the expected return for the market is 12 percent. What should be the required rates of return for each investment (using the CAPM)?

Security	Beta
A	1.50
B	0.82
C	0.60
D	1.15

3-7A. (*Capital Asset Pricing Model*) CSB, Inc., has a beta of 0.765. If the expected market return is 11.5 percent and the risk-free rate is 7.5 percent, what is the appropriate required return of CSB (using the CAPM)?

3-8A. (*Capital Asset Pricing Model*) The expected return for the general market is 12.8 percent, and the risk premium in the market is 4.3 percent. Tasaco, LBM, and Exxos have betas of 0.864, 0.693, and 0.575, respectively. What are the corresponding required rates of return for the three securities?

3-9A. (*Computing Holding-Period Returns*) From the price data below, compute the holding-period returns for Asman and Salinas.

Time	Asman	Salinas
1	$10	$30
2	12	28
3	11	32
4	13	35

How would you interpret the meaning of a holding-period return?

3-10A. (*Measuring Risk and Rates of Return*) Given the holding-period returns shown below, calculate the average returns and the standard deviations for the Zemin Corporation and for the market.

Month	Market	Zemin Corp.
1	4%	6%
2	2%	3%
3	1%	−1%
4	−2%	−3%
5	2%	5%
6	2%	0%

If Zemin's beta is 1.54, and the risk-free rate is 8 percent, what would be an appropriate required return for an investor owning Zemin? (Note: Since the above returns are based on monthly data, you will need to annualize the returns to make them compatible with the risk-free rate. For simplicity, you may convert from monthly to yearly returns by multiplying the average monthly returns by 12.)

How does Zemin's historical average return compare with the return you believe to be a "fair" return, given the firm's systematic risk?

3-11A. (*Portfolio Beta and Security Market Line*) You own a portfolio consisting of the following shares.

Security	Percentage of Portfolio	Beta	Expected Return
1	20%	1.00	16%
2	30%	0.85	14%
3	15%	1.20	20%
4	25%	0.60	12%
5	10%	1.60	24%

The risk-free rate is 7 percent. Also, the expected return on the market portfolio is 15.5 percent.

a. Calculate the expected return and the beta for your portfolio.

b. Given the information above, plot the security market line on paper. Plot the shares from your portfolio on your graph.

c. From your plot in part (b), which shares appear to be your "winners" and which ones appear to be "losers"?

d. Why should we consider our conclusions in part (c) to be less than certain?

STUDY PROBLEMS (SET B)

3-1B. (*Expected Rate of Return and Risk*) B. J. Gautney Enterprises is evaluating a security. One-year Treasury bills are currently paying 8.9 percent. Calculate the investment's expected return and its standard deviation. Should Gautney invest in this security?

Probability	Return
.15	6%
.30	5%
.40	11%
.15	14%

3-2B. (*Expected Rate of Return and Risk*) Kelly B. Stites, Inc., is considering an investment in one of two common shares. Given the information below, which investment is better, based upon risk (as measured by the standard deviation) and return?

Common Share A		Common Share B	
Probability	Return	Probability	Return
		.15	6%
.20	10%	.30	8%
.60	13%	.40	15%
.20	20%	.15	19%

3-3B. (*Expected Rate of Return and Risk*) Clevenger Manufacturing, Inc., has prepared the following information regarding two investments under consideration. Which investment should be accepted?

Common Share A		Common Share B	
Probability	Return	Probability	Return
.20	−2%	.10	4%
.50	19%	.30	7%
.30	25%	.40	12%
		.20	14%

3-4B. a. (*Required Rate of Return Using CAPM*) Compute a "fair" rate of return for the common shares of IBM given a beta of 1.5. The risk-free rate is 8 percent and the market portfolio (Toronto Stock Exchange 300 Index) has an expected return of 16 percent.

b. Why is the rate you have computed a "fair" rate?

3-5B. (*Estimating Beta*) The following figure illustrates the relationship between the holding-period returns for Bram, Inc., and the TSE 300 Index, estimate the firm's beta.

3-6B. (*Capital Asset Pricing Model*) Bobbi Manufacturing, Inc., is considering several investments. The rate on Treasury bills is currently 6.75 percent, and the expected return for the market is 12 percent. What should be the required rates of return for each investment (using the CAPM)?

Security	Beta
A	1.40
B	0.75
C	0.80
D	1.20

3-7B. (*Capital Asset Pricing Model*) Breckenridge, Inc., has a beta of 0.85. If the expected market return is 10.5 percent and the risk-free rate is 7.5 percent, what is the appropriate required return of Breckenridge (using the CAPM)?

3-8B. (*Capital Asset Pricing Model*) The expected return for the general market is 12.8 percent, and the risk premium in the market is 4.3 percent. NCNB, Toyota, and Macintosh have betas of 0.82, 0.57, and 0.68, respectively. What are the corresponding required rates of return for the three securities?

3-9B. (Computing Holding-Period Returns) From the price data below, compute the holding-period returns for O'Toole and Shamrock.

Time	O'Toole	Shamrock
1	$22	$45
2	24	50
3	20	48
4	25	52

How would you interpret the meaning of a holding-period return?

3-10B. (*Measuring Risk and Rates of Return*) Given the holding-period returns shown below, calculate the average returns and the standard deviations for the Sugita Corporation and for the market.

Month	Market	Sugita Corp.
1	1.50%	1.80%
2	1.00%	−0.50%
3	0.00%	2.00%
4	−2.00%	−2.00%
5	4.00%	5.00%
6	3.00%	5.00%

If Sugita's beta is 1.18, and the risk-free rate is 8 percent, what would be an appropriate required return for an investor owning Sugita? (Note: Since the above returns are based on monthly data, you will need to annualize the returns to make them compatible with the risk-free rate. For simplicity, you may convert from monthly to yearly returns by multiplying the average monthly returns by 12.)

How does Sugita's historical average return compare with the return you believe to be a "fair" return, given the firm's systematic risk?

3-11B. (*Portfolio Beta and Security Market Line*) You own a portfolio consisting of the following shares.

Security	Percentage of Portfolio	Beta	Expected Return
1	10%	1.00	12%
2	25%	0.75	11%
3	15%	1.30	15%
4	30%	0.60	9%
5	20%	1.20	14%

The risk-free rate is 8 percent. Also, the expected return on the market portfolio is 11.6 percent.

a. Calculate the expected return and the beta for your portfolio.

b. Given the information above, plot the security market line on paper. Plot the shares from your portfolio on your graph.

c. From your plot in part (b), which shares appear to be your "winners" and which ones appear to be "losers"?

d. Why should we consider our conclusions in part (c) to be less than certain?

SELF-TEST SOLUTIONS

SS-1.

(A) Probability $P(X_i)$	(B) Return (X_i)	Expected Return (X) (A) × (B)	Weighted Deviation $(X_i - \overline{X})^2 p(X_k)$
.10	−10%	−1%	52.9%
.20	5%	1%	12.8%
.30	10%	3%	2.7%
.40	25%	10%	57.6%
		$\overline{X} = 13\%$	$\sigma^2 = 126.0\%$
			$\sigma = 11.22\%$

From our studies in statistics, we know that if the distribution of returns was normal, then Universal could expect a return of 13 percent with a 67 percent possibility that this return would vary up or down by 11.22 percent between 1.78 percent (13% − 11.22%) and 24.22 percent (13% + 11.22%). However, the distribution is not normal, as is apparent from the probabilities.

SS-2. Security A 5% + .75(17% − 5%) = 14%

Security B 5% + .90(17% − 5%) = 15.8%

Security C 5% + 1.40(17% − 5%) = 21.8%

SS-3. Market:

$$\text{Average return} = \frac{2\% + 3\% + 1\% - 1\%}{4}$$

$$= 1.25\%$$

Standard deviation =

$$\sqrt{\frac{(2\% - 1.25\%)^2 + (3\% - 1.25\%)^2 + (1\% - 1.25\%)^2 + (-1\% - 1.25\%)^2}{4 - 1}}$$

$$= 1.71\%$$

Kaifu:

Average return $= \dfrac{4\% + 6\% + 0\% + 2\%}{4}$

$$= 3.00\%$$

Standard deviation =

$$\sqrt{\frac{(4\% - 3\%)^2 + (6\% - 3\%)^2 + (0\% - 3\%)^2 + (2\% - 3\%)^2}{4 - 1}}$$

$$= 2.58\%$$

SS-4.

Time	Share Price		Holding-Period Return
1	$10		
2	13	($13/$10) – 1	30.0%
3	11	($11/$13) – 1	–15.4%
4	15	($15/$11) – 1	36.4%

SS-5. Portfolio beta:

$$(.4 \times 1) + (.25 \times .75) + (.35 \times 1.3) = 1.04$$

Portfolio expected return:

$$(.4 \times 12\%) + (.25 \times 11\%) + (.35 \times 15\%) = 12.8\%$$

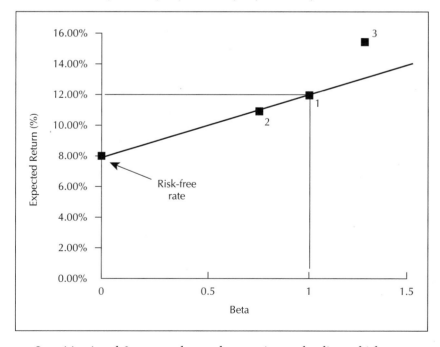

Securities 1 and 2 seem to be on the security market line, which suggests that they earn a fair return, given their systematic risk. Security 3, on the other hand, is earning more than a fair return (above the security market line). However, we may be seeing an illusion; it is possible to misspecify the security market line by using bad estimates in our data.

APPENDIX 3A: Review of Probability Distributions and Descriptive Statistics

ONLY ONE TO STUDY

Probability distributions illustrate the complete set of probabilities over all possible outcomes for that particular event. There are two general types of probability distributions—discrete and continuous. A discrete probability distribution is one in which a probability is assigned to each possible outcome in the set of all possible outcomes. For example, if we are considering a coin toss, there would be two possible outcomes, each with a .50 probability of occurring; if we were considering a horse race with 10 horses, there would be 10 possible outcomes, with the probability of each outcome depending on the speed of each horse. An investment opportunity with five possible outcomes, as shown in Table 3A-1, is another example of a discrete distribution.

This distribution is illustrated graphically in Figure 3A-1, giving us a picture of all the possible outcomes and the probabilities associated with them.

Note that the sum of all probabilities attached to all possible outcomes must add up to 1.0. This is because one of these outcomes must occur; otherwise all possible outcomes have not been identified.

STOP GO TO Pg 98 EXPECTED VALUE

Whereas in a discrete probability distribution probabilities are assigned to specific outcomes, in a continuous probability distribution there are an infinite number of possible outcomes, in which the probability of an event is related to a range of possible outcomes. The easiest way to illustrate a continuous distribution is graphically, as in Figure 3A-2. Probability in this case is measured by the area under the curve.

Thus, when provided with a continuous distribution, we can answer the question, "What is the probability that an outcome will fall within a certain range of values?" A discrete distribution, on the other hand, lets us answer the question, "What is the probability that a specific outcome will occur?" The key to understanding the difference between these questions—and the underlying differences between these classifications of distributions—is that for discrete distributions the number of possible outcomes is finite, while for continuous distributions the number is infinite.

Possible Outcome (X_1)	Probability of Occurrence $P(X_1)$
$ 5,000	0.10
$ 7,000	0.25
$ 8,000	0.30
$ 9,000	0.25
$11,000	0.10

1.0

TABLE 3A-1
A Discrete Probability Distribution

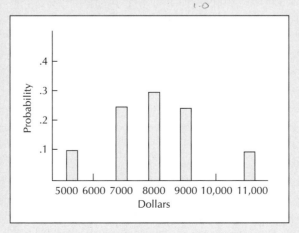

FIGURE 3A-1
A Discrete Probability Distribution

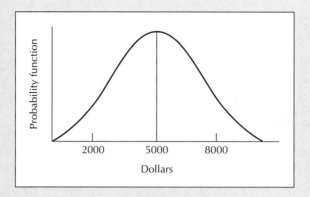

Continuous distributions are quite common and valuable, but in general they require a degree of calculus that might be confusing. Thus, in the remainder of the book we will be concerned primarily with discrete probability distributions.

Expected Value

The expected value of a distribution is the arithmetic mean or average of all possible outcomes, where those outcomes are weighted by the probability that each outcome will occur. Thus, the expected value, $\overline{X}$, can be calculated as follows:

$$\overline{X} = \sum_{i=1}^{N} X_i P(X_i) \qquad (3A\text{-}1)$$

where

N = the number of possible outcomes

X_i = the value of the ith possible outcome

$P(X_i)$ = the probability that the ith outcome will occur

To illustrate the computation of the expected value, consider the investment opportunity given in Table 3A-1. To determine the expected value of this distribution, we need only multiply each possible outcome by its probability of occurrence and add the products together as follows:

$$\begin{aligned}
\overline{X} &= \$5000(.10) + \$7000(.25) + \$8000(.30) \\
&\quad + \$9000(.25) + \$11,000(.10) \\
&= \$8000
\end{aligned}$$

When we are estimating cash flows that are to occur in the future, we cannot estimate them with certainty. The expected value provides us with only the mean of the probability distribution from which that future cash flow will come. While the expected value provides us with a measure of central tendency, it tells us nothing about the amount of dispersion contained in the probability distribution. To measure dispersion, we will examine the standard deviation and coefficient of variation.

Standard Deviation

The standard deviation provides a measure of the spread of the probability distribution. The larger the standard deviation, the greater the dispersion of the distribution. It is calculated by squaring the difference between each outcome and its expected value, weighting each value by its probability, adding all possible outcomes, and taking the square root of this sum. Thus, the standard deviation becomes

$$\sigma = \sqrt{\sum_{i=1}^{N} (X_i - \overline{X})^2 P(X_i)} \qquad (3A\text{-}2)$$

where
N = the number of possible outcomes

X_i = the value of the ith possible outcome

$\overline{X}$ = the expected value

$P(X_i)$ = the probability that the ith outcome will occur

The calculations for the standard deviation for the distribution given in Table 3A-1 are provided in Table 3A-2.

In the case of a normal distribution, the standard deviation gives us even more than a measure of the absolute dispersion of that distribution. In this case we can, by consulting a table of areas under the normal curve, determine the probability that the outcome will be above or below a specific value. For example, in a normal distribution there is a 68.3 percent probability that the outcome will be within one standard deviation (plus or minus) of the expected value and a 95.0 percent probability that it will be within two standard deviations. Thus, if we are looking at two normal distributions, one with an expected value of $1,000 and a standard deviation of $200 and the other with an expected value of $2,000 and a standard deviation of $300, we can conclude that the second distribution has more dispersion, and hence more absolute risk associated with it. This does not mean that the second distribution is less desirable, just that it has more absolute risk. While the standard deviation gives us a good measure of a distribution's absolute dispersion, it is also desirable to measure dispersion or risk relative to return to provide the manager with a relative measure of risk. This is the purpose of the coefficient of variation.

Coefficient of Variation ~ForGet.

The coefficient of variation provides us with a measure of the relative dispersion of a probability distribution—that is, the risk per unit of return. Mathematically, it is defined as the standard deviation divided by the expected value, or

$$\gamma = \frac{\sigma}{\overline{X}} \tag{3A-3}$$

This measure derives its value from the fact that using the standard deviation to compare the riskiness of two investments can be misleading when the investments are of unequal size.

For example, let us look at two normal distributions given in Table 3A-3. In this case distribution B has more absolute risk, as indicated by its standard deviation; however, distribution A has more risk associated with it relative to its expected value. The value of examining the relative risk can easily be seen when

Step 1: Calculate Differences $(X_i - \overline{X})$	Step 2: Square Differences $(X_i - \overline{X})^2$	Step 3: Squared Differences Times Probabilities $(X_i - \overline{X})^2 P(X_i)$
$ 5,000 − $8,000 = −$3,000	$9,000,000	$9,000,000(.10) = $900,000
7,000 − 8,000 = − 1,000	1,000,000	1,000,000(.25) = 250,000
8,000 − 8,000 = 0	0	0(.30) = 0
9,000 − 8,000 = 1,000	1,000,000	1,000,000(.25) = 250,000
11,000 − 8,000 = 3,000	9,000,000	9,000,000(.10) = 900,000

Step 4: Sum	Step 5: Take the Square Root
$\sum_{i=1}^{N} (X_i - \overline{X})^2 P(X_i) = \$2,300,000$	$\sigma = \sqrt{\sum_{i=1}^{N} (X_i - \overline{X})^2 P(X_i)} = \$1,517$

TABLE 3A-2
Calculation of the Standard Deviation for the Distribution in Table 3A-1

TABLE 3A-3			Investment A	Investment B
Coefficient of Variation	Expected value	$\overline{X}$	$1000	$2000
	Standard deviation	σ	$ 200	$ 300
	Coefficient of variation	$\sigma/\overline{X}$	0.20	0.15

examining distributions containing the same level of absolute risk or standard deviation but dramatically different levels of expected value. For example, consider two investments, both with standard deviations of $1,000, one having an expected value of $1,000, and the other an expected value of $1,000,000. In each case the absolute risk is the same, as measured by the standard deviation, but the relative risk is not. Thus, the use of the coefficient of variation along with the standard deviation is especially important when two investments of unequal size are being compared. To ignore the coefficient of variation in this case could lead to misconceptions as to the relative level of uncertainty contained in each investment.

APPENDIX 3B: Measuring a Security's Return and Risk

The Capital Asset Pricing Model (CAPM) draws heavily on our ability to measure a security's risk statistics, such as beta. We must determine an accurate beta for the CAPM to yield good results. An estimate of the appropriate required rate of return is only as accurate as the data used to obtain it.

As noted in this chapter, there are some difficulties in using the CAPM, most of which relate to empirical problems. Specifically, from where do we draw our data in making our estimates? Simply put, for us to use the model correctly, we need to know the investors' expectations about future returns. However, only historical rates of returns are available to us. Nevertheless, our best hope at seeing the future is by looking at the past. Essentially, we use the historical return data and hope that the past will closely reflect the investor's expectations about the future. Thus, we rely on historical returns when we compute the beta for a security or a portfolio.

To compute risk statistics, professional analysts typically use five years of monthly return data, or 60 months, and make certain adjustments to their computations. For instance, we know that betas over time tend to move toward a value of one. If the beta is, at the present, substantially greater than one, it will gradually decline over time, and betas that are substantially below one will tend to increase in future periods. So forecasters adjust for this observed tendency. However, for our purposes, we simply will use the historical return data of the past 12 months.

We now compute the risk statistics for Spar Aerospace's common share using historical returns for the 60 months ending December 1992. These returns, along with the corresponding returns for the TSE 300 Index, are shown in Table 3B-1.

We determine the beta for asset j which can take the form of a security or a portfolio by regressing its returns on the returns of the market portfolio. This relationship is described by the following equation:

$$R_{jt} = \alpha_j + \beta_j(R_{Mt}) + e_{jt}$$

where
R_{jt} = the monthly holding-period return for asset j in month t

α_j = alpha, the point where the regression line intercepts the vertical axis

β_j = beta for asset j; the slope of the regression line

Month and Year	Spar Aerospace		TSE 300 Index	
	Price $	Return %	Value	Return %
December 1987	16.25		3160.1	
January 1988	15.63	–3.85	3057.2	–3.26
February	14.5	–7.20	3204.8	4.83
March	16.75	15.52	3313.8	3.40
April	17.13	2.24	3339.8	0.78
May	18.25	6.57	3249.2	–2.71
June	19.00	4.11	3441.5	5.92
July	19.63	3.29	3376.7	–1.88
August	19.63	0.00	3285.8	–2.69
September	20.13	2.55	3283.7	–0.06
October	21.00	4.35	3395.5	3.40
November	16.75	–20.24	3294.7	–2.97
December	17.50	4.48	3390.0	2.89
January 1989	15.25	–12.86	3616.6	6.68
February	14.88	–2.43	3572.1	–1.25
March	14.88	0.00	3578.2	0.17
April	15.00	0.84	3627.9	1.39
May	13.63	–9.17	3707.4	2.19
June	12.88	–5.50	3760.9	1.44
July	13.00	0.97	3970.8	5.58
August	12.63	–2.88	4010.2	0.99
September	11.38	–9.90	3943.0	–1.68
October	10.00	–12.09	3918.6	–0.62
November	8.50	–15.00	3942.8	0.62
December	8.63	1.47	3969.8	0.68
January 1990	9.63	11.59	3704.4	–6.69
February	10.33	7.27	3686.7	–0.48
March	10.25	–0.73	3639.5	–1.28
April	8.25	–19.51	3340.9	–8.20
May	8.33	0.91	3582.0	7.22
June	9.25	11.11	3543.9	–1.06
July	10.25	10.81	3561.1	0.49
August	9.63	–6.10	3346.3	–6.03
September	8.25	–14.29	3159.4	–5.59
October	8.88	7.58	3081.3	–2.47
November	10.25	15.49	3151.0	2.26
December	10.88	6.10	3256.8	3.36
January 1991	12.13	11.49	3272.9	0.49
February	12.5	3.09	3462.4	5.79
March	14.38	15.00	3495.7	0.96
April	12.5	–13.04	3468.8	–0.77
May	12.63	1.00	3546.1	2.23
June	12.88	1.98	3465.8	–2.26
July	14.25	10.68	3539.6	2.13
August	15.75	10.53	3517.9	–0.61
September	14.38	–8.73	3387.9	–3.70
October	15.38	6.96	3515.8	3.78
November	16.00	4.07	3448.5	–1.91
December	16.00	0.00	3512.4	1.85

TABLE 3B-1

Monthly Holding-Period Returns, Spar Aerospace, and the TSE 300 Index December 1987– December 1992

Continued on page 102

TABLE 3B-1
Monthly Holding-Period
Returns, Spar Aerospace,
and the TSE 300 Index
December 1987–
December 1992
Continued from page 101

Month and Year	Spar Aerospace		TSE 300 Index	
	Price $	Return %	Value	Return %
January 1992	18.38	14.84	3596.1	2.38
February	18.25	–0.68	3582.0	–0.39
March	19.13	4.79	3412.1	–4.74
April	19.00	–0.65	3355.6	–1.66
May	18.25	–3.95	3387.9	0.96
June	15.50	–15.07	3387.7	–0.01
July	15.75	1.61	3443.4	1.64
August	16.75	6.35	3402.9	–1.18
September	16.38	–2.24	3297.9	–3.09
October	15.25	–6.87	3336.1	1.16
November	15.00	–1.64	3283.0	–1.59
December	15.75	5.00	3350.0	2.04

R_{Mt} = the return on the market portfolio in month t

e_{jt} = the error term; the difference between the actual return in month t and the expected return given the market's return (that is, the distance the actual return lies away from the regression line).

Our objective is to find the alpha and beta values that minimize the sum of the squares of the error terms. This type of calculation enables us to find the line that best fits the data; that is, it best describes the average relationship between the returns of asset j and the returns of the market portfolio. There are three ways for determining alpha and beta.

1. We could plot the return data on graph paper and then "eyeball" the regression line, trying to get what appears to be the best fit to the data. The point where the line crosses the vertical axis would indicate our estimate for the alpha value. We would then estimate the beta by measuring how steeply the line increases vertically (return of asset j) relative to a change on the horizontal axis (return of market portfolio). That is, we would find:

$$\beta_j = \frac{\text{Rise}}{\text{Run}} = \frac{\Delta R_{jt}}{\Delta R_{Mt}}$$

The obvious limitation with this approach is its potential for error since accuracy of the estimation depends in part on the sharpness of the eye. Your estimate would most likely be somewhat different from another person's, especially if the data did not have a tight fit.

2. The beta of asset j can be calculated from the following equation:

$$\beta_j = \frac{(\rho)(\sigma_j)(\sigma_M)}{(\sigma_M)^2} = \frac{(\rho)(\sigma_j)}{(\sigma_M)}$$

where ρ = the correlation coefficient of the regression of returns of asset j on returns of the market portfolio

σ_j = the standard deviation of the returns of asset j

σ_M = the standard deviation of the returns of the market portfolio

Table 3-3 shows that the standard deviations of returns of Spar Aerospace and the TSE 300 Index are 3.21 and 8.73, respectively. The correlation coefficient (ρ) of this regression equation is 0.23. Thus, the beta of Spar Aerospace can be computed by substituting these values in Equation (3B-1), as follows:

$$\beta = \frac{(\rho)(\sigma_j)}{(\sigma_M)} = \frac{(.23)(8.73)}{(3.21)} = 0.63$$

Thus, the beta for Spar Aerospace is 0.63.

3. We can also use a statistical package from a calculator (see Appendix E at the end of the book) or a computer spreadsheet to determine alpha and beta. This option is preferred because of the ability to view the original return data in order to check for accuracy in data entry and the ease of working with the calculations that are repetitive.

STUDY PROBLEMS (SET A)

3B-1. (*Risk and Return Statistics for a Security*) Compute the following statistics for Arka's common share: (1) average return, (2) standard deviation of the returns, (3) alpha, and (4) beta.

Yearly Holding-Period Returns		
Year	Arka	TSE 300
1990	10%	12%
1991	6%	7%
1992	18%	24%
1993	15%	18%

3B-2. (*Risk and Return Statistics for a Security*) Compute the following statistics for the common shares of Son Sen, Inc.: (1) average return, (2) standard deviation of the returns, (3) alpha, and (4) beta.

Yearly Holding-Period Returns		
Month	Son Sen	TSE 300
January	0.6%	0.9%
February	0.3	1.0
March	–1.5	–1.0
April	–0.7	0.0
May	1.9	3.0
June	0.5	–1.5
July	2.5	3.0
August	0.8	1.2
September	–2.5	–4.0
October	3.0	4.5
November	0.4	1.4
December	0.1	0.2

APPENDIX 3C: Measuring the Required Rate: The Arbitrage Pricing Model[26]

The basic theme of the arbitrage pricing model (APM) can be stated as follows:

1. Actual security returns vary from their expected amounts because of unanticipated changes in a number of basic economic forces, such as unexpected changes in industrial production, inflation rates, the term structure of interest rates, and the difference in interest rates between high- and low-risk bonds.[27]

2. Just as the CAPM defined a portfolio's systematic risk to be its sensitivity to the general-market returns (i.e., its beta coefficient), APM suggests that the risk of a security is reflected in its sensitivity to the unexpected changes in important economic forces.

3. Any two stocks or portfolios that have the same sensitivity to the meaningful economic forces (that is, the same relevant or systematic risk) must have the same expected return. Otherwise, we could replace some of the stocks in our portfolio with other stocks having the same sensitivities, but higher expected returns, and earn riskless profits.

4. We would expect portfolios that are highly sensitive to unexpected changes in macroeconomic forces to offer investors high expected returns. This relationship may be represented quantitatively as follows:

$$E(R_i) = R_f + (S_{i1})(RP_1) + (S_{i2})(RP_2) + \ldots + (S_{ij})(RP_j) + \ldots + (S_{im})(RP_m) \quad \text{(3C-1)}$$

where $E(R_i)$ = the expected return for stock or portfolio i

R_f = the risk-free rate

S_{ij} = the sensitivity of stock i returns to unexpected changes in economic force j

RP_j = the market risk premium associated with an unexpected change in the jth economic force

m = the number of relevant economic forces

To help understand the APM model, we will draw from the actual research of Bower, Bower, and Logue (BBL).[28] After computing monthly returns for 815 stocks from 1970 through 1979, BBL used a technique called factor analysis to study the general movement of monthly returns for the 815 stocks. The technique identified four factors that helped to explain the movement of the returns, and also used Equation (3C-1) to represent the risk-return relationship in an APM format. The actual model appears as follows:

Expected return for Stock i = 6.2% − 185.5%(S_{i1}) + 144.5%(S_{i2})
$\qquad\qquad\qquad\qquad$ + 12.4% (S_{i3}) − 274.4%(S_{i4})

The value of 6.2% in the equation is an estimate of the risk-free rate, as determined by the model; the remaining values, −185.5, ... −274.4, signify the

---

[26]The following description of the APM is taken in part from Dorothy H. Bower, Richard S. Bower, and Dennis E. Logue, "A Primer on Arbitrage Pricing Theory," *The Revolution in Corporate Finance*, eds. Joel M. Stern and Donald H. Chew, Jr. New York: Basil Blackwell, 1986, pp. 69–77.

[27]See R. Roll and S. Ross, "The Arbitrage Pricing Theory Approach to Strategic Portfolio Planning," *Financial Analysts Journal*, May–June 1984, pp. 14–26.

[28]Dorothy A. Bower, Richard S. Bower, and Dennis E. Logue, "Equity Screening Rates Using Arbitrage Pricing Theory," in C. F. Lee, ed., *Advances in Financial Planning*, Greenwich, CT: JAI Press, 1984.

market risk premiums for each of the four factors; and the $S_{i1}, \ldots, S_{i4}$ represent the sensitivities of stock i to the four factors.

The BBL factors are determined statistically from past return data and were not intuitively or economically identified. That is, the technique provides "factors" that tell us more about the movement in the returns than would any other factors.[29] Each factor could conceivably relate to a single economic variable; however, it is more likely that each factor represents the influence of several economic variables.[30]

Having specified the APM risk-return relationship, BBL then used the model to estimate the expected (required) rates of return for 17 stocks. This estimation required BBL to use regression analysis to study the relationships of the returns of the 17 stocks to the four factors. From this regression analysis, they were able to measure the sensitivity of each security's return to a particular factor. These "sensitivity coefficients" for a particular stock may then be combined with the APM model in Equation (3C-1) to estimate the investors' required rate of return.

Using 3 of the 17 stocks to demonstrate the calculation, the regression coefficients (sensitivity coefficients) for American Hospital Supply, CBS, and Western Union are shown below:

	Stock Sensitivity Coefficients (S)			
	Factor 1	Factor 2	Factor 3	Factor 4
American Hospital Supply	−0.050	0.010	0.040	0.020
CBS	−0.050	0.002	0.005	0.010
Western Union	−0.050	−0.020	−0.010	0.009

Using these stock sensitivity coefficients and the APM model, as developed by BBL, we can estimate the investors' expected (required) rate of return for each stock as follows:

$$\text{American Hospital Supply} = 6.2\% - 185.5\%(-0.050) + 144.5\%(0.010) \\ + 12.4\%(0.040) - 274.4\%(.020)$$

$$= 11.93\%$$

$$\text{CBS} = 6.2\% - 185.5\%(-0.050) + 144.5\%(0.002) \\ + 12.4\%(0.005) - 274.4\%(0.010)$$

$$= 13.08\%$$

$$\text{Western Union} = 6.2\% - 185.5\%(-0.050) + 144.5\%(-0.020) \\ + 12.4\%(-0.010) - 274.4\%(0.009)$$

$$= 9.99\%$$

We have now used two approaches for measuring the required rate of return (or expected rate of return) of investors: the CAPM and the APM. The capital asset pricing model (CAPM) is a single-index model that considers the general market to be the only important factor in setting the values of individual stocks. The arbitrage pricing model (APM), on the other hand, recognizes several macroeconomic factors in estimating returns (and values).

---

[29]A more detailed analysis of this material is provided by: N. Chen, "Some Empirical Tests of the Theory of Arbitrage Pricing," *Journal of Finance*, December 1983, 1393–1414; and Richard Roll, "A Critique of the Asset Pricing Theory's Tests," *Journal of Financial Economics*, March 1977, pp. 129–176.

[30]As noted earlier in the chapter, work is under way to determine the economic factors that most influence security returns. See R. Roll and S. Ross, "The Arbitrage Pricing Theory Approach to Strategic Portfolio Planning," *Financial Analysts Journal*, May–June 1984, pp. 14–26.

STUDY PROBLEMS

3C-1. (*Arbitrage Pricing Model*) Using the APM, along with the results of the Bower, Bower, and Logue research given in the chapter, estimate the appropriate required rates of return for the following three securities:

	Sensitivity Factor			
Security	Factor 1	Factor 2	Factor 3	Factor 4
A	−0.070	−0.020	0.010	0.003
B	−0.070	0.030	0.005	0.010
C	−0.070	−0.010	0.006	0.009

3C-2. **a.** (*Required Rate of Return Using APM*) If we use the arbitrage pricing model to measure investors' required rate of return, what is our concept of risk?

b. Using the results of the Bower, Bower, and Logue study of return variability, as captured in Equation (4C-1), calculate the investors' required rate of return for the following securities:

	Sensitivity Factor			
Security	Factor 1	Factor 2	Factor 3	Factor 4
A	−0.070	0.030	0.005	0.010
B	−0.070	−0.010	0.006	0.009
C	−0.050	0.004	−0.010	−0.007
D	−0.060	−0.007	−0.006	0.006

c. Assuming (i) a risk-free rate of 6.1 percent and (ii) an expected market return of 17.25 percent, estimate the investors' required rate of return for the four securities in part (b), using the CAPM.

Security	Beta
A	1.40
B	1.70
C	1.20
D	1.10

d. What might explain the differences in your answers to parts (b) and (c)?

Altman, Edward I. New York University, "Setting The Record Straight on Junk Bonds: A Review of the Research on Default Rates and Returns," *Journal of Applied Corporate Finance*, (Summer 1990), 82.

Black F., and M. Scholes. "The Pricing of Options and Corporate Liabilities," *Journal of Political Economy*, 81 (1973), 637–657.

Blume, Marshall E., Donald B. Keim, and Sandeep A. Patel. "Returns and Volatility of Low-Grade Bonds, 1977–1989," *The Journal of Finance* (March 1991), 49–74.

Bower, D., R. Bower, and D. Logue. "Arbitrage Pricing and Utility Stock Returns," *Journal of Finance* (September 1984), 1041–1054.

Brennan, M., and E. Schwartz. "Evaluating Natural Resource Investments," *The Journal of Business*, 58 (April 1985), 135–157.

Butler, J.S., and Barry Schachter. "The Investment Decision: Estimation Risk and Risk Adjusted Discount Rates," *Journal of Financial Management* (Winter 1989), 13.

Chen, N. "Some Empirical Tests of the Theory of Arbitrage Pricing," *Journal of Finance*, 38 (December 1983), 1393–1414.

Cochrane, John H. "Production-Based Asset Pricing and the Link Between Stock Returns and Economic Fluctuations," *The Journal of Finance* (March 1991), 209–238.

Hatch James E. and Robert W. White. *Canadian Stocks, Bonds, Bills, and Inflation: 1950–1987*. Charlottesville, Virginia: The Research Foundation of the Institute of Chartered Financial Analysts, 1988.

Haugen, Robert A., Eli Talmor, and Walter N. Torous. "The Effect of Volatility Changes on the Level of Stock Prices and Subsequent Expected Returns," *The Journal of Finance* (July 1991), 985–1008.

Ibbotson, R. G., and R. A. Sinquefield. *Stocks, Bonds, Bills and Inflations: Historical Return (1926–1987)*. Chicago: Dow Jones-Irwin, 1989.

Keim, D. "Size-Related Anomalies and Stock Market Seasonality: Further Empirical Evidence," *Journal of Financial Economics* (June 1983), 13–32.

Lanstein, R., and W. Sharpe. "Duration and Security Risk," *Journal of Financial and Quantitative Analysis* (November 1978), 653–668.

Levy, H. "Tests of Capital Asset Pricing Hypotheses," *Research in Finance*, 1 (1979), 115–223.

Macaulay, F. R. *Some Theoretical Problems Suggested by Movements of Interest Rates, Bond Yields, and Stock Prices Since 1856*. New York: National Bureau of Economic Research, 1938.

Markowitz, Harry M. "Foundations of Portfolio Theory," *The Journal of Finance* (June 1991), 469–478.

Martin, John, Samuel Cox, and Richard MacMinn. *The Theory of Finance: Evidence and Applications*, Chapters 15–17. Hinsdale, IL: The Dryden Press, 1988.

Modigliani, F., and G. Pogue. "An Introduction to Risk and Return," *Financial Analysts Journal* (March–April 1974 and May–June 1974), 68–80, 69–86.

Roll, R., and S. Ross. "The Arbitrage Pricing Theory Approach to Strategic Portfolio Planning," *Financial Analysts Journal* (May–June 1984), 14–26.

Rosenberg, B. "The Capital Asset Pricing Model and the Market Model," *Journal of Portfolio Management* (Winter 1981), 5–16.

Snow, Karl N. "Diagnosing Asset Pricing Models Using the Distribution of Asset Returns," *The Journal of Finance* (July 1991), 955–984.

Stewart, G. Bennett, III. "Announcing the Stern Stewart Performance 1,000: A New Way of Viewing Corporate America," *Journal of Applied Corporate Finance* (Summer 1990), 38.

In this chapter we examine the concepts and procedures for valuing financial assets, especially financial securities, such as bonds, preferred shares, and common shares. Since the financial manager's objective is to maximize the value of the firm's common shares, we need to understand the principles that underlie value. In fact, the Maxims of the French writer La Rouchefoucauld, written over three centuries ago, still speak to us: "The greatest of all gifts is the power to estimate things at their true worth."

The major objectives of this chapter include:

1. To examine various definitions of the term "value," including book value, liquidation value, market value, and intrinsic value.

2. To apply the concept of time value of money to single payments, annuities, streams of uneven cash flows, mortgage loans and perpetuities.

3. To determine the value of financial securities such as bonds, preferred shares, and common shares.

4. To examine the concept of the investor's expected rate of return, particularly as it relates to bonds, preferred shares, and common shares.

5. To examine a historical perspective of returns actually received by the "average investor" over the past decades.

6. The chapter concludes with appendices, in which we seek a deeper understanding of bond valuation, including the important concept of "duration," and examine the relationship between a firm's common share value and its earnings, which is often used as a guide by those needing to value a security.

DEFINITIONS OF VALUE

The term *value* is often used in different contexts, depending on the application being made. Examples of different uses of this term include book value, liquidation value, market value, and intrinsic value.

Book value is the value of an asset as shown on a firm's balance sheet. It represents a historical value rather than a current worth.[1] For example, the book value for a company's common shares is the sum of the capital shares value, the contributed surplus, and the retained earnings. The capital shares value and the contributed surplus are equal to the amount the company received when the securities were originally issued. Retained earnings are the amount of net income retained within the firm rather than being paid out as dividends to common shareholders. Thus, the retention of earnings is an indirect way for the shareholders to invest more money in the firm.[2] If we want to know the book value for each common share, we simply divide the total book value by the number of shares outstanding. For example, the book value for CAE Industries' common shares on March 31, 1990 was $4.93, computed as follows:

Common shares ($000)	$304,900
Retained earnings ($000)	170,189
Total book value of common ($000)	$475,089
Number of common shares outstanding	96,291,595
Book value per share ($475,089,000/96,291,595 shares)	$4.93

Liquidation value is the dollar sum that could be realized if an asset were sold individually and not as a part of a going concern. For example, if a product line is discontinued, the machinery used in its production might be sold. The sale price would be its liquidation value and would be determined independently of the firm's value. Similarly, if the firm's operations were discontinued and its assets were sold as a separate collection, the sales price would represent the firm's liquidation value.

The **market value** of an asset is the observed value for the asset in the marketplace. This value is determined by demand and supply forces working together in the marketplace, where buyers and sellers negotiate a mutually acceptable price for the asset. For instance, the range of market prices for which CAE Industries Ltd. traded during the fiscal year 1989–90 was $6.63 and $15.50. This price range was determined by a large number of buyers and sellers working through the Toronto Stock Exchange. In theory, a market price exists for all assets. However, many assets have no readily observable market price because trading seldom occurs. For instance, the market

---

[1] The book value of a firm will vary depending on the accounting practices used by the firm, and consequently may bear only a weak relationship to the firm's economic value.

[2] Note that 36% of CAE Industries' book value is attributable to the reinvestment of the firm's profits and 64% represent new investments in the firm.

price for the common shares of McCain Ltd., a New Brunswick-based family-owned firm, would be more difficult to establish than the market value of the Seagram company's common shares.

The **intrinsic value** of an asset can be defined as the present value of the asset's expected future cash flows. This value is also called the fair value, as perceived by the investor, given the amount, timing, and riskiness of future cash flows. In essence, intrinsic value is like the "value in the eyes of the investor." Given the risk, the investor determines the appropriate discount rate, sometimes called the capitalization rate, to use in computing the present or intrinsic value of the asset. Once the investor has estimated the intrinsic value of a security, this value can be compared with its market value. If the intrinsic value is greater than the market value, then the security is undervalued in the eyes of the investor. Should the market value exceed the investor's intrinsic value, then the security is overvalued.

We hasten to add that if the securities market is working efficiently, the market value and the intrinsic value of a security will be equal. That is, whenever a security's intrinsic value differs from its current market price, the competition among investors seeking opportunities to make a profit will quickly drive the market price back into equilibrium with intrinsic value. Thus, we may define an **efficient market** as one in which the values of all securities at any instant in time fully reflect all available information, which results in the market value and the intrinsic value being the same.[3] If the markets are truly efficient, it is extremely difficult for an investor to make extra profits from an ability to predict prices.

The idea of market efficiency has been the backdrop for an intense battle between professional investors and university professors. The academic community has contended that a blindfolded monkey throwing darts at the list of securities in the *Financial Post* could do as well as a professional money manager. Market professionals, on the other hand, retort that academicians are so immersed in research they could not recognize potential profits even if they were delivered to their offices. The war has been intense, but one that the student of finance should find intriguing.

Perspective in Finance
_____

Intrinsic value is the present value of expected future cash flows. This fact is true regardless of what type of asset we are valuing. If you remember only one thing from this chapter, remember that intrinsic value is the present value of expected future cash flows.

THE BASICS OF VALUATION

For our purposes, we will refer to the *value* of an asset as its *intrinsic value*, which is the present value of its expected future cash flows, where these cash flows are discounted back to the present using the investor's required rate of return. Value is affected by three elements:

1. The amount and timing of the asset's expected cash flows

_____

[3]Market efficiency is an equilibrium condition. This condition implies that intrinsic and market values are not equal at every instant, but these values are equal on average.

2. The riskiness of these cash flows

3. The investor's required rate of return for undertaking the investment

The first two factors are characteristics of the asset, while the required rate of return is the minimum rate necessary to attract an investor to purchase or hold a security. This rate must be high enough to compensate the investor for the risk perceived in the asset's future cash flows. These factors are depicted in Figure 4-1. As the figure shows, finding the value of an asset involves the following: (1) assessing the asset's characteristics, which include the amount and timing of the expected cash flows and the riskiness of these cash flows; (2) determining the investor's required rate of return, which embodies the investor's attitude about assuming risk and perception of the riskiness of the asset; and (3) discounting the expected cash flows back to the present, using the investor's required rate of return. We will look at each of these considerations.

Perspective in Finance

A key concept that underlies this material is the time value of money that is, a dollar today is worth more than a dollar received a year from now. Intuitively this idea is easy to understand. We are all familiar with the concept of interest, and this concept illustrates what economists call an opportunity cost of passing up the earning potential of a dollar today. This opportunity cost is the time value of money.

In evaluating and comparing investment proposals, we need to determine the value of cash flows from accepting these proposals. To do this, all dollar values must be made comparable; and, since a dollar received today is worth more than a dollar received in the future, we must move all dollar flows back to the present or out to a common future date. An understanding of the time value of money is essential to an understanding of financial management, whether basic or advanced. As a result, we will begin our analysis of valuation by examining simple financial assets, such as savings accounts, and then proceed to the valuation of more sophisticated financial instruments such as bonds, and preferred and common shares.

THE VALUATION OF SINGLE PERIOD PAYMENTS

Future Value

Most of us encounter the concept of future value or the compounding of interest at an early age. Anyone who has ever had a savings account at a commercial bank or trust company or purchased a Government of Canada savings bond has received compound interest. Compound interest occurs when interest paid on the investment during the first period is added to the principal and, during the second period, interest is earned on this new sum.

For example, suppose we place $100 in a savings account that pays 6 percent interest, compounded annually. How will our savings grow? At the end of the first year we have earned 6 percent, or $6 on our initial deposit of $100, giving us a total of $106 in our savings account. The future value of the investment is determined by the following equation:

$$FV_1 = PV_0(1 + i) \qquad (4\text{-}1)$$

where FV_1 = the future value of the investment at the end of one year

             i = the annual compound interest rate

      PV_0 = the present value or original amount invested at the beginning of the first year

In our example

$$FV_1 = PV_0(1 + i) \qquad (4\text{-}1)$$
$$= \$100(1 + .06)$$
$$= \$100(1.06)$$
$$= \$106$$

Carrying these calculations one period further, we find that we now earn the 6 percent interest on a principal of $106, which means we earn $6.36 in interest during the second year. Why do we earn more interest during the second year than we did during the first? Simply because we now earn interest on the sum of the original principal (or present value) and the interest we earned in the first year. In effect we are now earning interest on interest; this is the concept of compound interest. The future value of the investment in the second year is determined by the following equation:

$$FV_2 = FV_1(1 + i) \qquad (4\text{-}2)$$

which, for our example, gives

$$FV_2 = \$106(1.06)$$
$$= \$112.36$$

Looking back at Equation (4-1), we can see that FV_1, or $106, is actually equal to $PV_0(1 + i)$, or $100 (1 + .06). If we substitute these values into Equation (4-2), we get

$$FV_2 = PV_0(1 + i)(1 + i) \qquad (4\text{-}3)$$
$$= PV_0(1 + i)^2$$

Carrying this forward into the third year, we find that we enter the year with $112.36 and we earn 6 percent, or $6.74 in interest, giving us a total of $119.10 in our savings account. Expressing this mathematically:

$$FV_3 = FV_2(1 + i) \qquad (4\text{-}4)$$
$$= \$112.36(1.06)$$
$$= \$119.10$$

If we substitute the value in Equation (4-3) for FV_2 into Equation (4-4), we find

$$FV_3 = PV_0(1 + i)(1 + i)(1 + i) \qquad (4\text{-}5)$$
$$FV_3 = FV_2(1 + i)$$
$$FV_3 = PV_0(1 + i)^3$$

By now a pattern is beginning to be evident. We can generalize this formula to illustrate the value of our investment if it is compounded annually at a rate of i for n years to be[4]

$$FV_n = PV_0(1 + i)^n \qquad (4\text{-}6)$$

where FV_n = the future value of the investment at the end of n years

        n = the number of years during which the compounding occurs

        i = the annual interest rate

      PV_0 = the present value or original amount invested at the beginning of the first year

Table 4-1 illustrates how this investment of $100 would continue to grow for the first 10 years at a compound interest rate of 6 percent. It is easy to see that the amount of interest earned annually increases each year. Again, the reason is that each year interest is received on the sum of the original investment plus any interest earned in the past.

     When we examine the relationship between the number of years an initial investment is compounded for and its future value graphically, as shown in Figure 4-1, we see that we can increase the future value of an investment by increasing the number of years we let it compound or by compounding it at a higher interest rate. We can also see this by examining Equation (4-6), since an increase in either i or n while PV_0 is held constant will result in an increase in FV_n.

Perspective in Finance

Keep in mind that future cash flows are assumed to occur at the end of the time period during which they accrue. For example, if a cash flow of $100 occurs in time period 5, it is assumed to occur at the end of time period 5 which is also the beginning of time period 6. In addition, cash flows that occur in time t = 0 occur right now. These cash flows are already in present dollars.

Year	Beginning Value	Interest Earned	Ending Value
1	$100.00	$16.00	$106.00
2	106.00	6.36	112.36
3	112.36	6.74	119.10
4	119.10	7.15	126.25
5	126.25	7.57	133.82
6	133.82	8.03	141.85
7	141.85	8.51	150.36
8	150.36	9.02	159.38
9	159.38	9.57	168.95
10	168.95	10.13	179.08

TABLE 4-1
Illustration of Compound Interest Calculations

---

[4]The use of years as a unit of time is arbitrary. Any time period may be used. As a result, n is the number of periods and i is the rate per period.

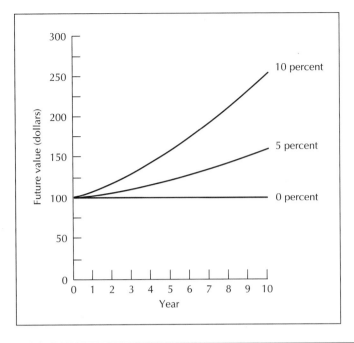

EXAMPLE

If we place $1,000 in a savings account paying 5 percent interest compounded annually, how much will our account accrue to in 10 years? Substituting $PV_0 = \$1000$, $i = 5$ percent, and $n = 10$ years into Equation (4-6), we get

$$FV_n = PV_0(1 + i)^n \qquad (4\text{-}6)$$
$$= \$1000(1 + .05)^{10}$$
$$= \$1000(1.62889)$$
$$= \$1628.89$$

Thus at the end of 10 years we will have $1,628.89 in our savings account. ■

As the determination of future value can be quite time-consuming when an investment is held for a number of years, tables have been compiled for the Future Value Interest Factor for i and n, ($FVIF_{i,n}$), which is defined as $(1 + i)^n$. Table 4-2 is an abbreviated compound interest or Future Value Interest Factor table. A more comprehensive version of this table appears in Appendix A in the back of this book. The $FVIF_{i,n}$ values could also be easily determined using a calculator. Note that the compounding factors given in these tables represent the value of $1 compounded at rate i at the end of the nth year. Thus, to calculate the future value of an initial investment we need only to determine the $FVIF_{i,n}$ using a calculator or the tables at the end of the text and multiply this by the initial investment. In fact, we can rewrite Equation (4-6) as follows:

$$FV_n = PV_0(FVIF_{i,n}) \qquad (4\text{-}6a)$$

EXAMPLE

If we invest $500 in the bank where it will earn 8 percent interest compounded annually, how much will it be worth at the end of seven years? Looking in

Table 4-2 in the row $n = 7$ and column $i = 8\%$, we find that the $FVIF_{8\%,7yr}$ has a value of 1.714. Substituting this in Equation (4-6), we find

$$FV_n = PV_0(1 + i)^n \qquad (4\text{-}6)$$
$$= \$500(1.714)$$
$$= \$857$$

Thus, we will have \$857 at the end of seven years. ∎

In the future we will find several uses for Equation (4-6); not only will we find the future value of an investment, but we can also solve for PV_0, i, or n. In any case, we will be given three of the four variables and will have to solve for the fourth.

Perspective in Finance

As you read through the chapter it is a good idea to solve the problems as they are presented. If you just read the problems, the principles behind them often do not sink in. The material presented in this chapter forms the basis for the rest of the course. Therefore a good command of the concepts underlying the time value of money is extremely important.[5]

EXAMPLE

How many years will it take for an initial investment of \$300 to grow to \$774 if it is invested at 9 percent compounded annually? In this problem we know the initial investment ($PV_0 = \$300$), the future value ($FV_n = \$774$), the compound growth rate ($i = 9\%$), and we are solving for the number of years it must compound for, n. Substituting the known values in Equation (4-6), we find

$$FV_n = PV_0(1 + i)^n \qquad (4\text{-}6)$$
$$\$774 = \$300(1 + .09)^n$$
$$2.58 = (1 + .09)^n$$

n	1%	2%	3%	4%	5%	6%	7%	8%	9%	10%
1	1.010	1.020	1.030	1.040	1.050	1.060	1.070	1.080	1.090	1.100
2	1.020	1.040	1.061	1.082	1.102	1.124	1.145	1.166	1.188	1.210
3	1.030	1.061	1.093	1.125	1.158	1.191	1.225	1.260	1.295	1.331
4	1.041	1.082	1.126	1.170	1.216	1.262	1.311	1.360	1.412	1.464
5	1.051	1.104	1.159	1.217	1.276	1.338	1.403	1.469	1.539	1.611
6	1.062	1.126	1.194	1.265	1.340	1.419	1.501	1.587	1.677	1.772
7	1.072	1.149	1.230	1.316	1.407	1.504	1.606	1.714	1.828	1.949
8	1.083	1.172	1.267	1.369	1.477	1.594	1.718	1.851	1.993	1.144
9	1.094	1.195	1.305	1.423	1.551	1.689	1.838	1.999	2.172	2.358
10	1.105	1.219	1.344	1.480	1.629	1.791	1.967	2.159	2.367	2.594
11	1.116	1.243	1.384	1.539	1.710	1.898	2.105	2.332	2.580	2.853
12	1.127	1.268	1.426	1.601	1.796	2.012	2.252	2.518	2.813	3.138
13	1.138	1.294	1.469	1.665	1.886	2.133	2.410	2.720	3.066	3.452
14	1.149	1.319	1.513	1.732	1.980	2.261	2.579	2.937	3.342	3.797
15	1.161	1.346	1.558	1.801	2.079	2.397	2.759	3.172	3.642	4.177

TABLE 4-2
FVIF$_{i,n}$ or the Compound Sum of \$1

---

[5]In 1624, Peter Minuit purchased Manhattan from the Indians for \$24 in "knickknacks" and jewellery. If banks had existed then and the sum was invested at 8% compounded annually at the end of 1624, it would be worth \$4.433 trillion at the end of 1993.

Thus we are looking for a value of 2.58 in the $FVIF_{i,n}$ table, and we know it must be in the 9% column. Looking down the 9% column for the value closest to 2.58, we find that it occurs in the $n = 11$ row. Thus, it will take 11 years for an initial investment of $300 to grow to $774 if it is invested at 9 percent compounded annually. ■

At what rate must $100 be compounded annually for it to grow to $179.10 in 10 years? In this case we know the initial investment ($PV_0 = \$100$), the future value of this investment at the end of n years ($FV_n = \$179.10$), and the number of years that the initial investment will compound for ($n = 10$ years). Substituting into Equation (4-6), we get

$$FV_n = PV_0(1 + i)^n \qquad (4\text{-}6)$$

$$\$179.10 = \$100(1 + i)^{10}$$

$$1.791 = (1 + i)^{10}$$

We know we are looking in the $n = 10$ row of the $FVIF_{i,n}$ table for a value of 1.791, and we find this in the $i = 6\%$ column. Thus, if we want our initial investment of $100 to accrue to $179.10 in 10 years, we must invest it at 6 percent. ■

Moving Money Through Time with the Aid of a Financial Calculator

Time value of money calculations can be made simple with the aid of a financial calculator. In solving time value of money problems with a financial calculator you will be given three or four variables and will have to solve for the unknown variable. Before presenting any solution using a financial calculator we will introduce the calculator's five most common keys. (In most time value of money problems, only four of these keys are relevant.) These keys are:

Menu Key	Description
N	Stores (or calculates) the total number of payments or compounding periods.
I/Y	Stores (or calculates) the interest or discount rate.
PV	Stores (or calculates) the present value of a cash flow or series of cash flows.
FV	Stores (or calculates) the future value, that is, the dollar amount of a final cash flow or the compound value of a single flow or series of cash flows.
PMT	Stores (or calculates) the dollar amount of each annuity payment deposited or recieved at the end of each year.

One thing you must keep in mind when using a financial calculator is that outflows generally have to be entered as negative numbers. In general, each problem will have two cash flows, one an outflow with a negative value and one an inflow with a positive value. The idea is that you deposit money in the bank at some point in time (an outflow), and at some other point in time you take money out of the bank (an inflow). Also, every calculator operates a bit differently with respect to entering variables. Needless to say, it is a good idea to familiarize yourself with exactly how your calculator functions.

As stated above, in any problem you will be given three or four variables. These variables will always include *N* and *I/Y*; in addition, two out of the final three variables, *PV*, *FV*, and *PMT*, will also be included. To solve a time value of money problem using a financial calculator, all you need to do is enter the appropriate numbers for three of the four variables and then press the key of the final variable to calculate its value. It is also a good idea to enter zero for any of the five variables not included in the problem in order to clear that variable.

Now let's solve the previous example using a financial calculator. We were trying to find at what rate must $100 be compounded annually for it to grow to $179.10 in ten years. The solution using a financial calculator would be as follows:

Step 1: Input Values of Known Variables

Data Input	Function Key	Description
10	N	Stores *N* = 10 years
100	+/− PV	Stores *PV* = −$100
179.10	FV	Stores *FV* = $179.10
0	PMT	Clears *PMT* = 0

Step 2: Calculate the Value of the Unknown Variable

Function Key	Answer	Description
CPT I/Y	6.00%	Calculates *I/Y* = 6.00%

NOTE: if you are using a TI BA II calculator, you must ensure that payments per year = 1.0 (2ⁿᵈ P/Y 1 ENTER).

Any of the problems in this chapter can easily be solved using a financial calculator; and the solutions to many examples using a financial calculator are provided in the margins. One final point: you will notice that solutions using the present-value tables versus solutions using a calculator may vary slightly—a result of rounding errors in the tables.

For further explanation see Appendix E at the end of the book. It provides a tutorial on the use of financial calculators, as well.

Perspective in Finance

The concepts of compound and present value will follow us through the remainder of this book. Not only will they allow us to determine the future value of any investment, but they will allow us to bring the benefits and costs from new investment proposals back to the present and thereby determine the value of the investment in today's dollars.

Future Value with Nonannual Periods

Until now we have assumed the compounding period was always annual; however, it need not be, as we can see by examining chartered banks and trust companies that compound on a quarterly, daily, and in some cases continuous basis. Fortunately, this adjustment of the compounding period

BASIC FINANCIAL MANAGEMENT IN PRACTICE

Andrew Tobias on the Power of Compounding

It was Homer who said that $1,000 invested at a mere 8 percent for 400 years would grow to $23 quadrillion—$5 million for every human on earth. (And you can't see any reason to save?) But, he said, the first 100 years are the hardest. (This was the late Sidney Homer, not Homer Homer—author of the classic A *History of Interest Rates*.)

What invariably happens is that long before the first 100 years are up, someone with access to the cache loses patience. The money burns a hole in his pocket. Or through his nose.

Doubtless that would have been true of the Correra fortune, too, had Domingos Faustino Correra not cut everyone out of his will for 100 years. That was in 1873, in Brazil. You could have gotten very tired waiting, but if you can establish that you are one of that misanthrope's 4,000-odd legitimate heirs, you may now have some money coming to you. Since 1873, Correra's estate has grown, by some estimates, to $12 billion.

Benjamin Franklin had much the same idea, only with higher purpose. Inventive to the end, he left $1,000 each to Boston and Philadelphia. The cities were to lend the money, at interest, to worthy apprentices. Then, after a century, they were to employ part of the fortune Franklin envisioned to construct some public work, while continuing to invest the rest.

One hundred ninety-two years later, when last I checked, Boston's funds exceeded $3 million, even after having been drained to build Franklin Union, and was being lent at interest to medical school students. Philadelphia's fund was smaller, but it, too, had been put to good use. All this from an initial stake of $2,000!

And then there was the king who held a chess tournament among the peasants—I may have this story a little wrong, but the point holds—and asked the winner what he wanted as his prize. The peasant, in apparent humility, asked only that a single kernel of wheat be placed for him on the first square of his chessboard, two kernels on the second, four on the third—and so forth. The king fell for it and had to import grain from Argentina for the next 700 years. Eighteen and a half million trillion kernels, or enough, if each kernel is a quarter-inch long (which it may not be; I've never seen wheat in its pre-English-muffin form), to stretch to the sun and back 391,320 times.

That was nothing more than one kernel's compounding at 100 percent per square for 64 squares. It is vaguely akin to the situation with our national debt.

Source: Andrew Tobias, *Money Angles*, New York: Linden Press, 1984, pp. 35–36.

follows the same format. If we invest our money for five years at 8 percent interest compounded semiannually, we are really investing our money for 10 six-month periods during which we receive 4 percent interest each period. If it is compounded quarterly, we receive 2 percent interest per period for 20 three-month periods. This process can easily be generalized, giving us the following equation to find the future value of an investment where interest is compounded in nonannual periods:

$$FV_n = PV_0 \left(1 + \frac{i}{m}\right)^{mn} \qquad (4\text{-}7)$$

where

FV_n = future value of the investment at the end of n years

n = number of years during which the compounding occurs

i = annual interest rate

PV_0 = present value or original amount invested at the beginning of the first year

m = the number of times compounding occurs during the year

In the case of continuous compounding, the value of m in Equation (4-7) is allowed to approach infinity. In fact, the effect of continuous compounding causes interest to earn interest immediately. As this happens, the value of $[1 + (i/m)]^{mn}$ approaches e^{in}, with e being defined as follows and having a value of approximately 2.71828:

$$e = \lim_{m \to \infty} \left(1 + \frac{1}{m}\right)^m \qquad (4\text{-}8)$$

where ∞ indicates infinity. Thus the future value of an investment compounded continuously for n years can be determined from the following equation:

$$FV_n = PV_0 e^{(i)(n)} \qquad (4\text{-}9)$$

where
- FV_n = the future value of the investment at the end of n years
- e = 2.71828
- n = the number of years during which the compounding occurs
- i = the annual interest rate
- PV_0 = the present value or original amount invested at the beginning of the first year

While continuous compounding appears quite complicated, it is used frequently and is a valuable theoretical concept. Continuous compounding takes on this importance because it allows interest to be earned on interest more frequently than any other compounding period. We can easily see the value of intra-year compounding by examining Table 4-3. Since interest is earned on interest more frequently as the length of the compounding period declines, there is an inverse relationship between the length of the compounding period and the effective annual interest rate.

TABLE 4-3
The Value of $100
Compounded at Various
Intervals

For One Year at i Percent				
$i =$	2%	5%	10%	15%
Compounded annually	$102.00	$105.00	$110.00	$115.00
Compounded semiannually	102.01	105.06	110.25	115.56
Compounded quarterly	102.02	105.09	110.38	115.87
Compounded monthly	102.02	105.12	110.47	116.08
Compounded weekly (52)	102.02	105.12	110.51	116.16
Compounded daily (365)	102.02	105.13	110.52	116.18
Compounded continuously	102.02	105.13	110.52	116.18

For 10 Years at i Percent				
$i =$	2%	5%	10%	15%
Compounded annually	$121.90	$162.89	$259.37	$404.56
Compounded semiannually	122.02	163.86	265.33	424.79
Compounded quarterly	122.08	164.36	268.51	436.04
Compounded monthly	122.12	164.70	270.70	444.02
Compounded weekly (52)	122.14	164.83	271.57	447.20
Compounded daily (365)	122.14	164.87	271.79	448.03
Compounded continuously	122.14	164.87	271.83	448.17

If we place \$100 in a savings account that yields 12 percent compounded quarterly, what will our investment grow to at the end of five years? Substituting $n = 5$, $m = 4$, $i = 12$ percent, and $PV_0 = \$100$ into Equation (4-7), we find

$$FV_5 = \$100 \left(1 + \frac{.12}{4}\right)^{(5)(4)}$$

$$= \$100(1 + .03)^{20}$$

$$= \$100(1.806)$$

$$= \$180.60$$

Thus, we will have \$180.60 at the end of five years. ∎

How much money will we have at the end of 20 years if we deposit \$1,000 in a savings account yielding 10 percent interest continuously compounded? Substituting $n = 20$, $i = 10$ percent, and $PV_0 = \$1000$ into Equation (4-9) yields

$$FV_{10} = \$1000(2.71828)^{(.10)(20)}$$

$$= \$1000(2.71828)^2$$

$$= \$1000(7.38905)$$

$$= \$7389.05$$

Thus, we will have \$7389.05 at the end of 20 years. ∎

Present Value

Up until this point we have been moving money forward in time. We know how much we have at the moment and are trying to determine how much that amount will grow to in a certain number of years when compounded at a specific rate. We are now going to look at the reverse question: What is the value in today's dollars of a sum of money to be received in the future? The answer to this question will help us determine the desirability of investment projects in Chapters 6 and 7. In this case we are moving money to be received in the future, back to the present. We will be determining the present value of a lump sum, which in simple terms is the current value of a future payment. What we will be doing is, in fact, nothing other than inverse compounding. The differences in these techniques come about merely from the investor's point of view. In compounding we used the compound interest rate and the initial investment; in determining the present value we use the discount rate and present value. Determination of the discount rate is the subject of Chapter 4 and can be defined as the rate of return available on an investment of equal risk to the investment that is being discounted. Other than that, the technique and the terminology remain the same, and the mathematics is simply reversed. In Equation (4-6) we were attempting to determine the future value of an initial investment. We now want to determine the initial investment or present value. By dividing both sides of Equation (4-6) by $(1 + i)^n$, we get

$$PV_0 = FV_n \left[\frac{1}{(1 + i)^n} \right] \tag{4-10}$$

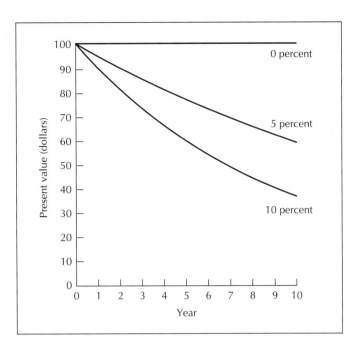

FIGURE 4-2
Present Value of $100 to Be
Received at a Future Date
and Discounted Back to
the Present at 0, 5, and
10 Percent

where FV_n = the future value of the investment at the end of n years

n = the number of years until the payment will be received[6]

i = the opportunity rate or discount rate

PV_0 = the present value of the future sum of money

Since the mathematical procedure for determining the present value is exactly the inverse of determining the future value, we also find that the relationships among n, i, and PV_0 are just opposite of those we observed in the future value. The present value of a future sum of money is inversely related to both the number of years until the payment will be received and the discount rate. Figure 4-2 illustrates this relationship.

Perspective in Finance

While the present value equation [Equation (4-10)] will be used extensively in evaluating new investment proposals, it should be stressed that the present value equation is actually the same as the future value or compounding equation [Equation (4-6)], where it is solved for PV_0.

EXAMPLE

What is the present value of $500 to be received 10 years from today if our discount rate is 6 percent? Substituting FV_{10} = $500, n = 10, and i = 6 percent into Equation (4-10), we find

$$PV_0 = \$500 \left[\frac{1}{(1 + .06)^{10}} \right]$$

---

[6]Note that a period does not need to be one year. Any period is allowed, with i being the rate per period and n the number of periods.

$$= \$500 \left(\frac{1}{1.791} \right)$$

$$= \$500(.558)$$

$$= \$279$$

Thus, the present value of the $500 to be received in 10 years is $279. ∎

To aid in the computation of present values, the Present Value Interest Factor for i and n, ($PVIF_{i,n}$), which is defined as $[1/(1 + i)^n]$ has been compiled for various combinations of i and n. The Present Value Interest Factors appear in Appendix B in the back of this book. An abbreviated version of Appendix B appears in Table 4-4. A close examination shows that the values in Table 4-4 are merely the inverses of those found in Appendix A. This, of course, is as it should be, as the values in Appendix A are $(1 + i)^n$ and those in Appendix B are $[1/(1 + i)^n]$. Now, to determine the present value of a sum of money to be received at some future date, we need only determine the value of the appropriate $PVIF_{i,n}$, by either using a calculator or consulting the tables and multiplying it by the future value. In fact, we can use our new notation and rewrite Equation (4-10) as follows:

$$PV_0 = FV_n(PVIF_{i,n}) \tag{4-10a}$$

EXAMPLE

What is the present value of $1,500 to be received at the end of 10 years if our discount rate is 8 percent? By looking in the $n = 10$ row and $i = 8\%$ column of Table 4-4, we find the value of $[1/(1 + .08)^{10}]$ is .463. Substituting this value into Equation (4-10), we find

$$PV_0 = \$1500(.463)$$

$$= \$694.50$$

Thus, the present value of this $1,500 payment is $694.50. ∎

TABLE 4-4
$PVIF_{i,n}$ or the Present Value of $1

n	1%	2%	3%	4%	5%	6%	7%	8%	9%	10%
1	.990	.980	.971	.962	.952	.943	.935	.926	.917	.909
2	.980	.961	.943	.925	.907	.890	.873	.857	.842	.826
3	.971	.942	.915	.889	.864	.840	.816	.794	.772	.751
4	.961	.924	.888	.855	.823	.792	.763	.735	.708	.683
5	.951	.906	.863	.822	.784	.747	.713	.681	.650	.621
6	.942	.888	.837	.790	.746	.705	.666	.630	.596	.564
7	.933	.871	.813	.760	.711	.655	.623	.583	.547	.513
8	.923	.853	.789	.731	.677	.627	.582	.540	.502	.467
9	.914	.837	.766	.703	.645	.592	.544	.500	.460	.424
10	.905	.820	.744	.676	.614	.558	.508	.463	.422	.386
11	.896	.804	.722	.650	.585	.527	.475	.429	.388	.350
12	.887	.789	.701	.625	.557	.497	.444	.397	.356	.319
13	.879	.773	.681	.601	.530	.469	.415	.368	.326	.290
14	.870	.758	.661	.577	.505	.442	.388	.340	.299	.263
15	.861	.743	.642	.555	.481	.417	.362	.315	.275	.239

Again, we only have one present-value-future-value equation; that is, Equations (4-6) and (4-10) are identical. We have introduced them as separate equations to simplify our calculations; in one case we are determining the value in future dollars and in the other case the value in today's dollars. In either case the reason is the same: In order to compare values on alternative investments and to recognize that the value of a dollar received today is not the same as that of a dollar received at some future date, we must measure the dollar values in dollars of the same time period. Since all present values are comparable, we can add and subtract the present value of inflows and outflows to determine the present value of an investment.

EXAMPLE

What is the present value of an investment that yields $500 to be received in five years and $1,000 to be received in 10 years if our discount rate is 4 percent? Substituting the values of $n = 5$, $i = 4$ percent, and $FV_5 = \$500$ and $n = 10$, $i = 4$ percent, and $FV_{10} = \$1000$ into Equation (4-10) and adding these values together, we find

$$PV_0 = \$500\left[\frac{1}{(1+.04)^5}\right] + \$1000\left[\frac{1}{(1+.04)^{10}}\right]$$

$$= \$500(.822) + \$1000(.676)$$

$$= \$411 + \$676$$

$$= \$1087$$

Again, present values are comparable because they are measured in the same time period's dollars. ∎

THE VALUATION OF ANNUITIES

An **annuity** is a series of equal dollar payments for a specified number of years. Because annuities occur frequently in finance—for example, as bond interest payments—we will treat them specially.[7] Although the future and the present value of an annuity can be dealt with using the methods we have just described, these processes can be time-consuming, especially for larger annuities. Thus, we have modified the equations and will deal directly with annuities.

The Future Value of Annuities

In determining the future value of an annuity, we are determining the value of an investment in which we deposited an equal sum of money at the end of each year for a certain number of years and allowed it to grow. Perhaps we are saving money for education, a new car, or a vacation home. In any case we want to know how much our savings will have grown by some point in the future.

Actually, we can find the answer by using Equation (4-6), our future value equation, and compounding each of the individual deposits to its

---

[7]Other examples of annuities include retirement payments, lottery disbursements, mortgage payments, and auto-loan payments.

future value. For example, if to provide for a college education we are going to deposit $500 at the end of each year for the next five years in a bank where it will earn 6 percent interest, how much will we have at the end of five years? Compounding each of these values using Equation (4-6), we find that we will have $2,818.50 at the end of five years.

$$FV_5 = \$500(1+.06)^4 + \$500(1+.06)^3 + \$500(1+.06)^2 + \$500(1+.06)^1 + \$500$$

$$= \$500(1.262) + \$500(1.191) + \$500(1.124) + \$500(1.060) + \$500$$

$$= \$631.00 + \$595.50 + \$562.00 + \$530.00 + \$500.00$$

$$= \$2818.50$$

From examining the mathematics involved and the graph of the movement of money through time in Table 4-5, we can see that this procedure can be generalized to

$$FV_n = PMT\left[\sum_{t=0}^{n-1}(1+i)^t\right] \qquad (4\text{-}11)$$

where FV_n = the future value of the annuity at the end of the nth year[8]

     PMT = the annuity payment deposited or received at the end of each year

     i = the annual interest rate

     n = the number of years for which the annuity will last

To simplify the process of determining the future value of an annuity, the Future Value Interest Factor for an Annuity for i and n, ($FVIFA_{i,n}$) is defined as

$$\left[\sum_{t=0}^{n-1}(1+i)^t\right]$$

and has been compiled for various combinations of n and i in Appendix C. An abbreviated version is given in Table 4-6. Using this new notation, we can rewrite Equation (4-11) as follows:

$$FV_n = PMT(FVIFA_{i,n}) \qquad (4\text{-}11a)$$

Solving the previous example to determine the value of $500 deposited at the end of each of the next five years in the bank at 6 percent interest after five

TABLE 4-5
Illustration of a Five-Year
$500 Annuity Compounded
at 6 Percent

Year	0	1	2	3	4	5
Dollar deposits at end of year		500	500	500	500	500
						$ 500.00
						530.00
						562.00
						595.50
						631.00
Future value of the annuity						$ 2818.50

[8]The future value of the annuity at the end of the nth year can also be expressed as follows:

$$FV_n = PMT\left[\frac{(1+i)^n - 1}{i}\right]$$

n	1%	2%	3%	4%	5%	6%	7%	8%	9%	10%
1	1.000	1.000	1.000	1.000	1.000	1.000	1.000	1.000	1.000	1.000
2	2.010	2.020	2.030	2.040	2.050	2.060	2.070	2.080	2.090	2.100
3	3.030	3.060	3.091	3.122	3.152	3.184	3.215	3.246	3.278	3.310
4	4.060	4.122	4.184	4.246	4.310	4.375	4.440	4.506	4.573	4.641
5	5.101	5.204	5.309	5.416	5.526	5.637	5.751	5.867	5.985	6.105
6	6.152	6.308	6.468	6.633	6.802	6.975	7.153	7.336	7.523	7.716
7	7.214	7.434	7.662	7.898	8.142	8.394	8.654	8.923	9.200	9.487
8	8.286	8.583	8.892	9.214	9.549	9.897	10.260	10.637	11.028	11.436
9	9.368	9.755	10.159	10.583	11.027	11.491	11.978	12.488	13.021	13.579
10	10.462	10.950	11.464	12.006	12.578	13.181	13.816	14.487	15.193	15.937
11	11.567	12.169	12.808	13.486	14.207	14.972	15.784	16.645	17.560	18.531
12	12.682	13.412	14.192	15.026	15.917	16.870	17.888	18.977	20.141	21.384
13	13.809	14.680	15.618	16.627	17.713	18.882	20.141	21.495	22.953	24.523
14	14.947	15.974	17.086	18.292	19.598	21.015	22.550	24.215	26.019	27.975
15	16.097	17.293	18.599	20.023	21.578	23.276	25.129	27.152	29.361	31.772

TABLE 4-6

$FVIFA_{i,n}$ or the Sum of an Annuity of $1 for n Years

CALCULATOR SOLUTION

Data Input	Function Key
5	N
6	I/Y
500	+/- PMT
0	PV

Function Key	Answer
CPT FV	2818.55*

*The difference between the two answers represents rounding error.

---

years, we would look in the $n = 5$ year row and $i = 6\%$ column and find the value of $FVIFA_{6\%,5yr}$ to be 5.637. Substituting this value into Equation (4-11a), we get

$$FV_5 = \$500(5.637)$$
$$= \$2818.50$$

This is the same answer we obtained earlier.

Rather than asking how much we will accumulate if we deposit an equal sum in a savings account each year, a more common question is how much we must deposit each year in order to accumulate a certain amount of savings. This problem frequently occurs with respect to saving for large expenditures and pension funding obligations.

For example, we may know that we need $10,000 for education in eight years; how much must we deposit at the end of each year in the bank at 6 percent interest in order to have the college money ready? In this case we know the values of n, i, and FV_n in Equation (4-11); what we do not know is the value of PMT. Substituting these example values in Equation (4-11), we find

$$\$10,000 = PMT\left[\sum_{t=0}^{8-1}(1+.06)^t\right]$$

$$\$10,000 = PMT(9.897)$$

$$\frac{\$10,000}{9.897} = PMT$$

$$PMT = \$1010.41$$

Thus, we must deposit $1,010.41 in the bank at the end of each year for eight years at 6 percent interest in order to accumulate $10,000 at the end of eight years.

CALCULATOR SOLUTION

Data Input	Function Key
8	N
6	I/Y
10,000	+/- FV
0	PV

Function Key	Answer
CPT PMT	1010.36*

*The difference between the two answers represents rounding error.

EXAMPLE

How much must we deposit in an 8 percent savings account at the end of each year in order to accumulate $5,000 at the end of 10 years? Substituting the values $FV_{10} = \$5000$, $n = 10$, and $i = 8$ percent into Equation (4-11), we find

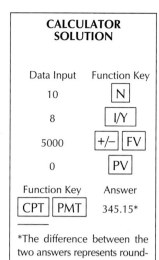
$$\$5000 = PMT\left[\sum_{t=0}^{10-1}(1+.08)^t\right]$$

$$\$5000 = PMT(14.487)$$

$$\frac{\$5000}{14.487} = PMT$$

$$PMT = \$345.14$$

Thus, we must deposit $345.14 per year for 10 years at 8 percent in order to accumulate $5,000. ■

Perspective in Finance

A time line often makes it easier to understand the time value of money problems. By visually plotting the flow of money you can better determine which formula to use. Arrows placed above the line are inflows, and arrows placed below the line represent outflows. One thing is certain, time lines reduce errors.

Present Value of an Annuity

Pension funds, insurance obligations, and interest received from bonds all involve annuities. To compare them, we need to know the present value of each. While we can find this by using the present-value table in Appendix B, this can be time-consuming, particularly when the annuity lasts for several years. For example, if we wish to know what $500 received at the end of the next five years is worth to us today given the appropriate discount rate of 6 percent, we can simply substitute the appropriate values into Equation (4-10), such that

$$PV_0 = \$500\left[\frac{1}{(1+.06)^1}\right] + \$500\left[\frac{1}{(1+.06)^2}\right] + \$500\left[\frac{1}{(1+.06)^3}\right]$$

$$+ \$500\left[\frac{1}{(1+.06)^4}\right] + \$500\left[\frac{1}{(1+.06)^5}\right]$$

$$= \$500(.943) + \$500(.890) + \$500(.840) + \$500(.792) + \$500(.747)$$

$$= \$2106.00$$

Thus, the present value of this annuity is $2,106.00. From examining the mathematics involved and the graph of the movement of these funds through time in Table 4-7, we see that this procedure can be generalized to

$$PV_0 = PMT\left[\sum_{t=1}^{n}\frac{1}{(1+i)^t}\right] \tag{4-12}$$

TABLE 4-7
Illustration of a Five-Year $500 Annuity Discounted Back to the Present at 6 Percent

Year	0	1	2	3	4	5
Dollars received at the end of year		500	500	500	500	500
	$ 471.50					
	445.00					
	420.00					
	396.00					
	373.50					
Present value of the annuity	$2106.00					

where, PMT = the annuity payments deposited or received at the end of each year

i = the annual interest or discount rate

PV_0 = the present value of the future annuity[9]

n = the number of years for which the annuity will last

To simplify the process of determining the present value of an annuity, the Present Value Interest Factor for an Annuity for i and n, ($PVIFA_{i,n}$) is defined as

$$\left[\sum_{t=1}^{n} \frac{1}{(1+i)^t} \right]$$

and has been compiled for various combinations of n and i in Appendix D with an abbreviated version is given in Table 4-8. Using this new notation, we can rewrite equation 4-12 as follows:

$$PV_0 = PMT(PVIFA_{i,n}) \qquad (4\text{-}12a)$$

Solving the previous example to find the present value of $500 received at the end of each of the next five years discounted back to the present at 6 percent, we look in the $n = 5$ year row and $i = 6\%$ column and find the $PVIFA_{6\%,5yr}$ to be 4.212. Substituting the appropriate values into Equation (4-12a), we find

$$PV_0 = \$500(4.212)$$

$$= \$2106$$

This, of course, is the same answer we calculated when we individually discounted each cash flow to the present. The reason is that we really only have one table; the Table 4-8 value for an n-year annuity for any discount rate i is

n	1%	2%	3%	4%	5%	6%	7%	8%	9%	10%
1	0.990	0.980	0.971	0.962	0.952	0.943	0.935	0.926	0.917	0.909
2	1.970	1.942	1.913	1.886	1.859	1.833	1.808	1.783	1.759	1.736
3	2.941	2.884	2.829	2.775	2.723	2.673	2.624	2.577	2.531	2.487
4	3.902	3.808	3.717	3.630	3.546	3.465	3.387	3.312	3.240	3.170
5	4.853	4.713	4.580	4.452	4.329	4.212	4.100	3.993	3.890	3.791
6	5.795	5.601	5.417	5.242	5.076	4.917	4.767	4.623	4.486	4.355
7	6.728	6.472	6.230	6.002	5.786	5.582	5.389	5.206	5.033	4.868
8	7.652	7.326	7.020	6.733	6.463	6.210	5.971	5.747	5.535	5.335
9	8.566	8.162	7.786	7.435	7.108	6.802	6.515	6.247	5.995	5.759
10	9.471	8.983	8.530	8.111	7.722	7.360	7.024	6.710	6.418	6.145
11	10.368	9.787	9.253	8.760	8.306	7.887	7.499	7.139	6.805	6.495
12	11.255	10.575	9.954	9.385	8.863	8.384	7.943	7.536	7.161	6.814
13	12.134	11.348	10.635	9.986	9.394	8.853	8.358	7.904	7.487	7.103
14	13.004	12.106	11.296	10.563	9.899	9.295	8.746	8.244	7.786	7.367
15	13.865	12.849	11.938	11.118	10.380	9.712	9.108	8.560	8.061	7.606

TABLE 4-8
$PVIFA_{i,n}$ or the Present Value of an Annuity of $1

[9]The present value of this future annuity can also be expressed as follows:

$$PV_0 = PMT \ \frac{1 - \left[\dfrac{1}{(1+i)^n} \right]}{i}$$

also influenced by the frequency of loan payments that the home-buyer chooses to make during the year. Canadian lending institutions have provided home-buyers with greater flexibility in developing their loan repayment schedules by offering packages that permit home-buyers to vary the frequency of the loan payments during the year—for example, weekly, bimonthly, monthly, quarterly and even semi-annually. Fortunately, the calculation to determine the amount of loan payment is similar to that of the annuity payment. However, we must adjust for the frequency of loan payments by using the effective interest rate which is calculated as follows:

$$k_{eff} = \left(1 + \frac{i}{m}\right)^{(m/f)} - 1 \qquad (4\text{-}13)$$

where k_{eff} = the effective interest rate for the frequency of payments during the year

f = the frequency of annuity payments during the year

i = the annual interest rate

m = the number of times compounding occurs during the year

Now the payment can be determined by substitution into the equation for the present value of an annuity as follows:

$$PV_0 = PMT \left[\sum_{t=1}^{(n)(f)} \frac{1}{(1+k_{eff})^t} \right] \qquad (4\text{-}14)$$

where PMT = the annuity payment required at the end of each period

f = the frequency of annuity payments during the year

n = the number of years for which the annuity will last

k_{eff} = the effective interest rate for the frequency of payments during the year

PV_0 = the present value of the annuity.

For example, suppose a home-buyer negotiates a home mortgage loan with his local bank over a 25-year period in order to purchase a $150,000 home. The local bank requires a 25 percent down payment on the purchase price and charges an annual interest rate of 9.80% for the loan. The home-buyer has decided to pay his loan payments on a monthly basis. The loan's terms are renegotiable after three years. Determine the amount of the monthly payment owed by the home-buyer.

The first step of this calculation is to determine the effective interest rate on a monthly basis since the frequency of the loan payment is being repaid on a monthly basis ($f = 12$).

$$k_{eff} = \left(1 + \frac{0.098}{2}\right)^{(2/12)} - 1$$

$$k_{eff} = (1 + .049)^{0.1667} - 1$$

$$k_{eff} = 0.80\% \text{ per month}$$

The second step is to determine the amount of the loan after the down payment is deducted. The down payment represents (.25)($150,000) or

$37,500; the home-buyer will require a loan of ($150,000 − $37,500) or $112,500.

The third step is to find the amount of the annuity payment that is required over the 300 months of the loan using the present value annuity formula:

$$112,500 = PMT \left[\sum_{t=1}^{(12)(25)} \frac{1}{(1 + 0.008)^t} \right]$$

$$PMT = \frac{112,500}{113.5515}$$

$$PMT = \$991.19 \text{ per month}$$

As shown in Table 4-11, the home-buyer will be required to pay a monthly payment of $991.19 over the next three years, at which time the home-buyer can renegotiate the loan terms.

Annuities Due

An annuity due is a series of equal payments deposited at the beginning of each period. For example, leasing is a long-term form of financing, which requires a series of payments to be deposited at the beginning of each period. In a similar manner, we can determine the present value or the future value of an annuity due. In determining the future value of an annuity due, we determine the value of an investment in which we deposit an equal sum of money at the beginning of each year for a certain number of years and allow it to grow. We now redo the earlier example in which we provide for a college education by depositing $500 at the beginning of each year for the next five years in a bank where it will earn 6 percent interest. How much will we have at the end of five years?

$$FV_5 = \$500(1 + .06)^5 + \$500(1 + .06)^4 + \$500(1 + .06)^3 + \$500(1 + .06)^2$$

$$+ \$500(1 + .06)^1$$

$$= \$500(1.338) + \$500(1.262) + \$500(1.191) + \$500(1.124) + \$500(1.060)$$

$$= \$669.00 + \$631.00 + \$595.50 + \$562.00 + \$530.00$$

$$= \$2987.50$$

Period	Beginning Balance	Amount of Payment	Interest	Amount of Repayment	Ending Balance
1	$112,500.00	$991.19	$900.54	$90.65	$112,409.35
2	112,409.35	991.19	899.81	91.38	112,317.97
3	112,317.97	991.19	899.08	92.11	112,225.86
4	112,225.86	991.19	898.34	92.85	112,133.01
.	.	.	.	.	.
.	.	.	.	.	.
.	.	.	.	.	.
297	3,886.66	991.19	31.11	960.08	2,926.59
298	2,926.59	991.19	23.43	967.76	1,958.82
299	1,958.82	991.19	15.68	975.51	983.32
300	983.32	983.32	7.87	983.32	0.00

TABLE 4-11
Home Mortgage Loan Amortization Schedule for the First Four Periods

Compounding each of these values using Equation (4-6), we find that we will have $2,987.50 at the end of five years.

From examining the mathematics involved and the graph of the movement of money through time in Table 4-12, we can see that this procedure can be generalized to

$$FV_n = PMT\left[\sum_{t=0}^{n-1}(1+i)^t\right][(1+i)] \tag{4-15}$$

or

$$FV_n = PMT(FVIFA_{i,n})(1+i) \tag{4-16}$$

To solve for our example, we use Equation (4-16) to find the future value of this annuity due

$$FV_n = \$500(FVIFA_{6\%,5})(1+.06)$$

$$FV_n = \$500(5.637)(1.06)$$

$$FV_n = \$2987.50$$

Thus, the future value of this annuity due is $2,987.50.

In determining the present value of an annuity due, we are determining today's value of a sum of equal payments which have been deposited at the beginning of each period. For example, if we wish to know what $500 received at the beginning of the next five years is worth to us today given the appropriate discount rate of 6 percent, we can simply substitute the appropriate values into Equation (4-10), such that

$$PV_0 = \$500 + \$500\left[\frac{1}{(1+.06)^1}\right] + \$500\left[\frac{1}{(1+.06)^2}\right]$$

$$+ \$500\left[\frac{1}{(1+.06)^3}\right] + \$500\left[\frac{1}{(1+.06)^4}\right]$$

$$= \$500 + \$500(.943) + \$500(.890) + \$500(.840) + \$500(.792)$$

$$= \$2232.50$$

Thus, the present value of this annuity due is $2,232.50. From examining the mathematics involved and the graph of the movement of these funds through time in Table 4-13, we see that this procedure can be generalized to

$$PV_0 = PMT\left[\sum_{t=1}^{n}\frac{1}{(1+i)^t}\right][(1+i)] \tag{4-17}$$

or

$$PV_0 = PMT(PVIFA_{i,n})(1+i) \tag{4-18}$$

TABLE 4-12
Illustration of a Five-Year $500 Annuity Due Compounded at 6 Percent

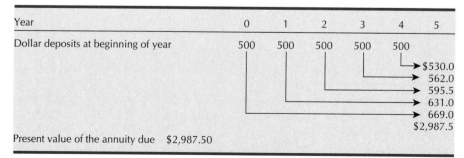

Year	0	1	2	3	4	5
Dollar deposits at beginning of year	500	500	500	500	500	
						$530.0
						562.0
						595.5
						631.0
						669.0
						$2,987.5

Present value of the annuity due $2,987.50

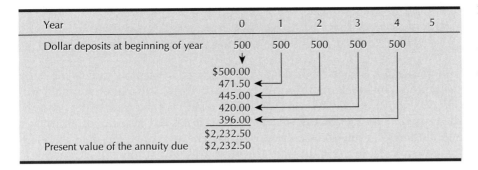

Year	0	1	2	3	4	5
Dollar deposits at beginning of year	500	500	500	500	500	
	$500.00					
	471.50					
	445.00					
	420.00					
	396.00					
	$2,232.50					
Present value of the annuity due	$2,232.50					

TABLE 4-13
Illustration of a Five-Year
$500 Annuity Due
Discounted at 6 Percent

To solve for our example, we use Equation (4-18) to find the present value of this annuity due

$$PV_0 = \$500(PVIFA_{6\%,5})(1 + .06)$$

$$= \$500(4.212)(1.06)$$

$$= 2232.50$$

Thus, the present value of this annuity due is $2,232.50

PERPETUITIES

A perpetuity is an annuity that continues forever; that is, every year from its establishment, this investment pays the same dollar amount. An example of a perpetuity is a preferred share that yields a constant dollar dividend infinitely. Determining the present value of a perpetuity is delightfully simple; we merely need to divide the constant flow by the discount rate.[10] For example, the present value of a $100 perpetuity discounted back to the present at 5 percent is $100/.05 = $2000. Thus, the equation representing the present value of a perpetuity is

$$PV_0 = \frac{PP}{i} \qquad (4\text{-}19)$$

where PV_0 = the present value of perpetuity

PP = the constant dollar amount provided by the perpetuity

i = the annual interest or discount rate

EXAMPLE

What is the present value of a $500 perpetuity discounted back to the present at 8 percent? Substituting $PP = \$500$ and $i = .08$ into Equation (4-19), we find

$$PV_0 = \frac{\$500}{.08} = \$6250$$

Thus, the present value of this perpetuity is $6,250. ∎

---

[10]The concept of valuing of a perpetuity is used to determine the intrinsic value of a preferred share.

PRESENT VALUE OF AN UNEVEN STREAM

Although some projects will involve a single cash outflow and a series of cash inflows of equal amounts, many projects will involve uneven cash flows over several years. For the analysis of projects we will be comparing not only the present value of cash flows between projects, but also the cash inflows and outflows within a particular project. Again we will be required to determine that project's present value. However, this will not be difficult because the present value of any cash flow is measured in today's dollars and thus can be compared, through addition for inflows and subtraction for outflows, to the present value of any other cash flow also measured in today's dollars. For example, suppose we wished to find the present value of the following cash flows:

Year	Cash Flow
1	$500
2	200
3	−400
4	500
5	500
6	500
7	500
8	500
9	500
10	500

If given a 6 percent discount rate, we would merely discount the flows back to the present and total them by adding in the positive flows and subtracting the negative ones. However, this problem is complicated by the annuity of $500 that runs from years 4 through 10. To accommodate this factor, we can first discount the annuity back to the beginning of period 4 (or end of period 3) by using the present-value-of-an-annuity table and get its present value at that point in time. We then use the present-value-of-a-single-flow table (Table 4-4) and discount the present value of this annuity at the end of period 3 back to the present. In effect we discount twice, first back to the end of period 3 then back to the present. This is shown graphically in Table 4-14 and numerically in Table 4-15. Thus, the present value of this uneven stream of cash flows is $2,657.94.

TABLE 4-14
Illustration of an Example of Present Value of an Uneven Stream Involving One Annuity Discounted to Present at 6 Percent

1. Present value of $500 received at the end of one year	=	$500(.943)	= $ 471.50
2. Present value of $200 received at the end of two years	=	$200(.890)	= 178.00
3. Present value of a $400 outflow at the end of three years	=	-$400(.840)	= -336.00
4. (a) Value at the end of year 3 of a $500 annuity, years 4 through 10:		$500(5.582)	= $2791.00
(b) Present value of $2791.00 received at the end of year 3		= $2791.00(.840)	= 2344.44
5. Total present value			= $2657.94

TABLE 4-15

Determination of Present Value of an Example with Uneven Stream Involving One Annuity Discounted to Present at 6 Percent

Year	0	1	2	3	4	5	6	7	8	9	10
Dollars received at the end of year		200	200	200	200	200	-300	500	500	500	500

$865.80
-223.80
$1773
1322.66
Total present value $1964.66

TABLE 4-16

Illustration of an Example of Present Value of an Uneven Stream Involving Two Annuities Discounted at 5 Percent

1. Present value of first annuity, years 1 through 5	=	$200(4.329)	= $ 865.80
2. Present value of $300 cash outflow	=	-300(.746)	= -223.80
3. (a) Value at end of year 6 of second annuity, years 7 through 10	=	$500(3.546)	= $1773.00
(b) Present value of $1773.00 received at the end of year 6	=	$1773.00(.746)	= 1322.66
4. Total present value			= $1964.66

TABLE 4-17

Determination of Present Value of an Example with Uneven Stream Involving Two Annuities Discounted at 5 Percent

EXAMPLE

What is the present value of an investment involving $200 received at the end of years 1 through 5, a $300 cash outflow at the end of year 6, and $500 received at the end of years 7 through 10 given a 5 percent discount rate? Here we have two annuities, one that can be discounted directly back to the present by multiplying it by the value of the $PVIFA_{5\%,5yr}$ and one that must be discounted twice to bring it back to the present. This second annuity must first be discounted back to the beginning of period 7 or end of period 6, by multiplying it by the value of the $PVIFA_{5\%,4yr}$; then, the present value of the annuity at the end of period 6 must be discounted back to the present, by multiplying it by the value of the $PVIFA_{5\%,6yr}$. To arrive at the total present value of this investment, we subtract the present value of the $300 cash outflow at the end of year 6 from the sum of the present value of the two annuities. Table 4-16 shows this graphically; Table 4-17 gives the calculations. Thus the present value of this series of cash flows is $1,964.66. ■

THE PROCESS OF VALUING FINANCIAL SECURITIES

The valuation process involves calculating the present value of an asset's expected future cash flows using the investor's required rate of return. The investor's required rate of return, R, is determined by the level of the risk-free rate of interest, R_f, and the risk premium, RP, that the investor feels is necessary to compensate for the risks assumed in owning the asset. Therefore, the basic security valuation model can be defined mathematically as follows:

$$V = \frac{C_1}{(1 + R)^1} + \frac{C_2}{(1 + R)^2} + ... + \frac{C_n}{(1 + R)^n} \qquad (4\text{-}20)$$

or

$$V = \sum_{t=1}^{n} \frac{C_t}{(1 + R)^t}$$

where V = the intrinsic value or present value of an asset producing expected future cash flows, C_t, in years 1 through n

R = the investor's required rate of return

Using Equation (4-20), there are three basic steps in the valuation process:

1. Estimate the C_t in Equation (4-20), which is the amount and timing of the future cash flows the security is expected to provide.

2. Determine R, the investor's required rate of return, using $R = R_f + RP$. We do this by evaluating the riskiness of the security's future cash flows and determining an appropriate risk premium, RP. We then observe the risk-free rate (such as the rate of interest on 3-month Treasury bills) and add the two together for the required rate of return.

3. Calculate the intrinsic value, V, as the present value of expected future cash flows discounted at the investor's required rate of return.

With these general principles of valuation as a foundation, we can investigate the procedures for valuing particular types of securities. Specifically, we will learn how to value bonds, preferred shares, and common shares.

BOND VALUATION

The process for valuing a bond requires first that we understand the terminology and institutional characteristics of a bond. More extensive coverage of the contractual provisions of a bond is provided in Chapter 19.

Perspective in Finance

The value of a bond is the present value of future interest payments to be received and the par or maturity value of the bond. Simply list these cash flows, use your discount rate of return, and find the value.

Terminology

When the Government of Canada or a corporation requires financing, one source is bonds. This type of financing instrument is simply a long-term promissory note issued by the borrower, promising to pay its holder a predetermined and fixed amount of interest each year. As a form of debt, a contract between the borrower and lender is executed, frequently called an indenture. Although the terms of the contract generally are extensive, incorporating detailed protective provisions for the creditor, only three items directly affect the cash flows from owning a bond: the bond's par value, maturity date, and the coupon rate of interest.

1. **Par value.** The amount which the firm is to pay on the maturity date is stated on the face of the bond. This amount, defined as the par value or face value, cannot be altered after the bond has been issued. Typically, the par value is set at $1,000. Hence, the issuing company contractually agrees to pay the investor this amount when the debt matures. The par value is essentially independent of the intrinsic value of the bond. Thus, while the price of the bond fluctuates in response to changing economic and market conditions, the par value remains constant.

2. **Maturity date.** As already suggested, a bond normally has a maturity date, at which time the borrowing organization is committed to repay the loan. At this time the holder of the security, assuming the company does not default on the obligation, is to receive cash in the amount of the par value.

3. **Coupon's nominal interest rate.** Besides paying the owner of the bond the par value at the maturity date, the borrower promises to pay a specified amount of interest each year. This amount of interest is stated either in terms of dollars, such as $90, or as a percent of the par value. In either instance the interest to be paid is inflexible. When the contractual agreement specifies the annual interest as a percent of par value, this percentage is known as the coupon's nominal interest rate or the contractual interest rate. For instance, if the terms of a $1,000 par value bond set the annual interest at $90, the nominal interest rate of the coupon is 9 percent, or $90 divided by $1,000. Furthermore, this rate should not be confused with the required rate of return.

Valuation Procedure

The valuation process for a bond, as depicted in Figure 4-3, requires knowledge of three essential elements: (1) the amount of the cash flows to be received by the investor, (2) the maturity date of the loan, and (3) the investor's required rate of return. The amount of cash flows is dictated by the periodic

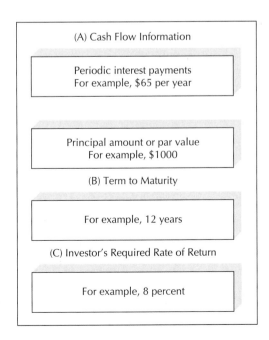

FIGURE 4-3
Data Requirements for Bond Valuation

(A) Cash Flow Information

Periodic interest payments
For example, $65 per year

Principal amount or par value
For example, $1000

(B) Term to Maturity

For example, 12 years

(C) Investor's Required Rate of Return

For example, 8 percent

INTERNATIONAL FINANCIAL MANAGEMENT

The Era of Global Corporate Valuation Has Arrived

Companies today are run by financial people, not by sales people, or production people, as they were in past eras. They are organized along product lines rather than regional lines. Strategic planning articles emphasize the importance of organizing globally, rather than into a North American region, a European region and so on.

Corporations today rely heavily on the increase in communications technology. They could not operate on a global basis without the communications capability available today. We are at the brink of computerized language translation, where even language barriers will become insignificant because we will be able to process foreign language financial reports automatically. There is also an integrated monetary policy. The Japanese monetary authorities may have more influence on North American money supply these days than the Federal Reserve.

In a global climate it is impossible to regulate securities. There is no way to protect North American investors when they wish to buy stocks in Japan, New Zealand, or London. Stock exchanges are going to become linked together. The corporate era relies on new global valuation characteristics, rather than the ones popular 10 or 20 years ago.

The North American markets have thus far been bound together by a common monetary climate, a common culture, and highly integrated trade. The institutional investors who were so strong in the recent past are losing ground to the corporate investors. The trend toward in-house money management has been in progress for more than a decade. Although institutional investors still write out the tickets, the major investment decisions are now being made by their clients. The corporate investor is taking back control of the funds for which they are responsible—and this represents a great deal of money. The corporate investor in North America has not gone global yet. They are dabbling in international securities in the old way, by picking stocks in local markets. They do not yet have integrated investment programs.

Each geographic and political region of the world has a different relationship among investment institutions, corporate management, and the government. In Europe, there is a managed environment between institutions and corporations; they have developed a very clear alliance, frequently with government cooperation. By and large, Europe has a very corporate-controlled climate. Inside information—for your own purposes—is quite common; it gives confidence and is a way of cementing relationships. It becomes the currency by which these affiliations thrive. But in reality, it is hard to determine what is inside information there. When everybody owns 21% of everybody else—everybody becomes an insider.

The Far East started out on an American model. Culturally, many of these systems did not take root. In Japan, of course, they are quite accustomed to the use of debt leverage. They also use a portfolio approach to investing, rather than a stock-selection approach.

Where Esteem Equals Cash Value

The most fascinating thing about Japanese investors is the information that they value. A recent study asked Japanese and American businessmen to rate a list of potential goals in order of importance. The list included such things as income, longevity, friendly relations with fellow workers, esteem, price, reputa-

---

interest to be received and by the par value to be paid at maturity. Given these elements, we can compute the value of the bond, or the present value.

> **EXAMPLE**

Assume that the Government of Canada issues an annual coupon bond,[11] having a maturity date of January 1st, 2000 and a stated nominal interest rate of 10.5% percent. The bonds were originally issued at a price of $1,000.

---

[11]In actuality, the Government of Canada remits the interest to its bondholders on a semi-annual basis such as January 15 and July 15. However, for the moment assume the interest is to be received annually. The effect of semiannual payments will be examined later.

tion, and quality. The Japanese rated esteem as the number one goal and income as least important. The Americans rated income as the most important goal and esteem as the least important. We should not be chauvinistic and say that our own notion of income maximization must be the primary goal of a Japanese investor. It seems perfectly clear that esteem can be just as important a valuation characteristic as income. Therefore, how can we subject the Japanese to what a friend of mine refers to as "the tyranny of the price/earnings ratio," when they do not subscribe to that notion at all?

In the global market, Latin America may be the most attractive region now. It offers some potentially exciting opportunities. Emerging market funds are gaining popularity, and Latin America seems to be emerging from its dark ages. One particularly appealing attribute is the region's lack of covariance with most of the other markets. The model of this region is close government and private control.

The market will become integrated because of these communication capabilities. The databases are becoming increasingly linked; eventually they will be consolidated into one or two strong databases. Deregulation, which is now a worldwide phenomenon, will accelerate this process. Competitive markets, in turn, will increase the likelihood of this trend toward deregulation. Cross-trading facilitates integrated markets. For example, today, Sony stock is traded in 18 markets. Equity prices will thrive in this climate, and be put to their best use.

The global market in this climate becomes countryless. Control is likely to be a major element, and currency will be dealt with as a separate characteristic. An elite set of global multinational companies is emerging today. These are companies with sales, production and ownership distributed across several countries.

As corporations are increasingly valued in a global context, a significant problem continues to be the dramatic differences in accounting practices among countries. One analyst (Paul Aron of Daiwa Securities) has suggested that Japanese company earnings are undervalued by at least 50% relative to US generally accepted accounting principles. Many companies are taking the initiative here, ahead of their accountants, by issuing annual reports in other countries, reconciled to their standards.

Companies which move quickly to achieve global stature, regardless of their size, will achieve the highest valuations at the hands of the broadest spectrum of possible investors.

These global investors are in our midst now, and have been for several years. They know, for example, that Americans will understand gold as a normal repository of value, and that the Japanese will learn to buy stocks on the dividend discount basis as this cross-cultural exchange takes place. The ultimate asset sheet in this global market will list all assets—common data for all—and have the flexibility to specify the currency mix of choice of the investor. The successful investor in this transitional phase is one who moves to the integrated standard first. Those who do not will give up profit because of their high-confidence, local-market biases. The profitable issuers will be listed in many markets; they will push for disclosure; they will consolidate control; they will use complex derivative instruments when profitable to issue; and most important, they will see the world as the smallest unit of financial market segmentation.

Source: An excerpt from: Dean LeBaron, "The Era of Global Corporate Valuation Has Arrived," *The Chief Financial Officer* (1988), pp. 100–101.

By 1993, however, since the investors' required rate of return had changed, the bond value was more than $1,000. In fact, in early 1993, investors were requiring a return of 8.25 percent for this type of security. At this time the value of the security was approximately $1,116, which can be calculated using the following three-step valuation procedure.

1. Estimate the amount and timing of the expected future cash flows. Two types of cash flows are received by the bondholder:

   a) Annual interest payments equal to the nominal interest rate times the face value of the bond. In this example the interest payments equal $105 or (.105)($1000). Assuming that 1992 interest payments have already been made, these cash flows will be received by the bondholder in each of the 7 years before the bond matures (2000 – 1993 = 7 years).

b) The face value of the bond of $1,000 to be received in 2000.

To summarize, the cash flows received by the bondholder are as follows:

1	2	3	4	5	6	7
$105	$105	$105	$105	$105	$105	$ 105
						+$1000
						$1105

2. Determine the investor's required rate of return by evaluating the riskiness of the bond's future cash flows. An 8.25 percent required rate of return for the Government of Canada bondholders is given.

3. Calculate the intrinsic value of the bond as the present value of the expected future interest and principal payments discounted at the investor's required rate of return. ∎

The present value of Government of Canada's bonds is found as follows:

$$\text{Bond value} = V_b = \frac{\$ \text{ interest in year 1}}{(1 + \text{required rate of return})^1}$$

$$+ \frac{\$ \text{ interest in year 2}}{(1 + \text{required rate of return})^2}$$

$$+ ... + \frac{\$ \text{ interest in year 7}}{(1 + \text{required rate of return})^7}$$

$$+ \frac{\$ \text{ par value of bond}}{(1 + \text{required rate of return})^7}$$

or, summing over the interest payments,

$$V_b = \underbrace{\sum_{t=1}^{7} \frac{\$ \text{ interest in year } t}{(1 + \text{required rate of return})^t}}_{\substack{\text{present value} \\ \text{of interest}}} + \underbrace{\frac{\$ \text{ par value of bond}}{(1 + \text{required rate of return})^7}}_{\substack{\text{present value} \\ \text{of par value}}} \quad (4\text{-}21)$$

Perspective in Finance

This equation is a restatement in a slightly different format of Equation (4-20). Recall that Equation (4-20) states that the value of an asset is the present value of future cash flows to be received by the investor.

Using I_t *to represent the interest payment in year* t, **M** *to represent the bond's maturity value, and* R_b *to equal the bondholder's required rate of return, we may express the value of a bond maturing in year* n *as follows:*

$$V_b = \sum_{t=1}^{n} \frac{\$I_t}{(1 + R_b)^t} + \frac{\$M}{(1 + R_b)^n} \quad (4\text{-}21a)$$

Since the interest payments I_t are an annuity for n years, and the maturity value is a one-time amount in year n, we can use the present-value factors in Appendixes B and D to solve for the present value of the bond as follows:

$$V_b = \$I_t\,[PVIFA_{R_b,n}] + \$M\,[PVIF_{R_b,n}] \qquad \text{(4-21b)}$$

For our Government of Canada bond,

$$V_b = \$105(5.162) + \$1000(.574)$$
$$= \$542.03 + \$574.12$$
$$= \$1,116.15$$

Thus, if investors consider 8.25 percent to be an appropriate required rate of return in view of the risk level associated with these Government of Canada bonds, paying a price of $1,116.15 would satisfy their return requirement.[12] We emphasize that the bondholder's required rate of return is the minimum rate of return that an investor must earn in order to invest in this type of financial instrument. In fact, the required rate of return is an opportunity cost which is determined by the rate of return from a comparable financial instrument in the market. In other words, the required rate of return is determined from the interest rates of bonds selling in market, which have the same risk characteristics and the same term-to-maturity. We describe an investor who is buying a bond at the required rate as buying the bond "at margin," since the investor is just willing to buy the bond at the market price and is not willing to pay a higher price for it.

Semiannual Interest Payments

In the preceding illustration, the coupons were assumed to be paid annually. However, companies typically forward an interest cheque to bondholders semiannually. For example, rather than disbursing $105 in interest at the conclusion of each year, Government of Canada pays $52.50 (half of $105) on January 1st and July 1st.

Several steps are involved in adapting Equation (4-21a) to recognize semiannual interest payments.[13] First, thinking in terms of "periods" instead of years, a bond with a life of n years paying coupons semiannually should be thought to have a life of $2n$ periods. In other words, a seven-year bond ($n = 7$) that remits its coupons on a semiannual basis actually makes 14 payments. Although the number of periods has doubled, the dollar amount of interest being sent to the investors for each period and the bondholders' required rate of return are half of the equivalent annual figures. I_t becomes $I_t/2$ and R_b is changed to $R_b/2$; thus, for semiannual compounding, Equation (4-21a) becomes

$$V_b = \sum_{t=1}^{2n} \frac{\dfrac{\$I_t}{2}}{\left(1 + \dfrac{R_b}{2}\right)^t} + \frac{\$M}{\left(1 + \dfrac{R_b}{2}\right)^{2n}} \qquad \text{(4-22)}$$

---

[12]Instead of using the present value tables in the appendix, it is easier to use a financial calculator. Also, the calculator is not as restrictive in that you are not limited to integer percentages. See Appendix E at the end of the text for a tutorial on using the Texas Instruments BAII Plus calculator.

[13]The logic for calculating the value of a semiannual coupon bond is similar to the material presented earlier in this Chapter, where compound interest with nonannual periods was discussed.

However, if the present-value tables are used, V_b is calculated as

$$V_b = \frac{\$I_t}{2}\left[PVIFA_{\frac{R_b}{2},2n}\right] + \$M\left[PVIF_{\frac{R_b}{2},2n}\right] \tag{4-22a}$$

EXAMPLE

To see the effect of semiannual coupon payments upon the value of a bond, assume the Government of Canada has issued a 9.75 percent, $1,000 bond. The debt is to mature in nine years, and the investor's required rate of return is currently 8.16 percent. If interest is paid semiannually, the number of periods is 18 (nine years × 2); the dollar interest to be received by the investor at the end of each six-month period is $48.75 ($97.50/2); and the required rate of return for six months is 4.08 percent (8.16 percent/2). Therefore, the valuation equation is

$$V_b = \sum_{t=1}^{18}\frac{\$48.75}{(1+.0408)^t} + \frac{\$1000}{(1+.0408)^{18}}$$

Equivalently,

$$V_b = \$48.75\,[PVIFA_{4.08\%,18}] + \$1,000\,[PVIF_{4.08\%,18}]$$

$$= \$48.75(12.577) + \$1000(.487)$$

$$= \$613.13 + \$486.87$$

$$= \$1,100.00$$

Thus, the value (present value) of a bond paying $48.75 semiannually, and $1,000 at maturity (six years), is $1,100.00, provided the investor's required rate of return is 8.16 percent.[14] ∎

CALCULATOR SOLUTION

Data Input	Function Key
18	N
4.08	I/Y
48.75	PMT
1000	FV

Function Key	Answer
CPT PV	−1099.99*

*The difference between the two answers represents rounding error.

Bondholder's Expected Rate of Return and Yield to Maturity

Mathematically, the internal rate of return (IRR) is the discount rate that equates the present value of the inflows with the present value of the outflows. The idea of comparing the present value of inflows to that of outflows is especially valuable when evaluating an investment project such as a security investment. For this type of security investment, the investor expectations of the actual rate of return from future cash flows are defined as the expected rate of return. For example, the expected rate of return implicit in the current bond price is the discount rate that equates the present value of the future cash flows with the current market price of the bond.[15] The Yield-To-Maturity (YTM) represents an estimate of the expected rate of return for a bond if the bond is held to maturity. Thus, when referring to bonds, the terms *expected rate of return* and *yield to maturity* are often used interchangeably when discussing the rate of return which equates the present value of

[14]A slightly different answer may result from differences in rounding.

[15]When we speak of computing an expected rate of return, we are not describing the situation very accurately. Expected rates of return are *ex ante* (before the fact) and are based upon "expected and unobservable future cash flows" and therefore can only be "estimated."

the future interest payments received until maturity to the current bond price. For a more in-depth understanding of bond valuation, see Appendix 4A at the end of the chapter.

To illustrate, consider the bonds of the Brister Corporation, which are selling for $1,140. The bonds carry a coupon interest rate of 9 percent and mature in 10 years.

In determining the expected rate of return implicit in the current market price, we need to find the rate that discounts the anticipated annual cash flows back to a present value of $1,140, the existing market price for the bond. Table 4-18 shows the method that should be used to estimate the YTM of the bond.

Solution: Pick an arbitrary discount rate and use it to determine the present value of the inflows. Compare the present value of the inflows with the initial outlay; if they are equal, you have determined the YTM. Otherwise, raise the discount rate if the present value of the inflows is larger than the initial outlay or lower the discount rate if the present value of the inflows is less than the initial outlay. Repeat this process until the YTM is found.

1. Try $i = 6$ percent:

$$V_b = \$90(PVIFA_{6\%,10}) + \$1,000(PVIF_{6\%,10})$$

$$= 90(7.3601) + 1000(.5584)$$

$$= 662.41 + 558.39$$

$$= \$1,220.80$$

2. Try $i = 8$ percent:

$$V_b = \$90(PVIFA_{8\%,10}) + \$1,000(PVIF_{8\%,10})$$

$$= 90(6.7101) + 1000(.4632)$$

$$= 603.91 + 463.19$$

$$= \$1,067.10$$

The actual rate can be more precisely approximated through interpolation as follows:

Discount rate	Present value
6%	$1,220.80
YTM	$1,140.16
8	$1,067.10

Initial outlay—$1140.16											
		↓									
year	0	1	2	3	4	5	6	7	8	9	10
		90	90	90	90	90	90	90	90	90	90
		$(1+i)^1$	$(1+i)^2$	$(1+i)^3$	$(1+i)^4$	$(1+i)^5$	$(1+i)^6$	$(1+i)^7$	$(1+i)^8$	$(1+i)^9$	$(1+i)^{10}$

TABLE 4-18
Computing the YTM for a Bond Without a Financial Calculator

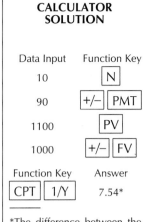

$$\frac{(YTM - 8\%)}{(8\% - 6\%)} = \frac{(1140.16 - 1067.10)}{(1067.10 - 1220.80)}$$

$$\frac{(YTM - 8\%)}{(2\%)} = \frac{(73.06)}{(-153.70)}$$

$$YTM - 8\% = (2\%)(-.475)$$

$$YTM = 7.05\%$$

Thus, the expected rate of return on the Brister Corporation's bonds for an investor who purchases the bonds for $1,140 is approximately 7 percent. A more precise answer can be obtained by using a calculator. ∎

PREFERRED SHARE VALUATION

Like a bondholder, the owner of a preferred share should receive a constant income from the investment in each period. However, the return from a preferred share comes in the form of dividends rather than interest. In addition, while bonds generally have a specific maturity date, most preferred shares are perpetuities (nonmaturing). In this instance, finding the value (present value) of a preferred share, V_p, with a level cash flow stream continuing indefinitely, may best be explained by an example.

EXAMPLE

To illustrate the valuation of a preferred share, consider the Royal Bank of Canada's preferred share issue. Once again we use the three-step valuation procedure.

1. Estimate the amount and timing of the receipt of the future cash flows the preferred share is expected to provide.

   Royal Bank of Canada's preferred share pays an annual dividend of $1.88. The shares do not have a maturity date; that is, they go to perpetuity.

2. Evaluate the riskiness of the preferred share's future dividends and determine the investor's required rate of return.

   The investor's required rate of return is assumed to equal 8.36 percent.

3. Calculate the intrinsic value of a preferred share, which is the present value of the expected dividends discounted at the investor's required rate of return.

The valuation model for a preferred share, V_p, is defined as follows:

$$V_p = \frac{\text{dividend in year 1}}{(1 + \text{required rate of return})^1}$$

$$+ \frac{\text{dividend in year 2}}{(1 + \text{required rate of return})^2}$$

$$+ \ldots + \frac{\text{dividend in infinity}}{(1 + \text{required rate of return})^\infty}$$

$$= \frac{D_1}{(1 + R_p)^1} + \frac{D_2}{(1 + R_p)^2} + \ldots + \frac{D_\infty}{(1 + R_p)^\infty}$$

$$V_p = \sum_{t=1}^{\infty} \frac{D_t}{(1 + R_p)^t} \qquad (4\text{-}23)$$

Since the dividends in each period are equal for preferred share, Equation (4-23) can be reduced to the following relationship.[16]

$$V_p = \frac{\text{annual dividend}}{\text{required rate of return}} = \frac{D}{R_p} \qquad (4\text{-}24)$$

Equation (4-24) represents the present value of an infinite stream of cash flows, where the cash flows are the same each year. We can determine the value of the Royal Bank's preferred shares using Equation (4-24), as follows:

$$V_p = \frac{D}{R_p} = \frac{\$1.88}{8.35} = \$22.51 \ \blacksquare$$

The Preferred Shareholder's Expected Rate of Return

In computing the preferred shareholder's expected rate we use the valuation equation for preferred shares. Earlier, Equation (4-24) specified the value of a preferred share, V_p, as

$$V_p = \frac{\text{annual dividend}}{\text{required rate of return}} = \frac{D}{R_p} \qquad (4\text{-}24)$$

Solving (4-24) for R_p,

$$R_p = \frac{\text{annual dividend}}{\text{value}} = \frac{D}{V_p} \qquad (4\text{-}25)$$

which simply indicates that the expected rate of return of a preferred security

---

[16]To verify this result, consider the following equation

(i) $\qquad V_p = \frac{D_1}{(1 + R_p)} + \frac{D_2}{(1 + R_p)^2} + \ldots + \frac{D_n}{(1 + R_p)^n}$

If we multiply both sides of this equation by $(1 + R_p)$, we have

(ii) $\qquad V_p(1 + R_p) = D_1 + \frac{D_2}{(1 + R_p)} + \ldots + \frac{D_n}{(1 + R_p)^{n-1}}$

Subtracting (i) from (ii) yields

$$V_p(1 + R_p - 1) = D_1 - \frac{D_n}{(1 + R_p)^n}$$

As n approaches infinity, $D_n/(1 + R_p)^n$ approaches zero. Consequently,

$$V_p R_p = D_1 \ \text{ and } \ V_p = \frac{D_1}{R_p}$$

Since $D_1 = D_2 = \ldots = D_n$, we need not designate the year. Therefore,

(iii) $\qquad V_p = \frac{D}{R_p}$

equals the dividend yield (dividend/price). For example, if the present market price of a preferred share is $50 and it pays a $3.64 dividend, the expected rate of return implicit in the present market price is

$$R_p = \frac{D}{V_p} = \frac{\$3.64}{\$50} = 7.28 \text{ percent}$$

Therefore, investors at the margin (who pay $50 per share for a preferred share that is paying $3.64 in annual dividends) are expecting a 7.28 percent rate of return.

Perspective in Finance

The value of a preferred share is the present value of all future dividends. But since most preferred shares are nonmaturing—the dividends continue to infinity—we have to come up with a shortcut for finding value.

COMMON SHARE VALUATION

The third and last security we will learn to value is the common share. Like both a bond and a preferred share, a common share's value is equal to the present value of all future cash flows expected to be received by the shareholder. However, in contrast to a bond, a common share does not guarantee interest income or a maturity payment at some specified time in the future. Nor does a common share entitle the holder to a predetermined constant dividend, as does a preferred share. For a common share, the dividend is based upon the profitability of the firm and upon management's decision to pay dividends or to retain the profits for reinvestment purposes. As a consequence, the dividend stream tends to increase with the growth in corporate earnings. Thus, the growth of future dividends is a prime distinguishing feature of a common share.

The Growth Factor in Valuing a Common Share

What is meant by the term "growth" when used in the context of valuing a common share? A company can grow in a variety of ways. It can become larger by borrowing money to invest in new projects. Likewise, it can issue new shares for expansion. Management could also acquire another company to merge with the existing firm; the firm's assets would clearly be increased. In all these cases, the firm is growing through the use of new financing, by issuing debt or common shares. While management could accurately say that the firm has grown, the original shareholders may or may not participate in this growth. Growth is being realized through the infusion of new capital.[17] The firm size has clearly increased, but unless the original investors increase their investment in the firm, they will own a smaller portion of the expanded business.

Another means of growing is internal growth, which requires that man-

[17]Growth in and of itself does not mean that we are creating value for shareholders. Only if we reinvest at a rate of return that is greater than the investor's required rate of return will growth cause an increase in the value of the firm. In fact, any investment at a rate less than the required rate of return for our investors causes the value of the firm to actually decline.

agement retain some or all of the firm's profits for reinvestment in the firm, resulting in the growth of future earnings and hopefully the value of the common shares. This process underlies the essence of potential growth for the firm's current shareholders, and what we may call the only "relevant growth," for our purposes in valuing a firm's common shares.[18]

EXAMPLE

To illustrate the nature of internal growth, assume that the return on equity for PepsiCo is 16 percent.[19] If PepsiCo's management decides to pay all the profits out in dividends to its shareholders, the firm will experience no growth internally. It might become larger by borrowing more money or issuing new shares, but internal growth will come only through the retention of profits. If, on the other hand, PepsiCo retained all the profits, the shareholders' investment in the firm will grow by the amount of profits retained, or by 16 percent. If, however, management kept only 50 percent of the profits for reinvestment, the common shareholders' investment would increase only by half of the 16 percent return on equity, or by 8 percent. Generalizing this relationship, we have

$$g = ROE \times r \tag{4-26}$$

where
g = the growth rate of future earnings and the growth in the common shareholders' investment in the firm

ROE = the return on equity (net income/common book value)

r = the company's percentage of profits retained, which is called the profit-retention rate[20]

Thus, if only 25 percent of the profits were retained by PepsiCo, we would expect the common shareholders' investment in the firm and the value of the share price to increase or grow by 4 percent; that is,

$$g = 16\% \times .25 = 4\% \blacksquare$$

In summary, common shareholders frequently rely upon share price as a source of return. If the company is retaining a portion of its earnings for reinvestment, future profits and dividends should grow. This growth should be reflected in an increased market price of the common share in future periods. Therefore, both types of return (dividends and price appreciation) are necessary in the development of a valuation model for common shares.

To explain this process, let us begin by examining how an investor might value a common share that is to be held for only one year.

---

[18]We are not arguing that the existing common shareholders never benefit from the use of external financing; however, such benefit is more evasive when dealing with efficient capital markets.

[19]The return on equity is the percentage return on the common shareholder's investment in the company, and is computed as follows:

$$\text{Return on equity} = \frac{\text{net income}}{(\text{common shares} + \text{contributed surplus} + \text{retained earnings})}$$

[20]The retention rate is also equal to (1 – the percentage of profits paid out in dividends). The percentage of profits paid out in dividends is often called the dividend-payout ratio.

Common Share Valuation—Single Holding Period

For an investor holding a common share for only one year, the value of the share should equal the present value of both the expected dividend to be received in one year, D_1, and the anticipated market price of the share at year-end, P_1. If R_c represents a common shareholder's required rate of return, the value of the security, V_c, would be

$$V_c = \text{present value of dividend } (D_1)$$
$$\qquad + \text{present value of market price } (P_1) \qquad (4\text{-}27)$$

$$= \frac{D_1}{(1 + R_c)} + \frac{P_1}{(1 + R_c)}$$

Suppose an investor is contemplating the purchase of RMI common shares at the beginning of this year. The dividend at year-end is expected to be $1.64 and the market price by the end of the year is projected to be $22. If the investor's required rate of return is 18 percent, the value of the security would be

$$V_c = \frac{\$1.64}{1 + .18} + \frac{\$22}{1 + .18}$$

$$= \$1.39 + \$18.64$$

$$= \$20.03$$

Once again we see that valuation is the same three-step process. First we estimate the expected future cash flows from common share ownership (a $1.64 dividend and a $22 end-of-year expected share price). Second, we estimate the investor's required rate of return after assessing the riskiness of the expected cash flows (assumed to be 18 percent). Finally, we discount the expected dividend and end-of-year share price back to the present at the investor's required rate of return.

Perspective in Finance

The intrinsic value of a common share is similar to that of a preferred share. Both these financial instruments have an intrinsic value which represents the present value of all future dividends. Furthermore, we have the same problem as we had with the valuation of preferred shares; that is, the difficulty of valuing cash flows that continue in perpetuity. So we must make some assumptions about the expected growth of future dividends. If, for example, we assume that dividends grow at a constant rate forever, we can then calculate the present value of the share.

Common Share Valuation—Multiple Holding Periods

Since common shares have no maturity date and are frequently held for many years, a multiple-holding-period valuation model is needed. The general common share valuation model can be defined as follows:

$$V_c = \frac{D_1}{(1 + R_c)^1} + \frac{D_2}{(1 + R_c)^2} + \ldots + \frac{D_n}{(1 + R_c)^n} + \ldots + \frac{D_\infty}{(1 + R_c)^\infty} \qquad (4\text{-}28)$$

Perspective in Finance

Equation (4-28) is a restatement in a slightly different format of Equation (4-20). Recall that Equation (4-20) states that the value of an asset is the present value of future cash flows to be received by the investor.

This equation simply indicates that we are discounting the dividend at the end of the first year, D_1, back one year, the dividend in the second year, D_2, back two years, ..., the dividend in the nth year back n years, ..., and the dividend in infinity back an infinite number of years. The required rate of return is R_c. In using Equation (4-28), note that the value of the share is being established at the beginning of the year, say January 1, 1994. The most recent past dividend D_0 would have been paid the previous day on December 31, 1993. Thus, if we purchased the share on January 1, the first dividend would be received in 12 months, on December 31, 1993, which is represented by D_0.

Fortunately, Equation (4-28) can be reduced to a much more manageable form if dividends grow each year at a constant rate, g. The "constant growth" common share valuation model is defined as follows:[21]

$$\text{common share value} = \frac{\text{dividend in year 1}}{(\text{required rate of return}) - (\text{growth rate})}$$

$$V_c = \frac{D_1}{R_c - g} \tag{4-29}$$

Consequently, the intrinsic value (present value) of a common share whose dividends grow at a constant annual rate can be calculated using Equation (4-29). Although the interpretation of this equation may not be intuitively obvious, we should remember that it solves for the present value of the future dividend stream growing at a rate, g, to infinity, assuming that R_c is greater than g.

---

[21]Where common share dividends grow at a constant rate of g every year, we can express the dividend in any year in terms of the dividend paid at the end of the previous year, D_0. For example, the expected dividend one year hence is simply $D_0(1 + g)$. Likewise, the dividend at the end of t years is $D_0(1 + g)^t$. Using this notation, the common share valuation Equation (4-28) can be rewritten as follows:

$$V_c = \frac{D_0(1+g)^1}{(1+R_c)^1} + \frac{D_0(1+g)^2}{(1+R_c)^2} + \ldots + \frac{D_0(1+g)^n}{(1+R_c)^n} + \ldots + \frac{D_0(1+g)^\infty}{(1+R_c)^\infty} \tag{4-28a}$$

If both sides of Equation (4-28a) are multiplied by $(1 + R_c)/(1 + g)$ and then Equation (4-28a) is subtracted from the product, the result is

$$\frac{V_c(1 + R_c)}{1 + g} - V_c = D_0 - \frac{D_0(1 + g)^\infty}{(1 + R_c)^\infty} \tag{4-28b}$$

If $R_c > g$, which normally should hold, $[D_0(1 + g)^\infty/(1 + R_c)^\infty]$ approaches zero. As a result,

$$\frac{V_c(1 + R_c)}{1 + g} - V_c = D_0$$

$$V_c\left(\frac{1 + R_c}{1 + g}\right) - V_c\left(\frac{1 + g}{1 + g}\right) = D_0$$

$$V_c\left[\frac{(1 + R_c) - (1 + g)}{1 + g}\right] = D_0$$

$$V_c(R_c - g) = D_0(1 + g)$$

$$V_c = \frac{D_1}{R_c - g}$$

Consider the valuation of a common share that paid a $2 dividend at the end of the last year and is expected to pay a cash dividend every year from now to infinity. Each year the dividends are expected to grow at a rate of 10 percent. Based upon an assessment of the riskiness of the common share, the investor's required rate of return is 15 percent. Using this information, we would compute the value of the common share as follows:

1. Since the $2 dividend was paid last year (actually yesterday), we must compute the next dividend to be received, that is, D_1, where

$$D_1 = D_0(1 + g)$$
$$= \$2(1 + .10)$$
$$= \$2.20$$

2. Now using Equation (4-29),

$$V_c = \frac{D_1}{R_c - g}$$
$$= \frac{\$2.20}{.15 - .10}$$
$$= \$44 \ \blacksquare$$

We have argued that the value of a common share is equal to the present value of all future dividends, which is without question a fundamental premise of finance. However, in practice, managers, along with many security analysts, often talk about the relationship between share value and earnings, rather than dividends. Appendix 4B provides some insights into the rationale and propriety of using earnings to value a firm's share. We encourage you to be very cautious in using earnings to value a share. Even though it may be a popular practice, the fact remains that investors look to the cash flows generated by the firm, not its earnings, for value. A firm's value truly is the present value of the cash flows it produces.

The Common Shareholder's Expected Rate of Return

The valuation equation for a common share was defined earlier as

$$\text{value} = \frac{\text{dividend in year 1}}{(1 + \text{required rate of return})^1}$$

$$+ \frac{\text{dividend in year 2}}{(1 + \text{required rate of return})^2}$$

$$+ ... + \frac{\text{dividend in year infinity}}{(1 + \text{required rate of return})^\infty}$$

$$V_c = \frac{D_1}{(1 + R_c)^1} + \frac{D_2}{(1 + R_c)^2} + ... + \frac{D_\infty}{(1 + R_c)^\infty} \qquad (4\text{-}28)$$

$$V_c = \sum_{t=1}^{\infty} \frac{D_t}{(1 + R_c)^t}$$

Owing to the difficulty of discounting to infinity, a key assumption was made that the dividends, D_t, increase at a constant annual compound growth rate of

g. If this assumption is valid, Equation (4-28) was shown to be equivalent to

$$\text{value} = \frac{\text{dividend in year 1}}{(\text{required rate of return} - \text{growth rate})}$$

$$V_c = \frac{D_1}{(R_c - g)} \qquad (4\text{-}29)$$

Thus, V_c represents the maximum value that an investor having a required rate of return of R_c would pay for a security having an anticipated dividend in year 1 of D_1 which is expected to grow in future years at rate g.[22] Solving Equation (4-28) for R_c, we can compute the expected rate of return for a common share implicit in its current market price as follows:

$$R_c = \underset{\substack{\uparrow \\ \text{dividend} \\ \text{yield}}}{\left(\frac{D_1}{V_c}\right)} + \underset{\substack{\uparrow \\ \text{annual} \\ \text{growth} \\ \text{rate}}}{g}$$

From this equation, the common shareholder's expected rate of return is equal to the dividend yield plus a growth factor. Although the growth rate, g, applies to the growth in the company's dividends, both the firm's earnings per share and its share price may also be expected to increase at the same rate. For this reason, g represents the annual percentage growth in the share price. In other words, the investors' expected rate of return is satisfied by receiving dividends, expressed as a percentage of the price of the share (dividend yield), and capital gains, as reflected by the percentage growth rate.[23]

We now compute the expected rate of return for a common share. Assume a firm's common share has a current market price of $44 and its dividends grow at a constant rate to infinity. If the expected dividend at the conclusion of this year is $2.20 and dividends and earnings are growing at a 10 percent annual rate (last year's dividend was $2), the expected rate of return implicit in the $44 share price is as follows:

$$R_c = \frac{\$2.20}{\$44} + 10\% = 15\%$$

EXPECTED RATES OF RETURN VS. REQUIRED RATES OF RETURN

Conceptually, each investor can have a different required rate of return for each individual security. However, the financial manager is interested in the

---

[22]At times the expected dividend at year-end (D_1) is not given. Instead we might only know the most recent dividend (paid yesterday), that is, D_0. If so, Equation (4-29) must be restated as follows:
$$V_0 = \frac{D_1}{(R_c - g)} = \frac{D_0(1 + g)}{(R_c - g)}$$

[23]If a firm's dividends, earnings per share, and share price increase at the same rate, the growth rate is equal to the firm's capital gains yield, which is expressed as follows: $g = (V_c - V_0)/V_c$. Hence, the investor's expected rate of return can now be determined as follows:

investor's expected rate of return = capital gains yield + dividend yield.
$$= \frac{(V_c - V_0)}{V_c} + \frac{D}{V_c}$$

BASIC FINANCIAL MANAGEMENT IN PRACTICE

Stock Prices Adjust Slowly to Earnings Jolt

Sometimes share prices do just the opposite of what you might expect from reading a company's earnings announcement. Each financial-reporting period sees hundreds of such "earnings surprises"—cases in which companies' reported earnings are stunningly different from what Wall Street's financial analysts predicted.

Although a company's share price quickly reacts to such earnings surprises, studies show that the full impact doesn't filter through for months. This is especially true for smaller, lesser known issues that aren't widely held by institutions.

Moreover, the more extreme the expectations that analysts have for a company, the bigger the impact of any unexpected turn in earnings. When the market's expectations are either very high or very low, an earnings surprise is likely to force a broad reassessment of the share, says Al Gould, senior vice president at Lynch, Jones & Ryan, a New York brokerage firm.

Helpful Factor

Shearson Lehman Brothers Inc. found that earnings surprises were a helpful factor in identifying shares that would outperform the market. In a Shearson study of 22 quantitative models used in evaluating share price movements since August 1985, a model based on earnings surprises was the third best in determining which shares would outshine the market average. Also, Shearson found that the companies in the top 20% in terms of having the most-positive earnings surprises saw their share prices gain an average of 80% by mid-May 1987— about twice the market's gain.

Research by Richard Rendleman and the late Henry Latane of the University of North Carolina and Charles Jones of North Carolina State University also indicates that share-price changes attributed to earnings surprises tend to be substantial. In the study, they sorted companies into 10 groups, ranging from those that had the most-positive earnings surprises to those that had the biggest earnings disappointments, between 1971 and 1980.

The researchers found that the share prices of the companies with the biggest positive surprises outperformed the market by an average of 5.6% in the three months after earnings were posted. For the group that had the biggest disappointments, share prices lagged the market by an average of 5.4%.

Several studies have shown that in most cases share prices only gradually adjust to earnings surprises. Profs. Jones, Rendleman and Latane's research, for instance, found that even if investors had waited a full month to react to a particular earnings surprise, they still could have captured more than 35% of the share-price change.

Gradual Correction

What's more, one earnings surprise tends to lead to another in the next quarter as analysts gradually raise estimates to account for the unexpected change in a company's fortune. A study by Thomas Kerrigan, president of Horizon Investment Research Inc., Boston, found that when analysts revise estimates upward in a given quarter, there is a 65% chance the same trend will appear in the next two quarters. For downward adjustments, the odds are 70% that the pattern will be repeated.

Mr. Gould says earnings surprises tend to repeat themselves because analysts are slow to acknowledge that their forecasts were incorrect. Most analysts "tend to rely heavily on management forecasts, which tend to be notoriously wrong," he says. When it comes time to adjust those estimates to actual earnings, the changes tend to be made in small increments.

No matter what an investor's basic strategy, studies indicate that the earnings-surprise approach can be included to improve returns. Drexel Burnham Lambert Inc. found that if this approach had been used from 1984 to 1986 with an institutional client's low price-earnings strategy—which already was outperforming the market—annual returns would have been improved by an average of six percentage points. Similar gains would have occurred with high-growth and small-capitalization strategies, Drexel found.

Source: An excerpt from: Barbara Donnelly, "Stock Prices Adjust Slowly to Earnings Jolt," *Wall Street Journal* (June 19, 1987), p. 19.

required rate of return for the firm's securities that is implied by the market prices of those securities. Market price, in a sense, reflects the consensus of all investors as to the expected rate of return.

For example, the Alpha Co. has a bond with a current market price of $1,000 that is maturing in one year; the bond's face value is $1,000 and it pays $100 per year in interest. Using the bond valuation model in Equation (4-21a):

$$V_b = \frac{\$I_1}{(1 + R_b)^1} + \frac{\$M}{(1 + R_b)^1} \qquad (4\text{-}21a)$$

we can solve for the investor's required rate of return implicit in the $1,000 market price of the bond. That is:

$$\$1000 = \frac{\$100}{(1 + R_b)^1} + \frac{\$1000}{(1 + R_b)^1}$$

Solving for R_b, we find that the $1,000 market price "implies" a required rate of return of 10 percent for investors at the margin—that is, investors who are just willing to purchase the bond for $1,000 but will not pay a higher price for it. For these investors, the required rate of return equals the expected rate of return reflected in the bond's current market price. In this instance, both equal 10 percent.[24]

In summary, the expected rate of return implied by a given market price equals the required rate of return for investors at the margin. For these investors, the expected rate of return is just equal to their required rate of return, and therefore they are willing to pay the current market price for the security. These investors' required rate of return is of particular significance to the financial manager, since it represents the cost of new financing to the firm.

SUMMARY

To make decisions, financial managers must compare the costs and benefits of alternatives that do not occur during the same time period. Whether for profitable investments or favourable interest rates, financial decision making requires the understanding of the time value of money. Managers who use the time value of money in all their financial calculations assure themselves of more logical decisions. The use of the time value of money ensures that all dollar values are comparable; since money has a time value, it moves all dollar flows either back to the present or out to a common future date. All time-value equations presented in this chapter originate from the single

---

[24]This 10 percent required return for the investor at the margin is used in Chapter 5 to measure the cost of new debt capital to the firm. That is, if the firm sells a bond for $1,000 and plans to repay the $1,000 plus $100 interest one year later, then the cost of borrowing equals 10 percent. This 10 percent cost of borrowing is also the required rate of return of the investor at the margin.

compounding equation: $FV_n = PV_0(1 + i)^n$. The formulae are used to deal simply with common financial situations—for example discounting single cash flows, compounding annuities, and discounting annuities. Table 4-19 provides a summary of these calculations.

TABLE 4-19
Summary of Time Value of Money Equations

Calculation	Equation	Related Table
Future value of a single payment	$FV_n = PV(1+i)^n = PV(FVIF_{i,n})$	Appendix A
Present value of a single payment	$PV = FV_n\left[\dfrac{1}{(1+i)^n}\right] = FV_n(PVIF_{i,n})$	Appendix B
Future value of an annuity	$FV_n = PMT\left[\displaystyle\sum_{t=0}^{n-1}(1+i)^t\right] = PMT(FVIFA_{i,n})$	Appendix C
Present value of an annuity	$PV = PMT\left[\displaystyle\sum_{t=1}^{n}\dfrac{i}{(1+i)^t}\right] = PMT(PVIFA_{i,n})$	Appendix D
Present value of a perpetuity	$PV = \dfrac{PP}{i}$	
Future value of a single payment with non-annual compounding	$FV_n = PV_0\left(1+\dfrac{i}{m}\right)^{(n)(m)}$	

where
FV_n = the future value of the investment at the end of the n years
n = the number of years for which the annuity will last
i = the annual interest or discount rate
PV_0 = the present value of the future sum of money
PMT = the annuity payments deposited or received at the end of each year
PP = the constant dollar amount provided by the perpetuity
m = the number of times compounding occurs during the year.

Valuation is an important process in financial management. An understanding of the concepts and computational procedures in valuing a security underlies sound decision-making. Valuation supports the financial manager's objective of maximizing the value of the firm's common shares.

For our purposes, *value* is the present value of future cash flows expected to be received from an investment discounted at the investor's required rate of return. In this context, the value of a security is a function of (1) the expected cash inflows from the asset, (2) the riskiness of the investment, and (3) the investor's required rate of return. In a world of uncertainty, returns are measured in terms of the expected cash flows anticipated from the security, a derivation of expected value takes into account possible future events and their probability.

Although the valuation of any security entails the same basic principles, the procedures used in each situation vary. For example, valuing a finite stream of cash flows involves computing the present value of the individual cash receipts for each period. An example of this type of valuation problem would be a bond that is scheduled to mature on a designated date. A second category of cash flow patterns involves an infinite cash flow stream, such as those from a preferred share or a common share. Although the underlying premise of valuation does not change—that is, value equals the present value of future cash flows—valuing such an asset requires a modification in the procedure. For securities with cash flows that are constant in each year, such as those from a preferred share, the present value equals the dollar amount of the annual dividend divided by the investor's required rate of return. Furthermore, for a common share where the future dividends are expected to increase at a constant growth rate, value may be given by the following equation:

$$\text{value} = \frac{\text{dividend in year one}}{(\text{required rate of return} - \text{growth rate})} \qquad (4\text{-}29)$$

We may also express the value of a common share as equal to the value of the dividend stream received from the existing assets plus the value of the dividend stream from the future reinvestment of earnings.

The expected rate of return on a security is the required rate of return of investors who are willing to pay the present market price for the security, but no higher price. This rate of return is important to the financial manager because it equals the required rate of return of the firm's investors. This rate is reached at the point where the present value of future cash flows to be received by the investor is just equal to the present market price of the security.

STUDY QUESTIONS

4-1. What is the time value of money? Why is it so important?

4-2. The processes of discounting and compounding are related. Explain this relationship.

4-3. How would an increase in the interest rate (i) or a decrease in the holding period (n) affect the future value (FV_n) of a sum of money? Explain why.

4-4. Suppose you were considering depositing your savings in one of three banks, all of which paid 5 percent interest; bank A compounded annually, bank B compounded semiannually, and bank C compounded continuously. Which bank would you choose? Why?

4-5. What is the relationship between the $PVIF_{i,n}$ and the $PVIFA_{i,n}$? What is the $PVIFA_{10\%,10}$? Add up the values of the $PVIF_{10\%,n}$ for $n = 1,...,10$. What is this value? Why do these values have the relationship they do?

4-6. What is an annuity? Give some examples of annuities. Distinguish between an annuity and a perpetuity.

4-7. What does continuous compounding mean?

4-8. What are the basic differences between book value, liquidation value, market value, and intrinsic value?

4-9. Explain the three factors that determine the value of an asset.

4-10. Explain the relationship between an investor's required rate of return and the value of a security.

4-11. Explain what the value of a security is.

4-12. **a.** How does a bond's par value differ from its market value?

   b. Explain the difference between the coupon interest rate and a bondholder's required rate.

4-13. The common shareholders receive two types of return from their investment. What are they?

4-14. State how the investor's required rate of return is computed.

4-15. Define the investor's expected rate of return.

SELF-TEST QUESTIONS

ST-1. (*Future Value*) You place $25,000 in a savings account paying annual interest of 8 percent for three years and then move it into a savings account that pays 10 percent interest compounded annually. How much will your money have grown at the end of six years?

ST-2. (*Future Value*) You purchase a boat for $35,000 and pay $5,000 down and agree to pay the rest over the next 10 years in 10 equal annual payments that include principal payments plus 13 percent compound interest on the unpaid balance. What will be the amount of each payment?

ST-3. (*Future Value Solving for* i) In order for an investment to grow eightfold in nine years, at what rate would it have to grow?

ST-4. (*Yield-to-Maturity*) You have the opportunity to buy a bond for $1,000 that will pay no interest during its 10-year life and have a value of $3,106 at maturity. What rate of return or yield does this bond pay?

ST-5. (*Bond Valuation*) Trico has issued annual coupon bonds which pay a nominal interest rate of 8 percent, have a par value of $1,000, and will mature in 20 years. If you require a return of 7 percent, what price would you be willing to pay for the bond? What happens if you pay more for the bond? What happens if you pay less for the bond?

ST-6. (*Bond Valuation*) Sunn Co. have issued semi-annual coupon bonds which pay a nominal interest rate of 8 percent on a $1,000 face value and mature in 7 years. If your required rate of return is 10 percent, what is the value of the bond? How would your answer change if these were annual coupon bonds?

ST-7. (*Bond Valuation*) Sharp Co. has issued annual coupon bonds which are selling in the market for $1,045. These 15-year bonds pay a nominal interest rate of 7 percent on a $1,000 par value. If they are purchased at the market price, what is the expected rate of return?

ST-8. (*Preferred Share Valuation*) The preferred share of Armlo pays a $2.75 dividend. What is the value of the share if your required return is 9 percent?

ST-9. (*Common Share Valuation*) Crosby Corporation's common share paid $1.32 in dividends last year and is expected to grow indefinitely at an annual 7 percent rate. What is the value of the share if you require an 11 percent return?

STUDY PROBLEMS (SET A)

4-1A. (*Future Value*) What will the following investments accumulate to?
  a. $5,000 invested for 10 years at 10 percent compounded annually
  b. $8,000 invested for 7 years at 8 percent compounded annually
  c. $775 invested for 12 years at 12 percent compounded annually
  d. $21,000 invested for 5 years at 5 percent compounded annually

4-2A. (*Future Value Solving for* n) How many years will it take for the following?
  a. $500 to grow to $1,039.50 if invested at 5 percent compounded annually
  b. $35 to grow to $53.87 if invested at 9 percent compounded annually
  c. $100 to grow to $298.60 if invested at 20 percent compounded annually
  d. $53 to grow to $78.76 if invested at 2 percent compounded annually

4-3A. (*Future Value Solving for* i) At what annual rate would the following have to be invested?
  a. $500 in order to grow to $1,948.00 in 12 years
  b. $300 in order to grow to $422.10 in 7 years

c. $50 in order to grow to $280.20 in 20 years

d. $200 in order to grow to $497.60 in 5 years

4-4A. (*Present Value*) What is the present value of the following future amounts?

    a. $800 to be received 10 years from now discounted back to present at 10 percent

    b. $300 to be received 5 years from now discounted back to present at 5 percent

    c. $1,000 to be received 8 years from now discounted back to present at 3 percent

    d. $1,000 to be received 8 years from now discounted back to present at 20 percent

4-5A. (*Future Value Annuity*) What is the accumulated sum of each of the following streams of payments?

    a. $500 a year for 10 years compounded annually at 5 percent

    b. $100 a year for 5 years compounded annually at 10 percent

    c. $35 a year for 7 years compounded annually at 7 percent

    d. $25 a year for 3 years compounded annually at 2 percent

4-6A. (*Present Value of an Annuity*) What is the present value of the following annuities?

    a. $2,500 a year for 10 years discounted back to the present at 7 percent

    b. $70 a year for 3 years discounted back to the present at 3 percent

    c. $280 a year for 7 years discounted back to the present at 6 percent

    d. $500 a year for 10 years discounted back to the present at 10 percent

4-7A. (*Future Value*) Mark Cox, who recently sold his Porsche, placed $10,000 in a savings account paying annual interest of 6 percent.

    a. Calculate the amount of money that will have accrued if he leaves the money in the bank for 1, 5, and 15 years.

    b. If he moves his money into an account that pays 8 percent or one that pays 10 percent, rework part (a) using these new interest rates.

    c. What conclusions can you draw from the relationship between interest rates, time, and future sums from the calculations you have done above?

4-8A. (*Future Value with Nonannual Periods*) Calculate the amount of money that will be in each of the following accounts at the end of the given deposit period:

Account	Amount Deposited	Annual Interest Rate	Compounding Period (Compounded Every N Months)	Deposit Period (Years)
Rod Wheeler	$ 1,000	10%	12	10
Bimbo Coles	95,000	12	1	1
Frankie Allen	8,000	12	2	2
Wayne Robinson	120,000	8	3	2
Jimmy Carruth	30,000	10	6	4
Del Curry	15,000	12	4	3

4-9A. (*Future Value with Nonannual Periods*)

    a. Calculate the future sum of $5,000, given that it will be held in the bank five years at an annual interest rate of 6 percent.

    b. Recalculate part (a) using a compounding period that is (1) semiannual and (2) bimonthly.

    c. Recalculate parts (a) and (b) for a 12 percent annual interest rate.

    d. Recalculate part (a) using a time horizon of 12 years (annual interest rate is still 6 percent).

e. With respect to the effect of changes in the stated interest rate and holding periods on future sums in parts (c) and (d), what conclusions do you draw when you compare these figures with answers found in parts (a) and (b)?

4-10A. (*Solving for* i *in Annuities*) Nicki Johnson, a sophomore mechanical engineering student, receives a call from an insurance agent, who believes that Nicki is an older woman ready to retire from teaching. He talks to her about several annuities that she could buy that would guarantee her an annual fixed income. The annuities are as follows:

Annuity	Initial Payment into Annuity (at t = 0)	Amount of Money Received per Year	Duration of Annuity (Years)
A	$50,000	$8,500	12
B	$60,000	$7,000	25
C	$70,000	$8,000	20

If Nicki could earn 11 percent on her money by placing it in a savings account, should she place it instead in any of the annuities? Which ones, if any? Why?

4-11A. (*Future Value*) Sales of a new finance book were 15,000 copies this year and were expected to increase by 20 percent per year. What are expected sales during each of the next three years? Graph this sales trend and explain.

4-12A. (*Future Value*) Reggie Jackson, formerly of the New York Yankees, hit 41 home runs in 1980. If his home run output grew at a rate of 10 percent per year, what would it have been over the following five years?

4-13A. (*Amortization of Home Mortgage Loan*) Todd Dodge purchased a new house for $80,000. He paid $20,000 down and agreed to pay the rest on a bi-monthly basis over the next 25 years. The bank charges a nominal interest rate of 9.75 percent for this type of loan and the terms of the loan can be renegotiated after five years. Determine what the bi-monthly payments will be equal to. (Note: Remember that the interest rate must be compounded semi-annually.)

4-14A. (*Solving for* PMT *in an Annuity*) To pay for your child's education you wish to have accumulated $15,000 at the end of 15 years. To do this you plan on depositing an equal amount into the bank at the end of each year. If the bank is willing to pay 6 percent compounded annually, how much must you deposit each year in order to obtain your goal?

4-15A. (*Solving for* i *in Compound Interest*) If you were offered $1,079.50 ten years from now in return for an investment of $500 currently, what annual rate of interest would you earn if you took the offer?

4-16A. (*Present Value and Future Value of an Annuity*) In 10 years you are planning on retiring and buying a house in Ovida, Florida. The house you are looking at currently costs $100,000 and is expected to increase in value each year at a rate of 5 percent. Assuming you can earn 10 percent annually on your investments, how much must you invest at the end of each of the next 10 years in order to be able to buy your dream home when you retire?

4-17A. (*Future Value*) The Aggarwal Corporation needs to raise $10 million to retire a $10 million mortgage that matures on December 31, 2002. To retire this mortgage, the company plans to put a fixed amount into an account at the end of each year for 10 years, with the first payment occurring on December 31, 1993. The Aggarwal Company expects to earn 9 percent annually on the money in this account. What equal annual contribution must it make to this account in order to accumulate the $10 million by December 31, 2002?

4-18A. (*Future Value with Nonannual Periods*) After examining the various personal loan rates available to you, you find that you can borrow funds from a finance company at 12 percent compounded monthly or from a bank at 13 percent compounded annually. Which alternative is the most attractive?

4-19A. (*Present Value of an Uneven Stream of Payments*) You are given three investment alternatives to analyze. The cash flows from these three investments are as follows:

End of Year	Investment A	Investment B	Investment C
1	$10,000		$10,000
2	10,000		
3	10,000		
4	10,000		
5	10,000	$10,000	
6		10,000	50,000
7		10,000	
8		10,000	
9		10,000	
10		10,000	10,000

Assuming a 20 percent discount rate, find the present value of each investment.

4-20A. (*Present Value*) The Kumar Corporation is planning on issuing bonds that pay no interest but can be converted into $1,000 at maturity, seven years from their purchase. In order to price these bonds competitively with other bonds of equal risk, it is determined that they should yield 10 percent, compounded annually. At what price should the Kumar Corporation sell these bonds?

4-21A. (*Perpetuities*) What is the present value of the following?

a. A $300 perpetuity discounted back to the present at 8 percent

b. A $1,000 perpetuity discounted back to the present at 12 percent

c. A $100 perpetuity discounted back to the present at 9 percent

d. A $95 perpetuity discounted back to the present at 5 percent

4-22A. (*Continuous Compounding*) What is the value of $500 after five years if it is invested at 10 percent compounded continuously? (If you don't have a calculator capable of solving this problem, simply set it up.)

4-23A. (*Solving for* n *with Nonannual Periods*) About how many years would it take for your investment to grow fourfold if it were invested at 16 percent compounded semiannually?

4-24A. (*Amortization of Home Mortgage Loan*) Eric Doe purchased a new house for $225,000. He paid $25,000 down and agreed to pay the rest on a bi-monthly basis over the next 25 years. The bank charges a nominal interest rate of 10.5 percent for this type of loan and the terms of the loan can be renegotiated after five years. Determine what the monthly payments will be equal to. (Note: Remember that the interest rate must be compounded semi-annually.)

4-25A. (*Complex Present Value*) How much do you have to deposit today so that beginning 11 years from now you can withdraw $10,000 a year for the next five years (periods 11 through 15) plus an additional amount of $20,000 in that last year (period 15)? Assume an interest rate of 6 percent.

4-26A. (*Loan Amortization*) On December 31, Beth Klemkosky bought a yacht for $50,000, paying $10,000 down and agreeing to pay the balance in 10 equal annual installments that include both the principal and 10 percent interest on the declining balance. How big would the annual payments be?

4-27A. (*Solving for* i *in an Annuity*) You lend a friend $30,000, which your friend will repay in five equal annual payments of $10,000, with the first payment to be received one year from now. What rate of return does your loan receive?

4-28A. (*Solving for* i *in Compound Interest*) You lend a friend $10,000, for which your friend will repay you $27,027 at the end of five years. What interest rate are you charging your "friend"?

4-29A. (*Loan Amortization*) A firm borrows $25,000 from the bank at 12 percent compounded annually to purchase some new machinery. This loan is to be repaid in equal annual installments at the end of each year over the next five years. How much will each annual payment be?

4-30A. (*Present Value Comparison*) You are offered $1,000 today, $10,000 in 12 years, or $25,000 in 25 years. Assuming that you can earn 11 percent on your money, which should you choose?

4-31A. (*Compound Annuity*) You plan on buying some property in Florida five years from today. To do this you estimate that you will need $20,000 at that time for the purchase. You would like to accumulate these funds by making equal annual deposits in your savings account, which pays 12 percent annually. If you make your first deposit at the end of this year and you would like your account to reach $20,000 when the final deposit is made, what will be the amount of your deposits?

4-32A. (*Complex Present Value*) You would like to have $50,000 in 15 years. To accumulate this amount you plan to deposit each year an equal sum in the bank, which will earn 7 percent interest compounded annually. Your first payment will be made at the end of the year.

  a. How much must you deposit annually to accumulate this amount?

  b. If you decide to make a large lump-sum deposit today instead of the annual deposits, how large should this lump-sum deposit be? (Assume you can earn 7 percent on this deposit.)

  c. At the end of five years you will receive $10,000 and deposit this in the bank toward your goal of $50,000 at the end of 15 years. In addition to this deposit, how much must you deposit in equal annual deposits in order to reach your goal? (Again assume you can earn 7 percent on this deposit.)

4-33A. (*Comprehensive Present Value*) You are trying to plan for retirement in 10 years, and currently you have $100,000 in a savings account and $300,000 in shares. In addition you plan on adding to your savings by depositing $10,000 per year in your savings account at the end of each of the next five years and then $20,000 per year at the end of each year for the final five years until retirement.

  a. Assuming your savings account returns 7 percent compounded annually while your investment in stocks will return 12 percent compounded annually, how much will you have at the end of 10 years? (Ignore taxes.)

  b. If you expect to live for 20 years after you retire, and at retirement you deposit all of your savings in a bank account paying 10 percent, how much can you withdraw each year after retirement (20 equal withdrawals beginning one year after you retire) in order to end up with a zero balance at death?

4-34A. (*Comprehensive Present Value*) You have just inherited a large sum of money and you are trying to determine how much you should save for retirement and how much you can spend now. For retirement you will deposit today (January 1, 1995) a lump sum in a bank account paying 10 percent compounded annually. You don't plan on touching this deposit until you retire in five years (January 1, 2000), and you plan on living for 20 additional years and then dropping dead on December 31, 2019. During your retirement you would like to receive income of $50,000 per year to be received the first day of each year, with the first payment on January 1, 2000, and the last payment on January 1, 2019. Complicating this objective is your desire to have one final three-year fling during which time you'd like to play golf in Europe. To finance this you want to receive $250,000 on January 1, 2016 and nothing on January 1, 2017, and January 1, 2018, as you will be on the road. In addition, after you pass on (January 1, 2020), you would like to have a total of $100,000 to leave to your children.

  a. How much must you deposit in the bank at 10 percent on January 1,

1995, in order to achieve your goal? (Use a time line in order to answer this question.)

b. What kinds of problems are associated with this analysis and its assumptions?

4-35A. (*Bond Valuation*) Calculate the value of an annual coupon bond that expects to mature in 12 years with a $1,000 face value. The coupon pays a nominal interest rate of 8 percent and the investors' required rate of return is 12 percent.

4-36A. (*Preferred Share Valuation*) What is the value of a preferred share where the dividend rate is 14 percent on a $100 par value? The appropriate discount rate for a share of this risk level is 12 percent.

4-37A. (*Bond Valuation*) Enterprise, Inc., has issued semi-annual coupon bonds which pay a nominal interest rate of 9 percent. The bonds mature in eight years and their par value is $1,000. If your required rate of return is 8 percent, what is the value of the bond? What is the value of this bond if coupons are distributed on an annual basis?

4-38A. (*Bond Valuation*) You are willing to pay $900 for a 10-year, annual coupon bond ($1,000 par value) that pays a nominal interest rate of 8 percent. What is your expected rate of return?

4-39A. (*Preferred Share Valuation*) Solitron's preferred share is selling for $42.16 and pays $1.95 in dividends. What is your expected rate of return if you purchase the security at the market price?

4-40A. (*Preferred Share Valuation*) You own 200 preferred shares of Somner Resources. Currently, a preferred share of Somner Resources sells for $40 and pays annual dividends of $3.40.

a. What is your expected return?

b. If you require an 8 percent return given the current price, should you sell or buy more shares?

4-41A. (*Common Share Valuation*) You intend to purchase a common share of Marigo at $50 per share, hold it one year, and sell after a dividend of $6 is paid. How much will the share price have to appreciate if your required rate of return is 15 percent?

4-42A. (*Common Share Valuation*) Made-It's common share currently sells for $22.50. The company's executives anticipate a constant growth rate of 10 percent and an end-of-year dividend of $2.

a. What is your expected rate of return?

b. If you require a 17 percent return, should you purchase the shares?

4-43A. (*Common Share Valuation*) Header Motor, Inc., paid a $3.50 dividend last year. At a growth rate of 5 percent, what is the value of a common share if the investors require a 20 percent rate of return?

4-44A. (*Common Share Valuation*) The common share of Zaldi Co. is selling for $32.84. This share recently paid dividends of $2.94 per share and has a projected growth rate of 9.5 percent. If you purchase the share at the market price, what is your expected rate of return?

4-45A. (*Common Share Valuation*) Honeywag's common share is expected to pay $1.85 in dividends next year, and the market price is projected to be $42.50 by year end. If the investor's required rate of return is 11 percent, what is the current value of the share?

4-46A. (*Common Share Valuation*) The market price for a Hobart common share is $43. The price at the end of one year is expected to be $48, and dividends for next year should be $2.84. What is the expected rate of return?

4-47A. (*Bond Valuation*) Exxon 20-year, annual coupon bonds pay a nominal interest rate of 9 percent on a $1,000 par value. If you buy the bonds at $945, what is your expected rate of return?

4-48A. (*Bond Valuation*) Zenith Co. has issued annual coupon bonds which mature in 12 years and pay a nominal interest rate of 7 percent on a par value of $1,000. If you purchase the bonds for $1,150, what is your expected rate of return?

4-49A. (*Bond Valuation*) National Steel 15-year, annual coupon bonds pay a nominal interest rate of 8 percent on a par value of $1,000. The market price of the bonds is $1,085, and your required rate of return is 10 percent.

a. Compute the bond's expected rate of return.

b. Determine the value of the bond to you, given your required rate of return.

c. Should you purchase the bond?

4-50A. (*Preferred Share Valuation*) Pioneer's preferred share is selling for $33 in the market and pays a $3.60 annual dividend.

a. What is the expected rate of return on the share?

b. If an investor's required rate of return is 10 percent, what is the value of the share for that investor?

c. Should the investor acquire the preferred share?

4-51A. (*Common Share Valuation*) The common share of NCP paid $1.32 in dividends last year. Dividends are expected to grow at an 8 percent annual rate for an indefinite number of years.

a. If NCP's current market price is $23.50, what is the share's expected rate of return?

b. If your required rate of return is 10.5 percent, what is the value of the share for you?

c. Should you make the investment?

4-52A. (*A Comprehensive Problem in Valuing Securities*) You are considering three investments. The first is an annual coupon bond that is selling in the market at $1,100. The bond pays a nominal interest rate of 13 percent on a par value of $1,000, and is scheduled to mature in 15 years. For bonds of this risk class, you believe that a 14 percent rate of return should be required. The second investment that you are analyzing is a preferred share ($100 par value) that sells for $90 and pays an annual dividend of $13. Your required rate of return for this share is 15 percent. The last investment is a common share that recently paid a $2 dividend. The firm's earnings per share have increased from $3 to $6 in 10 years, which also reflects the expected growth in dividends per share for the indefinite future. The share is selling for $20, and you think a reasonable required rate of return for the share is 20 percent.

a. Calculate the value of each security based on your required rate of return.

b. Which investment(s) should be accepted? Why?

c. 1. If your required rates of return changed to 12 percent for the bond, 14 percent for the preferred shares, and 18 percent for the common shares, how would your answers change to parts (a) and (b) above?

2. Assuming again that your required rate of return for the common share is 20 percent, but the anticipated growth rate changes to 12 percent, would your answers to (a) and (b) be different?

STUDY PROBLEMS (SET B)

4-1B. (*Future Value*) What will the following investments accumulate to?

a. $4,000 invested for 11 years at 9 percent compounded annually

b. $8,000 invested for 10 years at 8 percent compounded annually

c. $800 invested for 12 years at 12 percent compounded annually

d. $21,000 invested for 6 years at 5 percent compounded annually

4-2B. (*Future Value Solving for* n) How many years will it take for the following?

a. $550 to grow to $1,043.90 if invested at 6 percent compounded annually

b. $40 to grow to $88.44 if invested at 12 percent compounded annually

c. $110 to grow to $614.79 if invested at 24 percent compounded annually

d. $60 to grow to $78.30 if invested at 3 percent compounded annually

4-3B. (*Future Value Solving for* i) At what annual rate would the following have to be invested?

    a. $550 in order to grow to $1,898.60 in 13 years

    b. $275 in order to grow to $406.18 in 8 years

    c. $60 in order to grow to $279.66 in 20 years

    d. $180 in order to grow to $486.00 in 6 years

4-4B. (*Present Value*) What is the present value of the following future amounts?

    a. $800 to be received 10 years from now discounted back to present at 10 percent

    b. $400 to be received 6 years from now discounted back to present at 6 percent

    c. $1,000 to be received 8 years from now discounted back to present at 5 percent

    d. $900 to be received 9 years from now discounted back to present at 20 percent

4-5B. (*Future Value Annuity*) What is the accumulated sum of each of the following streams of payments?

    a. $500 a year for 10 years compounded annually at 6 percent

    b. $150 a year for 5 years compounded annually at 11 percent

    c. $35 a year for 8 years compounded annually at 7 percent

    d. $25 a year for 3 years compounded annually at 2 percent

4-6B. (*Present Value of an Annuity*) What is the present value of the following annuities?

    a. $3,000 a year for 10 years discounted back to the present at 8 percent

    b. $50 a year for 3 years discounted back to the present at 3 percent

    c. $280 a year for 8 years discounted back to the present at 7 percent

    d. $600 a year for 10 years discounted back to the present at 10 percent

4-7B. (*Future Value*) Mark Cox, who recently sold his Porsche, placed $20,000 in a savings account paying annual interest of 7 percent.

    a. Calculate the amount of money that will have accrued if he leaves the money in the bank for 1, 5, and 15 years.

    b. If he moves his money into an account that pays 9 percent or one that pays 11 percent, rework part (a) using these new interest rates.

    c. What conclusions can you draw from the relationship between interest rates, time, and future sums from the calculations you have done above?

4-8B. (*Future Value with Nonannual Periods*) Calculate the amount of money that will be in each of the following accounts at the end of the given deposit period:

Account	Amount Deposited	Annual Interest Rate	Compounding Period (Compounded Every N Months)	Deposit Period (Years)
Chuck Jones	$ 2,000	12%	2	2
Alonzo Spellman	50,000	12	1	1
Mark Bean	7,000	18	2	2
Steve Tovar	130,000	12	3	2
Ty Morrison	20,000	14	6	4
Roger Harper	15,000	15	4	3

4-9B. (*Future Value with Nonannual Periods*)

   a. Calculate the future sum of $6,000, given that it will be held in the bank five years at an annual interest rate of 6 percent.

   b. Recalculate part (a) using a compounding period that is (1) semiannual and (2) bimonthly.

   c. Recalculate parts (a) and (b) for a 12 percent annual interest rate.

   d. Recalculate part (a) using a time horizon of 12 years (annual interest rate is still 6 percent).

   e. With respect to the effect of changes in the stated interest rate and holding periods on future sums in parts (c) and (d), what conclusions do you draw when you compare these figures with answers found in parts (a) and (b)?

4-10B. (*Solving for* i *in Annuities*) Matt Denis, a sophomore mechanical engineering student, receives a call from an insurance agent who believes that Matt is an older man ready to retire from teaching. He talks to him about several annuities that he could buy that would guarantee him an annual fixed income. The annuities are as follows:

Annuity	Initial Payment into Annuity (at t = 0)	Amount of Money Received per Year	Duration of Annuity (Years)
A	$50,000	$8,500	12
B	$60,000	$7,000	25
C	$70,000	$8,000	20

   If Matt could earn 12 percent on his money by placing it in a savings account, should he place it instead in any of the annuities? Which ones, if any? Why?

4-11B. (*Future Value*) Sales of a new marketing book were 10,000 copies this year and were expected to increase by 15 percent per year. What are expected sales during each of the next three years? Graph this sales trend and explain.

4-12B. (*Future Value*) Reggie Jackson, formerly of the New York Yankees, hit 41 home runs in 1980. If his home run output grew at a rate of 12 percent per year, what would it have been over the following five years?

4-13B. (*Amortization of Home Mortgage Loan*) Doug Musgrave purchased a new house for $150,000. He paid $30,000 down and agreed to pay the rest on a bi-monthly basis over the next 15 years. The bank charges a nominal interest rate of 10 percent for this type of loan and the terms of the loan can be renegotiated after five years. Determine what the bi-monthly payments will be equal to. (Note: Remember that the interest rate must be compounded semiannually.)

4-14B. (*Solving for* PMT *in an Annuity*) To pay for your child's education you wish to have accumulated $25,000 at the end of 15 years. To do this you plan on depositing an equal amount into the bank at the end of each year. If the bank is willing to pay 7 percent compounded annually, how much must you deposit each year in order to obtain your goal?

4-15B. (*Solving for* i *in Compound Interest*) If you were offered $2,376.50 ten years from now in return for an investment of $700 currently, what annual rate of interest would you earn if you took the offer?

4-16B. (*Present Value and Future Value of an Annuity*) In 10 years you are planning on retiring and buying a house in Marco Island, Florida. The house you are looking at currently costs $125,000 and is expected to increase in value each year at a rate of 5 percent. Assuming you can earn 10 percent annually on your investments, how much must you invest at the end of each of the next 10 years in order to be able to buy your dream home when you retire?

4-17B. (*Future Value*) The Knutson Corporation needs to raise $15 million to retire a $15 million mortgage that matures on December 31, 2002. To retire this mortgage, the company plans to put a fixed amount into an account at the end of each year for 10 years, with the first payment occurring on December

31, 1993. The Knutson Company expects to earn 10 percent annually on the money in this account. What equal annual contribution must it make to this account in order to accumulate the $15 million by December 31, 2002?

4-18B. (*Future Value with Nonannual Periods*) After examining the various personal loan rates available to you, you find that you can borrow funds from a finance company at 24 percent compounded monthly or from a bank at 26 percent compounded annually. Which alternative is the most attractive?

4-19B. (*Present Value of an Uneven Stream of Payments*) You are given three investment alternatives to analyze. The cash flows from these three investments are as follows:

| | | Investment | |
End of Year	A	B	C
1	$15,000		$20,000
2	15,000		
3	15,000		
4	15,000		
5	15,000	$15,000	
6		15,000	60,000
7		15,000	
8		15,000	
9		15,000	
10		15,000	20,000

Assuming a 20 percent discount rate, find the present value of each investment.

4-20B. (*Present Value*) The Shin Corporation is planning on issuing bonds that pay no interest but can be converted into $1,000 at maturity, eight years from their purchase. In order to price these bonds competitively with other bonds of equal risk, it is determined that they should yield 9 percent, compounded annually. At what price should the Shin Corporation sell these bonds?

4-21B. (*Perpetuities*) What is the present value of the following?

a. A $400 perpetuity discounted back to the present at 9 percent

b. A $1,500 perpetuity discounted back to the present at 13 percent

c. A $150 perpetuity discounted back to the present at 10 percent

d. A $100 perpetuity discounted back to the present at 6 percent

4-22B. (*Continuous Compounding*) What is the value of $600 after five years if it is invested at 10 percent compounded continuously? (If you don't have a calculator capable of solving this problem, simply set it up.)

4-23B. (*Solving for* n *with Nonannual Periods*) About how many years would it take for your investment to grow sevenfold if it were invested at 10 percent compounded semiannually?

4-24B. (*Bond Values*) You are examining three bonds with par value of $1,000 (you receive $1,000 at maturity) and are concerned with what would happen to their market value if interest rates (or the market discount rate) changed. The three bonds are

Bond A—A bond with 7 years left to maturity that pays 10 percent per year compounded semiannually

Bond B—A bond with 3 years left to maturity that pays 10 percent per year compounded semiannually

Bond C—A bond with 20 years left to maturity that pays 10 percent per year compounded semiannually

What would be the value of these bonds if the market discount rate was

a. 10 percent per year compounded semiannually?

b. 4 percent per year compounded semiannually?

c. 16 percent per year compounded semiannually?

What observations can you make about these results?

4-25B. (*Complex Present Value*) How much do you have to deposit today so that beginning 11 years from now you can withdraw $10,000 a year for the next five years (periods 11 through 15) plus an additional amount of $15,000 in that last year (period 15)? Assume an interest rate of 7 percent.

4-26B. (*Loan Amortization*) On December 31, Matt Denis bought a yacht for $60,000, paying $15,000 down and agreeing to pay the balance in 10 equal annual installments that include both the principal and 9 percent interest on the declining balance. How big would the annual payments be?

4-27B. (*Solving for* i *in an Annuity*) You lend a friend $45,000, which your friend will repay in five equal annual payments of $9,000 with the first payment to be received one year from now. What rate of return does your loan receive?

4-28B. (*Solving for* i *in Compound Interest*) You lend a friend $15,000, for which your friend will repay you $37,313 at the end of five years. What interest rate are you charging your "friend"?

4-29B. (*Loan Amortization*) A firm borrows $30,000 from the bank at 13 percent compounded annually to purchase some new machinery. This loan is to be repaid in equal annual installments at the end of each year over the next four years. How much will each annual payment be?

4-30B. (*Present Value Comparison*) You are offered $1,000 today, $10,000 in 12 years, or $25,000 in 25 years. Assuming that you can earn 11 percent on your money, which should you choose?

4-31B. (*Compound Annuity*) You plan on buying some property in Florida five years from today. To do this you estimate that you will need $30,000 at that time for the purchase. You would like to accumulate these funds by making equal annual deposits in your savings account, which pays 10 percent annually. If you make your first deposit at the end of this year and you would like your account to reach $30,000 when the final deposit is made, what will be the amount of your deposits?

4-32B. (*Complex Present Value*) You would like to have $75,000 in 15 years. To accumulate this amount you plan to deposit each year an equal sum in the bank, which will earn 8 percent interest compounded annually. Your first payment will be made at the end of the year.

    a. How much must you deposit annually to accumulate this amount?

    b. If you decide to make a large lump-sum deposit today instead of the annual deposits, how large should this lump-sum deposit be? (Assume you can earn 8 percent on this deposit.)

    c. At the end of five years you will receive $20,000 and deposit this in the bank toward your goal of $75,000 at the end of 15 years. In addition to this deposit, how much must you deposit in equal annual deposits in order to reach your goal? (Again assume you can earn 8 percent on this deposit.)

4-33B. (*Comprehensive Present Value*) You are trying to plan for retirement in 10 years, and currently you have $150,000 in a savings account and $250,000 in stocks. In addition you plan on adding to your savings by depositing $8,000 per year in your savings account at the end of each of the next five years and then $10,000 per year at the end of each year for the final five years until retirement.

    a. Assuming your savings account returns 8 percent compounded annually while your investment in stocks will return 12 percent compounded annually, how much will you have at the end of 10 years? (Ignore taxes.)

    b. If you expect to live for 20 years after you retire, and at retirement you deposit all of your savings in a bank account paying 11 percent, how much can you withdraw each year after retirement (20 equal withdrawals beginning one year after you retire) in order to end up with a zero balance at death?

4-34B. (*Comprehensive Present Value*) You have just inherited a large sum of money and you are trying to determine how much you should save for retirement and how much you can spend now. For retirement you will deposit today (January 1, 1995) a lump sum in a bank account paying 10 percent compounded annually. You don't plan on touching this deposit until you retire in 5 years (January 1, 2000), and you plan on living for 20 additional years and then dropping dead on December 31, 2019. During your retirement you would like to receive income of $60,000 per year to be received the first day of each year, with the first payment on January 1, 2000, and the last payment on January 1, 2019. Complicating this objective is your desire to have one final three-year fling during which time you'd like to play tennis in Europe. To finance this you want to receive $300,000 on January 1, 2016, and nothing on January 1, 2017, and January 1, 2018, as you will be on the road. In addition, after you pass on (January 1, 2020), you would like to have a total of $100,000 to leave to your children.

a. How much must you deposit in the bank at 10 percent on January 1, 1995, in order to achieve your goal? (Use a time line in order to answer this question.)

b. What kinds of problems are associated with this analysis and its assumptions?

4-35B. (*Bond Valuation*) Calculate the value of an annual coupon bond that expects to mature in 10 years with a $1,000 face value. The coupon pays a nominal interest rate of 9 percent and the investors' required rate of return is 15 percent.

4-36B. (*Preferred Share Valuation*) What is the value of a preferred share where the dividend rate is 16 percent on a $100 par value? The appropriate discount rate for a share of this risk level is 12 percent.

4-37B. (*Bond Valuation*) Enterprise, Inc., has issued semiannual coupon bonds which pay a nominal interest rate of 10 percent. The bonds mature in 11 years and their par value is $1,000. If your required rate of return is 9 percent, what is the value of the bond? What is the value of this bond if coupons are distributed on an annual basis?

4-38B. (*Bond Valuation*) You are willing to pay $950 for an 8-year, annual coupon bond ($1,000 par value) that pays a nominal interest rate of 9 percent. What is your expected rate of return?

4-39B. (*Preferred Share Valuation*) Shewmaker's preferred share is selling for $55.16 and pays $2.35 in dividends. What is your expected rate of return if you purchase the security at the market price?

4-40B. (*Preferred Share Valuation*) You own 250 preferred shares of McCormick Resources. Currently, a preferred share of McCormick Resources sells for $38.50 and pays annual dividends of $3.24.

a. What is your expected return?

b. If you require an 8 percent return and given the current price, should you sell or buy more shares?

4-41B. (*Common Share Valuation*) You intend to purchase a common share of Bama, Inc., at $52.75, hold it one year, and sell after a dividend of $6.50 is paid. How much will the share price have to appreciate if your required rate of return is 16 percent?

4-42B. (*Common Share Valuation*) A common share of Blackburn & Smith's currently sells for $23. The company's executives anticipate a constant growth rate of 10.5 percent and an end-of-year dividend of $2.50.

a. What is your expected rate of return?

b. If you require a 17 percent return, should you purchase the share?

4-43B. (*Common Share Valuation*) Gilliland Motor, Inc., paid a $3.75 dividend last year. At a growth rate of 6 percent, what is the value of a common share if the investors require a 20 percent rate of return?

4-44B. (*Common Share Valuation*) A common share of Bouncy-Bob Moore Co. is selling for $33.84. This share recently paid dividends of $3 and has a projected growth rate of 8.5 percent. If you purchase the share at the market price, what is your expected rate of return?

4-45B. (*Common Share Valuation*) Honeywag's common share is expected to pay $1.85 in dividends next year, and the market price is projected to be $40 by year end. If the investors' required rate of return is 12 percent, what is the current value of the share?

4-46B. (*Common Share Valuation*) The market price for M. Simpson & Co.'s common share is $44. The price at the end of one year is expected to be $47, and dividends for next year should be $2. What is the expected rate of return?

4-47B. (*Bond Valuation*) Doisneau 20-year, annual coupon bonds pay a nominal interest rate of 10 percent on a $1,000 par value. If you buy the bonds at $975, what is your expected rate of return?

4-48B. (*Bond Valuation*) Hoyden Co. has issued annual coupon bonds which mature in 15 years and pay a nominal interest rate of 8 percent on a par value of $1,000. If you purchase the bonds for $1,175, what is your expected rate of return?

4-49B. (*Bond Valuation*) Fingen 14-year, annual coupon bonds pay a nominal interest rate of 9 percent on a par value of $1,000. The market price of the bonds is $1,100, and your required rate of return is 10 percent.

  a. Compute the bond's expected rate of return.

  b. Determine the value of the bond to you, given your required rate of return.

  c. Should you purchase the bond?

4-50B. (*Preferred Share Valuation*) Gree's preferred share is selling for $35 in the market and pays a $4 annual dividend.

  a. What is the expected rate of return on the share?

  b. If an investor's required rate of return is 10 percent, what is the value of the share for that investor?

  c. Should the investor acquire the preferred share?

4-51B. (*Common Share Valuation*) The common share of KPD paid $1 in dividends last year. Dividends are expected to grow at an 8 percent annual rate for an indefinite number of years.

  a. If KPD's current market price is $25, what is the share's expected rate of return?

  b. If your required rate of return is 11 percent, what is the value of the share for you?

  c. Should you make the investment?

4-52B. (*A Comprehensive Problem in Valuing Securities*) You are considering three investments. The first is an annual coupon bond that is selling in the market at $1,200. The bond pays a nominal interest rate of 14 percent on a par value of $1,000 and is scheduled to mature in 12 years. For bonds of this risk class, you believe that a 12 percent rate of return should be required. The second investment that you are analyzing is a preferred share ($100 par value) that sells for $80 and pays an annual dividend of $12. Your required rate of return for this share is 14 percent. The last investment is a common share that recently paid a $3 dividend. The firm's earnings per share have increased from $4 to $8 in 10 years, which also reflects the expected growth in dividends per share for the indefinite future. The share is selling for $25, and you think a reasonable required rate of return for the share is 20 percent.

  a. Calculate the value of each security based on your required rate of return.

  b. Which investment(s) should be accepted? Why?

  c. 1. If your required rates of return changed to 14 percent for the bond, 16 percent for the preferred shares, and 18 percent for the common shares, how would your answers change to parts (a) and (b) above?

    2. Assuming again that your required rate of return for the common share is 20 percent, but the anticipated growth rate changes to 12 percent, would your answers to (a) and (b) be different?

SS-1. This is a compound interest problem in which you must first find the future value of $25,000 growing at 8 percent compounded annually for three years and then allow that future value to grow for an additional three years at 10 percent. First, the value of the $25,000 after three years growing at 8 percent is

$$FV_3 = PV_0(1 + i)^n$$

$$FV_3 = \$25,000(1 + .08)^3$$

$$FV_3 = \$25,000(1.260)$$

$$FV_3 = \$31,500$$

Thus, after three years you have $31,500 and now this amount is allowed to grow for three years at 10 percent. Plugging this into Equation (4-6), $PV_0 = \$31,500$, $i = 10\%$, $n = 3$ years, and we solve for FV_3:

$$FV_3 = \$31,500(1 + .10)^3$$

$$FV_3 = \$31,500(1.331)$$

$$FV_3 = \$41,926.50$$

Thus, after six years the $25,000 will have grown to $41,926.50.

SS-2. This loan amortization problem is actually just a present-value-of-an-annuity problem in which we know the values of i, n, and PV_0 and are solving for A. In this case the value of i is 13 percent, n is 10 years, and PV_0 is $30,000. Substituting these values into Equation (4-12) we find

$$\$30,000 = A\left[\sum_{t=1}^{10} \frac{1}{(1 + .13)^t}\right]$$

$$\$30,000 = A(5.426)$$

$$\$5528.93 = A$$

SS-3. This is a simple compound interest problem in which FV_9 is eight times larger than PV_0. Here again three of the four variables are known: $n = 9$ years, $FV_9 = 8$, and $PV_0 = 1$ and we are solving for i. Substituting these values into Equation (4-6) we find

$$FV_9 = PV_0(1 + i)^n$$

$$8 = 1(1 + i)^9$$

$$8.00 = (1 + i)^9$$

Thus we are looking for a table value of 8 in the Future Value Table in Appendix A, which occurs in the 9-year row. If we look in the 9-year row for a value of 8.00, we find it in the 26% column (8.004). Thus, the answer is 26 percent.

SS-4.

$$FV_n = PV_0(1 + i)^n = PV(FVIF_{i,n})$$

$$\$3106 = \$1000(FVIF_{i,10})$$

$$3.106 = FVIF_{i,10}$$

Looking in the $n = 10$ row of Appendix A, we find a value of 3.106 in the 12% column. Therefore, $12\% = i$.

SS-5.

$$\text{Price } (P_0) = \sum_{t=1}^{20} \frac{\$80}{(1.07)^t} + \frac{\$1000}{(1.07)^{20}}$$

Thus,

$$\$80(10.594) = \$ \ 847.52$$
$$\$1000(0.258) = \$ \ 258.00$$
$$\text{price } (P_0) = \$1105.52$$

If you pay more for the bond, your required rate of return will not be satisfied. In other words, by paying an amount for the bond that exceeds $1,105.52, the expected rate of return for the bond is less than the required rate of return. If you have the opportunity to pay less for the bond, the expected rate of return exceeds the 7 percent required rate of return.

SS-6. If interest is paid semiannually:

$$\text{price } (P_0) = \sum_{t=1}^{14} \frac{\$40}{(1 + 0.05)^t} + \frac{\$1000}{(1 + 0.05)^{14}}$$

Thus,

$$\$40(9.899) = \$395.96$$
$$\$1000(0.505) = \$505.00$$
$$\text{price } (P_0) = \$900.96$$

If interest is paid annually:

$$\text{price } (P_0) = \sum_{t=1}^{7} \frac{\$80}{(1.10)^t} + \frac{\$1000}{(1.10)^7}$$

$$P_0 = \$80(4.868) + \$1000(0.513)$$
$$P_0 = \$902.44$$

SS-7.

$$\$1045 = \sum_{t=1}^{15} \frac{\$70}{(1 + R_b)^t} + \frac{\$1000}{(1 + R_b)^{15}}$$

At 6%: $\$70(9.712) + \$1000(0.417) = \$1096.84$

At 7%: $\$70(9.108) + \$1000(0.362) = \$1000.00$

Interpolation:

Expected rate of return: $R_b = 6\% + \dfrac{\$51.84}{\$96.84} (1\%) = 6.54\%$

CALCULATOR SOLUTION

Data Input	Function Key
15	N
70	+/− PMT
1000	+/− FV
1045	PV

Function Key	Answer
CPT I/Y	6.52

SS-8.

$$\text{price } (P_0) = \left(\frac{\text{dividend}}{\text{required rate of return}} \right) = \frac{\$2.75}{0.09} = \$30.56$$

SS-9.

$$\text{price } (P_0) = \left[\frac{\text{last year dividend } (1 + \text{growth rate})}{\text{required rate of return} - \text{growth rate}} \right]$$

$$= \frac{\$1.32 \ (1.07)}{0.11 - 0.07}$$

$$= \$35.31$$

APPENDIX 4A: More on Bond Valuation: Understanding Key Relationships

In the text of Chapter 4 we have learned to find the value of a bond (V_b), given (1) the amount of interest payments (I_t), (2) the maturity value (M), (3) the length of time to maturity (n years), and (4) the investor's required rate of return, R_b. We have also learned how to compute the expected rate of return, which also happens to be the current interest rate on the bond, given (1) the current market value (V_b), (2) the amount of interest payments (I_t), (3) the maturity value (M), and (4) the length of time to maturity (n years). These computations represent the basics of bond valuation; however, a more complete understanding of bond valuation requires that we examine five additional key relationships:

FIRST RELATIONSHIP

The value of a bond is inversely related to changes in the investor's present required rate of return (the current interest rate). That is, as interest rates increase (decrease), the value of the bond decreases (increases).

To illustrate, assume that an investor's required rate of return for a given bond is 12 percent. The bond has a par value of $1,000 and annual interest payments of $120, indicating a 12 percent coupon interest rate ($120 ÷ $1000 = 12%). Assuming a five-year maturity date, the bond would be worth $1,000, computed as follows:

$$V_b = \frac{I_1}{(1 + R_b)^1} + \ldots + \frac{I_n}{(1 + R_b)^n} + \frac{M}{(1 + R_b)^n}$$

$$V_b = \sum_{t=1}^{n} \frac{I_1}{(1 + R_b)^t} + \frac{M}{(1 + R_b)^n}$$

$$V_b = \sum_{t=1}^{n} \frac{\$120}{(1 + .12)^t} + \frac{\$1000}{(1 + .12)^5} \tag{4-17a}$$

$$V_b = \$120(PVIFA_{12\%,5}) + \$1000(PVIF_{12\%,5}) \tag{4-17b}$$

$$V_b = \$120(3.605) + \$1000(.567)$$

$$= \$432.60 + \$567.00$$

$$= \$999.60 \quad \$1000.00$$

If, however, the investor's required rate of return (going interest rate) increases from 12 to 15 percent, the value of the bond would decrease to $899.24:

$$V_b = \$120(PVIFA_{15\%,5}) + \$1000(PVIF_{15\%,5}) \tag{4-17b}$$

$$V_b = \$120(3.352) + \$1000(.497)$$

$$= \$402.24 + \$497.00$$

$$= \$899.24$$

On the other hand, if the investor's required rate of return decreases to 9 percent, the bond would increase in value to $1,116.80:

$$V_b = \$120(PVIFA_{9\%,5}) + \$1000(PVIF_{9\%,5}) \tag{4-17b}$$

$$V_b = \$120(3.890) + \$1000(.650)$$

$$= \$466.80 + \$650.00$$

$$= \$1116.80$$

This inverse relationship between the investor's required rate of return and the value of a bond is presented in Figure 4A-1. Clearly, as an investor demands a higher rate of return, the value of the bond decreases. The higher rate of return which the investor desires, can be achieved only by paying less for the bond. Conversely, a lower required rate of return yields a higher market value for the bond.

Changes in bond prices represent an element of uncertainty for the bond investor. If the current interest rate (required rate of return) changes, the price of the bond also fluctuates. An increase in interest rates causes the bondholder to incur a loss in market value. Since future interest rates and the resulting bond a change in the market value of a bond. However, the impact on value is greater for long-term bonds than it is for short-term bonds.

In Figure 4A-1 we observed the effect of interest rate changes on a five-year bond paying a 12 percent coupon interest rate. What if the bond did not mature until ten years from today instead of five years? Would the changes in market value be the same? Absolutely not. The changes in value would be more significant for the ten-year bond. For example, if we vary the current interest rates (the bondholder's required rate of return) from 9 percent to 12 percent and then to 15 percent, as we did earlier with the five-year bond, the values for both the five-year and the ten-year bonds would be as follows:

	Market Value for a 12% Coupon Rate Bond Maturing in	
Required Rate	5 Years	10 Years
9%	$1116.80	$1192.16
12	1000.00	1000.00
15	899.24	849.28

Using these values and the required rates, we can graph the changes in values for the two bonds relative to different interest rates. These comparisons are provided in Figure 4A-3. The figure clearly illustrates that the price of a long-term bond (say ten years) is more responsive or sensitive to interest rate changes than the price of a short-term bond (say five years).

The reason long-term bond prices fluctuate more than short-term bond prices in response to interest rate changes is simple. Assume an investor bought a ten-year bond yielding a 12 percent interest rate. If the current interest rate for bonds of similar risk increased to 15 percent, the investor would be locked into the lower rate for ten years. If, on the other hand, a shorter-term bond had been purchased, say one maturing in two years, the investor would have to accept the lower return for only two years and not the full ten years. At the end of year 2, the investor would receive the maturity value of $1,000 and could buy a bond offering the higher 15 percent rate for the remaining eight years. Thus, interest rate risk is determined, at least in part, by the length of time an investor is required to commit to an investment. However, the holder of a long-term bond may take some comfort from the fact that long-term interest rates are usually not as volatile as short-term rates. If the short-term rate changed one percentage point, for example, it would not be unusual for the long-term rate to change only .3 percentage points.

FIGURE 4A-3
Market Value of a 5-Year and a 10-Year Bond and Different Required Rates

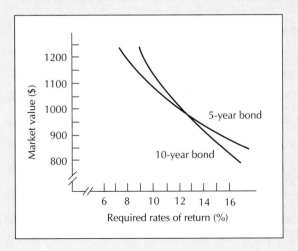

FIFTH RELATIONSHIP

The sensitivity of a bond's value to changing interest rates depends not only on the length of time to maturity, but also on the pattern of cash flows provided by the bond.

It is not at all unusual for two bonds with the same maturity to react differently to a change in interest rates. Consider two bonds, A and B, both with ten-year maturities and the same 10 percent interest rate. While the bonds are similar in terms of maturity date and the contractual interest rate, the structure of the interest payments is different for each bond. Bond A pays $100 interest annually, with the $1,000 principal being repaid at the end of the tenth year. Bond B is called a zero-coupon bond; it pays no interest until the bond matures. At that time the bondholder receives $1,593.70 in interest plus $1,000 in principal. The value of both bonds, assuming a market interest rate (required rate of return) of 10 percent, is $1,000. However, if interest rates fell to 6 percent, bond A's market value would be $1,294, compared with $1,447 for bond B. Why the difference? Both bonds have the same maturity, and each promises the same 10 percent rate of return. The answer lies in the differences in their cash flow patterns. Bond B's cash flows are received in the more distant future on average than are the cash flows for bond A. Since a change in interest rates always has a greater impact on the present value of later cash flows than on earlier cash flows (due to the effects of compounding), bonds with cash flows coming later on average will be more sensitive to interest rate changes than will bonds with earlier cash flows. This phenomenon was recognized in 1938 by Macaulay, who devised the concept of duration.

The **duration** of a bond is simply a measure of the responsiveness of its price to a change in interest rates. The greater the relative percentage change in a bond price in response to a given percentage change in the interest rate, the longer the duration. In computing duration, we consider not only the maturity or term over which cash flows are received but also the time pattern of interim cash flows. Specifically, duration is a weighted average time to maturity in which the weight attached to each year is the present value of the cash flow for that year. A measurement of duration may be represented as follows:

$$\text{duration} = \frac{\sum_{t=1}^{n} \dfrac{tC_t}{(1+R_b)^t}}{P_0} \qquad (4A\text{-}1)$$

where

t = the year the cash flow is to be received

n = the number of years to maturity

C_t = the cash flow to be received in year t

R_b = the bondholder's required rate of return

P_0 = the bond's present value

For our two bonds, A and B, duration would be calculated as follows:

$$\text{duration bond A} = \frac{\left[(1)\dfrac{\$100}{(1.1)^1} + (2)\dfrac{\$100}{(1.1)^2} + (3)\dfrac{\$100}{(1.1)^3} + \ldots + (9)\dfrac{\$100}{(1.1)^9} + (10)\dfrac{\$1100}{(1.1)^{10}}\right]}{\$1000}$$

$$= 6.759$$

$$\text{duration bond B} = \frac{\left[(1)\dfrac{0}{(1.1)^1} + (2)\dfrac{0}{(1.1)^2} + (3)\dfrac{0}{(1.1)^3} + \ldots + (9)\dfrac{0}{(1.1)^9} + (10)\dfrac{\$2593.70}{(1.1)^{10}}\right]}{\$1000}$$

$$= 10$$

Thus, while both bonds have the same maturity, 10 years, the zero coupon bond (bond B) is more sensitive to interest rate changes, as suggested by its higher duration, which in this instance equals its maturity.[25] (The negative sign has been added to the equation to remind us that values move inversely with changing interest rates.) The lesson learned: In assessing a bond's sensitivity to changing interest rates, the bond's duration is the appropriate measure, not the term to maturity.

SUMMARY

Certain key relationships exist in bond valuation. A brief summary of these factors would include the following:

1. A decrease in interest rates (required rates of return) will cause the value of a bond to increase; an interest rate increase will cause a decrease in value. The change in value caused by changing interest rates is called interest rate risk.

2. If the bondholder's required rate of return (current interest rate) equals the coupon interest rate, the bond will sell at par, or maturity value.

3. If the current interest rate exceeds the bond's coupon rate, the bond will sell below par value, or at a "discount."

4. If the current interest rate is less than the bond's coupon rate, the bond will sell above par value, or at a "premium."

5. Regardless of whether a bond is selling below or above par value, the value of the bond will gradually approach par value as the bond matures.

6. A bondholder owning a long-term bond is exposed to greater interest rate risk than when owning a short-term bond.

7. In understanding a bond's sensitivity to interest rate changes, we must consider not only the time to maturity, but also the time pattern of interim cash flows.

STUDY PROBLEMS

4A-1. (*Bond Valuation*) You own a bond that pays $100 in annual interest, with a $1,000 par value. It matures in 15 years. Your required rate of return is 12 percent.

   a. Calculate the value of the bond.

   b. How does the value change if your required rate of return (1) increases to 15 percent or (2) decreases to 8 percent?

   c. Explain the implications of your answers in part (b) as they relate to interest rate risk, premium bonds, and discount bonds.

   d. Assume that the bond matures in five years instead of 15 years. Recompute your answers in part (b).

   e. Explain the implications of your answers in part (d) as they relate to interest rate risk, premium bonds, and discount bonds.

[25]Maturity and duration are the same only for zero coupon bonds or securities that pay only one cash flow, and it occurs at maturity.

4A-2. (*Duration*) Calculate the value and the duration for the following bonds:

Bond	Years to Annual Maturity		
	Maturity	Interest	Value
P	5	$100	$1000
Q	5	70	1000
R	10	120	1000
S	10	80	1000
T	15	65	1000

Your required rate of return is 8 percent.

APPENDIX 4B: The Relationship Between Value and Earnings

In understanding the relationship between a firm's earnings and the market price of its share, it is helpful to look first at the relationship for a nongrowth firm and then expand our view to include the growth firm.

The Relationship Between Earnings and Value for the Nongrowth Company

When we speak of a nongrowth firm, we mean one that retains no profits for the purpose of reinvestment. The only investments made are for the purpose of maintaining status quo—that is, investing the amount of the depreciation taken on fixed assets so that the firm does do not lose its current earnings capacity. The result is both constant earnings and a constant dividends stream to the common shareholder, since we are paying all earnings out in the form of dividends (i.e., dividend in year t equals earnings in year t). This type of common share is essentially no different from a preferred share. Recalling from our earlier discussion about valuing a preferred share, we may value the nongrowth common share similarly, expressing our valuation in one of two ways:

$$\text{value of a nongrowth firm} = \frac{\text{earnings per share}_1}{\text{required rate of return}} \qquad \text{(4B-1)}$$

$$= \frac{\text{dividend per share}_1}{\text{required rate of return}} \qquad \text{(4B-2)}$$

or

$$V_{cng} = \frac{EPS_1}{R_c} = \frac{D_1}{R_c}$$

EXAMPLE

The Reeves Corporation expects its earnings per share this year to be $12, which is to be paid out in total to the investors in the form of dividends. If the investors have a required rate of return of 14 percent, the value of the share would be $85.71:

$$V_{cng} = \frac{\$12}{.14} = \$85.71$$

In this instance, the relationship between value and earnings per share is direct and unmistakable. If earnings per share increase (decrease) 10 percent, then the value of the share should increase (decrease) 10 percent. That is, the ratio of price to earnings will be a constant, as will the ratio of earnings to price. A departure from the constant relationship would occur only if the investors change their required rate of return, owing to a change in their perception about such things as risk or anticipated inflation. Thus, there is good reason to perceive a relationship between next year's earnings and share price for the nongrowth company. ∎

The Relationship Between Earnings and Value for the Growth Firm

Turning our attention now to the growth firm, one that does reinvest its profits back into the business, we will recall that our valuation model depended on dividends and earnings, for that matter, increasing at a constant growth rate. Returning to Equation (4-29), we valued a common share where dividends were expected to increase at a constant growth rate as follows:

$$\text{value} = \frac{\text{dividend}_1}{\text{required rate of return} - \text{growth rate}}$$

or

$$V_c = \frac{D_1}{R_c - g} \tag{4-29}$$

While Equation (4-25) is certainly the conventional way of expressing value of the growth share, it is not the only means. We could also describe the value of a share as the present value of the dividend stream provided from the firm's existing assets plus the present value of any future growth resulting from the reinvestment of future earnings. We could represent this concept notationally as follows:

$$V_c = \frac{EPS_1}{R_c} + PVDG, \tag{4B-3}$$

where EPS_1/R_c is the present value of the cash flow stream provided by the existing assets and $PVDG$ is the net present value of any dividend growth resulting from the reinvestment of future earnings. The first term, EPS_1/R_c, is immediately understandable given our earlier rationale about nongrowth shares. The second term, the present value of future dividend growth ($PVDG$), needs some clarification.

To begin our explanation of $PVDG$, let r equal the fraction of a firm's earnings that are retained in the business, which implies that the dividend in year 1 (D_1) would equal $(1 - r) \times EPS_1$. Next, assume that any earnings that are reinvested yield a rate of ROE (return on equity). Thus, from the earnings generated in year 1, we would be investing the percentage of earnings retained, r, times the firm's earnings per share, EPS_1, or $r \times EPS_1$. In return, we should expect to receive a cash flow in all future years equal to the expected return on our investment, ROE, times the amount of our investment, or $r \times EPS_1 \times$ ROE. Since the cash inflows represent an annuity continuing in perpetuity, the net present value from reinvesting a part of the firm's earnings in year 1 (NPV_1) would be equal to the present value of the new cash flows less the cost of the investment:

$$NPV_1 = \left(\frac{rEPS_1ROE}{R_c} \right) - rEPS_1 \tag{4B-4}$$

$$\underbrace{\phantom{\frac{rEPS_1ROE}{R_c}}}_{\substack{\text{present value} \\ \text{of increased} \\ \text{cash flows}}} \quad \underbrace{}_{\substack{\text{amount} \\ \text{of cash} \\ \text{retained and} \\ \text{reinvested}}}$$

If we continued to reinvest a fixed percentage of earnings each year and earned ROE on these investments, there would also be a net present value in all the following years. That is, we would have $NPV_2, NPV_3, NPV_4, ...NPV_\infty$. Also, since r

and ROE are both constant, the series of *NPV*s will increase at a constant growth rate of $r \times$ ROE. We may therefore use the constant-growth valuation model to value *PVDG* as follows:

$$PVDG = \frac{NPV_1}{R_c - g} \qquad (4B\text{-}5)$$

Thus, we may now establish the value of a common share as the sum of (1) a present value of a constant stream of earnings generated from the firm's assets already in place, and (2) the present value of an increasing dividend stream coming from the retention of profits. That is,

$$V_c = \frac{EPS_1}{R_c} + \frac{NPV_1}{R_c - g} \qquad (4B\text{-}6)$$

EXAMPLE

The Upp Corporation should earn $8 per share this year, of which 40 percent will be retained with the firm for reinvestment and 60 percent paid in the form of dividends to the shareholders. Management expects to earn an 18 percent return on any funds retained. Let us use both the constant-growth dividend model and the *PVDG* model to compute Upp's share value.

Constant-Growth Dividend Model

Since we are assuming that the firm's ROE will be constant and that management faithfully intends to retain 40 percent of earnings each year to be used for new investments, the dividend stream flowing to the investor should increase by 7.2 percent each year, which we know by solving for (r)(ROE), or $(.4)(18\%)$. The dividend for this year will be $4.80, which is the dividend-payout ratio of $(1 - r)$ times the expected earnings per share of $8 $(.60 \times \$8 = \$4.80)$. Given a 12 percent required rate of return for the investors, the value of the security may be shown to be $100.

$$V_c = \frac{D_1}{R_c - g} \qquad (4\text{-}25)$$

$$= \frac{\$4.80}{.12 - .072}$$

$$= \$100$$

PVDG Model

Restructuring the problem to compute separately the present value of the no-growth stream and the present value of future growth opportunities, we may again determine the value of the share to be $100. Solving first for value assuming a no-growth scenario,

$$V_{cng} = \frac{EPS_1}{R_c} \qquad (4B\text{-}1)$$

$$= \frac{\$8}{.12}$$

$$= \$66.67$$

We next estimate the value of the future growth opportunities coming from reinvesting corporate profits each year, which is

$$PVDG = \frac{NPV_1}{R_c - g} \qquad (4B\text{-}5)$$

Knowing R_c to be 12 percent and the growth rate to be 7.2 percent, we lack knowing only NPV_1, which can easily be determined using Equation (4B-4):

$$NPV_1 = \left(\frac{rEPS_1ROE}{R_c} \right) - rEPS_1 \qquad \text{(4B-4)}$$

$$= \left(\frac{(.4)(\$8)(.18)}{.12} \right) - (.4)(\$8)$$

$$= \$4.80 - \$3.20$$

$$= \$1.60$$

The *PVDG* may now be computed:

$$PVDG = \frac{\$1.60}{.12 - .072}$$

$$= \$33.33$$

Thus, the value of the combined streams is $100:

$$V_c = \$66.67 + \$33.33 = \$100 \ \blacksquare$$

From the preceding example, we see that the value of the growth opportunities represents a significant portion of the total value, 33 percent to be exact. Further, in looking at the *PVDG* model, we observe that value is influenced by the following: (1) the size of the firm's beginning earnings per share, (2) the percentage of profits retained, and (3) the spread between the return generated on new investments and the investor's required rate of return. The first factor relates to firm size; the second to management's decision about the investor's required rate of return. While the first two factors are not unimportant, the last one is the key to wealth creation by management. Simply because management retains profits does not mean that wealth is created for the shareholders. Wealth comes only if the return on equity from the investments, ROE, is greater than the investor's required rate of return, R_c. Thus, we should expect the market to assign value not only to the reported earnings per share for the current year, but also to the anticipated growth opportunities that have a marginal rate of return that exceeds the required rate of return of the firm's investors.

SELECTED REFERENCES

Arzac, Enrique R. "Do Your Business Units Create Shareholder Value?" *Harvard Business Review* (January–February 1986), 121–126.

Balachandran, Bala V., Nandu J. Nagarajan, and Alfred Rappaport. "Threshold Margins for Creating Economic Value," *Financial Management*, 15 (Spring 1986), 68–77.

Banz, Rolf W. "The Relationship Between Return and Market Value of Common Stocks," *Journal of Financial Economics*, 9 (March 1981), 3–18.

Basu, Snajoy. "The Relationship Between Earnings' Yield, Market Value and Return for NYSE Common Stocks: Further Evidence," *Journal of Financial Economics*, 12 (June 1983), 129–156.

Fuller, Russell J., and Chi-Cheng Hsia. "A Simplified Common Stock Valuation Model," *Financial Analysts Journal*, 40 (September–October 1984), 49–56.

Gordon, Myron. *The Investment, Financing and Valuation of the Corporation*. Homewood, IL: Richard D. Irwin, 1963.

Greynolds, Elbert B., Jr., Julius S. Aronofsky, and Robert J. Frame. *Financial Analysis Using Calculators: Time Value of Money*. New York: McGraw-Hill, 1980.

Hart, William L. *Mathematics of Investment*. 5th ed. Lexington, MA: D. C. Heath, 1975.

Hector, Gary. "What Makes Stock Prices Move?" *Fortune* (October 10, 1988), 69–76.

Hickman, Kent and Glenn H. Petry. "A Comparison of Stock Predictions Using Court Accepted Formulas, Dividend Discount, and P/E Models," *Journal of Financial Management* (Summer 1990), 76.

Malkiel, Burton G. *A Random Walk Down Wall Street*. New York: W. W. Norton, 1985.

Marsh, Terry A., and Robert C. Merton. "Dividend Variability and Variance Bounds Tests for the Rationality of Stock Market Prices," *American Economic Review* (June) 1986, 483–498.

Piper, Thomas R., and William E. Fruhan, Jr. "Is Your Stock Worth Its Market Price?" *Harvard Business Review* (May–June 1981), 124–132.

Rappaport, Alfred. *Creating Shareholder Wealth*. New York: The Free Press, 1986.

Reinganum, Marc R. "The Anatomy of a Stock Market Winner," *Financial Analysts Journal* (March–April 1988), 16–28.

Ryngaert, Michael D. "Firm Valuation, Takeover Defenses, and the Delaware Supreme Court," *Journal of Financial Management* (Autumn 1989), 20.

Shao, Stephen P. *Mathematics for Management and Finance*. 6th ed. Cincinnati: South-Western Publishing, 1990.

Shiller, Robert J. "Do Stock Prices Move Too Much to Be Justified by Subsequent Changes in Dividends," *American Economic Review* (June 1981), 421–436.

Timme, Stephen G., and Peter C. Eisemann. "On The Use of Consensus Forecasts of Growth in the Constant Growth Model: The Case of Electric Utilities," *Journal of Financial Management* (Winter 1989), 23.

Tobias, Andrew. *Money Angles*. New York: Linden Press, 1984.

Williams, John B. *The Theory of Investment Value*. Cambridge, MA: Harvard University Press, 1938.

CHAPTER 5

Cost of Capital

- The Concept of the Cost of Capital

- Factors Determining the Weighted Cost of Capital

- Assumptions of the Weighted Cost of Capital Model

- Computing the Weighted Cost of Capital

- Marginal Cost of Capital: A Comprehensive Example

- Required Rate of Return for Individual Projects:
  An Alternative Approach

- A Firm's Cost of Capital: Some Recent Evidence

Having studied risk and rates of return (Chapter 3) and the valuation of financial securities (Chapter 4), we are now ready to examine the firm's cost of capital. The cost of capital provides a fundamental connecting link between the firm's financing and investment decisions.[1] Figure 5-1 illustrates these relationships.

How a firm finances its assets affects its cost of capital, which in turn affects which investments the firm will accept. Also, the investments that are selected, depending upon their riskiness, may affect the firm's cost of capital and determine in part what financing options are available.

This chapter will examine the concepts behind the cost of capital, as well as the procedures for estimating the firm's cost of capital. For the time being, we assume that how the firm finances its investments is held constant. This assumption will be relaxed in Chapter 9 when we study the relationship between the firm's cost of capital and its financing decisions.

In this chapter, we will look at the following topics:

1. The basic concept underlying the cost of capital and the key factors influencing a corporation's cost of capital

2. The assumptions generally required in measuring and using a firm's overall or companywide cost of capital

3. The calculation of a corporation's overall cost of capital

4. An approach to measuring a project-specific required rate of return as an alternative to the firm's weighted cost of capital

5. An empirical study of the cost of capital of large firms, as estimated by the firm's managers.

---

[1]When determining the present value of cash flows, the term "cost of capital" may be used interchangeably with the firm's required rate of return, the hurdle rate, the discount rate, and the opportunity cost.

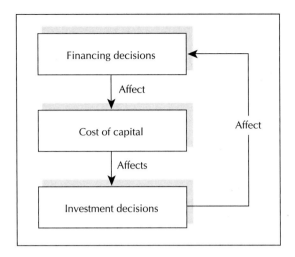

Perspective in Finance

The cost of capital is the rate that the firm must earn on its investments if it wants to keep the investors satisfied. A firm meets this objective by ensuring that its investors earn their required rate of return.

THE CONCEPT OF THE COST OF CAPITAL

A firm's **cost of capital** is the rate that must be earned in order to satisfy the firm's investors for a given level of risk.

If the firm earned exactly its cost of capital on an investment project, then we would expect the price of its common shares to remain unchanged following the acceptance of the project. However, if a rate different from the cost of capital was attained, we would expect the price of the shares to change. For example, in Figure 5-2 the internal rates of return for projects A,

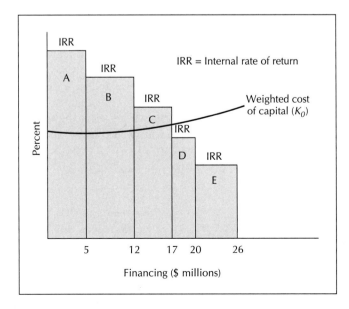

FIGURE 5-2
Investment and Financing
Schedules

TABLE 5-1
Salinas Corporation
Capital Structure

	Amount	Percentage of Capital Structure
Bonds (18% interest rate)	$ 600,000	30%
Preferred shares (10% dividend rate)	200,000	10%
Common shares	1,200,000	60%
Total liabilities and equity	$2,000,000	100%

B, and C exceed the firm's cost of capital, so accepting these projects would increase the value of the firm's common shares. In contrast, investing in projects D and E would lower the share value, which says that the best level of capital expenditures equals $17 million. Therefore, the cost of capital is the rate of return on investments that leaves the price of the firm's common shares unchanged. (As we will see later, we must assume that all the projects in Figure 5-2 are similar in terms of risk.)

Although we are trying to find the rate of return on an investment that leaves the common share's price unchanged, we must also consider the other sources of capital, such as debt and preferred shares. To illustrate, the Salinas Corporation's capital structure is presented in Table 5-1. The company is using three sources of capital: debt, preferred shares, and common shares. Management is considering a $200,000 investment opportunity with an expected internal rate of return of 14 percent. The current cost of the firm's capital (required rate of return) for each source of financing is shown below:[2]

	After-tax
Cost of debt capital	10%
Cost of preferred shares	12
Cost of common shares	16

Given this information, should the firm make the investment? The creditors and preferred shareholders would probably encourage us to undertake the project. However, since the 14 percent internal rate of return on the investment is less than the common shareholders' required rate of return, shareholders might argue that the investment should be forgone. What decision should the financial manager make?

To answer this question, we must know what percentage of the $200,000 is to be provided by each type of investor. If we intend to maintain the same capital structure mix as reflected in Table 5-1 (30 percent debt, 10 percent preferred shares, and 60 percent common shares), we could compute a weighted cost of capital, where the weights equal the percentage of capital to be financed by each source. Table 5-2 shows that the weighted cost of the individual sources of capital is 13.8 percent. From this calculation we would conclude that an investment offering at least a 13.8 percent return

---

[2]The underlying theme of the cost of capital tells us that investment and financing decisions should be based on the investor's marginal cost of capital and not on some criterion arbitrarily selected by management. By using the marginal cost of capital which has been determined in the financial markets, management imposes market discipline on its decisions. In addition. this type of approach ensures that market or intrinsic value is added to shareholder's wealth.

	Weights (Percentage of Financing)	After-tax Cost of Individual Sources	Weighted Cost
Debt	30%	10%	3.0%
Preferred shares	10	12	1.2%
Common shares	60	16	9.6%
	100%	Weighted cost of capital:	13.8%

TABLE 5-2
Salinas Corporation
Weighted Cost of Capital

would be acceptable to the company's investors. The investment should be undertaken, since the 14 percent rate of return more than satisfies all investors as indicated by a 13.8 percent weighted cost of capital. Again, the **weighted cost of capital** for a firm is equal to the cost of each source of financing (debt, preferred shares, and common shares) multiplied by the percentage of the financing provided by that source. Thus when we speak of a company's cost of capital, we mean its weighted cost of capital.

The Importance of Using a Weighted Cost of Capital

The weighted cost of capital may be fine in theory, but what if a company could borrow the entire amount needed for an investment in a new product line? Is it really necessary to use the weighted cost of capital, or would it be all right to make the decision based simply on the cost of the debt which provides the funding?

To answer these questions, we examine the following example. Management of the Poling Corporation believes it could earn 14 percent from purchasing $500,000 in new equipment, which would allow the firm to expand its sales base. Although the firm endeavors to maintain a capital structure with equal amounts of debt and equity, the bank is willing to loan the firm the entire $500,000 at an interest rate of 12 percent. The financial manager knows that the firm's earnings per share will increase if the firm earns a rate of return which exceeds the cost of financing or the cost of debt at 12 percent.

Poling's financial manager has also estimated the firm's cost of equity at 18 percent. However, management has decided to make the investment and finance it by borrowing the money from the bank at 12 percent.

The following year, management finds another investment opportunity costing $500,000, but with an expected internal rate of return of 17 percent which is better than the previous year's rate of return of 14 percent. However, this time the bank is unwilling to lend Poling any more money. The loan officer at the bank indicates that Poling has used up all of its debt capacity. The firm must now issue new common shares before the bank will be agreeable to fund any more loans. As a result, management decides to reject the investment since it does not earn the cost of equity of 18%.

What is the moral of the Poling example? Intuitively, we can see that Poling's management has made a mistake. The investment made by the firm in the first year has caused the firm to lose an opportunity to make a better investment decision in the second year.

We can conclude that a firm should never use a single cost of financing as the hurdle rate (discount rate) for making investment decisions. In this example the use of debt has caused the firm to implicitly use up some of its debt capacity for future investments and until the firm can complement the use of debt with equity, it will not be able to use more debt in the future.[3] Thus, financial managers should always use the weighted cost of capital and not an individual cost of funds, as the discount rate for investment decisions. We now examine in greater detail the weighted cost of capital.

Perspective in Finance

When we compute a firm's weighted cost of capital, we are simply calculating the average cost of money supplied by all investors, those being creditors and shareholders.

FACTORS DETERMINING THE WEIGHTED COST OF CAPITAL

To gain further insight into the meaning of the firm's cost of capital, we need to consider the elements in the business environment that cause a company's weighted cost of capital to be high or low.[4] Looking at Figure 5-2, we see four primary factors: general economic conditions, the marketability of the firm's securities (market conditions), operating and financing conditions within the company, and the amount of financing needed for new investments. These four variables also relate to our discussion in Chapter 3, where we separated an investor's required rate of return into risk-free rate of return and the risk premium. These two aspects of risk are also key ingredients in the firm's cost of capital.

Perspective in Finance

The cost of capital for a firm is driven by the demand for and supply of money in the economy and the riskiness of the firm.

Factor 1: General Economic Conditions

As discussed in Chapter 2, general economic conditions determine the demand for and supply of capital within the economy, as well as the level of expected inflation. This economic variable is reflected in the riskless rate of return. This rate represents the rate of return on risk-free investments, such as the interest rate on short-term Government of Canada T-Bills. In principle, as the demand for money in the economy changes relative to the supply, investors alter their required rate of return.[5] For example, if the demand for

---

[3]By financing entirely by debt, the firm has used some of its debt capacity, thereby denying the use of debt at some time in the future. Also, as more debt is used, the common shareholders require a higher rate of return because of the increase in financial risk to their investment. We will discuss in greater detail the effects of financial risk on return in Chapter 8.

[4]There is an inverse relationship between value and the cost of capital, given that all other conditions remain the same. For example, a decrease in the cost of capital or discount rate which is used to find the present value, causes the value of the cash flow stream to increase.

[5]The cost of capital is, in part, dependent on the demand and supply of money in the economy. The cost of capital is higher in Canada, where the supply of funds is less, than in other countries such as Japan, where the savings rate is higher.

money increases without an equivalent increase in the supply, lenders will raise their required interest rate. At the same time, if inflation is expected to deteriorate the purchasing power of the dollar, investors require a higher rate of return to compensate for this anticipated loss.[6]

Factor 2: Market Conditions

When an investor purchases a security with significant investment risk, the security must offer the investor an opportunity to earn additional returns to make the investment attractive. Essentially, as risk increases, the investor requires a higher rate of return. This increase is called a **risk premium**. An increase in the investor's required rate of return causes the firm's cost of capital to increase. Remember, we have defined risk as the potential variability of future returns. If the security is not readily marketable when the investor wants to sell, or even if a continuous demand for the security exists but the price varies significantly, an investor will require a relatively high rate of return. On the other hand, if a security is readily marketable and its price is reasonably stable, the investor will require a lower rate of return and the company's cost of capital will be lower.

Factor 3: Firm's Operating and Financing Decisions

Risk, or the variability of returns, also results from decisions made within the company. Risk resulting from these decisions is generally divided into two types: business risk and financial risk. **Business risk** is the variability in returns on assets and is affected by the company's investment decisions. **Financial risk** is the increased variability in returns to common shareholders as a result of financing with debt or preferred shares.[7] As business risk and financial risk increase or decrease, the investor's required rate of return (and the cost of capital) will move in the same direction.[8]

Factor 4: Amount of Financing

The last factor determining the firm's cost of funds is the level of financing the firm requires. As the financing requirements of the firm become larger, the weighted cost of capital increases for several reasons. For instance, as more securities are issued, additional issuing costs, or the cost incurred by the firm from issuing securities, will affect the percentage cost of the funds to the firm. Also, as management approaches the market for large amounts of capital relative to the firm's size, the investors' required rate of return may rise. Suppliers of capital become hesitant to grant relatively large sums without evidence of management's capability to absorb this capital into the business. This is typically "too much too soon." Also, as the size of the issue increases, there is greater difficulty in placing it in the market without reducing the price of the security, which also increases the firm's cost of capital.

---

[6]This effect was referenced earlier in Chapter 4 as the Fisher effect.

[7]During the 1980s, some North American firms issued large amounts of debt to finance growth through leveraged buy-outs. Consequently, the financial risk of these companies was increased dramatically. However, in computing the firm's weighted cost of capital, we assume that management does make such changes in the firm's capital structure.

[8]Both forms of risk, business and financial, are explained and illustrated in Chapter 8.

A Summary Illustration

To summarize, the important variables influencing a corporation's cost of capital include the following:

1. **General economic conditions.** This factor determines the risk-free rate or riskless rate of return.

2. **Marketability of a company's securities.** As the marketability of a security increases, investors' required rates of return decrease, lowering the corporation's cost of capital.

3. **Operating and financial decisions made by management.** If management accepts investments with high levels of risk or if it uses debt or preferred shares extensively, the firm's risk increases. Investors then require a higher rate of return, which causes a higher cost of capital to the company.

4. **Amount of financing needed.** Requests for larger amounts of capital increase the firm's cost of capital.

Figure 5-3 illustrates the cost of capital for a particular source. The risk-free rate, determined by the general economic conditions, is 9 percent. However, owing to the additional risks associated with the security, the firm has to earn an additional 7 percent to satisfy the investors' required rate of return of 16 percent.

ASSUMPTIONS OF THE WEIGHTED COST OF CAPITAL MODEL

In a complex business world, difficulties quickly arise in computing a corporation's cost of capital. For this reason, we make several simplifying assumptions.

Constant Business Risk

Business risk is defined as the potential variability of future returns on an investment. The level of business risk within a firm is determined by management's investment policies. As a result, both the investor's required rate of return on a firm's securities and the firm's cost of capital is a function of the firm's current business risk. If this risk level is altered, the corporation's investors will naturally change their required rates of return, which in turn modifies the cost of capital. However, the amount of change in the cost of capital resulting from a given increase or decrease in business risk is difficult to assess. For this reason, the cost of capital calculation assumes that any investment under consideration will not significantly change the firm's business risk. In other words, the cost of capital is an appropriate investment criterion only for an investment having a business risk level similar to that of existing assets.

Constant Financial Risk

Financial risk has been defined as the increased variability in returns on common shares resulting from the increased use of debt and preferred

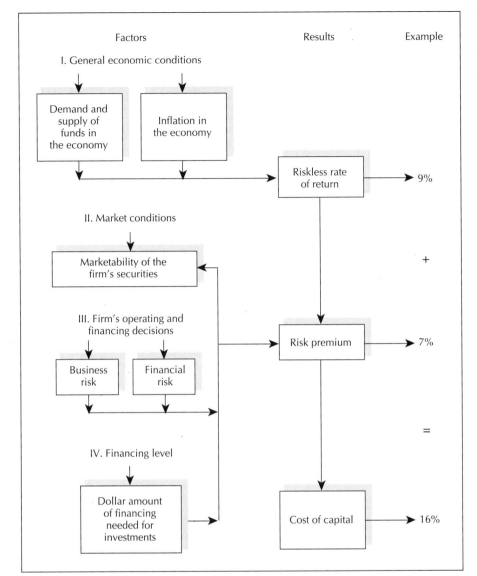

FIGURE 5-3
Primary Factors Influencing the Cost of a Particular Source of Capital

shares financing.[9] Also, financial risk relates to the threat of bankruptcy. As the percentage of debt in the capital structure increases, the possibility that the firm will be unable to pay interest and the principal balance is also increased. As a result, the level of financial risk in a company has an impact upon the investors' required rate of return. As the amount of debt rises, the common shareholders will increase their required rate of return. In other words, the costs of individual sources of capital are a function of the current financial structure. For this reason, the data used in computing the cost of capital are appropriate only if management continues to use the same financial mix. If the present capital structure consists of 40 percent debt, 10 percent preferred shares, and 50 percent common shares, this capital structure is assumed to be maintained in the financing of future investments.

---

[9]This concept is further explained in Chapter 8.

Constant Dividend Policy

A third assumption required in estimating the cost of capital relates to the corporation's dividend policy. For ease of computation, we generally assume that a firm's dividends are increasing at a constant annual growth rate. We also assume that this growth is a function of the firm's earning capabilities and not merely the result of paying out a larger percentage of the company's earnings. Thus, it is implicitly assumed that the dividend payout ratio (dividends/net income) is constant.

The assumptions of the weighted cost of capital model are quite restrictive. In practice, the financial manager may need a range of possible cost of capital values rather than a single-point estimate in order to perform an investment analysis. For example, it may be more appropriate to talk in terms of a 10 to 12 percent range as an estimate of the firm's cost of capital, rather than assuming that a precise number can be determined. In this chapter, however, our principal concern will be with calculating a single cost of capital figure.

Perspective in Finance

To compute a firm's weighted cost of capital, we must assume that the firm's financial mix will not change, that we will continue to invest in projects of about the same risk as we have done in the past, and that we will not change the percentage of earnings paid out in dividends to the shareholders.

COMPUTING THE WEIGHTED COST OF CAPITAL

A firm's weighted cost of capital is a composite of the individual costs of financing, weighted by the percentage of financing provided by each source. Therefore, a firm's weighted cost of capital is a function of (1) the individual costs of capital and (2) the makeup of the capital structure—the percentage of funds provided by debt, preferred shares, and common shares.[10] Also, as we noted earlier, the amount of funds needed affects the cost of capital. We will discuss this last consideration, the level of financing, later.

As we explain the procedures for computing a company's cost of capital, it is helpful to remember three basic steps:

1. Calculate the costs of capital for each individual source of financing used by the firm; these costs generally include debt, preferred shares, and common shares.

2. Determine the percentage of each source of financing in terms of their market value.

3. Using the individual costs and the capital structure percentages in the first two steps, compute an overall or weighted cost of capital for the various amounts of financing that might be needed.

[10]Examples of how a firm can lower its cost of capital include: offering incentives to customers to prepay for products that will be needed at a later date; using Government subsidies from foreign countries relating to the transfer of technology; and using joint ventures in foreign countries to lower the cost of equity.

The computations are not difficult if we understand our purpose: We want to calculate the firm's overall cost of capital. As a simple exercise, calculate the average age of students in a course where 40 percent are 19 years old, 50 percent are 20 years old, and 10 percent are 21 years old. We can easily find the average age to be 19.7 years by weighting each age by the percentage in each age category $[(40\%)(19) + (50\%)(20) + (10\%)(21)]$. In a similar way, the weighted cost of capital is estimated by weighing the cost of each individual source by the percentage of financing it provides. If we finance an investment by 40 percent debt at a 10 percent cost and 60 percent common equity at a cost of 18 percent, the weighted cost of capital is 14.8 percent $[(.40)(10\%) + (.60)(18\%) = 14.8\%]$. Thus, while the details become somewhat involved, the basic approach is relatively simple. Figure 5-4 summarizes the steps of this approach.

Determining Individual Costs of Capital

Companies have created a large variety of financing instruments in an attempt to attract new investors. However, our interest will be restricted to the three basic types of securities: debt, preferred shares, and common shares. In calculating their respective costs, the objective is to determine the rate of return the company must earn on its investments to satisfy investors' required rates of return after allowing for any issuing costs incurred in raising new funds. Also, since the cash flows used in capital-budgeting analysis (net present value, profitability index, and internal rate of return) are on an after-tax basis, the required rates of return should also be expressed on an after-tax basis.

Cost of Debt

The **cost of debt** may be defined as the rate that must be received from an investment in order to achieve the required rate of return for the creditors. In Chapter 4 the required rate of return for debt capital was found by a trial-and-error process or with the use of a financial calculator, where we solved for R_d in the following equation:

$$V_d = \frac{\$I_1}{(1 + R_d)^1} + \frac{\$I_2}{(1 + R_d)^2} + ... + \frac{\$I_n}{(1 + R_d)^n} + \frac{\$M}{(1 + R_d)^n} \qquad (5\text{-}1)$$

If we use the present value tables, the equation would be restated as follows:

$$V_d = \$I[PVIFA_{R_d,n}] + \$M[PVIF_{R_d,n}]$$

> **Remember: The firm's weighted cost of capital is calculated as follows:**
>
> 1. Compute the cost of capital for each and every source of financing, i.e., each source of debt, preferred shares, and common equity.
> 2. Determine the percentage of each source of financing in terms of their market value.
> 3. Calculate a weighted average of the costs of capital using the percentage of each source as the weights.

FIGURE 5-4
Computing the
Weighted Cost of Capital:
the Basic Steps

where

V_d = the market price of the debt

$\$I_t$ = the annual dollar interest paid to the investor

$\$M$ = the maturity value of the debt

R_d = the required rate of return of the debt holder

n = the number of years to maturity

Assume that an investor is willing to pay $908.32 for an annual coupon bond. The security pays a nominal interest rate of 8 percent on a par value of $1,000 and matures in 20 years. By trial and error, the investor's required rate of return is found to be 9 percent, which is the rate that sets the present value of the future interest payments and the maturity value equal to the price of the bond, or

$$\$908.32 = \sum_{t=1}^{20} \frac{\$80}{(1 + .09)^t} + \frac{\$1000}{(1 + .09)^{20}}$$

$$= \$908.32$$

However, if both brokerage commissions and legal or accounting fees are incurred in issuing the security, the company will not receive the full $908.32 market price. Both issuing expenses and interest expenses are considered by Revenue Canada as tax deductible expenses and can be written off as deductions against taxable income. As a result, the actual cost of these funds to the firm will be less than the investor's 9 percent required rate of return. In our example, suppose that management has determined that issuing expenses per $1,000 bond is $58.32. If the combined corporate tax rate is 50% for this firm, the after-tax cost of the issuing expenses is $(1 - .5)(\$58.32)$ or $29.16. If the after-tax issuing costs are deducted from the price of the bond, the net price after-tax of this bond would be $(\$908.32 - \$29.16)$ or $879.16. In addition, interest expenses are tax deductible to the firm. The firm pays $(1 - .5)(8\%)$ or 4% annual interest on a security that has $1,000 par value and matures in 20 years. As a result, the after-tax interest expense to the firm is $40. The net effect of these changes on Equation (5-1) is as follows:

$$NP_0 = \sum_{t=1}^{n} \frac{\$I_t(1-T)}{(1+K_d)^t} + \frac{\$M}{(1+K_d)^n} \tag{5-2}$$

where NP_0 represents the net price (after-tax) received by the firm from the debt, T equals the combined corporate tax rate, K_d equals the after-tax cost of debt, and the remaining variables retain their meaning from Equation (5-1). If in the present example the company nets $879.16 after-tax issuing costs, the equation should read

$$\$879.16 = \sum_{t=1}^{20} \frac{\$4}{(1 + K_d)^t} + \frac{\$1000}{(1 + K_d)^{20}}$$

$$= \$40[PVIFA_{K_d,20}] + \$1000[PVIF_{K_d,20}]$$

Solving for K_d in Equation (5-2) is achieved by trial and error when using the present-value tables or by using a financial calculator. If 5 percent is selected as a trial discount rate, a present value of $875.38 results. A choice of 4 percent as a trial discount rate gives a present value of $1,000.00. With this information, we may conclude that the after-tax cost of debt is between 4 and 5 percent. Therefore, we may approximate it by interpolating between these two rates. The computation is shown as follows:

Rate	Value		Differences in Values	
4%	$1000.00	} $120.84		} $3.78
K_d	879.16 net price			
5%	$875.38			

Solving for K_d by interpolation,

$$K_d = .04 + (0.97)(.05 - .04) = .0497 = 4.97\%$$

This problem can also be solved by the following approach. Since the company will not receive the full $908.32 market price, the effective cost of these funds is larger than the investor's 9 percent required rate of return. To adjust for this difference, we would simply use the market price less issuing costs in place of the market price in Equation (5-1). Thus, the equation becomes

$$P_0 - IC = \sum_{t=1}^{n} \frac{\$I_t}{(1 + k_d)^t} + \frac{\$M}{(1 + k_d)^n} \tag{5-3}$$

where P_0 represents the market price of the debt, IC represents the issuing costs of the new debt, k_d equals the before-tax cost of debt, and the remaining variables retain their meaning from Equation (5-1). If in the present example the company nets $850 after issuing costs, the equation should read

$$\$908.32 - \$58.32 = \$850 = \sum_{t=1}^{20} \frac{\$80}{(1 + k_d)^t} + \frac{\$1000}{(1 + k_d)^{20}}$$

$$= \$80(PVIFA_{k_d,20}) + \$1000(PVIF_{k_d,20})$$

Solving for k_d in Equation (5-3) can be achieved by trial and error or by using a financial calculator. If 10 percent is selected as a trial discount rate, a present value of $830.12 results. We know that the rate is above 9 percent because a 9 percent rate gave us a $908.32 value. We need the discount rate that gives us an $850 value. With this information, we may conclude that the before-tax cost of the debt capital is between 9 and 10 percent; therefore, we may approximate it by interpolating between these two rates. The computation may be shown as follows:

Rate	Value		Differences in Values	
9%	$908.32	} $58.32		} $78.20
k_d	850.00 proceeds			
10%	$830.12			

Solving for k_d by interpolation,

$$k_d = 0.09 + \left(\frac{\$58.32}{\$78.20}\right)(0.10 - 0.09) = 0.0975 = 9.75\%$$

We could also compute the before-tax cost of debt by using a financial calculator where $N = 20$, $PV = 850$ (−850 on some calculators), and $FV = 1,000$. Then press "I/Y" to solve for k_d. The result would be 9.79 percent (a slight rounding difference).

Thus, the company's cost of debt, before recognizing the tax deductibility of interest, is 9.75 percent. However, we want to know the after-tax cost of the debt, not the before-tax cost. Since interest is a tax-deductible expense, for every \$1 we pay in interest, we lower the firm's tax liability by \$1 times the tax rate. If our company has a combined corporate tax rate of 50 percent, then a dollar in interest means that we save \$.50 in taxes. Applying the same logic to our cost of debt, we may correctly conclude that the after-tax interest cost is found by multiplying the before-tax interest rate by [1 − (tax rate)]. If T is the company's combined corporate tax rate and k_d is the before-tax cost of debt, the after-tax cost of new debt financing, K_d, is found as follows:

$$K_d = k_d(1 - T) \tag{5-4}$$

If in the present example the corporation's tax rate is 50 percent, then the after-tax cost of debt is 4.88 percent:

$$K_d = 9.75\%(1 - .5) = 4.88\%$$

In summary, the firm must earn 4.88 percent on its borrowed capital after the payment of taxes.[11] In doing so, the investors will earn a 9 percent rate of return (their required rate) on the \$908.32 investment, the market price of the bond.

Cost of Preferred Shares

Determining the cost of preferred shares follows the same logic as the cost of debt computations. The objective is to find the rate of return that must be earned on the preferred shareholders' investment to satisfy their required rate of return.

In Chapter 4 the value of a preferred share, P_0, that is nonmaturing and promising a constant dividend per year was defined as follows:

$$P_0 = \frac{\text{dividend}}{\text{required rate of return for a preferred shareholder}} = \frac{D}{R_p} \tag{5-5}$$

From this equation, the required rate of return, R_p, is defined as

$$R_p = \frac{\text{dividend}}{\text{market price}} = \frac{D}{P_0} \tag{5-6}$$

If, for example, a preferred share pays \$1.50 in annual dividends and sells for \$15, the investors' required rate of return is 10 percent:

$$R_p = \frac{\$1.50}{\$15} = 10\%$$

Yet even if these preferred shareholders have a 10 percent required rate of return, the effective cost of this capital will be greater owing to the issuing costs incurred in issuing the security. In our example, a firm will net \$13.50 per share, the market price less the after-tax issuing costs, rather than the full \$15 market price. The cost of preferred shares, K_p, should be calculated using the net price received by the company. Therefore

$$K_p = \frac{\text{dividend}}{\text{net price}} = \frac{D}{NP_0} \tag{5-7}$$

[11]The slight difference in the after-tax cost of debt between both approaches represents a rounding error.

For the preceding example, the cost would be

$$K_p = \frac{\$1.50}{\$13.50} = 11.11\%$$

Since preferred share dividends are not tax-deductible, no adjustment for taxes is required. Thus, the firm must earn the cost of preferred capital after taxes have been paid, which for the preceding example was 11.1 percent.

Cost of Common Shares

While debt and preferred shares must be issued to receive any new money from these sources, common shareholders can provide additional capital in one of two ways. First, new common shares may be issued. Second, the earnings available to common shareholders can be retained, in whole or in part, within the company and used to finance future investments. Retained earnings represent the largest source of capital for most North American corporations. As much as 70 percent of a company's financing in any year may come from the profits retained within the business. To distinguish between these two sources, we will use the term **internal common equity** to designate the profits retained within the business for investment purposes, and **external common equity** to represent a new issue of common shares.

COST OF INTERNAL COMMON EQUITY ■ When managers are considering the retention of earnings as a means for financing an investment, they are serving in a fiduciary capacity. That is, the shareholders have entrusted the company assets to management. If the company's objective is to maximize the wealth of its common shareholders, management should retain the profits only if the company's investments within the firm are at least as attractive as the shareholders' next best investment opportunity.[12] Otherwise the profits should be paid out in dividends, thus permitting the investor to invest more profitably elsewhere.

How can management know the shareholders' alternative investment opportunities? Certainly identifying those specific investments is not feasible. However, the investors' required rate of return should be a function of competing investment opportunities. If the only other investment alternative of similar risk has a 12 percent return, one would expect a rational investor to set a minimum acceptable return on the investment at 12 percent. In other words, the investors' required rate of return should be equal to the expected rate of the best competing investment available. Thus, if the common shareholders' required rate of return is used as a minimum return for investments financed by common share investors, management may be assured that its investment policies are acceptable to the common shareholder.

In actually measuring the common shareholder's required rate of return, we will suggest three approaches: (1) the dividend-growth model, (2) the capital asset pricing model, and (3) the risk-premium approach.

The Dividend-Growth Model □ In Chapter 4, the value of a common share was found to be equal to the present value of the expected future dividends, discounted at the common shareholders' required rate of return. Since the

---

[12]Other factors may justify management's not adhering completely to this principle. These issues are examined when we discuss dividend policy in Chapter 10.

shares have no maturity date, these dividends extend to infinity. For an investor with a required rate of return of R_c, the value of a common share, P_0, promising dividends of D_t in year t would be

$$P_0 = \frac{D_1}{(1 + R_c)^1} + \frac{D_2}{(1 + R_c)^2} + \dots + \frac{D_n}{(1 + R_c)^n} + \dots + \frac{D_\infty}{(1 + R_c)^\infty} \quad (5\text{-}8)$$

Since the market price of the security, P_0, is known, the required rate of return of an investor purchasing the security at this price can be determined by estimating future dividends, D_t, and solving for R_c using Equation (5-8). Furthermore, if the dividends are increasing at a constant annual rate of growth[13] (g) that is less than R_c (the required rate), then R_c may be measured as follows:[14]

$$R_c = \left(\frac{\text{dividend in year 1}}{\text{market price}} \right) + \left(\begin{array}{c} \text{annual growth rate} \\ \text{in dividends} \end{array} \right) = \frac{D_1}{P_0} + g \quad (5\text{-}9)$$

To convert from the common investor's required rate of return in Equation (5-9) to the cost of internal common funds, no adjustment is required for taxes. Dividends paid to the firm's common shareholders are not tax-deductible; therefore, the cost is already on an after-tax basis. Also, issuing costs are not involved in computing the cost of internal common equity since the funds are already within the business. Thus, the investor's required rate of return, R_c, is the same as the cost of internal common equity, K_c.

EXAMPLE

To demonstrate the computation, the Talbot Corporation's common shareholders recently received a $2 dividend per share, and they expect dividends to grow at an annual rate of 10 percent. If the market price of the security is $50, the investor's required rate of return is

$$R_c = K_c = \frac{D_1}{P_0} + g \quad (5\text{-}9)$$

$$= \frac{\$2(1 + .10)}{\$50} + .10$$

$$= \frac{\$2.20}{\$50} + .10 = .144$$

$$= 14.4\%$$

Note that the forthcoming dividend, D_1, is estimated by taking the past dividend, $2, and increasing it by 10 percent, the expected growth rate. That is, $D_1 = D_0 (1.10) = \$2(1.10) = \$2.20$. ∎

The dividend-growth model has been a relatively popular approach for calculating the cost of equity. The primary difficulty, as you might expect, is esti-

[13]In the dividend-growth model, growth comes from the retention of earnings and is determined as follows: growth = percentage of earnings retained in the firm × return on equity.
[14]For additional explanation, see Chapter 4.

mating the expected growth rate in future dividends. One possible source of such expectations is investment advisory services such as Value Line. There are even services that collect and publish the forecasts of a large number of analysts. For instance, Institutional Broker's Estimate System (IBES) publishes earnings per share forecasts made by about 2,000 analysts on a like number of shares. While these forecasts are helpful in reducing the problems of the dividend-growth model, they cannot be considered completely accurate. Growth estimates are generally available only for about five years, and not for the indefinite future, as required by the constant-growth model. Also, the analysts usually state their forecasts in terms of earnings rather than dividends, which does not meet the strict requirements of the dividend-growth model. Even so, the earnings information is helpful, since dividend growth in the long run is dependent on earnings. Nevertheless, the analysts' forecasts are helpful because they provide direct measures of the expectations that determine values in the market.

The use of analysts' forecasts in conjunction with the dividend-growth model to compute required rates of return for the Standard and Poor's 500 shares has been studied by Harris.[15] Computing an average of the analysts' forecasts of five-year growth rates in EPS, Harris used this average as a proxy for the growth rate in dividends. Then, using the dividend-growth model, Equation (5-9), he estimated an average cost of equity for the S&P 500 shares. He next compared these required rates with the yields on U.S. Treasury bonds to see how much risk premium common shareholders were expecting. The analysis was conducted for each quarter from 1982 through 1984. Results of the Harris study are presented in Table 5-3. The findings suggest that common shareholders have required a return of between 17.26 and 20.08 percent on average each year for 1982 through 1984. For the three-year period, the average required rate of return was 18.41 percent. The average risk premiums of common shareholders each year, which are shown in the last column of Table 5-3, ranged from 4.28 percent to 7.16 percent, for an average of 6.16 percent. However, we should remember that these returns apply only for equity investments of average riskiness. As we well know, the risk of individual securities will differ from the average, as will the shareholders' required returns.

While the results in Table 5-3 look reasonable, the same computations for individual shares may not be as plausible, largely because of measurement errors that occur when only one or a few shares are analyzed. Moreover, the constant growth assumption of the model may be inconsistent with reality.

The CAPM Approach ☐ Drawing from Chapter 4, we can estimate the cost of equity using the capital asset pricing model (CAPM). Remember that investors should require a rate of return that at least equals the risk-free rate plus a risk premium appropriate for the level of systematic risk associated with the particular security. Using the CAPM, we may represent the equity required rate of return (cost of internal equity) as follows:

$$R_c = K_c = R_f + \beta(R_m - R_f) \tag{5-10}$$

---

[15]Robert Harris, "Using Analysts' Forecasts to Estimate Shareholder Required Returns," *Financial Management* (Spring 1986), pp. 58–67.

TABLE 5-3
Required Rates of Return
and Risk Premiums

	Government Bond Yield	S&P 500	
		Required Return	Risk Premium
1982			
Quarter 1	14.27	20.81	6.54
Quarter 2	13.74	20.68	6.94
Quarter 3	12.94	20.23	7.29
Quarter 4	10.72	18.58	7.86
Average	12.92	20.08	7.16
1983			
Quarter 1	10.87	18.07	7.20
Quarter 2	10.80	17.76	6.96
Quarter 3	11.79	17.90	6.11
Quarter 4	11.90	17.81	5.91
Average	11.34	17.88	6.54
1984			
Quarter 1	12.09	17.22	5.13
Quarter 2	13.21	17.42	4.21
Quarter 3	12.83	17.34	4.51
Quarter 4	11.78	17.05	5.27
Average	12.48	17.26	4.78
1982–1984 Average	12.25	18.41	6.16

Source: Robert Harris, "Using Analysts' Forecasts to Estimate Shareholder Required Returns," *Financial Management,* Spring 1986, p. 62.

where R_c, K_c = the required rate of return of the equity shareholders, and also the cost of internal equity capital

R_f = the risk-free rate

β = beta, or the measure of a share's systematic risk

R_m = the expected rate of return for the market as a whole— that is, the expected return for the "average security"

For example, assume the risk-free rate is 7 percent, the expected return in the market is 16 percent, and the beta for Talbot Corporation's common shares is .82. Then the cost of internal equity would be estimated as follows:

$$K_c = 7\% + .82(16\% - 7\%)$$

$$R_f \quad \beta \quad R_m \quad R_f$$

$$= 14.4\%$$

Perspective in Finance

The CAPM says that an investor's required rate of return is equal to the risk-free rate plus a risk premium, where the only risk of any importance is systematic risk. Systematic risk is measured by beta, which tells us how our shares respond to changes in the general market.

While using the CAPM appears relatively easy, its application is not entirely straightforward, particularly in the corporate setting. In estimating the risk-free rate, the market rate, and the security's beta, the goal is to describe the expectations in the minds of the investors, since it is these expectations that determine how assets are valued. Such a task is difficult. However, as indicated earlier, financial service companies now help provide information about investor expectations.

The Risk-Premium Approach □ Since we know that common shareholders will demand a return premium above the bondholder's required rate of return, we may state the cost of equity as follows:

$$K_c = K_d + RP_c \qquad\qquad (5\text{-}11)$$

where, as before, K_c and K_d represent the cost of internal common equity and debt, respectively. RP_c is the additional return premium common shareholders expect for assuming greater risk than bondholders. Since we can compute the cost of debt with some degree of confidence, the key to estimating the cost of equity is in knowing RP_c, the risk premium.

We again are in some difficulty, because we have no direct means of computing RP_c. We can only draw from our experience, which tells us that the risk premium of a firm's common shares relative to its own bonds has for the most part been between 3 and 5 percent. In times when interest rates are historically high, the premium is usually low. In years when interest rates are at historical lows, the premium has been higher. Using an average premium of 4 percent, we would approximate the cost of equity capital as follows:

$$K_c = K_d + 4\%$$

For a firm with A++ rated bonds that have a cost of 9 percent, the cost of equity would be estimated to be 13 percent (9 percent cost of debt plus the 4 percent average premium); a more risky company, with bonds that are rated B++ with a 13 percent cost, could expect its cost of equity to approximate 17 percent (13 percent + 4 percent).

The risk-premium approach is somewhat similar in concept to CAPM in that both recognize that common shareholders require a risk premium. The differences between the two approaches come from using different beginning points (CAPM uses the risk-free rate and the risk-premium approach uses the firm's cost of debt) and in how the risk premium is estimated. Both estimates of the risk premium involve subjectivity; however, CAPM has a more developed conceptual basis. Even so, the risk-premium approach is at times the best we can do, especially when the dividend-growth model and the CAPM give unreasonable estimates. Even if the dividend-growth and CAPM approaches are thought to fit the situation, the risk-premium technique gives us a good way to verify the reasonableness of our results.

COST OF NEW COMMON SHARES ■ If internal common equity does not provide all the equity capital needed for new investments, the firm may need to issue new common shares. Again, this capital should not be acquired from the investors unless the expected returns on the prospective investments exceed a rate sufficient to satisfy the shareholders' required rate of return. Since the required rate of return of common shareholders was measured using Equation (5-11), the only adjustment necessary is to consider the potential issuing costs incurred from issuing the shares. We recognize the issuing costs by reducing the market price of the shares by the after-tax issuing costs.[16] Thus, the cost of new common shares, K_{nc}, is

$$K_{nc} = \frac{D_1}{NP_0} + g \tag{5-12}$$

where NP_0 equals the net proceeds after-tax per share received by the company. Suppose that the after-tax issuing costs are 15 percent of the market price, the cost of capital for the new common shares, or external common, would be 15.18 percent, calculated as follows:

$$K_{nc} = \frac{\$2.20}{\$50 - .15(\$50)} + .10$$

$$= \frac{\$2.20}{\$42.50} + .10 = .1518$$

$$= 15.18\%$$

In this example, if management achieves a 15.18 percent return on the net capital received from common shareholders, it will satisfy the investors' required rate of return of 14.4 percent, as determined earlier by Equation (5-11).

Selection of Capital Structure Weights

The individual costs of capital will be different for each source of capital in the firm's capital structure. To use these costs of capital in our investment analyses, we must compute a composite or weighted average cost of capital. The weights for computing this overall cost should reflect the market values of the different sources in the corporation's financing mix. For instance, the balance sheet may indicate that creditors have financed 30 percent of the investments and that the common shareholders have provided the remaining 70 percent. These proportions represent an accounting perspective whereby the balance sheet carries debt and common shares at their book values. Remember that the book values of these financial instruments are the historical costs at which these instruments were issued in the past. However, the perspective in finance is to report the asset value in terms of its present value. Thus, we require a more accurate representation of the proportions of debt and common shares in the financing mix. To achieve this representation, we use the market values of both debt and common shares in determining their proportions in the firm's financing mix. Therefore, the firm's weighted cost of capital reflects the market values of the different sources of financing.

Several choices are available for selecting the financing weights for the weighted cost of capital. Theoretically, the actual mix to be used in financing the proposed investments should be used as the weights. But this approach presents a problem. The costs of capital for individual sources depend upon the firm's financial risk, which in turn is affected by its financial mix.[17] If

---

[16]For another approach to adjusting for flotation costs, see John R. Ezzell and R. Burr Porter, "Flotation Costs and the Weighted Average Cost of Capital," *Journal of Financial and Quantitative Analysis*, 11 (September 1976), 403–413.

[17]During the 1980s, many firms increased their use of debt. Relatively easy access to credit was used to fund office buildings, shopping centres, and housing developments. Many North American firms shifted financing from common shares to debt during the eighties. In addition, the increased debt caused interest payments to absorb a higher proportion of the firm's cash flows. Such large increases in debt have significantly altered the capital structure of most firms and impacted the level of financial risk.

BASIC FINANCIAL MANAGEMENT IN PRACTICE

What Does Equity Financing Really Cost?

Some companies, such as Union Carbide Corp. and UAL Corp., are borrowing heavily to buy their shares. The combination of greater debt and less equity has become preventive medicine for executives who want to keep their jobs. The final word in this struggle for control is the leveraged buyout. Management and private investors buy out all the other shareholders almost entirely with borrowed funds.

But the corporate dislike of equity financing is not just a consequence of merger mania. At first blush, issuing shares rather than bonds might appear to be a cheap way to raise money. After all, the only cost is paying the dividends on those new shares—and not all companies even pay them.

Equity capital is usually more expensive than debt. Just how much more is a matter of great debate among the experts. Says F. Gerard McGrath, a managing director of Prudential-Bache Securities Inc.: "We give clients three answers, and it almost doesn't matter which one they use as long as they understand the implications."

Those who look at the dividend payout as the key to determining the cost of equity point out that when a company floats shares, new shareholders have a claim not only on the current dividend but also on future dividends, which in all likelihood will grow. Suppose Stupendous Corp. stock sells at $25 a share and sports a current dividend of $1 a share. That's a 4% yield. The company expects dividends to grow at 10% a year into the future. So it will be paying out not only $1 in the future, but $1.10 next year and $1.21 the year after, and so on. For a shorthand method of figuring the total cost to the company using the dividend model, add the current yield, 4%, to the growth rate of future dividends, 10%. That means a cost of equity of 14%.

Some companies pay no dividends. But their cost of equity isn't zero, either. When a company sells shares, there may not be out-of-pocket dividend costs, but more people have a stake in the company. The new shareholders have the same claim on earnings as do the existing owners. To keep the share price from falling, the company must create additional earnings each year with the new shareholders' money. The rate that the company must earn on the new money is its "cost" of equity.

Go back to Stupendous Corp., and assume current earnings of $2 per share, and the same 10% growth rate for earnings, too. Divide the $2 by $25, to get the current earnings yield of 8%. Then add the 10% growth rate, which gives a cost of equity of 18%.

Some companies prefer to weigh the cost of equity using the so-called capital asset pricing model (CAPM). The CAPM method is based on the simple idea that the greater the risk in holding a share the greater the return investors must get. If the required return—dividends plus price appreciation—does not look like a reality, then investors will start dumping the shares. They will continue to sell, says the theory, until the share gets so low that it can achieve the expected return, but from a much lower level. Since all shareholders suffer if the share price falls, the real cost of equity capital to the corporation is, in effect, the expected return. If the company can meet the market's expectations, prices will not fall.

The CAPM says that the required return depends on interest rates, the risk of owning shares in general, and the risk in owning a specific company's shares. This calculation starts with a long-term, risk-free rate of return, a government bond. No one buys a share if they think that the total return will be less than that of a government bond.

More Volatile

Next comes the market risk premium. This premium varies, depending on such factors as the outlook for inflation, recession, and even investor sentiment toward shares. Historically this premium runs 4% to 7% a year. Let's use 6%, which means that to be in the stock market at all, investors want 6 percentage points over the risk-free rate.

Finally, there's the risk of owning a specific share, or "beta." This measures the share's volatility compared with the rest of the market. A beta of 1 means that a share's price moves in tandem with the overall market. A beta of 2 means it moves twice as much as the market. For Stupendous, say the beta is 1.15, which means the share is 15% more volatile than the market at large. Multiply the overall risk by Stupendous' beta, which produces 6.9%. Add that

Continued on page 202

management alters the present financial structure, the individual costs will change, making it more difficult to compute the cost of capital. Thus, we will assume that the company's financial mix is relatively stable and that these weights will closely approximate future financing. Although this assumption may not be strictly met in any particular year, firms frequently have a target capital structure (desired debt-equity mix), which is maintained over the long term. The target financing mix provides the appropriate weights to be used in calculating the firm's weighted cost of capital.

EXAMPLE

The Ash Company's current financing mix is contained in Table 5-4. The firm's chief financial officer, Tony Ash, does not want to alter the firm's financial risk, instead he chooses to maintain the same relative mix of capital in financing future investments. Thus, given our assumption of a constant financial mix, we will use these weights which represent market values of the different sources in computing Ash's weighted cost of capital. ∎

Computing the Weighted Cost of Capital

Let's now compute the weighted cost of capital for a firm, which is simply the weighted average of the individual costs, given the firm's financial mix. This calculation is best illustrated with our example.

From Table 5-4, we have estimated Ash's financial mix for the purpose of computing the firm's weighted or overall cost of capital. Let's further assume that management has computed the individual costs of capital for the firm, shown in Table 5-5. For the time being, we will restrict equity financing to the retained earnings available for reinvestment, or internally generated common equity. We are assuming Ash will not issue any new common shares. Therefore, the cost of new common shares is not relevant.

TABLE 5-4
Ash, Inc., Capital Structure

Investor Group	Amount of Funds Raised ($)[a]	Percentage of Total
Bonds	$1,750,000	35%
Preferred shares	250,000	5
Common shares	3,000,000	60%
Total new financing	$5,000,000	100%

[a]Funds raised represent market values.

BASIC FINANCIAL MANAGEMENT IN PRACTICE

Financing Corporate Canada In The 1990's

Looking ahead, Canadian companies must adapt not only to the central bankers' brave new world of price stability, but also global economic growth patterns that will differ markedly from those of the 1980's. Very slow growth in domestic demand is likely. Beyond the global slowdown of the early nineties, rapid growth will be largely found in unfamiliar, difficult markets. Slowdowns in demand always expose weak balance sheets and penalize those who have financed too aggressively. This is a material reality in an environment where the Bank of Canada will likely continue to pursue its goal of price stability within a moderate range.

Industrial Canada's Balance Sheet: 1978, 1988, and 1998

What does all this mean for the financial management of Corporate Canada? Comparing the aggregate balance sheet of large Canadian industrial corporations in 1978 with what it might look like in 1998 is instructive.

There has been a major reduction in working capital ratios during the last decade. Companies now routinely run their operations with less cash, lower receivables, and especially lower inventories. This trend will likely continue. Corporate treasurers, like their counterparts in physical operations, now have a bewildering array of new tools at their disposal. 'Just-in-time' delivery relates not only to assembly line parts, but also to cash in the payment stream.

Continued Financial Innovation: Implications

Securitization of receivables is now a hot topic. Commodity-linked securities, interest rate swaps and liquid futures and options markets are providing the capacity to restructure and transform the nature of the risks that the corporation must accept. These financial products are permitting corporate treasurers to manipulate the exposure of their companies to the economic factors intrinsic to their business, choosing which risks to accept and which to hedge. The financial markets are serving up a growing menu of these products at increasingly attractive prices.

Accounting standards are coming under great stress in this environment. The visible balance sheet does not necessarily give an accurate picture of a company's position when swaps, hedges, futures, and options are routinely employed to change one

form of risk into another. Regulators have become well aware of the degree to which companies can sidestep one country's taxes and regulations by nimbly shifting operations and assets to another. The result is already visible in heightened international coordination of tax and regulatory policies, but as usual, the bureaucrats are well behind the corporate innovators.

Fixed Assets

Fixed asset investment over the next decade is likely to be dominated by continuing strength in machinery and equipment purchases. As demand growth shifts even further toward export markets, and the pace of technological change continues to be very rapid, there must be a continuing focus on change and renewal. At the same time, tougher environmental regulation will accelerate obsolescence.

Investments in Affiliates

We predict 'investment in affiliates' will be the fastest-growing asset category of Canadian corporate balance sheets. Rising competition from abroad and greater business opportunities in foreign markets suggest that cross-border affiliations and associations will be useful and important. Marketing in one country, production in others, financial direction in a third: all this is becoming familiar. Since 1978, the share of corporate assets described as 'long-term equity investment in affiliated Canadian companies' has doubled, and the share of 'long-term equity investment in affiliated foreign companies' has tripled.

The Liability Side of the Balance Sheet

On the liability side, short-term bank loans are likely to continue to diminish in importance, as the working capital they support dwindles down. Thus while short-term bank financing will continue to play an important role during cyclical downturns, its secular trend continues to be downward. In the 'permanent finance' category, the key question is whether debt or equity will play an increased role over time. While profits decline and investment outlays continue to grow in the short term, corporations are financing with debt, causing the debt/equity ratio to rise in the short term.

Continued on page 204

203

Continued from page 203

Debt/Equity Ratios Unlikely To Trend Upwards

Our longer term view is that debt/equity ratios will not rise significantly during the 1990's. The average 1978 debt/equity ratio for (all, not just industrial) Canadian non-financial corporations was 0.86. In the midst of the 1982 recession, it climbed to 1.09. In the extended subsequent recovery, it was reduced back below 0.9. By 1991, given our forecast of slowing world growth, falling commodity prices and domestic disinflation, the ratio will likely have climbed to over 1.0 again. Longer term, we believe the corporate sector will want to make another assault on even lower debt ratios. We think that the ratio will be below 0.9 again in the late 1990's.

Major Upturn in Capital Availability Likely

Canada could become a major capital exporter before the end of the decade. Today, an excessive amount of domestic saving has to be devoted to financing the fiscal deficit. A further big chunk has been going to finance the house buying ambitions of the baby-boom generation. But these pressures will likely fall off over the next few years. Meanwhile, personal saving itself should increase at a healthy pace encouraged by major shifts in tax structure. The GST represents a shift from taxing personal income to taxing consumption.

Also, tax sheltered contribution rates to money-purchase pension plans and Registered Retirement Savings Plans (RRSPs) are soon to rise. And contractual saving, such as the rollover of investment income in trusteed pensions plans and RRSPs, continue to rise.

Much of New Canadian Financial Capital Will Be Risk-Seeking

Much of the large amounts of institutional money that will be available for investment, as well as some of the rapidly growing non-institutionally managed pools of capital based on self-directed RRSPs and closed-end mutual funds will be risk capital. One impetus is the trend toward relaxing investment restrictions on institutional investors through the adoption of 'prudent portfolio' pension investment rules. Also financial institutions and financial intermediaries, faced with intense competition, lower margins and the greater savings inflows, will be increasingly willing to consider higher-risk investment alternatives to achieve satisfactory returns.

For these reasons, we are likely to see very heavy participation by Canadian savers in equity finance for Canadian companies, more than they will in fact need to finance domestic operations. Fortunately, the government has recognized the desirability of encouraging international diversification by Canadian pension funds, permitting them to move over the next five years to place up to 20%, instead of only 10% of their portfolios in foreign assets.

Foreign Portfolio Investors Will Be a Factor Too

Canadian corporations have enjoyed relatively easy access to foreign capital markets. Earlier, we focused on the increasing role foreign direct investment will play in shaping Canadian corporate balance sheets. But it is wrong to ignore the role foreign portfolio investors could play. Currency hedging is increasingly cost-effective. Complex international swaps are now increasingly matter-of-course. So large corporations will increasingly access global markets for their financing in the 1990's.

Unregulated off-shore markets will from time to time provide attractive financing opportunities to those Canadian corporations with the credit quality to access them. Liquid markets in interest rate and currency swaps will facilitate financing abroad. In the 1980's, international markets provided very attractive sources of debt financing to Canadian corporations. In the 1990's, this availability of funding should extend to equities, a process that has already begun with the privatization initiatives in the U.K. and Europe.

A New Canadian Competitive Advantage: Risk Finance

We conclude that Canadian corporations will not be without some important competitive advantages as they face the demanding 1990's. They may not be world leaders in R&D or have special entries into some emerging new growth markets. But they do have access to a well-educated labour force, unbounded natural resources, strong infrastructure, and good international linkages to export markets. This article points to yet another emerging strength Canadian corporations have: good access to a broad range of risk finance. May they use it productively.

Source: An excerpt from "Financing Corporate Canada In The 1990's," by John Grant, Mary Webb and Peter Hendrick in *Canadian Investment Review*, 3 (Spring 1990), p. 9.

TABLE 5-5
After-tax Component Costs
of Capital for Ash, Inc.

Investor Group	After-Tax Component Costs
Bonds	7%
Preferred shares	13
Common equity	
Internally generated common	16
New common	18

(1) Investor Group	(2) Weight[a]	(3) Individual After-Tax Costs[b]	(4) Weighted Costs
Bonds	35%	7%	2.45%
Preferred shares	5	13	0.65
Common equity			
(internally generated)	60	16	9.60%
Weighted cost of capital (K_0)			12.70%

[a]Taken from the desired financing mix presented in Table 5-4.
[b]Taken from Table 5-5.

Table 5-6 combines the weights from Table 5-4 and the individual cost for each security from Table 5-5 into a single weighted cost of capital. Given that the assumptions of the weighted cost of capital concept are met and that common equity requirements can be satisfied internally, the company's weighted cost of capital is 12.7 percent. This rate is the firm's minimum acceptable rate of return for new investments.

We have now observed the process for measuring a firm's weighted cost of capital. We cannot overstate the importance of this calculation with respect to evaluating investment proposals. However, the limiting effects of our assumptions, such as the requirement of constant business and finance risk, reduces the level of confidence which we can place in the measurement techniques. At best, we can only approximate the firm's weighted cost of capital. Our approximation can be improved upon by testing our results over a reasonable range of values, as is done in sensitivity analyses.

We now examine the effects of the level of financing on the firm's cost of capital. In other words, as the firm continues to raise more capital for investment purposes, how is the cost of capital affected?

Level of Financing and the Weighted Cost of Capital

In the previous example, we assumed that no new common shares were to be issued. If new common shares are to be issued, the firm's weighted cost of capital will increase, because external equity capital has a higher cost than internal equity due to the issuing costs.

Generally the firm should use its cheapest sources of funds first, while maintaining its desired debt-equity mix. In other words, since internally generated funds cost less, they should be blended with debt until fully exhausted.

Beyond this point, the weighted cost of capital increases, since the firm has to rely on new shares for its equity financing. This basic concept is best explained through an example.[18]

The Crisp Corporation, an independent oil company, is contemplating three major capital investments this year. The first proposal is the acquisition of equipment used to examine geological formations. This new equipment should improve the success ratio in discovering productive oil and gas reserves. The second proposal requires an investment into water flooding equipment. This process involves the injection of large amounts of water into underground reserves, which permits a more efficient recovery of the minerals. The third proposal involves an investment into new and advanced drilling equipment which will offer cost savings in drilling for oil and gas. The costs and expected returns for these three possible investments are shown in Table 5-7. Management must decide which of these projects should be accepted.

If any of the proposed projects are accepted, the financing will consist of 50 percent debt and 50 percent common equity. Based upon the anticipated profits this year, the company should have $1,500,000 in profits for reinvestment (internally generated common equity). The costs of capital for each source of financing have been computed and are presented in Table 5-8.

The weighted cost of capital, K_0, would be calculated as follows:

$$K_0 = [(\text{percentage of debt financing}) \times (\text{cost of debt})] + \quad (5\text{-}13)$$
$$[(\text{percentage of common equity financing})$$
$$\times (\text{cost of common equity})]$$

If only internally generated common equity is utilized, the weighted cost of capital is 10 percent.

$$K_0 = [(50\%)(6\%) + (50\%)(14\%)] = 10 \text{ percent}$$

However, when new common shares are used rather than internally generated common equity, the weighted cost of capital is 12 percent:

$$K_0 = [(50\%)(6\%) + (50\%)(18\%)] = 12 \text{ percent} \blacksquare$$

TABLE 5-7
Crisp Corporation's
Investment Opportunities

	Investment Cost	Expected Internal Rate of Return
Geological equipment	$1,500,000	14%
Water flooding equipment	2,000,000	18
Drilling equipment	2,500,000	11

TABLE 5-8
Crisp Corporation's
Individual Costs of Capital

Source	Cost
Debt (after-tax)	6%
Internally generated common equity ($1,500,000)	14
New common shares	18

[18]Although we assume a constant debt-equity mix, we have no reason or need to assume a constant mix between internally generated equity and new common shares. Rather, we assume that we first use internal equity funds until exhausted; if more equity is needed, we issue new common shares.

Which weighted cost of capital should be used in evaluating the three investments?

To answer this question, we must first rank the projects in descending order by their respective internal rates of return. Second, we must calculate the level of total financing at which point our internally generated common equity is exhausted. In the Crisp Corporation example, $3 million in total new investments may be financed with debt and internally generated common equity, without having to change the present financial mix of 50 percent debt and 50 percent common equity and without having to issue common shares. The $3 million is determined by solving the following equation:

$$\begin{array}{ccc} \text{internally generated} & & \text{percentage} & & \text{total financing} \\ \text{common equity} & = & \text{of common} & \times & \text{from all} \\ \text{financing available} & & \text{equity financing} & & \text{sources} \end{array}$$

For the Crisp Corporation,

$$\$1,500,000 = 50\% \times \text{total financing}$$

which indicates that if Crisp has $1,500,000 in internally generated common equity, and management maintains a 50 percent debt ratio, Crisp will be able to finance $3 million of total investments without issuing new common shares. Equation (5-13) may be changed to solve directly for the amount of total financing:

$$\frac{\text{total financing}}{\text{from all sources}} = \frac{\text{internally generated common equity}}{\text{percentage of common equity financing}}$$

$$= \frac{\$1,500,000}{.50}$$

$$= \$3,000,000$$

Therefore, for a total investment level of $3 million or less, the firm's weighted cost of capital is expected to be 10 percent. Beyond this level of total financing our internally generated common equity is totally exhausted, and the weighted cost of capital increases to 12 percent. This reflects the increased cost of the common shares to be issued beyond the $3 million in total financing from both debt and common equity.

Figure 5-5 illustrates the relationship between the weighted costs of capital and the amount of financing being sought. The graph depicts the firm's **weighted marginal cost of capital**. The term *marginal* is used because the computed cost of capital shows the weighted cost of each additional dollar of financing. This marginal cost of capital represents the appropriate criterion for making investment decisions. Thus, the firm should continue to invest up to the point where the marginal rate of return earned on the new investment (IRR) equals the marginal cost of new capital. Figure 5-6 illustrates this comparison in which the firm's optimal investment schedule or capital budget is found to be $3,500,000. The company should invest in water flooding machinery and the geological equipment. However, since the weighted marginal cost of capital is greater than the expected internal rate of return of the drilling equipment, this investment should be rejected.

The Effect of New Financing on the Marginal Cost of Capital

Thus far, we have considered only the effect of increases of issuing new common shares on the weighted marginal cost of capital. Similar effects will

FIGURE 5-5
Crisp Corporation's
Weighted Marginal Cost of
Capital

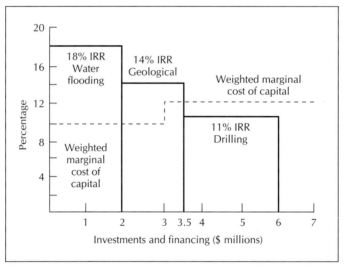

occur as the cost of any source of financing increases. If the 6 percent cost of debt capital for Crisp Corporation increased to 8 percent after the firm issued $2 million in bonds, an increase in the weighted marginal cost of capital would have occurred at the $4 million financing level from all sources. This break in the marginal cost of capital curve is determined as

$$\frac{\text{total financing available}}{\text{with the lower-cost debt}} = \frac{\text{total debt available at lower cost}}{\text{percentage of debt financing}} \quad (5\text{-}15)$$

$$= \frac{\$2,000,000}{.5}$$

$$= \$4,000,000$$

As a general rule, changes in the weighted marginal cost of capital will take place when the cost of an individual source increases. The break in the marginal cost of capital curve will occur at the dollar financing level in which

$$\frac{\text{total financing}}{\text{from all sources}} = \frac{\text{maximum amount of a lower-cost source of capital}}{\text{percentage financing provided by the source}} \quad (5\text{-}16)$$

Summary of Computations

1. Determine the percentage of financing to be used from each source of capital (debt, preferred shares, and common equity).

2. Compute the points on the marginal cost of capital curve where the weighted cost will increase.

3. Calculate the costs of each individual source of capital.

4. Compute the weighted cost of capital for the company, which will be different as the amount of financing increases.

5. Construct a graph that compares the internal rates of return with the weighted cost of capital, which will indicate which investments should be accepted.

MARGINAL COST OF CAPITAL: A COMPREHENSIVE EXAMPLE

To help bring together the principles for computing a firm's weighted cost of capital, consider J. N. Williams, Inc., a manufacturer of medical and surgical instruments. The firm's desired financing mix is presented in Table 5-9. Management attempts to maintain a relatively constant capital structure mix from year to year.

The most recent earnings per share (1993) was $8, which was twice the earnings per share in 1987, and this represents a growth rate of 12 percent.[19] Dividends and the market price of the firm's common shares have grown at the same rate. The dividend payout ratio, which equals the ratio of common dividends to earnings available to common, has been 50 percent, and J. Nathan Williams, president, intends to hold to this dividend policy in the future.[20] Five potential investments are being examined by the company for 1994. The costs and the expected internal rates of return for these projects are provided in Table 5-10. To finance these investments, Williams expects to have $500,000 from 1994 retained earnings available for reinvestment, and new security issues can be sold. The firm's current financing mix will be

Capital Structure	(%)
Total Liabilities and Equity Mix	
Bonds	30.0
Preferred shares	7.5
Common shares	62.5
Total liabilities and equity	100.0

TABLE 5-9
J. N. Williams, Inc., December 31, 1993

---

[19]This growth rate is computed by dividing the 1994 earnings per share by the 1988 earnings per share, $8/$4 = 2, which represents the compound interest factor for six years at 12 percent. That is, [EPS 1988 $(1 + g)^6$ = EPS 1994], or $4(1 + g)^6$ = $8; thus, $(1 + g)^6$ = $8/$4 = 2. Looking up a compound interest factor of two for six years in Appendix A, we find it corresponds to a growth rate of 12 percent. The same solution could be found by using the present value equation or even more easily by using a financial calculator.

[20]Dividend policy is discussed in Chapter 10.

TABLE 5-10
J. N. Williams, Inc., 1994
Investment Opportunities

Investment	Estimated Cost	Projected Internal Rates of Return
A	$ 450,000	22%
B	500,000	19
C	300,000	17
D	250,000	14
E	500,000	12
Total proposed budget	$2,000,000	

maintained and the firm's business risk should not change. The following information is available regarding the individual costs of capital:

1. **Bonds.** An amount not exceeding $240,000 could be issued in new bonds. The issue, after considering the effect of issuing costs, would have an effective before-tax cost of 13 percent. If additional debt is required, the effective yield would have to be increased to 16 percent. The combined corporate tax rate is 44 percent.

2. **Preferred shares.** New preferred shares could be issued by Williams with a par value of $50, paying $6 in annual dividends. The market price of the security is $45, but $1.80 per share in after-tax issuing costs would be incurred. Additional preferred shares can also be sold at $45; however, the issuing costs would be $3.33 per share.

3. **Common shares.** Common shares can be sold at the existing $75 market price. If the issue size is not greater than $375,000, a 15 percent after-tax issuing cost would result. For any additional common shares, the after-tax issuing costs would increase to 20 percent of the market price.

With the foregoing information and by using the following five steps, we can construct a weighted marginal cost of capital curve.

Step 1: Determine the financial mix. In Table 5-9, the desired financial mix for Williams was shown to be 30 percent in debt, 7.5 percent in preferred shares, and 62.5 percent in common equity. For Step 1, we assume that future financing will be made in the same proportions.

Step 2: Compute when costs will increase. With the above weights and knowing the amount of capital available at each cost, we can compute the points at which the marginal cost curve will occur. Remember that an increase in the weighted cost of capital occurs when one of the individual costs increases. For example, if the cost of debt rises, the weighted cost must also be higher. We need to know where these increases in weighted costs will occur. For Williams, Inc., we know that the cost of the bonds increases if we issue more than $240,000 in new bonds. If debt represents 30 percent of all sources, how much in total financing will be possible before this increase in debt financing (bonds) affects the weighted marginal cost of capital? Using Equation (5-16), we see that the weighted cost will increase when $800,000 in total capital has been raised, which is computed as follows:

$$\frac{\text{total financing available}}{\text{with the lower-cost debt}} = \frac{\text{total debt available at lower cost}}{\text{percentage of debt financing}}$$

$$= \frac{\$240,000}{.3}$$

$$= \$800,000$$

In other words, when we raise $800,000 in total financing and 30 percent is from debt, we will have used $240,000 in bonds (30 percent of $800,000). This same procedure must be followed for increases in the cost of preferred shares and for common equity, both for internally generated common equity and for new common shares. These calculations are shown in Table 5-11, and the results indicate two breaks in the curve. Increases in the marginal cost of capital curve occur as the amount of total financing reaches $800,000 (cost of debt and common equity simultaneously increase), and $1,400,000 (cost of preferred shares increase and cost of common equity increases). Figure 5-7 illustrates this result.

Debt	30.0%	$240,000
Preferred shares	7.5%	60,000
Common shares	62.5%	500,000
Total		$800,000

Step 3: *Calculate the cost of individual sources.* The next step requires computing the individual costs of capital, which is presented in Table 5-11. For debt the cost needs only to be adjusted by Williams's combined corporate income tax rate. For a 44 percent income tax rate, the 13 percent and 16 percent costs of debt have an effective

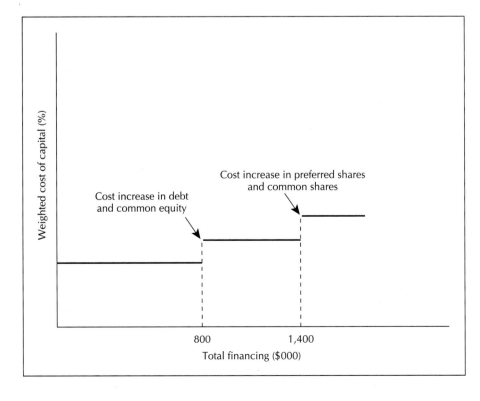

Source	Cost Calculations
I. Debt	after-tax cost of bonds = before-tax cost $(1 - \text{tax rate})$
(a) $0–240,000	$K_d = 13\% \ (1 - .44) = 7.3\%$
(b) Over $240,000	$K_d = 16\% \ (1 - .44) = 9.0\%$
II. Preferred shares	$\text{cost of preferred} = \left(\dfrac{\text{dividend per share}}{\text{market price less issuing costs}} \right)$
(a) $0–105,000	$K_p = \dfrac{\$6}{\$45 - \$1.80} = 13.9\%$
(b) Over $105,000	$K_p = \dfrac{\$6}{\$45 - \$3.33} = 14.4\%$
III. Common financing A. Internally generated common equity	$\text{cost of internal common} = \dfrac{\text{dividend in one year}}{\text{market price}} + \text{growth}$
$0-$500,000	$K_c = \dfrac{\$4(1 + .12)}{\$75} + .12 = 18.0\%$
B. New common shares	$\begin{matrix}\text{cost of new}\\ \text{common shares}\end{matrix} = \left(\dfrac{\text{dividend per share}}{\text{market price less issuing costs}} \right) + \text{growth}$
(a) $0–$375,000	$K_{nc} = \dfrac{\$4(1 + .12)}{\$75 - \$11.25} + .12 = 19.0\%$
(b) Over $375,000	$K_{nc} = \dfrac{\$4(1 + .12)}{\$75 - \$15} + .12 = 19.5\%$

after-tax cost of 7.3 percent and 9.0 percent, respectively. The cost of preferred shares, which equals the dollar dividend relative to the net price per share received by the company, equals 13.9 percent for the first $105,000 and 14.4 percent for any greater amounts. The cost of internally generated common equity equals the dividend yield (the forthcoming dividend per share/price) plus the expected growth in dividends. An annual compound growth rate of 12 percent is estimated from the past growth in earnings per share. The dividend yield plus the 12 percent growth rate produces an 18 percent cost of internally generated common equity. The cost of new common shares is easily determined by adjusting the required rate of return of the common shareholders by the issuing costs in issuing the shares. These calculations yield a cost of new common shares up to $375,000 of 19 percent, and 19.5 percent for amount exceeding $375,000.

Step 4: *Solve for the weighted marginal cost of capital.* With the preceding information, the weighted marginal costs of capital relative to the funds raised may be determined. Since the weighted cost of capital does not change for the first $800,000 in total financing, the weighted marginal cost of capital is determined by using the lowest costs of the individual sources. The weighted costs of financing up to $800,000 are calculated in Table 5-12. The percentage of capital that would be provided by each source is presented in column 2, and the cost of each individual source of capital appears in column 3 (taken from Table 5-11). Multiplying the weights (column 2) by

(1) Source	(2) Proportions	(3) Cost of Capital	(4) Weighted Cost of Capital (2 × 3)
Bonds	30.0%	7.3%	2.19%
Preferred shares	7.5%	13.9%	1.04%
Common equity	62.5%	18.0%	11.25%
	100.0%		
		Weighted cost of capital:	14.48%

(1) Source	(2) Proportions	(3) Cost of Capital	(4) Weighted Cost of Capital (2 × 3)
Bonds	30.0%	7.3%	2.19%
Preferred shares	7.5%	13.9%	1.04%
Common equity	62.5%	19.5%	12.19%
	100.0%		
		Weighted cost of capital:	15.42%

the individual costs (column 3) and summing the results produce a weighted cost of 14.48 percent. This cost applies to any amount of financing (including debt, preferred shares, and common equity) up to but not exceeding $800,000.

After the first $800,000 has been used to finance new investments, the cost of common equity will increase. The costs increase because we will have exceeded $240,000 in debt and $500,000 in common equity. Taking the increased costs from Table 5-11 for these two sources (cost of preferred shares has not changed), we calculate a weighted marginal cost of capital for an amount greater than $800,000, but not exceeding $1,400,000. This weighted cost would now be 15.42 percent, as is given in Table 5-13, where the new cost for common equity is shown in the boxes. Otherwise, the calculation is no different from the weighted cost of capital for less than $800,000.

Should the firm finance over $1,400,000, the weighted marginal cost of capital will again rise. Since we now need over $105,000 in preferred shares and $875,000 in common equity in order to raise more than $1,400,000 in total financing, the costs of preferred shares and common equity will increase. These new costs are presented in Table 5-14. They result in a final weighted cost of capital of 16.27 percent.

In summary, the weighted cost of capital for J. N. Williams, Inc., increases as the amount of money needed becomes larger, with the costs being as follows:

Total Financing	Weighted Cost
$0–$800,000	14.48%
$800,001–$1,400,000	15.42%
Over $1,400,000	16.27%

(1) Source	(2) Proportions	(3) Cost of Capital	(4) Weighted Cost of Capital (2 × 3)
Bonds	30.0%	9.0%	3.00%
Preferred shares	7.5%	14.4%	1.08%
Common equity	62.5%	19.5%	12.19%
	100.0%		
		Weighted cost of capital:	16.27%

Step 5: *Compare investment returns with weighted costs.* The weighted marginal costs of capital are to be used in determining whether to accept any or all of the investment prospects being reviewed by Williams. A ranking of the projects, taken from Table 5-10, and a comparison of the returns against the weighted costs of capital are given in Figure 5-8. As is evident from the figure, Williams's optimal capital budget for 1994 is $1,250,000. The particular investments that should be included in the budget are projects A and B, with the returns for projects C, D, and E falling short of the weighted cost of capital hurdle rate.

Perspective in Finance

For large strategic investments, which differ significantly from the company's previous investments, the company-wide cost of capital is an inappropriate measure of the opportunity cost of financing the investment. For these types of investments, we will need to develop a specific hurdle rate.

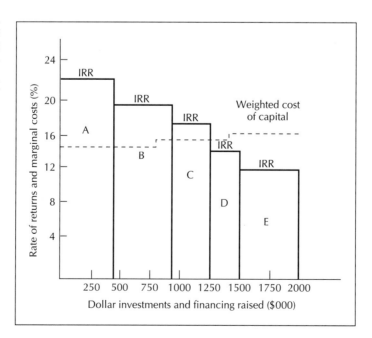

REQUIRED RATE OF RETURN FOR INDIVIDUAL PROJECTS: AN ALTERNATIVE APPROACH

Two basic assumptions were made in the preceding sections in computing the firm's weighted cost of capital as a cutoff rate for new capital investments. First, the riskiness of the project being evaluated is assumed to be similar to the riskiness of the company's existing assets. In other words, acceptance of the investment will not alter the firm's overall business risk. Second, future investments are assumed to be financed in the same proportions of debt, preferred shares, and common shares as past investments. Frequently these two assumptions are not met in practice. Firms often do make investments that have risk characteristics different from the firm's existing assets. The firm may also finance a given project with all debt, and then rely solely on equity for the next investment. Also, given the nature of an investment, the firm may be able to use more debt than what was possible for prior investments.

Figure 5-9 illustrates the problem that occurs from using the weighted cost of capital for projects having different levels of risk. The line which represents the firm's weighted cost of capital, K_0, does not allow for varying levels of project risk and is appropriate only for projects having a level of risk at point RL_0. The same figure illustrates the **risk-return line** which describes an increasing cost of capital with increasing levels of risk. In other words, we should use different costs of capital (required rates of return) for investments having different levels of risk. Investments A and B in Figure 5-9 illustrate any incorrect decisions that might result from the use of the firm's cost of capital as the cutoff rate for project acceptance where the risk inherent in A is below the firm's risk level of RL_0 and project B's risk exceeds RL_0. Investment A would be rejected and investment B accepted if the required rate being used were the weighted marginal cost of capital. However, if the

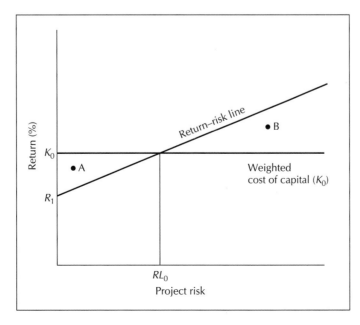

FIGURE 5-9
Return–Risk Relationship

return-risk line accurately measures the market return-risk relationship, investment A should be accepted and investment B rejected. Although the expected return for investment A is below the firm's weighted marginal cost of capital, the reduction in risk sufficiently justifies accepting the investment's lower expected return.

In determining a fair or appropriate rate of return for a given level of project risk, we will examine the different types of risk. We could think of risk as the total variability in returns for the investment, without regard for how it relates to the firm's other investments. This type of risk is called *project risk* or *risk in isolation*. We could alternatively think of the risk in terms of its contribution to the riskiness of the firm's portfolio of assets. Taking this contribution-to-firm approach, we would measure risk as the standard deviation of the returns for all the firm's assets taken together including the new project. A third option, and the one we choose to take is to see risk in terms of risk to shareholders. We assume that the firm's investors hold a diversified portfolio of investments and that we want our measure of risk to indicate how much incremental risk from the project is added to the investors' (not the firm's) diversified portfolio. In this situation, the Capital Asset Pricing Model (CAPM) provides us with a technique to evaluate a project. Using the CAPM, the required rate of return for the *j*th project may be expressed as follows:[21]

$$K_j = R_f + (R_m - R_f)\beta_j \tag{5-17}$$

where β_j (beta) identifies the volatility of the *j*th project returns relative to the investor's widely diversified portfolio. Thus, β_j represents the effect of the *j*th project upon the riskiness of the investor's portfolio, which is also the relevant risk used in the market to value the asset. As in Chapter 3, R_m and R_f represent the expected return for the diversified portfolio and for a risk-free asset, respectively.[22]

EXAMPLE

To illustrate the use of the capital asset pricing model for determining the required rate of return for a project, suppose that a firm is considering a capital investment with an expected return of 16 percent. Management believes that the riskiness of the project should be analyzed in terms of its contribution to the risk of a diversified investor's portfolio. The expected return for a diversified portfolio of assets, R_m, is 14 percent, and the risk-free rate, R_f, is

[21]For further explanation, see Ezra Solomon, "Measuring a Company's Cost of Capital," *Journal of Business* (October 1955), pp. 95–117; Steward C. Myers, "Interactions of Corporate Financing and Investment Decision—Implications for Capital Budgeting," *Journal of Finance* (March 1974), pp. 1–25; Richard S. Bower and Jeffrey M. Jenks, "Divisional Screening Rates," *Financial Management* (Autumn 1975), pp. 42–49; Donald I. Tuttle and Robert H. Litzenberger, "Leverage Diversification and Capital Market Effects on a Risk-Adjusted Capital Budgeting Framework," *Journal of Finance* (June 1968), pp. 427–443; and John D. Martin and David F. Scott, Jr., "Debt Capacity and the Capital Budgeting Decision," *Financial Management* (Summer 1976), pp. 7–14.

[22]For our purposes, we shall assume that the firm finances all its investments with equity. Thus, we need not be concerned with the problems that arise from having to adjust for different financing mixes. This issue is simply beyond the scope of our studies; however to see how it is done, refer to Thomas Conine and Maurry Tamarkin, "Divisional Cost of Capital Estimation: Adjusting For Financial Leverage," *Financial Management* (Spring 1985), pp. 54–58.

6 percent. Management has estimated that the beta for the project is 1.12 which indicates that a 1 percent change in the market portfolio's risk premium (that is, $R_m - R_f$) will produce an expected 1.12 percent change in the investment's risk premium ($K_j - R_f$). We may therefore estimate the appropriate required rate of return for the project, as follows:

$$K_j = R_f + (R_m - R_f)\beta_j \qquad (5\text{-}17)$$
$$= .06 + (.14 - .06)1.12 = .1496$$
$$= 14.96\%$$

Since the 16 percent expected return for the investment exceeds the required rate of return of 14.96 percent, the investment should be made. ∎

While conceptually attractive, the use of the capital asset pricing model in calculating a project required rate of return is difficult, owing to measurement problems. The primary difficulty lies in measuring the project's beta, or the systematic risk of the project. One approach to circumvent this problem is to use the beta of a "pure-play" firm as the project's beta or alternating by using selected accounting data for this purpose. In addition, the model maintains that the relevant risk is limited to the portion of the risk that the investor cannot eliminate through diversification. For this premise to hold, bankruptcy costs are assumed to equal zero if the firm falls. In reality, bankruptcy costs are generally significant. If a project increases significantly the probability of firm bankruptcy, total variability of project returns is the appropriate risk measure.

A FIRM'S COST OF CAPITAL: SOME RECENT EVIDENCE

An interesting survey of the 100 largest corporations listed on the New York Stock Exchange was conducted by Blume, Friend, and Westerfield.[23] In this survey, managers were asked to indicate various cost of capital figures. The results are reported in Table 5-15.

Of the 30 companies that responded to the survey, 10 were public utilities and 20 were nonfinancial corporations from a variety of industries. From the results, we can see that higher costs of capital prevailed when public utilities were excluded, which implies that public utilities are less risky. Even more significant, the results suggest that new common shares are slightly more expensive than internal common (retained earnings) and that internal common is four to five percentage points more costly than the before-tax cost of debt. We should also note that the weighted cost of capital, which falls around 12 to 13 percent, is at the bottom range of the cutoff or hurdle rate used to evaluate investments in plant and equipment. Thus, either new investments were considered more risky than existing investments or management is imposing capital rationing.

[23]Marshall E. Blume, Irwin Friend, and Randolph Westerfield, "Impediments to Capital Formation: Summary Report of a Survey of Nonfinancial Corporations," Working Paper Philadelphia: Wharton School, University of Pennsylvania, 1980, p. 6.

TABLE 5-15. Average Costs of Capital and Investment: Cutoff Rates for Plant and Equipment

Industries	After-tax Cost (%) Before-tax Cost-of-debt	New Common Equity	Retained Earnings	Debt	Weighted Cost	After-tax Cutoff Rate for Plant and Equipment Investments Least Risky	Most Risky
All industries	12.5%	17.2%	16.6%	6.4%	12.4%	12.9%	19.6%
All industries except public utilities	12.5	17.8	17.0	6.3	13.1	13.1	20.3

Source: Marshall E. Blume, Irwin Friend, and Randolph Westerfield, "Impediments to Capital Formation: Summary Report of a Survey of Nonfinancial Corporations," Working Paper, Philadelphia: Wharton School, University of Pennsylvania, 1980, p. 6.

In addition to the results summarized in Table 5-15, the authors found that

1. The dividend-growth model is the most frequently used method for estimating the cost of equity. However, the CAPM is also coming to be used with the dividend-growth model.

2. If management perceives the cost of a particular source to be excessive, it will rely more heavily on other sources. That is, how a firm finances its investments is affected by management's perception of the relative costs of each source of capital.

SUMMARY

The cost of capital is the rate of return that must be achieved on the company's projects in order to satisfy the investor's required rate of return. If the rate of return from the corporation's investments equals the cost of capital, the price of the shares should remain unchanged. In other words, the firm's cost of capital may be defined as the rate of return from an investment that will leave the company's share price unchanged. Therefore, the cost of capital, if certain assumptions are met, represents the minimum acceptable rate of return for new corporate investments.

The factors that affect a firm's cost of capital consist of four components. First, general economic conditions (as reflected in the demand and supply of funds in the economy), as well as inflationary pressures, affect the general level of interest rates. Second, the marketability of the firm's securities has an impact on the cost of capital. Any change in the marketability of a firm's shares will affect investors' required rate of return. These changes directly influence the firm's cost of capital. Third, the firm's operating and financial risks are reflected in its cost of capital. Finally, a relationship exists between a firm's cost of capital and the dollar amount of financing needed for future investments.

Cost of Individual Sources of Financing

The cost of debt is equal to the effective interest rate on new debt adjusted for the tax deductibility of both the firm's interest expense and the firm's issuing expense. The cost of preferred shares is equal to the effective dividend yield on new preferred shares. In making this computation, we should use the net price, the market price less the after-tax issuing costs, received by the company from the new issue. Thus,

$$\text{cost of preferred shares} = \frac{\text{annual dividend}}{\text{net price of preferred shares}} \qquad (5\text{-}7)$$

In calculating the cost of common equity, we distinguish between the costs of internally generated funds and the costs of new common shares. If historical data reasonably reflect the expectations of investors, the cost of internally generated capital is equal to the dividend yield on the common shares plus the anticipated percentage increase in dividends (and in the price of the share) during the forthcoming year. If, however, the common equity is to be acquired by issuing new common shares, the cost of common should recognize the effect of after-tax issuing costs. This alteration results in the following equation for the cost of new common shares:

$$\text{cost of new common} = \frac{\text{dividend in year 1}}{\text{market price} - \text{after-tax issuing cost}}$$
$$+ \text{ annual growth rate in dividends} \qquad (5\text{-}12)$$

where (market price − after-tax issuing cost) is equivalent to the net market price.

We may also compute the cost of equity by using the CAPM or the risk-premium technique.

Weighted Cost of Capital

A firm's weighted cost of capital is a composite of the individual costs of financing weighted by the percentage of financing provided by each source. In this chapter we have assumed that the firm is to finance future investments in the same proportions as past investments. The amount of each different source must be represented by its market value. Hence, the book values of the different sources must be converted to their market values in order to develop the weighting scheme.

Marginal Cost of Capital

Since the amount of financing has an impact upon the firm's weighted cost of capital, the expected return from an investment must be compared with the marginal cost of financing the project. If the cost of capital rises as the level of financing increases, we should use the marginal cost of capital, and not the average cost of all funds raised. Following the basic economic principle of marginal analysis, investments should be made to the point where marginal revenue (internal rate of return) equals the marginal cost of capital.

Measuring the Cost of Capital for Individual Projects

Owing to the limiting assumptions associated with an overall cost of capital for the firm, a single hurdle rate is not generally appropriate for all the investments a firm will analyze. In particular, if the risk associated with a specific investment is significantly different from the firm's existing assets, the weighted cost of capital should not be employed. In this context, a minimum acceptable rate of return that recognizes the different risk levels has to be used. To implement such an approach financial managers must identify the appropriate measure of risk; generally, an analysis of the project's systematic risk through the CAPM model is the best choice.

STUDY QUESTIONS

5-1. Define the term *cost of capital*.

5-2. Why do we calculate a firm's cost of capital?

5-3. In computing the cost of capital, which sources of capital do we consider?

5-4. In general, what factors determine a firm's cost of capital? In answering this question, identify the factors that are within management's control and those that are not.

5-5. What limitations exist in using the firm's cost of capital as an investment hurdle rate?

5-6. How does a firm's tax rate affect its cost of capital? What is the effect of the issuing costs associated with a new security issue?

5-7. **a.** Distinguish between internal common equity and new common shares.

    b. Why is a cost associated with internal common equity?

    c. Compare approaches that could be used in computing the cost of common equity.

5-8. Define the expression *marginal cost of capital*. Why is the marginal cost of capital an appropriate investment criterion?

5-9. How may we avoid the limitation of the weighted cost of capital approach when it requires that we assume business risk is constant?

5-10. What might we expect to see in practice in the relative costs of different sources of capital?

SELF-TEST PROBLEMS

ST-1. (*Individual Costs of Capital*) Compute the cost for the following sources of financing:

    a. A $1,000 par value bond with a market price of $970 and a coupon interest rate of 10 percent. After-tax issuing costs for a new issue would be approximately 5 percent. The bonds mature in 10 years and the combined corporate tax rate is 44 percent.

    b. A preferred share selling for $100 with an annual dividend payment of $8. If the company sells a new issue, the after-tax issuing cost will be $9 per share.

    c. Internally generated common equity totalling $4.8 million. The company's common share sells for $75 and the dividends per share were $9.80 last year. These dividends are expected to increase at an 8-percent growth rate into the indefinite future.

    d. New common shares where the most recent dividend was $9.80. The company's dividends per share should continue to increase at an 8 percent growth rate into the indefinite future. The market price of the share is currently $75; however, after-tax issuing of $6 per share is expected if the new shares are issued.

ST-2. (*Level of Financing*) The Argue Company has the following capital structure mix:

Debt	30%
Preferred shares	15
Common shares	55%
	100%

Assuming that management intends to maintain the above financial structure, what amount of total investments may be financed if the firm (a) restricts its common financing to the $200,000 that is available from internally generated common equity, or (b) uses $200,000 of internally generated common equity plus $300,000 in new common shares?

ST-3. (*Marginal Cost-of-Capital Curve*) The Zenor Corporation is considering three investments. The costs and expected returns of these projects are shown below:

Investment	Investment Cost	Internal Rate of Return
A	$165,000	17%
B	200,000	13
C	125,000	12

The firm would finance the projects by 40 percent debt and 60 percent common equity. The after-tax cost of debt is 7 percent. Internally generated common totaling $180,000 is available, and the common shareholders' required rate of return is 19 percent. If new shares are issued, the after-tax cost will be 22 percent.

a. Construct a weighted marginal cost of capital curve.

b. Which projects should be accepted?

ST-4. (*Weighted Cost of Capital*) David Osborn is the new vice-president-finance for Jozell Brister, Inc. He is preparing his recommendations for the firm's capital budget. With the information provided below, prepare a graph comparing the company's weighted cost of capital and the prospective investment returns. Which investments should be made?

Investment	Investment Cost	Rate of Return
A	$200,000	18%
B	125,000	16
C	150,000	12
D	275,000	10

The firm's capital structure consists of $2 million in debt, $500,000 in preferred shares, and $2.5 million in common equity. This capital mix is to be maintained for future investments.

The cost of debt (before-tax) is 14.14 percent.

The company's preferred shares each sell for $95 and pay a 14 percent dividend rate on a par value of $100. A new offering of this share would entail underwriting costs and a price discount after-tax of 8 percent of the present market price.

The common equity portion of the investments will be financed first by profits retained within the company of $150,000. If additional common financing is needed, new common shares can be issued at the $30 current price less after-tax issuing costs of $6 per share. Management expects to pay a dividend at the end of this year of $2.50, and dividends should increase at an annual rate of 9 percent thereafter. The firm's combined corporate tax rate is 44 percent.

ST-5. (*Individual Project—Required Return*) Scudder Corporation is evaluating three investments that have the expected returns and betas listed below. Managers want to determine the required rates of return of the projects using the capital asset pricing model. The expected return of a diversified portfolio is 15 percent. The rate on Government of Canada bonds is 8 percent. Which investments should they make?

Investment	Expected Return	Beta
A	18.8%	1.1
B	13.5	.90
C	15.0	.80

STUDY PROBLEMS (SET A)

5-1A. (*Individual or Component Costs of Capital*) Suppose that a firm has a combined corporate tax rate of 44 percent. Compute the cost for the following sources of financing:

a. A bond that has a $1,000 par value (face value) and a contract or coupon interest rate of 11 percent. A new issue would have an issuing cost of 5 percent of the $1,125 market value. The bonds mature in 10 years.

b. A new common share issue that paid a $3.27 dividend last year. The earnings per share have grown at a rate of 7 percent per year. This growth rate is expected to continue into the foreseeable future. The company maintains a constant dividend/earnings ratio of 30 percent. The price of this share is now $43.00, but 5 percent after-tax issuing costs are anticipated.

c. Internal common equity where the current market price of the common share is $43. The expected dividend this coming year should be $3.50, increasing thereafter at a 7 percent annual growth rate.

d. A preferred share issue paying a 9 percent dividend on a $150 par value. If a new issue is offered, after-tax issuing costs will be 12 percent of the current price of $175.

e. A bond selling to yield 12 percent after issuing costs, but prior to adjusting for the combined corporate tax rate of 44 percent. In other words, 12 percent is the rate that equates the net proceeds from the bond with the present value of the future cash flows (principal and interest).

5-2A. (*Individual or Component Costs of Capital*) Suppose that a firm has a combined corporate tax rate of 44%. Compute the cost for the following sources of financing:

a. A bond selling to yield 8 percent after issuing cost, but prior to adjusting for the combined corporate tax rate of 44 percent. In other words, 8 percent is the rate that equates the net proceeds from the bond with the present value of the future cash flows (principal and interest).

b. A new common share issue has recently paid a $1.05 dividend. The earnings per share have grown at a rate of 5 percent per year. This growth rate is expected to continue into the foreseeable future. The company maintains a constant dividend/earnings ratio of 40 percent. The price of this share is now $25, but 9 percent after-tax issuing costs are anticipated.

c. A bond that has a $1,000 par value (face value) and a contract or coupon interest rate of 12 percent. A new issue would net the company 90 percent of the $1,150 market value. The bonds mature in 20 years.

d. A preferred share issue paying a 7 percent dividend on a $100 par value. If a new issue is offered, the company can expect to receive a net price of $85 per share.

e. Internal common equity where the current market price of the common share is $25. The expected dividend this forthcoming year should be $1.10, increasing thereafter at a 5 percent annual growth rate.

5-3A. (*Cost of Equity*) Salte Corporation is issuing new common shares at a market price of $27. Dividends last year were $1.45 and are expected to grow at an annual rate of 6 percent forever. After-tax issuing costs will be 6 percent of market price. What is Salte's cost of equity?

5-4A. (*Cost of Preferred Shares*) The preferred shares of Walter Industries sell for $36 and pay $2.50 in dividends. The net price received from the security after tax issuing costs are deducted is $32.50. What is the cost of capital for the preferred shares?

5-5A. (*Cost of Debt*) Belton is issuing a $1,000 par value bond that pays 7 percent annual interest and matures in 15 years. Investors are willing to pay $958 for the bond. Issuing costs will be 11 percent of market value. The company is in a 44 percent tax bracket. What will be the firm's after-tax cost of debt on the bond?

5-6A. (*Cost of Debt*) The Zephyr Corporation is contemplating a new investment to be financed 33 percent from debt. The firm could sell new $1,000 par value bonds at a net price of $945. The coupon interest rate is 12 percent, and the bonds would mature in 15 years. If the company is in a 44 percent tax bracket, what is the after-tax cost of capital to Zephyr for bonds?

5-7A. (*Cost of Preferred Shares*) Your firm is planning to issue preferred shares. The share sells for $115; however, if new shares are issued, the company would receive a net price of $98. The par value of the share is $100 and the dividend rate is 14 percent. What is the cost of capital for the shares to your firm?

5-8A. (*Cost of Internal Equity*) Pathos Co.'s common shares are currently selling for $21.50. Dividends paid last year were $.70. After-tax issuing costs on new shares will be 10 percent of market price. The dividends and earnings per share are projected to have an annual growth rate of 15 percent. What is the cost of internal common equity for Pathos?

5-9A. (*Cost of Debt*) Sincere Stationery Corporation needs to raise $500,000 to improve its manufacturing plant. It has decided to issue a $1,000 par value bond with a 14 percent annual coupon rate and a 10-year maturity. If the investors require a 9 percent rate of return

a. Compute the market value of the bonds.

b. What will the net price be if issuing costs are 10.5 percent of the market price and the combined corporate tax rate is 44 percent?

c. How many bonds will the firm have to issue to receive the needed funds?

d. What is the firm's after-tax cost of debt?

5-10A. (*Cost of Debt*)

a. Rework problem 5-9A assuming a 10 percent coupon rate. What effect does changing the coupon rate have on the firm's after-tax cost of capital?

b. Why is there a change?

5-11A. (*Cost of Equity*) The common share for the Bestsold Corporation sells for $58. If a new issue is sold, the after-tax issuing cost is estimated to be 8 percent. The company pays 50 percent of its earnings in dividends, and a $4 dividend was recently paid. Earnings per share five years ago were $5. Earnings are expected to continue to grow at the same annual rate in the future as during the past five years. The firm's combined corporate tax rate is 44 percent. Calculate the cost of (a) internal common and (b) external common.

5-12A. (*Individual Project—Required Return*) Welton Corporation is evaluating two investments that have the expected returns and betas listed below. Managers want to determine the required rates of return of the projects using the capital asset pricing model. The expected return of a diversified portfolio is 16 percent. The rate on Government of Canada bonds is 7 percent. Which investments should they make?

Investment	Expected Return	Beta
A	15.7%	0.85
B	17.5	1.05

5-13A. (*Weighted Cost of Capital*) The capital structure for the Carion Corporation is provided below. The company plans to maintain its debt structure in the future. If the firm has a 5.5 percent cost of debt, a 13.5 percent cost of preferred shares, and an 18 percent cost of common shares, what is the firm's weighted cost of capital?

Capital Structure ($000)	
Bonds	$1083
Preferred shares	268
Common shares	3681
	$5032

5-14A. (*Individual Project—Required Return*) Hastings, Inc., is analyzing several investments. The expected returns and standard deviations of each project are tabulated below. The firm's cost of capital is 16.5 percent, and the standard deviation of the average project is 7 percent. The current rate on long-term Government of Canada bonds is 8.5 percent. Which investments should the firm accept?

Project	Investment's Expected Return	Standard Deviations of Returns
A	18.0%	7.0%
B	13.8	6.0
C	15.3	7.8
D	11.4	5.0

5-15A. (*Weighted Cost of Capital*) Calvert, Inc.'s capital structure is provided below. Issuing costs would be (a) 15 percent of market value for a new bond issue, (b) after-tax issuing costs of $1.21 per share for common shares, and (c) after-tax issuing costs of $2.01 per share for preferred shares. The dividends for common shares were $2.50 last year and are projected to have an annual growth rate of 6 percent. The firm is in a 44 percent tax bracket. What is the weighted cost of capital if the firm finances in the proportions shown below? Market prices are $1,035 for bonds, $19 for preferred shares, and $35 for common shares. There will be $500,000 of internal common available.

Calvert, Inc., Balance Sheet

Type of Financing	Percentage of Future Financing
Bonds (8%, $1000 par, 16-year maturity)	38%
Preferred shares (5000 shares outstanding, $50 par, $1.50 dividend)	15
Common shares	47
Total	100%

5-16A. (*Weighted Cost of Capital*) The Bach's Candy Corporation has determined the marginal costs of capital for debt after-taxes, preferred shares, and common equity as follows:

Source	Amount of Capital	Cost
Debt	$0–$175,000	4.8%
	$175,001–$300,000	5.5
	Over $300,000	6.0
Preferred shares	$0–50,000	10.0
	$50,001–$75,000	12.0
	Over $75,000	13.0
Common shares	$0–$400,000[a]	15.0
	$400,001–$750,000	18.0
	Over $750,000	22.0

[a]$400,000 is available from internally generated common equity.

The firm maintains a capital mix of 45 percent debt, 5 percent preferred shares, and 50 percent common equity. Construct Bach's weighted marginal cost of capital curve.

5-17A. (*Marginal Cost of Capital*) Mary Basett, Inc., a national advertising firm, is analyzing the following investment opportunities.

Investment	Investment Cost	Internal Rate of Return
A	$ 50,000	14.5%
B	$200,000	17.9
C	$325,000	15.6
D	$125,000	12.4
E	$400,000	10.9
F	$ 75,000	13.8

The information needed to calculate the firm's weighted marginal cost of capital is presented below. Construct Basset's weighted marginal cost of capital curve and decide which investments should be accepted.

Source	Percentage	Amount of Capital	After-tax Cost
Debt	40%	$0–$300,000	4.5%
		Over $300,000	6.0
Preferred shares	8	$0–50,000	9.5
		$50,001–$100,000	10.5
		Over $100,000	11.0
Common shares	52	$0–$520,000	16.0
		Over $520,000	18.0

5-18A. (*Weighted Cost of Capital*) Blacktop Chemical Co. is considering five investments. The cost of each of these investments is shown below. Retained earnings of $650,000 will be available for investment purposes, and management can issue the following securities:

1. **Bonds.** $270,000 can be issued at an after-issuing, before-tax cost of 8.5 percent. Over $270,000 the cost will be 9.75 percent.

2. **Preferred shares.** The shares can be issued at the prevailing market price. The firm incurs issuing costs of $1.55 per share up to an issue size of $90,000 and thereafter $2.80 per share.

3. **Common shares.** The shares will be issued at the market price. For an issue of $250,000 issuing costs will be $1 per share. For any additional issue of common shares, the issuing costs will be $1.75 per share.

The firm's combined tax rate is 44 percent. The firm's common share paid a dividend of $1.80 last year and is expected to grow at an annual rate of 9 percent. Market prices are $975 for bonds, $39 for preferred shares and $23 for common shares. Determine which projects should be accepted, based upon a comparison of the internal rate of return (IRR) of the investments and the weighted marginal cost of capital. The firm's capital structure at market value is shown below, and this mix is to be used for future investments.

Investment	Investment Cost	Internal Rate of Return
A	200,000	16.0%
B	650,000	12.0
C	115,000	9.0
D	875,000	10.0
E	180,000	15.0
Total	$2,020,000	

Capital Structure	Amount of Capital	Percentage of Financing
Bonds (9%, $1000, 18-year maturity)	$3,000,000	43%
Preferred shares (10%, $45 par, 30,000 shares outstanding)	1,350,000	20
Common shares	2,600,000	37
Total	$6,950,000	100%

5-19A. (*Weighted Cost of Capital*) Heard Ski, Inc., is a regional manufacturer of ski equipment. The firm's target financing mix appears as follows:

	Percentage
Debt	30%
Preferred shares	10
Common shares	60%
Total	100%

The firm's management is analyzing the following investment opportunities.

Investment	Investment Cost	Internal Rate of Return
A	$175,000	16.0%
B	$100,000	14.0
C	$125,000	12.0
D	$200,000	10.0
E	$250,000	9.0
F	$150,000	8.0

Using the accept-reject criterion, Paul Heard, president of the firm, has compiled the necessary data for computing the firm's weighted marginal cost of capital. The cost information indicates the following:

1. Debt can be raised at the following after-issuing, before-tax costs:

Amount	Cost
$0–$150,000	8.0%
$150,001–$225,000	9.0
Over $225,000	10.5

2. Preferred shares can be issued paying an annual dividend of $8.50. The par value of the stock is $100. Also, the market price of a preferred share is $100. If new shares were issued, the company would receive a net price of $80 on the first $75,000. Thereafter, the net amount received would be reduced to $75.

3. Common equity is provided first by internally generated funds. Profits for the year that should be available for reinvestment purposes are projected at $150,000. Additional common shares can be issued at the current $72 market price less 15 percent in issuing costs. However, a 20 percent issuing cost is expected if more than $225,000 in new common shares is issued. The dividend per share was $2.75 last year, and the long-term growth rate for dividends is 9 percent.

a. Given that the firm's combined tax rate is 44 percent, compute the firm's weighted marginal cost of capital at a financing level up to $1 million.

b. Construct a graph that presents the firm's weighted marginal cost of capital relative to the amount of financing.

c. What is the appropriate size of the capital budget, and which projects should be accepted?

STUDY PROBLEMS (SET B)

5-1B. (*Individual or Component Costs of Capital*) Suppose that a firm has a combined corporate tax rate of 44%. Compute the cost for the following sources of financing:

a. A bond that has a $1,000 par value (face value) and a contract or coupon interest rate of 12 percent. A new issue would have an issuing cost of 6 percent of the $1,125 market value. The bonds mature in 10 years.

b. New common shares will be issued with an expected dividend of $3.25. The earnings per share have grown at a rate of 7 percent per year. This growth rate is expected to continue into the foreseeable future. The company maintains a constant dividend/earnings ratio of 30 percent. The price of this share is now $43.50, but 5 percent after-tax issuing costs are anticipated.

c. Internal common equity where the current market price of the common share is $43.50. The expected dividend this coming year should be $3.25, increasing thereafter at a 7 percent annual growth rate.

d. A preferred share issue paying a 10 percent dividend on a $125 par value. If a new issue is offered, after-tax issuing costs will be 12 percent of the current price of $150.

e. A bond selling to yield 13 percent after issuing costs, but prior to adjusting for the combined corporate tax rate of 44 percent. In other words, 13 percent is the rate that equates the net proceeds from the bond with the present value of the future cash flows (principal and interest).

5-2B. (*Individual or Component Costs of Capital*) Suppose that a firm has a combined corporate tax rate of 44 percent. Compute the cost for the following sources of financing:

a. A bond selling to yield 9 percent after issuing cost, but prior to adjusting for the combined corporate tax rate of 44 percent. In other words, 9 percent is the rate that equates the net proceeds from the bond with the present value of the future cash flows (principal and interest).

b. A new common share issue has recently paid a $1.25 dividend. The earnings per share have grown at a rate of 6 percent per year. This growth rate is expected to continue into the foreseeable future. The company maintains a constant dividend/earnings ratio of 40 percent. The price of this share is now $30, but 9 percent after-tax issuing costs are anticipated.

c. A bond that has a $1,000 par value (face value) and a contract or coupon interest rate of 13 percent. A new issue would net the company 90 percent of the $1,125 market value. The bonds mature in 20 years.

d. A preferred share issue paying a 7 percent dividend on a $125 par value. If a new issue is offered, the company can expect to receive a net price of $90 per share.

e. Internal common equity where the current market price of the common share is $30. The expected dividend this forthcoming year should be $1.325, increasing thereafter at a 6 percent annual growth rate.

5-3B. (*Cost of Equity*) Falon Corporation is issuing new common shares at a market price of $28. Dividends last year were $1.30 and are expected to grow at an annual rate of 7 percent forever. After-tax issuing costs will be 6 percent of market price. What is Falon's cost of equity?

5-4B. (*Cost of Preferred Shares*) The preferred shares of Gator Industries sell for $35 and pays $2.75 in dividends. The net price received from the security after tax issuing costs are deducted, is $32.50. What is the cost of capital for the preferred shares?

5-5B. (*Cost of Debt*) Temple is issuing a $1,000 par value bond that pays 8 percent annual interest and matures in 15 years. Investors are willing to pay $950 for the bond. Issuing costs will be 11 percent of market value. The company is in a 44 percent tax bracket. What will be the firm's after-tax cost of debt on the bond?

5-6B. (*Cost of Debt*) The Walgren Corporation is contemplating a new investment to be financed 33 percent from debt. The firm could sell new $1,000 par value bonds at a net price of $950. The coupon interest rate is 13 percent, and the bonds would mature in 15 years. If the company is in a 44 percent tax bracket, what is the after-tax cost of capital to Walgren for bonds?

5-7B. (*Cost of Preferred Shares*) Your firm is planning to issue preferred shares. The share sells for $120; however, if new shares are issued, the company would receive a net price of only $97. The par value of the share is $100 and the dividend rate is 13 percent. What is the cost of capital for the shares to your firm?

5-8B. (*Cost of Internal Equity*) Oxford, Inc.'s common share is currently selling for $22.50. Dividends paid last year were $80. After-tax issuing costs on new shares will be 10 percent of market price. The dividends and earnings per share are projected to have an annual growth rate of 16 percent. What is the cost of internal common equity for Oxford?

5-9B. (*Cost of Debt*) Gillian Stationery Corporation needs to raise $600,000 to improve its manufacturing plant. It has decided to issue a $1,000 par value bond with a 15 percent annual coupon rate and a 10-year maturity. If the investors require a 10 percent rate of return

a. Compute the market value of the bonds.

b. What will the net price be if issuing costs are 11.5 percent of the market price and the firm's combined corporate tax rate is 44 percent?

c. How many bonds will the firm have to issue to receive the needed funds?

d. What is the firm's after-tax cost of debt?

5-10B. (*Cost of Debt*)

a. Rework Problem 5-9B assuming a 10 percent coupon rate. What effect does changing the coupon rate have on the firm's after-tax cost of capital?

b. Why is there a change?

5-11B. (*Cost of Equity*) The common shares for the Hetterbrand Corporation sell for $60. If a new issue is sold, the after-tax issuing cost is estimated to be 9 percent. The company pays 50 percent of its earnings in dividends, and a $4.5 dividend was recently paid. Earnings per share five years ago were $5. Earnings are expected to continue to grow at the same annual rate in the future as during the past five years. The firm's combined corporate tax rate is 44 percent. Calculate the cost of (a) internal common and (b) external common.

5-12B. (*Individual Project—Required Return*) Dellington Corporation is evaluating two investments that have the expected returns and betas listed below. Managers want to determine the required rates of return of the projects using the capital asset pricing model. The expected return of a diversified portfolio is 16 percent. The rate on Government of Canada bonds is 7 percent. Which investments should they make?

Investment	Expected Return	Beta
A	20.0%	1.25
B	16.2	.95

5-13B. (*Weighted Cost of Capital*) The capital structure for the Bias Corporation is provided below. The company plans to maintain its debt structure in the future. If the firm has a 6 percent cost of debt, a 13.5 percent cost of preferred shares, and a 19 percent cost of common shares, what is the firm's weighted cost of capital?

Capital Structure ($000)	
Bonds	$1100
Preferred shares	250
Common shares	3700
	$5050

5-14B. (*Individual Project—Required Return*) Badger, Inc., is analyzing several investments. The expected returns and standard deviations of each project are tabulated below. The firm's cost of capital is 16.5 percent, and the standard deviation of the average project is 7 percent. The current rate on long-term Government of Canada bonds is 8.5 percent. Which investments should the firm accept?

Project	Investment's Expected Return	Standard Deviations of Returns
A	20.0%	8.0%
B	16.2	6.8
C	15.0	7.0
D	11.2	6.1

5-15B. (*Weighted Cost of Capital*) R. Stewart, Inc.'s capital structure is provided below. Issuing costs would be (a) 13 percent of market value for a new bond issue, (b) after-tax issuing costs of $1.25 per share for common shares, and (c) after-tax issuing costs of $2.50 per share for preferred shares. The dividends for common shares were $3.25 last year and are projected to have an annual growth rate of 6 percent. The firm is in a 44 percent tax bracket. What is the weighted cost of capital if the firm finances in the proportions shown below? Market prices are $1,040 for bonds, $18 for preferred shares, and $30 for common shares. There will be $250,000 of internal common.

R. Stewart, Inc., Balance Sheet	
Type of Financing	**Percentage of Future Financing**
Bonds (8%, $1000 par, 16-year maturity)	38%
Preferred shares (5000 shares outstanding, $50 par, $1.50 dividend)	15
Common shares	47
Total	100%

5-16B. (*Weighted Cost of Capital*) The Hun Sen Corporation has determined the marginal costs of capital for debt after-taxes, preferred shares, and common equity as follows:

Source	Amount of Capital	Cost
Debt	$0–$200,000	6.0%
	$200,001–$350,000	7.5
	Over $350,000	9.0
Preferred shares	$0–70,000	11.0
	$70,001–$100,000	13.0
	Over $100,000	14.0
Common shares	$0–$500,000[a]	16.0
	$500,001–$750,000	20.0
	Over $750,000	22.0

[a]$500,000 is available from internally generated common equity.

The firm maintains a capital mix of 50 percent debt, 10 percent preferred shares, and 40 percent common equity. Construct Hun Sen's weighted marginal cost of capital curve.

5-17B. (*Marginal Cost of Capital*) TNC, Inc., a national advertising firm, is analyzing the following investment opportunities.

Investment	Investment Cost	Internal Rate of Return
A	$100,000	17.0%
B	$150,000	16.0
C	$325,000	15.0
D	$175,000	9.0
E	$420,000	14.0
F	$100,000	12.0

The information needed to calculate the firm's weighted marginal cost of capital is presented below. Construct TNC's weighted marginal cost of capital curve and decide which investments should be accepted.

Source	Percentage	Amount of Capital	After-tax Cost
Debt	45%	$0–$300,000	7.0%
		Over $300,000	8.0
Preferred shares	10	$0–$50,000	10.0
		$50,001–$100,000	11.0
		Over $100,000	13.0
Common shares	45	$0–$520,000	18.0
		Over $520,000	20.0

5-18B. (*Weighted Cost of Capital*) The Hannitin Co. is considering five investments. The cost of each of these investments is shown below. Retained earnings of $850,000 will be available for investment purposes, and management can issue the following securities:

1. **Bonds.** $350,000 can be issued at an after-issuing, before-tax cost of 9.0 percent. Over $350,000 the cost will be 10.75 percent.

2. **Preferred shares.** The shares can be issued at the prevailing market price. The firm incurs issuing costs of $1.75 per share up to an issue size of $100,000 and thereafter $2.40 per share.

3. **Common shares.** The shares will be issued at the market price. For an issue of $300,000 issuing costs will be $2 per share. For any additional issue of common shares, the issuing costs will be $2.75 per share.

The firm's combined tax rate is 44 percent. The firm's common share paid a dividend of $2.50 last year and is expected to grow at an annual rate of 10 percent. Market prices are $975 for bonds, $49 for preferred shares and $43 for common shares. Determine which projects should be accepted, based upon a comparison of the internal rate of return (IRR) of the investments and the weighted marginal cost of capital. The firm's capital structure at market value is shown below, and this mix is to be used for future investments.

Investment	Investment Cost	Internal Rate of Return
A	$ 250,000	21.0%
B	$ 700,000	17.0
C	$ 100,000	12.0
D	$ 500,000	13.0
E	$ 250,000	17.0
Total	$1,800,000	

Capital Structure	Amount of Capital	Percentage of Financing
Bonds (9%, $1000, 18-year maturity)	$2,800,000	35%
Preferred shares (10%, $45 par, 30,000 shares outstanding)	1,200,000	15
Common shares	4,000,000	50
Total	$8,000,000	100%

5-19B. (*Weighted Cost of Capital*) Dalton Ski, Inc., is a regional manufacturer of ski equipment. The firm's target financing mix appears as follows:

	Percentage
Debt	30%
Preferred shares	10
Common shares	60
Total	100%

The firm's management is analyzing the following investment opportunities.

Investment	Investment Cost	Internal Rate of Return
A	$175,000	16.0%
B	$100,000	14.0
C	$125,000	12.0
D	$200,000	10.0
E	$250,000	9.0
F	$150,000	8.0

Using the accept-reject criterion, Carter Dalton, president of the firm, has compiled the necessary data for computing the firm's weighted marginal cost of capital. The cost information indicates the following:

1. Debt can be raised at the following after-issuing, before-tax costs:

Amount	Cost
$0–$200,000	9.0%
$200,001–$300,000	10.0
Over $300,000	11.0

2. Preferred shares can be issued paying an annual dividend of $10. The par value of the stock is $100. Also, the market price of a preferred share is $100. If new shares were issued, the company would receive a net price of $90 on the first $100,000. Thereafter, the net amount received would be reduced to $85.

3. Common equity is provided first by internally generated funds. Profits for the year that should be available for reinvestment purposes are projected at $200,000. Additional common shares can be issued at the current $80 market price less 15 percent in issuing costs. However, a 20 percent issuing cost is expected if more than $250,000 in common shares is issued. The dividend per share was $4.00 last year, and the long-term growth rate for dividends is 12 percent.

a. Given that the firm's combined tax rate is 44 percent, compute the firm's weighted marginal cost of capital at a financing level up to $1 million.

b. Construct a graph that presents the firm's weighted marginal cost of capital relative to the amount of financing.

c. What is the appropriate size of the capital budget, and which projects should be accepted?

SELF-TEST SOLUTIONS

The following notations are used in this group of problems:

$$k_d = \text{the before-tax cost of debt}$$

$$K_d = \text{the after-tax cost of debt}$$

$$K_p = \text{the after-tax cost of preferred shares}$$

$$K_c = \text{the after-tax cost of internal common shares}$$

$$K_{nc} = \text{the after-tax cost of new common shares}$$

$$T = \text{the combined corporate tax rate}$$

$$D_t = \text{the dollar dividend per share, where } D_0 \text{ is the most recently paid dividend and } D_1 \text{ is the forthcoming dividend}$$

$$P_0 = \text{the value (present value) of a security}$$

$$NP_0 = \text{the value of a security less any issuing costs incurred in issuing the security}$$

SS-1. a.
$$\$921.50 = \sum_{t=1}^{10} \frac{\$100}{(1 + k_d)^t} + \frac{\$1000}{(1 + k_d)^{10}}$$

Rate	Value		
11%	$940.90	} $19.40	
k_d%	$921.50		} $53.90
12%	$887.00		

$$k_d = 0.11 + \left(\frac{\$19.40}{\$53.90}\right) 0.01 = 11.36\%$$

$$K_d = 11.36\% \, (1 - 0.44) = 6.36\%$$

b.
$$K_p = \frac{D}{NP_0}$$

$$K_p = \frac{\$8}{\$100 - \$9} = 8.79\%$$

c.

$$K_c = \frac{D_1}{P_0} + g$$

$$K_c = \frac{\$9.80(1 + .08)}{\$75} + 0.08 = 22.0\%$$

d.

$$K_{nc} = \frac{D_1}{NP_0} + g$$

$$K_{nc} = \frac{\$9.80(1 + .08)}{\$75 - \$6} + 0.08 = 23.0\%$$

SS-2.

$$\text{Dollar breaks} = \frac{\text{amount of financing at a given cost}}{\text{percentage of funds provided by the specific source}}$$

a. $\dfrac{\$100,000}{0.30} = \$333,333.33$

b. $\dfrac{\$150,000}{0.30} = \$500,000$

c. $\dfrac{\$40,000}{0.15} = \$266,667.67$

d. $\dfrac{\$90,000}{0.15} = \$600,000$

e. $\dfrac{\$200,000}{0.55} = \$363,636.36$

f. $\dfrac{\$500,000}{0.55} = \$909,090.91$

SS-3. a. The increase (break) in the weighted marginal cost of capital curve will occur resulting from the cost of debt:

$$\frac{\$120,000}{.40} = \$300,000$$

Increase from the cost of common:

$$\frac{\$180,000}{.60} = \$300,000$$

Weighted cost of capital (K_0) for

$0–$300,000 Total Financing

	Weights	Weighted Costs	Costs
Debt	40%	7%	2.80%
Common shares	60	19	11.40%
		$K_0 =$	14.20%

Over $300,000 Total Financing

	Weights	Weighted Costs	Costs
Debt	40%	11%	4.40%
Common shares	60	22	13.20%
		$K_0 =$	17.60%

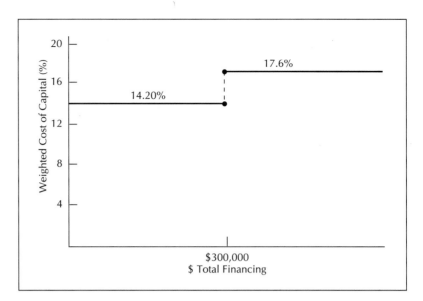

b. Only project A should be accepted.

SS-4. (1) Compute weights

	Capital Structure	Capital Mix (Weights)
Debt	$2,000,000	40%
Preferred shares	500,000	10
Common shares	2,500,000	50
	$5,000,000	100%

(2) Compute individual costs

Debt:
$0–$120,000:   14.14% (1 − .44) = 7.92%
over $120,000:   17.68% (1 − .44) = 9.90%

Preferred Shares:
$0–$50,000: $\dfrac{\$14}{\$95(1-.08)} = \dfrac{\$14}{\$87.40} = 16.02\%$

over $50,000: $\dfrac{\$14}{\$95(1-.11)} = \dfrac{\$14}{\$84.55} = 16.56\%$

Common Shares:
$0–$150,000: $\dfrac{\$2.50}{\$30} + .09 = .1733 = 17.33\%$

over $150,000 $\dfrac{\$2.50}{\$27} + .09 = .1826 = 18.26\%$

(3) Calculate the increase (break) in the weighted marginal cost of capital curve caused by an increase in the cost of common shares:

Debt = $\dfrac{\$120,000}{.40} = \$300,000$

Preferred Shares = $\dfrac{\$50,000}{.10} = \$500,000$

Common Shares = $\dfrac{\$150,000}{.50} = \$300,000$

(4) Construct the weighted cost of capital curve

$0–$300,000 Total Financing

	Individual Weights	Weighted Costs	Costs
Debt	40%	7.92%	3.17%
Preferred shares	10	16.02	1.60%
Common shares	50	17.33	8.67%
			$K_0 = 13.44\%$

At Least $300,001 But Not More Than $500,000

	Individual Weights	Weighted Costs	Costs
Debt	40%	9.90%	3.96%
Preferred shares	10	16.02	1.60%
Common shares	50	18.26	9.13%
			$K_0 = 14.69\%$

Over $500,000

	Individual Weights	Weighted Costs	Costs
Debt	40%	9.90%	3.96%
Preferred shares	10	16.56	1.66%
Common shares	50	18.26	9.13%
			$K_0 = 14.75\%$

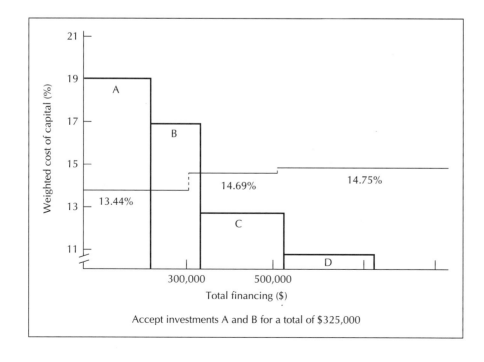

Accept investments A and B for a total of $325,000

SS-5.

Project	Required Rate of Return		Expected Return	Decision
A	$0.08 + (0.15 - 0.08)(1.1)$	$= 15.7\%$	18.8%	Accept
B	$0.08 + (0.15 - 0.08)(0.90)$	$= 14.3\%$	13.5%	Reject
C	$0.08 + (0.15 - 0.08)(0.80)$	$= 13.6\%$	15.0%	Accept

SELECTED REFERENCES

Amihud, Yakov, and Haim Mendelson. "Liquidity and Cost of Capital: Implications for Corporate Management," *Journal of Applied Corporate Finance* (Fall 1989), 65–73.

Ang, James S. "Weighted Average versus True Cost of Capital," *Financial Management*, 2 (Autumn 1973), 56–60.

Ang, James S., and Wilbur G. Lewellen. "Risk Adjustment in Capital Investment Project Evaluations," *Financial Management*, 11 (Summer 1982), 5–14.

Arditti, Fred D., and Haim Levy. "The Weighted Average Cost of Capital as a Cutoff Rate: A Critical Analysis of the Classical Textbook Weighted Average," *Financial Management*, 6 (Fall 1977), 24–34.

Beaver, William H., Paul Kettler, and Myron Scholes. "The Association between Market Determined and Accounting Determined Risk Measures," *Accounting Review* (October 1970), 654–682.

Blume, Marshall E., Irwin Friend, and Randolph Westerfield. "Impediments to Capital Formation: Summary Report of a Survey of Nonfinancial Corporations." Working Paper, Philadelphia: Wharton School, University of Pennsylvania, 1980.

Boudreaux, Kenneth, and Hugh W. Long. "The Weighted Average Cost of Capital as a Cutoff Rate: A Further Analysis," *Financial Management*, 8 (Summer 1979), 7–14.

Bowman, Robert G. "The Theoretical Relationship between Systematic Risk and Financial (Accounting) Variables," *Journal of Finance* (June 1979), 617–630.

Chambers, D. R., Robert S. Harris, and John J. Pringle. "Treatment of Financing Mix in Analyzing Investment Opportunities," *Financial Management*, 11 (Summer 1982), 24–41.

Chen, Carl R. "Time Series Analysis of Beta Stationarity and Its Determinants: A Case of Public Utilities," *Financial Management* (Autumn 1982), 64–70.

Conine, Thomas E., Jr., and Maury Tamarkin. "Division Cost of Capital Estimation: Adjusting for Leverage," *Financial Management*, 14 (Spring 1985), 54–58.

Cooley, Philip L. "A Review of the Use of Beta in Regulatory Proceedings," *Financial Management* (Winter 1981), 75–81.

Diamond, Douglas W., and Robert E. Verrecchia. "Disclosure, Liquidity, and the Cost of Capital," *The Journal of Finance* (September 1991), 1325–1360.

Durand, David. "Afterthoughts on a Controversy with MM, Plus New Thoughts on Growth and the Cost of Capital," *Journal of Financial Management* (Summer 1989), 12.

Elliott, J. Walter. "The Cost of Capital and U.S. Investment," *Journal of Finance*, 35 (September 1980), 981–1000.

Ezzell, John R., and R. Burr Porter. "Flotation Costs and the Weighted Average Cost of Capital," *Journal of Financial and Quantitative Analysis*, 11 (September 1976), 403–413.

Frankel, Jeffrey, A. "The Japanese Cost of Finance: A Survey," *Journal of Financial Management* (Winter 1991), 95.

Fuller, Russell J., and Halbert S. Kerr. "Estimating the Divisional Cost of Capital: An Analysis of the Pure-Play Technique," *Journal of Finance*, 36 (December 1981), 997–1009.

Gehr, Adam K., Jr. "Risk-Adjusted Capital Budgeting Using Arbitrage," *Financial Management*, 10 (Winter 1981), 14–19.

Gitman, Lawrence J., and Vincent A. Mercurio. "Cost of Capital Techniques Used by Major U.S. Firms: Survey and Analysis of Fortune's 1000," *Financial Management*, 11 (Winter 1982), 21–29.

Gordon, Myron J., and L. I. Gould. "The Cost of Equity Capital: A Reconsideration," *Journal of Finance*, 33 (June 1978), 849–861.

Gup, Benton E., and Samuel W. Norwood III. "Divisional Cost of Capital: A Practical Approach," *Financial Management*, 11 (Spring 1982), 20–24.

Harris, Robert S., and John J. Pringle. "A Note on the Implications of Miller's Argument for Capital Budgeting," *Journal of Financial Research* (Spring 1983), 13–23.

Miles, James A., and John R. Ezzell. "The Weighted Average Cost of Capital, Perfect Capital Markets, and Project Life: A Clarification," *Journal of Financial and Quantitative Analysis*, 15 (September 1980), 719–730.

Modigliani, F., and M. Miller. "The Cost of Capital, Corporation Finance, and the Theory of Investment," *American Economic Review*, 48 (June 1958), 261–296.

Nantell, Timothy J. and C. Robert Carlson. "The Cost of Capital as a Weighted Average," *Journal of Finance* (December 1975), 1343–1355.

Pettway, Richard H., and Bradford D. Jordon. "Diversification, Double Leverage, and the Cost of Capital," *Journal of Financial Research* (Winter 1982), 289–301.

Rosenberg, Barr, and Andrew Rudd. "The Corporate Use of Beta," *Issues in Corporate Risk Management*, New York: Stern, Stewart, Putman & Macklis, Inc., 1983, 42–45.

Scott, David F., Jr., and J. William Petty. "Determining the Cost of Common Equity Capital: The Direct Method," *Journal of Business Research*, 8 (March 1980), 89–103.

Van Horne, James C. "An Application of the Capital Asset Pricing Model to Divisional Required Returns," *Financial Management*, 9 (Spring 1980), 14–19.

CHAPTER 6

Capital Budgeting

- Guidelines to Capital Budgeting

- Competitive Markets and Profitable Projects—Where Do Profitable Projects Exist in Competitive Markets?

- Nondiscounted Cash Flow Criteria for Capital-Budgeting Decisions

- Discounted Cash Flow Criteria for Capital-Budgeting Decisions

- A Glance at Actual Capital-Budgeting Practices

In Chapter 4 we developed tools for comparing cash flows that occur in different time periods. This chapter will use these techniques in conjunction with additional decision rules to determine when to invest money in long-term assets, a process called **capital budgeting**. In evaluating capital investment proposals, we will compare the costs and benefits of each in a number of ways.[1] Some of these methods take into account the time value of money, others do not; but each of these methods is used frequently in the real world. As you will see, our preferred method of analysis will be the Net Present Value (NPV) method which compares the present value of inflows and outflows.

We will look first at the purpose and importance of capital budgeting. Next, since capital-budgeting techniques rely on cash flows as inputs, we will study how to determine these cash flows. Five capital-budgeting criteria will then be provided for evaluating capital investments, followed by a look at capital budgeting in practice.[2]

GUIDELINES TO CAPITAL BUDGETING

Capital budgeting is a decision-making process for investment in fixed assets; specifically, it involves measuring the incremental cash flows associ-

---

[1]How successful the manager and the business are depends upon how decisions among competing alternatives are made. This chapter develops a framework in which alternative courses of action can be analyzed.

[2]Examples of capital investments include the acquisition of another company, building a plant, introducing a new product, and purchasing equipment. One of the largest capital budgeting projects ever undertaken is the tunnel being built under the English Channel by the Eurotunnel Company. The original estimated cost of this project in 1987 when it was started was approximately $8 billion.

ated with investment proposals and evaluating the attractiveness of these cash flows relative to the project's cost.[3] Typically these investments involve rather large cash outlays at the outset and commit the firm to a particular course of action over a relatively long time period. Thus, if a capital-budgeting decision is incorrect, reversing it tends to be costly.

For example, about 30 years ago the Ford Motor Company's decision to produce the Edsel entailed an outlay of $250 million to bring the car to market and losses of approximately $200 million during the 2.5 years it was produced—in all, a $450 million mistake.[4] This type of decision is costly to reverse. Fortunately for Ford, it was able to convert Edsel production facilities to produce the Mustang, thereby avoiding an even larger loss.

Perspective in Finance

This chapter deals with decision rules for deciding when to invest in new projects. Before we can develop these rules we must be able to measure the benefits and costs of the new project by calculating cash flows. In reading over the upcoming section try not to look upon calculating cash flows as going down a checklist of possible sources of cash flows, but instead try to think about what cash flows are and what creates them.

In measuring cash flows, we will be interested in only the incremental cash flow after-tax that can be attributed to the project being evaluated.[5] A project proposal will present a forecast of expected cash inflows and cash outflows which must increase shareholder's wealth for the project to be accepted. Obviously, the worth of our decision depends upon the accuracy of our cash-flow estimates.

The measurement of cash flows will be affected by the type of project. The majority of projects encountered in a firm's capital budget are classified as either of two types: a replacement project or an expansion project. A replacement project involves the acquisition of a new asset for the purposes of either maintenance or cost reduction. The net cash flows of a replacement project will be measured in terms of the amount of net savings after taxes that accrues to the firm. An expansion project involves the acquisition of a new asset for the purpose of increasing production capacity. The net cash flows of an expansion project will be measured in terms of the amount of net operating income that accrues to the firm. Also encountered within the firm's capital budget are a small minority of projects called "soft projects". This type of project is difficult to evaluate by capital budgeting techniques because the measurement of either the expected cash inflow or the cash out-flow is imprecise; for example, the benefits to society of installing pollution control devices in factories.

To evaluate investment proposals, we must first set guidelines by which we measure the value of each proposal.

---

[3]The only relevant measure of a project's initial outlay is the market value of its assets. Historical costs measure book value and are not an appropriate measure of value for the decision-making with respect to maximizing shareholder's wealth.

[4]"The Edsel Dies, and Ford Regroups Survivors," *Business Week*, November 28, 1959, p. 27.

[5]Good capital budgeting decisions consider all relevant incremental cash flows. This decision process includes the consequences of not taking on the project. It also includes the value of opening up new options for the future. Unfortunately, while talking about this is easy, implementing it is not.

Cash Flows Rather Than Accounting Profits

We will use cash flows, not accounting profits, as our measurement tool. The firm receives and is able to reinvest cash flows, whereas accounting profits are shown when they are earned rather than when the money is actually in hand. Unfortunately, a firm's accounting profits and cash flows may not be timed to occur together. For example, capital expenses such as vehicles, plants and equipment, are depreciated over a number of years, with their annual depreciation subtracted from profit. Cash flow correctly reflects the timing of benefits and costs; that is, when the money is received, when it can be reinvested, and when it must be paid out.

Think Incrementally

Interestingly, calculating cash flow from a project may not be enough. Decision makers must ask: what new cash flows will the company as a whole receive if it takes on a given project? In fact, we may find that not all cash flows a firm expects from an investment proposal are incremental in nature. But, in measuring cash flows, the trick is to think incrementally. In doing so, we will see that only incremental cash flows after-tax matter. There are a number of things a firm must consider in its decision-making process.

Beware of Cash Flows Diverted from Existing Products

Assume for a moment that we are managers of a firm considering a new product line that might compete with one of our existing products and possibly reduce its sales. In determining cash flows associated with the proposed project, we should consider only the incremental sales brought to the company as whole. New product sales achieved at the cost of losing sales of other products in our line are not considered a benefit of adopting the new product.

Remember that we are only interested in sales dollars to the firm if this project is accepted as opposed to what the sales dollars would be if the project is rejected. Just moving sales from one product line to a new product line does not bring anything new into the company, but if sales are captured from our competitors or if sales that would have been lost to new competing products are retained then these are relevant incremental cash flows. In each case these are the incremental cash flows to the firm—looking at the firm as a whole with the new product versus without the new product.

Look for Incidental or Synergistic Effects

Although in some cases a new project may take sales away from a firm's current projects, in other cases a new effort may actually bring new sales to the existing line. For example, an airline may open a new route to a North American city. The new route not only means new tickets on this new route, but also means increasing ticket sales on connecting routes. If managers were to look only at the revenue from ticket sales from the new route, they would miss the incremental cash flow to the firm as a whole that results from taking on the new route. This called an incidental, or synergistic effect. As a result, a manager when analyzing the firm's bottom line must consider any cash flow to any part of the company that may result from the new project under consideration.

Work in Working Capital Requirements

Many times a new project will involve additional investment in working capital. This may take the form of new inventory to stock a sales outlet, additional investment in accounts receivable resulting from additional credit sales, or increased investment in cash to operate cash registers, and more. Working capital requirements are considered a cash flow even though they do not leave the company. Why is investment in inventory considered a cash outflow when the goods are still in the store? Because the firm does not have access to the inventory's cash value, the firm cannot use the money for other investments. Generally, working capital requirements are tied up over the life of the project. When the project terminates there is usually an offsetting cash inflow as the working capital is recovered.

Consider Incremental Expenses

Just as cash inflows from a new project are measured on an incremental basis, expenses should also be measured on an incremental basis. For example, the introduction of a new product line requires the training of sales staff and the cash flow after-tax associated with the training program must be considered a cash flow and charged to the project. If accepting a new project dictates that a production facility be re-engineered, the cash flow after-tax associated with the capital investment should be charged against the project. Again, any incremental cash flow after-tax affecting the company as a whole is a relevant cash flow—whether it is flowing in or flowing out.

Sunk Costs Are Not Incremental Cash Flows

Only cash flows that are affected by the decision making at the moment are relevant cash flows in capital budgeting. The manager must ask two questions: (1) Will this cash flow take place if the project is accepted? (2) Will this cash flow take place if the project is rejected? If the answers are yes to the first question and no to the second question, the cash flow is incremental. For example, let's assume you are considering the introduction of a new taste treat called Puddin' in a Shoe. You would like to do some test marketing before production. If you are considering the decision to test market and have not yet done so, the costs associated with the test marketing are relevant cash flows. On the other hand, if you have already test marketed, the cash flows involved in the test marketing are no longer relevant in project evaluation. It is a matter of timing. Regardless of what you may decide about future production, the cash flows allocated to marketing have already taken place. As a rule, any cash flows that are not part of the accept-or-reject decision should not be included in the capital budgeting analysis.

Account for Opportunity Costs

Now we will focus on the cash flows that are lost because assets already in place are now being used for a new project. This is the opportunity cost of doing business. For example, a product may use valuable floor space in a production facility. Although the cash flow is not obvious, the real question remains: What else could be done with this space? The space could have been rented out, or another product could have been stored there. The key point is that the opportunity costs have occurred because existing assets are now used for the new project and these opportunity costs must be included in the net cash flow of the new project.

Cash Flows from Changes in Overhead

Although we certainly want to include any incremental cash flows which are caused by changes from overhead expenses such as utilities and salaries, we also want to make sure that these are truly incremental cash flows. Many times, overhead expenses—heat, light, rent—would occur whether or not a given project is accepted. In many cases, expenses cannot be allocated to a specific project. Thus, we must determine whether or not these expenses are incremental cash flows and relevant to capital budgeting.

Ignore Interest Payments and Financing Flows

In evaluating new projects and determining cash flows, we must separate the investment decision from the financing decision. Interest payments and other financing cash flows that might result from raising funds to finance a project should not be considered incremental cash flows. If accepting a project means we have to raise new funds by issuing new bonds, interest charges associated with raising funds are not a relevant cash outflow. When we discount the incremental cash flows back to the present at the required rate of return, we are implicitly accounting for the cost of raising funds to finance the new project. In essence, the required rate of return reflects the cost of the funds needed to support the project. Managers must first determine the desirability of the project and then decide how best to finance it.

COMPETITIVE MARKETS AND PROFITABLE PROJECTS—WHERE DO PROFITABLE PROJECTS EXIST IN COMPETITIVE MARKETS?

At this point we are going to step back a bit and take a broad look at the capital-budgeting process. It is very easy to get caught up in the mechanics of capital budgeting without analyzing the process itself. Before moving on and examining the intricacies of capital budgeting we will examine where profitable projects come from.

In reality it is much easier evaluating profitable projects than it is finding them. If, for example, an industry is generating large profits, it will attract new entrants. The additional competition and added capacity should result in profits being driven down to the required rate of return. On the other hand, if an industry is returning profits below the required rate of return, then some participants in the market drop out, reducing capacity and competition; in turn, prices are driven back up. This is precisely what happened in the VCR video rental market in the mid-1980s. This market developed suddenly with the opportunity for excess profits. As a result, since there were no barriers to entry, this market was flooded with new entries in short time. By 1987 the resultant competition and price cutting produced losses for many firms in this industry, forcing them to flee the market. As the competition lessened with firms moving out of the video rental industry, profits again were able to rise to the point where the required rate of return could be earned on invested capital.

The point to all this is that in competitive markets extremely large profits simply do not exist for very long. Given this somewhat bleak scenario, how can we find the good projects—that is, the ones that return more than the required rate of return? The answer is that as long as the markets are competitive they will be hard to find. What we have to do is look to markets that are not perfectly competitive. The two most common ways of making the markets less competitive are to differentiate the product in some key way or to achieve a cost advantage that competitors cannot match which in turn discourages new entrants into the market.

Successful investments involve those that reduce competition by creating barriers to entry either through product differentiation or cost advantages. If products are differentiated, consumer choice is no longer made by price alone. As such, capital budgeting projects that involve product differentiation allow for the possibility of extremely large profits.

Product differentiation has long been used as a means of insulating a product from competition, thereby allowing prices to stay sufficiently high to support excess profits. For example, in the pharmaceutical industry patents have traditionally created competitive barriers. Products like SmithKline Beckman's Tagamet, used in the treatment of ulcers, and Hoffmann-La Roche's Valium, a tranquillizer, can protect themselves from direct competition.

Patents are one way of differentiating products. Service and quality have also been used successfully. For example, Caterpillar Tractor has long prided itself on the quality of its construction and earth-moving machinery. As a result, it has been able to securely hold on to its market. Similarly, some of the brand loyalty built up in recent years by Toyota and Honda Motors has been based upon quality.

The quality of service can also create product differentiation as witnessed by Domino's Pizza, and McDonald's. At McDonald's fast service, cleanliness, and consistency of product bring customers back. Regardless of how product differentiation occurs (focusing on service, advertising, the development of patents through R&D expenditures, or quality) the more the product is differentiated from competing products, the less competition it will have to face and thus the greater the possibility of extremely large profits.

Economies of scale and the ability to produce at a cost below competition can effectively detour new entrants to the market and thereby reduce competition. The retail hardware industry is one in which this is the case. In the hardware industry there are a number of fixed costs that are independent of the store's size or annual sales. For example, inventory costs, advertising expenses, and managerial salaries are essentially the same regardless of annual sales. As a result, the more sales can be built up, the lower the per sales dollar cost of inventory, advertising, and management. Restocking from warehouses also becomes more efficient as delivery trucks can now be used to full potential.

Regardless of how the cost advantage is created—by economies of scale, proprietary technology, or monopolistic control of raw materials—the cost advantage deters new entrants from the market while allowing production at below industry cost. Thus, investments aimed at creating a significant cost advantage have the potential to be accompanied by excess profits.

Thus, the key to locating profitable investment projects is to first understand how and where they exist in competitive markets. Once this is done the corporate philosophy must be directly aimed at creating or taking advantage of some imperfection in these markets—either through product differentiation or creation of a cost advantage—rather than looking to new markets or industries that appear to provide excess profits. In effect, any perfectly competitive industry that looks too good to be true, won't be for long.

NONDISCOUNTED CASH FLOW CRITERIA FOR CAPITAL-BUDGETING DECISIONS

We are now ready to consider the interpretation of cash flows. Cash flows represent the benefits generated from accepting a capital-budgeting proposal. In the remainder of this chapter, we will assume a given cash flow is generated by a project and will determine whether or not that project should be accepted or rejected.

We will consider five commonly used criteria for determining acceptability of investment proposals. The first two are the least sophisticated in that they do not incorporate the time value of money into their calculations; the final three do take it into account.

Nondiscounted Cash Flow Criterion 1: Payback Period

The payback period is the number of years needed to recover the initial cash outlay. As this criterion measures how quickly the project will return its original investment, it deals with cash flows rather than accounting profits. However, this criterion ignores the time value of money since it does not discount these cash flows back to the present. The accept-reject criterion involves whether or not the project's payback period is less than or equal to the firm's maximum desired payback period. For example, if a firm's maximum desired payback period is three years and an investment proposal requires an initial cash outlay of $10,000 and yields the following set of annual cash flows, what is its payback period? Should the project be accepted?

Year	Cash Flow After-Tax
1	$2000
2	4000
3	3000
4	3000
5	1000

In this case, after three years the firm will have recaptured $9,000 on an initial investment of $10,000, leaving $1,000 of the initial investment to be recouped. During the fourth year a total of $3,000 will be returned from this investment, and, assuming it will flow into the firm at a constant rate over the year, it will take one-third of the year ($1,000/$3,000) to recapture the remaining $1,000. Thus, the payback period on this project is three and a third years, which is more than the desired payback period. Using the payback period criterion, the firm would reject this project.

Although the payback period is used frequently, it does have some rather obvious drawbacks, which can best be demonstrated through the use of an example. Consider two investment projects, A and B, which involve an initial cash outlay of $10,000 each and produce the annual cash flows shown in Table 6-1. Both projects have a payback period of two years; therefore, in terms of the payback period criterion both are equally acceptable. However, if we had our choice, it is clear we would select A over B—for at least two reasons. First, regardless of what happens after the payback period, project A returns our initial investment to us earlier within the payback period. Thus, if there is a time value of money, the cash flows occurring within the payback period should not be weighted equally, as they are. In addition, all cash flows that occur after the payback period are ignored. This violates the principle that investors desire more in the way of benefits rather than less—a principle that is hard to deny, especially when we are talking about money.

Although these deficiencies limit the value of the payback period as a tool for investment evaluation, the payback period method does have several positive features. First, it deals with cash flows, as opposed to accounting profits, and therefore focuses on the true timing of the project's benefits and costs, even though these cash flows are not adjusted for the time value of money. Second, it is easy to visualize, quickly understood, and easy to calculate. Finally, while the payback period method does have serious deficiencies, it is often used as a rough screening device to eliminate projects whose returns do not materialize until later years. This approach emphasizes the earliest returns, which in all likelihood are less uncertain, and provides for the liquidity needs of the firm. Although these advantages of the payback

	A	B
Initial cash outlay	–$10,000	–$10,000
Annual net cash inflows:		
Year 1	6,000	5,000
2	4,000	5,000
3	3,000	0
4	2,000	0
5	1,000	0

TABLE 6-1
Payback Period
Example Projects

period are certainly significant, its disadvantages severely limit its value as a discriminating capital-budgeting criterion.

Nondiscounted Cash Flow Criterion 2: Accounting Rate of Return

The **accounting rate of return (AROR)** compares the average after-tax profits with the average dollar size of the investment.[6] The average profits figure is determined by adding up the after-tax profits generated by the investment over its life and dividing by the number of years. The average investment is determined by adding the initial outlay and the project's actual expected salvage value and dividing by two. This computation attempts to calculate the average value of an investment by simply averaging the initial and liquidation values. Thus, the accounting rate of return for an investment with an expected life of n years can be calculated as follows:

$$AROR = \frac{\sum_{t=1}^{n} (\text{accounting profit after tax}_t)/n}{(\text{initial outlay} + \text{expected salvage value})/2} \tag{6-1}$$

The accept-reject criterion associated with the accounting rate of return compares the calculated return with a minimum acceptable AROR level. If the AROR is greater than this minimum acceptable level, the project is accepted; otherwise it is rejected.

Consider an investment in new machinery that requires an initial outlay of $20,000 and has an expected salvage value of zero after five years. Assume that this machine, if acquired, will result in an increase in after-tax profits of $800 each year for five years. In this case the average accounting profit is $800, while the average investment is ($20,000 + 0)/2, or $10,000. For this example, the AROR would be $800/$10,000, or 8 percent.

This technique seems straightforward enough, but its limitations detract significantly from its value as a discriminating capital-budgeting criterion. To examine these limitations, let us first determine the AROR of three proposals, each with an expected life of five years. Assume that the initial outlay associated with each project is $10,000 and it will have an expected salvage value of zero in five years. The minimum acceptable AROR for this firm is 8 percent, and the annual accounting profits from the three proposals are given in Table 6-2. In each case, the average annual accounting profit is $500 and the average investment is $5,000—that is, ($10,000 + 0)/2. Therefore, the AROR is 10 percent for each project, which indicates that

TABLE 6-2
Annual Accounting Profits
After Tax

Year	A	B	C
1	$ 0	$500	$ 0
2	1000	500	0
3	500	500	0
4	500	500	0
5	500	500	2500

[6]Also known as the average rate of return method.

the AROR method does not do an adequate job of discriminating among these projects.

A casual examination leads us to the conclusion that project B is the best, as it yields its returns earlier than either project A or C. However, the AROR technique gives equal weight to all returns within the project's life without any regard for the time value of money. The second major disadvantage associated with the AROR method is that it deals with accounting profit figures rather than cash flows. For this reason it does not truly reflect the proper timing of the benefits.

In spite of the criticisms, the accounting rate of return has been a relatively popular tool for capital-budgeting analysis, primarily because it involves familiar terms that are easily accessible. Also it is easily understood. The AROR provides a measure of accounting profits per average dollar invested, and the intuitive appeal of this measurement has kept the method alive over the years.[7] For our purposes, the AROR is inadequate, as it does not treat cash flows and does not take account of the time value of money.

DISCOUNTED CASH FLOW CRITERIA FOR CAPITAL-BUDGETING DECISIONS

The final three capital-budgeting criteria to be examined base decisions on the investment's cash flows after adjusting for the time value of money. For the time being, the problem of incorporating risk into the capital-budgeting decision is ignored. This issue will be examined in Chapter 7. In addition, we will assume that the appropriate discount rate, required rate of return, or cost of capital is given. The determination of this rate was the topic of Chapter 5.

We will examine three discounted cash flow capital-budgeting techniques—net present value, profitability index, and internal rate of return.

Net Present Value

The **net present value (NPV)** of an investment proposal is equal to the present value of its annual net cash flows after tax less the investment's initial outlay. The net present value can be expressed as follows:

$$NPV = \sum_{t=1}^{n} \frac{CFAT_t}{(1 + k)^t} - IO \qquad (6\text{-}2)$$

where $CFAT_t$ = the annual cash flow after-tax in time period t (this can take on either positive or negative values)

k = the appropriate discount rate, that is, the required rate of return or cost of capital[8]

---

[7]It should be pointed out that the AROR will assess the rate of return based upon accounting information; thus, it is possible to analyze the ultimate effect of an alternative on the financial statements.

[8]The required rate of return or cost of capital is the rate of return necessary to justify raising funds to finance the project or, alternatively, the rate of return necessary to maintain the firm's current market price per share. These terms have been defined in Chapter 5.

$$IO = \text{the initial cash outlay}$$

$$n = \text{the project's expected life}$$

The project's net present value gives a measurement of the net value of an investment proposal in terms of today's dollars. Since all cash flows are discounted back to the present, comparing the difference between the present value of the annual cash flows and the investment outlay does not violate the time value of money assumption. The difference between the present value of the annual cash flows and the initial outlay determines the net present value of accepting the investment proposal in terms of today's dollars. Whenever the project's NPV is greater than or equal to zero, we will accept the project; and whenever there is a negative value associated with the acceptance of a project, we will reject the project. If the project's net present value is zero, then it returns the required rate of return and should be accepted. This accept-reject criterion is illustrated below:

$$NPV \geq 0.0 \qquad \text{Accept}$$
$$NPV < 0.0 \qquad \text{Reject}$$

The following example illustrates the use of the net present value capital-budgeting criterion.

EXAMPLE

A firm is considering new machinery, for which the cash flows after-tax are shown in Table 6-3. If the firm has a 12 percent required rate of return, the present value of the cash flow after-tax is $47,678, as calculated in Table 6-4. Furthermore, the net present value of the new machinery is $7,678. Since this value is greater than zero, the net present value criterion indicates that the project should be accepted. ■

Note that the worth of the net present value calculation is a function of the accuracy of cash flow predictions. Before the NPV criterion can be reasonably applied, incremental costs and benefits must first be estimated, including the initial outlay, the differential flows over the project's life, and the terminal cash flow.

In comparing the NPV criterion with those that we have already examined, we find it far superior. First of all, it deals with cash flows rather than accounting profits. In this regard it is sensitive to the true timing of the benefits resulting from the project. Moreover, recognizing the time value of money allows comparison of the benefits and costs in a logical manner. Finally, since projects are accepted only if a positive net present value is associated with them, the acceptance of a project using this criterion will increase the value of the firm, which is consistent with the goal of maximizing the shareholders' wealth.

The disadvantage of the NPV method stems from the need for detailed, long-term forecasts of the incremental cash flows accruing from the project's acceptance. In spite of this drawback, the net present value is the most theoretically correct criterion that we will examine. The following example provides an additional illustration of its application.

CALCULATOR SOLUTION*

Data Input	Function Key
40,000	+/− ENTER ↓
15,000	ENTER ↓
1	ENTER ↓
14,000	ENTER ↓
1	ENTER ↓
13,000	ENTER ↓
1	ENTER ↓
12,000	ENTER ↓
1	ENTER ↓
11,000	ENTER ↓
1	ENTER ↓
	NPV
12	ENTER ↓

Function Key	Answer
CPT	7674.63**

*Note: If you are using a TI BA II Plus calculator, you must first get the cash flow worksheet by pressing both CF and 2nd CLRWORK. To solve for the NPV, press the NPV button. For further explanation see Appendix E.

**The difference between the two answers represents rounding error.

	Cash Flow After-Tax
Initial outlay	–$40,000
Inflow year 1	15,000
Inflow year 2	14,000
Inflow year 3	13,000
Inflow year 4	12,000
Inflow year 5	11,000

TABLE 6-3
NPV Illustration of Investment in New Machinery

	Cash Flow After-tax	Factor at 12 Percent	Present Value
Inflow year 1	$15,000	.893	$13,395
Inflow year 2	14,000	.797	11,158
Inflow year 3	13,000	.712	9,256
Inflow year 4	12,000	.636	7,632
Inflow year 5	11,000	.567	6,237
Present value of cash flows			$47,678
Investment initial outlay			– 40,000
Net present value			$7,678

TABLE 6-4
Calculation for NPV Illustration of Investment in New Machinery

EXAMPLE

A firm is considering the purchase of a new computer system, which will cost $30,000 initially, to aid in credit billing and inventory management. The incremental cash flow after-tax resulting from this project are provided in Table 6-5. The required rate of return demanded by the firm is 10 percent. In order to determine the system's net present value, the three-year $15,000 cash flow annuity is first discounted back to the present at 10 percent. From Appendix D in the back of this book, we find that $PVIFA_{10\%,3yr}$ is 2.487. Thus, the present value of this $15,000 annuity is $37,305. ∎

Because the cash inflows have been discounted back to the present, they can now be compared with the initial outlay, since both of the flows are now stated in terms of today's dollars. Subtracting the initial outlay ($30,000) from the present value of the cash inflows ($37,305), we find that the system's net present value is $7,305. Since the NPV on this project is positive, the project should be accepted.

Profitability Index (Benefit/Cost Ratio)

The **profitability index (PI)**, or **benefit/cost ratio**, is the ratio of the present value of the future net cash flows to the initial outlay. While the net present

	Cash Flow After-Tax
Initial outlay	–$30,000
Year 1	15,000
Year 2	15,000
Year 3	15,000

TABLE 6-5
NPV Example Problem of a Computer System

value investment criterion gives a measure of the absolute dollar desirability of a project, the profitability index provides a relative measure of an investment proposal's desirability—that is, the ratio of the present value of its future net benefits to its initial cost. The profitability index can be expressed as follows:

$$\text{Profitability Index} = \frac{\sum_{t=1}^{n} \dfrac{CFAT_t}{(1 + k)^t}}{IO} \tag{6-3}$$

where $CFAT_t$ = the annual cash flow after-tax in time period t (this can take on either positive or negative values)

k = the appropriate discount rate; that is, the required rate of return or the cost of capital

IO = the initial cash outlay

n = the project's expected life

The decision criterion with respect to the profitability index is to accept the project if the PI is greater than or equal to 1.00, and to reject the project if the PI is less than 1.00.

$$PI \geq 1.0 \quad \text{Accept}$$
$$PI < 1.0 \quad \text{Reject}$$

Looking closely at this criterion, we see that it yields the same accept-reject decision as does the net present value criterion. Whenever the present value of the project's net cash flow is greater than its initial cash outlay, the project's net present value will be positive, signalling a decision to accept the project. When this is true, the project's profitability index will also be greater than 1, as the present value of the net cash flows (the PI's numerator) is greater than its initial outlay (the PI's denominator). While these two decision criteria will always yield the same decision, they will not necessarily rank acceptable projects in the same order. This problem of conflicting ranking will be dealt with at a later point.

Since the net present value and profitability index criteria are essentially the same, they have the same advantages over the other criteria examined. Both employ cash flows, recognize the timing of the cash flows, and are consistent with the goal of maximization of shareholders' wealth. The major disadvantage of both the profitability index and net present value criteria is that they require long, detailed cash flow forecasts.

EXAMPLE

A firm with a 10 percent required rate of return is considering investing in a new machine with an expected life of six years. The cash flows after-tax resulting from this investment are given in Table 6-6. Discounting the project's future net cash flows back to the present yields a present value of $53,667; dividing this value by the initial outlay of $50,000 gives a profitability index of 1.0733, as shown in Table 6-7. This tells us that the present value of the future benefits accruing from this project is 1.0733 times the level of the initial outlay. Since the profitability index is greater than 1.0, the project should be accepted. ∎

	Cash Flow After-Tax
Initial outlay	−$50,000
Inflow year 1	15,000
Inflow year 2	8,000
Inflow year 3	10,000
Inflow year 4	12,000
Inflow year 5	14,000
Inflow year 6	16,000

TABLE 6-6
Profitability Index (PI) Illustration of Investment in New Machinery

	Cash Flow After-tax	Factor at 10 Percent	Present Value
Initial outlay	−$50,000	1.0	−$50,000
Inflow year 1	15,000	0.909	13,635
Inflow year 2	8,000	0.826	6,608
Inflow year 3	10,000	0.751	7,510
Inflow year 4	12,000	0.683	8,196
Inflow year 5	14,000	0.621	8,694
Inflow year 6	16,000	0.564	9,024

TABLE 6-7
Calculation for PI Illustration of Investment in New Machinery

$$\text{Profitability Index} = \frac{\sum_{t=1}^{n} \frac{CFAT_t}{(1 + k)^t}}{IO}$$

$$= \frac{\$13,635 + \$6,608 + \$7,510 + \$8,196 + \$8,694 + \$9,024}{\$50,000}$$

$$= \frac{\$53,667}{\$50,000}$$

$$= 1.0733$$

Internal Rate of Return

The internal rate of return (IRR) attempts to answer this question: What rate of return does this project earn? For computational purposes, the **internal rate of return** is defined as the discount rate that equates the present value of the project's future net cash flows with the project's initial cash outlay. Mathematically, the internal rate of return is defined as the value IRR in the following equation:

$$IO = \sum_{t=1}^{n} \frac{CFAT_t}{(1 + IRR)^t} \tag{6-4}$$

where $CFAT_t$ = the annual cash flow after-tax in time period t (this can take on either a positive or negative value)

IO = the initial cash outlay

n = the project's expected life

IRR = the project's internal rate of return

The decision criterion associated with the internal rate of return is to accept the project if the internal rate of return is greater than or equal to the required rate of return. We reject the project if its internal rate of return is less than this required rate of return. This accept-reject criterion is illustrated below:

$$IRR \geq \text{required rate of return} \quad \text{Accept}$$
$$IRR < \text{required rate of return} \quad \text{Reject}$$

If the internal rate of return on a project is equal to the shareholders' required rate of return, then the project should be accepted. This is because the firm is earning the rate that its shareholders are requiring. However, the acceptance of a project with an internal rate of return below the investors' required rate of return will decrease the firm's stock price.

If the NPV is positive, the IRR must be greater than the required rate of return, k. Thus, all the discounted cash flow criteria are consistent and will give similar accept-reject decisions. In addition, since the internal rate of return is another discounted cash flow criterion, it exhibits the same general advantages and disadvantages as both the net present value and profitability index, and occasionally has an additional disadvantage of being tedious to calculate if a financial calculator is not available.[9]

Computing the IRR for Even Cash Flows

In this section, however, we are going to put our calculators aside and examine the mathematical process of calculating internal rates of return for a better understanding of internal rates of return.

The calculation of a project's internal rate of return can be either very simple or relatively complicated. As an example of straightforward solution, assume that a firm with a required rate of return of 10 percent is considering a project that involves an initial outlay of $45,555. If the investment is taken, the cash flow after-tax is expected to be $15,000 per annum over the project's four-year life.[10] In this case, the internal rate of return is equal to IRR in the following equation:

$$\$45,555 = \frac{\$15,000}{(1 + IRR)^1} + \frac{\$15,000}{(1 + IRR)^2} + \frac{\$15,000}{(1 + IRR)^3} + \frac{\$15,000}{(1 + IRR)^4}$$

From our discussion of the present value of an annuity in Chapter 4, we know that this equation can be reduced to

$$\$45,555 = \$15,000 \left[\sum_{t=1}^{4} \frac{1}{(1 + IRR)^t} \right]$$

Appendix D at the back of the book gives table values for the $PVIFA_{i,n}$ for various combinations of i and n, which further reduces this equation to

$$\$45,555 = \$15,000 \, (PVIFA_{IRR,n})$$

Dividing both sides by $15,000, this becomes

$$3.037 = PVIFA_{IRR,n}$$

CALCULATOR SOLUTION*

Data Input	Function Key
45,555	+/– ENTER ↓
15,000	ENTER ↓
4	ENTER ↓
	IRR

Function Key	Answer
CPT	12.01**

*Note: If you are using a TI BA II Plus calculator, you must first get the cash flow worksheet by pressing both CF and 2nd CLRWORK. To solve for IRR, press the IRR button. For further explanation see Appendix E.

**The difference between the two answers represents rounding error.

---

[9]In general, the IRR must be calculated by means of iteration since there is no explicit solution except in some special cases such as even cash flows.

[10]Even cash flows arise in many situations, such as in long-term leasing or loan amortization.

Hence, we are looking for a $PVIFA_{i,n}$ of 3.037 in the four-year row of Appendix D. This value occurs when i equals 12 percent, which means that 12 percent is the internal rate of return for the investment. Therefore, since 12 percent is greater than the 10 percent required return, the project should be accepted.

Computing the IRR for Uneven Cash Flows

Unfortunately, while solving for the IRR is quite easy when using a financial calculator or spreadsheet, it can be solved directly in the tables only when the future after-tax net cash flows are in the form of an annuity or a single payment. When a financial calculator is not available and these flows are in the form of an uneven series of flows, a trial-and-error approach is necessary. To do this, we first determine the present value of the future after-tax net cash flows using an arbitrary discount rate. If the present value of the future cash flows at this discount rate is larger than the initial outlay, the rate is increased; if it is smaller than the initial outlay, the discount rate is lowered, and the process begins again. This search routine is continued until the present value of the future cash flow after-tax is equal to the initial outlay. The interest rate that creates this situation is the internal rate of return.

To illustrate the procedure, consider an investment proposal that requires an initial outlay of $3,817 and returns $1,000 at the end of year 1, $2,000 at the end of year 2, and $3,000 at the end of year 3. In this case, the internal rate of return must be determined using trial and error. This process is presented in Table 6-8, in which an arbitrarily selected discount rate of 15 percent was chosen to begin the process. The trial-and-error technique slowly centres in on the project's internal rate of return of 22 percent. The project's internal rate of return is then compared with the firm's required rate of return, and if the IRR is the larger, the project is accepted.

EXAMPLE

A firm with a required rate of return of 10 percent is considering three investment proposals. Given the information in Table 6-9, management plans to calculate the internal rate of return for each project and determine which projects should be accepted.

Because project A is an annuity, we can easily calculate its internal rate of return by determining the $PVIFA_{i,n}$ necessary to equate the present value of the future cash flows with the initial outlay. This computation is done as follows:

$$IO = \sum_{t=1}^{n} \frac{CFAT_t}{(1 + IRR)^t}$$

$$\$10,000 = \sum_{t=1}^{4} \frac{\$3362}{(1 + IRR)^t}$$

$$\$10,000 = \$3362 \, (PVIFA_{IRR,4})$$

$$2.974 = PVIFA_{IRR,4}$$

We are looking in the four-year row of Appendix D, for a $PVIFA_{i,n}$ of 2.974, which occurs in the $i = 13$ percent column. Thus, 13 percent is the internal rate of return. Since this rate is greater than the firm's required rate of return of 10 percent, the project should be accepted.

Project B involves a single future cash flow of $13,605, resulting from

Initial outlay	–$ 3,817
Flow year	11,000
Flow year	22,000
Flow year	33,000

Solution: Pick an arbitrary discount rate and use it to determine the present value of the inflows. Compare the present value of the inflows with the initial outlay; if they are equal, you have determined the IRR. Otherwise, raise the discount rate if the present value of the inflows is larger than the initial outlay or lower the discount rate if the present value of the inflows is less than the initial outlay. Repeat this process until the IRR is found.

1. Try i = 15 percent:

	Net Cash Flows	Present Value Factor at 15 Percent	Present Value
Inflow year 1	$1000	.870	$ 870
Inflow year 2	2000	.756	1512
Inflow year 3	3000	.658	1974
Present value of inflows			$4356
Initial outlay			–$3817

2. Try i = 20 percent:

	Net Cash Flows	Present Value Factor at 20 Percent	Present Value
Inflow year 1	$1000	.833	$ 833
Inflow year 2	2000	.694	1388
Inflow year 3	3000	.579	1737
Present value of inflows			$3958
Initial outlay			–$3817

3. Try i = 22 percent:

	Net Cash Flows	Present Value Factor at 22 Percent	Present Value
Inflow year 1	$1000	.820	$ 820
Inflow year 2	2000	.672	1344
Inflow year 3	3000	.551	1653
Present value of inflows			$3817
Initial outlay			–$3817

CALCULATOR SOLUTION*

Data Input	Function Key
3817	+/– ENTER ↓
1000	ENTER ↓
1	ENTER ↓
2000	ENTER ↓
1	ENTER ↓
3000	ENTER ↓
1	ENTER ↓
	IRR

Function Key	Answer
CPT	21.98

*Note: If you are using a TI BA II Plus calculator, you must first get the cash flow worksheet by pressing both CF and 2nd CLRWORK. To solve for IRR, press the IRR button. For further explanation see Appendix E.

TABLE 6-9
Three IRR Investment
Proposal Examples

	A	B	C
Initial outlay	– $10,000	– $10,000	– $10,000
Inflow year 1	3,362	0	1,000
Inflow year 2	3,362	0	3,000
Inflow year 3	3,362	0	6,000
Inflow year 4	3,362	13,605	7,000

an initial outlay of $10,000; thus, its internal rate of return can be determined directly from the present-value table in Appendix B as follows:

$$IO = \sum_{t=1}^{n} \frac{CFAT_t}{(1 + IRR)^t}$$

$$\$10,000 = \sum_{t=1}^{4} \frac{\$13,605}{(1 + IRR)^t}$$

$$\$10,000 = \$13,605\,(PVIFA_{IRR,4})$$

$$0.735 = PVIFA_{IRR,4}$$

This tells us that we should look for a $PVIFA_{i,4yr}$ of .735 in the four-year row of Appendix B, which occurs in the $i = 8$ percent column. We may therefore conclude that 8 percent is the internal rate of return. Since this rate is less than the firm's required rate of return of 10 percent, project B should be rejected.

The uneven nature of the future cash flows associated with project C necessitates the use of the trial-and-error method. The internal rate of return for project C is equal to the value of IRR in the following equation:

$$\$10,000 = \frac{\$1000}{(1 + IRR)^1} + \frac{\$3000}{(1 + IRR)^2} + \frac{\$6000}{(1 + IRR)^3} + \frac{\$7000}{(1 + IRR)^4} \quad (6\text{-}5)$$

Arbitrarily selecting a discount rate of 15 percent and substituting it into Equation (6-5) for IRR reduces the right-hand side of the equation to $11,090, as shown in Table 6-10. Therefore, since the present value of the future cash flows is larger than the initial outlay, we must raise the discount rate in order to find the project's internal rate of return. Substituting 20 percent for the discount rate, the right-hand side of Equation (6-5) now becomes $9,763. As this is less than the initial outlay of $10,000, we must now decrease the discount rate. In other words, we know that the internal rate of return for this project is between 15 and 20 percent. Since the present value of the future flows discounted back to the present at 20 percent was only $237 too low, a discount rate of 19 percent is selected. As shown in Table 6-10, a discount rate of 19 percent reduces the present value of the future inflows down to $10,009, which is approximately the same as the initial outlay. Consequently, project C's internal rate of return is approximately 19 percent.[11] Since the internal rate of return is greater than the firm's required rate of return of 10 percent, this investment should be accepted. ■

-----

[11]If desired, the actual rate can be more precisely approximated through interpolation as follows:

	Discount Rate	Present Value
	19%	$10,009
	20	9,763
Difference	1%	$ 246

Proportion $9 is of $246 = $\dfrac{\$9}{\$246}$ = .0366

$$19\% + .0366\,(1\%) = 19.0366\%$$

TABLE 6-10
Computing the IRR for
Project C

1. Try i = 15 percent:

	Net Cash Flows	Present Value Factor at 15 Percent	Present Value
Inflow year 1	$1,000	.870	$ 870
Inflow year 2	3,000	.756	2,268
Inflow year 3	6,000	.658	3,948
Inflow year 4	7,000	.572	4,004
Present value of inflows			$11,090
Initial outlay			−$10,000

CALCULATOR SOLUTION*

Data Input	Function Key
10,000	+/− ENTER ↓
1000	ENTER ↓
1	ENTER ↓
3000	ENTER ↓
1	ENTER ↓
6000	ENTER ↓
1	ENTER ↓
7000	ENTER ↓
1	ENTER ↓
	IRR

Function Key	Answer
CPT	19.04

*Note: If you are using a TI BA II Plus calculator, you must first get the cash flow worksheet by pressing both CF and 2nd CLRWORK. To solve for IRR, press the IRR button. For further explanation see Appendix E.

2. Try i = 20 percent:

	Net Cash Flows	Present Value Factor at 20 Percent	Present Value
Inflow year 1	$1,000	.833	$ 833
Inflow year 2	3,000	.694	2,082
Inflow year 3	6,000	.579	3,474
Inflow year 4	7,000	.482	3,374
Present value of inflows			$ 9,763
Initial outlay			−$10,000

3. Try i = 19 percent:

	Net Cash Flows	Present Value Factor at 19 Percent	Present Value
Inflow year 1	$1,000	.840	$ 840
Inflow year 2	3,000	.706	2,118
Inflow year 3	6,000	.593	3,558
Inflow year 4	7,000	.499	3,493
Present value of inflows			$10,009
Initial outlay			−$10,000

Complications with the IRR: Multiple Rates of Return

While any project can have only one NPV and one PI, a single project under certain circumstances can have more than one IRR. The reason for this can be traced to the calculations involved in determining the IRR. Equation (6-4) states that the IRR is the discount rate that equates the present value of the project's future net cash flows with the project's initial outlay:

$$IO = \sum_{t=1}^{n} \frac{CFAT_t}{(1 + IRR)^t} \qquad (6\text{-}4)$$

However, since Equation (6-4) is a polynomial of a degree n, it has n solutions. Now if the initial outlay (IO) is the only negative cash flow and all the annual cash flows after-tax ($CFAT_t$) are positive, then all but one of these n solutions is either a negative or imaginary number and there is no problem.

But problems occur when there are sign reversals in the cash flow stream; in fact there can be as many solutions as there are sign reversals. Thus, a normal pattern with a negative initial outlay and positive annual after-tax cash flows (−, +, +, +,…, +) after that has only one sign reversal, hence only one positive IRR. However, a pattern with more than one sign reversal can have more than one IRR. Consider, for example, the following pattern of cash flows.[12]

	Cash Flow After-Tax
Initial outlay	−$ 1,600
Year 1	+$10,000
Year 2	−$10,000

In this pattern of cash flows there are two sign reversals, from −$1,600 to +$10,000 and then from +$10,000 to −$10,000, so there can be as many as two positive IRRs that will make the present value of the future cash flows equal to the initial outlay. In fact two internal rates of return solve this problem, 25 and 400 percent. Graphically what we are solving for is the discount rate that makes the project's NPV equal to zero; as Figure 6-1 illustrates, this occurs twice.

Which solution is correct? The answer is that neither solution is valid. While each fits the definition of IRR, neither provides any insight into the true project returns. What has happened is that the firm has borrowed or received $10,000 from the project at the end of year 1 and must return this sum at the end of year 2. The real question is this: What is the use of this $10,000 worth for one year? The answer depends upon what the investment opportunities are like to the firm. If they are 30 percent, then the value of receiving $10,000 at the end of year 1 and returning it at the end of year 2 is $3,000 received at the end of year 2, since this is what the firm would be left

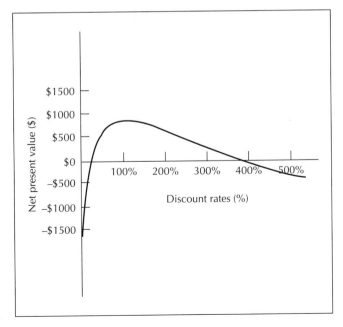

FIGURE 6-1
Multiple IRRs

[12]This example is taken from James H. Lorie and Leonard J. Savage, "Three Problems in Rationing Capital," *Journal of Business*, 28 (October 1955), pp. 229–239.

with. The internal rate of return on this (an initial outlay of $1,600 and a positive inflow of $3,000 at the end of year 2) is 37 percent. Thus, neither of the internal rates of return, 25 or 400 percent, was valid. In summary, when there is more than one sign reversal in the cash flow stream, the possibility of multiple IRRs exists, and the normal interpretation of the IRR loses its meaning.

Ethics in Capital Budgeting

While it may not seem obvious, ethics has a role in capital budgeting. Beech-Nut provides an example of how these rules have been violated in the past and what the consequences can be. No doubt this project appeared to have a positive net present value associated with it, but in fact, it cost Beech-Nut tremendously. The Ethics in Financial Management insert, "Bad Apple for Baby," provides a narrative of what took place.

ETHICS IN FINANCIAL MANAGEMENT

Bad Apple for Baby

It's a widely held, but hard to prove belief that a company gains because it is perceived as more socially responsive than its competitors. Over the years, the three major manufacturers of baby food—Gerber Products, Beech-Nut Nutrition and H. J. Heinz—had, with almost equal success, gone out of their way to build an image of respectability.

Theirs is an almost perfect zero-sum business. They know, at any given time, how many babies are being born. They all pay roughly the same price for their commodities, and their manufacturing and distribution costs are almost identical. So how does one company gain a market share edge over another, especially in a stagnant or declining market?

The answer for Beech-Nut was to sell a cheaper, adulterated product. Beginning in 1977, the company began buying a chemical concoction, made up mostly of sugar and water, and labelling it as apple juice. Sales of that product brought Beech-Nut an estimated $60 million between 1977 and 1982, while reducing material costs about $250,000 annually.

When various investigators tried to do something about it, the company stonewalled. Among other things, they shipped the bogus juice out of a plant in New York to Puerto Rico, to put it beyond the jurisdiction of federal investigators, and they even offered the juice as a give-away to reduce their stocks after they were finally forced to discontinue selling it.

In the end, the company pleaded guilty to 215 counts of introducing adulterated food into commerce and violating the Federal Food Drug and Cosmetic Act. The FDA fined Beech-Nut $2 million.

In addition, Beech-Nut's president, Neils Hoyvald, and its vice president of operations, John Lavery, were found guilty of similar charges. Each faces a year and one day in jail and a $100,000 fine. Both are now out on appeal on a jurisdiction technicality.

Why did they do it? The Fort Washington, Pa.-based company will not comment. But perhaps some portion of motive can be inferred from a report Hoyvald wrote to Nestle, the company which had acquired Beech-Nut in the midst of his coverup. "It is our feeling that we can report safely now that the apple juice recall has been completed. If the recall had been effectuated in early June [when the FDA had first ordered it], over 700,000 cases in inventory would have been affected…due to our many delays, we were only faced with having to destroy 20,000 cases."

One thing is clear: Two executives of a company with an excellent reputation breached a trust and did their company harm.

Since 1987, when the case was brought to a close, Beech-Nut's share of the overall baby food market has fallen from 19.1% to 15.8%. So what was gained in the past has been lost in the present, and perhaps for the future as well.

Source: Stephen Kindel, "Bad Apple for Baby," *Financial World*, June 27, 1989, p. 48.

A GLANCE AT ACTUAL CAPITAL-BUDGETING PRACTICES

The methods used in practice for capital budgeting are precisely those that we have described in this chapter. However, over the past 35 years the popularity of these methods has shifted rather dramatically. In the 1950s the payback period and AROR methods dominated capital budgeting, but through the 1960s and 1970s the discounted cash-flow decision techniques slowly displaced the nondiscounted techniques. This movement from the payback period and AROR to net present value and the internal rate of return is shown in Table 6-11, which indicates the growth in popularity of these techniques as reflected in surveys of practices over the years. Interestingly, while a large majority of firms use the NPV and IRR as their primary techniques, a large majority of firms also use the payback period as a secondary decision method for capital budgeting. In a sense they are using the payback period to control for risk. The logic behind this is that since the payback period dramatically emphasizes early cash flows, which are presumably more certain—that is, have less risk—than cash flows that occur later in a project's life, its use will lead to projects with more certain cash flows.

A reliance on the payback period came out even more dramatically in a recent study of the capital-budgeting practices of 12 large manufacturing firms.[13] Information for this study was gathered from interviews over one to three days in addition to an examination of the records of about 400 projects. This study revealed a number of things of interest. First, firms were typically found to categorize capital investments as mandatory (regulations and contracts, capitalized maintenance, replacement of antiquated equipment,

TABLE 6-11. Past Surveys of Capital-Budgeting Practices—Percent of Respondents Using Each Technique

Capital-Budgeting Technique	Klammer 1959	Klammer 1964	Klammer 1970	Kim and Farragher 1975	Gitman, Kim, and Farragher 1979	Blazouske, Carlin, and Kim 1980	Blazouske, Carlin, and Kim 1985	Kim, Crick, and Kim 1986
Primary method:								
NPV	5%	15%	27%	26%	19%	22%	25%	21%
IRR	8	17	30	37	49	38	40	49
Payback	34	24	12	15	12	25	19	19
AROR	34	30	26	10	8	11	9	8
Secondary method:								
NPV	2%	3%	7%	7%	8%	10%	11%	24%
IRR	1	2	6	7	8	7	13	15
Payback	18	21	32	33	39	41	44	35
AROR	4	9	11	3	3	10	9	19

Sources: Thomas Klammer, "Empirical Evidence of the Adoption of Sophisticated Capital Budgeting Techniques," *Journal of Business*, July 1972, pp. 387–397; S. H. Kim and E. J. Farragher, "Capital Budgeting Practices in Large Industrial Firms," *Baylor Business Studies*, November 1976, pp. 19–25; Lawrence J. Gitman and John R. Forrester, Jr., "Forecasting and Evaluation Practices and Performance: A Survey of Capital Budgeting," *Financial Management*, Fall 1977, pp. 66–71; J. D. Blazouske, Ian Carlin and S. H. Kim, "Current Capital Budgeting Practices in Canada," *CMA The Management Accounting Magazine*, March 1988, pp. 51–54; Suk H. Kim, T. Crick, and Sesung H. Kim, "Do Executives Practice What Academics Preach?" Management Accounting, November 1986, pp. 49–52.

---

[13]Marc Ross, "Capital Budgeting Practices of Twelve Large Manufacturers," *Financial Management*, 15 (Winter 1986), p. 15–22.

Project Size	Typical Boundaries	Primary Decision Site
Very small	Up to $100,000	Plant
Small	$100,000 to $1,000,000	Division
Medium	$1 million to $10 million	Corporate investment committee
Large	Over $10 million	CEO & board

TABLE 6-12
Project Size and
Decision-Making Authority

product quality) or discretionary (expanded markets, new businesses, cost cutting), with the decision-making process being different for mandatory and discretionary projects. Second, it was found that the decision-making process was different for projects of differing size. In fact, approval authority tended to rest in different locations, depending upon the size of the project. Table 6-12 provides the typical levels of approval authority.

The study also showed that while the discounted cash flow methods are used at most firms, the simple payback criterion was the measure relied upon primarily in one-third of the firms examined. The use of the payback period seemed to be even more common for smaller projects, with firms severely simplifying the discounted cash flow analysis and/or relying primarily on the payback period. Thus, while discounted cash flow decision techniques have become more widely accepted, their use depends to an extent upon the size of the project and where within the firm the decision is being made.

SUMMARY

The process of capital budgeting involves decision making with respect to investment in fixed assets. Specifically, we examined the measurement of incremental cash flows associated with a firm's investment proposals and the evaluation of those proposals. In measuring cash flows we focused on the incremental or differential after-tax cash flows attributed to the investment proposal.

We examined five commonly used criteria for determining the acceptance or rejection of capital-budgeting proposals. The first two methods, the payback period and accounting rate of return, are nondiscounted and do not incorporate the time value of money into their calculations. The discounted methods such as the net present value, profitability index, and internal rate of return, do account for the time value of money. These methods are summarized in Table 6-13.

TABLE 6-13
Capital-Budgeting Criteria

Nondiscounted Cash Flow Methods

1. Payback period = number of years required to recapture the initial investment

Accept if payback < maximum acceptable payback period
Reject if payback > maximum acceptable payback period

Advantages:
1. Uses cash flows.
2. Is easy to calculate and understand.
3. May be used as rough screening device.

Disadvantages:
1. Ignores the time value of money.
2. Ignores cash flows occurring after the pay-back period.

TABLE 6-13
Capital-Budgeting Criteria

2.

$$\text{Accounting rate of return} = \frac{\sum_{t=1}^{n} (\text{accounting profit after tax}_t)/n}{(\text{initial investment} + \text{expected salvage value})/2}$$

where n = project's expected life

Accept if $AROR$ > minimum acceptable rate of return

Reject if $AROR$ < minimum acceptable rate of return

Advantages:
1. Involves familiar, easily accessible terms.
2. Is easy to calculate and understand.

Disadvantages:
1. Ignores the time value of money.
2. Uses accounting profits rather than cash flows.

Discounted Cash Flow Methods

3. Net present value = present value of the annual cash flows after tax less the investment's initial outlay

$$NPV = \sum_{t=1}^{n} \frac{CFAT_t}{(1+k)^t} - IO$$

where, $CFAT_t$ = the annual after-tax cash flow in time period t (this can take on either positive or negative values)

k = the appropriate discount rate, that is, the required rate of return or the cost of capital[a]

IO = the initial cash outlay

n = the project's expected life

Accept if $NPV \geq 0.0$

Reject if $NPV < 0.0$

Advantages:
1. Uses cash flows.
2. Recognizes the time value of money.
3. Is consistent with the firm goal of shareholder wealth maximization.

Disadvantages:
1. Requires detailed long-term forecasts of the incremental benefits and costs.

4. Profitability index = the ratio of the present value of the future net cash flows to the initial outlay

$$\text{Profitability Index} = \frac{\sum_{t=1}^{n} \frac{CFAT_t}{(1+k)^t}}{IO}$$

Accept if $PI \geq 1.0$

Reject if $PI < 1.0$

Advantages:
1. Uses cash flows.
2. Recognizes the time value of money.
3. Is consistent with the firm goal of shareholder wealth maximization.

Disadvantages:
1. Requires detailed long-term forecasts of the incremental benefits and costs.

TABLE 6-13
Capital-Budgeting Criteria

5. Internal rate of return = the discount rate that equates the present value of the project's future net cash flows with the project's initial outlay

$$IO = \sum_{t=1}^{n} \frac{CFAT_t}{(1 + IRR)^t}$$

where IRR = the project's internal rate of return

Accept if $IRR \geq$ required rate of return
Reject if $IRR <$ required rate of return

Advantages:
1. Uses cash flows.
2. Recognizes the time value of money.

Disadvantages:
1. Requires detailed long-term forecasts of the incremental benefits and costs.
2. Can involve tedious calculations.
3. Possibility of multiple IRRs.

ªThe cost of capital is discussed in Chapter 5.

STUDY QUESTIONS

6-1. Why is the capital-budgeting decision such an important process? Why are capital-budgeting errors so costly?

6-2. Why do we focus on cash flows rather than accounting profits in making our capital-budgeting decisions? Why are we interested only in incremental cash flows rather than total cash flows?

6-3. If a project requires additional investment in working capital, how should this be treated in calculating cash flows?

6-4. How do sunk costs affect the determination of cash flows associated with an investment proposal?

6-5. What are the criticisms of the use of the payback period as a capital-budgeting technique? What are its advantages? Why is it so frequently used?

6-6. In some countries, expropriation of foreign investments is a common practice. If you were considering an investment in one of those countries, would the use of the payback period criterion seem more reasonable than it otherwise might? Why?

6-7. What are the criticisms of the use of the accounting rate of return as a capital-budgeting technique? What are its advantages?

6-8. Briefly compare and contrast the three discounted cash flow criteria. What are the advantages and disadvantages of the use of each of these methods?

SELF-TEST PROBLEM

ST-1. The B. Pari Corporation is considering signing a one-year contract with one of two computer-based marketing firms. While one is more expensive, it offers a more extensive program and thus will provide higher cash flows after-tax. Assume these two options are mutually exclusive and that the required rate of return is 12 percent. Given the following cash flows after tax:

Year	Option A	Option B
0	–$50,000	–$100,000
1	70,000	130,000

a. Calculate the net present value.

b. Calculate the profitability index.

c. Calculate the internal rate of return.

STUDY PROBLEMS (SET A)

6-1A. (*AROR Calculation*) Two mutually exclusive projects are being evaluated using the accounting rate of return. Each project has an initial cost of $20,000 and a salvage value of $4,000 after six years. Given the following information:

	Annual Accounting Profits After Tax	
Year	Project A	Project B
1	$ 2,000	$10,000
2	2,000	10,000
3	2,000	10,000
4	13,000	5,000
5	13,000	5,000
6	14,000	5,000

a. Determine each project's AROR.

b. Which project should be selected, using this criterion? Would you support that recommendation? Why or why not?

6-2A. (*IRR Calculation*) Determine the internal rate of return on the following projects:

a. An initial outlay of $10,000 resulting in a cash flow after tax of $1,993 at the end of each year for the next 10 years

b. An initial outlay of $10,000 resulting in a cash flow after tax of $2,054 at the end of each year for the next 20 years

c. An initial outlay of $10,000 resulting in a cash flow after tax of $1,193 at the end of each year for the next 12 years

d. An initial outlay of $10,000 resulting in a cash flow after tax of $2,843 at the end of each year for the next 5 years

6-3A. (*IRR Calculation*) Determine the internal rate of return on the following projects:

a. An initial outlay of $10,000 resulting in a single cash flow after tax of $17,182 after 8 years

b. An initial outlay of $10,000 resulting in a single cash flow after tax of $48,077 after 10 years

c. An initial outlay of $10,000 resulting in a single cash flow after tax of $114,943 after 20 years

d. An initial outlay of $10,000 resulting in a single cash flow after tax of $13,680 after 3 years

6-4A. (*IRR Calculation*) Determine the internal rate of return to the nearest percent on the following projects:

a. An initial outlay of $10,000 resulting in a cash flow after tax of $2,000 at the end of year 1, $5,000 at the end of year 2, and $8,000 at the end of year 3

b. An initial outlay of $10,000 resulting in a cash flow after tax of $8,000 at the end of year 1, $5,000 at the end of year 2, and $2,000 at the end of year 3

c. An initial outlay of $10,000 resulting in a cash flow after tax of $2,000 at the end of years 1 through 5 and $5,000 at the end of year 6

6-5A. (*Cash Flow—Capital-Budgeting Calculation*) The R. Boisjoly Chemical Corporation is considering the purchase of a new machine that costs $80,000. The expected life of this machine is three years, after which it will be discarded, having no value. The new machine is expected to produce cash flows after tax of $55,000 per year. The firm's required rate of return on this type of project is 10 percent. Given the above information, determine the following:

a. The net present value

b. The profitability index

c. The internal rate of return.

6-6A. (*Cash Flow—Capital-Budgeting Calculation*) The Mad Dog Hansen Electronic Components Corporation is considering the purchase of a new cash register at a cost of $40,000. This cash register is expected to have a life of six years, at which time the machine will be discarded, having no value. Material efficiencies resulting from the purchase would result in savings after-tax of $9,000 per year. The firm has a required rate of return of 20 percent, calculate

a. The net present value

b. The profitability index

c. The internal rate of return.

6-7A. (*NPV, PI, and IRR Calculations*) Brownsville Girl, Inc., is considering a major expansion of its product line and has estimated the following cash flows after tax associated with such an expansion. The initial outlay associated with the expansion would be $1,950,000 and the project would generate incremental cash flows after tax of $450,000 per year for six years. The appropriate required rate of return is 9 percent.

a. Calculate the net present value.

b. Calculate the profitability index.

c. Calculate the internal rate of return.

d. Should this project be accepted?

6-8A. (*NPV with Varying Required Rates of Return*) Big Steve's, makers of swizzle sticks, is considering the purchase of a new plastic stamping machine. This investment requires an initial outlay of $100,000 and will generate cash flows after tax of $18,000 per year for 10 years. For each of the listed required rates of return, determine the project's net present value.

a. The required rate of return is 10 percent.

b. The required rate of return is 15 percent.

c. Would the project be accepted under part (a) or (b)?

d. What is this project's internal rate of return?

6-9A. (*Internal Rate of Return Calculations*) Given the following cash flows after tax, determine the internal rate of return for projects A, B, and C.

	Project A	*Project B*	*Project C*
Initial Investment:	$50,000	$100,000	$450,000
Cash Inflows:			
Year 1	$10,000	25,000	200,000
Year 2	15,000	25,000	200,000
Year 3	20,000	25,000	200,000
Year 4	25,000	25,000	–
Year 5	30,000	25,000	–

6-1B. (*AROR Calculation*) Two mutually exclusive projects are being evaluated using the accounting rate of return. Each project has an initial cost of $35,000 and a salvage value of $7,000 after six years. Given the following information:

Annual Accounting Profits After Tax		
Year	Project A	Project B
1	$ 2,500	$10,500
2	2,500	10,500
3	2,500	10,500
4	13,000	5,000
5	13,000	5,000
6	14,000	5,000

a. Determine each project's AROR.

b. Which project should be selected, using this criterion? Would you support that recommendation? Why or why not?

6-2B. (*IRR Calculation*) Determine the internal rate of return on the following projects:

a. An initial outlay of $10,000 resulting in a single cash flow after tax of $19,926 after 8 years

b. An initial outlay of $10,000 resulting in a single cash flow after tax of $20,122 after 12 years

c. An initial outlay of $10,000 resulting in a single cash flow after tax of $121,000 after 22 years

d. An initial outlay of $10,000 resulting in a single cash flow after tax of $19,254 after 5 years

6-3B. (*IRR Calculation*) Determine the internal rate of return on the following projects:

a. An initial outlay of $10,000 resulting in a cash flow after tax of $2,146 at the end of each year for the next 10 years

b. An initial outlay of $10,000 resulting in a cash flow after tax of $1,960 at the end of each year for the next 20 years

c. An initial outlay of $10,000 resulting in a cash flow after tax of $1,396 at the end of each year for the next 12 years

d. An initial outlay of $10,000 resulting in a cash flow after tax of $3,197 at the end of each year for the next 5 years

6-4B. (*IRR Calculation*) Determine the internal rate of return to the nearest percent on the following projects:

a. An initial outlay of $10,000 resulting in a cash flow after tax of $3,000 at the end of year 1, $5,000 at the end of year 2, and $7,500 at the end of year 3

b. An initial outlay of $12,000 resulting in a cash flow after tax of $9,000 at the end of year 1, $6,000 at the end of year 2, and $2,000 at the end of year 3

c. An initial outlay of $8,000 resulting in a cash flow after tax of $2,000 at the end of years 1 through 5 and $5,000 at the end of year 6

6-5B. (*Cash Flow—Capital-Budgeting Calculation*) The R J Water, Inc., is considering the purchase of a new bottling machine that costs $150,000. The expected life of this machine is seven years, after which it will be discarded, having no value. The new machine is expected to produce cash flows after tax of $35,000 per year. The firm's required rate of return on this type of project is 13 percent. Given the above information, determine the following:

a. The net present value

b. The profitability index

c. The internal rate of return.

6-6B. (*Cash Flow—Capital-Budgeting Calculation*) The P J Corporation is considering the purchase of a new wrapping machine at a cost of $160,000. This new machine is expected to have a life of six years, at which time the machine will be discarded, having no value. Material efficiencies resulting from the purchase would result in savings after-tax of $25,000 per year. The firm has a required rate of return on this type of project of 15 percent, calculate

a. The net present value

b. The profitability index

c. The internal rate of return.

6-7B. (*NPV, PI, and IRR Calculations*) Anderson, Inc., is considering a major expansion of its product line and has estimated the following cash flows after tax associated with such an expansion. The initial outlay associated with the expansion would be $2,500,000 and the project would generate incremental cash flows after tax of $750,000 per year for six years. The appropriate required rate of return is 11 percent.

a. Calculate the net present value.

b. Calculate the profitability index.

c. Calculate the internal rate of return.

d. Should this project be accepted?

6-8B. (*Internal Rate of Return Calculations*) Given the following cash flows after tax, determine the internal rate of return for projects A, B, and C.

	Project A	Project B	Project C
Initial Investment:	$75,000	$95,000	$395,000
Cash Inflows:			
Year 1	$10,000	25,000	150,000
Year 2	10,000	25,000	150,000
Year 3	30,000	25,000	150,000
Year 4	25,000	25,000	–
Year 5	30,000	25,000	–

SELF-TEST SOLUTION

SS-1. **a.**

$$NPV_A = \frac{\$70,000}{(1 + .12)^1} - \$50,000$$

$$= \$70,000(.893) - \$50,000$$

$$= \$62,510 - \$50,000$$

$$= \$12,510$$

$$NPV_B = \frac{\$130,000}{(1 + .12)^1} - \$100,000$$

$$= \$130,000(.893) - \$100,000$$

$$= \$116,090 - \$100,000$$

$$= \$16,090$$

b.

$$\text{Profitability Index (A)} = \frac{\$62,510}{\$50,000}$$

$$= 1.2502$$

$$\text{Profitability Index (B)} = \frac{\$116,090}{\$100,000}$$

$$= 1.1609$$

c.

$$\$50,000 = \$70,000(PVIF_{i,1yr})$$

$$.7143 = PVIF_{i,1yr}$$

Looking for the value of $PVIF_{i,1yr}$ in Appendix B at the back of the book, a value of .714 is found in the 40 percent column. Thus, the IRR is 40 percent.

$$\$100,000 = \$130,000(PVIF_{i,1yr})$$

$$.7692 = PVIF_{i,1yr}$$

Looking for a value of $PVIF_{i,1yr}$ in Appendix B, a value of .769 is found in the 40 percent column. Thus is IRR is 30 percent.

SELECTED REFERENCES

Agmon, Tamir. "Capital Budgeting and Unanticipated Changes in the Exchange Rate," *Advances In Financial Planning and Forecasting*, 5 (1990) Part II, 295–314.

Alpin, Richard D., and George L. Casler. *Capital Investment Analysis*. Columbus, OH: Grid, 1973.

Bacon, Peter W. "The Evaluation of Mutually Exclusive Investments," *Financial Management*, 6 (Summer 1977), 55–64.

Bernhard, Richard H. "Mathematical Programming Models for Capital Budgeting—A Survey, Generalization and Critique," *Journal of Financial and Quantitative Analysis*, 4 (June 1969), 111–158.

Bierman, Harold, Jr. "A Reconciliation of Present Value Capital Budgeting and Accounting," *Financial Management*, 6 (Summer 1977), 52–54.

Bierman, Harold, Jr., and Seymour Smidt. *The Capital Budgeting Decision*, 6th ed. New York: Macmillan, 1984.

Bodie, Zvi. "Compound Interest Depreciation in Capital Investment," *Harvard Business Review*, 60 (May–June 1982), 58–60.

Cheung, Joseph K. and John Heaney. "A Contingent Claim Integration of Cost-Volume-Profit Analysis with Capital Budgeting," *Contemporary Accounting Research*, 6 (1990) Part II, 738–760.

Dorfman, Robert. "The Meaning of Internal Rates of Return," *Journal of Finance*, 36 (December 1981), 1011–1021.

Dudley, Carlton L., Jr. "A Note on Reinvestment Assumptions in Choosing between Net Present Value and Internal Rate of Return," *Journal of Finance*, 27 (September 1972), 907–915.

Folger, H. Russell. "Ranking Techniques and Capital Rationing," Accounting Review, 47 (January 1972), 134–143.

Gitman, Lawrence J., and John R. Forrester, Jr. "Forecasting and Evaluation Practices and Performance: A Survey of Capital Budgeting," *Financial Management*, 6 (Fall 1977), 66–71.

Haka, Susan F., Lawrence A. Gordan, and George F. Pinches. "Sophisticated Capital Budgeting Selection Techniques and Firm Performance," *Accounting Review*, 60 (October 1985), 651–669.

Herbst, Anthony. "The Unique, Real Internal Rate of Return: Caveat Emptor!" *Journal of Financial and Quantitative Analysis*, 13 (June 1978), 363–370.

Hoskins, Colin G., and Glen A. Mumey. "Payback: A Maligned Method of Asset Ranking?" *Engineering Economist*, 25 (Fall 1979), 53–65.

Ingersoll, Jonathan E. and Stephan A. Ross. "Waiting to Invest: Investment and Uncertainty," *Journal of Business*, 65 (1992), 1–29.

Jean, William H. *Capital Budgeting: The Economic Evaluation of Investment Projects*. Scranton, PA: International Textbook, 1969.

Jessell, Kenneth A. and Daniel E. McCarty. "A Note on Marginal Analysis, NPV Criterion and Wealth Maximization," *Journal of Financial Education*, 16 (1987), 12–15.

Keane, Simon M. "The Internal Rate of Return and the Reinvestment Fallacy," *Journal of Accounting and Business Studies*, 15 (June 1979), 48–55.

Kim, Suk H. "Capital Budgeting Practices in Large Corporations and Their Impact on Over-all Profitability," *Baylor Business Studies* (November–December 1978, January 1979), 48–66.

267

Kim, Suk H., and E. J. Farragher. "Capital Budgeting Practices in Large Industrial Firms," *Baylor Business Studies* (November 1976), 19–25.

Kim, Suk H., and Larry Guin. "A Summary of Empirical Studies on Capital Budgeting Practices," *Business and Public Affairs*, 13 (Fall 1986), 21–25.

Kim, Suk H., Trevor Crick, and Sesung H. Kim. "Do Executives Practice What Academics Teach?" *Management Accounting*, 33 (November 1986), 49–52.

Klammer, Thomas. "The Association of Capital Budgeting Techniques with Firm Performance," *Accounting Review* (April 1973), 535–564.

Kwan, Clarence C. Y., and Yufei Yuan. "Optimal Sequential Selection in Capital Budgeting: A Shortcut," *Financial Management*, 17 (Spring 1988), 54–59.

Logue, Dennis E., and T. Craig Tapley. "Performance Monitoring and the Timing of Cash Flows," *Financial Management*, 14 (Autumn 1985), 34–39.

Lorie, James H., and Leonard J. Savage. "Three Problems in Rationing Capital," *Journal of Business*, 28 (October 1955), 229–239.

Mao, James C. T. "The Internal Rate of Return as a Ranking Criterion," *Engineering Economist*, 11 (Winter 1966), 1–13.

McConnell, John J., and Chris J. Muscarella. "Corporate Capital Expenditure Decisions and the Market Value of the Firm," *Journal of Financial Economics*, 14 (September 1985), 399–422.

Mehta, Dileep R., Michael D. Curley, and Hung-Gay Fung. "Inflation Cost of Capital and Capital Budgeting Procedures," *Financial Management*, 13 (Winter 1984), 48–54.

Merrett, A. J., and Allen Sykes. *Capital Budgeting and Company Finance*. London: Longmans, 1966.

Miller, Edward M. "The Competitive Market Assumption and Capital Budgeting Criteria," *Financial Management*, 16 (Winter 1987), 22–28.

Myers, Stewart C. "Notes on an Expert System for Capital Budgeting," *Financial Management*, 17 (Autumn 1988), 23–31.

Narayanan, M. P. "Observability and the Payback Criterion," *Journal of Business*, 58 (July 1985), 309–323.

Osteryoung, Jerome. *Capital Budgeting: Long-Term Asset Selection*. 2nd ed., Columbus, OH: Grid, 1979. 65.

Petty, J. William, and Oswald D. Bowlin. "The Financial Manager and Quantitative Decision Models," *Financial Management*, 4 (Winter 1976), 32–41.

Petty, J. William, David F. Scott, Jr., and Monroe M. Bird. "The Capital Expenditure Decision-Making Process of Large Corporations," *Engineering Economist*, 20 (Spring 1975), 159–172.

PonArul, Richard. "Treatment of Flotation Cost of Equity in Capital Budgeting," *Journal of Financial Education*, 19 (1990), 44–45.

Porter, Michael E. *Competitive Advantage*. New York: Free Press, 1985.

Quirin, G. David, and John C. Wiginton. *Analyzing Capital Expenditures*. Homewood, IL: Richard D. Irwin, 1981.

Rappaport, Alfred, and Robert A. Taggart, Jr. "Evaluation of Capital Expenditure Proposals under Inflation," *Financial Management*, 11 (Spring 1982), 5–13.

Rosenblatt, Meir J. "A Survey and Analysis of Capital Budgeting Decision Process in Multi-Division Firms," *Engineering Economist*, 25 (Summer 1980), 259–273.

Ross, Marc. "Capital Budgeting Practices of Twelve Large Manufacturers," *Financial Management*, 15 (Winter 1986), 15–22.

Sarnat, Marshall, and Haim Levy. "The Relationship of Rules of Thumb to the Internal Rate of Return: A Restatement and Generalization," *Journal of Finance*, 24 (June 1969), 479–490.

Schall, Laurence D., Gary L. Sundem, and William R. Geljsbeek, Jr. "Survey and Analysis of Capital Budgeting Methods," *Journal of Finance*, 33 (March 1978), 281–287.

Schnell, James S., and Roy S. Nicholosi. "Capital Expenditure Feedback: Project Reappraisal," *Engineering Economist*, 19 (Summer 1974), 253–261.

Schwab, Bernhard, and Peter Lusztig. "A Comparative Analysis of the Net Present Value and the Benefit-Cost Ratios as Measures of the Economic Desirability of Investments," *Journal of Finance*, 24 (June 1969), 507–516.

Solomon, Ezra. "The Arithmetic of Capital-Budgeting Decisions," *Journal of Business*, 29 (April 1956), 124–129.

Statman, Meir, and David Caldwell. "Applying Behavioral Finance to Capital Budgeting: Project Terminations," *Financial Management*, 16 (Winter 1987), 7–15.

Statman, Meir, and Tyzoon T. Tyebjee. "Optimistic Capital Budgeting Forecasts," *Financial Management*, 14 (Autumn 1985), 27–33.

Teichroew, Daniel, Alexander A. Robichek, and Michael Montalbano. "An Analysis of Criteria for Investment and Financing Decisions under Certainty," *Management Science*, 12 (November 1965), 151–179.

Thompson, Arthur A., Jr. *Economics of the Firm: Theory and Practice*. Englewood Cliffs, NJ: Prentice-Hall, 1989.

Turner, Leslie D. "Improved Measures of Manufacturing Maintenance in a Capital Budgeting Context: An Application of Data Envelopment Analysis Efficiency Measures," *Journal of Management Accounting Research*, 2 (1990), 127–133.

Viscione, Jerry, and John Neuhauser. "Capital Expenditure Decisions in Moderately Sized Firms," *Financial Review* (1974), 16-23.

Weaver, James B. "Organizing and Maintaining a Capital Expenditure Program," *Engineering Economist*, 20 (Fall 1974), 1–36.

Weaver, Samuel C., Donald Peters, Roger Cason, and Joe Daleiden. "Capital Budgeting: Panel Discussions on Corporate Investments," *Financial Management*, 18 (Spring 1989), 10–17.

Weingartner, H. Martin. *Mathematical Programming and the Analysis of Capital Budgeting Problems*. Copyright H. Martin Weingartner, 1963.

Woods, John C., and Maury R. Randall. "The Net Present Value of Future Investment Opportunities: Its Impact on Shareholder Wealth and Implications for Capital Budgeting Theory," *Financial Management*, 18 (Summer 1989), 85–92.

CHAPTER 7

Advanced Topics in Capital Budgeting

- Capital Budgeting for Expansion Projects
- Capital Budgeting for Replacement Projects
- Risk and Capital Budgeting
- Methods for Incorporating Risk into Capital Budgeting
- Other Approaches to Evaluating Risk in Capital Budgeting
- Other Sources and Measures of Risk
- Inflation and Capital-Budgeting Decisions
- Capital Rationing
- Project Ranking

In the previous chapter we discussed criteria which should be used to evaluate a firm's investment projects. However, the application of these criteria to capital-budgeting decisions was based upon the following assumptions: no tax regulations for depreciation; each project has the same risk level; no inflation; and, no dollar limit for capital spending. In this chapter, we remove these assumptions and examine the discounted cash flow criteria for capital-budgeting decisions.

In this chapter the following topics will be examined:

1. We apply the discounted cash flow criteria to expansion and replacement projects. These criteria require us to determine cash flows which adhere to tax regulations that enable firms to write off the investment value of depreciable assets. The values of cash flows over the project's life are determined using two different approaches.

2. Next, we remove the assumption that each project has the same level of risk and examine the capital-budgeting decision with uncertainty. Several methods are introduced to incorporate risk into the capital-budgeting technique. In addition, we examine the impact of inflation on the capital budgeting decision.

3. Finally, we examine the capital budgeting decision for a situation in which there is a choice among a number of acceptable projects or there is a limit to the capital budget; that is, capital rationing is imposed. In these situations managers must assign different rankings to the projects according to the discounted cash flow criterion being used. As a result, the issues of capital rationing and project ranking are examined so as to determine how they affect capital-budgeting decisions.

In examining the discounted cash flow criteria for capital-budgeting decisions, we showed that these criteria were superior to nondiscounted cash flow criteria because they used the concept of cash flows and accounted for the time value of money. As a result, we now apply these criteria to capital budgeting decisions for expansion and replacement projects.

CAPITAL BUDGETING FOR EXPANSION PROJECTS

An expansion project for manufacturing and processing firms generally requires the acquisition of new assets for either initiating a production line or increasing the existing production capacity. The decision criteria for evaluating expansion projects are dependent upon how accurately we measure the net cash flows of the project. To facilitate the measurement of cash flows during the project's life, we arbitrarily divide the project into three periods: the initial period when the project set-up costs are incurred, the operating period when the project incurs both revenues and expenses for manufacturing the product, and the final period when the project is terminated. As a result of dividing the project into three periods, we can now separate the net cash flows of an expansion project into one of three categories: (1) the initial outlay, (2) the incremental net cash flows over the project's operating life, (3) the terminal cash flow. In introducing these cash flow categories, we first determine what factors influence each category of cash flow and then determine the value of these cash flows to shareholders of the firm.

Initial Outlay

The most important component of the initial outlay for an expansion project is the immediate cash outflow required to purchase an asset and to put it into operating order. Revenue Canada designates the purchase cost of an asset to the firm as the asset's capital cost.[1] The capital cost of an asset also includes any costs associated with acquiring or putting the asset into working order, such as shipping fees, installation costs, special engineering costs, and any incremental administrative costs such as accounting expenses.

The initial outlay must also include any opportunity costs that are associated with the implementation of the project. For example, the firm should include the fair market value of any land that is owned by the firm but is being used for the project. Furthermore, any lost revenues (e.g., parking fees) from this land should also be included as an opportunity cost to the firm. The initial outlay also includes any nonexpense cash outlays. If we are considering a new sales outlet, there might be incremental cash flows associated with the investment in working capital such as any increases in inventory or cash which are necessary to operate the sales outlet. While these cash flows

---

[1]The Income Tax Act, Section 13(7.1), refers to the deemed capital cost of depreciable property as the capital cost of the asset net of any investment tax credit or governmental assistance.

TABLE 7-1	1. Capital cost of asset
Summary of Calculation of	2. Opportunity costs
Initial Outlay Incremental	3. Incremental nonexpense outlays incurred (for example, working capital investments)
Cash Flow After-Tax	4. Incremental cash expenses on an after-tax basis (for example, training expenses)
	5. In a replacement decision, the cash flow associated with the sale of the old machine

are not included in the cost of the asset or even expensed on the books, they must be included in our analysis. In addition, the initial outlay will include investment tax credits and any cash expenses on an after tax basis, such as any training expenses associated with operating the new asset.

Obviously, determining the initial outlay is a complex calculation. Table 7-1 summarizes some of the more common calculations involved in determining the initial outlay. This list is by no means exhaustive, but it should help simplify the calculations involved in the example that follows.[2]

Perspective in Finance

At this point we should note that the incremental nature of the cash flow is of great importance. In many cases if the project is not accepted, then "status quo" for the firm will simply not continue. In estimating incremental cash flows we must be realistic in choosing our base case. The reading in Basic Financial Management in Practice, "Using the Right Base Case," deals with precisely this question.

EXAMPLE

In order to clarify the calculation of the initial outlay, consider an example of a manufacturing company in the electronic components sector. Assume that this company has a combined corporate tax rate of 45 percent with a 15 percent required rate of return or cost of capital. Management is considering the expansion of a manufacturing line by purchasing a $500,000 hand-operated assembly machine. To put the new machine in running order, it is necessary to pay shipping charges of $30,000 and installation charges of $30,000. The new machine will require an increase in goods-in-progress inventory of $50,000 and its expected useful life is ten years.

The capital cost of the new machine would be the $500,000 purchase cost plus the $30,000 shipping and the $30,000 installation fees, for a total of $560,000. An incremental outflow occurs with the increased investment in inventory. The increase in goods-in-process inventory of $50,000 must also be considered part of the initial outlay, with an offsetting inflow of $50,000 corresponding to the recapture of this inventory occurring at the termination of the project. In effect, the firm invests $50,000 in inventory now, resulting in an initial cash outlay, and liquidates this inventory in ten years, resulting in a cash inflow at the end of the project. The total outlays associated with the new machine are $560,000 for its capital cost and $50,000 in investment in inventory, for a total of $610,000. Thus, the net initial outlay associated with this project is $610,000. These calculations are summarized in Table 7-2. ■

[2]The evaluation of new projects should also look at the strategic options provided by a new investment. In light of the opening up of borders in Europe in 1992, many companies based their investment decision in part on the access to the marketing and distribution channels.

Incremental Net Cash Flows over the Project's Operating Life

In considering an investment proposal, we must determine the net cash flows generated from a project during the operating period. Again, we emphasize that the cash flows being measured must be incremental. As a

---

BASIC FINANCIAL MANAGEMENT IN PRACTICE

I. Patrick Barwise, Paul Marsh, and Robin Wensley on Using the Right Base Case

Finance theory assumes that a project will be evaluated against its base case, that is, what will happen if the project is not carried out. Managers tend to explore fully the implications of adopting the project but usually spend less time considering the likely outcome of not making the investment. Yet unless the base case is realistic, the incremental cash flows—the difference between the "with" and the "without" scenarios—will mislead.

Often companies implicitly assume that the base case is simply a continuation of the status quo, but this assumption ignores market trends and competitor behavior. It also neglects the impact of changes the company might make anyway, like improving operations management.

Using the wrong base case is typical of product launches in which the new product will likely erode the market for the company's existing product line. Take Apple Computer's introduction of the Macintosh SE. The new PC had obvious implications for sales of earlier generation Macintoshes. To analyze the incremental cash flows arising from the new product, Apple would have needed to count the lost contribution from sales of its existing products as a cost of the launch.

Wrongly applied, however, this approach would equate the without case to the status quo: it would assume that without the SE, sales of existing Macintoshes would continue at their current level. In the competitive PC market, however, nothing stands still. Competitors like IBM would likely innovate and take share away from the earlier generation Macintoshes—which a more realistic base case would have reflected. Sales of existing products would decline even in the base case.

Consider investments in the marketing of existing brands through promotions, media budgets, and

the like. They are often sold as if they were likely to lead to ever-increasing market share. But competitors will also be promoting their brands, and market shares across the board still have to add up to 100%. Still, such an investment is not necessarily wasted. It may just need a more realistic justification: although the investment is unlikely to increase sales above existing levels, it may prevent sales from falling. Marketers who like positive thinking may not like this defensive argument, but it is the only argument that makes economic sense in a mature market.

In situations like this, when the investment is needed just to maintain market share, the returns may be high in comparison with the base case, but the company's reported profits may still go down. Senior managers are naturally puzzled at apparently netting only 5% on a project that had promised a 35% return.[3] Without the investment, however, the profit picture would have looked even worse, especially in the longer term.

Some projects disappoint for other reasons. Sometimes the original proposals are overoptimistic, partly because the base case is implicit or defined incorrectly. That is, if managers are convinced that the investment is sound and are frustrated because the figures fail to confirm their intuition, they may over-inflate projections of sales or earnings. But misstating the base case and then having to make unrealistic projections are unlikely to cancel each other out; they merely cloud the analysis.

---

[3]Joseph L. Bower, *Managing the Resource Allocation Process*, Boston: Harvard Business School Press, 1986, p. 13.

TABLE 7-2
Calculation of Initial Outlay
for Example Problem

Outflows:	
Purchase price	$500,000
Shipping fee	30,000
Installation fee	30,000
Capital cost of machine	$560,000
Increased investment in inventory	50,000
Total outflows	$610,000
Inflows:	
None	– 0
Net initial outlay	$610,000

result, the incremental net cash flow occurring over the life of an expansion project includes the following items: increases in operating revenues, labour or material savings, and reductions in selling expenses. Incremental increases in any overhead items such as utilities, heat, light, and executive salaries must be included in the determination of incremental operating expenses.

Another important consideration in determining the net operating cash flows is the effect of depreciation for tax purposes on the firm's taxes payable. For the purposes of accounting, depreciation and depletion are recognized on the balance sheet as an allocation of the cost of a depreciable asset or a natural resource over its useful life. In other words, accounting depreciation or depletion expenses are non-cash expenses and are generally included in operating expenses. For the purposes of finance, we are only interested in determining cash expenses. As a result, non-cash expenses such as the accounting expenses of depreciation and depletion must be added back to operating expenses in order to obtain real flows of cash from operations.

Perspective in Finance

The analysis of an investment proposal for tax purposes requires that we determine the effect of depreciation on taxable income. For purposes of taxes, depreciation expenses are called capital cost allowances and they decrease the firm's taxable income. In other words, the effect of capital cost allowance on taxable income causes a decrease in the firm's taxes which in turn increases the firm's profits. However, for the purposes of finance, the analysis of projects requires that we maximize shareholders' wealth. In fact, projects are chosen on the basis of how much economic wealth is transferred from the project to the firm. Because the emphasis in financial decision-making is to increase the shareholder's economic wealth, management will choose a project on the basis of how much economic wealth it generates and not on the basis of the amount of tax savings generated from the project. Nevertheless, we must bear in mind that although the capital cost allowance is not a cash flow item, the permitted write-off in terms of a capital cost allowance does have a tax effect on the project's cash flows. As a result, our decision-making process should account for the tax effects of capital cost allowance, but only to the extent that it provides a more accurate basis to evaluate the project's cash flows.

Depreciation Methods for Tax Purposes

Revenue Canada permits a taxpayer to write off the value of depreciable assets by using the capital cost allowance system. For the purposes of taxes, the portion of the asset's value being written off is called a *capital cost allowance.* In other words, capital cost allowances are the equivalent of depreciation expenses for accounting purposes. To understand how the capital cost allowance system functions, we first define some of the system's terms such as asset classes and undepreciated capital cost.

Revenue Canada has classified all depreciable assets into groups, called asset classes, which specify both the method of depreciation and the rate at which the asset can be written off. The majority of depreciable assets belong to asset classes which require the use of the declining balance method to write off the asset's value.[4] Some of the major asset classes and their depreciation methods are shown in Table 7-3.

A small number of depreciable assets are classified in asset classes which use methods other than the declining balance method. For example, asset class 14 contains limited life intangibles such as patents, franchises, concessions, or licenses. Revenue Canada requires that these assets be written off over their legal life using a straight-line method of depreciation. Other examples of depreciation methods include asset classes 24, 27 and 34 which permit the asset to be fully written off over three years. The capital cost allowances are determined from the following capital cost allowance rates: 25 percent in the first year, 50 percent in the second year, and 25 percent in the third year.

Class	Summary of Items	Method and CCA Rate
1	Buildings or other structures including components parts acquired by taxpayer after 1987	Declining Balance Method at 4 percent
3	Buildings or other structures including components parts acquired by taxpayer before 1987	Declining Balance Method at 5 percent
8	Kilns, vats, electrical equipment acquired after May 25, 1976 or equipment not included in another class	Declining Balance Method at 20 percent
9	Aircraft acquired May 25, 1976	Declining Balance Method at 25 percent
10	General purpose electronic data-processing equipment, systems software, electronic communications control equipment and automotive equipment	Declining Balance Method at 30 percent
12	Books of a lending library, chinaware, cutlery, linen, uniforms, computer software acquired after May 25, 1976	100 percent
13	Leasehold interests	Straight-line method over unexpired term of lease (i.e., 5yr < unexpired term < 40yr)
14	Patents, Franchises, Concessions or Licenses for a limited period	Remaining legal life
29	Property acquired by a taxpayer before 1988 to be used directly or indirectly by him or her in Canada primarily in manufacturing or processing of goods for sale or lease	25 percent 1st year 50 percent 2nd year 25 percent 3rd year
39	Property acquired by a taxpayer after February 1992 that is not included in class 29	Declining Balance Method at 30 percent

TABLE 7-3
Depreciation Methods of the Major Asset Classes

[4]The declining balance method of depreciation encourages more noncash expenses to occur in the earlier years of the project. As a result, the declining balance method is used to minimize taxable income and thereby postpone taxes. This advantage is somewhat reduced for asset classes which require that the half-net amount rule be applied to the asset's *UCC.*

For tax purposes, Revenue Canada defines Undepreciated Capital Cost (UCC) of an asset, as the capital cost of the asset net of any capital cost allowances claimed by the firm. The UCC of the asset class is the sum of UCCs for each asset in the class net of any capital cost allowances for assets in the asset class.

Revenue Canada allows a taxpayer to claim any amount of capital cost allowance up to a maximum which is determined from the capital cost allowance rate of each asset class and the UCC of the asset at the beginning of the year. The amount of capital cost that is written off in a year is known as the capital cost allowance for tax purposes. A taxpayer is only permitted to claim a capital cost allowance on assets that are in productive use. For the purposes of capital budgeting, we are only interested in the assets purchased for the project. As a result, we determine the amount of capital cost allowance (CCA) which can be claimed for an asset as follows:

$$CCA = (UCC_n)(d) \qquad (7\text{-}1)$$

where
CCA = amount of capital cost allowance to be written off for the asset in year n

UCC_n = undepreciated capital cost of an asset at the beginning of year n

d = capital cost allowance rate

For most assets, Revenue Canada requests that in the first year of productive use the half-net amount rule be used to determine the amount of capital cost allowance. This rule requires that 50 percent of the net amount, the difference between any cost of purchase and any proceeds from disposition of assets within the asset class during the year, be added to the undepreciated capital cost at the beginning of the first year. The remaining 50 percent of the net amount is added to the undepreciated capital cost at the end of the first year. No half-net amount rule is applied to asset class 14.

To illustrate the declining balance method of depreciation, consider the firm which is purchasing the hand-operated assembly machine. This newly installed machine has a capital cost of $560,000. The assembly machine is one of several assets in asset class 39 which uses a declining balance method of depreciation at a capital cost allowance rate of 30 percent. In the machine's first year of productive use, the maximum amount of capital cost allowance that can be claimed by the firm is $84,000, the product of the capital cost allowance rate of 30 percent and 50 percent of the net amount (.50 × $560,000) or $280,000.

For purposes of finance, it is easier to think of the amount of depreciation expense for tax purposes in terms of tax shields. A tax shield is determined as follows:

$$\text{tax shield} = (CCA)(T) \qquad (7\text{-}2)$$

where
CCA = capital cost allowance

T = the firm's combined tax rate

In the first year, the firm inherits a tax shield of $37,800, the product of the capital cost allowance ($84,000) and the combined corporate tax rate (45%). The capital cost allowances and the tax shields for the 10 years of economic life are shown in Table 7-4.

In the first year of the project, the capital cost allowance from the

Year	Undepreciated Capital Cost Beginning	Capital Cost Allowance	Tax Shields	Undepreciated Capital Cost End
1	$280,000	$ 84,000	$37,800	$476,000
2	476,000	142,800	64,260	333,200
3	333,200	99,960	44,982	233,240
4	233,240	69,972	31,487	163,268
5	163,268	48,980	22,041	114,288
6	114,288	34,286	15,429	80,001
7	80,001	24,000	10,800	56,001
8	56,001	16,800	7,560	39,201
9	39,201	11,760	5,292	27,441
10	27,441	8,232	3,704	19,208

TABLE 7-4
Schedule for Capital Cost Allowances and Tax Shields

depreciation of the new machine will be based on the undepreciated capital cost which is adjusted for the half-net amount rule. Thus, the undepreciated capital cost at the beginning of the first year is $280,000, the product of the undepreciated capital cost ($560,000) and the adjustment for the half-net amount rule (50%). The capital cost allowance is $84,000, the product of the undepreciated capital cost ($280,000) and capital cost allowance rate (30%). At the end of the first year, the undepreciated capital cost is $476,000, the sum of undepreciated capital cost at the beginning of the year less the capital cost allowance ($560,000 – $84,000) and the other half of the adjustment for half-net amount rule ($280,000). The undepreciated capital cost at the beginning of the second year is $476,000, the undepreciated capital cost at the end of the first year. The capital cost allowance for the second year is $142,800, the product of the undepreciated capital cost at the beginning of the second year ($476,000) and the capital cost allowance rate (30%). The undepreciated capital cost at the end of the second year is $333,200, the difference between the undepreciated capital cost at the beginning of the year ($476,000) and the capital cost allowance ($142,800). This procedure for the second year is repeated to determine the annual undepreciated capital costs and the capital cost allowance for the useful life of the asset.

We now examine how the firm uses tax shields to determine the net operating cash flow for capital budgeting purposes. For an expansion project the net operating cash flow is the sum of the project's net operating income and the tax shields generated from the depreciation of the project's assets. We summarize the calculation for net operating cash flow as follows:[5]

	Incremental Operating Revenues
Deduct:	Incremental Operating Expenses (includes
	accounting depreciation and depletion expenses)
Add:	Accounting Depreciation and Depletion Expenses
	Net Operating Revenue
Deduct:	Tax on Net Operating Revenue
	Net Operating Income
Add:	Tax Shields from Depreciation & Depletion
	Net Operating Cash Flow After-Tax

[5]This relationship can also be described as follows:

Net Operating Cash Flows = (Net Operating Revenue)$(1 - T)$ + $(CCA)(T)$

where T is the combined corporate tax rate and CCA is the capital cost allowances.

Any increase in interest payments incurred as a result of issuing bonds to finance the project should not be included in net operating cash flows, since the costs of funds needed to support the project are implicitly accounted for by discounting the project back to the present using the required rate of return—the rate of return a project must earn to justify raising funds to finance it. Table 7-5 lists some of the factors that might be involved in determining a project's incremental cash flows.

EXAMPLE

Suppose that the new hand-operated assembly machine from the previous example requires one full-time operator who will be paid an annual salary of $35,000 with fringe benefits of $5,000 per year. The operation of this machine is expected to require variable overtime of $10,000 per year. In addition, the cost of defects is expected to increase by $5,000 per year, whereas the maintenance cost is expected to increase by $10,000 annually. For accounting purposes, the hand-operated assembly machine will be depreciated over 10 years using the straight-line method. Finally, management estimates that the annual operating revenue will increase by $275,000. Table 7-6 shows the calculation to determine the net operating income for the operating period.

The annual net operating income is $115,500, the difference between the annual net operating revenue ($210,000) and taxes ($94,500). Note that the annual net operating revenue is the difference between incremental operating revenues and incremental operating expenses net of the accounting depreciation expense. The adjustment of adding back accounting depreciation expense is required since depreciation is a non-cash expense. Table 7-7 shows the net operating cash flows after taxes over the useful life of the asset.

TABLE 7-5 Summary of Calculation of Incremental Net Cash Flows on an After-Tax Basis	1. Added revenue offset by increased expenses 2. Labour and material savings 3. Increases in overhead incurred 4. Tax shields from depreciation and depletion expenses 5. Do not include interest expenses if the project is financed by issuing debt, as this is accounted for in the required rate of return

TABLE 7-6
Calculation of the Annual Net Operating Income for an Expansion Project

Revenue:	
Incremental operating revenue	$275,000
Costs:	
Salary	35,000
Variable overtime	5,000
Fringe benefits	10,000
Defects	5,000
Maintenance expense	10,000
Accounting depreciation	56,000
Incremental operating expenses (including accounting depreciation)	121,000
Add: Accounting depreciation	56,000
Net operating revenue before taxes	$210,000
Taxes (@45%)	94,500
Net operating income	$115,500

Year	Net Operating Income	Tax Shield	Cash Flow After Tax
1	$115,500	$37,800	$153,300
2	115,500	64,260	179,760
3	115,500	44,982	160,482
4	115,500	31,487	146,987
5	115,500	22,041	137,541
6	115,500	15,429	130,929
7	115,500	10,800	126,300
8	115,500	7,560	123,060
9	115,500	5,292	120,792
10	115,500	3,704	119,204

TABLE 7-7
Net Operating Cash Flow After-Taxes Over the Useful Life of the Asset

Thus, the net operating cash flow after tax for the first year of operation is $153,300, the sum of the net operating income after taxes ($115,500) and the tax shield from depreciation ($37,800) of the new machine. ■

Terminal Cash Flow

The calculation of the terminal cash flow must be representative of the economic value of the project when it is terminated by the firm. Cash flows associated with the project's termination generally include the salvage value of the project, any tax effects caused by the salvage value, taxable gains associated with its sale, and any recaptured expenses from the initial outlay.

Generally, the most important terminal cash flow that a manager will add to the cash flows of the project in its last year is the salvage value of the asset. However, the time value of this cash flow must be determined by discounting the salvage value (SV) by the project's required rate of return.

$$PV(SV_n) = \left[\frac{SV_n}{(1 + k)^n}\right]$$ (7-3)

where SV_n = salvage value of the asset in year n

n = year in which the asset is salvaged

k = required rate of return on the project

When a project is terminated, the sale of assets will create one of two possible cases for tax purposes.

Case 1: Asset Class Kept Open □ This case is frequently encountered by a firm since an asset is sold to terminate the project but the sale does not terminate the asset class. For tax purposes, Revenue Canada requires that the firm subtract the salvage value of the asset from the undepreciated capital cost of the class. However, for purposes of capital budgeting, the sale of the asset causes the firm to forgo any future tax shields which it would inherit by continuing to own the asset. The sale of the asset at the end of the year of the project requires that the firm determine the value of all tax shields which it forgoes from the salvage year to time infinity. The amount of tax shields inherited in one year is determined as follows:

Annual tax shield $= (UCC_n)(d)(T)$ (7-4)

To determine the value of the tax shields from the year of salvage to time infinity, we apply the principles used to value a perpetuity. In this case, we are determining the value of a series of tax shields which extend from period n to infinity. The value of these lost tax shields to the project at $t = n$ is determined as follows:

$$\text{Value of lost tax shields} = \frac{(UCC_n - SV_n)(d)(T)}{(k + d)} \qquad (7\text{-}5)$$

It is important to note here that these tax shields are lost to the project but not to the firm. In fact, these tax shields have value for the firm until the asset class is terminated. The appropriate discount rate for the valuation of these lost tax shields is the project's required rate of return which is adjusted by the CCA rate. This discount rate reflects the appropriate risk level for a firm's investment into the tax shields from this type of project.

Case 2: Asset Class Terminated □ The sale of an asset can cause both the project and the asset class to be terminated. For tax purposes, Revenue Canada requires that the firm adjust its taxable income for either a recaptured depreciation or a terminal loss. These adjustments depend on whether the UCC_n of the asset class is greater or smaller than the lesser of the salvage value or the capital cost of the asset. The adjustments are made as follows:

SCENARIO (I) $SV_n > UCC_n$ ■ If the salvage value is greater than the undepreciated capital cost of the asset class, the firm has written off the asset too rapidly. In this situation, Revenue Canada requires that the firm report a recaptured depreciation because the asset class is being terminated.

The amount of recaptured depreciation to be reported is determined from the difference between the undepreciated capital cost of the asset class and the lesser of either the salvage value (SV_n) or the original capital cost (C_0) of the asset to be salvaged.

$$\text{Recaptured depreciation} = UCC_n - \text{Lesser of:} \left\{ \begin{array}{l} C_0 \\ SV_n \end{array} \right.$$

The recaptured depreciation is added to the firm's taxable income since both the salvage value and the original capital cost are greater than the UCC_n of the asset class. If the firm has written off the asset too rapidly for the purposes of capital budgeting, the firm is required to subtract the portion of tax shields which the firm is not entitled to claim from the cash flows of the project. The value of these tax shields is discounted by the project's required rate of return to determine their present value. The present value of the tax shields from terminating the asset class under this scenario is determined as follows:

$$\begin{array}{l} PV(\text{tax shields from} \\ \text{recaptured depreciation}) \end{array} = \left[\frac{(\text{Recaptured depreciation})(d)(T)}{(1 + k)^n} \right] \qquad (7\text{-}6)$$

Since the lesser of either the salvage value or the capital cost is greater than UCC_n of the asset class, the amount will be negative, indicating that these tax shields will be subtracted from the cash flows of the project.

SCENARIO (II) $SV_n < UCC_n$ ■ In this scenario, the firm has written off the asset too slowly such that the salvage value is less than the undepreciated capital cost of the asset class. In this situation, Revenue Canada allows the firm to report a terminal loss because the asset class is being terminated.

The amount of terminal loss to be reclaimed is determined from the difference between the undepreciated capital cost (UCC_n) of the asset class and the salvage value (SV_n) of the asset to be salvaged.

$$\text{Terminal loss} = UCC_n - SV_n$$

The terminal loss is subtracted from the firm's taxable income since the salvage value is less than the UCC_n of the asset class. If the firm has written off the asset too slowly for purposes of capital budgeting, the firm would add the portion of tax shields which the firm should have used to the cash flows of the project. The value of these tax shields is discounted by the project's required rate of return to determine their present value. The present value of the tax shields from terminating the asset class under this scenario is determined as follows:

$$PV(\text{tax shields from terminal loss}) = \left[\frac{(UCC_n - SV_n)(d)(T)}{(1 + k)^n} \right] \quad (7\text{-}7)$$

Since the salvage value is less than UCC_n, the amount will be positive, which indicates that these tax shields will be added to the cash flows of the project.

Scenario (iii) $UCC_n = SV_n$ ■ In this scenario, the salvage value of the asset equals the UCC_n of the asset class and no adjustment to the tax shields is required.

The sale of the assets when terminating a project may also cause the firm to incur a capital gain which must be included in the terminal cash flow. Revenue Canada requires that corporations report three quarters of the capital gain as taxable income.[6]

In addition to the cash flows from the salvage value, there may be cash flows associated with the termination of the project. For example, at the close of a strip-mining operation, the mine must be refilled in an ecologically acceptable manner. Finally, any working capital outlay required at the initiation of the project—for example, increased inventory needed for the operation of a new plant—will be recaptured at the termination of the project. In effect, the increased inventory required by the project can be liquidated when the project expires. For example, the amount of recaptured inventory expense would be determined as follows:

$$PV(\text{recaptured expenses from initial outlay}) = \frac{(\text{inventory expense})}{(1 + k)^n} \quad (7\text{-}8)$$

Table 7-8 provides a sample list of some of the factors that might affect a project's terminal cash flow.

EXAMPLE

The hand-held assembly machine is expected to have a salvage value of $50,000 at the end of ten years of useful life. The sale of the hand-held

---

[6]Capital gains incurred by corporations are not eligible for the lifetime capital gains exemption of $100,000.

1. The salvage value of the project
2. Recaptured capital cost allowance or terminal loss associated with the termination of the asset class
3. Cash outlays associated with the project's termination
4. Recapture of nonexpense outlays that occurred at the project's initiation (for example, working capital investment)

assembly machine is not expected to terminate the asset class for tax purposes. In addition, the firm will recapture the inventory expense at the end of the tenth year. Determine the firm's terminal cash flow.

To solve for the terminal cash flow of this project, we first determine the present value of the salvage value.

$$PV(SV_n) = \frac{SV_n}{(1 + k)^n}$$

$$= \frac{50,000}{(1.15)^{10}}$$

$$= 12,359$$

The second step is to determine the lost tax shields to the project because the asset is being salvaged.

$$PV(\text{Lost tax shields}) = \frac{\dfrac{(UCC_n - SV_n)(d)(T)}{(k + d)}}{(1 + k)^n}$$

$$= \frac{\dfrac{(19,208 - 50,000)(.30)(.45)}{(.15 + .30)}}{(1 + .15)^{10}}$$

$$= -2,283$$

Finally, we determine the amount of recaptured inventory expense which will be claimed by the firm when terminating the project.

$$PV(\text{Recaptured expenses of initial outlay}) = \frac{\text{inventory expenses}}{(1 + k)^n}$$

$$= \frac{50,000}{(1.15)^{10}}$$

$$= 12,359$$

Thus, the terminal cash flow is $90,762 and its present value is $22,435. ■

Determining Net Present Value

The project's net present value (NPV) can now be determined from the present value of each of the project's annual net cash flows. The calculation would require that the net operating cash flows over the life of the project be added to the terminal cash flow and then subtracted from the initial outlay. The following equation shows this procedure:

$$NPV = PV(\text{net operating cash flows}) + PV(\text{terminal cash flow}) - IO \qquad (7\text{-}9)$$

FIGURE 7-1. Cash Flow Diagram

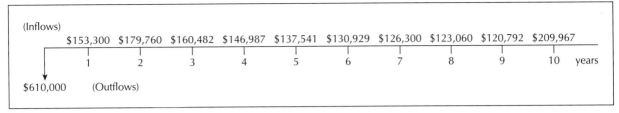

This equation can be rewritten as follows:

$$NPV = \sum_{t=1}^{n} \frac{CFAT_t}{(1+k)^t} - IO \qquad (7\text{-}10)$$

The firm should accept the project if the NPV is positive, reject the project if NPV is negative and be indifferent to accepting or rejecting the project if NPV is zero.

A simple tool which effectively illustrates the cash flows of this project is the cash flow diagram in Figure 7-1.

The NPV of this project is determined by discounting the annual net cash flow at the project's required rate of return over the ten years of project life. The equation for NPV is shown as follows:

$$NPV = \frac{\$153,300}{(1.15)^1} + \frac{\$179,760}{(1.15)^2} + \frac{\$160,482}{(1.15)^3} + \frac{\$146,987}{(1.15)^4} +$$

$$\frac{\$137,541}{(1.15)^5} + \frac{\$130,929}{(1.15)^6} + \frac{\$126,300}{(1.15)^7} +$$

$$\frac{\$123,060}{(1.15)^8} + \frac{\$120,792}{(1.15)^9} + \frac{\$209,967}{(1.15)^{10}} - \$610,000$$

$$NPV = \$147,722$$

Thus, the firm should accept the project of purchasing the hand-held assembly machine which has a positive NPV.

Determining the Net Present Value: The Annuity Approach

The net present value of a project can also be determined by applying principles which we used to value annuities and perpetuities. This approach separates the project's cash flows into components such as the project's annual net operating incomes and tax shields from depreciation, which can be valued using the same principles used to value either an annuity or a perpetuity of cash flows. The present value of each of these cash flows' components is then used to determine the net present value of the project.

First we examine the annuity which represents the annual net operating incomes which occur over the life of the project. The present value of this annuity is determined as follows:

$PV(\text{Net operating income}) = (\text{annual net operating income})(PVIFA_{k,n})$ (7-11)

The second component of the project's cash flows represents the tax shields from depreciation of the newly purchased asset. Most assets are written off for tax purposes using the declining balance method of depreciation. This particular method depreciates the capital cost (C_0) over an infinite number of years. An infinite series of tax shields which decrease at a constant rate can be valued as a perpetuity.[7] The present value of the tax shields from the purchase of an asset is determined as follows:

$$PV(\text{Tax shields of purchased asset}) = \left[\frac{(C_0)(d)(T)}{(k + d)} \right] \qquad (7\text{-}12)$$

However, Revenue Canada requires that the undepreciated capital cost of a new asset in asset class 39 be adjusted for the half-net amount rule. As a result of this adjustment, the present value of the adjusted tax shields from the purchase of an asset is determined as follows:

$$PV\left(\begin{array}{c}\text{Adjusted tax}\\\text{shields of purchased asset}\end{array}\right) = \left[\frac{(C_0)(d)(T)}{(k + d)} \right]\left[\frac{1 + (.5)(k)}{(1 + k)} \right] \qquad (7\text{-}13)$$

The firm is only permitted to use for capital budgeting purposes those tax shields which occur over the useful life of the asset. Once the asset is sold, any future tax shield generated by the asset cannot be used by this firm for capital budgeting purposes. These future tax shields represent a series of an infinite number of tax shields which decrease at a constant rate. Again, this type of series is valued as a perpetuity and its value at $t = n$ is determined as follows when the asset class is kept open:

$$(\text{Value of lost tax shields at } t = n) = \left[\frac{(SV_n)(d)(T)}{(k + d)} \right] \qquad (7\text{-}14)$$

---

[7]In the case of a declining balance method of depreciation whereby the capital cost of the asset is written off at a constant CCA rate (d), we can express the tax shield (TS) in any year in terms of the tax shield paid at the end of the previous year, $(C_0)(T)(d)(1 - d)^{-1}$. For example, the expected tax shield one year hence is simply $(C_0)(T)(d)(1 - d)^{-1}(1 + g)$ where $g = -d$. Likewise, the tax shield at the end of t years is $(C_0)(T)(d)(1 - d)^{-1}(1 + g)^t$. Using this notation, the valuation equation of tax shields inherited by the firm can be rewritten as follows:

$$V_{TS} = \frac{(C_0)(T)(d)(1 - d)^{-1}(1 - d)^1}{(1 + k)^1} + \frac{(C_0)(T)(d)(1 - d)^{-1}(1 - d)^2}{(1 + k)^2} + \ldots$$

$$\frac{(C_0)(T)(d)(1 - d)^{-1}(1 - d)^n}{(1 + k)^n} + \ldots \frac{(C_0)(T)(d)(1 - d)^{-1}(1 - d)^\infty}{(1 + k)^\infty}$$

If both sides of the equation are multiplied by $(1 + k)/(1 - d)$ and then the equation is subtracted from the product, the result is

$$\frac{V_{TS}(1 + k)}{(1 - d)} - V_{TS} = (C_0)(T)(d)(1 - d)^{-1} - \frac{(C_0)(T)(d)(1 - d)^{-1}(1 - d)^\infty}{(1 + k)^\infty}$$

If $k > g$ where $g = -d$, which normally should hold, $[(C_0)(T)(d)(1 - d)^{-1}(1 + g)/(1 + k)]$ approaches zero. As a result,

$$\frac{V_{TS}(1 + k)}{(1 - d)} - V_{TS} = (C_0)(T)(d)(1 - d)^{-1}$$

$$V_{TS}\left(\frac{1 + k}{1 - d}\right) - V_{TS} = \left(\frac{1 - d}{1 - d}\right) = (C_0)(T)(d)(1 - d)^{-1}$$

$$V_{TS}\left[\frac{(1 + k) - (1 - d)}{1 - d}\right] = (C_0)(T)(d)(1 - d)^{-1}$$

$$V_{TS}(k + d) = (C_0)(T)(d)(1 - d)^{-1}(1 - d)$$

$$V_{TS} = \frac{(C_0)(T)(d)}{(k + d)}$$

The value of this series of tax shields has been determined when the asset is salvaged and does not represent their present value.

In order to adjust for their present value we discount this series of tax shields by the project's required rate of return as follows:

$$PV(\text{Lost tax shields}) = \left[\frac{(SV_n)(d)(T)}{(k + d)} \right]\left[\frac{1}{(1 + k)^n} \right] \tag{7-15}$$

For capital budgeting purposes, we define the inherited tax shields from the purchased asset at $t = 0$, as the difference between the present value of the tax shields from purchasing the asset and the present value of the tax shields forgone by the sale of the asset. The present value of tax shields over the useful life of the asset is determined as follows:

$$PV\left(\begin{array}{c}\text{Inherited tax}\\\text{shields of purchased asset}\end{array}\right) = \left[\frac{(C_0)(d)(T)}{(k + d)} \right]\left[\frac{1 + (.5)(k)}{(1 + k)} \right] -$$

$$\left[\frac{(SV_n)(d)(T)}{(k + d)} \right]\left[\frac{1}{(1 + k)^n} \right] \tag{7-16}$$

In most cases, the firm will terminate a project, but will not close an asset class for tax purposes. As a result, we determine the present value of the tax shields over the useful life of the asset by using the salvage value. However, in some cases both the project and the asset class will be terminated. We adjust the present value of the tax shields over the useful life of the asset by replacing the salvage value with the undepreciated capital cost (UCC_n) in the equation as follows:

$$PV\left(\begin{array}{c}\text{Inherited tax}\\\text{shields of purchased asset}\end{array}\right) = \left[\frac{(C_0)(d)(T)}{(k + d)} \right]\left[\frac{1 + (.5)(k)}{(1 + k)} \right] -$$

$$\left[\frac{(UCC_n)(d)(T)}{(k + d)} \right]\left[\frac{1}{(1 + k)^n} \right] \tag{7-17}$$

The undepreciated capital cost (UCC_n) at the end of any year, n, can be determined by constructing a schedule for capital cost allowances and tax shields as shown in Table 7-4. However, the UCC_n at the end of any year, n, can also be determined through the following equation:

$$UCC_n = \left[C_0 \right]\left[1 - \left(\frac{d}{2} \right) \right]\left[(1 - d)^{n - 1} \right] \tag{7-18}$$

where UCC_n = undepreciated capital cost at end of the firm's taxation year n

        C_0 = capital cost

        d = capital cost allowance rate

        n = firm's taxation year

In addition to this change, we must also make the adjustment to the project's cash flows for either a recaptured depreciation or a terminal loss in the following manner:

SCENARIO (I) $SV_n > UCC_n$ ■ In this scenario, the firm has written off the asset too rapidly such that the salvage value is greater than the undepreciated capital cost of the asset class. In this situation, Revenue Canada requires the firm to report recaptured depreciation because the asset class is being terminated. The present value of the tax shields from terminating the asset class under this scenario is determined as follows:

$$PV\left(\begin{array}{c}\text{tax shields of}\\\text{recaptured depreciation}\end{array}\right) = \frac{(\text{Recaptured depreciation})(d)(T)}{(1 + k)^n} \quad (7\text{-}19)$$

Since the lesser of either the salvage value or the capital cost is greater than UCC_n, the amount will be negative which indicates that these tax shields will be subtracted from the cash flows of the project.

SCENARIO (II) $SV_n < UCC_n$ ■ In this scenario, the firm has written off the asset too slowly such that the salvage value is less than the undepreciated capital cost of the asset class. In this situation, Revenue Canada requires the firm to report a terminal loss because the asset class is being terminated. The present value of the tax shields from terminating the asset class under this scenario is determined as follows:

$$PV(\text{tax shields of terminal loss}) = \frac{(UCC_n - SV_n)(d)(T)}{(1 + k)^n} \quad (7\text{-}20)$$

Since the salvage value is less than UCC_n, the amount will be positive which indicates that these tax shields will be added to the cash flows of the project.

SCENARIO (III) $UCC_n = SV_n$ ■ In this scenario, the salvage value of the asset equals the UCC_n of the asset class and no adjustment to the tax shields is required.

The last step in our procedure is to include all other terms, such as the present value of the salvage value and any recaptured expense from the initial outlay, in the NPV equation. The NPV equation for the project is determined as follows:

$$\begin{aligned}NPV = \; &PV(\text{Project's Net Operating Income}) + \\ &PV(\text{Inherited tax shields of purchased asset}) + \\ &PV(\text{Salvage Value}) + \\ &PV(\text{Adjustment for the termination of the asset class}) + \\ &PV(\text{Recapture of Inventory expense}) - IO \quad (7\text{-}21)\end{aligned}$$

EXAMPLE

Using the annuity approach, we will now redo the previous example in which a firm is considering the purchase of a hand-held assembly machine.

1st Step: The annual net operating income for the project has been determined to be $115,500 as shown in Table 7-6. The present value of the series of annual net operating incomes over the 10 years of useful life of the asset is determined as follows:

$$PV(\text{net operating income}) = (\text{annual net operating income})(PVIFA_{15\%, 10yr})$$
$$= (115,500)(5.0188)$$
$$= 579,668$$

Thus, the present value of the net operating incomes over the 10 years of the project is $579,668.

2nd Step: The present value of the tax shields over the useful life of the asset is determined from the difference between the present value of the tax shields from purchasing the asset and the present value of the tax shields forgone by the sale of the asset at $t = 0$. Given a capital cost (C_0) of $560,000, a combined corporate tax rate (T) of 45%, a capital cost allowance rate (d) of 30% and the project's required rate of return, k, of 15%, the present value of the adjusted tax shields from purchasing the asset is determined as follows:

$$PV \left(\begin{array}{c} \text{Adjusted tax} \\ \text{shields of purchased asset} \end{array} \right) = \left[\frac{(C_0)(d)(T)}{(k + d)} \right] \left[\frac{1 + (.5)(k)}{(1 + k)} \right]$$

$$= \left[\frac{(560,000)(.30)(.45)}{(.15 + .30)} \right] \left[\frac{1 + (.5)(.15)}{(1 + .15)} \right]$$

$$= [168,000][.9348]$$

$$= 157,046$$

Thus, the present value of the tax shields from purchasing the asset is $157,046.

Given the salvage value of $50,000, the present value of the tax shields forgone by the sale of the asset at $t = 0$, when the asset class is kept open, is determined as follows:

$$PV(\text{Lost tax shields}) = \left[\frac{(SV_n)(d)(T)}{(k + d)} \right] \left[\frac{1}{(1 + k)^n} \right]$$

$$= \left[\frac{(50,000)(.30)(.45)}{(.15 + .30)} \right] \left[\frac{1}{(1 + .15)^{10}} \right]$$

$$= [15,000][.2472]$$

$$= 3,708$$

Thus, the present value of the tax shields forgone by the sale of the asset at $t = 0$ is $3,708.

We can now determine the present value of the tax shields over the useful life of the asset as follows:

$$PV \left(\begin{array}{c} \text{Inherited tax} \\ \text{shields of purchased asset} \end{array} \right) = \left[\frac{(C_0)(d)(T)}{(k + d)} \right] \left[\frac{1 + (.5)(k)}{(1 + k)} \right] -$$

$$\left[\frac{(SV_n)(d)(T)}{(k + d)} \right] \left[\frac{1}{(1 + k)^n} \right]$$

$$= 157,046 - 3,708$$

$$= 153,338$$

Thus, the present value of the tax shields over the useful life of the asset is $153,338.

3rd Step: The present value of the salvage value is determined as follows:

$$PV(\text{Salvage Value}) = (SV_n)(PVIF_{15\%,10yr})$$
$$= (50,000)(.2472)$$
$$= 12,359$$

Thus, the present value of the salvage value is $12,359.

4th Step: The present value of any recaptured expense from the initial outlay is determined as follows:

$$PV(\text{Recaptured expenses of initial outlay}) = (\text{inventory expenses})(PVIF_{15\%,10yr})$$
$$= (50,000)(.2472)$$
$$= 12,359$$

Thus, the present value of any recaptured expense from the initial outlay is $12,359.

5th Step: The NPV equation for this problem is determined as follows:

$$NPV = PV(\text{Project's Net Operating Income}) +$$
$$PV(\text{Inherited tax shields of purchased asset}) +$$
$$PV(\text{Salvage Value}) +$$
$$PV(\text{Recapture of Inventory expense}) - IO$$

$$NPV = (\$115,500)(5.0188) + [(168,000)(.9348)] - [(15,000)(.2472)] +$$
$$(\$50,000)(.2472) + (\$50,000)(.2472) - \$610,000$$

$$NPV = \$147,722$$

Given the asset class is kept open, the NPV of this project is $147,722. Since the NPV is positive, the firm should accept the project. ∎

Suppose in the above example, the asset class is terminated when the asset is sold for $50,000. This situation represents the first scenario in which the asset class is terminated. The UCC_n of the asset class is determined as follows:

$$UCC_n = \left[C_0\right]\left[1-\left(\frac{d}{2}\right)\right]\left[(1-d)^{n-1}\right]$$
$$UCC_{10} = \left[560,000\right]\left[1-\left(\frac{.30}{2}\right)\right]\left[(1-.30)^{10-1}\right]$$
$$= 19,208$$

Thus, the UCC_{10} of the asset class is $19,208.

The present value of the tax shields over the useful life of the asset when the asset class is closed, is determined as follows:

$$PV\left(\begin{array}{c}\text{inherited tax shields}\\\text{of purchased asset}\end{array}\right) = \left[\frac{(C_0)(d)(T)}{(k+d)}\right]\left[\frac{1+(.5)(k)}{(1+k)}\right] -$$
$$\left[\frac{(UCC_n)(d)(T)}{(k+d)}\right]\left[\frac{1}{(1+k)^n}\right]$$
$$= \left[\frac{(560,000)(.30)(.45)}{(.15+.30)}\right]\left[\frac{1+(.5)(.15)}{(1+.15)}\right] -$$
$$\left[\frac{(19,208)(.30)(.45)}{(.15+.30)}\right]\left[\frac{1}{(1+.15)^{10}}\right]$$
$$= 157,046 - 1,424$$
$$= 155,622$$

Thus, the present value of tax shields over the useful life of the asset is $155,622.

Since the asset class is being closed, an adjustment to the tax shields is required. In this scenario, the salvage value is greater than the UCC_n such that the asset was written off too rapidly and the firm is required to report recaptured depreciation. The value of the recaptured depreciation is determined as follows:

$$PV(\text{tax shields from recaptured depreciation}) =$$

$$\left[\frac{(UCC_n - \text{Lesser of either: \{Salvage value or Original capital cost\}})(d)(T)}{(1 + k)^n} \right]$$

$$= \frac{(19{,}208 - 50{,}000)(.30)(.45)}{(1.15)^{10}}$$

$$= -1{,}028$$

Since the adjustment is negative, the firm would recognize the amount as recaptured depreciation. In this case the recaptured depreciation of $1,028 is subtracted from the cash flows of the project. The effect of terminating the asset class on the NPV is shown in Table 7-9.

This same example can be redone whereby the asset class is terminated when the asset is sold for $0. This situation illustrates the second scenario in which the asset class is terminated and the salvage value of the asset is less than the UCC_n. Again, the UCC_n of the asset class is $19,208 and the present value of the tax shields over the useful life of the asset is $155,622. If the salvage value is less than the UCC_n, the firm has written off the asset too slowly and the firm would report a terminal loss for tax purposes. The value of the terminal loss is determined as follows:

$$PV(\text{Tax shields of terminal loss}) = \frac{(UCC_n - SV_n)(d)(T)}{(1 + k)^n}$$

$$= \frac{(19{,}208 - 0)(.30)(.45)}{(1 + .15)^{10}}$$

$$= 641$$

In this case the terminal loss of $641 is added to the cash flows of the project. The effect of the terminating the asset class on the NPV is shown in Table 7-9.

Present Value of Cash Flows	Asset Class Kept Open	Recaptured Depreciation	Terminal Loss
Net operating incomes after tax	$579,668	$579,668	$579,668
Tax shields over useful life of asset	153,338	$155,622	$155,622
Salvage value	12,359	$12,359	$0
Tax shields adjustment for terminating the asset class	0	–$1,028	$641
Recapture of inventory expense	12,359	$12,539	$12,539
NPV	$147,722	$149,160	$138,470

CAPITAL BUDGETING FOR REPLACEMENT PROJECTS

We now examine replacement projects which involve the acquisition of a new asset to replace an older, less efficient asset. To evaluate whether to accept or reject a replacement project, we will use the annuity approach to determine the NPV of the project. However, the replacement project differs from the expansion project because the net cash flows of a replacement project will be measured in terms of the amount of net savings after taxes that accrues to the firm. In addition to the cash flows which we described for the initial outlay of an expansion project, we also consider the cash flow associated with the selling price of the old asset and the tax shields lost from the sale of the old asset.

Although the old asset is sold, the asset class remains open during the first year of the replacement project. We use the concept of incremental capital cost to adjust for the tax shields lost because of the sale of the old machine. The incremental capital cost of the new machine is calculated as the difference between the capital cost of the new machine and the current salvage value of the old machine.

$$\Delta C_0 = C_{0,\text{new}} - SV_{0,\text{old}} \tag{7-22}$$

Table 7-1 provides a summary of the considerations which are used in determining the initial outlay of a replacement project.

The incremental net operating cash flows occurring over the life of a replacement project also include items such as increases in operating revenues, labour or material savings, and reductions in selling expenses. The net operating cash flow over the life of the project is the sum of the project's annual net operating incomes and the tax shields generated from the depreciation of the project's assets. The annual net operating cash flow is determined as follows:

	Incremental Operating Savings
Deduct:	Incremental Operating Expenses (includes accounting depreciation and depletion expenses)
Add:	Depreciation and Depletion Expenses
	Net Operating Savings before taxes
Deduct:	Tax on Net Operating Savings
	Net Operating Savings after taxes
Add:	Tax Shields from Depreciation and Depletion
	Net Operating Cash Flow

Table 7-5 summarizes some of the factors used in determining the net operating cash flows of a replacement project.

The series of annual net operating savings after tax can be valued as an annuity. The present value of this annuity is determined as follows:

$$PV\left(\begin{array}{c}\text{net operating}\\\text{savings after taxes}\end{array}\right) = \left(\begin{array}{c}\text{annual net}\\\text{operating savings after taxes}\end{array}\right)\left(PVIFA_{k,n}\right)$$

The approach of valuing tax shields inherited by the firm over the life of the replacement project is similar to that of the expansion project. However, we adjust the annuity for the change we made to the incremental capital cost. This change to the incremental capital cost affects the calculation for ΔUCC_n as follows:

$$\Delta UCC_n = \left[\Delta C_0\right]\left[1 - \left(\frac{d}{2}\right)\right]\left[(1 - d)^{n-1}\right] \tag{7-23}$$

In addition, we must treat the salvage value of the new asset as an incremental cash flow by considering the salvage value of the old asset if it were not replaced. This consideration is an example of an opportunity cost for a replacement project. As a result, the incremental salvage value (ΔSV_n) for the new asset is determined as follows:

$$\Delta SV_n = SV_{n,\text{new}} - SV_{n,\text{old}} \tag{7-24}$$

We now examine the adjustments which have to be made to the tax shields because of the changes to both the capital cost and salvage value of the new asset. The incremental capital cost and the incremental salvage value of an asset affect the present value of the tax shields over the life of a project when the asset is kept open. We determine the present value these tax shields over the life of the project as follows:

$$PV\left(\begin{array}{c}\text{Inherited tax shields} \\ \text{of purchased asset}\end{array}\right) = \left[\frac{(\Delta C_0)(d)(T)}{(k + d)}\right]\left[\frac{1 + (.5)(k)}{(1 + k)}\right] - \left[\frac{(\Delta SV_n)(d)(T)}{(k + d)}\right]\left[\frac{1}{(1 + k)^n}\right] \tag{7-25}$$

A similar adjustment is made to the present value of the tax shields over the life of the project when the asset class is closed. We determine the present value of these tax shields over the life of the project as follows:

$$PV\left(\begin{array}{c}\text{Inherited tax shields} \\ \text{of purchased asset}\end{array}\right) = \left[\frac{(\Delta C_0)(d)(T)}{(k + d)}\right]\left[\frac{1 + (.5)(k)}{(1 + k)}\right] - \left[\frac{(\Delta UCC_n)(d)(T)}{(k + d)}\right]\left[\frac{1}{(1 + k)^n}\right] \tag{7-26}$$

We also adjust the tax shields from terminating the project as follows:

$$PV(\text{Tax shields of terminal loss}) = \left[\frac{(\Delta UCC_n - \Delta SV_n)(d)(T)}{(1 + k)^n}\right] \tag{7-27}$$

Finally, we include the recapture of any expense from the initial outlay such as inventory expenses, in the NPV equation. The NPV equation for a replacement project is determined as follows:

$$\begin{aligned}NPV = {}&PV(\text{Project's Net Operating Savings after taxes}) + \\ &PV(\text{Inherited tax shields of purchased asset}) + \\ &PV(\text{Incremental Salvage Value}) + \\ &PV(\text{Adjustment for the termination of the asset class}) + \\ &PV(\text{Recapture of Inventory expense}) - IO\end{aligned} \tag{7-28}$$

In order to clarify the annuity approach for determining the Net Present Value of a replacement project, we consider an example of a company that has a combined corporate tax rate of 45 percent. This company is considering the purchase of a $30,000 machine which will replace an existing machine that has been used for gas and oil drilling. Both of these machines are classified in asset class 28 for tax purposes. Revenue Canada requires that assets in this asset class be written off using the declining balance method of depreciation at a CCA rate of 30 percent. Five years ago, the existing machine had a capital cost of $20,000. However, the existing machine can now be sold to a scrap dealer for $15,000. The existing machine is expected to have a salvage value of zero in five years, while the new machine is expected to be salvaged for $8,000 in five years. To put the new machine in running order, it is necessary to pay shipping charges of $2,000 and installation charges of $3,000. Because the new machine will work faster than the existing one, it will require an increase in goods-in-progress inventory of $5,000.

The purchase of the new machine is expected to reduce salaries by $10,000 per year and fringe benefits by $1,000 annually. These benefits accrue to the firm because it will take only one person to operate the new machine, whereas the old machine requires two operators. In addition, the cost of defects will fall from $8,000 per year to $3,000. However, maintenance expenses will increase by $4,000 annually.

The sale of the new machine in five years is not expected to terminate the asset class for tax purposes. The firm's required rate of return on this type of project is 12 percent. Determine whether the firm should accept or reject this replacement project.

We now solve the NPV for this project using the annuity approach:

Step 1: We must first determine the initial outlay made by the firm. In this example, the firm's initial outlay is the sum of the capital cost and the incremental investment in inventory expenses. The capital cost of the new machine is the $30,000 purchase cost plus the $2,000 shipping and the $3,000 installation fees, for a total of $35,000. Since the replacement of the existing machine with a new machine occurs within the same year, the asset class will remain open for tax purposes. An incremental cash outflow occurs with the increased investment in inventory. The increase in goods-in-process inventory of $5,000 must also be considered part of the initial outlay, with an offsetting inflow of $5,000 corresponding to the recapture of this inventory occurring at the termination of the project. In effect, the firm invests $5,000 in inventory now, resulting in an initial cash outlay, and liquidates this inventory in five years, resulting in a cash inflow at the end of the project. The total outlay associated with the new machine is $35,000 for its capital cost and $5,000 in investment in inventory, for a total of $40,000. This is somewhat offset by the sale of the existing machine for $15,000. Thus, the net initial outlay associated with this project is $25,000. These calculations are summarized in Table 7-10.

Step 2: We now determine the present value of the net operating savings after-taxes. The annual net operating savings after taxes is the difference between the net operating savings before taxes and taxes payable on these savings. Table 7-11 shows the calculation for the annual net operating savings which occur over the life of the project.

The present value of the series of annual net operating savings after taxes is determined as follows:

TABLE 7-10

Calculation of Initial Outlay for Example Problem

Outflows:	
Purchase price	$30,000
Shipping fee	2,000
Installation fee	3,000
Capital cost of machine	$35,000
Increased investment in inventory	5,000
Total outflows	$40,000
Inflows:	
Salvage value of old machine	−15,000
Net initial outlay	$25,000

Note: Assume that the asset class remained open with the purchase of the new machine.

TABLE 7-11

Schedule for the Annual Net Operating Savings After Tax

Savings:	
Reduced Salary	$10,000
Reduced Fringe Benefits	1,000
Reduced Defects	5,000
Costs:	
Increased Maintenance Costs	4,000
Net Operating Savings before taxes	$12,000
Taxes (@45%)	5,400
Net Operating Savings after taxes	$ 6,600

$$PV \left(\begin{array}{c} \text{net operating} \\ \text{savings after taxes} \end{array} \right) = \left(\begin{array}{c} \text{annual net} \\ \text{operating savings after taxes} \end{array} \right) \left(PVIFA_{12\%,5yr} \right)$$

$$= (6,600)(3.6048)$$

$$= 23,792$$

Thus the present value of the net operating savings after taxes is $23,792.

Step 3: We now determine the present value of the incremental salvage value. In our example, the new machine is expected to salvage for $8,000 at the end of five years of useful life. If the existing machine is not replaced by the new machine, the existing machine is expected to have no salvage value at the end of five years of additional useful life. As a result, we determine the present value of the incremental salvage value as follows:

$$PV(\text{incremental salvage value}) = \frac{(SV_{new} - SV_{old})}{(1 + k)^n}$$

$$= \frac{(8,000 - 0)}{(1.12)^5}$$

$$= 4,539$$

Thus, the present value of the incremental salvage value is $4,539.

Step 4: The present value of the tax shields occurring over the useful life of the asset is affected by both the incremental capital cost and the incremental salvage value of the new machine when the asset class is kept open. In this example, the incremental capital cost is $20,000 and the incremental salvage value is $8,000. As a result, the present value of the tax shields occurring over the life of the asset is determined as follows:

A. Initial Outlay
   1. Capital cost of asset
   2. Opportunity costs
   3. Incremental nonexpense outlays incurred (for example, working-capital investments)
   4. Incremental cash expenses on an after-tax basis (for example, training expenses)
   5. In a replacement decision, the cash flow associated with the sale of the old machine

B. Incremental Cash Flows over the Project's Life
   1. Added revenue offset by increased expenses
   2. Labour and material savings
   3. Increases in overhead incurred
   4. Tax shields from depreciation and depletion expenses
   5. Do not include interest expenses if the project is financed by issuing debt, as this is accounted for in the required rate of return

C. Terminal Cash Flow
   1. The salvage value of the project
   2. Recaptured capital cost allowance or terminal loss associated with the termination of the asset class
   3. Cash outlays associated with the project's termination
   4. Recapture of nonexpense outlays that occurred at the project's initiation (for example, working capital investment)

$$
\begin{aligned}
PV \left(\begin{matrix} \text{Inherited tax shields} \\ \text{of purchased asset} \end{matrix} \right) &= \left[\frac{(\Delta C_0)(d)(T)}{(k + d)} \right]\left[\frac{1 + (.5)(k)}{(1 + k)} \right] - \\
&\quad \left[\frac{(\Delta SV_n)(d)(T)}{(k + d)} \right]\left[\frac{1}{(1 + k)^n} \right] \\
&= \left[\frac{(20,000)(.30)(.45)}{(.30 + .12)} \right]\left[\frac{1 + (.5)(.12)}{(1 + .12)} \right] - \\
&\quad \left[\frac{(8,000)(.30)(.45)}{(.30 + .12)} \right]\left[\frac{1}{(1 + .12)^5} \right] \\
&= [6,429][.9464] - [2,571][.5674] \\
&= 6,084 - 1,459 \\
&= 4,625
\end{aligned}
$$

Thus the present value of the tax shields occurring over the useful life of the asset is \$4,625.

Step 5: We also must determine the present value of any recaptured expense from the initial outlay. In this example the initial investment in inventory expense of \$5,000 must be recaptured by the firm. We determine the present value of any recaptured expense from the initial outlay as follows:

$$
\begin{aligned}
PV \left(\begin{matrix} \text{Recaptured expenses} \\ \text{of initial outlay} \end{matrix} \right) &= \left(\text{inventory expenses} \right)\left(PVIF_{12\%, 5yr} \right) \\
&= (5,000)(0.5674) \\
&= 2,837
\end{aligned}
$$

Thus, the present value of the recaptured expense from the initial outlay is \$2,837.

Step 6: The NPV equation for this replacement project is determined as follows:

$$NPV = PV(\text{Project's Net Operating Savings after taxes}) +$$
$$PV(\text{Inherited tax shields of purchased asset}) +$$
$$PV(\text{Incremental Salvage Value}) +$$
$$PV(\text{Recapture of Inventory expense}) - IO$$

$$= 23{,}792 + 4{,}625 + 4{,}539 + 2{,}837 - 25{,}000$$

$$= 10{,}793$$

Thus, the NPV of this replacement project is $10,793. The firm should accept this replacement project since the NPV is positive. ■

RISK AND CAPITAL BUDGETING

Up to this point we have ignored risk in the capital budgeting decision; in fact, we have discounted expected cash flows back to the present and ignored any uncertainty that is associated with the discount factor.[8] In reality the future cash flows associated with the introduction of a new sales outlet or a new product are estimates of what is expected to happen in the future, not necessarily what will happen in the future.[9] In effect, the cash flows we have discounted back to the present have only been our best estimate of the expected future cash flows.[10] A cash flow diagram based on the possible outcomes of an investment proposal rather than the expected values of these outcomes appears in Figure 7-2.

In this section we will assume that risk exists; consequently, we do not know beforehand what cash flows will actually result from a new project.

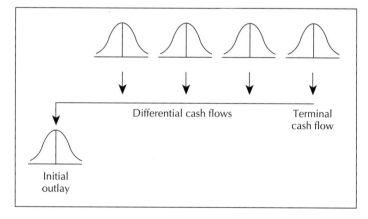

FIGURE 7-2
Cash Flow Diagram Based on Possible Outcomes

---

[8]It is assumed that all cash flows mentioned here are after taxes.

[9]The capital budgeting process is dynamic and must constantly adjust to new forecasts of future cash flows. As the project moves forward, some uncertainty is resolved leading to estimates of future cash flows and subsequent cash re-evaluations of the project. A good example of a project bouncing back and forth between acceptable and unacceptable is the Quebec Hydro electric power project in Northern Quebec. While much of the uncertainty surrounding the decision to go or not to go with this project is centred on environmental concerns and demand forecasts, it still provides a good example of re-evaluating and reforecasting distribution of future events.

[10]Sometimes the risk associated with a project can be in the estimation of the initial outlay. The Eurotunnel project was initiated in 1987 at a cost of $8 billion. By April of 1990 the cost overruns had pushed the estimate to $12.33 billion and at one point in early 1990 had caused a freeze on bank credit, putting the project in jeopardy.

However, we do have expectations concerning the possible outcomes and are able to assign probabilities to these outcomes. Stated another way, although we do not know what the cash flows resulting from the acceptance of a new project will be, we can formulate the probability distributions from which the flows will be drawn.

What Measure of Risk is Relevant in Capital Budgeting?

Before we begin our discussion of how to adjust for risk, it is important to determine just what type of risk we are to adjust for. In capital budgeting, a project's risk can be looked at in three levels. First there is total risk, which is a project's risk that ignores the fact that much of this risk will be diversified away as the project is combined with the firm's other projects and assets. Second, we have the project's contribution to the risk of the firm. This type of risk represents the amount of risk that the project contributes to the firm as a whole. This measure considers the fact that some of the project's risk will be diversified away as the project is combined with the firm's other projects and assets, but ignores the effect of any diversification by the firm's shareholders. Finally, there is systematic risk, which is the risk of the project from the point of view of a well diversified shareholder. This measure considers the fact that some of a project's risk will be diversified away by shareholders as they combine this security with other securities in their portfolio. Figure 7-3 illustrates the three levels of risk.

Should we be interested in total project risk? The answer is no. Perhaps the easiest way to understand why not is to look at an example. Let's take the case of research and development projects at Johnson & Johnson. Each year Johnson & Johnson takes on hundreds of new R&D projects, knowing that they only have about a 10 percent probability of being successful. If they are successful, the profits can be enormous; if they fail, the investment is lost. If we examined these R&D projects individually and measured their total proj-

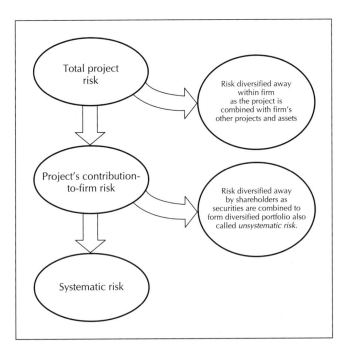

FIGURE 7-3
Looking at Three Measures of a Project's Risk

ect risk, we would have to judge them to be enormously risky. However, if we consider the effect of the diversification that comes about from taking on several hundred independent R&D projects a year, all with about a 10 percent chance of success, we can see that these R&D projects do not add much in the way of risk to Johnson & Johnson. In short, since much of a project's risk is diversified away within the firm, total project risk is an inappropriate measure of the meaningful level of risk of a capital budgeting project.

Should we be interested in the project's contribution to the risk of the firm? Once again, the answer is no, provided investors are well-diversified and there is no chance of bankruptcy. From our earlier discussion of risk in Chapter 3, we saw that as a shareholder combined a security with other securities to form a diversified portfolio, much of the risk of this security would be diversified away. Thus, all that affects the shareholders is the systematic risk of the project, and as such is all that is theoretically relevant for capital budgeting.

Measuring Risk for Capital Budgeting Purposes and a Dose of Reality—Is Systematic Risk All There Is?

According to the CAPM, systematic risk is the only relevant risk for capital budgeting purposes. The use of systematic risk in evaluating capital budgeting decisions is complicated by the fact that the firm may have undiversified shareholders, including owners of small corporations. For these types of investors, the relevant measure of risk is the project's contribution to firm risk.

The possibility of bankruptcy also affects our view of what measure of risk is relevant. In the real world there is a cost associated with bankruptcy. First, if the firm fails, its assets in general cannot be sold for their true economic value. Moreover, the amount of money actually available for distribution to shareholders is further reduced by liquidation and legal fees that must be paid. Finally, the opportunity cost associated with the delays related to the legal process further reduces the funds available to the shareholder. Since costs are associated with bankruptcy, any reduction in the probability of a firm's bankruptcy has a very real value associated with it.

Indirect costs of bankruptcy also affect other areas of the firm including production, sales, and the quality and efficiency of management. For example, firms with a higher probability of bankruptcy may have a more difficult time in recruiting and retaining quality managers because jobs with that firm are viewed as being less than secure. Suppliers also may be less willing to sell on credit. Finally, customers may lose confidence and fear that the firm may not be around to honour the warranty or to supply the spare parts for the product in the future. In other words, as the probability of bankruptcy increases, the eventual bankruptcy may become self-fulfilling as potential customers and suppliers flee. Thus, the influence that a project has on possible bankruptcy costs which are incurred by a firm causes the project's contribution to the firm's risk to be a relevant measure of risk.

Finally, problems in measuring a project's systematic risk make its implementation extremely difficult. As we will see later on in this chapter, it is much easier talking about a project's systematic risk than measuring it.

Given all of these considerations, what do we use? The answer is that we will address both measures. We know in theory that systematic risk is correct. We also know that bankruptcy costs and undiversified shareholders violate the assumptions of the theory, which brings us back to the concept of a project's contribution to the firm's risk. Still, the concept of systematic risk holds value for capital budgeting decisions because shareholders are being compensated for taking on this type of risk. As such, we will concern ourselves with both the project's contribution to the firm's risk and the project's systematic risk without making any specific allocation of importance between the two for capital budgeting purposes.

METHODS FOR INCORPORATING RISK INTO CAPITAL BUDGETING

In the preceding chapter we ignored any risk differences between projects. This omission simplifies matters but it is not valid; different investment projects do, in fact, contain different levels of risk. We will now look at several methods for incorporating risk into the analysis. The first technique, the certainty equivalent approach, attempts to incorporate the manager's utility function into the analysis. The second technique, the risk-adjusted discount rate, is based on the notion that investors require higher rates of return on more risky projects.

Certainty Equivalent Approach

The **certainty equivalent approach** involves a direct attempt to allow the decision maker to incorporate utility function into the analysis. The financial manager is allowed to substitute the certain dollar amount that he or she feels is equivalent to the expected but risky cash flow offered by the investment for that risky cash flow in the capital-budgeting analysis. In effect, a set of riskless cash flows is substituted for the original risky cash flows.

To illustrate the concept of a certainty equivalent, let us look at a simple coin toss. Assume you can play the game only once and if it comes out heads, you win $10,000, and if it comes out tails you win nothing. Obviously, you have a 50 percent chance of winning $10,000 and a 50 percent chance of winning nothing, with an expected value of $5,000. Thus, $5,000 is your uncertain expected value outcome. The certainty equivalent then becomes the amount you would demand in order to make you indifferent with regard to playing and not playing the game. If you are indifferent with respect to receiving $3,000 for certain and not playing the game, then $3,000 is the certainty equivalent.

In order to simplify future calculations and problems, let us define certainty equivalent coefficients (α_t) that represent the ratio of the certain outcome to the risky outcome, between which the financial manager is indifferent. In equation form, α_t can be represented as follows:

$$\alpha_t = \frac{\text{certain cash flow after tax}_t}{\text{risky cash flow after tax}_t} \tag{7-29}$$

Thus, the alphas can vary between 0, in the case of extreme risk, and 1, in the case of certainty. To obtain the value of the equivalent certain cash flow, we need only multiply the risky cash flow and the α_t. When this is done, we are indifferent with respect to the certain and the risky cash flows. In the preceding example of the simple coin toss, the certain cash flow was $3,000, while the risky cash flow was \$5,000 (the expected value of the coin toss); thus, the certainty equivalent coefficient is 3000/5000 = .6. In summary, by multiplying the certainty equivalent coefficient (α_t) times the expected but risky cash flow, we can determine an equivalent certain cash flow.

Once this risk is taken out of the project's cash flows, those cash flows are discounted back to the present at the risk-free rate of interest, and the project's net present value or profitability index is determined. If the internal rate of return is calculated, it is then compared with the risk-free rate of interest rather than the firm's required rate of return in determining whether or not it should be accepted or rejected. The certainty equivalent method can be summarized as follows:

$$NPV = \sum_{t=1}^{n} \frac{\alpha_t CFAT_t}{(1 + R_f)^t} - IO \qquad (7\text{-}30)$$

where
α_t = the certainty equivalent coefficient in time period t

$CFAT_t$ = the annual expected cash flow after tax in time period t

IO = the initial cash outlay

n = the project's expected life

R_f = the risk-free interest rate[11]

Let us examine a graphic presentation of the concept of certainty equivalents to illustrate its meaning. Assume that we can plot annual cash flows in risk-return space and that $CFAT_1$ and $CFAT_2$ in Figure 7-4 represent the location of the annual net cash flows during years 1 and 2. If I_1 and I_2 represent indifference curves of the decision maker, then $\alpha_1 CFAT_1$ and $\alpha_2 CFAT_2$ represent riskless equivalents of $CFAT_1$ and $CFAT_2$. As is evident

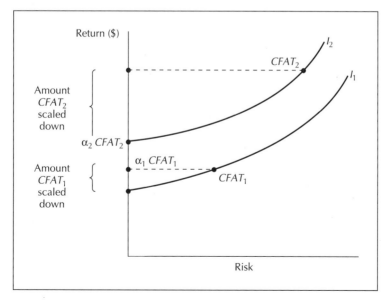

FIGURE 7-4
Certainty Equivalents

---

[11]Note that the risk-free interest rate is used to discount back the cash flows to the present and the risk of the cash flows is obtained by the estimation of the certainty equivalent coefficient.

from Figure 7-4, $CFAT_2$ is riskier than $CFAT_1$, and thus is scaled down more. The degree to which the risky cash flows are scaled down—that is, how small the α_t is—will depend upon the following:

1. The amount of risk or dispersion associated with the subjective probability distribution assigned to the expected annual cash flow—the more risk, the lower the α_t values

2. The decision maker's feelings about the attractiveness of the distribution's form—the more attractive the distribution, the higher the α_t values

3. The extent to which the random variations in the annual cash flows from this project are expected to cancel out with variations in flows from other projects—the more variations that are cancelled out, the higher the α_t values.[12]

The certainty equivalent approach can be summarized as follows:

Step 1: Risk is removed from the cash flows by substituting equivalent certain cash flows for the risky cash flows. If the certainty equivalent coefficient (α_t) is given, this is done by multiplying each risky cash flow by the appropriate α_t value.

Step 2: These riskless cash flows are then discounted back to the present at the riskless rate of interest.

Step 3: The normal capital-budgeting criteria are then applied, except in the case of the internal rate of return criterion, where the project's internal rate of return is compared with the risk-free rate of interest rather than the firm's required rate of return.

EXAMPLE

A firm with a 10 percent required rate of return is considering building new research facilities with an expected life of five years. The initial outlay associated with this project involves a certain cash outflow of $120,000. The expected cash inflows and certainty equivalent coefficients, α_t, are as follows:

Year	Expected Cash Flow After Tax	Certainty Equivalent Coefficient, α_t
1	$10,000	.95
2	20,000	.90
3	40,000	.85
4	80,000	.75
5	80,000	.65

The risk-free rate of interest is 6 percent. What is the project's net present value?

To determine the net present value of this project using the certainty equivalent approach, we must first remove the risk from the future cash flows. We do so by multiplying each expected cash flow by the corresponding certainty equivalent coefficient, α_t.

[12]These last two types of risk—risk associated with non-normal distributions and risk in a portfolio concept—will be dealt with more fully later in the chapter.

Expected Cash Flow After Tax	Certainty Equivalent Coefficient, α_t	$\alpha_t \times$ (Expected Cash Flow After Tax) = Equivalent Riskless Cash Flow After Tax
$10,000	.95	$ 9,500
20,000	.90	18,000
40,000	.85	34,000
80,000	.75	60,000
80,000	.65	52,000

The equivalent riskless cash flows are then discounted back to the present at the riskless interest rate, not the firm's required rate of return. The required rate of return would be used if this project had the same level of risk as a typical project for this firm. However, these equivalent cash flows have no risk at all; hence, the appropriate discount rate is the riskless rate of interest. The equivalent riskless cash flows can be discounted back to present at the riskless rate of interest, 6 percent, as follows:

Year	Equivalent Riskless Cash Flow After Tax	Present Value Factor at 6 Percent	Present Value
1	$ 9,500	.943	$ 8,958.50
2	18,000	.890	16,020.00
3	34,000	.840	28,560.00
4	60,000	.792	47,520.00
5	52,000	.747	38,844.00

$NPV = -\$120,000 + \$8958.50 + \$16,020 + \$28,560 + \$47,520 + \$38,844$
$= \$19,902.50$

Applying the normal capital-budgeting decision criteria, we find that the project should be accepted, as its net present value is greater than zero. ∎

Risk-Adjusted Discount Rates

The use of risk-adjusted discount rates is based on the assumption that investors demand higher returns for more risky projects. This assumption is also important to the CAPM. Figure 7-5 illustrates the relationship between risk and return.[13]

The required rate of return on any investment should include compensation for delaying consumption. As a result, the required rate of return is equal to the risk-free rate of return, plus compensation for any risk taken on. If the risk associated with the investment is greater than the risk involved in a typical endeavour, the discount rate is adjusted upward to compensate for this added risk. Once the firm determines the appropriate required rate of return for a project with a given level of risk, the cash flows are discounted back to the present at the risk-adjusted discount rate. Then the normal capital-budgeting criteria are applied, except in the case of the internal rate of return. In this particular case the hurdle rate becomes the risk-adjusted

---

[13]Note that this relationship does not represent a continuous distribution but a discrete relationship between risk and return. In a continuous distribution, the probability of a range of outputs is given by the area under the curve over that range. However, for a continuous distribution, the probability of a return taking on a particular value, say 15%, is zero.

FIGURE 7-5
Risk–Return Relationship

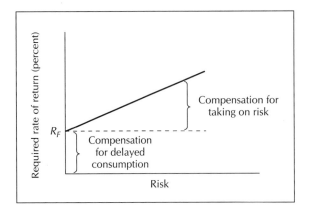

discount rate. Expressed mathematically, the net present value using the risk-adjusted discount rate becomes[14]

$$NPV = \sum_{t=1}^{n} \frac{CFAT_t}{(1 + i^*)^t} - IO \qquad (7\text{-}31)$$

where $CFAT_t$ = the annual expected cash flow after tax in time period t

         IO = the initial cash outlay

         i^* = the risk-adjusted discount rate

         n = the project's expected life

The logic behind the risk-adjusted discount rate stems from the idea that if the level of risk in a project is different from that in the typical firm project, then management must incorporate the shareholders' probable reaction to this new endeavour into the decision-making process. If the project has more risk than a typical project, then a higher required rate of return should apply. Otherwise, marginal projects will lower the firm's share price—that is, reduce shareholders' wealth. This will occur as the market raises its required rate of return on the firm to reflect the addition of a more risky project, while the incremental cash flows resulting from the acceptance of the new project are not large enough to fully offset this change. By the same logic, if the project has less than normal risk, a reduction in the required rate of return is appropriate. Thus, the risk-adjusted discount method attempts to apply more stringent standards—that is, require a higher rate of return—to projects that will increase the firm's risk level. This is because these projects will lead shareholders to demand a higher required rate of return to compensate for the higher risk level of the firm. If this adjustment is not made, the marginal projects containing above-average risk could actually lower the firm's share price.[15]

[14]Cash outflows as well as cash inflows, when not known with certainty, should be adjusted for risk. For example, the Eurotunnel project's initial outlay was spread over 5 years and had a good deal of uncertainty concerning what the actual cost would be. These cash outflows should also have been adjusted for uncertainty when evaluating the project.

[15]Risk adjustment is not a precise process. Although we may feel confident in saying that a specific project contains more or less risk than a typical project, we do not have a precise formula to tell us exactly how much to adjust the discount rate.

A toy manufacturer is considering the introduction of a line of fishing equipment with an expected life of five years. In the past, this firm has been quite conservative in its investment in new products, sticking primarily to standard toys. In this context, the introduction of a line of fishing equipment is considered an abnormally risky project. Management feels that the normal required rate of return for the firm of 10 percent is not sufficient. Instead, the minimum acceptable rate of return on this project should be 15 percent. The initial outlay would be $110,000, and the expected cash flows after tax from this project are as given below:

Year	Expected Cash Flow After Tax
1	$30,000
2	30,000
3	30,000
4	30,000
5	30,000

Discounting this annuity back to the present at 15 percent yields a present value of the future cash flows of $100,560. Since the initial outlay on this project is $110,000, the net present value becomes –$9,440, and the project should be rejected. If the normal required rate of return of 10 percent had been used as the discount rate, the project would have been accepted with a net present value of $3,730.

In practice, when the risk-adjusted discount rate is used, projects are generally grouped according to purpose, or risk class; then the discount rate pre-assigned to that purpose or risk class is used.[16] For example, a firm with a required rate of return of 12 percent might use the following rate-of-return categorization:

Project	Required Rate of Return
Replacement decision	12%
Modification or expansion of existing product line	15
Project unrelated to current operations	18
Research and development operations	25

The purpose of this categorization of projects is to make their evaluation easier, but it also makes the evaluation less meaningful since the calculations for required rate of return are made on an arbitrary basis. The tradeoffs involved in the classification above are obvious: time and effort are minimized, but only at the cost of precision.

---

[16]Many firms actually calculate different risk-adjusted discount rates for different company divisions. Again, this procedure is far from exact, but it does recognize that different divisions have different costs of capital and different projects being considered by each division have different levels of risk.

Certainty Equivalent vs. Risk-Adjusted Discount Rate Methods

The primary difference between the certainty equivalent approach and the risk-adjusted discount rate approach involves the point at which the adjustment for risk is incorporated into the calculations. The certainty equivalent penalizes or adjusts downward the value of the expected annual cash flows, $CFAT_t$, which results in a lower net present value for a risky project. The risk-adjusted discount rate, on the other hand, leaves the cash flows at their expected value and adjusts the required rate of return, i, upward to compensate for added risk. In either case the project's net present value is being adjusted downward to compensate for additional risk. The computational differences are illustrated in Table 7-13.

TABLE 7-13
Computational Steps in the Certainty Equivalent and Risk-Adjusted Discount Rate Methods

Certainty Equivalent	*Risk-Adjusted Discount Rate*
STEP 1: Adjust the expected cash flows after tax, $CFAT_t$, downward for risk by multiplying them by the corresponding certainty equivalent, risk-coefficient, α_t.	STEP 1: Adjust the discount rate upward for risk.
STEP 2: Discount the certainty equivalent, riskless, cash flows after tax back to the present using the risk-free rate of interest.	STEP 2: Discount the expected cash flows after tax back to present using the risk-adjusted discount rate.
STEP 3: Apply the normal decision criteria, except in the case of the internal rate of return, where the riskfree rate of interest replaces the required rate of return as the hurdle rate.	STEP 3: Apply the normal decision criteria, except in the case of the internal rate of return, where the risk-adjusted discount rate replaces the required rate of return as the hurdle rate.

In addition to the difference in point of adjustment for risk, the risk-adjusted discount rate makes the implicit assumption that risk becomes greater as we move further out in time. While this is not necessarily a good or bad assumption, we should be aware of it and understand it. Let's look at an example in which the risk-adjusted discount rate is used and then determine what certainty equivalent coefficients, α_t, would be necessary to arrive at the same solution.

EXAMPLE

Assume that a firm with a required rate of return of 10 percent is considering introducing a new product. This product has an initial outlay of $800,000, an expected life of 15 years, and cash flows after tax of $100,000 each year during its life. Because of the increased risk associated with this project, management is requiring a 15 percent rate of return. Let us also assume that the risk-free rate of return is 6 percent.

If the firm chose to use the certainty equivalent method, the certainty equivalent cash flows after tax would be discounted back to the present at 6 percent, the risk-free rate of interest. The present value of the $100,000 cash flow after tax occurring at the end of the first year discounted back to present at 15 percent is $87,000. The present value of this $100,000 flow discounted back to the present at the risk-free rate of 6 percent is $94,300.

BASIC FINANCIAL MANAGEMENT IN PRACTICE

Bennett Stewart on the Calculation of a Business Risk Index Used in Setting a Firm's Required Rate of Return

The calculation of the Business Risk Index focuses on a series of ratios grouped into four Risk Factors. The four Risk Factors found to be most important are:

1. Operating Risk
2. The Risk in Achieving Profitable Growth
3. Asset Management
4. Size and Diversity of Operations

Each of these is discussed in more detail in the following sections.

Operating Risk

The first set of ratios measures the risk in achieving a predictable level of operating profitability over time. It gauges investors' confidence (or lack thereof) in predicting future rates of return on capital already employed. When a unit's profitability is judged to be more unpredictable than that of other companies in the industry, its risk index, and thus its required return, are adjusted upward.

Risk in Achieving Profitable Growth

Our research demonstrates that unrealized investment opportunities create an additional risk for investors. As the perceived value of future investments changes, this leads to dramatic movements in stock prices and great risk for investors. For example, as IBM's success in personal computers became apparent, investors marked down the likely value from Digital Equipment Corporation's (DEC's) participation in the office of the future. The result: DEC's stock price fell by nearly $30. Similar dramatic stock price movements have been experienced by Apple Computer, Genentech, and Peoplexpress. The common attributes are rapid growth, great profit potential, and high P/E multiples.

It is precisely these attributes that our statistical research revealed as conveying high business risk. Accordingly, a single measure of risk is derived by weighting the unit's rate of return and growth rate. A business unit whose combined score is higher than that of its business peers will be deemed to have a higher price-earnings ratio and more risk in achieving continued profitable growth.

Asset Quality

The Risk Factor that measures the quality of a company's assets has four components: Working Capital Management, Plant Intensity, Plant Newness, and Useful Plant Life. Maintaining low and stable levels of working capital—inventory and receiv-ables, less payables and accruals—relative to competitors demonstrates a superior budgeting and control capability. Managing working capital effectively also provides an additional source of cash during recessions and, in expansionary cycles, minimizes the need for external capital to grow. This is viewed positively by investors and results in a reduction in the company's BRI.

The extent to which a company is more plant-intensive than other companies in its business suggests that management has established a dominant position through a low-cost production capability. The fact that management is willing to commit a large amount of fixed capital is an indication of management confidence that results in a reduction in the Risk Index.

Also, the newer the plant, the less is the perceived risk in a company's assets. Older plants, because of their higher operating cost, generally are the first to be shut down in a recession, only to be reopened in expansionary times. As a result, companies operating older, less efficient plants will experience more volatile returns over a business cycle than companies with new plants. Thus, they are penalized with a higher risk index.

A related characteristic is useful plant life. Having to replace important assets frequently exposes the company to risk, and is a sign of rapid and often unpredictable technological change. In contrast, longer-lived assets are viewed by investors as providing operating stability and, hence, serve to reduce risk.

Size and Diversity

Absolute size of assets and the diversification of earnings sources tend to stabilize a company's performance. The size of the company often suggests the degree of market power it has in its industry, the length of its track record, all factors generally associated with lower business risk. Also, geographic diversification is viewed as mitigating overall business risk. The reason is that a company's investment in other countries reduces investors' exposure to business cycles in the United States.

Source: Bennett Stewart, "Commentary: A Framework for Setting Required Rates of Return by Line of Business," in *Six Roundtable Discussions of Corporate Finance with Joel Stern*, ed. Donald H. Chew, Jr. New York; Quorum Books, 1986.

TABLE 7-14
Certainty Equivalent
Coefficients Yielding the
Same Results as the
Risk-Adjusted Discount Rate
of 15 Percent in the
Illustrative Example

Year	1	2	3	4	5	6	7	8	9	10
α_t:	.9226	.8494	.7833	.7222	.6653	.6128	.5654	.5215	.4797	.4427

Thus, if the certainty equivalent approach were used, a certainty equivalent coefficient, α_1, of .9226 would be necessary to produce a present value of $87,000. In other words, the same results can be obtained in the first year by using the risk-adjusted discount rate and adjusting the discount rate up to 15 percent or by using the certainty equivalent approach and adjusting the expected cash flows by a certainty equivalent coefficient of .9226.

Under the risk-adjusted discount rate, the present value of the $100,000 cash flow occurring at the end of the second year becomes $75,600, and to produce an identical present value under the certainty equivalent approach a certainty equivalent coefficient of .8494 would be needed. Following this through for the life of the project yields the certainty equivalent coefficients given in Table 7-14.

What does this analysis suggest? It indicates that if the risk-adjusted discount rate method is used, we are adjusting downward the value of future cash flows that occur further in the future more severely than earlier cash flows. We can easily see this by comparing Equations (7-30) and (7-31). The net present value using the risk-adjusted discount rate is expressed as

$$NPV = \sum_{t=1}^{n} \frac{CFAT_t}{(1 + i^*)^t} - IO \tag{7-31}$$

and the certainty equivalent net present value is measured by

$$NPV = \sum_{t=1}^{n} \frac{\alpha_t CFAT_t}{(1 + R_f)^t} - IO \tag{7-30}$$

Thus, for the net present values under each approach to be equivalent, the following must be true:

$$\frac{CFAT_t}{(1 + i^*)^t} = \frac{\alpha_t CFAT_t}{(1 + R_f)^t} \tag{7-32}$$

Solving for α_t yields

$$\alpha_t = \frac{(1 + R_f)^t}{(1 + i^*)^t} = \left(\frac{1 + R_f}{1 + i^*} \right)^t \tag{7-33}$$

Thus, since R_f and i^* are constants and i^* is greater than R_f, the value of α_t, or $[(1 + R_f)/(1 + i^*)]^t$, must decrease as t increases for the present values under each approach to be equivalent. This is exactly what we concluded from Table 7-14. ∎

In summary, the use of the risk-adjusted discount rate assumes that risk increases over time and that cash flows occurring further in the future should be more severely penalized.

Perspective in Finance

If performed properly, either of these methods can do a good job of adjusting for risk. However, by far, the most popular method of risk adjustment is the risk-adjusted discount rate. The reason for the popularity of the risk-adjusted discount rate over the certainty equivalent approach is purely and simply its ease of implementation.

The Risk-Adjusted Discount Rate and Measuring a Project's Systematic Risk

When we initially talked about systematic risk or beta, we were talking about measuring it for the entire firm. As you recall, while we could estimate a firm's beta using historical data, we did not have complete confidence in our results. As we will see, estimating the appropriate level of systematic risk for a single project is even more fraught with difficulties. To truly understand what it is that we are trying to do and the difficulties that we will encounter let us step back a bit and examine systematic risk and the risk adjustment for a project.

What we are trying to do is to use the CAPM to determine the level of risk and the appropriate risk-return tradeoffs for a particular project. We will then take the expected return on this project and compare it to the risk-return tradeoffs suggested by the CAPM to determine whether or not the project should be accepted. If the project appears to be a typical one for the firm, using the CAPM to determine the appropriate risk-return tradeoffs and then judging the project against them may be a warranted approach. But if the project is not a typical project, what do we do? Historical data generally does not exist for a new project. In fact, for some capital investments (for example, a truck or a new building) historical data would not have much meaning. What we need to do is make the best out of a bad situation. We either (1) use historical accounting data, if available, to substitute for historical price data in estimating systematic risk, or (2) attempt to find a substitute firm in the same industry as the capital-budgeting project and use the substitute firm's estimated systematic risk as a proxy for the project's systematic risk.

Beta Estimation Using Accounting Data

When we are dealing with a project that is identical to the firm's other project, we need only estimate the level of systematic risk for the firm and use that estimate as a proxy for the project's risk. Unfortunately, when projects are not typical of the firm this approach does not work. For example, when R. J. Reynolds introduces a new food through one of its food products divisions, this new product most likely carries with it a different level of systematic risk than is typical for Reynolds as a whole.

To get a better approximation of the systematic risk level on this project we will estimate the level of systematic risk for the food division and use that as a proxy for the project's systematic risk. Unfortunately, historical stock price data are available only for the company as a whole, and as you recall historical stock return data are generally used to estimate a firm's beta. Thus, we are forced to use accounting return data rather than historical stock return data for the division to estimate the division's systematic risk. To estimate a project's beta using accounting data we need only run a time series regression of the division's return on assets (net income/total assets) on the market index (the TSE 300 Index). The regression coefficient from this equation would be the project's accounting beta and would serve as an approximation for the project's true beta or measure of systematic risk. Alternatively, a multiple regression model based on accounting data could be developed to explain betas. The results of this model could then be applied to firms which are not publicly traded to estimate their betas.

How good is the accounting beta technique? It certainly is not as good as a direct calculation of the beta. In fact, the correlation between the accounting beta and the beta calculated on historical stock return data is only about 0.6; however, better luck has been experienced with multiple regression models used to predict betas. Unfortunately, in many cases there may not be any realistic alternative to the calculation of the accounting beta. Owing to the importance of adjusting for a project's risk, the accounting beta method is a preferred alternative than to doing nothing.

The Pure Play Method for Estimating a Project's Beta

Whereas the accounting beta method attempts to directly estimate a project or division's beta, the pure play method attempts to identify publicly traded firms that are engaged solely in the same business as the project or division. Once the proxy or pure play firm is identified, its systematic risk is determined and then used as a proxy for the project or division's level of systematic risk. What we are doing is looking for a publicly traded firm on the outside that looks like our project and using that firm's required rate of return to judge our project. In doing so we are presuming that the systematic risk and the capital structure of the proxy firm are identical to those of the project.[17]

In using the pure play method it should be noted that a firm's capital structure is reflected in its beta. When the capital structure of the proxy firm is different from that of the project's firm, some adjustment must be made for this difference. While not a perfect approach, it does provide some insights as to the level of systematic risk a project might have.

OTHER APPROACHES TO EVALUATING RISK IN CAPITAL BUDGETING

Simulation

Another method for evaluating the effects of risk on an investment decision is through the use of **simulation**. Whereas the certainty equivalent and risk-adjusted discount rate approaches provided us with a single value for the risk-adjusted net present value, a simulation approach gives us a probability distribution for the investment's net present value or internal rate of return. Simulation imitates the performance of the project under evaluation. This is done by randomly selecting observations from each of the assumed probability distributions for factors that affect the outcome of the project, combining those observations to determine the final output of the project, and contin-

[17]While portfolio betas tend to be stable, individual betas are not necessarily stable and not always meaningful. In fact, many individual securities have coefficients of determination of 10 percent or less, indicating that the characteristic line with a slope of beta explains only 10 percent or less of the variability of the security's returns.

uing with this process until a representative record of the project's probable outcome is assembled.

The easiest way to develop an understanding of the computer simulation process is to follow through an example simulation for an investment project evaluation. Suppose a chemical producer is considering an extension to its processing plant. The simulation process is portrayed in Figure 7-6.

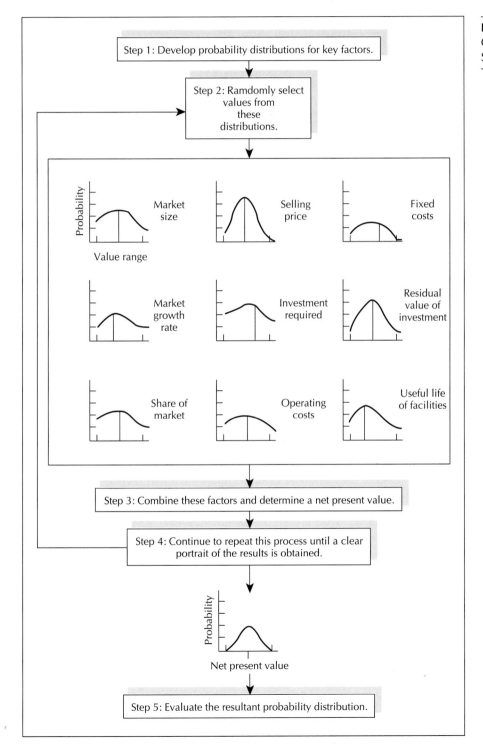

FIGURE 7-6
Capital-Budgeting
Simulation

First the probability distributions are determined for all the factors that affect the project's returns; in this case, let us assume there are nine such variables:

1. Market size

2. Selling price

3. Market growth rate

4. Share of market (which results in physical sales volume)

5. Investment required

6. Residual value of investment

7. Operating costs

8. Fixed costs

9. Useful life of facilities

Then the computer randomly selects one observation from each of the probability distributions, according to its chance of actually occurring in the future. These nine observations are combined, and a net present value or internal rate of return figure is calculated. This process is repeated as many times as desired, until a representative distribution of possible future outcomes is assembled. Thus, the inputs to a simulation include all the principal factors affecting the project's profitability, and the simulation output is a probability distribution of net present values or internal rates of return for the project. The decision maker bases the decision on the full range of possible outcomes. The project is accepted if the decision maker feels that enough of the distribution lies above the normal cutoff criteria (*NPV* > 0, *IRR* > required rate of return).

Suppose that the output from the simulation of a chemical producer's project is as given in Figure 7-7. This output provides the decision maker with the probability of different outcomes occurring in addition to the range of possible outcomes. Sometimes called **scenario analysis**, this examination identifies the range of possible outcomes under the worst, best, and most likely case. The firm's management will examine the distribution to determine the project's level of risk, and then make the appropriate adjustment.

You'll notice that while the simulation approach helps us to determine the amount of total risk that a project has, it does not differentiate between systematic and unsystematic risk. Since systematic risk cannot be diversified away for free, the simulation approach does not provide a complete method

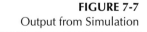

FIGURE 7-7
Output from Simulation

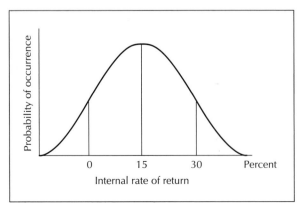

of assessment. However, it does provide important insights as to the total risk level of a given investment project. Now we will look briefly at how the simulation approach can be used to perform sensitivity analysis.

Sensitivity Analysis Through the Simulation Approach

Sensitivity analysis involves determining how the distribution of possible net present values or internal rates of return for a particular project is affected by a change in one particular input variable. This is done by changing the value of one input variable while holding all other input variables constant. The distribution of possible net present values or internal rates of return that is generated is then compared with the distribution of possible returns generated before the change was made to determine the effect of the change. For this reason, sensitivity analysis is commonly called **"What if?" Analysis**.

For example, the chemical producer that was considering a possible expansion to its plant may wish to determine the effect of a more pessimistic forecast of the anticipated market growth rate. After the more pessimistic forecast replaces the original forecast in the model, the simulation is rerun. The two outputs are then compared to determine how sensitive the results are to the estimate of the revised market growth rate.

By modifying assumptions made about the values and ranges of the input factors and rerunning the simulation, management can determine how sensitive the outcome of the project is to these changes. If the output appears to be highly sensitive to one or two of the input factors, financial managers may then wish to spend additional time refining those input estimates to make sure they are accurate.

Probability Trees

A **probability tree** is a graphic exposition of the sequence of possible outcomes; it presents the decision maker with a schematic representation of the problem in which all possible outcomes are illustrated. Moreover, the computations and results of the computations are shown directly on the tree, so that the information can be easily understood.

To illustrate the use of a probability tree, suppose a firm is considering an investment proposal that requires an initial outlay of $1 million and will yield resultant cash flows for the next two years. Table 7-15 shows that we have assumed that there are three possible outcomes during the first year. Figure 7-8 illustrates each of these three possible alternatives on the probability tree as one of the three possible branches.

The second step in the probability tree is to continue drawing branches in a similar manner so that each of the possible outcomes during the second year is represented by a new branch. For example, if outcome 1 occurs in year 1, a 20 percent chance of a $300,000 cash flow and an 80 percent chance of a $600,000 cash flow in year 2 have been projected. Two branches would

	Probability		
	.5	.3	.2
	Outcome 1	Outcome 2	Outcome 3
Cash flow after tax	$600,000	$700,000	$800,000

TABLE 7-15
Possible Outcomes in Year 1

FIGURE 7-8
First Stage of a Probability
Tree Diagram

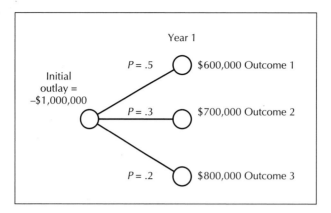

TABLE 7-16
Conditional Outcomes and
Probabilities for Year 2

	If Outcome 1		If Outcome 2		If Outcome 3	
Year 1	$CFAT_1 = \$600,000$		$CFAT_1 = \$700,000$		$CFAT_1 = \$800,000$	
	Then		**Then**		**Then**	
Year 2	$CFAT_2$	Probability	$CFAT_2$	Probability	$CFAT_2$	Probability
	$300,000	.2	$300,000	.2	$400,000	.2
	600,000	.8	500,000	.3	600,000	.7
			700,000	.5	800,000	.1

be sent out from the outcome 1 node, reflecting these two possible outcomes. The cash flows that occur if outcome 1 takes place and the probabilities associated with them are called **conditional outcomes** and **conditional probabilities** because they can occur only if outcome 1 occurs during the first year. Finally, to determine the probability of the sequence of a $600,000 flow in year 1 and a $300,000 outcome in year 2, the probability of the $600,000 flow (.5) is multiplied by the conditional probability of the second flow (.2), telling us that this sequence has a 10 percent chance of occurring; this probability is called its **joint probability**. Letting the values in Table 7-16 represent the conditional outcomes and their respective conditional probabilities, we can complete the probability tree, as shown in Figure 7-9.

The financial manager, by examining the probability tree, is provided with the expected internal rate of return for the investment, the range of possible outcomes, and a listing of each possible outcome with the probability associated with it. In this case, the expected internal rate of return is 14.74 percent, and there is a 10 percent chance of incurring the worst possible outcome with an internal rate of return of –7.55 percent. There is a 2 percent probability of achieving the most favourable outcome, an internal rate of return of 37.98 percent.

Decision making with probability trees does not mean simply the acceptance of any project with an internal rate of return greater than the firm's required rate of return, because the project's required rate of return has not yet been adjusted for risk. As a result, the financial decision maker must examine the entire distribution of possible internal rates of return and then, based on that examination, decide, given her or his aversion to risk, if enough of this distribution is above the appropriate (risk-adjusted) required rate of return to warrant acceptance of the project. Thus, the probability tree allows the manager to quickly visualize the possible future events, their

FIGURE 7-9 Probability Tree

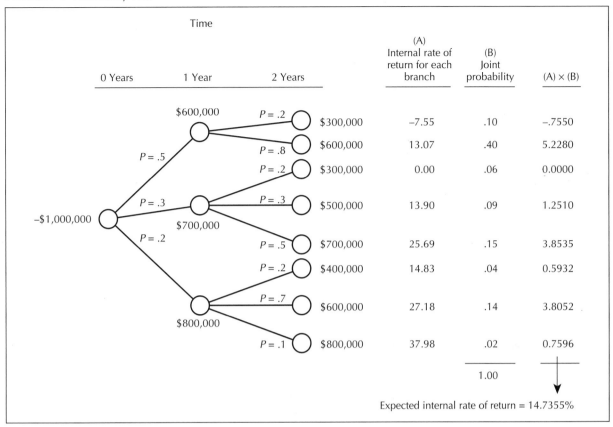

probabilities, and their outcomes. In addition, the calculation of the expected internal rate of return and enumeration of the distribution should aid the financial manager in determining the risk level of the project.

OTHER SOURCES AND MEASURES OF RISK

Time Dependence of Cash Flows

Up to this point, in all approaches other than the probability tree we have assumed that the cash flow in one period is independent of the cash flow in the previous period. While this assumption is appealing because of its simplifying nature, in many cases it is also invalid. For example, if a new product is introduced and the initial public reaction is poor, resulting in low initial cash flows, then cash flows in future periods are likely to be low. An extreme example of this is Ford's experience with the Edsel. Poor consumer acceptance and sales in the first year were followed by even poorer results in the second year. If the Edsel had been received favourably during its first year, it quite likely would have done well in the second year. The end effect of time dependence of cash flows is to increase the risk of the project over time. That is, since large cash flows in the first period lead to large cash flows in the second period, and low cash flows in the first period lead to low cash flows in the second period, the probability distribution of possible net present values tends to be wider than if the cash flows were not dependent over time. The greater the degree of correlation between flows over time, the greater will be the dispersion of the probability distribution.

Skewness

In all previous approaches other than simulation and probability trees, we have assumed that the distributions of net present values for projects being evaluated are normally distributed. This assumption is not always valid. When it is true, the standard deviation provides an adequate measure of the distribution's dispersion; however, when the distribution is not normally distributed, reliance on the standard deviation can be misleading.

A distribution that is not symmetric is said to be **skewed**. A skewed distribution has either a longer "tail" to the right or to the left. For example, if a distribution is skewed to the right, most values will be clustered around the left end, and the distribution will appear to have a long tail on the right end of the range of values. Graphic illustrations of skewed distributions are presented in Figure 7-10.

The difficulty associated with skewed distributions arises from the fact that the use of the expected value and standard deviation alone may not be enough to differentiate properly between two distributions. For example, the two distributions shown in Figure 7-11 have the same expected value and the same standard deviation; however, distribution A is skewed to the left while B is skewed to the right. If a financial manager were given a choice between these two distributions, assuming they are mutually exclusive, he or she would most likely choose distribution B, because it involves less chance of a negative net present value. Thus, skewness can affect the level of risk and the desirability of a distribution.

FIGURE 7-10
Examples of Skewed
Distributions

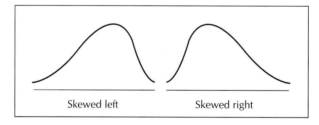

FIGURE 7-11
Two Distributions with
Identical Expected Values
and Standard Deviations but
Different Skewness

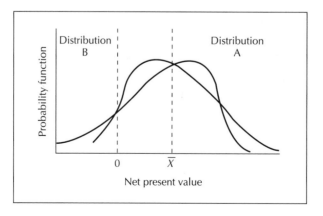

INFLATION AND CAPITAL-BUDGETING DECISIONS

It is always important to consider the effect of inflation in capital-budgeting decisions. While every project is affected a little differently by inflation, there are four general ways in which inflation can affect capital-budgeting decisions:

1. Increased inflation will cause the required rate of return on the project to rise. As cash flows received in the future will buy less with increased inflation, investors will demand a higher required rate of return on funds invested. This is called the Fisher Effect and was referred to in Chapter 2. It states that the required rate of return on a project is

$$R_j = R_j{}^* + \rho$$

where R_j is the required rate of return in nominal terms, $R_j{}^*$ is the required rate of return in real terms, and ρ is the weighted average anticipated inflation rate over the life of the project.[18]

2. Both anticipated cash inflows and outflows could be affected by inflation. Inflation may well affect materials, wages, sales, and administrative expenses, while also affecting the selling price of the item being produced. It is obviously impossible to generalize on exactly how it will affect these items for all projects, but it is safe to assume it could have a significant impact on both cash inflows and outflows.

3. The salvage value of the project could also be affected by inflation. Again, it is impossible to generalize on exactly what the relationship will be on all capital-budgeting projects.

4. The fact that depreciation charges do not change with inflation also distorts capital-budgeting decisions. Since depreciation charges are based upon original costs rather than replacement costs, they are not affected by inflation. As such, if inflation increases while depreciation remains constant, a smaller percentage of the cash inflows is sheltered by depreciation and thus a larger percentage is taxed. The end result of this is that the real cash flows decline over time as taxes increase faster than inflation because everything but depreciation is free to rise with inflation.

How can financial managers adjust capital-budgeting decisions for inflation? They must anticipate and include any effects of expected inflation in the cash flow estimates and also include it in the estimate of the required rate of return. Since it does affect the magnitude of the cash flows, it must be allowed for in order to produce an appropriate capital-budgeting decision.

In the previous chapter we have focused solely on the decision-making process that is required for a single capital-budgeting project. Sometimes, financial managers may have to choose among a number of acceptable projects. At other times the number of projects that can be accepted, or the total

---

[18]Actually $(1 + R_j) = (1 + R_j{}^*)(1 + \rho)$; thus, $R_j = R_j{}^* + \rho + R_j{}^*\rho$. However, since $R_j{}^*\rho$ is assumed to be extremely small and inconsequential, it is generally dropped from consideration.

budget, is limited; that is, capital rationing is imposed. In these cases, managers may assign different rankings which depend upon the discounted cash flow criterion being used. In this chapter we will examine the reasons for these differences. We will explore the rationale behind capital rationing and project ranking and the ways in which they affect capital budgeting decisions. We will then turn our attention to the problem of capital budgeting under uncertainty. In discussing capital-budgeting techniques in the preceding chapter, we implicitly assumed the level of risk associated with each investment proposal was the same. In this chapter, we will lift that assumption and examine various ways in which risk can be incorporated into the capital-budgeting decision.

CAPITAL RATIONING

The use of our capital-budgeting decision rules which were developed in Chapter 6 implies that the size of the capital budget is determined by the availability of acceptable investment proposals. However, a firm may place a limit on the dollar size of the capital budget. This situation is called **capital rationing**.

Using the internal rate of return as the firm's decision rule, the firm accepts all projects with an internal rate of return greater than the firm's required rate of return. This rule is illustrated in Figure 7-12, where projects A through E would be chosen. However, when capital rationing is imposed, the dollar size of the total investment is limited by the budget constraint. In Figure 7-12 the budget constraint of $X precludes the acceptance of an attractive investment, project E. This situation obviously contradicts prior decision rules. Moreover, the solution of choosing the projects with the highest internal rate of return is complicated by the fact that some projects may be indivisible; for example, it is meaningless to recommend that half a computer be acquired.

Perspective in Finance

It is always somewhat uncomfortable to deal with problems associated with capital rationing because, under capital rationing, projects with positive net present values are rejected. This is a situation that violates the goal of the firm

---

FIGURE 7-12
Projects Ranked by IRR

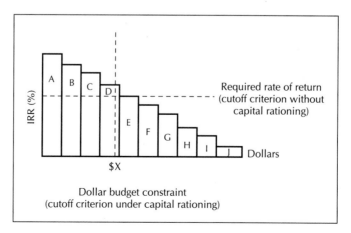

of shareholder wealth maximization. However, in the real world capital rationing does exist, and managers must deal with it. When firms impose capital constraints, they are recognizing that they do not have the ability to profitably handle more than a certain number or dollar value of new projects. In this case, perhaps a better approach would be to recalculate the incremental cash flows associated with the marginal project.

Rationale for Capital Rationing

We will first ask why capital rationing exists and whether or not it is rational. In general, three principal reasons are given for imposing a capital-rationing constraint. First, management may feel that market conditions are temporarily adverse. In the seventies this reason was frequently given. At that time interest rates were at an all-time high, and share prices were depressed. Second, there may be a shortage of qualified managers to direct new projects; this circumstance can occur when projects are of a highly technical nature and qualified managers are simply not available. Third, there may be intangible considerations. For example, the management may simply fear debt, wishing to avoid interest payments at any cost. Or perhaps the issuing of common shares may be limited to preserve the current owners' strict voting control over the company or to maintain a stable dividend policy.

Despite strong evidence that capital rationing exists in practice, the question remains as to its effect on the firm. In brief, the effect is negative, and its degree depends upon the severity of the rationing. If the rationing is minor and brief, then the firm's share price will not suffer to any great extent. In this case, any capital rationing can probably be excused, although it should be noted that any capital rationing which rejects projects with positive net present values is contrary to the firm's goal of maximization of shareholders' wealth. If capital rationing is a result of the firm's decision to limit dramatically the number of new projects or to limit total investment to internally generated funds, then this policy will eventually have a significantly negative effect on the firm's share price. For example, a lower share price will eventually result from lost competitive advantage if, owing to a decision to limit its capital budget arbitrarily, a firm fails to upgrade its products and manufacturing process.

Capital Rationing and Project Selection

If the firm decides to impose a capital constraint on investment projects, it must set an appropriate decision criterion to select the set of projects with the highest net present value subject to the capital constraint. This guideline may preclude merely taking the highest-ranked projects in terms of the profitability index or the internal rate of return. If the projects shown in Figure 7-12 are divisible, the last project accepted may be only partially accepted. Although partial acceptances may be possible in some cases, the indivisibility of most capital investments prevents it. If a project is a sales outlet or a truck, it may be meaningless to purchase half a sales outlet or half a truck.

To illustrate this procedure, consider a firm with a budget constraint of $1 million and five indivisible projects available to it, as given in Table 7-17. If the highest-ranked projects were taken, projects A and B would be taken first. At that point there would not be enough funds available to take project C; hence, projects D and E would be taken. However, a higher total net present value is provided by the combination of projects A and C. Thus projects A and C should be selected from the set of projects available. This illustrates

TABLE 7-17
Capital-Rationing Example
of Five Indivisible Projects

Project	Initial Outlay	Profitability Index	Net Present Value
A	$200,000	2.4	$280,000
B	200,000	2.3	260,000
C	800,000	1.7	560,000
D	300,000	1.3	90,000
E	300,000	1.2	60,000

our guideline: to select the set of projects that maximizes the firm's net present value.

PROJECT RANKING

In the past, we have proposed that all projects with a positive net present value, a profitability index greater than 1.0, or an internal rate of return greater than the required rate of return be accepted, assuming there is no capital rationing. However, this acceptance is not always possible. In some cases, in which two projects are judged acceptable by the discounted cash flow criteria, it may be necessary to select only one of them, as they are mutually exclusive. **Mutually exclusive projects** occur when a set of investment proposals perform essentially the same task; acceptance of one will necessarily mean rejection of the others. For example, a company considering the installation of a computer system may evaluate three or four systems, all of which may have positive net present values; but the acceptance of one system will automatically mean rejection of the others. In general, to deal with mutually exclusive projects, we will simply rank them by means of the discounted cash flow criteria and select the project with the highest ranking. On occasion, however, problems of conflicting ranking may arise.

Problems in Project Ranking

There are three general types of ranking problems—the size disparity problem, the time disparity problem, and the unequal lives problem. Each involves the possibility of conflict in the ranks yielded by the various discounted cash flow capital-budgeting criteria. As noted in the previous chapter, when one discounted cash flow criterion gives an accept signal, they will all give an accept signal, but they will not necessarily rank all projects in the same order. In most cases this disparity is not critical; however, for mutually exclusive projects the ranking order is important.

Size Disparity

The **size disparity problem** occurs when mutually exclusive projects of unequal size are examined. This problem is most easily illustrated with the use of an example.

EXAMPLE

Suppose that a firm with a cost of capital of 10 percent is considering two mutually exclusive projects, A and B. Project A involves a $200 initial outlay

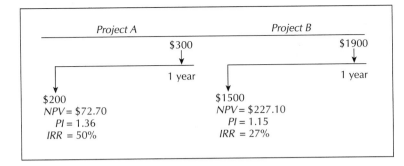

FIGURE 7-13
Size Disparity Ranking
Problem

and cash inflow of $300 at the end of one year, while project B involves an initial outlay of $1,500 and a cash inflow of $1,900 at the end of one year. The net present value, profitability index, and internal rate of return for these projects are given in Figure 7-13.

In this case, if the net present value criterion is used, project B should be accepted, while if the profitability index or the internal rate of return criterion is used, project A should be chosen. The question now becomes: which project is better? The answer depends on whether or not capital rationing exists. Without capital rationing, project B is better because it provides the largest increase in shareholders' wealth; that is, it has a larger net present value. If there is a capital constraint, the problem then focuses on what can be done with the additional $1,300 that is freed if project A is chosen (costing $200, as opposed to $1,500). If the firm can earn more on project A plus the project financed with the additional $1,300 than it can on project B, then project A and the marginal project should be accepted. In effect, we are attempting to select the set of projects that maximizes the firm's NPV. Thus, if the marginal project has a net present value greater than $154.40, selecting it plus project A with a net present value of $72.70 will provide a net present value greater than $227.10, the net present value for project B. ■

In summary, whenever the size disparity problem results in conflicting rankings between mutually exclusive projects, the project with the largest net present value will be selected, provided there is no capital rationing. When capital rationing exists, the firm should select the set of projects with the largest net present value.

Time Disparity

The **time disparity problem** and the conflicting rankings that accompany it result from the differing re-investment assumptions made by the net present value and internal rate of return decision criteria. The NPV criterion assumes that cash flows over the life of the project can be re-invested at the required rate of return or cost of capital, while the IRR criterion implicitly assumes that the cash flows over the life of the project can be re-invested at the internal rate of return. Again, this problem may be illustrated through the use of an example.

EXAMPLE

Suppose a firm with a required rate of return or cost of capital of 10 percent and with no capital constraints is considering the two mutually exclusive

FIGURE 7-14
Time Disparity Ranking
Problem

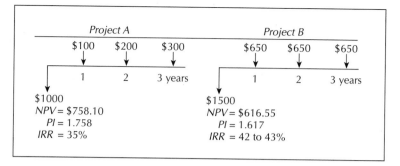

projects illustrated in Figure 7-14. The net present value and profitability index indicate that project A is the better of the two, while the internal rate of return indicates that project B is better. Project B receives its cash flows after tax earlier than project A, and the different assumptions made as to how these flows can be reinvested result in the difference in rankings. Which criterion should be followed depends upon which re-investment assumption is used. The net present value criterion is preferred in this case because it makes the most acceptable assumption for the wealth-maximizing firm. It is certainly the most conservative assumption that can be made, since the required rate of return is the lowest possible reinvestment rate. Moreover, as we have already noted, the net present value method maximizes the value of the firm and the shareholders' wealth. ∎

Unequal Lives

The final ranking problem to be examined centres on the question of whether or not it is appropriate to compare mutually exclusive projects with different life spans.

EXAMPLE

Suppose a firm with a 10 percent required rate of return is faced with the problem of replacing an aging machine and is considering two replacement machines, one with a three-year life and one with a six-year life. The relevant cash flow information for these projects is given in Figure 7-15.

Examining the discounted cash flow criteria, we find that the net present value and profitability index criteria indicate that project B is the better project, while the internal rate of return favours project A. This inconsistency in ranking is caused by the different life spans of the projects being compared. In this case the decision is a difficult one because the projects are not comparable.

The problem of incomparability of projects with different lives arises because future profitable investment proposals may be rejected without being included in the analysis. This can easily be seen in a replacement problem such as the present example, in which two mutually exclusive machines with different lives are being considered. In this case a comparison of the net present values alone on each of these projects would be misleading. If the project with the shorter life were taken, at its termination the firm could replace the machine and receive additional benefits, while acceptance of the project with the longer life would exclude this possibility, a possibility that is not included in the analysis. The key question thus becomes: Does today's investment decision include all future profitable investment proposals in its analysis? If not, the projects are not comparable. In this case, if project B is

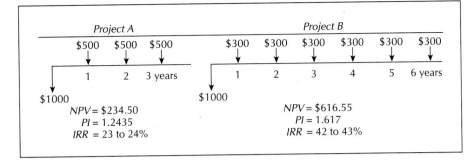

FIGURE 7-15
Unequal Lives Ranking
Problem

taken, then the project that could have been taken after three years when project A terminates is automatically rejected without being included in the analysis. Thus, acceptance of project B not only forces rejection of project A, but also forces rejection of any replacement machine that might have been considered for years 4 through 6 without including this replacement machine in the analysis.

There are several methods to deal with this situation. The first option is merely to assume that the cash inflows from the shorter-lived investment will be re-invested at the cost of capital until the termination of the longer-lived asset. While this approach is the simplest, merely calculating the net present value, it actually ignores the problem at hand—that of allowing for participation in another replacement opportunity with a positive net present value. The proper solution thus becomes the projection of re-investment opportunities into the future—that is, making assumptions about possible future investment opportunities. Unfortunately, while the first method is too simplistic to be of any value, the second is extremely difficult, requiring extensive cash flow forecasts. The final technique for confronting the problem is to assume that re-investment opportunities in the future will be similar to the current ones. The two most common ways of doing this are by creating a replacement chain to equalize life spans or calculating the project's Equivalent Annual Annuity (EAA). Using a replacement chain, the present example would call for the creation of a two-chain cycle for project A—that is, we assume that project A can be replaced with a similar investment at the end of three years. Thus, project A would be viewed as two A projects occurring back to back, as illustrated in Figure 7-16. The net present value on this replacement chain is $426.50, which is comparable with project B's net present value. Therefore, project A should be accepted because the net present value of its replacement chain is greater than the net present value of project B. ■

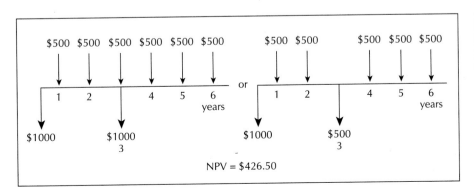

FIGURE 7-16
Replacement Chain
Illustration: Two A Projects

Unequal Lives—The Equivalent Annual Annuity (EAA) Approach

One problem with replacement chains is that depending upon the life of each project, it can be quite difficult to come up with equivalent lives. For example, if the two projects had 7- and 13-year lives, a replacement chain of 91 years would be needed to establish equivalent lives. In this case, it is easier to determine the project's EAA. A project's EAA is simply an annuity cash flow that yields the same present value as the project's NPV. To calculate a project's EAA we need only calculate a project's NPV and then divide that number by the $PVIFA_{k,n}$ to determine the dollar value of an n-year annuity that would produce the same NPV as the project. This can be done in two steps as follows:

Step 1: Calculate the project's NPV. In Figure 7-16, we determined that project A had an NPV of 234.50 and project B had an NPV of $306.50.

Step 2: Calculate the EAA. The EAA is determined by dividing each project's NPV by the $PVIFA_{k,n}$ where k is the required rate of return and n is the project's life. This determines the level of an annuity cash flow that would produce the same NPV as the project. For project A the $PVIFA_{k,n}$ is equal to 2.487 and the $PVIFA_{k,n}$ for project B is equal to 4.355. Dividing each project's NPV by the appropriate $PVIFA_{k,n}$, we determine the EAA for each project:

$$EAA_A = \frac{NPV_A}{PVIFA_{k,n}}$$
$$= \frac{\$234.50}{2.487}$$
$$= \$94.29$$

$$EAA_B = \frac{NPV_B}{PVIFA_{k,n}}$$
$$= \frac{\$306.29}{4.355}$$
$$= \$70.38$$

How do we interpret the EAA? For a project with an n-year life, it tells us what the dollar value is of an n-year annual annuity that would provide the same NPV as the project. Thus, for project A it means that a three-year annuity of $94.29 given a discount rate of 10 percent, would produce an NPV the same as project A's NPV which is $234.50. We can now compare the EAAs directly to determine which project is better. We can do this because we now have found the level of annual annuity that produces an NPV equivalent to the project's NPV. Since they are both annual annuities, they are comparable. An easy way to see this is to use the EAA's to create infinite life replacement chains. To do this we need only calculate the present value of an infinite stream or perpetuity of equivalent annual annuities. This is done by using the present value of an annuity formula, that is, simply dividing the equivalent annual annuity by the appropriate discount rate. In this case we find:

$$NPV_{A,\infty} = \frac{\$94.29}{.10} = \$942.90$$

$$NPV_{B,\infty} = \frac{\$70.38}{.10} = \$703.80$$

Here we calculated the present value of an infinite life replacement chain. Since the EAA method provides the same results as the infinite life replacement chain, it really doesn't matter which method you prefer to use.

This chapter introduced a number of complications into the capital-budgeting process. We first examined how cash flows for both an expansion project and a replacement project are determined for capital budgeting. The effect of taxes payable on cash flows was examined by determining the amount of tax shields inherited by the firm from the depreciation of assets. Tax shields do not affect cash flows directly, but reduce taxes payable which in turn increases cash flows. The evaluation of cash flows after tax for the purposes of capital budgeting has enabled us to develop two different approaches to determine the NPV of a project.

We also covered the problem of incorporating risk into the capital-budgeting decision. First we explored just what type of risk to adjust for: total project risk, the project's contribution to the firm's risk, or the project's systematic risk. In theory, systematic risk is the appropriate risk measure, but bankruptcy costs and the issue of undiversified shareholders (small business owners) support the use of a project's contribution to the firm's risk as the appropriate risk measure. Both measures of risk are valid, and we avoid making any specific allocation of importance between the two measures in capital budgeting.

Several commonly used methods for incorporating risk into capital budgeting are: (1) the certainty equivalent method, (2) risk-adjusted discount rates, (3) simulation, and (4) probability trees. The certainty equivalent approach involves a direct attempt to incorporate the decision maker's utility function into the analysis. Under this method, cash flows are adjusted downward by multiplying them by certainty equivalent coefficients, α_t, which transform the risky cash flows into equivalent certain cash flows in terms of desirability. A project's net present value using the certainty equivalent method for adjusting for risk becomes

$$NPV = \sum_{t=1}^{n} \frac{\alpha_t CFAT_t}{(1 + R_f)^t} - IO$$

The risk-adjusted discount rate involves an upward adjustment of the discount rate to compensate for risk. This method is based on the concept that investors demand higher returns for more risky projects.

The simulation and probability-tree methods are used to provide information as to the location and shape of the distribution of possible outcomes. Decisions could be based directly upon these methods, or they could be used to determine input into either certainty equivalent or risk-adjusted discount method approaches.

We examined capital rationing and the problems it can create by imposing a limit on the dollar size of the capital budget. Furthermore, capital rationing does not lead to the goal of maximization of shareholder's wealth.

Finally, we discussed the problems associated with the evaluation of mutually exclusive projects. Mutually exclusive projects occur when a set of investment proposals perform essentially the same task. In general, we rank mutually exclusive projects by means of the discounted cash flow criteria and select the project with the highest ranking. Conflicting rankings may arise due to the size disparity problem, the time disparity problem, and unequal lives. The problem of incomparability of projects with different lives is not simply a result of the different lives; rather, it arises because future profitable investments proposals may be rejected without being included in the analysis. Replacement chains and equivalent annual annuities (EAA) were presented as possible solutions to this problem.

STUDY QUESTIONS

7-1. If depreciation is not a cash flow expense, does it affect the level of cash flows from a project in any way?

7-2. Compare and contrast the cash flows of an expansion project and of a replacement project.

7-3. Explain how capital cost allowances influence cash flows for capital budgeting purposes.

7-4. Explain the difference between terminal loss and recaptured depreciation.

7-5. Often government action to push or slow down the economy is implemented by altering the capital-budgeting decision-making process of the firm. How might the following changes affect capital-budgeting decisions?

    a. A movement by the Bank of Canada to reduce interest rates

    b. A change in the tax laws which increases the capital cost allowance rate

    c. A change in tax laws that prohibits installation costs to be included in the calculation of the capital cost

7-6. In Chapter 6 we examined the payback period capital-budgeting criterion. Often this capital-budgeting criterion is used as a risk-screening device. Explain the rationale behind its use.

7-7. The use of the risk-adjusted discount rate assumes that risk increases over time. Justify this assumption.

7-8. What are the similarities and differences between the risk-adjusted discount rate and certainty equivalent methods for incorporating risk into the capital-budgeting decision?

7-9. What is the value of using the probability-tree technique for evaluating capital-budgeting projects?

7-10. Explain how simulation works. What is the value in using a simulation approach?

7-11. What does time dependence of cash flows mean? Why might cash flows be time dependent? Give some examples.

7-12. What does skewness mean? If a distribution is skewed, how does this affect the significance of its standard deviation and mean?

7-13. Through the diversification effect, the total risk of a portfolio can be reduced. How does this happen? How does the correlation between returns on the various projects affect this process?

7-14. What are mutually exclusive projects? Why might the existence of mutually exclusive projects cause problems in the implementation of the discounted cash flow capital-budgeting criteria?

7-15. Why do firms practice capital rationing for the purposes of capital budgeting?

7-16. How should managers compare two mutually exclusive projects of unequal size? Would your approach change if capital rationing existed?

7-17. What causes the time disparity ranking problem? What reinvestment rate assumptions are associated with the net present value and internal rate of return capital-budgeting criteria?

7-18. When might two mutually exclusive projects having unequal lives be incomparable? How should managers deal with this problem?

ST-1. The Scotty Gator Corporation of Meadville, maker of Scotty's electronic components, is considering the replacement of one of its existing hand-operated assembly machines with a new fully-automated machine. This replacement project would mean the elimination of one employee, generating salary and benefit savings. Given the following information, determine the cash flows after tax associated with this replacement project.

Existing situation:	One full-time machine operator—salary and benefits, $25,000 per year
	Cost of maintenance—$2000 per year
	Cost of defects—$6000
	Capital cost of old machine—$50,000
	Depreciation method—declining balance method
	CCA rate—30 percent
	Expected life—4 years
	Machine's age—two years old
	Expected salvage value in two years—$4,000
	Current salvage value—$5000
	Combined corporate tax rate—45 percent
Proposed situation:	Fully automated machine
	Cost of machine—$60,000
	Installation fee—$3,000
	Shipping fee—$3,000
	Cost of maintenance—$3,000 per year
	Cost of defects—$3,000 per year
	Expected life—two years
	Expected salvage value—$20,000
	Depreciation method—declining balance method
	CCA rate—30 percent
	Required rate of return—15 percent

Assume that the asset class is kept open after the sale of the fully automated machine.

ST-2. Given the cash flow information in problem ST-1 and a required rate of return of 15 percent, complete the following for the new, fully automated machine:

a. Net present value

b. Profitability index

c. Internal rate of return

Should this project be accepted?

ST-3. The N. Sen Corp. is considering two mutually exclusive projects. Both require an initial outlay of $25,000 and will operate for five years. The probability distributions associated with each project for years 1 through 5 are given below:

Net Cash Flow After Tax, Years 1–5

Project A		Project B	
Probability	Cash Flow After Tax	Probability	Cash Flow After Tax
.20	$10,000	.20	$ 6,000
.60	15,000	.60	18,000
.20	20,000	.20	30,000

Since project B is the riskier of the two projects, the management of N. Sen has decided to apply a required rate of return of 18 percent to its evaluation, but only a 12 percent required rate of return to project A.

a. Determine the expected value of each project's net cash flows after tax.

b. Determine each project's risk-adjusted net present value.

ST-4. G. Norohna and Co. is considering two mutually exclusive projects. The expected values for each project's net cash flows after tax are given below.

Year	Project A	Project B
0	–$300,000	–$300,000
1	100,000	200,000
2	200,000	200,000
3	200,000	200,000
4	300,000	300,000
5	300,000	400,000

The company has decided to evaluate these projects using the certainty equivalent method. The certainty equivalent coefficients for each project's net cash flows after tax are given below.

Year	Project A	Project B
0	1.00	1.00
1	.95	.90
2	.90	.80
3	.85	.70
4	.80	.60
5	.75	.50

Given that this company's normal required rate of return is 15 percent and the after-tax risk-free rate is 8 percent, which project should be selected?

STUDY PROBLEMS (SET A)

7-1A. (*Capital Gains*) The J. Harris Corporation is considering the sale of its only assembly machine in asset class 39. This machine had a capital cost of $30,000 three years ago. The expected life of the machine when purchased was 10 years after which it is expected to have a salvage value of zero. Revenue Canada requires that assets in this asset class be written off using a declining balance method at a CCA rate of 30 percent. This assembly machine would now sell for $35,000. Assume that the firm has a 45 percent combined corporate tax rate.

a. What would be the taxes associated with this sale?

b. If the old machine were sold for $25,000, what would be the taxes associated with this sale?

c. If the old machine were sold for $15,000, what would be the taxes associated with this sale?

d. If the old machine were sold for $12,000, what would be the taxes associated with this sale?

7-2A. (*Expansion Project—Capital-Budgeting Calculation*) The R. Boisjoly Chemical Corporation is considering the purchase of a new machine that has a capital cost of $80,000. The new machine is classified in asset class 8 for tax purposes. Revenue Canada requires that assets in this asset class be written off using the declining balance method at a CCA rate of 20 percent. The expected life of this machine is two years, after which it can be sold for $50,000. The asset class will be kept open after the sale of the asset. This new machine will produce net operating revenues (excluding accounting depreciation) of $55,000 per year. The firm's combined corporate tax rate is 45 percent, and firm's required rate of return is 10 percent. Given the above information, determine the following:

a. The net present value

b. The profitability index

c. The internal rate of return.

7-3A. (*Expansion Project—Capital-Budgeting Calculation*) The C. Duncan Chemical Corporation is considering the purchase of a new machine that has a capital cost of $200,000. The new machine is classified in asset class 39 for tax purposes. Revenue Canada requires that assets in this asset class be written off using the declining balance method at a CCA rate of 30 percent. The expected life of this machine is two years, after which it can be sold for $50,000. The asset class will remain open after the sale of the asset. This new machine will produce net operating revenues (excluding accounting depreciation) of $90,000 per year. The firm's combined corporate tax rate is 45 percent, and the firm's required rate of return is 15 percent. Find the following:

a. The net present value

b. The profitability index

c. The internal rate of return.

7-4A. (*Expansion Project—Capital-Budgeting Calculation*) The Woodchuck Corporation is considering the purchase of a new machine that has a capital cost of $450,000. The new machine is classified in asset class 8 for tax purposes. Revenue Canada requires that assets in this asset class be written off using the declining balance method at a CCA rate of 20 percent. The expected life of this machine is four years, after which it can be sold for $150,000. The asset class will be terminated after the sale of the asset. This new machine will produce net operating revenues (excluding accounting depreciation) of $115,000 per year. The firm's combined corporate tax rate is 45 percent, and the firm's required rate of return is 10 percent. Given the above information, determine the following:

a. The net present value

b. The profitability index

c. The internal rate of return.

7-5A. (*Expansion Project—Capital-Budgeting Calculation*) The Labelit Corporation is considering the purchase of a new printing machine that costs $450,000. In order to get the automated machine in running order, there would be a $5,000 shipping fee and a $10,000 installation charge. In addition, the new machine will require an investment in raw materials and goods-in-process inventories of $5,000. This increase in inventory cost of $5,000 will be recovered at the end of the five-year project. The new machine is classified in asset class 8 for tax purposes. Revenue Canada requires that assets in this asset class be written off using the declining balance method at a CCA rate of 20 percent. The expected life of this machine is five years, after which it can be sold for $150,000. The asset class will be terminated after the sale of the asset. This new machine will produce incremental operating revenues of $325,000 and incremental operating expenses of $210,000 (including accounting depreciation of $93,000) per year. The firm's combined corporate tax rate is 45 percent, and the firm's required rate of return is 10 percent. Given the above information, determine the following:

a. The net present value

b. The profitability index

c. The internal rate of return.

7-6A. (*Replacement Project—Capital-Budgeting Calculation*) The Mad Dog Hansen Electronic Components Corporation is considering the replacement of its existing machine with a new automated machine. The existing machine was purchased and installed at a capital cost of $30,000 three years ago. The existing machine when purchased had an expected life of six years, at which time the machine was expected to have a salvage value of zero. Both machines belong to asset class 8. Revenue Canada requires that assets in this asset class be written off using the declining balance method at a CCA rate of 20 percent. The new automated machine being considered has a capital cost of $80,000 and an expected life of three years. The new machine is expected to salvage for $4,000 in three years and the asset class will be kept open. Material efficiencies resulting from the replacement would result in savings of $30,000 per year before depreciation taxes. Currently, the old machine could be sold for $15,000. The firm's combined corporate tax rate is 45 percent, and the firm has a required rate of return of 20 percent. Calculate the following:

a. The net present value

b. The profitability index

c. The internal rate of return.

7-7A. (*Replacement Project—Capital-Budgeting Calculation*) The L. Knutson Company, a manufacturer of electronic components in the 45 percent combined corporate tax-rate bracket, is considering the purchase of a new, fully automated machine to replace an older, manually operated one. Both machines belong to asset class 8. Revenue Canada requires that these types of machines be written off using a declining balance method at a CCA rate of 20 percent.

The old machine had an expected life of 10 years, at which time the salvage value was expected to be zero. After five years of productive use the old machine can now be sold for $25,000. It took one employee to operate the old machine, and he earned $15,000 per year in salary and $2,000 per year in fringe benefits. The annual costs of maintenance and defects associated with the old machine were $7,000 and $3,000, respectively. Ten years ago, the old machine had a capital cost of $40,000. The replacement machine being considered has a purchase price of $50,000. The salvage value of this new machine is expected to be $10,000 after five years, and the asset class will continue to remain open. In order to get the automated machine in running order, there would be a $3,000 shipping fee and a $2,000 installation charge. In addition, because the new machine would work faster than the old one, investment in raw materials and goods-in-process inventories would need to be increased by a total of $5,000. This increase in inventory cost of $5,000 will be recovered at the end of the five-year project. The annual costs of maintenance and defects on the new machine would be $2,000 and $4,000, respectively. The acquisition of the new machine caused the firm to incur an additional $5,000 in administrative costs in the form of accounting costs. Finally, in order to purchase the new machine, it appears the firm would have to borrow an additional $20,000 at 10 percent interest from its local bank, resulting in additional interest payments of $2,000 per year. The required rate of return on projects of this kind is 20 percent.

a. What is the project's initial outlay?

b. What are the differential cash flows after tax over the project's life?

c. What is the terminal cash flow?

d. Draw a cash flow diagram for this project.

e. What is its net present value?

f. What is its profitability index?

g. What is its internal rate of return?

h. Should the project be accepted? Why or why not?

7-8A. (*Cash Flow Calculations*) The Winky Corporation, maker of electronic components, is considering the replacement of a hand-operated machine used in the manufacture of electronic components with a new, fully automated machine. Given the following information, determine the after-tax cash flows associated with this replacement project. Assume that both machines belong to asset class 39 for tax purposes.

Existing situation:	Two full-time machine operators—salaries $10,000 each per year
	Cost of maintenance—$5,000 per year
	Cost of defects—$5,000
	Capital cost of old machine—$30,000
	Expected life—10 years
	Machine's age—7 years old
	Expected salvage value—$0
	Depreciation method—declining balance method
	CCA rate—30 percent
	Current salvage value—$10,000
	Combined corporate tax rate—45 percent
Proposed situation:	Fully automated machine
	Cost of machine—$55,000
	Installation fee—$5,000
	Cost of maintenance—$6,000 per year
	Cost of defects—$2,000 per year
	Expected life—3 years
	Expected salvage value—$0
	Depreciation method—declining balance method
	CCA rate—30 percent
	Required rate of return—15 percent

Assume the asset class will be terminated with the sale of the automated machine after 3 years

7-9A. (*Capital-Budgeting Calculation*) Given the cash flow information in problem 7-8A and a required rate of return of 15 percent, compute the following for the automated machine:

a. Net present value

b. Profitability index

c. Internal rate of return

Should this project be accepted?

7-10A. (*Capital Rationing*) The Cowboy Hat Company of Dawson Creek is considering seven capital investment proposals, for which the funds available are limited to a maximum of $12 million. The projects are independent and have the following costs and profitability indexes associated with them:

Project	Cost	Profitability Index
A	$4,000,000	1.18
B	3,000,000	1.08
C	5,000,000	1.33
D	6,000,000	1.31
E	4,000,000	1.19
F	6,000,000	1.20
G	4,000,000	1.18

a. Under strict capital rationing, which projects should be selected?

b. Is this an optimal strategy?

7-11A. (*Unequal Lives Ranking Problem*) The B. T. Knight Corporation is considering two mutually exclusive pieces of machinery that perform the same task. The two alternatives available provide the following set of cash flows after tax:

Year	Equipment A	Equipment B
0	–$20,000	–$20,000
1	12,590	6,625
2	12,590	6,625
3	12,590	6,625
4		6,625
5		6,625
6		6,625
7		6,625
8		6,625
9		6,625

Equipment A has an expected life of three years, while equipment B has an expected life of nine years. Assume a required rate of return of 15 percent.

a. Calculate each project's payback period.

b. Calculate each project's net present value.

c. Calculate each project's internal rate of return.

d. Are these projects comparable?

e. Compare these projects using replacement chains. Which project should be selected? Support your recommendation.

7-12A. (*Time Disparity Ranking Problem*) The R. Rogers Corporation is considering two mutually exclusive projects. The cash flows after tax associated with those projects are as follows:

Year	Project A	Project B
0	–$50,000	–$50,000
1	15,625	0
2	15,625	0
3	15,625	0
4	15,625	0
5	15,625	$100,000

The required rate of return on these projects is 10 percent.

a. What is each project's payback period?

b. What is each project's net present value?

c. What is each project's internal rate of return?

d. What has caused the ranking conflict?

e. Which project should be accepted? Why?

7-13A. (*Size Disparity Ranking Problem*) The D. Dorner Farms Corporation is considering purchasing one of two fertilizer-herbicides for the upcoming year. The more expensive of the two is the better and will produce a higher yield. Assume these projects are mutually exclusive and that the required rate of return is 10 percent. Given the following cash flows after tax:

Year	Project A	Project B
0	–$500	–$5,000
1	700	6,000

a. Calculate the net present value.

b. Calculate the profitability index.

c. Calculate the internal rate of return.

d. If there is no capital-rationing constraint, which project should be selected? If there is a capital-rationing constraint, how should the decision be made?

·7-14A. (*Risk-Adjusted NPV*) The Goblu Corporation is evaluating two mutually exclusive projects, both of which require an initial outlay of $100,000. Each project has an expected life of five years. The probability distributions associated with the annual net cash flows after tax from each project are given below:

	Net Cash Flow After Tax, Years 1–5		
	Project A		Project B
Probability	Cash Flow After Tax	Probability	Cash Flow After Tax
.10	$35,000	.10	$10,000
.40	40,000	.20	30,000
.40	45,000	.40	45,000
.10	50,000	.20	60,000
		.10	80,000

The normal required rate of return for Goblu is 10 percent, but since these projects are riskier than most, they are requiring a higher-than-normal rate of return on them. On project A they are requiring a 12 percent, and on project B a 13 percent rate of return.

a. Determine the expected value for each project's net cash flows after tax.

b. Determine each project's risk-adjusted net present value.

c. What other factors might be considered in deciding between these projects?

7-15A. (*Certainty Equivalents*) The V. Coles Corp. is considering two mutually exclusive projects. The expected values for each project's net cash flows after tax are given below:

Year	Project A	Project B
0	–$1,000,000	–$1,000,000
1	500,000	500,000
2	700,000	600,000
3	600,000	700,000
4	500,000	800,000

The management has decided to evaluate these projects using the certainty equivalent method. The certainty equivalent coefficients for each project's net cash flows after tax are given below:

Year	Project A	Project B
0	1.00	1.00
1	.95	.90
2	.90	.70
3	.80	.60
4	.70	.50

Given that this company's normal required rate of return is 15 percent and the risk-free rate is 5 percent, which project should be selected?

7-16A. (*Certainty Equivalents*) Neustal, Inc., has decided to use the certainty equivalent method in determining whether or not a new investment should be made. The expected net cash flows after tax associated with this investment and the estimated certainty equivalent coefficients are as follows:

Year	Expected Values for Cash Flows After Tax	Certainty Equivalent Coefficients
0	-$90,000	1.00
1	25,000	0.95
2	30,000	0.90
3	30,000	0.83
4	25,000	0.75
5	20,000	0.65

Given that Neustal's normal required rate of return is 18 percent and that the risk-free rate is 7 percent, should this project be accepted?

7-17A. (*Risk-Adjusted Discount Rates and Risk Classes*) The G. Wolfe Corporation is examining two capital-budgeting projects with five-year lives. The first, project A, is a replacement project; the second, project B, is a project unrelated to current operations. The G. Wolfe Corporation uses the risk-adjusted discount rate method and groups projects according to purpose and then uses a required rate of return or discount rate that has been pre-assigned to that purpose or risk class. The expected net cash flows after tax for these projects are given below:

	Project A	Project B
Initial Investment:	$250,000	$400,000
Cash Inflows:		
Year 1	$ 30,000	$135,000
Year 2	40,000	135,000
Year 3	50,000	135,000
Year 4	90,000	135,000
Year 5	130,000	135,000

The purpose/risk classes and pre-assigned required rates of return are as follows:

Purpose	Required Rate of Return
Replacement decision	12%
Modification or expansion of existing product line	15
Project unrelated to current operations	18
Research and development operations	20

Determine the project's risk-adjusted net present value.

7-18A. (*Certainty Equivalents*) "Nacho" Nachtmann Company uses the certainty equivalent approach when it evaluates risky investments. The company presently has two mutually exclusive investment proposals, with an expected life of four years each, to choose from with money it received from the sale of part of its toy division to another company. The expected net cash flows after tax are given below:

Year	Project A	Project B
0	-$50,000	-$50,000
1	15,000	20,000
2	15,000	25,000
3	15,000	25,000
4	45,000	30,000

The certainty equivalent coefficients for the net cash flows after tax are as follows:

Year	Project A	Project B
0	1.00	1.00
1	.95	.90
2	.85	.85
3	.80	.80
4	.70	.75

Which of the two investment proposals should be chosen, given that the risk-free rate of return is 6 percent?

7-19A. (*Probability Trees*) The M. Solt Corporation is evaluating an investment proposal with an expected life of two years. This project will require an initial outlay of $1,200,000. The resultant possible net cash flows after tax are given below:

Possible Outcomes in Year 1

	Probability		
	.6	.3	.1
	Outcome 1	Outcome 2	Outcome 3
Net Cash flow after tax =	$700,000	$850,000	$1,000,000

Conditional Outcomes and Probabilities for Year 2

If CFAT$_1$ = $700,000		If CFAT$_1$ = $850,000		If CFAT$_1$ = $1,000,000	
CFAT$_2$	Probability	CFAT$_2$	Probability	CFAT$_2$	Probability
$ 300,000	.3	$ 400,000	.2	$ 600,000	.1
700,000	.6	700,000	.5	900,000	.5
1,100,000	.1	1,100,000	.2	1,100,000	.4
		1,300,000	.1		

a. Construct a probability tree representing the possible outcomes.

b. Determine the joint probability of each possible sequence of events taking place.

c. What is the expected IRR of this project?

d. What is the range of possible IRRs for this project?

7-20A. (*Probability Trees*) V. Janjigian, Inc., is considering expanding its operations into computer-based basketball games. Janjigian feels that there is a three-year life associated with this project, and it will initially involve an investment of $100,000. It also feels there is a 60 percent chance of success and a cash flow after tax of $100,000 in year 1 and a 40 percent chance of "failure" and a $10,000 cash flow after tax in year 1. If the project "fails" in year 1, there is a 60 percent chance that it will produce net cash flows after tax of only $10,000 in years 2 and 3. There is also a 40 percent chance that it will really fail and Janjigian will earn nothing in year 2 and get out of this line of business, with the project terminating and no net cash flow after tax occurring in year 3. If, on the other hand, this project succeeds in the first year, then net cash flows after tax in the second year are expected to be $200,000, $175,000, or $150,000 with probabilities of .30, .50, and .20, respectively. Finally, if the project succeeds in the third and final year of operation, the net cash flows after tax are expected to be either $30,000 more or $20,000 less than they were in year 2, with an equal chance of occurrence.

a. Construct a probability tree representing the possible outcomes.

b. Determine the joint probability of each possible sequence of events.

c. What is the expected IRR?

d. What is the range of possible IRRs for this project?

7-21A. (*Probability Trees*) The E. Swank Corporation is considering an investment project with an expected life of two years. The initial outlay on this project would be $600,000, and the resultant possible net cash flows after tax are given below:

Possible Outcomes in Year 1

	Probability		
	.4	.4	.3
	Outcome 1	Outcome 2	Outcome 3
Net Cash flow after tax =	$300,000	$350,000	$450,000

Conditional Outcomes and Probabilities for Year 2

If $CFAT_1 = \$300,000$		If $CFAT_1 = \$350,000$		If $CFAT_1 = \$450,000$	
$CFAT_2$	Probability	$CFAT_2$	Probability	$CFAT_2$	Probability
$200,000	.3	$250,000	.2	$ 300,000	.2
300,000	.7	450,000	.5	500,000	.5
		650,000	.3	700,000	.2
				1,000,000	.1

a. Construct a probability tree representing the possible outcomes.

b. Determine the joint probability of each possible sequence of events taking place.

c. What is the expected IRR of this project?

d. What is the range of possible IRRs for this project?

7-22A. (*Cash Flow—Capital-Budgeting Calculation*) The Beamer Corp. is considering the expansion of its highly technical construction facilities. The construction will take a total of four years until it is completed and ready for operation. The following data and assumptions describe the proposed expansion:

1. In order to make this expansion feasible, installation expenditures of $200,000 must be made immediately to ensure that the construction facilities are competitively efficient ($t = 0$).

2. At the end of the first year the land will be purchased and construction on stage 1 of the facilities will begin, involving a cash outflow of $150,000 for the land and $300,000 for the construction facilities. For tax purposes, the construction facilities belong to asset class 1. Revenue Canada requires that assets in this asset class be written off using a declining balance method at a CCA rate of 4 percent.

3. Stage 2 of the construction will involve a $300,000 cash outflow at the end of year 2. This cash outlay was used for the purchase of a processing machine. For tax purposes, the processing machine belongs to asset class 39. Revenue Canada requires that assets in this asset class be written off using a declining balance method at a CCA rate of 30 percent.

4. At the end of year 3, when production begins, inventory will be increased by $50,000.

5. At the end of year four, the first sales from operation of the new plant is estimated at $800,000 and continues at that level for 10 years (with the final flow from sales occurring at the end of year 13).

6. Annual operating costs on these sales include $100,000 of fixed operating costs per year and variable operating costs equal to 40 percent of sales.

7. When the plant is closed, it is expected that the processing machine will salvage at $30,000 and asset class 39 will be terminated. The construction facilities are expected to salvage for $50,000 and asset class 1 will also be terminated.

8. When the plant is closed, the land will be sold for $200,000 ($t = 13$).

9. The company is in the 45-percent combined corporate tax-rate bracket. Given a 12 percent required rate of return, what is the NPV of this project? Should it be accepted?

7-23A. (*Cash Flow—Capital-Budgeting Calculation*) The Steel Mill Corporation of Asbury Park must replace its executive jet and is considering two mutually exclusive planes as replacements. As far as it is concerned, both planes are identical and each will provide annual benefits, before maintenance, taxes, and depreciation, of $40,000 per year for the life of the plane; however, the costs on each are decidedly different. The first is a Steel Mills and costs $94,000. It has an expected life of seven years and will require major maintenance at the end of year 4. The annual maintenance costs are $8,000 for the first three years, $25,000 in year 4, and $10,000 for years 5 through 7. Its salvage value at the end of year 7 is $24,000.

The other plane is a Honeybilt Jet costing $100,000 and also having an expected life of seven years. Its maintenance expenses are expected to be $9,000 the first four years, rising to $18,000 annually for years 5 through 7. In years 3 and 5 the jet engine must be overhauled at an expense of $15,000 each time; this overhaul expense is in excess of the maintenance expenses. Finally, at the end of year 7 this jet will have a salvage value of $30,000. Both planes being considered belong to asset class 9. Revenue Canada requires that assets in this asset class 9 be written off using the declining balance method at a CCA rate of 25 percent. At the end of year 7, the asset class will remain open. Given a 45 percent combined corporate tax rate and a 10 percent required rate of return, what is the NPV on each jet? Which should be taken?

STUDY PROBLEMS (SET B)

7-1B. (*Capital Gains Tax*) The R. T. Kleinman Corporation is considering the sale of its only assembly machine in asset class 39. This machine had a capital cost of $40,000 three years ago. The expected life of the machine when purchased was 10 years, after which it is expected to have a salvage value of zero. Revenue Canada requires that assets in this asset class be written off using a declining balance method at a CCA rate of 30 percent. This assembly machine would now sell for $45,000. Assume that the firm has a 45 percent combined corporate tax rate.

a. What would be the taxes associated with this sale?

b. If the old machine were sold for $30,000, what would be the taxes associated with this sale?

c. If the old machine were sold for $15,000, what would be the taxes associated with this sale?

7-2B. (*Expansion Project—Capital-Budgeting Calculation*) The Kensinger Corporation is considering the purchase of a new machine that has a capital cost of $300,000. The new machine is classified in asset class 39 for tax purposes. Revenue Canada requires that assets in this asset class be written off using the declining balance method at a CCA rate of 30 percent. The expected life of this machine is four years, after which it can be sold for $75,000. The asset class will remain open after its sale. Because of reductions in defects and material savings, the new machine will produce cash benefits of $110,000 per year before depreciation and taxes. The firm's combined corporate tax rate is 45 percent, and the firm's required rate of return is 15 percent. Find:

a. The net present value

b. The profitability index

c. The internal rate of return.

7-3B. (*Expansion Project—Capital-Budgeting Calculation*) The Boiling Chemical Corporation is considering the purchase of a new machine that has a capital cost of $100,000. The new machine is classified in asset class 8 for tax purposes. Revenue Canada requires that assets in this asset class be written off using the declining balance method at a CCA rate of 20 percent. The expected life of this machine is five years, after which it can be sold for $80,000. The asset class will be kept open after the sale of the asset. As a result of reductions in defects and material savings, the new machine will produce cash benefits of $85,000 per year before depreciation and taxes. The firm's combined corporate tax rate is 45 percent, and the firm's required rate of return is 10 percent. Given the above information, determine the following:

a. The net present value

b. The profitability index

c. The internal rate of return.

7-4B. (*Expansion Project—Capital-Budgeting Calculation*) The BJ Manufacturing Corporation is considering the purchase of a new machine that has a capital cost of $500,000. The new machine is classified in asset class 8 for tax purposes. Revenue Canada requires that assets in this asset class be written off using the declining balance method at a CCA rate of 20 percent. The expected life of this machine is four years, after which it can be sold for $110,000. The asset class will be terminated after its sale. This new machine will produce net operating revenues (excluding accounting depreciation) of $145,000 per year. The firm's combined corporate tax rate is 45 percent, and the firm's required rate of return is 10 percent. Given the above information, determine the following:

a. The net present value

b. The profitability index

c. The internal rate of return.

7-5B. (*Expansion Project—Capital-Budgeting Calculation*) The Printit Corporation is considering the purchase of a new printing machine that costs $400,000. In order to get the automated machine in running order, there would be a $5,000 shipping fee and a $10,000 installation charge. In addition, the new machine will require an investment in raw materials and goods-in-process inventories of $5,000. This increase in inventory cost of $5,000 will be recovered at the end of the five-year project. The new machine is classified in asset class 8 for tax purposes. Revenue Canada requires that assets in this asset class be written off using the declining balance method at a CCA rate of 20 percent. The expected life of this machine is five years, after which it can be sold for $100,000. The asset class will be terminated after the sale of the asset. This new machine will produce incremental operating revenues of $365,000 and incremental operating expenses of $240,000 (including accounting depreciation of $83,000) per year. The firm's combined corporate tax rate is 45 percent, and the firm's required rate of return is 10 percent. Given the above information, determine the following:

a. The net present value

b. The profitability index

c. The internal rate of return.

7-6B. (*Replacement Project—Capital-Budgeting Calculation*) The G. Rod Electronic Components Corporation is considering the replacement of its existing machine with a new automated machine. The existing machine was purchased and installed at a capital cost of $25,000 three years ago. The existing machine when purchased had an expected life of six years, at which time the machine was expected to have a salvage value of zero. Both machines belong to asset class 8. Revenue Canada requires that assets in this asset class be written off using the declining balance method at a CCA rate of 20 percent. The new automated machine being considered has a capital cost of $75,000 and an expected life of three years. The new machine is expected to salvage for $4,000 in three years and at that time the asset class will be terminated. Material efficiencies resulting from the replacement would result in savings of $40,000 per year before taxes.

Currently, the old machine could be sold for $15,000. The firm's combined corporate tax rate is 45 percent, and the firm has a required rate of return of 20 percent. Calculate the following:

a. The net present value

b. The profitability index

c. The internal rate of return.

7-7B. (*Comprehensive Cash Flow—Capital-Budgeting Calculation*) The L. Bellich Company, a manufacturer of electronic components in the 45-percent combined corporate tax-rate bracket, is considering the purchase of a new, fully automated machine to replace an older, manually operated one. Both machines belong to asset class 8. Revenue Canada requires that these types of machines be written off using a declining balance method at a CCA rate of 20 percent.

The old machine had an expected life of 10 years, at which time the salvage value was expected to be zero. After five years of productive use, the old machine can now be sold for $30,000. It took one person to operate the old machine, and he earned $14,000 per year in salary and $6,000 per year in fringe benefits. The annual costs of maintenance and defects associated with the old machine were $6,000 and $2,000, respectively. Ten years ago, the old machine had a capital cost of $37,500. The replacement machine being considered has a purchase price of $40,000. The salvage value of the new machine is expected to be $15,000 after five years, and the asset class will continue to remain open. In order to get the automated machine in running order, there would be a $6,000 shipping fee and a $4,000 installation charge. In addition, because the new machine would work faster than the old one, investment in raw materials and goods-in-process inventories would need to be increased by a total of $7,000. This increase in inventory costs will be recovered at the end of the 5-year project. The annual costs of maintenance and defects on the new machine would be $1,000 and $1,000, respectively. The acquisition of the new machine requires an additional $5,000 in administrative costs in the form of accounting costs. Finally, in order to purchase the new machine, it appears the firm would have to borrow an additional $25,000 at 10 percent interest from its local bank, resulting in additional interest payments of $2,500 per year. The required rate of return on projects of this kind is 20 percent.

a. What is the project's initial outlay?

b. What are the differential cash flows after tax over the project's life?

c. What is the terminal cash flow?

d. Draw a cash flow diagram for this project.

e. What is its net present value?

f. What is its profitability index?

g. What is its internal rate of return?

h. Should the project be accepted? Why or why not?

7-8B. (*Cash Flow Calculations*) The J. R. Woolridge Corporation, maker of electronic components, is considering the replacement of a hand-operated machine used in the manufacture of electronic components with a new, fully automated machine. Given the following information, determine the cash flows after tax associated with this replacement project. Assume that both machines belong to asset class 39 for tax purposes.

Existing situation: Two full-time machine operators salaries—$12,000 each per year
Cost of maintenance—$6,000 per year
Cost of defects—$5,000
Capital cost of old machine—$40,000
Expected life—10 years
Machine's age—7 years old
Expected salvage value—$0
Depreciation method—declining balance method
CCA rate—30 percent

Current salvage value—$10,000
Combined corporate tax rate—45 percent

Proposed situation: Fully automated machine

Cost of machine—$55,000
Installation fee—$5,000
Cost of maintenance—$6,000 per year
Cost of defects—$2,000 per year
Expected life—3 years
Expected salvage value—$0
Depreciation method—declining balance method
CCA rate 30—percent
Required rate of return—15 percent

Assume the asset class will be terminated with the sale of the automated machine after 3 years.

7-9B. (*Capital-Budgeting Calculation*) Given the cash flow information in problem 7-8B and a required rate of return of 17 percent, compute the following for the automated machine:

a. Net present value

b. Profitability index

c. Internal rate of return.

Should this project be accepted?

7-10B. (*Size Disparity Ranking Problem*) The Unk's Farms Corporation is considering purchasing one of two fertilizer-herbicides for the upcoming year. The more expensive of the two is the better and will produce a higher yield. Assume these projects are mutually exclusive and that the required rate of return is 10 percent. Given the following net cash flows after tax:

Year	Project A	Project B
0	–$650	–$4,000
1	800	5,500

a. Calculate the net present value.

b. Calculate the profitability index.

c. Calculate the internal rate of return.

d. If there is no capital-rationing constraint, which project should be selected? If there is a capital-rationing constraint, how should the decision be made?

7-11B. (*Time Disparity Ranking Problem*) The Z. Bello Corporation is considering two mutually exclusive projects. The cash flows after tax associated with those projects are as follows:

Year	Project A	Project B
0	–$50,000	–$50,000
1	16,000	0
2	16,000	0
3	16,000	0
4	16,000	0
5	16,000	$100,000

The required rate of return on these projects is 11 percent.

a. What is each project's payback period?

b. What is each project's net present value?

c. What is each project's internal rate of return?

d. What has caused the ranking conflict?

e. Which project should be accepted? Why?

7-12B. (*Unequal Lives Ranking Problem*) The Battling Bishops Corporation is considering two mutually exclusive pieces of machinery that perform the same task. The two alternatives available provide the following set of cash flows after tax:

Year	Equipment A	Equipment B
0	−$20,000	−$20,000
1	13,000	6,500
2	13,000	6,500
3	13,000	6,500
4		6,500
5		6,500
6		6,500
7		6,500
8		6,500
9		6,500

Equipment A has an expected life of three years, while equipment B has an expected life of nine years. Assume a required rate of return of 14 percent.

a. Calculate each project's payback period.

b. Calculate each project's net present value.

c. Calculate each project's internal rate of return.

d. Are these projects comparable?

e. Compare these projects using replacement chains. Which project should be selected? Support your recommendation.

7-13B. (*Capital Rationing*) The Taco Toast Company is considering seven capital investment proposals, for which the funds available are limited to a maximum of $12 million. The projects are independent and have the following costs and profitability indexes associated with them:

Project	Cost	Profitability Index
A	$4,000,000	1.18
B	3,000,000	1.08
C	5,000,000	1.33
D	6,000,000	1.31
E	4,000,000	1.19
F	6,000,000	1.20
G	4,000,000	1.18

a. Under strict capital rationing, which projects should be selected?

b. Is this an optimal strategy?

7-14B. (*Risk-Adjusted NPV*) The Cake-O-Las Corporation is considering two mutually exclusive projects. Each of these projects requires an initial outlay of $10,000 and will operate for five years. The probability distributions associated with each project for years 1 through 5 are given as follows:

Net Cash Flow After Tax, Years 1–5			
Project A		Project B	
Probability	Net Cash Flow After Tax	Probability	Net Cash Flow After Tax
.20	$5,000	.20	$ 3,000
.60	6,000	.60	7,000
.20	7,000	.20	11,000

Since project B is the riskier of the two projects, the management of Cake-O-Las Corporation has decided to apply a required rate of return of 18 percent to its evaluation but only a 13 percent required rate of return to project A.

a. Determine the expected value of each project's net cash flow after tax.

b. Determine each project's risk-adjusted net present value.

c. What other factors might be considered in deciding between these two projects?

7-15B. (*Risk-Adjusted NPV*) The Dorf Corporation is evaluating two mutually exclusive projects, both of which require an initial outlay of $125,000. Each project has an expected life of five years. The probability distributions associated with the annual net cash flows from each project are given below:

Net Cash Flow After Tax, Years 1-5			
Project A		*Project B*	
Probability	Net Cash Flow After Tax	Probability	Net Cash Flow After Tax
.10	$40,000	.10	$20,000
.40	45,000	.20	40,000
.40	50,000	.40	55,000
.10	55,000	.20	70,000
		.10	90,000

The normal required rate of return for Dorf is 10 percent, but since these projects are riskier than most, Dorf is requiring a higher-than-normal rate of return on them. It is requiring an 11 percent rate of return on project A and a 13 percent rate of return on project B.

a. Determine the expected value for each project's net cash flows after tax.

b. Determine each project's risk-adjusted net present value.

c. What other factors might be considered in deciding between these projects?

7-16B. (*Certainty Equivalents*) The Temco Corp. is considering two mutually exclusive projects. The expected values for each project's net cash flows after tax are given below:

Year	Project A	Project B
0	–$1,000,000	–$1,000,000
1	600,000	600,000
2	750,000	650,000
3	600,000	700,000
4	550,000	750,000

Temco has decided to evaluate these projects using the certainty equivalent method. The certainty equivalent coefficients for each project's net cash flows after tax are given below:

Year	Project A	Project B
0	1.00	1.00
1	.90	.95
2	.90	.75
3	.75	.60
4	.65	.60

Given that this company's normal required rate of return is 15 percent and the risk-free rate is 5 percent, which project should be selected?

7-17B. (*Certainty Equivalents*) Perumperal, Inc., has decided to use the certainty equivalent method in determining whether or not a new investment should be made. The expected net cash flows after tax associated with this investment and the estimated certainty equivalent coefficients are as follows:

Year	Expected Values for Cash Flows After Tax	Certainty Equivalent Coefficients
0	–$100,000	1.00
1	30,000	0.95
2	25,000	0.90
3	30,000	0.83
4	20,000	0.75
5	25,000	0.65

Given that Perumperal's normal required rate of return is 18 percent and that the risk-free rate is 8 percent, should this project be accepted?

7-18B. (*Risk-Adjusted Discount Rates and Risk Classes*) The Kick 'n' MacDonald Corporation is examining two capital-budgeting projects with five-year lives. The first, project A, is a replacement project; the second, project B, is a project unrelated to current operations. The Kick 'n' MacDonald Corporation uses the risk-adjusted discount rate method and groups projects according to purpose and then uses a required rate of return or discount rate that has been pre-assigned to that purpose or risk class. The expected net cash flows after tax for these projects are given below:

	Project A	Project B
Initial Investment:	$300,000	$450,000
Cash Inflows:		
Year 1	$ 30,000	$130,000
Year 2	40,000	130,000
Year 3	50,000	130,000
Year 4	80,000	130,000
Year 5	120,000	130,000

The purpose/risk classes and pre-assigned required rates of return are as follows:

Purpose	Required Rate of Return
Replacement decision	13%
Modification or expansion of existing product line	16
Project unrelated to current operations	18
Research and development operations	20

Determine the project's risk-adjusted net present value.

7-19B. (*Certainty Equivalents*) The M. Jose Company uses the certainty equivalent approach when it evaluates risky investments. The company presently has two mutually exclusive investment proposals, with an expected life of four years each, to choose from with money it received from the sale of part of its toy division to another company. The expected net cash flows after tax are given below:

Year	Project A	Project B
0	–$75,000	–$75,000
1	20,000	25,000
2	20,000	30,000
3	15,000	30,000
4	50,000	25,000

The certainty equivalent coefficients for the net cash flows after tax are as follows:

Year	Project A	Project B
0	1.00	1.00
1	.90	.95
2	.85	.85
3	.80	.80
4	.70	.75

Which of the two investment proposals should be chosen, given that the risk-free rate of return is 7 percent?

7-20B. (*Probability Trees*) The Buckeye Corporation is evaluating an investment proposal with an expected life of two years. This project will require an initial outlay of $1,300,000. The resultant possible net cash flows after tax are given below:

Possible Outcomes in Year 1

	Probability		
	.6	.3	.1
	Outcome 1	Outcome 2	Outcome 3
Net Cash flow after tax =	$750,000	$900,000	$1,500,000

Conditional Outcomes and Probabilities for Year 2

If $CFAT_1 = \$750,000$		If $CFAT_1 = \$900,000$		If $CFAT_1 = \$1,500,000$	
$CFAT_2$	Probability	$CFAT_2$	Probability	$CFAT_2$	Probability
$ 300,000	.10	$400,000	.2	$ 600,000	.3
700,000	.50	700,000	.5	900,000	.6
1,100,000	.40	900,000	.2	1,100,000	.1
				1,300,000	.1

a. Construct a probability tree representing the possible outcomes.

b. Determine the joint probability of each possible sequence of events taking place.

c. What is the expected IRR of this project?

d. What is the range of possible IRRs for this project?

7-21B. (*Probability Trees*) The OSUCOWBOYS Corporation is considering an investment project with an expected life of two years. The initial outlay on this project would be $700,000, and the resultant possible net cash flows after tax are given as follows:

Possible Outcomes in Year 1

	Probability		
	.4	.4	.4
	Outcome 1	Outcome 2	Outcome 3
Net Cash flow after tax =	$325,000	$350,000	$475,000

Conditional Outcomes and Probabilities for Year 2

If $CFAT_1 = \$325,000$		If $CFAT_1 = \$350,000$		If $CFAT_1 = \$475,000$	
$CFAT_2$	Probability	$CFAT_2$	Probability	$CFAT_2$	Probability
$200,000	.3	$250,000	.2	$ 300,000	.2
350,000	.7	400,000	.5	550,000	.5
		650,000	.3	600,000	.2
				1,000,000	.1

    a. Construct a probability tree representing the possible outcomes.

    b. Determine the joint probability of each possible sequence of events taking place.

    c. What is the expected IRR of this project?

    d. What is the range of possible IRRs for this project?

7-22B. (*Probability Trees*) Mac's Buffaloes, Inc., is considering expanding its operations into computer-based basketball games. Mac's Buffaloes feels that there is a three-year life associated with this project, and it will initially involve an investment of $120,000. It also feels there is a 70 percent chance of success and a net cash flow after tax of $100,000 in year 1 and a 30 percent chance of "failure" and a $10,000 net cash flow after tax in year 1. If the project "fails" in year 1, there is a 60 percent chance that it will produce net cash flows after tax of only $10,000 in years 2 and 3. There is also a 40 percent chance that it will really fail and Mac's Buffaloes will earn nothing in year 2 and get out of this line of business, with the project terminating and no net cash flow after tax occurring in year 3. If, on the other hand, this project succeeds in the first year, then net cash flows after tax in the second year are expected to be $225,000, $180,000, or $140,000 with probabilities of .30, .50, and .20, respectively. Finally, if the project succeeds in the third and final year of operation, the net cash flows after tax are expected to be either $30,000 more or $20,000 less than they were in year 2, with an equal chance of occurrence.

    a. Construct a probability tree representing the possible outcomes.

    b. Determine the joint probability of each possible sequence of events.

    c. What is the expected IRR?

    d. What is the range of possible IRRs for this project?

7-23B. (*Cash Flow—Capital-Budgeting Calculation*) The Hokie Tech Corp. is considering expanding its highly technical construction facilities. The construction will take a total of four years until it is completed and ready for operation. The following data and assumptions describe the proposed expansion:

    1. In order to make this expansion feasible, installation expenditures of $175,000 must be made immediately to ensure that the construction facilities are competitively efficient ($t = 0$).

    2. At the end of the first year the land will be purchased and construction on stage 1 of the facilities will begin, involving a cash outflow of $100,000 for the land and $300,000 for the construction facilities. For tax purposes, the construction facilities belong to asset class 1. Revenue Canada requires that assets in this asset class be written off using a declining balance method at a CCA rate of 4 percent.

    3. Stage 2 of the construction will involve a $300,000 cash outflow at the end of year 2. This cash outlay was used for the purchase of a processing machine. For tax purposes, the processing machine belongs to asset class

39. Revenue Canada requires that assets in this asset class be written off using a declining balance method at a CCA rate of 30 percent.

4. At the end of year 3, when production begins, inventory will be increased by $50,000.

5. At the end of year four, the first sales from operation of the new plant is estimated at $800,000 and continues at that level for 10 years (with the final flow from sales occurring at the end of year 13).

6. Annual operating costs on these sales include $100,000 of fixed operating costs per year and variable operating costs equal to 35 percent of sales.

7. When the plant is closed, it is expected that the processing machine will salvage at $35,000 and asset class 39 will be terminated. The construction facilities are expected to salvage for $50,000 and asset class 1 will also be terminated.

8. When the plant is closed, the land will be sold for $225,000 ($t = 13$).

9. The company is in the 45-percent combined corporate tax-rate bracket. Given a 12 percent required rate of return, what is the NPV of this project? Should it be accepted?

7-24B. (*Cash Flow—Capital-Budgeting Calculation*) The M. Jose Corporation of Ontario must replace its executive jet and is considering two mutually exclusive planes as replacements. As far as it is concerned, both planes are identical and each will provide annual benefits, before maintenance, taxes, and depreciation, of $50,000 per year for the life of the plane; however, the costs on each are decidedly different. The first is a Lays Jet and costs $94,000. It has an expected life of seven years and will require major maintenance at the end of year 4. The annual maintenance costs are $7,500 for the first three years, $25,000 in year 4, and $12,000 for years 5 through 7. Its salvage value at the end of year 7 is $24,000.

The other plane is a Honeybilt Jet costing $100,000 and also having an expected life of seven years. Its maintenance expenses are expected to be $9,000 the first four years, rising to $18,000 annually for years 5 through 7. In years 3 and 5 the jet engine must be overhauled at an expense of $13,000 each time; this overhaul expense is in excess of the maintenance expenses. Finally, at the end of year 7 this jet will have a salvage value of $30,000. Both planes being considered belong to asset class 9. Revenue Canada requires that assets in asset class 9 be written off using the declining balance method at a CCA rate of 25 percent. At the end of year 7, the asset class will remain open. Given a 45 percent combined corporate tax rate and a 10 percent required rate of return, what is the NPV on each jet? Which should be taken?

CASE PROBLEM

HARDING PLASTIC MOLDING COMPANY

CAPITAL BUDGETING: RANKING PROBLEMS

On January 11, 1991, the finance committee of Harding Plastic Molding Company (HPMC) met to consider eight capital-budgeting projects. Present at the meeting were Robert L. Harding, president and founder, Susan Jorgensen, comptroller, and Chris Woelk, head of research and development. Over the past five years, this committee has met every month to consider and make final judgment on all proposed capital outlays brought up for review during the period.

Harding Plastic Molding Company was founded in 1965 by Robert L. Harding to produce plastic parts and molding for the Oshawa automakers. For the first 10 years of operations, HPMC worked solely as a subcontractor for the automakers, but since then has made strong efforts to diversify in an attempt to avoid the cyclical problems faced by the auto industry. By 1991, this diversification attempt had led HPMC into the production of over 1,000 different items, including kitchen utensils, camera housings, and phonographic and recording equipment. It also led to an increase in sales of 800 percent during the 1975–1991 period. As this dramatic increase in sales was paralleled by a corresponding increase in production volume, HPMC was forced, in late 1989, to expand production facilities. This plant and equipment expansion involved capital expenditures of approximately $10.5 million and resulted in an increase of production capacity of about 40 percent. Because of this increased production capacity, HPMC has made a concerted effort to attract new business and consequently has recently entered into contracts with a large toy firm and a major discount department store chain. While non-auto-related business has grown significantly, it still only represents 32 percent of HPMC's overall business. Thus, HPMC has continued to solicit nonautomotive business, and as a result of this effort and its internal research and development, the firm has four sets of mutually exclusive projects to consider at this month's finance committee meeting.

Over the past 10 years, HPMC's capital-budgeting approach has evolved into a somewhat elaborate procedure in which new proposals are categorized into three areas: profit, research and development, and safety. Projects falling into the profit or research and development areas are evaluated using present value techniques, assuming a 10 percent opportunity rate; those falling into the safety classification are evaluated in a more subjective framework. Although research and development projects have to receive favourable results from the present value criteria, there is also a total dollar limit assigned to projects of this category, typically running about $750,000 per year. This limitation was imposed by Harding primarily because of the limited availability of quality researchers in the plastics industry. Harding felt that if more funds than this were allocated, "we simply couldn't find the manpower to administer them properly." The benefits derived from safety projects, on the other hand, are not in terms of cash flows after tax; hence, present value methods are not used at all in their evaluation. The subjective approach used to evaluate safety projects is a result of the pragmatically difficult task of quantifying the benefits from these projects into dollar terms. Thus, these projects are subjectively evaluated by a management-worker committee with a limited budget. All eight projects to be evaluated in January are classified as profit projects.

The first set of projects listed on the meeting's agenda for examination involve the utilization of HPMC's precision equipment. Project A calls for the production of vacuum containers for thermos bottles produced for a large discount hardware chain. The containers would be manufactured in five different size and colour combinations. This project would be carried out over a three-year period, for which HPMC would be guaranteed a minimum return plus a percentage of the sales. Project B involves the manufacture of inexpensive photographic equipment for a national photography outlet. Although HPMC currently has excess plant capacity, each of these projects would utilize precision equipment of which the excess capacity is limited. Thus, adopting either project would tie up all precision facilities. In addition, the purchase of new equipment would be both prohibitively expensive and involve a time delay of approximately two years, thus making these projects mutually exclusive. (The cash flows after tax associated with these two projects are given in Exhibit 1.)

The second set of projects involves the renting of computer facilities over a one-year period to aid in customer billing and perhaps inventory control. Project C entails the evaluation of a customer billing system proposed by Advanced Computer Corporation. Under this system all the bookkeeping and billing presently being done by HPMC's accounting department would be done by Advanced. In addition to saving costs involved in bookkeeping, Advanced would provide a more efficient billing system and do a credit analysis of delinquent customers, which could be used in the future for in-depth credit analysis. Project D is proposed by International Computer Corporation and includes a billing system similar to that offered by Advanced and, in addition, an inventory control system that will keep track of all raw materials and parts in stock and reorder when necessary, thereby reducing the likelihood of material stockouts, which has become more and more frequent over the past three years. (The cash flows after tax for these projects are given in Exhibit 2.)

The third decision that faces the financial directors of HPMC involves a newly developed and patented process for molding hard plastics. HPMC can either manufacture and market the equipment necessary to mold such plastics or it can sell the patent rights to Polyplastics Incorporated, the world's largest producer of plastics products. (The cash flows after tax for projects E and F are shown in Exhibit 3.) At present, the process has not been fully tested, and if HPMC is going to market it itself, it will be necessary to complete this testing and begin production of plant facilities immediately. On the other hand, the selling of these patent rights to Polyplastics would involve only minor testing and refinements, which could be completed within the year. Thus, a decision as to the proper course of action is necessary immediately.

The final set of projects up for consideration revolve around the replacement of some of the machinery. HPMC can go in one of two directions. Project G suggests the purchase and installation of moderately priced, extremely efficient equipment with an expected life of five years; project H advocates the purchase of a similarly priced, although less efficient, machine with a life expectancy of 10 years. (The cash flows after tax for these alternatives are shown in Exhibit 4.)

As the meeting opened, debate immediately centered on the most appropriate method for evaluating all the projects. Harding suggested that as the projects to be considered were mutually exclusive, perhaps their usual capital-budgeting criteria of net present value was inappropriate. He felt that, in examining these projects, perhaps they should be more concerned with relative profitability or some measure of yield. Both Jorgensen and Woelk agreed with Harding's point of view, with Jorgensen advocating a profitability index approach and Woelk preferring the use of the internal rate of return. Jorgensen argued that the use of the profitability index would provide a benefit-cost ratio, directly implying relative profitability. Thus, they merely need to rank these projects and select those with the highest profitability index. Woelk agreed with Jorgensen's point of view, but suggested that the calculation of an internal rate of return would also give a measure of profitability and

EXHIBIT 1
Harding Plastic Molding Company

	Cash Flows After Tax	
Year	Project A	Project B
0	–$ 75,000	–$75,000
1	10,000	43,000
2	30,000	43,000
3	100,000	43,000

EXHIBIT 2
Harding Plastic Molding Company

	Cash Flows After Tax	
Year	Project C	Project D
0	–$ 8,000	–$20,000
1	11,000	25,000

EXHIBIT 3
Harding Plastic Molding Company

	Cash Flows After Tax	
Year	Project E	Project F
0	–$ 30,000	–$271,500
1	210,000	100,000
2		100,000
3		100,000
4		100,000
5		100,000
6		100,000
7		100,000
8		100,000
9		100,000
10		100,000

EXHIBIT 4
Harding Plastic Molding Company

	Cash Flows After Tax	
Year	Project G	Project H
0	–$500,000	–$500,000
1	225,000	150,000
2	225,000	150,000
3	225,000	150,000
4	225,000	150,000
5	225,000	150,000
6		150,000
7		150,000
8		150,000
9		150,000
10		150,000

perhaps be somewhat easier to interpret. To settle the issue, Harding suggested that they calculate all three measures, as they would undoubtedly yield the same ranking.

From here the discussion turned to an appropriate approach to the problem of differing lives among mutually exclusive projects E and F, and G and H. Woelk argued that there really was not a problem here at all, that as all the cash flows after tax from these projects can be determined, any of the discounted cash flow methods of capital budgeting will work well. Jorgensen argued that although this was true, some compensation should be made for the fact that the projects being considered did not have equal lives.

QUESTIONS

1. Was Harding correct in stating that the NPV, PI, and IRR necessarily will yield the same ranking order? Under what situations might the NPV, PI, and IRR methods provide different rankings? Why is it possible?

2. What are the NPV, PI, and IRR for projects A and B? What has caused the ranking conflicts? Should project A or B be chosen? Might your answer change if project B is a typical project in the plastic molding industry? For example, if projects for HPMC generally yield approximately 12 percent, is it logical to assume that the IRR for project B of approximately 33 percent is a correct calculation for ranking purposes? (*Hint:* Examine the reinvestment rate assumption.)

3. What are the NPV, PI, and IRR for projects C and D? Should project C or D be chosen? Does your answer change if these projects are considered under a capital constraint? What return on the marginal $12,000 not employed in project C is necessary to make one indifferent to choosing one project over the other under a capital-rationing situation?

4. What are the NPV, PI, and IRR for projects E and F? Are these projects comparable even though they have unequal lives? Why? Which project should be chosen? Assume that these projects are not considered under a capital constraint.

5. What are the NPV, PI, and IRR for projects G and H? Are these projects comparable even though they have unequal lives? Why? Which project should be chosen? Assume that these projects are not considered under a capital constraint.

SELF-TEST SOLUTIONS

SS-1: *STEP 1:* First calculate the initial cash outlay.

Initial Outlay	
Outflows:	
Cost of machine	$60,000
Installation fee	3,000
Shipping fee	3,000
Inflows:	
Salvage value—old machine	–5,000
Initial cash outlay	$61,000

STEP 2: Calculate the incremental cash flows after tax over the project's life.

Schedule for Annual Net Operating Cash Flows After Tax

	Year	
	1	2
Savings:		
Reduced Salary	$25,000	$25,000
Reduced Defects	3,000	3,000
Costs:		
Increased Maintenance	−1,000	−1,000
Net Savings Before Taxes	$27,000	$27,000
Taxes (@45%)	−12,150	−12,150
Net Savings after Taxes	$14,850	$14,850
Tax Shields from Depreciation	4,118	7,000
Net Cash Flows After Tax	$18,968	$21,850

Schedule for Capital Cost Allowances and Tax Shields

Year	UCC (Beg)	Capital Cost Allowance	Tax Shields	UCC (End)
1	$30,500	$ 9,150	$4,118	$51,850
2	51,850	15,555	7,000	36,295

STEP 3: Calculate the terminal cash flow.

Salvage value—new machine	$20,000
Tax shield adjustment	4,889[a]
Terminal cash flow	$24,889

$$^a \left[\frac{(\$36,295 - \$20,000)(.30)(.45)}{(.30+.15)} \right] = \$4,889$$

Summary

	Year		
	0	1	2
Initial Outlay	−$61,000		
Net Operating Cash Flow		$18,968	$21,850
Salvage Value			20,000
Tax Shield Adjustment			4,889
Net Annual Cash Flow	−$61,000	$18,968	$46,739

SS-2: a. 1st Approach:

$$NPV = \frac{\$18,968}{(1.15)^1} + \frac{\$46,739}{(1.15)^2} - \$61,000$$

$$= \$16,494 + \$35,341 - \$61,000$$

$$= -\$9,165$$

2nd Approach:

$$NPV = PV(\text{Project's Net Savings after Taxes}) +$$
$$PV(\text{Tax shields from Depreciation}) + PV(\text{Salvage Value}) - IO$$

$$= (\$14,850)(1.6257) +$$

$$\left[\frac{(\$61,000)(.30)(.45)}{(.30+.15)} \right] \left[\frac{1.075}{1.15} \right] -$$

$$\left[\frac{(\$20,000)(.30)(.45)}{(.30+.15)}\right]\left[\frac{1}{(1.15)^2}\right]+$$

$$(\$20,000)(.7561) - \$61,000$$

$$= \$24,142 + \$17,107 - \$4,537 + \$15,122 - \$61,000$$

$$= -\$9,165$$

b.

$$\text{Profitability Index} = \frac{\sum_{t=1}^{n} \dfrac{CFAT_t}{(1+k)^t}}{IO}$$

$$= \frac{\$51,832}{\$61,000}$$

$$= 0.8497$$

c. Through linear interpolation, upper and lower boundaries for IRR can be estimated by substitution in the following equations

$$NPV = \sum_{t=1}^{n} \frac{CFAT_t}{(1+IRR)^t} - IO$$

$$NPV = \frac{\$18,968}{(1+IRR)^1} + \frac{\$46,738}{(1+IRR)^2} - \$61,000$$

From linear interpolation we find that the value of IRR occurs between 3 and 4 percent. As a result, the project's internal rate of return is less than the firm's required rate of return of 15 percent, and the project should not be accepted.

Thus, the project should be rejected since the NPV is negative, the PI is less than 1.0, and the IRR is less than the required rate of return of 15 percent.

SS-3. a.

$$\overline{X} = \sum_{i=1}^{N} X_i P(Xi)$$

$$\overline{X}_A = 0.20(\$10,000) + 0.60(\$15,000) + 0.20(\$20,000)$$

$$= \$2,000 + \$9,000 + \$4,000$$

$$= \$15,000$$

$$\overline{X}_B = 0.20(\$6,000) + 0.60(\$18,000) + 0.20(\$30,000)$$

$$= \$1,200 + \$10,800 + \$6,000$$

$$= \$18,000$$

b.

$$NPV = \sum_{t=1}^{n} \frac{CFAT_t}{(1+i^*)^t} - IO$$

$$NPV_A = \$15,000(3.605) - \$25,000$$

$$= \$54,075 - \$25,000$$

$$= \$29,075$$

$$NPV_B = \$18,000(3.127) - \$25,000$$

$$= \$56,286 - \$25,000$$

$$= \$31,286$$

SS-4. Project A:

Year	(A) Expected Cash Flow After Tax	(B)	(A · B) (Expected Cash Flow) × (α_t)	Present Value Factor at 8%	Present Value
0	−$300,000	1.00	−$300,000	1.000	−$300,000
1	100,000	.95	95,000	0.926	87,970
2	200,000	.90	180,000	0.857	154,260
3	200,000	.85	170,000	0.794	134,980
4	300,000	.80	240,000	0.735	176,400
5	300,000	.75	225,000	0.681	153,225
				NPV_A =	$406,835

Project B:

Year	(A) Expected Cash Flow After Tax	(B)	(A · B) (Expected Cash Flow) × (α_t)	Present Value Factor at 8%	Present Value
0	−$300,000	1.00	−$300,000	1.000	−$300,000
1	200,000	.90	180,000	0.926	166,680
2	200,000	.80	160,000	0.857	137,120
3	200,000	.70	140,000	0.794	111,160
4	300,000	.60	180,000	0.735	132,300
5	400,000	.50	200,000	0.681	136,200
				NPV_B =	$383,460

Thus, project A should be selected since it has the higher NPV.

SELECTED REFERENCES

Aggarwal, Raj and Luc A. Soenen. "Project Exit Value as a Measure of Flexibility and Risk Exposure," *Engineering Economist*, 35 (Fall 1989), 39–54.

Balachandran, Bala V., Nandu J. Nagarajan, and Alfred Rappaport. "Threshold Margins for Creating Economic Value," *Financial Management*, 15 (Spring 1986), 68–77.

Bierman, Harold, Jr., and Vithala R. Rao. "Investment Decisions with Sampling," *Financial Management*, 7 (Autumn 1978), 19–24.

Brennan, Michael J. "Latent Assets," *Journal of Finance*, 45 (July 1990), 709–30.

Brennan, Michael J. and Eduardo S. Schwartz. "A New Approach to Evaluating Natural Resource Investments," *Midland Corporate Finance Journal*, 3 (Spring 1985), 37–47.

Butler, J. S. and Barry Schachter. "Estimation Risk Adjusted Discount Rates," *Financial Management*, 18 (Winter 1989), 13–22.

Bonini, Charles P. "Capital Investment under Uncertainty with

Abandonment Options," *Journal of Financial and Quantitative Analysis*, 12 (March 1977), 39–54.

Breen, William J., and Eugene M. Lerner. "Corporate Financial Strategies and Market Measures of Risk and Return," *Journal of Finance*, 28 (May 1973), 339–351.

Carter, E. Eugene. *Portfolio Aspects of Corporate Capital Budgeting*. Lexington, MA: D. C. Heath, 1974.

Cozzolina, John M. "A New Method of Risk Analysis," *Sloan Management Review*, 20 (Spring 1979), 53–65.

Dixit, Avinash. "Entry and Exit Decisions under Uncertainty," *Journal of Political Economy*, 97 (June 1989), 620–38.

Galai, Dan, and Ronald W. Masulis. "The Option Pricing Model and the Risk Factor of Stock," *Journal of Financial Economics*, 3 (January–March 1976), 66–69.

Grayson, C. Jackson, Jr. *Decisions under Uncertainty: Drilling Decisions by Oil and Gas Operators*. Boston: Division of Research, Harvard Business School, 1960.

Greer, Willis R., Jr. "Capital Budgeting Analysis with the Timing of Events Uncertain," *Accounting Review*, 45 (January 1970), 103-114.

Hayes, Robert H. "Incorporating Risk Aversion into Risk Analysis," *Engineering Economist*, 20 (Winter 1975), 99–121.

Hertz, David B. "Investment Policies that Pay Off," *Harvard Business Review*, 46 (January–February 1968), 96–108.

Hillier, Frederick S. "A Basic Model for Capital Budgeting of Risky Interrelated Projects," *Engineering Economist*, 17 (Fall 1971), 1–30.

Hodder, James E., and Henry E. Riggs. "Pitfalls in Evaluating Risky Projects," *Business Review*, 63 (January–February 1985), 128-135.

Jarrett, Jeffrey E. "An Abandonment Decision Model," *Engineering Economist*, 19 (Fall 1973), 35–46.

Keeley, Robert, and Randolph Westerfield. "A Problem in Probability Distribution Techniques for Capital Budgeting," *Journal of Finance*, 27 (June 1972), 703–709.

Levy, Haim, and Marshall Sarnat. *Capital Investment and Financial Decisions.* Englewood Cliffs, NJ: Prentice-Hall, 1976.

Lewellen, Wilbur G., and Michael S. Long. "Simulation versus Single-Value Estimates in Capital Expenditure Analysis," *Decision Sciences*, 3 (1972), 19–33.

Magee, J. F. "How to Use Decision Trees in Capital Investment," *Harvard Business Review*, 42 (September–October 1964), 79–96.

Marshuetz, Richard J. "How American Can Allocates Capital," *Harvard Business Review*, 63 (January–February 1985), 82–91.

Osteryoung, Jerome S., Elton Scott, and Gordon S. Roberts. "Selecting Projects with the Coefficient of Variation," *Financial Management*, 6 (Summer 1977), 65–70.

Petty, J. William, David F. Scott, Jr., and Monroe M. Bird. "The Capital Expenditure Decision-Making Process of Large Corporations," *Engineering Economist*, 20 (Spring 1975), 159–172.

Robichek, Alexander A. "Interpreting the Results of Risk Analysis," *Journal of Finance*, 30 (December 1975), 1384–1386.

Salazar, Rudolfo C., and Subrata K. Sen. "A Simulation Model of Capital Budgeting under Uncertainty," *Management Science*, 15 (December 1968), 161–179.

Schall, Lawrence D., and Gary L. Sundem. "Capital Budgeting Methods and Risk: A Further Analysis," *Financial Management*, 9 (Spring 1980), 7–11.

Schall, Lawrence D., Gary L. Sundem, and William R. Geijsbeek, Jr. "Survey and Analysis of Capital Budgeting Methods," *Journal of Finance*, 33 (March 1978), 281–287.

Sick, Gordon A. "A Certainty-Equivalent Approach to Capital Budgeting," *Financial Management*, 15 (Winter 1986), 23–32.

Spahr, Ronald W., and Stanley A. Martin. "Project Pricing in Limited Diversification Portfolios," *Engineering Economist*, 26 (Spring 1981), 207–222.

PART THREE

Financial Structure
and Dividend
Policy Decisions

CHAPTER 8

Analysis and Impact of Leverage

- Business Risk and Financial Risk

- Breakeven Analysis

- Operating Leverage

- Financial Leverage

- Combining Operating and Financial Leverage

Our work in Chapters 4 and 6 allowed us to develop an understanding of how financial assets are valued in the marketplace. Drawing on the tenets of valuation theory, we presented various approaches to measuring the cost of funds to the business organization. This chapter will also present concepts that relate to the valuation process and the cost of capital. These concepts will assist us in examining the chapter's objective, the planning of the firm's financing mix.

The cost of capital provides a direct link between the formulation of the firm's asset structure and its financial structure. This is illustrated in Figure 8-1. Recall that the cost of capital is a basic input to the time-adjusted capital-budgeting models. Therefore, the cost of capital affects both the process of capital budgeting and the process of selecting assets. The cost of capital is affected, in turn, by the composition of the right-hand side of the firm's balance sheet—that is, its financial structure.

This chapter will examine tools that can be useful aids to the financial manager in determining the firm's proper financial structure. First, we will review the technique of breakeven analysis. This review provides the foundation for the relationships to be highlighted in the remainder of the chapter. We will then examine the concept of operating leverage, some consequences of the firm's use of financial leverage, and the impact on the firm's earnings stream under various degrees of operating leverage and financial leverage. Our immediate tasks are to distinguish two types of risk that confront the firm and to clarify some key terminology that will be used throughout this and the subsequent chapter.

Perspective in Finance

In this chapter we become more precise in assessing the causes of variability in the firm's expected revenue streams. Business risk occurs as a result of the

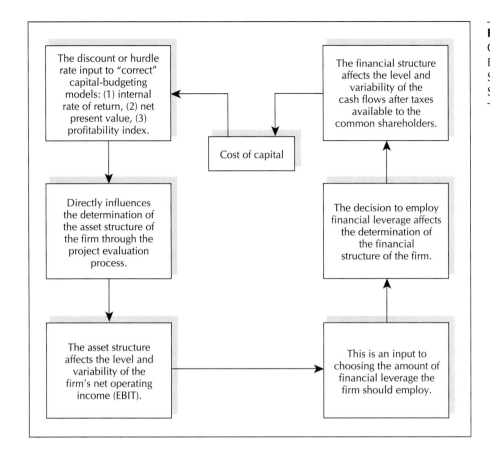

FIGURE 8-1
Cost of Capital as a Link
Between the Firm's Asset
Structure and Financial
Structure

firm's investment decisions. For example, the composition of the firm's assets determines its exposure to business risk. This type of risk is described by what appears on the left-hand side of the company's balance sheet. Financial risk occurs as a result of the choices used to arrange the right-hand side of the company's balance sheet. The choice to use more financial leverage means that the firm will experience greater exposure to financial risk. The tools developed here will help you quantify the firm's business and financial risk. A solid understanding of these tools will make you a better financial manager.

BUSINESS RISK AND FINANCIAL RISK

In studying capital-budgeting techniques we referred to **risk** as the likely variability associated with expected cash flows. As our attention is now focused on the firm's financing decision rather than its investment decision, it is useful to separate the income stream variations attributable to (1) the company's exposure to business risk[1] and (2) its decision to incur financial risk.

Business risk refers to the relative dispersion (variability) in the firm's expected earnings before interest and taxes (EBIT).[2] Figure 8-2 shows a sub-

---

[1]Examples of firms that have a low degree of business risk include electric power corporations, whereas examples of firms that have a high degree of business risk include computer software companies.

[2]If what the accountants call "other income" and "other expenses" are equal to zero, then EBIT is equal to net operating income. These terms will be used interchangeably.

FIGURE 8-2
Subjective Probability
Distribution of Next Year's
EBIT

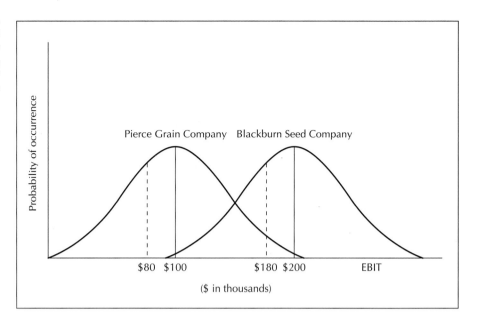

jectively estimated probability distribution of next year's EBIT for the Pierce Grain Company and the same type of projection for Pierce's larger competitor, the Blackburn Seed Company. The expected value of EBIT for Pierce is $100,000, with an associated standard deviation of $20,000. If next year's EBIT for Pierce fell one standard deviation short of the expected $100,000, the actual EBIT would equal $80,000. Blackburn's expected EBIT is $200,000, and the size of the associated standard deviation is $20,000. The standard deviation for the expected level of EBIT is the same for both firms. We would say that Pierce's degree of business risk exceeds Blackburn's owing to its larger coefficient of variation of expected EBIT, as follows:

$$\text{Pierce's coefficient of variation of expected EBIT} = \frac{\$20,000}{\$100,000} = .20$$

$$\text{Blackburn's coefficient of variation of expected EBIT} = \frac{\$20,000}{\$200,000} = .10$$

The relative dispersion in the firm's EBIT stream, measured here by its expected coefficient of variation, is the residual effect of several causal influences. Dispersion in operating income does not cause business risk; rather, this dispersion which we call business risk is the result of several influences. Some of these are listed in Table 8-1, along with an example of each particular attribute. Notice that the company's cost structure, product demand characteristics, and intra-industry competitive position all affect its business risk exposure. Such business risk is a direct result of the firm's investment decision. It is the firm's asset structure, after all, that gives rise to both the level and variability of its operating profits.[3]

Financial risk, on the other hand, is a direct result of the firm's financing decision. In the context of selecting a proper financing mix, this risk applies to (1) the additional variability in earnings available to the firm's common shareholders and (2) the additional chance of insolvency borne by

[3]Portfolio theory suggests that shareholders can diversify away much of the business risk through the choice of the assets in their portfolios.

Business Risk Attribute	Example[a]
1. Sensitivity of the firm's product demand to general economic conditions	If GNP declines, does the firm's sales level decline by a greater percentage?
2. Degree of competition	Is the firm's market share small in comparison with other firms that produce and distribute the same product(s)?
3. Product diversification	Is a large proportion of the firm's sales revenue derived from a single major product or product line?
4. Operating leverage	Does the firm utilize a high level of operating leverage resulting in a high level of fixed costs?
5. Growth prospects	Are the firm's product markets expanding and (or) changing, making income estimates and prospects highly volatile?
6. Size	Does the firm suffer a competitive disadvantage due to lack of size in assets, sales, or profits that translates into (among other things) difficulty in tapping the capital market for funds?

[a]Affirmative responses indicate greater business risk exposure.

TABLE 8-1
The Concept of
Business Risk

the common shareholder caused by the use of financial leverage.[4] **Financial leverage** means financing a portion of the firm's assets with securities bearing a fixed (limited) rate of return in hopes of increasing the ultimate return to the common shareholders. The decision to use debt or preferred shares in the financial structure of the corporation means that those who own the common shares of the firm are exposed to financial risk. Any given level of variability in EBIT will be magnified by the firm's use of financial leverage, and such additional variability will be embodied in the variability of earnings available to the common shareholder and earnings per share.[5] If these magnifications are negative, the common shareholder has a higher chance of insolvency than would have existed had the use of fixed charge securities (debt and preferred shares) been avoided.

The closely related concepts of business and financial risk are crucial to the problem of financial structure design. This follows from the impact of these types of risk on the variability of the earnings stream flowing to the company's common shareholders. In the rest of this chapter we will study techniques that permit a precise assessment of the earnings stream variability caused by (1) operating leverage and (2) financial leverage. We have already defined financial leverage. Table 8-1 shows that the business risk of the enterprise is influenced by the use of what is called operating leverage. **Operating leverage** refers to the occurrence of fixed operating costs in the firm's income stream. To understand the nature and importance of operating leverage, we need to draw upon the basics of cost-volume-profit analysis or breakeven analysis.

---

[4]Note that the concept of financial risk used here differs from that used in our examination of cash and marketable securities management in Chapter 14.

[5]Sometimes a firm's management is burdened with financial problems because of its policy towards high financial risk, even though management may have a good track record. For example, the Campeau Corporation used huge amounts of debt to acquire Allied Stores and Federated Department Stores. This type of financial decision made life very uncomfortable for the operating side of this company.

Perspective in Finance

The breakeven analysis concepts presented in the next section are often covered in many of your other classes such as basic accounting principles and managerial economics. This just shows you how important and accepted this tool is within the realm of business decision making. The "Objective and Uses" section below identifies five typical uses of the breakeven model. You can probably add an application or two of your own. Hotels and motels, for instance, know exactly what their breakeven occupancy rate is. This breakeven occupancy rate gives them an operating target. This operating target, in turn, often becomes a crucial input to the hotel's advertising strategy. You may not want to become a financial manager—but you do want to understand how to compute breakeven points.

BREAKEVEN ANALYSIS

The technique of breakeven analysis is familiar to legions of people in business. It is usefully applied in a wide array of business settings, including both small and large organizations. This tool is widely accepted by the business community for two reasons: it is based on straightforward assumptions and companies have found the information gained from the breakeven model beneficial in decision-making situations.

Objective and Uses

The objective of breakeven analysis is to determine the breakeven quantity of output by studying the relationships among the firm's cost structure, volume of output, and profit. Alternatively, the firm ascertains the breakeven level of sales dollars that corresponds to the breakeven quantity of output. We will develop the fundamental relationships by concentrating on units of output. Then, we will extend the procedure to calculate the breakeven sales level.

What is meant by the breakeven quantity of output? It is that quantity of output, denominated in units, that results in an EBIT level equal to zero. Use of the breakeven model, therefore, enables the financial officer (1) to determine the quantity of output that must be sold to cover all operating costs, as distinct from financial costs, and (2) to calculate the EBIT that will be achieved at various output levels.

There are many actual and potential applications of the breakeven approach. Some of these include:

1. **Capital expenditure analysis.** As a complementary technique to discounted cash flow evaluation models, the breakeven model locates in a rough way the sales volume needed to make a project economically beneficial to the firm. It should not be used to replace the time-adjusted evaluation techniques.

2. **Pricing policy.** The sales price of a new product can be set to achieve a target EBIT level. Furthermore, should market penetration be a prime objective, a price could be set that would cover slightly more than the variable costs of production and provide only a partial contribution to the recovery of fixed costs. The negative EBIT at several possible sales prices can then be studied.

3. **Labour contract negotiations.** The effect of increased variable costs resulting from higher wages on the breakeven quantity of output can be analyzed.

4. **Cost structure.** The choice of reducing variable costs at the expense of incurring higher fixed costs can be evaluated. Management might decide to become more capital-intensive by performing tasks in the production process through use of equipment rather than labour. Application of the breakeven model can indicate what the effects of this tradeoff will be on the breakeven point for the given product.

5. **Financing decisions.** Analysis of the firm's cost structure will reveal the proportion that fixed operating costs bear to sales. If this proportion is high, the firm might reasonably decide not to add any fixed financing costs on top of the high fixed operating costs.

Essential Elements of the Breakeven Model

To implement the breakeven model, we must separate the production costs of the company into two mutually exclusive categories: fixed costs and variable costs. You will recall from your study of basic economics that in the long run all costs are variable. Breakeven analysis, therefore, is a short-run concept.

Assumed Behaviour of Costs

Fixed Costs □ **Fixed costs**, also referred to as **indirect costs**, do not vary in total amount as sales volume or the quantity of output changes over some relevant range of output.[6] Total fixed costs are independent of the quantity of product produced and equal to some constant dollar amount. As the production volume increases, the fixed cost per unit of product decreases because the fixed costs are being spread over larger and larger quantities of output. Figure 8-3 illustrates the behaviour of total fixed costs with respect to the company's relevant range of output. This total is shown to be unaffected by the quantity of product that is manufactured and sold. Over some other relevant output range, the amount of total fixed costs might be higher or lower for the same company.

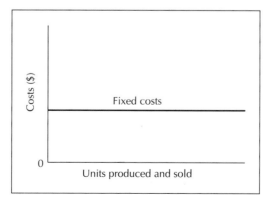

FIGURE 8-3
Fixed Cost Behaviour over the Relevant Range of Output

---

[6]A firm would normally produce several products in the same plant. As a result, some fixed costs will be allocated across a number of different end products. The method of assigning the fixed costs to the products will vary with company practice; typical approaches are to allocate on the basis of labour inputs, square footage used in the production process, or even by selling price.

In a manufacturing setting, some specific examples of fixed costs are:

1. Administrative salaries
2. Depreciation
3. Insurance
4. Lump sums spent on intermittent advertising programs
5. Property taxes
6. Rent

Variable Costs □ Variable costs are sometimes referred to as **direct costs**. **Variable costs** are fixed per unit of output but vary in total as output changes. Total variable costs are computed by taking the variable cost per unit and multiplying it by the quantity produced and sold. The breakeven model assumes proportionality between total variable costs and sales. Thus, if sales rise by 10 percent, it is assumed that variable costs will rise by 10 percent. Figure 8-4 illustrates the behaviour of total variable costs with respect to the company's relevant range of output. Total variable costs are seen to depend on the quantity of product that is manufactured and sold. Notice that if zero units of the product are manufactured, then variable costs are zero but fixed costs are greater than zero. This implies that some contribution to the coverage of fixed costs occurs as long as the selling price per unit exceeds the variable cost per unit. This helps explain why some firms will operate a plant even when sales are temporarily depressed—that is, to provide some increment of revenue toward the coverage of fixed costs.

For a manufacturing operation, some examples of variable costs include:

1. Direct labour
2. Direct materials
3. Energy costs (fuel, electricity, natural gas) associated with the production area
4. Freight costs for products leaving the plant
5. Packaging
6. Sales commissions

More on Behaviour of Costs □ No one really believes that all costs behave as neatly as we have illustrated the fixed and variable costs in Figures 8-3 and

FIGURE 8-4
Variable Cost Behaviour over the Relevant Range of Output

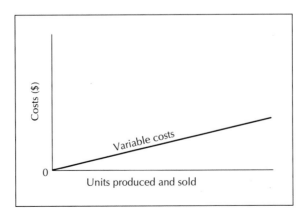

8-4. Nor does any law or accounting principle dictate that a certain element of the firm's total costs always be classified as fixed or variable. This will depend on each firm's specific circumstances. One firm's energy costs may be predominantly fixed, whereas another firm's energy costs may vary with output.[7]

Furthermore, some costs may be fixed for a while, then rise sharply to a higher level as a higher output is reached, remain fixed, and then rise again with further increases in production. Such costs may be termed either (1) **semivariable** or (2) **semifixed**. The label is your choice, since both are used in industrial practice. An example might be the salaries paid production supervisors. Should output be cut back by 15 percent for a short period, the management of the organization is not likely to lay off 15 percent of the supervisors. Similarly, commissions paid to salespeople often follow a stepwise pattern over wide ranges of success. This sort of cost behaviour is shown in Figure 8-5.

To implement the breakeven model and deal with such a complex cost structure, the financial manager must (1) identify the most relevant output range for planning purposes and then (2) approximate the cost effect of semivariable items over this range by segregating a portion of them to fixed costs and a portion to variable costs. In an actual business application the analyst who deals with semivariable items will spend considerably more time allocating costs to fixed and variable categories than in carrying out the actual breakeven calculations.

Total Revenue and Volume of Output

Besides fixed and variable costs, the essential elements of the breakeven model include total revenue from sales and volume of output. Total revenue means sales dollars and is equal to the selling price per unit multiplied by the quantity sold. The volume of output refers to the firm's level of operations and may be indicated either as a unit quantity or as sales dollars.

Finding the Breakeven Point

Finding the breakeven point in terms of units of production can be accomplished in several ways. All approaches require the essential elements of the

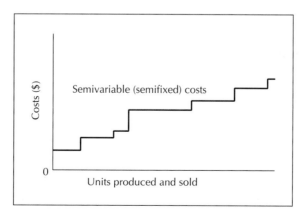

FIGURE 8-5
Semivariable Cost Behaviour over the Relevant Range of Output

---

[7]In a greenhouse operation, where plants are grown (manufactured) under strictly controlled temperatures, heat costs will tend to be fixed whether the building is full or only half full of seedlings. In a metal stamping operation, where levers are being produced, there is no need to heat the plant to as high a temperature when the machines are stopped and the workers are not there. In this latter case, the heat costs will tend to be variable.

breakeven model just described. The breakeven model is a simple adaptation of the firm's income statement expressed in the following analytical format:[8]

$$\text{sales} - (\text{total variable cost} + \text{total fixed cost}) = \text{profit} \qquad (8\text{-}1)$$

On a units of production basis, it is necessary to introduce (1) the price at which each unit is sold and (2) the variable cost per unit of output. Because the profit item studied in breakeven analysis is EBIT, we will use that acronym instead of the word "profit." In terms of units, the income statement shown in Equation (8-1) becomes the breakeven model by setting EBIT equal to zero:

$$\left(\begin{array}{c}\text{sales price} \\ \text{per unit}\end{array}\right)\left(\begin{array}{c}\text{units} \\ \text{sold}\end{array}\right) - \left[\left(\begin{array}{c}\text{variable cost} \\ \text{per unit}\end{array}\right)\left(\begin{array}{c}\text{units} \\ \text{sold}\end{array}\right) + \left(\begin{array}{c}\text{total fixed} \\ \text{cost}\end{array}\right)\right]$$
$$= \text{EBIT} = \$0 \qquad (8\text{-}2)$$

We must now determine the number of units that must be produced and sold in order to satisfy Equation (8-2)—that is, to arrive at an EBIT = $0. This can be done by (1) trial-and-error analysis, (2) contribution margin analysis, or (3) algebraic analysis. Each approach will be illustrated using the same set of circumstances.

The Problem Situation

Even though the Pierce Grain Company manufactures several different products, the product mix for this company is rather constant if examined over a lengthy period. This allows management to conduct its financial planning by use of a "normal" sales price per unit and "normal" variable cost per unit. The "normal" sales price and variable cost per unit are calculated from the constant product mix. The assumption for this calculation is that the product mix is considered as one product. The selling price is $10 and the variable cost is $6. Total fixed costs for the firm are $100,000 per year. What is the breakeven point in units produced and sold for the company during the coming year?

Trial-and-Error Analysis

The most cumbersome approach to determining the firm's breakeven point is to employ the trial-and-error technique illustrated in Table 8-2. The process simply involves the arbitrary selection of an output level and the calculation of a corresponding EBIT amount. When the level of output is found that results in an EBIT = $0, the breakeven point has been located. Notice that Table 8-2 is just Equation (8-2) in worksheet form. For the Pierce Grain Company, total operating costs will be covered when 25,000 units are manufactured and sold. This tells us that if sales equal $250,000, the firm's EBIT will equal $0.

Contribution Margin Analysis

Unlike trial and error, use of the contribution margin technique permits direct computation of the breakeven quantity of output. The **contribution**

[8]Note that: Sales − Variable costs = Contribution to overhead and profits.

TABLE 8-2. The Pierce Grain Company Sales, Cost, and Profit Schedule

	(1) *Units Sold*	*(2)* *Unit Sales Price*	*(3)=(1) × (2)* *Sales*	*(4)* *Unit Variable Cost*	*(5)=(1) × (4)* *Total Variable Cost*	*(6)* *Total Fixed Cost*	*(7)=(5)+(6)* *Total Cost*	*(8)=(3) − (7)* *EBIT*
1.	10,000	$10	$100,000	$6	$ 60,000	$100,000	$160,000	–$60,000
2.	15,000	10	150,000	6	90,000	100,000	190,000	–40,000
3.	20,000	10	200,000	6	120,000	100,000	220,000	–20,000
4.	25,000	10	250,000	6	150,000	100,000	250,000	0
5.	30,000	10	300,000	6	180,000	100,000	280,000	20,000
6.	35,000	10	350,000	6	210,000	100,000	310,000	40,000

Input Data
Unit sales price = $10
Unit variable cost = $6
Total fixed cost = $100,000

Output Data
Breakeven point in units = 25,000 units produced and sold
Breakeven point in sales = $250,000

margin is the difference between the unit selling price and unit variable costs, as follows:

$$\begin{array}{l} \text{Unit sales price} \\ - \ \underline{\text{Unit variable cost}} \\ = \ \underline{\underline{\text{Unit contribution margin}}} \end{array}$$

The use of the word "contribution" in the present context means contribution to the coverage of fixed operating costs. For the Pierce Grain Company, the unit contribution margin is

$$\begin{array}{lr} \text{Unit sales price} & \$10 \\ \text{Unit variable cost} & \underline{-6} \\ \text{Unit contribution margin} & \underline{\underline{\$\ 4}} \end{array}$$

If the annual fixed costs of $100,000 are divided by the unit contribution margin of $4, we find the breakeven quantity of output for Pierce Grain is 25,000 units. With much less effort, we have arrived at the identical result found by trial and error. Figure 8-6 portrays the contribution margin technique for finding the breakeven point.

Algebraic Analysis

To explain the algebraic method for finding the breakeven output level we need to adopt the following notation. Let

Q = the number of units sold

Q_B = the breakeven level of Q

P = the unit sales price

F = total fixed costs anticipated over the planning period

V = the unit variable cost

Equation (8-2), the breakeven model, is repeated below as Equation (8-2a) with the model symbols used in place of words. The breakeven model is then

FIGURE 8-6
Contribution Margin
Approach to Breakeven
Analysis

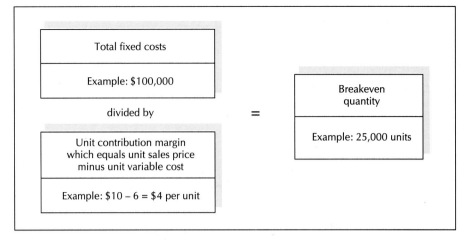

solved for Q, the number of units that must be sold in order that EBIT will equal $0. We label the breakeven point quantity Q_B.

$$(P \cdot Q) - [(V \cdot Q) + F] = EBIT = \$0 \qquad (8\text{-}2a)$$

$$(P \cdot Q) - (V \cdot Q) - F = \$0$$

$$Q(P - V) = F$$

$$Q_B = \frac{F}{P - V} \qquad (8\text{-}3)$$

Observe that Equation (8-3) says: divide total fixed operating costs, F, by the unit contribution margin, $P - V$, and the breakeven level of output, Q_B, will be obtained. The contribution margin analysis is nothing more than Equation (8-3) in different garb.

Application of Equation (8-3) permits direct calculation of Pierce Grain's breakeven point, as follows:

$$Q_B = \frac{F}{P - V} = \frac{\$100,000}{\$10 - \$6} = 25,000 \text{ units}$$

The Breakeven Point in Sales Dollars

In dealing with the multi-product firm, it is convenient to compute the breakeven point in terms of sales dollars rather than units of output.[9] Sales, in effect, become a common denominator associated with a particular product mix. Furthermore, an outside analyst may not have access to internal unit cost data. He or she may, however, be able to obtain annual reports for the firm. If the analyst can separate the firm's total costs as identified from its annual reports into their fixed and variable components, he or she can calculate a general breakeven point in sales dollars.

We will illustrate the procedure using the Pierce Grain Company's cost structure, contained in Table 8-2. Suppose that the information on line 5 of

[9]This approach is also useful if we relax one of the basic assumptions of the breakeven analysis and allow price to vary over some output range; in this form, price is a function of the volume produced and assumed to be sold.

Sales	$300,000	**TABLE 8-3**
Less: Total variable costs	180,000	The Pierce Grain Company
Revenue before fixed costs	$120,000	Analytical Income Statement
Less: Total fixed costs	100,000	
EBIT	$ 20,000	

Table 8-2 is arranged in the format shown in Table 8-3. We will refer to this type of financial statement as an **analytical income statement**. This distinguishes it from audited income statements published, for example, in the annual reports of public corporations. If we are aware of the simple mathematical relationships on which cost-volume-profit analysis is based, we can use Table 8-3 to find the breakeven point in sales dollars for the Pierce Grain Company.

First, let us explore the logic of the process. Recall from Equation (8-1) that

$$\text{sales} - (\text{total variable cost} + \text{total fixed cost}) = \text{EBIT}$$

If we let total sales = S, total variable cost = VC, and total fixed cost = F, the above relationship becomes

$$S - (VC + F) = \text{EBIT}$$

Since variable cost per unit of output and selling price per unit are assumed constant over the relevant output range in breakeven analysis, the ratio of total sales to total variable cost, VC/S, is a constant for any level of sales. This permits us to rewrite the previous expression as

$$S - \left[\left(\frac{VC}{S}\right)S\right] - F = \text{EBIT}$$

and

$$S\left(1 - \frac{VC}{S}\right) - F = \text{EBIT}$$

At the breakeven point, however, EBIT = 0, and the corresponding breakeven level of sales can be represented as S^*. At the breakeven level of sales, we have

$$S^*\left(1 - \frac{VC}{S}\right) - F = 0$$

or

$$S^*\left(1 - \frac{VC}{S}\right) = F$$

Therefore,

$$S^* = \frac{F}{1 - \dfrac{VC}{S}} \qquad (8\text{-}4)$$

The application of Equation (8-4) to Pierce Grain's analytical income statement[10] in Table 8-3 permits the breakeven sales level for the firm to be directly computed, as follows:

$$S^* = \frac{\$100,000}{1 - \dfrac{\$180,000}{\$300,000}}$$

$$= \frac{\$100,000}{1 - .60} = \$250,000$$

Notice that this is indeed the same breakeven sales level for Pierce Grain that is indicated on line 4 of Table 8-2.

Graphic Representation, Analysis of Input Changes, and Cash Breakeven Point

In making a presentation to management, it is often effective to display the firm's cost-volume-profit relationships in the form of a chart. Even those individuals who truly enjoy analyzing financial problems find figures and equations dry material at times. Furthermore, by quickly scanning the basic breakeven chart, the manager can approximate the EBIT amount that will prevail at different sales levels.

Such a chart has been prepared for the Pierce Grain Company. Figure 8-7 has been constructed for this firm using the input data contained in Table 8-2. Total fixed costs of $100,000 are added to the total variable costs associated with each production level to form the total costs line. When 25,000 units of product are manufactured and sold, the sales line and total costs line intersect. This means, of course, that the EBIT that would exist at that volume of output is zero. Beyond 25,000 units of output, notice that sales revenues exceed the total costs line. This causes a positive EBIT. This positive EBIT or profits is labelled "original EBIT" in Figure 8-7.

The unencumbered nature of the breakeven model makes it possible to quickly incorporate changes in the requisite input data and generate the revised output. Suppose a favourable combination of events causes Pierce Grain's fixed costs to decrease by $25,000. This would put total fixed costs for the planning period at a level of $75,000 rather than the $100,000 originally forecast. Total costs, being the sum of fixed and variable costs, would be lower by $25,000 at all output levels. The revised total costs line in Figure 8-7 reflects Pierce Grain's reduction in fixed costs. Under these revised conditions, the new breakeven point in units would be as follows:

$$Q_B = \frac{\$75,000}{\$10 - \$6} = 18,750 \text{ units}$$

The revised breakeven point of 18,750 units is identified in Figure 8-7, along with the revised EBIT amounts that would prevail at differing output and sales levels. The chart clearly indicates that at any specific production and sales level, the revised EBIT would exceed the original EBIT. This must be the case, as the revised total costs line lies below the original total costs line over the entire relevant output range. The effect on the breakeven point

---

[10]The derivation of Equation (8-4) requires that we assume VC/S is constant over the relevant output range.

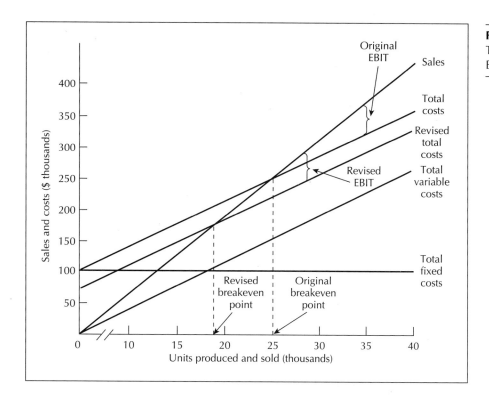

FIGURE 8-7
The Pierce Grain Company's
Breakeven Chart

caused by other changes in (1) the cost structure or (2) the pricing policy can be analyzed in a similar fashion.

The data in Figure 8-7 can be used to demonstrate another version of basic cost-volume-profit analysis. This can be called **cash breakeven analysis**. If the company's fixed or variable cost estimates contain allowance for any noncash expenses, then the resultant breakeven point is higher on an accounting profit basis than on a cash basis. This means the firm's production and sales levels do not have to be as great to cover the cash costs of manufacturing the product.

What are these noncash expenses? The largest and most significant is depreciation expense. Another category is prepaid expenses. Insurance policies are at times paid to cover a three-year cycle. Thus, the time period for which the breakeven analysis is being performed might not involve an actual cash outlay for insurance coverage.

For purposes of illustration, assume that noncash expenses for Pierce Grain amount to $25,000 over the planning period and that all these costs are fixed. We can compare the revised total costs line in Figure 8-7, which implicitly assumes a lower fixed cash cost line, with the sales revenue line to find the cash breakeven point. Provided Pierce Grain can produce and sell 18,750 units over the planning horizon, revenues from sales will be equal to cash operating costs.

Perspective in Finance

The "limitations" of the breakeven models that we have examined are really the underlying assumptions of the models. All models rest upon some set of assumptions and knowing those assumptions is requisite to effective application of the technique. This does not mean the tool is of no value in decision making; it only means that you need to be aware of exactly what you are doing when you use the tool to make a business decision. If you can explain the assumptions to someone else, you can effectively use the technique.

Limitations of Breakeven Analysis

Earlier we identified some of the applications of breakeven analysis. This technique is a useful tool in many settings. It must be emphasized, however, that breakeven analysis provides a beneficial guide to managerial action, not the final answer. The use of cost-volume-profit analysis has limitations, which should be kept in mind.[11] These include the following:

1. The cost-volume-profit relationship is assumed to be linear. This is realistic only over narrow ranges of output.

2. The total revenue curve (sales curve) is presumed to increase linearly with the volume of output. This implies any quantity can be sold over the relevant output range at that single price. To be more realistic, it is necessary in many situations to compute several sales curves and corresponding breakeven points at differing prices.

3. A constant production and sales mix is assumed. Should the company decide to produce more of one product and less of another, a new breakeven point would have to be found. Only if the variable cost-to-sales ratios were identical for products involved would the new calculation be unnecessary.

4. The breakeven chart and the breakeven computation are static forms of analysis. Any alteration in the firm's cost or price structure dictates that a new breakeven point be calculated. Breakeven analysis is more helpful, therefore, in stable industries than in dynamic ones.

5. From the perspective of finance, the analysis of accounting costs does not consider the timing and the riskiness of cash outflows made by the firm. For example, how much should the business report costs for depreciation, given the timing difference between the accounting methods of depreciation and the methods used for the capital cost allowance system.

OPERATING LEVERAGE

Operating leverage occurs if fixed operating costs are present in the firm's cost structure. Fixed operating costs do not include interest charges incurred from the firm's use of debt financing. Those costs will be incorporated into the analysis when financial leverage is discussed.

So operating leverage arises from the firm's use of fixed operating costs. But what is operating leverage? **Operating leverage** is the responsiveness of the firm's EBIT to fluctuations in sales. By continuing to draw upon our data for the Pierce Grain Company, we can illustrate the concept of operating leverage. Table 8-4, contains data for a case in which a possible fluctuation occurs in the firm's sales level. It is assumed here that Pierce

[11]The utilities industry and the hotel and lodging industry are examples of industries in which the breakeven analysis is likely to be very useful because of the stable cost and pricing structure. In contrast, the computer industry and related software industry are examples of industries which do not show long-term stability in their cost and pricing structure.

Item	Base Sales Level, t	Forecast Sales Level, t + 1
Sales	$300,000	$360,000
Less: Total variable costs	180,000	216,000
Revenue before fixed costs	$120,000	$144,000
Less: Total fixed costs	100,000	100,000
EBIT	$ 20,000	$ 44,000

Grain is currently operating at an annual sales level of $300,000. This is referred to in the tabulation as the base sales level at t (time period zero). The question is: How will Pierce Grain's EBIT level respond to a positive 20 percent change in sales? A sales volume of $360,000, referred to as the forecast sales level at $t + 1$, reflects the 20 percent sales rise anticipated over the planning period. Assume that the planning period is one year.

Operating leverage relationships are derived within the mathematical assumptions of cost-volume-profit analysis. In the present example, this means that Pierce Grain's variable cost-to-sales ratio of .6 will continue to hold during time period $t + 1$, and the fixed costs will hold steady at $100,000.

Given the forecasted sales level for Pierce Grain and its cost structure, we can measure the responsiveness of EBIT to the upswing in volume. Notice in Table 8-4 that EBIT is expected to be $44,000 at the end of the planning period. The percentage change in EBIT from t to $t + 1$ can be measured as follows:

$$\text{percentage change in EBIT} = \frac{\$44,000_{t+1} - \$20,000_t}{\$20,000_t}$$

$$= \frac{\$24,000}{\$20,000}$$

$$= 120\%$$

We know that the projected fluctuation in sales amounts to 20 percent of the base period, t, sales level. This is verified below:

$$\text{percentage change in sales} = \frac{\$360,000_{t+1} - \$300,000_t}{\$300,000_t}$$

$$= \frac{\$60,000}{\$300,000}$$

$$= 20\%$$

By relating the percentage fluctuation in EBIT to the percentage fluctuation in sales, we can calculate a specific measure of operating leverage.[12] Thus, we have

$$\begin{array}{l} \text{degree of operating leverage} \\ \text{from the base sales level(s)} \end{array} = DOL_s = \frac{\text{percentage change in EBIT}}{\text{percentage change in sales}} \quad (8\text{-}5)$$

---

[12]The degree of operating leverage (DOL) is an elasticity equation which has the general form:

$$\text{Elasticity coefficient} = \frac{\% \text{ change in some dependent variable}}{\% \text{ change in some independent variable}}$$

Applying Equation (8-5) to our Pierce Grain data gives

$$DOL_{\$300,000} = \frac{120\%}{20\%} = 6 \text{ times}$$

Unless we understand what the specific measure of operating leverage tells us, the fact that we may know it is equal to six times is nothing more than sterile information. For Pierce Grain, the inference is that for any percentage fluctuation in sales from the base level, the percentage fluctuation in EBIT will be six times as great. If Pierce Grain expected only a 5 percent rise in sales over the coming period, a 30 percent rise in EBIT would be anticipated as follows:

$$(\text{percentage change in sales}) \times (DOL_s) = \text{percentage change in EBIT}$$

$$(5\%) \times (6) = 30\%$$

We will now return to the postulated 20 percent change in sales. What if the direction of the fluctuation is expected to be negative rather than positive? What is in store for Pierce Grain? Unfortunately for Pierce Grain, but fortunately for the analytical process, we will see that the operating leverage measure holds in the negative direction as well. This situation is displayed in Table 8-5.

At the $240,000 sales level, which represents the 20 percent decrease from the base period, Pierce Grain's EBIT is expected to be –$4,000. How sensitive is EBIT to this sales change? The magnitude of the EBIT fluctuation is calculated as[13]

$$\text{percentage change in EBIT} = \frac{-\$4,000_{t+1} - \$20,000_t}{\$20,000_t}$$

$$= \frac{-\$24,000}{\$20,000}$$

$$= -120\%$$

Making use of our knowledge that the sales change was equal to –20 percent permits us to compute the specific measure of operating leverage as

$$DOL_{\$300,000} = \frac{-120\%}{-20\%} = 6 \text{ times}$$

What we have seen, then, is that the degree of operating leverage measure works in the positive or negative direction. A negative change in production

TABLE 8-5
The Concept of Operating
Leverage: A Decrease in
Pierce Grain Company Sales

Item	Base Sales Level, t	Forecast Sales Level, t + 1
Sales	$300,000	$240,000
Less: Total variable costs	180,000	144,000
Revenue before fixed costs	$120,000	$ 96,000
Less: Total fixed costs	100,000	100,000
EBIT	$ 20,000	$ –4,000

[13]Some students have conceptual difficulty in computing these percentage changes when negative amounts are involved. Notice by inspection in Table 8-5 that the difference between an EBIT amount of +$20,000 at t and –$4,000 at $t + 1$ is –$24,000.

volume and sales can be magnified severalfold when the effect on EBIT is calculated.

To this point our calculations of the degree of operating leverage have required two analytical income statements: one for the base period and a second for the subsequent period that incorporates the possible sales alteration. This cumbersome process can be simplified. If unit cost data are available to the financial manager, the relationship can be expressed directly in the following manner:

$$DOL_s = \frac{Q(P - V)}{Q(P - V) - F} \qquad (8\text{-}6)$$

Observe in Equation (8-6) that the variables were all previously defined in our algebraic analysis of the breakeven model. Recall that Pierce sells its product at $10 per unit, the unit variable cost is $6, and total fixed costs over the planning horizon are $100,000. Still assuming that Pierce is operating at a $300,000 sales volume, which means output (Q) is 30,000 units, we can find the degree of operating leverage by application of Equation (8-6):

$$DOL_{\$300,000} = \frac{30,000(\$10 - \$6)}{30,000(\$10 - \$6) - \$100,000} = \frac{\$120,000}{\$20,000} = 6 \text{ times}$$

Whereas Equation (8-6) requires us to know unit cost data to carry out the computations, the next formulation we examine does not. If we have an analytical income statement for the base period, then Equation (8-7) can be employed to find the firm's degree of operating leverage:

$$DOL_s = \frac{\text{revenue before fixed costs}}{\text{EBIT}} = \frac{S - VC}{S - VC - F} \qquad (8\text{-}7)$$

Use of Equation (8-7) in conjunction with the base period data for Pierce Grain shown in either Table 8-4 or 8-5 gives

$$DOL_{\$300,000} = \frac{\$120,000}{\$20,000} = 6 \text{ times}$$

The three versions of the operating leverage measure all produce the same result. Data availability will sometimes dictate which formulation can be applied. The crucial consideration, though, is that you grasp what the measurement tells you. For Pierce Grain, a 1 percent change in sales will produce a 6 percent change in EBIT.[14]

Perspective in Finance

Before we complete our discussion of operating leverage and move on to the subject of financial leverage, ask yourself "which type of leverage is more under the control of management?" You will probably (and correctly) come to the conclusion that the firm's managers have less control over its operating cost structure and almost complete control over its financial structure. What the firm actually produces, for example, will determine to a significant degree the

---

[14]Note that each of the underlying parameters can be assessed in terms of its effect on DOL.

division between fixed and variable costs. There is more room for substitution among the various sources of financial capital than there is among the labour and real capital inputs that enable the firm to meet its production requirements. Thus, you can anticipate more arguments over the choice to use a given degree of financial leverage than the corresponding choice over operating leverage use.

Implications

As the firm's scale of operations moves in a favourable manner above the breakeven point, the degree of operating leverage at each subsequent (higher) sales base will decline. In short, the greater the sales level, the lower the degree of operating leverage. This is demonstrated in Table 8-6 for the Pierce Grain Company. At the breakeven sales level for Pierce Grain, the degree of operating leverage is undefined, since the denominator in any of the computational formulas is zero. Notice that beyond the breakeven point of 25,000 units, the degree of operating leverage declines. It will decline at a decreasing rate and asymptotically approach a value of 1.00. As long as some fixed operating costs are present in the firm's cost structure, however, operating leverage exists, and the degree of operating leverage (DOL_s) will exceed 1.00. Operating leverage is present, then, whenever the firm faces the following situation:

$$\frac{\text{percentage change in EBIT}}{\text{percentage change in sales}} > 1.00$$

The data in Table 8-6 are presented in graphic form in Figure 8-8.

The greater the firm's degree of operating leverage, the more its profits will vary with a given percentage change in sales. Thus, operating leverage is definitely an attribute of the business risk that confronts the company. From Table 8-6 and Figure 8-8 we have seen that the degree of operating leverage falls as sales increase past the firm's breakeven point. The sheer size and operating profitability of the firm, therefore, affect and can lessen its business risk exposure.

A manager who is considering an alteration in the firm's cost structure will benefit from an understanding of the operating leverage concept. It might be possible to replace part of the labour force with capital equipment (machinery). A possible result is an increase in fixed costs associated with the new machinery and a reduction in variable costs attributable to a lower labour bill. This conceivably could raise the firm's degree of operating leverage at a specific sales base. If the prospects for future sales increases are high, then increasing the degree of operating leverage might be a prudent decision. The opposite conclusion will be reached if sales prospects are unattractive.

TABLE 8-6

The Pierce Grain Company Degree of Operating Leverage Relative to Different Sales Bases

Units Produced and Sold	Sales Dollars	DOL$_s$
25,000	$ 250,000	Undefined
30,000	300,000	6.00
35,000	350,000	3.50
40,000	400,000	2.67
45,000	450,000	2.25
50,000	500,000	2.00
75,000	750,000	1.50
100,000	1,000,000	1.33

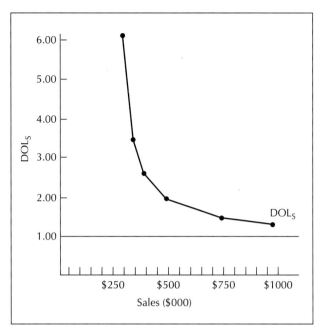

Perspective in Finance

As you are introduced to the topic of "financial leverage" keep in mind that this is one of the most crucial policy areas on which a financial executive spends his or her time. We describe and measure here what happens to the firm's earnings per share when financial risk is assumed. Try to understand this effect. We demonstrate how to actually measure this effect in the next section. By now you should be realizing that variability of all types—be it in an earnings stream or in stock returns—is a central element of financial thought and the practice of financial management.

BASIC FINANCIAL MANAGEMENT IN PRACTICE

Using Operating Leverage to Increase Small Business Profits

In a manufacturing company, two types of leverage generally exist: operating leverage and financial leverage.

Operating leverage or "first-level leverage" measures the effect of a sales variation on the net operating income. With operating leverage, the percentage change in the operating income exceeds that of sales volume.

Financial leverage or "second-level leverage" measures the effect of a variation of the net operating income on the earnings per share.

In the following discussion, we are dealing mainly with operating leverage. If we ignore financial leverage, it is simply because it has more limited use in smaller companies than in larger companies. With regard to the debt-equity ratio, it is generally the lenders rather than the owners who decide on the financial ratio to observe and the latter's room to manoeuvre is therefore fairly limited.

How to Visualize Your Operating Leverage

The manager of a small or medium-sized business can realize a number of advantages from the proper

Continued on page 374

373

Continued from page 373

interpretation of his or her company's break-even point (B/P) graph.

For example, let us see what information can be obtained from analyzing and comparing the graphs of Companies A, B, C, and D (see Table 1). First of all, if we use their sales as a yardstick, we have to take into consideration that we are comparing companies of identical size.

We can easily see that the B/P and sales of Companies A, B, C are identical ($750,000 and $1 million) but the profits are 5%, 10%, and 15% due solely to the operating leverage.

A second, just as important observation is the increase in operating risk for companies whose fixed costs are higher. For example, if the forecast sales of $1 million are reduced to $600,000, Company A will lose $30,000, Company B, $60,000, and Company C, $90,000.

Taking a close look at Company's D graph, we can see that the company will record operating losses if its revenues fall below $874,300. And here we have to carry our line of reasoning further, as this company has three types of revenue which produce different profit ratios. The $874,300 break-even point is determined from an average profit of 45.75% when Product 1 accounts for 80% of revenues, Product 2 for 15%, and Product 3 for 5%. Since the profit ratios are quite different, it becomes obvious that any change in the composition or mix of revenues will have an effect on the break-even point.

On the basis of these preliminary observations, we can already conclude that a principal advantage of using a break-even point graph for a small or medium-sized business is that it enables it to set objectives that will guarantee the best profitability possible, given the company's business plan (its resources, size, industry segment, etc.). The B/P graph also allows us to forecast the important controls on which the business will have to focus. For example:

- Company A will first have to control its variable costs well.

- Company B will also have to monitor its fixed costs.

- Companies C and D will have to control their fixed costs regularly and also ensure that their sales objectives are met, in view of the much greater leverage and risk for these two types of companies.

By pursuing this line of reasoning, we can deduce

that a work stoppage in Companies C and D will be more costly than in Companies A and B.

And what about incentives the small and medium-sized business manager can use to have a positive impact on the attainment of company's objectives? Bonuses, premiums, incentives, various types of participation, etc. obtainable from the break-even point, will certainly be welcome in Companies C and D if emphasis is placed on profitability.

Industry Segment Image

The size of the small or medium-sized business apart, we can also identify our business with its industrial segment and establish a certain relationship between the available external ratios and the business's own organizational structure.

For example, if my company operates as a sub-contractor in the automobile's parts, wood, clothing, or other industries, it is highly probable that my B/P will look like Company A's graph. Hence, I will want to concentrate on controlling my costs, in view of the marginal profitability.

The structure of Company B's B/P is the same as that of most small and medium-sized manufacturing businesses. All businesses that have a gross profit of between 20% and 30% have a graph that is similar to this company's B/P. They therefore have to monitor their fixed and variable costs constantly.

Companies C and D have a fixed cost graph line that can represent at least four different types of businesses:

1. Businesses that are high in capital investments (fixed assets) representing high maintenance, insurance, financing, and depreciation costs.

2. Businesses that are heavy on human resources with fixed compensation (salesmen on salary, engineers, appraisers, specialists, stylists, etc.).

3. Companies that specialize in research and development.

4. Small and medium-sized businesses that take care of their own distribution to individuals, which increases their distribution and administration costs.

These businesses will have to keep close track of changes in their fixed costs and place the emphasis on achieving sales and profitability objectives. Of course, these categories of businesses also need to stress "quality". The "marketing" approach should help them to absorb high fixed costs more quickly.

Continued on page 376

Table 1

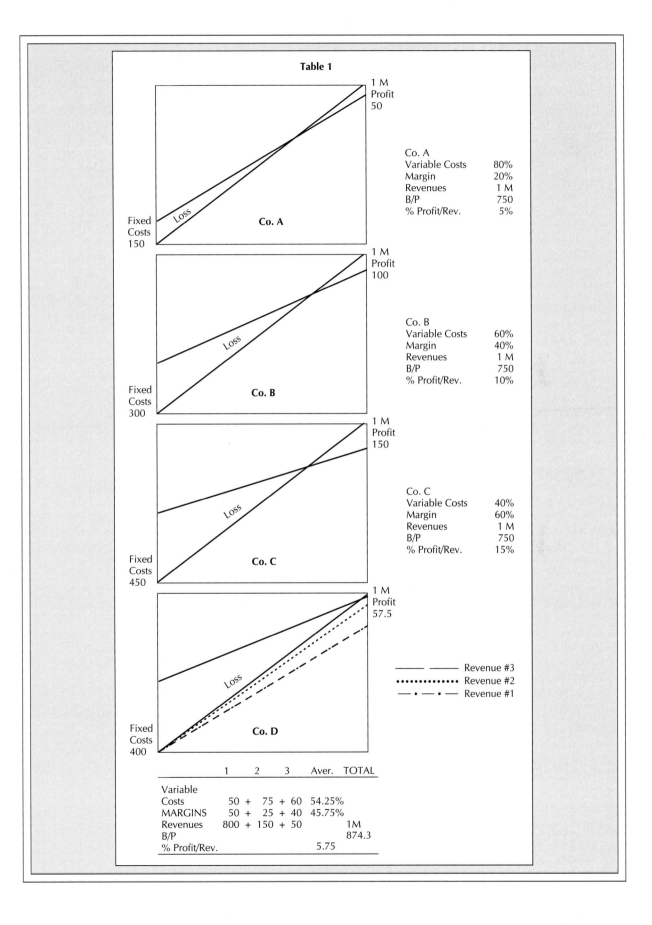

1 M
Profit
50

Co. A
Variable Costs 80%
Margin 20%
Revenues 1 M
B/P 750
% Profit/Rev. 5%

Fixed Costs 150

Loss

Co. A

1 M
Profit
100

Co. B
Variable Costs 60%
Margin 40%
Revenues 1 M
B/P 750
% Profit/Rev. 10%

Fixed Costs 300

Loss

Co. B

1 M
Profit
150

Co. C
Variable Costs 40%
Margin 60%
Revenues 1 M
B/P 750
% Profit/Rev. 15%

Fixed Costs 450

Loss

Co. C

1 M
Profit
57.5

Fixed Costs 400

Loss

Co. D

— — Revenue #3
•••••••• Revenue #2
— • — • Revenue #1

	1		2		3	Aver.	TOTAL
Variable Costs	50	+	75	+	60	54.25%	
MARGINS	50	+	25	+	40	45.75%	
Revenues	800	+	150	+	50		1M
B/P							874.3
% Profit/Rev.						5.75	

Continued from page 376

How to Ensure Follow-up

The best method to employ to ensure follow-up between the B/P graph and reality is undoubtedly the variable costing (direct costing) method, simply because this method draws its inspiration from the same line of reasoning that we apply when we wish to draw a B/P graph.

From the standpoint of affordability, however, the small manufacturing business will use a very different approach from that followed by a medium-sized business. The accountant in a small business can hardly go into the amount of detail and will not have the analyses and related reports available as that of a more developed organization.

Small Business

To determine the profit ratio obtained and the burden of fixed costs from period to period, the small manufacturing business will have to have an accounting plan that is comparable to direct costing. This plan must make it possible to draw up interim statements as required that will unambiguously show the profits achieved by revenue category (product or customer) and the corresponding fixed cost burden.

It will obviously be easier for a small business that mass produces to use standards for determining its costs and evaluate regularly. The small business that does custom work needs to make controlling its labour for each order manufactured a priority (e.g., printing).

Given the personnel constraints in small business, it is not realistic to require too elaborate reports from the person in charge of the accounting information. He or she generally has to support the employer in other areas of daily management and obviously has less time for accounting duties. The production of interim statements, accompanied by a profit analysis (either per order, per product, or per customer), should allow the business to achieve acceptable follow-up with the forecast objectives. Data processing is now increasingly accessible to this type of business.

Medium-Sized Business

We are referring here to a manufacturing business that is generally better structured. This type of business often has experienced managers, each with a clearly defined role. They generally use data processing in their management.

In addition to regular interim financial statements, the business comptroller or management accountant will be able to provide additional information related to the statements. The directors will be able to know the hourly contributions obtained either by product, customer or machine, depending on the type of operation of the production equipment.

This information will obviously have to be interpreted correctly in terms of effective and efficient management.

When the product is for current consumption, the cycle of the products will have to be taken into account before drawing conclusions about the profit ratio obtained (principally if the ratio is low). The decision will depend on the answer to the question: "Are we at the beginning or the end of the cycle?"

The use of flexible budgets in mass production plants will take on its full significance. The explanation of the variances will become a variable aid for decision-making. The medium-sized business that produces by order and by bid will profit from knowing the variations between the actual and the estimated.

Omnipresent Tools

In addition to the close relationship between the B/P graph and the variable costs (direct costing) graph, they have another dimension in common. Both are highly recommended for short-term management.

With or without tariff barriers, with or without free trade, these tools will always be with us because they are based on behavior of the costs (fixed or variable) from which a B/P chart can be drawn and our business's leverage can be visualized.

According to a National Association of Accountants study, the use of the direct costing method (variable costs) has contributed to the making of better decisions. In reality, it is only an extension of the B/P chart into day-to-day management.

Source: Adapted from C. Lortie, "Using operating leverage to increase small business profits," *CMA Management Accounting Magazine*, 63(9) (November 1989), pp. 32–34. Reprinted from *CMA* magazine by permission of the Society of Management Accountants of Canada.

FINANCIAL LEVERAGE

We have defined **financial leverage** as the practice of financing a portion of the firm's assets with securities bearing a fixed rate of return in hope of increasing the ultimate return to the common shareholders. In the present discussion we focus on the responsiveness of the company's earnings per share to changes in its EBIT. For the time being, then, the return to the common shareholder being concentrated upon is earnings per share. We are not saying that earnings per share is the appropriate criterion for all financing decisions. In fact, the weakness of such a contention will be examined in the next chapter. The effect of financial leverage on the firm earnings can be examined by concentrating on an earnings per share criterion.

Let us assume that the Pierce Grain Company is in the process of getting started. The firm's potential owners have calculated that $200,000 is needed to purchase the necessary assets to conduct the business. Three possible financing plans have been identified for raising the $200,000; they are presented in Table 8-7. In plan A no financial risk is assumed: the entire $200,000 is raised by selling 2,000 common shares. In plan B a moderate amount of financial risk is assumed: 25 percent of the assets are financed with a debt issue that carries an 8 percent annual interest rate. Plan C would use the most financial leverage: 40 percent of the assets would be financed with a debt issue costing 8 percent.[15]

Table 8-8 presents the impact of financial leverage on earnings per share associated with each fund-raising alternative. If EBIT should increase from $20,000 to $40,000, then earnings per share would rise by 100 percent under plan A. The same positive fluctuation in EBIT would occasion an earnings per share rise of 125 percent under plan B, and 147 percent under plan C. In plans B and C the 100 percent increase in EBIT (from $20,000 to $40,000) is magnified to a greater than 100 percent increase in earnings per

---

TABLE 8-7
The Pierce Grain Company Possible Financial Structures

Plan A: 0% debt			
	Total debt	$	0
	Common equity		200,000 [a]
Total assets	$200,000	Total liabilities and equity	$200,000
Plan B: 25% debt at 8% interest rate			
	Total debt	$	50,000
	Common equity		150,000 [b]
Total assets	$200,000	Total liabilities and equity	$200,000
Plan C: 40% debt at 8% interest rate			
	Total debt	$	80,000
	Common equity		120,000 [c]
Total assets	$200,000	Total liabilities and equity	$200,000

[a]2,000 common shares outstanding
[b]1,500 common shares outstanding
[c]1,200 common shares outstanding

---

[15]In actual practice, moving from a 25 to a 40 percent debt ratio would probably result in a higher interest rate on the additional bonds. That effect is ignored here to let us concentrate on the ramifications of using different proportions of debt in the financial structure.

TABLE 8-8

The Pierce Grain Company
Analysis of Financial
Leverage at Different EBIT
Levels

(1) EBIT	(2) Interest	(3) = (1) − (2) EBT	(4) = (3) × .5 Taxes	(5) = (3) − (4) Net Income to Common	(6) Earnings per Share
Plan A: 0% debt; $200,000 common equity; 2000 shares					
$ 0	$ 0	$ 0	$ 0	$ 0	$ 0
20,000	0	20,000	10,000	10,000	5.00 ⎫ 100%
40,000	0	40,000	20,000	20,000	10.00 ⎭
60,000	0	60,000	30,000	30,000	15.00
80,000	0	80,000	40,000	40,000	20.00
Plan B: 25% debt; 8% Interest rate; $150,000 common equity; 1500 shares					
$ 0	$4,000	$ (4,000)	$ (2,000)ᵃ	$ (2,000)	$ (1.33)
20,000	4,000	16,000	8,000	8,000	5.33 ⎫ 125%
40,000	4,000	36,000	18,000	18,000	12.00 ⎭
60,000	4,000	56,000	28,000	28,000	18.67
80,000	4,000	76,000	38,000	38,000	25.33
Plan C: 40% debt; 8% Interest rate; $120,000 common equity; 1200 shares					
$ 0	$6,400	$ (6,400)	$ (3,200)ᵃ	$ (3,200)	$ (2.67)
20,000	6,400	13,600	6,800	6,800	5.67 ⎫ 147%
40,000	6,400	33,600	16,800	16,800	14.00 ⎭
60,000	6,400	53,600	26,800	26,800	22.33
80,000	6,400	73,600	36,800	36,800	30.67

ᵃThe negative tax bill recognizes the deduction arising from the loss carryback and carryforward provision of the Income Tax Act. See Chapter 2.

share. The firm is employing financial leverage, and exposing its owners to financial risk, when the following situation exists:

$$\frac{\text{percentage change in earnings per share}}{\text{percentage change in EBIT}} > 1.00$$

By following the same general procedures that allowed us to analyze the firm's use of operating leverage, we can lay out a precise measure of financial leverage. Such a measure deals with the sensitivity of earnings per share to EBIT fluctuations. The relationship can be expressed as

$$\begin{array}{l}\text{degree of}\\ \text{financial leverage from} = \text{DFL}_{EBIT} = \dfrac{\text{percentage change in earnings per share}}{\text{percentage change in EBIT}}\\ \text{base EBIT level}\end{array} \quad (8\text{-}8)$$

Use of Equation (8-8) with each of the financing choices outlined for Pierce Grain is shown below. The base EBIT level is $20,000 in each case.

$$\text{Plan A:} \qquad \text{DFL}_{\$20,000} = \frac{100\%}{100\%} = 1.00 \text{ time}$$

$$\text{Plan B:} \qquad \text{DFL}_{\$20,000} = \frac{125\%}{100\%} = 1.25 \text{ times}$$

$$\text{Plan C:} \qquad \text{DFL}_{\$20,000} = \frac{147\%}{100\%} = 1.47 \text{ times}$$

Like operating leverage, the degree of financial leverage concept performs in the negative direction as well as the positive. Should EBIT fall by 10 percent, the Pierce Grain Company would suffer a 12.5 percent decline in earnings per share under plan B. If plan C were chosen to raise the necessary financial capital, the decline in earnings would be 14.7 percent. Observe that the greater the degree of financial leverage, the greater the fluctuations (positive or negative) in earnings per share. The common shareholder is required to endure greater variations in returns when the firm's management chooses to use more financial leverage rather than less. The degree of financial leverage measure allows the variation to be quantified.

Rather than taking the time to compute percentage changes in EBIT and earnings per share, the degree of financial leverage can be found directly, as follows:

$$\text{DFL}_{EBIT} = \frac{\text{EBIT}}{\text{EBIT} - I} \tag{8-9}$$

In Equation (8-9) the variable, I, represents the total interest expense incurred on all the firm's contractual debt obligations. If six bonds are outstanding, I is the sum of the interest expense on all six bonds. If the firm has preferred shares in its financial structure, the dividend on such issues must be inflated to a before-tax basis and included in the computation of I.[16] In this latter instance, I is in reality the sum of all fixed financing costs.

Equation (8-9) has been applied to each of Pierce Grain's financing plans (Table 8-8) at a base EBIT level of $20,000. The results are as follows:

Plan A: $\quad \text{DFL}_{\$20,000} = \dfrac{\$20,000}{\$20,000 - 0} = 1.00 \text{ time}$

Plan B: $\quad \text{DFL}_{\$20,000} = \dfrac{\$20,000}{\$20,000 - \$4000} = 1.25 \text{ times}$

Plan C: $\quad \text{DFL}_{\$20,000} = \dfrac{\$20,000}{\$20,000 - \$6400} = 1.47 \text{ times}$

As you have probably suspected, the measures of financial leverage shown above are identical to those obtained by use of Equation (8-8).[17] This will always be the case.

Perspective in Finance

The effect on the earnings stream available to the firm's common shareholders from combining operating and financial leverage in large degrees is dramatic. When the use of both leverage types is indeed heavy, a large sales increase will result in a very large rise in earnings per share. Be aware, though, that the very same thing happens in the opposite direction should the sales change be negative! Piling heavy financial leverage use upon a high degree of operating leverage, then, is a very risky way to do business. This is why you will find leveraged buyouts are not concentrated in heavy, durable goods industries. The firms in such industries have major (real) capital spending requirements. Rather, the

---

[16]Suppose (1) preferred dividends of $4,000 are paid annually by the firm and (2) it faces a combined corporate tax rate of 45 percent rate. How much must the firm earn before taxes to make the $4,000 payment out of after-tax earnings? Since preferred dividends are not tax-deductible to the paying company, we have $4000/(1 − .45) = $7,272.73. Note that from a financial policy viewpoint, corporate debt financing is less expensive than preferred share and common share financing, because the interest cost of debt financing is generally tax deductible.

[17]The degree of financial leverage (DFL) increases as the interest costs (I) to the firm increase. Further, as EBIT increases, DFL decreases (holding interest costs constant).

firms favoured in leveraged buyouts will be those with comparatively low levels of operating leverage; retail operations are good examples. As a result, many national retail chains and department stores have been involved in leveraged buyouts during the past few years. The leveraged buyout, by its very nature, translates into a high degree of financial leverage use.

COMBINING OPERATING AND FINANCIAL LEVERAGE

Changes in sales revenues cause greater changes in EBIT. Additionally, changes in EBIT translate into larger variations in both earnings per share (EPS) and total earnings available to the common shareholders (EAC), if the firm chooses to use financial leverage. It should be no surprise, then, to find out that combining operating and financial leverage causes rather large variations in earnings per share. This entire process is visually displayed in Figure 8-9.

Since the risk associated with possible earnings per share is affected by the use of combined or total leverage, it is useful to quantify the effect. For an illustration, we refer once more to the Pierce Grain Company. The cost structure identified for Pierce Grain in our discussion of breakeven analysis still holds. Furthermore, assume that plan B, which carried a 25 percent debt ratio, was chosen to finance the company's assets. Table 8-9 shows the combined leverage analysis for the Pierce Grain Company.

In Table 8-9 an increase in output for Pierce Grain from 30,000 to 36,000 units is analyzed. This increase represents a 20 percent rise in sales revenues. From our earlier discussion of operating leverage and the data in Table 8-9, we can see that this 20 percent increase in sales is magnified into a 120 percent rise in EBIT. From this base sales level of $300,000 the degree of operating leverage is 6 times.

The 120 percent rise in EBIT induces a change in earnings per share and earnings available to the common shareholders of 150 percent. The degree of financial leverage is therefore 1.25 times.

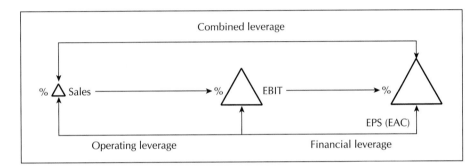

FIGURE 8-9
Leverage and Earnings Fluctuations

Item	Base Sales Level, t	Forecast Sales Level, t + 1	Selected Percentage Changes
Sales	$300,000	$360,000	+20
Less: Total variable costs	180,000	216,000	
Revenue before fixed costs	$120,000	$144,000	
Less: Total fixed costs	100,000	100,000	
EBIT	$ 20,000	$ 44,000	+120
Less: Interest expense	4,000	4,000	
Earnings before taxes (EBT)	$ 16,000	$ 40,000	
Less: Taxes at 50%	8,000	20,000	
Net income	$ 8,000	$ 20,000	+150
Less: Preferred dividends	0	0	
Earnings available to common (EAC)	$ 8,000	$ 20,000	+150
Number of common shares	1,500	1,500	
Earnings per share (EPS)	$ 5.33	$ 13.33	+150

TABLE 8-9
The Pierce Grain Company Combined Leverage Analysis

$$\text{Degree of operating leverage} = \text{DOL}_{\$300,000} = \frac{120\%}{20\%} = 6 \text{ times}$$

$$\text{Degree of financial leverage} = \text{DFL}_{\$20,000} = \frac{150\%}{120\%} = 1.25 \text{ times}$$

$$\text{Degree of combined leverage} = \text{DCL}_{\$300,000} = \frac{150\%}{20\%} = 7.50 \text{ times}$$

The upshot of the analysis is that the 20 percent rise in sales has been magnified to 150 percent, as reflected by the percentage change in earnings per share. The formal measure of combined leverage can be expressed as follows:

$$\left(\begin{array}{c} \text{degree of} \\ \text{combined leverage from} \\ \text{the base sales level} \end{array}\right) = \text{DCL}_s = \left(\frac{\text{percentage change in}}{\text{percentage change in sales}}\right) \quad (8\text{-}10)$$

This equation was used in the bottom portion of Table 8-9 to determine that the degree of combined leverage from the base sales level of $300,000 is 7.50 times. Pierce Grain's use of both operating and financial leverage will cause any percentage change in sales (from the specific base level) to be magnified by a factor of 7.50 when the effect on earnings per share is computed. A 1 percent change in sales, for example, will result in a 7.50 percent change in earnings per share.

Notice that the degree of combined leverage is actually the product (not the simple sum) of the two independent leverage measures. Thus, we have

$$(\text{DOL}_s) \times (\text{DFL}_{EBIT}) = \text{DCL}_s$$
$$\text{or} \qquad (6) \times (1.25) = 7.50 \text{ times} \qquad (8\text{-}11)$$

It is possible to ascertain the degree of combined leverage in a direct fashion, without determining any percentage fluctuations or the separate leverage values. We need only substitute the appropriate values into Equation (8-12):[18]

$$\text{DCL}_s = \frac{Q(P - V)}{Q(P - V) - F - I} \qquad (8\text{-}12)$$

The variable definitions in Equation (8-12) are the same ones that have been employed throughout this chapter. Use of Equation (8-12) with the information in Table 8-9 gives

$$\text{DCL}_{\$300,000} = \frac{\$30,000(\$10 - \$6)}{\$30,000(\$10 - \$6) - \$100,000 - \$4000}$$
$$= \frac{\$120,000}{\$16,000}$$
$$= 7.5 \text{ times}$$

Implications

The total risk exposure the firm assumes can be managed by combining operating and financial leverage in different degrees. Knowledge of the various leverage measures assists the financial officer in determining the proper level of overall risk that should be accepted. If a high degree of business risk is inherent to the specific line of commercial activity, then a low posture

[18]As was the case with the degree of financial leverage metric, the variable, I, in the combined leverage measure must include the before-tax equivalent of any preferred dividend payments when preferred shares are in the financial structure.

with regard to financial risk would minimize additional earnings fluctuations stemming from sales changes. On the other hand, the firm that by its very nature incurs a low level of fixed operating costs might choose to use a high degree of financial leverage in the hope of increasing earnings per share and the rate of return on the common equity investment.

SUMMARY

In this chapter we began to study the process of arriving at an appropriate financial structure for the firm. Tools that can assist the financial manager in this task were examined. We were mainly concerned with assessing the variability in the firm's residual earnings stream (either earnings per share or earnings available to the common shareholders) induced by the use of operating and financial leverage. This assessment built upon the tenets of breakeven analysis.

Breakeven Analysis

Breakeven analysis permits the financial manager to determine the quantity of output or the level of sales that will result in an EBIT level of zero. This means that the firm has neither a loss nor a profit before any tax consideration. The effect of price changes, cost structure changes, or volume changes upon profits (EBIT) can be studied. To make the technique operational, it is necessary that the firm's costs be classified as fixed or variable. Not all costs fit neatly into one of these two categories. Over short planning horizons, though, the preponderance of costs can be assigned to either the fixed or variable classification. Once the cost structure has been identified, the breakeven point can be found by use of (1) trial-and-error analysis, (2) contribution margin analysis, or (3) algebraic analysis.

Operating Leverage

Operating leverage is the responsiveness of the firm's EBIT to changes in sales revenues. It arises from the firm's use of fixed operating costs. When fixed operating costs are present in the company's cost structure, changes in sales are magnified into even greater changes in EBIT. The firm's degree of operating leverage from a base sales level is the percentage change in EBIT divided by the percentage change in sales. All types of leverage are two-edged swords. When sales decrease by some percentage, the negative impact upon EBIT will be even larger.

Financial Leverage

A firm employs financial leverage when it finances a portion of its assets with securities bearing a fixed rate of return. The presence of debt and/or preferred shares in the company's financial structure means that it is using financial leverage. When financial leverage is used, changes in EBIT translate into larger changes in earnings per share. The concept of the degree of financial leverage dwells on the sensitivity of earnings per share to changes in EBIT. The degree of financial leverage from a base EBIT level is defined as the percentage change in earnings per share divided by the percentage change in EBIT. All other things equal, the more fixed-charge securities the firm employs in its financial structure, the greater its degree of financial leverage. Clearly, EBIT can rise or fall. If it falls, and financial leverage is used, the firm's shareholders endure negative changes in earnings per share that are larger than the relative decline in EBIT. Again, leverage is a two-edged sword.

Combining Operating and Financial Leverage

Firms use operating and financial leverage in various degrees. The joint use of operating and financial leverage can be measured by computing the degree of combined leverage, defined as the percentage change in earnings per share divided by the percentage change in sales. This measure allows the financial manager to ascertain the effect on total leverage caused by adding financial leverage on top of operating leverage. Effects can be dramatic, because the degree of combined leverage is the product of the degrees of operating and financial leverage. Table 8-10 summarizes the salient concepts and calculation formats discussed in this chapter.

TABLE 8-10. Summary of Leverage Concepts and Calculations

Technique	Description or Concept	Calculation	Text Reference
Breakeven Analysis			
1. Breakeven point quantity	Total fixed costs divided by the unit contribution margin	$Q_B = \dfrac{F}{P - V}$	(8-3)
2. Breakeven sales level	Total fixed costs divided by 1 minus the ratio of total variable costs to the associated level of sales	$S^* = \dfrac{F}{1 - \dfrac{VC}{S}}$	(8-4)
Operating Leverage			
3. Degree of operating leverage	Percentage change in EBIT divided by the percentage change in sales; or revenue before fixed costs divided by revenue after fixed costs	$DOL_s = \dfrac{Q(P - V)}{Q(P - V) - F}$	(8-6)
Financial Leverage			
4. Degree of financial leverage	Percentage change in earnings per share divided by the percentage change in EBIT; or EBIT divided by EBT.[a]	$DFL_{EBIT} = \dfrac{EBIT}{EBIT - I}$	(8-9)
Combined Leverage			
5. Degree of combined leverage	Percentage change in earnings per share divided by the percentage change in sales; or revenue before fixed costs divided by EBT.[a]	$DCL_s = \dfrac{Q(P - V)}{Q(P - V) - F - I}$	(8-12)

[a]The use of EBT here presumes no preferred dividend payments. In the presence of preferred dividend payments replace EBT with earnings available to common shares (EAC).

STUDY QUESTIONS

8-1. Distinguish between business risk and financial risk. What gives rise to, or causes, each type of risk?

8-2. Define the term *financial leverage*. Does the firm use financial leverage if preferred shares is present in the capital structure?

8-3. Define the term *operating leverage*. What type of effect occurs when the firm uses operating leverage?

8-4. What is the difference between the (ordinary) breakeven point and the cash breakeven point? Which will be the greater?

8-5. A manager in your firm decides to employ breakeven analysis. Of what shortcomings should this manager be aware?

8-6. What is meant by total risk exposure? How may a firm move to reduce its total risk exposure?

8-7. If a firm has a degree of combined leverage of 3.0 times, what does a negative sales fluctuation of 15 percent portend for the earnings available to the firm's common share investors?

8-8. Breakeven analysis assumes linear revenue and cost functions. In reality these linear functions over large output and sales levels are highly improbable. Why?

SELF-TEST PROBLEMS

ST-1. (*Breakeven Point*) You are a hard-working analyst in the office of financial operations for a manufacturing firm that produces a single product. You have developed the following cost structure information for this company. All of it pertains to an output level of 10 million units. Using this information, find the breakeven point in units of output for the firm.

Return on operating assets	= 30%
Operating asset turnover	= 6 times
Operating assets	= $20 million
Degree of operating leverage	= 4.5 times

ST-2. (*Leverage Analysis*) You have developed the following analytical income statement for your corporation. It represents the most recent year's operations, which ended yesterday.

Sales	$20,000,000
Variable costs	12,000,000
Revenue before fixed costs	$ 8,000,000
Fixed costs	5,000,000
EBIT	$ 3,000,000
Interest expense	1,000,000
Earnings before taxes	$ 2,000,000
Taxes (0.50)	1,000,000
Net income	$ 1,000,000

Your supervisor in the financial studies office has just handed you a memorandum that asked for written responses to the following questions:

a. At this level of output, what is the degree of operating leverage?

b. What is the degree of financial leverage?

c. What is the degree of combined leverage?

d. What is the firm's breakeven point in sales dollars?

e. If sales should increase by 30 percent, by what percent would earnings before taxes (and net income) increase?

f. Prepare an analytical income statement that verifies the calculations from part (e) above.

ST-3. (*Fixed Costs and the Breakeven Point*) Bonaventure Manufacturing expects to earn $210,000 next year after taxes. Sales will be $4 million. The firm's single plant is located on the outskirts of Lockport, N.S. The firm manufactures a combined bookshelf and desk unit used extensively in college dormitories. These units sell for $200 each and have a variable cost per unit of $150. Bonaventure experiences a combined corporate tax rate of 30 percent.

a. What are the firm's fixed costs expected to be next year?

b. Calculate the firm's breakeven point in both units and dollars.

STUDY PROBLEMS (SET A)

8-1A. (*Breakeven Point and Operating Leverage*) Some financial data for each of three firms are given below:

	Jake's Lawn Chairs	Sarasota Sky Lights	Jefferson Wholesale
Average selling price per unit	$32.00	$875.00	$97.77
Average variable cost per unit	$17.38	$400.00	$87.00
Units sold	18,770	2,800	11,000
Fixed costs	$120,350	$850,000	$89,500

a. What is the profit for each company at the indicated sales volume?

b. What is the breakeven point in units for each company?

c. What is the degree of operating leverage for each company at the indicated sales volume?

d. If sales were to decline, which firm would suffer the largest relative decline in profitability?

8-2A. (*Leverage Analysis*) You have developed the following analytical income statement for your corporation. It represents the most recent year's operations, which ended yesterday.

Sales	$45,750,000
Variable costs	22,800,000
Revenue before fixed costs	$22,950,000
Fixed costs	9,200,000
EBIT	$13,750,000
Interest expense	1,350,000
Earnings before taxes	$12,400,000
Taxes (0.50)	6,200,000
Net income	$ 6,200,000

Your supervisor in the controller's office has just handed you a memorandum asking for written responses to the following questions:

a. At this level of output, what is the degree of operating leverage?

b. What is the degree of financial leverage?

c. What is the degree of combined leverage?

d. What is the firm's breakeven point in sales dollars?

e. If sales should increase by 25 percent, by what percent would earnings before taxes (and net income) increase?

8-3A. (*Breakeven Point and Operating Leverage*) Footwear Inc. manufactures a complete line of men's and women's dress shoes for independent merchants. The average selling price of its finished product is $180 per pair. The variable cost for the same pair of shoes is $126. Footwear Inc. incurs fixed costs of $540,000 per year.

    a. What is the breakeven point in pairs of shoes for the company?

    b. What is the dollar sales volume the firm must achieve in order to reach the breakeven point?

    c. What would be the firm's profit or loss at the following pairs of production sold: 12,000 pairs of shoes? 15,000 pairs of shoes? 20,000 pairs of shoes?

    d. Find the degree of operating leverage for the production and sales levels given in part (c).

8-4A. (*Breakeven Point and Operating Leverage*) Zeylog Corporation manufactures a line of computer memory-expansion boards used in microcomputers. The average selling price of its finished product is $180 per unit. The variable cost for these same units is $110. Zeylog incurs fixed costs of $630,000 per year.

    a. What is the breakeven point in units for the company?

    b. What is the dollar sales volume the firm must achieve in order to reach the breakeven point?

    c. What would be the firm's profit or loss at the following units of production sold: 12,000 units? 15,000 units? 20,000 units?

    d. Find the degree of operating leverage for the production and sales levels given in part (c).

8-5A. (*Breakeven Point and Operating Leverage*) Some financial data for each of three firms are shown below:

	Blacksburg Furniture	Lexington Cabinets	Williamsburg Colonials
Average selling price per unit	$15.00	$400.00	$40.00
Average variable cost per unit	$12.35	$220.00	$14.50
Units sold	75,000	4,000	13,000
Fixed costs	$35,000	$100,000	$70,000

    a. What is the profit for each company at the indicated sales volume?

    b. What is the breakeven point in units for each company?

    c. What is the degree of operating leverage for each company at the indicated sales volume?

    d. If sales were to decline, which firm would suffer the largest relative decline in profitability?

8-6A. (*Fixed Costs and the Breakeven Point*) A & B Beverages expects to earn $50,000 next year after taxes. Sales will be $375,000. The company's average product sells for $27 a unit. The variable cost per unit is $14.85. The company experiences a corporate tax rate of 45 percent.

    a. What are the company's fixed costs expected to be next year?

    b. Calculate the company's breakeven point in both units and dollars.

8-7A. (*Breakeven Point and Profit Margin*) Ms Thompson is planning to open a new wholesaling operation. Her target operating profit margin is 26 percent. Her unit contribution margin will be 50 percent of sales. Average annual sales are forecast to be $3,250,000.

    a. How large can fixed costs be for the wholesaling operation and still allow the 26 percent operating profit margin to be achieved?

    b. What is the breakeven point in dollars for the firm?

8-8A. (*Leverage Analysis*) You have developed the following analytical income statement for your corporation. It represents the most recent year's operations, which ended yesterday.

Sales	$30,000,000
Variable costs	13,500,000
Revenue before fixed costs	$16,500,000
Fixed costs	8,000,000
EBIT	$ 8,500,000
Interest expense	1,000,000
Earnings before taxes	$ 7,500,000
Taxes (0.50)	3,750,000
Net income	$ 3,750,000

Your supervisor in the controller's office has just handed you a memorandum that asked for written responses to the following questions:

a. At this level of output, what is the degree of operating leverage?

b. What is the degree of financial leverage?

c. What is the degree of combined leverage?

d. What is the firm's breakeven point in sales dollars?

e. If sales should increase by 25 percent, by what percent would earnings before taxes (and net income) increase?

8-9A. (*Breakeven Point*) You are a hard-working analyst in the office of financial operations for a manufacturing firm that produces a single product. You have developed the following cost structure information for this company. All of it pertains to an output level of 10 million units. Using this information, find the breakeven point in units of output for the firm.

Return on operating assets	= 25%
Operating asset turnover	= 5 times
Operating assets	= $20 million
Degree of operating leverage	= 4 times

8-10A. (*Breakeven Point and Operating Leverage*) Allison Radios manufactures a complete line of radio and communication equipment for law enforcement agencies. The average selling price of its finished product is $200 per unit. The variable cost for these same units is $125. Allison Radios incurs fixed costs of $620,000 per year.

a. What is the breakeven point in units for the company?

b. What is the dollar sales volume the firm must achieve in order to reach the breakeven point?

c. What would be the firm's profit or loss at the following units of production sold: 12,000 units? 15,000 units? 20,000 units?

d. Find the degree of operating leverage for the production and sales levels given in part (c).

8-11A. (*Breakeven Point and Operating Leverage*) Some financial data for each of three firms are shown below:

	Oviedo Seeds	Gainesville Sod	Athens Peaches
Average selling price per unit	$14.00	$200.00	$25.00
Average variable cost per unit	$11.20	$130.00	$17.50
Units sold	100,000	10,000	48,000
Fixed costs	$25,000	$100,000	$35,000

a. What is the profit for each company at the indicated sales volume?

b. What is the breakeven point in units for each company?

c. What is the degree of operating leverage for each company at the indicated sales volume?

d. If sales were to decline, which firm would suffer the largest relative decline in profitability?

8-12A. (*Fixed Costs and the Breakeven Point*) D. Q. Kirk Inc., expects to earn $40,000 next year after taxes. Sales will be $400,000. The micro-brewery sells only kegs of beer for $20 a keg. The variable cost per keg is $8. This manufacturing company experiences a combined corporate tax rate of 17 percent.

a. What are the company's fixed costs expected to be next year?

b. Calculate the firm's breakeven point in both units and dollars.

8-13A. (*Fixed Costs and the Breakeven Point*) Albert's Cooling Equipment hopes to earn $80,000 next year after taxes. Sales will be $2 million. The firm's single plant is located on the edge of Slippery Rock, N.B., and manufactures only small refrigerators. These are used in many of the dormitories found on college campuses. The refrigerators sell for $80 per unit and have a variable cost of $56. Albert's has a combined corporate tax rate of 45 percent.

a. What are the firm's fixed costs expected to be next year?

b. Calculate the firm's breakeven point both in units and dollars.

8-14A. (*Breakeven Point and Selling Price*) Gerry's Tool and Die Company will produce 200,000 units next year. All of this production will be sold as finished goods. Fixed costs will total $300,000. Variable costs for this firm are relatively predictable at 75 percent of sales.

a. If Gerry's Tool and Die wants to achieve an earnings before interest and taxes level of $240,000 next year, at what price per unit must it sell its product?

b. Based upon your answer to part (a), set up an analytical income statement that will verify your solution.

8-15A. (*Breakeven Point and Selling Price*) Parks Castings, Inc., will manufacture and sell 200,000 units next year. Fixed costs will total $300,000, and variable costs will be 60 percent of sales.

a. The firm wants to achieve an earnings before interest and taxes level of $250,000. What selling price per unit is necessary to achieve this result?

b. Set up an analytical income statement to verify your solution to part (a).

8-16A. (*Breakeven Point and Profit Margin*) A recent business graduate is planning to open a new wholesaling operation. His target operating profit margin is 28 percent. His unit contribution margin will be 50 percent of sales. Average annual sales are forecast to be $3,750,000.

a. How large can fixed costs be for the wholesaling operation and still allow the 28 percent operating profit margin to be achieved?

b. What is the breakeven point in dollars for the firm?

8-17A. (*Operating Leverage*) Rocky Mount Metals Company manufactures an assortment of wood-burning stoves. The average selling price for the various units is $500. The associated variable cost is $350 per unit. Fixed costs for the firm average $180,000 annually.

a. What is the breakeven point in units for the company?

b. What is the dollar sales volume the firm must achieve in order to reach the breakeven point?

c. What is the degree of operating leverage for a production and sales level of 5,000 units for the firm? (Calculate to three decimal places.)

d. What will be the projected effect upon earnings before interest and taxes if the firm's sales level should increase by 20 percent from the volume noted in part (c)?

8-18A. (*Breakeven Point and Operating Leverage*) The Rockland Recreation Company manufactures a full line of lawn furniture. The average selling price of a finished unit is $25. The associated variable cost is $15 per unit. Fixed costs for Rockland average $50,000 per year.

   a. What is the breakeven point in units for the company?

   b. What is the dollar sales volume the firm must achieve in order to reach the breakeven point?

   c. What would be the company's profit or loss at the following units of production sold: 4,000 units? 6,000 units? 8,000 units?

   d. Find the degree of operating leverage for the production and sales levels given in part (c).

   e. What is the effect on the degree of operating leverage as sales rise above the breakeven point?

8-19A. (*Fixed Costs*) Harting Heat Treating forecasts that next year its fixed costs will total $120,000. Its only product sells for $12 per unit, of which $7 is a variable cost. The management of Harting Heat Treating is considering the purchase of a new machine that will lower the variable cost per unit to $5. The new machine, however, will add to fixed costs through an increase in depreciation expense. How large can the addition to fixed costs be in order to keep the firm's breakeven point in units produced and sold unchanged?

8-20A. (*Operating Leverage*) The management of Harting Heat Treating did not purchase the new piece of equipment (see Problem 8-19A). Using the existing cost structure, calculate the degree of operating leverage at 30,000 units of output. Comment on the meaning of your answer.

8-21A. (*Leverage Analysis*) An analytical income statement for Harting Heat Treating is shown below. It is based upon an output (sales) level of 40,000 units. You may refer to the original cost structure data in Problem (8-19A).

Sales	$480,000
Variable costs	280,000
Revenue before fixed costs	$200,000
Fixed costs	120,000
EBIT	$ 80,000
Interest expense	30,000
Earnings before taxes	$ 50,000
Taxes	25,000
Net income	$ 25,000

   a. Calculate the degree of operating leverage at this output level.

   b. Calculate the degree of financial leverage at this level of EBIT.

   c. Determine the combined leverage effect at this output level.

8-22A. (*Breakeven Point*) You are employed as a financial analyst for a single-product manufacturing firm. Your supervisor has made the following cost structure information available to you, all of which pertains to an output level of 1,600,000 units.

Return on operating assets	= 15%
Operating asset turnover	= 5 times
Operating assets	= $3 million
Degree of operating leverage	= 8 times

Your task is to find the breakeven point in units of output for the firm.

8-23A. (*Fixed Costs*) Percy's Printing Services is forecasting fixed costs next year of $300,000. The firm's single product sells for $20 per unit and incurs a variable cost per unit of $14. The firm may acquire some new binding equipment that would lower variable cost per unit to $12. The new equipment, however, would add to fixed costs through the price of an annual maintenance agreement on the new equipment. How large can this increase in fixed costs be and still keep the firm's present breakeven point in units produced and sold unchanged?

8-24A. (*Leverage Analysis*) Your firm's cost analysis supervisor supplies you with the following analytical income statement and requests answers to the four questions listed below the statement.

Sales	$12,000,000
Variable costs	9,000,000
Revenue before fixed costs	$ 3,000,000
Fixed costs	2,000,000
EBIT	$ 1,000,000
Interest expense	200,000
Earnings before taxes	$ 800,000
Taxes	400,000
Net income	$ 400,000

a. At this level of output, what is the degree of operating leverage?

b. What is the degree of financial leverage?

c. What is the degree of combined leverage?

d. What is the firm's breakeven point in sales dollars?

8-25A. (*Leverage Analysis*) You are supplied with the following analytical income statement for your firm. It reflects last year's operations.

Sales	$16,000,000
Variable costs	8,000,000
Revenue before fixed costs	$ 8,000,000
Fixed costs	4,000,000
EBIT	$ 4,000,000
Interest expense	1,500,000
Earnings before taxes	$ 2,500,000
Taxes	1,250,000
Net income	$ 1,250,000

a. At this level of output, what is the degree of operating leverage?

b. What is the degree of financial leverage?

c. What is the degree of combined leverage?

d. If sales should increase by 20 percent, by what percent would earnings before taxes (and net income) increase?

e. What is your firm's breakeven point in sales dollars?

8-26A. (*Sales Mix and the Breakeven Point*) Crash Components produces four lines of auto accessories for the major Windsor automobile manufacturers. The lines are known by the code letters A, B, C, and D. The current sales mix for Crash and the contribution margin ratio (unit contribution margin divided by unit sales price) for these product lines are as follows:

Product Line	Percent of Total Sales	Contribution Margin Ratio
A	33.33%	40%
B	41.67	32
C	16.67	20
D	8.33	60

Total sales for next year are forecast to be $120,000. Total fixed costs will be $29,400.

a. Prepare a table showing (1) sales, (2) total variable costs, and (3) the total contribution margin associated with each product line.

b. What is the aggregate contribution margin ratio indicative of this sales mix?

c. At this sales mix, what is the breakeven point in dollars?

8-27A. (*Sales Mix and the Breakeven Point*) Because of production constraints, Crash Components (see Problem 8-26A) may have to adhere to a different sales mix for next year. The alternative plan is outlined below:

Product Line	Percent of Total Sales
A	25%
B	36.67
C	33.33
D	5

a. Assuming all other facts in Problem 8-26A remain the same, what effect will this different sales mix have on Crash's breakeven point in dollars?

b. Which sales mix will Crash's management prefer?

STUDY PROBLEMS (SET B)

8-1B. (*Breakeven Point and Operating Leverage*) Avitar Corporation manufactures a line of computer memory-expansion boards used in microcomputers. The average selling price of its finished product is $175 per unit. The variable cost for these same units is $115. Avitar incurs fixed costs of $650,000 per year.

a. What is the breakeven point in units for the company?

b. What is the dollar sales volume the firm must achieve in order to reach the breakeven point?

c. What would be the firm's profit or loss at the following units of production sold: 10,000 units? 16,000 units? 20,000 units?

d. Find the degree of operating leverage for the production and sales levels given in part (c).

8-2B. (*Breakeven Point and Operating Leverage*) Some financial data for each of three firms are given below:

	Durham Furniture	Raleigh Cabinets	Charlotte Colonials
Average selling price per unit	$20.00	$435.00	$35.00
Average variable cost per unit	$13.75	$240.00	$15.75
Units sold	80,000	4,500	15,000
Fixed costs	$40,000	$150,000	$60,000

a. What is the profit for each company at the indicated sales volume?

b. What is the breakeven point in units for each company?

c. What is the degree of operating leverage for each company at the indicated sales volume?

d. If sales were to decline, which firm would suffer the largest relative decline in profitability?

8-3B. (*Fixed Costs and the Breakeven Point*) Cypress Books expects to earn $55,000 next year after taxes. Sales will be $400,008. The company's average product sells for $28 a unit. The variable cost per unit is $18. The company experiences a combined tax rate of 45 percent.

   a. What are the company's fixed costs expected to be next year?

   b. Calculate the company's breakeven point in both units and dollars.

8-4B. (*Breakeven Point and Profit Margin*) Ms Neeley is planning to open a new wholesaling operation. Her target operating profit margin is 28 percent. Her unit contribution margin will be 45 percent of sales. Average annual sales are forecast to be $3,750,000.

   a. How large can fixed costs be for the wholesaling operation and still allow the 28 percent operating profit margin to be achieved?

   b. What is the breakeven point in dollars for the firm?

8-5B. (*Leverage Analysis*) You have developed the following analytical income statement for your corporation. It represents the most recent year's operations, which ended yesterday.

Sales	$40,000,000
Variable costs	16,000,000
Revenue before fixed costs	$24,000,000
Fixed costs	10,000,000
EBIT	$14,000,000
Interest expense	1,150,000
Earnings before taxes	$12,850,000
Taxes	3,750,000
Net income	$ 9,100,000

Your supervisor in the controller's office has just handed you a memorandum asking for written responses to the following questions:

   a. At this level of output, what is the degree of operating leverage?

   b. What is the degree of financial leverage?

   c. What is the degree of combined leverage?

   d. What is the firm's breakeven point in sales dollars?

   e. If sales should increase by 20 percent, by what percent would earnings before taxes (and net income) increase?

8-6B. (*Breakeven Point*) You are a hard-working analyst in the office of financial operations for a manufacturing firm that produces a single product. You have developed the following cost structure information for this company. All of it pertains to an output level of 7 million units. Using this information, find the breakeven point in units of output for the firm.

Return on operating assets	= 25%
Operating asset turnover	= 5 times
Operating assets	= $20 million
Degree of operating leverage	= 4 times

8-7B. (*Breakeven Point and Operating Leverage*) Matthew Electronics manufactures a complete line of radio and communication equipment for law enforcement agencies. The average selling price of its finished product is $175 per unit. The variable cost for these same units is $140. Matthew incurs fixed costs of $550,000 per year.

   a. What is the breakeven point in units for the company?

   b. What is the dollar sales volume the firm must achieve in order to reach the breakeven point?

   c. What would be the firm's profit or loss at the following units of production sold: 12,000 units? 15,000 units? 20,000 units?

d. Find the degree of operating leverage for the production and sales levels given in part (c).

8-8B. (*Breakeven Point and Operating Leverage*) Some financial data for each of three firms are given below:

	Farm City Seeds	Empire Sod	Golden Peaches
Average selling price per unit	$15.00	$190.00	$28.00
Average variable cost per unit	$11.75	$145.00	$19.00
Units sold	120,000	9,000	50,000
Fixed costs	$30,000	$110,000	$33,000

a. What is the profit for each company at the indicated sales volume?

b. What is the breakeven point in units for each company?

c. What is the degree of operating leverage for each company at the indicated sales volume?

d. If sales were to decline, which firm would suffer the largest relative decline in profitability?

8-9B. (*Fixed Costs and the Breakeven Point*) Keller Inc., expects to earn $38,000 next year after taxes. Sales will be $420,002. The company's average product sells for $17 a unit. The variable cost per unit is $9. The company experiences a combined corporate tax rate of 45 percent.

a. What are Keller's fixed costs expected to be next year?

b. Calculate the firm's breakeven point in both units and dollars.

8-10B. (*Fixed Costs and the Breakeven Point*) Mini-Kool hopes to earn $70,000 next year after taxes. Sales will be $2,500,000. The firm's single plant manufactures only small refrigerators. These are used in many recreational campers. The refrigerators sell for $75 per unit and have a variable cost of $58. Mini-Kool experiences a combined corporate tax rate of 45 percent.

a. What are the firm's fixed costs expected to be next year?

b. Calculate the firm's breakeven point both in units and dollars.

8-11B. (*Breakeven Point and Selling Price*) Heritage Chain Company will produce 175,000 units next year. All of this production will be sold as finished goods. Fixed costs will total $335,000. Variable costs for this firm are relatively predictable at 80 percent of sales.

a. If Heritage Chain wants to achieve an earnings before interest and taxes level of $270,000 next year, at what price per unit must it sell its product?

b. Based upon your answer to part (a), set up an analytical income statement that will verify your solution.

8-12B. (*Breakeven Point and Selling Price*) Thomas Appliances, will manufacture and sell 190,000 units next year. Fixed costs will total $300,000, and variable costs will be 75 percent of sales.

a. The firm wants to achieve an earnings before interest and taxes level of $250,000. What selling price per unit is necessary to achieve this result?

b. Set up an analytical income statement to verify your solution to part (a).

8-13B. (*Breakeven Point and Profit Margin*) A recent business graduate is planning to open a new wholesaling operation. His target operating profit margin is 25 percent. His unit contribution margin will be 60 percent of sales. Average annual sales are forecast to be $4,250,000.

a. How large can fixed costs be for the wholesaling operation and still allow the 25 percent operating profit margin to be achieved?

b. What is the breakeven point in dollars for the firm?

8-14B. (*Operating Leverage*) The B. H. Williams Company manufactures an assortment of wood-burning stoves. The average selling price for the various units is $475. The associated variable cost is $350 per unit. Fixed costs for the firm average $200,000 annually.

a. What is the breakeven point in units for the company?

b. What is the dollar sales volume the firm must achieve in order to reach the breakeven point?

c. What is the degree of operating leverage for a production and sales level of 6,000 units for the firm? (Calculate to three decimal places.)

d. What will be the projected effect upon earnings before interest and taxes if the firm's sales level should increase by 13 percent from the volume noted in part (c)?

8-15B. (*Breakeven Point and Operating Leverage*) The Palm Patio Company manufactures a full line of lawn furniture. The average selling price of a finished unit is $28. The associated variable cost is $17 per unit. Fixed costs for Palm Patio average $55,000 per year.

a. What is the breakeven point in units for the company?

b. What is the dollar sales volume the firm must achieve in order to reach the breakeven point?

c. What would be the company's profit or loss at the following units of production sold: 4,000 units? 6,000 units? 8,000 units?

d. Find the degree of operating leverage for the production and sales levels given in part (c).

e. What is the effect on the degree of operating leverage as sales rise above the breakeven point?

8-16B. (*Fixed Costs*) Tropical Sun projects that next year its fixed costs will total $135,000. Its only product sells for $13 per unit, of which $6 is a variable cost. The management of Tropical is considering the purchase of a new machine that will lower the variable cost per unit to $5. The new machine, however, will add to fixed costs through an increase in depreciation expense. How large can the addition to fixed costs be in order to keep the firm's breakeven point in units produced and sold unchanged?

8-17B. (*Operating Leverage*) The management of Tropical Sun did not purchase the new piece of equipment (see Problem 8-16B). Using the existing cost structure, calculate the degree of operating leverage at 40,000 units of output. Comment on the meaning of your answer.

8-18B. (*Leverage Analysis*) An analytical income statement for Tropical Sun is shown below. It is based upon an output (sales) level of 50,000 units. You may refer to the original cost structure data in Problem (8-16B).

Sales	$650,000
Variable costs	300,000
Revenue before fixed costs	$350,000
Fixed costs	135,000
EBIT	$215,000
Interest expense	60,000
Earnings before taxes	$155,000
Taxes	70,000
Net income	$ 85,000

a. Calculate the degree of operating leverage at this output level.

b. Calculate the degree of financial leverage at this level of EBIT.

c. Determine the combined leverage effect at this output level.

8-19B. (*Breakeven Point*) You are employed as a financial analyst for a single-product manufacturing firm. Your supervisor has made the following cost structure information available to you, all of which pertains to an output level of 1,700,000 units.

Return on operating assets	= 16%
Operating asset turnover	= 6 times
Operating assets	= $3.25 million
Degree of operating leverage	= 9 times

Your task is to find the breakeven point in units of output for the firm.

8-20B. (*Fixed Costs*) Saskatoon Silkscreen is forecasting fixed costs next year of $375,000. The firm's single product sells for $25 per unit and incurs a variable cost per unit of $13. The firm may acquire some new binding equipment that would lower variable cost per unit to $11. The new equipment, however, would add to fixed costs through the price of an annual maintenance agreement on the new equipment. How large can this increase in fixed costs be and still keep the firm's present breakeven point in units produced and sold unchanged?

8-21B. (*Leverage Analysis*) Your firm's cost analysis supervisor supplies you with the following analytical income statement and requests answers to the four questions listed below the statement.

Sales	$13,750,000
Variable costs	9,500,000
Revenue before fixed costs	$ 4,250,000
Fixed costs	3,000,000
EBIT	$ 1,250,000
Interest expense	250,000
Earnings before taxes	$ 1,000,000
Taxes	430,000
Net income	$ 570,000

a. At this level of output, what is the degree of operating leverage?

b. What is the degree of financial leverage?

c. What is the degree of combined leverage?

d. What is the firm's breakeven point in sales dollars?

8-22B. (*Leverage Analysis*) You are supplied with the following analytical income statement for your firm. It reflects last year's operations.

Sales	$18,000,000
Variable costs	7,000,000
Revenue before fixed costs	$11,000,000
Fixed costs	6,000,000
EBIT	$ 5,000,000
Interest expense	1,750,000
Earnings before taxes	$ 3,250,000
Taxes	1,250,000
Net income	$ 2,000,000

a. At this level of output, what is the degree of operating leverage?

b. What is the degree of financial leverage?

c. What is the degree of combined leverage?

d. If sales should increase by 15 percent, by what percent would earnings before taxes (and net income) increase?

e. What is your firm's breakeven point in sales dollars?

8-23B. (*Sales Mix and the Breakeven Point*) Wayne Automotive produces four lines of auto accessories for the major Ontario automobile manufacturers. The lines are known by the code letters A, B, C, and D. The current sales mix for

Wayne and the contribution margin ratio (unit contribution margin divided by unit sales price) for these product lines are as follows:

Product Line	Percent of Total Sales	Contribution Margin Ratio
A	25.67%	40%
B	41.33	32
C	19.67	20
D	13.33	60

Total sales for next year are forecast to be $150,000. Total fixed costs will be $35,000.

a. Prepare a table showing (1) sales, (2) total variable costs, and (3) the total contribution margin associated with each product line.

b. What is the aggregate contribution margin ratio indicative of this sales mix?

c. At this sales mix, what is the breakeven point in dollars?

8-24B. (*Sales Mix and the Breakeven Point*) Because of production constraints, Wayne Automotive (see Problem 8-23B) may have to adhere to a different sales mix for next year. The alternative plan is outlined below:

Product Line	Percent of Total Sales
A	33.33%
B	41.67
C	16.67
D	8.33

a. Assuming all other facts in Problem 8-23B remain the same, what effect will this different sales mix have on Wayne's breakeven point in dollars?

b. Which sales mix will Wayne's management prefer?

CASE PROBLEM

HAMILTON GENERAL PRODUCERS

BREAKEVEN ANALYSIS, OPERATING LEVERAGE, FINANCIAL LEVERAGE

Hamilton General Producers (HGP) is a medium-sized public corporation that until recently consisted of two divisions. The Retail Furniture Group (RFG) has eight locations in the Ontario area, mostly concentrated around Toronto. These retail outlets generate sales of contemporary, traditional, and early American furniture. In addition, casual and leisure furniture lines are carried by the stores. The other (old) division of HGP is its Concrete Group (CG). The CG operates three plants in the Hull area of western Quebec. These plants produce precast concrete wall panels and concrete stave farm silos. The company headquarters of HGP is located in Hamilton, Ontario. This community touches Lake Ontario and is about 40 miles west of Toronto. Since Hamilton is almost equidistant from Toronto and Niagara Falls and is a connecting hub for several major highways, it makes a sensible spot for the firm's home offices.

HGP was started 10 years ago as Hamilton Producers by its current president and board chairman, Anthony Toscano. During the firm's existence it has enjoyed periods of both moderate and strong growth in sales, assets, and earnings. Key managerial decisions have always been dominated by Toscano, who openly boasts of the fact that his company has never suffered through a year of negative earnings despite the often cyclical nature of both the retail furniture (RFG) and concrete (CG) divisions.

Recently Mr. Toscano decided to acquire a third division for his firm. The division manufactures special machinery for the seafood processing industry and is appropriately called the Seafood Industry Group (SIG). The financial settlement for the acquisition took place yesterday. Currently, the SIG consists of one manufacturing plant in Port Hope. A single product is to be manufactured, assembled, and shipped from the facility. That product, however, represents a design breakthrough and carries with it a projected contribution margin ratio of .4000. This is greater than that enjoyed by either of HGP's other two divisions.

HGP's manufacturing operation in Hamilton will produce a new machine called "The Picker." The Picker was invented and successfully tested by Ben Pinkerton, the major shareholder and manager of a small seafood processing firm in Port Hope, Ontario. Pinkerton plans and supervises all operations at Eastern Shore Processors. Eastern Shore specializes in freezing and pasteurizing New Zealand mussel meat. Freezing and pasteurizing procedures have been a boon to the seafood industry, for they permit the processor to retain a product without spoilage in hopes of higher prices at a later date. In comparing his industry to that of agriculture, Pinkerton aptly states: "The freezer is our grain elevator."

The seafood processing industry is characterized by a notable lack of capital equipment and a corresponding heavy use of human labour. Pinkerton will tell you that at Eastern Shore Processors a skilled mussel meat picker will produce about 30 pounds of meat per day. No matter how skilled the human picker, however, he will leave about 5 pounds of meat per day in the top piece of the mussel shell. This past year, after five years of trying, Pinkerton perfected a machine that would recover about 30 percent of this otherwise lost meat. In exchange for cash, Eastern Shore Processors sold all rights to The Picker to HGP. Thus, Toscano established the SIG and immediately made plans to manufacture The Picker.

Recent income statements for the older divisions of HGP are contained in Exhibits 1 and 2. Toscano has now decided to assess more fully the probable impact of the decision to establish the SIG on the financial condition of HGP. Toscano knew that such figures should have been generated prior to the decision to enter this special field, but his seasoned judgment led him to a quick choice. He has requested several pieces of information, detailed below, from his chief financial officer.

EXHIBIT 1

Hamilton General Producers Retail Furniture Group Income Statement, December 31, Last Year

Sales	$12,000,000
Variable costs	7,920,000
Revenue before fixed costs	$ 4,080,000
Fixed costs	2,544,000
EBIT	$ 1,536,000
Interest expense	192,000
Earnings before taxes	$ 1,344,000
Taxes	672,000
Net income	$ 672,000

EXHIBIT 2

Hamilton General Producers Concrete Group Income Statement, December 31, Last Year

Sales	$8,000,000
Variable costs	5,920,000
Revenue before fixed costs	$2,080,000
Fixed costs	640,000
EBIT	$1,440,000
Interest expense	80,000
Earnings before taxes	$1,360,000
Taxes	680,000
Net income	$ 680,000

QUESTIONS AND PROBLEMS

1. Using last year's results, determine the breakeven point in dollars for HGP (i.e., before investing in the new SIG). The breakeven point is defined here in the traditional manner where EBIT = $0. (*Hint*: Use an aggregate contribution margin ratio in your analysis.)

2. Using last year's results, determine what volume of sales must be reached in order to cover all before-tax costs.

3. Next year's sales for the SIG are projected to be $4,000,000. Total fixed costs will be $640,000. This division will have no outstanding debt on its balance sheet. HGP uses a 50 percent tax rate in all its financial projections. Using the format of Exhibits 1 and 2, construct a pro forma income statement for the SIG.

4. After the SIG begins operations, what will be HGP's breakeven point in dollars (a) as traditionally defined and (b) reflecting the coverage of all before-tax costs? Base the new sales mix on last year's sales performance for the older divisions plus that anticipated next year for the SIG. Using your answer to part (b) of this question, construct an analytical income statement demonstrating that earnings before taxes = $0.

5. Using next year's anticipated sales volume for HGP (including the SIG), compute (a) the degree of operating leverage, (b) the degree of financial leverage, and (c) the degree of combined leverage. Comment on the meaning of each of these statistics.

6. Using projected figures, determine whether acquisition of the SIG will increase or decrease the vulnerability of HGP's earnings before interest and taxes (EBIT) to cyclical swings in sales. Show your work.

7. Review the key assumptions of cost-volume-profit analysis.

SELF-TEST SOLUTIONS

SS-1: *STEP 1.* Compute the operating profit margin:

$$(\text{margin}) \times (\text{turnover}) = \text{return on operating assets}$$

$$(\text{M}) \times (6) = 0.30$$

$$\text{M} = \frac{0.30}{6} = 0.05$$

STEP 2. Compute the sales level associated with the given output level:

$$\frac{\text{sales}}{\$20,000,000} = 6$$

$$\text{sales} = \$120,000,000$$

STEP 3. Compute EBIT:

$$(.05)(\$120,000,000) = \$6,000,000 = \text{EBIT}$$

STEP 4. Compute revenue before fixed costs. Since the degree of operating leverage is 4.5 times, revenue before fixed costs (RBF) is 4.5 times EBIT, as follows:

$$\text{RBF} = (4.5)\,(\$6,000,000) = \$27,000,000$$

STEP 5. Compute total variable costs:

$$(\text{sales}) - (\text{total variable costs}) = \$27,000,000$$

$$\$120,000,000 - (\text{total variable costs}) = \$27,000,000$$

$$\text{total variable costs} = \$93,000,000$$

STEP 6. Compute total fixed costs:

$$\text{RBF} - \text{fixed costs} = \text{EBIT}$$

$$\$27,000,000 - \text{fixed costs} = \$6,000,000$$

$$\text{Fixed costs} = \$21,000,000$$

STEP 7. Find the selling price per unit (P), and the variable cost per unit (V):

$$P = \frac{\text{sales}}{\text{output in units}} = \frac{\$120,000,000}{10,000,000} = \$12.00$$

$$V = \frac{\text{total variable costs}}{\text{output in units}} = \frac{\$93,000,000}{10,000,000} = \$9.30$$

STEP 8. Compute the breakeven point:

$$Q_B = \frac{F}{P - V} = \frac{\$21,000,000}{\$12.00 - \$9.30}$$

$$= \frac{\$21,000,000}{\$2.70} = 7,777,778 \text{ units}$$

The firm will break even when it produces and sells 7,777,778 units.

SS-2: a. $\dfrac{\text{Revenue before fixed costs}}{\text{EBIT}} = \dfrac{\$8,000,000}{\$3,000,000} = 2.67$ times

b. $\dfrac{\text{EBIT}}{\text{EBIT} - I} = \dfrac{\$3,000,000}{\$2,000,000} = 1.50$ times

c. $DCL_{\$20,000,000} = (2.67)(1.50) = 4.00$ times

d.
$$S^* = \frac{F}{1 - \dfrac{VC}{S}} = \frac{\$5,000,000}{1 - \dfrac{\$12M}{\$20M}} =$$

$$\frac{\$5,000,000}{1 - 0.60} = \frac{\$5,000,0000}{0.40} = \$12,500,000$$

e. $(30\%)(4.00) = 120\%$

f.

Sales	$26,000,000
Variable costs	15,600,000
Revenue before fixed costs	$10,400,000
Fixed costs	5,000,000
EBIT	$ 5,400,000
Interest expense	1,000,000
Earnings before taxes	$ 4,400,000
Taxes (0.50)	2,200,000
Net income	$ 2,200,000

We know that sales have increased by 30 percent to $26 million from the base sales level of $20 million.

Let us focus now on the change in earnings before taxes. We can compute that change as follows:

$$\frac{\$4,400,000 - \$2,000,000}{\$2,000,000} = \frac{\$2,400,000}{\$2,000,000} = 120\%$$

Since the tax rate was held constant, the percentage change in net income will also equal 120 percent. The fluctuations implied by the degree of combined leverage measure are therefore accurately reflected in this analytical income statement.

SS-3. a.

$$[(P \cdot Q) - [V \cdot Q + (F)]]\,(1 - T) = \$210{,}000$$

$$[(\$4{,}000{,}000) - (\$3{,}000{,}000) - F]\,(.7) = \$210{,}000$$

$$(\$1{,}000{,}000 - F)\,(.7) = \$210{,}000$$

$$\$700{,}000 - .7F = \$210{,}000$$

$$F = \$700{,}000$$

Fixed costs next year, then, are expected to be $700,000.

b.

$$Q_B = \frac{F}{P - V} = \frac{\$700{,}000}{\$50} = 14{,}000 \text{ units}$$

$$S^* = \frac{F}{1 - \dfrac{VC}{S}} = \frac{\$700{,}000}{1 - .75} = \frac{\$700{,}000}{.25} = \$2{,}800{,}000$$

The firm will break even (EBIT = 0) when it sells 14,000 units. With a selling price of $200 per unit, the breakeven sales level is $2,800,000.

SELECTED REFERENCES

Adar, Zvi, Amir Barnea, and Baruch Lev. "A Comprehensive Cost-Volume-Profit Analysis under Uncertainty," *Accounting Review*, 52 (January 1977), 137–149.

Berkovitch, Elazar, and E. Han Kim. "Financial Contracting and Leverage Induced Over and Under-Investment Incentives," *The Journal of Finance*, 45 (July 1990), 765–94.

Bowlin, Oswald D., John D. Martin, and David F. Scott, Jr. *Guide to Financial Analysis*. Chapter 11. 2nd ed. New York: McGraw-Hill, 1990.

Brigham, Eugene F., and T. Craig Tapley. "Financial Leverage and Use of the Net Present Value Investment Criterion: A Reexamination," *Financial Management*, 14 (Summer 1985), 48–52.

Choi, Jongmoo J., Frank J. Fabozzi, and Uzi Yaari. "Optimum Corporate Leverage with Risky Debt: A Demand Approach," *Journal of Financial Research*, 12 (Summer 1989), 129–142.

Chung, Kee H. "The Impact of the Demand Volatility and Leverages on the Systematic Risk of Common Stocks," *Journal of Business Finance and Accounting*, 16 (Summer 1989), 343–360.

Clark, John J., Margaret T. Clark, and Andrew G. Verzilli. "Strategic Planning and Sustainable Growth," *Columbia Journal of World Business*, 20 (Fall 1985), 51.

Conine, Thomas E., Jr. "A Pedagogical Note on Cash Break-even Analysis," *Journal of Business Finance and Accounting*, 14 (Autumn 1987), 437–441.

Dammon, Robert M., and Lemma W. Senbet. "The Effect of Taxes and Depreciation on Corporate Investment and Financial Leverage," *Journal of Finance*, 43 (June 1988), 357–374.

Dugan, Michael T., and Keith A. Shriver. "The Effects of Estimation Period, Industry, and Proxy on the Calculation of the Degree of Operating Leverage," *The Financial Review*, 24 (February 1989), 109–122.

Gamble, Richard H. "Deleveraging: Relief from a Big Debt Hangover," *Corporate Cashflow*, 12 (January 1991), 24–30.

Gahlon, James M., and James A. Gentry. "On the Relationship between Systematic Risk and the Degrees of Operating and Financial Leverage," *Financial Management*, 11 (Summer 1982), 15–23.

Ghandi, J. K. S. "On the Measurement of Leverage," *Journal of Finance*, 21 (December 1966), 715–726.

Gilbert, Nathaniel. "Living on Leverage: Can U.S. Business Survive Its Passion for Debt?" *Management Review*, 79 (April 1990), 50–55.

Golbe, Devra L., and Barry Schachater. "The Net Present Value Rule and an Algorithm for Maintaining a Constant Debt-Equity Ratio," *Financial Management*, 14 (Summer 1985), 53–58.

Gritta, Richard D. "The Effect of Financial Leverage on Air Carrier Earnings: A Break-Even Analysis," *Financial Management*, 8 (Summer 1979), 53–60.

Gupta, Atul, and Leonard Rosenthal. "Ownership Structure, Leverage, and Firm Value: The Case of Leveraged Recapitalizations," *Financial Management*, 20 (Autumn 1991), 69–83.

Haslem, John A. "Leverage Effects on Corporate Earnings," *Arizona Business Review*, 19 (March 1970), 7–11.

Helfert, Erich A. *Techniques of Financial Analysis*. Chapter 6. 5th ed. Homewood, IL: Richard D. Irwin, 1982.

Higgins, Robert C. *Analysis for Financial Management*, Chapter 7. Homewood, IL: Richard D. Irwin, 1984.

Hunt, Pearson. "A Proposal for Precise Definitions of Trading on the Equity and Leverage," *Journal of Finance*, 16 (September 1961), 377–386.

Jaedicke, Robert K., and Alexander A. Robichek. "Cost-Volume-Profit Analysis under Conditions of Uncertainty," *Accounting Review*, 39 (October 1964), 917–926.

Janjigian, Vahan. "The Leverage Changing Consequences of Convertible Debt Financing," *Financial Management*, 16 (Autumn 1987), 15–21.

Leibowitz, Martin L., and Stanley Kogelman. "The Franchise Factor for Leveraged Firms," *Financial Analysts Journal*, 47 (November–December 1991), 29–43.

Leibowitz, Martin L., Stanley Kogelman, and Eric B. Lindenberg. "A Shortfall Approach to the Creditor's Decision: How Much Leverage Can a Firm Support?" *Financial Analysts Journal*, 46 (May–June, 1990), 43–52.

Lev, Baruch. "On the Association between Operating Leverage and Risk," *Journal of Financial and Quantitative Analysis*, 9 (September 1974), 627–642.

Lewellen, Wilbur G., and William A. Kracaw. "Inflation, Corporate Growth, and Corporate Leverage," *Financial Management*, 16 (Winter 1987), 29–36.

Lortie, Conrad. "Using Operating Leverage to Increase Small Business Profits," *CMA Management Accounting Magazine*, 63(9) (November 1989), 32–34.

McConoughey, Deborah J. "Breakeven Analysis for Maturity Decisions in Cash Management," *Journal of Cash Management*, 5 (January–February 1985), 18–21.

Miller, Merton H. "Leverage," *The Journal of Finance*, 46 (June 1991), 479–88.

O'Brien, Thomas J., and Vanderheiden, Paul A. "Empirical Measurement of Operating Leverage for Growing Firms," *Financial Management*, 16 (Spring 1987), 45–53.

Osteryoung, Jerome S., and Daniel E. McCarty. *Analytical Techniques for Financial Management*, Chapter 11. Columbus, OH: Grid, 1980.

Percival, John R. "Operating Leverage and Risk," *Journal of Business Research*, 2 (April 1974), 223–227.

Phillips, Aaron L. "An Empirical Study of Asset Size, Financial Leverage, and Stock Market Anomalies," *Akron Business and Economic Review*, 20 (Fall 1989), 40–54.

Prezas, Alexandros P. "Effects of Debt on the Degree of Operating and Financial Leverage," *Financial Management*, 16 (Spring 1987), 39–44.

Reinhardt, U. E. "Break Even Analysis for Lockheed's Tri Star: An Application of Financial Theory," *Journal of Finance*, 28 (September 1973), 821–838.

Remolona, Eli M. "Understanding International Differences in Leverage Trends," *Federal Reserve Bank of New York Quarterly Review*, 15 (Spring 1990), 31–42.

Shalit, Sol S. "On the Mathematics of Financial Leverage," *Financial Management*, 4 (Spring 1975), 57–66.

Shashua, Leon, and Yaaqov Goldschmidt. "Break-even Analysis Under Inflation," *Engineering Economist*, 32 (Winter 1987), 79–88.

Siegel, Frederick W., and James P. Hoban. "Measuring Risk Aversion: Allocation, Leverage, and Accumulation," *Journal of Financial Research*, 14 (Spring 1991), 27–35.

Sullivan, Timothy G. "Market Power, Profitability and Financial Leverage," *Journal of Finance*, 29 (December 1974), 1407–1414.

Thode, Stephen F., Ralph E. Drtina, and James A. Largay III. "Operating Cash Flows: A Growing Need for Separate Reporting," *Journal of Accounting, Auditing and Finance*, 1 (Winter 1986), 46–57.

Tsurumi, Yoshi, and Hiroki Tsurumi. "Value-Added Maximizing Behavior of Japanese Firms and Roles of Corporate Investment and Finance," *Columbia Journal of World Business*, 20 (Spring 1985), 29–35.

Viscione, Jerry A. *Financial Analysis: Principles and Procedures*. Chapter 4. Boston: Houghton Mifflin, 1977.

Wiggins, James B. "The Relation between Risk and Optimal Debt Maturity and the Value of Leverage," *Journal of Financial and Quantitative Analysis*, 25 (September 1990), 377–86.

Zimmer, Steven A. "Event Risk Premia and Bond Market Incentives for Corporate Leverage," *Federal Reserve Bank of New York Quarterly Review*, 15 (Spring 1990), 15–30.

CHAPTER 9

Planning the Firm's Financing Mix

- A Glance at Capital-Structure Theory

- Basic Tools of Capital-Structure Management

- A Glance at Actual Capital-Structure Management

In this chapter we direct our attention to the determination of an appropriate financing mix for the firm. First, we must distinguish between financial structure and capital structure. **Financial structure** is the mix of all items that appear on the right-hand side of the company's balance sheet. **Capital structure** is the mix of the long-term sources of funds used by the firm.[1] The relationship between financial and capital structure can be expressed through the following equation:

$$\text{(financial structure)} - \text{(current liabilities)} = \text{capital structure} \quad \text{(9-1)}$$

Prudent **financial structure design** requires answers to the following two questions:

1. What should be the maturity composition of the firm's sources of funds; in other words, how should a firm divide its total source of funds between short- and long-term components?

2. In what proportions relative to the total should the various forms of permanent financing be utilized?

The major influence on the maturity structure of the financing plan is the nature of the assets owned by the firm. A company heavily committed to real capital investment, represented primarily by fixed assets on its balance sheet, should finance those assets with permanent (long-term) types of financial capital. Furthermore, the permanent portion of the firm's investment in current assets should likewise be financed with permanent capital. Alternatively, assets held on a temporary basis are to be financed

---

[1]For the purposes of finance, capital structure should be expressed in terms of market value and not book value.

TABLE 9-1
Balance Sheet

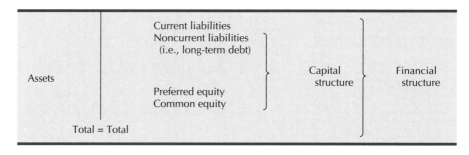

with temporary sources.[2] The present discussion assumes that the bulk of the company's current liabilities are comprised of temporary capital.

This **hedging concept** is discussed in both Chapters 13 and 16. Accordingly, our focus in this chapter is an answer to the second of the two questions noted above—this process is usually called *capital-structure management.*

The objective of capital-structure management is to mix the permanent sources of funds used by the firm in a manner that will maximize the company's common share price. Alternatively, this objective may be viewed as a search for the funds mix that will minimize the firm's composite cost of capital. We can call this proper mix of funds sources the **optimal capital structure**.

Table 9-1 looks at Equation (9-1) in terms of a simplified balance sheet format. It helps us visualize the overriding problem of capital-structure management. The sources of funds that give rise to financing fixed costs (long-term debt and preferred equity) must be combined with common equity in the proportions most suitable to the investing marketplace. If that mix can be found, then holding all other factors constant, the firm's common share price will be maximized.

While Equation (9-1) quite accurately indicates that the corporate capital structure may be viewed as an absolute dollar amount, the real capital structure problem is one of balancing the array of funds sources in a proper manner. Our use of the term *capital structure* emphasizes this latter problem of relative magnitude, or proportions.

The rest of this chapter will cover three main areas. First, we discuss the theory of capital structure to provide a perspective. Second, we examine the basic tools of capital structure management. We conclude with a real-world look at actual capital-structure management.

Perspective in Finance

It pays to understand the essential components of capital structure theory. The assumption of excessive financial risk can put the firm into bankruptcy proceedings. Some argue that the decision to use little financial leverage results in an undervaluation of the firm's shares in the marketplace. Financial managers must know how to find the area of optimum financial leverage use which will enhance share value, all other considerations held constant. Thus, grasping the theory will make you better able to formulate a sound financial-structure policy.

[2]The matching of asset and liability maturities is known as the matching principle and its implications will be discussed in greater detail in Chapter 13.

A GLANCE AT CAPITAL-STRUCTURE THEORY

An enduring controversy within financial theory concerns the effect of financial leverage on the overall cost of capital to the enterprise. The heart of the argument may be stated in the form of a question:[3]

> Can the firm affect its overall cost of funds, either favourably or unfavourably, by varying the mixture of financing sources used?

This controversy has taken many elegant forms in the finance literature (see "Suggested References" at the end of this chapter). Most of these presentations appeal more to academics than financial management practitioners. To emphasize the ingredients of capital structure theory that have practical applications for business financial management, we will pursue an intuitive, or nonmathematical, approach to reach a better understanding of the underpinnings of this **cost of capital–capital-structure argument**.

The Importance of Capital Structure

It makes economic sense for the firm to strive to minimize the cost of using financial capital. Both capital costs and other costs, such as manufacturing costs, share a common characteristic in that they potentially reduce the size of the cash dividend that could be paid to common shareholders.

We saw in Chapter 4 that the ultimate value of common shares depends in part on the returns investors expect to receive from holding these shares. Cash dividends comprise all (in the case of an infinite holding period) or part (in the case of a holding period less than infinity) of these expected returns. Now, hold constant all factors that could affect share price except capital costs. If these capital costs could be kept at a minimum, the dividend stream flowing to the common shareholders would be maximized. This, in turn, would maximize the firm's common share price.

If the firm's cost of capital can be affected by its capital structure, then capital-structure management is clearly an important subset of business financial management.

The Analytical Setting

The essentials of the capital structure controversy are best highlighted within a framework that economists would call a "partial equilibrium analysis." In a partial equilibrium analysis changes that do occur in a number of factors and have an impact upon a certain key item are ignored in order to study the effect of changes in a main factor upon that same item of interest. Here, two items are simultaneously of interest: (1) K_0, the firm's weighted cost of capital, and (2) P_0, the market price of the firm's common share. The firm's use of financial leverage is the main factor that is allowed to vary in the analysis. This means that important financial decisions, such as investment policy and dividend policy, are held constant throughout the discussion. We are concerned with the effect of changes in the financing mix on share price and capital costs.

Our analysis will be facilitated if we adopt a simplified version of the basic dividend valuation model presented in Chapter 4 in our study of valua-

---

[3]The question can also be stated as follows: Can firm value be affected by the design of the company's capital structure? This type of question recognizes that all cost-of-capital estimation techniques have a valuation underpinning.

tion principles and in Chapter 5 in our assessment of the cost of capital. That model is shown below as Equation (9-2):

$$P_0 = \sum_{t=1}^{\infty} \frac{D_t}{(1 + K_c)^t} \tag{9-2}$$

where P_0 = the current price of the firm's common share

   D_t = the cash dividend per share expected by investors during period t

   K_c = the cost of common equity capital

We can strip away some complications by making the following assumptions concerning the valuation process implicit in Equation (9-2):

1. Cash dividends paid will not change over the infinite holding period. Thus, $D_1 = D_2 = D_3 = ... = D_\infty$. There is no expected growth by investors in the dividend stream.

2. The firm retains none of its current earnings. This means that all of each period's per-share earnings are paid to shareholders in the form of cash dividends. The firm's dividend payout ratio is 100 percent. Cash dividends per share in Equation (9-2), then, also equal earnings per share for the time period.

Under these assumptions, the cash dividend flowing to investors can be viewed as a level payment over an infinite holding period. The payment stream is perpetual, and according to the mathematics of perpetuities, Equation (9-2) reduces to Equation (9-3), where E_t represents earnings per share during time period t.

$$P_0 = \frac{D_t}{K_c} = \frac{E_t}{K_c} \tag{9-3}$$

In addition to the suppositions noted above, the analytical setting for the discussion of capital-structure theory includes the following assumptions:

1. Corporate income is not subject to any taxation. The major implication of removing this assumption is discussed later.

2. Capital structures consist of only shares and bonds. Furthermore, the degree of financial leverage used by the firm is altered by the issuance of common shares with the proceeds used to retire existing debt, or the issuance of debt with the proceeds used to repurchase shares. This permits leverage use to vary but maintains constancy of the total book value of the firm's capital structure.

3. The expected values of all investors' forecasts of the future levels of net operating income (EBIT) for each firm are identical. Say that you forecast the average level of EBIT to be achieved by General Motors of Canada over a very long period ($n \rightarrow \infty$). Your forecast will be the same as our forecast, and both will be equal to the forecasts of all other investors interested in General Motors common shares. In addition, we do not expect General Motors' EBIT to grow over time. Each year's forecast is the same as any other year's. This is consistent with our assumption underlying Equation (9-3), where the firm's dividend stream is not expected to grow.

4. Securities are traded in perfect or efficient financial markets. This means that transaction costs and legal restrictions do not impede any investors' incentives to execute portfolio changes that they expect will increase their wealth. Information is freely available. Moreover, corporations and individuals that are equal credit risks can borrow funds at the same rates of interest.

This completes our description of the analytical setting. We now discuss three differing views on the relationship between use of financial leverage and common share value.

Perspective in Finance

The discussion and illustrations of the two "extreme" positions on the importance of capital structure that follow are meant to highlight the critical differences between differing viewpoints. This is not to say that the markets really behave in strict accordance with either position—they don't. The point is to identify polar positions on how things might work. Then by relaxing various restrictive assumptions, a more useful theory of how financing decisions are actually made becomes possible. That results in the third, or "moderate," view.

Extreme Position 1: The Independence Hypothesis (NOI Theory)[4]

The crux of this position is that the firm's weighted cost of capital, K_0, and common share price, P_0, are both independent of the degree to which the company chooses to use financial leverage. In other words, no matter how

[4]The net operating income and net income capitalization methods, which are referred to here as "extreme positions 1 and 2," were first presented in comprehensible form by Durand. (See David Durand, "Costs of Debt and Equity Funds for Business: Trends and Problems of Measurement," *Conference on Research in Business Finance.* New York: National Bureau of Economic Research, 1952, reprinted in *The Management of Corporate Capital*, Ezra Solomon, ed. New York: Free Press, 1959, pp. 91–116.) The leading proponents of the independence hypothesis in its various forms are Professors Modigliani and Miller. (See Franco Modigliani and Merton H. Miller, "The Cost of Capital, Corporation Finance and the Theory of Investment," *American Economic Review*, 48 (June 1958), pp. 261–297; Franco Modigliani and Merton H. Miller, "Corporate Income Taxes and the Cost of Capital: A Correction," *American Economic Review*, 53 (June 1963), pp. 433–443; and Merton H. Miller, "Debt and Taxes," *Journal of Finance*, 32 (May 1977), pp. 261–275.)

modest or excessive the firm's use of debt financing, its common share price will not be affected. Let us illustrate the mechanics of this point of view.

Suppose that Rix Camper Manufacturing Company has the following financial characteristics:

Expected level of net operating income	(EBIT) = $2,000,000
Common shares outstanding	= 2,000,000 shares
Common share price, P_0	= $10 per share
Expected level of net operating income	(EBIT) = $2,000,000
Dividend payout ratio	= 100 percent

Currently the firm uses no financial leverage; its capital structure consists entirely of common equity. Earnings per share and dividends per share equal $1 each. When the capital structure is all common equity, the cost of common equity, K_c, and the weighted cost of capital, K_0, are equal. If Equation (9-3) is restated in terms of the cost of common equity, we have for Rix Camper

$$K_c = \frac{D_t}{P_0} = \frac{\$1}{\$10} = 10\%$$

Now, the management of Rix Camper decides to use some debt capital in its financing mix. The firm sells $8 million worth of long-term debt at an interest rate of 6 percent. With no taxation of corporate income, this 6 percent interest rate is the cost of debt capital, K_d. The firm uses the proceeds from the sale of the bonds to repurchase 40 percent of its outstanding common shares. After the capital-structure change has been accomplished, Rix Camper Manufacturing Company has the financial characteristics displayed in Table 9-2.

Based on the predicted data above we notice that the recapitalization (capital structure change) of Rix Camper will result in a dividend paid to owners that is 26.7 percent higher than it was when the firm used no debt in its capital structure. Will this higher dividend result in a lower weighted cost of capital to Rix and a higher common share price? According to the principles of the independence hypothesis, the answer is "No."

The independence hypothesis suggests that the total market value of the firm's outstanding securities is unaffected by the manner in which the right-hand side of the balance sheet is arranged. That is, the sum of the market value of outstanding debt plus the sum of the market value of outstanding common equity will always be the same regardless of how much or little debt is actually used by the company. If capital structure has no impact on the total market value of the company, then that value is arrived at by the

Capital-Structure Information	
Common shares outstanding = 1,200,000	
Bonds at 6 percent = $8,000,000	
Earnings Information	
Expected level of net operating income (EBIT) =	$2,000,000
Less: Interest expense	480,000
Earnings available to common shareholders	$1,520,000
Earnings per share (E_t)	$1.267
Dividends per share (D_t)	$1.267
Percentage change in both earnings per share and dividends per share relative to the unlevered capital structure	26.7 percent

marketplace's capitalizing (discounting) the firm's expected net operating income stream.

$$V_U = \frac{NOI}{K_c^U} \tag{9-3}$$

where V_U = the value of the unlevered firm

NOI = the expected level of net operating income

K_c^U = the cost of equity of the unlevered firm

K_0 = the weighted cost of capital

For the Rix Camper Manufacturing Company, the firm's value is determined as follows:

$$V_U = \frac{\$2,000,000}{0.10} = \$20,000,000$$

Therefore, the independence hypothesis rests upon what is called the **net operating income (NOI) approach to valuation**.

The format is a very simple one, and the market value of the firm's common shares turns out to be a residual of the valuation process. Recall that before Rix Camper's recapitalization, the total market value of the firm was $20 million (2,000,000 common shares times $10 per share). The firm's cost of common equity, K_c, and its weighted cost of capital, K_0, were each equal to 10 percent. The composite discount rate, K_0, is used to arrive at the market value of the firm's securities. After the recapitalization, we have for Rix Camper

Expected level of net operating income Capitalized at K_0 = 10 percent	$ 2,000,000
= Market value of debt and equity	$20,000,000
− Market value of the new debt	8,000,000
= Market value of the common shares	$12,000,000

With this valuation format, what is the market price of each common share? Since we know that 1,200,000 common shares are outstanding after the capital structure change, the market price per share is $10 ($12,000,000/1,200,000). This is exactly the market value per share, P_0, that existed before the change.

Now, if the firm is using some debt that has an explicit cost of 6 percent, K_d, and the weighted (composite) cost of capital, K_0, is still 10 percent, it stands to reason that the cost of common equity, K_c, has risen above its previous level of 10 percent. What will the cost of common equity be in this situation? As we did previously, we can take Equation (9-3) and restate it in terms of K_c, the cost of common equity. After the recapitalization, the cost of common equity for Rix Camper is shown to rise to 12.67 percent:

$$K_c = \frac{D_t}{P_0} = \frac{\$1.267}{\$10} = 12.67\%$$

The cost of common equity for Rix Camper is 26.7 percent higher than it was before the capital structure shift. Notice in Table 9-2 that this is exactly equal to the percentage increase in earnings and dividends per share that accompanies the same capital structure adjustment. This highlights a fundamental relationship that is an integral part of the independence hypothesis. It concerns the perceived behaviour in the firm's cost of common equity as expected dividends (earnings) increase relative to a financing mix change:

$$\text{percentage change in } K_c = \text{percentage change in } D_t$$

In this framework the use of a greater degree of financial leverage may result in greater earnings and dividends, but the firm's cost of common equity will rise at precisely the same rate as the earnings and dividends do. Thus, the inevitable tradeoff between the higher expected return in dividends and earnings (D_t and E_t) and increased risk that accompanies the use of debt financing manifests itself in a linear relationship between the cost of common equity (K_c) and financial leverage use. This view of the relationship between the firm's cost of funds and its financing mix is shown graphically in Figure 9-1. Figure 9-2 relates the firm's share price to its financing mix under the same set of assumptions.

In Figure 9-1 the firm's overall cost of capital, K_0, is shown to be unaffected by an increased use of financial leverage.[5] If more debt is used in the capital structure, the cost of common equity will rise at the same rate that additional earnings are generated. This will keep the weighted cost of capital to the corporation unchanged. Figure 9-2 shows that since the cost of capital will not change with the leverage use, neither will the firm's share price.

FIGURE 9-1
Capital Costs and Financial Leverage: No Taxes—The Independence Hypothesis (NOI Theory)

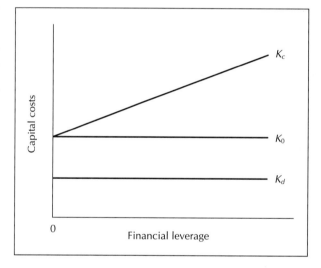

FIGURE 9-2
Share Price and Financial Leverage: No Taxes—The Independence Hypothesis (NOI Theory)

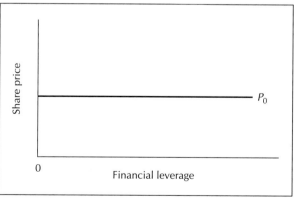

[5]The firm's overall cost of capital is unaffected by the increase in financial leverage:
$$K_0 = (.4)(6.00\%) + (.6)(12.67\%) = 10\%.$$

Debt financing, then, has two costs—its **explicit cost of capital**, K_d, calculated according to the formats outlined in Chapter 5, and an implicit cost. The **implicit cost of debt** is the change in the cost of common equity brought on by using financial leverage (additional debt). The real cost of debt is the sum of these explicit and implicit costs. In general, the real cost of any source of capital is its explicit cost, plus the change that it induces in the cost of any other source of funds.

Followers of the independence hypothesis argue that the use of financial leverage brings a change in the cost of common equity large enough to offset the benefits of higher dividends to investors. Debt financing is not as cheap as it first appears to be. This will keep the weighted cost of funds constant. The implication for management is that one capital structure is as good as any other; financial officers should not waste time searching for an optimal capital structure. One capital structure, after all, is as beneficial as any other, because all result in the same weighted cost of capital.

Extreme Position 2: The Dependence Hypothesis (NI Theory)

The dependence hypothesis is at the opposite pole from the independence hypothesis. It suggests that both the weighted cost of capital, K_0, and common share price, P_0, are affected by the firm's use of financial leverage. No matter how modest or excessive the firm's use of debt financing, both its cost of debt capital, K_d, and cost of equity capital, K_c, will not be affected by capital structure management. Since the cost of debt is less than the cost of equity, greater financial leverage will lower the firm's weighted cost of capital indefinitely. Greater use of debt financing will thereby have a favourable effect on the company's common-share price. By returning to the Rix Camper situation, we can illustrate this point of view.

The same capital structure shift is being evaluated. That is, management will market $8 million of new debt at a 6 percent interest rate and use the proceeds to purchase its own common shares. Under this approach the market is assumed to capitalize (discount) the expected earnings available to the common shareholders in order to arrive at the aggregate market value of the common shares. The market value of the firm's common equity is not a residual of the valuation process. After the recapitalization, the firm's cost of common equity, K_c, will still be equal to 10 percent. Thus, a 10 percent cost of common equity is applied in the following format:

	Expected level of net operating income	$ 2,000,000
−	Interest expense	480,000
=	Earnings available to common shareholders capitalized at K_C = 10 percent	$ 1,520,000
=	Market value of the common shares	$15,200,000
+	Market value of the new debt	8,000,000
=	Market value of debt and equity	$23,200,000

When we assume that the firm's capital structure consists only of debt and common equity, earnings available to the common shareholders is synonymous with net income. In the valuation process outlined above, it is net income that is actually capitalized to arrive at the market value of the common equity. Because of this, the dependence hypothesis is also called the **net income approach to valuation**.

Notice that the total market value of the firm's securities has risen to $23,200,000 from the $20 million level that existed before the firm moved from the unlevered to the levered capital structure.[6] The per-share value of the common shares is also shown to rise under this valuation format. With 1,200,000 shares outstanding, the market price per share is $12.67 ($15,200,000/1,200,000).

This increase in the share price to $12.67 represents a 26.7 percent rise over the previous level of $10 per share. This is exactly equal to the percentage change in earnings per share and dividends per share calculated in Table 9-1. This permits us to characterize the dependence hypothesis in a very succinct fashion:

percentage change in K_c = 0 percent < percentage change in D_t
(over all degrees of leverage)

percentage change in P_0 = percentage change in D_t

The dependence hypothesis suggests that the explicit and implicit costs of debt are one and the same. The use of more debt does not change the firm's cost of common equity.[7] Using more debt, which is explicitly cheaper than common equity, will lower the firm's weighted cost of capital, K_0. If you take the market value of Rix Camper's common share according to the net income theory of $15,200,000 and express it as a percent of the total market value of the firm's securities, you get a market value weight of .655 ($15,200,000/$23,200,000). In a similar fashion, the market value weight of Rix Camper's debt is found to be .345 ($8,000,000/$23,200,000). After the capital structure adjustment, the firm's weighted cost of capital becomes

$$K_0 = (.345)(6.00\%) + (.655)(10.00\%) = 8.62\%$$

So, changing the financing mix from all equity to a structure including both debt and equity lowered the weighted cost of capital from 10 percent to 8.62 percent. The ingredients of the dependence hypothesis are illustrated in Figures 9-3 and 9-4.

The implication for management from Figures 9-3 and 9-4 is that the firm's weighted cost of capital, K_0, will decline as the debt-to-equity ratio increases. This also implies that the company's common-share price will rise with increased leverage use. Since the cost of capital decreases continuously with leverage, the firm should use as much leverage as is possible. Next, we will move toward reality in the analytical setting of our capital structure discussion. This is accomplished by relaxing some of the major assumptions that surrounded the independence and dependence hypotheses.

A Moderate Position: Corporate Income Is Taxed and Firms May Fail

In general, an analysis of extreme positions may be useful in that you are forced to sharpen your thinking not only about the poles, but also the situations that span the poles. In microeconomics the study of perfect competi-

---

[6]Although the aggregate equity value decreases by only $4.8 million ($20.0 – $15.2); at the same time, the value of the debt claim has increased from zero to $8 million. As a result, the value of the firm increases from $20 million to $23.2 million.

[7]The NI model assumes that the choice to use debt does not affect the cost of common equity. In practice this may be true over certain ranges of leverage use. Note that some firms do increase their debt usage and maintain a given bond rating.

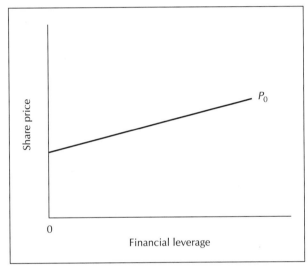

tion and monopoly provides a better understanding of the business activity
that occurs in the wide area between these two model markets. In a similar
fashion, the study of the independence and dependence hypotheses of the
importance of capital structure helps us formulate a more informed view of
the possible situations between those polar positions.

We turn now to a description of the cost of capital–capital-structure
relationship that has rather wide appeal to both business practitioners and
academics. This moderate view (1) admits to the fact that interest expense is
tax deductible and (2) acknowledges that the probability of the firm's suffering bankruptcy costs are directly related to the company's use of financial
leverage.

Tax Deductibility of Interest Expense

This portion of the analysis recognizes that corporate income is subject to
taxation. Furthermore, we assume that interest expense is tax deductible for
purposes of computing the firm's tax bill. In this environment the use of debt
financing should result in a higher total market value for the firm's outstanding securities. We will see why subsequently.

We continue with our Rix Camper Manufacturing Company example. In the case of no taxes and all equity financing, the value of the firm to the shareholders was determined as follows:

$$V_U = \frac{NOI}{K_c^U} \tag{9-3}$$

$$= \frac{\$2,000,000}{0.10}$$

$$= \$20 \text{ million}$$

Furthermore, the total cash distribution to the shareholders is $2 million in cash dividends. In the second case of no taxes with debt and equity financing, the value of the levered firm is determined by the following equation:

$$V_L = S_L + B_0 \tag{9-4}$$

$$= \frac{(NOI - I)}{K_c^L} + B_0$$

$$= \frac{(\$2,000,000 - \$480,000)}{0.1267} + \$8,000,000$$

$$= \$20,000,000$$

Again, the sum of cash dividends paid to common shareholders and the interest expense paid to bondholders is $2 million. Thus, both the value of the firm and the sum of the cash flows paid to contributors of debt and equity capital are not affected by the financing mix of the firm.

When corporate income is taxed by Revenue Canada, however, the sum of the cash flows made to all contributors of financial capital is affected by the firm's financing mix. Table 9-3 illustrates this point.

If Rix Camper makes the capital-structure adjustment identified in the preceding sections of this chapter, the total payments to equity and debt holders will be $240,000 greater than under the all-common-equity capitalization. Where does this $240,000 come from? The government's take, through taxes collected, is lower by that amount. This difference, which flows to the Rix Camper security holders, is called the **tax shield** on interest. In general, it may be calculated as follows:

$$PV(\text{interest tax shields}) = \frac{(R_d)(M)(T)}{K_d} \tag{9-5}$$

where R_d = the interest rate paid on the debt

M = the principal amount of the debt

TABLE 9-3 Rix Camper Company Cash Flows to All Investors— The Case of Taxes		Unlevered Capital Structure	Levered Capital Structure
	Expected level of net operating income	$2,000,000	$2,000,000
	Less: Interest expense	0	480,000
	Earnings before taxes	$2,000,000	$1,520,000
	Less: Taxes at 50%	1,000,000	760,000
	Earnings available to common shareholders	$1,000,000	$ 760,000
	Expected payments to *all* security holders	$1,000,000	$1,240,000

$$T = \text{the firm's combined tax rate}$$

$$K_d = \text{the required yield on the firm's debt}$$

If we assume that both the interest rate paid on the firm's debt (R_d) and the required yield on the firm's debt (K_d) are equal, Equation (9-5) is simplified as follows:

$$PV(\text{interest tax shields}) = (M)(T) \qquad (9\text{-}6)$$

The moderate position on the importance of capital structure presumes that the tax shield must have value in the marketplace. Accordingly, this tax benefit will increase the total market value of the firm through the following equation:

$$V_L = V_U + PV(\text{interest tax shields}) \qquad (9\text{-}7)$$

$$= V_U + (M)(T)$$

$$= \frac{(NOI)(1-T)}{K_c^U} + (M)(T)$$

Financial leverage does affect firm value. Because the cost of capital is just the other side of the valuation coin, financial leverage also affects the firm's weighted cost of capital. Can the firm increase firm value indefinitely and lower its cost of capital continuously by using more and more financial leverage? Common sense would tell us "No!" So would most financial managers and academicians. The acknowledgment of bankruptcy costs provides one possible rationale.

Likelihood of Firm Failure

The probability that the firm will be unable to meet the financial obligations identified in its debt contracts increases as more debt is employed. The highest costs would be incurred if the firm actually went into bankruptcy proceedings. Here, assets would be liquidated. If we admit that these assets might sell for something less than their perceived market values, equity investors and debt holders could both suffer losses. Other problems accompany bankruptcy proceedings. Lawyers and accountants have to be hired and paid. Managers must spend time preparing lengthy reports for those involved in the legal action.

Milder forms of financial distress also have their costs. As their firm's financial condition weakens, creditors may take action to restrict normal business activity. Suppliers may not deliver materials on credit. Profitable capital investments may have to be forgone, and dividend payments may even be interrupted. At some point the expected cost of default will be large enough to outweigh the tax shield advantage of debt financing.[8] The firm will turn to other sources of financing, mainly common equity. At this point the real cost of debt is thought to be higher than the real cost of common equity.

Moderate View: Saucer-Shaped Cost of Capital Curve

This moderate view of the relationship between financing mix and the firm's cost of capital is depicted in Figure 9-5. The result is a saucer-shaped (or

---

[8]Even this argument that the tradeoff between bankruptcy costs and the tax shield benefit of debt financing can lead to an optimal structure has its detractors. See Robert A. Haugen and Lemma W. Senbet, "The Insignificance of Bankruptcy Costs to the Theory of Optimal Capital Structure," *Journal of Finance*, 33 (May 1978), pp. 383–393.

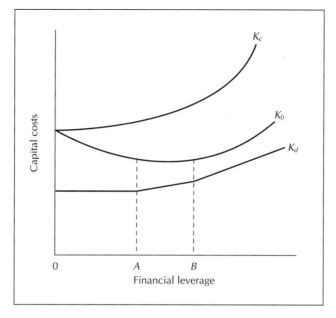

U-shaped) weighted cost of capital curve, K_0.[9] The firm's average cost of equity, K_c, is seen to rise over all positive degrees of financial leverage use. For a while the firm can borrow funds at a relatively low cost of debt, K_d. Even though the cost of equity is rising, it does not rise at a fast enough rate to offset the use of the less expensive debt financing. Thus, between points 0 and A on the financial-leverage axis, the weighted cost of capital declines and the share price increases.

Eventually, the threat of financial distress causes the cost of debt to increase. In Figure 9-5 this increase in the cost of debt shows up in the average cost of debt curve, K_d, at point A. Between points A and B, mixing debt and equity funds produces an average cost of capital that is (relatively) flat. The firm's **optimal range of financial leverage** lies between points A and B. All capital structures between these two points are optimal because they produce the lowest weighted cost of capital. As we said in the introduction to this chapter, finding this optimal range of financing mixes is the objective of capital structure management.

Point B signifies the firm's debt capacity. **Debt capacity** is the maximum proportion of debt the firm can include in its capital structure and still maintain its lowest cost of capital. Beyond point B, additional fixed-charge capital can be attracted only at very costly interest rates. At the same time, this excessive use of financial leverage would cause the firm's cost of equity to rise at a faster rate than previously. The weighted cost of capital would then rise quite rapidly, and the firm's share price would decline.

This version of the moderate view as it relates to the firm's share price is characterized below. The notation is the same as that found in our discussion of the independence and dependence hypotheses.

[9]In reality these cost curves, just as valuations, are unique to each firm. This makes "the" optimal capital structure difficult to estimate. As a result, we settle for identifying an optimal range of leverage use.

1. Between points 0 and A:
   $0 <$ percentage change in $P_0 <$ percentage change in D_t

2. Between points A and B:
   percentage change in $P_0 = 0$

3. Beyond point B:
   percentage change in $P_0 < 0$

Perspective in Finance

Given the same task or assignment, it is quite likely that you will do it better for yourself than for someone else. If you are paid well enough, you might do the job about as effectively for that other person. Once you receive compensation, your work will be evaluated by someone. This process of evaluation is called "monitoring" within most discussions on agency costs.

This describes the heart of what is called the "agency problem." The large size of North American firms has caused the owners and managers of these firms to become (for the most part) separate groups of individuals. An inherent conflict exists, therefore, between managers and shareholders for whom managers act as agents in carrying out their objectives (for example, corporate goals). The following discussion relates the agency problem to the financial decision-making process of the firm.

Firm Value and Agency Costs

In Chapter 1 of this text we mentioned "the agency problem." Recall that the agency problem gives rise to agency costs, which tend to occur in business organizations because ownership and management control are often separate. Thus, the firm's managers can be properly thought of as agents for the firm's shareholders.[10] To ensure that agent-managers act in the shareholders' best interests requires that they have (1) proper incentives to do so and (2) that their decisions are monitored. The incentives usually take the form of executive compensation plans and managerial "perks." For example, perks may take the form of a bloated support staff, country club memberships, luxurious corporate planes, or other amenities of a similar nature. Monitoring requires that certain costs be borne by the shareholders, such as (1) bonding the managers, (2) auditing financial statements, (3) structuring the organization in unique ways that limit useful managerial decisions, and (4) reviewing the costs and benefits of managerial perks. This list is indicative, not exhaustive. The main point is that monitoring costs are ultimately covered by the owners of the company—its common shareholders.

---

[10]Economists have studied the problems associated with control of the corporation for decades. An early, classic work on this topic was A. A. Berle, Jr., and G. C. Means, *The Modern Corporation and Private Property*, New York: Macmillan, 1932. The recent emphasis in corporate finance and financial economics stems from the important contribution of Michael C. Jensen and William H. Meckling, "Theory of the Firm: Managerial Behavior, Agency Costs and Ownership Structure," *Journal of Financial Economics*, 3 (October 1976), pp. 305–360. Professors Jensen and Smith have analyzed the bondholder-shareholder conflict in a very clear style. See Michael C. Jensen and Clifford W. Smith, Jr., "Stockholder, Manager, and Creditor Interests: Applications of Agency Theory," in *Recent Advances in Corporate Finance*, eds. Edward I. Altman and Marti G. Subrahmanyam, Homewood, IL: Richard D. Irwin, 1985, pp. 93–131. An entire volume dealing with agency problems, including those of capital-structure management, is Amir Barnea, Robert A. Haugen, and Lemma W. Senbet, *Agency Problems and Financial Contracting*, Englewood Cliffs, NJ: Prentice-Hall, 1985.

BASIC FINANCIAL MANAGEMENT IN PRACTICE

Financial Managers and Theory

Earlier in this chapter we discussed a moderate view of capital structure theory. The saucer-shaped cost of capital curve implied by this theory (Figure 9-5) predicts that managers will add debt to the firm's current capital structure if leverage is below the firm's optimal level of debt. Conversely, managers will add equity if leverage is above the firm's optimal level of debt. In either case, both of these financing activities lower the cost of capital of the firm and increase shareholder's wealth.

A recent survey of chief financial officers of the top (largest) non-financial, non-regulated U.S. firms addressed these predicted activities. Of the 800 firms surveyed, 117 responded for a response rate of 14.6 percent. These decision makers were asked how their firms would respond if confronted with certain specific financing activities.

It should be noted that the moderate view does not distinguish between internal equity (retained earnings and depreciation) and external equity (the sale of common shares). The questions posed to the financial managers, however, do make the distinction. Based on our financial asset valuation models, common equity is generally considered the most expensive source of funds, exceeding the costs of both debt and preferred shares. The cost of external equity exceeds internal equity by the addition of flotation costs (Recall our discussion in Chapter 5 on these relationships).

Addressing the downward sloping portion of the cost of capital curve, managers were asked what their financing choice would be if (1) the firm has internal funds sufficient for investment requirements (capital budgeting needs), but (2) the debt ratio is below the level preferred by the firm. The moderate theory predicts that managers will add debt to the firm's capital structure in this situation. However, Table 9-4 indicates that 81 percent of the respondents said they would use internal equity to finance their investments. Only 17 percent suggested that

they would use long-term debt, and 11 percent selected short-term debt. In this situation, most managers indicated they would choose to use the most expensive internal equity rather than the (seemingly) less expensive debt for investments.

Similarly, when internal funds are sufficient for new investment and the debt level exceeds the firm's optimum range of debt, managers again chose to use internal equity in 81 percent of the responses. Seventeen percent would issue new equity if market conditions were favourable. Since the debt level is currently excessive, the moderate theory would predict that external equity would be added to minimize the cost of capital. Instead, most firms preferred to fund investments with their internal funds. This is a prevalent tendency in corporate North America.

Responses to the preceding questions imply that, if managers follow the financing activity prescribed by the moderate view, it is only after the internal funds have been exhausted.[11] Since these internal funds are relatively expensive (compared with debt), their use as the initial financing option indicates that either: (1) managers do not view their financing goal to be the minimization of the firm's cost of capital, or (2) the explicit and implicit costs of new security issues are understated. If this is actually the case, internal funds may be the least expensive sources of funds from the perspective of financial managers.[12]

The chief financial officers were also asked what their financing decision would be under these conditions: (1) the firm requires external funds, (2) financial debt exceeds the desired level, and (3) equity markets are underpricing the firm's shares. Table 9-4 summarizes the responses to this question.

In this difficult situation, Table 9-4 shows that 68 percent of the managers indicated that they

Continued on page 419

---

[11]These observations are consistent with the findings of Donaldson which indicated that a pecking order existed for financial policy: (1) use internal funds first, until these have been exhausted; (2) to the extent that external funds must be relied upon, issue debt first, the less risky the better; (3) issue common shares only as a last resort, after all debt capacity has been exhausted. These rules for financial policy form the basis of the pecking order hypothesis which offers an alternative view of capital-structure theory.

[12]The suggestion that internal funds may be the least expensive source of funds to financial managers would also be an example of the agency problem that exists between shareholders/owners and managers of the firm.

Continued from page 418

would reduce their investment plans. In effect, managers would reduce their capital budgets. The primary reasons for this type of investment restriction were: (1) maximize shareholder's wealth, (2) control the firm's exposure to risk.

The next favoured choice (28 percent) was the use of short-term debt with a possible reduction of investment. This suggests that managers attempt to wait out difficult market conditions by adopting short-term solutions. The timing of security issues with favourable market conditions is a major objective of financial managers which is entirely consistent with the optimal capital structure range defined under the moderate theory (Figure 9-5).

Table 9-4 indicates that only four percent of the respondents indicated that they would issue equity despite the underpricing of the firm's shares. Thirteen percent of the firms indicated that they would attempt to correct the adverse pricing by providing the market with adequate information before attempting to issue equity. Another 13 percent of the respondents indicated that they would add long-term debt which moved the debt level beyond the optimal range.

A small percentage (4 percent) of the executives stated that they would obtain the needed funds by reducing the cash dividend payout. To managers, the shareholders' cash dividend payment is quite important. Firms prefer to forgo profitable projects rather than to reallocate the shareholders' expected cash dividends to investment. Dividend policies are extensively discussed in Chapter 10.

You can see that our ability as analysts to predict financing choices, as opposed to prescribing them, is far from perfect. In many instances managers appear to react as suggested by popular capital structure theories. In other instances, though, managers either are rejecting some aspects of the theories or the theories need more work. Understanding these aberrations is useful to the analyst.

A thorough grounding in both the theory of financing decisions and in the tools of capital structure management will assist you in making sound choices and ask some very perceptive questions when faced with a decision-making situation.

Source: Derived from David F. Scott, Jr., and Nancy Jay, "Financial Managers and Capital Structure Theories," Working Paper 9203, Orlando, FL: Dr. Phillips Institute for the Study of American Business Activity, University of Central Florida, March 1992.

TABLE 9-4. Managers and Theory: Some Responses

Question

Your firm requires external funds to finance the next period's capital investments. The use of financial leverage exceeds the level preferred by the firm. Equities markets are underpricing your securities. Would your firm:

Choices	Responses
Reduce your investment plans?	68%
Obtain short-term debt?	28%
Attempt to provide the market with adequate information to correctly price your securities before issuing equity?	13%
Issue long-term debt?	13%
Issue equity anyway	4%
Reduce your dividend payout?	4%

Capital structure management also gives rise to agency costs. Agency problems stem from conflicts of interest, and capital structure management encompasses a natural conflict between shareholders and bondholders. Acting in the shareholders' best interests might cause management to invest in extremely risky projects. Existing investors in the firm's bonds could logically take a dim view of such an investment policy. A change in the risk structure of the firm's assets would change the business risk exposure of the firm. This could lead to a downward revision of the bond rating the firm currently enjoys. A lowered bond rating in turn would lower the current market value of the firm's bonds. Clearly, bondholders would be unhappy with this result.

To reduce this conflict of interest, the creditors (bond investors) and shareholders may agree to include several protective covenants in the bond contract. These bond covenants are discussed in more detail in Chapter 19, but essentially they may be thought of as restrictions on managerial decision

FIGURE 9-6
Agency Costs of Debt: The
Tradeoffs

No Protective Bond Covenants	Many Protective Bond Covenants
High interest rates	Low interest rates
Low monitoring costs	High monitoring costs
No lost operating efficiencies	Many lost operating efficiencies

making. Typical covenants restrict payment of cash dividends on common shares, limit the acquisition or sale of assets, or limit further debt financing. To make sure that the protective covenants are complied with by management means that monitoring costs are incurred. Like all monitoring costs, they are borne by common shareholders. Further, like many costs, they involve the analysis of an important tradeoff.

Figure 9-6 displays some of the tradeoffs involved with the use of protective bond covenants. Note (in the left panel of Figure 9-6) that the firm might be able to sell bonds that carry no protective covenants only by incurring very high interest rates. With no protective covenants, there are no associated monitoring costs. Also, there are no lost operating efficiencies, such as being able to move quickly to acquire a particular company in the acquisitions market. Conversely, the willingness to submit to several covenants could reduce the explicit cost of the debt contract, but would involve incurring significant monitoring costs and losing some operating efficiencies (which also translates into higher costs). When the debt issue is first sold, then, a tradeoff will be arrived at between incurring monitoring costs, losing operating efficiencies, and enjoying a lower explicit interest cost.

Next, we have to consider the presence of monitoring costs at low levels of leverage and at higher levels of leverage. When the firm operates at a low debt-to-equity ratio, there is little need for creditors to insist on a long list of bond covenants. The financial risk is just not there to require that type of activity. The firm will likewise benefit from low explicit interest rates when leverage is low. When the debt-to-equity ratio is high, however, it is logical for creditors to demand a great deal of monitoring. This increase in agency costs will raise the implicit cost (the true total cost) of debt financing. It seems logical, then, to suggest that monitoring costs will rise as the firm's use of financial leverage increases. Just as the likelihood of firm failure (financial distress) raises a company's overall cost of capital (K_0), so do agency costs. On the other side of the coin, this means that total firm value (the total market value of the firm's securities) will be lower owing to the presence of agency costs. Taken together, the presence of agency costs and the costs associated with financial distress argue in favour of the concept of an optimal capital structure for the individual firm.

This discussion can be summarized by introducing Equation (9-5) for the market value of the levered firm.

$$\begin{array}{ccccc} \text{market value of} & = & \text{market value of} & + & \text{present value} \\ \text{levered firm} & & \text{unlevered firm} & & \text{of tax shields} \end{array}$$

$$\qquad\qquad\qquad\qquad\qquad\qquad\qquad\qquad (9\text{-}8)$$

$$- \left(\begin{array}{ccc} \text{present value} & & \text{present value} \\ \text{of financial} & + & \text{of agency} \\ \text{distress costs} & & \text{costs} \end{array} \right)$$

The relationship expressed in Equation (9-8) is presented graphically in Figure 9-7. There we see that the tax shield effect is dominant until point *A* is reached. After point *A*, the rising costs of the likelihood of firm failure (financial distress) and agency costs cause the market value of the levered firm to decline.[13] The objective for the financial manager here is to find point *B* by using all of his or her analytical skill; this must also include a good dose of seasoned judgment. At point *B* the actual market value of the levered firm is maximized, and its weighted cost of capital (K_0) is at a minimum. The implementation problem is that the precise costs of financial distress and monitoring can only be estimated by subjective means; a definite mathematical solution is not available. Thus, planning the firm's financing mix always requires good decision-making by management.

Agency Costs, Free Cash Flow, and Capital Structure

In 1986, Professor Michael C. Jensen further extended the concept of agency costs into the area of capital structure management. The contribution revolves around a concept that Jensen labels "free cash flow."

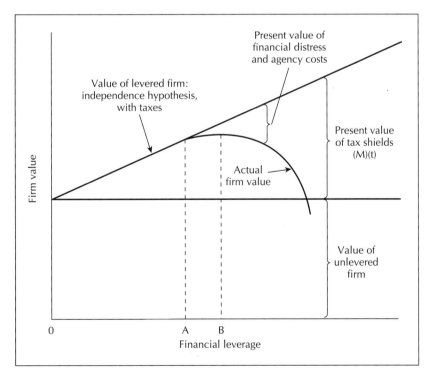

FIGURE 9-7
Firm Value Considering Taxes, Agency Costs, and Financial Distress Costs

[13]Note that point *A* in Figure 9-7 could represent the point where a B++ bond rate firm may lie. Since the firm has used its perceived optimal debt capacity, any further leverage use will be severely penalized.

Professor Jensen defines free cash flow as follows:[14]

> Free cash flow is cash flow in excess of that required to fund all projects that have positive net present values when discounted at the relevant cost of capital.

Jensen indicated that substantial free cash flow can lead to misbehaviour by managers and poor decisions that are not in the best interests of the firm's common shareholders. In other words, managers have an incentive to hold on to the free cash flow and have "fun" with it, rather than "disgorging" it, say, in the form of higher cash dividend payments.

But, all is not lost. This leads to what Jensen calls his "control hypothesis" for debt creation. This means that by levering up, the firm's shareholders will enjoy increased control over their management team. For example, if the firm issues new debt and uses the proceeds to retire outstanding common shares, then management is obligated to pay out cash to service the debt—this simultaneously reduces the amount of free cash flow available to management with which to have fun.

We can also refer to this motive for financial leverage use as the "threat hypothesis." Management works under the threat of financial failure—therefore, according to the "free cash flow theory of capital structure," it works more efficiently. This is supposed to reduce the agency costs of free cash flow—which will in turn be recognized by the marketplace in the form of greater returns on the common shares.

Note that the free cash flow theory of capital structure does not give a theoretical solution to the question of just how much financial leverage is enough. Nor does it suggest how much leverage is too much. It is a way of thinking about why shareholders and their boards of directors might use more debt to control management behaviour and decisions. The basic decision tools of capital-structure management still have to be utilized. They will be presented later in this chapter.

Professor Ben Bernanke indicates that not all analysts totally buy into the control hypothesis for debt creation (See "Basic Financial Management in Practice"). Bernanke reviews Jensen's free cash flow theory and also comments on the buildup in corporate leverage that has occurred in recent years.

Managerial Implications

Where does our examination of capital structure theory leave us? The upshot is that the determination of the firm's financing mix is centrally important to the financial manager. The firm's shareholders are affected by capital structure decisions.

At the very least, and before bankruptcy costs and agency costs become detrimental, the tax shield effect will cause the shares of a levered firm to sell at a higher price than they would if the company had avoided debt financing. Owing to both the risk of failure and agency costs that accompany the excessive use of leverage, the financial manager must exercise caution in the use of fixed-charge capital. This problem of searching for the optimal range of use of financial leverage is our next task.[15]

---

[14]Michael C. Jensen, "Agency Costs of Free Cash Flow, Corporate Finance, and Takeovers," *American Economic Review*, 76 (May 1986), pp. 323–329.

[15]The relationship between capital structure and enterprise valuation by the marketplace continues to stimulate considerable research output. The complexity of the topic is reviewed in Stewart C. Myers, "The Capital Structure Puzzle," *Journal of Finance*, 39 (July 1984), pp. 575–592. Ten useful papers are contained in *Corporate Capital Structures in the United States*, ed. Benjamin M. Friedman, Chicago: National Bureau of Economic Research and The University of Chicago Press, 1985.

BASIC FINANCIAL MANAGEMENT IN PRACTICE

Ben Bernanke on the Free Cash Flow Theory of Capital Structure and the Buildup in Corporate Debt

Introduction

The idea is that the financial structure of firms influences the incentives of "insiders" (managers, directors, and large shareholders with some operational interest in the business) and that, in particular, high levels of debt may increase the willingness of insiders to work hard and make profit-maximizing decisions. This incentive-based approach makes a valuable contribution to our understanding of a firm's capital structure. But while this theory might explain why firms like to use debt in general, does it explain why the use of debt has increased so much in recent years?

Michael Jensen, a founder and leading proponent of the incentive-based approach to capital structure, argues that it can. Jensen focuses on a recent worsening of what he calls the "free cash flow" problem. Free cash flow is defined as the portion of a corporation's cash flow that it is unable to invest profitably within the firm. Companies in industries that are profitable but no longer have much potential for expansion—the U.S. oil industry, for example—have a lot of free cash flow.

Why is free cash flow a problem? Jensen argues that managers are often tempted to use free cash flow to expand the size of the company, even if the expansion is not profitable. This is because managers feel that their power and job satisfaction are enhanced by a growing company; so given that most managers' compensation is at best weakly tied to the firm's profitability, Jensen argues that managers will find it personally worthwhile to expand even into money-losing operations. In principle, the board of directors and shareholders should be able to block these unprofitable investments; however, in practice, the fact that the management typically has far more information about potential investments than do outside directors and shareholders makes it difficult to second-guess the managers' recommendations.

How More Leverage Can Help

The company manager with lots of free cash flow may attempt to use that cash to increase his power and perquisites, at the expense of the shareholders. Jensen argues that the solution to the free-cash-flow problem is more leverage. For example, suppose that management uses the free cash flow of the company, plus the proceeds of new debt issues, to repur-

chase stock from the outside shareholders—that is, to do a management buyout. This helps solve the free-cash-flow problem in several ways. The personal returns of the managers are now much more closely tied to the profits of the firm, which gives them incentives to be more efficient. Second, the re-leveraging process removes the existing free cash from the firm, so that any future investment projects will have to be financed externally; thus, future projects will have to meet the market test of being acceptable to outside bankers or bond purchasers. Finally, the high interest payments implied by re-leveraging impose a permanent discipline on the managers; in order to meet these payments, they will have to ruthlessly cut money-losing operations, avoid questionable investments, and take other efficiency-promoting actions.

According to Jensen, a substantial increase in free-cash-flow problems—resulting from deregulation, the maturing of some large industries, and other factors—is a major source of the recent debt expansion. Jensen also points to a number of institutional factors that have promoted increased leverage. These include relaxed restrictions on mergers, which have lowered the barriers to corporate takeovers created by the antitrust laws, and increased financial sophistication, such as the greatly expanded operations of takeover specialists like Drexel Burnham Lambert Inc. and the development of the market for "junk bonds." Jensen's diagnosis is not controversial: it's quite plausible that these factors, plus changing norms about what constitutes an "acceptable" level of debt, explain at least part of the trend toward increased corporate debt. One important piece of evidence in favour of this explanation is that net equity issues have been substantially negative since 1983. This suggests that much of the proceeds of the new debt issues is being used to repurchase outstanding shares. This is what we would expect if corporations are attempting to re-leverage their existing assets, rather than using debt to expand their asset holdings. However, the implied conclusion—that the debt buildup is beneficial overall to the economy—is considerably more controversial.

Continued on page 424

Continued from page 423

Criticisms of the Incentive-Based Rationale for Increased Debt

Jensen and other advocates of the incentive-based approach to capital structure have made a cogent theoretical case for the beneficial effects of debt finance, and many architects of large-scale restructurings have given improved incentives and the promise of greater efficiency as a large part of the rationale for increased leverage. The idea that leverage is beneficial has certainly been embraced by the stock market: even unsubstantiated rumours of a potential leveraged buy-out (LBO) have been sufficient to send the stock price of the targeted company soaring, often by 40 percent or more. At a minimum, this indicates that stock market participants believe that higher leverage increases profitability. Proponents of restructuring interpret this as evidence that debt is good for the economy.

There are, however, criticisms of this conclusion. First, the fact that the stock market's expectations of company profitability rise when there is a buy-out is not proof that profits will rise in actuality. It is still too soon to judge whether the increased leverage of the 1980s will lead to a sustained increase in profitability. One might think of looking to historical data for an answer to this question. But buy-outs in the 1960s and 1970s were somewhat different in character from more recent restructurings, and, in any case, the profitability evidence on the earlier episodes is mixed.

Even if the higher profits expected by the stock market do materialize, there is contention over where they are likely to come from. The incentive-based theory of capital structure says they will come from improved efficiency. But some opponents have argued that the higher profits will primarily reflect transfers to the shareholders from other claimants on the corporation—its employees, customers, suppliers, bondholders, and the government. Customers may be hurt if takeovers are associated with increased monopolization of markets. Bondholders have been big losers in some buyouts, as higher leverage has increased bankruptcy risk and thus reduced the value of outstanding bonds. The government may have lost tax revenue, as companies, by increasing leverage, have increased their interest deductions (although there are offsetting effects here, such as the taxes paid by bought-out shareholders on their capital gains). The perception that much of the profits associated with re-leveraging and buyouts comes from "squeezing" existing beneficiaries of the corporation explains much of the recent political agitation to limit these activities.

The debt buildup can also be criticized from the perspective of incentive-based theories themselves. Two points are worth noting: first, the principal problem that higher leverage is supposed to address is the relatively weak connection between firms' profits and managers' personal returns, which reduces managers' incentives to take profit-maximizing actions. But if this is truly the problem, it could be addressed more directly—without subjecting the company to serious bankruptcy risk—simply by changing managerial compensation schemes to include more profit-based incentives.

The Downside of Debt Financing

Increased debt is not the optimal solution to all incentive problems. For example, it has been shown, as a theoretical proposition, that managers of debt-financed firms have an incentive to choose riskier projects over safe ones; this is because firms with fixed-debt obligations enjoy all of the upside potential of high-risk projects but share the downside losses with the debt holders, who are not fully repaid if bad investment outcomes cause the firm to fail.

That high leverage does not always promote efficiency can be seen when highly leveraged firms suffer losses and find themselves in financial distress. When financial problems hit, the need to meet interest payments may force management to take a very short-run perspective, leading them to cut back production and employment, cancel even potentially profitable expansion projects, and sell assets at fire-sale prices. Because the risk of bankruptcy is so great, firms in financial distress cannot make long-term agreements; they lose customers and suppliers who are afraid they cannot count on an ongoing relationship, and they must pay wage premiums to hire workers.

These efficiency losses, plus the direct costs of bankruptcy (such as legal fees), are the potential downside of high leverage.

Source: Ben Bernanke, "Is There Too Much Corporate Debt?" *Business Review*, Federal Reserve Bank of Philadelphia (September–October 1989), pp. 5–8.

BASIC FINANCIAL MANAGEMENT IN PRACTICE

Thrifty Canadian Firms Are Fighting Fit: StatCan

Canadian businesses enter the 1990s saving and investing more than almost any of their competitors in the industrialized world, a news report by Statistics Canada says.

The study suggests to some observers that the businesses may be better prepared to compete globally than often thought, despite a recent fall in profits and the high Canadian dollar.

After profits were trampled in the 1981–82 recession, firms responded by rapidly rebuilding their balance sheets and embarking on an investment boom that has raised business spending to its largest proportion of gross domestic product on record, StatCan's economists note.

Keeping Retained Earnings

Retained earnings by Canadian business as a proportion of GDP averaged 3.51% between 1982 and 1987, higher than any of the five largest industrialized economies.

"They're obviously trying to keep retained earnings at a very high level. When profits eased in 1989, they sharply cut back on dividend payments in an attempt to keep up cash flow," said Philip Cross, chief of current analysis at StatCan.

Ruth Getter, senior economist at Toronto Dominion Bank said the report confirms her own research that suggests Canadian firms are far better prepared to compete in the 1990s than they normally get credit for.

"We do not give our business people enough credit," Getter said.

"Since the recession, and certainly since free trade discussions began, [they] have been preparing and have done an excellent job of improving their productive capacity and ability to compete."

Getter said the high C$ over 1989, despite reducing profits and exports, has also enabled firms to import capital goods much more cheaply during the investment boom.

She added: "Ironically, perhaps the high C$ has enforced competitiveness. When you see your profit margins being cut, you try to cut costs and become more productive."

Cross said the rise in retained earnings as a proportion of GDP was originally a reaction to the devastation wreaked by the debt overhang of corporations going into the 1990 recession.

"There's a very determined effort that we are not going to leave ourselves in this position again."

StatCan notes that the ratio of Canadian business debt to equity fell steadily to 1.37 in 1987 from 1.45 in 1981.

Since this time the debt to equity ratio has risen slightly as firms replaced declining earnings with borrowing to maintain investment.

International Phenomenon

More recently, firms have been more driven by the need to compete globally, in which the free trade agreement is just one factor, Cross said.

"Its part of an international phenomenon. Business investment has been at extremely high levels in Europe. It's not all driven by international trade considerations," he added. "Obviously, we're having a lot of growth in the energy sector. Some of it is just driven by the need to build more capacity in Canada."

Source: Adapted from: Greg Ip, "Thrifty Canadian Firms Are Fighting Fit: StatCan." *Financial Post*, 3(29) (March 22 1990), p. 52.

Perspective in Finance

You have now developed a workable knowledge of capital-structure theory. This makes you better equipped to search for your firm's optimal capital structure. Several tools are available to help you in this search process and simultaneous-

ly help you make prudent financing choices. These tools are decision-oriented. They assist us in answering this question: "The next time we need $20 million, should we issue common shares or sell long-term bonds?"

BASIC TOOLS OF CAPITAL-STRUCTURE MANAGEMENT

Recall from Chapter 8 that the use of financial leverage has two effects upon the earnings stream flowing to the firm's common shareholders. For clarity of exposition Tables 8-7 and 8-8 are repeated here as Tables 9-5 and 9-6. Three possible financing mixes for the Pierce Grain Company are contained in Table 9-5, and an analysis of the corresponding financial leverage effects is displayed in Table 9-6.

The first financial leverage effect is the added variability in the earnings-per-share stream that accompanies the use of fixed-charge securities in the company's capital structure. By means of the degree-of-financial-leverage measure (DFL_{EBIT}) we explained how this variability can be quantified. The firm that uses more financial leverage (rather than less) will experience larger relative changes in its earnings per share (rather than smaller) following EBIT fluctuations. Assume that Pierce Grain elected financing plan C rather than plan A. Plan C is highly levered and plan A is unlevered. A 100 percent increase in EBIT from $20,000 to $40,000 would cause earnings per share to rise by 147 percent under plan C, but only 100 percent under plan A. Unfortunately, the effect would operate in the negative direction as well. A given change in EBIT is magnified by the use of financial leverage. This magnification is reflected in the variability of the firm's earnings per share.

The second financial leverage effect concerns the level of earnings per share at a given EBIT under a given capital structure. Refer to Table 9-6. At the EBIT level of $20,000, earnings per share would be $5, $5.33, and $5.67 under financing arrangements A, B, and C, respectively. Above a critical level

---

TABLE 9-5
The Pierce Grain Company
Possible Capital Structures

Plan A: 0% debt			
		Total debt	$ 0
		Common equity	200,000 [a]
Total assets	$200,000	Total liabilities and equity	$200,000
Plan B: 25% debt at 8% interest rate			
		Total debt	$ 50,000
		Common equity	150,000 [b]
Total assets	$200,000	Total liabilities and equity	$200,000
Plan C: 40% debt at 8% interest rate			
		Total debt	$ 80,000
		Common equity	120,000 [c]
Total assets	$200,000	Total liabilities and equity	$200,000

[a] 2,000 common shares outstanding
[b] 1,500 common shares outstanding
[c] 1,200 common shares outstanding

(1)	(2)	(3) = (1) – (2)	(4) = (3) × .5	(5) = (3) – (4)	(6)
				Net Income	Earnings
EBIT	Interest	EBT	Taxes	to Common	per Share
Plan A: 0% debt; $200,000 common equity; 2000 shares					
$ 0	$ 0	$ 0	$ 0	$ 0	$ 0
20,000	0	20,000	10,000	10,000	5.00 ⎤ 100%
40,000	0	40,000	20,000	20,000	10.00 ⎦
60,000	0	60,000	30,000	30,000	15.00
80,000	0	80,000	40,000	40,000	20.00
Plan B: 25% debt; 8% Interest rate; $150,000 common equity; 1500 shares					
$ 0	$4,000	$ (4,000)	$ (2,000)[a]	$ (2,000)	$ (1.33)
20,000	4,000	16,000	8,000	8,000	5.33 ⎤ 125%
40,000	4,000	36,000	18,000	18,000	12.00 ⎦
60,000	4,000	56,000	28,000	28,000	18.67
80,000	4,000	76,000	38,000	38,000	25.33
Plan C: 40% debt; 8% Interest rate; $120,000 common equity; 1200 shares					
$ 0	$6,400	$ (6,400)	$ (3,200)[a]	$ (3,200)	$ (2.67)
20,000	6,400	13,600	6,800	6,800	5.67 ⎤ 147%
40,000	6,400	33,600	16,800	16,800	14.00 ⎦
60,000	6,400	53,600	26,800	26,800	22.33
80,000	6,400	73,600	36,800	36,800	30.67

TABLE 9-6
The Pierce Grain Company Analysis of Financial Leverage at Different EBIT Levels

[a]The negative tax bill recognizes the deduction arising from the loss carryback and carryforward provision of the Income Tax Act. See Chapter 2.

of EBIT, the firm's earnings per share will be higher if greater degrees of financial leverage are employed. Conversely, below some critical level of EBIT, earnings per share will suffer at greater degrees of financial leverage. Whereas the first financial-leverage effect is quantified by the degree-of-financial-leverage measure (DFL_{EBIT}), the second is quantified by what is generally referred to as EBIT-EPS analysis. EPS refers, of course, to earnings per share. The rationale underlying this sort of analysis is simple. Earnings is one of the key variables that influences the market value of the firm's common shares. The effect of a financing decision on EPS, then, should be understood because the decision will probably affect the value of the shareholders' investment.

EBIT-EPS Analysis

EXAMPLE

Assume that plan B in Table 9-6 is the existing capital structure for the Pierce Grain Company. Furthermore, the asset structure of the firm is such that EBIT is expected to be $20,000 per year for a very long time. A capital investment is available to Pierce Grain that will cost $50,000. Acquisition of this asset is expected to raise the projected EBIT level to $30,000, permanently. The firm can raise the needed cash by (1) selling 500 common shares at $100 each or (2) selling new bonds that will net the firm $50,000 and carry an interest rate of 8.5 percent. These capital structures and corresponding EPS amounts are summarized in Table 9-7.

At the projected EBIT level of $30,000, the EPS for the common shares and debt alternatives are $6.50 and $7.25, respectively. Both are considerably

TABLE 9-7. The Pierce Grain Company Analysis of Financing Choices

Part A: Capital Structures

Existing Capital Structure		With New Common Share Financing		With New Debt Financing	
Long-term debt at 8%	$ 50,000	Long-term debt at 8%	$ 50,000	Long-term debt at 8%	$ 50,000
Common shares	150,000	Common shares	200,000	Long-term debt at 8.5%	50,000
				Common shares	150,000
Total liabilities and equity	$200,000	Total liabilities and equity	$250,000	Total liabilities and equity	$250,000
Common shares outstanding	1,500	Common shares outstanding	2,000	Common shares outstanding	1,500

Part B: Projected EPS Levels

	Existing Capital Structure	With New Common Share Financing	With New Debt Financing
EBIT	$20,000	$30,000	$30,000
Less: Interest expense	4,000	4,000	8,250
Earnings before taxes (EBIT)	$16,000	$26,000	$21,750
Less: Taxes at 50%	8,000	13,000	10,875
Net Income	$ 8,000	$13,000	$10,875
Less: Preferred dividends	0	0	0
Earnings available to common	$ 8,000	$13,000	$10,875
EPS	$ 5.33	$ 6.50	$ 7.25

above the $5.33 that would occur if the new project were rejected and the additional financial capital were not raised. Based on a criterion of selecting the financing plan that will provide the highest EPS, the bond alternative is favoured. But what if the basic business risk to which the firm is exposed causes the EBIT level to vary over a considerable range? Can we be sure that the bond alternative will always have the higher EPS associated with it? The answer, of course, is "No." When the EBIT level is subject to uncertainty, a graphic analysis of the proposed financing plans can provide useful information to the financial manager. ■

Graphic Analysis

The EBIT-EPS analysis chart allows the decision maker to visualize the impact of different financing plans on EPS over a range of EBIT levels. The relationship between EPS and EBIT is linear. All we need, therefore, to construct the chart is two points for each alternative. Part B of Table 9-7 already provides us with one of these points. The answer to the following question for each choice gives us the second point: At what EBIT level will the EPS for the plan be exactly zero? If the EBIT level just covers the plan's financing costs (on a before-tax basis), then EPS will be zero. For the share plan, an EPS of zero is associated with an EBIT of $4,000. The $4,000 is the interest expense incurred under the existing capital structure. If the bond plan is elected, the interest costs will be the present $4,000 plus $4,250 per year arising from the new debt issue. An EBIT level of $8,250, then, is necessary to provide a zero EPS with the bond plan.

The EBIT-EPS analysis chart representing the financing choices available to the Pierce Grain Company is shown as Figure 9-8. EBIT is charted on the horizontal axis and EPS on the vertical axis. The intercepts on the horizontal axis represent the before-tax equivalent financing charges related to

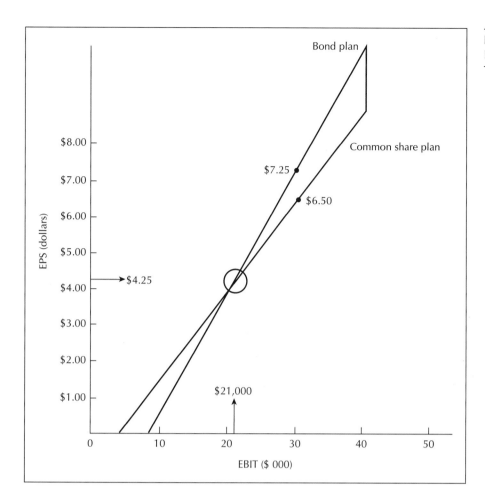

FIGURE 9-8
EBIT-EPS Analysis Chart

each plan. The straight lines for each plan tell us the EPS amounts that will occur at different EBIT amounts.

Notice that the bond-plan line has a steeper slope than the share-plan line. This ensures that the lines for each financing choice will intersect. Above the intersection point, EPS for the plan with greater leverage will exceed that for the plan with lesser leverage. The intersection point, encircled in Figure 9-8, occurs at an EBIT level of $21,000 and produces EPS of $4.25 for each plan. When EBIT is $30,000, notice that the bond plan produces EPS of $7.25 and the share plan, $6.50. Below the intersection point, EPS with the share plan will exceed that with the more highly levered bond plan. The steeper slope of the bond-plan line indicates that with greater leverage, EPS is more sensitive to EBIT changes. This same concept was discussed in Chapter 8 when we derived the degree of financial leverage measure.

Computing Indifference Points

The point of intersection in Figure 9-8 is called the EBIT-EPS indifference point. It identifies the EBIT level at which the EPS will be the same regardless of the financing plan chosen by the financial manager. This indifference point, sometimes called the breakeven point, has major implications for financial planning. At EBIT amounts in excess of the EBIT indifference level, the more heavily levered financing plan will generate a higher EPS. At EBIT amounts below the EBIT indifference level, the financing plan involving less leverage will generate a higher EPS. It is important, then, to know the EBIT indifference level.

We can find it graphically, as in Figure 9-8. At times it may be more efficient, though, to calculate the indifference point directly. This can be done by using the following equation:

$$\underset{S_s}{\underbrace{\frac{(\text{EBIT} - I)(1 - t) - P}{S_s}}_{\textit{EPS: Share Plan}}} = \underset{S_b}{\underbrace{\frac{(\text{EBIT} - I)(1 - t) - P}{S_b}}_{\textit{EPS: Bond Plan}}} \qquad (9\text{-}9)$$

where S_s and S_b are the number of common shares outstanding under the share and bond plans, respectively, I is interest expense, t is the firm's income tax rate, and P is preferred dividends paid. In the present case P is zero, because there are no preferred shares outstanding. If preferred shares are associated with one of the financing alternatives, keep in mind that the preferred dividends, P, are not tax deductible. Equation (9-9) does take this fact into consideration.

For the present example, we calculate the indifference level of EBIT as

$$\frac{(\text{EBIT} - \$4000)(1 - 0.5) - 0}{2000} = \frac{(\text{EBIT} - \$8250)(1 - 0.5) - 0}{1500}$$

When the expression above is solved for EBIT, we obtain $21,000. If EBIT turns out to be $21,000, then EPS will be $4.25 under both plans.

Uncommitted Earnings per Share and Indifference Points

The calculations that permitted us to solve for Pierce Grain's EBIT-EPS indifference point made no explicit allowance for the repayment of the bond principal. This procedure is not that unrealistic. It only presumes the debt will be perpetually outstanding. This means that when the current bond issue matures, a new bond issue will be floated. The proceeds from the newer issue would be used to pay off the maturity value of the older issue.

Many bond contracts, however, require that sinking fund payments be made to a bond trustee. A **sinking fund** is a real cash reserve that is used to provide for the orderly and early retirement of the principal amount of the bond issue. Most often the sinking fund payment is a mandatory fixed amount and is required by a clause in the bond indenture. Sinking fund payments can represent a sizable cash drain on the firm's liquid resources.[16] Moreover, sinking fund payments are a return of borrowed principal, so they are not tax-deductible to the firm.

Because of the potentially serious nature of the cash drain caused by sinking fund requirements, the financial manager might be concerned with the uncommitted earnings per share (UEPS) related to each financing plan. The calculation of UEPS recognizes that sinking fund commitments have been honoured. UEPS can be used, then, for discretionary spending—such as the payment of cash dividends to common shareholders or investment in capital facilities.

[16]As the sinking fund retires the bond issue faster, the issue is typically viewed as less risky than a non-sinking fund issue.

If we let *SF* be the sinking fund payment required in a given year, the EBIT-UEPS indifference point can be calculated as

$$\underset{\text{UEPS: Share Plan}}{\underbrace{\frac{(\text{EBIT} - I)(1 - t) - P - SF}{S_s}}} = \underset{\text{UEPS: Bond Plan}}{\underbrace{\frac{(EBIT - I)(1 - t) - P - SF}{S_b}}} \qquad (9\text{-}10)$$

If several bond issues are already outstanding, then *I* in Equations (9-9) and (9-10) for the share plan consists of the sum of their related interest payments. For the bond plan, *I* would be the sum of existing plus new interest charges. In Equation (9-10) the same logic applies to the sinking fund variable, *SF*. The indifference level of EBIT based on UEPS will always exceed that based on EPS.

A Word of Caution

Above the EBIT-EPS indifference point, a more heavily levered financial plan promises to deliver a larger EPS. Strict application of the criterion of selecting the financing plan that produces the highest EPS might have the firm issuing debt most of the time it raised external capital. Our discussion of capital-structure theory taught us the dangers of that sort of action.

The primary weakness of EBIT-EPS analysis is that it disregards the implicit costs of debt financing. The effect of the specific financing decision on the firm's cost of common equity capital is totally ignored. Investors should be concerned with both the level and variability of the firm's expected earnings stream. EBIT-EPS analysis considers only the level of the earnings stream and ignores the variability (riskiness) inherent in it. Thus, this type of analysis must be used in conjunction with other basic tools in reaching the objective of capital-structure management.

Comparative Leverage Ratios

In Chapter 11 we will explore the overall usefulness of financial ratio analysis. Leverage ratios are one of the categories of financial ratios identified in that chapter. We emphasize here that the computation of leverage ratios is one of the basic tools of capital-structure management.

Two types of leverage ratios must be computed when a financing decision faces the firm. We call these **balance sheet leverage ratios** and **coverage ratios**. The firm's balance sheet provides the required accounts for computing the balance sheet leverage ratios. In various forms these balance sheet ratios compare the firm's use of funds supplied by creditors with those supplied by owners.

The accounts required to calculate the coverage ratios generally come from the firm's income statement. At times the external analyst may have to consult balance sheet information to construct some of these needed estimates. On a privately placed debt issue, for example, some fraction of the current portion of the firm's long-term debt might have to be used as an estimate of that issue's sinking fund. Coverage ratios provide estimates of the firm's ability to service its financing contracts. High coverage ratios, compared with a standard, imply unused debt capacity.

A Worksheet

Table 9-8 is a sample worksheet used to analyze financing choices. The objective of the analysis is to determine the effect each financing plan will have on key financial ratios. The financial officer can compare the existing level of each ratio with its projected level, taking into consideration the contractual commitments of each alternative.

In reality we know that EBIT might be expected to vary over a considerable range of outcomes. For this reason the coverage ratios should be calculated several times, each at a different level of EBIT. If this is accomplished over all possible values of EBIT, a probability distribution for each coverage ratio can be constructed. This provides the financial manager with much more information than simply calculating the coverage ratios based on the expected value of EBIT.

Industry Norms

The comparative leverage ratios calculated according to the format laid out in Table 9-8, or in a similar format, have additional utility to the decision maker if they can be compared with some standard. Generally, corporate financial analysts, investment dealers, commercial bank loan officers, and bond-rating agencies rely upon industry classes from which to compute "normal" ratios. Although industry groupings may actually contain firms whose basic business risk exposure differs widely, the practice is entrenched in North American business behaviour.[17] At the very least, then, the financial officer must be interested in industry standards because almost everybody else is.

Several published studies indicate that capital structure ratios vary in a significant manner among industry classes.[18] For example, random sampling of the common equity ratios of large retail firms seem to differ statistically from those of major steel producers. The major steel producers use financial leverage to a lesser degree than do the large retail organizations. On the whole, firms operating in the same industry tend to exhibit capital-structure ratios that cluster around a central value, which we call a *norm*. Business risk will vary from industry to industry. As a consequence, the capital structure norms will vary from industry to industry.

This is not to say that all companies in the industry will maintain leverage ratios "close" to the norm. For instance, firms that are very profitable may display high coverage ratios and high balance sheet leverage ratios. The moderately profitable firm, though, might find such a posture unduly risky. Here the usefulness of industry normal leverage ratios is clear. If the firm chooses to deviate in a material manner from the accepted values for the key ratios, it must have a sound reason.

Companywide Cash Flows: What Is the Worst That Could Happen?

In Chapter 11 we will note that liquidity ratios are designed to measure the ability of the firm to pay its bills on time. Financing charges are just another

---

[17] An approach to grouping firms based on several component measures of business risk, as opposed to ordinary industry classes, is reported in John D. Martin, David F. Scott, Jr., and Robert F. Vandell, "Equivalent Risk Classes: A Multidimensional Examination," *Journal of Financial and Quantitative Analysis*, 14 (March 1979), pp. 101–118.

[18] See, for example, Eli Schwartz and J. Richard Aronson, "Some Surrogate Evidence in Support of the Concept of Optimal Financial Structure," *Journal of Finance*, 22 (March 1967), pp. 10–18; David F. Scott, Jr., "Evidence on the Importance of Financial Structure," *Financial Management*, 1 (Summer 1972), pp. 45–50; and David F. Scott, Jr., and John D. Martin, "Industry Influence on Financial Structure," *Financial Management*, 4 (Spring 1975), pp. 67–73.

TABLE 9-8. Comparative Leverage Ratios: Worksheet for Analyzing Financing Plans

Ratios	Computation Method	Existing Ratio	Ratio with New Common Share Financing	Ratio with New Debt Financing
Balance sheet leverage ratios				
1. Debt ratio	$\dfrac{\text{total liabilities}}{\text{total assets}}$	_____ %	_____ %	_____ %
2. Long-term debt to total capitalization	$\dfrac{\text{long-term debt}}{\text{long-term debt + net worth}}$	_____ %	_____ %	_____ %
3. Total liabilities to net worth	$\dfrac{\text{total liabilities}}{\text{net worth}}$	_____ %	_____ %	_____ %
4. Common equity ratio	$\dfrac{\text{common equity}}{\text{total assets}}$	_____ %	_____ %	_____ %
Coverage ratios				
1. Times interest earned	$\dfrac{\text{EBIT}}{\text{annual interest expense}}$	_____ times	_____ times	_____ times
2. Times burden covered	$\dfrac{\text{EBIT interest + sinking fund}}{\text{interest} + \dfrac{\text{sinking fund}}{1-t}}$	_____ times	_____ times	_____ times
3. Cash flow overall coverage ratio	$\dfrac{\text{EBIT + lease expense + depreciation}}{\text{interest + lease expense} + \dfrac{\text{preferred dividends}}{1-t} + \dfrac{\text{principal payments}}{1-t}}$	_____ times	_____ times	_____ times

type of bill that eventually comes due for payment. Interest charges, preferred dividends, lease charges, and principal payments all must be paid on time, or the company risks being caught in bankruptcy proceedings. To a lesser extent, dispensing with financing charges on an other than timely basis can result in severely restricted business operations. We have just seen that coverage ratios provide a measure of the safety of one general class of payment—financing charges. Coverage ratios, then, and liquidity ratios are very close in concept.

A more comprehensive method is available for studying the impact of capital-structure decisions on corporate cash flows. The method is simple but nonetheless very valuable. It involves the preparation of a series of cash budgets under (1) different economic conditions and (2) different capital structures.[19] The net cash flows under these different situations can be examined to determine if the financing requirements expose the firm to a degree of default risk too high to bear.

In work that has been highly acclaimed, Donaldson has suggested that the firm's debt-carrying capacity (defined in the broad sense here to include preferred dividend payments and lease payments) ought to depend upon the

---

[19]Cash budget preparation is discussed in Chapter 12.

net cash flows the firm could expect to receive during a recessionary period.[20] In other words, target capital structure proportions could be set by planning for the "worst that could happen." An example will be of help.

Suppose that a recession is expected to last for one year.[21] Moreover, the end of the year represents the bottoming-out, or worst portion of the recession. Equation (9-11) defines the cash balance, CB_r, the firm could expect to have at the end of the recession period.[22]

$$CB_r = C_0 + (C_s + OR) - (P_a + RM + \ldots + E_n) - FC \qquad (9\text{-}11)$$

where
C_0 = the cash balance at the beginning of the recession

C_s = collection from sales

OR = other cash receipts

P_a = payroll expenditures

RM = raw material payments

E_n = the last of a long series of expenditures over which management has little control (nondiscretionary expenditures)

FC = fixed financial charges associated with a specific capital structure

If we let the net of total cash receipts and nondiscretionary expenditures be represented by NCF_r, then Equation (9-11) can be simplified to

$$CB_r = C_0 + NCF_r - FC \qquad (9\text{-}12)$$

The inputs to Equation (9-12) come from a detailed cash budget. The variable representing financing costs, FC, can be changed in accordance with several alternative financing plans to ascertain if the net cash balance during the recession, CB_r, might fall below zero.

Suppose that some firm typically maintains $500,000 in cash and marketable securities. This amount would be on hand at the start of the recession period. During the economic decline, the firm estimates that its net cash flows from operations, NCF_r, will be $2 million. If the firm currently finances its assets with an unlevered capital structure, its cash balance at the worst point of the recession would be

$$CB_r = \$500,000 + \$2,000,000 - \$0 = \$2,500,000$$

This procedure allows us to study many different situations.[23] Assume that the same firm is considering a shift in its capitalization such that annual

---

[20]Refer to Gordon Donaldson, "New Framework for Corporate Debt Policy," *Harvard Business Review*, 40 (March–April 1962), pp. 117–131; Gordon Donaldson, Corporate Debt Capacity, Boston: Division of Research, Graduate School of Business Administration, Harvard University, 1961, Chap. 7; and Gordon Donaldson, "Strategy for Financial Emergencies," *Harvard Business Review*, 47 (November–December 1969), pp. 67–79.

[21]The analysis can readily be extended to cover a recessionary period of several years. All that is necessary is to calculate the cash budgets over a similar period.

[22]For the most part, the present notation follows that of Donaldson.

[23]It is not difficult to improve the usefulness of this sort of analysis by applying the technique of simulation to the generation of the various cash budgets. This facilitates the construction of probability distributions of net cash flows under differing circumstances. Simulation was discussed in Chapter 7.

interest and sinking-fund payments will be $2,300,000. If a recession occurred, the firm's cash balance at the end of the adverse economic period would be

$$CB_r = \$500,000 + \$2,000,000 - \$2,300,000 = \$200,000$$

The firm ordinarily maintains a liquid asset balance of $500,000. Thus, the effect of the proposed capital structure on the firm's cash balance during adverse circumstances might seem too risky for management to accept. When the chance of being out of cash is too high for management to bear, the use of financial leverage has been pushed beyond a reasonable level. According to this tool, the appropriate level of financial leverage is reached when the chance of being out of cash is exactly equal to that which management will assume.

A GLANCE AT ACTUAL CAPITAL-STRUCTURE MANAGEMENT

In this chapter we have discussed (1) the concept of an optimal capital structure, (2) the search for an appropriate range of financial leverage, and (3) the fundamental tools of capital structure management. We now examine the opinions and practices of financial executives which work in the area of capital structure management.

Cheung, Roy and Gordon have surveyed Canadian financial managers about their firms' capital structure practices.[24] Each of these financial managers worked for companies listed on the Financial Post Survey of Industrials. The results of this survey indicated that 72 percent of these financial managers thought that their firm's common equity would be maximized at a particular debt ratio. This type of response is consistent with the results of other surveys (Scott and Johnson, 1982 and Walsh, 1972) which indicated that managers believe there is an optimum capital structure for the corporation. One respondent summarized his opinion on optimum capital structure of a firm as follows:

> In my opinion, there is an optimum capital structure for companies. However, this optimum capital structure will vary by individual companies, industries, and then is subject to changing economies, by money markets, earnings trends, and prospects...the circumstances and the lenders will determine an optimum at different points in time.[25]

This survey and others consistently point out that (1) financial officers set target debt ratios for their companies, and (2) the values for those ratios are influenced by a conscious evaluation of the basic business risk to which the firm is exposed.

---

[24]Joseph K. Cheung, S. Paul Roy and Irene Gordon, "Financing Policies of Large Canadian Corporations," *CMA Management Accounting Magazine*, 63(4) (May 1989), pp. 26–31.
[25]Francis J. Walsh, Jr., *Planning Corporate Capital Structures*, New York: The Conference Board, 1972, p. 14.

Target Debt Ratios

Selected comments from financial executives of large international companies point to the widespread use of target debt ratios. A vice-president and treasurer of the American Telephone and Telegraph Company (AT&T) described his firm's debt ratio policy in terms of a range:

> All of the foregoing considerations led us to conclude, and reaffirm for a period of many years, that the proper range of our debt was 30% to 40% of total capital. Reasonable success in meeting financial needs under the diverse market and economic conditions that we have faced attests to the appropriateness of this conclusion.[26]

Cheung, Roy and Gordon have reported that only 11% of the Canadian firms surveyed have target ratios greater than 50%; the most popular target range among firms is 40–50%, with 21–50% being the most predominant.[27] These authors also reported that the predominant factor in establishing target ratios among Canadian industrial companies was the desire to maintain financial flexibility.[28] Other factors which were mentioned in this study were: the need to maintain a minimum credit rating on the firm's long-term debt, the concern for covenant violation and share price maximization. A similar survey of American companies mentioned the following influences on the level of the target debt ratio: the ability of the firm to meet financing charges, maintaining a desired bond rating, providing an adequate borrowing reserve, and exploiting the advantage of financial leverage.[29]

Who Sets Target Debt Ratios?

From the discussion above, we know that firms do use target debt ratios in arriving at financing decisions. But what is the relative influence of external parties on the firm setting these target ratios? Table 9-9 summarizes the results of Cheung, Roy, and Gordon which indicate that managers ranked commercial bankers first as an outside party which influenced the setting of target ratios. Other parties which were ranked by managers were investment bankers and comparative ratios; trade creditors and security analysts were thought to have little or no influence in determining the target financial structure. The role of the investment bankers (dealers) in this country's capital market system is explored in some detail in Chapter 17.

Debt Capacity

Previously in this chapter we noted that the firm's debt capacity is the maximum proportion of debt that it can include in its capital structure and still maintain its lowest weighted cost of capital. It is of interest to have some understanding of how financial executives make the concept of debt capacity

---

[26]John J. Scanlon, "Bell System Financial Policies," *Financial Management*, 1 (Summer 1972), pp. 16–26.

[27]Joseph K. Cheung, S. Paul Roy and Irene Gordon, "Financing Policies of Large Canadian Corporations," *CMA Management Accounting Magazine*, 63(4) (May 1989), pp. 26–31.

[28]We emphasize the following ideas on capital structure design: First, there exists empirical support for the assertion that firms identify and attempt to move toward target debt (leverage) ratios. Managers tell us this is so, and survey studies have confirmed the tendency. Second, there is also empirical support for the assertion that firms prefer internal finance before using external finance and debt is preferred to equity financing. The second assertion is now often referred to as the "pecking order theory" of capital structure.

[29]Francis J. Walsh, *Planning Corporate Capital Structures*, New York: The Conference Board, 1972, p. 17.

Type of Influence	Rank 1	Rank 2	Rank 3
Investment bankers	15	25	24
Commercial bankers	30	21	18
Trade creditors supplies	0	6	9
Outside security analysts	8	20	22
Comparative ratios	18	24	24
Other	29	4	3
Total	100%	100%	100%

TABLE 9-9
External Influences on the Determination of Target Financial Structure

Source: Joseph K. Cheung, S. Paul Roy and Irene Gordon, "Financing Policies of Large Canadian Corporations," *CMA Management Accounting Magazine*, 63(4) (May 1989), p. 27.

Standard or Method	1,000 Largest Corporations (Percent Using)
Target percent of total capitalization (long-term debt to total capitalization)	27%
Long-term debt to net worth ratio (or its inverse)	14
Long-term debt to total assets	2
Interest (or fixed charge) coverage ratio	6
Maintain bond ratings	14
Restrictive debt covenants	4
Most adverse cash flow	4
Industry standard	3
Other	10
No response	16
Total	100%

TABLE 9-10
Definitions of Debt Capacity in Practice

Source: Derived from David F. Scott, Jr., and Dana J. Johnson, "Financing Policies and Practices in Large Corporations," *Financial Management*, 11 (Summer 1982), pp. 51–59.

operational. Table 9-10 is adapted from a survey of the 1,000 largest industrial firms in the United States (as ranked by total sales dollars) and involves the responses from 212 financial executives. These executives defined debt capacity in a wide variety of ways. The most popular approach was as a target percentage of total capitalization.

Twenty-seven percent of the respondents thought of debt capacity in this manner. Forty-three percent of the participating executives remarked that debt capacity is defined in terms of some balance-sheet-based financial ratio (see the first three items in Table 9-10). Maintaining a specific bond rating was also indicated to be a popular approach to implementing the debt capacity concept.

Financial Leverage

Cheung, Roy and Gordon have examined how managers rank measures of financial leverage in terms of their importance.[30] These financial measures were derived from the both the balance sheet and the income statement.

---

[30]Joseph K. Cheung, S. Paul Roy and Irene Gordon. "Financing Policies of Large Canadian Corporations," *CMA Management Accounting Magazine*, 63(4) (May 1989), p. 26–31.

These measures can also be used to determine the desired debt-equity mix of the firm. The results of this survey indicated that firms prefer to use the long-term debt to total capitalization ratio which is derived from the balance sheet to measure financial leverage. Other measures of financial leverage which were preferred by these firms include: long-term debt to net worth ratio, times interest earned and cash flow coverage ratio.

Table 9-11 presents some results from a study of financial structure tendencies over the 1970–1986 period. The 100 largest nonfinancial corporations were studied in selected years with regard to several financial leverage measures.

Size was based on the book value of total assets. Two of those measures are shown in Table 9-11. Part A of the table shows the coverage and long-term debt to total capitalization ratios for all 100 firms for the selected years. Part B of the table shows the results for only those firms that existed across all years of the study. This means 47 firms from the 1970 list also existed in identifiable form in 1986. The second ratio in each panel was measured at book value.

Two main points can be made. First, there is a definite, observed weakening in interest coverage ratios since 1970. We can offer, then, that the likelihood of firm failure has increased over the past two decades for the sample firms. Second, the long-term debt to total capitalization ratios are rather stable over the period. Other researchers have noted this same set of relationships. They are not contradictory—it merely emphasizes that more than one approach has to be taken to assess leverage use. The debt and stock metrics have grown at about the same rates over time—but earnings available to service the interest payments on the debt have lagged.

Most analysts agree that the next recession will be a real (tough) test of recent capital-structure policies. We can see how crucial the analysis of financial risk is both to the firm and to the aggregate economy.[31]

Business Cycles

Effective financial managers—those who assist in creating value for the firm's shareholders—are quite perceptive about and in constant communica-

TABLE 9-11
Indicators of Financial
Leverage Use

Part A: 100 Largest (by total assets) Nonfinancial Corporations				
Year/Ratio	1986	1980	1975	1970
Coverage ratio (times)	4.98	8.64	7.85	9.09
Long-term debt to total capitalization (%)	31.9	26.3	30.9	31.2
Part B: 47 "Survivors" of the 100 Largest Nonfinancial Corporations				
Year/Ratio	1986	1980	1975	1970
Coverage ratio (times)	3.91	8.91	9.97	13.22
Long-term debt to total capitalization (%)	30.4	26.0	27.8	26.1

Source: Derived from David F. Scott, Jr., and Nancy Jay, "Leverage Use in Corporate America," Working Paper 9011, Orlando, FL: Dr. Phillips Institute for the Study of American Business Activity, University of Central Florida, January 1990.

[31]Ben Bernanke, "Is There Too Much Corporate Debt?" *Business Review*, Federal Reserve Bank of Philadelphia (September–October 1989), 10. Similar findings on increased leverage use are found in Margaret Mendenhall Blair, "A Surprising Culprit Behind the Rush to Leverage," *The Brookings Review* (Winter 1989/90), 19–26.

tion with the financial marketplace. When market conditions change abruptly, company financial policies and decisions must adapt to the new conditions. However, there are some firms that do a better job of adjusting than others. Companies that are slow to adapt to changes in the aggregate business environment face a lower level of cash flow generation and increased risk of financial distress.

Changes in the aggregate business environment are often referred to as *business cycles*. There are many useful definitions of such cycles. For example, Dr. Fischer Black, a former finance professor and later an executive with the well-known investment banking firm of Goldman, Sachs and Co., defined business cycles as follows:[32]

> Business cycles are fluctuations in economic activity. Business cycles show up in virtually all measures of economic activity—output, income, employment, unemployment, retail sales, new orders by manufacturers, even housing starts. When times are good, they tend to be good all over; and when times are bad, they tend to be bad all over.

A slightly different but compatible definition of business cycles that we will use is the following:

> Business cycles are a series of commercial adjustments to unanticipated, new information. These adjustments are accentuated by both public and private sector decisions. When these decisions, on balance, are correct the economy expands. When these decisions, on balance, are incorrect, the economy contracts.

Since 1950, Canada has endured nine recessions. Recessions are the contractionary or negative phase of the entire business cycle.

Typically, different stages of the business cycle induce a different set of relationships in the financial markets. These different relationships are reflected in the different capital-structure decisions managers make. For example, relationships between interest rates and equity prices may differ sharply over different phases of the cycle. Some phases of the cycle favour the issuance of debt securities over equity instruments, and vice versa. Complicating the decision-making process for the manager is the fact that financial relationships will be dissimilar over each cycle.[33]

The recession that began in 1990 has produced its own set of unique financial characteristics. Accordingly, financial managers altered their firm's capital structures in response to new information that included capital cost relationships in the financial markets. For example, managers began to reverse the financial leverage buildup that occurred in the 1980s. Whereas in the early 1990s, corporations began to take advantage of an improved market for common equities and brought to the marketplace substantial amounts of new common-share issues.

---

[32]Fischer Black, "The ABCs of Business Cycles," *Financial Analysts Journal*, 37 (November/December 1981), pp. 75–80. Dr. Black touched upon similar and other far-reaching points in his compelling presidential address to the American Finance Association; see Fischer Black, "Noise," *Journal of Finance*, 41 (July 1986), pp. 529–543.

[33]Available discussions and studies on the relationship between business cycles and corporate financing patterns are not plentiful. One such study is Robert A. Taggart, Jr., "Corporate Financing: Too Much Debt," *Financial Analysts Journal*, 42 (May/June 1986), pp. 35–42.

BASIC FINANCIAL MANAGEMENT IN PRACTICE

Yes, Managers, There is Still a Business Cycle

There are a number of ways in which managers may be able to profitably counter the business cycle.

First, inventory. The optimal time to begin reducing inventory levels is not when the recession hits; if inventories are reduced in anticipation of a slowdown, then carrying and associated costs are minimized and the organization does not experience the trauma of a knee-jerk inventory adjustment. Interestingly, one of the bright spots of the current recession is the relatively low inventory levels that most manufacturers, retailers and wholesalers were carrying when the economy turned down; this is in sharp contrast to 1981–82 when a huge inventory overhang played a major role in making that recession so bad.

Managers should reduce inventory in anticipation of contraction; they should accordingly expand in anticipation of expansion. Profits are maximized if product and capacity are available when the market wants them, but this requires foresight and planning. Organizations that count on building inventory after the expansion has commenced will miss those major opportunities that generally occur in the early months of expansion.

Second, accounts receivable. Bad debt losses track the business cycle. Debtors are more likely to encounter difficulties servicing their obligations in contractions than expansions. Managers can capitalize on this tendency by tightening credit conditions ahead of contraction and easing ahead of expansion. Optimal accounts receivable management requires careful consideration of the business cycle.

Third, cash. John Keynes mused at length on the counter-cyclical management of the liquid part of the balance sheet. When the economy is strong and security values are high, managers should increase liquidity so they might capitalize on the lower asset values that usually accompany the business cycle's inevitable downturn; the reverse similarly applies. Most people do not appreciate that John Keynes was far more than a theoretical economist; he was an extraordinary successful investor who relied heavily on the contrarian notion of buying and selling against the crowd. To some, John Keynes is the father of contrarian investing.

Fourth, investment. Managers who do not invest ahead of the business cycle in the state-of-the-art plant, equipment, machinery, research, development and training needed to assure internationally competitive workplaces, work processes and employees, will be surpassed. The time to put the facilities in place for the next expansion is many months or even years before it begins; similarly, the time to ease up to position for the next contraction is well before it begins. Few decisions are more important to an organization's long term prosperity than those involving investment; the business cycle is an important consideration in investment decision making.

Fifth, mergers and acquisitions. There is a popular one-liner to the effect that the stock market has correctly forecast 12 of the last four recessions. The stock market is not perfect but it does tend to peak and trough several months before the economy does. Correctly anticipating the business cycle is crucial to merger and acquisition success. The time to act on mergers and acquisitions is before the crowd moves equity prices to levels that make deals marginal.

Sixth, payables. The dull business of payables management is given short shrift at many organizations, but few organizations would not benefit from a review of payable policies, procedures and practices. When the cycle is turning down, payables management can be very important, especially if an organization is in jeopardy. Artfully using funds provided suppliers and even employees can be the difference in making it through rough spots. One thing is certain: the cash represented by the bills that an organization pays is not available for other purposes; when the economy is turning down, the precarious firm should assure it is making the right payments.

Seventh, debt. The common thread through most corporate crises is the inability to meet required payments associated with borrowed capital. Debt policy that misreads the business cycle can be lethal. In the face of contraction, managers should be reducing fixed charges by paying down debt, particularly short term debt. Heading into recession is no time to be commencing major debt-financed expansion programs; it is also no time to be seriously mismatching the balance sheet by financing longer term assets with short term liabilities. One of the most important management functions is synchronizing the liability side of the balance sheet with the business cycle.

The current downturn graphically illustrates the consequences of debt policies that misread the

Continued on page 441

Continued from page 440

business cycle. Bankruptcies are skyrocketing; debt beleaguered lenders have turned credit tap off to all but the most creditworthy; the old notion that bridge financing through downturns would always be available to at least average balance sheets has died; the willingness of lenders to make funds available has become a major factor in this recession; for those who did not see the credit crunch coming and position their balance sheets accordingly, the road back is going to be rough.

Eighth, cost control. In today's fiercely competitive business world, few enterprises will prosper without relentless control of costs. At no time is cost control more important than heading into a downturn. Managers who wait for recession to eliminate waste, duplication and excess may find it too late. Nothing exposes ineffective management like the unexpected arrival of recession.

Ninth, promotion. Counter-cyclical promotion policy can pay huge dividends to the firm that calls the business cycle correctly. The time to have the marketplace enthusiastically aware of your product is when the economy is growing and confidence is high. Just as it takes nerve to spend on promotion when business conditions are soft, promotion spending is easiest to justify when the economy is peaking, and probably represents a highly inefficient use of the scarce promotion dollar. Correctly projecting the business cycle is key to maximizing promotion effectiveness.

Finally, product development. The time to

have new products in the marketplace is when consumers are willing to buy. As with promotion spending, managers often find it difficult to convince the board of directors of the merits of product development spending in a downturn, but if it is not done in the downturn, success in the upturn is unlikely. Similarly, the optimal time to spend on product development is not when contraction is near.

It Is Worth Trying to Assess the Business Cycle

Although economists have identified numerous business cycles, managers do not find it easy to identify where their given industry is in what cycle; a bit of luck probably beats all the analytical ammunition that can be mustered, but it is nonetheless useful for managers to attempt business cycle forecasting.

The exercise of trying, on a systematic basis, to assess the business cycle has organizational benefits regardless of how the predictions themselves prove out. It is hard to think of an important managerial decision that is not seriously impacted by how an enterprise fits through time in the phases of the economy. If nothing else, managers will be ahead if they come away from the current recession with new-found respect for the business cycle; the extraordinary 1982 to 1990 boom to the contrary, the business cycle clearly matters, and clearly should not be ignored and assumed away.

Source: John S. McCallum, "Yes, Managers, There is Still a Business Cycle," *Business Quarterly*, 56(1) (Summer 1991), pp. 38–40.

Business Risk

The single most important factor that should affect the firm's financing mix is the underlying nature of the business in which it operates. In Chapter 8 we defined business risk as the relative dispersion in the firm's expected stream of EBIT. If the nature of the firm's business is such that the variability inherent in its EBIT stream is high, then it would be unwise to impose a high degree of financial risk on top of this already uncertain earnings stream.

Corporate executives are likely to point this out in discussions of capital-structure management. A financial officer in a large steel firm related:

> The nature of the industry, the marketplace, and the firm tend to establish debt limits that any prudent management would prefer not to exceed. Our industry is capital intensive and our markets tend to be cyclical.... The capability to service debt while operating in the environment described dictates a conservative financial structure.[34]

[34]Walsh, *Planning Corporate Capital Structures*, p. 18.

Notice how that executive was concerned with both his firm's business risk exposure and its cash flow capability for meeting any financing costs. The AT&T financial officer referred to earlier also has commented on the relationship between business and financial risk:

> In determining how much debt a firm can safely carry, it is necessary to consider the basic risks inherent in that business. This varies considerably among industries and is related essentially to the nature and demand for an industry's product, the operating characteristics of the industry, and its ability to earn an adequate return in an unknown future.[35]

It appears clear that the firm's capital structure cannot be properly designed without a thorough understanding of its commercial strategy.

SUMMARY

This chapter examines the firm's financing mix and emphasizes the importance of managing the firm's permanent sources of funds—that is, its capital structure. The objective of capital structure management is to arrange the company's sources of funds so that the price of its common share will be maximized, all other factors held constant.

Capital Structure Theory

Can the firm affect its weighted cost of capital by altering its financing mix? Attempts to answer this question have comprised a significant portion of capital structure theory for over three decades. Extreme positions show that the firm's share price is either unaffected or continually affected as the firm increases its reliance upon leverage-inducing funds. In the real world, an operating environment where interest expense is tax-deductible and market imperfections operate to restrict the amount of fixed-income obligations a firm can issue, most financial officers and financial academics subscribe to the concept of an optimal capital structure. The optimal capital structure minimizes the firm's weighted cost of capital. Searching for a proper range of financial leverage, then, is an important financial management activity.

Complicating the manager's search for an optimal capital structure are conflicts that lead to agency costs. A natural conflict exists between shareholders and bondholders (the agency costs of debt). To reduce excessive risk taking by management on behalf of shareholders, it may be necessary to include several protective covenants in bond contracts that serve to restrict managerial decision-making.

Another type of agency cost is related to free cash flow. For example, managers have the incentive to hold on to free cash flow and enjoy it, rather than paying it out in the form of higher cash dividend payments. This conflict between managers and shareholders leads to the concept of the free cash flow theory of capital structure. This same theory is also known as the control hypothesis and the threat hypothesis. The ultimate resolution of these agency costs affects the specific form of the firm's capital structure.

[35]Scanlon, "Bell System Financial Policies," p. 19.

The Tools of Capital-Structure Management

The decision to use senior securities in the firm's capitalization causes two types of financial leverage effects. The first is the added variability in the earnings per share stream that accompanies the use of fixed-charge securities. We explained in Chapter 8 how this could be quantified by use of the degree of financial leverage metric. The second financial leverage effect relates to the level of earnings per share (EPS) at a given EBIT under a specific capital structure. We rely upon EBIT-EPS analysis to measure this second effect. Through EBIT-EPS analysis the decision maker can inspect the impact of alternative financing plans on EPS over a full range of EBIT levels.

A second tool of capital-structure management is the calculation of comparative leverage ratios. Balance sheet leverage ratios and coverage ratios can be computed according to the contractual stipulations of the proposed financing plans. Comparison of these ratios with industry standards enables the financial officer to determine if the firm's key ratios are materially out of line with accepted practice.

A third tool is the analysis of corporate cash flows. This process involves the preparation of a series of cash budgets that consider different economic conditions and different capital structures. Useful insight into the identification of proper target capital-structure ratios can be obtained by analyzing projected cash flow statements that assume adverse operating circumstances.

Capital Structure Practices

Surveys indicate that the majority of financial officers in large firms believe in the concept of an optimal capital structure. The optimal capital structure is approximated by the identification of target debt ratios. The targets reflect the firm's ability to service fixed financing costs and also consider the business risk to which the firm is exposed.

Several studies have provided information on who sets or influences the firm's target leverage ratios. The firm's own management group and staff of analysts are the major influence, followed in importance by investment dealers. Studies also show that executives operationalize the concept of debt capacity in many ways. The most popular approach was to maintain financial flexibility. Other factors which were mentioned in this study were: the need to maintain a minimum credit rating on the firm's long-term debt, the concern for covenant violation, and share price maximization.

Financing policies change in significant ways over time. For example during the 1980s, most studies confirm that North American companies "levered up" when compared with past decades. Specifically, interest coverage ratios deteriorated during the 1980s when compared with the 1970s.

The early 1990s are displaying a reversal of this trend. Effective financial managers have a sound understanding of the business cycle. The recession that started in 1990 produced a unique set of financial characteristics that led financial managers to reverse the buildup of leverage in the 1980s and bring substantial amounts of new common shares to the marketplace.

Other studies of managers' financing tendencies suggest that (1) a tremendous preference for the use of internally generated equity to finance investments exists, (2) firms prefer to forgo seemingly profitable projects rather than reduce shareholders' expected cash dividends to finance a greater part of the capital budget, and (3) security issues are timed with favourable market conditions.

STUDY QUESTIONS

9-1. Define the following terms:
   a. Financial structure
   b. Capital structure
   c. Optimal capital structure
   d. Debt capacity

9-2. What is the primary weakness of EBIT-EPS analysis as a financing decision tool?

9-3. What is the objective of capital-structure management?

9-4. Distinguish between (a) balance sheet leverage ratios and (b) coverage ratios. Give two examples of each and indicate how they would be computed.

9-5. Why might firms whose sales levels change drastically over time choose to use debt only sparingly in their capital structures?

9-6. What condition would cause capital-structure management to be a meaningless activity?

9-7. What does the term "independence hypothesis" mean as it applies to capital structure theory?

9-8. Who have been the foremost advocates of the independence hypothesis?

9-9. A financial manager might say that the firm's weighted cost of capital is saucer-shaped or U-shaped. What does this mean?

9-10. Define the EBIT-EPS indifference point.

9-11. What is uncommitted earnings per share (UEPS)?

9-12. Explain how industry norms might be used by the financial manager in the design of the company's financing mix.

9-13. Define the term "free cash flow"?

9-14. What is meant by the free cash flow theory of capital structure?

9-15. Why should the financial manager be familiar with the business cycle?

SELF-TEST PROBLEMS

ST-1. (*Analysis of Recessionary Cash Flows*) The management of Story Enterprises is considering an increase in its use of financial leverage. The proposal on the table is to sell $6 million of bonds that would mature in 20 years. The interest rate on these bonds would be 12 percent. The bond issue would have a sinking fund attached to it requiring that one-twentieth of the principal be retired each year. Most business economists are forecasting a recession that will affect the entire company in the coming year. Story's management has been saying, "If we can make it through this, we can make it through anything." The firm prefers to carry an operating cash balance of $750,000. Cash collections from sales next year will total $3 million. Miscellaneous cash receipts will be $400,000. Raw material payments will be $700,000. Wage and salary costs will be $1,200,000 on a cash basis. On top of this, Story will experience nondiscretionary cash outlays of $1.2 million, including all tax payments. The firm faces a combined tax rate of 45 percent.

   a. At present, Story is unlevered. What will be the total fixed financial charges the firm must pay next year?

   b. If the bonds are issued, what is your forecast for the firm's expected cash balance at the end of the recessionary year (next year)?

   c. As Story's financial consultant, do you recommend that it issue the bonds?

ST-2. (*Assessing Leverage Use*) Some financial data and the appropriate industry norm for three companies are shown in the following table:

Measure	Firm X	Firm Y	Firm Z	Industry Norm
Total debt to total assets	20%	30%	10%	30%
Times interest and preferred dividend coverage	8 times	16 times	19 times	8 times
Price/earnings ratio	9 times	11 times	9 times	9 times

    a. Which firm appears to be employing financial leverage to the most appropriate degree?

    b. In this situation, which "financial leverage effect" appears to dominate the market valuation process?

ST-3. (*EBIT-EPS Analysis*) Four engineers from Martin-Bowing Company are leaving that firm in order to form their own corporation. The new firm will produce and distribute computer software on a national basis. The software will be aimed at scientific markets and at businesses desiring to install comprehensive information systems. Private investors have been lined up to finance the new company. Two financing proposals are being studied. Both of these plans involve the use of some financial leverage; however, one is much more highly levered than the other. Plan A requires the firm to sell bonds with an effective interest rate of 14 percent. One million dollars would be raised in this manner. In addition, under plan A, $5 million would be raised by selling common shares at $50 each. Plan B also involves raising $6 million. This would be accomplished by selling $3 million of bonds at an interest rate of 16 percent. The other $3 million would come from selling common shares at $50 each. In both cases the use of financial leverage is considered to be a permanent part of the firm's capital structure, so no fixed maturity date is used in the analysis. The firm considers a 50 percent tax rate appropriate for planning purposes.

    a. Find the EBIT indifference level associated with the two financing plans, and prepare an EBIT-EPS analysis chart.

    b. Prepare an analytical income statement that demonstrates that EPS will be the same regardless of the plan selected. Use the EBIT level found in part (a).

    c. A detailed financial analysis of the firm's prospects suggests that long-term EBIT will be above $1,188,000 annually. Taking this into consideration, which plan will generate the higher EPS?

    d. Suppose that long-term EBIT is forecast to be $1,188,000 per year. Under plan A, a price/earnings ratio of 13 would apply. Under plan B, a price/earnings ratio of 11 would apply. If this set of financial relationships does hold, which financing plan would you recommend be implemented?

    e. Again, assume an EBIT level of $1,188,000. What price/earnings ratio applied to the EPS of plan B would provide the same share price as that projected for plan A? Refer to your data from part (d).

STUDY PROBLEMS (SET A)

9-1A. (*EBIT-EPS Analysis*) A group of college professors have decided to form a small manufacturing corporation. The company will produce a full line of contemporary furniture. Two financing plans have been proposed by the investors. Plan A is an all common equity alternative. Under this arrangement 1,000,000 common shares will be sold to net the firm $20 per share. Plan B involves the use of financial leverage. A debt issue with a 20-year maturity period will be privately placed. The debt issue will carry an interest rate of 10 percent and the principal borrowed will amount to $6 million. In addition, $14 million will be issued in common shares at a price of $20 per share. The corporate tax rate is 50 percent.

a. Find the EBIT indifference level associated with the two financing proposals.

b. Prepare an analytical income statement that proves EPS will be the same regardless of the plan chosen at the EBIT level found in part (a).

c. Prepare an EBIT-EPS analysis chart for this situation.

d. If a detailed financial analysis projects that long-term EBIT will always be close to $2,400,000 annually, which plan will provide for the higher EPS?

9-2A. (*Capital-Structure Theory*) Deep End Pools & Supplies has an all-common-equity capital structure. Some financial data for the company are shown below:

Common shares outstanding	= 900,000
Common share price, P_0	= $30 per share
Expected level of EBIT	= $5,400,000
Dividend payout ratio	= 100 percent

In answering the following questions, assume that corporate income is not taxed.

a. Under the present capital structure, what is the total value of the firm?

b. What is the cost of common equity capital, K_c? What is the weighted cost of capital, K_0?

c. Now, suppose Deep End sells $1.5 million of long-term debt with an interest rate of 8 percent. The proceeds are used to retire outstanding common shares. According to the net operating income theory (the independence hypothesis), what will be the firm's cost of common equity after the capital-structure change?

    1. What will be the dividend per share flowing to the firm's common shareholders?

    2. By what percentage has the dividend per share changed owing to the capital-structure change?

    3. By what percentage has the cost of common equity changed owing to the capital-structure change?

    4. What will be the weighted cost of capital after the capital-structure change?

9-3A. (*EBIT-EPS Analysis*) Four recent liberal arts graduates have interested a group of venture capitalists in backing a small business enterprise. The proposed operation would consist of a series of retail outlets that would distribute and service a full line of vacuum cleaners and accessories. These stores would be located in Alberta. Two financing plans have been proposed by the graduates. Plan A is an all common equity capital structure. Two million dollars would be raised by selling 80,000 common shares. Plan B would involve the use of long-term debt financing. One million dollars would be raised by marketing bonds with an interest rate of 12 percent. Under this alternative another $1 million would be raised by selling 40,000 common shares. With both plans, then, $2 million is needed to launch the new firm's operations. The debt funds raised under plan B are considered to have no fixed maturity date, in that this proportion of financial leverage is thought to be a permanent part of the company's capital structure. The fledgling executives have decided to use a 22 percent tax rate in their analysis.

a. Find the EBIT indifference level associated with the two financing proposals.

b. Prepare an analytical income statement that proves EPS will be the same regardless of the plan chosen at the EBIT level found in part (a).

9-4A. (*EBIT-EPS Analysis*) Three recent graduates of the computer science program are forming a company to write and distribute software for various personal computers. Initially, the corporation will operate in southern

Ontario. Twelve serious prospects for retail outlets have already been identified and committed to the firm. The firm's software products have been tested and displayed at several trade shows and computer fairs in the perceived operating region. All that is lacking is adequate financing to continue with the project. A small group of private investors in the Toronto area is interested in financing the new company. Two financing proposals are being evaluated. The first (plan A) is an all-common-equity capital structure. Two million dollars would be raised by selling common shares at $20 per share. Plan B would involve the use of financial leverage. One million dollars would be raised selling bonds with an effective interest rate of 11 percent (per annum). Under this second plan, the remaining $1 million would be raised by selling common shares at the $20 price per share. The use of financial leverage is considered to be a permanent part of the firm's capitalization, so no fixed maturity date is needed for the analysis. A 22 percent tax rate is appropriate for the analysis.

a. Find the EBIT indifference level associated with the two financing plans.

b. A detailed financial analysis of the firm's prospects suggests that the long-term EBIT will be above $300,000 annually. Taking this into consideration, which plan will generate the higher EPS?

c. Suppose the long-term EBIT is forecast to be $300,000 per year. Under plan A, a price/earnings ratio of 19 would apply. Under plan B, a price/earnings ratio of 15 would apply. If this set of financial relationships does hold, which financing plan would you recommend?

9-5A. (*EBIT-EPS Analysis*) Three recent liberal arts graduates have interested a group of venture capitalists in backing a new business enterprise. The proposed operation would consist of a series of retail outlets to distribute and service a full line of personal computer equipment. These stores would be located in New Brunswick. Two financing plans have been proposed by the graduates. Plan A is an all-common-equity structure. Three million dollars would be raised by selling 75,000 common shares. Plan B would involve the use of long-term debt financing. One million dollars would be raised by marketing bonds with an effective interest rate of 15 percent. Under this alternative, another $2 million would be raised by selling 50,000 common shares. With both plans, then, $3 million is needed to launch the new firm's operations. The debt funds raised under plan B are considered to have no fixed maturity date, in that this proportion of financial leverage is thought to be a permanent part of the company's capital structure. The fledgling executives have decided to use a 22 percent tax rate in their analysis, and they have hired you on a consulting basis to do the following:

a. Find the EBIT indifference level associated with the two financing proposals.

b. Prepare an analytical income statement that proves EPS will be the same regardless of the plan chosen at the EBIT level found in part (a).

9-6A. (*EBIT-EPS Analysis*) Two recent graduates of the computer science program are forming a company to write, market, and distribute software for various personal computers. Initially, the corporation will operate in Western Canada. Twelve serious prospects for retail outlets in these different provinces have already been identified and committed to the firm. The firm's software products have been tested and displayed at several trade shows and computer fairs in the perceived operating region. All that is lacking is adequate financing to continue the project. A small group of private investors in Vancouver are interested in financing the new company. Two financing proposals are being evaluated. The first (plan A) is an all-common-equity capital structure. Four million dollars would be raised by selling common shares at $40 per share. Plan B would involve the use of financial leverage. Two million dollars would be raised by selling bonds with an effective interest rate of 16 percent (per annum). Under this second plan, the remaining $2 million would be raised by selling common shares at the $40 price per share. This use of financial leverage is considered to be a permanent part of the firm's capitalization, so no fixed maturity date is needed for the analysis. A 50 percent tax rate is appropriate for the analysis.

a. Find the EBIT indifference level associated with the two financing plans.

b. Prepare an analytical income statement that proves EPS will be the same regardless of the plan chosen at the EBIT level found in part (a).

c. A detailed financial analysis of the firm's prospects suggests that long-term EBIT will be above $800,000 annually. Taking this into consideration, which plan will generate the higher EPS?

d. Suppose that long-term EBIT is forecast to be $800,000 per year. Under plan A, a price/earnings ratio of 12 would apply. Under plan B, a price/earnings ratio of 10 would apply. If this set of financial relationships does hold, which financing plan would you recommend be implemented?

9-7A. (*Analysis of Recessionary Cash Flows*) The management of PEI Produce is considering an increase in its use of financial leverage. The proposal on the table is to sell $10 million of bonds that would mature in 20 years. The interest rate on these bonds would be 15 percent. The bond issue would have a sinking fund attached to it requiring that one-twentieth of the principal be retired each year. Most business economists are forecasting a recession that will affect the entire economy in the coming year. PEI's management has been saying, "If we can make it through this, we can make it through anything." The firm prefers to carry an operating cash balance of $1 million. Cash collections from sales next year will total $4 million. Miscellaneous cash receipts will be $300,000. Raw material payments will be $800,000. Wage and salary costs will total $1.4 million on a cash basis. On top of this, PEI will experience nondiscretionary cash outflows of $1.2 million including all tax payments. The firm faces a 50 percent tax rate.

a. At present, PEI is unlevered. What will be the total fixed financial charges the firm must pay next year?

b. If the bonds are issued, what is your forecast for the firm's expected cash balance at the end of the recessionary year (next year)?

c. As PEI's financial consultant, do you recommend that it issue the bonds?

9-8A. (*EBIT-EPS Analysis*) Four recent business school graduates have interested a group of venture capitalists in backing a small business enterprise. The proposed operation would consist of a series of retail outlets that would distribute and service a full line of energy-conservation equipment. These stores would be located in Alberta. Two financing plans have been proposed by the graduates. Plan A is an all-common-equity capital structure. Three million dollars would be raised by selling 60,000 common shares. Plan B would involve the use of long-term debt financing. One million dollars would be raised by marketing bonds with an interest rate of 10 percent. Under this alternative another $2 million would be raised by selling 40,000 common shares. With both plans, then, $3 million is needed to launch the new firm's operations. The debt funds raised under plan B are considered to have no fixed maturity date, in that this proportion of financial leverage is thought to be a permanent part of the company's capital structure. The fledgling executives have decided to use a 22 percent tax rate in their analysis.

a. Find the EBIT indifference level associated with the two financing proposals.

b. Prepare an analytical income statement that proves EPS will be the same regardless of the plan chosen at the EBIT level found in part (a).

9-9A. (*EBIT-EPS Analysis*) A group of college professors have decided to form a small manufacturing corporation. The company will produce a full line of contemporary furniture. Two financing plans have been proposed by the investors. Plan A is an all-common-equity alternative. Under this arrangement 1,400,000 common shares will be sold to net the firm $10 per share. Plan B involves the use of financial leverage. A debt issue with a 20-year maturity period will be privately placed. The debt issue will carry an interest rate of 8 percent and the principal borrowed will amount to $4 million. The corporate tax rate is 50 percent.

a. Find the EBIT indifference level associated with the two financing proposals.

b. Prepare an analytical income statement that proves EPS will be the same regardless of the plan chosen at the EBIT level found in part (a).

c. Prepare an EBIT-EPS analysis chart for this situation.

d. If a detailed financial analysis projects that long-term EBIT will always be close to $1,800,000 annually, which plan will provide for the higher EPS?

9-10A. *(EBIT-EPS Analysis)* The professors in problem 9-9A contacted a financial consultant to provide them with some additional information. They felt that in a few years the shares of the firm would be publicly traded over-the-counter, so they were interested in the consultant's opinion as to what the share price would be under the financing plan outlined in problem 9-9A. The consultant agreed that the projected long-term EBIT level of $1,800,000 was reasonable. He also felt that if plan A were selected, the marketplace would apply a price/earnings ratio of 12 times to the company's share; for plan B he estimated a price/earnings ratio of 10 times.

a. According to this information, which financing alternative would offer a higher share price?

b. What price/earnings ratio applied to the EPS related to plan B would provide the same share price as that projected for plan A?

c. Comment upon the results of your analysis of problems 9-9A and 9-10A.

9-11A. *(Analysis of Recessionary Cash Flows)* Cavalier Agriculture Supplies is undertaking a thorough cash flow analysis. It has been proposed by management that the firm expand by raising $5 million in the long-term debt markets. All of this would be immediately invested in new fixed assets. The proposed bond issue would carry an 8 percent interest rate and have a maturity period of 20 years. The bond issue would have a sinking fund provision that one-twentieth of the principal would be retired annually. Next year is expected to be a poor one for Cavalier. The firm's management feels, therefore, that the upcoming year would serve well as a model for the worst possible operating conditions that the firm can be expected to encounter. Cavalier ordinarily carries a $500,000 cash balance. Next year sales collections are forecast to be $3 million. Miscellaneous cash receipts will total $200,000. Wages and salaries will amount to $1 million. Payments for raw materials used in the production process will be $1,400,000. In addition, the firm will pay $500,000 in nondiscretionary expenditures including taxes. The firm faces a 50 percent tax rate.

a. Cavalier currently has no debt or preferred shares outstanding. What will be the total fixed financial charges that the firm must meet next year?

b. What is the expected cash balance at the end of the recessionary period (next year), assuming the debt is issued?

c. Based on this information, should Cavalier issue the proposed bonds?

9-12A. *(Assessing Leverage Use)* Some financial data for three corporations are displayed below:

Measure	Firm A	Firm B	Firm C	Industry Norm
Debt ratio	20%	25%	40%	20%
Times burden covered	8 times	10 times	7 times	9 times
Price/earnings ratio	9 times	11 times	6 times	10 times

a. Which firm appears to be excessively levered?

b. Which firm appears to be employing financial leverage to the most appropriate degree?

c. What explanation can you provide for the higher price/earnings ratio enjoyed by firm B as compared with firm A?

9-13A. *(Assessing Leverage Use)* Some financial data and the appropriate industry norm are shown in the following table:

Measure	Firm X	Firm Y	Firm Z	Industry Norm
Total debt to total assets	35%	30%	10%	35%
Times interest and preferred dividend coverage	7 times	14 times	16 times	7 times
Price/earnings ratio	8 times	10 times	8 times	8 times

a. Which firm appears to be using financial leverage to the most appropriate degree?

b. In this situation which "financial leverage effect" appears to dominate the market's valuation process?

9-14A. (*Capital-Structure Theory*) Titian Textiles has an all-common-equity capital structure. Pertinent financial characteristics for the company are shown below:

Common shares outstanding	= 1,000,000
Common share price, P_0	= $20 per share
Expected level of EBIT	= $5,000,000
Dividend payout ratio	= 100 percent

In answering the following questions, assume that corporate income is not taxed.

a. Under the present capital structure, what is the total value of the firm?

b. What is the cost of common equity capital, K_c? What is the weighted cost of capital, K_0?

c. Now, suppose that Titian Textiles sells $1 million of long-term debt with an interest rate of 8 percent. The proceeds are used to retire outstanding common shares. According to net-operating-income theory (the independence hypothesis), what will be the firm's cost of common equity after the capital structure change?

   1. What will be the dividend per share flowing to the firm's common shareholders?

   2. By what percent has the dividend per share changed owing to the capital-structure change?

   3. By what percent has the cost of common equity changed owing to the capital-structure change?

   4. What will be the weighted cost of capital after the capital structure change?

9-15A. (*Capital-Structure Theory*) Easy Blend Auto Parts has an all-common-equity capital structure. Some financial data for the company are shown below:

Common shares outstanding	= 600,000
Common share price, P_0	= $40 per share
Expected level of EBIT	= $4,200,000
Dividend payout ratio	= 100 percent

In answering the following questions, assume that corporate income is not taxed.

a. Under the present capital structure, what is the total value of the firm?

b. What is the cost of common equity capital, K_c? What is the weighted cost of capital, K_0?

c. Now, suppose Easy Blend sells $1 million of long-term debt with an interest rate of 10 percent. The proceeds are used to retire outstanding common shares. According to the net operating income theory (the independence hypothesis), what will be the firm's cost of common equity after the capital-structure change?

   1. What will be the dividend per share flowing to the firm's common shareholders?

2. By what percentage has the dividend per share changed owing to the capital-structure change?

3. By what percentage has the cost of common equity changed owing to the capital-structure change?

4. What will be the weighted cost of capital after the capital-structure change?

9-16A. (*EBIT-EPS Analysis*) Victoria Golf Equipment is analyzing three different financing plans for a newly formed subsidiary. The plans are described below:

Plan A	Plan B	Plan C
Common shares: $100,000	Bonds at 9%: $20,000 Common shares: $80,000	Preferred shares at 9%: $20,000 Common shares: $80,000

In all cases the common shares will be sold to net Victoria $10 per share. The subsidiary is expected to generate an average EBIT per year of $22,000. The management of Victoria places great emphasis on EPS performance. Income is taxed at a 50 percent rate.

a. Where feasible, find the EBIT indifference levels between the alternatives.

b. Which financing plan do you recommend that Victoria pursue?

STUDY PROBLEMS (SET B)

9-1B. (*EBIT-EPS Analysis*) Three recent graduates of the computer science program at the University of Toronto are forming a company to write and distribute software for various personal computers. Initially, the corporation will operate in southern Ontario. Twelve serious prospects for retail outlets have already been identified and committed to the firm. The firm's software products have been tested and displayed at several trade shows and computer fairs in the perceived operating region. All that is lacking is adequate financing to continue with the project. A small group of private investors in the Toronto area are interested in financing the new company. Two financing proposals are being evaluated. The first (plan A) is an all common equity capital structure. Three million dollars would be raised by selling common shares at $20 per share. Plan B would involve the use of financial leverage. Two million dollars would be raised selling bonds with an effective interest rate of 11 percent (per annum). Under this second plan, the remaining $1 million would be raised by selling common shares at the $20 price per share. The use of financial leverage is considered to be a permanent part of the firm's capitalization, so no fixed maturity date is needed for the analysis. A 22 percent tax rate is appropriate for the analysis.

a. Find the EBIT indifference level associated with the two financing plans.

b. A detailed financial analysis of the firm's prospects suggests that the long-term EBIT will be above $450,000 annually. Taking this into consideration, which plan will generate the higher EPS?

c. Suppose the long-term EBIT is forecast to be $450,000 per year. Under plan A, a price/earnings ratio of 19 would apply. Under plan B, a price/earnings ratio of 12.39 would apply. If this set of financial relationships does hold, which financing plan would you recommend?

9-2B. (*EBIT-EPS Analysis*) Three recent liberal arts graduates have interested a group of venture capitalists in backing a new business enterprise. The proposed operation would consist of a series of retail outlets to distribute and service a full line of personal computer equipment. These stores would be located in New Brunswick. Two financing plans have been proposed by the graduates. Plan A is an all-common-equity structure. Four million dollars would be raised by selling 80,000 common shares. Plan B would involve the use of long-term debt financing. Two million dollars would be raised by marketing bonds with an effective interest rate of 16 percent. Under this alternative, another $2 million would be raised by selling 50,000 common shares. With both plans, then, $4 million is needed to launch the new firm's operations. The debt funds raised under plan B are considered to have no fixed maturity date, in that this proportion of financial leverage is thought to be a permanent part of the company's capital structure. The fledgling executives have decided to use a 22 percent tax rate in their analysis, and they have hired you on a consulting basis to do the following:

a. Find the EBIT indifference level associated with the two financing proposals.

b. Prepare an analytical income statement that proves EPS will be the same regardless of the plan chosen at the EBIT level found in part (a).

9-3B. (*EBIT-EPS Analysis*) Two recent graduates of the computer science program are forming a company to write, market, and distribute software for various personal computers. Initially, the corporation will operate in Western Canada. Eight prospects for retail outlets in these different provinces have already been identified and committed to the firm. The firm's software products have been tested. All that is lacking is adequate financing to continue the project. A small group of private investors are interested in financing the new company. Two financing proposals are being evaluated. The first (plan A) is an all-common-equity capital structure. Three million dollars would be raised by selling common shares at $40 per share. Plan B would involve the use of financial leverage. One million dollars would be raised by selling bonds with an effective interest rate of 14 percent (per annum). Under this second plan, the remaining $2 million would be raised by selling common shares at the $40 price per share. This use of financial leverage is considered to be a permanent part of the firm's capitalization, so no fixed maturity date is needed for the analysis. A 50 percent tax rate is appropriate for the analysis.

a. Find the EBIT indifference level associated with the two financing plans.

b. Prepare an analytical income statement that proves EPS will be the same regardless of the plan chosen at the EBIT level found in part (a).

c. A detailed financial analysis of the firm's prospects suggests that the long-term EBIT will be above $750,000 annually. Taking this into consideration, which plan will generate the higher EPS?

d. Suppose that long-term EBIT is forecast to be $750,000 per year. Under plan A, a price/earnings ratio of 12 would apply. Under plan B, a price/earnings ratio of 9.836 would apply. If this set of financial relationships does hold, which financing plan would you recommend be implemented?

9-4B. (*Analysis of Recessionary Cash Flows*) The management of Calgary Collectibles (CC) is considering an increase in its use of financial leverage. The proposal on the table is to sell $11 million of bonds that would mature in 20 years. The interest rate on these bonds would be 16 percent. The bond issue would have a sinking fund attached to it requiring that one-twentieth of the principal be retired each year. Most business economists are forecasting a recession that will affect the entire economy in the coming year. CC's management has been saying, "If we can make it through this, we can make it through anything." The firm prefers to carry an operating cash balance of $500,000. Cash collections from sales next year will total $3.5 million. Miscellaneous cash receipts will be $300,000. Raw material payments will be $800,000. Wage and salary costs will total $1.5 million on a cash basis. On top of this, CC will experience nondiscretionary cash outflows of $1.3 million including all tax payments. The firm faces a 50 percent tax rate.

a. At present, CC is unlevered. What will be the total fixed financial charges the firm must pay next year?

b. If the bonds are issued, what is your forecast for the firm's expected cash balance at the end of the recessionary year (next year)?

c. As CC's financial consultant, do you recommend that it issue the bonds?

9-5B. (*EBIT-EPS Analysis*) Four recent business school graduates have interested a group of venture capitalists in backing a small business enterprise. The proposed operation would consist of a series of retail outlets that would distribute and service a full line of energy-conservation equipment. These stores would be located in Alberta. Two financing plans have been proposed by the graduates. Plan A is an all-common-equity capital structure. Five million dollars would be raised by selling 75,000 common shares. Plan B would involve the use of long-term debt financing. Two million dollars would be raised by marketing bonds with an interest rate of 12 percent. Under this alternative, another $3 million would be raised by selling 55,000 common shares. With both plans, then, $5 million is needed to launch the new firm's operations. The debt funds raised under plan B are considered to have no fixed maturity date, in that this proportion of financial leverage is thought to be a permanent part of the company's capital structure. The fledgling executives have decided to use a 22 percent tax rate in their analysis.

   a. Find the EBIT indifference level associated with the two financing proposals.

   b. Prepare an analytical income statement that proves EPS will be the same regardless of the plan chosen at the EBIT level found in part (a).

9-6B. (*EBIT-EPS Analysis*) A group of college professors have decided to form a small manufacturing corporation. The company will produce a full line of contemporary furniture. Two financing plans have been proposed by the investors. Plan A is an all common equity alternative. Under this arrangement 1,200,000 common shares will be sold to net the firm $10 per share. Plan B involves the use of financial leverage. A debt issue with a 20-year maturity period will be privately placed. The debt issue will carry an interest rate of 9 percent and the principal borrowed will amount to $3.5 million. The corporate tax rate is 50 percent.

   a. Find the EBIT indifference level associated with the two financing proposals.

   b. Prepare an analytical income statement that proves EPS will be the same regardless of the plan chosen at the EBIT level found in part (a).

   c. Prepare an EBIT-EPS analysis chart for this situation.

   d. If a detailed financial analysis projects that long-term EBIT will always be close to $1,500,000 annually, which plan will provide for the higher EPS?

9-7B. (*EBIT-EPS Analysis*) The professors in Problem 9-6B contacted a financial consultant to provide them with some additional information. They felt that in a few years the shares of the firm would be publicly traded over-the-counter, so they were interested in the consultant's opinion as to what the share price would be under the financing plan outlined in Problem 9-6B. The consultant agreed that the projected long-term EBIT level of $1,500,000 was reasonable. He also felt that if plan A were selected, the marketplace would apply a price/earnings ratio of 13 times to the company's share; for plan B he estimated a price earnings ratio of 11 times.

   a. According to this information, which financing alternative would offer a higher share price?

   b. What price/earnings ratio applied to the EPS related to plan B would provide the same share price as that projected for plan A?

   c. Comment upon the results of your analysis of Problems 9-6B and 9-7B.

9-8B. (*Analysis of Recessionary Cash Flows*) Seville Cranes, Inc., is undertaking a thorough cash flow analysis. It has been proposed by management that the firm expand by raising $6 million in the long-term debt markets. All of this would be immediately invested in new fixed assets. The proposed bond issue would carry a 10 percent interest rate and have a maturity period of 20 years. The bond issue would have a sinking fund provision that one-twentieth of the principal would be retired annually. Next year is expected to be a poor one for Seville. The firm's management feels, therefore, that the upcoming year would serve well as a model for the worst possible operating conditions that the firm can be expected to encounter. Seville ordinarily carries a $750,000 cash balance. Next year sales collections are forecast to be $3.5 million. Miscellaneous cash receipts will total $200,000. Wages and salaries will amount to $1.2 million. Payments for raw materials used in the production process will be $1,500,000. In addition, the firm will pay $500,000 in nondiscretionary expenditures including taxes. The firm faces a 50 percent tax rate.

a. Seville currently has no debt or preferred shares outstanding. What will be the total fixed financial charges that the firm must meet next year?

b. What is the expected cash balance at the end of the recessionary period (next year), assuming the debt is issued?

c. Based on this information, should Seville issue the proposed bonds?

9-9B. (*Assessing Leverage Use*) Some financial data for three corporations are displayed below:

Measure	Firm A	Firm B	Firm C	Industry Norm
Debt ratio	15%	20%	35%	25%
Times burden covered	9 times	11 times	6 times	9 times
Price/earnings ratio	10 times	12 times	5 times	10 times

a. Which firm appears to be excessively levered?

b. Which firm appears to be employing financial leverage to the most appropriate degree?

c. What explanation can you provide for the higher price/earnings ratio enjoyed by firm B as compared with firm A?

9-10B. (*Assessing Leverage Use*) Some financial data and the appropriate industry norm are shown in the following table:

Measure	Firm X	Firm Y	Firm Z	Industry Norm
Total debt to total assets	40%	35%	10%	35%
Times interest and preferred dividend coverage	8 times	13 times	16 times	7 times
Price/earnings ratio	8 times	11 times	8 times	8 times

a. Which firm appears to be using financial leverage to the most appropriate degree?

b. In this situation which "financial leverage effect" appears to dominate the market's valuation process?

9-11B. (*Capital-Structure Theory*) Whittier Optical Labs has an all-common-equity capital structure. Pertinent financial characteristics for the company are shown below:

Common shares outstanding	= 1,000,000
Common share price, P_0	= $22 per share
Expected level of EBIT	= $4,750,000
Dividend payout ratio	= 100 percent

In answering the following questions, assume that corporate income is not taxed.

a. Under the present capital structure, what is the total value of the firm?

b. What is the cost of common equity capital, K_c? What is the weighted cost of capital, K_0?

c. Now, suppose that Whittier sells $1 million of long-term debt with an interest rate of 9 percent. The proceeds are used to retire outstanding common shares. According to net-operating-income theory (the independence hypothesis), what will be the firm's cost of common equity after the capital-structure change?

   1. What will be the dividend per share flowing to the firm's common shareholders?

   2. By what percentage has the dividend per share changed owing to the capital-structure change?

   3. By what percentage has the cost of common equity changed owing to the capital-structure change?

   4. What will be the weighted cost of capital after the capital-structure change?

9-12B. (*Capital-Structure Theory*) Fernando Hotels has an all-common-equity capital structure. Some financial data for the company are shown below:

Common shares outstanding	= 575,000
Common share price, P_0	= $38 per share
Expected level of EBIT	= $4,500,000
Dividend payout ratio	= 100 percent

In answering the following questions, assume that corporate income is not taxed.

   a. Under the present capital structure, what is the total value of the firm?

   b. What is the cost of common equity capital, K_c? What is the weighted cost of capital, K_0?

   c. Now, suppose Fernando sells $1.5 million of long-term debt with an interest rate of 11 percent. The proceeds are used to retire outstanding common shares. According to the net operating income theory (the independence hypothesis), what will be the firm's cost of common equity after the capital-structure change?

   1. What will be the dividend per share flowing to the firm's common shareholders?

   2. By what percent has the dividend per share changed owing to the capital-structure change?

   3. By what percent has the cost of common equity changed owing to the capital-structure change?

   4. What will be the weighted cost of capital after the capital-structure change?

9-13B. (*EBIT-EPS Analysis*) Mount Rosemead Health Services, Inc., is analyzing three different financing plans for a newly formed subsidiary. The plans are described below:

Plan A	Plan B		Plan C	
Common shares:	Bonds at 10%:	$50,000	Preferred shares at 10%:	$50,000
$150,000	Common shares:	$100,000	Common shares:	$100,000

In all cases the common shares will be sold to net Mount Rosemead $10 per share. The subsidiary is expected to generate an average EBIT per year of $36,000. The management of Mount Rosemead places great emphasis on EPS performance. Income is taxed at a 50 percent rate.

   a. Where feasible, find the EBIT indifference levels between the alternatives.

   b. Which financing plan do you recommend that Mount Rosemead pursue?

SELF-TEST SOLUTIONS

SS-1. a. FC = interest + sinking fund

$$FC = (\$6,000,000)(.12) + \left(\frac{\$6,000,000}{20} \right)$$

$$FC = \$720,000 + \$300,000 = \$1,020,000$$

b. $CB_r = C_0 + NCF_r - FC$

where $C_0 = \$750,000$

$$FC = \$1,020,000$$

and

$$NCF_r = \$3,400,000 - \$3,100,000 = \$300,000$$

so

$$CB_r = \$750,000 + \$300,000 - \$1,020,000$$

$$CB_r = \$30,000$$

c. We know that the firm has a preference for maintaining a cash balance of $750,000. The joint impact of the recessionary economic environment and the proposed issue of bonds would put the firm's recessionary cash balance (CB_r) at $30,000. Since the firm desires a minimum cash balance of $750,000 ($C_0$), the data suggest that the proposed bond issue should be postponed.

SS-2. a. Firm Y seems to be using financial leverage to the most appropriate degree. Notice that its price/earnings ratio of 16 times exceeds that of firm X (at 9 times) and firm Z (also at 9 times).

b. The first financial leverage effect refers to the added variability in the earnings per share stream caused by the use of leverage-inducing financial instruments. The second financial leverage effect concerns the level of earnings per share at a specific EBIT associated with a specific capital structure.

Beyond some critical EBIT level, earnings per share will be higher if more leverage is used. Based on the company data provided, the marketplace for financial instruments is weighing the second leverage effect more heavily. Firm Z, therefore, seems to be under-levered (is operating below its theoretical leverage capacity).

SS-3. a.

Plan A		Plan B
EPS: Less-Levered Plan		EPS: More-Levered Plan
$\dfrac{(EBIT - I)(1 - t) - P}{S_A}$	$=$	$\dfrac{(EBIT - I)(1 - t) - P}{S_B}$
$\dfrac{(EBIT - \$140,000)(1 - 0.5)}{100,000 \text{ (shares)}}$	$=$	$\dfrac{(EBIT - \$480,000)(1 - 0.5)}{60,000 \text{ (shares)}}$
$\dfrac{0.5\,EBIT - \$70,000}{10}$	$=$	$\dfrac{0.5\,EBIT - \$240,000}{6}$
$EBIT = \$990,000$		

b. The EBIT-EPS analysis chart for Martin-Bowing is presented in Figure 9-9.

FIGURE 9-9
EBIT-EPS Analysis Chart for
Martin-Bowing

	Plan A	Plan B
EBIT	$990,000	$990,000
I	140,000	480,000
EBT	$850,000	$510,000
T (.5)	425,000	255,000
NI	$425,000	$255,000
P	0	0
EAC	$425,000	$255,000
÷ No. of common shares	100,000	60,000
EPS	$ 4.25	$ 4.25

  c. Since $1,188,000 exceeds the calculated indifference level of $990,000, the more highly levered plan (plan B) will produce the higher EPS.

  d. At this stage of the problem it is necessary to compute earnings per share (EPS) under each financing alternative. Then the relevant price/earnings ratio for each plan can be applied to project the common share price for the plan at a specific EBIT level.

	Plan A	Plan B
EBIT	$1,188,000	$1,188,000
I	140,000	480,000
EBT	$1,048,000	$ 708,000
T (.5)	524,000	354,000
NI	$ 524,000	$ 354,000
P	0	0
EAC	$ 524,000	$ 354,000
÷ No. of common shares	100,000	60,000
EPS	$ 5.24	$ 5.90
× P/E ratio	13	11
= Projected share price	$ 68.12	$ 64.90

Notice that the greater riskiness of plan B results in the market applying a lower price/earnings multiple to the expected EPS. Therefore, the investors would actually enjoy a higher share price under plan A ($68.12) than they would under plan B ($64.90).

e. Here, we want to find the price/earnings ratio that would equate the common share prices for both plans at an EBIT level of $1,188,000. All we have to do is take plan B's EPS and relate it to plan A's share price. Thus:

$$\$5.90\left(\frac{P}{E}\right) = \$68.12$$

$$\left(\frac{P}{E}\right) = \frac{\$68.12}{\$5.90} = 11.546.$$

A price/earnings ratio of 11.546 when applied to plan B's EPS would give the same share price as that of plan A ($68.12).

SELECTED REFERENCES

Altman, Edward I. "Corporate Bankruptcy Potential, Stockholder Returns, and Share Valuation," *Journal of Finance*, 24 (December 1969), 887–900.

Barges, Alexander. *The Effect of Capital Structure on the Cost of Capital*. Englewood Cliffs, NJ: Prentice-Hall, 1963.

Barnea, Amir, Robert A. Haugen, and Lemma W. Senbet. "Market Imperfections, Agency Problems, and Capital Structure: A Review," *Financial Management*, 10 (Summer 1981), 7–22.

Barton, Sidney L., Ned C. Hill, and Srinivasan Sundaram. "An Empirical Test of Stakeholder Theory Predictions of Capital Structure," *Financial Management*, 18 (Spring 1989), 36–44.

Baskin, Jonathan. "An Empirical Investigation of the Pecking Order Hypothesis," *Financial Management*, 18 (Spring 1989), 26–35.

Baumol, William, and Burton G. Malkiel. "The Firm's Optimal Debt-Equity Combination and the Cost of Capital," *Quarterly Journal of Economics*, 81 (November 1967), 547–578.

Baxter, Nevins D. "Leverage, Risk of Ruin, and the Cost of Capital," *Journal of Finance*, 22 (September 1967), 395–404.

Belkaoui, Ahmed. "A Canadian Survey of Financial Structure," *Financial Management*, 4 (Spring 1975), 74–79.

Bhandari, Laxmi Chard. "Debt/Equity Ratio and Expected Common Stock Returns: Empirical Evidence," *Journal of Finance*, 43 (June 1988), 507–528.

Bhide, Amar. "Why Not Leverage Your Company to the Hilt?" *Harvard Business Review*, 66 (May/June 1988), 92–98.

Billingsley, Randall S., Robert E. Lamy, and G. Rodney Thompson. "The Choice Among Debt, Equity, and Convertible Bonds," *Journal of Finance*, 11 (Spring 1988), 43–56.

Bowen, Robert M., Lane A. Daley, and Charles C. Huber, Jr. "Evidence on the Existence and Determinants of Inter-Industry Differences in Leverage," *Financial Management*, 11 (Winter 1982), 10–20.

Brick, Ivan E., and S. Abraham Ravid. "Interest Rate Uncertainty and the Optimal Debt Maturity Structure," *Journal of Financial and Quantitative Analysis*, 26 (March 1991), 63–82.

Brigham, Eugene F., and Myron J. Gordon. "Leverage, Dividend Policy, and the Cost of Capital," *Journal of Finance*, 23 (March 1968), 85–104.

Castanias, Richard. "Bankruptcy Risk and Optimal Capital Structure," *Journal of Finance*, 38 (December 1983), 1617–1635.

Chang, Rosita P. and S. Ghon Rhee. "The Impact of Personal Taxes on Corporate Dividend Policy and Capital Structure Decisions," *Financial Management*, 19 (Summer 1990), 21–35.

Cherry, Richard T., and Larry W. Spradley. "Further Tests of Industry Influence on Capital Structure," *The Review of Business and Economic Research*, 25 (Spring 1990), 58–66.

Chatterjee, Sris, and James H. Scott, Jr. "Explaining Differences in Corporate Capital Structure: Theory and New Evidence," *Journal of Banking and Finance*, 13 (May 1989), 283–310.

Cheung, Joseph K., S. Paul Roy and Irene Gordon. "Financing Policies of large Canadian Corporations," *CMA Managemnt Account Magazine*, 63(4) (May 1989), 26–31.

Collins, J. Markham, and William S. Sekely. "The Relationship of Headquarters Country and Industry Classification to Financial Structure," *Financial Management*, 12 (Autumn 1983), 45–51.

Conine, Thomas E. "Debt Capacity and the Capital Budgeting Decision: A Comment," *Financial Management*, 9 (Spring 1980), 20–22.

Cornell, Bradford, and Alan C. Shapiro. "Corporate Stakeholders and Corporate Finance," *Financial Management*, 16 (Spring 1987), 5–14.

Donaldson, Gordon. *Corporate Debt Capacity*. Boston: Division of Research, Graduate School of Business Administration, Harvard University, 1961. April 1962, 117–131.

Donaldson, Gordon. "New Framework for Corporate Debt Policy," *Harvard Business Review*, 40 (March–April 1962), 117–31.

Donaldson, Gordon. "Strategy for Financial Emergencies," *Harvard Business Review*, 47 (November–December 1962), 67–79.

Durand, David. "Costs of Debt and Equity Funds for Business: Trends and Problems of Measurement," *Conference on Research in Business Finance*. New York: National Bureau of Economic Research, 1952, 215–247.

Easterwood, John C., and Palani-Rajan Kadapakkam. "The Role of Private and Public Debt in Corporate Capital Structures," *Financial Management*, 20 (Autumn 1991), 49–57.

Ellis, Charles D. "New Framework for Analyzing Capital Structure," *Financial Executive*, 37 (April 1969), 75–86.

Emery, Douglas R., and Adam K. Gehr, Jr. "Tax Options, Capital Structure, and Miller Equilibrium: A Numerical Illustration," *Financial Management*, 17 (Summer 1988), 30–40.

Ferri, Michael G., and Wesley H. Jones. "Determinants of Financial Structure: A New Methodological Approach," *Journal of Finance*, 34 (June 1979), 631–644.

Fischer, Edwin O., Robert Heinkel, and Josef Zechner. "Dynamic Capital Structure Choice: Theory and Tests," *Journal of Finance*, 44 (March 1989), 19–40.

Fletcher, Ralph H., Jr. and Stephan D. Gray. "Private Placements' Big Screen Success," *Corporate Cashflow*, 11 (March 1990), 32–37.

Green, Richard C., and Eli Talmor. "Asset Substitution and the Agency Costs of Debt Financing," *Journal of Banking and Finance*, 10 (October 1986), 391–399.

Greenfield, Robert L., Maury R. Randall, and John C. Woods. "Financial Leverage and Use of the Net Present Value Criterion," *Financial Management*, 12 (Autumn 1983), 40–44.

Hamada, Robert S. "The Effect of the Firm's Capital Structure on the Systematic Risk of Common Stocks," *Journal of Finance*, 27 (May 1972), 435–452.

Harris, John M., Jr., Rodney L. Roenfeldt, and Philip L. Cooley. "Evidence of Financial Leverage Clienteles," *Journal of Finance*, 38 (September 1983), 1125–1132.

Harris, John M., Jr., Rodney L. Roenfeldt and Philip L. Cooley. "Evidence of Financial Leverage Clienteles," *Journal of Finance*, 38 (September 1983), 1125–32.

Harris, Milton and Artur Raviv. "Capital Structure and the Informational Role of Debt," *Journal of Finance*, 45 (June 1990), 321–49.

Harris, Milton and Artur Raviv. "The Theory of Capital Structure," *The Journal of Finance*, 46 (March 1991), 297–355.

Haubrich, Joseph G. "Optimal Financial Structure in Exchange Economies," *International Economic Review*, 29 (May 1988), 217–236.

Haugen, Robert A., and Lemma W. Senbet. "The Insignificance of Bankruptcy Costs to the Theory of Optimal Capital Structure," *Journal of Finance*, 33 (May 1978), 383–393.

Hong, Hai, and Alfred Rappaport. "Debt Capacity, Optimal Capital Structure, and Capital Budgeting," *Financial Management*, 7 (Autumn 1978), 7–11.

Huggins, Nancy J. "Where Can the Middle Market Find Capital?" *Financial Executive*, 7 (May/June 1991), 24–29.

Israel, Ronen. "Capital Structure and the Market for Corporate Control: The Defensive Role of Debt Financing," *The Journal of Finance*, 46 (September 1991), 1391–1409.

Jalilvand, Abolhassan, and Robert S. Harris. "Corporate Behavior in Adjusting to Capital Structure and Dividend Targets: An Econometric Study," *Journal of Finance*, 39 (March 1984), 127–145.

Jensen, Michael C., and William E. Meckling. "Theory of the Firm: Managerial Behavior, Agency Costs and Ownership Structure," *Journal of Financial Economics*, 3 (October 1976), 305–360.

Kane, Alex, Alan J. Marcus, and Robert L. McDonald. "Debt Policy and the Rate of Return Premium to Leverage," *Journal of Financial and Quantitative Analysis*, 20 (December 1985), 479–499.

459

Kidwell, David S., M. Wayne Marr, and Joseph P. Ogden. "The Effect of a Sinking Fund on the Reoffering Yields of New Public Utility Bonds," *The Journal of Financial Research*, 12 (Spring 1989), 1–14.

Kim, E. Han. "A Mean-Variance Theory of Optimal Financial Structure and Corporate Debt Capacity," *Journal of Finance*, 33 (March 1978), 45–64.

Kim, Moon K., and Chunchi, Wu. "Effects of Inflation on Capital Structure," The Financial Review, 23 (May 1988), 183–200.

Lewellen, Wilbur G. *The Cost of Capital*. Dubuque, IA: Kendall/Hunt Publishing Company, 1976.

Lewellen, Wilbur G., and Douglas R. Emery. "Corporate Debt Management and the Value of the Firm," *Journal of Financial and Quantitative Analysis*, 21 (December 1986), 415–426.

Litzenberger, Robert H. "Some Observations on Capital Structure and the Impact of Recent Recapitalizations on Share Prices," *Journal of Financial and Quantitative Analysis*, 21 (March 1986), 59–71.

Marsh, Paul. "The Choice between Equity and Debt: An Empirical Study," *Journal of Finance*, 37 (March 1982), 121–144.

Martin, John D., and David F. Scott, Jr. "A Discriminant Analysis of the Corporate Debt-Equity Decision," *Financial Management*, 3 (Winter 1974), 71–79.

Melnyk, Z. Lew. "Cost of Capital as a Function of Financial Leverage," *Decision Sciences*, 1 (July–October 1970), 327–356.

Miller, Merton H. "Debt and Taxes," *Journal of Finance*, 32 (May 1977), 261–275.

Modigliani, Franco, and Merton H. Miller. "Corporate Income Taxes and the Cost of Capital: A Correction," *American Economic Review*, 53 (June 1963), 433–443.

Myers, Stewart C. "Determinants of Corporate Borrowing," *Journal of Financial Economics*, 5 (1977), 147–175.

Picker, Ida. "Getting Smarter About Debt," *Institutional Investor*, 24 (February 1990), 87–90.

Park, Sang Young, and Joseph Williams. "Taxes, Capital Structure, and Bond Clienteles," *Journal of Business*, 58 (April 1985), 203–224.

Piper, Thomas R., and Wolf A. Weinhold. "How Much Debt Is Right for Your Company?" *Harvard Business Review*, 60 (July–August 1982), 106–114.

Pringle, John J. "Price/Earnings Ratios, Earnings per Share, and Financial Management," *Financial Management*, 2 (Spring 1973), 34–40.

Ravid, S. Abraham. "On Interactions of Production and Financial Decisions," *Financial Management*, 17 (Autumn 1988), 87–99.

Roderick, Pamela H. "Cracking the Debt Market: Tough Nut, Cheap Funds," *Corporate Cashflow*, 12 (August 1991), 24–30.

Rogers, Ronald C., and James E. Owens. "Equity for Debt Exchanges and Stockholder Wealth," *Financial Management*, 14 (Autumn 1985), 18–26.

Schall, Lawrence D. "Firm Financial Structure and Investment," *Journal of Financial and Quantitative Analysis*, 6 (June 1971), 925–942.

Schwartz, Eli, and J. Richard Aronson. "Some Surrogate Evidence in Support of the Concept of Optimal Capital Structure," *Journal of Finance*, 22 (March 1967), 10–18.

Scott, David F., Jr. "Evidence on the Importance of Financial Structure," *Financial Management*, 1 (Summer 1972), 45–50.

Scott, David F., Jr., and Dana J. Johnson. "Financing Policies and Practices in Large Corporations," *Financial Management*, 11 (Summer 1982), 51–59.

Scott, David F., Jr., and John D. Martin. "Industry Influence on Financial Structure," *Financial Management*, 4 (Spring 1975), 67–73.

Scott, James H., Jr. "A Theory of Optimal Capital Structure," *Bell Journal of Economics*, 7 (Spring 1976), 33–54.

Senbet, Lemma A., and Robert A. Taggert, Jr. "Capital Structure Equilibrium under Market Imperfections and Incompleteness," *Journal of Finance*, 39 (March 1984), 93–103.

Shrieves, Ronald E., and Mary M. Pashley. "Evidence on the Association Between Mergers and Capital Structure," *Financial Management*, 13 (Autumn 1984), 39–48.

Solomon, Ezra. "Leverage and the Cost of Capital," *Journal of Finance*, 18 (May 1963), 273–279.

Stulz, Renew M., and Herb Johnson. "An Analysis of Secured Debt," *Journal of Financial Economics*, 14 (December 1985), 501–521.

Taggart, Robert A. "Capital Budgeting and the Financing Decision: An Exposition," *Financial Management*, 6 (Summer 1977), 59–64.

Titman, Sheridan. "The Effect of Forward Markets on the Debt-Equity Mix of Investor Portfolios and the Optimal Capital Structure of Firms," *Journal of Financial and Quantitative Analysis*, 20 (March 1985), 19–27.

Titman, Sheridan, and Roberto Wessels. "The Determinants of Capital Structure Choice," *Journal of Finance*, 43 (March 1988), 1–20.

Walsh, Francis J., Jr. *Planning Corporate Capital Structures*. New York: The Conference Board, 1972.

Zechner, Josef, and Peter Swoboda. "The Critical Implicit Tax Rate and Capital Structure," *Journal of Banking and Finance*, 10 (October 1986), 327–341.

CHAPTER 10

Dividend Policy and Internal Financing

- Key Terms

- Does Dividend Policy Affect Share Price?

- The Dividend Decision in Practice

- Dividend Payment Procedures

- Stock Dividends and Stock Splits

- Share Repurchases

We know that maximizing shareholders' wealth in a firm is the primary goal in financial decision making. The "success" or "failure" of a management decision is determined by its impact on the common share price. We observed that the company's investment (Chapters 5, 6, and 7) and financing decisions (Chapters 8 and 9) can increase the value of the firm. As we examine the firm's dividend and internal financing policies, we return to the same basic question: Can management influence the price of the firm's share through its dividend policy? This chapter will examine the following six objectives in order to answer this question:

1. Study the relationship between a corporation's dividend policy and the market price of its common share.

2. Present practical considerations that may be important to the firm's dividend policy.

3. Review the types of dividend policy that corporations frequently use.

4. Examine the procedures that a company will follow to administer the dividend payment.

5. Examine the use of noncash dividends (stock dividends and stock splits).

6. Explain the use of share repurchases.

KEY TERMS

Before taking up the particular issues relating to dividend policy, we must understand several key terms and interrelationships.

A firm's dividend policy can be described in terms of two basic charac-

FIGURE 10-1
Dividend-Retention-
Financing Tradeoffs

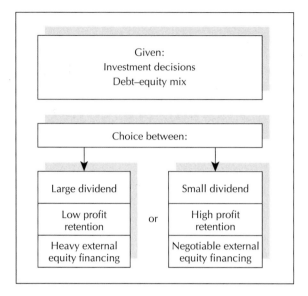

teristics. First, the **dividend payout ratio** indicates the amount of dividends paid relative to the company's earnings. For instance, if the dividend per share is $2 and the earnings per share is $4, the payout ratio is 50 percent ($2/$4). The second characteristic of a firm's dividend policy relates to the *stability* of the dividends over time. As will be observed later in the chapter, dividend stability may be almost as important to the investor as the amount of dividends received.

The financial manager faces an important tradeoff in formulating a firm's dividend policy. The decision to pay a large dividend means that the firm will retain little, if any, profits, which results in heavy reliance on external equity financing. Conversely, the decision to pay a small dividend payment is equivalent to high profit retention with less need for externally generated equity funds. Both these cases assume that management has already decided how much to invest and the debt-equity mix to be used in financing these investments. A summary of these tradeoffs, which are fundamental to our discussion, are illustrated in Figure 10-1.

DOES DIVIDEND POLICY AFFECT SHARE PRICE?[1]

The fundamental question to be resolved in our study of the firm's dividend policy may be stated simply: "What is a sound rationale or motivation for dividend payments?" If we believe our objective should be to maximize the

---

[1]The concepts of this section draw heavily from Donald H. Chew, Jr. (ed.), *Six Roundtable Discussions of Corporate Finance with Joel Stern*, "Do Dividends Matter? A Discussion of Corporate Dividend Policy," New York: Quorum Books, 1986, pp. 67-101; and a book of readings edited by Joel M. Stern and Donald H. Chew, Jr., *The Revolution in Corporate Finance*, New York: Basil Blackwell, 1986. Specific readings included Merton Miller, "Can Management Use Dividends to Influence the Value of the Firm?" pp. 299-303; Richard Brealey, "Does Dividend Policy Matter?" pp. 304-309; and Michael Rozeff, "How Companies Set Their Dividend Payout Ratios," pp. 320-326.

market value of the common shares, we may restate the question as follows: "Given the firm's capital-budgeting and borrowing decisions, what is the effect of the firm's dividend policies on the share price?" "Does a high dividend payment decrease share value, increase it, or make no real difference?"

At first glance, we might reasonably conclude that a firm's dividend policy is important. We have already (in Chapter 4) defined the value of a share to be equal to the present value of future dividends. How can we now suggest that dividends are not important? Why do so many companies pay dividends, and why is space in prominent Canadian finance newspapers devoted to dividend announcements? Based upon intuition, we could quickly conclude that dividend policy is important. However, we might be surprised to learn that the dividend question has been a controversial issue for well over three decades. It has even been called the "dividend puzzle."[2]

Three Basic Views

Some would argue that the amount of the dividend is irrelevant, and any time spent on the decision is a waste of energy. Others contend that a high dividend will result in a high share price. Still others take the view that dividends actually hurt the share value. Let us look at these three views in turn.

View 1: Dividend Policy Is Irrelevant

Much of the controversy about the dividend issue is based on the time-honoured arguments between the academic and professional communities. Experienced practitioners perceive share price changes as resulting from dividend announcements, whereas professors argue that most dividend policies have not been carefully defined, and as a result the perceived relationship between dividend announcements and share prices is an illusion.[3]

The position that dividends are not important rests on two preconditions. First, we assume that investment and borrowing decisions have already been made, and that these decisions will not be altered by the amount of any dividend payments. Second, "perfect" capital markets are assumed to exist, which means that (1) investors can buy and sell shares without incurring any transaction costs, such as brokerage commissions; (2) companies can issue shares without any cost of doing so; (3) there are no corporate or personal taxes; (4) complete information about the firm is readily available; and (5) there are no conflicts of interest between managements and shareholders.

The first assumption—that we have already made the investment and financing decisions—simply keeps us from confusing the issues. We want to know the effect of dividend decisions on a stand-alone basis, without mixing in other decisions. The second assumption of perfect capital markets allows us to study the effect of dividend decisions in isolation, much like a physicist studies motion in a vacuum to avoid the influence of friction.

Given these assumptions, the effect of a dividend decision on share price may be stated unequivocally: There is no relationship between dividend policy and share value. One dividend policy is as good as another one. Under

---

[2]See Fischer Black, "The Dividend Puzzle," *Journal of Portfolio Management*, 2 (Winter 1976), pp. 5–8.

[3]For an excellent presentation of this issue, see Merton Miller, "Can Management Use Dividends to Influence the Value of the Firm?" in *The Revolution in Corporate Finance*, edited by Joel M. Stern and Donald H. Chew, Jr. New York: Basil Blackwell, 1986, pp. 299–305.

this hypothesis, the investor is concerned only with total returns which come from the firm's investment decisions; they are indifferent whether these returns come from capital gains or dividend income. Given the firm's investment policy, they recognize that the firm's dividend decision is really a choice of financing strategy. The principles which enable a firm to grow through its investments have been discussed in Chapter 4. A firm may choose either to use its own profits or to issue more equity and pay more dividends. In the first case, shareholders should receive their return as capital gains since the value of the shares should increase; in the second case, shareholders should receive their return as dividends. The nature of the return is the only difference: total returns should be about the same. Thus, to argue that paying dividends can make shareholders better off is to argue that paying out cash with one hand and taking it back with the other hand is a worthwhile activity for management.

The firm's dividend payout could affect share price if the shareholder has no other way to receive income from the investment. In this case shareholders will sell their shares since capital markets have been assumed to be efficient. In the case that the firm pays a dividend, the investor could eliminate any dividend received, in whole or in part, by using the dividend to purchase shares. The investor can thus personally create any desired dividend stream, no matter what dividend policy is chosen by management. The dividend policy is therefore an inconsequential activity for management.

AN EXAMPLE OF DIVIDEND IRRELEVANCE ■ To demonstrate the argument that dividends may not matter, come to the Land of Ez (pronounced "ease"), where the environment is quite simple. First, the king, being a kind soul, has imposed no income taxes on his subjects. Second, investors can buy and sell securities without paying any sales commissions. In addition, when a company issues new securities (shares or bonds), there are no flotation costs. Furthermore, the Land of Ez is completely computerized, so that all information about firms is instantaneously available to the public at no cost. Next, all investors realize that the value of a company is a function of its investment opportunities and its financing decisions. Therefore, the dividend policy offers no new information about either the firm's ability to generate earnings or the riskiness of its earnings. Finally, all firms are owned and managed by the same parties; thus, we have no potential conflict between owners and managers. To summarize, in the Land of Ez:

1. There is no income tax on the investor's income; nor is there a tax on gains realized from holding common shares.

2. Security markets are considered to be perfect:

   a. The investors incur no brokerage commissions.

   b. Firms can issue securities at no cost.

   c. Information is free and equally available to all investors.

   d. A particular dividend policy has no effect in determining the firm's capability to generate profits.

   e. Security prices equal the present value of the expected future cash flows accruing to their owners.

   f. There is no possible conflict between owners and managers, since they are the same.

Within this financial utopia, would a change in a corporation's dividend stream have any effect upon the price of the firm's shares? The answer is

"No." To illustrate, consider Dowell Venture, Inc., a corporation that received a charter at the end of 1993 to conduct business in the Land of Ez. The firm is to be financed by common shares only. Its life is to extend for only two years (1994 and 1995), at which time it will be liquidated.

Table 10-1 presents Dowell Venture's balance sheet at the time of its incorporation, as well as the projected cash flows from the short-term venture. The anticipated cash flows are based upon an expected return on investment of 20 percent, which is exactly what the common shareholders require as a rate of return on their investment in the firm's shares.

At the end of 1994 an additional investment of $300,000 will be required, which may be financed by (1) retaining $300,000 of the 1994 profits, or (2) issuing new common shares, or (3) some combination of both of these. In fact, two dividend plans for 1994 are under consideration. The investors would receive either $100,000 or $250,000 in dividends. If $250,000 is paid out of 1994's $400,000 in earnings, the company would be required to issue $150,000 in new shares to make up the difference in the total amount of funds needed of $300,000 and the $150,000 that is retained. Table 10-2 depicts these two dividend plans and the corresponding new share issue. Our objective in analyzing the data is to answer this question: Which dividend plan is preferable to the investors? In answering this question, we must take three steps: (1) Calculate the amount and timing of the dividend stream for the original investors. (2) Determine the present value of the dividend stream for each dividend plan. (3) Select the dividend alternative providing the higher value to the investors.

Step 1: Computing the Dividend Streams. The first step in this process is presented in Table 10-3. The dividends in 1994 (line 1, Table 10-3) are readily apparent from the data in Table 10-2. However, the amount of the dividend to be paid to the present shareholders in 1995 has to be calculated. To do so, we assume that investors receive (1) their original investments (line 2, Table 10-3), (2) any funds retained within the business in 1994 (line 3, Table 10-3), and (3) the profits for 1995 (line 4, Table 10-3). However, if additional shareholders invest in the company, as with plan 2, the dividends to be paid to these investors must be subtracted from the total available dividends (line 6, Table 10-3). The remaining dividends (line 7, Table 10-3) represent the

	December 31, 1993	
Total assets	$2,000,000	
Common shares (100,000 shares)	$2,000,000	
	1994	*1995*
Projected cash available from operations for paying DIVIDENDS or for REINVESTING	$400,000	$460,000

TABLE 10-1
Dowell Venture, Inc., Financial Data

	Plan 1	*Plan 2*
Internally generated cash flow	$400,000	$400,000
Dividend for 1994	100,000	250,000
Cash available for reinvestment	$300,000	$150,000
Amount of investment in 1994	300,000	300,000
Additional external financing required	$ 0	$150,000

TABLE 10-2
Dowell Venture, Inc., 1994 Proposed Dividend Plans

465

	Plan 1		Plan 2	
	Total Amount	Amount Per Share[a]	Total Amount	Amount Per Share[a]
Year 1 (1994)				
(1) Dividend Year 2 (1995)	$ 100,000	$ 1.00	$ 250,000	$ 2.50
Total dividend consisting of:				
(2) Original investment:				
(a) Old investors	$2,000,000		$2,000,000	
(b) New investors	0		150,000	
(3) Retained earnings	300,000		150,000	
(4) Profits for 1995	460,000		460,000	
(5) Total dividend to all investors in 1994	$2,760,000		$2,760,000	
(6) Less dividends to new investors:				
(a) Original investment	0		(150,000)	
(b) Profits for new investors (20% of $150,000 investment)	0		(30,000)	
(7) Liquidating dividends available to original investors in 1995	$2,760,000	$27.60	$2,580,000	$25.80

[a]Number of original shares outstanding equals 100,000.

amount that current shareholders will receive in 1995. Therefore, the amounts of the dividend may be summarized as follows:

Dividend Plan	Year 1	Year 2
1	$1.00	$27.60
2	2.50	25.80

Step 2: Determining the Present Value of the Cash Flow Streams. For each of the dividend payment streams the resulting common share value is

$$\text{share price (plan 1)} = \frac{\$1.00}{(1 + .20)} + \frac{\$27.60}{(1 + .20)^2} = \$20$$

$$\text{share price (plan 2)} = \frac{\$2.50}{(1 + .20)} + \frac{\$25.80}{(1 + .20)^2} = \$20$$

Therefore, the two approaches provide the same end product; that is, the market price of Dowell Venture's common share is $20 regardless of the dividend policy chosen.

Step 3: Select the Best Dividend Plan. If the objective is to maximize the shareholders' wealth, either plan is equally acceptable. Alternatively, shifting the dividend payments between years by changing the dividend policy does not affect the value of the security. Thus, only if investments are made with expected returns exceeding 20 percent will the value of the share increase. In other words, the only wealth-creating activity in the Land of Ez, where companies are financed entirely by equity, is management's investment decisions.

View 2: High Dividends Increase Share Value

The belief that a firm's dividend policy is unimportant implicitly assumes that an investor should use the same required rate of return, whether income comes through capital gains or through dividends. However, dividends are more predictable than capital gains; management can control dividends, but it cannot dictate the price of the share. Investors are less certain of receiving income from capital gains than from dividends. The incremental risk associated with capital gains relative to dividend income implies a higher required rate for discounting a dollar of capital gains than for discounting a dollar of dividends. In other words, we would value a dollar of expected dividends more highly than a dollar of expected capital gains. We might, for example, require a 14 percent rate of return for a share that pays its entire return from dividends, but a 20 percent return for a high-growth share that pays no dividend. In so doing, we would give a higher value to the dividend income than we would to the capital gains. This view, which says dividends are more certain than capital gains, has been called the "bird-in-the-hand" theory.

The position that dividends are less risky than capital gains, and should therefore be valued differently, is not without its critics. If we hold to our basic decision not to let the firm's dividend policy influence its investment and capital-mix decisions, the company's operating cash flows, both in expected amount and variability, are unaffected by its dividend policy. Since the dividend policy has no impact on the volatility of the company's overall cash flows, it has no impact on the riskiness of the firm.

Increasing a firm's dividend does not reduce the basic riskiness of the share; rather, if a dividend payment requires management to issue new shares, it only transfers risk and ownership from the current owners to new owners. We would have to acknowledge that the current investors who receive the dividend trade an uncertain capital gain for a "safe" asset (the cash dividend). However, if risk reduction is the only goal, the investor could have kept the money in the bank and not bought the shares in the first place.

We might find fault with this "bird-in-the-hand" theory, but there is still a strong perception among many investors and professional investment advisors that dividends are important. They frequently argue their case based upon their own personal experience. For example, one investment advisor who is an advocate of dividend policy stated the following:

> In advising companies on dividend policy, we're absolutely sure on one side that the investors in companies like the utilities and the banks want dividends. We're absolutely sure on the other side that...the high-technology companies should have no dividends. For the high earners—the ones that have a high rate of return like 20 percent, or more than their cost of capital—we think they should have a low payout ratio. We think a typical industrial company which earns its cost of capital—just earns its cost of capital—probably should be in the average [dividend payout] range of 40 to 50 percent.[4]

View 3: Low Dividends Increase Share Value

The third view of how dividends affect share price proposes that dividends actually hurt the investor. This argument has largely been based on the difference in tax treatment for dividend income and capital gains. Unlike the investors in the great Land of Ez, most other investors do pay income taxes. For these taxpayers, the objective is to maximize the after-tax return on investment relative to the risk assumed. This objective is realized by minimizing the effective tax rate on the income and, whenever possible, by deferring the payment of taxes.

---

[4]Donald H Chew, Jr. (ed.) "Do Dividends Matter? A Discussion of Corporate Dividend Policy," in *Six Roundtable Discussions of Corporate Finance with Joel Stern*, New York: Quorum Books, 1986, 83–84.

Tax Reform legislation has changed the tax treatment of capital gains and dividends for individuals. Revenue Canada requires an individual to be taxed on only 75 percent of capital gains realized from the sale of capital property for 1990 and subsequent years. Furthermore, each individual is eligible for a lifetime capital gains deduction of $100,000. With respect to dividends, Revenue Canada requires an individual's dividend income to be grossed up by 25 percent and taxed at individual's marginal tax rate. However, an individual is eligible to claim a dividend tax credit of 13.33 percent on the grossed-up amount. This dividend tax credit is used to reduce the taxes payable of an individual. Nevertheless, the use of the capital gains deduction offers the individual a higher after-tax return for the first $100,000 of investment income than the after-tax return offered from the use of the dividend tax credit.

If an individual's lifetime capital gains deduction is exhausted, the after-tax return from dividend income will be greater than that of capital gains for investment income.[5] However, we should note that taxes on dividend income are paid in the year of receipt; whereas, taxes on price appreciation (capital gains) are deferred until the share is actually sold. Thus, when it comes to tax considerations, most investors will still prefer the retention of a firm's earnings as opposed to the payment of cash dividends. If earnings are retained within the firm, the share price increases, but the increase is not taxed until the shares are sold.

To summarize, when it comes to taxes, we want to maximize our after-tax return, as opposed to the before-tax return. As a result, investors try to defer taxes whenever possible. Shares that allow tax deferral (low dividends—high capital gains) will possibly sell at a premium relative to shares that require us to pay taxes immediately (high dividends—low capital gains). In this way, the two shares may provide comparable after-tax returns. This suggests that a policy of paying low dividends will result in a higher share price. That is, high dividends hurt investors, while low dividends and high retention help investors. This is the logic of advocates of the low-dividend policy.

Improving Our Thinking

We have now looked at three views on dividend policy. Which is right? The argument that dividends are irrelevant is difficult to refute, given the perfect market assumptions. However, in the real world, it is not always easy to feel

---

[5]Examples of the effective tax rates for different amounts of investment income for 1992 are shown below:

Investment Income	Effective tax rate[a]	
	Capital gain	Dividend
$32,000	9.7%[b]	4.3%[c]
40,000	10.6	6.7
90,000	16.4	14.0

[a] The tax calculation assumed no other type of income, federal tax and surtax rates for 1992, and a personal tax credit of $1,098.

[b] The tax calculation assumed that the personal capital gains exemption of $100,000 is exhausted and 75% of the capital gains is taxable.

[c] The tax calculation assumed a gross-up of 25% and a dividend tax credit of 13.33% on grossed-up taxable income.

comfortable with such an argument. On the other hand, the high-dividend philosophy, which measures risk by how we split the firm's cash flows between dividends and retention, is not particularly appealing when studied carefully. The third view, which is essentially a tax argument against high dividends, is persuasive, given the lifetime capital gains deduction of $100,000 for an individual. This type of deduction provides preferential tax treatment on income derived from capital gains as compared to income derived from dividends. Furthermore, even if the individual has exhausted the lifetime capital gains deduction, the "deferral advantage" of capital gains is still alive and well. However, if low dividends are so advantageous and generous dividends are so hurtful, why do companies continue to pay dividends?[6] It is difficult to believe that managers would forgo such an easy opportunity to benefit their shareholders. What are we missing?

The need to find the missing elements in our "dividend puzzle" has not been ignored. In an effort to gain a better understanding of this puzzle, we need to improve our thinking and/or to gather more evidence about the topic. While no single definitive answer has yet been found that is acceptable to all, a number of plausible extensions have been developed. Several of the more popular additions include (1) the residual dividend theory, (2) the clientele effect, (3) information effects, (4) agency costs, and (5) expectations theory.

The Residual Dividend Theory

Within the Land of Ez, companies were blessed with professional consultants who were essentially charitable in nature; they did not seek any compensation when they helped a firm through the process of issuing shares. (Even in the Land of Ez, managers needed help from investment dealers, accountants, and attorneys to sell a new issue.) In reality, the process is quite expensive, and may cost as much as 20 percent of the dollar issue size.[7]

If a company incurs flotation costs, they may have a direct bearing upon the dividend decision. As a result of the high flotation costs, a firm must issue a larger amount of securities in order to receive the amount required for investment. For example, if $300,000 is needed to finance proposed investments, an amount exceeding the $300,000 will have to be issued to offset flotation costs incurred in the sale of the new share issue. This means, very simply, that new equity capital raised through the sale of common shares will be more expensive than capital raised through the retention of earnings.

Flotation costs eliminate our indifference between financing by internal capital and by new common shares. Earlier, the company could pay dividends and issue common shares or retain profits. However, internal financing is preferred to the high flotation costs. Dividends are paid only if profits are not completely used for investment purposes; that is, only when there are "residual earnings" after the financing of new investments. This policy is called the **residual dividend theory**.[8]

---

[6]In fact, most successful companies pay dividends. Furthermore, most financial managers think dividend policy is important. See H. Kent Baker, Gail E. Farrelly, and Richard B. Edelman, "A Survey of Management Views on Dividend Policy," *Financial Management*, (Autumn 1985), pp. 78–84

[7]We discuss the costs of issuing securities in Chapter 17.

[8]The residual dividend theory is consistent with the "pecking order" theory of finance as described by Stewart Myers, "The Capital Structure Puzzle," *The Journal of Finance* (July 1984), 575–592.

BASIC FINANCIAL MANAGEMENT IN PRACTICE

Excerpts from "Do Dividends Matter? A Discussion of Corporate Dividend Policy"

January 6, 1982

Joseph T. Willett, Moderator: I would like to welcome the participants and guests to this discussion, the subject of which is Corporate Dividend Policy. The general questions we want to address are these: Does dividend policy matter? And if so, why and how does it matter? Certain people argue that the theory of finance, combined with the treatment of dividends under U.S. tax law, would suggest that low dividends benefit investors. Others argue that because of the demand by some investors for current income, high dividends benefit investors. In the presence of these widely held views, I think it is fair to say that most carefully executed research has revealed no consistent relationship between dividends and share prices. From these studies, the market collectively appears to be "dividend neutral." That is, while individual investors may have preferences between dividends and capital gains, the results suggest neither a preference for nor an aversion to dividends. Which, of course, doesn't satisfy either the pro-dividend or anti-dividend group. Amid all this confusion, one observation stands out: nearly all successful firms pay dividends. And, furthermore, dividend policy is an important concern of most chief financial officers and financial managers generally. These facts of corporate practice, in light of all the evidence on the subject, present us with a puzzle—one which has continued to baffle the academic finance profession. In a paper written in 1976, entitled "The Dividend Puzzle," Fischer Black of MIT—one of the most widely respected researchers in the field—posed the question: "What should the individual investor do about dividends in his portfolio? What should the corporation do about dividend policy?"

Joel Stern: I'd like to point out that the major reason why people like Fischer Black believe they don't know the answer to the question of the appropriate dividend policy is this: the evidence that has been accumulated in the academic community by serious researchers—by people that we have a lot of respect for, who are on the faculties of the premiere business schools—almost without exception, these academics find that there is no evidence to suggest that investors at the margin, where prices are set, have any preference for dividends over capital gains. This supports the point of view that the price-setting, marginal investor is "dividend-neutral," which means that a dollar of dividends gained is equal to a dollar of capital gains returned, while being indifferent how that return was divided between dividends and price appreciation. There is a second point of view, that has been expressed recently in research, which shows that investors who receive dividends cannot undo the harmful tax consequences of receiving that dividend. And, as a result, the market is actually "dividend averse," marking down prices of shares that pay cash dividends, so that the pretax returns that investors earn are high enough such that, post-tax, the returns are what they would have been had the company not paid cash dividends in the first place. But there is no creditable evidence that I am aware of—none that has been accepted by the academic finance community—that shows that investors prefer dividends over capital gains.

If the evidence that has been published to date says that investors are dividend neutral or dividend averse, then how is it that somebody with the esteem of Fischer Black can come along and say: "We don't know what the right dividend policy is." The problem is that he is what we call a "positive economist." That doesn't mean that he is an economist who is positive about things. It means that he says the job of the economist is to account for what we see around us. He believes that markets behave in a sensible fashion at the margin; that under the guidance of the dominant price-setting investors, the market behaves in a rational manner, making the right choices for itself. Therefore, he is saying that there must be a reason why almost all companies for all time have been paying cash dividends. If a few companies paid dividends for all time, or almost all companies paid dividends only occasionally, then one could make the case that it is possible dividends are really not important. But, if we find that almost all companies pay dividends for almost all time, there must be a good reason why they are paying the dividends. Therefore, who are we, as financial advisors, to say to a company, "No, don't pay cash dividends. After all, it won't harm you very much despite the fact that almost all companies are paying cash dividends"? That wouldn't make very much sense.

Source: Donald H. Chew, Jr. (ed.), "Do Dividends Matter? A Discussion of Corporate Dividend Policy," *Six Roundtable Discussions of Corporate Finance with Joel Stern*. New York: Quorum Books, 1986, pp. 67–101.

With the assumption of no flotation costs removed, the firm's dividend policy would be as follows:

1. Maintain the optimum debt ratio in financing future investments.

2. Accept an investment if the net present value is positive. That is, the expected rate of return exceeds the cost of capital.

3. Finance the equity portion of new investments first by internally generated funds. Only after this capital is fully utilized should the firm issue new common shares.

4. If any internally generated funds still remain after making all investments, pay dividends to the investors. However, if all internal capital is needed for financing the equity portion of proposed investments, pay no dividend.

EXAMPLE

Assume that the Krista Corporation finances 40 percent of its investments with debt and the remaining 60 percent with common equity. Two million dollars have been generated from operations and may be used to finance the common equity portion of new investments or to pay common dividends. The firm's management is considering five investment opportunities. Figure 10-2 illustrates the expected rate of return for these investments, along with the firm's weighted marginal cost of capital curve. From the information contained in the figure, we would accept projects A, B, and C, requiring $2.5 million in total financing. Therefore, $1 million in new debt (40% of $2.5 million) would be needed, with common equity providing $1.5 million (60% of $2.5 million). In this instance the dividend payment decision would be to pay $500,000 in dividends, which is the residual or remainder of the $2 million internally generated capital.

To illustrate further, consider the dividend decision if project D had also been acceptable. If this investment were added to the firm's portfolio of

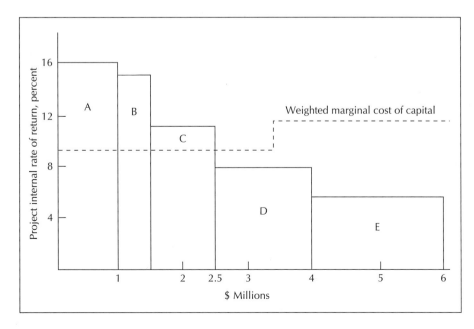

FIGURE 10-2
Krista Corporation
Investment Schedule

proposed capital expenditures, then $4 million in new financing would be needed. Debt financing would constitute $1.6 million (40% × $4 million) and common equity would provide the additional $2.4 million (60% × $4 million). Since only $2 million is available internally, $400,000 in new common shares would be issued. The residual available for dividends would be zero, and no dividend would be paid. ∎

In summary, dividend policy is influenced by (1) the company's investment opportunities, (2) the capital-structure mix, and (3) the availability of internally generated capital. In the Krista Corporation example, dividends were paid only after all acceptable investments had been financed. This logic, called the residual dividend theory, implies that the dividends to be paid should equal the equity capital remaining after financing investments. According to this theory, dividend policy is a passive influence, having by itself no direct influence on the market price of the common shares.

The Clientele Effect

What if the investors living in the Land of Ez did not like the dividend policy chosen by Dowell's management? No problem. They could simply satisfy their personal income preferences by purchasing or selling securities when the dividends received did not satisfy their current needs for income. If an investor did not view the dividends received in any given year to be sufficient, he or she could simply sell a portion of shares, thereby "creating a dividend." In addition, if the dividend were larger than the investor desired, he or she could purchase shares with the "excess cash" created by the dividend. However, once we leave the Land of Ez, we find that such adjustments in share ownership are not cost-free. For example, an investor who buys or sells shares incurs the following costs: brokerage fees, taxes on the cash dividends, and the cost of acquiring information needed to make the decision to buy or sell the shares. Finally, some institutional investors, such as university endowment funds, are precluded from selling shares and "spending" the proceeds.

As a result of these considerations, investors may not be too inclined to buy shares that require them to "create" a dividend stream more suitable to their purposes. Rather, if investors do in fact have a preference between dividends and capital gains, we could expect them to seek firms that have a dividend policy consistent with these preferences. They would, in essence, "sort themselves out" by buying shares that satisfy their preferences for dividends and/or capital gains. Individuals and institutions that need current income would be drawn to companies that have high dividend payouts. Other investors, such as wealthy individuals, would much prefer holding securities that offer no or small dividend income but large capital gains because of the lifetime capital gains deduction and the "deferral advantage" of capital gains. In other words, there would be a **clientele effect**: Firms draw a given clientele, given their stated dividend policy.

The possibility that clienteles of investors exist might lead us to believe that the firm's dividend policy matters. However, unless there is a greater aggregate demand for a particular policy than the market can satisfy, dividend policy is still unimportant: one policy is as good as the other. As a result of the clientele effect, a firm should avoid making capricious changes in their dividend policy. Given that the firm's investment decisions are already made, the level of the dividend is still unimportant. The change in the policy matters only when it requires clientele to shift to another company.

The Information Effect

The investor in the Land of Ez would argue with considerable persuasion that a firm's value is determined strictly by its investment and financing decisions, and that the dividend policy has no impact on value. Yet we know from experience that a large, unexpected change in dividends can have a significant impact on the share price. For instance, in 1988 TransCanada Pipelines Ltd. cut its dividend from $1.12 to $0.67, or a 39 percent decline. Despite management's insistence that the reduction was necessary because of the company's acquisition of Encor Energy Corporation, the response of the market to the dividend announcement caused the share price to decrease from $15.50 to $13.75, a decline of 11 percent. Other more dramatic reactions in North American markets to dividend announcements include the following: in November of 1990, Occidental Petroleum cut its dividend from $2 to $1, and the response of the market to the dividend announcement caused the share price to decrease from about $32 to $12; in July of 1984, ITT cut its dividend from $.69 to $.25, and the response of the market to the dividend announcement caused the share price to decrease from $31 to $21.13, a 32 percent decline. Thus, how can we suggest that dividend policy matters little, when we can cite numerous such examples of a change in dividend affecting the share price, especially when the change is negative?[9]

Market response to dividend announcements must be examined for its cause, that is, for its information content. In effect investors may understand the announcement of a change in dividend policy as a signal about the firm's financial condition, especially its earning power.[10] Thus, a dividend increase that is larger than expected "signals" to investors that management expects significantly higher earnings in the future. Conversely, a dividend decrease, or even a less than expected increase, "signals" that management is forecasting less favourable future earnings.

Some would argue that management frequently has inside information about the firm that it cannot make available to investors. This difference in accessibility to information between management and investors, called **information asymmetry**, may result in a lower share price than would occur under conditions of certainty. However, a regularly increasing dividend may be interpreted by an investor that management is making a commitment to continue these cash flows to the shareholders for the foreseeable future. If we recognize the fact that increasing dividends impinge on management's flexibility, we can conclude that management is not concealing some negative information about the company. So in a risky marketplace, dividends become a means to minimize any "drag" on the share price that might come from differences in the level of information available to managers and investors.

Dividends may therefore be important only as a communication tool; management may have no other credible way to inform investors about future earnings, or at least no convincing way that is less costly.

---

[9]Unanticipated changes in dividends do have an impact on share price. However, the price change is most likely the consequence of the investor using the dividend change as "new information" about the company.

[10]It is possible that dividends are used by investors as a proxy for a measure of risk. We know that high-dividend-paying companies are often less risky and lower-dividend-paying firms frequently have greater risk. However, it is difficult to measure the causal relationship between dividend decisions and shareholder value, because of other seemingly unrelated factors.

Agency Costs

Let us return again to the Land of Ez. We had avoided any potential conflict between the firm's investors and managers by assuming them to be one and the same. With only a cursory look at the real marketplace, we can see that managers and investors are typically not the same people, and as noted in the preceding section, these two groups do not have the same access to information about the firm. If the two groups are not the same, we must then assume that management is dedicated to maximizing shareholder wealth.[11] In other words, we are making a presupposition that the market values of companies with separate owners and managers will not differ from those of owner-managed firms.

Two possibilities should help managers see things as the equity investors see them: (1) Low market values may attract takeover bids; and (2) a competitive labour market may allow investors to replace uncooperative managers. That is, if management is not sensitive to the need to maximize shareholder wealth, new investors may buy the shares, take "control" of the firm, and remove management.[12] If current management is being less than supportive of the owners, these owners can always seek other managers who will work in the investors' best interest. If these two market mechanisms worked perfectly without any cost, the potential conflict would be nonexistent. In reality, however, conflicts may still exist, and the share price of a company owned by investors who are separate from management may be less than the share value of a closely held firm. The difference in price is the cost of the conflict to the owners, which has come to be called **agency costs**.[13]

Recognizing the possible problem, management, acting independently or at the insistence of the board of directors, frequently takes action to minimize the cost associated with the separation of ownership and management control. Such action, which in itself is costly, includes auditing by independent accountants, assigning supervisory functions to the company's board of directors, creating covenants in lending agreements that restrict management's powers, and providing inventive compensation plans for management that help "bond" the management with the owners.

A firm's dividend policy may be perceived by owners as a tool to minimize agency costs. Assuming that the payment of a dividend requires management to issue shares to finance new investments, new investors will be attracted to the company only if management provides convincing information that the capital will be used profitably. Thus, the payment of dividends indirectly results in a closer monitoring of management's investment activities. In this case, dividends may make a meaningful contribution to the value of the firm.

Expectations Theory[14]

A common thread throughout much of our discussion of dividend policy, particularly as it relates to information effects, is the word "expected." We

---

[11]This issue was addressed briefly in Chapter 1.

[12]The "corporate control hypothesis," especially as it relates to companies merging or being acquired, has generated a great amount of interest in recent years. For example, see the April 1983 issue of *Journal of Financial Economics*.

[13]See M. C. Jenson, and W. H. Meckling, "Theory of the Firm: Managerial Behavior, Agency Costs, and Ownership Structure," *Journal of Financial Economics*, (October 1976), pp. 305–360.

[14]Much of the thoughts in this section came from Merton Miller, "Can Management Use Dividends to Influence the Value of the Firm?" in *The Revolution in Corporate Finance*, edited by Joel M. Stern, and Donald H. Chew, Jr., New York: Basil Blackwell, 1986, pp. 299–303.

should not overlook the significance of this word when we are making any financial decision within the firm. No matter what the decision area, how the market price responds to management's actions is not determined entirely by the action itself; it is also affected by investors' expectations about the ultimate decision to be made by management.

As the time approaches for management to announce the amount of the next dividend, investors form expectations as to how much that dividend will be. These expectations are based on a number of factors internal to the firm, such as past dividend decisions, current and expected earnings, investment strategies, and financing decisions. They also consider such things as the condition of the general economy, the strength or weakness of the industry at the time, and possible changes in government policies.

When the actual dividend decision is announced, the investor compares the actual decision with the expected decision. If the amount of the dividend is as expected, even if it represents an increase from prior years, the market price of the share will remain unchanged. However, if the dividend is higher or lower than expected, investors will re-assess their perceptions about the firm. They will question the meaning of the unexpected change in the dividend. They may use the unexpected dividend decision as a clue about unexpected changes in earnings; that is, the unexpected dividend change has information content about the firm's earnings and other important factors. In short, management's actual decision about the firm's dividend policy may not be terribly significant, unless it departs from investors' expectations. If there is a difference between actual and expected dividends, we will more than likely see a movement in the share price.

The Empirical Evidence

Our search for an answer to the question of dividend relevance has been less than successful. We have given it our best thinking, but still no single definitive position has emerged. Maybe we could gather evidence to show the relationship between dividend practices and security prices. We might also inquire into the perceptions of financial managers who make decisions about dividend policies, with the idea that their beliefs affect their decision-making process. Then we could truly know that dividend policy is important or that it does not matter.

To test the relationship between dividend payments and security prices, we could compare a firm's dividend yield (dividend/share price) and the share's total return. The following question can then be asked: "Do shares that pay high dividends provide higher or lower returns to investors?" Such tests have been conducted with the use of highly sophisticated statistical techniques.[15] Despite the use of these extremely powerful analytical tools, which involve intricate and complicated procedures, the results have been mixed.[16]

---

[15]Some of the difficulties which occur in this type of research include: (1) the inability to disentangle the effect of the dividend decision from other influences and (2) the need to know the investor's expected returns for holding the shares in order to test the relationship between dividend policy and the share price. However, the investor's expectations are unknown, forcing us to rely on historical returns in any testing of relationships.

[16]See F. Black and M. Scholes, "The Effects of Dividend Yield and Dividend Policy on Common Stock Prices and Returns," *Journal of Financial Economics*, 1 (May 1974), pp. 1–22; P. Hess, "The Ex-Dividend Behavior of Stock Returns: Further Evidence on Tax Effects," *Journal of Finance*, 37 (May 1982), pp. 445–456; R. H. Litzenberger and K. Ramaswamy, "The Effect of Personal Taxes and Dividends on Capital Asset Prices: Theory and Empirical Evidence," *Journal of Financial Economics*, 7 (June 1979), pp. 163–195; and M. H. Miller and M. Scholes, "Dividends and Taxes: Some Empirical Evidence," *Journal of Political Economy*, 90 (1982), pp. 1118–1141.

However, over long periods of time, the results have given a slight advantage to the low-dividend shares; that is, shares that pay lower dividends appear to have higher prices. The findings are far from conclusive, however, owing to the relatively large standard errors of the estimates. The apparent differences may be the result of random sampling error and not real differences. We simply have been unable to disentangle the effect of dividend policy from other influences.

Several reasons may be given for our inability to get conclusive results. First, to be accurate, we would need to know the amount of dividends investors expected to receive. Since these expectations cannot be observed, we can only use historical data, which may or may not relate to current expectations. Second, most empirical studies have assumed a linear relationship between dividend payments and share prices. The actual relationship may be nonlinear, possibly even discontinuous. Whatever the reasons, the evidence to date is inconclusive and the vote is still out.

Since our statistical prowess does not provide any conclusive evidence, let's turn to our last hope. What do the financial managers of the world believe about the relevance of dividend policy? While we may not conclude that a manager's opinion is necessarily the "final word on the matter," having these insights is helpful. If financial managers believe that dividends matter and act consistently in accordance with that conviction, they could influence the relationship between share value and dividend policy.

To help us gain some understanding of managements' perceptions, we examine a study by Baker, Farrelly, and Edelman, which surveyed financial executives at 318 firms listed on the New York Stock Exchange.[17] The study, conducted in 1983, is summarized in Table 10-4. In looking at the Baker, Farrelly, and Edelman results, the evidence favours the relevance of dividend

TABLE 10-4
Management Opinion Survey on Dividends

Statement of Managerial Beliefs	Level of Managers' Agreement		
	Agree-ment	No Opinion	Disagree-ment
1. A firm's dividend payout ratio affects the price of the common share.	61	33	6
2. Dividend payments provide a signalling device of future prospects.	52	41	7
3. The market uses dividend announcements as information for assessing security value.	43	51	6
4. Investors have different perceptions of the relative riskiness of dividends and retained earnings.	56	42	2
5. Investors are basically indifferent with regard to returns from dividends versus those from capital gains.	6	30	64
6. A shareholder is attracted to firms that have dividend policies appropriate to the shareholder's particular tax environment.	44	49	7
7. Management should be responsive to its shareholders' preferences regarding dividends.	41	49	10

Source: Adapted from H. Kent Baker, Gail E. Farrelly, and Richard B. Edelman, "A Survey of Management Views on Dividend Policy," *Financial Management* (Autumn 1985), p. 81.

[17]H. Kent Baker, Gail E. Farrelly, and Richard B. Edelman, "A Survey of Management Views on Dividend Policy," *Financial Management* (Autumn 1985), pp. 78–84.

policy, but not overwhelmingly so. For the most part, managers are divided between believing that dividends are important and having no opinion in the matter.

Regarding the question about the price-dividend relationship, Baker et al. asked the financial managers straight up, "Does the firm's dividend policy affect the price of the common shares?" Slightly more than 60 percent of the responses were affirmative, which is significant, but there were still almost 40 percent who had no opinion or disagreed. Thus, we could conclude that the majority of managers think that dividends matter, but they have no mandate in the matter. Similarly, when asked if dividends provide informational content about the firm's future (Questions 2 and 3), the managers are basically split between "no opinion" and "agreement." When asked about the tradeoff between dividends and capital gains (Questions 4 and 5), almost two-thirds of the managers thought shareholders have a preference for dividends or capital gains, with a lesser number (56 percent) believing that investors perceive the relative riskiness of capital gains and dividends to be different. Interestingly enough, though, almost half of the managers felt no clear responsibility to be responsive to shareholders' preferences. Finally, Statement 6 suggests that the majority of managers are not "true believers" in the concept of a clientele effect. Specifically, 56 percent of the financial executives either had no opinion or did not believe that shareholders are attracted to firms that have dividend policies appropriate to the shareholders' particular tax environment.

What Are We to Conclude?

We have now looked carefully at the importance of a firm's dividend policy as management seeks to increase the shareholders' wealth. We have gone to great lengths to gain insight and understanding from our best thinking. We have even drawn from the empirical evidence on hand to see what the findings suggest.

From our examination of the empirical evidence, the following conclusions would appear reasonable:

1. As a firm's investment opportunities increase, the dividend payout ratio should decrease. In other words, an inverse relationship should exist between the amount of investments with an expected rate of return that exceeds the cost of capital and the dividends remitted to investors. Since flotation costs are incurred with raising external capital, the retention of internally generated equity financing is preferable to selling shares in terms of the wealth of the current common shareholders.

2. The firm's dividend policy appears to be important; however, appearances may be deceptive. The real issue may be the firm's expected earning power and the riskiness of these earnings. Investors may be using the dividend payment as a source of information about the company's expected earnings. Management's actions regarding dividends may carry greater weight than a statement by management that earnings will be increasing.

3. Any influence that dividends have on share price may be attributed to the investor's desire to minimize and/or defer taxes and from the role of dividends in minimizing agency costs.

4. The expectations theory indicates to management that it must maintain a consistent dividend policy. The firm's dividend policy might effective-

ly be treated as a long-term residual. Rather than projecting investment requirements for a single year, management could anticipate financing needs for several years. Based upon the expected investment opportunities during the planning horizon, the firm's debt-equity mix, and the funds generated from operations, a target dividend payout ratio could be established. If internal funds remained after projection of the necessary equity financing, dividends would be paid. However, the planned dividend stream should distribute residual capital evenly to investors. Conversely, if over the long term the entire amount of internally generated capital is needed for reinvestment in the company, then no dividend should be paid.

THE DIVIDEND DECISION IN PRACTICE

Financial managers will take into consideration the concepts set forth in this chapter to select the firm's dividend policy. While these concepts do not provide an equation that explains the key relationships, they certainly give us a more complete view of the finance world, which can only help us make better decisions. Other considerations of a more practical nature affect the decision-making process for a firm's dividend policy.

Other Practical Considerations

A large number of considerations may influence a firm's decision about its dividends, some of them unique to that company. Some of the more general considerations are given below.

Legal Restrictions

Certain legal restrictions may limit the amount of dividends a firm may pay. These legal constraints fall into two categories. First, statutory restrictions may prevent a company from paying dividends. The distribution of dividends is permitted by the Canada Business Corporation Act if a company meets the conditions of a solvency test which requires that either before or after the dividend payment (1) the firm is able to pay its liabilities and (2) the firm's assets have a realizable value not less than the aggregate of its liabilities and equity capital.

The second type of legal restriction is unique to each firm and results from restrictions in debt and preferred-share contracts. To minimize their risk, investors frequently impose restrictive provisions upon management as a condition to their investment in the company. These constraints may include the provision that dividends may not be declared prior to the debt being repaid. Also, the corporation may be required to maintain a given amount of working capital. Preferred shareholders may stipulate that common dividends may not be paid when any preferred dividends are delinquent.

Liquidity Position

Contrary to common opinion, the mere fact that a company shows a large amount of retained earnings in the balance sheet does not indicate that cash is available for the payment of dividends. The firm's current position in liquid assets, including cash, is basically independent of the retained earnings account. Historically, a company with sizable retained earnings has been successful in generating cash from operations. Yet these funds are typically either reinvested in the company within a short time period or used to pay maturing debt. Thus, a firm may be extremely profitable and still be cash

---

BASIC FINANCIAL MANAGEMENT IN PRACTICE

Dividends Must Be Adequately Funded

Companies make money in order to distribute it, eventually, to their shareholders. Their is no benefit from making an investment in a company if the profits are neither distributed nor reinvested wisely.

If the business is successful, some of the money must be kept by the company to maintain its market position, its productivity, and in some cases, to comply with legal and social obligations. Still more money may be retained if the company has opportunities to reinvest it more profitably than the shareholders can manage on their own. Beyond that, the profits should be distributed. The choice is a simple one of allocating capital where it can be best used: by the company or by its owners.

Normally, companies tell their shareholders they intend to pay a fixed portion of their after-tax income as dividends. This is typically about 40%.

To be sure, net income is important, but a better starting point would be cash flow from operations—earnings before deducting non-cash charges.

These charges include depreciation (an accounting approximation for the wear and tear on machinery, equipment and buildings), amortization of intangible assets (which usually arise from a business acquisition), and increases in deferred taxes.

Obligatory Expenditures

Operating cash flow is sometimes treated as if were freely disposable income; it is not. To arrive at the cash flow figure, we must also deduct those obligatory expenditures that a company must make to enable it to at least maintain its existing productive capability and market position. After these expenditures are subtracted from operating cash flow, what remains is available for expansion, for new acquisitions and to pay dividends. This is called available cash earnings.

Operating cash flow will invariably be greater than earnings, but often available cash earnings are not. Indeed, in capital intensive businesses, available cash earnings are frequently zero or even negative. Throughout most of the 1980s, for example, Stelco Inc. enjoyed a large and positive operating cash flow. But its available cash earnings, after pro-

viding for its substantial cash investments, was either negative or at least not large enough to cover its dividends. In 1990, the company endured a substantial loss. If we look at 1989, after-tax income was $94 million and operating cash flow was $250 million; but capital needs totalled $285 million, so available cash earnings were really a negative $35 million. In addition, even though the company had negative cash earnings, it still saw fit to pay cash dividends of $35 million to its common shareholders. Although earnings and operating cash flow appeared to cover the dividend, the available cash earnings clearly did not. This had been true during the previous four years as well.

Debt Increased

It is this point that highlights how important it is to look at available cash earnings. Stelco paid out more than $165 million in dividends in the years 1986–1990. It had to borrow to pay these dividends. It did not eliminate the dividend until late in 1990, by which time its debt had increased substantially. The borrowing required just to pay the dividend was an important ingredient in the deterioration of the financial position.

One of the few aspects of dividend policy which is universally agreed on is that a dividend rate, once established, should not be cut. Unless the regular dividend is set at a level within the reasonably expected available cash flow, the company will be borrowing to pay the dividend at the best of times; when earnings drop, the dividend may have to be eliminated to avoid placing a financial hardship on the company. In this scenario, no one benefits.

On the other hand, companies that focus on cash earnings and formulate dividend policy consistent with the availability of cash earnings are allocating the capital in the most economically efficient manner. They are thereby demonstrating their loyalty to and respect for their shareholders. It is these companies which create real economic value.

Source: R. Fogler, "Dividends must be adequately funded," *Financial Post Daily*, February 21, 1992, p. 11.

poor. Since dividends are paid with cash, and not with retained earnings, the firm must have cash available for dividends to be paid. Hence, the firm's liquidity position has a direct bearing on its ability to pay dividends.

Absence or Lack of Other Sources of Financing

As already noted, a firm may (1) retain profits for investment purposes and/or (2) pay dividends and issue new debt or equity securities to finance investments. For many small or new companies, this second option is not realistic. These firms do not have access to the capital markets, so they must rely more heavily upon internally generated funds. As a consequence, the dividend payout ratio is generally much lower for a small or newly established firm than for a large, publicly owned corporation.

Earnings Predictability

A company's dividend payout ratio depends to some extent upon the predictability of the firm's profits over time. If earnings fluctuate significantly, management cannot rely on internally generated funds to meet future needs. When profits are realized, the firm may retain larger amounts to ensure that money is available when needed. Conversely, a firm with a stable earnings trend will typically pay a larger portion of its earnings out in dividends. This company has less concern about the availability of profits to meet future capital requirements.

Ownership Control

For many large corporations, control through the ownership of common shares is not an issue. However, for many small and medium-sized companies, maintaining voting control takes a high priority. If the present common shareholders are unable to participate in a new offering, issuing new shares is unattractive, in that the control of the current shareholders is diluted. The owners might prefer that management finance new investments with debt and through profits rather than by issuing new common shares. This firm's growth is then constrained by the amount of debt capital available and by the company's ability to generate profits.

Inflation

Before the late 1970s, inflationary pressures had not been a significant problem for either consumers or businesses. However, over the last two decades, the deterioration of the dollar's purchasing power has had a direct impact upon the replacement of fixed assets. For most firms, the funds generated from depreciation are used to finance the replacements of fixed assets that have become worn and obsolete. During a period of inflation, the cost of replacing equivalent equipment increases and the depreciation funds are insufficient. These cost increases require a greater retention of profits which implies that dividends will be adversely affected.

Alternate Dividend Policies

Regardless of a firm's long-term dividend policy, most firms choose one of the following dividend payment patterns:

1. **Constant dividend payout ratio.** In this policy, the percentage of earnings paid out in dividends is held constant. Although the dividend-to-earnings ratio is stable, the dollar amount of the dividend naturally fluctuates from year to year as profits vary.

FIGURE 10-3. Corporate Earnings and Dividends

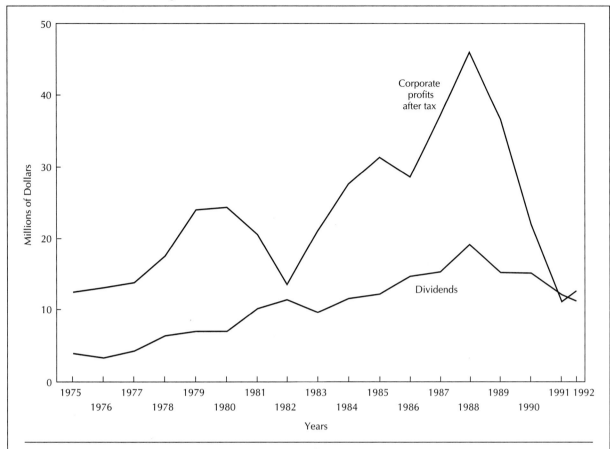

Source: Statistics Canada, National Income and Expenditure Accounts, Catalogue 13-001, Various issues 1977–1992. Reproduced with the permission of the Minister of Industry, Science and Technology, 1993.

2. **Stable dollar dividend per share.** This policy maintains a relatively stable dollar dividend over time. An increase in the dollar dividend usually does not occur until management is convinced that the higher dividend level can be maintained in the future. Management also will not reduce the dollar dividend until the evidence clearly indicates that a continuation of the present dividend cannot be supported.

3. **Small, regular dividend plus a year-end extra.** A corporation following this policy pays a small regular dollar dividend plus a year-end extra dividend in prosperous years. The extra dividend is declared toward the end of the fiscal year, when the company's profits for the period can be estimated. Management's objective is to avoid the connotation of a permanent dividend. However, this purpose may be defeated if recurring "extra" dividends come to be expected by investors. Ford Motor of Canada Ltd. and Budd Canada Inc. are examples of firms that in recent years have employed the low stable dividend plus an extra dividend at the end of the year.

Of the three dividend policies, the stable dollar dividend is by far the most common. Figure 10-3 illustrates the general tendency of companies to pay stable, but increasing, dividends, even though the profits fluctuate significantly. In a study by Lintner, corporate managers were found to be reluctant to change the dollar amount of the dividend in response to "temporary" fluctuations in earnings from year to year. This aversion was particularly evident when it came to decreasing the amount of the dividend from the previous level.[18] Smith explained stable dividends in terms of his "increasing-stream hypothesis of dividend policy."[19] He proposed that dividend stability is essentially a smoothing of the dividend stream in order to minimize the effect of other types of company reversals. Thus, corporate managers make every effort to avoid a dividend cut, attempting instead to develop a gradually increasing dividend series over the long-term future.[20] However, if a dividend reduction is absolutely necessary, the cut should be large enough to reduce the probability of future cuts.[21]

As an example of a stable dividend policy, Figure 10-4 compares the Bank of Montreal's earnings per share and dividends per share for 1974 through 1991. Ignoring 1989, when earnings were exceptionally low, the firm has, on average, paid approximately 42 percent of its earnings out in dividends. The historical dividends and earnings patterns for the firm clearly demonstrate management's hesitancy to change dividends in response to short-term fluctuations in earnings.[22]

Perspective in Finance

We don't know much with certitude about dividend policy and its impact on the firm's share price, but we do know that managers hate, even despise, the thought of cutting the dividend. It will be done only as a last resort. Count on it.

DIVIDEND PAYMENT PROCEDURES

After the firm's dividend policy has been structured, several procedural details must be arranged.[23] For instance, how frequently are dividend payments to be made? If a shareholder sells the shares during the year, who is entitled to the dividend? To answer these questions, we need to understand the dividend payment procedures.

Generally, companies pay dividends on a quarterly basis. To illustrate, Scott Paper pays $0.40 per share in annual dividends. However, the firm

---

[18]John Lintner, "Distribution of Income of Corporations Among Dividends, Retained Earnings, and Taxes," *American Economic Review*, 46 (May 1956), 97–113.

[19]Keith V. Smith, "Increasing-Stream Hypothesis of Corporate Dividend Policy," *California Management Review*, 15 (Fall 1971), 56–64.

[20]Boards of directors, as a general rule, view the dividend as a fixed cost. Once they raise it, they will not cut it, unless there is no other alternative.

[21]In examining this issue, the financial manager should answer the following questions: (1) Should management dare to decrease the dividend to provide equity capital for financing future investments? and (2) If a decrease in dividends were to be made, how should this decision be communicated to the market?

[22]The empirical evidence suggests that the following variables have a significant impact on management's dividend policy. In other words, the next dividend to be paid will largely be the result of (1) management's target dividend-payout ratio; (2) the current earnings per share; (3) the amount of the prior dividends paid, with the more recent dividend being weighted more heavily than earlier dividends; and (4) management's expectations about future earnings per share.

[23]Given that the dividend policy may be important because of its informational content, management ought to be as concerned about how the announcement is communicated as it is about the actual announcement.

FIGURE 10-4. Earnings per Share and Dividends per Share for the Bank of Montreal

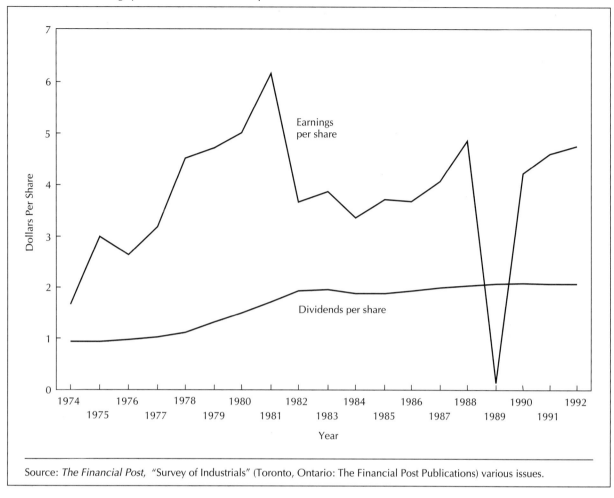

Source: *The Financial Post*, "Survey of Industrials" (Toronto, Ontario: The Financial Post Publications) various issues.

actually issues a $0.10 quarterly dividend for a total yearly dividend of $0.40 ($0.10 × 4 quarters).

The final approval of a dividend payment comes from the board of directors. As an example, Canadian Pacific Ltd., on March 9, 1992, announced that holders of record as of March 27 would receive a $0.08 dividend. The dividend payment was to be made on April 28. March 9 is the **declaration date**—the date when the dividend is formally declared by the board of directors. The **date of record**, March 27, designates when the share transfer books are to be closed. Investors shown to own the share on this date receive the dividend. If a notification of a transfer is recorded subsequent to March 27, the new owner is not entitled to the dividend. However, a problem could develop if the share were sold on March 26, one day prior to the record date. Time would not permit the sale to be reflected on the shareholder list by the March 27 date of record. To avoid this problem, stock brokerage companies have uniformly decided to terminate the right of ownership to the dividend four working days prior to the record date. This prior date is the **ex-dividend date**. Therefore, any acquirer of the Canadian Pacific shares on March 23 or thereafter does not receive the dividend. Finally, the company mails the dividend check to each investor on April 28, the **payment date**.

INTERNATIONAL FINANCIAL MANAGEMENT

Dividend Pay-Outs: Different Practices in Different Countries

How much of the earnings do most firms pay out in dividends? It depends on the country. As shown in the graph here, British firms pay out a lot more than German and Japanese companies.

Sources: Datastream; BZW; IDD Information Services; Securities Data Company; Paribas, Referenced in *The Economist*, January 25, 1992, p. 73.

STOCK DIVIDENDS AND STOCK SPLITS

An integral part of dividend policy is the use of **stock dividends** and **stock splits**. Both involve issuing new shares of stock on a pro rata basis to the current shareholders, while the firm's assets, its earnings, and the risk assumed and the investor's percentage of ownership in the company remain unchanged. The only definite result from either a stock dividend or stock split is the increase in the number of shares outstanding.

To illustrate the effect of a stock dividend, assume that the Katie Corporation has 100,000 shares outstanding.[24] The firm's after-tax profits are $500,000, or $5 in earnings per share. At present, the company's shares are selling at a price/earnings multiple of 10, or $50 per share. Management is planning to issue a 20 percent stock dividend, so that a shareholder owning 10 shares would receive two additional shares. We might immediately conclude that this investor is being given an asset (two shares) worth $100; consequently, his or her personal worth should increase by $100. This

[24]The logic of this illustration is equally applicable to a stock split.

conclusion is erroneous. The firm will be issuing 20,000 new shares (100,000 shares × 20 percent). Since the $500,000 in after-tax profits does not change, the new earnings per share will be $4.167 ($500,000/120,000 shares). If the price/earnings multiple remains at 10, the market price of the share after the dividend should fall to $41.67 ($4.167 earnings per share × 10). The investor now owns 12 shares worth $41.67, which provides a $500 total value; thus he or she is neither better nor worse off than before the stock dividend.

This example may make us wonder why a corporation would even bother with a stock dividend or stock split if no one benefits. However, before we study the rationale for such distributions, we should understand the differences between a stock split and a stock dividend.

Stock Dividend versus Split

The only difference between a stock dividend and a stock split relates to their respective accounting treatment. Stated differently, there is absolutely no difference on an economic basis between a stock dividend and a stock split. Both represent a proportionate distribution of additional shares to the present shareholders.

The accounting treatment for a dividend in common shares requires the issuing firm to capitalize the "market value" of the dividend.[25] In other words, the dollar amount of the dividend is transferred from retained earnings to the common shares account. This procedure may best be explained by an example. Assume that the L. Bernard Corporation is preparing to issue a 15 percent dividend in common shares. Table 10-5 presents the equity portion of the firm's balance sheet prior to the distribution. The market price for the share has been $14. Thus, the 15 percent stock dividend increases the number of shares by 150,000 (1,000,000 shares × 15 percent). The "market value" of this increase is $2,100,000 (150,000 shares × $14 market price). To record this transaction, $2,100,000 would be transferred from retained earnings, resulting in a $2,100,000 increase in the value of common shares. Table 10-6 shows the revised balance sheet.

What if the management of L. Bernard Corporation changed the plan and decided to split the stock two-for-one? In other words, a 100 percent increase in the number of shares would result. In accounting for the split, the changes to be recorded are (1) the increase in the number of shares and

Common Equity:	
Common shares (1,000,000 shares outstanding)	$10,000,000
Retained earnings	15,000,000
Total equity	$25,000,000

TABLE 10-5
L. Bernard Corporation Balance Sheet Before Stock Dividend

Common Equity:	
Common shares (1,150,000 shares outstanding)	$12,100,000
Retained earnings	12,900,000
Total equity	$25,000,000

TABLE 10-6
L. Bernard Corporation Balance Sheet After Stock Dividend

---

[25]*CICA Handbook*, 1540.20–21.

10-1A. (*Flotation Costs and Issue Size*) Your firm needs to raise $10 million. Assuming that after-tax issuing costs are expected to be $15 per share and that the market price of the share is $120, how many shares would have to be issued? What is the dollar size of the issue?

10-2A. (*Flotation Costs and Issue Size*) If after-tax issuing costs for a common share issue are 18 percent, how large must the issue be so that the firm will net $5,800,000? If the shares sell for $85 each, how many shares must be issued?

10-3A. (*Residual Dividend Theory*) Terra Cotta finances new investments by 40 percent debt and 60 percent equity. The firm needs $640,000 for financing new investments. If retained earnings equal $400,000, how much money will be available for dividends in accordance with the residual dividend theory?

10-4A. (*Stock Dividend*) RCB has 2 million common shares outstanding. Net income is $550,000, and the P/E ratio for the share is 10. Management is planning a 20 percent stock dividend. What will be the price of the share after the stock dividend? If an investor owns 100 shares prior to the stock dividend, does the total value of his or her shares change? Explain.

10-5A. (*Dividends in Perfect Markets*) The management of Harris, Inc., is considering two dividend policies for the years 1994 and 1995, one and two years away. In 1996 the management is planning to liquidate the firm. One plan would pay a dividend of $2.50 in 1994 and 1995 and a liquidating dividend of $45.75 in 1996. The alternative would be to pay out $4.25 in dividends in 1994, $4.75 in dividends in 1995, and a final dividend of $40.66 in 1996. The required rate of return for the common shareholders is 18 percent. Management is concerned about the effect of the two dividend streams on the value of the common share.

a. Assuming perfect markets, what would be the effect?

b. What factors in the real world might change your conclusion reached in part (a)?

10-6A. (*Long-Term Residual Dividend Policy*) Stetson Manufacturing, Inc., has projected its investment opportunities over a five-year planning horizon. The cost of each year's investment and the amount of internal funds available for re-investment for that year are given below. The firm's debt-equity mix is 35 percent debt and 65 percent equity. There are currently 100,000 common shares outstanding.

a. What would be the dividend each year if the residual dividend theory were used on a year-to-year basis?

b. What target stable dividend can Stetson establish by using the long-term residual dividend theory over the future planning horizon?

c. Why might a residual dividend policy applied to the five years as opposed to individual years be preferable?

Year	Cost of Investments	Internal Funds Available for Reinvestment or for Dividends
1	$350,000	$250,000
2	475,000	450,000
3	200,000	600,000
4	980,000	650,000
5	600,000	390,000

10-7A. (*Stock Split*) You own 5 percent of the Trexco Corporation's common shares, which most recently sold for $98 prior to a two-for-one stock split announcement. Before the split there are 25,000 common shares outstanding.

a. Relative to now, what will be your financial position after the stock split? (Assume the share price falls proportionately.)

b. The executive vice-president in charge of finance believes the price will only fall 40 percent after the split because she feels the price is above the optimal price range. If she is correct, what will be your net gain?

10-8A. (*Dividend Policies*) The earnings for Crystal Cargo, Inc., have been predicted for the next five years and are listed below. There are 1 million shares outstanding. Determine the yearly dividend per share to be paid if the following policies are enacted:

a. Constant dividend payout ratio of 50 percent.

b. Stable dollar dividend targeted at 50 percent of the earnings over the five-year period.

c. Small, regular dividend of $.50 per share plus a year-end extra when the profits in any year exceed $1,500,000. The year-end extra dividend will equal 50 percent of profits exceeding $1,500,000.

Year	Profits After Taxes
1	$1,400,000
2	2,000,000
3	1,860,000
4	900,000
5	2,800,000

10-9A. (*Repurchase of Shares*) The Dunn Corporation is planning to pay dividends of $500,000. There are 250,000 shares outstanding, with an earnings per share of $5. The share should sell for $50 after the ex-dividend date. If instead of paying a dividend, management decides to repurchase shares,

a. What should be the repurchase price?

b. How many shares should be repurchased?

c. What if the repurchase price is set below or above your suggested price in part (a)?

d. If you own 100 shares, would you prefer that the company pay the dividend or repurchase shares?

10-10A. (*Flotation Costs and Issue Size*) D. Butler Inc. needs to raise $14 million. Assuming that after-tax issuing costs are expected to be 10 percent of the market price and that the market price of the share is $95, how many shares would have to be issued? What is the dollar size of the issue?

10-11A. (*Residual Dividend Theory*) Terra Cotta finances new investments with 70 percent debt and the rest in equity. The firm needs $1.2 million for financing a new acquisition. If retained earnings are $450,000, how much money will be available for dividends in accordance with the residual dividend theory?

10-12A. (*Stock Split*) You own 20 percent of Rainy Corporation which recently sold common shares for $86 prior to a two-for-one stock-split announcement. Before the split there are 80,000 common shares outstanding.

a. Relative to now, what will be your financial position after the stock split? (Assume the share price falls proportionately.)

b. The executive vice-president in charge of finance believes the price will fall only 45 percent after the split, because she feels the price is above the optimal price range. If she is correct, what will be your net gain?

STUDY PROBLEMS (SET B)

10-1B. (*Flotation Costs and Issue Size*) Your firm needs to raise $12 million. Assuming that after-tax issuing costs are expected to be $17 per share and that the market price of the share is $115, how many shares would have to be issued? What is the dollar size of the issue?

10-2B. (*Flotation Costs and Issue Size*) If after-tax issuing costs for a common share issue are 14 percent, how large must the issue be so that the firm will net $6,100,000? If the share sells for $76 per share, how many shares must be issued?

10-3B. (*Residual Dividend Theory*) Steven Miller finances new investments by 35 percent debt and 65 percent equity. The firm needs $650,000 for financing new investments. If retained earnings equal $375,000, how much money will be available for dividends in accordance with the residual-dividend theory?

10-4B. (*Stock Dividend*) DCA has 2.5 million common shares outstanding. Net income is $600,000, and the P/E ratio for the share is 10. Management is planning an 18 percent stock dividend. What will be the price of the share after the stock dividend? If an investor owns 120 shares prior to the stock dividend, does the total value of his or her shares change? Explain.

10-5B. (*Dividends in Perfect Markets*) The management of Montford, Inc., is considering two dividend policies for the years 1994 and 1995, one and two years away. In 1993 the management is planning to liquidate the firm. One plan would pay a dividend of $2.55 in 1994 and 1995 and a liquidating dividend of $45.60 in 1996. The alternative would be to pay out $4.35 in dividends in 1994, $4.70 in dividends in 1995, and a final dividend of $40.62 in 1996. The required rate of return for the common shareholders is 17 percent. Management is concerned about the effect of the two dividend streams on the value of the common shares.

   a. Assuming perfect markets, what would be the effect?

   b. What factors in the real world might change your conclusion reached in part (a)?

10-6B. (*Long-Term Residual Dividend Policy*) Wells Manufacturing, Inc., has projected its investment opportunities over a five-year planning horizon. The cost of each year's investment and the amount of internal funds available for re-investment for that year are given below. The firm's debt-equity mix is 40 percent debt and 60 percent equity. There are currently 125,000 common shares outstanding.

   a. What would be the dividend each year if the residual dividend theory were used on a year-to-year basis?

   b. What target stable dividend can Wells establish by using the long-term residual dividend theory over the future planning horizon?

   c. Why might a residual dividend policy applied to the five years as opposed to individual years be preferable?

Year	Cost of Investments	Internal Funds Available for Reinvestment or for Dividends
1	$360,000	$225,000
2	450,000	440,000
3	230,000	600,000
4	890,000	650,000
5	600,000	400,000

10-7B. (*Stock Split*) You own 8 percent of the Standlee Corporation's common shares, which most recently sold for $98 per share prior to a two-for-one stock split announcement. Before the split there are 30,000 common shares outstanding.

   a. Relative to now, what will be your financial position after the stock split? (Assume the share price falls proportionately.)

   b. The executive vice-president in charge of finance believes the price will fall only 45 percent after the split, because she feels the price is above the optimal price range. If she is correct, what will be your net gain?

10-8B. (*Dividend Policies*) The earnings for Carlson Cargo, Inc., have been predicted for the next five years and are listed below. There are 1 million shares outstanding. Determine the yearly dividend per share to be paid if the following policies are enacted:

a. Constant dividend payout ratio of 40 percent.

b. Stable dollar dividend targeted at 40 percent of the earnings over the five-year period.

c. Small, regular dividend of $.50 per share plus a year-end extra when the profits in any year exceed $1,500,000. The year-end extra dividend will equal 50 percent of profits exceeding $1,500,000.

Year	Profits After Taxes
1	$1,500,000
2	2,000,000
3	1,750,000
4	950,000
5	2,500,000

10-9B. (*Repurchase of Shares*) The B. Phillips Corporation is planning to pay dividends of $550,000. There are 275,000 shares outstanding, with earnings per share of $6. The share should sell for $45 after the ex-dividend date. If instead of paying a dividend, management decides to repurchase shares,

a. What should be the repurchase price?

b. How many shares should be repurchased?

c. What if the repurchase price is set below or above your suggested price in part (a)?

d. If you own 100 shares, would you prefer that the company pay the dividend or repurchase shares?

10-10B. (*Flotation Costs and Issue Size*) D.B. Fool, Inc., needs to raise $16 million. Assuming that after-tax issuing costs are expected to be 12 percent of the market price and that the market price of the share is $100, how many shares would have to be issued? What is the dollar size of the issue?

10-11B. (*Residual Dividend Theory*) Mabness Inc. finances new investments with 65 percent debt and the rest in equity. The firm needs $1.5 million for financing a new acquisition. If retained earnings are $525,000, how much money will be available for dividends in accordance with the residual dividend theory?

10-12B. (*Stock Split*) You own 25 percent of The Star Corporation which recently sold common shares for $90 prior to a two-for-one stock split announcement. Before the split, there are 90,000 common shares outstanding.

a. Relative to now, what will be your financial position after the stock split? (Assume the share price falls proportionately.)

b. The executive vice-president in charge of finance believes the price will fall only 45 percent after the split, because she feels the price is above the optimal price range. If she is correct, what will be your net gain?

SELF-TEST SOLUTIONS

SS-1. Dividend per share $= 35\% \times \$8.20$

$$= \$2.87$$

Dividends:

1 year $= \$2.87 (1 + 0.12)$

$$= \$3.21$$

5 years $= \$2.87 (1 + 0.12)^5$

$$= \$2.87 (1.762)$$

$$= \$5.06$$

SS-2. a. Investments A, B, and C will be accepted, requiring $1,150,000 in total financing. Therefore, 40 percent of $1,150,000 or $460,000 in new debt will be needed, and common equity will have to provide $690,000. The remainder of the $750,000 internal funds will be $60,000, which will be paid out in dividends.

b. Assuming a 10 percent cost of capital, all four investments would be accepted, requiring total financing of $1,550,000. Equity would provide 60 percent, or $930,000 of the total, which would not leave any funds to be paid out in dividends. New common would have to be issued.

SS-3. a. If a 15 percent stock dividend is issued, the financial statement would appear as follows:

Robson Corporation	
Debt	$1,800,000
Common equity	
Common shares (115,000 shares)	230,000
Contributed surplus	670,000
Retained earnings	600,000
	$3,300,000

b. A two-for-one split would result in a 100 percent increase in the number of shares. Since the total value remains at $200,000, the new per share value is $1 ($200,000/200,000 shares). The new financial statement would be as follows:

Robson Corporation	
Debt	$1,800,000
Common equity	
Common shares (100,000 shares)	200,000
Contributed surplus	400,000
Retained earnings	900,000
	$3,300,000

SELECTED REFERENCES

Asquith, Paul, and David Mullins. "The Impact of Initiating Dividend Payments on Shareholders' Wealth," *Journal of Business*, 56 (January 1983), 77–99.

Asquith, Paul, and David Mullins. "Signalling with Dividends, Stock Repurchases, Equity Issues," *Financial Management*, 15 (Autumn 1986), 27–45.

Baker, H. K., G. E. Farrelly, and R. B. Edelman. "A Survey of Management's Views on Dividend Policy," *Financial Management* (Autumn 1985), 78–84.

Benesh, G. A., A. J. Keown, and J. M. Pinkerton. "An Examination of the Market Reaction to Substantial Shifts in Dividend Policy," *Journal of Financial Research* (Summer 1984), 131–142.

Black, F. "The Dividend Puzzle," *Journal of Portfolio Management*, 2 (Winter 1976).

Black, F., and M. Scholes. "The Effects of Dividend Yield and Dividend Policy on Common Stock Prices and Returns," *Journal of Financial Economics*, 1 (May 1974), 1–22.

Blume, Marshal E. "Stock Returns and Dividend Yields: Some More Evidence," *Review of Economics and Statistics*, 62 (November 1980), 567–577.

Brickley, James A. "Shareholder Wealth, Information Signalling, and the Specially Designated Dividend: An Empirical Study," *Journal of Financial Economics*, 12 (1983), 287–309.

Chang, Rosita P., and S. Ghon Rhee. "The Impact of Personal Taxes on Corporate Dividend Policy and Capital Structure

Decisions," *Journal of Financial Management* (Summer 1990), 21.

Crutchley, Claire E. and Robert S. Hansen. "A Test of the Agency Theory of Managerial Ownership, Corporate Leverage, and Corporate Dividends," *Journal of Financial Management* (Winter 1989), 36.

Dielman, T., and Henry Oppenheimer. "An Examination of Investor Behavior during Periods of Large Dividend Changes," 19 (June 1984), 197–216.

Dyl, E. A., and J. R. Hoffmeister. "A Note on Dividend Policy and Beta," *Journal of Business Finance and Accounting* (Spring 1986), 107–115.

Eades, K. M. "Empirical Evidence on Dividends as a Signal of Firm Value," *Journal of Financial and Quantitative Analysis* (November 1982), 471–500.

Feldstein, M., and J. Green. "Why Do Companies Pay Dividends?" National Bureau of Economic Research, Conference Paper No. 54 (October 1980).

Gonedes, N. "Corporate Signalling, External Accounting and Capital Market Equilibrium: Evidence on Dividends, Income, and Extraordinary Items," *Journal of Accounting Research* (Spring 1978), 26–79.

Grinblatt, M. S., R. W. Masulis, and S. Titman. "The Valuation Effects of Stock Splits and Stock Dividends," *Journal of Financial Economics*, 13 (December 1984), 461–490.

Hakansson, Nils H. "To Pay or Not to Pay Dividends," *Journal of Finance*, 37 (May 1982), 415–428.

Hess, P. "The Ex-Dividend Behavior of Stock Returns: Further Evidence on Tax Effects," *Journal of Finance*, 37 (May 1982), 445–456.

John, Kose and Larry L. Lang. "Insider Trading around Dividend Announcements: Theory and Evidence," *The Journal of Finance* (September 1991), 1361–1390.

Lintner, J. "Distribution of Incomes of Corporations Among Dividends, Retained Earnings, and Taxes," *American Economic Review*, 46 (May 1956), 97–113.

Litzenberger, R. H., and K. Ramaswamy. "The Effect of Personal Taxes and Dividends on Capital Asset Prices: Theory and Empirical Evidence," *Journal of Financial Economics*, 7 (June 1979), 163–195.

Michaely, Roni. "Ex-Dividend Day Stock Price Behavior: The Case of the 1986 Tax Reform Act," *The Journal of Finance* (July 1991), 845–860.

Miller, M. H. "Behavioral Rationality: The Case of Dividends," *Journal of Business*, 59 (October 1986), 5451–5468.

Miller, M. H. "The Informational Content of Dividends," in *Macroeconomics: Essays in Honor of Franco Modigliani*, ed. J. Bossons, R. Dornbusch, and S. Fischer. Cambridge, MA: MIT Press, 1987.

Miller, M. H., and Franco Modigliani. "Dividend Policy, Growth, and the Valuation of Shares," *Journal of Business*, 34 (October 1961), 411–433.

Miller, M. H., and M. Scholes. "Dividends and Taxes: Some Empirical Evidence," *Journal of Political Economy*, 90 (1982), 1118–1141.

Miller M. H., and K. Rock. "Dividend Policy under Asymmetric Information," *Journal of Finance*, 40 (September 1985), 1031–1051.

Morgan, I. G. "Dividends and Capital Asset Prices," *Journal of Finance*, 37 (September 1982), 1071–1086.

Penman, S. H. "The Predictive Content of Earnings Forecasts and Dividends," *Journal of Finance* (September 1983), 1181–1199.

Shefrin, H., and M. Statman. "Explaining Investor Preference for Cash Dividends," *Journal of Financial Economics*, 13 (June 1984), 253–282.

Talmor, Eli and Sheridan Titman. "Taxes and Dividend Policy," *Journal of Financial Management* (Summer 1990), 32.

Woolridge, J. R. "Dividend Changes and Security Prices," *Journal of Finance*, 38 (December 1983), 1607–1615.

Woolridge, J. R. "Stock Dividends as Signals," *Journal of Financial Research*, 6 (Spring 1983), 1–12.

PART FOUR

Financial Analysis, Planning, and Control

Financial analysis is the assessment of a firm's past, present, and anticipated future financial condition. The objectives of financial analysis are to determine the firm's financial strengths and to identify its weaknesses. For example, a firm's financial analyst may perform an internal financial analysis to determine the firm's liquidity position or to measure its past earnings performance. Alternatively, a financial analyst from a brokerage firm may perform a financial analysis from arm's length of the firm in an effort to determine the firm's creditworthiness or investment potential. Regardless of who is performing the analysis, the tools used in financial analysis are basically the same.

Financial ratios are the principal tools of financial analysis, since they can be used to answer a variety of questions regarding a firm's financial well-being. For example, a commercial bank-loan officer considering an application for a six-month loan might want to know whether the applicant firm is solvent or liquid; a potential investor in the firm's common shares might want to know how profitable the firm has been; and an internal financial analyst might want to know whether the firm can reasonably afford to borrow all or part of the funds needed to finance a planned expansion. Answers to these questions can be obtained through the use of financial ratios.

We begin our discussion of financial analysis with an overview of the firm's financial statements. These include the balance sheet, income statement, and statement of changes in financial position. We also examine the schedule of operating cash flows which enables us to determine the effect of the firm's primary business on cash flows. Then we will provide a survey of key financial ratios that can be used to assess the firm's financial position.

BASIC FINANCIAL STATEMENTS

In Chapter 2 we discussed the fact that corporate and noncorporate enterprises report their financial position and performance through the use of two basic financial statements: the **balance sheet** and the **income statement**. In accordance with generally accepted accounting practice, however, firms normally report a third statement. This statement is the **statement of changes in financial position**. Since financial analysts frequently make use of this statement we will discuss it in the pages that follow.

The balance sheet and income statement for Jimco, Inc., are found in Tables 11-1 and 11-2, respectively. Appendix 1A contains a discussion of the

TABLE 11-1
Jimco, Inc., Balance Sheet
December 31, 1993 ($000)

Assets		
Current assets:		
Cash	$ 1,400	
Marketable securities—at cost (market value, $320)	300	
Accounts receivable	10,000	
Inventories	12,000	
Prepaid expenses	300	
Total current assets		$24,000
Fixed assets:		
Land	2,000	
Plant and equipment	$12,300	
Less: Accumulated depreciation	7,300	
Net plant and equipment	5,000	
Total fixed assets		7,000
Total assets		$31,000

Liabilities and Owners' Equity		
Current liabilities:		
Accounts payable	$3,000	
Notes payable, 9%, due March 1, 1994	3,400	
Accrued salaries, wages, and other expenses	3,100	
Current portion of long-term debt	500	
Total current liabilities		$10,000
Long-term liabilities:		
Deferred income taxes	1,500	
First mortgage bonds, 7%, due January 1, 1994	6,300	
Debentures, 8½%, due June 30, 2000	2,900	
Total long-term liabilities		10,700
Owners' equity:		
Common shares	100	
Contributed surplus	2,000	
Retained earnings	8,200	
Total owners' equity		10,300
Total liabilities and owners' equity		$31,000

TABLE 11-2
Jimco, Inc., Statement of
Income for the Year Ended
December 31, 1993 ($000
except per-share data)

Net sales		$51,000
Cost of goods sold		(38,000)
Gross profit		$13,000
Operating expenses		
Selling expenses	$3,100	
Depreciation expense	500	
General and administrative expense	5,400	(9,000)
Net operating income (NOI)		$ 4,000
Interest expense		(1,000)
Earnings before taxes (EBT)		$ 3,000
Income taxes[a]		(1,200)
Net income (NI)		$ 1,800
Disposition of net income		
Common share dividends		$ 300
Change in retained earnings		1,500
Per-share data (dollars)		
Number of common shares		100,000 shares
Earnings per common share ($1,800,000/100,000 shares)		$ 18
Dividends per common share ($300,000/100,000 shares)		$ 3

[a]A tax rate of 40 percent on all income is assumed here for simplicity.

balance sheet and income statement. We will use the information contained in these statements to derive the statement of changes in financial position.

Perspective in Finance

The double-entry system of accounting used in this country dates back to about 3600 B.C., with the first published work describing the double-entry accounting system in 1494 by Luca Pacioli in Venice. Although the details of the double-entry system can be overwhelming to the novice, the mathematical content of the basic financial statements is straightforward, as we see below:

1. Balance sheet or statement of financial position:

$$Assets = Liabilities + Owners' \ Equity$$

2. Income statement or statement of results from operations:

$$Revenues + Gains - Expenses - Losses = Income$$

3. Statement of changes in financial position:

$$Cash \ Inflow - Cash \ Outflow = Change \ in \ Cash$$

Statement of Changes in Financial Position

The CICA committee on accounting standards has defined the objective of the statement of changes in financial position to be that of providing information about the operating, financing and investing activities of an enterprise and the effects of those activities on cash resources.[1] Other suitable titles for this

[1]*CICA Handbook*, Statement of Changes in Financial Position, 1540.01.

statement include: "Cash flow statement," "Statement of operating, financing and investment activities," or "Statement of changes in cash resources."

For the purposes of financial reporting, the **statement of changes in financial position** emphasizes the availability to the firm of liquid resources such as cash and its cash equivalents.[2] As a result, this statement is structured to reflect the cash flows involved in the operating, financing, and investing activities of the firm. These three activities of the firm include items such as: cash flows resulting from discontinued operations; cash flows from extraordinary items, outlays for acquisition and proceeds on disposal of assets, the issue and redemption of debt, share capital, and the payment of dividends.

Preparing the Statement of Changes in Financial Position

The preparation the statement of changes in financial position for 1993 requires the use of comparative balance sheets for the current year and last year as shown in Table 11-3. The purpose of comparing accounts of the balance sheet is to determine the effect of changes in the accounts on the firm's cash balance. For example, a decrease in the level of accounts receivable over the period would normally denote an increase in the cash level of the firm, since the firm would have collected more dollars from its credit accounts than it created through new credit sales. In general, a decrease in an asset balance indicates an increase in the firm's cash balance or a source of cash flow. Furthermore, an increase in a liability account signals that the net additional borrowing took place in the firm's cash balance. An increase in the levels of the common and preferred shares accounts would also increase in the firm's cash balance. In contrast, a decrease in the level of the accounts payable over the period would normally indicate a decrease in the cash level of the firm, since the firm is paying its creditors immediately and is not making use of short-term credit. In general, a decrease in the liability balance would indicate a decrease in the firm's cash balance or a use of cash flow.

The column entitled "changes" in Table 11-3 provides the basis for determining Jimco's sources and uses of cash flows. Note that cash decreased by $100,000 during the year. Since this change in cash is explained by the statement of changes in financial position, we will ignore it for the time being. Marketable securities did not change; thus, no source or use of cash flows was provided. The accounts receivable balance increased by $1,500,000, indicating that more credit sales were made during the period than were collected. Hence, the firm used cash flows to invest in accounts receivable. Likewise, inventories and prepaid expenses increased by $700,000 and $100,000, respectively, indicating uses of cash flows. In addition, Jimco increased plant and equipment by $1,100,000, which constitutes still another use of cash flows.[3] Note that the increase in accumulated depreciation of $500,000 equals depreciation expense for the period.

---

[2]Cash equivalents are defined as short-term, highly liquid investments that are readily convertible into known amounts of cash and are so near to their maturity that they pose an insignificant risk of changes in value because of changes in interest rates.

[3]The use of funds attributed to the purchase of plant and equipment can also be obtained from an analysis of the change in the net plant and equipment account. For Jimco, Inc., this can be accomplished as follows:

Net plant and equipment (1993)		$5,000
Plus:	Depreciation expense for the period	500
		5,500
Less:	Net plant and equipment (1992)	(4,400)
	Net purchase (sale) of plant and equipment	$1,100

Assets			
	1992	1993	Changes
Current assets:			
Cash	$ 1,500	$ 1,400	$ (100)
Marketable securities	300	300	—
Accounts receivable	8,500	10,000	1,500
Inventories	11,300	12,000	700
Prepaid expenses	200	300	100
Total current assets	$21,800	$24,000	$2,200
Fixed assets:			
Land	$ 2,000	$ 2,000	$ —
Plant and equipment	11,200	12,300	1,100
Less: Accumulated depreciation	(6,800)	(7,300)	(500)
Net plant and equipment	4,400	5,000	600
Total fixed assets	6,400	7,000	600
Total assets	$28,200	$31,000	$2,800

Liabilities and Owners' Equity			
	1992	1993	Changes
Current liabilities:			
Accounts payable	$ 3,200	$ 3,000	$ (200)
Notes payable	900	3,400	2,500
Accrued salaries, wages, and other expenses	3,800	3,100	(700)
Current portion of long-term debt	500	500	—
Total current liabilities	$ 8,400	$10,000	$1,600
Long-term liabilities			
Deferred income taxes	$ 1,400	$ 1,500	$100
First mortgage bonds	6,600	6,300	(300)
Debenture bonds	3,000	2,900	(100)
Total long-term liabilities	$11,000	$10,700	$ (300)
Owners' equity:			
Common shares	$ 100	$ 100	—
Contributed surplus	2,000	2,000	—
Retained earnings	6,700	8,200	1,500
Total owners' equity	$ 8,800	$10,300	$1,500
Total liabilities and owners' equity	$28,200	$31,000	$2,800

Looking at the changes in the firm's liabilities, we note first that accounts payable decreased by $200,000. This indicates that the firm paid off more accounts payable than it created during the year. This constitutes a use of cash flows. Notes payable increased by $2,500,000, signalling a source of cash flows from short-term borrowing. The accrued salaries, wages, and other expense accounts decreased by $700,000 during the period, which indicates a use of cash flows. Deferred income taxes increased by $100,000 (source). Both the first mortgage bonds and the debenture bonds decreased for the period by $300,000 and $100,000, respectively. Both decreases constitute uses of cash flows for the period.

The common shares and contributed surplus accounts did not change for the period, indicating no new shares were issued and none was repurchased. Jimco's retained earnings increased by $1,500,000. This represents the net income for 1993 of $1,800,000 less common share dividends of

$300,000. Since net income is included as a source of cash flows (as a part of cash flows provided by operations) and dividends are a use of cash flows, the change in the retained earnings account is not used directly in preparing the statement of changes in financial position.

To summarize, sources and uses are determined by analyzing the changes in the balance sheet accounts between two points in time (for example, between December 31, 1992, and December 31, 1993). However, the change in accumulated depreciation in the balance sheet is disregarded. In place of this change, we show the depreciation expense for the year as a source of cash flows. Also, the change in retained earnings is not included directly in the statement. Since the change in retained earnings equals net income less dividends paid, we prefer to list these latter items separately in place of the change in retained earnings.

In defining the format for the statement of changes in financial position, the cash flows are classified into three categories (operating activities, investment activities, financing activities). The focus of this statement is on cash plus cash equivalents. Table 11-4 illustrates the Statement of Changes in Financial Position for the year ended December 31, 1993.

A review of Jimco's statement of changes in financial position for 1993 indicates that the firm realized a $1,800 positive cash flow from its financing activities, which was $100 less than the cash outflow experienced from the firm's operating activities plus its investments in plant, machinery, and equipment. Thus, the statement of changes in financial position provides the analyst with a useful tool for determining where the firm obtained cash during a prior period and how that cash was spent.

Cash flows from operating activities		
Net income (from the statement of income)	$1800	
Add (deduct) to reconcile net income to net cash flow		
Increase in accounts receivable	(1500)	
Increase in inventories	(700)	
Increase in prepaid expenses	(100)	
Depreciation expense	500	
Decrease in accounts payable	(200)	
Decrease in accrued wages	(700)	
Increase in deferred income taxes	100	
Net cash inflow from operating activities		($800)
Cash flows from investing activities		
Cash inflows		
Cash outflows		
Purchase of plant and equipment	($1100)	
Net cash outflow from investment activities		($1100)
Cash flows from financing activities		
Cash inflows		
Increase in notes payable	$2500	
Cash outflows		
Decrease in mortgage bonds	(300)	
Decrease in debenture bonds	(100)	
Common dividends	(300)	
Net cash inflow from financing activities		$1800
Effect of foreign exchange rates		-0-
Net increase (decrease) in cash during the period		($100)
Cash balance at the beginning of the period	$1500	
Cash balance at the end of the period	$1400	

TABLE 11-4
Jimco, Inc., Statement of Changes in Financial Position for the Year Ended December 31, 1993 ($000)

TABLE 11-5
Schedule for Operating
Cash Flows

Cash flows from operating activities	
Cash inflows from operating activities:	
From customers (Sales + Beginning A/R – Ending A/R)	$ 49,500
Cash outflows from operating activities:	
Cash paid to suppliers (Cost of Goods Sold + Beginning A/P – Ending A/P + Beginning Inventory – Ending Inventory)	($38,900)
Cash paid for remaining expenses (Selling + Gen. Adm. Expense + Beginning Accrued Expenses – Ending Accrued Expenses + Ending Prepaid Expenses – Beginning Prepaid Expenses)	($9,300)
Cash paid for interest expense (Interest Expense + Beginning Accrued Interest Expense – Ending Accrued Interest Expense)	($1,000)
Cash paid for income tax (Income Tax Liability + Beginning Deferred Taxes – Ending Deferred Taxes)	($1,100)
Net cash inflow (outflow) from operating activities	($800)

The financial analyst may also wish to isolate the cash flows occurring from operations as shown in Table 11-5. Such a summary enables the analyst to determine the effect of the firm's primary business on cash flows.

Perspective in Finance

Mathematically, a financial ratio is nothing more than a ratio whose numerator and denominator are comprised of financial data. Sound simple? Well, in concept it is. The objective in using a ratio when analyzing financial information is simply to standardize the information being analyzed so that comparisons can be made between ratios of different firms or possibly the same firm at different points in time. So try to keep this in mind as you read through the discussion of financial ratios. All we are doing is trying to standardize financial data so that we can make comparisons with industry norms or other standards.

FINANCIAL RATIOS

Financial ratios give the analyst a way of making meaningful comparisons of a firm's financial data at different points in time and with other firms. For example, the inventories for a firm with $10 million in annual sales would be expected to be larger than those for a comparable firm with sales of only $5 million. However, the ratio of sales to inventory might be similar for the two firms. Financial ratios represent an attempt to standardize financial information to facilitate meaningful comparisons.

Financial ratios provide the basis for answering some very important questions concerning the financial well-being of the firm. Examples include the following:

1. *How liquid is the firm?* Liquidity refers to the firm's ability to meet maturing obligations and to convert assets into cash. This factor is obviously very important to the firm's creditors.

2. *Is management generating sufficient profits from the firm's assets?* Since the primary purpose for purchasing an asset is to produce profits, the analyst often seeks an indication of the adequacy of the profits being realized. If the level of profits appears insufficient in relation to the investment, an investigation into the reasons for the inferior returns is in order.

3. *How does the firm's management finance its investments?* These decisions have a direct impact upon the returns provided to the common shareholders.

4. *Are the common shareholders receiving sufficient returns on their investment?* The objective of the financial manager is to maximize the value of the firm's common shares, and the level of an investor's return relative to their investment is a key factor in determining that value.

The mathematics skills underlying ratio analysis are quite simple. However, the use and interpretation of financial ratios require a great deal of skill in order to answer questions and to make decisions. The balance of this chapter will be devoted to a discussion of financial ratios and their use in financial analysis.

Using Financial Ratios

The interpretation of financial information which is obtained from the use of financial ratios, is dependent on the perspective of the analyst. For example, a firm's financial analyst may perform an internal financial analysis to determine the firm's liquidity position, its debt capacity or to measure its past earnings performance. Alternatively, a financial analyst from an investment dealer may perform a financial analysis from a position of arm's length in an effort to determine the firm's creditworthiness or investment potential. Regardless of who is performing the analysis, the tools used in financial analysis are basically the same, but their interpretation will be different depending on the perspective of the analyst. Furthermore, a financial analyst will improve the interpretation of the financial information by comparing the firm's financial ratios with a standard or norm. Two types of norms are commonly used. The first type consists of similar ratios for the same firm from previous financial statements. An analysis based upon comparisons of this type is commonly referred to as a **trend analysis**. A second type of norm comes from the ratios of other firms that are considered comparable in their general characteristics to the subject firm—generally this involves the use of published industry average ratios.

There are several widely used sources of industry average ratios. Average ratios for Canadian industries are published annually by sources such as Leibowitz and Statistics Canada. Leibowitz coordinates the publication of 32 key ratios for different industries annually; the financial data of this publication is supplied by Statistics Canada. In the United States, Dun and Bradstreet publishes on an annual basis a set of 14 key ratios for each of the 125 lines of business. Robert Morris Associates also publishes on an annual basis a set of 16 key ratios for over 350 lines of business. Table 11-6 gives an example of standard ratios for the dairy industry in Canada.

The ratio norms in Table 11-6 are classified by firm size to provide the basis for more meaningful comparisons. Thus, a firm with total assets of less than $1 million would not be compared with firms having a much larger asset base. Note also that common size financial statements are reported as well as 32 key ratios. The common size balance sheet simply represents each asset, liability, and owner's equity account as a percent of total assets, whereas each entry in the income statement is reported as a percent of total income. Thus, ratios are effectively related to the entries in the balance sheet and the entries in the income statement. In addition, the use of these ratios over the four quartiles of the year will give the analyst some idea as to how much variation exists within the industry in regard to each ratio.

TABLE 11-6
Industry Average Ratios,
1990

Dairy Industry Asset Size Number of Corporations	<250K[a] 63	>249K–1M 67	>1M–5M 75	>5M–10M 16	>10M–25M 9	>25M 21
Assets	%	%	%	%	%	%
Cash and equivalents	20.5	1.7	6.5	0.4	4.1	0.5
Accounts receivables—(net)	21.9	26.0	25.4	23.5	19.6	18.8
Inventory	15.1	19.2	13.8	14.9	15.1	23.1
All other current	16.4	2.9	7.5	4.2	10.4	12.0
Total current	74.0	49.9	53.2	43.0	49.2	54.4
Total fixed assets (net)	23.3	49.6	44.2	46.1	48.5	35.3
Other assets	2.7	0.7	2.6	10.8	2.3	10.3
Total assets	100.0	100.0	100.0	100.0	100.0	100.0
Liabilities						
Bank loans	0.0	7.6	2.9	13.8	8.0	3.5
Accounts payable	61.6	16.2	26.2	18.7	27.0	21.3
Other current liabilities	9.6	4.9	9.4	5.8	5.1	6.9
Total current	71.2	28.5	38.5	38.3	40.1	31.7
Deferred income	0.0	0.7	2.2	1.0	0.1	0.2
Due shareholders or affiliates	0.0	22.1	9.2	3.3	5.5	9.7
Long-term bank loans	0.0	5.7	0.9	8.2	0.0	0.9
Mortgages, bonds and other debt	1.4	8.8	10.1	11.0	10.7	7.9
LESS: current long-term debt	0.0	1.0	1.4	1.9	0.2	1.1
Other liabilities	0.0	0.7	2.3	2.8	4.4	5.3
Total non-current liabilities	1.4	36.9	23.3	24.6	20.3	22.8
Total liabilities	72.6	65.6	61.9	62.9	60.5	54.5
Total equity	27.4	34.4	38.1	37.2	39.5	45.5
Total liabilities & equity	100.0	100.0	100.0	100.0	100.0	100.0
Income data						
Net sales	98.1	99.9	99.5	99.8	99.5	99.4
Other income	1.9	0.1	0.5	0.2	0.5	0.6
Total income	100.0	100.0	100.0	100.0	100.0	100.0
Gross profit	20.2	25.4	19.0	13.4	18.1	16.7
Materials	77.5	71.6	75.2	80.3	76.0	75.9
Salaries and wages	9.9	12.0	11.7	7.3	10.5	9.4
Repairs and maintenance	1.1	1.6	0.8	0.7	0.4	0.1
Rent	0.8	0.4	0.0	0.2	0.2	0.2
Interest	0.0	0.8	0.4	0.7	0.7	0.7
Depreciation, depletion and amortization	1.1	2.0	1.7	1.8	1.7	1.2
Other expenses	6.9	7.5	6.3	7.2	8.5	7.8
Total expenses	97.7	96.1	96.2	98.2	97.9	95.3
Net profit before taxes and non-recurring items	2.3	3.9	3.8	1.8	2.1	4.7
Non-recurring items	0.0	0.0	0.5	0.0	0.6	0.0
Net Income before taxes	2.3	3.9	4.3	1.8	2.7	4.7
Income taxes						
Current	0.8	1.1	1.2	0.5	0.6	1.7
Deferred	0.0	0.5	0.2	0.1	0.1	0.2
Net Income after taxes	1.0	2.0	2.0	1.0	2.0	2.0

Continued on page 509

Dairy Industry Asset Size Number of Corporations	<250Kᵃ 63	>249K–1M 67	>1M–5M 75	>5M–10M 16	>10M–25M 9	>25M 21
Ratios	%	%	%	%	%	%
Current assets to current liabilities Times	1.04	1.75	1.38	1.12	1.23	1.72
Current assets less inventory to current liabilities Times	0.83	1.08	1.02	0.74	0.85	0.99
Working capital to total assets %	2.74	21.38	14.65	4.73	9.08	22.70
Total liabilities to equity %	265.00	115.65	130.66	155.41	134.33	98.80
Inventory to working capital %	550.00	89.66	94.20	14.55	166.12	101.76
Sales to working capital Times	128.50	15.45	21.52	52.84	28.66	12.99
Sales to inventory Times	23.36	17.23	22.85	16.80	17.25	12.77
Sales to fixed assets Times	15.12	6.65	7.13	5.41	5.36	8.36
Total revenue to total assets Times	3.59	3.31	3.17	2.50	2.62	2.97
Collection period Days	22.72	28.79	29.38	34.42	27.45	23.20
Depreciation to cash earnings %	42.86	47.37	36.56	61.18	46.15	30.58
Depreciation to total expenses %	1.17	2.09	1.78	1.82	1.76	1.29
Accumulated depreciation to gross depreciable assets %	79.78	45.59	43.80	38.90	41.44	47.78
Long term debt to equity %	5.00	23.91	20.30	42.89	23.17	13.96
Current liabilities to equity %	260.00	50.43	81.35	94.69	89.17	57.41
Fixed assets to total assets %	23.29	49.63	44.21	46.13	48.54	35.30
Fixed assets to equity %	85.00	87.83	93.371	14.01	107.83	63.99
Inventory to total assets %	15.07	19.16	13.80	14.86	15.08	23.10
Cost of sales to sales %	79.77	74.63	81.04	86.58	81.89	83.33
Cash earnings to sales %	2.72	4.24	4.71	2.92	3.75	4.03
Net profit before taxes on capital employed %	28.57	17.87	19.57	7.10	9.27	20.50
Net profit before taxes on equity %	30.00	22.61	25.41	10.83	12.33	25.40
Net profit before taxes on total income %	2.29	3.86	3.79	1.75	2.12	4.72
Net profit before taxes on total assets %	8.22	12.78	12.03	4.38	5.55	14.01
Net profit after taxes on capital employed %	19.05	10.31	15.32	4.60	8.77	12.09
Net profit after taxes on equity %	20.00	13.04	19.89	7.01	11.67	14.97
Net profit after taxes on total income %	1.53	2.23	2.97	1.13	2.01	2.78
Net profit after taxes on capital employed %	5.48	7.37	9.42	2.84	5.25	8.26
Provision for income taxes to pre-tax profit %	33.33	42.31	31.28	35.29	26.32	40.17
Salaries and wages to sales %	10.12	12.05	11.75	7.30	10.58	9.46
Salaries and wages to total expenses %	10.16	12.52	12.16	7.41	10.75	9.87
Interest expenses to total expenses %	0.00	0.85	0.45	0.73	0.67	0.75

ᵃK = thousands, M = millions.

Source: A. Leibowitz, *Financial Survey of Canadian Business Performance*, 1990 ed., CCH Canadian Limited. Data supplied by Statistics Canada. Reproduced with the permission of the Minister of Industry, Science and Technology, 1993.

TABLE 11-6
Industry Average Ratios, 1990
Continued from page 508

Categories of Financial Ratios

There are four basic categories of financial ratios. Each category represents an important aspect of the firm's financial condition. The categories consist of liquidity, efficiency, leverage, and profitability ratios. In an attempt to explain each category of ratios from the perspective of an analyst who is examining the investment potential of Jimco, Inc., the financial ratios from each category will be determined from 1993 financial statements of Jimco, Inc. Jimco's balance sheet and income statement were presented in Tables 11-1 and 11-2, respectively.

Jimco, Inc., is involved in the manufacturing of dairy products. The firm has been in business for more than 20 years and is considered by its competitors to be well managed.

Liquidity Ratios

Liquidity ratios provide the basis for answering the question: Does the firm have sufficient cash and near-cash assets to pay its bills on time?

Current liabilities represent the firm's maturing financial obligations. The firm's ability to repay these obligations when due depends largely on whether it has sufficient cash together with other assets that can be converted into cash before the current liabilities mature. The firm's current assets are the primary sources of funds needed to repay current and maturing financial obligations. Thus, the current ratio is a logical measure of liquidity.

CURRENT RATIO ■ The **current ratio** is computed as follows:

$$\text{current ratio} = \frac{\text{current assets}}{\text{current liabilities}} \qquad (11\text{-}1)$$

$$= \frac{\$24,000,000}{\$10,000,000}$$

$$= 2.40 \text{ times}$$

industry average = 2.01 times

For 1993 Jimco's current assets were 2.40 times larger than its current liabilities. Although no firm plans to liquidate a major portion of its current assets to meet its matching current liabilities, this ratio does indicate the margin of safety (the liquidity) of the firm.

Jimco's current ratio is higher than the median industry ratio of 2.01.[4] Thus, Jimco's current ratio indicates greater short-term liquidity than that of other firms in the industry.

ACID TEST OR QUICK RATIO ■ Since inventories and other current liabilities such as pre-paid expenses are generally the least liquid of the firm's assets, it may be desirable to remove them from the numerator of the current ratio, thus obtaining a more refined liquidity measure. For Jimco, the **acid test ratio** is computed as follows:

---

[4]Note that 1992 industry ratios are used in the analysis, since more recent information was not available at the time of writing. The analyst will find that published industry averages are generally a year behind, owing to the time required to collect and publish them.

$$\text{acid test ratio} = \frac{(\text{current assets} - \text{inventories} - \text{pre-paid expenses})}{\text{current liabilities}} \qquad (11\text{-}2)$$

$$= \frac{\$11,700,000}{\$10,000,000}$$

$$= 1.17 \text{ times}$$

industry average $= 0.61$

Once again Jimco's acid test ratio is higher than the ratio for its industry of 0.61. Thus, on the basis of its current and acid test ratios, Jimco offers no visible evidence of a liquidity problem.

Efficiency Ratios

Efficiency ratios provide the basis for assessing how effectively the firm is using its resources to generate sales. For example, a firm that produces $8 million in sales using $4 million in assets is certainly using its resources more efficiently than a similar firm that has $6 million invested in assets.

Efficiency ratios can be defined for each asset category in which a firm invests. Our discussion will include a limited number of key efficiency ratios, related to accounts receivable, inventories, net fixed assets, and total assets.

AVERAGE COLLECTION PERIOD RATIO ■ The **average collection period ratio** serves as the basis for determining how rapidly the firm's credit accounts are being collected. The lower this number is, other things being the same, the more efficient the firm is in managing its investment in accounts receivable. We can also think of this ratio in terms of the number of daily credit sales contained in accounts receivable. For example, the average collection period is equal to the accounts receivable balance divided by the firm's average daily credit sales. Computing the ratio for Jimco, we find

$$\text{average collection period} = \frac{\text{accounts receivable}}{\left(\dfrac{\text{annual credit sales}}{365}\right)} \qquad (11\text{-}3)$$

$$= \frac{\$10,000,000}{\left(\dfrac{\$51,000,000}{365}\right)}$$

$$= 71.57$$

industry average $= 23.21$ days

Therefore, on average, Jimco collects its credit sales every 71.57 days.

The accounts receivable turnover ratio is often interchanged with the average collection period ratio, since it contains the same information. For Jimco this ratio would be equal to

$$\text{accounts receivable turnover} = \frac{\text{credit sales}}{\text{accounts receivable}} \qquad (11\text{-}4)$$

$$= \frac{\$51,000,000}{\$10,000,000} = 5.10 \text{ times}$$

Thus, Jimco is turning its accounts receivable over at a rate of 5.10 times per year. This easily translates into an average collection period of 71.57 days.

For example, if Jimco's receivables turnover is 5.10 times in a 365-day year, then its average collection period must be 365/5.10 = 71.57 days.

The industry norm for the receivables turnover ratio is 15.73 times, which translates into an average collection period of 365/15.73 = 23.21 days. In terms of both standards Jimco does not compare favourably with the industry norm. This could indicate the presence of some slow-paying accounts, which calls for analysis in greater depth.[5] Before performing such an analysis, it is necessary to know whether Jimco's credit terms are longer than those of other firms in the industry. For example, if Jimco allows its customers terms calling for payment in 72 days when 23 days is the industry norm, then the longer average collection period is to be expected.

INVENTORY TURNOVER RATIO ■ The effectiveness or efficiency with which a firm is managing its investment in inventories is reflected in the number of times that its inventories are turned over (replaced) during the year. The **inventory turnover ratio** is defined as follows:

$$\text{inventory turnover} = \frac{\text{cost of goods sold}}{\text{inventories}} \qquad (11\text{-}5)$$

$$= \frac{\$38,000,000}{\$12,000,000}$$

$$= 3.17 \text{ times}$$

$$\text{industry average} = 8.64 \text{ times}$$

Thus, Jimco turns over its inventories 3.17 times per year.[6] When quarterly or monthly information is available, an average inventory figure should be used in order to eliminate the influence of any seasonality in inventory levels from the ratio.

Jimco's inventory turnover ratio of 3.17 does not compare favourably with the industry norm of 8.64 times. In other words, Jimco invests significantly more in inventories per dollar of sales than does the average firm in its industry.

FIXED ASSET TURNOVER RATIO ■ To measure the efficiency with which the firm utilizes its investment in fixed assets, we calculate the **fixed asset turnover ratio** as follows:

$$\text{fixed asset turnover} = \frac{\text{sales}}{\text{net fixed assets}} \qquad (11\text{-}6)$$

$$= \frac{\$51,000,000}{\$7,000,000}$$

$$= 7.286 \text{ times}$$

$$\text{industry average} = 8.36 \text{ times}$$

---

[5]Although it will not be discussed here, one tool for further assessing the liquidity of a firm's receivables is an *aging of accounts receivable schedule*. Such a schedule identifies the number and dollar value of accounts outstanding for various periods. For example, accounts that are less than 10 days old, 11 to 20 days, and so forth might be examined. Still another way to construct the schedule would involve analyzing the length of time to eventual collection of accounts over a past period. For example, how many accounts were outstanding less than 10 days when collected, between 10 and 20 days, and so forth.

[6]Some analysts prefer the use of sales in the numerator of the inventory turnover ratio. However, cost of goods sold is used here, since inventories are stated at cost, and to use sales in the numerator would add a potential source of distortion to the ratio when comparisons are made across firms that have different "markups" on their cost of goods sold.

Thus, Jimco has a larger investment in fixed assets relative to its sales volume than is the case for the industry norm.

TOTAL ASSET TURNOVER RATIO ■ The **total asset turnover ratio** indicates how many dollars in sales the firm squeezes out of each dollar it has invested in assets. For Jimco, we calculate this ratio as follows:

$$\text{total asset turnover} = \frac{\text{sales}}{\text{total assets}} \qquad (11\text{-}7)$$

$$= \frac{\$51,000,000}{\$31,000,000}$$

$$= 1.645 \text{ times}$$

$$\text{industry average} = 2.95 \text{ times}$$

Jimco's total asset turnover ratio compares well with the industry norm of 2.95. This ratio indicates that compared with other firms in its industry, Jimco's management has efficiently utilized its resources in generating sales.

Since total assets equals the sum of fixed and current assets, we can use our turnover ratios for both total and fixed assets to analyze the efficiency with which the firm manages its investment in current assets. For example, since Jimco's total asset turnover is higher than the industry norm, the lower than average fixed asset turnover indicates that Jimco's investment in current assets must be smaller, in relation to sales, than the industry norm.

Leverage Ratios

Leverage ratios provide the basis for answering two questions: How has the firm financed its assets? and Can the firm afford the level of fixed charges associated with its use of non-owner-supplied funds such as bond interest and principal repayments? The first question is answered through the use of balance sheet leverage ratios, the second by using income statement based on ratios, or simply coverage ratios.

At this point we will review the concept of leverage. As related to financial ratios the term will be used to mean financial leverage.[7] Financial leverage results when a firm obtains financing for its investments from sources other than the firm's owners. For a corporation, this means funds from any source other than the common shareholders. Thus, **financial leverage** is leverage that results from the firm's use of debt financing, financial leases, and preferred shares. These sources of financing share a common characteristic: They all require a fixed cash payment or return for their use. For example, debt requires contractually set interest and principal payments, leases require fixed rental payments, and preferred shares usually require a fixed cash dividend. This requirement provides the basis for the leverage in financial leverage. If the firm earns a return higher than the return which is required by the suppliers of leverage funds, then the excess goes to the common shareholders. However, should the return earned fall below the required return, then the common shareholders must make up the difference out of the returns on their invested funds. This, in a nutshell, is the concept of financial leverage.

[7]The concept of leverage was discussed more fully in Chapter 8.

BALANCE SHEET LEVERAGE RATIOS ■ These ratios provide the basis for answering the question, Where did the firm obtain the financing for its investments? The label **balance sheet leverage ratios** is used to indicate that these ratios are computed using information from the balance sheet alone.

Debt Ratio □ The **debt ratio** measures the extent to which the total assets of the firm have been financed using borrowed funds. For Jimco, the ratio is computed as follows:

$$\text{debt ratio} = \frac{\text{total liabilities}}{\text{total assets}} \quad \text{or}$$

$$= \frac{(\text{current liabilities} + \text{noncurrent liabilities})}{\text{total assets}} \quad (11\text{-}8)$$

$$= \frac{(\$10{,}000{,}000 + \$10{,}700{,}000)}{\$31{,}000{,}000}$$

$$= .668, \text{ or } 66.8\%$$

industry average = 54.9%

Thus, Jimco has financed approximately 67 percent of its assets with borrowed funds. This compares with only 54.9 percent for the industry. Note that this ratio can be found by using a common size balance sheet. Simply sum the percent of total assets financed by current liabilities, long-term debt, and all other noncurrent liabilities. Jimco has relied on the use of nonowner financing to a far greater extent than the average firm in its industry. This, in turn, will mean that Jimco may have difficulty trying to borrow additional funds in the future.

Long-Term Debt to Total Capitalization □ The **long-term debt** to **total capitalization ratio** indicates the extent to which the firm has used long-term debt in its permanent financing. Total capitalization represents the sum of all the permanent sources of financing used by the firm, including long-term debt, preferred shares, and common equity. For Jimco, the ratio is computed as follows:

$$\frac{\text{long-term debt to}}{\text{total capitalization}} = \frac{\text{Long-term (noncurrent) liabilities}}{(\text{long-term debt} + \text{preferred shares} + \text{common equity})}$$

$$= \frac{\$10{,}700{,}000}{(\$10{,}700{,}000 + 10{,}300{,}000)} \quad (11\text{-}9)$$

$$= .509, \text{ or } 50.9\%$$

industry average = 33.41%

Therefore, Jimco has obtained a little more than half its permanent financing from debt sources.

Once again referring to a common size balance sheet for an industry norm, note that current liabilities account for 31.7 percent of total assets; thus, permanent financing is equal to $(1 - .317)$, or 68.3 percent of total assets. Furthermore, long-term debt accounts for 22.8 percent of total assets; thus it accounts for $22.8/68.3 = 33.4$ percent of the firm's total capitalization. It is evident that Jimco uses far more long-term debt in its total capitalization than is characteristic of its industry.

One final point about lease financing should be made concerning balance sheet leverage ratios. Since most firms must include the present value of long-term financial lease agreements in the assets and liabilities of the balance sheet, it is now possible to assess their impact on the firm's balance sheet leverage ratios.[8] Annual lease payments generally are contained in footnotes to the firm's financial statements; thus, their effect on the firm's coverage ratios, which are discussed next, can be assessed.

COVERAGE RATIOS ■ These ratios are a second category of leverage ratios, and they are used to measure the firm's ability to cover the finance charges associated with its use of financial leverage. They provide the basis for answering the question of whether the firm has used too much financial leverage.

Times Interest Earned Ratio □ The **times interest earned ratio** indicates the firm's ability to meet its interest payments out of its annual operating earnings. The ratio measures the number of times the firm is covering its interest. Jimco's ratio is computed as follows:[9]

$$\text{times interest earned} = \frac{\begin{array}{c}\text{net operating income (NOI) or}\\ \text{earnings before interest and taxes (EBIT)}\end{array}}{\text{annual interest expense}} \qquad (11\text{-}10)$$

$$= \frac{\$4,000,000}{\$1,000,000}$$

$$= 4.00 \text{ times}$$

$$\text{industry average} = 7.62 \text{ times}$$

This ratio is much lower than the industry norm of 7.62 times, which is not surprising in light of Jimco's higher than average use of financial leverage. However, it appears that Jimco's earnings could be improved in order to afford the higher use of financial leverage.

Cash Flow Overall Coverage Ratio □ The purpose of this ratio is to compare the cash flow (from net operating income) available to meet fixed financial commitments against the cash flow requirements of these obligations. The financial commitments to be recognized include interest, lease payments, preferred dividends, and debt principal repayments. The cash available to pay these obligations equals net operating income plus depreciation. We also add lease payments to operating income plus depreciation, since lease payments have been deducted from revenues to calculate net operating income.[10] We adjust debt principal repayment and preferred share

---

[8]The Accounting committee of the CICA has asserted that a lease which transfers substantially all of the benefits and risks incident to the ownership of property should be accounted for as an acquisition of an asset and the occurrence of an obligation by the lessee. As a result, many firms are now forced to include the value of their lease agreements directly in the balance sheet rather than treat them as operating leases which are reported in footnotes to the balance sheet. Chapter 18 discusses lease accounting further.

[9]The interchangeable use of EBIT and NOI presumes there was no "other" income earned by the firm. If the presence of other nonoperating income is thought to be transitory, then NOI should be used; if not, then EBIT is appropriate.

[10]Lessors have frequently used the argument that lease financing is "off-balance sheet" and does not impact the firm's borrowing capacity. This argument is flawed in two major respects. First, all financial leases must be capitalized and incorporated into the firm's balance sheet. Second, lease payment commitments do impact the firm's cash flow ability to support additional borrowing.

dividends that are not tax deductible to a before-tax basis, since we need to compute the amount of before-tax cash flows that are required to make these payments. For instance, we might assume that Jimco's current portion of long-term debt ($500,000) equals the principal repayment for the period. However, to pay $500,000 using after-tax income, we would have to earn $833,333 before taxes. For example, $833,333 income less taxes at a 40 percent rate ($333,333 = .40 × $833,333) leaves $500,000 after taxes to make the principal repayment. For preferred share dividends and debt principal repayment, we have to make the following adjustments:

$$\frac{\text{before-tax cost of}}{\text{preferred share dividends}} = \frac{\text{preferred share dividend}}{(1 - \text{combined corporate tax rate})}$$

$$\frac{\text{before-tax debt principal}}{\text{repayment requirement}} = \frac{\text{principal repayment}}{(1 - \text{combined corporate tax rate})}$$

We can now compute Jimco's cash flow coverage ratio, as follows:

$$\text{cash flow overall coverage ratio} = \frac{\begin{array}{c}\text{net operating income +}\\ \text{lease expense + depreciation}\end{array}}{\begin{array}{c}\text{interest + lease expense +}\\ \text{preferred dividends/}\\ (1 - \text{combined corporate tax rate}) +\\ \text{principal payments/}\\ (1 - \text{combined corporate tax rate})\end{array}} \quad (11\text{-}11)$$

$$= \frac{\$(4{,}000{,}000 + 500{,}000)}{\$1{,}000{,}000 + \dfrac{500{,}000}{(1-0.40)}}$$

$$= \frac{\$4{,}500{,}000}{\$1{,}833{,}333} = 2.45 \text{ times}$$

Thus, Jimco's operating earnings were 4.00 times its interest expense, whereas the firm's operating cash flows were only 2.45 times its total finance charges.

One further refinement may be desirable in the cash flow overall coverage ratio. This relates to the coverage of any common dividends the firm wishes to pay. For example, should Jimco desire to pay dividends to common shareholders totalling $300,000, then the firm must earn $300,000/ (1 − .40) = $500,000 of income on a before-tax basis. Adding this figure for common dividends to the firm's existing finance charges reduces the coverage ratio to 1.93 times. This second version of the coverage ratio is particularly useful when the firm analyzes alternative sources of long-term financing and wishes to maintain a stable dividend payment to its common shareholders.

Summarizing the results of Jimco's leverage ratios, we have made two basic observations: first, Jimco has utilized more nonowner financing than is characteristic of its industry; second, Jimco's earnings could be improved in order to afford the higher use of financial leverage.

Profitability Ratios

As we have discussed, financial ratios help us answer some very important questions about the effectiveness of the firm's management of its resources to produce profits. Specifically, **profitability ratios** can be used to answer such questions as these: How much of each sales dollar was management able to convert into profits? How much profit did the firm earn on each dollar of assets under its control? For discussion purposes we will divide profitability ratios into two groups: profitability in relation to sales and profitability in relation to investment.

PROFITABILITY IN RELATION TO SALES ■ These ratios can be used to assess the ability of the firm's management to control the various expenses involved in generating sales. The profit ratios discussed here are commonly referred to as profit margins and include the gross profit margin, operating profit margin, and net profit margin.

Gross Profit Margin □ The **gross profit margin** is calculated as follows:

$$\text{gross profit margin} = \frac{\text{gross profit}}{\text{net sales}} \qquad (11\text{-}12)$$

$$= \frac{\$13,000,000}{\$51,000,000}$$

$$= .255, \text{ or } 25.5\%$$

$$\text{industry average} = 16.67\%$$

Thus Jimco's gross profit constitutes 25.5 percent of firm sales. This margin reflects the firm's markup on its cost of goods sold as well as the ability of management to minimize the firm's cost of goods sold in relation to sales (and the method for determining that cost).

Jimco's gross profit margin appears to be greater than the industry norm of 16.67 percent. Note that the gross profit margin reflects both the level of Jimco's cost of goods sold and the size of the firm's markup on those costs, or its pricing policy.

Operating Profit Margin □ Moving down the income statement, the next profit figure encountered is net operating income (or earnings before interest and taxes—EBIT). This profit figure serves as the basis for computing the **operating profit margin**. For Jimco this profit margin is found as follows:

$$\text{operating profit margin} = \frac{\text{net operating income}}{\text{sales}} \qquad (11\text{-}13)$$

$$= \frac{\$4,000,000}{\$51,000,000}$$

$$= .0784, \text{ or } 7.84\%$$

$$\text{industry average} = 5.47\%$$

The operating profit margin reflects the firm's operating expenses as well as its cost of goods sold. Therefore, this ratio serves as an overall measure of operating effectiveness.

Jimco's operating profit margin is greater than the industry norm of 5.47 percent. Thus, Jimco's operating expenses per dollar of sales are below the industry norm.

Net Profit Margin □ The final profit margin considered involves the net after-tax profits of the firm as a percent of sales. For Jimco the **net profit margin** is computed as follows:

$$\text{net profit margin} = \frac{\text{net income}}{\text{sales}} \qquad (11\text{-}14)$$

$$= \frac{\$1,800,000}{\$51,000,000}$$

$$= .035, \text{ or } 3.5\%$$

$$\text{industry average} = 2.00\%$$

Therefore, $.035 of each sales dollar is converted into profits after taxes. Note that this profit margin reflects the firm's cost of goods sold, operating expenses, finance charges (interest expense), and taxes. For the industry, profits before taxes are 3.48 percent of sales. Assuming that firms on the average pay approximately 42.6 percent of their taxable earnings in taxes, this produces a net profit margin of $.0348(1 - .426) = .020$, or 2.00 percent. Hence, Jimco's net profit margin is above the norm for its industry. In the next category of profitability ratios we investigate the firm's total investment and the return on the investment of the common shareholders.

PROFITABILITY IN RELATION TO INVESTMENT ■ This category of profitability ratios attempts to measure firm profits in relation to the invested funds used to generate those profits. Thus, these ratios are very useful in assessing the overall effectiveness of the firm's management.

Operating Income Return on Investment □ The **operating income return on investment** reflects the rate of return on the firm's total investment before interest and taxes. For Jimco, this return measure is computed as follows:

$$\text{operating income return on investment} = \frac{\text{net operating income}}{\text{total assets}}$$

$$= \frac{\$4,000,000}{\$31,000,000} \qquad (11\text{-}15)$$

$$= .129, \text{ or } 12.9\%$$

$$\text{industry average} = 16.13\%$$

Jimco's management produced a 12.9 percent return on its total assets before interest and taxes have been paid.[11] As a benchmark to determine whether leverage is favourable or unfavourable, the 12.9 percent rate of return can be compared with the cost of borrowed funds. If the firm is borrowing at a cost less than 12.9 percent, then leverage is favourable and will result in higher after-tax earnings to its shareholders.[12]

---

[11]Intangible assets are often subtracted from total assets in an effort to measure the firm's return on invested capital. The lack of physical qualities of intangible assets makes evidence of their existence elusive, their value often difficult to estimate, and their useful lives indeterminable. However, since Jimco has no intangible assets, no adjustment is necessary.

[12]The concept of leverage was fully developed earlier in Chapter 8. Very simply, when a firm borrows money that requires a fixed return, then the return to the common shareholders will be enhanced only if the return the firm earns on these borrowed funds exceeds their cost. For the firm as a whole the operating income rate of return measures the before-tax-and-interest rate of return on the firm's investment. This rate must exceed the cost of borrowed funds for the firm as a whole to experience favourable financial leverage. The favourableness of financial leverage is determined by the effect of its use on earnings per share to the firm's common shareholders.

This rate of return is useful in assessing operating effectiveness of the firm's management. The operating return on investment does not reflect the influence of the firm's use of financial leverage. Neither the numerator (operating income) nor the denominator (total assets) is affected by the way in which the firm has financed its assets. Thus, it provides a measure of management's effectiveness in making operating decisions as opposed to financing decisions.

If the industry norm for this ratio is not readily available, we can calculate one, using the information given there. Sales divided by total assets equals 2.95; and the operating profit margin is 5.47 percent of sales for the industry. Using the following relationship, we derive an industry norm of 16.13 percent. Thus, Jimco's operating rate of return compares favourably with the industry norm.

$$\left(\frac{\text{operating income}}{\text{sales}}\right) \times \left(\frac{\text{sales}}{\text{total assets}}\right) = \left(\frac{\text{operating income}}{\text{total assets}}\right) \quad (11\text{-}16)$$

$$0.0547 \quad \times \quad 2.95 \quad = \quad .1613, \text{ or } 16.13\%$$

In deriving the industry norm for the operating income return on investment ratio, we have identified a very useful relationship between operating profit margin and the ratio of sales divided by total assets (which we earlier referred to as total asset turnover). For example, a firm's rate of return on investment is a function of (1) how much profit it squeezes out of each dollar of sales (as reflected in its operating profit margin), and (2) how much it has invested in assets to produce those sales (as reflected in the total asset turnover ratio). Jimco's above-average operating profit margin, combined with its higher than average turnover of total investment in assets, produces an operating income return on investment that is above its industry norm.

Return on Total Assets or Return on Investment ☐ The **return on total assets** or **return on investment ratio** relates after-tax income to the firm's total investment in assets. For Jimco, this ratio is found as follows:

$$\text{return on total assets} = \frac{\text{net income}}{\text{total assets}} \quad (11\text{-}17)$$

$$= \frac{\$1,800,000}{\$31,000,000}$$

$$= .058, \text{ or } 5.8\%$$

$$\text{industry average} = 5.9\%$$

Again total assets are used in an attempt to measure total investment. In this analysis an industry norm was obtained in a manner similar to that used with the operating rate of return. For example,

$$\text{return on total assets} = \frac{\text{net income}}{\text{sales}} \times \frac{\text{sales}}{\text{total assets}} \quad (11\text{-}18)$$

Earlier the net income to sales ratio for the industry was estimated to be 2.0 percent. Using the industry's sales to total assets ratio of 2.95 produces an industry norm for return on total assets of .020 × 2.95 = .0590, or 5.90

percent. Thus, Jimco provides a very good return on its total investment when compared to other firms in its industry.[13]

Return on Equity □ The **return on equity ratio** measures the rate of return earned on the shareholder's investment. Jimco earned the following rate of return for its shareholders:

$$\text{return on common equity} = \frac{\text{net income available to common}}{\text{common equity}} \quad (11\text{-}19)$$

$$= \frac{\$1,800,000}{\$10,300,000}$$

$$= .175, \text{ or } 17.5\%$$

$$\text{industry average} = 13.08\%$$

The following relationship can be used to derive an industry norm from the return on total assets ratio and the debt ratio:

$$\text{return on common equity} = \frac{\text{return on total assets}}{(1 - \text{debt ratio})} \quad (11\text{-}20)$$

Recall that the debt ratio is simply total liabilities divided by total assets. The industry norm for the return on equity ratio is found as follows:

$$= \frac{0.059}{(1 - .549)}$$

$$= 0.1308 \text{ or } 13.08\%$$

Thus, Jimco's 17.5 percent return compares favourably with that of the industry. This higher than average return reflects both the firm's above-average profit margins (reflected in the firm's operating and net profit margins) and its above-average use of financial leverage (as reflected in its debt ratio).

In summary, Jimco has slightly below-average return on its assets; however, the firm has above-average profits in relation to its sales. This factor results from the firm's above-average operating and net profit margins and the fact that Jimco utilized more leverage than the norm for its industry.

Trend Analysis

We noted earlier that a firm's financial ratios can be compared with two types of standards and have discussed industry norms as the basis for comparison. Now, we will demonstrate the use of trend comparisons. Figure 11-1 illustrates graphs of Jimco's current ratio, acid-test ratio, debt ratio, and return on total asset ratio for the past five years.

Surveying the trend in Jimco's liquidity ratios reveals that Jimco's current and acid-test ratios compare very favourably with their respective indus-

---

[13]The return on investment defined as the ratio of net income to total assets has long been a widely used measure with an inappropriate investment base and can produce misleading signals. The problem relates to the fact that the net income does not include interest expense, which is the return paid to the firm's creditors who financed a portion of the firm's investments. The problem can be resolved in one of two ways. First, if the analyst is interested in evaluating the performance of the firm with respect to its total asset investment, then the operating income rate of return discussed earlier is appropriate. On the other hand, if the analyst is specifically interested in how well the firm's shareholders have fared, then the return on common equity is the appropriate ratio to use.

INTERNATIONAL FINANCIAL MANAGEMENT

Suppose that you want to analyze and compare the financial health of a group of North American companies and Dutch companies. Can you calculate a set of ratios for each of the two sets of firms and compare one set to the other? In general the answer is no. The following are examples of international accounting differences: (1) in the Netherlands assets are valued at their economic worth or replacement value rather than historical cost as is generally the case in North America and (2) intangible assets, such as goodwill from a consolidation that occurs in North America, must be amortized and expensed against reported income over a period of no more than 40 years. In Germany, the maximum amortization period is five years, while in Great Britain goodwill does not have to be expensed against reported income at all but can be charged directly against retained earnings on the firm's balance sheet. These differences in accounting practice can have a significant impact on the firm's reported earnings where all else is held constant. Finally, in Japan, income smoothing is permitted because firms are allowed to make discretionary changes in such items as depreciation and bad debts. These are just a few cases that make accounting practices across international borders difficult.

The need for uniform standards is widely recognized and the financial accounting community has long supported a move toward uniform international standards. As far back as 1973, the International Accounting Standards Committee (IASC) was formed to promote uniformity and to narrow the areas of divergence among participating nations. International accounting practices still vary widely and comparisons of firms across international borders remain difficult.

try norms from a creditor's perspective. However, the firm's management may want to question whether too much of the firm's assets are being tied up in liquid assets which yield a low return.

Jimco's debt ratio appears to have declined slightly over the past five years, with moderate interim fluctuations. However, no material change in the ratio appears to have occurred over the period. In light of Jimco's current use of leverage, however, any further increases in this ratio may be unwarranted.

Finally, the return on total assets ratio for the past five years depicts the relatively volatile nature of Jimco's business, with returns ranging from 4 percent in 1990 to 10 percent in 1992. However, based upon Jimco's return on total assets ratio for 1993 and that of the industry, it would appear that Jimco has done as well or better than the median for its industry.

Summary of Jimco's Financial Ratios

Table 11-7 summarizes Jimco's financial ratios, as well as the corresponding industry norms. Each ratio is evaluated in relation to the appropriate norm. Briefly, the results of those comparisons are as follows:

1. Jimco's liquidity position is much better than the industry.

2. Jimco has made extensive use of financial leverage. In fact, the firm has financed 67 percent of its assets with nonowner funds.

3. The firm cannot afford any further use of financial leverage, as is indicated by the times interest earned ratio.

4. The firm must re-examine its policies for accounts receivable and inventory management, as indicated by both the average collection period and the inventory turnover ratios.

5. Jimco's profit margins are better than the respective industry norms; however, the firm has not been able to convert these profit margins

into better than average rates of return on investment. This resulted from the higher than average sales per dollar invested in assets as reflected in Jimco's efficiency ratios.

6. Finally, Jimco has benefited from the favourable use of financial leverage. The firm earned a favourable 17.5 percent return on the investment of its common shareholders, compared with 13.08 percent for the industry.

FIGURE 11-1. Trend Analysis Illustration

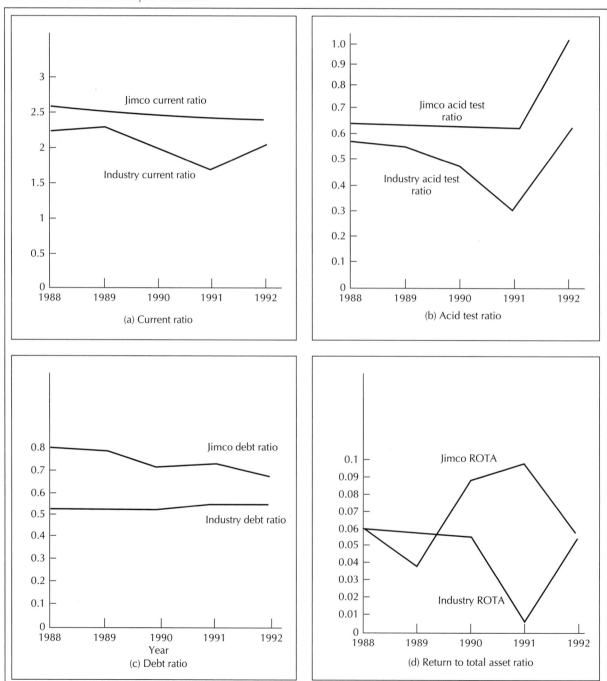

TABLE 11-7. Summary of Ratios for Jimco, Inc.

Ratio	Formula	Calculation	Industry Average	Evaluation
Liquidity ratios				
1. Current ratio	Current assets/current liabilities	$24,000,000/10,000,000 = 2.40 times	2.01 times	Excellent
2. Acid test ratio	(Current assets − inventories − pre-paid expenses)/current liabilities	$11,700,000/10,000,000 = 1.17 times	0.61 times	Good
Efficiency ratios				
3. Average collection period	Average accounts receivable/ (annual credit sales/365)	$10,000,000/(51,000,000/365) = 71.57 days	23.21 days	Poor
4. Inventory turnover	Cost of goods sold/ending inventory	$38,000,000/12,000,000 = 3.17 times	8.64 times	Poor
5. Fixed asset turnover	Sales/fixed assets	$51,000,000/7,000,000 = 7.286 times	8.36 times	Satisfactory
6. Total asset turnover	Sales/total assets	$51,000,000/31,000,000 = 1.645 times	2.95 times	Good
Leverage ratios				
7. Debt ratio	Total liabilities/total assets	$20,700,000/31,000,000 = 66.8%	54.90%	Satisfactory
8. Long-term debt to total capitalization	Long-term debt/total capitalization	$10,700,000/21,000,000 = 50.9%	33.41%	Satisfactory
9. Times interest earned	Net operating income/annual interest expense	$4,000,000/1,000,000 = 4.00 times	7.62 times	Poor
10. Cash flow overall	(NOI + lease expense + depreciation interest + lease expense + principal payments/ (1 − tax rate)	$4,500,000/1,833,333 = 2.45 times	N.A.[a]	—
Profitability ratios				
11. Gross profit margin	Gross profit/sales	$13,000,000/51,000,000 = 25.5%	16.67%	Excellent
12. Operating profit margin	Net operating income/sales	$4,000,000/51,000,000 = 7.84%	5.47%	Satisfactory
13. Net profit margin	Net income/sales	$1,800,000/51,000,000 = 3.5%	2.00%	Good
14. Operating income return on investment	Net operating income/total assets	$4,000,000/31,000,000 = 12.9%	16.13%	Satisfactory
15. Return on total assets	Net income/total assets	$1,800,000/31,000,000 = 5.8%	5.90%	Satisfactory
16. Return on common equity	Net income available to common/common equity	$1,800,000/10,300,000 = 17.5%	13.08%	Good

[a]Norm was not available.

AN INTEGRATED FORM OF FINANCIAL ANALYSIS BASED ON EARNING POWER

Table 11-7 presents an alternative format for analyzing financial ratios. This alternative format focuses on the firm's earning power as measured by two of the firm's profitability ratios: the operating income return on investment and the return on common equity. This method of financial analysis is particularly well suited to internal analyses carried out by the firm's management. The reason is that the analysis focuses directly on firm profitability, which in turn reflects how well the firm is being managed. In addition, the analysis of earning power is a valuable guide to analyze the firm's ability to manage effectively its financial assets from the common shareholder's perspective.

The analysis of a firm's earning power involves a two-stage procedure designed to answer two basic questions:

Stage 1: How effective has the firm's management been in generating sales using the total assets of the firm and converting those sales into operating profits?

Stage 2: How effective has the firm's management been in forming a financial structure that increases the returns to the common shareholders? Here we analyze the effect of the firm's financing decisions (that is, the mixture of debt and owner financing used by the firm) on the rate of return earned on the common shareholder's investment.

Figure 11-2 provides a template for carrying out the first stage of the analysis of Jimco's earning power. We focus our attention on the ratio of operating income return on investment. This ratio reflects the rate of return earned on the firm's investment in assets and before giving any consideration to how they have been financed. Note that the operating income return on investment can be broken down into the product of two ratios,

$$\frac{\text{Operating Income}}{\text{Return on Investment}} = \left(\frac{\text{Operating Income}}{\text{Sales}}\right) \times \left(\frac{\text{Sales}}{\text{Total Assets}}\right)$$

$$= \frac{\text{Operating Income}}{\text{Total Assets}}$$

Figure 11-2 simply lays out the relationships that underlie the operating profit margin and total asset turnover ratios. The left-hand branch of the figure shows the determinants of the operating profit margin and the right-hand branch details the determinants of the total asset turnover ratio.

A total of seven ratios are calculated in the first stage of the analysis of Jimco's earning power. The first is the operating income return on investment (Step 1). Step 2 involves calculating the operating profit margin, which, along with the total asset turnover (Step 4), determines the operating income return on investment. Step 3 involves calculation of the gross profit margin, which provides the basis for assessing the impact of cost of goods sold on the operating profit margin calculated in Step 2. Steps 5, 6, and 7 involve the calculation of the fixed asset turnover, accounts receivable turnover, and inventory turnover ratios, which provide the basis for a detailed analysis of the determinants of the total asset turnover ratio (calculated in Step 4).

Note that by following the steps in Figure 11-2, the analyst is led through a detailed analysis of the determinants of the operating income return on investment. Each successive step provides the basis for understanding more about the determinants of this rate of return. For example, the total asset turnover ratio is one of the two basic determinants of the operating income return on investment (the other is the operating profit margin). By analyzing the fixed asset turnover ratio in conjunction with the total asset turnover, the analyst can determine whether fixed or current assets caused the total asset turnover ratio to deviate from the industry average. Furthermore, the accounts receivable turnover and inventory turnover ratios can be analyzed to determine the effect of the level of investment in these assets on total asset turnover, and, consequently, the observed operating income return on investment.

FIGURE 11-2. Analyzing Earning Power: Stage 1 (Analyzing the Operating Income Return on Investment)

Step	Ratio	Formula	Calculation	Industry	Evaluation
1	Operating income return on investment	$\dfrac{\text{Net operating income}}{\text{Total assets}}$	$\dfrac{\$\,4{,}000{,}000}{\$31{,}000{,}000} = 12.9\%$	16.13%	Poor
2	Operating profit margin	$\dfrac{\text{Net operating income}}{\text{Sales}}$	$\dfrac{\$\,4{,}000{,}000}{\$51{,}000{,}000} = 7.84\%$	5.47%	Satisfactory
3	Gross profit margin	$\dfrac{\text{Gross profit}}{\text{Sales}}$	$\dfrac{\$13{,}000{,}000}{\$51{,}000{,}000} = 25.5\%$	16.67%	Excellent
4	Total asset turnover	$\dfrac{\text{Sales}}{\text{Total assets}}$	$\dfrac{\$51{,}000{,}000}{\$31{,}000{,}000} = 1.645$ times	2.95 times	Good
5	Fixed asset turnover	$\dfrac{\text{Sales}}{\text{Fixed assets}}$	$\dfrac{\$51{,}000{,}000}{\$\,7{,}000{,}000} = 7.286$ times	8.36 times	Satisfactory
6	Accounts receivable turnover	$\dfrac{\text{Credit sales}}{\text{Accounts receivable}}$	$\dfrac{\$51{,}000{,}000}{\$10{,}000{,}000} = 5.10$ times	15.73 times	Poor
7	Inventory turnover	$\dfrac{\text{Cost of goods sold}}{\text{Inventories}}$	$\dfrac{\$38{,}000{,}000}{\$12{,}000{,}000} = 3.17$ times	10.64 times	Poor

Figure 11-3 provides a template for use in analyzing the effect of the firm's financing decisions on the return earned on the common shareholder's investment. The analysis presented in Figure 11-3 depends on the following basic relationship:

$$\text{Return on Common Equity} = \frac{\text{Net Income Available to Common Shareholders}}{\text{Common Equity}}$$

The analysis begins with the operating income return on investment ratio, which was the subject of the analysis in Figure 11-2. Next, Step 9 involves calculation of the return on total assets. This ratio is then adjusted for the influence of the firm's use of financial leverage in order to calculate the return on common equity. In Step 10 we measure the rate of return earned on the common shareholders' investment in the firm, which reflects both the firm's operating and financing decisions.

The 10-step procedure outlined in Figures 11-2 and 11-3 connects the return earned on common equity to the firm's use of financial leverage and

FIGURE 11-3. Analyzing Earning Power: Stage 2 (The Return Earned on the Common Shareholder's Investment)

Step	Ratio	Formula	Calculation	Industry	Evaluation
8	Operating income Return on investment	$\dfrac{\text{Net operating income}}{\text{Total assets}}$	$\dfrac{\$\,4{,}000{,}000}{\$31{,}000{,}000} = 12.9\%$	16.13%	Poor
9	Return on total assets	$\dfrac{\text{Net income}}{\text{Total assets}}$	$\dfrac{\$\,1{,}800{,}000}{\$31{,}000{,}000} = 5.8\%$	5.9%	Satisfactory
10	Return on common equity	$\dfrac{\text{Net income available to common}}{\text{Common equity}}$	$\dfrac{\$\,1{,}800{,}000}{\$10{,}300{,}000} = 17.5\%$	13.08%	Good

the operating profitability. The operating rate of return ratio was shown to be determined by the firm's profit margins on sales (Steps 2 and 3) and the sales to asset relationship (Steps 4 through 7). The real value of this approach to financial analysis is its ability to demonstrate the interrelationships between the return earned on the owners' investment in the firm and a wide variety of financial attributes of the firm. The analyst is provided with a "roadmap" to follow in determining how successful the firm's management has been in managing its resources to maximize the return earned on the owners' investment. In addition, the analyst can determine why that particular return was earned.

Limitations of Ratio Analysis

The analyst who works with financial ratios must be aware of the limitations involved in their use. The following list includes some of the more important pitfalls that may be encountered in computing and interpreting financial ratios:

1. It is sometimes difficult to identify the industry category to which a firm belongs when the firm engages in multiple lines of business.

2. Published industry averages are only approximations and provide the user with general guidelines rather than scientifically determined averages of the ratios of all or even a representative sample of the firms within the industry. For example, Robert Morris Associates prepares a cautionary statement in conjunction with its published industry ratios (See, *Basic Financial Management in Practice*).

3. Accounting practices differ widely among firms and can lead to differences in computed ratios. For example, the use of last-in, first-out (LIFO) in inventory valuation can, in a period of rising prices, lower the firm's inventory account and increase its inventory turnover ratio as compared to that of a firm that utilizes first-in, first-out (FIFO). In addition, firms may choose different methods of depreciating their fixed assets.

4. Financial ratios can be too high or too low. For example, a current ratio that exceeds the industry norm may signal the presence of excess liquidity, which results in a lowering of overall profits in relation to the firm's investment in assets. On the other hand, a current ratio that falls below the norm indicates the possibility that the firm has inadequate liquidity and may at some future date be unable to pay its bills on time.

5. An industry average may not provide a desirable target ratio or norm. At best, an industry average provides a guide to the financial position of the average firm in the industry. However, Table 11-6 does provide industry norms according to size of firm, which enables a more meaningful comparison of ratios.[14]

6. Many firms experience seasonality in their operations. Thus, balance sheet entries and their corresponding ratios will vary with the time of year when the statements are prepared. To avoid this problem, an aver-

---

[14]A recent study (Rose and Cunningham, 1991) indicates the need to carefully consider the choice of an industry norm. In fact, your analysis may require you to construct your own norm from, say, a list of four or five firms in a particular industry that might provide the most appropriate standard of comparison for the firm being analyzed.

BASIC FINANCIAL MANAGEMENT IN PRACTICE

Industrial ratios and statement studies data be regarded only as general guidelines and not as absolute industry norms. For example, Robert Morris Associates (RMA) provide several reasons why the data may not be fully representative of a given industry:

(1) The financial statements used in the Statement Studies are not selected by any random or statistically reliable method. RMA member banks voluntarily submit the raw data they have available each year provided that the companies' total assets are less than $250 million, except for contractors' statements which have no upper size limit.

(2) Many companies have varied product lines; however, the Statement Studies categorize them by their primary product Standard Industrial Classification (SIC) number only.

(3) Some of our industry samples are rather small in relation to the total number of firms in a given industry. A relatively small sample can increase the changes that some of our composites do not fully represent an industry.

(4) There is the chance that an extreme statement can be present in a sample, causing a disproportionate influence on the industry composite.

This is particularly true in a relatively small sample.

(5) Companies within the same industry may differ in their method of operations which in turn can directly influence their financial statements. Since they are included in our sample, too, these statements can significantly affect our composite calculations.

(6) Other considerations that can result in variations among different companies engaged in the same general line of business are different labour markets; geographical location; different accounting methods; quality of products handled; sources and methods of financing; and terms of sale.

For these reasons, RMA does not recommend the Statement Studies figures be considered as absolute norms for a given industry. Rather the figures should be used only as general guidelines and in addition to the other methods of financial analysis. RMA makes no claim as to the representativeness of the figures printed in this book.

Source: Robert Morris Associates, One Liberty Place, Philadelphia, PA 19103. © 1991 by Robert Morris Associates. Reprinted with permission.

age account balance should be used (for several months or quarters during the year) rather than the year-end total. For example, an average of month-end inventory balance might be used to compute a firm's inventory turnover ratio when the firm is subject to a significant seasonality in its sales (and correspondingly in its investment in inventories).

Given their limitations, financial ratios provide the analyst with a very useful tool for assessing a firm's financial condition. The analyst should, however, be aware of these potential weaknesses when performing a ratio analysis. In many cases, the real importance of analyzing financial ratios is the framework that is provided for asking questions about the firm.

SUMMARY

Basic Financial Statements

Three basic financial statements are commonly used to describe the financial condition and performance of the firm: the balance sheet, the income statement, and the statement changes in financial position. The balance sheet provides a picture of the firm's assets, liabilities, and owners' equity on a particular date, whereas the income statement reflects the net revenues from the firm's operations over a given period. The statement of changes in financial position combines information from both the balance sheet and income statement to describe sources and uses of cash for a given period in the firm's history.

Financial Ratios

Financial ratios are the principal tool of financial analysis. Sometimes referred to as benchmarks, ratios standardize financial information so that comparisons of firms of varying sizes can be made. Ratio analysis should be designed to provide information for the specific needs of an analyst.

Financial ratios are of four main kinds: (1) liquidity, (2) efficiency, (3) leverage, and (4) profitability ratios. The financial statements of Jimco, Inc., demonstrate the computation of a sample listing of ratios from each category. The set of possible ratio calculations is limited only by the analyst's imagination, and those discussed here represent only one possible listing that can be used in performing a financial analysis.

Analyzing Financial Ratios

Two methods were demonstrated for analyzing financial ratios. The first involved trend analysis for the firm over time; the second involved making ratio comparisons with industry ratios. A set of industry ratios was presented and used in the analysis of a company. In addition, an integrated form of financial analysis based upon earning power focused the user's attention on the underlying determinants of a firm's profitability.

STUDY QUESTIONS

11-1. The basic financial statements of an organization consist of the balance sheet, income statement, and statement of changes in financial position. Describe the nature of each and explain how their functions differ.

11-2. Why is it that the preferred shareholders' equity section of the balance sheet changes only when new shares are sold, whereas the common equity section changes from year to year regardless of whether new shares are bought or sold?

11-3. Discuss two reasons why net income for a particular period does not necessarily reflect a firm's cash flow during that period.

11-4. The four basic groups of financial ratios are liquidity, efficiency, leverage, and profitability ratios. Discuss the nature of each group and list two example ratios that you would use to measure that aspect of a firm's financial condition.

11-5. Discuss briefly the two sources of standards or norms that can be used in performing ratio analyses.

11-6. Where can the analyst obtain industry norms? What limitations does the use of industry average ratios suffer from? Discuss briefly.

SELF-TEST PROBLEMS

ST-1. (*Ratio Analysis and Short-term Liquidity*) Ray's Tool and Supply Company has been expanding its level of operations for the past two years. The firm's sales have grown rapidly as a result of the expansion in the economy. However, Ray's is a privately held company, and the only source of available funds it has is a line of credit with the firm's bank. The company needs to expand its inventories to meet the needs of its growing customer base but also wishes to maintain a current ratio of at least 3 to 1. If Ray's current assets are $6,000,000 and its current ratio is now 4 to 1, how much can it expand its inventories (financing the expansion with its line of credit) before the target current ratio is violated?

ST-2. (*Ratio Analysis of Loan Request*) On February 3, 1994, Mr. Jerry Simmons, chief financial officer for M & G Industries, contacted the firm's bank regarding a loan. The loan was to be used to repay notes payable and to finance current assets. Mr. Simmons wanted to repay the loan plus interest in one year. Upon receiving the loan request, the bank asked that the firm supply it with complete financial statements for the past two years. These statements are presented below:

M & G Industries Balance Sheets at the End of Calendar Year

	1992	1993
Cash	$ 9,000	$ 500
Accounts receivable	12,500	16,000
Inventories	29,000	45,500
Total current assets	$ 50,500	$ 62,000
Land	20,000	26,000
Buildings and equipment	70,000	100,000
Less: Allowance for depreciation	28,000	38,000
Total fixed assets	$ 62,000	$ 88,000
	$112,500	$150,000
Accounts payable	$ 10,500	$ 22,000
Bank notes	17,000	47,000
Total current liabilities	$ 27,500	$ 69,000
Long-term debt	28,750	22,950
Common shares	31,500	31,500
Retained earnings	24,750	26,550
	$112,500	$150,000

M & G Industries Income Statements for Years Ending December 31

	1992	1993
Sales	$125,000	$160,000
Cost of goods sold	75,000	96,000
Gross profit	$ 50,000	$ 64,000
Operating expense:		
Fixed cash operating expense	21,000	21,000
Variable operating expense	12,500	16,000
Depreciation	4,500	10,000
Total operating expense	38,000	47,000
Earnings before interest and taxes	$ 12,000	$ 17,000
Interest	3,000	6,100
Earnings before taxes	$ 9,000	$ 10,900
Taxes	4,500	5,450
Net income	$ 4,500	$ 5,450

a. Based upon the preceding statements, complete the following table.

M & G Industries Ratio Analysis

	Industry Averages	Actual 1992	Actual 1993
Current ratio	1.80		
Acid test ratio	.70		
Average collection period[a]	37 days		
Inventory turnover[a]	2.50 times		
Debt to total assets	58%		
Long-term debt to total capitalization	33%		
Times interest earned	3.8 times		
Gross profit margin	38%		
Operating profit margin	10%		
Net profit margin	3.5%		
Total asset turnover	1.14 times		
Fixed asset turnover	1.40 times		
Operating income return on investment	11.4%		
Return on total assets	4.0%		
Return on common equity	9.5%		

[a]Based on a 365-day year and on end-of-year figures.

b. Analyze Mr. Simmons' loan request. Would you grant the loan? Explain.

ST-3. (Statement of Changes in Financial Position)

a. Prepare a statement of changes in financial position for M & G Industries for 1993, using information given in Self-Test Problem ST-2.

b. How does this statement supplement your ratio analysis from Self-Test Problem ST-2? Explain.

STUDY PROBLEMS (SET A)

11-1A. (*Ratio Analysis*) The Mitchem Marble Company has a target current ratio of 2 to 1 but has experienced some difficulties financing its expanding sales in the past few months. At present the current ratio of 2.5 to 1 is based upon current assets of $2.5 million. If Mitchem expands its receivables and inventories using its short-term line of credit, how much additional funding can it borrow before its current ratio standard is reached?

11-2A. (*Ratio Analysis*) The balance sheet and income statement for the J. P. Robard Mfg. Company are as follows:

Balance Sheet ($000)

Cash	$ 500
Accounts receivable	2000
Inventories	1000
Current assets	$3500
Net fixed assets	$4500
Total assets	$8000
Accounts payable	$1100
Accrued expenses	600
Short-term notes payable	300
Current liabilities	$2000
Long-term debt	$2000
Owners' equity	$4000
	$8000

Income Statement ($000)	
Net sales (all credit)	$8000
Cost of goods sold	(3300)
Gross profit	$4700
Operating expenses[a]	(3000)
Net operating income	$1700
Interest expense	(367)
Earnings before taxes	$1333
Income taxes (40%)	(533)
Net income	$ 800

[a]Including depreciation expense of $500 for the year.

Calculate the following ratios:

Current ratio	Gross profit margin
Debt ratio	Operating profit margin
Times interest earned	Net profit margin
Average collection period	Operating return on investment
Inventory turnover	Return on total assets
Fixed asset turnover	Return on common equity
Total asset turnover	

11-3A. (*Analyzing Profitability*) The R. M. Smithers Corporation earned a net profit margin of 5 percent based on sales of $10 million and total assets of $5 million last year.

  a. What was Smithers's rate of return on total assets?

  b. During the coming year the company president has set a goal of attaining a 12 percent return on total assets. How much must firm sales rise, other things being the same, for the goal to be achieved? (State your answer as an annual growth rate in sales.)

  c. If Smithers finances 30 percent of its assets by borrowing, what was its return on common equity for last year? What will it be next year if the return on total asset goal is achieved?

11-4A. (*Using Financial Ratios*) The Brenmar Sales Company had a gross profit margin of 30 percent and sales of $9 million last year. Seventy-five percent of the firm's sales are on credit while the remainder are cash sales. Brenmar's current assets equal $1,500,000, its current liabilities $300,000, and it has $100,000 in cash plus marketable securities.

  a. If Brenmar's accounts receivable are $562,500, what is its average collection period?

  b. If Brenmar reduces its average collection period to 20 days, what will be its new level of accounts receivable?

  c. Brenmar's inventory turnover ratio is 9 times. What is the level of Brenmar's inventories?

11-5A. (*Ratio Analysis of Loan Request*) Pamplin, Inc., has recently applied for a loan from the National Bank to be used to expand the firm's inventory of soil pipe used in construction and agriculture. This expansion is predicted on expanded sales predicted for the coming year. Pamplin's financial statements for the two most recent years are as follows:

Pamplin, Inc., Balance Sheet at 12/31/92 and 12/31/93		
Assets		
	12/31/92	12/31/93
Cash	$ 200	$ 150
Accounts receivable	450	425
Inventory	550	625
Current assets	1200	1200

	2200	2600
Plant and equipment	2200	2600
Less: Accumulated depreciation	(1000)	(1200)
Net plant and equipment	1200	1400
Total assets	$2400	$2600

Liabilities and Owners' Equity

	1992	1993
Accounts payable	$ 200	$ 150
Notes payable—current (9%)	0	150
Current liabilities	200	600
Bonds	600	600
Owners' equity		
Common shares	300	300
Contributed surplus	600	600
Retained earnings	700	800
Total owners' equity	1600	1700
Total liabilities and owners' equity	$2400	$2600

Pamplin, Inc., Income Statement
Year Ended 12/31/92 and 12/31/93

Income Statement	1992	1993
Sales	$1200	$1450
Cost of goods sold	700	850
Gross profit	$ 500	$ 600
Operating expenses	30	40
Depreciation	220	200
Net operating income	$ 250	$ 360
Interest expense	50	60
Net income before taxes	$ 200	$ 300
Taxes (40%)	80	120
Net income	$ 120	$ 180

a. Compute the following ratios for Pamplin, Inc., from the financial statements provided above:

	1992	1993	Industry Norm
Current ratio			5.0 ×
Acid test (quick) ratio			3.0 ×
Inventory turnover			2.2 ×
Average collection period			90 days
Debt ratio			.33
Times interest earned			7.0 ×
Total asset turnover			0.75 ×
Fixed asset turnover			1.0 ×
Operating profit margin			.20
Net profit margin			.12
Return on total assets			.09

b. Based on your answer in (a) above, what are Pamplin's financial strengths and weaknesses?

c. Would you make the loan? Why or why not?

11-6A. (*Statement of Changes in Financial Position*) Prepare a statement of changes in financial position for Pamplin, Inc., for the year ended December 31, 1993 (Problem 11-5A).

11-7A. (*Statement of Changes in Financial Position*) (a) Prepare a statement of changes in financial position for the Waterhouse Co. in the year 1993. (b) What were the firm's primary sources and uses of cash?

	1992	1993
Cash	$ 75,000	$ 82,500
Receivables	102,000	90,000
Inventory	168,000	165,000
Prepaid expenses	12,000	13,500
Fixed assets	325,500	468,000
Accumulated depreciation	94,500	129,000
Patents	61,500	52,500
	$649,500	$742,500

	1992	1993
Accounts payable	$124,500	$112,500
Taxes payable	97,500	105,000
Mortgage payable	150,000	—
Preferred shares	—	225,000
Contributed surplus—preferred	—	6,000
Common shares	225,000	225,000
Retained earnings	52,500	69,000
	$649,500	$742,500

Additional Information:

1. The only entry in the accumulated depreciation account is the depreciation expense for the period.

2. The only entries in the retained earnings account are for dividends paid in the amount of $18,000 and for the net income for the year.

3. The income statement for 1993 is as follows:

Sales	$187,500
Cost of sales[a]	141,000
Gross profit	46,500
Operating expenses	12,000
Net income	$ 34,500

[a]Includes depreciation expense of $34,500.

11-8A. (*Review of Financial Statements*) Prepare a balance sheet and income statement at December 31, 1993, for the Sharpe Mfg. Co. from the scrambled list of items below.

Accounts receivable	$120,000
Machinery and equipment	700,000
Accumulated depreciation	236,000
Notes payable—current	100,000
Net sales	800,000
Inventory	110,000
Accounts payable	90,000
Long-term debt	160,000
Cost of goods sold	500,000
Operating expenses	280,000

Common shares		320,000
Cash		96,000
Retained earnings—prior year		?
Retained earnings—current year		?

11-9A. (*Financial Ratios—Investment Analysis*) The annual sales for Salco, Inc., were $4.5 million last year. The firm's end-of-year balance sheet appeared as follows:

Current assets	$ 500,000	Liabilities	$1,000,000
Net fixed assets	$1,500,000	Owners' equity	$1,000,000
	$2,000,000		$2,000,000

The firm's income statement for the year was as follows:

Sales	$4,500,000
Less: Cost of goods sold	(3,500,000)
Gross profit	1,000,000
Less: Operating expenses	(500,000)
Net operating income	500,000
Less: Interest expense	(100,000)
Earnings before taxes	400,000
Less: Taxes	(200,000)
Net income	$ 200,000

a. Calculate Salco's total asset turnover, operating profit margin, and operating income return on investment.

b. Salco plans to renovate one of its plants, which will require an added investment in plant and equipment of $1 million. The firm will maintain its present debt ratio of .5 when financing the new investment and expects sales to remain constant, while the operating profit margin will rise to 13 percent. What will be the new operating income return on investment for Salco after the plant renovation?

c. Given that the plant renovation in part (b) occurs and Salco's interest expense rises by $50,000 per year, what will be the return earned on the common shareholders' investment? Compare this rate of return with that earned before the renovation.

11-10A. (*Statement of Changes in Financial Position*) The consolidated balance sheets of the TMU Processing Company are presented below for June 1, 1992, and May 31, 1993 (in millions of dollars). TMU earned $14 million after taxes during the year ended May 31, 1993, and paid common dividends of $10 million.

	June 1, 1992	May 31, 1993	Change
Cash	$ 10	$ 8	
Accounts receivable	12	22	
Inventories	8	14	
Current assets	$ 30	$ 44	
Gross fixed assets	100	110	
Less: Accumulated depreciation	(40)	(50)	
Net fixed assets	$ 60	$ 60	
Total assets	$ 90	$104	
Accounts payable	$ 12	$ 9	
Notes payable	7	7	

Long-term debt	11	24
Common shares	20	20
Retained earnings	40	44
Total liabilities and owners' equity	$ 90	$104

a. Prepare a statement of changes in financial position for TMU Processing Company.

b. Summarize your findings.

11-11A. (*Comprehensive Financial Analysis Problem*) The T. P. Jarmon Company manufactures and sells a line of exclusive sportswear. The firm's sales were $600,000 for the year just ended, and its total assets exceed $400,000. The company was started by Mr. Jarmon just 10 years ago and has been profitable every year since its inception. The chief financial officer for the firm, Brent Vehlim, has decided to seek a line of credit from the firm's bank totalling $80,000. In the past the company has relied on its suppliers to finance a large part of its needs for inventory. However, in recent months tight money conditions have led the firm's suppliers to offer sizable cash discounts to speed up payments for purchases. Mr. Vehlim wants to use the line of credit to supplant a large portion of the firm's payables during the summer months, which are the firm's peak seasonal sales period.

The firm's two most recent balance sheets were presented to the bank in support of its loan request. In addition, the firm's income statement for the year just ended was provided to support the loan request. These statements are found below:

T. P. Jarmon Company Balance Sheets
for 12/31/92 and 12/31/93

Assets

	1992	1993
Cash	$ 15,000	$ 14,000
Marketable securities	6,000	6,200
Accounts receivable	42,000	33,000
Inventory	51,000	84,000
Prepaid rent	1,200	1,100
Total current assets	$115,200	$138,300
Net plant and equipment	286,000	270,000
Total assets	$401,200	$408,300

Liabilities and Shareholders' Equity

	1992	1993
Accounts payable	$ 48,000	$ 57,000
Notes payable	15,000	13,000
Accruals	6,000	5,000
Total current liabilities	$ 69,000	$ 75,000
Long-term debt	$160,000	$150,000
Common shareholders' equity	$172,200	$183,300
Total liabilities and equity	$401,200	$408,300

T. P. Jarmon Company Income Statement
for the Year Ended 12/31/93

Sales	$600,000
Less: Cost of goods sold	460,000
Gross profits	$140,000

Less: Expenses		
General and administrative	$30,000	
Interest	10,000	
Depreciation	30,000	
Total		70,000
Profit before taxes		$ 70,000
Less: Taxes		27,100
Profits after taxes		$ 42,900
Less: Cash dividends		31,800
To retained earnings		$ 11,110

Jan Fama, associate credit analyst for the National Bank of was assigned the task of analyzing Jarmon's loan request.

a. Calculate the financial ratios for 1993 corresponding to the industry norms provided below:

Ratio	Norm	Jarmon's Ratio	Evaluation
Current ratio	1.8 times		
Acid test ratio	.9 times		
Debt ratio	.5		
Long-term debt to total capitalization	.7		
Times interest earned	10 times		
Average collection period	20 days		
Inventory turnover (based on COGS)	7 times		
Return on total assets	8.4%		
Gross profit margin	25%		
Net profit margin	7%		
Operating return on investment	16.8%		
Operating profit margin	14%		
Total asset turnover	1.2 times		
Fixed asset turnover	1.8 times		

b. Which of the ratios reported above in the industry norms do you feel should be most crucial in determining whether the bank should extend the line of credit? What strengths and weaknesses are apparent from your analysis of Jarmon's financial ratios?

c. Based upon the ratio analysis you performed in part (b), would you recommend approval of the loan request? Discuss.

d. Prepare a statement of changes in financial position for Jarmon covering the year ended December 31, 1993. How does this statement directly support your ratio analysis of Jarmon?

e. Perform an analysis of Jarmon's earning power using the procedure laid out in Figures 11-2 and 11-3.

CASE PROBLEM

L. M. MYERS, INC.

FINANCIAL ANALYSIS

L. M. Myers, Inc., is one of the three largest grain exporters in North America. The firm also engages in soybean processing and several other related activities. During fiscal 1992–1993 Myers derived 72.1 percent of its sales from its exporting activities, 14.8 percent from agriproducts, and the remainder from chemical and consumer products. Myers' nonexport sales are derived almost completely from soybean processing activities, including the production and sale of a number of food ingredients. One of the most promising soybean derivatives produced by the company is a newly developed meat substitute called "Prosoy." At present Prosoy is marketed almost strictly as a ground beef substitute; however, plans are under way to market the product in a number of other forms resembling familiar cuts of meat, such as bacon and even roasts. The success that the company has enjoyed with Prosoy in its initial three years of production promises to make soybean processing an even more important segment of the firm's overall sales. Other soybean-related products produced by the firm include a number of derivatives used in animal and poultry feeds. Myers' export business primarily involves corn, wheat, and some soybeans. The principal investment made by the firm related to its exporting operations involves a chain of grain elevators at strategic locations along the seacoast. These elevators are used to store grain and load it onto ships, which deliver it all over the world.

For the fiscal year just ended Myers experienced an overall sales growth of 10 percent. This increase represented a mere 5 percent increase in export-related activities and a whopping 20 percent increase in sales related to soybean processing. This and other factors have led the company to make a commitment to expand its processing capacity by $20 million during the next three years. The firm plans to finance the expansion through an $11 million bond issue and through the retention of earnings.

Owing to the seasonal nature of its export business, Myers has had to borrow heavily during the harvest months to finance seasonal inventory buildups and then repay the loans as sales are made throughout the year. In the past the company has arranged with a group of banks for a line of credit (discussed in Chapter 16) sufficient to meet its credit needs; however, in recent years this arrangement has become increasingly more cumbersome as the firm's total needs for funds have grown. This and cost considerations have led Myers' financial vice-president, James Graham, to consider the possibility of raising all or at least a part of the firm's credit needs through a commercial paper issue (discussed in Chapter 16). Mr. Graham is somewhat concerned about his firm's creditworthiness in light of the industry norms generally used by banks and other creditors. His concern relates to the fact that Myers has never issued commercial paper and the belief that only the most creditworthy of borrowers can successfully use the commercial paper market to raise funds.

a. Using the financial statements for Myers presented below, complete the calculation of the financial ratios contained in Exhibit 1.

b. Based upon your calculated ratios and the associated industry norms, what is your financial analysis of Myers?

L. M. Myers, Inc., Balance Sheets for Years Ended December 31 ($000)

Assets		
	1992	*1993*
Cash	$ 11,451	$ 12,844
Accounts receivable	64,199	52,599
Marketable securities	—	33,995
Inventories	69,814	75,366
Deferred income taxes	2,948	2,750
Prepaid expenses	1,089	1,794
Total current assets	$149,501	$179,348
Investments and advances	11,681	12,012
Other assets	14,509	3,735
Net property and equipment	118,810	153,856
Total assets	$294,501	$348,951

Liabilities and Shareholders' Equity		
	1992	*1993*
Accounts payable	$ 34,327	$ 35,099
Notes payable	14,544	20,907
Accrued income and other taxes	28,526	40,112
Other accrued expenses	19,854	22,299

Total current liabilities	$ 97,251	$118,417
Long-term debt	75,817	67,006
Cumulative preferred shares	582	565
Common shares	26,596	26,812
Contributed surplus	2,030	2,606
Retained earnings	92,225	133,545
Total shareholders' equity	121,433	163,528
Total liabilities and shareholders' equity	$294,501	$348,951

L. M. Myers, Inc., Income Statements for Years Ended December 31 ($000)

	1992	1993
Sales (net)	$706,457	$777,104
Less: Cost of goods sold	(637,224)	(662,093)
Gross profit	$ 69,233	$115,011
Operating expenses:		
Selling and administrative expenses	(17,612)	(17,804)
Labour expense	(9,418)	(15,263)
Depreciation	(6,976)	(7,428)
Miscellaneous operating expenses	(1,887)	(2,011)
Total	($ 35,893)	($ 42,506)
Net operating income	$ 33,340	$ 72,505
Interest income	512	2,012
	33,852	74,517
Less: Interest expense	(9,127)	(8,408)
Earnings before taxes	$ 24,725	$ 66,109
Less: Taxes payable	(5,440)	(25,232)
Net income	$ 19,285	$ 40,877
Less: Preferred dividends	(58)	(56)
Net earnings available to common	$ 19,227	$ 40,821

EXHIBIT 1
Financial Ratios for L. M. Myers, Inc.

Ratio	1992	1993	Industry Norm[a]
Acid test ratio			1.00 ×
Current ratio			1.61 ×
Average collection period[b]			30.00 days
Inventory turnover[b]			10.1 ×
Debt ratio			49.1%
Long-term debt to total capitalization			31.0%
Times interest earned			5.87 ×
Cash flow overall coverage ratio			7.42
Total asset turnover			2.1 ×
Gross profit margin			11.7%
Operating profit margin			7.6%
Operating income return on investment			14.75%
Return on total assets			8.45%
Return on common equity			21.39%

[a]These industry norms pertain to Myers' grain export operations, which comprised over 70 percent of the firm's sales for 1992. Also, the industry averages are applicable to both 1992 and 1993.

[b]Compute using end-of-year figures and assuming all sales are credit sales.

11-1B. (*Ratio Analysis*) The Allendale Office Supply Company has a target current ratio of 2 to 1 but has experienced some difficulties financing its expanding sales in the past few months. At present the current ratio of 2.75 to 1 is based upon current assets of $3.0 million. If Allendale expands its receivables and inventories using its short-term line of credit, how much additional funding can it borrow before its current ratio standard is reached?

11-2B. (*Ratio Analysis*) The balance sheet and income statement for the Simsboro Paper Company are as follows:

Balance Sheet ($000)

Cash	$1000
Accounts receivable	1500
Inventories	1000
Current assets	$3500
Net fixed assets	$4500
Total assets	$8000
Accounts payable	$1000
Accrued expenses	600
Short-term notes payable	200
Current liabilities	$1800
Long-term debt	2100
Owners' equity	$4100
	$8000

Income Statement ($000)

Net sales (all credit)	$7500
Cost of goods sold	(3000)
Gross profit	$4500
Operating expenses[a]	(3000)
Net operating income	$1500
Interest expense	(367)
Earnings before taxes	$1133
Income taxes (40%)	(415)
Net income	$680

[a]Including depreciation expense of $500 for the year.

Calculate the following ratios:

Current ratio	Gross profit margin
Debt ratio	Operating profit margin
Times interest earned	Net profit margin
Average collection period	Operating return on investment
Inventory turnover	Return on total assets
Fixed asset turnover	Return on common equity
Total asset turnover	

11-3B. (*Analyzing Profitability*) The R. M. Smithers Corporation earned a net profit margin of 6 percent based on sales of $11 million and total assets of $6 million last year.

a. What was Smithers' rate of return on total assets?

b. During the coming year the company president has set a goal of attaining a 13 percent return on total assets. How much must firm sales rise, other things being the same, for the goal to be achieved? (State your answer as an annual growth rate in sales.)

c. If Smithers finances 25 percent of its assets by borrowing, what was its return on common equity for last year? What will it be next year if the return on total asset goal is achieved?

11-4B. (*Using Financial Ratios*) Edgar Smith, Inc., had a gross profit margin of 25 percent and sales of $9.75 million last year. Seventy-five percent of the firm's sales are on credit while the remainder are cash sales. The company's current assets equal $1,550,000, its current liabilities $300,000, and it has $150,000 in cash plus marketable securities.

a. If Smith's accounts receivable are $562,500, what is its average collection period?

b. If Smith reduces its average collection period to 20 days, what will be its new level of accounts receivable?

c. Smith's inventory turnover ratio is 8 times. What is the level of the firm's inventories?

11-5B. (*Ratio Analysis of Loan Request*) The J. B. Champlin Corporation has experienced two consecutive years of improved sales and foresees the need to increase its investment in inventories and receivables to meet yet a third year of increased sales. Champlin's President, J. B. Champlin, Jr., recently approached the company's bank to discuss the possibility of extending the firm's line of credit to cover the firm's projected future funds requirements. The financial statements for the firm are found below:

J. B. Champlin Corporation, Balance Sheet at 12/31/92 and 12/31/93 ($000)

Assets

	1992	1993
Cash	$ 225	$ 175
Accounts receivable	450	430
Inventory	575	625
Total current assets	$1250	$1230
Plant and equipment	2200	2500
Less: Accumulated depreciation	(1000)	(1200)
Net plant and equipment	1200	1300
Total assets	$2450	$2530

Liabilities and Shareholders' Equity

	1992	1993
Accounts payable	$ 250	$ 115
Notes payable—current (9%)	0	115
Current liabilities	250	230
Bonds	600	600
Owners' equity		
Common shares	300	300
Contributed surplus	600	600
Retained earnings	700	800
Total owners' equity	1600	1700
Total liabilities and equity	$2450	$2530

J. B. Champlin Corporation Income Statement
Year Ended 12/31/92 and 12/31/93

	1992	1993
Sales	$1250	$1450
Cost of goods sold	700	875
Gross profit	$ 550	$ 575
Operating expenses	30	45
Depreciation	220	200
Net operating income	$ 300	$ 330
Interest expense	50	60
Net income before taxes	$ 250	$ 270
Taxes (40%)	100	108
Net income	$ 150	$ 162

a. Compute the following ratios for Champlin from the financial statements provided above:

	1992	1993	Industry Norm
Current ratio			5.0
Acid test (quick) ratio			3.0
Inventory turnover			2.2
Average collection period			90 days
Debt ratio			.33%
Times interest earned			7.0 ×
Total asset turnover			.75 ×
Fixed asset turnover			1.0 ×
Operating profit margin			20%
Net profit margin			12%
Return on total assets			9%

b. Based on your answer in (a) above, what are Champlin's financial strengths and weaknesses?

c. Would you make the loan? Why or why not?

11-6B. (*Statement of Changes in Financial Position*) Prepare a statement of changes in financial position for Champlin for the year ended December 31, 1993 (Problem 11-5B).

11-7B. (*Statement of Changes in Financial Position*) (a) Prepare a statement of changes in financial position for Cramer, Inc., for 1993. (b) What were the firm's primary sources and uses of cash?

Cramer, Inc., for 1993

	1992	1993
Cash	$ 76,000	$ 82,500
Receivables	100,000	91,000
Inventory	168,000	163,000
Prepaid expenses	11,500	13,500
Fixed assets	325,500	450,000
Accumulated depreciation	94,500	129,000
Patents	61,500	52,500
	$648,000	$723,500

	1992	1993
Accounts payable	$123,000	$ 93,500
Taxes payable	97,500	105,000
Mortgage payable	150,000	—
Preferred shares	—	225,000
Contributed surplus—preferred	—	6,000
Common shares	225,000	225,000
Retained earnings	52,500	69,000
	$648,000	$723,500

Additional Information:

1. The only entry in the accumulated depreciation account is the depreciation expense for the period.

2. The only entries in the retained earnings account are for dividends paid in the amount of $20,000 and for the net income for the year.

3. The income statement for 1993 is as follows:

Sales	$190,000
Cost of sales[a]	140,000
Gross profit	50,000
Operating expenses	13,500
Net income	$ 36,500

[a]Includes depreciation of $34,500.

11-8B. (*Basic Financial Statements*) Prepare a balance sheet and income statement at December 31, 1993, for the Sabine Mfg. Co. from the scrambled list of items below.

Accounts receivable	$150,000
Machinery and equipment	700,000
Accumulated depreciation	236,000
Notes payable—current	90,000
Net sales	900,000
Inventory	110,000
Accounts payable	90,000
Long-term debt	160,000
Cost of goods sold	550,000
Operating expenses	280,000
Common shares	320,000
Cash	90,000
Retained earnings—prior year	?
Retained earnings—current year	?

11-9B. (*Financial Ratios—Investment Analysis*) The annual sales for Salco, Inc., were $5,000,000 last year. The firm's end-of-year balance sheet appeared as follows:

Current assets	$ 500,000	Liabilities	$1,000,000
Net fixed assets	$1,500,000	Owners' equity	$1,000,000
	$2,000,000		$2,000,000

period. Step 2: Estimate the levels of investment in current and fixed assets that are necessary to support the projected sales. Step 3: Determine the firm's financing needs throughout the planning period.

The Cash Flow Cycle

The entire firm's operations can be visualized through the use of a **cash flow cycle diagram**. The diagram, as shown in Figure 12-1, depicts the firm's operations as a large pump that pushes cash through various reservoirs such as inventories and accounts receivable and dispenses cash for taxes, interest and principal payments on debt, and cash dividends to the shareholders. The problem in financial forecasting is one of predicting cash inflows and outflows and the corresponding financial needs of the firm. The firm's needs are related to the size of the various reservoirs that hold cash. These reservoirs of cash represent the various assets in which the firm must make investments in order to produce the expected level of sales.

Tracing the Cash Flow Cycle

Since the firm's cash flow cycle is a continuous process, we will find it useful for illustrative purposes to consider the first cycle of a new firm. The process begins with the firm's cash reservoir, which consists initially of the owner's investment (funds raised through the issuance of shares) and funds borrowed from creditors. This cash is used to acquire plant and equipment, as well as supplies and materials. It is also used to pay wages and salaries, to pay for utilities such as heat and power, and to replace materials, plant, and

FIGURE 12-1. Cash Flow Diagram

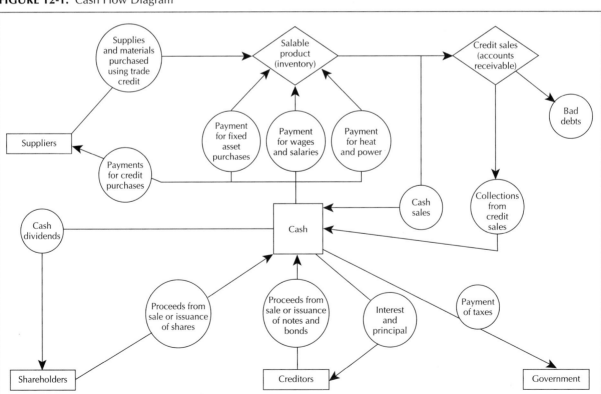

BASIC FINANCIAL MANAGEMENT IN PRACTICE

Cash Flow Rates Flawed

In these uncertain times, cash flow per share may seem like the best measure of what's really going on at a company.

But investor beware. Canada has no standard for calculating this ratio. In the U.S., the Securities and Exchange Commission won't allow cash flow per share information to be disclosed in annual reports because the ratios aren't comparable between companies.

The Ontario Securities Commission recently asked the Canadian Institute of Chartered Accountants to put cash flow per share, which is not dealt with in the *CICA Handbook*, on their agenda.

Until a standard measure is developed, the OSC wants issuers to present cash flow per share calculations in the notes, not in the face of the financial statements.

The real estate industry is one place where cash flow per share is an investment yardstick.

Maybe that's why the Canadian Institute for Public Real Estate Companies has issued a set of accounting rules which set some parameters for this calculation—take earnings from operations and add back noncash deductions such as depreciation, amortization, and deferred income taxes.

By contrast, in the oil and gas industry there are several different measures, such as discretionary cash flow per share, where the company makes adjustments for capitalized costs.

"Cash flow per share is a big headache," said one analyst. "We calculate our own cash flow from operations, which excludes extraordinary items such as cash from the sale of operations or dividends from an associated company."

Accountants may have to look at the whole idea of cash flow measurement and its presentation in the financial statements.

One would like to know the cash inflows and outflows. In other words, to be able to follow the flow of receipts from customers and payments to suppliers. Apparently, cash flow is not as straightforward as it sounds.

Source: Adapted from B. Critchley and S. Gittins, "Cash Flow Rates Flawed," *The Financial Post* (May 23, 1991) p. 44.

---

equipment that are used or worn out in the process of making the firm's product. These expenditures make up the cost of goods sold for the firm's sellable product. Sales are then made either for cash or on credit (with some leakage for bad debt losses). To this cash flow stream are added cash inflows resulting from the sale of assets such as equipment, land, or securities. In the final phase of the cycle, cash is dispersed to pay obligations to suppliers for materials purchased on credit, income taxes to the government, interest and principal to the firm's creditors, and cash dividends to the firm's owners. Finally, any cash not paid in dividends is reinvested in the firm and becomes a part of the owners' investment.

Forecasting Cash Flows

The problem of financial forecasting, to summarize, consists of predicting future sales, which in turn provides the basis for predicting the level of investment in inventories, receivables, plant, and equipment required to support the firm's projected sales. Through the use of the cash budget, the information from these projections is combined to provide an estimate of the firm's future financing needs.

Sales Forecast

The key ingredient in the firm's planning process is the **sales forecast**. This projection will generally be derived using information from a number of sources. At a minimum, the sales forecast for the coming year would reflect (1) any past trend in sales that is expected to carry through into the new year and (2) the influence of any events that might materially affect that trend.[1] An example of the latter would be the initiation of a major advertising campaign or a change in the firm's pricing policy.

Forecasting Financial Variables

Traditional financial forecasting takes the sales forecast as a given and estimates its impact on the firm's various expenses, assets, and liabilities. The most commonly used method for making these projections is the percent of sales method.

Percent of Sales Method of Financial Forecasting

The **percent of sales method** involves estimating the level of an expense, asset, or liability for a future period as a percent of the sales forecast. The percentage used can come from the most recent financial statement item as a percent of current sales, from an average computed over several years, from the judgment of the analyst, or from some combination of these sources.

Figure 12-2 presents a complete example of the use of the percent of sales method of financial forecasting. In that example, each item in the firm's balance sheet that varies with sales is converted to a percentage of 1993 sales. The forecast of the new balance for each item is then calculated by multiplying this percentage by the $12 million in projected sales for the 1994 planning period. This method of forecasting future financing is not as precise or detailed as the method which uses the cash budget; however, it offers a relatively low-cost and easy-to-use first approximation of the firm's financing needs for a future period. The cash budget method will be examined later on in this chapter.

Note that in the example in Figure 12-2 both current and fixed assets are assumed to vary with the level of firm sales. This means that the firm does not have sufficient productive capacity to absorb a projected increase in sales. Thus, if sales were to rise by $1, fixed assets would rise by $.40, or 40 percent of the projected increase in sales. Note that if the fixed assets the firm presently owns had been sufficient to support the projected level of new sales, these assets should not be allowed to vary with sales. If this were the case, then fixed assets would not be converted to a percent of sales and would be projected to remain unchanged for the period being forecast.

Also, we note that accounts payable and accrued expenses are the only liabilities allowed to vary with sales. Both these accounts might reasonably be expected to rise and fall with the level of firm sales; hence the use of the percent of sales forecast. Since these two categories of current liabilities normally vary directly with the level of sales, they are often referred to as **spontaneous sources of financing**. Chapter 13 examines in greater detail working-capital management and the various sources of financing. Notes payable, long-term debt, common shares, and contributed surplus are not assumed to vary directly with the level of firm sales. These sources of financ-

---

[1]A complete discussion of forecast methodologies is outside the scope of this book. The interested reader will find the following references helpful: F. Gerard Adams, *The Business Forecasting Revolution*, Oxford: Oxford University Press, 1986; C. W. J. Granger, *Forecasting in Business and Economics*, 2nd ed. Boston, Mass.: Academic Press, Inc., 1989; and Paul Newbold and Theodore Bos, *Introductory Business Forecasting*, Cincinnati, Ohio: South-Western Publishing Co., 1990.

	Present (1993)	Percent of Sales (1993 Sales = $10 M)	Projected (Based on 1994 Sales = $12 M)	
		Assets		
Current assets	$2 M	$2 M/$10 M = 20%	0.2 X $12 M =	$2.4 M
Net fixed assets	4 M	$4 M/$10 M = 40%	0.4 X $12 M =	4.8 M
Total	$6 M			$7.2 M
		Liabilities and Owners' Equity		
Accounts payable	$1.0 M	$1 M/$10 M = 10%	0.10 X $12 M =	$1.2 M
Accrued expenses	1.0 M	$1 M/$10 M = 10%	0.10 X $12 M =	$1.2 M
Notes payable	0.5 M	NA[a]	no change	0.5 M
Long-term debt	$2.0 M	NA[a]	no change	2.0 M
Total liabilities	$4.5 M			$4.9 M
Common shares	$0.1 M	NA[a]		$0.1 M
Contributed surplus	0.2 M	NA[a]		$0.2 M
Retained earnings	1.2 M		1.2 M + [.05 X $12 M X (1 - .5)] = 1.5 M[b]	
Common equity	$1.5 M			$1.8 M
Total	$6.0 M	Total financing provided	$6.7 M	
		Discretionary financing needed		0.5 M[c]
		Total		$7.2 M

FIGURE 12-2

Using the Percent of Sales Method to Forecast Future Financing Requirements

[a]Not applicable. These account balances are assumed not to vary with sales.
[b]Projected retained earnings equals the beginning level ($1.2 M) plus projected net income less any dividends paid. In this case net income is projected to equal 5 percent of sales, and dividends are projected to equal half of net income: $.05 \times \$12 M \times (1 - .5) = \$300,000$.
[c]Discretionary financing needed equals projected total assets ($7.2 M) less projected total liabilities ($4.9M) less projected common equity ($1.8 or $7.2 M – 4.9 – 1.8 M = $500,000.

ing are termed discretionary, in that the firm's management must make a conscious decision to seek additional financing using any one of them. Finally, we note that the level of retained earnings does vary with estimated sales. The predicted change in the level of retained earnings equals the difference in estimated after-tax profits (projected net income) of $600,000 and common share dividends of $300,000.

Thus, using the example from Figure 12-2, we estimate that firm sales will increase from $10 M to $12 M, which will cause the firm's needs for total assets to rise to $7.2 M. These assets will then be financed by $4.9 M in existing liabilities plus spontaneous liabilities, $1.8 M in owner funds including $300,000 in retained earnings from next year's sales, and, finally, $500,000 in discretionary financing, which can be raised by issuing notes payable, selling bonds, offering an issue of shares, or some combination of these sources.

In summary, we can estimate the firm's needs for discretionary financing, using the percent of sales method of financial forecasting, by following a four-step procedure:

Step 1: Convert each asset and liability account that varies directly with firm sales to a percent of current year's sales.

EXAMPLE

$$\frac{\text{current assets}}{\text{sales}} = \frac{\$2 M}{\$10 M} = .2 \text{ or } 20\%$$

Step 2: Project the level of each asset and liability account in the balance sheet using its percent of sales multiplied by projected sales or by leaving the account balance unchanged where the account does not vary with the level of sales.

EXAMPLE

$$\frac{\text{projected}}{\text{current assets}} = \text{projected sales} \times \frac{\text{current assets}}{\text{sales}} = \$12\ M \times .2 = 2.4\ M\ \blacksquare$$

Step 3: Project the level of new retained earnings available to help finance the firm's operations. This equals projected net income for the period less planned dividends from common shares.

EXAMPLE

$$\text{projected addition to retained earnings} =$$

$$\text{projected sales} \times \frac{\text{net income}}{\text{sales}} \times \left(1 - \frac{\text{cash dividends}}{\text{net income}}\right)$$

$$= \$12\ M \times .05 \times [1 - .5] = \$300,000 \qquad \blacksquare$$

Step 4: Project the firm's need for discretionary financing as the projected level of total assets less projected liabilities and owners' equity.

EXAMPLE

$$\text{discretionary financing needed} =$$

$$\text{projected total assets} - \text{projected total liabilities} - \text{projected owners' equity}$$

$$= \$7.2\ M - \$4.9\ M - \$1.8\ M = \$500,000 \qquad \blacksquare$$

As we noted earlier, the principal virtue of the percent of sales method of financial forecasting is its simplicity.[2] To obtain a more precise estimate of the amount and timing of the firm's future financing needs, we require a cash budget. The percent of sales method of financial forecasting does provide a very useful, low-cost forerunner to the development of the more detailed cash budget, which the firm will ultimately use to estimate its financing needs.

Perspective in Finance

Are you beginning to wonder exactly where finance comes into financial forecasting? To this point financial forecasting looks for all the world like financial statement forecasting. The reason for this is the fact that we have adopted the accountant's model of the firm, the balance sheet, as the underlying structure of the financial forecast. The key to financial forecasting is the identification of the firm's anticipated future financing requirements which is identified as the "plug figure" and balances a pro forma balance sheet.

---

[2]Although a linear type of relationship may describe a firm's inventory requirements for sales very close to the level used in estimating "%" sales, it can be a very poor predictor for large changes in sales. An improvement in this estimator might include an intercept term or in some cases a nonlinear model might be appropriate, i.e., $Y = a + b(\text{sales}) + c(\text{sales})^2$. Models of this type can be easily estimated and incorporated into financial planning using financial spreadsheet software.

FINANCIAL PLANNING AND BUDGETING

Financial forecasts are put to use in constructing financial plans. These plans culminate in the preparation of a cash budget and a set of pro forma statements for a future period in the firm's operations.

Budget Functions

A **budget** is simply a forecast of future events. For example, students preparing for final exams make use of time budgets, which help them allocate their limited preparation time among their courses. Students also must budget their financial resources among competing uses, such as books, tuition, food, rent, clothes, and extracurricular activities.

Budgets perform three basic functions for the user. First, they indicate the amount and timing of the firm's needs for future financing. Second, they provide the basis for taking corrective action in the event that budgeted figures do not match actual or realized figures. Third, budgets provide the basis for performance evaluation. Plans are carried out by people, and budgets provide benchmarks that can be used to evaluate the performance of those responsible for carrying out those plans and, in turn, controlling their actions. Thus, budgets are valuable aids in both planning and control aspects of the firm's financial management.

In the pages that follow, we will develop an example budgetary system for a retailing firm. The primary emphasis will be on the cash budget and pro forma financial statements. These statements provide the information needed for a detailed estimate for the firm's future financing requirements.

The Budgetary System

Although our interest in financial planning focuses on the cash budget, a number of other budgets provide the basis for its preparation. This system of budgets allows planning for each source of cash flow, both inflow and outflow, that will affect the firm throughout the planning period. In general, a business will utilize four types of budgets: physical budgets, cost budgets, profit budgets, and cash budgets. Figure 12-3 presents an overview of the budgetary system.

Physical budgets include budgets for physical items as opposed to financial items. For example, physical budgets are used for unit sales, personnel, unit production, inventories, and physical facilities. Management use these budgets as the basis for generating cost and profit budgets. **Cost budgets** are prepared for every major expense category of the firm. For example, a manufacturing firm would prepare cost budgets for manufacturing or production cost, selling cost, administrative cost, financing cost, and research and development cost. These cost budgets along with the sales budget provide the basis for preparing a profit budget. Finally, converting all the budget information to a cash basis provides the information required to prepare the cash budget.

The Cash Budget

The cash budget represents a detailed plan of future cash flows and is composed of four elements: cash receipts, cash disbursements, net change in cash for the period, and new financing needed.

FIGURE 12-3
The Budget System

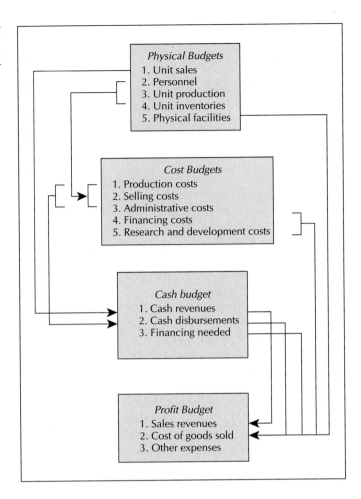

To demonstrate the construction and use of the cash budget, consider Salco Furniture Company, Inc., a regional distributor of household furniture. Salco's sales are highly seasonal, peaking in the months of March through May. Roughly 30 percent of Salco's sales are collected one month after the sale, 50 percent two months after the sale, and the remainder during the third month following the sale.

Salco attempts to pace its purchases with its forecast of future sales. Purchases generally equal 75 percent of sales and are made two months in advance of anticipated sales. Payments are made in the month following purchases. For example, June sales are estimated at $100,000, thus April purchases are .75 × $100,000 = $75,000. Correspondingly, payments for purchases in May equal $75,000. Wages, salaries, rent, and other cash expenses are recorded in Table 12-1, which gives Salco's cash budget for the six-month period ended in June 1994. Additional expenditures are recorded in the cash budget related to the purchase of equipment in the amount of $14,000 during February and the repayment of a $12,000 loan in May. In June Salco will pay $7,500 interest on its $150,000 in long-term debt for the period of January–June 1994. Interest on the $12,000 short-term note repaid in May for the period January through May equals $600 and is paid in May.

Salco presently has a cash balance of $20,000 and wants to maintain a minimum balance of $10,000. Additional borrowing necessary to maintain that minimum balance is estimated in the final section of Table 12-1. Borrowing takes place at the beginning of the month in which the funds are needed. Interest on borrowed funds equals 12 percent per annum, or 1 percent per month, and is paid in the month following the one in which funds are borrowed. Thus, interest on funds borrowed in January will be paid in February equal to 1 percent of the loan amount outstanding during January.

The financing-needed line on Salco's cash budget indicates that the firm will need to borrow $36,350 in February, $65,874 in March, $86,633 in April, and $97,599 in May. Only in June will the firm be able to reduce its borrowing to $79,875. Note that the cash budget indicates not only the amount of financing needed during the period, but also when the funds will be needed. ■

Fixed Versus Flexible Budgets

The cash budget given in Table 12-1 for Salco, Inc., is an example of a **fixed budget**. Cash flow estimates are made for a single set of monthly sales estimates. Thus, the estimates of expenses and new financing needed are meaningful only for the level of sales for which they were computed. To avoid this limitation, several budgets corresponding to different sets of sales estimates

---

[3]This section is based on Essam Mahmoud, "Accuracy in Forecasting: A survey," *Journal of Forecasting*, 3(2) (1984), pp. 139–59; Reed Moyer, "The Futility of Forecasting," *Long Range Planning* (February 1984), pp. 65–72; and Ronald Bailey, "Them That Can Do, Them That Can't, Forecast," *Forbes* (December 26, 1988), pp. 94–100.

Worksheet	Oct.	Nov.	Dec.
Sales	$55,000	$62,000	$50,000
Collections:			
First month (30%)			
Second month (50%)			
Third month (20%)			
Total			
Purchases			$56,250
Payments (one-month lag)			
Cash receipts:			
Collections			
Cash disbursements:			
Purchases			
Wages and salaries			
Rent			
Other expenses			
Interest expense on existing debt ($12,000 note and $150,000 in long-term debt)			
Taxes			
Purchase of equipment			
Loan repayment ($12,000 note due in May)			
Total disbursements:			
Net monthly charge			
Plus: Beginning cash balance			
Less: Interest on short-term borrowing			
Equals: Ending cash balance—no borrowing			
Financing needed[a]			
Ending cash balance			
Cumulative borrowing			

[a]The amount of financing that is required to raise the firm's ending cash balance up to its $10,000 desired cash balance.

can be prepared. Such a flexible budget fulfills two basic needs: first, it gives information regarding the range of the firm's possible financing needs, and second it provides a standard against which to measure the performance of subordinates who are responsible for the various cost and revenue items contained in the budget.

This second function deserves some additional comment. The obvious problem that arises relates to the fact that costs vary with the actual level of sales experienced by the firm. Thus, if the budget is to be used as a standard for performance evaluation or control, it must be constructed to match realized sales and production figures. This can involve much more than simply "adjusting cost figures up or down in proportion to the deviation of actual from planned sales." That is, costs may not vary in strict proportion to sales, just as inventory levels may not vary as a constant percent of sales. Thus, preparation of a flexible budget involves re-estimating all the cash expenses that would be incurred at each of several possible sales levels. This process might utilize a variant of the percent of sales method discussed earlier or apply a regression method to the forecasting problem.[4]

[4]An excellent discussion of the financial forecasting problem in general is found in George G. C. Parker, "Financial Forecasting," in *Handbook of Corporate Finance*, ed. E. I. Altman. New York: Wiley, 1986, 2.1–2.37.

Jan.	Feb.	Mar.	Apr.	May	June	July	Aug.
$60,000	$75,000	$88,000	$100,000	$110,000	$100,000	$80,000	$75,000
15,000	18,000	22,500	26,400	30,000	33,000		
31,000	25,000	30,000	37,500	44,000	50,000		
11,000	12,400	10,000	12,000	15,000	17,600		
$57,000	55,400	62,500	75,900	89,000	100,600		
66,000	75,000	82,500	75,000	60,000	56,250		
56,250	66,000	75,000	82,500	75,000	60,000		
$57,000	55,400	62,500	75,900	89,000	100,600		
$56,250	66,000	75,000	82,500	75,000	60,000		
3,000	10,000	7,000	8,000	6,000	4,000		
4,000	4,000	4,000	4,000	4,000	4,000		
1,000	500	1,200	1,500	1,500	1,200		
				600	7,500		
		4,460			5,200		
	14,000						
				12,000			
$64,250	94,500	91,660	96,000	99,100	81,900		
$(7,250)	(39,100)	(29,160)	(20,100)	(10,100)	18,700		
20,000	12,750	10,000	10,000	10,000	10,000		
—	—	(364)	(659)	(866)	(976)		
12,750	(26,350)	(19,524)	(10,759)	(966)	27,724		
—	36,350	29,524	20,759	10,966	(17,724)[b]		
$12,750	10,000	10,000	10,000	10,000	10,000		
—	36,350	65,874	86,633	97,599	79,875		

[b]Negative financing needed simply means the firm has excess cash that can be used to retire a part of its short-term borrowing from prior months.

Budget Period

There are no strict rules for determining the length of the budget period. However, as a general rule it should be long enough to show the effect of management policies, yet short enough so that estimates can be made with reasonable accuracy. Applying this rule of thumb to the Salco example in Table 12-1 indicates that the six-month budget period is probably too short, in that it is not known whether the planned operations of the firm will be successful over the coming fiscal year. That is, for most of the first six-month period the firm is operating with a cash flow deficit. If this does not reverse in the latter six months of the year, then a re-evaluation of the firm's plans and policies is clearly in order.

Longer-range budgets are also prepared in the form of the capital-expenditure budget. This budget details the firm's plans for acquiring plant and equipment over a 5-year, 10-year, or even longer period. Furthermore, firms often develop comprehensive long-range plans extending up to 10 years into the future. These plans are generally not as detailed as the annual cash budget, but they do consider such major components as sales, capital expenditures, new product development, capital funds acquisition, and employment needs.

Pro Forma Financial Statements

The final stage in the budgeting process involves construction of a set of **pro forma financial statements** depicting the end result of the planning period's operations. Salco, Inc., is used to demonstrate the construction of the pro forma income statement and balance sheet. To do this, we need Salco's cash budget (found in Table 12-1) and its beginning balance sheet, which depicts the financial condition of the firm at the start of the planning period (see Table 12-2).

The Pro Forma Income Statement

The **pro forma income statement** represents a statement of planned profit or loss for a future period. For Salco a six-month pro forma income statement is constructed from the information contained in the cash budget found in Table 12-1. The final statement is presented in Table 12-3.

Net sales, found by summing the six monthly sales projections (January through June) from Table 12-1, total $533,000. Cost of goods sold is computed as 75 percent of sales, or $399,750. This figure could also have been found by summing purchases for November through April, which represent items sold from January through June. Recall that purchases are made two months in advance, so that items sold in January through June were purchased in November through April.

Depreciation expense cannot be obtained from the cash budget, since it does not constitute a cash flow. Thus, this expense must be determined from the depreciation schedules of Salco's plant and equipment. On its existing fixed assets Salco has an annual depreciation expense of $17,200. In addi-

TABLE 12-2
Salco Furniture Co., Inc.,
Balance Sheet
December 31, 1993

Assets		
Current assets		
Cash	$ 20,000	
Accounts receivable	104,400	
Inventories	101,250	
Total current assets		$225,650
Fixed assets		
Net plant and equipment		180,000
Total assets		$405,650

Liabilities and Owners' Equity		
Current liabilities		
Accounts payable	$ 56,250	
Notes payable (due in May 1994)	12,000	
Taxes payable	4,460	
Total current liabilities		$ 72,710
Noncurrent liabilities		
Long-term debt		150,000
Shareholders' equity		
Common shares	$ 20,000	
Contributed surplus	50,000	
Retained earnings	112,940	
Total owners' equity		182,940
Total liabilities and owners' equity		$405,650

Sales	(from cash budget—Table 12-1)		$533,000
Cost of goods sold	(75% of sales)		(399,750)
Gross profit	(calculation)		$133,250
Operating Expenses			
Depreciation	[($17,200/2) + $230]	$ 8,830	
Wages and salaries	(from cash budget—Table 12-1)	38,000	
Rent	(from cash budget—Table 12-1)	24,000	
Other expenses	(from cash budget—Table 12-1)	6,900	(77,730)
Net operating income	(calculation)		$55,520
Interest expense	(calculation—see text footnote 5)		(11,764)
Earnings before taxes	(calculation)		$43,756
Income taxes payable	(40%)		(17,502)
Net income	(calculation)		$26,254

TABLE 12-3
Salco Furniture Co., Inc., Pro Forma Income Statement for the Six-Month Period Ended June 30, 1994

tion, the $14,000 piece of equipment purchased at the end of February will be depreciated over a 15-year life toward a $3,650 salvage value. Using straight-line depreciation and depreciating the asset for four months of the budget period, we find this amounts to roughly $230. Thus, total depreciation expense for the period is $8,830 [or ($17,200/2) + $230].

Wages and salaries, rent, and other expenses are found by summing the relevant cash flow items from the cash budget for the months of January through June. This assumes, of course, that all these expenses are paid at the end of each month in which they are earned, rent is not paid in advance, and all other expenses are paid on a monthly basis except interest on short-term borrowing, which is paid in the month following its occurrence. Wages and salaries total $38,000, rent expense equals $24,000, and other expenses are expected to be $6,900.

Subtracting the above operating expenses from gross profit leaves a net operating income of $55,520. Interest expense of $11,764 is then deducted from net operating income to obtain earnings before taxes of $43,756.[5] Total income taxes payable are found using a 40 percent corporate income tax rate. For Salco this equals a tax expense for the period of $17,502. Finally, subtracting the estimated taxes from earnings before taxes indicates net income for the period of $26,254.

Net Cash Flow Versus Net Income

The difference in the cash and accrual bases of accounting for corporate income is vividly demonstrated in the cash budget and pro forma income statements for the period. On a cash flow basis the firm has a substantial net negative cash flow, while on an accrual basis the firm earned $26,254. The difference, of course, relates to when revenues and expenses are accounted for or recognized in the two statements. In the cash budget revenues and expenses are included in the months in which cash is actually received or disbursed. In the income statement revenues and expenses are included in

---

[5]Total interest expense incurred (but not necessarily paid) during the period equals $7,500 on long-term debt plus $600 on the $12,000 note repaid in May, plus the sum of all interest incurred during the budget period on short-term borrowing. Note that we include $364 for February, $659 for March, and so forth, plus $799 for June, which was incurred but not paid until July.

the month in which the corresponding sale took place, which usually is not the same month in which cash is received. The income statement is therefore prepared on an accrual basis. See Appendix 1A for added discussion of the accrual basis of accounting.

The Pro Forma Balance Sheet

We can construct the pro forma balance sheet for Salco by using information from the cash budget (Table 12-1); the December 31, 1993, balance sheet (Table 12-2); and the pro forma income statement (Table 12-3). Salco's pro forma balance sheet for June 30, 1994, is presented in Table 12-4. Estimates of the individual statement entries are provided below.[6]

Ending cash from the cash budget, $10,000, becomes the cash entry in Salco's pro forma balance sheet. The accounts receivable balance is found as follows:

Accounts receivable (12/31/93) (from Table 12-2)	$104,400
+ Credit sales (from Table 12-1)	533,000
− Collections (from Table 12-1)	(440,400)
Accounts receivable (6/30/94) (calculation)	$197,000

The beginning balance for accounts receivable is taken from the December 31, 1993, balance sheet (Table 12-2), and credit sales and collections are obtained by summing across the relevant cash budget monthly totals. Inventories are determined in a similar manner:

Inventories (12/31/93) (from Table 12-2)	$101,250
+ Purchases (from Table 12-1)	414,750
− Cost of goods sold (from Table 12-3)	(399,750)
Inventories (6/30/94) (calculation)	$116,250

Purchases were found by summing relevant monthly figures from the cash budget for all six months of the budget period; and cost of goods sold was taken from the pro forma income statement in Table 12-3. The net plant and equipment figure is found as follows:

Net plant and equipment (12/31/93) (from Table 12-2)	$180,000
+ Purchases of plant and equipment (from Table 12-1)	14,000
− Depreciation expense (from Table 12-3)	(8,830)
Net plant and equipment (6/30/94) (calculation)	$185,170

Purchases of plant and equipment are reflected in the cash budget, and depreciation expense is taken from the pro forma income statement. The only changes that took place during the period involved the $14,000 purchase and depreciation expense of $8,830, leaving a net balance of $185,170. Total assets for Salco are therefore expected to be $508,420.

The liability accounts are estimated using the same basic methodology used in finding asset balances. Accounts payable is found as follows:

[6]The cash flow from operating activities can be estimated from the schedule of net operating cash flows or the statement of changes in financial position; both techniques were examined in Chapter 11.

	Assets	
Current assets		
Cash	$ 10,000	
Accounts receivable	197,000	
Inventories	116,250	
Total current assets		$323,250
Fixed assets		
Net plant and equipment		185,170
Total assets		$508,420

TABLE 12-4
Salco Furniture Co., Inc.,
Pro Forma Balance Sheet,
June 30, 1994

	Liabilities and Owners' Equity	
Current liabilities		
Accounts payable	$ 56,250	
Interest payable	799[a]	
Notes payable[b]	79,875	
Taxes payable	12,302	
Total current liabilities		$149,226
Noncurrent liabilities		
Long-term debt		150,000
Shareholders' equity		
Common shares	$ 20,000	
Contributed surplus	50,000	
Retained earnings	139,194	
Total owners' equity		209,194
Total liabilities and owners' equity		$508,420

[a]This contains the $799 in interest incurred on June's total borrowing of $77,875, but which will not be paid until July.
[b]Cumulative borrowing for the period was assumed to take the form of notes payable. This figure is taken from the cumulative borrowing row of cash budget contained in Table 12-1.

Accounts payable (12/31/93) (from Table 12-2)	$ 56,250
+ Purchases (from Table 12-1)	414,750
− Payments (from Table 12-1)	(414,750)
Accounts payable (6/30/94) (calculation)	$ 56,250

During June the firm had total borrowing of $77,875, on which it owes $799 in interest. However, since interest is not paid in the month in which the expense is incurred, this interest liability still exists at the end of June. We can analyze the ending balance for interest payable as follows:

Interest payable (12/31/93)	$ 0
+ Interest expense (see footnote 5)	11,764
− Interest paid	10,965
Interest payable (6/30/94)	$ 799

Again, purchases and payments were taken from the cash budget for each of the six months of the budget period. Notes payable are found as follows:

Notes payable (12/31/93) (from Table 12-2)	$12,000
+ Borrowing (6/30/89) (from Table 12-1)	79,875
− Repayments (from Table 12-1)	(12,000)
Notes payable (6/30/94) (calculation)	$79,875

Here it is assumed that the total new financing needed during the period ($79,875) would be raised through notes payable. Salco's use of short-term financing may or may not be desirable, as we shall see in Chapter 13 when we discuss working-capital management. An accrued interest expense item of $799 is created as a result of interest expense in that amount that was incurred during June on short-term borrowing but will not be paid until July. Next, compute taxes payable as follows:

Taxes payable (12/31/93) (from Table 12-2)	$ 4,460
+ Tax liability for the period (from Table 12-3)	17,502
− Tax payments made during the period (from Table 12-1)	(9,660)
Taxes payable (6/30/94) (calculation)	$12,302

Long-term debt, common shares, and contributed surplus remain unchanged for the period, as no new shares or long-term debt was issued nor was any repurchased or retired. Finally, the retained earnings balance is found as follows:

Retained earnings (12/31/93) (from Table 12-2)	$112,940
+ Net income for the period (from Table 12-3)	26,254
− Cash dividends (from Table 12-1)	0
Retained earnings (6/30/94) (calculation)	$139,194

Since no common dividends were paid (none were considered in the cash budget—Table 12-1), the new retained earnings figure is $139,194.

Salco's management may now wish to perform a financial analysis using the newly prepared pro forma statements. Such an analysis would provide the basis for evaluating the firm's planned financial performance over the next six months. It would entail use of a set of ratios such as those discussed in Chapter 11, which could be compared with prior-year figures and industry averages. If this analysis identified any potential weakness, the firm could take steps to correct it before it became reality.

Financial Control

The pro forma statements just prepared can be used to monitor or control the firm's financial performance. One approach would involve preparing pro forma statements for each month during the planning period. Actual operating results for each month's operations could then be compared with the projected or pro forma figures. This type of analysis would provide an early warning system to detect financial problems as they develop. In particular, by comparing actual monthly (or even weekly) operating results with projected revenue and expense items (from pro forma income statements), the financial manager can maintain a very close watch on the firm's overall profitability and take an active role in determining the firm's overall performance for the planning period.

Financial Planning and Budgeting: Closing Comments

Two aspects of pro forma statements should be emphasized. First, these figures represent single-point estimates of each of the items in the entire system of budgets and the resulting pro forma statements. Although these may be the best estimates as to what the future will hold for Salco, at least two additional sets of estimates may be desired, corresponding to the very worst set of circumstances that the firm might face and the very best. These extremes provide the necessary input for formulating contingency financing plans, should a deviation from the expected figures occur. Second, notes payable was used as a plug figure for additional financing needed. The actual source of financing selected will depend on a number of factors, including (1) the length of the period for which the financing will be needed, (2) the cost of alternative sources of funds, and (3) the preferences of the firm's management regarding the use of debt versus equity. These factors will be further investigated in Chapter 16, when we discuss short-term financing.

COMPUTERIZED FINANCIAL PLANNING

In recent years a number of developments in both computer hardware (machines) and software (programs) have reduced the tedium of the planning and budgeting process immensely. These developments include the introduction of "user friendly" or "easy to use" computer programs that are specialized for application to financial planning.

Financial planning software packages (sometimes referred to as electronic spreadsheets) were first made popular on large mainframe computers. These packages allow even a computer novice to utilize a personal computer to construct budgets and forecasts. The real advantage of the computer occurs if there is a need for different scenarios to be evaluated quickly and at a low cost in labour-hours.

Another major development that has had a significant impact on the extent to which computers are used in the planning and budgeting process is the advent of the microcomputer. For mere hundreds of dollars the financial analyst's desk can contain the computing power it took hundreds of thousands of dollars to buy just a decade ago. The development of financial planning software has parallelled the development of microcomputer technology. The number of spreadsheet packages has mushroomed over the past five years. These packages generally sell for less than $500 and usually include graphics programs as well as elementary database management capabilities.[7] The appendix offers an example spreadsheet exercise.

---

[7]The number and variety of financial spreadsheet programs has expanded dramatically since the introduction of the original Visi-Calc program. These include Lotus 123 and Excel among others. In addition, there is a growing set of products referred to as "expert systems," which attempt to mimic the decisions of experts. To date these efforts have produced a limited number of financial applications software related to such things as the capital-budgeting decision (discussed in Chapter 6), but they offer an opportunity to expand the capabilities of the financial manager of the future.

SUMMARY

This chapter has developed the role of forecasting within the context of the firm's financial planning efforts. Forecasts of the firm's sales revenues and related expenses provide the basis for projecting future financing needs. The most popular method for forecasting variables is the percent of sales method.

Forecasts of firm sales and expenses were used to develop the cash budget for the planning period, which was then used to estimate the firm's future financing needs. In this chapter all needed financing was supplied through short-term notes. However, in Chapters 16 and 19 we will look more closely at sources of financing. Chapter 16 deals with the choice between current or short-term financing versus long-term financing, Chapter 19 with the choice among long-term sources (bonds, preferred shares, and common shares).

Pro forma financial statements provide the user with the basis for (1) evaluating the results of the firm's financial plans and (2) controlling the firm's operations during the planning period.

STUDY QUESTIONS

12-1. Discuss the shortcomings of the percent of sales method of financial forecasting.

12-2. Explain how a fixed cash budget differs from a variable or flexible cash budget.

12-3. What two basic needs does a flexible (variable) cash budget serve?

12-4. What would be the probable effect on a firm's cash position of the following events?
  a. Rapidly rising sales
  b. A delay in the payment of payables
  c. A more liberal credit policy on sales (to the firm's customers)
  d. Holding larger inventories

12-5. How long should the budget period be? Why would a firm not set a rule that all budgets be for a 12-month period?

12-6. A cash budget is usually thought of as a means of planning for future financing needs. Why would a cash budget also be important for a firm that had excess cash on hand?

12-7. Explain why a cash budget would be of particular importance to a firm that experiences seasonal fluctuations in its sales.

12-8. Is there a difference between estimated net profit after taxes for a period and the estimated net addition to the cash balance? Explain.

SELF-TEST PROBLEMS

ST-1. (*Financial Forecasting*) Use the percent of sales method to prepare a pro forma income statement for Calico Sales Co., Inc. Projected sales for next year equal $4 million. Cost of goods sold equal 70 percent of sales, administrative expense equals $500,000, and depreciation expense is $300,000. Interest expense equals $50,000 and income is taxed at a rate of 40 percent. The firm plans to spend $200,000 during the period to renovate its office facility and will retire $150,000 in notes payable. Finally, selling expense equals 5 percent of sales.

ST-2. (*Pro Forma Statements and Liquidity Analysis*) The balance sheet for Odom Manufacturing Company on December 31, 1993, is found below:

Odom Manufacturing Co. Balance Sheet December 31, 1993

Cash	$ 250,000	Accounts payable	$ 850,000
Accounts receivable	760,000	Notes payable	550,000
Inventory	860,000	Current liabilities	$1,400,000
Current assets	$1,870,000	Long-term debt	800,000
Property, plant, and equipment	1,730,000	Common shares	600,000
		Retained earnings	800,000
Total assets	$3,600,000	Total liabilities and shareholders' equity	$3,600,000

The Treasurer of Odom Manufacturing wishes to borrow $500,000, the funds from which would be applied in the following manner:

1. $100,000 to reduce accounts payable
2. $75,000 to retire current notes payable
3. $175,000 to expand existing plant facilities
4. $80,000 to increase inventories
5. $70,000 to increase cash on hand

Repayment of the $500,000 will be in 20 years with interest paid annually.

a. Assuming that the loan is obtained, prepare a pro forma balance sheet for Odom Manufacturing that reflects the use of the loan proceeds.

b. Did the firm's liquidity improve after the loan was obtained and the proceeds were dispensed in the above manner? Why or why not?

ST-3. (*Cash Budget*) Stauffer, Inc., has estimated sales and purchase requirements for the last half of the coming year. Past experience indicates that it will collect 20 percent of its sales in the month of the sale, 50 percent of the remainder one month after the sale, and the balance in the second month following the sale. Stauffer prefers to pay for half its purchases in the month of the purchase and the other half the following month. Labour expense for each month is expected to equal 5 percent of that month's sales, with cash payment being made in the month in which the expense is incurred. Depreciation expense is $5,000 per month; miscellaneous cash expenses are $4,000 per month and are paid in the month incurred. General and administrative expenses of $50,000 are recognized and paid monthly. A $60,000 truck is to be purchased in August and is to be depreciated on a straight-line basis over 10 years with no expected salvage value. The company also plans to pay a $9,000 cash dividend to shareholders in July. The company feels that a minimum cash balance of $30,000 should be maintained. Any borrowing will cost 12 percent annually, with interest paid in the month following the month in which the funds are borrowed. Borrowing takes place at the beginning of the month in which the need for funds arises. For example, if during the month of July the firm should need to borrow $24,000 to maintain its $30,000 desired minimum balance, then $24,000 will be taken out on July 1 with interest owed for the entire month of July. Interest for the month of July would then be paid on August 1. Sales and purchase estimates are shown below. Prepare a cash budget for the months of July and August (cash on hand 6/30 was $30,000, while sales for May and June were $100,000 and purchases were $60,000 for each of these months).

Month	Sales	Purchases
July	$120,000	$50,000
August	150,000	40,000
September	110,000	30,000

12-1A. (*Financial Forecasting*) Sambonoza Enterprises projects its sales next year to be $4 million and expects to earn 5 percent of that amount after taxes. The firm is currently in the process of projecting its financing needs and has made the following assumptions (projections):

1. Current assets will equal 20 percent of sales while fixed assets will remain at their current level of $1 million.
2. Common equity is presently $0.8 million, and the firm pays out half its after-tax earnings in dividends.
3. The firm has short-term payables and trade credit that normally equal 10 percent of sales and has no long-term debt outstanding.

What are Sambonoza's financing needs for the coming year?

12-2A. (*Financial Forecasting—Percent of Sales*) Tulley Appliances, Inc., projects next year's sales to be $20 million. Current sales are at $15 million based on current assets of $5 million and fixed assets of $5 million. The firm's net profit margin is 5 percent after taxes. Tulley forecasts that current assets will rise in direct proportion to the increase in sales but fixed assets will increase by only $100,000. At present Tulley has $1.5 million in accounts payable plus $2 million in long-term debt (due in 10 years) outstanding and common equity (including $4 million in retained earnings) totalling $6.5 million. Tulley plans to pay $500,000 in dividends from common shares next year.

a. What are Tulley's total financing needs (i.e., total assets) for the coming year?
b. Given the firm's projections and dividend payment plans, what are its discretionary financing needs?
c. Based upon the projections given and assuming the $100,000 expansion in fixed assets will occur, what is the largest increase in sales the firm can support without having to resort to the use of discretionary sources of financing?

12-3A. (*Pro Forma Balance Sheet Construction*) Use the following industry average ratios to construct a pro forma balance sheet for the V. M. Willet Co.

Total asset turnover	2.0 times
Average collection period (assume a 365-day year)	9.125 days
Fixed asset turnover	5.0 times
Inventory turnover (based on cost of goods sold)	3.0 times
Current ratio	2.0 times
Sales (all on credit)	$4.0 million
Cost of goods sold	75% of sales
Debt ratio	50%

Cash		Current liabilities	
Accounts receivable		Long-term debt	
Net fixed assets	$_____	Common shares plus retained earnings	
	$_____		$_____

12-4A. (*Cash Budget*) The Sharpe Corporation's projected sales for the first eight months of 1994 are as follows:

January	$ 90,000	May	$300,000
February	120,000	June	270,000
March	135,000	July	225,000
April	240,000	August	150,000

Of Sharpe's sales, 10 percent is for cash, another 60 percent is collected in the month following sale, and 30 percent is collected in the second month following sale. November and December sales for 1993 were $220,000 and $175,000, respectively.

Sharpe purchases its raw materials two months in advance of its sales equal to 60 percent of their final sales price. The supplier is paid one month after it makes delivery. For example, purchases for April sales are made in February and payment is made in March.

In addition, Sharpe pays $10,000 per month for rent and $20,000 each month for other expenditures. Tax prepayments of $22,500 are made each quarter, beginning in March.

The company's cash balance at December 31, 1993, was $22,000; a minimum balance of $15,000 must be maintained at all times. Assume that any short-term financing needed to maintain cash balance would be paid off in the month following the month of financing if sufficient funds are available. Interest on short-term loans (12%) is paid monthly. Borrowing to meet estimated monthly cash needs takes place at the beginning of the month. Thus, if in the month of April the firm expects to have a need for an additional $60,500, these funds would be borrowed at the beginning of April with interest of $605 (.12 × 1/12 × $60,500) owed for April and paid at the beginning of May.

a. Prepare a cash budget for Sharpe covering the first seven months of 1994.

b. Sharpe has $200,000 in notes payable due in July that must be repaid or renegotiated for an extension. Will the firm have ample cash to repay the notes?

12-5A. (*Financial Forecasting—Pro Forma Statements*) The Bell Retailing Company has been engaged in the process of forecasting its financing needs over the next quarter and has made the following forecasts of planned cash receipts and disbursements:

1. Historical and predicted sales:

Historical		Predicted	
April	$ 80,000	July	$130,000
May	100,000	August	130,000
June	120,000	September	120,000
		October	100,000

2. The firm incurs and pays a monthly rent expense of $3,000.

3. Wages and salaries for the coming months are estimated as follows: with payments coinciding with the month in which the expense is incurred.

July	$18,000
August	18,000
September	16,000

4. Of the firm's sales, 40 percent is collected in the month of sale, 30 percent one month after sale, and the remaining 30 percent two months after sale.

5. Merchandise is purchased one month before the sales month and is paid for in the month it is sold. Purchases equal 80 percent of sales.

6. Tax prepayments are made on the calendar quarter, with a prepayment of $1,000 in July based on earnings for the quarter ended June 30.

7. Utilities for the firm average 2 percent of sales and are paid in the month of their occurrence.

8. Depreciation expense is $12,000 annually.

9. Interest on a $40,000 bank note (due in November) is payable at an 8 percent annual rate in September for the three-month period just ended.

10. The firm follows a policy of paying no cash dividends.

Based on the above, supply the following items:

a. Prepare a monthly cash budget for the three-month period ended September 30, 1994.

b. If the firm's beginning cash balance for the budget period is $5,000 and this is its minimum desired balance, determine when and how much the firm will need to borrow during the budget period. The firm has an $80,000 line of credit with its bank with interest (12 percent annual) paid monthly (for example, for a loan taken out at the end of December, interest would be paid at the end of January and every month thereafter so long as the loan was outstanding).

c. Prepare a pro forma income statement for Bell covering the three-month period ended September 30, 1994. Use a 40 percent tax rate.

d. Given the following balance sheet dated June 30, 1994, and your pro forma income statement from (c), prepare a pro forma balance sheet for September 30, 1994.

Bell Manufacturing Co. Balance Sheet June 30, 1994			
Cash	$ 5,000	Accounts payable	$104,000
Accounts receivable	102,000	Bank notes (8%)	40,000
Inventories	114,000	Accrued taxes	1,000
Current assets	221,000	Current liabilities	145,000
Net fixed assets	120,000	Common shares	100,000
		Contributed surplus	28,400
		Retained earnings	67,600
Total assets	$341,000	Total liabilities and capital	$341,000

12-6A. (*Forecasting Accounts Receivable*) Sampkin Mfg. is evaluating the effects of extending trade credit to its out-of-province customers. In the past, Sampkin has given credit to local customers but has insisted on cash upon delivery from customers in the bordering province of Manitoba. At present Sampkin's average collection period is 35 days based upon total sales; that is, including both its $900,000 in-province credit sales and its $300,000 out-of-province cash sales, the firm's accounts receivable balance is 35 days.

$$\text{average collection period} = \frac{\text{accounts receivable}}{\frac{\text{sales}}{365}}$$

$$= \frac{\$115,068}{\frac{\$1,200,000}{365}} = 35 \text{ days}$$

a. Calculate Sampkin's average collection period based upon credit sales alone.

b. If Sampkin extends credit to its out-of-province customers, it expects total credit sales to rise to $1,500,000. If the firm's average collection period remains the same, what will be the new level of accounts receivable?

12-7A. (*Forecasting Accounts Receivable*) The Ace Traffic Company sells its merchandise on credit terms of 2/10, net 30 (2 percent discount if payment is made within 10 days or the net amount is due in 30 days). Only a part of the firm's customers take the trade discount, so that the firm's average collection period is 20 days.

a. Based upon estimated sales of $405,556, project Ace's accounts receivable balance for the coming year.

b. If Ace changes its cash discount terms to 1/10, net 30, it expects its average collection period will rise to 28 days. Estimate Ace's accounts receivable balance based on the new credit terms and expected sales of $405,556.

12-8A. (*Percent of Sales Forecasting*) Which of the following accounts would most likely vary directly with the level of firm sales? Discuss each briefly.

	Yes	No
Cash	_____	_____
Marketable securities	_____	_____
Accounts payable	_____	_____
Notes payable	_____	_____
Plant and equipment	_____	_____
Inventories	_____	_____

12-9A. (*Financial Forecasting—Percent of Sales*) The balance sheet of the Thompson Trucking Company (TTC) is found below:

Thompson Trucking Company Balance Sheet
January 31, 1993 ($ millions)

Current assets	$10	Accounts payable	$ 5
Net fixed assets	15	Notes payable	0
Total	$25	Bonds payable	10
		Common equity	10
		Total	$25

TTC had sales for the year ended 1/31/93 of $50 million. The firm follows a policy of paying all net earnings out to its common shareholders in cash dividends. Thus, TTC generates no funds from its earnings that can be used to expand its operations (assume that depreciation expense is just equal to the cost of replacing worn-out assets.)

a. If TTC anticipates sales of $80 million during the coming year, develop a pro forma balance sheet for the firm for 1/31/93. Assume that current assets vary as a percent of sales, net fixed assets remain unchanged, accounts payable vary as a percent of sales, and use notes payable as a balancing entry.

b. How much "new" financing will TTC need next year?

c. What limitations does the percent of sales forecast method suffer from? Discuss briefly.

12-10A. (*Financial Forecasting—Discretionary Financing Needed*) The most recent balance sheet for the Armadillo Dog Biscuit Co. is shown in the table below. The company is about to embark on an advertising campaign, which is expected to raise sales from the present level of $5 million to $7 million by the end of next year. The firm is presently operating at full capacity and will have to increase its investment in both current and fixed assets to support the projected level of new sales. In fact, the firm estimates that both categories of assets will rise in direct proportion to the projected increase in sales.

The firm's net profits were 6 percent of the current year's sales but are expected to rise to 7 percent of next year's sales. To help support its anticipated growth in asset needs next year, the firm has suspended plans to pay cash dividends to its shareholders. In years past a $1.50 per share dividend has been paid annually.

Armadillo Dog Biscuit Co., Inc. ($ millions)

	Present Level	Percent of Sales	Projected Level
Current assets	$2.0		
Net fixed assets	$3.0		
Total	$5.0		

Accounts payable	$0.5
Accrued expenses	$0.5
Notes payable	—
Current liabilities	$1.0
Long-term debt	$2.0
Common shares	$0.5
Retained earnings	$1.5
Common equity	$2.0
Total	$5.0

Armadillo's payables and accrued expenses are expected to vary directly with sales. In addition, notes payable will be used to supply the added funds needed to finance next year's operations that are not forthcoming from other sources.

a. Fill in the table and project the firm's needs for discretionary financing. Use notes payable as the balancing entry for future discretionary financing needed.

b. Compare Armadillo's current ratio and debt ratio (total liabilities/total assets) before the growth in sales and after. What was the effect of the expanded sales on these two dimensions of Armadillo's financial condition?

c. What difference, if any, would have resulted if Armadillo's sales had risen to $6 million in one year and $7 million only after two years? Discuss only; no calculations required.

12-11A. (*Financial Forecasting—Changing Credit Policy*) Island Resorts, Inc., has $400,000 invested in receivables throughout much of the year. It has annual credit sales of $3,650,000 and a gross profit margin of 80 percent.

a. What is Island Resorts' average collection period? [*Hint:* Recall that average collection period = accounts receivable/(credit sales/365).]

b. By how much would Island Resorts be able to reduce its accounts receivable if it were to change its credit policies in a way that reduced its average collection period to 30 days without affecting annual credit sales?

12-12A. (*Forecasting Discretionary Financing Needs*) Fishing Charter, Inc., estimates that it invests 30 cents in assets for each dollar of new sales. However, 5 cents in profits are produced by each dollar of additional sales, of which 1 cent can be reinvested in the firm. If sales rise from their present level of $5 million by $500,000 next year, and the ratio of spontaneous liabilities of sales is .15, what will be the firm's need for discretionary financing? (*Hint:* In this situation you do not know what the firm's existing level of assets is, nor do you know how they have been financed. Thus, you must estimate the change in financing needs and match this change with the expected changes in spontaneous liabilities, retained earnings, and other sources of discretionary financing.)

12-13A. (*Cash Budget*) The Cramer Enterprise projected sales for the first eight months of 1994 are as follows:

January	$100,000	May	$275,000
February	140,000	June	250,000
March	150,000	July	200,000
April	250,000	August	120,000

Of Cramer's sales, 20 percent is for cash, another 50 percent is collected in the month following sale, and 30 percent is collected in the second month following sale. November and December sales for 1993 were $220,000 and $175,000, respectively.

Cramer purchases its raw materials two months in advance of its sales equal to 65 percent of their final sales price. The supplier is paid one month after it makes delivery. For example, purchases for April sales are made in February and payment is made in March.

In addition, Cramer pays $10,000 per month for rent and $20,000 each month for other expenditures. Tax prepayments of $22,500 are made each quarter, beginning in March.

The company's cash balance at December 31, 1993, was $22,000; a minimum balance of $20,000 must be maintained at all times. Assume that any short-term financing needed to maintain cash balance would be paid off in the month following the month of financing if sufficient funds are available. Cramer has arranged with its bank the use of short-term credit at an interest rate of 12 percent per annum (1 percent per month) to be paid monthly. Borrowing to meet estimated monthly cash needs takes place at the beginning of the month but interest is not paid until the end of the following month. If in the month of April the firm expects to have a need for an additional $50,000, these funds would be borrowed at the beginning of April with interest of $500 (= .01 × $50,000) in interest during May. Finally, Cramer follows a policy of repaying any outstanding short-term loans in any month in which its cash balance exceeds the minimum desired balance of $20,000.

a. Cramer needs to know what its cash requirements will be for the next six months so that it can renegotiate the terms of its short-term credit agreement with its bank, if necessary. To evaluate this problem the firm plans to evaluate the impact of a 20% variation in its monthly sales effort. Prepare a six-month cash budget for Cramer and use it to evaluate the firm's cash needs.

b. Cramer has $200,000 in notes due in July. Will the firm have sufficient cash to repay the notes?

CASE PROBLEM

LINCOLN PLYWOOD, INC.

FINANCIAL FORECASTING

Lincoln Plywood, Inc. (LPI), owns and operates a plywood fabricating plant in Northern British Columbia. LPI's primary product is 4 × 8 sheets of pine plywood used in the construction industry. The plywood is formed out of thin sheets of wood that are "peeled" from pine logs bought in the region. A number of varieties of thicknesses and grades of plywood can be made in LPI's plant, ranging from 1/4-inch sheets used as panelling in new homes to 3/4-inch sheets used in framing and heavy industrial applications. LPI's sales have grown rapidly over the past 10 years at an average of 10 percent per year. This growth has resulted from the housing boom that occurred during this period and in particular the very rapid rate of regional growth in the central British Columbia.

The firm's management has been pleased with the growth in sales; however, during the past six months it has begun to experience some cash flow problems that appear to have gotten out of control (LPI's current balance sheet is shown below). The firm's controller, James Christian, is aware of the decline in the firm's cash position and plans to correct the problem as soon as an appropriate course of action can be identified. One factor that he feels is surely making the problem worse is the firm's credit and collections policy. In particular, LPI recently "liberalized" its credit terms in an effort to stimulate demand in the face of stiffening competition. The full effect of the change is not known, but Christian plans to address that problem when he makes his projection of cash needs for the coming year.

Lincoln Plywood, Inc., Balance Sheet for December 31, 19X1

Assets

Cash		$ 125,000
Accounts receivable	$ 517,500	
Less: Allowance for bad debts	7,500	510,000
Inventories		725,000
Current assets		$1,360,000
Plant and equipment	$2,320,000	
Less: Accumulated depreciation	(1,280,000)	
Net plant and equipment		1,040,000
Total assets		$2,400,000

Liabilities and Owners' Equity

Accounts payable	$ 30,000
Accrued taxes	50,000
Accrued expenses	270,000
Current liabilities	$ 350,000
Common shares	$ 400,000
Retained earnings	1,650,000
Common equity	$2,050,000
Total liabilities and owner's equity	$2,400,000

LPI's cash cycle is a relatively simple one. The firm purchases timber, processes that timber by turning it into various types of plywood products, sells the timber on credit, and collects its credit sales. The cash flow problem the firm currently faces is partly a result of its increasing the term over which credit sales can be repaid. In fact, following its recent liberalization of credit terms, the firm estimates that only 10 percent of its customers will pay within the month of the sale, 46 percent of the total will be collected in one month, and all but 2 percent of sales will be collected in the second month following the sale. Bad debt expense is estimated at 1 percent of sales in the income statement.

Christian plans to make a monthly cash budget for LPI spanning the next six months (January through June) and has already projected firm sales as follows:

Month	Projected Sales
January	$500,000
February	300,000
March	250,000
April	525,000
May	800,000
June	250,000

The monthly sales estimates reflect a long-established seasonality in the firm's sales. However, the firm's purchases of timber are not closely matched to its sales. The harvest of timber is heavily seasonal due to the problems associated with getting the timber out of the woods during the rainy winter months. Since LPI contracts up to eight months in advance for its timber purchases, it has a very good idea as to what its expenditures for timber will be over the six-month planning horizon. Specifically, LPI has contracted to make the following timber purchases:

Month	Purchase Contracts
January	$120,000
February	120,000
March	200,000
April	300,000

May	550,000
June	600,000

LPI's standard purchase contract calls for cash payment 30 days following the delivery, and its purchases during December were only $20,000. Timber purchases are added to the firm's inventories at cost plus a processing cost equal to half the cost of the timber. Thus, for the month of December LPI increased its inventories by a total of $30,000 and this is the outstanding balance of accounts payable for December. This balance will be paid in full in January.

In addition to its timber purchases, LPI plans to acquire a new chipping machine used to convert waste resulting from its processing of the timber to chips of wood that are then sold to paper mills, which convert the chips to paper stock. The new machine will cost $400,000 and will be purchased and paid for in June (payment will actually be made as late as possible in June). The firm also plans to acquire a new forklift truck in February which will cost $60,000. The purchase will be paid for in March. LPI's monthly depreciation expense for January is $15,000 but will increase by $1,000 per month in February because of the purchase of the forklift, and it will increase again in July by $8,000 per month because of the purchase of the chipper.

Christian estimates the firm's general and administrative expense to be $70,000 per month, with payment being made in the month of the expense's occurrence. The firm also has a category called miscellaneous cash expenses, which is estimated to be at $20,000 per month and paid monthly. Although LPI has no formal policy with regard to its minimum cash balance, Christian feels that a $100,000 balance is the minimum he would like to have over the planning horizon. Finally, LPI plans to make a cash dividend payment to stockholders at the end of March and June equal to $100,000 and will also make quarterly tax payments of $50,000 in the months of January and April. (For planning purposes, a 30 percent tax rate is used in estimating LPI's tax liability.)

QUESTIONS

1. Prepare a month-by-month cash budget for LPI for the next six months. You may assume that any borrowing that must be undertaken will cost 1 percent interest per month, with interest paid the month following the month in which borrowing takes place. Assume borrowing is at the beginning of the month. November and December sales for the current year were $350,000 and $400,000, respectively.

2. Prepare pro forma income statements for the three-month periods ended with March and June. You may assume that inventories consist of materials and related labour expense. Cost of goods sold equal 75 percent of sales and are comprised of materials and related labour.

3. Prepare a pro forma balance sheet for LPI for the end of March and June. You may assume that accrued expenses and common shares do not change over the six-month planning period.

4. Given LPI's financing requirements for the period, what suggestions do you have for James Christian for raising the necessary funds? Discuss your reasons for the stated plans.

STUDY PROBLEMS (SET B)

12-1B. (*Financial Forecasting*) Simpson Inc. projects its sales next year to be $5 million and expects to earn 6 percent of that amount after taxes. The firm is currently in the process of projecting its financing needs and has made the following assumptions (projections):

1. Current assets will equal 15 percent of sales while fixed assets will remain at their current level of $1 million.

2. Common equity is presently $0.7 million, and the firm pays out half its after-tax earnings in dividends.

3. The firm has short-term payables and trade credit which normally equal 11 percent of sales and has no long-term debt outstanding.

What are Simpon Inc.'s financing needs for the coming year?

12-2B. (*Financial Forecasting—Percent of Sales*) Carson Enterprises is in the midst of its annual planning exercise. Bud Carson, the owner, is a mechanical engineer by education and has only modest skills in financial planning. In fact, the firm has operated in the past on a "crisis" basis with little attention being paid to the firm's financial affairs until a problem arose. This worked reasonably well for several years until the firm's growth in sales created a serious cash flow shortage last year. Bud was able to convince the firm's bank to come up with the needed funds but an outgrowth of the agreement was that the firm would begin to make forecasts of its financing requirements annually. To support its first such effort Bud has made the following estimates for next year: Sales are currently $18 million with projected sales of $25 million for next year. The firm's current assets equal $7 million, while its fixed assets are $6 million. The best estimate Bud can make is that current assets will equal the current proportion of sales while fixed assets will rise by $100,000. At the present time the firm has accounts payable of $1.5 million, $2 million in long-term debt which is due in 10 years, and common equity totalling $9.5 million (including $4 million in retained earnings). Finally, Carson plans to continue paying its dividend of $600,000 next year.

a. What are Carson's total financing needs (i.e., total assets) for the coming year?

b. Given the firm's projections and dividend payment plans, what are its discretionary financing needs?

c. Based upon the projections given and assuming the $100,000 expansion in fixed assets will occur, what is the largest increase in sales the firm can support without having to resort to the use of discretionary sources of financing?

12-3B. (*Pro Forma Balance Sheet Construction*) Use the following industry average ratios to construct a pro forma balance sheet for the V. M. Willet Co.

Total asset turnover	2.5 times
Average collection period (assume a 365-day year)	10.139 days
Fixed asset turnover	6.0 times
Inventory turnover (based on cost of goods sold)	4.0 times
Current ratio	3.0 times
Sales (all on credit)	$5.0 million
Cost of goods sold	80% of sales
Debt ratio	60%

Cash		Current liabilities	
Accounts receivable		Long-term debt	
		Common shares plus retained earnings	
Net fixed assets	$ _____		_____
	$ _____		$ _____

12-4B. (*Cash Budget*) The Sharpe Corporation's projected sales for the first eight months of 1994 are as follows:

January	$100,000	May	$275,000
February	110,000	June	250,000
March	130,000	July	235,000
April	250,000	August	160,000

Of Sharpe's sales, 20 percent is for cash, another 60 percent is collected in the month following sale, and 20 percent is collected in the second month following sale. November and December sales for 1993 were $220,000 and $175,000, respectively.

Sharpe purchases its raw materials two months in advance of its sales equal to 70 percent of their final sales price. The supplier is paid one month after it makes delivery. For example, purchases for April sales are made in February and payment is made in March.

In addition, Sharpe pays $10,000 per month for rent and $20,000 each month for other expenditures. Tax prepayments of $23,000 are made each quarter, beginning in March.

The company's cash balance at December 31, 1993, was $22,000; a minimum balance of $25,000 must be maintained at all times. Assume that any short-term financing needed to maintain cash balance would be paid off in the month following the month of financing if sufficient funds are available. Interest on short-term loans (12 percent) is paid monthly. Borrowing to meet estimated monthly cash needs takes place at the beginning of the month. Thus, if in the month of April the firm expects to have a need for an additional $60,500, these funds would be borrowed at the beginning of April with interest of $605 (.12 × 1/12 × $60,500) owed for April and paid at the beginning of May.

a. Prepare a cash budget for Sharpe covering the first seven months of 1994.

b. Sharpe has $250,000 in notes payable due in July that must be repaid or renegotiated for an extension. Will the firm have ample cash to repay the notes?

12-5B. (*Financial Forecasting—Pro Forma Statements*) In the Spring of 1993 Cherill Adison, the chief financial analyst for Jarrett Sales Company, found herself faced with a major financial forecasting exercise. She had joined the firm about three months ago and was just beginning to feel comfortable with her new duties when she was called into her supervisor's office about 3:30 p.m. on a Friday afternoon. It seems that Margaret Simpson, the analyst who had been in charge of the firm's annual financial planning exercise, had taken maternity leave and would not be available to help prepare the firm's projected financing needs for the coming quarter. The job fell in her lap and it needed to be completed by Monday at 2:00 p.m. when the company president met with the executive committee to work out their plans for requesting a limit for the firm's line of credit with its bank for the next quarter. After reviewing Ms. Simpson's files Cherill found that the task might not be so difficult as she had first thought. In fact, the critical forecasts had been compiled and were contained in the file. In addition, Cherill found some carefully documented assumptions that she could use to compile the necessary forecast. This information is found below:

1. Historical and predicted sales:

	Historical		Predicted
April	$ 80,000	July	$140,000
May	110,000	August	120,000
June	120,000	September	120,000
		October	100,000

2. The firm incurs and pays a monthly rent expense of $2,500.

3. Wages and salaries for the coming months are estimated as follows (with payments coinciding with the month in which the expense is incurred):

July	$20,000
August	18,000
September	13,000

4. Of the firm's sales, 40 percent is collected in the month of sale, 30 percent one month after sale, and the remaining 30 percent two months after sale.

5. Merchandise is purchased one month before the sales month and is paid for in the month it is sold. Purchases equal 80 percent of sales.

6. Tax prepayments are made on the calendar quarter, with a prepayment of $1,000 in July based on earnings for the quarter ended June 30.

7. Utilities for the firm average 2 percent of sales and are paid in the month of their occurrence.

8. Depreciation expense is $13,000 annually.

9. Interest on a $40,000 bank note (due in November) is payable at an 8 percent annual rate in September for the three-month period just ended.

10. The firm follows a policy of paying no cash dividends.

Based on the above, supply the following items:

a. Prepare a monthly cash budget for the three-month period ended September 30, 1993.

b. If the firm's beginning cash balance for the budget period is $5,000 and this is its minimum desired balance, determine when and how much the firm will need to borrow during the budget period. The firm has an $80,000 line of credit with its bank with interest (12 percent annual) paid monthly (for example, for a loan taken out at the end of December, interest would be paid at the end of January and every month thereafter so long as the loan was outstanding).

c. Prepare a pro forma income statement for Jarrett covering the three-month period ended September 30, 1993. Use a 40 percent tax rate.

d. Given the following balance sheet dated June 30, 1993, and your pro forma income statement from (c), prepare a pro forma balance sheet for September 30, 1993.

Jarrett Sales Co. Balance Sheet June 30, 1993

Cash	$ 5,000	Accounts payable	$104,000
Accounts receivable	102,000	Bank notes (8%)	40,000
Inventories	114,000	Accrued taxes	1,000
Current assets	221,000	Current liabilities	145,000
Net fixed assets	120,000	Common shares	100,000
		Contributed surplus	28,400
		Retained earnings	67,600
Total assets	$341,000	Total liabilities and capital	$341,000

12-6B. (*Forecasting Accounts Receivable*) Sam's Mfg. Co. is evaluating the effects of extending trade credit to its out-of-province customers. In the past Sam's has given credit to local customers but has insisted on cash upon delivery from customers in the bordering province of Manitoba. At present Sam's average collection period is 35 days based upon total sales; that is, including both its $700,000 in-province credit sales and its $250,000 out-of-province cash sales, the firm's accounts receivable balance is 35 days.

$$\text{average collection period} = \frac{\text{accounts receivable}}{\dfrac{\text{sales}}{365}}$$

$$= \frac{\$91,096}{\dfrac{\$950,000}{365}} = 35 \text{ days}$$

a. Calculate Sam's average collection period based upon credit sales alone.

b. If Sam's extends credit to its out-of-province customers, it expects total credit sales to rise to $1,750,000. If the firm's average collection period remains the same, what will be the new level of accounts receivable?

12-7B. (*Forecasting Accounts Receivable*) The Carter Distribution Company sells its merchandise on credit terms of 2/10, net 30 (2 percent discount if payment is made within 10 days or the net amount is due in 30 days). Only a part of the firm's customers take the trade discount, so that the firm's average collection period is 20 days.

a. Based upon estimated sales of $500,000, project Carter's accounts receivable balance for the coming year.

b. If Carter changes its cash discount terms to 1/10, net 30, it expects its average collection period will rise to 28 days. Estimate Carter's accounts receivable balance based on the new credit terms and expected sales of $500,000.

12-8B. (*Percent of Sales Forecasting*) Which of the following accounts would most likely vary directly with the level of firm sales? Discuss each briefly.

	Yes	No
Cash	_____	_____
Marketable securities	_____	_____
Accounts payable	_____	_____
Notes payable	_____	_____
Plant and equipment	_____	_____
Inventories	_____	_____

12-9B. (*Financial Forecasting—Percent of Sales*) The balance sheet of the Taylor Drilling Company (TDC) is found below:

Taylor Drilling Company Balance Sheet
January 31, 1993 ($ millions)

Current assets	$15	Accounts payable	$10
Net fixed assets	15	Notes payable	0
Total	$30	Bonds payable	10
		Common equity	10
		Total	$30

TDC had sales for the year ended 1/31/93 of $60 million. The firm follows a policy of paying all net earnings out to its common shareholders in cash dividends. Thus, TDC generates no funds from its earnings that can be used to expand its operations (assume that depreciation expense is just equal to the cost of replacing worn-out assets).

a. If TDC anticipates sales of $80 million during the coming year, develop a pro forma balance sheet for the firm for 1/31/93. Assume that current assets vary as a percent of sales, net fixed assets remain unchanged, accounts payable vary as a percent of sales, and use notes payable as a balancing entry.

b. How much "new" financing will TDC need next year?

c. What limitations does the percent of sales forecast method suffer from? Discuss briefly.

12-10B. (*Financial Forecasting—Discretionary Financing Needed*) Symbolic Logic Corporation (SLC) is a technological leader in the application of surface mount technology in the manufacture of printed circuit boards used in the personal computer industry. The firm has recently patented an advanced version of its original path-breaking technology and expects sales to grow from their present level of $5 million to $8 million by the end of the coming year. Since the firm is at present operating at full capacity it expects to have to increase its investment in both current and fixed assets in proportion to the predicted increase in sales.

flows, they do not enter the income statement directly. These expenditures affect expenses for the period's income statement only through their effect on depreciation and interest expense. A cash budget would indicate the full cash impact of the renovation and debt retirement expenditures.

SS-2. **a.**

Odom Manufacturing Co. Pro Forma Balance Sheet

Cash	$ 320,000	Accounts payable	$ 750,000
Accounts receivable	760,000	Notes payable	475,000
Inventory	940,000	Total current liabilities	$1,225,000
Total current assets	$2,020,000	Long-term debt	1,300,000
Property, plant, and equipment	$1,905,000	Common shares	600,000
		Retained earnings	800,000
Total assets	$3,925,000	Total liabilities and shareholders' equity	$3,925,000

b. In order to assess whether or not the firm's liquidity position has improved with the securing of the $500,000 loan, its current financial position must be compared with its position before the loan was granted.

	Position Before Loan	Position After Loan
Current ratio	1.34	1.65
Acid test ratio	0.72	0.88

These two ratios indicate that there has been an improvement in Odom's liquidity position and that the firm was justified in seeking the loan and in allocating the funds as previously described.

SS-3.

	May	June	July	Aug.
Sales	$100,000	$100,000	$120,000	$150,000
Purchases	60,000	60,000	50,000	40,000
Cash Receipts:				
Collections from month of sale (20%)	20,000	20,000	24,000	30,000
1 month later (50% of uncollected amount)		40,000	48,000	48,000
2 months later (balance)			40,000	40,000
Total receipts			$104,000	$118,000
Cash Disbursements:				
Payments for purchases—				
From 1 month earlier			$ 30,000	$ 25,000
From current month			$ 25,000	20,000
Total			$ 55,000	$ 45,000
Miscellaneous cash expenses			4,000	4,000
Labour expense (5% of sales)			6,000	7,500
General and administrative expense ($50,000 per month)			50,000	50,000
Truck purchase			0	60,000
Cash dividends			9,000	—
Total disbursements			(124,000)	(166,500)
			(20,000)	(48,500)
Plus: Beginning cash balance			30,000	30,000
Less: Interest on short-term borrowing (1% of prior month's borrowing)				(200)

Equals: Ending cash balance— without borrowing	10,000	(18,700)
Financing needed to reach target cash balance	20,000	48,700
Cumulative borrowing	20,000	68,700

APPENDIX 12A: Microcomputers and Spreadsheet Software in Financial Planning

We have briefly discussed the role of personal computers and spreadsheet software in financial planning within this chapter. The purpose of this appendix is to illustrate how a financial planning model can be constructed and used. First, we examine how to design effective spreadsheets.

HOW TO DESIGN AN EFFECTIVE SPREADSHEET MODEL

Back in the dark ages of computing, when we had to program computers using languages such as Fortran, Cobol and Pascal, we were told to "flow chart" our programs. These flow charts were like outlines that organize the programmer's work so others could more easily follow it. A current equivalent of flow charting can be of great use to spreadsheet users. The particular methodology was devised by Urschel (1987) and is summarized in the following box.[8]

Designing a Spreadsheet

Block One: Assumptions. These are the variables that are the object of *what if* analysis.

Block Two: Inputs. The data used in the model.

Block Three: Calculations. The mechanical section of the model containing intermediate computations but not the final output of the model.

Block Four: Bottom Line. The final results of the model.

The four blocks provide a useful structure for the person building the spreadsheet model. They also make it easy for others to interpret and use the model. We will illustrate this recommended structure in the development of the spreadsheet model for the cash budgeting that follows.

SPREADSHEET MODELLING EXERCISE

Cramer Enterprises has projected its sales for the first eight months of 1993 as follows:

---

[8]W. Urschel, "Worksheets by Design," *PC World* (September 1987).

January	$100,000	May	$275,000
February	140,000	June	250,000
March	150,000	July	200,000
April	250,000	August	120,000

Cramer collects 20 percent of its sales in the month of the sale, 50 percent is collected in the month following the sale, and the remaining 30 percent is collected two months following the sale. During November and December of 1992, Cramer's sales were $220,000 and $175,000, respectively.

Cramer purchases raw materials two months in advance of its sales equal to 65 percent of those sales. The supplier is paid one month after delivery. Thus, purchases for April sales are made in February and payment is made in March.

In addition, Cramer pays $10,000 per month for rent and $20,000 each month for other expenditures. Tax prepayments of $22,500 are made each quarter beginning in March. The company's cash balance at December 31, 1992 was $22,000 and a minimum balance of $20,000 must be maintained at all times to satisfy the firm's bank line of credit agreement. Cramer has arranged with its bank for the short-term credit at an interest rate of 12 percent per annum (1 percent per month) to be paid monthly. Borrowing to meet estimated monthly cash needs takes place at the beginning of the month but interest is not paid until the end of the following month. Consequently, if the firm were to need to borrow $50,000 during the month of April then it would pay $500 (.01 × $50,000) in interest during May. Finally, Cramer follows a policy of repaying any outstanding short-term debt in any month in which its cash balance exceeds the minimum desired balance of $20,000.

Cramer faces two related problems. First, the firm needs to know what its cash requirements will be for the next six months so that it can renegotiate the terms of its short-term credit agreement with its bank, if necessary. Second, Cramer has a $200,000 note due June 30th and needs to determine whether it will have sufficient cash to repay the loan.

Sample Spreadsheet Model

Table 12A-1 contains the cash budget for Cramer spanning the first six months of 1993. The model is composed of four blocks following the procedure discussed earlier. Note that the first block contains all those elements which the analyst might wish to use in performing a sensitivity analysis of the final outcome. The second section contains raw data inputs, the third consists of intermediate calculations necessary to support the bottom line results found in block four.

A quick analysis of the results indicate the following: Cramer will not need to borrow until March when it will need an additional $27,500 followed in April when its total borrowing needs rise to $97,025. In May the firm is able to retire $31,530 of its short-term borrowing and by June it is able to retire all of the seasonal debt it borrowed over the planning period. However, the firm's projected cash balance for June is only $33,850 which is insufficient to retire the $200,000 by June 30th.

At this point you may want to explore the sensitivity of the cash requirement of the firm to changes in projected level of sales. In the Assumptions block of the model you will see a variable called "Sales Expansion %". This variable allows us to increase our January through September sales forecasts by an arbitrary percentage and then see the impact of the change on the firm's cash requirements. For example, decreasing sales by 20% or increasing them by 20% has the following impact on the firm's projected level of borrowing for the months of March, April, and May:

Sales Expansion	Cumulative Borrowing Needs		
%	March	April	May
–20%	2,900	45,229	25,681
–10%	15,200	71,127	45,588
0%	27,500	97,025	65,495
10%	39,800	122,923	85,402
20%	52,100	148,821	105,309

The effect of changes in projected sales on Cramer's cumulative borrowing needs is dramatic. A ±20% variation in sales estimates leads to an increase in the maximum level of borrowing for the planning period from $45,229 to $148,821. This is but one type of sensitivity analysis that Cramer might want to perform. The real value of having a spreadsheet model of the financial forecasting problem comes in the ease with which the user can perform such analyses.

CELL FORMULAE IN THE MODEL

Table 12A-2 contains the model's cell formulae for Blocks 3 and 4 and the month of January. Note that this spreadsheet was done using the Excel spreadsheet program, however the cell formulae would differ only slightly for Lotus 123. The principal difference that you would see in Table 12A-2 related to the fact for Lotus formulae begin with a "+" or "−" rather than "=". Of course, there are other differences in the two programs and we will point out one of them in the following discussion.

TABLE 12A-1. Cramer Enterprises, Inc., Cash Budget: January–June 1993

	A	B	C	D	E	F	G	H	I
1									
2									
3									
4									
5	Block 1: Assumptions								
6									
7	Minimum Cash Balance		20,000						
8	Beginning Cash Balance		22,000						
9									
10	Sales Expansion %		0.00%		Annual Interest				
11	Purchases as a % Sales		65%		Rate	12.00%			
12									
13	Collections:	Current Mo.	1 Mo. Later	2 Mo. Later					
14		20%	50%	30%					
15									
16	Block 2: Inputs								
17									
18	Historical Sales and Base Case Sales Predictions for Future Sales								
19	January	100,000		May	275,000				
20	February	140,000		June	250,000				
21	March	150,000		July	200,000				
22	April	250,000		August	120,000				

Table 12A-1 Continued on page 586

	A	B	C	D	E	F	G	H	I
23									
24	Block 3: Calculation								
25									
26									
27		November	December	January	February	March	April	May	June
28		220,000	175,000	100,000	140,000	150,000	250,000	275,000	250,000
29	Collections								
30	Month of sales			20,000	28,000	30,000	50,000	55,000	50,000
31	First Month			87,500	50,000	70,000	75,000	125,000	137,500
32	Second Month			66,000	52,500	30,000	42,000	45,000	75,000
33	Total collections			173,500	130,500	130,000	167,000	225,000	262,500
34	Purchases	65,000	91,000	97,500	162,500	178,750	162,500	130,000	97,500
35	Payments		65,000	91,000	97,500	162,500	178,750	162,500	130,000
36									
37	*Cash Budget for January through June*			January	February	March	April	May	June
38									
39	*Cash Receipts*			173,500	130,500	130,000	167,000	225,000	262,500
40	(collections)								
41	Cash Disbursements								
42	Payments for Purchases			91,000	97,500	162,500	178,750	162,500	130,000
43	Rent			10,000	10,000	10,000	10,000	10,000	10,000
44	Other Expenditures			20,000	20,000	20,000	20,000	20,000	20,000
45	Tax Deposits					22,500			22,500
46	Interest on S-T						275	970	655
47	Borrowing								
48	*Total Disbursements*			121,000	127,500	215,000	209,025	193,470	183,155
49									
50	*Net Monthly Change*			52,500	3,000	−85,000	−42,025	31,530	79,345
51									
52	Block 4: Bottom Line								
53									
54	Beginning Cash Balance			22,000	74,500	77,500	−7,500	20,000	20,000
55	Ending Cash (No Borrowing)			74,500	77,500	−7,500	−49,525	51,530	99,345
56	Needed (No Borrowing)			0	0	27,500	69,525	0	0
57	Loan Repayment			0	0	0	0	31,530	65,495
58	Ending Cash Balance			74,500	77,500	20,000	20,000	20,000	33,850
59	Cumulative Borrowing			0	0	27,500	97,025	65,495	0
60									

TABLE 12A-2. Cell Formulae for the Cramer Cash Budget Problem for November Through January

	A	B	C	D
23				
24	Block 3: Calculations			
25				
26				
27		November	December	January
28		220000	175000	=B19*(1+$C$10)
29	Collections			
30	Month of Sales			=$B$14*D28
31	First month			=$C$14*C28
32	Second month			=$D$14*B28
33	Total collections			=$D$26+D31+D32
34	Purchases	=$C$11*D28	=$C$11*E28	=$C$11*F28
35	Payments		=B34	=C34
36				
37	*Cash Budget*			January
38				
39	*Cash Receipts*			=D33
40	(collections)			
41	Cash Disbursements			
42	Payments for Purchases			=D35
43	Rent			10000
44	Other Expenditures			20000
45	Tax Deposits			
46	Interest on S-T			
47	Borrowing			
48	*Total Disbursements*			=SUM(D42..D47)
49				
50	*Net Monthly Change*			=D39-D48
51				
52	Block 4: Bottom Line			
53				
54	Beginning Cash Balance			=$C$8
55	Ending Cash (No Borrowing)			=D50+D54
56	Needed (Borrowing)			=IF(D55-$C$7>0,0,$C$7-D55
57	Loan Repayment			=IF((AND(C59>0,D55>$C$7)),MIN(C59,D55-$C$7),0)
58	Ending Cash Balance			=D50+D54+D56
59	Cumulative Borrowing			=D56

Perhaps the most interesting cell formulae in the spreadsheet model is found in Block 4 of the model where the debt repayment for the month is calculated. The cell formula for cell D53 is the following:

$$= IF((AND(C55>0,D51>\$C\$7)),MIN(C55,D51-\$C\$7),0)$$

This statement calculates the debt repayment. Note that the loan repayment is only made if two conditions are met. The firm is that the cumulative borrowing be greater than zero (C55>0) and, second, that the firm has excess cash on hand which can be used to repay a portion of the debt (D51>\$C\$7). If both these conditions are satisfied then the debt repayment is set equal to the minimum of the amount of short-term debt owed (cell C55) or the amount of excess cash over and above the desired minimum balance (D51−\$C\$7). The corresponding cell formula using Lotus 123 is slightly different and appears as follows:

$$@IF((C55>0\#AND\#D51>\$C\$7),@MIN(C55,D51-\$C\$7),0)$$

The result is the same in both instances, however. The cell formulae used in this example demonstrate that you can incorporate fairly sophisticated logic into your spreadsheet model.

SELECTED REFERENCES

Beyer, William E. "Liquidity Measurement in Corporate Forecasting," *Journal of Cash Management* (November–December 1988), 14–16.

Carleton, W. T. "An Analytical Model for Long-Range Financial Planning," *Journal of Finance*, 25 (May 1970), 291–315.

Carleton, W. T., C. L. Dick, and D. H. Downes. "Financial Policy Models: Theory and Practice," *Journal of Financial and Quantitative Analysis*, 8 (December 1973), 691–710.

Chambers, John C., Satinder K. Mullick, and Donald D. Smith. "How to Choose the Right Forecasting Technique," *Harvard Business Review*, 49 (July–August 1971), 45–74.

Francis, J. C., and D. R. Rowell. "A Simultaneous Equation Model of the Firm for Financial Analysis and Planning," *Financial Management* (Spring 1978), 29–44.

Parker, G. G. C., and E. L. Segura. "How to Get a Better Forecast," *Harvard Business Review*, 49 (March–April 1971), 99–109.

Seed, A. H., III. "Measuring Financial Performance in an Inflationary Environment," *Financial Executive* (January 1982), 40–50.

Weston, J. Fred. "Forecasting Financial Requirements," *Accounting Review*, 33 (July 1958), 427–440.

PART FIVE

Working Capital
Management

CHAPTER *13* *Introduction to Working-Capital Management*

- Managing Current Assets

- Managing the Firm's Use of Current Liabilities

- Appropriate Level of Working Capital

Traditionally, **working capital** has been defined as the firm's investment in current assets. **Current assets** are comprised of all assets that the firm expects to convert into cash within the year, including cash, marketable securities, accounts receivable, and inventories. Managing the firm's working capital, however, has come to mean more than simply managing the firm's investment in current assets. In fact, a more descriptive title for this chapter might be Net Working-Capital Management, where **net working capital** refers to the difference in the firm's current assets and its current liabilities:

$$\text{net working capital} = \text{current assets} - \text{current liabilities} \qquad (13\text{-}1)$$

Thus, in managing the firm's net working capital we are concerned with managing the firm's liquidity. This entails considering two related problems:

1. Managing the firm's investment in current assets;

2. Managing the firm's use of short-term or current liabilities.

Perspective in Finance

This chapter provides the basic principles underlying the analysis of each of these problems. These principles are then applied in each of the following chapters in this section. Specifically, Chapter 14 discusses the management of the firm's investment in cash and marketable securities, and Chapter 15 addresses the problems associated with managing the firm's investments in accounts receivable and inventories. Finally, Chapter 16 presents a discussion of sources of short-term or current liabilities and their role in the sound financial management of the firm.

MANAGING CURRENT ASSETS

We have examined the management of fixed-asset investments in Chapters 6 and 7. In each of these chapters the underlying principle was that investments were expected to generate future benefits. In this chapter a firm's investment into its accounts receivable and inventory will also be expected to generate future benefits. However, the firm will trade off some of these future benefits in order to establish a position of greater liquidity. Thus, our interest in the firm's investment decisions relates to their effects on the firm's net working capital and consequently its liquidity. The following chapters investigate the decision-making process in managing the firm's investment in specific current asset categories (cash and marketable securities in Chapter 14 and accounts receivable and inventories in Chapter 15).

Other things remaining the same, the greater the firm's investment in current assets, the greater its liquidity. As a means of increasing its liquidity, the firm may choose to invest additional funds in cash and/or marketable securities. Such action involves a tradeoff, however, since these assets earn little or no return. The firm thus finds that it can reduce its risk of illiquidity only by reducing its overall return on invested funds, and vice versa.

The Risk-Return Tradeoff from Investing in Current Assets

The **risk-return tradeoff** involved in managing the firm's liquidity via investing in marketable securities is illustrated in the following example. Firms A and B are identical in every respect but one: Firm B has invested $10,000 in marketable securities, which has been financed with common equity. That is, the firm sold common shares and raised $10,000. The balance sheets and net incomes of the two firms are shown in Table 13-1. Note that Firm A has a current ratio of 2.5 (reflecting net working capital of $30,000) and earns a 10 percent return on its total assets. Firm B, with its larger investment in marketable securities, has a current ratio of 3 and has net working capital of $40,000. Since the marketable securities earn a return of only 6 percent before taxes (3 percent after taxes with a 50 percent tax rate), Firm B earns only 9.6 percent on its total investment. Thus, investing in current assets, and, in particular, in marketable securities, does have a favourable effect on liquidity, but it also has an unfavourable effect on the firm's rate of return earned on invested funds. The risk-return tradeoff involved in holding more cash and marketable securities, therefore, is one of added liquidity versus reduced profitability.

MANAGING THE FIRM'S USE OF CURRENT LIABILITIES

The second and final determinant of the firm's net working capital relates to its use of current versus long-term debt. In this case, the firm faces a risk-return tradeoff. Other things remaining the same, the greater the firm's reliance upon

Balance Sheets		
	Firm A	Firm B
Cash	$ 1,000	$ 1,000
Marketable securities		10,000
Accounts receivable	19,000	19,000
Inventories	30,000	30,000
Current assets	$ 50,000	$ 60,000
Net fixed assets	100,000	100,000
Total	$150,000	$160,000
Current liabilities	$ 20,000	$ 20,000
Long-term debt	30,000	30,000
Common equity	100,000	110,000
Total	$150,000	$160,000
Net income	$ 15,000	$ 15,300[a]
Current ratio [current assets/current liabilities]	$\frac{\$50,000}{\$20,000} = 2.5$ times	$\frac{\$60,000}{\$20,000} = 3.0$ times
Net working capital [current assets/current liabilities]	$ 30,000	$ 40,000
Return on total assets [net income/total assets]	$\frac{\$15,000}{\$150,000} = 10\%$	$\frac{\$15,300}{\$160,000} = 9.6\%$

[a]During the year firm B held $10,000 in marketable securities, which earned a 6 percent return or $600 for the year. After paying taxes at a rate of 50 percent, the firm netted a $300 return on this investment.

short-term debt or current liabilities in financing its asset investments, the lower will be its liquidity. On the other hand, the use of current liabilities offers some very real advantages to the user in that they can be less costly than long-term financing, and they provide the firm with a flexible means of financing its fluctuating needs for assets. We will discuss each of the advantages and disadvantages associated with the use of current liabilities as a source of financing. In addition, we will give an example to demonstrate the risk-return tradeoff associated with the use of current versus long-term liabilities.

Advantages of Current Liabilities

Flexibility

Current liabilities offer the firm a flexible source of financing. They can be used to match the timing of a firm's needs for short-term financing. If, for example, a firm needs funds for a three-month period during each year to finance a seasonal expansion in inventories, then a three-month loan can provide substantial cost savings over a long-term loan (even if the interest rate on short-term financing should be higher). The fact that the use of long-term debt in this situation involves borrowing for the entire year rather than for the period when the funds are needed increases the amount of interest the firm must pay. This brings us to the second advantage generally associated with the use of short-term financing.

Interest Cost

In general, interest rates on short-term debt are lower than on long-term debt for a given borrower. This relationship was introduced in Chapter 2 and is referred to as the **term structure of interest rates**. For a given firm, the term structure might appear as follows:

Loan Maturity	Interest Rate
3 months	9.00%
6 months	9.25
1 year	9.80
3 years	10.20
5 years	10.90
10 years	11.40
30 years	12.80

Note that this term structure reflects the rates of interest applicable to a given borrower at a particular point in time; it would not, for example, describe the rates of interest available to another borrower or even those applicable to the same borrower at a different point in time.

Disadvantages of Current Liabilities

The use of current liabilities or short-term debt as opposed to long-term debt subjects the firm to a greater risk of illiquidity for two reasons.[1] First, short-term debt, due to its very nature, must be repaid or rolled over more often, and so it enhances the possibility that the firm's financial condition might deteriorate to a point where the needed funds might not be available.[2]

A second disadvantage of short-term debt is the uncertainty of interest costs from year to year. For example, where a firm borrows during a six-month period each year to finance a seasonal expansion in current assets, it might incur a different rate of interest each year. This rate reflects the current rate of interest at the time of the loan, as well as the lender's perception of the firm's riskiness. If fixed rate long-term debt were used, the interest cost would be known for the entire period of the loan agreement.

The Risk-Return Tradeoff from Using Current Liabilities

Consider the risk-return characteristics of firm X and firm Y, whose balance sheets and income statements are given in Table 13-2. Both firms had the same seasonal needs for financing throughout the past year. In December they each required $40,000 to finance a seasonal expansion in accounts receivable. In addition, during the four-month period beginning with August and extending through November, both firms needed $20,000 to support a seasonal buildup in inventories. Firm X financed its seasonal expansion in accounts receivable using $40,000 in long-term debt carrying an annual interest rate of 10 percent. Firm Y, on the other hand, satisfied its seasonal expansion in accounts receivable using short-term borrowing on which it

---

[1]Most current liabilities are financed with working-capital loans from banks. Many working capital loans have provisions that require the borrower to be debt-free over some period of the lending cycle.

[2]The dangers of such a policy are readily apparent in the experiences of firms that have experienced insolvency. For example, Olympia and York Developments Ltd. had to retire its program of selling commercial paper during the first quarter of 1992 because the company was experiencing a liquidity crisis.

Balance Sheets

	Firm X	Firm Y
Current assets	$ 60,000	$ 60,000
Net fixed assets	140,000	140,000
Total	$200,000	$200,000
Accounts payable	$ 20,000	$ 20,000
Notes payable	—	40,000
Current liabilities	$ 20,000	$ 60,000
Long-term debt	40,000	—
Common equity	140,000	140,000
Total	$200,000	$200,000

Income Statements

	Firm X	Firm Y
Net operating income	$44,000	$44,000
Less: Interest expense	4,000[a]	900[b]
Earnings before taxes	40,000	43,100
Less: Taxes (50%)	20,000	21,550
Net income	$20,000	$21,550

Current ratio $\left[\dfrac{\text{current assets}}{\text{current liabilities}}\right]$ $\dfrac{\$60,000}{\$20,000} = 3 \text{ times}$ $\dfrac{\$60,000}{\$60,000} = 1 \text{ time}$

Net working capital $\quad\quad\quad\quad\quad\quad\quad\quad\quad\quad \$40,000 \quad\quad\quad\quad\quad\quad\quad\quad \$0$
[current assets – current liabilities]

Return on total assets $\left[\dfrac{\text{net income}}{\text{total assets}}\right]$ $\dfrac{\$20,000}{\$200,000} = 10\%$ $\dfrac{\$21,550}{\$200,000} = 10.8\%$

[a]Firm X paid interest during the entire year on $40,000 in long-term debt at a rate of 10 percent. Its interest expense for the year was .10 × $40,000 = $4,000.

[b]Firm Y paid interest on $40,000 for one month and on $20,000 for four months at 9 percent interest during the year. Thus, Firm Y's interest expense for the year equals $40,000 × .09 × 1/12 plus $20,000 × .09 × 4/12, or $300 + $600 = $900.

paid 9 percent interest. Since firm Y borrowed only when it needed the funds and did so at the lower rate of interest on short-term debt, its interest expense for the year was only $900, whereas firm X incurred $4,000 in annual interest expense.[3]

The end result of the two firms' financing policies is evidenced in their current ratio, net working capital, and return on total assets, which appear at the bottom of Table 13-2. Firm X, using long-term rather than short-term debt, has a current ratio of 3 times and $40,000 in net working capital, whereas firm Y's current ratio is only 1, which represents zero net working capital. However, owing to its lower interest expense, firm Y was able to earn 10.8 percent on its invested funds, whereas firm X produced a 10 percent return. Thus, a firm can reduce its risk of illiquidity through the use of long-term debt at the expense of a reduction in its return on invested funds. Once again we see that the risk-return tradeoff involves an increased risk of illiquidity versus increased profitability.

[3]Interest expense calculations are found in the footnotes to Table 13-2.

BASIC FINANCIAL MANAGEMENT IN PRACTICE

How Firms Manage Their Working Capital

So how do firms manage their working capital? The following table provides aggregate percent of assets for six different industries and two time periods. The first column of percentages under each Canadian industry reflects the average for the corresponding industry for 1990 and the second column corresponds to 1986.

Current assets for the firms of these industries and years averaged 40.6 percent of total assets while current liabilities averaged 32.9 percent and long-term debt was only 18.9 percent. There is substantial variation in the relative importance of current assets across industries with electrical appliances—retail and book publishing having the highest percent of assets invested in current assets and hotels and restaurants having the lowest. With the exception of the hotel and restaurant industry current liabilities are greater than long-term debt.

So what can we conclude? First, current assets are a major component of a firm's investment and can constitute as much as 75% of the firm's assets. Second, most firms maintain current ratios greater than one although this relationship varies both across industries and over time. Finally, long-term debt is frequently a less important source of financing (measured in terms of its percent of assets) than current liabilities. The message then is this. Working capital management is extremely important to the firm's financial well being and deserves serious consideration!

Source: Industry averages are from: Statistics Canada "Detailed Balance Sheet Statistics for 182 Industries," (Corporation Financial Statistics, Catalogue 61-207, 1987) and Avery Leibowitz, "Financial Survey of Canadian Business Performance" (CCH Canadian Ltd., Don Mills, 1990). Reproduced with the permission of Minister of Industry, Science, and Technology, 1993.

	Electronic Appliances Retail		Book Publishing		Air Transport		Petroleum Refining		Gas Stations		Hotels Restaurants	
	1990	1986	1990	1986	1990	1986	1990	1986	1990	1986	1990	1986
Current Assets	76.2	62.8	59.4	63.2	26.1	25.3	30.1	24.1	43.6	43.7	17.8	14.7
Current Liabilities	45.9	45.5	46.3	46.3	26.9	26.3	18.9	17.6	35.8	35.2	26.6	23.4
Long-Term Debt	7.5	8.1	1.9	3.9	33.8	32.3	7.7	13.0	22.5	22.8	34.5	38.7

APPROPRIATE LEVEL OF WORKING CAPITAL

Managing the firm's net working capital (that is, its liquidity) has been shown to involve simultaneous and interrelated decisions regarding investment in current assets and use of current liabilities. Fortunately, a guiding principle exists that can be used as a benchmark for the firm's working-capital policies: the **hedging principle**, or **principle of self-liquidating debt**. This principle provides a guide to the maintenance of a level of liquidity sufficient for the firm to meet its maturing obligations on time.[4]

___

[4]A value-maximizing approach to the management of the firm's liquidity would involve assessing the value of the benefits derived from increasing the firm's investment in liquid assets and weighing them against the added costs to the firm's owners resulting from investing in low-yielding current assets. Unfortunately, the benefits derived from increased liquidity relate to the expected costs of bankruptcy to the firm's owners, and these costs are "unmeasurable" by existing technology. Thus, a "valuation" approach to liquidity management exists only in the theoretical realm.

Perspective in Finance

In Chapter 9 we discussed the firm's financing decision in terms of the choice between debt and equity sources of financing. However, there is yet another critical dimension of the firm's financing decision. This relates to the maturity structure of the firm's debt. How should the decision be made as to whether to use short-term or current debt or longer maturity debt? This is one of the fundamental questions addressed in this chapter and one that is critically important to the financial success of the firm. Basically, the hedging principle is one possible rule of thumb for guiding a firm's debt maturity financing decisions. This principle states that financing maturity should follow the cash-generating characteristics of the asset being financed. For example, an asset that is expected to provide cash flows over an extended period of time such as five years should, in accordance with the hedging principle, be financed with debt instruments that have a pattern of similar cash flow requirements. Note that if the hedging principle is followed, the firm's debt will "self liquidate" since the assets being financed will generally provide sufficient cash to retire the debt as it comes due.

Hedging Principle

Very simply, the hedging principle involves matching the cash-flow-generating characteristics of an asset with the maturity of the source of financing used to finance its acquisition. For example, a seasonal expansion in inventories, according to the hedging principle, should be financed with a short-term loan or current liability. The rationale underlying the rule is straightforward. Funds are needed for a limited period of time, and when that time has passed, the cash needed to repay the loan will be generated by the sale of the extra inventory items. Obtaining the needed funds from a long-term source (longer than one year) would mean that the firm would still have the funds after the inventories they helped finance had been sold. In this case the firm would have "excess" liquidity, which it either holds in cash or invests in low-yield marketable securities until the seasonal increase in inventories occurs again and the funds are needed. This would result in an overall lowering of firm profits, as we saw earlier in the example presented in Table 13-2.

Consider a second example in which a firm purchases a new conveyor belt system, which is expected to produce cash savings to the firm by eliminating the need for two labourers and, consequently, their salaries. This amounts to an annual savings of $14,000, while the conveyor belt costs $150,000 to install and will last 20 years. If the firm chooses to finance this asset with a one-year note, then it will not be able to repay the loan from the cash flow generated by the asset. In accordance with the hedging principle, the firm should finance the asset with a source of financing that more nearly matches the expected life and cash-generating characteristics of the asset.[5] In this case, a 15- to 20-year loan would be more appropriate.

---

[5]The maturity-matching concept is roughly equivalent to an immunization strategy based upon the concept of duration. Immunization provides protection from interest rate exposure, while the maturity-matching concept as it is applied to working capital management is intended to match up operating cash flows with cash flow requirements of the firm's financing sources. Maturity matching does not insure the firm against the risks of uncertain cash flow shortfalls but attempts simply to match up the expected cash flow producing capacity of the firm's assets with the cash flow requirements of the assets being financed.

Permanent and Temporary Assets

The notion of maturity matching in the hedging principle can be most easily understood when we think in terms of the distinction between permanent and temporary investments in assets as opposed to the more traditional fixed and current asset categories. A **permanent investment** in an asset is an investment that the firm expects to hold for a period longer than one year. Note that we are referring to the period of time the firm plans to hold an investment, and not the useful life of the asset. For example, permanent investments are made in the firm's minimum level of current assets, as well as in its fixed assets. **Temporary investments**, on the other hand, are comprised of current assets that will be liquidated and not replaced within the current year. Thus, some part of the firm's current assets is permanent and the remainder is temporary. For example, a seasonal increase in level of inventories is a temporary investment; the buildup in inventories will be eliminated when it is no longer needed.

Spontaneous, Temporary, and Permanent Sources of Financing

Since total assets must always equal the sum of spontaneous, temporary, and permanent sources of financing, the hedging approach provides the financial manager with the basis for determining the sources of financing to use at any point in time.

Now, what constitutes a temporary, permanent, and spontaneous source of financing? Temporary sources of financing consist of current liabilities. Short-term notes payable (discussed in Chapter 16) constitute the most common example of a temporary source of financing. Examples of notes payable include unsecured bank loans, commercial paper, and loans secured by accounts receivable and inventories. Permanent sources of financing include intermediate-term loans (discussed in Chapter 18), long-term debt, preferred shares, and common equity (discussed in Chapter 19).

Trade credit and other types of accounts payable are spontaneous sources of financing which expand or contract as a result of the level of a firm's business activity. For example, as the firm acquires materials for its inventories, the firm's suppliers will provide trade credit to the firm on demand. Once trade credit is granted, this source of financing is said to occur spontaneously with increasing or decreasing levels of business activity. Trade credit appears on the firm's balance sheet as accounts payable, and the size of the accounts payable balance varies directly with the firm's purchases of inventory items. In turn, inventory purchases are related to anticipated sales. Thus, part of the financing needed by the firm is spontaneously provided in the form of trade credit.

In addition to trade credit, wages and salaries payable, accrued interest, and accrued taxes also provide valuable sources of spontaneous financing. These expenses accrue throughout the period until they are paid. For example, if a firm has a wage expense of $10,000 a week and pays its employees monthly, then its employees effectively provide financing equal to $10,000 by the end of the first week following a payday, $20,000 by the end of the second week, and so forth. Since these expenses generally arise in direct conjunction with the firm's ongoing level of operations, they too are referred to as *spontaneous*.

Hedging Principle: Graphic Illustration

The hedging principle can now be stated very succinctly—Asset needs of the firm not financed by spontaneous sources should be financed in accordance with this rule: Permanent asset investments are financed with permanent sources, and temporary investments are financed with temporary sources.

The hedging principle is depicted in Figure 13-1. Total assets are broken down into temporary and permanent asset investment categories. The firm's permanent investment in assets is financed by the use of permanent sources of financing (intermediate- and long-term debt, preferred shares, and common equity) or spontaneous sources (trade credit and other accounts payable).[6] Its temporary investment in assets is financed with temporary (short-term) debt.

Modifications to the Hedging Principle

Figures 13-2 and 13-3 depict two modifications of the strict hedging approach to working-capital management. In Figure 13-2 the firm follows a more cautious plan whereby permanent sources of financing exceed permanent assets in the trough of the asset cycle so that excess cash is available (which must be invested in marketable securities).[7] Note that the firm actually has excess liquidity during the low ebb of its asset cycle, and thus faces a lower risk of being caught short of cash than a firm that follows the pure hedging approach. However, the firm also increases its investment in relatively low-yielding assets so that its return on investment is diminished (recall the example from Table 13-1).

FIGURE 13-1
Hedging Financing Strategy

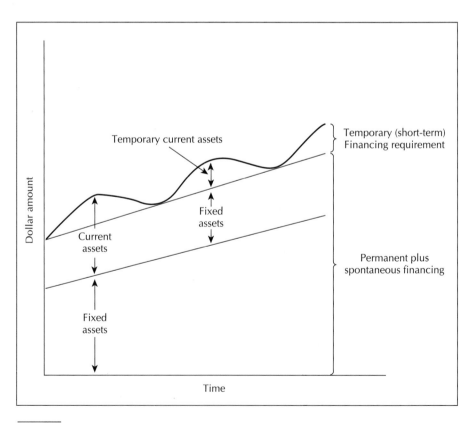

[6]For illustration purposes, spontaneous sources of financing are treated as if their amount were fixed. In practice, of course, spontaneous sources of financing fluctuate with the firm's purchases and its expenditures for wages, salaries, taxes, and other items that are paid on a delayed basis.

[7]Marketable securities and cash management are discussed in Chapter 14.

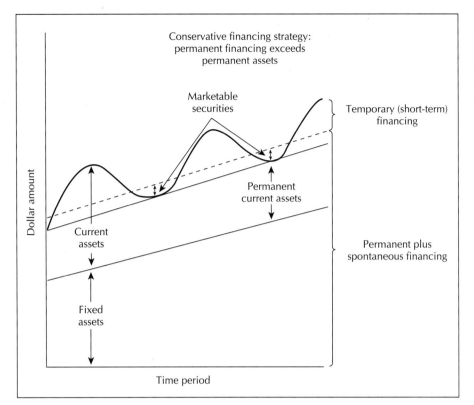

FIGURE 13-2
Conservative Financing Strategy: Spontaneous Plus Permanent Sources of Financing Exceed Permanent Assets

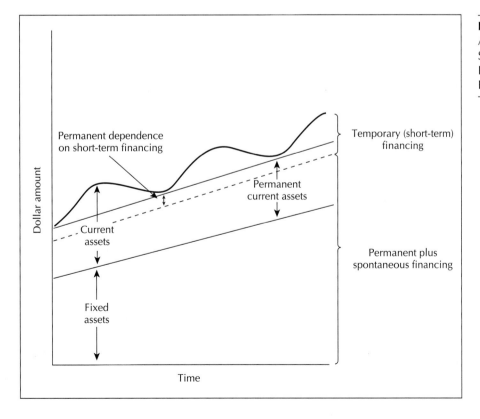

FIGURE 13-3
Aggressive Financing Strategy: Permanent Reliance on Short-Term Financing

In contrast, Figure 13-3 depicts a firm that continually finances a part of its permanent asset needs with temporary or short-term funds and thus follows a more aggressive strategy in managing its working capital. Even when its investment in asset needs is lowest, the firm must still rely on short-term or temporary financing. Such a firm would be subject to increased risks of a cash shortfall in that it must depend on a continual rollover or replacement of its short-term debt with more short-term debt. The benefit derived from following such a policy relates to the possible savings resulting from the use of lower-cost short-term debt (as opposed to long-term debt—recall the example presented in Table 13-2).

Most firms will not exclusively follow any one of the three strategies outlined here in determining their reliance on short-term credit. Instead, a firm will at times find itself overly reliant on permanent financing and thus holding excess cash; at other times it may have to rely on short-term financing throughout an entire operating cycle. The hedging approach does, however, provide an important benchmark that can be used to guide decisions regarding the appropriate use of short-term credit.

SUMMARY

Working-capital management involves managing the firm's liquidity, which, in turn, involves managing (1) the firm's investment in current assets and (2) its use of current liabilities. Each of these problems involves risk-return tradeoffs. Investing in current assets reduces the firm's risk of illiquidity at the expense of lowering its overall rate of return on its investment in assets. Furthermore, the use of long-term sources of financing enhances the firm's liquidity while reducing its rate of return on assets.

The hedging principle, or principle of self-liquidating debt, is a benchmark for working-capital decisions. Basically, this principle involves matching the cash-flow-generating characteristics of an asset with the cash flow requirements of the source of funds used to finance its acquisition.

Chapters 14 and 15 discuss the problems involved in managing the firm's investment in current assets. This includes the management of cash, marketable securities, accounts receivable, and inventories. Chapter 16 discusses short-term financing. Two basic problems are encountered in attempting to manage the firm's use of short-term financing: (1) How much short-term financing should the firm use? (2) What specific sources should be selected? This chapter has addressed the first of these questions with the hedging or self-liquidating-debt principle. The answer to the second question involves analyzing the relative costs of the available sources of short-term credit, an issue addressed at length in Chapter 16.

STUDY QUESTIONS

13-1. Define and contrast the terms *working capital* and *net working capital*.

13-2. Discuss the risk-return relationship involved in the firm's asset investment decisions as it pertains to working-capital management.

13-3. What advantages and disadvantages are generally associated with the use of short-term debt? Discuss.

13-4. Explain what is meant by the statement "The use of current liabilities as opposed to long-term debt subjects the firm to a greater risk of illiquidity."

13-5. Define the hedging principle. How can this principle be used in the management of working capital?

13-6. Define the following terms:

a. Permanent asset investments

b. Temporary asset investments

c. Permanent sources of financing

d. Temporary sources of financing

e. Spontaneous sources of financing

SELF-TEST PROBLEMS

ST-1. (*Investing in Current Assets and the Return on Common Equity*) Walker Enterprises is presently evaluating its investment in working capital for the coming year. Specifically, the firm is analyzing its level of investment in current assets. The firm projects that it will have sales of $4,000,000 next year, and its fixed assets are projected to total $1,500,000. The firm pays interest at a rate of 10 percent on its short- and long-term debt (which is managed by the firm so as to equal a target of 40 percent of assets). The firm projects its earnings before interest and taxes to be 15 percent of sales and faces a 30 percent tax rate.

a. If Walker decides to follow a working-capital strategy calling for current assets equal to 40 percent of sales, what will be the firm's return on common equity?

b. Answer (a) for a current asset to sales ratio of 60 percent.

c. Throughout our analysis we have assumed that the rate of return earned by the firm on sales is independent of its investment in current assets. Is this a valid assumption?

ST-2. (*Using Marketable Securities to Increase Liquidity*) The balance sheet for the Simplex Mfg. Co. is presented below for the year ended December 31, 19X3:

Simplex Mfg. Co. Balance Sheet December 31, 19X3		
Cash	$10,000	
Accounts receivable	50,000	
Inventories	40,000	
Total current assets		$100,000
Net fixed assets		100,000
Total		$200,000
Current liabilities		$ 60,000
Long-term liabilities		40,000
Common equity		100,000
Total		$200,000

During 19X3 the firm earned net income after taxes of $20,000 based on net sales of $400,000.

a. Calculate Simplex's current ratio, net working-capital position, and return on total assets ratio (net income/total assets) using the above information.

b. The vice-president for finance at Simplex is considering a plan for enhancing the firm's liquidity. The plan involves raising $20,000 in common equity and investing in marketable securities that will earn 8 percent before taxes and 4.8 percent after taxes. Calculate Simplex's current ratio, net working capital, and return on total asset ratio after the plan has been implemented. (*Hint:* Net income will now become $20,000, plus .048 times $20,000, or $20,960.)

c. Will the plan proposed in (b) enhance firm liquidity? Explain.

d. What effect does the plan proposed in (b) have on firm profitability? Explain.

ST-3. (*Using Long-Term Debt to Increase Liquidity*) On April 30, 19X3, the Jamax Sales Company had the following balance sheet and income statement for the year just ended:

Jamax Sales Company Balance Sheet April 30, 19X3

Current assets		$100,000
Net fixed assets		200,000
Total		$300,000
Accounts payable	$30,000	
Notes payable (14%)[a]	40,000	
Total		$ 70,000
Long-term debt (10%)		100,000
Common equity		130,000
Total		$300,000

Partial Income Statement for the year ended April 30, 19X3

Net operating income	$72,800
Less: Interest expense[b]	12,800
Earnings before taxes	$60,000
Less: Taxes (50%)	30,000
Net income	$30,000

---

[a]The short-term notes are outstanding during the latter half of the firm's fiscal year in response to the firm's seasonal need for funds.

[b]Total interest expense for the year consists of 14% interest on the firm's $40,000 note for a six-month period (.14 × $40,000 × 1/2), $2,800, plus 10% of the firm's $100,000 long-term note for a full year (.10 × $100,000), or $10,000. Thus, total interest expense for the year is $2,800, plus $10,000 or $12,800.

a. Calculate Jamax's current ratio, net working capital, and return on total assets.

b. The treasurer of Jamax was recently advised by the firm's investment dealer that its current ratio was considered below par. In fact, a current ratio of 2.00 was considered to be a sign of a healthy liquidity position. In response to this news the treasurer devised a plan wherein the firm would issue $40,000 in 13 percent long-term debt and pay off its short-term notes payable. This long-term note would be outstanding all year long, and when the funds were not needed to finance the firm's seasonal asset needs, they would be invested in marketable securities earning 8 percent before taxes. If the plan had been in effect last year, other things being the same, what would have been the firm's current ratio, net working capital, and return on total assets ratio? [*Hint:* The firm's net income with the change would have been $29,600.]

c. Did Jamax's liquidity improve to the desired level (based on a desired current ratio of 2.0)?

d. How was the firm's profitability in relation to total investment affected by the change in financial policy?

13-1A. (*Investing in Current Assets and the Return on Common Equity*) In June the MacMinn Company began planning for the coming year. A primary concern is its working-capital management policy. In particular, the firm's management is considering the effects of its investment in current assets on the return earned on common shareholders' equity. The firm projects that it will have sales of $8,000,000 next year, and its fixed assets are projected to total $2,000,000. It pays interest at a rate of 12 percent on its short- and long-term debt (which is managed by the firm so as to equal a target of 30 percent of assets). Finally, the firm projects its earnings before interest and taxes to be 15 percent of sales and faces a 30 percent tax rate.

    a. If MacMinn decides to follow a working-capital strategy calling for current assets equal to 40 percent of sales, what will be the firm's return on common equity?

    b. Answer (a) for a current-asset-to-sales ratio of 60 percent.

    c. Throughout our analysis we have assumed that the rate of return earned by the firm on sales is independent of its investment in current assets. Is this a valid assumption?

13-2A. (*Managing Firm Liquidity*) On September 30, 19X3, the balance sheet and income statement for Trecor Mfg. Company appeared as follows:

Trecor Mfg. Company Balance Sheet
September 30, 19X3

Current assets	$ 500,000
Net fixed assets	500,000
Total	$1,000,000
Accounts payable	$ 100,000
Notes payable (17%)[a]	400,000
Total	$ 500,000
Long-term debt (12%)	100,000
Common equity	400,000
Total	$1,000,000

[a]Short-term notes are used to finance a three-month seasonal expansion in Trecor's asset needs. This period is the same for every year and extends from July through September with the note being due October 1.

Trecor Mfg. Company Income Statement
September 30, 19X3

Net operating income	$195,666
Less: Interest expense[b]	(29,000)
Earnings before taxes	166,666
Less: Taxes (40%)	(66,666)
Net income	$100,000

[b]Interest expense was calculated as follows:

Notes payable (.17 × $400,000 × 1/4 year)	= $17,000
Long-term debt (.12 × $100,000 × 1 year)	= 12,000
Total	= $29,000

a. Calculate the current ratio, net working capital, return on total assets, and return on common equity ratio for Trecor.

b. Assume that you have just been hired as financial vice-president of Trecor. One of your first duties is to assess the firm's liquidity position. Based upon your analysis, you plan to issue $400,000 in common shares and use the proceeds to retire the firm's notes payable. Recalculate the ratios from (a) and assess the change in the firm's liquidity.

c. Given your actions in (b), assume now that in the future you will finance your three-month seasonal need for $400,000 using a long-term bond issue that will carry an interest cost of 15 percent. (Note that during the time the funds are needed your current assets increase by $400,000 because of increased inventories and receivables.) In addition, you estimate that during the nine months you do not need the funds, they can be invested in marketable securities to earn a rate of 10 percent. Recalculate the financial ratios from (a) for 19X4 where all revenues and nonfinance expenses are expected to be the same as in 19X3. Analyze the results of your plan.

13-3A. (*Managing Firm Liquidity*) Re-analyze (c) of problem 13-2A assuming that a three-month short-term note is used as opposed to the bonds. The note carries a rate of 15 percent per annum.

13-4A. (*The Hedging Principle*) H. O. Hielregal, Inc., estimates that its current assets are about 25 percent of sales. The firm's current balance sheet is presented below:

H. O. Hielregal Balance Sheet
December 31, 19X3 ($ millions)

Current assets	$2.0	Trade credit and	
Fixed assets	2.8	accounts payable	$ .8
		Long-term debt	1.0
Total	$4.8	Common equity	3.0
		Total	$4.8

Hielregal pays out all of its net income in cash dividends to its shareholders. Trade credit and accounts payable equal 10 percent of the firm's sales.

a. Based on the following five-year sales forecast, prepare five end-of-year pro forma balance sheets that indicate "additional financing needed" for each year as a balancing account. Fixed assets are expected to increase by $0.2 million each year.

Year	Predicted Sales ($ Millions)
19X4	10
19X5	11
19X6	13
19X7	14
19X8	15

b. Develop a financing policy for Hielregal using your answer to (a) above that is consistent with the following goals:

1. A minimum current ratio of 2.0 and a maximum of 3.0.

2. A debt-to-total-assets ratio of 35–45 percent. You may issue new common shares to raise equity funds.

13-1B. (*Investing in Current Assets and the Return on Common Equity*) The managers of Tharp's Tarps, Inc., are considering a possible change in their working-capital management policy. Specifically, they are concerned with the effect of their investment in current assets on the return earned on common shareholders' equity. They expect sales of $7,000,000 next year, and their fixed assets are projected to total $2,000,000. The firm pays 11 percent interest on both short- and long-term debt (which is managed by the firm so as to equal a target of 30 percent of assets) and faces a 30 percent tax rate. Finally, the firm projects its earnings before interest and taxes to be 15 percent of sales.

    a. If management follows a working-capital strategy calling for current assets equal to 50 percent of sales, what will be the firm's return on common equity?

    b. Answer (a) for a current-asset-to-sales ratio of 40 percent.

    c. Is it reasonable to assume, as we did, that the rate of return earned by the firm on sales is independent of its investment in current assets?

13-2B. (*Managing Firm Liquidity*) As of September 30, 19X1, the balance sheet and income statement of No-Soy Foods, Inc., appeared as follows:

No-Soy Foods, Inc.
Balance Sheet September 30, 19X1

Current assets	$ 625,000
Net fixed assets	400,000
Total	$1,025,000
Accounts payable	$ 125,000
Notes payable (17%)[a]	400,000
Total	$ 525,000
Long-term debt (12%)	100,000
Common equity	400,000
Total	$1,025,000

[a]Short-term notes are used to finance a three-month seasonal expansion in No-Soy Foods asset needs. This period is the same for every year and extends from July through September with the note being due October 1.

No-Soy Foods, Inc. Income Statement
September 30, 19X1

Net operating income	$195,666
Less: Interest expense[b]	(29,000)
Earnings before taxes	166,666
Less: Taxes (40%)	(66,666)
Net income	$100,000

[b]Interest expense was calculated as follows:

Notes payable (.17 × $400,000 × 1/4 year)	= $17,000
Long-term debt (.12 × $100,000 × 1 year)	= 12,000
Total	= $29,000

a. Calculate the current ratio, net working capital, return on total assets, and return on common equity ratio for No-Soy.

b. Assume that you have just been hired as financial vice-president of No-Soy. One of your first duties is to assess the firm's liquidity position. Based upon your analysis, you plan to issue $400,000 in common shares and use the proceeds to retire the firm's notes payable. Recalculate the ratios from (a) and assess the change in the firm's liquidity.

c. Given your actions in (b), assume now that in the future you will finance your three-month seasonal need for $450,000 using a long-term bond issue that will carry an interest cost of 15 percent. (Note that during the time the funds are needed your current assets increase by $450,000 because of increased inventories and receivables.) In addition, you estimate that during the nine months you do not need the funds, they can be invested in marketable securities to earn a rate of 10 percent. Recalculate the financial ratios from (a) for 19X2 where all revenues and nonfinance expenses are expected to be the same as in 19X1. Analyze the results of your plan.

13-3B. (*Managing Firm Liquidity*) Re-analyze (c) of Problem 13-2B assuming that a three-month short-term note is used as opposed to the bonds. The note carries a rate of 15 percent per annum.

13-4B. (*The Hedging Principle*) B. A. Freeman, Inc., successfully sells bail bond franchises throughout the country. Its founder, Mr. Freeman, estimates current assets to be 30 percent of sales. The firm's current balance sheet is as follows:

B. A. Freeman Balance Sheet
December 31, 19X3 ($ millions)

Current assets	$2.0	Trade credit and	
Fixed assets	2.8	accounts payable	$ .8
		Long-term debt	1.0
Total	$4.8	Common equity	3.0
		Total	$4.8

Freeman pays out all of its net income in cash dividends to its shareholders. Trade credit and accounts payable equal 10 percent of the firm's sales.

a. Based on the following five-year sales forecast, prepare five end-of-year pro forma balance sheets that indicate "additional financing needed" for each year as a balancing account. Fixed assets are expected to increase by $.3 million each year.

Year	Predicted Sales ($ Millions)
19X2	10
19X3	11
19X4	13
19X5	14
19X6	15

b. Develop a financing policy for Freeman using your answer to (a) that is consistent with the following goals:

1. A minimum current ratio of 2.5 and a maximum of 3.5.

2. A debt-to-total-assets ratio of 35–45 percent. You may issue new common shares to raise equity funds.

SS-1. a. Walker's pro forma balance sheet for next year will appear as follows:

Current assets	$1,600,000	Debt (40% of assets)	$1,240,000
Fixed assets	1,500,000	Owner's equity	1,860,000
Total	$3,100,000	Total	$3,100,000

Projected earnings are calculated as follows:

Sales	$4,000,000
EBIT (15%)	600,000
Interest	(124,000)
EBT	$ 476,000
Taxes	(142,800)
Net income	$ 333,200

Thus, the firm's return on common equity is

$$\frac{\$333,200}{\$1,860,000} = 17.9\%$$

SS-1. b. Under this scenario, Walker's pro forma balance sheet for next year will appear as follows:

Current assets	$2,400,000	Debt (40% of assets)	$1,560,000
Fixed assets	1,500,000	Owner's equity	2,340,000
Total	$3,900,000	Total	$3,900,000

Projected earnings are calculated as follows:

Sales	$4,000,000
EBIT (15%)	600,000
Interest	(156,000)
EBT	$ 444,000
Taxes	(133,200)
Net income	$ 310,800

Thus, the firm's return on common equity is

$$\frac{\$310,800}{\$3,900,000} = 13.3 \text{ percent}$$

c. One would expect that the firm would earn some positive return from investing in current assets. For example, the firm could hold some of its current assets in marketable securities earning some positive rate of return. Note, however, that as long as these current assets earn a rate of return less than the cost of financing the investment, the rate of return on the common shareholders' equity will decrease with increased investment in current assets.

CHAPTER *14* *Cash and Marketable Securities Management*

- Why a Company Holds Cash
- Variations in Liquid Asset Holdings
- Cash Management Objectives and Decisions
- Collection and Disbursement Procedures
- Electronic Funds Transfer
- Evaluating Costs of Cash-Management Services
- Composition of Marketable Securities Portfolio
- A Glance at Actual Cash-Management Practices

Chapter 13 introduced the concept of working-capital management. Now we will consider the various elements of the firm's working capital in some depth. This chapter and Appendix 14A centre on the formulation of financial policies for management of cash and marketable securities. We explore three major areas: (1) management techniques used to favourably influence cash receipts and disbursements patterns, (2) sensible investment possibilities that enable the company productively to employ excess cash balances, and (3) some straightforward models that can assist financial managers in deciding on how much cash to hold. Appendix 14A presents these models.

First it will be helpful to distinguish among some terms. **Cash** is the currency and coin the firm has on hand in petty cash drawers, in cash registers, or in chequing accounts at the various commercial banks where its demand deposits are maintained. **Marketable securities** are those security investments the firm can quickly convert into cash balances. Most firms in Canada tend to hold marketable securities with very short maturity periods—less than one year. No law, of course, dictates that instruments with longer terms to maturity must be avoided. Rather, the decision to keep the average maturity quite short is based upon some sound business reasoning, which will be discussed later. Marketable securities are also referred to as **near cash** or **near-cash assets** because they can be turned into cash in a short period of time. Taken together, cash and near cash are known as **liquid assets**.

Perspective in Finance

It is useful to think of the firm's cash balance as a reservoir that rises with cash inflows and falls with cash outflows. Any nonfinancial firm, such as Northern Telecom, desires to minimize its cash balances consistent with meeting its financial obligations in a timely manner.

Holding too much cash—what analysts tend to call "excess cash"—results in

610

a loss of profitability to the firm. The auto manufacturer, for example, is not in business to build up its cash reservoir. Rather, it wants to manage its cash balance in order to maximize its financial returns—this will enhance shareholder wealth.

Our emphasis in this chapter is to learn how to effectively manage the firm's cash and marketable securities investments. We begin with a review of the basic cash flow process and the motives that economic units have for holding cash balances. In recent years the financial function of cash management has grown to the extent that trade associations and professional certifications exist just for this function. The cash management function is usually considered part of treasury management in the company.

WHY A COMPANY HOLDS CASH

A thorough understanding of why and how a firm holds cash requires an accurate conception of how cash flows into and through the enterprise. Figure 14-1 depicts the process of cash generation and disposition in a typical manufacturing setting. The arrows designate the direction of the flow—that is, whether the cash balance increases or decreases.

Cash Flow Process

The firm experiences irregular increases in its cash holdings from several external sources. Funds can be obtained in the financial markets from the

FIGURE 14-1. The Cash Generation and Disposition Process sale of securities, such as bonds, preferred shares, and common shares, or the firm can enter into nonmarketable debt contracts with lenders such as commercial banks. These irregular cash inflows do not occur on a daily basis. They tend to be episodic; the financing arrangements that give rise to them are effected at wide intervals. The reason is that external financing contracts usually involve huge sums of money stemming from a major need identified by the company's management, and these needs do not occur every day. For example, a new product might be at the development stage, or a plant expansion might be required to provide added productive capacity.

In most organizations the financial manager responsible for cash management also controls the transactions that affect the firm's investment in marketable securities. As excess cash becomes temporarily available, marketable securities are purchased. When cash is in short supply, a portion of the marketable securities portfolio is liquidated.

Whereas the irregular cash inflows are from external sources, the other main sources of cash to the firm arise from internal operations and occur on a more regular basis. Over long periods, the largest receipts come from accounts receivable collections and to a lesser extent from direct cash sales of finished goods. Many manufacturing concerns also generate cash on a regular basis through the liquidation of scrap or obsolete inventory. In the automobile industry, large and costly machines called chip crushers grind waste metal into fine scrap which brings considerable revenue to the major producers. At various times fixed assets may also be sold, thereby generating some cash inflow. This is not a large source of funds except in unusual situations where, for instance, a complete plant renovation may be taking place.

Apart from the investment of excess cash in near-cash assets, the cash balance decreases for three key reasons. First, on an irregular basis withdrawals are made to (1) pay cash dividends on preferred and common shares, (2) meet interest requirements on debt contracts, (3) repay the principal borrowed from creditors, (4) buy the firm's own shares in the financial markets for use in executive compensation plans or as an alternative to paying a cash dividend, and (5) pay tax bills. Again, by an "irregular basis" we mean items not occurring on a daily or frequent schedule. Second, the company's capital expenditure program designates that fixed assets be acquired at various intervals. Third, inventories are purchased on a regular basis to ensure a steady flow of finished goods off the production line. Note that the arrow linking the investment in fixed assets with the inventory account is labelled *depreciation*. This indicates that a portion of the cost of fixed assets is charged against the products coming off the assembly line. This cost is subsequently recovered through the sale of the finished goods inventory, since the product selling price will be set by management to cover all the costs of production, including depreciation.

The variety of influences that constantly affect the cash balance held by the firm can be synthesized in terms of the classic motives for holding cash, as identified in the literature of economic theory.

Motives for Holding Cash

In a classic economic treatise John Maynard Keynes segmented the firm's, or any economic unit's, demand for cash into three categories: (1) the transactions motive, (2) the precautionary motive, and (3) the speculative motive.[1]

[1] John Maynard Keynes, *The General Theory of Employment, Interest, and Money* (New York: Harcourt Brace Jovanovich, 1936).

Transactions Motive

Balances held for transactions purposes allow the firm to dispense with cash needs that arise in the ordinary course of doing business. In Figure 14-1, transactions balances would be used to meet the irregular outflows as well as the planned acquisition of fixed assets and inventories.

The relative amount of transactions cash held is significantly affected by the industry in which the firm operates. If revenues can be forecast to fall within a tight range of outcomes, then the ratio of cash and near cash to total assets will be less for the firm than if the prospective cash inflows might be expected to vary over a wide range. It is well known that utilities can forecast cash receipts quite accurately, because of stable demand for their services. This enables the firm to stagger its billings throughout the month and to time them to coincide with planned expenditures. Inflows and outflows of cash are thus synchronized. We would expect the cash holdings of utility firms relative to sales or assets to be less than those associated with a major clothing retailer which has a more variable demand.

Firms competing in the same industry may experience notably different strains on their cash balances. Transactions balances for the juice processing industry are influenced by a seasonal factor. During the summer and autumn months, most juice processors within Canada will incur a large part of their operating expenses for raw materials and labour necessary for picking, grading and processing of fruits. As a result, juice processors in Canada will suffer sizable cash drains throughout the summer and autumn seasons. Cash balances for juice processors in Canada will therefore be expected to be relatively higher during the summer and autumn seasons than that of juice processors operating in more southerly areas of the United States where processing may occur on annual basis.

The Precautionary Motive

Precautionary balances are a buffer stock of liquid assets. This motive for holding cash relates to the maintenance of balances to be used to satisfy possible, but as yet indefinite, needs.

In our discussion of transactions balances, we saw that cash flow predictability could affect a firm's cash holdings through synchronization of receipts and disbursements. Cash flow predictability also has a material influence on the firm's demand for cash through the precautionary motive. The airline industry provides a typical illustration. Air passenger carriers are plagued with a high degree of cash flow uncertainty. The weather, rising fuel costs, and continual strikes by operating personnel make cash forecasting difficult for any airline. The upshot of this problem is that because of all the things that might happen, the minimum cash balances desired by the management of the air carriers tend to be large.

In addition to cash flow predictability, the precautionary motive for holding cash is affected by access to external funds.[2] Especially important are cash sources that can be tapped on short notice. Good banking relationships and established lines of credit can reduce the need to keep cash on hand. This unused borrowing power obviates somewhat the need to invest in precautionary balances.

---

[2]According to Keynes, the precautionary motive for holding cash would be greatly increased in the absence of financial markets.

In actual business practice, the precautionary motive is met to a large extent by the holding of a portfolio of liquid assets, not just cash. Notice in Figure 14-1 the two-way flow of funds between the company's holdings of cash and marketable securities. In large corporate organizations, funds may flow either into or out of the marketable securities portfolio on a daily basis. In this type of organization, the precautionary motive will be met by investment in marketable securities because some actual rate of return can be earned on the near-cash assets as compared to a zero rate of return available on cash holdings.

The Speculative Motive

Cash is held for speculative purposes in order to take advantage of potential profit-making situations.[3] Construction firms that build private dwellings will at times accumulate cash in anticipation of a significant drop in lumber costs. If the price of building supplies does drop, the companies that built up their cash balances stand to profit by purchasing materials in large quantities. This will reduce their cost of goods sold and increase their net profit margin. Generally, the speculative motive is the least important component of a firm's preference for liquidity. The transactions and precautionary motives account for most of the reasons why a company holds cash balances.

VARIATIONS IN LIQUID ASSET HOLDINGS

Decisions that concern the amounts of liquid assets to hold rest with the financial manager responsible for cash management. A number of factors that can be expected to influence the financial manager's investment in cash or liquid assets have just been reviewed. Not all these factors affect every firm. Moreover, factors that do affect many companies do so in differing degrees. Since cash management choices have different risk-bearing preferences, we might expect that holdings of liquid assets among industries and firms show considerable variation.

Table 14-1 shows that both utility industries, telephone, telegraph and cable systems and electric power hold a small proportion of its total assets in the form of liquid assets—7.3% and 3.4% respectively. Both of these utility industries operate in an environment where cash flows are highly predictable relative to other industries. Table 14-1 suggests that industries which compete in a more risky global arena, such as retailing of motor vehicles or the manufacturing of paper, boxes, and bags, there is considerable variation in the holding of cash and liquid assets. This type of variation can be attributed to factors such as the state of the economy, management credit policies and management's risk preferences. For example, in the early nineties the North American economy fell into a period of recession. During this period most consumers postponed the purchases of large-ticket items such as cars and trucks. The difficulty of accurately predicting sales demand in the retailing of motor vehicles caused many retailers to carry more of their assets as liquid assets. Companies continually adjust their liquid asset

[3]Likewise Keynes indicated that the speculative motive for holding cash will increase with the existence of financial markets.

	Cash and Equivalents[a] %	Total Liquid Assets[a] %
Electric Power	0.006	3.4
Telephone, Telegraph and Cable Systems	0.084	7.3
Food Stores—Retailing	4.86	8.7
Publishing	2.73	25.8
Paint and Varnish Manufacturing	.99	27.8
Electrical Wire and Cable—Manufacturing	1.21	22.6
Paper, Boxes and Bags Manufacturing	1.6	22.9
Motor Vehicles—Retailing	2.4	11.3
Hollinger Inc.	6.92	21.1
Toronto Sun Publishing Corp.	2.31	15.2

[a]Expressed as a percentage of total assets.
Source: Avery Leibowitz, *Financial Survey of Canadian Business Performance*, 1990 ed. (Don Mills, CCH Canadian Limited, 1991) and *The Financial Post*, "Survey of Industrials 1991," (Toronto, The Financial Post Publishing Inc., 1991).

TABLE 14-1
Liquid Asset Positions of Selected Industries and Firms for 1990 (%)

positions to meet operating needs and to respond to the real investment requirements of strategic plans.

Table 14-1 also suggests that it takes more than a knowledge of the industry class in which a firm operates to understand its cash management policies. For example, in the newspaper industry, Hollinger Inc. and Toronto Sun Publishing Corp. had holdings of liquid assets of 21.1% and 15.2% respectively. In fact, Hollinger Inc. had a greater cash holdings (6.9%) as compared with the cash holding (2.3%) of Toronto Sun Publishing Corp. The management of these newspaper companies perceive their liquidity needs quite differently. Different corporate strategies and different risk-bearing preferences with respect to the chances of running out of cash cause variations in levels of liquidity investment.

The examples given above showing liquid asset holdings of some specific industries and firms are only snapshots at a fixed point in time. In fact, assets are acquired, wasted, and sold every day. We must view the management of cash and liquid assets as a dynamic process. The flow of cash as depicted in Figure 14-1 never ceases. The cash inflows and outflows affecting the size of the firm's cash reservoir occur simultaneously. To ensure effective management of the firm's cash flows, managers must define a cash management system that has clearly defined objectives.

Perspective in Finance

Any company can benefit from a properly designed cash-management system. If you identify what you believe to be a superbly run business organization, the odds are that firm has in place a sound cash-management system. Before we explore several cash-management techniques, it is necessary to introduce (1) the risk-return tradeoff, (2) the objectives, and (3) the decisions that comprise the centre of the cash-management process. Keep in mind that the billion-dollar company will save millions each year by grasping these concepts —while the small and mid-sized organization may actually enhance its overall chances of survival. The following section provides the rationale and structure for knowing about all of the techniques and financial instruments discussed in the remainder of the chapter.

CASH MANAGEMENT OBJECTIVES AND DECISIONS

The Risk-Return Tradeoff

A companywide cash management program must be concerned with minimizing the firm's risk of insolvency. In the context of cash management, the term **insolvency** describes the situation where the firm is unable to meet its maturing liabilities on time. In such a case the company is **technically insolvent** in that it lacks the necessary liquidity to make prompt payment on its current debt obligations. A firm could avoid this problem by carrying large cash balances to pay the bills that come due. Production, after all, would soon come to a halt should payments for raw material purchases be continually late or omitted entirely. The firm's suppliers would just cut off further shipments. In fact, fear of irritating a key supplier by being past due on the payment of a trade payable does cause some financial managers to invest in too much liquidity.

The management of the company's cash position, however, is one of those problem areas in which you are criticized if you don't and criticized if you do. True, the production process will eventually be halted should too little cash be available to pay bills. If excessive cash balances are carried, the value of the enterprise in the financial marketplace will be suppressed because of the large cost of income forgone. The explicit return earned on idle cash balances is zero.

The financial manager must strike an acceptable balance between holding either too much cash or too little cash. This is the focal point of the risk-return tradeoff. A large cash investment minimizes the chances of insolvency, but penalizes company profitability. A small cash investment frees excess balances for investment in both marketable securities and longer-lived assets; this enhances company profitability and the value of the firm's common shares, but increases the chances of running out of cash.

The Objectives

The risk-return tradeoff can be reduced to two prime objectives for the firm's cash-management system:

1. Enough cash must be on hand to meet the disbursal needs that arise in the course of doing business.
2. Investment in idle cash balances must be reduced to a minimum.

Evaluation of these operational objectives, and a conscious attempt on the part of management to meet them, gives rise to the need for some typical cash-management decisions.

The Decisions

Two conditions would allow the firm to operate for extended periods with cash balances near or at a level of zero: (1) a completely accurate forecast of net cash flows over the planning horizon and (2) perfect synchronization of cash receipts and disbursements.

Cash flow forecasting is the initial step in any effective cash-management program. This is usually accomplished by the finance function's evaluation of data supplied by the marketing and production functions in the company. The cash budget is used to forecast the cash flows over the planning period. Although cash-budgeting procedures were explained in Chapter 12, we emphasize that the net cash flows pinpointed in the formal cash budget are estimates, subject to considerable variation. A totally accurate cash flow projection is an ideal, not a reality.

Our discussion of the cash flow process depicted in Figure 14-1 showed that inflows and outflows are not synchronized. Some inflows and outflows are irregular; others are more continual. Some finished goods are sold directly for cash, but more likely the sales will be on account. The receivables, then, will have to be collected before a cash inflow is realized. Raw materials have to be purchased, but several suppliers are probably used, and each may have its own payment date. Further, no law of doing business fixes receivable collections to coincide with raw material payments dates. So the second criterion that would permit a firm to operate with extremely low cash balances is not met in actual practice either.

Given that the firm will, as a matter of necessity, invest in some cash balances, certain types of decisions related to the size of those balances dominate the cash-management process. These include decisions that answer the following questions:

1. What can be done to speed up cash collections and slow down or better control cash outflows?

2. What should be the composition of a marketable securities portfolio?

3. How should investment in liquid assets be split between actual cash holdings and marketable securities?

The remainder of this chapter dwells on the first two of these three questions. The third is explored in Appendix 14A.

Perspective in Finance

Although the sheer number of cash collection and payment techniques is large, the concepts upon which those techniques rest are quite simple. Controlling the cash inflow and outflow is a major theme of treasury management. But, within the confines of ethical management, the cash manager is always thinking (1) "How can I speed up the firm's cash receipts?" and (2) "How can I slow down the firm's cash payments and not irritate too many important constituencies, such as suppliers?"

The critical point is that cash saved becomes available for investment elsewhere in the company's operations, and at a positive rate of return this will increase total profitability. Grasping the elements of cash management requires that you understand the concept of cash float. We address the concept of float and float reduction early in the discussion on collection and disbursement procedures.

COLLECTION AND DISBURSEMENT PROCEDURES

The efficiency of the firm's cash-management program can be enhanced by knowledge and use of various procedures aimed at (1) accelerating cash receipts and (2) improving the methods used to disburse cash. We will see that greater opportunity for corporate profit improvement lies with the cash receipts side of the funds flow process, although it would be unwise to ignore opportunities for favourably affecting cash-disbursement practices.

Managing the Cash Inflow[4]

A **float** refers to the delay that a firm incurs from the processing of payments within the payment cycle. The reduction of float lies at the centre of the many approaches employed to speed up cash receipts. Float (or total float) has four elements as follows:

1. **Mail float** is caused by the time lapse from the moment a customer mails a remittance cheque until the firm begins to process it.

2. **Processing float** is caused by the time required for the firm to process remittance cheques before they can be deposited in the bank.

3. **Transit** or **banking float** is caused by the time necessary for a deposited cheque to clear through the commercial banking system and become usable funds to the company. The introduction of same-day settlement to the Canadian Payments Association (CPA) Act enables credit for cheques deposited on the day received so that the depositor can use the money immediately.[5]

4. **Disbursing float** derives from the fact that funds are available in the company's bank account until its payment cheque has cleared through the banking system. Typically, funds available in the firm's banks exceed the balances indicated on its own books (ledgers).

We will use the term *float* to refer to the total of the four elements just described. Float reduction can yield considerable benefits in terms of usable funds that are released for company use and returns produced on such freed-up balances. As an example, for the year 1992 Northern Telecom reported total revenues of $8.5211 billion. The amount of usable funds that would be released if Northern Telecom could achieve a one-day reduction in float can be approximated by dividing annual revenues (sales) by the number of days in a year.[6] In this case one day's freed-up balances would be

$$\frac{annual\ revenues}{365\ days}$$

$$= \frac{\$8,521,100,000}{365}$$

$$= \$23,345,479$$

---

[4]The discussions on cash receipt and disbursement procedures draw heavily from the following sources: S. Sarpkaya, *Modern Cash Management*, 2nd ed. (Don Mills, CCH Canadian Ltd., 1991) and from the management of the Canadian Imperial Bank of Commerce.

[5]The Bank of Canada and the Canadian Payments Association provide cheque-clearing facilities for deposit-taking institutions. The cheque-clearing system is referred to as the "Canadian Payments System" in Canada. This term will be used several times in this chapter. The objective of the Canadian Payments System is to ensure that the proper amount of funds is available in a customer's chequing account for the collecting bank, trust, or Caisse Populaire. The Bank of Canada will only then transfer the appropriate credit to the collecting bank's account. A computerized network between clearing centres situated in major regions of the country and the Bank of Canada reduces the transit float by providing same-day settlement of cheques.

[6]Frederick W. Searby, "Use Your Hidden Cash Resources," *Harvard Business Review*, 46 (March–April 1968), 71–80.

If these released funds, which represent one day's sales, of approximately $23.3 million could be invested to return 8 percent a year, then the annual value of the one-day float reduction would be

(sales per day) × (assumed yield) = $23,345,479 × .08 = $1,867,638

It is clear that effective cash management can yield impressive opportunities for profit improvement. Let us look now at specific techniques for reducing float.

The Lock-Box Arrangement

The lock-box system is the most widely used commercial banking service for expediting cash gathering. Such a system speeds up the conversion of receipts into usable funds by reducing both mail and processing float. For large corporations that receive cheques from all parts of the country, float reductions of two to four days are not unusual.

Figure 14-2 illustrates an elementary, but typical, cash collection system for a hypothetical firm. It also shows the origin of mail float, processing float, and transit float. In this system the customer places with Canada post his or her remittance cheque with Canada Post, which is then delivered to the firm's headquarters. This causes the mail float. On the cheque's arrival at the firm's headquarters (or local collection centre), general accounting personnel must go through the bookkeeping procedures needed to prepare them for local deposit. The cheques are then deposited. These procedures cause the processing float. Once Canadian dollar cheques are deposited with a branch bank, the Canadian banking system provides processing on the same

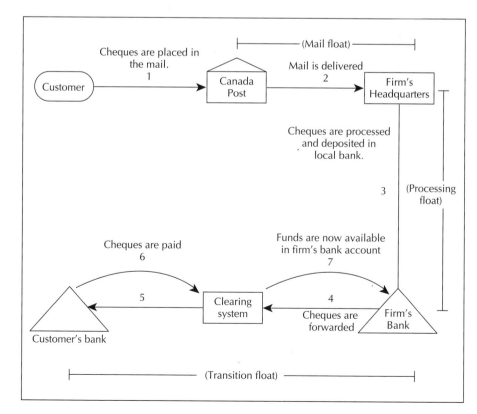

FIGURE 14-2
An Ordinary Cash-Gathering System

day that they are received by the bank.[7] In fact, all cheques, money orders, drafts, travellers' cheques, and other electronically transacted payments are paid immediately at the clearing point; same-day value for items deposited is a standard banking practice in Canada. Final settlement of payment occurs through the clearing centres of the Canadian payments system. The clearing centres of the Bank of Canada are located in the major cities of Canada, such as Halifax, Quebec City, Montreal, Ottawa, Toronto, Winnipeg, Regina, Calgary, and Vancouver. In general, final settlement of the transaction occurs on the day of deposit or at the latest on the next business day. This cheque-clearing system represents the transit float. However, the policy of same-day settlement at major Canadian banks, credit unions, and trust and loan companies has substantially reduced this type of float.

The lock-box arrangement shown in Figure 14-3 is based on a simple procedure. The firm's customers are instructed to mail their remittance cheques not to company headquarters or regional offices, but to a numbered Post Office box. The bank that is providing the lock-box service is authorized to open the box, collect the mail, process the cheques, and deposit the cheques directly into the company's account.

Typically a large bank will collect payments from the lock box at one- to two-hour intervals, 365 days of the year. During peak business hours, the bank may increase the frequency of pick-up of mail.

Once the mail is received at the bank, the cheques will be examined, totalled, photocopied, and microfilmed. A deposit form is then prepared by the bank, and each batch of processed cheques is forwarded to the collection department for clearance. Funds deposited in this manner are usually available for company use in one business day or less.

FIGURE 14-3
A Simple Lock-Box System

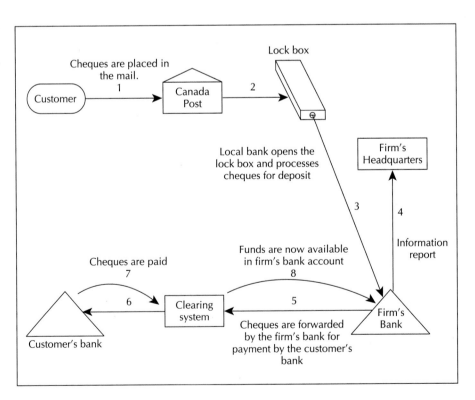

[7]Sarpkaya, S. *Modern Cash Management*, 2nd ed. (Don mills, CCH Canada Ltd., 1991).

The bank can notify the firm via some type of telecommunications system that the same day deposits have been made according to their specified amounts. At the conclusion of each day all cheque photocopies, invoices, deposit slips, and any other documents included with the remittances are mailed to the firm.

Note that the firm that receives cheques from all over the country will have to use several lock boxes to take full advantage of a reduction in mail float. The firm's major bank should be able to offer as a service a detailed lock-box study, analyzing the company's receipt patterns to determine the proper number and location of lock-box receiving points.[8]

The two systems described by Figures 14-2 and 14-3 are summarized in Table 14-2. There, the step numbers refer to those shown in Figure 14-2 (the ordinary system). Furthermore, Table 14-2 assumes that the customer and the firm's headquarters or its collection centre are located in different cities. This causes the lag of two working days before the firm actually receives the remittance cheque. We notice at the bottom of Table 14-2 that the installation of the lock-box system can result in funds being credited to the firm's bank account a full four working days faster than is possible under the ordinary collection system.

Previously in this chapter we calculated the 1992 sales per day for Northern Telecom to be $23.3 million and assumed that firm could invest its excess cash in marketable securities to yield 8 percent annually. If Northern Telecom could speed up its cash collections by four days, as the hypothetical firm did in Table 14-2, the results would be startling. The gross annual savings to Northern Telecom (apart from operating the lock-box system) would amount to $7.5 million, as follows:

$$\text{(sales per day)} \times \text{(days of float reduction)} \times \text{(assumed yield)}$$

$$= \$23{,}345{,}479 \times (4) \times .08 = \$7{,}470{,}553$$

As you might guess, the prospects for generating revenues of this magnitude are important not only to the firms involved, but also to commercial banks that offer lock-box services.

In summary, the benefits of a lock-box arrangement are these:

1. **Increased working cash.** The time required for converting receivables into available funds is reduced. This frees up cash for use elsewhere in the enterprise.

2. **Elimination of clerical functions.** The bank takes over the tasks of receiving, endorsing, totalling, and depositing cheques. With less handling of receipts by employees, better audit control is achieved and the chance of documents becoming lost is reduced.

3. **Early knowledge of dishonoured cheques.** Should a customer's cheque be uncollectible because of lack of funds, it is returned, usually by special handling, to the firm.

---

[8]Several quantitative studies have examined the problem of identifying the optimal locations and numbers of lock boxes, these include: Batlin, C. A., and Susan Hinko. "Lockbox Management and Value Maximization," *Financial Management*, 10 (Winter 1981), 39–44; Ferguson, Daniel M. "Optimize Your Firm's Lockbox Selection System," *Financial Executive*, 51 (April 1983), 8–12, 14–15, 18–19; and Nauss, Robert M., and Robert E. Markland, "Solving Lock Box Location Problems," *Financial Management*, 8 (Spring 1979), 21–27.

Step Numbers	Ordinary System and Time		Advantage of Lock Box
1	Customer writes cheque and places it in the mail	1 Day	
2	Mail is delivered to firm's headquarters	2 Days	Mail will not have to travel as far. Result: save 1 day
3	Accounting personnel process the cheques and deposit them in the firm's local bank	2 Days	Bank personnel prepare cheques for deposit. Result: save 2 days
4 and 5	Cheques are forwarded for payment through the cheque clearing system	1 Day	As the lock boxes are located near the clearing centres of the Canadian Payments System, and the standard banking practice in Canada of same-day value for items deposited, will reduce the transit float.
6 and 7	The firm receives notice from its bank that the cheques have cleared and the funds are now "good"	1 Day	Result: save 1 day
	Total working days	7 Days	Overall result: Save 4 working days

These benefits are not free. Usually, the bank levies a charge for each cheque processed through the system. The benefits derived from the acceleration of receipts must exceed the incremental costs of the lock-box system, or the firm would be better off without it. Companies that find the average size of their remittances to be quite small, for instance, might avoid a lock-box plan. One major bank has pointed out that for companies with less than $500,000 in average monthly sales or with customer remittance cheques averaging less than $1,000, the lock-box approach would probably not yield a great enough benefit to offset its costs. Later in this chapter a straightforward method for assessing the desirability of a specific cash-management service, such as the lock-box arrangement, will be illustrated.

Acceptance of Payments of Accounts

Another commercial banking service used for cash gathering is the acceptance of payments of accounts system which has been designed for public utilities, municipalities, and corporate retail organizations. Most Canadian banks offer through their branch banks the service of collecting the payments of an account. In such a case, the individual's banking account is debited for the payment and the funds are transferred to the corporation's account. For example, Bell Canada customers use this type of payment system when paying their telephone bills at their branch banks or automated teller machines.

The user of the acceptance of payments of accounts will benefit from a reduction in clerical labour costs, an acceleration of incoming cash flows from conversion of receivables and a reduction of the mail float. Furthermore, the corporation's customer benefits from the convenience of paying at their branch bank.

Pre-authorized Payments

For some firms the use of pre-authorized payments (PAP) system can be an even more effective way of converting receipts into working cash. The PAP system uses an electronic debit feature to collect a large volume of recurring payments of fixed or variable amounts from the same customer. The bank account of most financial institutions in Canada will be debited for the customer's specified payment on the due date and the bank account of the user of the PAP system will be credited for the collected funds on the due date. This type of cash management service has proved useful to insurance companies, consumer credit firms, leasing enterprises and charitable and religious organizations. The objective of this system is to reduce both mail and processing float. In relation to either the typical cash-gathering system (Figure 14-2) or the lock-box system (Figure 14-3), we note that the customer no longer (1) physically writes his or her own cheque or (2) deposits such a cheque in the mail. The exchange of payments between the user of PAPs and the customer is performed electronically and such an exchange is controlled by strict rules issued by the Canadian Payments Association. Paper input in the form of pre-authorized cheques is still acceptable by this payment system, with cheques being processed and cleared through the inter-bank clearing system.

The operation of a PAP system is illustrated in Figure 14-4. It involves the following sequence of events:

1. The firm's customers give authorization for payments to be charged to their respective demand deposit accounts.

2. All corporate customers which use pre-authorized debits must be sponsored by members of the inter-bank indemnity agreement of the Canadian Bankers Association. This agreement protects the payer and the payer's bank against erroneous debits without requiring the financial institution to hold authorization.

3. The firm prepares a magnetic tape that contains all appropriate information about the regular payments.

4. At each processing cycle (monthly, weekly, semi-monthly) the corporation retains a hard copy listing of all tape data for control purposes. Usually, the payments that are about to be printed will be deposited in the firm's demand deposit account, so a deposit ticket will also be forwarded to the bank.

5. Upon receipt of the tape, the bank will produce the payments, deposit them to the firm's account, forward them for clearing through the commercial banking system, and return a control report to the firm.

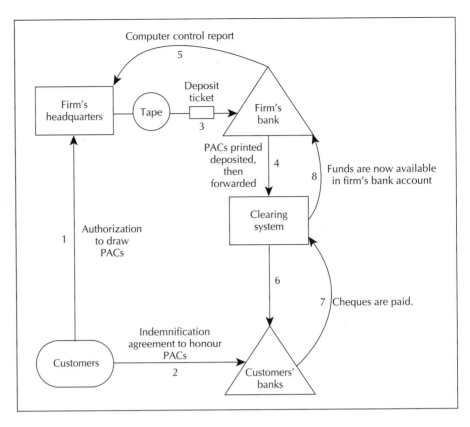

For firms that can take advantage of a PAP system, the benefits include these:

1. **Highly predictable cash flows.**

2. **Reduced expenses.** Billing and postage costs are eliminated, and the clerical processing of customer payments is significantly reduced.

3. **Customer preference.** Many customers prefer not to be bothered with a regular billing. With a PAP system the payment is even made if he or she is on vacation or otherwise out of town.

4. **Increased working cash.** Mail float and processing float can be dramatically reduced in comparison with other payment processing systems.

Deposit Consolidation Service

In an effort to accelerate collections, many companies have established multiple collection centres. Regional lock-box networks are one type of approach to strategically located collection points. Even without lock boxes, firms may have numerous sales outlets throughout the country and collect cash over the counter. This requires many local bank accounts to handle daily deposits. Rather than have funds sitting in these multiple bank accounts in different geographic regions of the country, most firms will regularly transfer the surplus balances to one or more concentration accounts. Centralizing the firm's pool of cash provides the following benefits:

1. **Lower levels of excess cash.** Desired cash balance target levels are set for each regional bank. These target levels consider both compensating balance requirements and necessary working levels of cash. Cash in

excess of the target levels can be transferred regularly to the concentration account for deployment by the firm's top-level management.

2. **Better control.** With more cash held in fewer accounts, stricter control over available cash is achieved. Quite simply, there are fewer problems to keep track of. The bank providing these consolidating services will prepare sophisticated reports that detail companywide movements of funds into and out of the central cash pool.

3. **More efficient investments in near-cash assets.** The coupling of information from the firm's cash forecast with data on available funds supplied by the concentration banks allows the firm to quickly transfer cash to the marketable securities portfolio.

This type of consolidating service enables funds to be transferred automatically and electronically to the firm's concentration account from financial institutions across North America. The deposits of customers are consolidated into the firm's concentration account through either an integrated on-line computer network of branch banks in Canada or via a telephone data collection facility for deposits.[9] If Canadian dollar deposits are made in Canada prior to an agreed time, the firm will benefit from the Canadian Payments association's policy of same-day credit. For American deposits made in the United States, the firm will be credited the funds according the policy of the American clearing system which credits the funds when they become available. This system is depicted in Figure 14-5. Both the mail and processing floats are reduced for the transfer of regional deposits to the firm's concen-

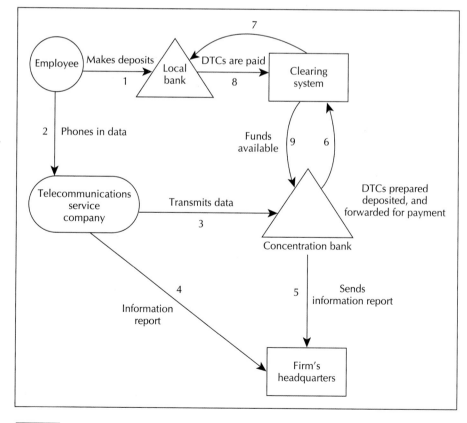

FIGURE 14-5
Automated Depository Transfer Cheque System (DTC)

[9]Sarpkaya, S., *Modern Cash Management*, 2nd ed. (Don Mills, CCH Canadian Ltd., 1991).

tration account. For example, the local company employee makes the daily deposit as usual. This employee does not, however, manually fill out the preprinted depository transfer cheque; instead, he or she telephones the deposit information to a regional data collection centre. Various data collection centres will accumulate information throughout the day on the firm's regional deposits. Then, at specified cutoff times the deposit information from all local offices is transmitted to the bank providing the consolidating services. At this point the bank will consolidate the debits and credits to the firm's concentration account and provide customer and internal control reports on the daily activity of the concentration account.

The electronic transfer of debits by an on-line computerized network of Canadian branch banks provides a more efficient means of moving funds as compared to the traditional use of depository transfer cheques which has been used to move funds from local bank accounts to concentration accounts. The depository transfer cheque itself is an unsigned, nonnegotiable instrument. It is payable only to the bank of deposit (the concentration bank in our discussion) for credit to the firm's specific account. An authorization form is filed by the firm with each bank from which it might withdraw funds. This form instructs the bank to pay the depository transfer cheques without any signature. The transfer cheques are placed into the commercial bank cheque-clearing process and presented to the firm's local bank for payment. When paid by the local bank, the funds become available in the concentration account for company use.

Funds Transfer Service

The fastest way to move cash between banks is by use of the on-line computerized payment service which is offered by most Canadian branch banks. This service reduces the transit float and provides the firm with same-day value. Funds moved in this manner, then, immediately become usable funds or "good funds" to the firm at the receiving bank. The proper authorization of a customer's branch bank can process electronically all payments in either Canadian or international currencies.[10] For example, a company's headquarters would authorize a branch bank to transfer regularly a payment of $100,000 every Tuesday and Thursday to the firm's concentration bank.

Managing the Cash Outflow

Significant techniques and systems for improving the firm's management of cash disbursements include (1) zero balance accounts, (2) payable-through drafts, and (3) remote disbursing. The first two offer markedly better control over companywide payments, and as a secondary benefit they may increase disbursement float. In Canada, payment systems which aim at increasing the disbursement float are not effective because both the Canadian payments system and the computerized branch bank system ensure same-day processing of payments. However, in the United States there are systems, such as remote disbursing, which aim solely at increasing the disbursement float.

Zero Balance Accounts

Large corporations that operate multiple branches, divisions, or subsidiaries often maintain numerous bank accounts (in different banks) for the purpose

[10]Other examples of fund transfer systems or wire transfers include Western Union which has locations across North America and SWIFT (Society of Worldwide Interbank Financial Telecommunication) which specializes in international transfers.

of making timely operating disbursements. It does make good business sense for payments for purchased parts that go into, say, an automobile transmission to be made by the Transmission and Chassis Division of the auto manufacturer rather than its central office. The Transmission and Chassis Division originates such purchase orders, receives and inspects the shipment when it arrives at the plant, authorizes payment, and writes the appropriate cheque. To have the central office involved in these matters would be a waste of company time.

What tends to happen, however, is that with several divisions utilizing their own disbursal accounts, excess cash balances build up in outlying banks and rob the firm of earning assets. Zero balance accounts are used to alleviate this problem. The objectives of a zero balance account system are (1) for the firm to achieve better control over its cash payments, (2) to reduce excess cash balances held in regional banks for disbursing purposes, and (3) to increase disbursing float.

Zero balance accounts permit centralized control (at the headquarters level) over cash outflows while maintaining divisional disbursing authority. Under this system the firm's authorized employees, representing their various divisions, continue to write cheques on their individual accounts. Note that the numerous individual disbursing accounts are now all located in the same concentration bank. Actually, these separate accounts contain no funds at all, thus their appropriate label, "zero balance." These accounts have all the characteristics of regular demand deposit accounts including separate titles, numbers, and statements.

Figure 14-6 illustrates a zero balance account disbursing system. The firm is assumed to have three operating divisions, each with its own zero balance account (ZBA). The system works as follows. The firm's authorized agents write their payment cheques as usual against their specific accounts (Step 1). These cheques clear through the banking system in the usual way. On a daily basis cheques will be presented to the firm's concentration bank (the drawee bank) for payment. As the cheques are paid by the bank, negative (debit) balances will build in the proper disbursing accounts (Step 2). At the end of each day the negative balances will be restored to a zero level by means of credits to the zero balance accounts (Step 3); a corresponding reduction in funds is made against the firm's concentration (master) demand deposit account (also Step 3). Each morning a report is electronically forwarded to corporate headquarters reflecting the balance in the master account as well as the previous day's activity in each zero balance account (Step 4). Using the report, the financial manager in charge of near-cash investments is ready to initiate appropriate transactions.

Managing the cash outflow through use of a zero balance account system offers the following benefits to the firm with many operating units:

1. Centralized control over disbursements is achieved, even though payment authority continues to rest with operating units.

2. Management time spent on superficial cash-management activities is reduced. Exercises such as observing the balances held in numerous bank accounts, transferring funds to those accounts short of cash, and reconciling the accounts demand less attention.

3. Excess balances held in outlying accounts can be reduced.

4. The costs of cash management can be reduced, as wire transfers to build up funds in outlying disbursement accounts are eliminated.

financial manager will want the cash quickly and will not want to accept a large price concession in order to convert the securities.[13] Thus, in the formulation of preferences for the inclusion of particular instruments in the portfolio, the manager must consider (1) the time period needed to sell the security and (2) the likelihood that the security can be sold at or near its prevailing market price. The latter element, here, means that "thin" markets, where relatively few transactions take place or where trades are accomplished only with large price changes between transactions, will be avoided.

Taxability

The tax treatment of a firm's income which is received from its security investments, does not affect the ultimate mix of the marketable securities portfolio as much as the criteria mentioned earlier. This is because the interest income from most instruments suitable for inclusion in the portfolio is taxable at both the federal and provincial levels. Still, the taxability of interest income and capital gains is seriously evaluated by some corporate treasurers.

Capital gains enjoy a preferential tax treatment as compared to interest income. Under such circumstances, bonds selling at a discount from their face value may be attractive investments to tax-paying firms. Should a high level of interest rates currently exist, the market prices of debt issues that were issued in the past at low coupon rates will be depressed. This, as we said previously, brings their yield to maturity up to that obtainable on a new issue. Part of the yield to maturity on a bond selling at a discount is a capital gain, or the difference between the purchase price and the maturity value. Hence, the return after tax that is earned could be higher than that derived from a comparable issue carrying a higher coupon but selling at par. We say *could be higher*, as the marketplace is rather efficient and recognizes this feature of taxability; consequently, bonds sold at a discount will provide a lower yield than issues that have similar risk characteristics but larger coupons. For short periods, though, a firm might find a favourable yield advantage by purchasing bonds sold at a discount.

Yields

The final selection criterion that we mention is a significant one—the yields that are available on the different financial assets suitable for inclusion in the near-cash portfolio. By now it is probably obvious that the factors of (1) financial risk, (2) interest rate risk, (3) liquidity, and (4) taxability all influence the available yields on financial instruments. The yield criterion involves an evaluation of the risks and benefits inherent in all of these factors. If a given risk is assumed, such as lack of liquidity, a higher yield may be expected on the non-liquid instruments.

Figure 14-8 summarizes our framework for designing the firm's marketable securities portfolio. The four basic considerations are shown to influence the yields available on securities. The financial manager must focus on the risk-return tradeoffs identified through analysis. Coming to grips with these tradeoffs will enable the financial manager to determine the proper marketable securities mix for the company. Let us look now at the marketable securities prominent in firms' near-cash portfolios.

---

[13]The high demand by corporate treasurers for short-term instruments will generally keep these instruments more liquid than long-term maturity instruments.

Considerations	→	Influence	→	Focus Upon	→	Determine
Financial risk		Yields		Risk vs. return		Marketable
Interest rate risk				preferences		securities mix
Liquidity						
Taxability						

FIGURE 14-8
Designing the Marketable
Securities Portfolio

Marketable Security Alternatives[14]

Government of Canada Treasury Bills

Table 14-5 shows that the Government of Canada treasury bills are the best-known and most popular short-term investment. The Government of Canada treasury bill is a non-interest bearing, discount security that the Bank of Canada sells in order to raise money for the Government of Canada. Since treasury bills are sold on a discount basis, the investor does not receive actual interest payments. The actual dollar return is the difference between the purchase price and the face (par) value of the bill less any transaction costs. However, for comparison purposes with other securities, the return of a treasury bill can be expressed on a true yield basis. The true yield is the annualized rate of interest which is compounded to the frequency of the bill's term-to-maturity. For example, suppose three-month treasury bills are issued on a true yield basis of 6.93%. This yield implies that the interest rate on a quarterly basis is (6.93 × 1/4) or 1.73 percent. As a result, a $1,000 treasury bill has a present value over a period of one quarter of ($1000/(1 + .0173)) or $982.99. In fact, the Government of Canada will be

TABLE 14-5. Volume of Selected Money Market Instruments, 1981–1992 (millions of dollars)

End of Year	Government of Canada Treasury Bills	Government of Canada Bonds Less than 3 Years	Provincial, Municipal Treasury Bills and Notes	Bankers' Acceptances	Commercial Paper	Sales Paper and Consumer Loan Company Paper	Term and Notice Deposits and GICs
1981	20,700	16,594	2,067	6,591	9,314	3,501	55,081
1982	25,725	19,037	3,903	12,647	7,696	1,821	55,618
1983	39,025	17,952	5,297	13,954	9,915	2,372	51,748
1984	49,675	20,061	6,950	13,982	11,341	2,975	54,511
1985	59,400	19,744	7,418	17,007	10,125	4,049	52,879
1986	69,700	23,956	9,943	24,896	10,298	6,102	54,616
1987	74,200	26,701	11,445	31,115	12,017	7,335	62,965
1988	95,100	31,734	10,255	40,191	16,377	8,729	68,375
1989	120,550	36,149	11,921	43,666	19,029	9,898	80,750
1990	135,400	42,216	14,164	44,109	21,851	9,004	90,340
1991	147,600	48,228	13,992	36,151	25,199	6,464	92,450
1992	159,450	54,616	17,694	21,970	25,069	5,971	105,035

Source: *Bank of Canada Review*, various issues (1981–1993).

---

[14]The discussions on market security alternatives draw heavily from the following sources: S. Sarpkaya, *Modern Cash Management*, 2nd ed. (Don Mills, CCH Canadian Ltd., 1991) and from G.F. Boreham, *Money, Banking, and Finance* (Toronto, Holt, Reinehart and Winston of Canada, Ltd., 1988).

obliged to pay $1,000 after the quarter has expired for every $928.99 of investment in three-month treasury bills by the investor, today.

At present bills are regularly offered with maturities of three months, six months, and one year. The three-month, six-month, and one-year treasury bills are auctioned weekly by the Bank of Canada. Every Tuesday the Bank of Canada invites both the banks and investment dealers to submit bids to buy treasury bills. The allotment of treasury bills is distributed according to the highest price submitted by bidders. This type of auction process enables the Bank of Canada to set their weekly Bank rate at one quarter of one percentage point above the latest average rate for three-month treasury bills. Any variation in the Bank rate of the Bank of Canada will influence the level of interest rates set by financial institutions.

Treasury bills are marketed by the Bank of Canada only in bearer form. They are purchased, therefore, without the investor's name on them. This attribute makes them easily transferable from one investor to the next. Of prime importance to the corporate treasurer is the fact that a very active secondary market exists for bills. After a treasury bill has been acquired by the firm, should the need arise to turn it into cash, a group of securities dealers stand ready to purchase it. This highly developed secondary market for treasury bills not only makes them extremely liquid, but also allows the firm to buy treasury bills with maturities of a week or even less. This type of flexibility in maturity of treasury bills enables a cash manager to plan for the payments on projects and the distribution of dividend payments.

As treasury bills have the full financial backing of the Government of Canada, they are, for all practical purposes, risk-free. This negligible financial risk and high degree of liquidity makes the yields lower than those obtainable on other marketable securities.

Since a treasury bill is a non-interest-bearing security which is sold at a discount, Revenue Canada requires that for tax purposes the discount be treated as business income for corporations and as interest income for individuals.

Short-Term Government Bonds

The Government of Canada not only issues medium-term (3–10 years) and long-term bonds (over 10 years) but also issues short-term bonds that mature in less than three years. The obligations of the Government of Canada are direct and guaranteed which provide investors with a safe return. As a result, the secondary market is active with the most recent issues being more liquid. The preference of investors for short-term bonds is due to the fluctuations in the levels of interest rates over the last 15 years.

The Bank of Canada acts as an agent of the Government of Canada for the process of underwriting new issues. Government of Canada bonds provide semi-annual interest coupons and are generally issued in the following denominations: $1,000; $5,000; $25,000; $100,000; and $1,000,000. New issues are either offered in allotments to a group of primary distributors or are sold at auctions every three months in a process similar to that of selling Government of Canada treasury bills. The group of primary distributors comprise both the chartered banks and the investment dealers.

Both provincial and municipal governments of Canada issue short-term bonds and paper in the money market. Generally, these types of governments use this market to cover short-term lending programs or to meet current expenditures in anticipation of tax revenues. The provinces also issue treasury bills which are sold on a discount basis in denominations of

$100,000. Both the yield and liquidity of these types of short-term obligations are determined by the credit standing of the government. In this case, the credit standing of the government is a reflection of debt burden, prospects of local economy, taxing power, and per capita income of the residents. Provincial and municipal short-term obligations provide higher returns than similar federal government issues. However, provincial and municipal government obligations are not as liquid as federal debt obligations because the issues are generally small in size or are private placements such that only a few investment dealers are required to be involved in the underwriting of the issue.

Bank-Issued Securities

The chartered banks of Canada issue several types of short-term investment securities to their customers. These securities include: bearer term deposit notes, deposit receipts, Eurodollar negotiable certificates of deposit, inter-bank deposit receipts, swapped deposits, special call loans, corporate certificates of deposit, and bankers' acceptances. Each of these instruments is customized to either the specific needs of their clients or the needs of the banks themselves. For example, the bearer term deposit notes are instruments that offer money market dealers a prime credit rating with a competitive rate of return for activities such as short selling; whereas, the special day loans provide chartered banks with a means to finance investment dealers. The most important of these instruments in terms of dollar volume are bankers' acceptances and corporate certificates of deposit.

BANKERS' ACCEPTANCES ■ **Bankers' acceptances** are among the least understood instruments suitable for inclusion in the firm's marketable securities portfolio. The role of bankers' acceptances in Canada's financial system has increased to such an extent that this instrument is the underlying security for financial interest futures which are sold on the Montreal Futures Exchange. Generally, an acceptance is a draft (order to pay) that has been accepted by a specific bank. Once accepted, the draft becomes a negotiable financial instrument that can be traded in the marketplace. For example, the following sequence of events demonstrates its use in international transactions:

1. A retailer in Toronto wants to import a shipment of stereo equipment from Tokyo. He goes to his commercial bank, which examines his credit standing and finds it satisfactory.

2. The importer's commercial bank sends the Tokyo exporter a letter of credit (a sophisticated reference letter) which authorizes the exporter to draw a draft on the Toronto commercial bank.[15] In the meantime, the importer has signed a contract with his bank agreeing to pay the bank the amount of the draft plus a commission in time for the bank to honour the draft at maturity.

3. Having received the letter of credit, the exporter draws a time draft on the Toronto bank for the amount of the sale price and releases the stereo equipment for shipment. He retains possession of critical docu-

---

[15]In fact, this money instrument is called an "acceptance" because the bank "accepts" the responsibility of repaying the loan. This is why the letter of credit is an important document to the bank.

ments associated with the sale, such as the bill of lading, the transfer of title to the merchandise, and insurance papers.

4. The exporter will probably not want to wait several months for his funds, so he will obtain cash at once by selling (discounting) the draft with his bank in Tokyo at less than its face value. The shipping documents are turned over to the Tokyo bank.

5. The Tokyo bank will forward the draft and shipping documents to its correspondent bank in Canada. The correspondent bank will present the draft to the importer's Toronto bank for acceptance.

6. The Toronto bank (the drawee bank) will observe that the draft was authorized by its own letter of credit, will detach all shipping documents, and will stamp the draft "accepted." At this time, and not before, the bankers' acceptance is created. It is now a negotiable instrument, payable to the bearer.

7. The maturity period of the acceptance will be pre-arranged between the firm importing the stereo equipment and its Toronto bank. When the draft is presented for acceptance, the maturity period begins, as most drafts are "sight drafts." This means, for instance, that if the maturity period is to be 90 days, the 90-day period begins after the drawee bank accepts the draft.

8. After accepting the draft, the Toronto bank will notify its customer (the importer) that he can pick up the shipping documents, which will enable him to take possession of his stereo equipment. In exchange for the shipping documents, the drawee bank will obtain a signed document from the importer (a trust receipt) giving the bank a security interest in the goods. The importer can take title to the goods, sell them, and pay the Toronto bank the face value of the acceptance (plus the stipulated service fee) shortly before its maturity.

9. The correspondent bank in Canada, which now holds the acceptance, will be instructed by the Tokyo bank to take either of two courses of action: (1) hold the acceptance until it matures as an investment or (2) immediately sell the acceptance in the market and credit its deposit account.

10. This latter course of action makes acceptances available to corporate treasurers for inclusion in near-cash portfolios.

Any chartered bank will issue bankers' acceptances once a customer's line of credit is established. These financial instruments are sold in multiples of $100,000 that normally mature in 30 to 90 days. A well-developed secondary market exists for bankers' acceptances. Furthermore, the credit quality of these financial instruments is enhanced since both the names of the accepting bank and the issuer appear on the draft.[16] The income generated from investing in bankers' acceptances is fully taxable at both federal and provincial levels. Owing to their greater financial risk and lesser liquidity, acceptances provide investors a yield advantage over treasury bills. However, the bankers' acceptances of chartered banks are a very safe investment, making the yield advantage over treasuries worth looking at from the firm's vantage point.

---

[16]Bankers' acceptances are referred to among practitioners as a form of "two-name paper." This stems from the fact that should the bank default on the instrument, the holder (investor) can seek payment from the drawer of the acceptance.

CORPORATE CERTIFICATES OF DEPOSIT ■ A **certificate of deposit**, CD, is a non-marketable term note issued at par, generally in blocks of $100,000. These invested funds earn a fixed rate of interest. CDs are offered by banks on a basis differing from treasury bills; that is, they are not sold at a discount. Rather, when the certificate matures, the owner receives the full amount deposited plus the earned interest. CDs are generally offered in terms ranging from a few days to one year. CDs are registered in the name of the original investor and their terms are non-negotiable. Withdrawal of the investment funds before the maturity date causes the investor to incur an interest penalty. The income received from an investment in CDs is subject to taxation at all government levels. In recent years CD yields have been above those available on bankers' acceptances. To accommodate the individual investor with limited funds, the banks offer certificates of deposit with smaller denominations.

Commercial Paper

Commercial paper refers to short-term, unsecured promissory notes sold by large businesses to raise cash. These are sometimes described in the popular financial press as short-term corporate IOUs. Because they are unsecured, the issuing side of the market is dominated by large corporations, which typically maintain sound credit ratings. The issuing (borrowing) firm can sell the paper to a dealer who will in turn sell it to the investing public; if the firm's reputation is solid, the paper can be sold directly to the ultimate investor. The denominations in which commercial paper can be bought vary over a wide range. The usual denominations are $25,000, $50,000, $100,000, $250,000, $500,000, and $1 million.

Commercial paper can be purchased with maturities that range from overnight to 365 days. These notes are generally sold on a discount basis in bearer form, although paper is available at times that is interest-bearing and can be made payable to the order of the investor. The return on commercial paper is fully taxable to the investor at all levels of government. Because of its lack of marketability, commercial paper in past years consistently provided a yield advantage over other near-cash assets of comparable maturity. Over any time period, then, CD yields may be slightly above the rates available on commercial paper.

For practical purposes, financial managers must be concerned with the limited secondary market for commercial paper. On occasion, a dealer or finance company (the borrower) will redeem a note prior to its contract maturity date, but this is not a regular procedure. Thus, when the corporation evaluates commercial paper for possible inclusion in its marketable securities portfolio, it should plan to hold it to maturity.

Repurchase Agreements

Repurchase agreements (repos) are legal contracts that involve the actual sale of securities by a money market dealer to the lender, with a commitment on the part of the money market dealer to repurchase the securities at the contract price plus a stated interest charge. The securities sold to the lender are Government of Canada treasury bills or other government securities.

Why might the corporation with excess cash prefer to buy repurchase agreements rather than a given marketable security? There are two major reasons. First, the original maturities of the instruments being sold can, in effect, be adjusted to suit the particular needs of the investing corporation.

The cash-acceleration plan presented by the managers of the Bank of Nova Scotia involves both a lock-box system and concentration banking. The Bank of Nova Scotia would be the firm's only concentration bank. Lock boxes would be established in (1) Victoria, (2) Ottawa, (3) Montreal, and (4) Halifax. This would reduce funds tied up by mail float to 2.5 days. Processing float would be eliminated. Funds would then be transferred twice each business day by means of automated depository transfer cheques from branch banks of the Bank of Nova Scotia in Victoria, Ottawa, and Montreal. Each depository transfer cheque (ADTC) costs $22. These transfers will occur all 270 business days of the year. Each cheque processed through the lock-box system will cost Ball Kitchens $.20.

a. What amount of cash balances will be freed if Ball Kitchens adopts the system proposed by the Bank of Nova Scotia?

b. What is the opportunity cost of maintaining the current banking arrangement?

c. What is the projected annual cost of operating the proposed system?

d. Should Ball Kitchens adopt the new system? Compute the net annual gain or loss associated with adopting the system.

14-10A. (*Buying and Selling Marketable Securities*) Saturday Knights Live Products, Inc., has $1 million in excess cash that it might invest in marketable securities. In order to buy and sell the securities, however, the firm must pay a transactions fee of $30,000.

a. Would you recommend purchasing the securities if they yield 11 percent annually and are held for

1. One month?

2. Two months?

3. Three months?

4. Six months?

5. One year?

b. What minimum required yield would the securities have to return for the firm to hold them for three months (what is the breakeven yield for a three-month holding period)?

14-11A. (*Concentration Banking*) Terri Textiles, located in Quebec, manufactures and distributes textile products on a nationwide basis. The firm has always used a centralized billing system. Terri Textiles has annual credit sales of $365 million. The National Bank has approached Terri Textiles with an offer to establish and operate a concentration banking system for the company. Terri Textiles already has an established line of credit with this same bank. The National Bank says it will operate the system on a flat fee basis of $200,000 per year. A detailed analysis done by the bank's cash-management services division shows conclusively that two days in mail float and one day in processing float can be eliminated. Since Terri Textiles borrows almost continuously from the National Bank, the value of the float reduction would be applied against the line of credit. The borrowing rate on the line of credit is set at an annual rate of 15 percent. In addition, because of a reduction in clerical help, the new system will save the firm $50,000 per year in processing costs. Terri Textiles uses a 365-day year in analyses of this sort. Should Terri Textiles accept the bank's offer to install the new system?

14-12A. (*Lock-Box System*) Hamilton Foundry specializes in the manufacture of aluminum and steel castings, which are used for numerous automobile parts. All of the firm's output is shipped to 10 warehouses near major auto assembly plants across Canada. The Bank of Montreal is Hamilton Foundry's lead bank and has just completed a study of Hamilton Foundry's cash collection system. Overall, the Bank of Montreal estimates that it can reduce Hamilton Foundry's total float by 2.5 days with the installation of a lock-box arrangement in each of the firm's 10 regions. The lock-box arrangement would cost each region $300 per month. Any funds freed up would be added to the firm's marketable securities portfolio and would yield 10.5 percent on an annual basis. Annual sales average $5,475,000 for each regional office. The firm and the bank use a 365-day year in their analyses. Should Hamilton Foundry's management approve the use of the proposed system?

14-13A. (*Valuing Float Reduction*) Griffey Manufacturing Company is forecasting that next year's gross revenues from sales will be $890 million. The senior treasury analyst for the firm expects the marketable securities portfolio to earn 9.60 percent over this same time period. A 365-day year is used in all the firm's financial procedures. What is the value to the company of one day's float reduction?

14-14A. (*Costs of Services*) The Leblanc Lumber Company may install a lock-box system in order to speed up its cash receipts. On an annual basis, Leblanc Lumber receives $60 million of remittances by cheque. The firm will record and process 18,000 cheques over the year. The National Bank will administer the system for a unit cost of $.30 per cheque. Cash that is freed by the use of this system can be invested to yield 8 percent on an annual before-tax basis. A 365-day year is used for analysis purposes. What reduction in cheque collection time is necessary for Leblanc Lumber to be neither better nor worse off for having adopted the proposed system?

14-15A. (*Costs of Services*) Mustang Ski-Wear, Inc., is investigating the possibility of adopting a lock-box system as a cash receipts acceleration device. In a typical year this firm receives remittances totalling $12 million by cheque. The firm will record and process 6,000 cheques over this same time period. The National Bank has informed the management of Mustang that it will expedite cheques and associated documents through the lock-box system for a unit cost of $.20 per cheque. Mustang's financial manager has projected that cash freed by adoption of the system can be invested in a portfolio of near-cash assets that will yield an annual before-tax return of 7 percent. Mustang financial analysts use a 365-day year in their procedures.

    a. What reduction in cheque collection time is necessary for Mustang to be neither better nor worse off for having adopted the proposed system?

    b. How would your solution to (a) be affected if Mustang could invest the freed balances only at an expected annual return of 4.5 percent?

    c. What is the logical explanation for the difference in your answers to (a) and (b)?

14-16A. (*Valuing Float Reduction*) The Columbus Tool and Die Works will generate $18 million in credit sales next year. Collections occur at an even rate, and employees work a 270-day year. At the moment, the firm's general accounting department ties up five days' worth of remittance cheques. An analysis undertaken by the firm's treasurer indicates that new internal procedures can reduce processing float by two days. If Columbus Tool invests the released funds to earn 8 percent, what will be the annual savings?

14-17A. (*Lock-Box System*) Penn Steelworks is a distributor of cold-rolled steel products to the automobile industry. All its sales are on a credit basis, net 30 days. Sales are evenly distributed over its 10 sales regions throughout Canada. Delinquent accounts are no problem. The company has recently undertaken an analysis aimed at improving its cash-management procedures. Penn determined that it takes an average of 3.2 days for customers' payments to reach the head office in Hamilton from the time they are mailed. It takes another full day in processing time prior to depositing the cheques with a local bank. Annual sales average $4,800,000 for each regional office. Reasonable investment opportunities can be found yielding 7 percent per year. To alleviate the float problem confronting the firm, the use of a lock-box system in each of the 10 regions is being considered. This would reduce mail float by 1.2 days. One day in processing float would also be eliminated, plus a full day in transit float. The lock-box arrangement would cost each region $250 per month.

    a. What is the opportunity cost to Penn Steelworks of the funds tied up in mailing and processing? Use a 365-day year.

    b. What would the net cost or savings be from use of the proposed cash-acceleration technique? Should Penn adopt the system?

14-18A. (*Valuing Float Reduction*) Next year P. F. Anderson Motors expects its gross revenues from sales to be $80 million. The firm's treasurer has projected that its marketable securities portfolio will earn 6.50 percent over the coming budget year. What is the value of one day's float reduction to the company? Anderson Motors uses a 365-day year in all of its financial analysis procedures.

14-19A. (*Cash Receipts Acceleration System*) Peggy Pierce Designs, Inc., is a vertically integrated, national manufacturer and retailer of women's clothing. Currently, the firm has no coordinated cash-management system. However, a proposal from the Royal Bank aimed at speeding up cash collections is being examined by several of Pierce's corporate executives.

The firm currently uses a centralized billing procedure, which requires that all cheques be mailed to the Edmonton head office for processing and eventual deposit. Under this arrangement all the customers' remittance cheques take an average of five business days to reach the head office. Once in Edmonton, another two days are required to process the cheques for ultimate deposit with the Royal Bank.

The firm's daily remittances average $1 million. The average cheque size is $2,000. Pierce Designs currently earns 6 percent annually on its marketable securities portfolio.

The cash acceleration plan proposed by managers of the Royal Bank involves both a lock-box system and concentration banking. The Royal Bank would be the firm's only concentration bank. Lock boxes would be established in (1) Vancouver, (2) Toronto, (3) Montreal, and (4) Edmonton. This would reduce funds tied up by mail float to three days, and processing float will be eliminated. Funds would then be transferred twice each business day by means of automated depository transfer cheques from branch banks of the Royal Bank in Vancouver, Toronto, and Montreal. Each depository transfer cheque (ADTC) costs $15. These transfers will occur all 270 business days of the year. Each cheque processed through the lock-box system will cost $.18.

a. What amount of cash balances will be freed if Pierce Designs, Inc., adopts the system suggested by the Royal Bank?

b. What is the opportunity of maintaining the current banking setup?

c. What is the projected annual cost of operating the proposed system?

d. Should Pierce adopt the new system? Compute the net annual gain or loss associated with adopting the system.

14-20A. (*Marketable Securities Portfolio*) The Alex Daniel Shoe Manufacturing Company currently pays its employees on a weekly basis. The weekly wage bill is $500,000. This means that on the average the firm has accrued wages payable of ($500,000 + $0)/2 = $250,000.

Alex Daniel, Jr., works as the firm's senior financial analyst and reports directly to his father, who owns all of the firm's common shares. Alex Daniel, Jr., wants to move to a monthly wage payment system. Employees would be paid on the Wednesday of every fourth week. The younger Daniel is fully aware that the labour union representing the company's workers will not permit the monthly payments system to take effect unless the workers are given some type of fringe benefit compensation.

A plan has been worked out whereby the firm will make a contribution to the cost of life insurance coverage for each employee. This will cost the firm $35,000 annually. Alex Daniel, Jr., expects the firm to earn 7 percent annually on its marketable securities portfolio.

a. Based on the projected information, should Daniel Shoe Manufacturing move to the monthly wage payment system?

b. What annual rate of return on the marketable securities portfolio would enable the firm to just break even on this proposal?

14-21A. (*Valuing Float Reduction*) The Cowboy Bottling Company will generate $12 million in credit sales next year. Collections of these credit sales will occur evenly over this period. The firm's employees work 270 days a year. Currently, the firm's processing system ties up four days' worth of remittance cheques. A recent report from a financial consultant indicated procedures that will enable Cowboy Bottling to reduce processing float by two full days. If Cowboy invests the released funds to earn 6 percent, what will be the annual savings?

14-22A. (*Valuing Float Reduction*) Montgomery Woodcraft is a large distributor of woodworking tools and accessories to hardware stores, lumber yards, and tradesmen. All its sales are on a credit basis, net 30 days. Sales are evenly distributed over its 12 sales regions throughout Canada. There is no problem with delinquent accounts. The firm is attempting to improve its cash-management procedures. Montgomery recently determined that it took an average of 3.0 days for customers' payments to reach their office from the time they were mailed and another day for processing before payments could be deposited. Annual sales average $5,200,000 for each region, and investment opportunities can be found to return 9 percent per year. What is the opportunity cost to the firm of the funds tied up in mailing and processing? In your calculations use a 365-day year.

14-23A. (*Lock-Box System*) To mitigate the float problem discussed above, Montgomery Woodcraft is considering the use of a lock-box system in each of its regions. By so doing, it can reduce the mail float by 1.5 days and receive the other benefits of a lock-box system. It also estimates that transit float could be reduced to half its present duration of two days. Use of the lock-box arrangement in each of its regions will cost $300 per month. Should Montgomery Woodcraft adopt the system? What would the net cost or savings be?

14-24A. (*Accounts Payable Policy and Cash Management*) Bradford Construction Supply Company is suffering from a prolonged decline in new construction in its sales area. In an attempt to improve its cash position, the firm is considering changes in its accounts payable policy. After careful study it has determined that the only alternative available is to slow disbursements. Purchases for the coming year are expected to be $37.5 million. Sales will be $65 million, which represents about a 20 percent drop from the current year. Currently, Bradford discounts approximately 25 percent of its payments at 3/10, net 30, and the balance of accounts are paid in 30 days. If Bradford adopts a policy of payment in 45 days or 60 days, how much can the firm gain if the annual opportunity cost of investment is 12 percent? What will be the result if this action causes Bradford Construction suppliers to increase their prices to the company by 0.5 percent to compensate for the 60-day extended term of payment? In your calculations, use a 365-day year and ignore any compounding effects related to expected returns.

14-25A. (*Interest Rate Risk*) Two years ago your corporate treasurer purchased for the firm a 20-year bond at its par value of $1,000. The coupon rate on this security is 8 percent. Interest payments are made to bondholders once a year. Currently, bonds of this particular risk class are yielding investors 9 percent. A cash shortage has forced you to instruct your treasurer to liquidate his bond.

  a. At what price will your bond be sold? Assume annual compounding.

  b. What will be the amount of your gain or loss over the original purchase price?

  c. What would be the amount of your gain or loss had the treasurer originally purchased a bond with a four-year rather than a 20-year maturity? (Assume all characteristics of the bonds are identical except their maturity periods.)

  d. What do we call this type of risk assumed by your corporate treasurer?

14-26A. (*Marketable Securities Portfolio*) Red Raider Feedlots has $4 million in excess cash to invest in a marketable securities portfolio. Its broker will charge $10,000 to invest the entire $4 million. The president of Red Raider wants at least half of the $4 million invested at a maturity period of three months or less; the remainder can be invested in securities with maturities not to exceed six months. The relevant term structure of short-term yields follows:

Maturity	Available Yield (Annual)
One month	6.2%
Two months	6.4%
Three months	6.5%
Four months	6.7%
Five months	6.9%
Six months	7.0%

a. What should be the maturity periods of the securities purchased with the excess $4 million in order to maximize the before-tax income from the added investment? What will be the amount of the income from such an investment?

b. Suppose that the president of Red Raider relaxes his constraint on the maturity structure of the added investment. What would be your profit-maximizing investment recommendation?

c. If one-sixth of the excess cash is invested in each of the maturity categories shown above, what would be the before-tax income generated from such an action?

14-27A. (*Forecasting Excess Cash*) The C. K. S. Stove Company manufactures wood-burning stoves in the Pacific Northwest. Despite the recent popularity of this product, the firm has experienced a very erratic sales pattern. Owing to volatile weather conditions and abrupt changes in new housing starts, it has been extremely difficult for the firm to forecast its cash balances. Still, the company president is disturbed by the fact that the firm has never invested in any marketable securities. Instead, the liquid asset portfolio has consisted entirely of cash. As a start toward reducing the firm's investment in cash and releasing some of it to near-cash assets, a historical record and projection of corporate cash holdings is needed. Over the past five years sales have been $10 million, $12 million, $11 million, $14 million, and $19 million, respectively. Sales forecasts for the next two years are $23 and $21 million. Total assets for the firm are 60 percent of sales. Fixed assets are the higher of 50 percent of total assets or $4 million. Inventory and receivables amount to 70 percent of current assets and are held in equal proportions.

a. Prepare a worksheet that details the firm's balance sheets for each of the past five years and for the forecast periods.

b. What amount of cash will the firm have on hand during each year for short-term investment purposes?

STUDY PROBLEMS (SET B)

14-1B. (*Buying and Selling Marketable Securities*) Universal Concrete Company has generated $700,000 in excess cash that it could invest in marketable securities. In order to buy and sell the securities, the firm will pay total transactions fees of $25,000.

a. Would you recommend purchasing the securities if they yield 11.5 percent annually and are held for

1. One month?
2. Two months?
3. Three months?
4. Six months?
5. One year?

b. What minimum required yield would the securities have to return for the firm to hold them for two months (i.e., what is the breakeven yield for a two-month holding period)?

14-2B. (*Cash Receipts Acceleration System*) Kobrin Door & Glass, Inc., is a buyer and distributor of doors used in the home building industry. The firm has grown very quickly since it was established eight years ago. Kobrin Door has managed to increase sales and profits at a rate of about 18 percent annually, despite moderate economic growth at the national level. Until recently, the company paid little attention to cash-management procedures. Charles Kobrin, the firm's president, said: "With our growth—who cares?" Bending to the suggestions of several analysts in the firm's finance group, Kobrin did agree to have a proposal prepared by the National Bank in Moncton. The objective of the proposal is to accelerate the firm's cash collections.

At present, Kobrin Door uses a centralized billing procedure. All cheques are mailed to the Moncton office headquarters for processing and eventual deposit. Under this arrangement, all customers' remittance cheques take an average of five business days to reach the Moncton office. Once in Moncton, another two days are needed to process the cheques for deposit with the National Bank.

Daily cash remittances at Kobrin Door average $800,000. The average cheque size is $4,000. The firm currently earns 9.5 percent annually on its marketable securities portfolio.

The cash-acceleration plan presented by the managers of the National Bank involves both a lock-box system and concentration banking. The National Bank would be the firm's only concentration bank. Lock boxes would be established in (1) Victoria, (2) Toronto, (3) Montreal, and (4) Moncton. This would reduce funds tied up in mail float to 3.5 days. Processing float would be totally eliminated. Funds would then be transferred twice each business day by means of automated depository transfer cheques from local banks in Victoria, Toronto, and Montreal to the National Bank. Each depository transfer cheque (ADTC) costs $30. These transfers will occur all 270 business days of the year. Each cheque processed through the lock box will cost Kobrin Door $.40.

a. What amount of cash balances will be freed if Kobrin Door adopts the system proposed by the National Bank?

b. What is the opportunity cost of maintaining the current banking arrangement?

c. What is the projected annual cost of operating the proposed system?

d. Should Kobrin Door & Glass adopt the system? Compute the net annual gain or loss associated with adopting the system.

14-3B. (*Concentration Banking*) Smith & Tucker (S&T) Enterprises operates in Ontario. The firm manufactures and distributes quality furniture on a nationwide basis. The firm presently uses a centralized billing system. S&T has annual credit sales of $438 million. Royal Bank has presented an offer to operate a concentration banking system for the company. S&T already has an established line of credit with the Royal Bank. The Royal Bank says it will operate the system on a flat fee basis of $300,000 per year. The analysis done by the bank's cash-management services division suggests that two days in mail float and one day in processing float can be eliminated.

Since S&T borrows almost continuously from the Royal Bank, the value of the float reduction would be applied against the line of credit. The borrowing rate on the line of credit is set at an annual rate of 11 percent. Further, because of a reduction in clerical help, the new system will save the firm $68,000 in processing costs. S&T uses a 365-day year in analyses of this sort. Should S&T accept the bank's offer to install the new system?

14-4B. (*Lock-Box System*) Regency Components is located in Montreal. The firm manufactures components used in a variety of electrical devices. All the firm's finished goods are shipped to five regional warehouses across Canada.

The Bank of Montreal is Regency Components' lead bank and has recently completed a study of Regency's cash-collection system. The Bank of Montreal estimates that it can reduce Regency's total float by 3.0 days with the installation of a lock-box arrangement in each of the firm's five regions.

The lock-box arrangement would cost each region $600 per month. Any funds freed up would be added to the firm's marketable securities portfolio and would yield 11.0 percent on an annual basis. Annual sales average

$10,000,000 for each regional office. The firm and the bank use a 365-day year in their analyses. Should Regency Components' management approve the use of the proposed system?

14-5B. (*Costs of Services*) The Hallmark Technology Company of Scarborough may install a lock-box system in order to speed up its cash receipts. On an annual basis, Hallmark receives $50 million in remittances by cheque. The firm will record and process 20,000 cheques over the year. The Royal Bank will administer the system at a cost of $.37 per cheque. Cash that is freed up by use of the system can be invested to yield 9 percent on an annual before-tax basis. A 365-day year is used for analysis purposes. What reduction in cheque collection time is necessary for Hallmark to be neither better nor worse off for having adopted the proposed system?

14-6B. (*Cash Receipts Acceleration System*) Lee Collins Woodcrafts Corp. is a medium-sized manufacturer, buyer, and installer of quality kitchen equipment and apparatus. The firm, which was established five years ago, has grown very quickly. Despite some rough economic times that included two recessions in three years, Collins Woodcrafts has managed to increase sales and profits at an approximate rate of 20 percent annually. Until recently, the firm paid no attention to its cash-management procedures. Lee Collins, the company's president, just said, "We are too busy growing to worry about those trivial things." Bending to the pleas of several analysts in the firm's finance group, Collins did agree to have a proposal prepared by the Bank of Nova Scotia. The objective of the proposal is to speed up the firm's cash collections.

At present, Collins Woodcrafts uses a centralized billing procedure. All cheques are mailed to the Halifax headquarters office for processing and eventual deposit. Under this arrangement all of the customers' remittance cheques take an average of four business days to reach the Halifax office. Once in Halifax, another two days are needed to process the cheques for deposit with the Bank of Nova Scotia.

The daily cash remittances of Collins Woodcrafts average $450,000. The average cheque size is $2,000. The firm currently earns 8.5 percent annually on its marketable securities portfolio.

The cash-acceleration plan presented by the managers of the Bank of Nova Scotia involves both a lock-box system and concentration banking. The Bank of Nova Scotia would be the firm's only concentration bank. Lock boxes would be established in (1) Victoria, (2) Ottawa, (3) Montreal, and (4) Halifax. This would reduce funds tied up by mail float to 2.5 days. Processing float would be eliminated. Funds would then be transferred twice each business day by means of automated depository transfer cheques from local banks in Victoria, Ottawa, and Montreal to the Bank of Nova Scotia. Each depository transfer cheque (ADTC) costs $25. These transfers will occur all 270 business days of the year. Each cheque processed through the lock-box system will cost Collins Woodcrafts $.25.

a. What amount of cash balances will be freed if Collins Woodcrafts adopts the system proposed by the Bank of Nova Scotia?

b. What is the opportunity cost of maintaining the current banking arrangement?

c. What is the projected annual cost of operating the proposed system?

d. Should Collins Woodcrafts adopt the new system? Compute the net annual gain or loss associated with adopting the system.

14-7B. (*Buying and Selling Marketable Securities*) Western Photo Corp. has $1 million in excess cash that it might invest in marketable securities. In order to buy and sell the securities, however, the firm must pay a transactions fee of $35,000.

a. Would you recommend purchasing the securities if they yield 10 percent annually and are held for

1. One month?

2. Two months?

3. Three months?

4. Six months?

5. One year?

b. What minimum required yield would the securities have to return for the firm to hold them for three months (i.e., what is the breakeven yield for a three-month holding period)?

14-8B. (*Concentration Banking*) Block Music Company, located in Ottawa, manufactures and distributes musical instruments on a nationwide basis. The firm has always used a centralized billing system. Block Music has annual credit sales of $375,000 million. The National Bank has approached Block Music with an offer to establish and operate a concentration banking system for the company. Block already has an established line of credit with this same bank. National Bank says it will operate the system on a flat fee basis of $150,000 per year. A detailed analysis done by the bank's cash-management services division shows conclusively that two days in mail float and one day in processing float can be eliminated. Since Block borrows almost continuously from the National Bank, the value of the float reduction would be applied against the line of credit. The borrowing rate on the line of credit is set at an annual rate of 16 percent. In addition, because of a reduction in clerical help, the new system will save the firm $40,000 per year in processing costs. Block uses a 365-day year in analyses of this sort. Should Block Music accept the bank's offer to install the new system?

14-9B. (*Lock-Box System*) Metrocorp is located on the outskirts of Toronto. The firm specializes in the manufacture of aluminum and steel castings, which are used for numerous automobile parts. All of the firm's output is shipped to 10 warehouses near major auto assembly plants across Canada. The Royal Bank is Metrocorp's lead bank and has just completed a study of Metrocorp's cash collection system. Overall, the Royal Bank estimates that it can reduce Metrocorp's total float by 2.5 days with the installation of a lock-box arrangement in each of the firm's 10 regions. The lock-box arrangement would cost each region $300 per month. Any funds freed up would be added to the firm's marketable securities portfolio and would yield 10.0 percent on an annual basis. Annual sales average $4,475,000 for each regional office. The firm and the bank use a 365-day year in their analyses. Should Metrocorp's management approve the use of the proposed system?

14-10B. (*Valuing Float Reduction*) Brady Consulting Services is forecasting that next year's gross revenues from sales will be $900 million. The senior treasury analyst for the firm expects the marketable securities portfolio to earn 9.5 percent over this same time period. A 365-day year is used in all the firm's financial procedures. What is the value to the company of one day's float reduction?

14-11B. (*Costs of Services*) The Discount Storage Co. may install a lock-box system in order to speed up its cash receipts. On an annual basis, Discount receives $55 million of remittances by cheque. The firm will record and process 20,000 cheques over the year. The National Bank will administer the system for a unit cost of $.30 per cheque. Cash that is freed by the use of this system can be invested to yield 8 percent on an annual before-tax basis. A 365-day year is used for analysis purposes. What reduction in cheque collection time is necessary for Discount Storage to be neither better nor worse off for having adopted the proposed system?

14-12B. (*Costs of Services*) Colour Communications is investigating the possibility of adopting a lock-box system as a cash receipts acceleration device. In a typical year this firm receives remittances totalling $10 million by cheque. The firm will record and process 7,000 cheques over this same time period. The Bank of Nova Scotia has informed the management of Colour Communications that it will expedite cheques and associated documents through the lock-box system for a unit cost of $.30 per cheque. Colour Communications' financial manager has projected that cash freed by adoption of the system can be invested in a portfolio of near-cash assets that will yield an annual before-tax return of 7 percent. Colour Communications' financial analysts use a 365-day year in their procedures.

a. What reduction in cheque collection time is necessary for Colour

Communications to be neither better nor worse off for having adopted the proposed system?

b. How would your solution to (a) be affected if Colour Communications could invest the freed balances only at an expected annual return of 4.5 percent?

c. What is the logical explanation for the difference in your answers to (a) and (b)?

14-13B. (*Valuing Float Reduction*) Campus Restaurants, Inc., will generate $17 million in credit sales next year. Collections occur at an even rate, and employees work a 270-day year. At the moment, the firm's general accounting department ties up four days' worth of remittance cheques. An analysis undertaken by the firm's treasurer indicates that new internal procedures can reduce processing float by two days. If Campus invests the released funds to earn 9 percent, what will be the annual savings?

14-14B. (*Lock-Box System*) Alpine Systems is a distributor of refrigerated storage units to the meat products industry. All its sales are on a credit basis, net 30 days. Sales are evenly distributed over its 10 sales regions throughout Canada. Delinquent accounts are no problem. The company has recently undertaken an analysis aimed at improving its cash-management procedures. Alpine determined that it takes an average of 3.2 days for customers' payments to reach the head office in Edmonton from the time they are mailed. It takes another full day in processing time prior to depositing the cheques with a local bank. Annual sales average $5,000,000 for each regional office. Reasonable investment opportunities can be found yielding 8 percent per year. To alleviate the float problem confronting the firm, the use of a lock-box system in each of the 10 regions is being considered. This would reduce mail float by 1.0 days. One day in processing float would also be eliminated, plus a full day in transit float. The lock-box arrangement would cost each region $225 per month.

a. What is the opportunity cost to Alpine Systems of the funds tied up in mailing and processing? Use a 365-day year.

b. What would the net cost or savings be from use of the proposed cash-acceleration technique? Should Alpine adopt the system?

14-15B. (*Valuing Float Reduction*) Next year Concept Realty expects its gross revenues from sales to be $90 million. The firm's treasurer has projected that its marketable securities portfolio will earn 6.50 percent over the coming budget year. What is the value of one day's float reduction to the company? Concept Realty uses a 360-day year in all of its financial analysis procedures.

14-16B. (*Cash Receipts Acceleration System*) Carter's Bicycles, Inc., is a vertically integrated, national manufacturer and retailer of racing bicycles. Currently, the firm has no coordinated cash-management system. However, a proposal from the Royal Bank aimed at speeding up cash collections is being examined by several of Carter's corporate executives.

The firm currently uses a centralized billing procedure, which requires that all cheques be mailed to the Edmonton head office for processing and eventual deposit. Under this arrangement all the customers' remittance cheques take an average of four business days to reach the head office. Once in Edmonton, another 1.5 days are required to process the cheques for ultimate deposit at the Royal Bank.

The firm's daily remittances average $1 million. The average cheque size is $2,000. Carter's currently earns 7 percent annually on its marketable securities portfolio.

The cash-acceleration plan proposed by managers of the Royal Bank involves both a lock-box system and concentration banking. The Royal Bank would be the firm's only concentration bank. Lock boxes would be established in (1) Vancouver, (2) Toronto, (3) Montreal, and (4) Edmonton. This would reduce funds tied up by mail float to three days, and processing float will be eliminated. Funds would then be transferred twice each business day by means of automated depository transfer cheques from branch banks of the Royal Bank in Vancouver, Toronto, and Montreal. Each depository transfer cheque (ADTC) costs $16. These transfers will occur all 270 business days of the year. Each cheque processed through the lock-box system will cost $0.22.

    a. What amount of cash balances will be freed if Carter's Bicycles adopts the system suggested by the Royal Bank?

    b. What is the opportunity of maintaining the current banking setup?

    c. What is the projected annual cost of operating the proposed system?

    d. Should Carter's adopt the new system? Compute the net annual gain or loss associated with adopting the system.

14-17B. (*Marketable Securities Portfolio*) Katz Jewelers currently pays its employees on a weekly basis. The weekly wage bill is $500,000. This means that on the average the firm has accrued wages payable of ($500,000 + $0)/2 = $250,000.

    Harry Katz works as the firm's senior financial analyst and reports directly to his father, who owns all of the firm's common shares. Harry Katz wants to move to a monthly wage payment system. Employees would be paid on the Wednesday of every fourth week. The younger Katz is fully aware that the labour union representing the company's workers will not permit the monthly payments system to take effect unless the workers are given some type of fringe benefit compensation.

    A plan has been worked out whereby the firm will make a contribution to the cost of life insurance coverage for each employee. This will cost the firm $40,000 annually. Harry Katz expects the firm to earn 8 percent annually on its marketable securities portfolio.

    a. Based on the projected information, should Katz Jewelers move to the monthly wage payment system?

    b. What annual rate of return on the marketable securities portfolio would enable the firm just to break even on this proposal?

14-18B. (*Valuing Float Reduction*) Magic Hardware Stores, Inc., will generate $12 million in credit sales next year. Collections of these credit sales will occur evenly over this period. The firm's employees work 270 days a year. Currently, the firm's processing system ties up 4.5 days' worth of remittance cheques. A recent report from a financial consultant indicated procedures that will enable Magic Hardware to reduce processing float by two full days. If Magic invests the released funds to earn 7 percent, what will be the annual savings?

14-19B. (*Valuing Float Reduction*) True Locksmith is a large distributor of residential locks to hardware stores, lumber yards, and tradesmen. All its sales are on a credit basis, net 30 days. Sales are evenly distributed over its 10 sales regions throughout Canada. There is no problem with delinquent accounts. The firm is attempting to improve its cash-management procedures. True Locksmith recently determined that it took an average of 3.0 days for customers' payments to reach their office from the time they were mailed, and another day for processing before payments could be deposited. Annual sales average $5,000,000 for each region, and investment opportunities can be found to return 9 percent per year. What is the opportunity cost to the firm of the funds tied up in mailing and processing? In your calculations use a 365-day year.

14-20B. (*Lock-Box System*) To mitigate the float problem discussed above, True Locksmith is considering the use of a lock-box system in each of its regions. By so doing, it can reduce the mail float by 1.5 days and receive the other benefits of a lock-box system. It also estimates that transit float could be reduced to half its present duration of two days. Use of the lock-box arrangement in each of its regions will cost $350 per month. Should True Locksmith adopt the system? What would the net cost or savings be?

14-21B. (*Accounts Payable Policy and Cash Management*) Meadowbrook Paving Company is suffering from a prolonged decline in new development in its sales area. In an attempt to improve its cash position, the firm is considering changes in its accounts payable policy. After careful study it has determined that the only alternative available is to slow disbursements. Purchases for the coming year are expected to be $40 million. Sales will be $65 million, or

$$P = (D)(S)(i) \text{ [see Equation 14-2]}$$

$$\$0.25 = (D)(\$1750)(.0002192)$$

$$0.6517 \text{ days} = D$$

Creative Fashion Designs therefore will experience a financial gain if it implements the lock-box system and by doing so will speed up its collections by more than 0.6517 days.

b. Here the daily opportunity cost of carrying cash is

$$\frac{0.055}{365} = 0.0001507 \text{ per day}$$

For Creative Fashion Designs to break even, should it choose to install the lock-box system, cash collections must be accelerated by 0.9480 days, as follows:

$$\$0.25 = (D)(\$1750)(.0001507)$$

$$0.9480 \text{ days} = (D)$$

c. The breakeven cash-acceleration period of 0.9480 days is greater than the 0.6517 days found in (a). This is due to the lower yield available on near-cash assets of 5.5 percent annually, versus 8.0 percent. Since the alternative rate of return on the freed-up balances is lower in the second situation, more funds must be invested to cover the costs of operating the lock-box system. The greater cash-acceleration period generates this increased level of required funds.

SS-2. a. Reduction in mail float:

$$(2.0 \text{ days})(\$200,000) = \$400,000$$

$$+ \text{ reduction in processing float:}$$

$$(2.5 \text{ days})(\$200,000) = 500,000$$

$$= \text{ total float reduction} = \$900,000$$

b. The opportunity of maintaining the present banking arrangement is

$$\left(\begin{array}{c}\text{forecast yield on marketable} \\ \text{securities portfolio}\end{array}\right) \cdot \left(\begin{array}{c}\text{total float} \\ \text{reduction}\end{array}\right)$$

$$(.106)(\$900,000) = \$95,400$$

c. The average number of cheques to be processed each day through the lock-box arrangement is

$$\frac{\text{daily remittances}}{\text{average cheque size}} = \frac{\$200,000}{\$800} = 250 \text{ cheques}$$

The resulting cost of the lock-box system on an annual basis is

$$(250 \text{ cheques})(\$0.25)(270 \text{ days}) = \$16,875$$

Next, we must calculate the estimated cost of the automated depository transfer cheque (ADTC) system. The Royal Bank will not contribute to the cost of the ADTC arrangement because it is the lead concentration bank and thereby receives the transferred data. This means that Artie Kay's Komputer Shops will be charged for six ADTCs (three locations @ 2 cheques each) each business day. Therefore, the ADTC system costs

$$(6 \text{ daily transfers})(\$20 \text{ per transfer})(270 \text{ days}) = \$32,400$$

We now have the total cost of the proposed system:

Lock-box cost	$16,875
ADTC cost	32,400
Total cost	$49,275

d. Our analysis suggests that Artie Kay's Komputer Shops should adopt the proposed cash receipts acceleration system. The projected net annual gain is $46,125 as follows:

Projected return on freed balances	$95,400
Less: Total cost of new system	49,275
Net annual gain	$46,125

SS-3. a. Here we must calculate the dollar value of the estimated return for each holding period and compare it with the transactions fee to determine if a gain can be made by investing in the securities. Those calculations and the resultant recommendations follow:

	Recommendation
1. $2,000,000 (.12) (1/12) = $20,000 < $45,000	No
2. $2,000,000 (.12) (2/12) = $40,000 < $45,000	No
3. $2,000,000 (.12) (3/12) = $60,000 > $45,000	Yes
4. $2,000,000 (.12) (6/12) = $120,000 > $45,000	Yes
5. $2,000,000 (.12) (12/12) = $240,000 > $45,000	Yes

b. Let (%) be the required yield. With $2 million to invest for three months we have

$$\$200,000 \ (\%) \ (3/12) = \$45,000$$

$$\$200,000 \ (\%) \ (3/12) = \$180,000$$

$$\$200,000 \ (\%) \ (3/12) = \$180,000/2,000,000 = 9\%$$

The breakeven yield, therefore, is 9%.

APPENDIX 14A: Cash-Management Models: The Split Between Cash and Near Cash

In this appendix we continue our discussion of the management of the firm's cash position. We have dwelled upon the overall objectives of company cash management, described some actual liquid asset holdings of selected industries and firms, and overviewed a wide array of cash-collection and disbursement procedures.

     We now consider the problem of properly dividing the firm's liquid asset holdings between cash and near cash.

LIQUID ASSETS: CASH VERSUS MARKETABLE SECURITIES

Through use of the cash-budgeting procedures outlined in Chapter 12, the financial manager can pinpoint time periods when funds will be in either short or excess supply. If a shortage of funds is expected, then alternative avenues of financing must be explored. On the other hand, the cash-budget projections might indicate that large, positive net cash balances in excess of immediate transactions needs will be forthcoming. In this more pleasant situation the financial manager ought to decide on the proper split of the expected cash balances between actual cash holdings and marketable securities. To hold all of the expected cash balances as actual balances would needlessly penalize the firm's profitability.

The ensuing discussion centres on various methods by which the financial manager can develop useful cash balance level benchmarks.

Benchmark 1: When Cash Need Is Certain

A basic method for indicating the proper average amount of cash to have on hand involves use of the economic order quantity concept so familiar in discussions of inventory management (Chapter 15).[20] The objective of this analysis is to balance the lost income that the firm suffers from holding cash rather than marketable securities against the transactions costs involved in converting securities into cash. The rudiments of this decision model can easily be introduced by the use of an illustration.

Suppose that the firm knows with certainty that it will need $250,000 in cash for transactions purposes over the next two months and that this much cash is currently available. This transactions demand for cash will be represented by the variable T. Let us assume, for purposes of this illustration, that when the firm requires cash for its transactions needs it will sell marketable securities in any one of five lot sizes, ranging from $30,000 to $70,000. These cash conversion (order) sizes, C, are identified in line 1 of Table 14A-1.

Line 2 shows the number of times marketable securities will be turned into cash over the next two months if a particular order size is utilized. For example, should it be decided to liquidate securities in amounts of $40,000, then the number of cash conversions needed to meet transactions over the next two months is $250,000/$40,000 = 6.25. In general, the number of cash withdrawals from the near-cash portfolio can be represented as T/C.

Next, we assume that the firm's cash payments are of constant amounts and are made continually over the two-month planning period. This implies that the firm's cash balance behaves in the sawtooth manner shown in Figure 14A-1. The assertion of regularity and constancy of payments allows the firm's average cash balance over the planning period to be measured as $C/2$ (see Figure 14A-1). When marketable securities are sold and cash flows into the demand deposit account, the cash balance is equal to C. As payments are made on a regular and constant basis, the cash balance is reduced to a level of zero. The average cash balance over the period is then

$$\frac{C + 0}{2} = \frac{C}{2}$$

[20]The roots of a quantitative treatment of the firm's cash balance as just another type of inventory are found in William J. Baumol, "The Transactions Demand for Cash: An Inventory Theoretic Approach," *Quarterly Journal of Economics*, 66 (November 1952), pp. 545–556.

TABLE 14A-1
Determination of the Optimal Cash Order Size

	$30,000	$40,000	$50,000	$60,000	$70,000
1. Cash conversion size (the dollar amount of marketable securities that will be sold to replenish the cash balance)	$30,000	$40,000	$50,000	$60,000	$70,000
2. Number of cash order per time period (the time period is two months in this example) ($250,000 ÷ line 1)	8.33	6.25	5.00	4.17	3.57
3. Average cash balance (line 1 ÷ 2)	$15,000	$20,000	$25,000	$30,000	$35,000
4. Interest income forgone (line 3 × .01)	$150.00	$200.00	$250.00	$300.00	$350.00
5. Cash conversion cost ($50 × line 2)	$416.50	$312.50	$250.00	$208.50	$178.50
6. Total cost of ordering and holding cash (line 4 + line 5)	$566.50	$512.50	$500.00	$508.50	$528.50

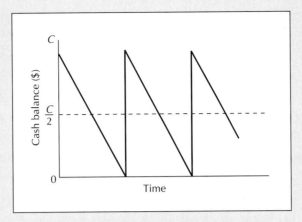

The average cash balances corresponding to the different cash conversion sizes in our example are noted in line 3 of Table 14A-1.

Line 4 measures the opportunity cost of earnings forgone based upon holding the average cash balance recorded on line 3. If the annual yield available on marketable securities is 6 percent, then over the two-month period we are analyzing, the forfeited interest rate is $.06/6 = .01$.[21] Multiplying each average cash balance, $C/2$, by the .01 interest rate, i, available over the two-month period produces the opportunity costs entered on line 4.

The very act of liquidating securities, unfortunately, is not costless. Transacting conversions of marketable securities into cash can involve any of the following activities, which require the time of company employees as well as direct payment by the firm for various services:

1. Assistant treasurer's time to order the trade.

2. Long-distance phone calls to effect the trade.

3. Secretarial time to type authorization letters, make copies of the letters, and forward the letters to the company treasurer.

4. Treasurer's time to read, approve, and sign the documents that authorize the trade.

5. General accountant's time to record and audit the transaction.

6. The value of fringe benefits incurred on the above times.

7. The brokerage fee on each transaction.

Suppose that the firm has properly studied the transaction costs, similar to those enumerated above, and finds they are of a fixed amount, b, per trade equal to $50. The transaction cost variable, b, is taken to be independent of the size of a particular securities order. Multiplying the transaction cost of $50 per trade by the number of cash orders that will take place during the planning period produces line 5. In general, the cash conversion cost (transaction cost) is equal to $b(T/C)$.

We are now down to the last line in Table 14A-1. This is the sum total of the income lost by holding cash rather than marketable securities and the cash-ordering costs. Line 6, then, is the total of lines 4 and 5. The inventory model seeks to minimize these total costs associated with holding cash balances.

---

[21]If we were studying a one-month planning period, rather than the two-month period being discussed, the annual yield would have to be stated on a monthly basis or $.06/12 = .005$.

Table 14A-1 tells us, if cash is ordered on five occasions in $50,000 sizes over the two-month period, the total costs of holding an average cash balance of $25,000 will be $500. This is less than the total costs associated with any other cash conversion size.

At the beginning of the two-month planning horizon, all of the $250,000 available for transactions purposes need not be held in the firm's demand deposit account. To minimize the total costs of holding cash, only $50,000 should immediately be retained to transact business. The remaining $200,000 should be invested in income-yielding securities and then turned into cash as the firm's disbursal needs dictate.

It is useful to put our discussion of the inventory model for cash management into a more general form. Summarizing the definitions developed in the illustration, we have

C = The amount per order of marketable securities to be converted into cash

i = the interest rate per period available on investments in marketable securities

b = the fixed cost per order of converting marketable securities into cash

T = the total cash requirements over the planning period

TC = the total costs associated with maintenance of a particular average cash balance

As just pointed out, the total costs (TC) of having cash on hand can be expressed as

$$TC = i\left(\frac{C}{2}\right) + b\left(\frac{T}{C}\right) \tag{14A-1}$$

total interest income forgone   total ordering costs

If Equation (14A-1) is applied to the $50,000 cash conversion size column in Table 14A-1, the total costs can be computed in a direct fashion as follows:

$$TC = .01\left(\frac{\$50,000}{2}\right) + 50\left(\frac{\$250,000}{\$50,000}\right)$$

$$= \$250 + \$250 = \$500$$

You can see that the $500 total cost is the same as was found deductively in Table 14A-1. The optimal cash conversion size, C^*, can be found by use of Equation (14A-2):

$$C^* = \sqrt{\frac{2bT}{i}} \tag{14A-2}$$

When the data in our example are applied to Equation (14A-2), the optimal cash order size is found to be

$$C^* = \sqrt{\frac{2(5)(250,000)}{.01}} = \$50,000$$

This solution to our example problem is displayed graphically in Figure 14A-2. Notice that the optimal cash order size of $50,000 occurs at the minimum point of the total cost curve associated with keeping cash on hand.

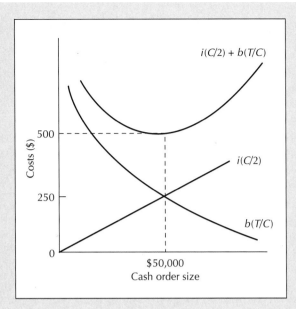

FIGURE 14A-2
Solution to the Inventory Model for Cash Management

Inventory Model Implications

The solution to Equation (14A-2) tells the financial manager that the optimal cash order size, C^*, varies directly with the square root of the order costs, bT, and inversely with the yield, i, available on marketable securities. Notice that as transactions requirements, T, increase, owing perhaps to an augmented sales demand, the optimal cash order size does not rise proportionately.

   The model also indicates that as interest rates rise on near-cash investments, the optimal cash order size decreases, with the effect dampened by the square-root sign as Equation (14A-2) suggests. With higher yields to be earned on the marketable securities portfolio, the financial manager will be more reluctant to make large withdrawals because of the interest income that will be lost.

   Some final perspectives on the use of the economic order quantity model in cash management can be obtained by reviewing the assumptions upon which it is derived. Among the more important of these assumptions are the following:

   1. Cash payments over the planning period are (a) of a regular amount, (b) continuous, and (c) certain.

   2. No unanticipated cash receipts will be received during the analysis period.

   3. The interest rate to be earned on investments remains constant over the analysis period.

   4. Transfers between cash and the securities portfolio may take place any time at a fixed cost, regardless of the amount transferred.

Clearly, the strict assumptions of the inventory model will not be completely realized in actual business practice. For instance, the amount and timing of cash payments will not be known with certainty; nor are cash receipts likely to be as discontinuous or lumpy as is implied. If relaxation of the critical assumptions is not so prohibitive as to render the model useless, then a benchmark for possible managerial action is provided. The model's output is not intended to be a precise and inviolable rule. On the other hand, if the assumptions of the model cannot be reasonably approximated, the financial manager must look elsewhere for possible guides that indicate a proper split between cash and marketable securities.

Benchmark 2: When Cash Balances Fluctuate Randomly

It is entirely possible that the firm's cash balance pattern does not at all resemble that indicated in Figure 14A-1. The assumptions of certain regularity and constancy of cash payments may be unduly restrictive when applied to some organizations.[22] Rather, the cash balance might behave more like the jagged line shown in Figure 14A-3. In this figure it is assumed that the firm's cash balance changes in an irregular fashion from day to day. The changes are unpredictable; that is, they are random. Further, let us suppose the chances that a cash balance change will be either (1) positive or (2) negative are equal at .5 each.

As cash receipts exceed expenditures, the cash balance will move upward until it hits an upper control limit, *UL*, expressed in dollars. This occurs at point *A* in Figure 14A-3. At such time, the financial manager will initiate an investment in marketable securities equal to *UL* – *RP* dollars, where *RP* is the cash return point.

If cash payments exceed receipts, the cash balance will move downward until it hits a lower control limit, *LL*. This situation is noted by point *B* in Figure 14A-3. When this occurs, the financial manager will sell marketable securities equal to *RP* – *LL* dollars. This will restore the cash balance to the return point, *RP*.

To make this application of control theory to cash management operational, we must determine the upper control limit, *UL*, the lower control limit, *LL*, and the cash return point, *RP*. For the present case where a net cash increase is as likely to occur as a net cash decrease, use of the following variables will allow computation of the cash return point, *RP*.[23]

b = the fixed cost per order of converting marketable securities into cash

i = the daily interest rate available on investments in marketable securities

σ^2 = the variance of daily changes in the firm's expected cash balances (this is a measure of volatility of cash flow changes over time)

FIGURE 14A-3
Randomly Fluctuating Cash Balances

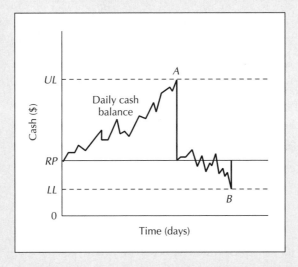

---

[22]This discussion is based upon Merton H. Miller and Daniel Orr, "A Model of the Demand for Money by Firms," *Quarterly Journal of Economics*, 80 (August 1966), pp. 413–435.

[23]Situations where the probabilities of cash increases and decreases are not equal are extremely difficult to evaluate within the framework of the Miller-Orr decision model. See Miller and Orr, "A Model of the Demand for Money by Firms," *Quarterly Journal of Economics*, 80 (August 1966), pp. 427–429 and 433–435.

The optimal cash return point, RP, can be calculated as follows:

$$RP = \sqrt[3]{\frac{3b\sigma^2}{4i}} + LL \qquad (14A\text{-}3)$$

The upper control limit, UL, can be computed quite simply:

$$UL = 3RP - 2LL \qquad (14A\text{-}4)$$

The actual value for the lower limit, LL, is set by management. In business practice a minimum is typically established below which the cash balance is not permitted to fall. Among other things, it will be affected by (1) the firm's banking arrangements, which may require compensating balances, and (2) management's risk-bearing tendencies.

To illustrate use of the model, suppose that the annual yield available on marketable securities is 9 percent. Over a 360-day year, i becomes $.09/360 = .00025$ per day. Assume that the fixed cost, b, of transacting a marketable securities trade is $50. Moreover, the firm has studied its past cash balance levels and has observed that the standard deviation, s, in daily cash balance changes is equal to $800. The firm sees no reason why this variability should change in the future. It is the firm's policy to maintain $1,000 in its demand deposit account (LL) at all times. Finally, the firm has established that each day's actual cash balance is random. The equations that comprise this control limit system can be applied to provide guidelines for cash-management policy.

The optimal cash return point for transactions purposes becomes

$$RP = \sqrt[3]{\frac{3(50)(800)^2}{4(.00025)}} + 1000 = (4579 + 1000) = \$5579$$

The upper cash balance limit that will trigger a transfer of cash to marketable securities is

$$UL = 3(5579) - 2(1000) = \$14,737$$

The cash balance control limits derived from this example are graphed in Figure 14A-4. Should the cash balance bump against the upper limit of $14,737 (point A), then the financial manager is instructed to buy $9,158 of marketable securities. At the other extreme, if the cash balance should drop to the lower limit of $1,000 (point B), then the financial manager is instructed to sell $4,579

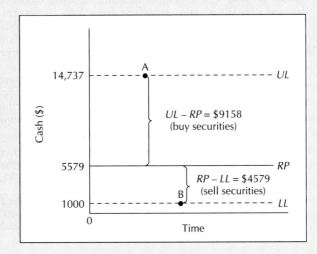

FIGURE 14A-4
Control Limit Model

making a credit decision would be a mistake. If extending a customer credit means that the customer may become a regular customer in the future, it may be appropriate to take a risk that otherwise would not be prudent. In effect, our goal is to ensure that all cash flows affected by the decision at hand are considered, not simply the most immediate cash flows.

FIGURE 15-2. Credit "Scorecard"

Telephone   Score

Home	Relative	None				
5	1	0				

Living quarters

Own home no mortgage	Own home mortgage	Rent a house	Live with someone	Rent an apartment	Rent a room	
5	1	0	1	0	0	

Bank accounts

None	1	More than 1				
0	4	6				

Years at present address

Under 1/2	1/2-2	3-7	8 or more			
0	1	3	4			

Size of family including customer

1	2	3-6	7 or more			
2	4	3	0			

Monthly income

Under $700	$701-$900	$901-$1200	$1201-$1500	More than $1500		
0	1	2	6	8		

Length of present employment

Under 1/2 year	1/2-2 years	3-7 years	8 years or more			
0	1	2	4			

Percent of selling price on credit

Under 50	50-69	70-84	85-99			
5	3	1	0			

Interview discretionary point (+5 to −5)

Total

Credit scorecard

_____
(Customer's name)

_____
(Street address)

_____
(City, Province, Postal Code)

_____
(Home/Office telephone)

_____
(Credit scorer)

Credit scorecard evaluation

Dollar amount: $0-$2000

0-18	19-21	22 or more
Reject	Refer to main credit	Accept

Dollar amount: $2001-$5000

0-21	22-24	25 or more
Reject	Refer to main credit	Accept

Dollar amount: more than $5000

0-23	26-27	27 or more
Reject	Refer to main credit	Accept

If a previous loan customer, were payments received promptly?   Yes ☐   No* ☐

Are you willing to take reponsibility for authorizing this loan?   Yes ☐   No* ☐

*Refer to main credit if answer to either question is *No.*

Collection Efforts—Decision Variable

The key to maintaining control over collection of accounts receivable is the fact that the probability of default increases with the age of the account. Thus, control of accounts receivable focuses on the control and elimination of past-due receivables. One common way of evaluating the current situation is **ratio analysis**. The financial manager can determine whether or not accounts are under control by examining the average collection period, the ratio of receivables to assets, the ratio of credit sales to receivables (called the *accounts receivable turnover ratio*), and the amount of bad debts relative to sales over time, the financial manager can determine whether or not receivables are drifting out of control. In addition, the manager can use a schedule to determine the amount of aging of accounts receivable. Such a schedule provides a breakdown both in dollars and in percentage terms of the proportion of receivables that are past due. A comparison of the current aging of receivables with past data provides the manager with even more control over receivables. Table 15-2 shows an example of an aging account or schedule.

Table 15-3 provides a ranking of measures used in monitoring accounts receivable compiled in a survey of Fortune 500 Companies. This survey indicates that the aging account or schedule along with the accounts receivable turnover ratio and average collection period, which are actually variations of each other, serve as the primary tools used in monitoring the payment behaviour of customers.

Once the delinquent accounts have been identified, the firm will make an effort to collect them. For example, the firm can send a past-due letter, called a dunning letter, if payment is not received on time, followed by an additional dunning letter in a more serious tone if the account becomes 3 weeks past due, followed after 6 weeks by a telephone call. Finally, if the account becomes 12 weeks past due, it might be turned over to a collection agency. Again, a direct tradeoff exists between collection expenses and lost

Age of Accounts Receivable (Days)	Dollar Value (00)	Percent of Total
0–30	$2340	39%
31–60	1500	25
61–90	1020	17
91–120	720	12
Over 120	420	7%
Total	$6000	100%

TABLE 15-2
Aging Account

Measure	Number of Responses	Percentage Assigning Rank			
		1	2	3	4
Accounts receivable turnover	52	9.6%	26.9%	63.5%	
Collection period	77	33.8	50.6	15.6	
Aging schedule	92	69.6	27.2	2.2	1.1%
Other	5	20.0	80.0		

TABLE 15-3
Ranking of Measures Used in Monitoring Payment Behaviour of Customers, 1988

Source: K. V. Smith and B. Belt, "Working Capital Management in Practice: An Update," Working Paper No. 951 (West Lafayette, IN: Krannert Graduate School of Management, Purdue University, 1989).

goodwill on one hand and noncollection of accounts on the other. This type of tradeoff is always part of making the decision.

Thus far, we have discussed the importance and role of accounts receivable in the firm and then examined the determinants of the size of the investment in accounts receivable. We have focused on the credit and collection policies since these are the only discretionary variables for management. In examining these decision variables, we have simply described their traits. These variables are analyzed in a decision-making process called marginal or incremental analysis.

Credit Policy Changes: The Use of Marginal or Incremental Analysis

Changes in credit policy involve direct tradeoffs between costs and benefits. When credit policies are eased, sales and profits from customers are expected to also increase. On the other hand, easing credit policies can also involve an increase in bad debts, additional funds tied up in both accounts receivable and inventory, and additional costs from customers taking a cash discount. Given these costs, when is it appropriate for the firm to change its credit policy? The answer is when the increased sales generate enough in the way of new profit to more than offset the increased costs associated with the change. Determining whether this is so is the job of marginal or incremental analysis. In general, there are three categories of changes in credit policy that a firm can consider: a change in the risk class of the customer, the collection process, or a change in the discount terms. The following example illustrates a change in credit policy.

EXAMPLE

Assume that Denis Electronics currently has annual sales, all credit, of $8 million and an average collection period of 30 days. The current level of bad debts is $240,000 and the firm's opportunity cost or required rate of return is 15 percent. Further assume that the firm produces only one product, with variable costs equalling 75 percent of the selling price. The company is considering a change in the credit terms—the current terms of net 30 to 1/30 net 60. If this change is made it is expected that half of the customers will take the discount and pay on the 30th day while the other half will not take the discount and pay on the 60th day. This will increase the average collection period from 30 days to 45 days. The major reason Denis Electronics is considering this change is that it will generate additional sales of $1,000,000. Although the sales from these new customers will generate new profits, they will also generate more bad debts. The level of bad debts on original sales will remain constant, but the level of bad debts on the new sales will be 6 percent of those sales. In addition, the new sales will require an increase in the level of average inventory from $1,000,000 to $1,025,000. ■

General Procedure

Marginal or incremental analysis involves a comparison of the incremental profit contribution (or benefits) from new sales with the incremental costs resulting from the change in credit policy. If the benefits outweigh the costs, the change is made. If not, the credit policy remains as it is. The following procedure shows the four steps for performing marginal or incremental analysis on a change in credit policy:

Step 1: Estimate the change in profit.

Step 2: Estimate the cost of additional investment in accounts receivable and inventory.

Step 3: Estimate the cost of the discount (if a change in the cash discount is enacted).

Step 4: Compare the incremental revenues with the incremental costs. To simplify the analysis, Table 15-4 provides a summary of the relevant information concerning Denis's proposed credit change and Table 15-5 provides the results of the incremental analysis.

In Step 1 of the analysis, the additional profits less bad debts from the new sales are $190,000. In Step 2, the additional investment in accounts receivable and inventory is determined to be $458,340. Since the pre-tax required rate of return is 15 percent, the company's required rate of return on this investment is $72,501. In Step 3, the cost of introducing a cash discount is determined to be $45,000. Finally, in Step 4 the benefits and costs are compared, and the net change in pre-tax profits is determined to be $72,499. Thus, a change to the present credit policy is warranted.

In summary, the logic behind this approach to credit policy is to examine the incremental or marginal benefits from such a change and to compare these with the incremental or marginal costs. If the change promises more benefits than costs, the change should be made. If the incremental costs are greater than the benefits, the proposed change should not be made. Figure 15-3 illustrates this process: the point where marginal costs equal marginal benefits occurs at credit policy A.

Perspective in Finance

The calculations associated with the incremental analysis of a change in credit policy illustrate the changes that take place when the credit policy is adjusted. On the positive side, a loosening of the credit policy should increase sales. On

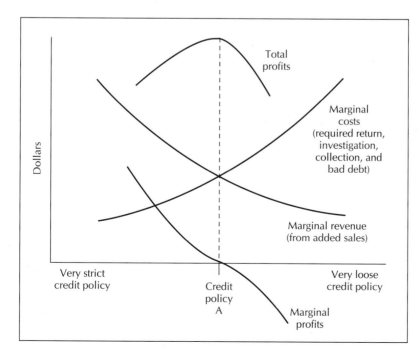

FIGURE 15-3
Credit Policy and Profits

TABLE 15-4 Denis Electronics: Relevant Information for Incremental Analysis		
New sales level (all credit):	$9,000,000
Original sales level (all credit):	$8,000,000
Contribution Margin:	25%
Percent bad debt losses on new sales:	6%
New average collection period:	45 days
Original average collection period:	30 days
Additional investment in inventory:	$25,000
Pre-tax required rate of return:	15%
New percent cash discount:	1%
Percent of customers taking the cash discount:	50%

TABLE 15-5
Denis Electronics: Incremental Analysis of a Change in Credit Policy

Step 1: *Estimate the change in profit.* This is equal to the increased sales times the profit contribution on those sales less any additional bad debts incurred.

= (Incremental sales × Contribution Margin) −
(Incremental sales × Percent bad debt losses on new sales)

= ($1,000,000 × .25) − ($1,000,000 × .06)

= $190,000

Step 2: *Estimate the cost of any additional investment in accounts receivable and inventory.* This involves first calculating the change in the investment in accounts receivable: the new and the original levels of investment in accounts receivable are calculated by multiplying the daily sales level times the average collection period. The additional investment in inventory is added to this, and the sum is then multiplied by the pre-tax required rate of return.

= (Additional accounts receivable + Additional inventory) ×
(Pre-tax required rate of return)

First, calculate the additional investment in accounts receivable:

= [(New level of daily sales) × (New average collection period)] −
[(Original level of daily sales) × (Original average collection period)]

$$= \left[\left(\frac{\$9,000,000}{365}\right) \times 45\right] - \left[\left(\frac{\$8,000,000}{365}\right) \times 30\right]$$

= $458,340

Second, the sum of additional investments in accounts receivable and inventory is multiplied by the pre-tax required rate of return:

= ($458,340 + $25,000) × .15

= $72,501

Step 3: *Estimate the change in the cost of the cash discount (if a change in the cash discount is enacted).* This is equal to the new level of sales times the new percent cash discount, less the original level of sales, times the original percent cash discount, times the percent of customers taking the discount.

= [(New level of sales) × (New percent cash discount) ×
(Percent of customers taking discount)] − [(Original level of sales) ×
(Original percent cash discount) × (Percent of customers taking discount)]

= [($9,000,000 × .01 × .50)] − [($8,000,000 × .00 × .00)]

= $45,000

Step 4: *Compare the incremental revenues with the incremental costs:*

Net change in pre-tax profits = (Change in profits) − (Cost of new investment in
accounts receivable and inventory +
Cost of change in cash discount)

= (Step 1) − (Step 2 + Step 3)

= $190,000 − ($72,501 + $45,000)

= $72,499

the negative side, bad debts, investment in accounts receivable and inventory, and costs associated with the cash discount all increase. The decision then boils down to whether the incremental benefits outweigh the incremental costs.

INVENTORY MANAGEMENT

Inventory management involves the control of assets that are produced to be sold in the normal course of the firm's operations. The general categories of inventory include raw materials inventory, work in process inventory, and finished goods inventory. The importance of inventory management to the firm depends upon the extent of the inventory investment.[7] For an average firm, approximately 6.4 percent of all industries' assets are in the form of inventory and 13.2 percent of non-financial industries' assets are in the form of inventory. Table 15-6 shows that inventory as a percentage of total assets varies widely from industry to industry. For example, it is much more important in the motor vehicles, parts and accessories, and tires, where inventories make up 23.4 percent of total assets, than in the accommodation, food and beverage, educational, health and recreational services, where the average investment in inventory is only 2.9 percent of total assets.

Purposes and Types of Inventory

The purpose of carrying inventories is to uncouple the operations of the firm—that is, to make each function of the business independent of each other function—so that delays or shutdowns in one area do not affect the production and sale of the final product. Since production shutdowns result in increased costs, and since delays in delivery can lose customers, the management and control of inventory are important duties of the financial manager.

Industry	*Inventory Relative to Total Assets (%)*
All industries	6.4
Non-financial industries	13.2
Consumer goods and services	34.0
Building materials and construction	12.9
Motor vehicles, parts and accessories, and tires	24.7
Other transportation equipment	34.5
Household appliances and electrical products	28.7
Electronic equipment and computer services	11.8
Printing, publishing and broadcasting	4.1
Chemicals, chemical products, and textiles	18.3
Wood and Paper	13.0
Food—retail	20.4
Accommodation, food and beverage, educational, health, and recreational services	2.8

TABLE 15-6
Inventory as a Percentage of Total Assets for Major Industries

Source: Statistics Canada, *Quarterly Financial Statistics for Enterprises*, Cat. No. 61-008, Fourth quarter, 1992. Reproduced with the permission of the Minister of Industry, Science and Technology.

———

[7]The optimal inventory policy is specific to the firm; similar to optimal capital structure decision.

The decision-making process for an investment in inventory involves a basic tradeoff between risk and return. The risk is that if the level of inventory is too low, the various functions of business do not operate independently, and delays in production and customer delivery can result. The return results because reduced inventory investment saves money. As the size of inventory increases, storage and handling costs are expected to increase. However, the required return on capital invested in inventory is also expected to increase. Therefore, a firm will reduce the risk of running out of inventory by increasing its level of inventory, but at the cost of increasing inventory expenses. To better illustrate the uncoupling function that inventories perform, we will look at several general types of inventories.

Raw Materials Inventory

Raw materials inventory consists of basic materials purchased from other firms to be used in the firm's production operations. These goods may include steel, lumber, petroleum, or manufactured items such as wire, ball bearings, or tires that the firm does not produce itself. Regardless of the type of raw materials, all manufacturing firms by definition maintain a raw materials inventory. Its purpose is to uncouple the production function from the purchasing function—that is, to make these two functions independent of each other, so that delays in shipment of raw materials do not cause production delays. In the event of a delay in shipment, the firm can satisfy its need for raw materials by liquidating its inventory.

Work in Process Inventory

Work in process inventory consists of partially finished goods requiring additional work before they become finished goods. The more complex and lengthy the production process, the larger the investment in work in process inventory. The purpose of work in process inventory is to uncouple the various operations in the production process so that machine failures and work stoppages in one operation will not affect the other operations. Assume, for example, there are 10 different production operations, each one involving the piece of work produced in the previous operation. If the machine performing the first production operation breaks down, a firm with no work in process inventory will have to shut down all 10 production operations. Yet if a firm has such inventory, the remaining 9 operations can continue by drawing the input for the second operation from inventory rather than directly from the output of the first operation.

Finished Goods Inventory

The **finished goods inventory** consists of goods on which the production has been completed but that are not yet sold. The purpose of a finished goods inventory is to uncouple the production and sales functions so that it is not necessary to produce the good before a sale can occur—sales can be made directly out of inventory. For example, in the auto industry, customers would not buy from a dealer who made them wait weeks or months when another dealer could fill the order immediately.

Stock of Cash

Although we have already discussed cash management at some length in Chapter 14, it is worthwhile to mention cash again in the light of inventory management. This is because the **stock of cash** carried by a firm is simply a special type of inventory. In terms of uncoupling the various operations of the firm, the purpose of holding a stock of cash is to make the payment of bills independent of the collection of accounts due. When cash is kept on hand, bills can be paid without prior collection of accounts.

As we examine and develop inventory economic ordering quantity (EOQ) models, we will see a striking resemblance between the EOQ inventory and EOQ cash model; in fact, except for a minor redefinition of terms, they will be exactly the same.

Inventory-Management Techniques

The importance of effective inventory management is directly related to the size of the investment in inventory. Since, on average, approximately 6.1 percent of a firm's assets are tied up in inventory, effective management of these assets is essential to the goal of shareholder wealth maximization. To control the investment in inventory, management must solve two problems: the order quantity problem and the order point problem.

The Order Quantity Problem

The order quantity problem involves determining the optimal order size for an inventory item given its expected usage, carrying costs, and ordering costs. Aside from a change in some of the variable names, it is exactly the same as the inventory model for cash management (EOQ model) presented in Chapter 14.

The EOQ model attempts to determine the order size that will minimize total inventory costs. It assumes that

$$\begin{matrix} \text{total} \\ \text{inventory costs} \end{matrix} = \begin{matrix} \text{total} \\ \text{carrying costs} \end{matrix} + \begin{matrix} \text{total} \\ \text{ordering costs} \end{matrix} \qquad (15\text{-}4)$$

Assuming that inventory is allowed to fall to zero and then is immediately replenished (this assumption will be lifted when we discuss the order point problem), the average inventory becomes $Q/2$, where Q is inventory order size in units.[8] Figure 15-4 illustrates the average inventory level.

If the average inventory is $Q/2$ and the carrying cost per unit is C, then carrying costs become:

$$\begin{matrix} \text{total} \\ \text{carrying costs} \end{matrix} = \left(\begin{matrix} \text{average} \\ \text{inventory} \end{matrix} \right) \left(\begin{matrix} \text{carrying cost} \\ \text{per unit} \end{matrix} \right) \qquad (15\text{-}5)$$

$$= \left(\frac{Q}{2} \right) C \qquad (15\text{-}6)$$

where Q = the inventory order size in units

           C = carrying costs per unit

The carrying costs on inventory include insurance fees, employee salaries associated with inventory storage, property taxes, warehouse or storage

---

[8]The assumption of inventory being replenished immediately enables us to exclude from the model any term for losses in sales from not having enough inventory.

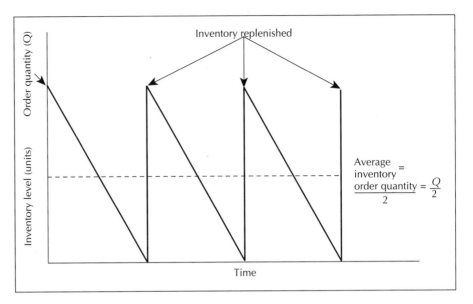

FIGURE 15-4
Inventory Level and the Replenishment Cycle

costs, wages for those who operate the warehouse, and costs associated with inventory shrinkage, obsolescence, and spoilage. Thus, carrying costs include both real cash flows and opportunity costs associated with having funds tied up in inventory.[9]

The ordering costs incurred are equal to the ordering costs per order times the number of orders.[10] If we assume total demand over the planning period is S and we order in lot sizes of Q, then S/Q represents the number of orders over the planning period. If the ordering cost per order is O, then

$$\begin{matrix} \text{total} \\ \text{ordering costs} \end{matrix} = \begin{pmatrix} \text{number} \\ \text{of orders} \end{pmatrix} \begin{pmatrix} \text{ordering cost} \\ \text{per order} \end{pmatrix} \qquad (15\text{-}7)$$

$$= \left(\frac{S}{Q}\right) O \qquad (15\text{-}8)$$

where S = total demand in units over the planning period

O = ordering cost per order

Thus, total costs in Equation (15-4) become

$$\text{total costs} = \left(\frac{Q}{2}\right) C + \left(\frac{S}{Q}\right) O \qquad (15\text{-}9)$$

Figure 15-5 illustrates this equation.

---

[9]The opportunity cost associated with having funds tied up in inventory is represented by the required rate of return on investment in inventory.

[10]Ordering costs include: the cost of placing an order; the production set-up costs; shipping and handling costs; and quantity discount costs. An example of set-up costs in production is the cost of resetting stamping machines in the auto industry. Note that quantity discount costs are negative costs received if the purchase (order) size is at least a specified level or more.

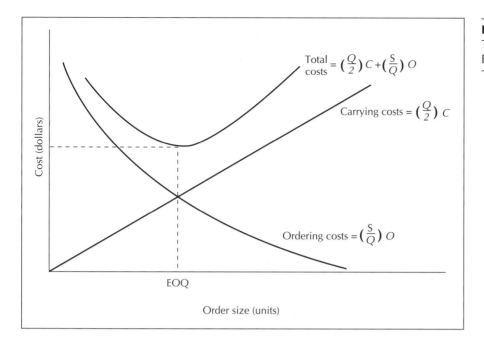

FIGURE 15-5
Total Cost and
EOQ Determination

What we are looking for is the ordering size, Q^*, that provides the minimum total costs. By manipulating Equation (15-9), we find that the optimal value of Q—that is, the economic ordering quantity (EOQ)—is[11]

$$Q^* = \sqrt{\frac{2SO}{C}} \qquad (15\text{-}10)$$

The use of the EOQ model can best be illustrated through an example.

EXAMPLE

Suppose a firm expects total demand (S) for its product over the planning period to be 5,000 units, while the ordering cost per order (O) is $200, and

---

[11]This result can be obtained through calculus.

$$\text{total cost } (TC) = \left(\frac{Q}{2}\right)C + \left(\frac{S}{Q}\right)O$$

The first derivative with respect to Q defines the slope of the total cost curve. Setting this derivative equal to zero specifies the minimum point (zero slope) on the curve. Thus,

$$\frac{dTC}{dQ} = \frac{C}{2} - \frac{SO}{Q^2} = O$$

$$Q^2 = \frac{2SO}{C}$$

$$Q^* = \sqrt{\frac{2SO}{C}}$$

To verify that a minimum point is being found, rather than a maximum point where the slope would also equal zero, we check for a positive second derivative:

$$\frac{d^2TC}{dQ^2} = \frac{2SO}{Q^3} \geq 0$$

The second derivative must be positive, since SO and Q can only take on positive values; hence, this is a minimum point.

the carrying cost per unit (C) is \$2. Substituting these values into Equation (15-10) yields

$$Q^* = \sqrt{\frac{2 \cdot 5000 \cdot 200}{2}} = \sqrt{1,000,000} = 1000 \text{ units}$$

Thus, if this firm orders in 1,000-unit lot sizes, it will minimize its total inventory costs. ∎

Examination of EOQ Assumptions

Despite the fact that the model tends to yield quite good results, there are major weaknesses in the EOQ model associated with several of its assumptions. If the model's assumptions are violated, the EOQ model can generally be modified to accommodate the situation. The model's assumptions are as follows:

1. **Constant or uniform demand.** Although the EOQ model assumes constant demand, demand may vary from day to day. If demand is stochastic—that is, not known in advance—the model must be modified through the inclusion of a safety stock.

2. **Constant unit price.** The inclusion of variable prices resulting from quantity discounts can be handled quite easily through a modification of the original EOQ model, redefining total costs and solving for the optimum order quantity.

3. **Constant carrying costs.** Unit carrying costs may vary substantially as the size of the inventory rises, perhaps decreasing because of economies of scale or storage efficiency or increasing as storage space runs out and new warehouses have to be rented. This situation can be handled through a modification in the original model similar to the one used for variable unit price.

4. **Constant ordering costs.** While this assumption is generally valid, its violation can be accommodated by modifying the original EOQ model in a manner similar to the one used for variable unit price.

5. **Instantaneous delivery.** If delivery is not instantaneous, which is generally the case, the original EOQ model must be modified through the inclusion of a safety stock. Safety stock represents any amount of inventory that is held to accommodate any unusually large and unexpected usage during the delivery time.

6. **Independent orders.** If multiple orders result in cost savings by reducing paperwork and transportation cost, the original EOQ model must be further modified. While this modification is somewhat complicated, special EOQ models have been developed to deal with it.[12]

These assumptions illustrate the limitations of the basic EOQ model and the ways in which it can be modified to compensate for them. An understanding of the limitations and assumptions of the EOQ model enables the financial manager to make more effective inventory decisions.[13]

---

[12]For example, R. J. Tersire, *Material Management and Inventory Control* (New York: Elsevier–North Holland, 1976).

[13]Much of the recent criticism of the EOQ model has been based upon the inability of such a system to respond quickly to rapidly changing demand. For example, the 800-ton presses used to stamp out automobile panels take about four hours to set up. If we assume that set-up costs are equivalent to ordering costs, the EOQ model predicts that at least 10,000 identical panels must be produced before the presses be reset. It is estimated that at least two weeks of production would be required for this type of output. Unfortunately, batch sizes this large make it impossible to respond rapidly to changing demands.

The Order Point Problem

The two most limiting assumptions—those of constant or uniform demand and instantaneous delivery—are dealt with through the inclusion of safety stock. The decision on how much safety stock to hold is generally referred to as the order point problem; that is, how low should inventory be depleted before it is reordered?

Two factors go into the determination of the appropriate order point: (1) the procurement or delivery-time stock and (2) the safety stock desired. Figure 15-6 illustrates the process involved in order point determination. We observe that the order-point problem can be decomposed into its two components, the **delivery-time stock**—that is, the inventory needed between the order date and the receipt of the inventory ordered—and the safety stock. Thus, the order point is reached when inventory falls to a level equal to the delivery-time stock plus the safety stock.

$$\begin{array}{l} \text{inventory order point} \\ \text{[order new inventory when} \\ \quad \text{the level of inventory} \\ \quad \text{falls to this level]} \end{array} = (\text{delivery-time stock}) + (\text{safety stock}) \quad (15\text{-}11)$$

As a result of constantly carrying safety stock, the average level of inventory increases. Whereas before the inclusion of safety stock the average level of inventory was equal to EOQ/2, now it will be

$$\text{average inventory} = \frac{\text{EOQ}}{2} + \text{safety stock} \quad (15\text{-}12)$$

In general, several factors simultaneously determine how much delivery-time stock and safety stock should be held. First, the efficiency of the replenishment system affects how much delivery-time stock is needed. Since the delivery-time stock is the expected inventory usage between ordering and receiving inventory, efficient replenishment of inventory would reduce the need for delivery-time stock.

The uncertainty surrounding both the delivery time and the demand for the product affects the level of safety stock needed. The more certain the

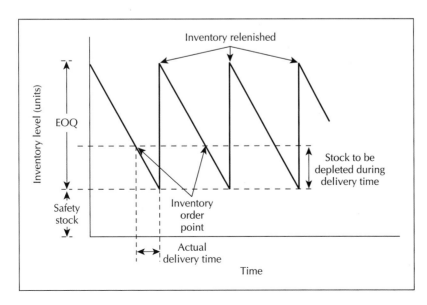

FIGURE 15-6
Order Point Determination

patterns of these inflows and outflows from the inventory, the less safety stock required. In effect, if these inflows and outflows are highly predictable, then there is little chance of any stock-out occurring. However, if they are unpredictable, it becomes necessary to carry additional safety stock to prevent unexpected stock-outs.[14]

The safety margin desired also affects the level of safety stock held. If it is a costly experience to run out of inventory, the safety stock held will be larger than it would be otherwise. If running out of inventory and the subsequent delay in supplying customers result in strong customer dissatisfaction and the possibility of lost future sales, then additional safety stock is necessary.[15] A final determinant is the cost of carrying additional inventory, in terms of both the handling and storage costs and the opportunity cost associated with the investment in additional inventory. Very simply, the greater the costs, the smaller the safety stock.

The determination of the level of safety stock involves a basic tradeoff between the risk of stock-out, resulting in possible customer dissatisfaction and lost sales, and the increased costs associated with carrying additional inventory.

Inflation and EOQ

Inflation affects the EOQ model in two major ways. First, while the EOQ model can be modified to assume constant price increases, often major price increases occur only once or twice a year and are announced ahead of time. If this is the case, the EOQ model may lose its applicability and may be replaced with **anticipatory buying**—that is, buying in anticipation of a price increase in order to secure the goods at a lower cost. Of course, as with most decisions, there are tradeoffs. The costs are the added carrying costs associated with the inventory. The benefits, of course, come from buying at a lower price. The second way inflation affects the EOQ model is through increased carrying costs. As inflation pushes interest rates up, the cost of carrying inventory increases. In our EOQ model this means that C increases, which results in a decline in Q^*, the optimal economic order quantity:

$$\downarrow Q^* = \sqrt{\frac{2SO}{C\uparrow}} \qquad (15\text{-}13)$$

Reluctance to stock large inventories because of high carrying costs became particularly prevalent during the late 1970s and early 1980s when inflation and interest rates were at high levels.

JUST-IN-TIME INVENTORY CONTROL

The **just-in-time inventory control system** is more than just an inventory control system, it is a production and management system. Not only is

---

[14]Note that with a safety stock, costs will rise over what they were without a safety stock. Thus, demand uncertainty creates an additional cost to the firm.

[15]Safety stock costs include: lost sales due to stock-outs; costs associated with production stoppages owing to stock-outs; lost future sales as customers find new sources for the item during stock-out periods.

inventory cut down to a minimum, but the time and physical distance between the various production operations are also reduced. In addition management is willing to trade off costs to develop close relationships with suppliers and promote speedy replenishment of inventory in return for the ability to hold less safety stock.

The just-in-time inventory control system was originally developed in Japan by Taiichi Okno, a vice-president of Toyota. Originally the system was called the *kanban* system after the cards placed in the parts bins which were used to call for a new supply. The idea behind the system is that the firm should keep a minimum level of inventory on hand, relying on suppliers to furnish parts "just in time" for them to be assembled. This is in direct contrast to the traditional inventory philosophy of North American firms, which is sometimes referred to as a "just in case" system, which keeps healthy levels of safety stocks to ensure that production will not be interrupted. While large inventories may not be a bad idea when interest rates are low, when interest rates are high, as they have been in recent years, they become very costly.

While the just-in-time inventory system is intuitively appealing, it has not proved easy to implement. Successful implementation of this system has been limited by the construction of plants that have too much space for storage and not enough access doors and loading docks to receive inventory. However, the just-in-time inventory system has forced the firm to change its relationship with its suppliers. Since the firm relies on suppliers to deliver high-quality parts and materials immediately, it must have a close long-term relationship with them. Despite the difficulties of implementation, many North American firms are committed to moving toward a just-in-time system. Using its own version of the Japanese inventory control system, General Motors of Canada has implemented the synchronous manufacturing system which has reduced the monthly average inventory level by 3 percent in 1990 over 1989. In this case, Woodbridge Foam corporation provides seats to GM's Sainte Therese car assembly plant. This type of inventory system has enabled the Sainte Therese plant to eliminate the stocking of car seats in their inventory.

While the just-in-time system does not at first appear to bear much of a relationship to the EOQ model, it simply alters some of the assumptions of the model with respect to delivery time and ordering costs and draws out the implications. Actually, it is just a new approach to the EOQ model that tries to produce the lowest average level of inventory possible. If we look at the average level of inventory as defined by the EOQ model, we find it to be:

$$\text{average inventory} = \frac{\sqrt{\dfrac{2SO\downarrow}{C}}}{2} + \text{safety stock}$$

The just-in-time system attacks this equation in two places. First, by locating inventory supplies in convenient locations, laying out plants in such a way that it is inexpensive and easy to unload new inventory shipments, and computerizing the inventory order system, the cost of ordering new inventory, O, is reduced. Second, by developing a strong relationship with suppliers located in the same geographical area and setting up restocking strategies that cut time, the safety stock is also reduced. The philosophy behind the just-in-time inventory system is that the benefits associated with reducing inventory and delivery time to a bare minimum through adjustment in the EOQ model will more than offset the costs associated with the increased possibility of stock-outs.[16]

SUMMARY

The size of the investment in accounts receivable depends upon three factors: the percentage of credit sales to total sales, the level of sales, and the credit and collection policies. However, only the credit and collection policies are decision variables open to the financial manager. The policies that the financial manager has control over include the terms of sale, the quality of customer, and the collection efforts.

While the typical firm has fewer assets tied up in inventory than it does in accounts receivable, inventory management and control is still an important function of the financial manager. The purpose of holding inventory is to make each function of the business independent of the other functions— that is, to uncouple the firm's operations. Inventory-management techniques primarily involve questions of how much inventory should be ordered and when the order should be placed. The answers directly determine the average level of investment in inventory. The EOQ model is employed in answering the first of these questions. This model attempts to calculate the order size that minimizes the sum of the inventory carrying and ordering costs.

---

[16]Part of the inspiration for employing the Just-In-Time inventory system (besides increasing the ability to respond to changing demand) was the argument that costs other than carrying and ordering or set-up costs were affected by the batch size, namely, quality of the finished product, amount of waste, and the motivation of the workers. All these factors, proponents of the Just-In-Time system, contributed to increased costs as the batch size increased.

The order point problem attempts to determine how low inventory can drop before it is reordered. The order point is reached when the inventory falls to a level equal to the delivery-time stock plus the safety stock. In solving for the level of safety stock, the financial manager must tradeoff between the risk of running out of inventory and the increased costs associated with carrying additional inventory.

The just-in-time inventory control system lowers inventory by reducing the time and distance between the various production functions. The idea behind the system is that the firm should keep a minimum level of inventory on hand and rely upon suppliers to furnish parts "just-in-time" for them to be assembled.

STUDY QUESTIONS

15-1. What factors determine the size of the investment a firm makes in accounts receivable? Which of these factors are under the control of the financial manager?

15-2. What do the following trade credit terms mean?

    a. 1/20, net 50

    b. 2/30, net 60

    c. net 30

    d. 2/10, 1/30, net 60

15-3. What is the purpose of the use of an aging account in the control of accounts receivable? Can this same function be performed through ratio analysis? Why or why not?

15-4. If a credit manager experienced no bad debt losses over the past year, would this be an indication of proper credit management? Why or why not?

15-5. What is the purpose of credit scoring?

15-6. What are the risk-return tradeoffs associated with adopting a more liberal trade credit policy?

15-7. Explain the purpose of marginal analysis.

15-8. What is the purpose of holding inventory? Name several types of inventory and describe their purpose.

15-9. Can cash be considered a special type of inventory? If so, what functions does it attempt to uncouple?

15-10. In order to control investment in inventory effectively, what two questions must be answered?

15-11. What are the major assumptions made by the EOQ model?

15-12. What are the risk-return tradeoffs associated with inventory management?

15-13. How might inflation affect the EOQ model?

SELF-TEST PROBLEMS

ST-1. (*EOQ Calculations*) A local gift shop is attempting to determine how many sets of wine glasses to order. The store feels it will sell approximately 800 sets in the next year at a price of $18 per set. The wholesale price that the store pays per set is $12. Costs for carrying one set of wine glasses are estimated at $1.50 per year while ordering costs are estimated at $25.00.

    a. What is the economic order quantity for the sets of wine glasses?

b. What are the annual inventory costs for the firm if it orders in this quantity? (Assume constant demand and instantaneous delivery and thus no safety stock is carried.)

ST-2. (*EOQ Calculations*) Given the following inventory information and relationships for the F. Beamer Corporation:

1. Orders can be placed only in multiples of 100 units.
2. Annual unit usage is 300,000. (Assume a 50-week year in your calculations.)
3. The carrying cost is 30 percent of the purchase price of the goods.
4. The purchase price is $10 per unit.
5. The ordering cost is $50 per order.
6. The desired safety stock is 1,000 units. (This does not include delivery-time stock.)
7. Delivery time is two weeks.

Given this information,

a. What is the optimal EOQ level?

b. How many orders will be placed annually?

c. At what inventory level should a reorder be made?

STUDY PROBLEMS (SET A)

15-1A. (*Trade Credit Discounts*) Determine the effective annualized cost of forgoing the trade credit discount on the following terms:

a. 1/10, net 20

b. 2/10, net 30

c. 3/10, net 30

d. 3/10, net 60

e. 3/10, net 90

f. 5/10, net 60

15-2A. (*Altman Model*) The following ratios were supplied by six loan applicants. Given this information and the credit-scoring model developed by Altman [Equation (15-3)], which loans have a high probability of defaulting next year and thus should be avoided?

	EBIT ——— Total Assets	Sales ——— Total Assets	Market Value of Equity ——— Book Value of Debt	Earnings ——— Total Assets	Working Capital ——— Total Assets
Applicant 1	.2	.2	1.2	.3	.5
Applicant 2	.2	.8	1.0	.3	.8
Applicant 3	.2	.7	.6	.3	.4
Applicant 4	.1	.4	1.2	.4	.4
Applicant 5	.3	.7	.5	.4	.7
Applicant 6	.2	.5	.5	.4	.4

15-3A. (*Ratio Analysis*) Assuming a 365-day year, calculate what the average investment in inventory would be for a firm, given the following information in each case:

a. The firm has sales of $600,000, a gross profit margin of 10 percent, and an inventory turnover ratio of 6.

b. The firm has a cost of goods sold figure of $480,000 and an average age of inventory of 40.56 days.

c. The firm has a cost of goods sold figure of $1,150,000 and an inventory turnover ratio of 5.

d. The firm has a sales figure of $25 million, a gross profit margin of 14 percent, and an average age of inventory of 45 days.

15-4A. (*Marginal Analysis*) the Bandwagonesque Corporation is considering relaxing its current credit policy. Currently, the firm has annual sales (all credit) of $5 million and an average collection period of 60 days (assume a 365-day year). Under the proposed change the trade credit terms would be changed from net 60 days to net 90 days and credit would be extended to a more risky class of customer. It is assumed that bad debt losses on current customers will remain at their current level. Under this change, it is expected that sales will increase to $6,000,000. Given the following information, should the firm adopt the new policy?

New sales level (all credit):	$6,000,000
Original sales level (all credit):	$5,000,000
Contribution margin:	20%
Percent bad debt losses on new sales:	8%
New average collection period:	90 days
Original average collection period:	60 days
Additional investment in inventory:	$50,000
Pre-tax required rate of return:	15%

15-5A. (*Marginal Analysis*) The Foxbase Alpha Corporation is considering a major change in credit policy. The new credit policy requires extending credit to a riskier class of customer and extending their credit period from net 30 days to net 45 days. They do not expect bad debt losses on their current customers to change. Given the following information, should they go ahead with the change in credit policy?

New sales level (all credit):	$12,500,000
Original sales level (all credit):	$11,000,000
Contribution margin:	20%
Percent bad debt losses on new sales:	9%
New average collection period:	45 days
Original average collection period:	30 days
Additional investment in inventory:	$75,000
Pre-tax required rate of return:	15%

15-6A. (*Marginal Analysis*) Nirvana Inc. has annual sales of $5 million. All sales are credit and the current credit terms are 1/50, net 70. The company is studying the possibility of relaxing credit terms to 2/60, net 90 in hopes of securing new sales. Management does not expect bad debt losses on the current customers to change under the new credit policy. Given the following information, should the firm go ahead with the change in credit policy?

New sales level (all credit):	$8,000,000
Original sales level (all credit):	$7,000,000
Contribution margin:	25%
Percent bad debt losses on new sales:	8%
New average collection period:	75 days
Original average collection period:	60 days
Additional investment in inventory:	$50,000
Pre-tax required rate of return:	15%
New percent cash discount:	2%
Percent of customers taking the cash discount:	50%
Old percent cash discount:	1%
Percent of customers taking the old cash discount:	50%

15-7A. (*EOQ Calculations*) A downtown bookstore is trying to determine the optimal order quantity for a popular novel just printed in paperback. The store feels that the book will sell at four times its hardback figures. It would therefore sell approximately 3,000 copies in the next year at a price of $1.50. The store buys the book at a wholesale figure of $1. Costs for carrying the book are estimated at $.10 a copy per year, and it costs $10 to order more books.

    a. Determine the economic order quantity.

    b. What would be the total costs for ordering the books 1, 4, 5, 10, and 15 times a year?

    c. What questionable assumptions are being made by the EOQ model?

15-8A. (*EOQ Calculations*) The local hamburger fast-food restaurant purchases 20,000 boxes of hamburger rolls every month. Order costs are $50 an order, and it costs $.25 a box for storage.

    a. What is the optimal order quantity of hamburger rolls for this restaurant?

    b. What questionable assumptions are being made by the EOQ model?

15-9A. (*EOQ Calculations*) A local car manufacturing plant has a $75 per-unit per-year carrying cost on a certain item in inventory. This item is used at a rate of 50,000 per year. Ordering costs are $500 per order.

    a. What is the economic order quantity for this item?

    b. What are the annual inventory costs for this firm if it orders in this quantity? (Assume constant demand and instantaneous delivery.)

15-10A. (*EOQ Calculations*) Swank Products is involved in the production of camera parts and has the following inventory, carrying, and storage costs:

    1. Orders must be placed in round lots of 200 units.

    2. Annual unit usage is 500,000. (Assume a 50-week year in your calculations.)

    3. The carrying cost is 20 percent of the purchase price.

    4. The purchase price $2 per unit.

    5. The ordering cost is $90 per order.

    6. The desired safety stock is 15,000 units. (This does not include delivery time stock.)

    7. The delivery time is one week.

Given the above information

    a. Determine the optimal EOQ level.

    b. How many orders will be placed annually?

    c. What is the inventory order point? (That is, at what level of inventory should a new order be placed?)

    d. What is the average inventory level?

15-11A. (*EOQ Calculations*) Regina Distributors has determined the following inventory information and relationships:

    1. Orders can be placed only in multiples of 200 units.

    2. Annual unit usage is 500,000 units. (Assume a 50-week year in your calculations.)

    3. The carrying cost is 10 percent of the purchase price of the goods.

    4. The purchase price is $5 per unit.

    5. The ordering cost is $100 per order.

    6. The desired safety stock is 5,000 units. (This does not include delivery time stock.)

    7. Delivery time is four weeks.

Given this information

    a. What is the EOQ level?

b. How many orders will be placed annually?

c. At what inventory level should a reorder be made?

d. Now assume the carrying costs are 50 percent of the purchase price of the goods and recalculate (a), (b), and (c). Are these the results you anticipated?

15-12A. (*Comprehensive EOQ Calculations*) Knutson Products, Inc., is involved in the production of airplane parts and has the following inventory, carrying, and storage costs:

1. Orders must be placed in round lots of 100 units.

2. Annual unit usage is 250,000. (Assume a 50-week year in your calculations.)

3. The carrying cost is 10 percent of the purchase price.

4. The purchase price is $10 per unit.

5. The ordering cost is $100 per order.

6. The desired safety stock is 5,000 units. (This does not include delivery time stock.)

7. The delivery time is one week.

Given the above information

a. Determine the optimal EOQ level.

b. How many orders will be placed annually?

c. What is the inventory order point? (That is, at what level of inventory should a new order be placed?)

d. What is the average inventory level?

e. What would happen to the EOQ if annual unit sales doubled (all other unit costs and safety stocks remaining constant)? What is the elasticity of EOQ with respect to sales? (That is, what is the percent change in EOQ divided by the percent change in sales?)

f. If carrying costs double, what would happen to the EOQ level? (Assume the original sales level of 250,000 units.) What is the elasticity of EOQ with respect to carrying costs?

g. If the ordering costs double, what would happen to the level of EOQ? (Again assume original levels of sales and carrying costs.) What is the elasticity of EOQ with respect to ordering costs?

h. If the selling price doubles, what would happen to the EOQ? What is the elasticity of EOQ with respect to selling price?

STUDY PROBLEMS (SET B)

15-1B. (*Trade Credit Discounts*) Determine the effective annualized cost of forgoing the trade credit discount on the following terms:

a. 1/5, net 20

b. 2/20, net 90

c. 1/20, net 100

d. 4/10, net 50

e. 5/20, net 100

f. 5/30, net 50

15-2B. (*Altman Model*) The following ratios were supplied by six loan applicants. Given this information and the credit-scoring model developed by Altman [Equation (15-3)], which loans have a high probability of defaulting next year and thus should be avoided?

	EBIT	Sales	Market Value of Equity	Earnings	Working Capital
	Total Assets	Total Assets	Book Value of Debt	Total Assets	Total Assets
Applicant 1	.3	.4	1.2	.3	.5
Applicant 2	.2	.6	1.3	.4	.3
Applicant 3	.2	.7	.6	.3	.2
Applicant 4	.1	.5	.8	.5	.4
Applicant 5	.5	.7	.5	.4	.6
Applicant 6	.2	.4	.2	.4	.4

15-3B. (*Ratio Analysis*) Assuming a 365-day year, calculate what the average investment in inventory would be for a firm, given the following information in each case.

a. The firm has sales of $550,000, a gross profit margin of 10 percent, and an inventory turnover ratio of 5.

b. The firm has a cost of goods sold figure of $480,000 and an average age of inventory of 35 days.

c. The firm has a cost of goods sold figure of $1,250,000 and an inventory turnover ratio of 6.

d. The firm has a sales figure of $25 million, a gross profit margin of 15 percent, and an average age of inventory of 50 days.

15-4B. (*Marginal Analysis*) The Hyndford Street Corporation is considering relaxing its current credit policy. Currently, the firm has annual sales (all credit) of $6 million and an average collection period of 40 days (assume a 365-day year). Under the proposed change the trade credit terms would be changed from net 40 days to net 90 days and credit would be extended to a more risky class of customer. It is assumed that bad debt losses on current customers will remain at their current level. Under this change, it is expected that sales will increase to $7,000,000. Given the following information, should the firm adopt the new policy?

New sales level (all credit):	$7,000,000
Original sales level (all credit):	$6,000,000
Contribution margin:	20%
Percent bad debt losses on new sales:	8%
New average collection period:	90 days
Original average collection period:	40 days
Additional investment in inventory:	$40,000
Pre-tax required rate of return:	15%

15-5B. (*Marginal Analysis*) The Northern Muse Corporation is considering a major change in credit policy. The new credit policy requires extending credit to a riskier class of customer and extending their credit period from net 30 days to net 50 days. They do not expect bad debt losses on their current customers to change. Given the following information, should they go ahead with the change in credit policy?

New sales level (all credit):	$18,000,000
Original sales level (all credit):	$17,000,000
Contribution margin:	20%
Percent bad debt losses on new sales:	8%
New average collection period:	50 days
Original average collection period:	30 days
Additional investment in inventory:	$60,000
Pre-tax required rate of return:	15%

15-6B. (*Marginal Analysis*) Nirvana Inc. has annual sales of $10 million. All sales are credit and the current credit terms are 1/30, net 60. The company is studying the possibility of relaxing credit terms to 2/60, net 90 in hopes of securing new sales. Management does not expect bad debt losses on the current customers to change under the new credit policy. Given the following information, should the firm go ahead with the change in credit policy?

New sales level (all credit):	$10,500,000
Original sales level (all credit):	$10,000,000
Contribution margin:	25%
Percent bad debt losses on new sales:	8%
New average collection period:	75 days
Original average collection period:	45 days
Additional investment in inventory:	$60,000
Pre-tax required rate of return:	15%
New percent cash discount:	2%
Percent of customers taking the cash discount:	50%
Old percent cash discount:	1%
Percent of customers taking the old cash discount:	50%

15-7B. (*EOQ Calculations*) A downtown bookstore is trying to determine the optimal order quantity for a popular novel just printed in paperback. The store feels that the book will sell at four times its hardback figures. It would therefore sell approximately 3,500 copies in the next year at a price of $1.50. The store buys the book at a wholesale figure of $1. Costs for carrying the book are estimated at $.20 a copy per year, and it costs $9 to order more books.

   a. Determine the economic order quantity.

   b. What would be the total costs for ordering the books 1, 4, 5, 10, and 15 times a year?

   c. What questionable assumptions are being made by the EOQ model?

15-8B. (*EOQ Calculations*) The local hamburger fast-food restaurant purchases 21,000 boxes of hamburger rolls every month. Order costs are $55 an order, and it costs $.20 a box for storage.

   a. What is the optimal order quantity of hamburger rolls for this restaurant?

   b. What questionable assumptions are being made by the EOQ model?

15-9B. (*EOQ Calculations*) A local car manufacturing plant has a $70 per-unit per-year carrying cost on a certain item in inventory. This item is used at a rate of 55,000 per year. Ordering costs are $500 per order.

   a. What is the economic order quantity for this item?

   b. What are the annual inventory costs for this firm if it orders in this quantity? (Assume constant demand and instantaneous delivery.)

15-10B. (*EOQ Calculations*) Swank Products is involved in the production of camera parts and has the following inventory, carrying, and storage costs:

   1. Orders must be placed in round lots of 200 units.

   2. Annual unit usage is 600,000. (Assume a 50-week year in your calculations.)

   3. The carrying cost is 15 percent of the purchase price.

   4. The purchase price is $3 per unit.

   5. The ordering cost is $90 per order.

   6. The desired safety stock is 15,000 units. (This does not include delivery time stock.)

   7. The delivery time is one week.

Given the above information

a. Determine the optimal EOQ level.

b. How many orders will be placed annually?

c. What is the inventory order point? (That is, at what level of inventory should a new order be placed?)

d. What is the average inventory level?

15-11B. (*EOQ Calculations*) Regina Distributors has determined the following inventory information and relationships:

    1. Orders can be placed only in multiples of 200 units.

    2. Annual unit usage is 500,000 units. (Assume a 50-week year in your calculations.)

    3. The carrying cost is 9 percent of the purchase price of the goods.

    4. The purchase price is $5 per unit.

    5. The ordering cost is $75 per order.

    6. The desired safety stock is 5,000 units. (This does not include delivery time stock.)

    7. Delivery time is four weeks.

Given this information

a. What is the EOQ level?

b. How many orders will be placed annually?

c. At what inventory level should a reorder be made?

d. Now assume the carrying costs are 50 percent of the purchase price of the goods and recalculate (a), (b), and (c). Are these the results you anticipated?

15-12B. (*Comprehensive EOQ Calculations*) Good Gravy Products, Inc., is involved in the production of tractor parts and has the following inventory, carrying, and storage costs:

    1. Orders must be placed in round lots of 100 units.

    2. Annual unit usage is 300,000. (Assume a 50-week year in your calculations.)

    3. The carrying cost is 10 percent of the purchase price.

    4. The purchase price is $12 per unit.

    5. The ordering cost is $100 per order.

    6. The desired safety stock is 4,000 units. (This does not include delivery time stock.)

    7. The delivery time is one week.

Given the above information

a. Determine the optimal EOQ level.

b. How many orders will be placed annually?

c. What is the inventory order point? (That is, at what level of inventory should a new order be placed?)

d. What is the average inventory level?

e. What would happen to the EOQ if annual unit sales doubled (all other unit costs and safety stocks remaining constant)? What is the elasticity of EOQ with respect to sales? (That is, what is the percent change in EOQ divided by the percent change in sales?)

f. If carrying costs double, what would happen to the EOQ level? (Assume the original sales level of 250,000 units.) What is the elasticity of EOQ with respect to carrying costs?

g. If the ordering costs double, what would happen to the level of EOQ? (Again assume original levels of sales and carrying costs.) What is the elasticity of EOQ with respect to ordering costs?

h. If the selling price doubles, what would happen to EOQ? What is the elasticity of EOQ with respect to selling price?

SS-1. **a.** The economic order quantity is

$$Q^* = \sqrt{\frac{2SO}{C}}$$

where, SOC = total demand in units over the planning period

O = ordering cost per order

C = carrying costs per unit

Substituting the values given in the self-test problem into the EOQ equation we get

$$Q^* = \sqrt{\frac{2 \cdot 800 \cdot 25}{1.50}}$$

$$= \sqrt{26,667}$$

$$= 163 \text{ units per order}$$

Thus, 163 units should be ordered each time an order is placed. Note that the EOQ calculations take place based upon several limiting assumptions such as constant demand, constant unit price, and constant carrying costs, which may influence the final decision.

b. Total costs = carrying costs + ordering costs

$$= \left(\frac{Q}{2}\right)C + \left(\frac{S}{Q}\right)O$$

$$= \left(\frac{163}{2}\right)\$1.50 + \left(\frac{800}{163}\right)\$25$$

$$= \$122.25 + \$122.70$$

$$= \$244.95$$

Note that carrying costs and ordering costs are the same (other than a slight difference caused by having to order in whole rather than fractional units). This is because the total costs curve is at its minimum when ordering costs equal carrying costs, as shown in Figure 15-5.

SS-2. **a.**

$$EOQ = \sqrt{\frac{2SO}{C}}$$

$$= \sqrt{\frac{2(300,000)(50)}{3}}$$

$$= 3,162 \text{ units, but since orders must be placed in } 100\text{-unit lots, the effective EOQ becomes 3,200 units}$$

b.

$$\frac{\text{Total usage}}{\text{EOQ}} = \frac{300,000}{3,200} = 93.75 \text{ orders per year}$$

c. Inventory order point = delivery time + safety stock

$$= \frac{2}{50} \times 300,000 + 1,000$$

$$= 12,000 + 1,000$$

$$= 13,000 \text{ units}$$

SELECTED REFERENCES

Altman, Edward I. "Financial Ratios, Discriminate Analysis and the Prediction or Corporate Bankruptcy," *Journal of Finance*, 23 (September 1968), 589–609.

Ammer, Dean S. "Materials Management as a Profit Center," *Harvard Business Review*, 47 (January–February 1969), 72–89.

Atkins, Joseph C., and Yong H. Kim. "Comment and Correction: Opportunity Cost in the Evaluation of Investment in Accounts Receivable," *Financial Management*, 6 (Winter 1977), 71–74.

Beranek, William. "Financial Implications of Lot-Size Inventory Models," *Harvard Business Review*, 47 (January–February 1969), 72–90.

Brennan, Michael, J., Vojislav Maksimovic and Josef Zechner. "Vendor Financing," *The Journal of Finance*, 43 (December 1988), 1127–41.

Brick, Ivan E., and William K. H. Fung. "The Effect of Taxes on the Trade Credit Decision," *Financial Management*, 13 (Summer 1984), 24–30.

Brooks, Leroy D. "Risk-Return Criteria and Optimal Inventory Stocks," *Engineering Economist*, 25 (Summer 1980), 275–299.

Brosky, John J. *The Implicit Cost of Trade Credit and Theory of Optimal Terms of Sale*. New York: Credit Research Foundation, 1969.

Buffa, Elwood S. *Modern Production Management*. Chap. 11. 5th ed. Santa Barbara, CA: Wiley, 1977.

Carpenter, Michael D., and Jack E. Miller. "A Reliable Framework for Monitoring Accounts Receivable," *Financial Management*, 8 (Winter 1979), 37–40.

Celec, Stephen E., and Joe D. Icerman. "A Comprehensive Approach to Accounts Receivable," *Financial Management*, 15 (Spring 1980), 23–34.

Dyl, Edward A. "Another Look at the Evaluation of Investments in Accounts Receivable," *Financial Management*, 6 (Winter 1977), 67–70.

Emery, Gary W. "A Pure Financial Explanation for Trade Credit," *Journal of Financial and Quantitative Analysis*, 19 (September 1984), 271–285.

Greer, Carl C. "The Optimal Credit Acceptance Policy," *Journal of Financial and Quantitative Analysis*, 2 (December 1967), 399–415.

Halloren, John A., and Howard P. Lanser. "The Credit Policy Decision in an Inflationary Environment," *Financial Management*, 10 (Winter 1981), 31–38.

Herbst, Anthony F. "Some Empirical Evidence on the Determinants of Trade Credit at the Industry Level of Aggregation," *Journal of Financial and Quantitative Analysis*, 9 (June 1974), 377–394.

Hill, Ned C., and Kenneth D. Riener. "Determining the Cash Discount in the Firm's Credit Policy," *Financial Management*, 8 (Spring 1979), 68–73.

Hillier, Frederick S., and Gerald J. Lieberman. *Introduction to Operations Research*. Chap. 11. San Francisco: Holden-Day, 1974.

Kim, Yong H., and Joseph C. Atkins. "Evaluating Investments in Accounts Receivable: A Wealth Maximization Framework," *Journal of Finance*, 33 (May 1978), 403–412.

Kim, Yong H. and Kee H. Chung. "An Integrated Evaluation of Investment in Inventory and Credit," *Journal of Business Finance and Accounting*, 17 (1990), 381–90.

Lane, Sylvia. "Submarginal Credit Risk Classification," *Journal of Financial and Quantitative Analysis*, 7 (January 1972), 1379–1385.

Long, Michael S. "Credit Screening System Selection," *Journal of Financial and Quantitative Analysis*, 11 (June 1976), 313–328.

Mao, James, C. T. "Controlling Risk in Accounts Receivable Management," *Journal of Business Finance & Accounting*, 1 (Autumn 1974), 395–403.

Marrah, George G. "Managing Receivables," *Financial Executive*, 38 (July 1970), 40–44.

Mehta, Dileep. "The Formulation of Credit Policy Models," *Management Science*, 15 (October 1968), 30–50.

Mian, Shedzad L. and Clifford Smith. "Accounts Receivable Management Policy: Theory and Evidence," *Journal of Finance*, 47 (March 1992), 169–200.

Oh, John S. "Opportunity Cost in the Evaluation of Investment in Accounts Receivable," *Financial Management*, 6 (Summer 1976), 32–36.

Sachdeva, Kanwal S. "Accounts Receivable Decisions in a Capital Budgeting Framework," *Financial Management*, 10 (Winter 1981), 45–49.

Schiff, Michael. "Credit and Inventory Management," *Financial Executive*, 40 (November 1972), 28–33.

Smith, David E. *Quantitative Business Analysis*. Chaps. 14 and 15. Santa Barbara, CA: Wiley, 1977.

Smith, Keith V. *Management of Working Capital*. 2nd ed. New York: West Publishing, 1980.

Smith, Keith V., and Brian Belt. "Working Capital Management in Practice: An Update," Working Paper No. 951 (West Lafayette, IN: Krannert Graduate School of Management, Purdue University, 1989).

Snyder, Arthur. "Principles of Inventory Management," *Financial Executive*, 32 (April 1964), 16–19.

Soldofsky, Robert M. "A Model for Accounts Receivable Management," *N.A.A. Bulletin* (January 1966), 55–58.

Srinivasan, Venkat and Yong H. Kim. "Granting: A Comprehensive Analysis of Classification Procedures," *Journal of Finance*, 42 (July 1987), 665–81.

Vander Weide, J., and S. F. Maier. *Managing Corporate Liquidity*. New York: Wiley, 1985.

Walia, Tirlochan S. "Explicit and Implicit Cost of Changes in the Level of Accounts Receivable and the Credit Policy Decision of the Firm," *Financial Management*, 6 (Winter 1977), 75–78.

Welshans, Merle T. "Using Credit for Profit Making," *Harvard Business Review*, 45 (January–February 1967), 141–156.

Weston, J. Fred, and Pham D. Tuan. "Comment on Analysis of Credit Policy Changes," *Financial Management*, 9 (Winter 1980), 59–63.

Wrightsman, Dwayne. "Optimal Credit Terms for Accounts Receivable," *Quarterly Review of Economics and Business*, 9 (Summer 1969), 59–66.

The Effective Annual Rate Formula

The simple RATE calculation does not consider compound interest. To account for the influence of compounding, we can use the following equation:

$$EAR = \left(1 + \frac{r}{m}\right)^m - 1 \qquad (16\text{-}3)$$

where EAR is the **effective annual rate**, r is the nominal rate of interest per year (12 percent in the above example) and m is the number of compounding periods within a year [$m = 1/\text{TIME} = 1/(3/12) = 4$ in the example above]. Thus, the effective annual rate of interest on the example problem, considering compounding, is

$$EAR = \left(1 + \frac{0.12}{4}\right)^4 - 1 = 0.126 = 12.6\%$$

Compounding effectively raises the cost of short-term credit. Since compounding is commonly used in business transactions,[2] the effective annual cost will be used in future calculations.

SOURCES OF SHORT-TERM CREDIT

Short-term credit sources can be classified into two basic groups: unsecured and secured. **Unsecured** loans include all those sources that have as their security only the lender's faith in the ability of the borrower to repay the funds when due. There are three major sources of unsecured short-term credit: trade credit, unsecured bank loans, and commercial paper. **Secured** loans involve the pledge of specific assets as collateral in the event the borrower defaults in payment of principal or interest. Commercial banks, finance companies, and factors are the primary suppliers of secured credit. The principal sources of collateral include accounts receivable and inventories.

Unsecured Sources: Accrued Wages and Taxes

Since most businesses pay their employees only periodically (weekly, biweekly, or monthly), firms accrue a wages payable account that is, in essence, a loan from the firm's employees. For example, if the wage expense for a manufacturing firm is $450,000 per week and it pays its employees monthly, then by the end of a four-week month the firm will owe its employees $1.8 million in wages for services they have already performed during the month. Consequently, the employees finance their own efforts through waiting a full month for payment.

Similarly, firms are required by Revenue Canada to make monthly income tax payments for their estimated monthly tax liability. This means that the firm has the use of the tax monies it owes based upon monthly deductions. In addition, the firm pays sales taxes and withholding (income) taxes for its employees on a deferred basis. The longer the period of time that the firm holds the tax payments, the greater the amount of financing they provide.

[2]A similar expression was used in Chapter 15 to estimate the effective cost of passing up discounts on trade credit.

Note that these sources of financing occur spontaneously with increases or decreases in the level of firm sales. For example, as a firm's sales increase so do its labour expense, goods and services tax, and income tax. Consequently, these accrued expense items provide the firm with automatic or spontaneous sources of financing.

Trade Credit

Trade credit provides one of the most flexible sources of short-term financing available to the firm. In Chapter 13 we noted that trade credit is a primary source of spontaneous financing. That is, trade credit arises spontaneously with the firm's purchases. To arrange for credit the firm need only place an order with one of its suppliers. The supplier checks the firm's credit and, if it is good, sends the merchandise. The purchasing firm then pays for the goods in accordance with the supplier's credit terms.

Credit Terms and Cash Discounts

Very often the credit terms offered with trade credit involve a cash discount for early payment. For example, a supplier might offer terms of 2/10, net 30, which means that a 2 percent discount is offered for payment within 10 days or the full amount is due in 30 days. Thus, a 2 percent penalty is involved for not paying within 10 days or for delaying payment from the tenth to the thirtieth day (that is, for 20 days). The effective annual cost of not taking the cash discount can be quite severe. Using a $1 invoice amount, the effective annual cost of passing up the discount period using the above credit terms and our EAR equation can be estimated:

$$EAR = \left(1 + \frac{\$0.02}{\$0.98}\right)^{365/20} - 1 = .4576 = 45.76\%$$

Note that the 2 percent cash discount is the interest cost of extending the payment period an additional 20 days. Note also that the principal amount of the credit is $.98. This amount constitutes the full principal amount as of the tenth day of the credit period, after which time the cash discount is lost. The effective annual cost of passing up the 2 percent discount for two days is quite expensive: 45.76 percent. Furthermore, once the discount period has passed, there is no reason to pay before the final due date (the thirtieth day). Table 16-1 lists the effective annual cost of a number of alternative credit terms. Note that the cost of trade credit varies directly with the size of the cash discount and inversely with the length of time between the end of the discount period and the final due date.

Stretching on Trade Credit

Some firms that use trade credit engage in a practice called stretching of trade accounts. This practice involves delaying payments beyond the pre-

Credit Terms	Effective Annual Rate
2/10, net 60	15.89%
2/10, net 90	9.66
3/20, net 60	32.04
6/10, net 90	32.62

TABLE 16-1
Effective Annual Rates of Interest on Selected Trade Credit Terms

713

scribed credit period. For example, a firm might purchase materials under credit terms of 3/10, net 60; however, when faced with a shortage of cash, the firm might extend payment to the eightieth day. Continued violation of trade terms would eventually lead to a loss of credit. However, for short periods, and at infrequent intervals, stretching offers the firm a potentially useful source of short-term credit.

Advantages of Trade Credit

As a source of short-term financing, trade credit has a number of advantages. First, trade credit is conveniently obtained as a normal part of the firm's operations. Second, no formal agreements are generally involved in extending credit. Furthermore, the amount of credit extended expands and contracts with the needs of the firm; this is why it is classified as a spontaneous source of financing (Chapter 13).

Unsecured Sources: Bank Credit

Commercial banks provide unsecured short-term credit in two basic forms: lines of credit and transaction loans (notes payable).[3] Maturities of both types of loans are usually one year or less, with rates of interest depending on the creditworthiness of the borrower and the level of interest rates in the economy as a whole.

Line of Credit

A line of credit is generally an informal agreement or understanding between the borrower and the bank as to the maximum amount of credit that the bank will provide the borrower at any one time. Under this type of agreement there is no legal commitment on the part of the bank to provide the stated credit. In a revolving credit agreement, which is a variant of this form of financing, a legal obligation is involved. The line of credit agreement generally covers a period of one year corresponding to the borrower's fiscal year.[4] Thus, if the borrower is on a July 31 fiscal year, its lines of credit will be based on the same annual period.

CREDIT TERMS ■ Lines of credit generally do not involve fixed rates of interest; instead they state that credit will be extended at 0.5 percent over prime or some other spread over the bank's prime rate.[5] Furthermore, the agreement usually does not spell out the specific use that will be made of the funds beyond a general statement, such as for working-capital purposes. Figure 16-1 illustrates a letter of agreement to extend a line of credit.

Lines of credit usually require that the borrower maintain a minimum balance in the bank throughout the loan period, which is called a **compensating balance**. This type of required balance (which can be stated as a percent of the line of credit or the loan amount) increases the effective annual

---

[3]This type of bank loan is frequently referred to simply as a working capital loan.

[4]The principal distinction between a revolving line of credit and open line of credit is maturity. An open line is for less than one year while a revolving line is usually for three to five years, after which time the remaining balance can often be converted into a term loan. The revolving credit agreement is generally represented by a formal agreement; whereas, an open line agreement can either be formal or informal.

[5]The "prime rate of interest" represents the rate that a bank charges its most creditworthy borrowers.

FIGURE 16-1
Letter of Agreement to
Extend a Line of Credit

July 14, 19XX

Ms. Rebecca Swank
Vice President and Treasurer
Nuland Manufacturing Company

Dear Ms. Swank:

Following an analysis of your request, we have decided to extend to you a line of
credit for working capital purposes in the amount of $300,000. The credit is
extended for your current fiscal year ending July 31, 19XX. Borrowings under this
line will be at our prime rate prevailing at the time.

This credit is subject only to maintaining the firm's financial position.

Sincerely,

Francis L. Prince
Executive Vice President

cost of the loan to the borrower unless a deposit balance equal to or greater
than the compensating balance is ordinarily maintained in the bank.

The effective annual cost of short-term bank credit can be estimated
using the EAR equation. Consider the following example:

EXAMPLE

M&M Beverage Company has a $300,000 line of credit that requires a
compensating balance equal to 10 percent of the loan amount. The rate paid
on the loan is 12 percent per annum, $200,000 is borrowed for a six-month
period, and the firm does not, at present, have a deposit with the lending
bank. The dollar cost of the loan includes the interest expense and, in addition, the opportunity cost of maintaining an idle cash balance equal to the
10 percent compensating balance. To accommodate the cost of the compensating balance requirement, assume that the added funds will have to be borrowed and simply left idle in the firm's chequing account. Thus, the amount
actually borrowed (B) will be larger than the $200,000 needed. In fact, the
needed $200,000 will comprise 90 percent of the total borrowed funds due to
the 10 percent compensating balance requirement, hence $.90B = \$200,000$,
such that $B = \$222,222$. Thus, interest is paid on a $222,222 loan ($222,222 \times
.12 \times .5 = \$13,333.32$), of which only $200,000 is available for use by the
firm. The effective annual cost of credit therefore is

$$EAR = \left(1 + \frac{\$13,333.33}{\$200,000}\right)^{365/182} - 1 = 1.1382 - 1 = 13.82\%$$

BASIC FINANCIAL MANAGEMENT IN PRACTICE

How Do Banks Lend Money?

It is often quipped that a banker is a man who lends you an umbrella when it is fair, and takes it away when it rains. Actually, bankers utilize two very basic approaches to lending money. The first is commonly referred to as secured lending which can be loosely translated to mean lending on the borrower's assets, and the second is cash flow lending.

Secured lending involves lending money based upon the borrower's assets as collateral. In *The Merchant of Venice* Shylock demanded a pound of flesh as security for a loan. In practice banks accept a wide variety of objects as collateral. In any case to be acceptable as collateral the object must have three basic attributes: (i) It must first be worth at least as much as the amount being lent. Of course the worth of any asset is not always known with certainty nor is it assured that its worth will remain constant over the term of the loan. For these reasons banks will vary the percentage of the value of the collateral they will lend in response to their assessment of the riskiness of the collateral asset's value. For instance, if the borrower has a portfolio of government securities that it wants to use as collateral then the bank might advance a loan of up to 90 percent of the face value of these securities while it might loan as little as 20 percent against the estimated worth of the firm's work in progress inventories. (ii) To be good collateral it must be relatively easy to take possession of the asset. Here it helps if the collateral is not too mobile. For example, following the collapse of the shipping industry beginning in 1982 bankers found themselves with over $10 billion in bad debts which required that they quite literally search the ports of the world in search of their floating security. (iii) Finally, collateral must be easily identified. This requirement is actually an important element of item (ii) above. For example, although banks do make loans based on blanket liens against all or a portion (for example, inventories) of a firm's assets they prefer not to since it is more difficult to determine just what assets they hold claim to in the event of default.

An alternative to asset based loans, banks also engage in *cash flow lending* or loans based upon the supposed ability of the debtor to repay the loan. The key to this type of lending is a good estimate of the borrower's normal free cash flow that can serve as the basis for creditors. One commonly used basis for assessing this free cash flow is the sum of the firm's net profit after tax, its depreciation expense and its interest charges. The idea here is that this sum is the amount of cash the firm could use to meet its principal and interest charges. The ratio of the firm's free cash flow to its interest and principal expenses is generically referred to as the firm's interest cover. What constitutes an acceptable interest cover will vary with the nature of the firm's business with riskier businesses demanding a higher coverage ratio.

All of this sounds very scientific and quantifiable to this point. However, we know from the history of bank failures and crises that the lending process is fraught with uncertainty. In the end there is no substitute for common sense.

Source: "How Banks Lend," *The Economist* (February 4, 1989), pp. 78–79.

If the firm normally maintains at least $20,000 (or 10 percent of the needed funds) in a demand deposit with the lending bank, then the cost of the credit is

$$EAR = \left(1 + \frac{\$12,000}{\$200,000}\right)^{365/182} - 1 = 1.1239 - 1 = 12.39\% \blacksquare$$

In the M&M Beverage Company example the loan required the payment of principal ($222,222) plus interest ($13,333.32) at the end of the six-month loan period. Frequently, bank loans will be made on a discount basis. That is, the loan interest will be deducted from the loan amount before the funds are transferred to the borrower. Extending the M&M Beverage Company example to consider discounted interest involves reducing the loan proceeds

($200,000) in the previous example by the amount of interest for the full six months ($13,333.32). The effective annual rate of interest on the loan is now:

$$EAR = \left(1 + \frac{\$13,333.33}{\$200,000 - \$13,333.33}\right)^{365/182} - 1 = 1.1484 - 1 = 14.84\%$$

The effect of discounting interest was to raise the cost of the loan from 13.82 to 14.84 percent. This results from the fact that the firm pays interest on the same amount of funds as before ($222,222); however, this time it gets the use of $13,333.32 less, or $200,000 - $13,333.32 = $186,666.68.[6]

Transaction Loans

Still another form of unsecured short-term bank credit can be obtained in the form of **transaction loans**. Here the loan is made for a specific purpose.[7] This is the type of loan that most individuals associate with bank credit. The loan is obtained by signing a promissory note.

Unsecured transaction loans are very similar to a line of credit with regard to cost, term to maturity, and compensating balance requirements. In both instances commercial banks often require that the borrower clean up its short-term loans for a 30- to 45-day period during the year.[8] This means, very simply, that the borrower must be free of any bank debt for the stated period. The purpose of such a requirement is to ensure that the borrower is not using short-term bank credit to finance a part of its permanent needs for funds.

Unsecured Sources: Commercial Paper

Only the largest and most creditworthy companies are able to use **commercial paper**, which is simply a short-term *promise to pay* that is sold in the market for short-term debt securities.[9]

Credit Terms

The maturity of this credit source is generally six months or less, although some issues carry 9-month maturities. The interest rate on commercial paper is generally slightly lower (one-half to one percent) than the prime rate on commercial bank loans. Furthermore, the interest cost on commercial paper is determined on a discount basis.

---

[6]If M&M needs the use of a full $200,000 then it will have to borrow more than $222,222 to cover both the compensating balance requirement and the discounted interest. In fact, the firm will have to borrow some amount B such that

$$B - .10B - \left(.12 \times \frac{1}{2}\right)B = \$200,000$$

$$B = \frac{\$200,000}{.84} = \$238,095$$

The cost of credit remains the same at 14.84 percent, as we see below:

$$EAR = \left(1 + \frac{\$14,285.70}{\$238,095.70 - \$23,810 - \$14,285.70}\right)^{365/180} - 1 = 1.1484 - 1 = .1484 \ or \ 14.84\%$$

[7]Transaction loans are usually made to finance a nonrecurring purchase.

[8]The "clean-up" provision is very appropriate for those firms that have seasonal patterns in their business (for example, hotels or restaurants in certain vacation areas).

[9]A limited discussion of commercial paper is presented here; the topic is discussed in detail in Chapter 6.

New issues of commercial paper are either placed directly (sold by the issuing firm directly to the investing public) or dealer placed. Dealer placement involves the use of a commercial paper dealer, who sells the issue for the issuing firm. Many major companies, such as Marlborough Properties, Sobey Stores and Eaton's issue their commercial paper. The volume of direct versus dealer placements favours that of direct placements. Dealers are used primarily by industrial firms that either make only infrequent use of the commercial paper market or have difficulty placing the issue because of their small size.

Commercial Paper as a Source of Short-Term Credit

A number of advantages accrue to the user of commercial paper:

1. **Interest rate.** Commercial paper rates are generally lower than rates on bank loans and comparable sources of short-term financing. Figure 16-2 displays historical rates of interest on short-term bank credit and commercial paper.

2. **Compensating balance requirement.** No minimum balance requirements are associated with commercial paper. However, issuing firms usually find it desirable to maintain lines of credit agreements sufficient to back up their short-term financing needs in the event that a new issue of commercial paper cannot be sold or an outstanding issue cannot be repaid when due.

FIGURE 16-2. Historical Rates of Interest on Selected Financial Instruments

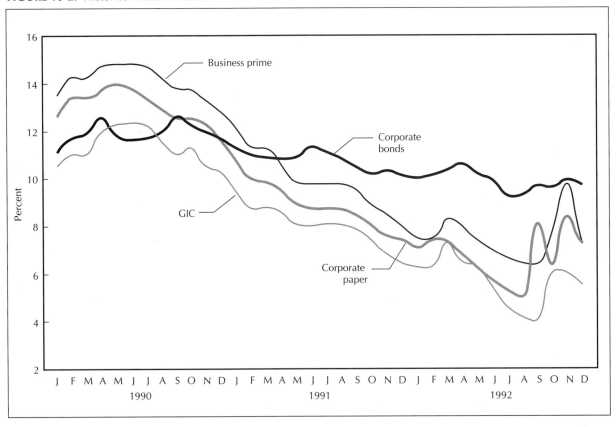

3. **Amount of credit.** Commercial paper offers the firm with very large credit needs a single source for all its short-term financing. Loan restrictions placed on the financial institutions by the regulatory authorities may cause a firm to obtain the necessary funds from a number of financial institutions.

4. **Prestige.** Since it is widely recognized that only the most creditworthy borrowers have access to the commercial paper market, its use signifies a firm's credit status.

Using commercial paper for short-term financing, however, involves a very important risk. That is, the commercial paper market is highly impersonal and denies even the most creditworthy borrower any flexibility in terms of repayment. When bank credit is used, the borrower has someone with whom he or she can work out any temporary difficulties that might be encountered in meeting a loan deadline. This flexibility simply does not exist for the user of commercial paper.

Estimating the Cost of Commercial Paper

The cost of commercial paper can be estimated using the simple effective annual cost of credit equation (EAR). The key points to remember are that commercial paper interest is usually discounted and that if a dealer is used to place the issue, a fee is charged. Even if a dealer is not used, the issuing firm will incur costs associated with preparing and placing the issue, which also must be considered in estimating the cost of credit.

EXAMPLE

The EPG Mfg. Company uses commercial paper regularly to support its needs for short-term financing. The firm plans to sell $100 million in 9-month-maturity paper on which it expects to have to pay discounted interest at an annual rate of 12 percent per annum. In addition, EPG expects to incur a cost of approximately $100,000 in dealer placement fees and other expenses of issuing the paper. The effective annual cost of credit to EPG can be calculated as follows:

$$EAR = \left[1 + \frac{(\$9,000,000 + \$100,000)}{(\$100,000,000 - \$100,000 - \$9,000,000)} \right]^{365/273} - 1$$

$$= 1.1361 - 1 = 13.61\%$$

where the interest cost is calculated as $100 million × .12 × 273/365 = $9 million. Thus, the effective annual cost of credit to EPG is 13.61 percent. ∎

Secured Sources: Accounts Receivable Loans

Secured sources of short-term credit have certain assets of the firm pledged as collateral to secure the loan. Upon default of the loan agreement, the lender has first claim to the pledged assets in addition to its claim as a general creditor of the firm. Hence the secured credit agreement offers an added margin of safety to the lender.

Generally, a firm's receivables are among its most liquid assets. For this reason they are considered by many lenders to be prime collateral for a secured loan. Two basic procedures can be used in arranging for financing based on receivables: pledging and factoring.

Pledging Accounts Receivable

Under the **pledging** arrangement the borrower simply pledges accounts receivable as collateral for a loan obtained from either a commercial bank or a finance company. The amount of the loan is stated as a percent of the face value of the receivables pledged. If the firm provides the lender with a general line on its receivables, then all of the borrower's accounts are pledged as security for the loan. This method of pledging is simple and inexpensive. However, since the lender has no control over the quality of the receivables being pledged, it will set the maximum loan at a relatively low percent of the total face value of the accounts, generally ranging downward from a maximum of around 75 percent.

Still another approach to pledging involves the borrower's presenting specific invoices to the lender as collateral for a loan. This method is somewhat more expensive in that the lender must assess the creditworthiness of each individual account pledged; however, given this added knowledge, the lender will be willing to increase the loan as a percent of the face value of the invoices. In this case the loan might reach as high as 85 or 90 percent of the face value of the pledged receivables.

CREDIT TERMS ■ Accounts receivable loans generally carry an interest rate 2 to 5 percent higher than the bank's prime lending rate. Finance companies charge an even higher rate. In addition, the lender will usually charge a handling fee stated as a percent of the face value of the receivables processed, which may be as much as 1 to 2 percent of the face value.

EXAMPLE

The A. B. Good Company sells electrical supplies to building contractors on terms of net 60. The firm's average monthly sales are $100,000; thus, its average receivables balance is $200,000 over the firm's two-month credit terms. The firm pledges all its receivables to a local bank, which in turn advances up to 70 percent of the face value of the receivables at 3 percent over prime and with a 1 percent processing charge on all receivables pledged. A. B. Good follows a practice of borrowing the maximum amount possible, and the current prime rate is 10 percent.

The effective annual cost of using this source of financing for a full year is computed as follows:

$$EAR = \left[1 + \frac{(\$3,033 + \$2,000)}{\$140,000} \right]^{365/60} - 1 = 1.2397 - 1 = 23.97\%$$

where the total dollar cost of the loan consists of both the 2-month interest expense (.13 × (2/12) × .70 × $200,000 = $3,033) and the annual processing fee (.01 × $100,000 × 2 months = $2,000). The amount of credit extended is .70 × $200,000 = $140,000. Note that the processing charge applies to all receivables pledged. Thus, the A. B. Good Company pledges $100,000 each month on which a 1 percent fee must be paid, for a total monthly charge of $1,000. ■

The lender, in addition to making advances or loans, may be providing certain credit services to the borrower. For example, the lender may provide billing and collection services. The value of these services should not be considered a part of the cost of credit. In the preceding example, A. B. Good Company may save credit department expenses of $850 per month by pledging all its accounts and letting the lender provide those services. In this case, the cost of short-term credit is only

$$EAR = \left[1 + \frac{(\$3{,}033 + 2{,}000 - \$1{,}700)}{\$140{,}000} \right]^{365/60} - 1 = 1.1539 - 1 = 15.39\%$$

ADVANTAGES AND DISADVANTAGES OF PLEDGING ■ The primary advantage of pledging as a source of short-term credit is the flexibility it provides the borrower. Financing is available on a continuous basis. The new accounts created through credit sales provide the collateral for the financing of new production. Furthermore, the lender may provide credit services that eliminate or at least reduce the need for similar services within the firm. The primary disadvantage associated with this method of financing is its cost, which can be relatively high compared with other sources of short-term credit, owing to the level of the interest rate charged on loans and the processing fee on pledged accounts.

Factoring Accounts Receivable

Factoring receivables involves the outright sale of a firm's accounts to a financial institution called a **factor**. A factor is a financial institution that acquires the receivables of other firms. The factor may be a commercial finance company that engages solely in the factoring of receivables (known as an **old line factor**) or it may be a commercial bank. The factor, in turn, bears the risk of collection and, for a fee, services the accounts. The fee is stated as a percent of the face value of all receivables factored (usually from 1 to 3 percent).

The factor typically does not make payment for factored accounts until the accounts have been collected or the credit terms have been met. Should the firm wish to receive immediate payment for its factored accounts, it can borrow from the factor, using the factored accounts as collateral. The maximum loan the firm can obtain is equal to the face value of its factored accounts less the factor's fee (1 to 3 percent) less a reserve (6 to 10 percent) less the interest on the loan. For example, if $100,000 in receivables is factored, carrying 60-day credit terms, a 2 percent factor's fee, a 6 percent reserve, and interest at 1 percent per month on advances, then the maximum loan or advance the firm can receive is computed as follows:

Face amount of receivables factored	$100,000
Less: Fee (.02 × $100,000)	(2,000)
Reserve (.06 × $100,000)	(6,000)
Interest (.01 × $92,000 × 2 months)	(1,840)
Maximum advance	$ 90,160

Note that interest is discounted and calculated based upon a maximum amount of funds available for advance ($92,000 = $100,000 − $2000 − $6000). Thus, the effective annual cost of credit can be calculated as follows:

$$EAR = \left[1 + \frac{(\$1840 + \$2000)}{\$90{,}160} \right]^{365/60} - 1 = .2888 = 28.88\%$$

Secured Sources: Inventory Loans

Inventory loans provide a second source of security for short-term secured credit. The amount of the loan that can be obtained depends on both the mar-

BASIC FINANCIAL MANAGEMENT IN PRACTICE

The Ins and Outs of Factoring

Getting In

Factors are necessarily selective in the companies they agree to take on as clients. Detailed negotiations take place with prospective clients and their financial advisers; two key items of information that the factor will require are:

- Audited accounts for the past year and the current management accounts.

- A list of the customers and a monthly turnover projection for each.

Commencement date. Once agreement has been reached a date will be arranged for the factor to assume responsibility for the sales ledger.

Introducing the service. At the start of the factoring arrangement, it is useful for the client to send a letter to customers explaining the introduction of the factor. Where appropriate, the factor may speak personally to some customers.

Invoices. Once factoring starts, clients will be encouraged to invoice their customers immediately a valid debt has been created, passing copies of invoices to the factor or, in some cases, passing the invoices to the factor for mailing. Clients must ensure that their invoicing procedure is efficient, with the terms and conditions clearly stated so that they will be understood by customers.

Factoring. With recourse and non-recourse factoring, clients may only draw on a financial facility within the credit limits agreed for each customer. These credit limits must be monitored constantly to ensure they are realistic.

Credit cover. In the case of non-recourse factoring, clients must ensure they have credit approval from the factor before delivering the goods or providing the service. They must seek credit cover for new customers before delivery, and should monitor the level of credit cover on existing customers to ensure that it is adequate.

Management accounts. During the course of the year, a factor will ask to see its client's management accounts, usually at about quarterly intervals, in order to monitor the progress of the business.

Day-to-day operation. A number of routine procedures and associated documentation will be employed in the operation of the factoring arrangement, depending on the precise system of the factor concerned. Factors will usually supply a concise set of operating instructions to guide the client.

Getting Out

Companies should not be inhibited from entering into factoring arrangements for fear that they may find it difficult to discontinue the service. Indeed they may wish to discontinue for a variety of reasons. For instance:

- Acquisition by a larger parent who does not wish to factor.

- Change in the pattern of business, resulting for example in a significant reduction in customers.

- Replacement from another source of funding at present being taken from the factor.

- Generation of increased profits rendering factoring unnecessary.

A factoring agreement will almost certainly contain a clause relating to the notice requirement—usually about three months on either side. On deciding to withdraw from factoring, clients will need to address themselves to just three principal matters:

- The availability of funds to finance the buying back of the outstanding debts from the factor.

- The setting up of a sales ledger system and the acquisition of necessary sales ledger administration, credit control and collection staff, to be effective from the agreed handing-over date.

- Credit insurance arrangements to replace the credit cover at present provided by the factor in the case of a non-recourse agreement.

Factors have no wish to hold clients to agreements if their services are no longer needed. Indeed they will provide every assistance to effect a smooth change-over when client wishes to terminate the arrangement.

Source: Michael Maberly, "Factoring: A Catalyst for Growth and Profits," *Accountancy*, Institute of Chartered Accountants 97 (April 1986), pp. 122–124.

ketability and perishability of the inventory. Some items, such as raw materials (grains, oil, lumber, and chemicals), are excellent sources of collateral, since they can easily be liquidated. Other items, such as work in process inventories, provide very poor collateral because of their lack of marketability.

There are several methods by which inventory can be used to secure short-term financing. These include a floating or blanket lien, chattel mortgage, field warehouse receipt, and terminal warehouse receipt.

Floating Lien Agreement

Under a **floating lien** agreement the borrower gives the lender a lien against all its inventories. This provides the simplest but least secure form of inventory collateral. The borrowing firm maintains full control of the inventories and continues to sell and replace them as it sees fit. Obviously, this lack of control over the collateral greatly dilutes the value of this type of security to the lender. Correspondingly, loans made with floating liens on inventory as collateral are generally limited to a relatively modest fraction of the value of the inventories covered by the lien. In addition, floating liens usually include future as well as existing inventories.

Chattel Mortgage Agreements

The lender can increase its security interest by having specific items of inventory identified (by serial number or otherwise) in the security agreement. Such an arrangement is provided by a **chattel mortgage**. The borrower retains title to the inventory but cannot sell the items without the lender's consent. This type of agreement is costly to implement, because specific items of inventory must be identified. It is used only for major items of inventory such as machine tools or other capital assets.

Field Warehouse Financing Agreements

Increased lender control over inventories used as loan collateral can be obtained through the use of a **field warehouse agreement**. Here the inventories used as collateral are physically separated from the firm's other inventories and placed under the control of a third-party field warehousing firm. Inventories are not removed from the borrower's premises, but are placed under the control of a third party who is responsible for protecting the security interests of the lender. This arrangement is particularly useful when large, bulky items are used as collateral. For example, a refinery might use a part of its inventory of fuel oil to secure a short-term bank loan. Under a field warehousing agreement the oil reserves would be set aside in specific tanks or storage vessels, which would be controlled (monitored) by a field warehousing concern.

The warehousing firm, upon receipt of the inventory, takes full control of the collateral. This means that the borrower is no longer allowed to use or sell the inventory items without the consent of the lender. The warehousing firm issues a warehouse receipt for the merchandise, which carries title to the goods represented therein. The receipt may be negotiable, in which case title can be transferred through sale of the receipt, or nonnegotiable, whereby title remains with the lender. In a negotiable receipt arrangement the warehouse concern will release the goods to whoever holds the receipt, whereas a nonnegotiable receipt allows the goods to be released only on the written consent of the lender.

The cost of such a loan can be quite high, since the services of the field warehouse company must be paid for by the borrower.

The M. M. Richards Company follows a practice of obtaining short-term credit based on its seasonal finished goods inventory. The firm builds up its inventories of outdoor furniture throughout the winter months for sale in spring and summer. Thus, for the two-month period ended March 31, it uses its fall and winter production of furniture as collateral for a short-term bank loan. The bank lends the company up to 70 percent of the value of the inventory at 14 percent interest plus a fixed fee of $2,000 to cover the costs of a field warehousing arrangement. During this period the firm usually has about $200,000 in inventories, which it borrows against. The annual effective annual cost of the short-term credit is therefore

$$EAR = \left[1 + \frac{(\$3,222 + \$2,000)}{\$140,000} \right]^{365/60} - 1 = .2495 = 24.95\%$$

where the financing cost consists of two months' interest ($140,000 × .14 × 60/365 = $3,222) plus the field warehousing fee of $2,000. ∎

Terminal Warehouse Agreements

The **terminal warehouse agreement** differs from the field warehouse agreement in only one respect. Here the inventories pledged as collateral are transported to a public warehouse that is physically removed from the borrower's premises. The lender has an added degree of safety or security because the inventory is totally removed from the borrower's control. Once again the cost of this type of arrangement is increased because the warehouse firm must be paid by the borrower and the inventory must be transported to and eventually from the public warehouse.

The same warehouse receipt procedure described earlier for field warehouse loans is used. Again, the cost of this type of financing can be quite high.

SUMMARY

There are two basic issues involved in managing the firm's use of short-term financing. The first of these is determining the level of short-term financing the firm should use. This question was first addressed in Chapter 13 through the use of the hedging principle of working-capital management. Basically, this principle suggests that short-term financing be used to finance temporary or short-term investments in assets. In this chapter we have sought to answer the second question: How should the financial manager select a source of short-term financing?

Three basic factors provide the key considerations in selecting a source of short-term financing: (1) the effective annual cost of credit, (2) the availability of financing in the amount and for the time needed, and (3) the effect of the use of credit from a particular source on the cost and availability of other sources of credit.

The various sources of short-term credit can be categorized into two groups: unsecured and secured. Unsecured credit offers no specific assets as security for the loan agreement. The primary sources include trade credit, lines of credit and unsecured transaction loans from commercial banks, and commercial paper. Secured credit is generally provided to business firms by commercial banks, finance companies, and factors. The most popular sources of security involve the use of accounts receivable and inventories. Loans secured by accounts receivable include pledging agreements in which a firm pledges its receivables as security for a loan, and factoring agreements in which the firm sells the receivables to a factor. A primary difference in these two arrangements relates to the ability of the lender to seek payment from the borrower in the event that the accounts used as collateral become uncollectible. In a pledging arrangement the lender retains the right of recourse in the event of default, whereas in factoring a lender is generally is without recourse.

Loans secured by inventories can be made using one of several types of security arrangements. Among the most widely used are the floating lien, chattel mortgage, field warehouse agreement, and terminal warehouse agreement. The form of agreement used will depend on the type of inventories being pledged as collateral and the degree of control the lender wishes to exercise over the loan collateral.

STUDY QUESTIONS

16-1. What distinguishes short-term, intermediate-term, and long-term debt?

16-2. What considerations should be used in selecting a source of short-term credit? Discuss each.

16-3. How can the formula "interest = principal × rate × time" be used to estimate the annual approximate cost of short-term credit?

16-4. How does compounding influence the calculation of the effective annual cost of short-term credit?

16-5. There are three major sources of unsecured short-term credit. List and discuss the distinguishing characteristics of each.

16-6. What is meant by the following trade credit terms: 2/10, net 30? 4/20, net 60? 3/15, net 45?

16-7. Define the following:
   a. Line of credit
   b. Commercial paper
   c. Compensating balance
   d. Prime rate

16-8. List and discuss four advantages of the use of commercial paper.

16-9. What "risk" is involved in the firm's use of commercial paper as a source of short-term credit? Discuss.

16-10. List and discuss the distinguishing features of the principal sources of secured credit based upon accounts receivable.

16-11. List and discuss the distinguishing features of the primary sources of secured credit based upon inventories.

SELF-TEST PROBLEMS

ST-1. (*Analyzing the Cost of a Commercial Paper Offering*) The Marilyn Sales Company is a wholesale machine tool broker which has gone through a recent expansion of its activities resulting in a doubling of its sales. The company has determined that it needs an additional $200 million in short-term funds to finance peak season sales during roughly six months of the year. Marilyn's treasurer has recommended that the firm utilize a commercial paper offering to raise the needed funds. Specifically, he has determined that a $200 million offering would require 10 percent interest (paid in advance or discounted) plus a $125,000 placement fee. The paper would carry a six-month maturity. What is the effective annual cost of credit?

ST-2. (*Analyzing the Cost of Short-Term Credit*) The Samples Mfg. Co. provides specialty steel products to the oil industry. Although the firm's business is highly correlated with the cyclical swings in oil exploration activity, it also experiences some significant seasonality. The firm is currently concerned with the seasonality in its need for funds. The firm needs $500,000 for the two-month July–August period each year, and as a result the company's vice president of finance is currently considering the following three sources of financing:

a. Establish a line of credit with the Bank of Montreal. The bank has agreed to provide Samples with the needed $500,000, carrying an interest rate of 14 percent with interest discounted and a compensating balance of 20 percent of the loan balance. Samples does not have a bank account with the Bank of Montreal and would have to establish one to satisfy the compensating balance requirement.

b. Samples can forgo its trade discounts over the two months of July and August when the funding will be needed. The firm's discount terms are 3/15, net 30, and the firm averages $500,000 in trade credit purchases during July and August.

c. Finally, Samples could enter into a pledging arrangement with a local finance company. The finance company has agreed to extend Samples the needed $500,000, if it pledges $750,000 in receivables. The finance company has offered to advance the $500,000, with 12 percent annual interest payable at the end of the two-month loan term. In addition, the finance company will charge a one-half of one percent fee based on pledged receivables to cover the cost of processing the company's accounts (this fee is paid at the end of the loan period). Analyze the effective annual cost of each of the alternative sources of credit and select the best one. Note that a total of $500,000 will be needed for a two-month period (July–August) each year.

ST-3. (*Analyzing the Cost of Short-Term Credit*) The treasurer of the Lights-a-Lot Mfg. Company is faced with three alternative bank loans. The firm wishes to select the one that minimizes its cost of credit on a $200,000 note that it plans to issue in the next 10 days. Relevant information for the three loan configurations is found below:

a. An 18 percent rate of interest with interest paid at year-end and no compensating balance requirement.

b. A 16 percent rate of interest but carrying a 20 percent compensating balance requirement. This loan also calls for interest to be paid at year-end.

c. A 14 percent rate of interest that is discounted plus a 20 percent compensating balance requirement.

Analyze the effective annual cost of each of these alternatives. You may assume that the firm would not normally maintain any bank balance that might be used to meet the 20 percent compensating balance requirements of alternatives (b) and (c).

STUDY PROBLEMS (SET A)

16-1A. (*Estimating the Cost of Bank Credit*) Paymaster Enterprises has arranged to finance its seasonal working-capital needs with a short-term bank loan. The loan will carry a rate of 12 percent per annum with interest paid in advance (discounted). In addition, Paymaster must maintain a minimum demand deposit with the bank of 10 percent of the loan balance throughout the term of the loan. If Paymaster plans to borrow $100,000 for a period of three months, what is the effective annual cost of the bank loan?

16-2A. (*Estimating the Cost of Commercial Paper*) On February 3, 199X, the Western Company plans a commercial paper issue of $20 million. The firm has never used commercial paper before but has been assured by the firm placing the issue that it will have no difficulty raising the funds. The commercial paper will carry a 270-day maturity and will require interest based upon a rate of 11 percent per annum. In addition, the firm will have to pay fees totalling $200,000 in order to bring the issue to market and place it. What is the effective annual cost of the commercial paper issue to Western?

16-3A. (*Cost of Trade Credit*) Calculate the effective annual cost of the following trade credit terms where payment is made on the net due date.

    a. 2/10, net 30

    b. 3/15, net 30

    c. 3/15, net 45

    d. 2/15, net 60

16-4A. (*Annual Percentage Rate*) Compute the cost of the trade credit terms in Problem 16-3A using the annual approximate rate method.

16-5A. (*Cost of Short-Term Financing*) The R. Morin Construction Company needs to borrow $100,000 to help finance the cost of a new $150,000 hydraulic crane used in the firm's commercial construction business. The crane will pay for itself in one year and the firm is considering the following alternatives for financing its purchase:

    Alternative A—The firm's bank has agreed to lend the $100,000 at a rate of 14 percent. Interest would be discounted, and a 15 percent compensating balance would be required. However, the compensating balance requirement would not be binding on R. Morin, since the firm normally maintains a minimum demand deposit (chequing account) balance of $25,000 in the bank.

    Alternative B—The equipment dealer has agreed to finance the equipment with a one-year loan. The $100,000 loan would require payment of principal and interest totalling $116,300.

    a. Which alternative should R. Morin select?

    b. If the bank's compensating balance requirement were to necessitate idle demand deposits equal to 20 percent of the loan, what effect would this have on the cost of the bank loan alternative?

16-6A. (*Cost of Short-Term Bank Loan*) On July 1, 199X, the Southwest Forging Corporation arranged for a line of credit with the bank. The terms of the agreement called for a $100,000 maximum loan with interest set at 1 percent over prime. In addition, the firm has to maintain a 20 percent compensating balance in its demand deposit throughout the year. The prime rate is currently 12 percent.

    a. If Southwest normally maintains a $20,000-to-$30,000 balance in its chequing account with the bank, what is the effective annual cost of credit through the line-of-credit agreement where the maximum loan amount is used for a full year?

    b. Recompute the effective annual cost of credit to Southwest if the firm will have to borrow the compensating balance and it borrows the maximum possible under the loan agreement. Again, assume the full amount of the loan is outstanding for a whole year.

16-7A. (*Cost of Commercial Paper*) Tri-Lite Enterprises plans to issue commercial paper for the first time in the firm's 35-year history. The firm plans to issue $500,000 in 180-day maturity notes. The paper will carry a $10^{1/4}$ percent rate with discounted interest and will cost Tri-Lite $12,000 (paid in advance) to issue.

    a. What is the effective annual cost of credit to Tri-Lite?

b. What other factors should the company consider in analyzing whether to issue the commercial paper?

16-8A. (*Cost of Accounts Receivable*) Johnson Enterprises, Inc., is involved in the manufacture and sale of electronic components used in small AM-FM radios. The firm needs $300,000 to finance an anticipated expansion in receivables due to increased sales. Johnson's credit terms are net 60, and its average monthly credit sales are $200,000. In general, the firm's customers pay within the credit period; thus, the firm's average accounts receivable balance is $400,000.

Chuck Idol, Johnson's comptroller, approached the firm's bank with a request for a loan for the $300,000 using the firm's accounts receivable as collateral. The bank offered to make the loan at a rate of 2 percent over prime plus a 1 percent processing charge on all receivables pledged ($200,000 per month). Furthermore, the bank agreed to lend up to 75 percent of the face value of the receivables pledged.

a. Estimate the effective annual cost of the receivables loan to Johnson where the firm borrows the $300,000. The prime rate is currently 11 percent.

b. Idol also requested a line of credit for $300,000 from the bank. The bank agreed to grant the necessary line of credit at a rate of 3 percent over prime and required a 15 percent compensating balance. Johnson currently maintains an average demand deposit of $80,000. Estimate the effective annual cost of the line of credit to Johnson.

c. Which source of credit should Johnson select? Why?

16-9A. (*Cost of Factoring*) MDM, Inc., is considering factoring its receivables. The firm has credit sales of $400,000 per month and has an average receivables balance of $800,000 with 60-day credit terms. The factor has offered to extend credit equal to 90 percent of the receivables factored less interest on the loan at a rate of $1\frac{1}{2}$ percent per month. The 10 percent difference in the advance and the face value of all receivables factored consists of a 1 percent factoring fee plus a 9 percent reserve, which the factor maintains. In addition, if MDM, Inc., decides to factor its receivables, it will sell them all, so that it can reduce its credit department costs by $1,500 a month.

a. What is the effective annual cost of borrowing the maximum amount of credit available to MDM, Inc., through the factoring agreement?

b. What considerations other than cost should be accounted for by MDM, Inc., in determining whether or not to enter the factoring agreement?

16-10A. (*Inventory Financing*) In June of each year the Arlyle Publishing Company builds up its inventories for fall sales. The company has explored the possibility of a field warehouse security agreement as collateral for an inventory loan from its bank during the three summer months. During these months inventories average $400,000. The field warehouse arrangement will cost Arlyle a flat fee of $2,000 a month on all its inventory regardless of the amount the firm borrows. The bank has agreed to lend up to 70 percent of the value of the inventory at a rate of 14 percent.

a. If Arlyle borrows $200,000 using the inventory loan for June through August, what is the effective annual cost of credit?

b. What is the effective annual cost of borrowing $280,000 for the June through August period?

16-11A. (*Cost of Secured Short-Term Credit*) The Sean-Janeow Import Co. needs $500,000 for the three-month period ending September 30, 199X. The firm has explored two possible sources of credit.

1. S-J has arranged with its bank for a $500,000 loan secured by accounts receivable. The bank has agreed to advance S-J 80 percent of the value of its pledged receivables at a rate of 11 percent plus a 1 percent fee based on all receivables pledged. S-J's receivables average a total of $1 million year-round.

2. An insurance company has agreed to lend the $500,000 at a rate of 9 percent per annum, using a loan secured by S-J's inventory of salad oil.

A field warehouse agreement would be used, which would cost S-J $2,000 a month.

Which source of credit should S-J select? Explain.

16-12A. (*Cost of Short-Term Financing*) You plan to borrow $20,000 from the bank to pay for inventories for a gift shop you have just opened. The bank offers to lend you the money at 10 percent annual interest for the six months the funds will be needed.

    a. Calculate the effective annual rate of interest on the loan.

    b. In addition, the bank requires you to maintain a 15 percent compensating balance in the bank. Since you are just opening your business, you do not have a demand deposit at the bank that can be used to meet the compensating balance requirement. This means that you will have to put 15 percent of the loan amount from your own personal money (which you had planned to use to help finance the business) in a chequing account. What is the effective annual cost of the loan now?

    c. In addition to the compensating balance requirement in (b), you are told that interest will be discounted. What is the effective annual rate of interest on the loan now?

16-13A. (*Cost of Factoring*) A factor has agreed to lend the JVC Corporation working capital on the following terms. JVC's receivables average $100,000 per month and have a 90-day average collection period (note that accounts receivable average $300,000 because of the 90-day average collection period). The factor will charge 12 percent interest on any advance (1 percent per month paid in advance), will charge a 2 percent processing fee on all receivables factored, and will maintain a 20 percent reserve. If JVC undertakes the loan it will reduce its own credit department expenses by $2,000 per month. What is the effective annual rate of interest to JVC on the factoring arrangement? Assume that the maximum advance is taken.

16-14A. (*Opportunity Cost of Decreasing Wages Payable*) In June of this year the AMB Manufacturing Company negotiated a new union contract with its employees. One of the provisions of the new contract involved increasing the frequency of its wage payments from once a month to once every two weeks. AMB's biweekly payroll averages $250,000 and the firm's opportunity cost of funds is 12 percent per annum.

    a. What is the annual dollar cost of this new wage payment scheme to AMB?

    b. What is the maximum percentage increase in wages that AMB would have been willing to accept in lieu of the increased frequency of wage payments?

STUDY PROBLEMS (SET B)

16-1B. (*Estimating the Cost of Bank Credit*) Dee's Christmas Trees, Inc. is evaluating options for financing its seasonal working-capital needs. A short-term loan from a bank would carry a 14 percent annual interest rate, with interest paid in advance (discounted). If this option is chosen, Dee's would also have to maintain a minimum demand deposit equal to 10 percent of the loan balance, throughout the term of the loan. If Dee's needs to borrow $125,000 for the upcoming three months before Christmas, what is the effective annual cost of the loan?

16-2B. (*Estimating the Cost of Commercial Paper*) Duro Auto Parts would like to exploit a production opportunity overseas, and is seeking additional capital to finance this expansion. The company plans a commercial paper issue of $15 million on February 3, 199X. The firm has never issued commercial paper before, but has been assured by the investment dealer placing the issue that it will have no difficulty raising the funds, and that this method of financing is the least expensive option, even after the $150,000 placement fee. The issue will carry a 270-day maturity and will require interest based on an annual rate of 12 percent. What is the effective annual cost of the commercial paper issue to Duro?

16-3B. (*Cost of Trade Credit*) Calculate the effective annual cost of the following trade credit terms where payment is made on the net due date.

    a. 2/10, net 30

    b. 3/15, net 30

    c. 3/15, net 45

    d. 2/15, net 60

16-4B. (*Annual Percentage Rate*) Compute the cost of the trade credit terms in Problem 16-3B using the annual approximate rate method.

16-5B. (*Cost of Short-Term Financing*) Vitra Glass Company needs to borrow $150,000 to help finance the cost of a new $225,000 kiln to be used in the production of glass bottles. The kiln will pay for itself in one year and the firm is considering the following alternatives for financing its purchase:

> **Alternative A**—The firm's bank has agreed to lend the $150,000 at a rate of 15 percent. Interest would be discounted, and a 16 percent compensating balance would be required. However, the compensating balance requirement would not be binding on Vitra, since the firm normally maintains a minimum demand deposit (chequing account) balance of $25,000 in the bank.

> **Alternative B**—The kiln dealer has agreed to finance the equipment with a one-year loan. The $150,000 loan would require payment of principal and interest totaling $163,000.

    a. Which alternative should Vitra select?

    b. If the bank's compensating balance requirement were to necessitate idle demand deposits equal to 20 percent of the loan, what effect would this have on the cost of the bank loan alternative?

16-6B. (*Cost of Short-Term Bank Loan*) Lola's Ice Cream recently arranged for a line of credit with the bank. The terms of the agreement called for a $100,000 maximum loan with interest set at 2.0 percent over prime. In addition, Lola's must maintain a 15 percent compensating balance in its demand deposit throughout the year. The prime rate is currently 12 percent.

    a. If Lola's normally maintains a $15,000-to-$25,000 balance in its chequing account with the bank, what is the effective annual cost of credit through the line-of-credit agreement where the maximum loan amount is used for a full year?

    b. Recompute the effective annual cost of credit to Lola's Ice Cream if the firm has to borrow the compensating balance and it borrows the maximum possible under the loan agreement. Again, assume the full amount of the loan is outstanding for a whole year.

16-7B. (*Cost of Commercial Paper*) Luft, Inc., recently acquired production rights to an innovative sailboard design but needs funds to pay for the first production run, which is expected to sell briskly. The firm plans to issue $450,000 in 180-day maturity notes. The paper will carry an 11 percent rate with discounted interest and will cost Luft $13,000 (paid in advance) to issue.

    a. What is the effective annual cost of credit to Luft?

    b. What other factors should the company consider in analyzing whether to issue the commercial paper?

16-8B. (*Cost of Accounts Receivable*) TLC Enterprises, Inc., is a wholesaler of toys and curios. The firm needs $400,000 to finance an anticipated expansion in receivables due to increased sales. TLC's credit terms are net 60, and its average monthly credit sales are $250,000. In general, the TLC's customers pay within the credit period; thus, the firm's average accounts receivable balance is $500,000.

Kelly Leaky, TLC's comptroller, approached the firm's bank with a request for a loan for the $400,000 using the firm's accounts receivable as collateral. The bank offered to make the loan at a rate of 2 percent over prime plus a 1 percent processing charge on all receivables pledged ($250,000 per month). Furthermore, the bank agreed to lend up to 75 percent of the face value of the receivables pledged.

    a. Estimate the effective annual cost of the receivables loan to TLC where the firm borrows the $400,000. The prime rate is currently 11 percent.

    b. Leaky also requested a line of credit for $400,000 from the bank. The bank agreed to grant the necessary line of credit at a rate of 3 percent over prime and required a 15 percent compensating balance. TLC currently maintains an average demand deposit of $100,000. Estimate the effective annual cost of the line of credit to TLC.

    c. Which source of credit should TLC select? Why?

16-9B. (*Cost of Factoring*) To increase profitability, a management consultant has suggested to the Dal Molle Fruit Company that it consider factoring its receivables. The firm has credit sales of $300,000 per month and has an average receivables balance of $600,000 with 60-day credit terms. The factor has offered to extend credit equal to 90 percent of the receivables factored less interest on the loan at a rate of $1\frac{1}{2}$ percent per month. The 10 percent difference in the advance and the face value of all receivables factored consists of a 1 percent factoring fee plus a 9 percent reserve, which the factor maintains. In addition, if Dal Molle, decides to factor its receivables, it will sell them all, so that it can reduce its credit department costs by $1,400 a month.

    a. What is the effective annual cost of borrowing the maximum amount of credit available to Dal Molle, through the factoring agreement?

    b. What considerations other than cost should be accounted for by Dal Molle, in determining whether or not to enter the factoring agreement?

16-10B. (*Inventory Financing*) In anticipation of summer sales, Ol' Trusty Barbecues, Inc., builds up inventories each year in March. The company has explored the possibility of a field warehouse security agreement as collateral for an inventory loan from its bank during the three spring months. During these months inventories average $400,000. The field warehouse arrangement will cost Ol' Trusty a flat fee of $2,000 a month on all its inventory regardless of the amount the firm borrows. The bank has agreed to lend up to 70 percent of the value of the inventory at a rate of 14 percent.

    a. If Ol' Trusty borrows $250,000 using the inventory loan for March through May, what is the effective annual cost of credit?

    b. What is the effective annual cost of borrowing $180,000 for the March through May period?

16-11B. (*Cost of Secured Short-Term Credit*) DST, Inc., a producer of inflatable river rafts, needs $400,000 for the three-month summer season, ending September 30, 199X. The firm has explored two possible sources of credit.

    1. DST has arranged with its bank for a $400,000 loan secured by accounts receivable. The bank has agreed to advance DST 80 percent of the value of its pledged receivables at a rate of 11 percent plus a 1 percent fee based on all receivables pledged. DST's receivables average a total of $1 million year-round.

    2. An insurance company has agreed to lend the $400,000 at a rate of 10 percent per annum, using a loan secured by DST's inventory. A field warehouse agreement would be used, which would cost DST $1,500 a month.

Which source of credit should DST select? Explain.

16-12B. (*Cost of Secured Short-Term Financing*) You are considering a loan of $25,000 to finance inventories for a janitorial supply store that you plan to open. The bank offers to lend you the money at 11 percent annual interest for the six months the funds will be needed.

    a. Calculate the effective annual rate of interest on the loan.

    b. In addition, the bank requires you to maintain a 15 percent compensating balance in the bank. Since you are just opening your business, you do not have a demand deposit at the bank that can be used to meet the compensating balance requirement. This means that you will have to put 15 percent of the loan amount from your own personal money (which you had planned to use to help finance the business) in a chequing account. What is the effective annual cost of the loan now?

    c. In addition to the compensating balance requirement in (b), you are told that interest will be discounted. What is the effective annual rate of interest on the loan now?

16-13B. (*Cost of Financing*) Tanglewood Roofing Supply, Inc., has agreed to borrow working capital from a factor on the following terms: Tanglewood's receivables average $150,000 per month and have a 90-day average collection period (note that accounts receivable average $450,000 because of the 90-day average collection period). The factor will charge 13 percent interest on any advance (1 percent per month paid in advance), will charge a 2 percent processing fee on all receivables factored, and will maintain a 15 percent reserve. If Tanglewood undertakes the loan it will reduce its own credit department expenses by $2,000 per month. What is the effective annual rate of interest to Tanglewood on the factoring arrangement? Assume that the maximum advance is taken.

16-14B. (*Opportunity Cost of Decreasing Wages Payable*) In June of this year Becker Services, Inc., negotiated a new union contract with its employees. One of the provisions of the new contract involved increasing the frequency of its wage payments from once a month to once every two weeks. Becker's biweekly payroll averages $300,000 and the firm's opportunity cost of funds is 11 percent per annum.

    a. What is the annual dollar cost of this new wage payment scheme to Becker?

    b. What is the maximum percentage increase in wages that Becker would have been willing to accept in lieu of the increased frequency of wage payments?

SELF-TEST SOLUTIONS

SS-1. The discounted interest cost of the commercial paper issue is calculated as follows:

$$\text{Interest expense} = .10 \times \$200 \text{ million} \times \frac{6}{12} = \$10 \text{ million}$$

The effective annual cost of credit can now be calculated as follows:

$$EAR = \left(1 + \frac{\$10,000,000 + \$125,000}{\$200,000,000 - \$125,000 - \$10,000,000}\right)^{12/6} - 1 = 0.1095 = 10.95\%$$

SS-2. **a.** Interest for two months = $.14 \times .16667 \times \$500,000 = \$11,667$

    Loan proceeds (for $500,000 loan) = $\$500,000 - (.2 \times \$500,000 + \$11,667)$

$$= \$388,333$$

$$EAR = \left(1 + \frac{\$11,667}{\$388,333}\right)^{12/2} - 1 = 0.1944 = 19.44\%$$

Note that Samples would actually have to borrow more than the needed $500,000 in order to cover the compensating balance requirement. However, as we demonstrated earlier, the effective annual cost of credit will not be affected by adjusting the loan amount for interest expense changes accordingly.

SS-1. **b.** The estimation of the cost of forgoing trade discounts is generally quite straightforward; however, in this case the firm actually stretches its trade credit for purchases made during July beyond the due date by an additional 30 days. If it is able to do this without penalty, then the firm effectively forgoes a 3 percent discount for not paying within 15 days and does not pay for an additional 45 days (60 days less the discount period of 15 days). Thus, for the July trade credit, Samples' cost is calculated as follows:

$$EAR = \left(1 + \frac{0.03}{0.97}\right)^{365/45} - 1 = 0.2803 = 28.03\%$$

However, for the August trade credit the firm actually pays at the end of the credit period (the 30th day), so that the cost of trade credit becomes

$$EAR = \left(1 + \frac{0.03}{0.97}\right)^{365/15} - 1 = 1.0984 = 109.84\%$$

c. Interest for two months = $.12 \times 212 \times \$500,000 = \$10,000$

Pledging fee = $.005 \times \$750,000 = \$3750$

$$EAR = \left(1 + \frac{\$10,000 + \$3,750}{\$500,000}\right)^{12/2} - 1 = .1768 = 17.68\%$$

SS-3. a.

$$EAR = \left[1 + \frac{(.18 \times \$200,000)}{\$200,000}\right]^1 - 1 = .18 = 18.00\%$$

b.

$$EAR = \left[1 + \frac{(.16 \times \$200,000)}{\$200,000 - (.16 \times \$200,000)}\right]^1 - 1 = .20 = 20.00\%$$

c.

$$EAR = \left[1 + \frac{(.14 \times \$200,000)}{\$200,000 - (.14 \times \$200,000) - (.20 \times \$200,000)}\right]^1 - 1$$

$$= .2121 = 21.21\%$$

Alternative (a) offers the lower-cost service of financing, although it carries the highest stated rate of interest. The reason for this, of course, is that there is no compensating balance requirement nor is interest discounted for this alternative.

SELECTED REFERENCES

Besley, S., and J. S. Osteryoung. "Survey of Current Practices in Establishing Trade-Credit Limits," *Financial Review* (February 1985), 70–81.

Brosky, John J. *The Implicit Cost of Trade Credit and Theory of Optimal Terms of Sale*, New York: Credit Research Foundation, 1969.

D'Agostino, R. S. "Accounts Receivable Loans—Worthless Collateral?" *Journal of Commercial Bank Lending*, 52 (July 1970), 34–42.

Daniels, F., S. Legg, and E. C. Yuelle. "Accounts Receivable and Related Inventory Financing," *Journal of Commercial Bank Lending*, 52 (July 1970), 38–53.

Emery, G. W. "A Pure Financial Explanation for Trade Credit," *Journal of Financial and Quantitative Analysis*, 19 (September 1984), 271–286.

Hill, Ned C., Robert A. Wood and Dale R. Sorenson. "Factors Influencing Credit Policy: A Survey," *Journal of Cash Management*, 1 (December 1981), 38–47.

Korsvik, W. J., and C. O. Mailburg. *The Loan Officer's Handbook*. Homewood, IL: Dow Jones-Irwin, 1986.

Loosigian, Allan M. "Hedging Commercial Paper Borrowing Costs with Treasury Bill Futures," *Journal of Cash Management*, 2 (June 1982), 50–57.

Kim, Y. H., and J. C. Atkins. "Evaluating Investment in Accounts Receivable: A Wealth Maximizing Framework." *Journal of Finance* (May 1978), 403–412.

Nadler, Paul S. "Compensating Balances and the Prime at Twilight," *Harvard Business Review*, 50 (January–February 1972), 112–120.

Pizzo, T. V. "Factoring as a Management Tool," *Credit and Financial Management* (December 1979), 16–18.

The importance of the Toronto Stock Exchange in the Canadian financial market is demonstrated by its 53 percent share of the total trading volume during 1992.[10] This trading volume represents a value of 76,161 million dollars. Both the Vancouver Stock Exchange and the Montreal Stock Exchange recorded 28.3 and 12.2 percent share of the total trading volume in Canada during 1992. The trading volume of the Vancouver Stock Exchange represented 3,572 million dollars of value traded in Canada. This amount contrasts with the 21,063 million dollars that the Montreal Stock Exchange traded in value during 1992. The Alberta Stock Exchange plays a smaller role in Canadian equity market in that it captured only 6.3 percent, or 980 million dollars, of the total trading volume.

The business of an exchange, including securities transactions, is conducted by its members. Members are said to occupy "seats." Major brokerage firms own seats on the exchanges. An officer of the firm is designated to be the member of the exchange, and this membership permits the brokerage firm to use the facilities of the exchange to effect trades. The price of seats on the exchange can range from $50,000 in 1992 to as high as $370,000 in October of 1987.[11] This price range for an exchange seat reflects the unsettled nature of the markets during economic slowdowns.

STOCK EXCHANGE BENEFITS ■ Both corporations and investors enjoy several benefits provided by the existence of organized security exchanges. These include the following:

1. **Providing a continuous market.** This may be the most important function of an organized security exchange. A continuous market provides a series of continuous security prices. Price changes from trade to trade tend to be smaller than they would be in the absence of organized markets. The reasons are that there is a relatively large sales volume in each security, trading orders are executed quickly, and the range between the price asked for a security and the offered price tends to be narrow. The result is that price volatility is reduced. This enhances the liquidity of security investments and makes them more attractive to potential investors. While it is difficult to prove, it seems logical that this market feature probably reduces the cost of capital to corporations.

2. **Establishing and publicizing fair security prices.** An organized exchange permits security prices to be set by competitive forces. They are not set by negotiations off the floor of the exchange, where one party might have a bargaining advantage. The bidding process flows from the supply and demand underlying each security. This means the specific price of a security is determined in the manner of an auction. In addition, the security prices determined at each exchange are widely publicized. Just read the pages of most newspapers, and the information is available to you. By contrast, the prices and resulting yields on the private placements of securities are more difficult to obtain.

3. **Helping business raise new capital.** Because a continuous secondary market exists where prices are competitively determined, it is easier for firms to float new security offerings successfully. This continuous pric-

---

[10]Gail Lem, "Exchanges See Better Year," *Globe and Mail* (January 9, 1993) p. B5.
[11]Barry Critchley and Susan Gittins, "TSE Seat Prices Reflect Hard Times," *The Financial Post* (June 7, 1991) p. 44.

ing mechanism also facilitates the determination of the offering price of a new issue. This means that comparative values are easily observed.

LISTING REQUIREMENTS ■ To receive the benefits provided by an organized exchange, the firm must seek to have its securities listed on the exchange. An application for listing must be filed and a fee paid. The requirements for listing vary from exchange to exchange; those of the TSE are stringent. The general criteria for listing fall into these categories: (1) profitability; (2) size, (3) market value, and (4) public ownership. To give you the flavour of an actual set of listing requirements, those set forth by the TSE are displayed in Table 17-6.

Over-the-Counter Markets

Many publicly held firms do not meet the listing requirements of major stock exchanges. Others may want to avoid the (1) reporting requirements and (2) fees required to maintain listing. As an alternative, their securities may trade in the over-the-counter markets. On the basis of sheer numbers (not dollar volume), more securities are traded over-the-counter than on organized exchanges. As far as secondary trading in corporate bonds is concerned, the over-the-counter markets are where the action is. In a typical year, more than 90 percent of corporate bond business takes place over-the-counter.

Most over-the-counter transactions are done through a loose network of security traders who are known as broker-dealers and brokers. Brokers do not purchase securities for their own account, whereas dealers do. Broker-dealers stand ready to buy and sell specific securities at selected prices. They are said to "make a market" in those securities. Their profit is the spread or difference between the price they will pay for a security (bid price) and the price at which they will sell the security (asked price).

PRICE QUOTES ■ In 1986 the Ontario Securities Commission established an over-the-counter trading system, called the Canadian Over-the-counter Automated Trading System (COATS). However in 1991, the Toronto Stock exchange assumed administrative responsibility and changed the name to the Canadian Dealing Network Inc. (CDN). The trading system is a telecommunications system that provides a national information link among the brokers and dealers operating in the over-the-counter markets. Subscribing traders use computer terminals which enable them to obtain representative bids and ask prices for securities traded over-the-counter. Canadian Dealing Network Inc. provides a quotation system, not a transactions system. The final trade is still consummated by direct negotiation between traders.

Profitability
Pre-tax cash flow for the most recent year must be at least $400,000.
Size
Net tangible assets must be at least $1 million. Industrial companies with profits of less than $100,000 need to have net tangible assets of $5 million. Mineral exploration companies must have net tangible assets of $2 million.
Market Value
The market value of publicly held stock must be at least $1,000,000.
Public Ownership
There must be at least 1,000,000 publicly held common shares. There must be at least 300 holders of 100 shares or more. Newly listed companies must have a public float of $2 million.

TABLE 17-6
TSE Listing Requirements

CDN price quotes for Canadian unlisted stocks are published daily in the *Globe and Mail* or the *Financial Post*. In the United States, the National Quotation Bureau publishes daily "pink sheets," which contain prices on over-the-counter securities; these sheets are available in the offices of most security dealers.

Perspective in Finance

We touched briefly on the underwriting industry and the investment dealer earlier in this chapter when we described various methods for transferring financial capital (see Figure 17-2). The investment dealer is to be distinguished from the commercial banker in that the former's organization is not a permanent deposit-taking organization for funds. However, deregulation of the investment industry in this country enables commercial banks to perform more functions and services that have belonged almost exclusively to the investment dealers industry. For the moment, it is important for you to learn about the role of the investment dealer in the funding of commercial activity.

THE INVESTMENT DEALER

Most corporations do not raise long-term capital frequently. The activities of working-capital management go on daily, but attracting long-term capital is, by comparison, episodic. The sums involved can be huge, so these situations are considered of great importance to financial managers. And since most managers are unfamiliar with the subtleties of raising long-term funds, they will enlist the help of an expert. That expert is an investment dealer.

Definition

The **investment dealer** is a financial specialist involved as an intermediary in the merchandising of securities. He or she acts as a "middleman" by facilitating the flow of savings from those economic units that want to invest to those units that want to raise funds. We use the term "investment dealer" to refer both to a given individual and to the organization for which such a person works. Although these firms are called "investment dealers," they perform no deposit-taking or lending functions. Just what is the role of this middleman? That is most easily understood in terms of the basic functions of an investment dealer.

Functions

The investment dealer performs three basic functions: (1) underwriting, (2) advising, and (3) distributing.

Underwriting

The term **underwriting** is borrowed from the field of insurance. It means "assuming a risk." The investment dealer assumes the risk of selling a security issue at a satisfactory price.[12] A satisfactory price is one that will generate a profit for the investment dealer.

---

[12]This "assumed" risk can be of varied degrees. The investment dealer may assume total risk (a firm commitment for the entire security issue), some risk (a standby agreement), or no risk (a best efforts agreement).

The procedure goes like this. The managing investment dealer and its syndicate will buy the security issue from the corporation in need of funds. The syndicate is a group of other investment dealers who are invited to help buy and resell the issue. The managing investment dealer is the firm that originated the business because its corporate client decided to raise external funds. On a specific day, the firm that is raising capital is presented with a cheque in exchange for the securities being issued. At this point the underwriting syndicate owns the securities. The corporation has its cash and can proceed to use it. The firm is now immune from the possibility that the security markets might turn sour. If the price of the newly issued security falls below that paid to the firm by the syndicate, the syndicate will suffer a loss. The syndicate, of course, hopes that the opposite situation will result. Its objective is to sell the new issue to the investing public at a price per security greater than its cost.

Advising

The investment dealer is an expert in the issuance and marketing of securities. The expertise of an investment dealer includes an understanding of prevailing market conditions and an ability to relate those conditions to the particular type of security that should be sold at a given time. Business conditions may be pointing to a future increase in interest rates. The investment dealer might advise the firm to issue its bonds in a timely fashion to avoid the higher yields that are forthcoming. The dealer can analyze the firm's capital structure and make recommendations as to what general source of capital should be issued. In many instances the firm will invite its investment dealer to sit on the board of directors. This permits the dealer to observe corporate activity and make recommendations on a regular basis.[13]

Distributing

Once the syndicate owns the new securities, it must get them into the hands of the ultimate investors. This is the distribution or selling function of investment banking. The investment dealer may have branch offices across both Canada and the United States, or it may have an informal arrangement with several security dealers who regularly buy a portion of each new offering for final sale. It is not unusual to have 100 to 600 dealers involved in the selling effort across North America. The syndicate can properly be viewed as the security wholesaler, while the dealer organization can be viewed as the security retailer.

Distribution Methods[14]

Several methods are available to the corporation for placing new security offerings in the hands of final investors. The investment dealer's role is different in each of these. Sometimes, in fact, it is possible to bypass the investment dealer. These methods are described in this section. Private placements, because of their importance, are treated separately later in the chapter.

---

[13]Investment dealers have access to more information since they are frequently in the market and have staff to accumulate and analyze relevant data. On this basis, investment dealers are able to price and sell advice.

[14]The discussion on distribution methods draws heavily on material from James E. Hatch and Michael J. Robinson, *Investment Management*, 2nd ed. (Scarborough, Ontario: Prentice-Hall Canada, 1989).

Public Offering

The most prevalent method of distributing securities in both Canada and the United States is the public offering. The public offering of securities is either negotiated with a specific investment dealer or the offering is auctioned off among several investment dealers. In each case, the issuing institution reduces the risk of selling new securities to the public by negotiating the underwriting of the new issue with an investment dealer. The objective of the underwriting agreement is to determine the type and the price of the securities to be sold to the public. Once the terms of the underwriting agreement are negotiated between the two parties, the investment dealer buys the firm's securities and then resells them to the public. In this type of underwriting arrangement, the investment provides the firm with its expertise in the issuing, marketing, and selling of the securities.

The issuing institution may use the auction process to choose the investment dealer which underwrites and distributes the new securities issue. This type of auction process is commonly used by the Government of Canada and provincial governments to issue government bonds. The investment dealers willing to pay the greatest dollar amount per new security will win the competitive bid. The argument in favour of competitive bids is that any undue influence of the investment dealer over the firm is mitigated and the price received by the firm for each security should be higher. Thus, we would intuitively suspect that the cost of capital in a competitive bid situation would be less than in a negotiated purchase situation. Evidence on this question, however, is mixed.[15] One problem with the competitive bid purchase as far as the fundraising firm is concerned is that the benefits gained from the advisory function of the investment dealer are lost.

Commission or Best-Efforts Basis

In some cases, the investment dealer acts as an agent rather than as a principal in the distribution process. The securities are not underwritten. The investment dealer attempts to sell the issue in return for a fixed commission on each security actually sold. Unsold securities are returned to the corporation. This arrangement is typically used for more speculative issues. The issuing firm may be smaller or less established than the investment dealer would like. Because the underwriting risk is not passed on to the investment dealer, this distribution method is less costly to the issuer than a public offering. On the other hand the investment dealer only has to give it his or her "best effort." A successful sale is not guaranteed.

Privileged Subscription or Rights Offerings

Occasionally, the firm may feel that a distinct market already exists for its new securities. When a new issue is marketed to a definite and select group of investors, it is called a **privileged subscription**. Three target markets are typically involved: (1) current shareholders, (2) employees, or (3) customers. Of these, distributions directed at current shareholders are the most prevalent. Such offerings, called rights offerings, are discussed in detail in Chapter 19. In a privileged subscription the investment dealer may act only as a selling agent. It is also possible that the issuing firm and the investment dealer

[15]Gary D. Tallman, David F. Rush, and Ronald W. Melicher, "Competitive versus Negotiated Underwriting Cost of Regulated Industries," *Financial Management*, 3 (Summer 1974), pp. 49–55.

might sign a standby agreement, which would obligate the investment dealer to underwrite the securities that are not accepted by the privileged investors.

Bought Deal

In certain cases, an underwriter or a group of underwriters can negotiate the sale of an entire issue with large institutional or retail investors before the issue comes to market. Since the underwriter has assured itself of reselling the securities when they are bought from the issuing firm, the distribution method is called a **bought deal**. The success of this type of distribution method is dependent on the terms of the securities issue and the reputations of both the issuing firm and the underwriter.

The Public Offering Process

The public offering is the distribution method most likely to be used by the private corporation. It makes sense, then, to cover in some detail the sequence of events that comprise the negotiated underwriting.

1. **Selection of an investment dealer.** The firm initiates the fundraising process by choosing an investment dealer. On some occasions a third party, called a finder, may direct the firm to a specific investment dealer. Typically, the finder receives a fee from the fundraising firm if an underwriting agreement is eventually signed. Use of a finder is one way of gaining access to a quality investment dealer.

2. **Preunderwriting conferences.** A series of preunderwriting conferences are held between the firm and the investment dealer. Key items discussed are (1) the amount of capital to be raised, (2) whether the capital markets seem to be especially receptive at this time to one type of financing instrument over another, and (3) whether the proposed use of the new funds appears reasonable. At these conferences, confirmation is obtained that a flotation will occur and the particular investment dealer will manage the underwriting. The investment dealer then undertakes a complete financial analysis of the corporation and assesses its future prospects. The final outcome of the preunderwriting conferences is the **tentative underwriting agreement**. This agreement details (1) the approximate price the investment dealer will pay for the securities and (2) the upset price. The upset price is a form of escape mechanism for the benefit of the issuing firm. If the market price of the firm's securities should drop in a significant fashion just before the new securities are to be sold, the price the investment dealer is to pay the firm might drop below the upset price. In this situation the new offering would be aborted.

3. **Formation of the underwriting syndicate.** An underwriting syndicate is a temporary association of investment dealers formed to purchase a security issue from a corporation for subsequent resale, hopefully at a profit to the underwriters. The syndicate is formed for very sound reasons. First, the managing investment dealer probably could not finance the entire underwriting itself. Second, the use of a syndicate reduces the risk of loss to any single underwriter. Third, the use of a syndicate widens the eventual distribution effort. Each underwriter has its own network of security dealers who purchase a portion of the participation in the offering. Most syndicates contain 5 to 20 investment dealers. Since each dealer has its own distribution network, the selling group

can often consist of 100 to 600 dealers across North America. All members of the syndicate sign the agreement which binds them to certain performance standards, provides detail as to their participation (amount they can purchase) in the offering and determines their liability for any portion of the issue unsold by their fellow underwriters.

4. **Registering the securities.** Most provinces in Canada have enacted legislation through their Securities Acts to protect investors against fraud, to ensure fair conduct within the marketplace, and to encourage full and true disclosure by corporations. Each of these provinces has also empowered its own Securities Commission to oversee the regulations of the Securities Act. For example in Ontario, a new public issue cannot be offered to prospective investors before the new issue is registered with the Ontario Securities Commission (OSC). However, for well-established firms, the registration process has been streamlined to make the process more expedient. We will now examine both the long-form registration and the short-form registration processes.

a) Long-form registration process

The distribution of a new issue of securities across Canada requires that the firm comply with the regulations of the Securities Acts in each of the provinces where the security is to be distributed. To facilitate the process of meeting all the regulations of each province, the firm would generally register the issue where distribution will be the greatest, for example Ontario. The Ontario Securities Act dictates that a registration statement must be submitted to the OSC; the objective of this statement is disclosure of all facts relevant to the new issue that will permit an investor to make an informed decision. The OSC itself does not judge the investment quality of securities. The registration statement is a lengthy document containing (1) historical, (2) financial, and (3) administrative facts about the firm. The details of the new offering are presented, as well as the proposed use of the funds that are being raised. During a three- to six-week waiting period, the OSC examines the statement for errors or omissions. While this examination process is being carried out, the underwriting syndicate cannot offer the security for sale. Part of the package presented to the OSC for scrutiny is a document called a **prospectus**. Once approved, it is the official advertising vehicle for the offering. During the waiting period a **preliminary prospectus**, outlining the important features of the new issue, may be distributed to potential investors. The preliminary prospectus contains no selling price information or offering date. In addition, a stamped red-ink statement on the first page tells the reader that the document is not an official offer to sell the securities. In the jargon of finance, this preliminary prospectus is called a **red herring**. Once the registration statement is approved by the OSC, a series of provincial agreements enable the security issue to be registered with the provincial Security Commissions and to be offered for sale in all provinces provided the prospectus is made available to all concerned parties.

b) Prompt Offering Qualification System (POP System)

In 1982, security regulators agreed to implement the POP system which streamlines the process of public distribution of securities to Canadian capital markets. The POP system streamlines the procedures for a public offering through the use of a short-form prospectus. However, issuing firms must satisfy the following conditions to be eligible for distribution of securities by the POP system:

- must satisfy the reporting period test which requires an issuing firm to have reported for at least 36 months;
- must satisfy the public float test which requires an issuing firm to have an aggregate market value of Canadian listed equity shares held by non-insiders of at least $75 million or more outstanding during the last calendar month of the issuer's most recently completed financial year;
- must satisfy the requirements of securities legislation for provinces or territories where securities will be distributed;
- must satisfy either of the top three categories of recognized ratings organizations for issues of investment grade non-convertible debt securities and preferred shares.[16]

The compliance of the issuing firm to these conditions enables the public offering to be cleared by the security regulators within 7–10 days of filing the short-form prospectus. This type of delay contrasts to the 30 to 45 days required for the traditional long-form prospectus. Investor's risk is reduced by the strict disclosure rules which require firms using the short-form prospectus method to file financial information with security regulators on annual basis. Such eligibility conditions ensure that the transactions of an issuing firm are reported by the financial media and analyzed by financial specialists for their financial information content.

The POP system can be used for the public offering of common shares, as well as for the public offerings of preferred shares and investment grade non-convertible debt securities. The latter two securities may be offered under more relaxed conditions; for example, the issuing firms of preferred shares may be required to satisfy the reporting period test but not have to satisfy the public float test.

5. **Formation of the selling group.** In order to distribute the securities to final investors, a **selling group** is formed. The dealers comprising the selling group purchase portions of the new issue from the syndicate members with whom they regularly do business. A dealer of the selling group pays a higher price than that paid by the syndicate member, but less than the offering price to the investing public. The responsibilities and rewards of the selling group are outlined in the selling group agreement. Formation of the selling group completes the distribution network for the new offering. The structure of such a network is illustrated in Figure 17-2.

6. **The due diligence meeting.** This is a "last-chance" gathering to get everything in order before taking the offering to the public. Usually, all members of the syndicate are present, along with key officers of the issuing firm. Any omissions from the prospectus should be corrected at this meeting. Most important, the final price to be paid by the syndi-

---

[16]Sean Sadler, Rene Sorell, and Richard Balfour, "Proposed Changes To The POP System," *Mergers and Acquisitions In Canada* (February 1992) pp. 5–7.

FIGURE 17-2
Distributing New Securities

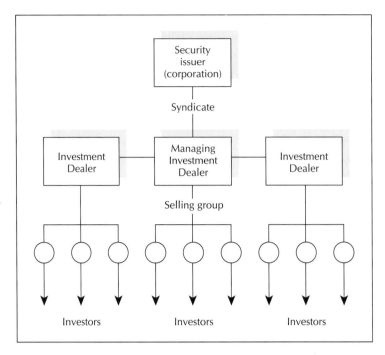

cate to the firm is settled at this meeting. As we said earlier, if the issue represents additional common shares, the underwriting price may be a fixed amount below the closing price of the firm's outstanding shares on the day prior to the new offering. Capital market conditions are discussed, and the security's offering price to the public is set in light of those conditions. The "go ahead" is given to print the final prospectus, which now contains all relevant price information. The offering is usually made the day after the meeting.

7. **Price-pegging.** Once the issue has been offered for sale, the managing underwriter attempts to mitigate downward price movements in the secondary market for the security by placing orders to buy at the agreed-upon public offering price. The objective is to stabilize the market price of the issue so it can be sold at the initial offering price. The syndicate manager's intention to perform this price maintenance operation must be disclosed in the registration statement.

8. **Syndicate termination.** A contractual agreement among the underwriters identifies the duration of the syndicate. Pragmatically, the syndicate is dissolved when the issue has been fully subscribed. If the demand for the issue is great, it may be sold out in a few days. If the issue lingers on the market, without much buyer interest, the remaining inventory may be sold at the existing secondary market price. The name of the game in underwriting is not margin, but turnover. Should the issue go sour, the underwriters will quickly absorb the loss and get on to the next underwriting project.

Industry Leaders

Investment dealers in Canada provide underwriting services for both domestic and international issues of debt and equity financing. Domestic issues include both public offerings and private placements. In addition, federal crown corporations, municipalities, provincial governments, and corporations use Canadian investment dealers for underwriting debt issues. As an example of the magnitude of financings in the early nineties, RBC Dominion Securities Inc. lead the industry as a manager of $9.4 billion worth of financings: $3.6 billion of corporate issues and $5.8 billion of provincial issues.[17]

BASIC FINANCIAL MANAGEMENT IN PRACTICE

Investment Banking and Commercial Banking

One of the more important events that has affected our financial markets is the deregulation of the investment industry. The following article describes some of the realities that chartered banks have faced since legislation was enacted in 1987.

Banks Face More Uncertainty on Brokerage Front

Back in 1987, after finally getting permission to own securities dealers, four of the country's five largest chartered banks lost little time buying into some of the country's largest investment houses. Shortly after four of the five major Canadian banks entered the securities business in the late 1980s, the brokerage industry took a nosedive. In 1990, possibly the worst year in its history, the securities industry lost $226 million. And although the industry turned things around with a profit of $338 million in 1991, uncertain times are still ahead.

But Mike Andrews, associate director for financial service research at the Conference Board of Canada in Ottawa, says as long as bankers remain bullish on their investments, they'll wait it out.

"[Restructuring] is inevitable in any business," says Peter Godsoe, Toronto-based president and chief operating officer of the Bank of Nova Scotia. "The industry is constantly renewing itself as new firms evolve and others rationalize."

Many changes have been made since 1987, and more are on the way. But experts agree that the banks' infusion of equity into the industry did much to strengthen it.

"The banks injected a fair bit of capital into the industry," Andrews says. "If the banks weren't there, its hard to say what would have happened."

New Relationship

His report, *The Canadian Securities Industry: A Decade of Transition*, says regulatory capital grew $1 billion in 1987 to $2.5 billion, thanks to the banks' purchase of ownership in the largest security firms.

The new relationship between banks and their securities subsidiaries is hardly one way. Andrews notes that it gives banks greater access to capital markets, while their subsidiaries gain a foothold in the credit market. Together, it gives them more clout in the competitive market.

Godsoe adds that as financial markets move toward greater integration of product and services, "we had no choice but to develop better skills in [shares] distribution and underwriting". And having ScotiaMcLeod Inc., a wholly owned subsidiary since 1988, on board helps. "We continue to build [our businesses] in the U.S., Europe, and the Far East," he says. When clients require more than banking services, they can be referred to the brokerage firm, which operates independently of its parent. In Canada, "we have transferred some operations from the bank—mostly in short-term trading—to ScotiaMcLeod because they have greater expertise in that area." A discount brokerage service, offered through another unit, Scotia Securities Inc., uses ScotiaMcLeod's "expertise in processing and running the back office, and that makes us more competitive."

Paul Taylor, executive vice-president of treasury and investment banking, at Royal Bank of Canada, which bought 75% of RBC Dominion Securities Inc. (DS) in 1988, is similarly pleased with the bank's investment in DS. "It's improved our knowledge of the investment industry and market. [The DS team] were more advanced in operations, such as bond trading, providing corporate acquisition advice, right down the line. So we chose to leave that business in their group."

Big Players Now Bigger

Industry analysts note that with the new ownership structure, big players have become bigger, middle

Continued on page 758

---

[17]*The Financial Post*, "1991 A Big Year For The Underwriters" (June 29, 1992) p. 13.

757

Continued from page 757

size firms have all but disappeared, replaced by boutique firms that address niche markets.

However, Charles Winograd, chairman and chief executive officer of Richardson Greenshields of Canada Ltd., in Toronto, notes that competition from bankers can hurt small players. "Banks are suppliers of capital to brokerage business," he adds. While there hasn't been much reason for concern, "its never a comfortable situation when you're dependent on your competitor for capital." The smaller the player, the greater the discomfort. While bank-owned securities firms can now use their parent's extensive retail outlets to push their own sales, it isn't a major concern to independents, Winograd says.

The issue is whether they can get the right people to offer competent investment advice at those outlets. Taylor notes that while some DS investment advisors have moved into various bank premises across Canada, "we don't think it's necessary or logical to have stockbrokers in all the banks' outlets." For the most part, the way the industry has operated hasn't changed much, mainly because the new players have retained the same managers to run their companies.

"All you've done is altered ownership," says Charles Caty, president of the Toronto-based Investment Dealers Association. In most cases, "management of these subsidiaries are still run by the securities people, not bankers. The banks were buying management [skills], and so long as they perform, they'll keep the management."

Source: Adapted from: Miriam Cu-Uy-Gam, "Banks Face More Uncertainty On Brokerage Front," *The Financial Post* (September 14, 1992) p. s21.

PRIVATE PLACEMENTS

Private placements offer an alternative to the sale of securities to the public or to a restricted group of investors through a privileged subscription. Any type of security can be privately placed (directly placed). However, the private placement market is clearly dominated by debt issues.

In arranging a private placement the firm may either avoid the use of an investment dealer and work directly with the investing institutions or engage the services of an investment dealer. If the firm does not use an investment dealer, of course, it does not have to pay a fee. On the other hand, investment dealers can provide valuable advice in the private placement process. They are usually in contact with several major institutional investors; thus, the investment dealer will know if a firm is in a position to invest in a proposed offering, and can help with evaluating the terms of the new issue.

Private placements have both advantages and disadvantages as compared with those of public offerings. The financial manager must carefully evaluate both sides of the question. The advantages associated with private placements are these:

1. **Speed.** The firm usually obtains funds more quickly through a private placement than a public offering.

2. **Reduced flotation costs.** Underwriting and distribution costs are lower than those of public offerings because it is not necessary to file a long-form prospectus.

3. **Financing flexibility.** In a private placement, the firm deals on a face-to-face basis with a small number of investors. This means that the terms of the issue can be tailored to meet the specific needs of the company. For example, all of the funds need not be taken by the firm at

once. In exchange for a commitment fee the firm can "draw down" against the established amount of credit with the investors. This provides some insurance against capital market uncertainties, and the firm does not have to borrow the funds if the need does not arise. There is also the possibility of renegotiation. The terms of the debt issue can be altered. The term to maturity, the interest rate, or any restrictive covenants can be discussed among the affected parties.

The following disadvantages of private placements must be evaluated:

1. **Interest costs.** It is generally conceded that interest costs on private placements exceed those of public issues. Whether this disadvantage is enough to offset the reduced flotation costs associated with a private placement is a determination that the financial manager must make. There is some evidence that on smaller issues, say $500,000 as opposed to $30 million, the private placement alternative would be preferable.[18]

2. **Restrictive covenants.** Dividend policy, working-capital levels, and the raising of additional debt capital may all be affected by provisions in the private-placement debt contract. That is not to say that such restrictions are always absent in public debt contracts. Rather, the financial officer must be alert to the tendency for these covenants to be especially burdensome in private contracts.

Until 1990 Canadian access to the U.S. private placement market was considered expensive because U.S. security laws restricted the resale of privately sold securities. In April of 1990 the U.S. Securities and Exchange Commission passed a security law enabling a large institution to resell debt securities.[19] As a result, large Canadian corporations are using the private placement market to place corporate debt in the U.S. capital markets. For example, both CP Forest Products and Hees International have used the private placement market to issue U.S. $102 million and U.S. $200 million in corporate debt in the early nineties. The most likely Canadian companies to use the U.S. private placement market are companies with U.S. revenues that can use the U.S. debt as a hedge against currency fluctuations. The major investors in private placements are large financial institutions. Based on the volume of securities purchased, the three most important investor groups are (1) life insurance companies, (2) registered retirement funds, and (3) private pension funds.

FLOTATION COSTS

The firm raising long-term capital incurs two types of **flotation costs**: (1) the underwriter's spread and (2) issuing costs. Of these two costs, the underwriter's spread is the larger. The underwriter's spread is simply the difference between the gross and net proceeds from a given security issue expressed as a percent of the gross proceeds. The issue costs include (1)

---

[18]John D. Rea and Peggy Brockschmidt, "The Relationship Between Publicly Offered and Privately Placed Corporate Bonds," *Monthly Review*, Federal Reserve Bank of Kansas City (November 1973), p. 15.

[19]Jacquie McNish, "Canadians Look To U.S. As Source Of Cheap Capital," *Globe and Mail*, (December 5, 1991) pp. B1, B2.

printing and engraving, (2) legal fees, (3) accounting fees, (4) trustee fees, and (5) several other miscellaneous components. The two most significant issue costs are printing and engraving and legal fees.

Flotation costs vary according to the type of security issued and the size of the issue. For example, the costs associated with issuing common shares are notably greater than the costs associated with preferred share offerings. In turn, costs of preferred shares exceed those of bonds. Furthermore, flotation costs (expressed as a percent of gross proceeds) decrease as the size of the security issue increases.

This variation in flotation costs indicates that these costs are sensitive to the risks involved in successfully distributing a security issue. Common shares are riskier to own than corporate bonds. Underwriting risk is, therefore, greater with common shares than with bonds. Thus, flotation costs just mirror these risk relationships. Furthermore, a portion of the flotation costs is fixed. Legal fees and accounting costs are good examples. So, as the size of the security issue rises, the fixed component is spread over a larger gross proceeds base. As a consequence, average flotation costs vary inversely with the size of the issue.

Perspective in Finance

Since late 1986, there has been a renewal of public interest in the rules which regulate the North American financial markets. The concern was raised because of a massive insider trading scandal that made the name "Ivan F. Boesky" one of almost universal recognition—but, unfortunately, in a negative sense. This event was followed by the October 19, 1987, crash of the equity markets. More recently, in early 1990, the investing community (both institutional and individual) became increasingly concerned over a weakening in the so-called "junk bond market" and the collapse of the real estate market. The upshot of all of this enhanced awareness is a new appreciation of the crucial role that security regulation plays in the financial system. The basics are presented below.

REGULATION

The regulation of securities is legislated both federally and provincially through the Canada Business Corporation Act and provincial acts which administer security, commodity, futures, and deposits regulation. For example in Ontario, the Ontario Securities Commission (OSC) has both administrative and enforcive responsibility over the Securities and Commodity Futures Acts.[20] However, the actual regulation is administered through self-regulatory organizations such as the Toronto Stock Exchange (TSE) and the Toronto Futures Exchange (TFE) and the Investment Dealers Association of Canada (IDA). These self-regulatory organizations impose financial and trading rules on their members which are enforced through independent audits and compliance checks. The OSC will oversee the self-regulatory organizations to ensure the following activities:

1. Licensing and registration of persons and firms trading in securities and commodity futures contracts.

[20]Ontario Securities Commission, "Annual Report For The Ontario Securities Commission" (Toronto, Queen's Printer for Ontario, 1991) p. 6.

2. Review of prospectuses and other disclosure documents
3. Enforcement of the Securities Act and the Commodity Futures Act.[21]

The introduction of new issues on the Toronto Stock Exchange is governed by the Securities Act of Ontario. The intent of the act is important. It aims to provide potential investors with accurate, truthful disclosure about the firm and the new securities being offered to the public. This does not prevent firms from issuing highly speculative securities. The OSC says nothing whatsoever about the possible investment worth of a given offering. It is up to the investor to separate the junk from the jewels. The OSC does have the legal power and responsibility to enforce the Securities Act.

Full public disclosure is achieved by the requirement that the issuing firm file a registration statement with the OSC containing requisite information. The statement details particulars about the firm and the new security being issued. During a minimum 21-day waiting period, the OSC examines the submitted document. In numerous instances the 21-day wait has been extended by several weeks. The OSC can ask for additional information that was omitted in order to clarify the original document. The OSC can also order that the offering be stopped.

During the registration process a preliminary prospectus (the red herring) may be distributed to potential investors. When the registration is approved, the final prospectus must be made available to the prospective investors. The prospectus is actually a condensed version of the full registration statement. If, at a later date, the information in the registration statement and the prospectus is found to be lacking, purchasers of the new issue who incurred a loss can sue for damages. Officers of the issuing firm and others who took part in the registration and marketing of the issue may suffer both civil and criminal penalties.

Recent changes in the regulation of the Canadian equity market have ensured that Canadian firms have access to foreign sources of capital. The following article discusses one of these important regulatory developments.

Secondary Market Regulations

The trading of securities on the secondary market is regulated by the Securities Exchange, for example the Toronto Stock Exchange, and the provincial Securities Acts. The policy of the Toronto Stock Exchange concerning persons investing in securities listed on this exchange is to ensure equal access to information that may affect their investment decisions. Thus, both the Toronto Stock Exchange and the OSC require companies listed on the exchange to provide timely disclosure of material information concerning their business and affairs. Other powers which the OSC has to fulfill its mandate for effective regulation are:

- to investigate;
- to suspend, to cancel or impose terms on registration, or reprimand registrants;
- to grant or deny exemptions from provisions concerning prospectuses, registration, take-over bids or issuer bids;
- to cease trading of any security;

[21]Ibid.

BASIC FINANCIAL MANAGEMENT IN PRACTICE

Canadian Equity Markets: Taking Advantage of Change

The emerging global economy is challenging many industries, and the securities business is no exception. In recent years, international equity trading has been encouraged by a number of factors, including the evolution of technology and the deregulation/regulation of security markets. One measure of this trend is the surge in gross cross-border equity flows: the value of overall trading in domestic shares conducted in the domestic market by or on behalf of foreign non-residents rose from U.S. $73 billion in 1979 to $1.44 trillion in 1990.

For Canadian corporations, the implications of this development are varied. As barriers fall in the global equity market, large corporations are benefiting from improved access to foreign capital. Many mid-sized and small firms, however, still find it difficult to tap international markets. Thus the Canadian securities industry faces a twofold challenge: to ensure that Canadian companies benefit from new opportunities for access to foreign capital, and to maintain a viable domestic securities market for Canadian corporations in an increasingly competitive global environment.

Regulatory Changes

One important step toward increasing access to foreign capital is the Multi Jurisdictional Disclosure System (MJDS). Five years in the making, MJDS was negotiated by the U.S. Securities and Exchange Commission (SEC) and the Canadian provincial securities regulators. Essentially, the system allows large Canadian and U.S. issuers to do public offerings of their securities in another country using the disclosure documents required at home.

Since its implementation in July 1991, a number of Canadian corporations have used MJDS. An example is Magna International Inc., which offered an equity issue in the United States and Canada using MJDS. Because of the agreement, Magna was able to offer the issue in both countries without a U.S. SEC review, by using documents vested by the Ontario Securities Commission and other provincial regulators. Magna officials say the new system allowed the company to access the U.S. market faster and less expensively than before. In addition, Magna notes that although MJDS has only recently come into effect, U.S. underwriters had no difficulty marketing the issue using Canadian-style documents.

Experiences like these show that MJDS can help Canadian companies to obtain a foreign source of capital at a competitive price, and to quickly take advantage of favourable market conditions in the United States. Although at present the system is being used mainly by companies like Magna, which have previously sought capital abroad, the coming years likely will see a growing use of MJDS by Canadian corporations that might not otherwise have made offerings in the United States.

Despite the success of this arrangement, no initiatives are yet in place to extend the benefits of regulatory harmonization to smaller corporations seeking financing in countries other than the United States. Although the International Organization of Securities Commissions (IOSCO) contemplates the possible development of a system analogous to MJDS for a large group of countries including Canada, such a project is unlikely to bear fruit for many years.

Source: Adapted from: K. Michael Edwards, "Canadian Equity Markets: Taking Advantage of Change," *Canadian Business Review* (Spring, 1992) pp. 26–28.

- to freeze funds or apply to courts for the appointment of receivers;
- to order audits of registrants, reporting issuers, mutual fund custodians and clearing houses of commodity futures and stock exchanges;
- to grant relief from financial reporting requirements; and
- to grant relief from proxy solicitation and insider reporting requirements.[22]

[22]Ibid.

This chapter centred on the market environment in which corporations raise long-term funds, including the structure of the Canadian financial markets, the institution of investment banking, and the various methods for distributing securities.

The Mix of Corporate Securities Sold

When corporations go to the capital market for cash, the most favoured financing method is debt. The corporate debt markets clearly dominate the equity markets when new funds are raised. The Canadian tax system inherently favours debt capital as a fund-raising method. In an average year over the 1971–1992 period, bonds and notes made up 59 percent of external cash that was raised.

Why Financial Markets Exist

The function of financial markets is to allocate savings efficiently in the economy to the ultimate demander (user) of the savings. In a financial market the forces of supply and demand for a specific financial instrument are brought together. The wealth of an economy would not be as great as it is without a fully developed financial market system.

Financing Business

Every year households are a net supplier of funds to the financial markets. The nonfinancial business sector is always a net borrower of funds. Both life insurance companies and private pension funds are important buyers of corporate securities. In the economy, savings are ultimately transferred to the business firm seeking cash by means of (1) the direct transfer, (2) the indirect transfer using the investment dealer, or (3) the indirect transfer using the financial intermediary.

Components of the Canadian Financial Market System

Corporations can raise funds through public offerings or private placements. The public market is impersonal in that the security issuer does not meet the ultimate investors in the financial instruments. In a private placement, the securities are sold directly to a limited number of institutional investors.

The primary market is the market for new issues. The secondary market represents transactions in currently outstanding securities. Both the money and capital markets have primary and secondary sides. The money market refers to transactions in short-term debt instruments. The capital market, on the other hand, refers to transactions in long-term financial instruments. Trading in the money and capital markets can take place in either the organized security exchanges or the over-the-counter market. The money market is exclusively an over-the-counter market.

The Investment Dealer

The investment dealer is a financial specialist involved as an intermediary in the merchandising of securities. He or she performs the functions of

(1) underwriting, (2) advising, and (3) distributing. Major methods for the public distribution of securities include (1) the public offering, (2) the commission or best-efforts basis, (3) privileged subscriptions, and (4) bought deal. The bought deal may bypass the use of an investment dealer. The public offering provides the greatest amount of investment underwriting services to the corporate client.

Private Placements

Privately placed debt provides an important market outlet for corporate bonds. Major investors in this market are (1) life insurance firms, (2) retirement funds, and (3) private pension funds. Several advantages and disadvantages are associated with private placements. The financial officer must weigh these attributes and decide if a private placement is preferable over a public offering.

Flotation Costs

Flotation costs consist of the underwriter's spread and issuing costs. The flotation costs of common shares exceed those of preferred shares, which, in turn, exceed those of debt. Moreover, flotation costs as a percent of gross proceeds are inversely related to the size of the security issue.

Regulation

The primary market for new issues is regulated at the provincial level by their Securities Acts. A national distribution of securities must meet the regulations of every province before it can be sold to the public. A firm that is distributing a new issue of securities for the first time must use the long-form registration process to register the issue with the provincial Security Commissions. However, large and well-established firms may use the Prompt Offering Qualification System (POP System) to register a security issue instead of the long-form registration process which is more costly and time-consuming. Secondary market trading is also regulated by the provincial Securities Acts. In Canada, members of the secondary market are self-regulated. The Security Acts empower their Security Commissions to oversee the self-regulatory organizations to ensure the licensing and registration of persons and firms trading in securities and commodity futures contracts, to review prospectuses and other disclosure documents, and to enforce the regulations of the Securities Acts and the Commodity Futures Act.

STUDY QUESTIONS

17-1. What are financial markets? What function do they perform? How would an economy be worse off without them?

17-2. Define in a technical sense what we mean by "financial intermediary." Give an example of your definition.

17-3. Distinguish between the money and capital markets.

17-4. What major benefits do corporations and investors enjoy because of the existence of organized security exchanges?

17-5. What are the general categories examined by an organized exchange in determining whether an applicant firm's securities can be listed on it? (Specific numbers are not needed here, but rather "areas" of investigation.)

17-6. Why do you think most secondary market trading in bonds takes place over-the-counter?

17-7. What is an investment dealer, and what major functions does he or she perform?

17-8. Explain the Prompt Offering Qualification System (POP System).

17-9. Why is an investment dealer syndicate formed?

17-10. Why might a large corporation want to raise long-term capital through a private placement rather than a public offering?

17-11. As a recent business school graduate, you work directly for the corporate treasurer. Your corporation is going to issue a new security and is concerned with the probable flotation costs. What tendencies about flotation costs can you relate to the treasurer?

17-12. You own a group of five clothing stores, all located in southern Ontario. You are about to market $200,000 worth of new common shares. Your shares trade over-the-counter. The shares will be sold only to Ontario residents. Your financial advisor informs you that the issue must be registered with the OSC. Is the advisor correct?

17-13. When corporations raise funds, what type of financing vehicle (instrument or instruments) is most favoured?

17-14. What is the major (most significant) savings-surplus sector in the Canadian economy?

17-15. Identify three distinct ways that savings are ultimately transferred to business firms in need of cash.

SELECTED REFERENCES

Affleck-Graves, John, and Robert E. Miller. "Regulatory and Procedural Effects on the Underpricing of Initial Public Offering," *The Journal of Financial Research*, 12 (Fall 1989), 183–192.

Amling, Frederick. *Investments: An Introduction to Analysis and Management.* 5th ed. Englewood Cliffs, NJ: Prentice-Hall, 1984.

Asquith, Paul, and David W. Mullins, Jr. "Equity Issues and Offering Dilution," *Journal of Financial Economics*, 15 (January–February 1986), 61–89.

Bae, Sung C. and Haim Levy. "The Valuation of Firm Commitment Underwriting Contracts for Seasoned New Equity Issues: Theory and Evidence," *Financial Management*, 19 (Summer 1990), 48–59.

Barry, Christopher B., Chris J. Muscarella, and Michael R. Vetsuypens. "Underwriting Warrants, Underwriter Compensation, and the Costs of Going Public," *Journal of Financial Economics*, 29 (March 1991), 113–35.

Ben-Horim, Moshe, Shalom Hoch-man, and Oded Palmon. "The Impact of the 1986 Tax Reform Act on Corporate Financial Policy," *Financial Management*, 16 (Autumn 1987), 29–35.

Bhagat, S., M. Wayne Marr, and G. Rodney Thompson. "The Rule 415 Experiment: Equity Markets," *Journal of Finance*, 40 (December 1985), 1385–1401.

Bloch, Ernest. "Pricing a Corporate Bond Issue: A Look Behind the Scenes," *Essays in Money and Credit*, 72–76. New York: Federal Reserve Bank of New York, 1964.

Booth, James R., and Richard L. Smith, II. "Capital Raising, Underwriting and the Certification Hypothesis," *Journal of Financial Economics*, 15 (January–February 1986), 261–281.

Bower, Nancy L. "Firm Value and the Choice of Offering Method in Initial Public Offerings," *Journal of Finance*, 44 (July 1989), 647–662.

Brown, Keith C., and Donald J. Smith. "Recent Innovation in Interest Rate Risk Management and the Reintermediation of Commercial Banking," *Financial Management*, 13 (Winter 1988), 45–58.

Carter, Richard B. and Frederick H. Dark. "The Use of the Over Allotment Option in Initial Public Offerings," *Financial Management*, 19 (Autumn 1990), 55–64.

Cohan, A. B. *Private Placements and Public Offerings: Market Shares Since 1945.* Chapel Hill: University of North Carolina Press, 1961.

Collins, Bruce M. and Frank J. Fabozzi. "A Methodology for Measuring Transaction Costs," *Financial Analyst Journal*, 47 (March–April 1991), 27–36.

Conroy, Robert M., and Robert L. Winkler. "Market Structure: The Specialist as Dealer and Broker," *Journal of Banking and Finance*, 10 (March 1986), 21–36.

Cooper, S. Kerry, Donald R. Fraser, and Gene C. Uselton. *Money, the Financial System, and Economic Policy.* Reading, MA: Addison-Wesley, 1983.

Dougall, Herbert E., and Jack E. Gaumnitz. *Capital Markets and Institutions*. 4th ed. Englewood Cliffs, NJ: Prentice-Hall, 1980.

Duchessi, Peter, Shawky Hang, and John P. Seagle. "A Knowledge-Engineered System for Commercial Loan Decisions," *Financial Management*, 17 (Autumn 1988), 57–65.

Eckbo, B. Espen. "Valuation Effects of Corporate Debt Offerings," *Journal of Financial Economics*, 15 (January–February 1986), 119–151.

Ederington, Louis H. "Negotiated versus Competitive Underwritings of Corporate Bonds," *Journal of Finance*, 31 (March 1976), 17–28.

Edmister, Robert O. *Financial Institutions, Markets and Management*. 2nd ed. New York: McGraw-Hill, 1986.

Fabozzi, Frank J., and Frank G. Zarb, eds. *Handbook of Financial Markets*. Homewood, IL: Dow Jones-Irwin, 1981.

Feldstein, Martin, ed. *The American Economy in Transition*. Chicago: University of Chicago Press, 1980.

Friedman, Benjamin M., ed. *The Changing Roles of Debt and Equity in Financing U.S. Capital Formation*. Chicago: University of Chicago Press, 1982.

Furst, Richard W. "Does Listing Increase the Market Price of Common Stocks?" *Journal of Business*, 43 (April 1970), 174–180.

Goulet, Waldemar M. "Price Changes, Managerial Actions and Insider Trading at the Time of Listing," *Financial Management*, 3 (Spring 1974), 30–36.

Gup, Benton E. *Financial Intermediaries*. 2nd ed. Boston: Houghton Mifflin, 1980.

Hansell, Saul. "The Six-Month Corporate Underwriting Sweepstakes," *Institutional Investors*, 24 (September 1991), 87–88.

Hansen, Robert S., Beverly R. Fuller, and Vahan Janjigian. "The Over-Allotment Option and Equity Financing Costs: An Empirical Investigation," *Financial Management*, 16 (Summer 1987), 24–32.

Hatch, James E. and Michael J. Robinson. *Investment Management in Canada*. 2nd ed. Scarborough, Ont., Prentice-Hall Canada, 1989.

Haubrich, Joseph G. "Financial Intermediation: Delegated Monitoring and Long-Term Relationships," *Journal of Banking and Finance*, 13 (March 1989), 9–20.

Hayes, Samuel L., III. "Investment Banking: Power Structure in Flux," *Harvard Business Review*, 49 (March–April 1971), 136–152.

Henning, Charles N., William Pigott, and Robert H. Scott. *Financial Markets and the Economy*. 4th ed. Englewood Cliffs, NJ: Prentice-Hall, 1984.

Houston, Arthur L., Jr., and Carol Olson Houston. "Financing With Preferred Stock," *Financial Management*, 17 (Autumn 1990), 42–54.

Humphrey, Joseph J. H. "Investment Banking—1989," *Journal of Cash Management*, 9 (September–October 1989), 26–34.

Johnson, James M., and Robert E. Miller. "Investment Banker Prestige and the Underpricing of Initial Public Offerings," *Financial Management*, 17 (Summer 1988), 19–29.

Johnson, Keith B., Gregory T. Morton, and M. Chapman Findlay III. "An Empirical Analysis of the Flotation Cost of Corporate Securities, 1971–1972," *Journal of Finance*, 30 (June 1975), 1129–1133.

Kwast, Myron L. "The Impact of Underwriting and Dealing on Bank Returns and Risks," *Journal of Banking and Finance*, 13 (March 1989), 101–126.

Light, J. O., and William L. White. *The Financial System*. Homewood, IL: Richard D. Irwin, 1979.

Logue, Dennis E., and John R. Lindvall. "The Behavior of Investment Bankers: An Econometric Investigation," *Journal of Finance*, 29 (March 1974), 203–215.

Logue, Dennis E., John R. Lindvall, and Robert A. Jarrow. "Negotiation vs. Competitive Bidding in the Sale of Securities by Public Utilities," *Financial Management*, 7 (Autumn 1978), 31–39.

Marr, M. Wayne, and G. Rodney Thompson. "Rule 415: Preliminary Empirical Results," Working Paper No. 24, Department of Finance, Virginia Polytechnic Institute and State University, October 1983.

Miller, Robert E., and Frank K. Reilly. "An Examination of Mispricing, Returns, and Uncertainty for Initial Public Offerings," *Financial Management*, 16 (Autumn 1987), 29–35.

Ratner, David L. *Securities Regulation in a Nutshell*. St. Paul, MN: West Publishing, 1978.

Retkwa, Rosalyn. "Cultivating Equity: Growing New Capital in a Post-Debt Era," *Corporate Cashflow*, 11 (February 1990), 29–31.

Rose, Peter S., and Donald R. Fraser. *Financial Institutions*. 3rd ed. Dallas: Business Publications, 1984.

Ross, Stephen A. "Institutional Markets, Financial Marketing, and Financial Innovation," *Journal of Finance*, 44 (July 1989), 541–556.

Seward, James K. "Corporate Financial Policy and the Theory of Financial Intermediation," *The Journal of Finance*, 45 (June 1990), 29–31.

Sharpe, William F., Gordon J. Alexander and David J. Fowler. Investments. 1st ed. Scarborough: Ont., Prentice-Hall Canada, 1993.

Smith, Clifford W., Jr. "Investment Banking and the Capital Acquisition Process," *Journal of Financial Economics*, 15 (January–February 1986), 3–29.

Strebel, Paul. "Managing the Information Cost of Financing," *Columbia Journal of World Business*, 21 (Summer 1986), 39–45.

766

Stulz, René M. "Managerial Discretion and Optimal Financing Policies," *Journal of Financial Economics*, 26 (July 1990), 3–27.

Tallman, Gary D., David R. Rush, and Ronald W. Melicher. "Competitive versus Negotiated Underwriting Cost of Regulated Industries," *Financial Management*, 3 (Summer 1974), 49–55.

Van Horne, James C. *Financial Market Rates and Flows*. 2nd ed. Englewood Cliffs, NJ: Prentice-Hall, 1984.

Welch, Ivo. "Seasonal Offerings, Imitation Costs, and the Underpricing of Initial Public Offerings," *Journal of Finance*, 44 (June 1989), 421–450.

West, Richard R., and Seha M. Tinic. "Corporate Finance and the Changing Stock Market," *Financial Management*, 3 (Autumn 1974), 14–23.

Wiesen, Jeremy L. *Regulating Transactions in Securities*. St. Paul, MN: West Publishing, 1975.

Zent, Charles H. "Pricing an IPO: An Accurate Way to Set Share Value When Going Public," *Corporate Cashflow*, 11 (February 1990), 32–35.

CHAPTER 18

Term Loans and Leases

- Term Loans

- Leases

For discussion purposes we generally categorize the sources of financing available to the business firm into three groups, distinguished by their terms-of-maturity. These maturities are not exact but represent generally accepted guidelines for categorizing sources of financing. Short-term sources of financing, which have a maturity of one year or less, were discussed in Chapter 16. Intermediate-term financing, which includes all financing arrangements whose final maturities are longer than one year but no longer than ten years, is the subject of this chapter. Long-term financing, which is defined as all forms of financing with final maturities longer than ten years, is discussed in Chapters 19 and 20.

Perspective in Finance

The principal sources of intermediate-term financing are term loans and leases. We will look first at the primary sources of term loans and their characteristics. Then we will discuss lease financing, including (1) the types of leasing arrangements, (2) the accounting treatment of financial leases, (3) the lease versus purchase decision, and (4) the potential benefits from leasing.

TERM LOANS

Term loans generally share three common characteristics: They (1) have maturities of 1 to 10 years, (2) are repaid in periodic installments (such as quarterly, semiannual, or annual payments) over the life of the loan, and (3) are usually secured by a chattel mortgage on equipment or a mortgage on real property. The principal suppliers of term credit are commercial banks, insurance companies, and to a lesser extent pension funds.

We will consider briefly some of the more common characteristics of term loan agreements.

Maturities

Commercial banks generally restrict their term lending to 1- to 5-year maturities. Insurance companies and pension funds with their longer-term liabilities generally make loans with 5- to 15-year maturities.[1] Thus, the term lending activities of commercial banks actually complement rather than compete with those of insurance companies and pension funds. In fact, commercial banks very often cooperate with both insurance companies and pension funds in providing term financing for very large loans.

Collateral

Term loans are generally backed by some form of collateral. Shorter-maturity loans are frequently secured with a chattel mortgage, or a mortgage on machinery and equipment, or with securities such as shares and bonds. Longer-maturity loans are frequently secured by mortgages on real estate.

Restrictive Covenants

In addition to requiring collateral, the lender in a term loan agreement often places restrictions on the borrower such that, if these restrictions are violated, the loan immediately becomes due and payable. These restrictive covenants are designed to prohibit the borrower from engaging in any activities that would increase the likelihood of loss on the loan. Some of the more common restrictions are discussed below.

1. **Working-capital requirement.** This restriction requires that the borrower maintains a minimum amount of working capital. Very often this restriction takes the form of a minimum current ratio, such as 2 to 1 or $3\frac{1}{2}$ to 1, or a minimum dollar amount of net working capital. The actual requirement would reflect the norm for the borrower's industry, as well as the lender's desires.

2. **Additional borrowing.** Generally this type of restriction requires the lender's approval before any additional debt can be issued. Furthermore, a restriction on additional borrowing is often extended to long-term lease agreements, which are discussed later in this chapter.

3. **Periodic financial statements.** A standard covenant in most term loan agreements includes a requirement that the borrower supply the lender with financial statements on a regular basis. These generally include annual or quarterly income statements and balance sheets.

4. **Management.** Term loan agreements sometimes include a provision that requires prior approval by the lender of major personnel changes. In addition, the borrower may be required to insure the lives of certain key personnel, naming the lender as beneficiary.

We have presented only a partial listing of restrictions commonly found in term loan agreements. The number and form of such provisions are limited

---

[1] Term loan agreements may also have a "recapture clause" that requires the borrower to pay back the loan faster if the borrower does better than anticipated in terms of sales, profitability, or some other measure of performance.

only by the imagination of the parties involved. It should be noted, however, that restrictive covenants are subject to negotiation. An agreement reflects the relative bargaining strengths of the borrower and lender. Marginal borrowers are more likely to find their loan agreements burdened with restrictive covenants than more creditworthy borrowers.

Term loan agreements can be very technical and are generally tailored to the situation. Therefore, it is difficult to generalize about their content. However, many banks rely on worksheets or checksheets to aid in the preparation of the document.

Repayment Schedules

Term loans are generally repaid with periodic installments, which include both an interest and a principal component. Thus, the loan is repaid over its life with equal annual, semiannual, or quarterly payments.

To illustrate how the repayment procedure works, let us assume that a firm borrows $15,000, which is to be repaid in five annual installments. The loan will carry an 8 percent rate of interest, and payments will be made at the end of each of the next five years. The following diagram shows the cash flows to the lender:

The $15,000 cash flow at time period zero is placed in parentheses to indicate an outflow of cash by the lender, whereas the annual installments, A_1 through A_5, represent cash inflows (of course, the opposite is true for the borrower). The lender must determine the annual installments that will give an 8 percent return on the outstanding balance over the life of the loan. This problem is very similar to the internal rate of return problem encountered in Chapter 6, where we discussed capital-budgeting decisions. There we had to determine the rate of interest that would make the present value of a stream of future cash flows equal to some present sum. Here we want to determine the future cash flows whose present value, when discounted at 8 percent, is equal to the $15,000 loan amount. Thus, we must solve for those values of A_1 through A_5 whose present value when discounted at 8 percent is $15,000. In equation form,

$$\$15,000 = \sum_{t=1}^{5} \frac{A_t}{(1 + .08)^t} \tag{18-1}$$

Where we assume equal annual installments, A, for all five years, we can solve for A_t as follows:

$$\$15,000 = A_t \sum_{t=1}^{5} \frac{1}{(1 + .08)^t}$$

where

$$A_t = \frac{\$15,000}{\displaystyle\sum_{t=1}^{5} \frac{1}{(1 + .08)^t}} \tag{18-2}$$

The $15,000 loan is divided by the present value factor for a five-year annuity carrying an 8 percent rate of interest. Thus,

$$A_t = \frac{\$15,000}{3.993} = \$3756.57$$

If the borrower makes payments of $3,756.57 each year, then the lender will receive an 8 percent return on the outstanding loan balance. To verify this assertion, check Table 18-1, which contains the principal and interest components of the annual loan payments. We see that the installments of $3,756.57 truly provide the lender with an 8 percent return on the outstanding balance of a $15,000 loan.

Eurodollar Loans

Eurodollar loans are intermediate term loans made by major international banks to businesses and are based upon foreign deposits that are normally denominated in U.S. dollars. These loans are generally made in amounts ranging from $1 million to $1.5 billion with the rate based on a certain amount above the London Interbank Offered Rate (LIBOR). The rate on these loans is adjusted periodically (generally every six months) and there is a wide range of maturities. Eurodollar lending has become a major source of commercial lending with the total volume of lending being measured in trillions of dollars.[2]

TABLE 18-1
Term Loan Amortization Schedule

End of Year t	Installment Payment[a] A_t	Interest[b] I_t	Principal Repayment[c] P_t	Remaining Balance[d] RB_t
0	—	—	—	$15,000.00
1	$3,756.57	$1,200.00	$2,556.57	12,443.43
2	3,756.57	995.47	2,761.10	9,682.33
3	3,756.57	774.59	2,981.98	6,700.35
4	3,756.57	536.03	3,220.54	3,479.81
5	3,756.57	278.38	3,478.19	1.62[e]

[a]The annual installment payment, A_t, is found as follows:

$$A_t = \frac{\$15,000}{\sum\limits_{t=1}^{5} \dfrac{1}{(1+.08)^t}} = 3756.57$$

[b]Annual interest expense is equal to 8 percent of the outstanding loan balance. Thus, for year 1 the interest expense, I_1, is found as follows:

$$I_1 = .08(\$15,000) = \$1200$$

[c]Principal repayment for year t, P_t, is the difference in the loan payment, A, and interest for the year. Thus, for year 1 we compute:

$$P_1 = A_1 - I_1 = \$3756.57 - \$1200 = \$2556.57$$

[d]The remaining balance of the end of year 1, RB_1, is the difference in the remaining balance for the previous year, RB_0, and the principal payment in year 1, P_1. Thus, at the end of year 1,

$$RB_1 = RB_0 - P_1 = \$15,000 - \$2556.57 = \$12,443.43$$

[e]The $1.62 difference in RB_4 and P_5 is due to rounding error.

[2]For a description of the workings of the Eurodollar market see E. W. Reed, R. V. Cotter, E. K. Gill, and R. K. Smith, *Commercial Banking*, 3rd ed. (Englewood Cliffs, NJ: Prentice-Hall, 1984).

Project Financing

The demand for large amounts of capital to finance development projects has provided an incentive for lending institutions to organize as a group for the purposes of financing. Generally, a bank will lead a syndicate of lending institutions to finance a specific development project. Projects that are suitable for this type of financing include: off-shore oil exploration projects, construction of high-rise office towers, and residential development projects. The formation of a syndicate ensures that the level of default risk is reduced to an acceptable level for each lending institution. In addition, the syndicate will require further protection for the loan through the use of the project's assets as collateral and the use of protective covenants within the lending contract to ensure orderly repayment of principal and loan interest. In most cases of project financing, equity participation will occur through a parent corporation setting-up a subsidiary corporation to run the project. The project's cash flows are earned by the subsidiary corporation and may be distributed to the parent corporation through dividends. An example of this type of arrangement is the joint venture between Nova Scotia Resources Ltd., a Crown corporation owned by the Nova Scotia Government, and LASMO Nova Scotia, a subsidiary of LASMO PLC which is the British parent company that specializes in oil exploration and production. Profits earned by LASMO Nova Scotia would be distributed to the parent company, LASMO PLC, as intercorporate dividends.[3]

Perspective in Finance

Leasing provides an alternative to buying an asset in order to acquire its services. Although some leases involve maturities of more than 10 years, most do not. Thus, lease financing is classified as a source of intermediate term credit. Today, virtually any type of asset can be acquired through a lease agreement.

LEASES

We begin our discussion by defining the major types of lease arrangements. Next we briefly review the history and describe the present accounting practices for leasing. We examine the lease versus purchase decision, and we conclude by investigating the potential benefits of leasing.

Types of Lease Arrangements

There are three major types of lease agreements: direct leasing, sale and leaseback, and leveraged leasing. Most lease agreements fall into one of these categories. However, the particular lease agreement can take one of two forms. (1) The **financial lease** constitutes a noncancellable contractual commitment on the part of the firm leasing the asset (the lessee) to make a series of payments to the firm that actually owns the asset (the lessor) for use of the asset. (2) The **operating lease** differs from the financial lease only with respect to its cancellability. An operating lease can be cancelled after proper notice to the lessor any time during its term. Thus, operating leases are by

[3]Jennifer Henderson, "Offshore Oil Begins To Flow," *The Financial Post* (June 6, 1992), p. 6.

their very nature sources of short-term financing. The balance of this chapter is concerned with the financial lease, which provides the firm with a form of intermediate-term financing most comparable to debt financing.

Direct Leasing

In a **direct lease** the firm acquires the services of an asset it did not previously own. Direct leasing is available through a number of financial institutions, including manufacturers, banks, finance companies, independent leasing companies, and special purpose leasing companies.[4] In the lease arrangement, the lessor purchases the asset and leases it to the lessee. In the case of the manufacturer lessor, however, the acquisition step is not necessary.

Sale and Leaseback

A **sale and leaseback** arrangement arises when a firm sells land, buildings, or equipment that it already owns to a lessor and simultaneously enters into an agreement to lease the property back for a specified period under specific terms. The lessor involved in the sale and leaseback varies with the nature of the property involved and the lease period. When land is involved and the corresponding lease is long term, the lessor is generally a life insurance company. If the property consists of machinery and equipment, then the maturity of the lease will probably be intermediate term and the lessor could be an insurance company, commercial bank, or leasing company.

The lessee firm receives cash in the amount of the sales price of the assets sold and the use of the asset over the term of the lease. In return, the lessee must make periodic rental payments through the term of the lease and give up any salvage or residual value to the lessor.

Net and Net-Net Leases

In the jargon of the leasing industry, a financial lease can take one of two basic forms: a net lease or a net-net lease. In a **net lease** agreement the lessee firm assumes the risk and burden of ownership over the term of the lease. That is, the lessee must maintain the asset, as well as pay insurance and taxes on the asset. A **net-net lease** requires that the lessee meet all the requirements of a net lease as well as return the asset, still worth a pre-established value, to the lessor at the end of the lease term.

Leveraged Leasing

In the leasing arrangements discussed thus far, only two participants have been identified: the lessor and lessee. In a **leveraged lease** a third participant is added. The added party is the lender who helps finance the acquisition of the asset to be leased. From the point of view of the lessee there is no difference in a leveraged lease, direct lease, or sale and leaseback arrangement. However, with a leveraged lease, the method of financing used by the lessor in acquiring the asset receives special consideration. The lessor will generally supply equity funds to 20 to 30 percent of the purchase price and borrow the remainder from a third-party lender, which may be a commercial bank or insurance company. In some arrangements the lessor firm sells bonds, which are guaranteed by the lessee. This guarantee serves to reduce the risk and thus the cost of the debt. The majority of financial leases are leveraged leases.

---

[4]Many leasing companies specialize in the leasing of a single type of asset. For example, a number of firms lease computers exclusively, and others lease only automobiles.

Accounting for Leases

The Accounting Standards Committee of the C.I.C.A. has asserted that "a lease that transfers substantially all of the benefits and risks of ownership to that of the lease, is in substance an acquisition of an asset and an obligation by the lessee and a sale or financing by the lessor."[5] To verify that a lease transfers substantially all of the benefits and risks of ownership, the lease must meet one or more of the following conditions:

1. The lease transfers ownership of the property to the lessee by the end of the lease term.

2. The lease contains a bargain repurchase option.

3. The lease term is equal to 75 percent or more of the estimated economic life of the leased property.

4. The present value of the minimum lease payments equals or exceeds 90 percent of the excess of the fair value of the leased property, at the commencement of the lease.[6]

If a lease meets these conditions, it is a capital lease and must be included in the balance sheet of the lessee.[7] All other lease agreements are classified as operating leases for accounting purposes and are included in the footnotes of the financial statements of the lessee.[8]

Figure 18-1 contains an example balance sheet for the Alpha Mfg. Company. Alpha has entered into capital leases whose payments have a present value of $4 million. Note that the asset "leased property" is matched by a liability, "capital lease obligations." The specific entries recorded for the lease obligation equal the present value of minimum lease payments the firm must pay over the term of the lease. The discount rate used is the lower of the lessee's incremental borrowing rate or the lessor's implicit interest rate (where that rate can be determined).

The Lease Versus Purchase Decision

The lease versus purchase decision is a hybrid capital-budgeting problem that forces the analyst to consider the consequences of alternative forms of

FIGURE 18-1
Alpha Mfg. Company Balance Sheet December 31, 1993 ($ millions)

Assets:	
Current assets	$14
Plant and equipment	20
Leased property (capital leases)	4
Total	$38
Liabilities and shareholders' equity:	
Current liabilities	8
Long-term debt	9
Capital lease obligations	4
Shareholders' equity	17
Total	$38

[5]Canadian Institute of Chartered Accountants, "Leases," *CICA Handbook* 3605.05.
[6]Canadian Institute of Chartered Accountants, "Leases," *CICA Handbook* 3605.06.
[7]Canadian Institute of Chartered Accountants, "Leases," *CICA Handbook* 3605.20–3605.28.
[8]Canadian Institute of Chartered Accountants, "Leases," *CICA Handbook* 3605.31–3605.33.

financing on the investment decision. When we discussed capital budgeting in Chapter 6 and the cost of capital in Chapter 5, we assumed that all new financing would be undertaken in accordance with the firm's optimal capital structure. When analyzing an asset that is to be leased, the analysis must be altered to consider financing through leasing as opposed to the use of the more traditional debt and equity sources of funds. Thus, the lease versus purchase decision requires a standard capital-budgeting type of analysis, as well as an analysis of two alternative financing packages. The lease-purchase decision involves the analysis of two basic issues:

1. Should the asset be purchased using the firm's optimal financing mix?
2. Should the asset be financed using a financial lease?

The answer to the first question can be obtained through an analysis of the project's net present value (NPV) following the method laid out in Chapter 7. However, regardless of whether the asset should or should not be purchased, it may be advantageous for the firm to lease it. That is, the cost savings accruing through leasing might be great enough as to offset a negative net present value resulting from the purchase of an asset. For example, the Alpha Mfg. Co. is considering the acquisition of a new computer-based inventory and payroll system. The computed net present value of the new system based upon normal purchase financing is –$40, indicating that acquisition of the system through purchasing or ownership is not warranted. However, an analysis of the cost savings resulting from leasing the system (referred to here as the net advantage of leasing—NAL) indicates that the lease alternative will produce a present value cost saving of $60 over normal purchase financing. Therefore, the net present value of the system if leased is $20 (the net present value if leased equals the NPV of a purchase plus the net advantage of leasing, or – $40 + $60). Thus, the system's services should be acquired via the lease agreement.

In the pages that follow we will (1) review briefly the concept of a project's net present value, which we will refer to as the net present value of purchase, or NPV(P); (2) introduce a model for estimating the net present value advantage of leasing over normal purchase financing, which we will refer to as the net advantage of lease financing, or NAL; (3) present a flow chart that can be used in performing lease-purchase analyses based upon NPV(P) and NAL; and (4) provide a comprehensive example of a lease-purchase analysis.

The Lease-Purchase Algorithm

Answers to both questions posed above can be obtained using the two equations found in Table 18-2. The first equation is simply the net present value of purchasing the proposed project, discussed in Chapters 6 and 7. The second equation determines the net present value advantage of leasing (NAL). NAL represents an accumulation of the cash flows (both inflows and outflows) associated with leasing as opposed to purchasing the asset. Specifically, through leasing the firm avoids certain operating expenses, O_t, but incurs the after-tax rental expense, $R_t(1 – T)$. By leasing, furthermore, the firm loses the tax-deductible expense associated with depreciation, $T(CCA_t)$. Finally, the firm does not receive the salvage value from the asset, SV_n, if it is leased, but it does not have to make the initial cash outlay to purchase the asset, IO. Thus, NAL reflects the cost savings associated with leasing, net of the opportunity costs of not purchasing.

Note that the after-tax cost of new debt is used to discount the NAL cash flows other than the salvage value, SV_n. This is justified on the basis

TABLE 18-2
The Lease-Purchase Model

Equation One—Net present value of purchase [*NPV(P)*]:

$$NPV(P) = \sum_{t=1}^{n} \frac{CFAT_t}{(1+K)^t} - IO \qquad (18\text{-}3)$$

where $CFAT_t$ = the annual cash flow after-tax in period t resulting from the asset's purchase (note that $CFAT_n$ also includes any salvage value expected from the project and the tax effects which occur from the termination of the asset class).

K = the firm's weighted cost of capital applicable to the project being analyzed and the particular mix of financing used to acquire the project.

IO = the initial cash outlay required to purchase the asset in period zero (now).

n = the productive life of the project.

Equation Two—Net Advantage of Leasing (*NAL*):

$$NAL = \sum_{t=1}^{n} \frac{O_t(1-T) - R_t(1-T) - I_t(T) - T(CCA_t)}{(1+r_b)^t} - \frac{SV_n}{(1+K_s)^n} + \frac{(UCC_n - SV_n)(d)(T)}{(1+K_s)^n} - IO \qquad (18\text{-}4)$$

where O_t = any net operating income incurred in period t that are incurred only where the asset is purchased. Most often this consists of maintenance expenses and insurance that would be paid by the lessor

R_t = the annual rental for period t

T = the combined tax rate on corporate income

CCA_t = capital cost allowance (depreciation) in period t for the asset

SV_n = the salvage value of the asset expected in year n

K_s = the discount rate used to find the present value of SV_n. This rate should reflect the risk inherent in the estimated SV_n. For simplicity the weighted cost of capital (K) is often used as a proxy for this rate. Also, note that this rate is the same one used to discount the salvage value in $NPV(P)$.

UCC_n = the undepreciated capital cost of the asset class in year n

IO = the purchase price of the asset, which is not paid by the firm in the event the asset is leased

r_b = the after-tax rate of interest on borrowed funds (i.e., $r_b = r(1-T)$ where r is the before-tax borrowing rate for the firm). This rate is used to discount the relatively certain cash flow after-tax savings that accrue through the leasing of the asset.

Note: This analysis makes the implicit assumption that a dollar of lease financing is equivalent to a dollar of loan. This form of equivalence is only one of several that might be used. The interested reader is referred to A. H. Ofer, "The Evaluation of the Lease Versus Purchase Alternatives," *Financial Management*, 5 (Summer 1976), pp. 67–74.

that the affected cash flows are very nearly riskless and certainly no more risky than the interest and principal accruing to the firm's creditors (which underlie the rate of interest charged to the firm for its debt).[9] Since SV_n is

---

[9]The argument for using the firm's borrowing rate to discount these tax shelters goes as follows: The tax shields are relatively free of risk in that their source (depreciation, interest, rental payments) can be estimated with a high degree of certainty. There are, however, two sources of uncertainty with regard to these tax shelters: (1) the possibility of a change in the firm's tax rate and (2) the possibility that the firm might become bankrupt at some future date. If we attach a very low probability to the likelihood of a reduction in the tax rate, then the prime risk associated with these tax shelters is the possibility of bankruptcy wherein they would be lost forever (certainly, all tax shelters after the date of bankruptcy would be lost). We now note that the firm's creditors also faced the risk of the firm's bankruptcy when they lent the firm funds at the rate r. If this rate, r, reflects the market's assessment of the firm's bankruptcy potential as well as the time value of money, then it offers an appropriate rate for discounting the interest shelters generated by the firm. Note also that the O_t cash flows are generally estimated with a high degree of certainty (in the case where they represent insurance premiums they may be contractually set) such that r_b, the interest rate after taxes, is appropriate as a discount rate here also.

not a risk-free cash flow but depends upon the market price for the leased asset in year n, a rate higher than r, the interest rate before taxes, is appropriate. Since the salvage value of the leased asset was discounted using the weighted cost of capital when determining $NPV(P)$, we again use this rate here when calculating NAL.

Figure 18-2 contains a flow chart that can be used in performing lease purchase analyses. The analyst first calculates $NPV(P)$. If the project's net present value is positive, then the left-hand branch of Figure 18-2 should be followed. Tracing through the left branch we now compute NAL. If NAL is positive, the lease alternative offers a positive present-value cost advantage over normal purchase financing in which case the asset should be leased. Should NAL be negative, then the purchase alternative should be selected. Return to the top of Figure 18-2 once again. This time we assume that $NPV(P)$ is negative and the analyst's attention is directed to the right-hand side of the flow chart. The only hope for the project's acceptance at this point is a favourable set of lease terms. In this circumstance the project would be acceptable and thus leased only if NAL were large enough to offset the nega-

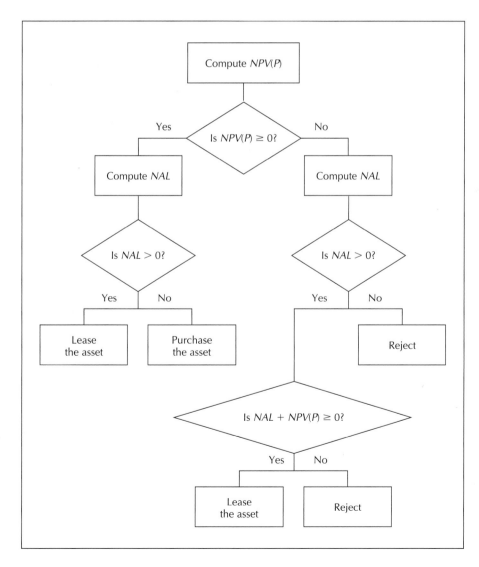

FIGURE 18-2
Lease-Purchase Analysis

tive $NPV(P)$ [that is, where NAL was greater than the absolute value of $NPV(P)$ or, equivalently, where $NAL + NPV(P) \geq 0$].[10]

Case Problem in Lease-Purchase Analysis

The Waynesboro Plastic Molding Company (WPM) is now deciding whether to purchase an automatic casting machine. The machine will cost $15,000 and for tax purposes will be depreciated at the CCA rate of 30 percent using a declining balance method of depreciation. The machine's expected useful life is five years and is expected to have a salvage value of $2,100 at the end of the five years.[11] The asset class will be terminated after the machine is salvaged. For accounting purposes, the firm will depreciate the machine over a five-year period using a straight line depreciation method. Over the next five years, the project is expected to generate annual operating revenues of $16,000 per year and annual operating expenses of $4,000 (including accounting depreciation). WPM has a combined corporate tax rate of 50 percent and a target debt ratio of 40 percent for projects of this type. Finally, WPM estimates that its after-tax cost-of-capital for projects of similar risk is 12 percent and it can borrow funds at a before-tax rate of 8 percent.

COMPUTING $NPV(P)$—SHOULD THE ASSET BE PURCHASED? ■ The first step in analyzing the lease-purchase problem involves computing the net present value under the purchase alternative. The relevant cash flow computations are presented in Table 18-3.

The annual cash flows after-tax are discounted at the weighted cost of capital of 12 percent. Table 18-4 shows that the NPV of the project is the sum

TABLE 18-3
Computing Project Annual Cash Flows After-Tax ($CFAT_t$) Associated with Asset Purchase

Year:	1	2	3	4	5
Operating revenue	$16,000	$16,000	$16,000	$16,000	$16,000
Operating expense (including accounting depreciation)	($ 4,000)	(4,000)	(4,000)	(4,000)	(4,000)
Accounting depreciation	$ 3,000	3,000	3,000	3,000	3,000
Net operating revenue	$15,000	15,000	15,000	15,000	15,000
Taxes	($ 7,500)	(7,500)	(7,500)	(7,500)	(7,500)
Net operating income	$ 7,500	7,500	7,500	7,500	7,500
Tax shields[a]	$ 1,125	1,913	1,339	937	656
Cash flows after-tax	$ 8,625	9,413	8,839	8,437	8,156

[a] The schedule for tax shields is determined as follows:

Year	UCC(beg)	CCA	Tax Shields	UCC(end)
1	$ 7,500.00	$2,250.00	$1,125.00	$12,750.00
2	12,750.00	3,825.00	1,912.50	8,925.00
3	8,925.00	2,677.50	1,338.75	6,247.50
4	6,247.50	1,874.25	937.13	4,373.25
5	4,373.25	1,311.98	655.99	3,061.28

[10] That is, $NAL = NPV(L) - NPV(P)$, where $NPV(L)$ is the net present value of the asset if leased. Thus, the sum of $NPV(P)$ and NAL is the net present value of the asset if leased. See Lawrence D. Schall, "The Lease-or-Buy and Asset Acquisition Decisions," *Journal of Finance*, 29 (September 1974), pp. 1203–1214, for a development of net present value of leasing and purchasing equations.

[11] The problem example is a modification of the well-known example from R. W. Johnson and W. G. Lewellen, "Analysis of the Lease-or-Buy Decision," *Journal of Finance*, 27 (September 1972), pp. 815–823.

TABLE 18-4
Calculating $NPV(P)$

Year t	Annual Cash Flow $CFAT_t$	Discount Factor for 12 Percent	Present Value
1	$8,625	.893	$7,702
2	9,413	.797	7,502
3	8,839	.712	6,293
4	8,437	.636	5,366
5	8,156	.567	4,624
5 (Salvage—SV_n)	2,100	.567	1,191
5 (Tax Shield Adjustment)	343[a]	.567	195
Initial cash flow			−15,000
		$NPV(P)$	$17,873

[a] Tax shield adjustment $= \dfrac{(UCC_n - SV_n)(d)(T)}{(K + d)} = \dfrac{(\$3061 - \$2100)(.30)(.50)}{(.12 + .30)} = \$343$

The project's $NPV(P)$ is a positive $17,873, indicating that the asset should be acquired.

of the discounted cash flows, the present value of the salvage value, the tax effects caused by the termination of the asset class and the initial cash outlay.

The second question concerns whether the asset should be leased. This can be answered by considering the net advantage to leasing (NAL).

The calculation to determine NAL involves solving Equation (18-4) presented earlier in Table 18-2. To do this, we first estimate all those cash flows that are to be discounted at the firm's after-tax cost of debt, r_b. These include $O_t(1 - T)$, $R_t(1 - T)$, $I_t(T)$ and $CCA_t(T)$.

The operating expenses associated with the asset that will be paid by the lessor if we lease—that is, the O_t—generally consist of certain maintenance expenses and insurance. WPM estimates them to be $1,000 per year over the life of the project. The annual rental or lease payments, R_t, are given and equal $3,800.

The interest tax shelter lost because the asset is leased and not purchased must now be estimated. This tax shelter is lost because the firm does not borrow any money if it enters into the lease agreement. Table 18-1 contains the principal and interest components for a $15,000 loan. Note that the interest column supplies the needed information for the interest tax shelter that is lost if the asset is leased, I_t.[12]

The next steps in calculating NAL involve the determination of the present value of the salvage value and the present value of any forgone tax shields from the termination of the asset class. Since the asset is the only one in the asset class and the salvage value (SV_n) is less than the undepreciated

---

[12]Technically the firm does not lose the interest tax shelter on a $15,000 loan if it leases. In fact, the firm would lose the tax shelter on only that portion of the $15,000 purchase price that it would have financed by borrowing, for example, 40 percent of the $15,000 investment, or $6,000. However, if the firm leases the $15,000 asset, it has effectively used 100 percent levered (nonowner) financing. This means that the leasing of this project uses not only its 40 percent allotment of levered (debt) financing, but an additional 60 percent as well. Thus, by leasing the $15,000 asset the lessee forfeits the interest tax shelter on a 40 percent or $6,000 loan plus an additional 60 percent of the $15,000 purchase price, or an additional $9,000 loan. In total, leasing has caused the firm to forgo the interest tax savings on a loan equal to 100 percent of the leased asset's purchase price. Once again, we note that this analysis presumes $1 of lease financing is equivalent to $1 of loan financing. See Note to Table 18-2.

capital cost (UCC$_n$), the firm would normally benefit from the terminal loss when disposing of the asset. However, in the case of leasing, the lessee does not have ownership of the asset. As a result, the lessee cannot claim the benefits of both the salvage value and the terminal loss. Thus, the terms for the salvage value and the terminal loss[13] are subtracted from the benefits of leasing in Equation (18-4). The computation of *NAL* is shown in Table 18-5.

The resulting *NAL* is a positive $272, which indicates that leasing is preferred to purchasing. In fact, WPM will increase shareholder's value by $272 if it chooses to lease rather than purchase the asset.

Note that the lease payments used in this example were made at the end of each year. In practice, most lease payments are made at the beginning

TABLE 18-5. Computing the Net Advantage to Leasing (*NAL*)

Overview: To solve for *NAL* we use Equation (18-4), which was discussed in Table 18-2. This equation contains three terms and is repeated below for convenience.

$$NAL = \sum_{t=1}^{n} \frac{O_t(1 - T) - R_t(1 - T) - I_t(T) - T(CCA_t)}{(1 + r_b)^t} - \frac{SV_n}{(1 + K_s)^n} - \frac{(UCC_n - SV_n)(d)(T)}{(1 + K_s)^n} - IO \qquad (18\text{-}4)$$

Step 1:

$$\text{Solving for Term 1} = \sum_{t=1}^{n} \frac{O_t(1 - T) - R_t(1 - T) - I_t(T) - T(CCA_t)}{(1 + r_b)^t}$$

Year	After-tax Operating Expenses Paid by Lessor[a]		After-tax Lease Expense[b]		Tax Shelter on Loan Interest[c]		Tax Shelter on Depreciation[d]	Total	Discount Factor at 4 Percent		Present Value
t	$O_t(1 - T)$	−	$R_t(1 - T)$	−	$I_t(T)$	−	$CCA_t(T)$	= SUM ×	DF	=	PV
1	$500		$1900		$600		$1125	−$3125	.962		−$3006
2	500		1900		498		1913	−3811	.925		−3525
3	500		1900		387		1339	−3126	.889		−2779
4	500		1900		268		937	−2605	.855		−2227
5	500		1900		140		656	−2196	.822		−1805
									Sum of present value		−$13,342

Step 2:

$$\text{Solving for Term 2} = \frac{-SV_n}{(1 + K_s)^n} = \frac{-\$2100}{(1 + .12)^5} = -\$2100 \times .5674^e = -\$1,191$$

Step 3:

$$\text{Term 3} = -\left[\frac{(UCC_n - SV_n)(d)(T)}{(K_s + d)}\right]\left[\frac{1}{(1 + K_s)^n}\right] = -\left[\frac{(3062 - 2100)(.30)(.50)}{(.12 + .30)}\right]\left[.5674\right] = -\$195$$

Step 4:
$$\text{Term 4} = IO = \$15,000$$

Step 5:
$$\text{Calculate } NAL = \text{Term 1} - \text{Term 2} - \text{Term 3} + \text{Term 4}$$
$$= -\$13,342 - \$1,191 - \$195 + \$15,000 = \$272$$

[a]After-tax lessor-paid operating expenses are found by $O_t(1 - T) = \$1000(1 - 0.5) = \$500$.
[b]After-tax rent expense for year 1 is computed as follows: $R_t(1 - T) = \$4200(1 - 0.5) = \$2100$.
[c]The values of interest expense were calculated in Table 18-1 for a $15,000 loan. For year 1 the interest rate tax shelter is $0.5 \times \$1200 = \$600$.
[d]The tax shelter from depreciation is found as follows: $(CCA_t)T = \$2250 \times 0.5 = \$1,125$.
[e]K_s was estimated to be the same as the firm's weighted cost of capital, 12 percent.

[13]If the asset class remains open, the term for any forgone tax shields from depreciation is not included in Equation (18-4).

of each year. A series of constant payments made at the beginning of the year can be valued in terms of an annuity due.[14] The effect of paying leasing payments at the beginning of each year causes the computation for *NAL* to change. We examine this effect by redoing the previous example, as follows:

Step 1: Solving for Term 1: Present Value of After-Tax Lease Payments.

Year	After-tax Operating Expenses Paid by Lessor	After-tax Rental Expense	Tax Shelter on Loan Interest	Tax Shelter on Depreciation[d]	Total	Discount Factor at 4 Percent	Present Value
t	$O_t(1-T)$	$-\ R_t(1-T)$	$-\ I_t(T)$	$-\ CCA_t(T)$	$=$ SUM	$\times$ DF	$=$ PV
0	$ 0	$1900	$ 0	$ 0	–$1900	1.000	–$1900
1	500	1900	600	1125	–3125	.962	–3006
2	500	1900	498	1913	–3811	.925	–3525
3	500	1900	387	1339	–3126	.889	–2779
4	500	1900	268	937	–2605	.855	–2227
5	500	0	140	656	–296	.822	–243
						Sum of present value	–$13,680

Step 2:

$$\text{Solving for Term 2} = \frac{-SV_n}{(1+K_s)^n} = \frac{-\$2100}{(1+.12)^5} = -\$2100 \times .567 = -\$1,191$$

Step 3:

$$\text{Term 3} = -\left[\frac{(UCC_n - SV_n)(d)(T)}{(K_s + d)}\right]\left[\frac{1}{(1+K_s)^n}\right] = -\left[\frac{(3062 - 2100)(.30)(.50)}{(.12+.30)}\right]\left[.5674\right] = -\$195$$

Step 4: $\text{Term 4} = IO = \$15,000$

Step 5: $\text{Calculate } NAL = \text{Term 1} - \text{Term 2} - \text{Term 3} + \text{Term 4}$
                    $= -\$13,680 - \$1,191 - \$195 + \$15,000 = -\$66$

We adjust for the change from a regular annuity to an annuity due by including –$1,900 as the discounted cash flow at time $t = 0$ and changing the discounted cash flow for the fifth year to –$1,629 (–$243 + –$1,191 + –$195). In this example in which payments are made at the beginning of the year, the *NAL* is –$66 (– $13,680 – $1,191 – $195 + $15,000). According to our lease or purchase decision-making strategy which was illustrated in Figure 18-2, the asset should not be leased since the *NPV(P)* is positive but the *NAL* is negative.

To summarize the procedure used to analyze the lease or purchase decision: first, the project's net present value was computed. This analysis produced a positive *NPV(P)* equal to $17,873, which indicated that the asset should be purchased. Upon computing the net advantage to leasing, we found that leasing is the preferred method of financing when lease payments are made at the end of the year. However, the asset should be purchased if the leasing payments are made at the beginning of the year.

---

[14]We have examined the concept of annuity due in Chapter 4. You can easily verify this result as follows: Note first that changing from a regular annuity to an annuity due affects only the first and last annuity payments. In this example, this means that the first lease payment of $2,100 (after tax) is paid immediately such that its present value is $2,100. However, the final lease payment is now made at the beginning of year 4. The present value of the after-tax lease payment in the fifth year is $128 ($156 × .822), the present value of the sum between the tax shelters from depreciation and the after-tax operating expenses paid by the lessor at the end of the year.

Potential Benefits from Leasing[15]

A number of purported advantages have been associated with leasing as opposed to debt financing. These benefits include flexibility and convenience, lack of restrictions, avoiding the risk of obsolescence, conservation of working capital, 100 percent financing, tax savings, and availability of credit. However, before we discuss the relative merits of each purported advantage, we review briefly the economic character of leasing and purchasing.

Figure 18-3 illustrates the participants and transactions involved in leasing (the right-hand side of the figure) and purchasing (the left-hand side). In purchasing, the asset is financed via the sale of securities and the purchaser acquires title to the asset (including both the use and salvage value of the asset). In leasing, the lessee acquires the use value of the asset but uses the lessor as an "intermediary" to finance and purchase the asset. The key feature of leasing as opposed to purchasing is the interjection of a financial intermediary (the lessor) into the scheme used to acquire the asset's services. Thus, the basic question that arises in lease-purchase analysis is one of "Why does adding another financial intermediary (the lessor) save the lessee money?" Some of the "traditional" answers to this question are discussed below. As you read through each, simply remember that the lessee is "hiring" the lessor to perform the functions associated with ownership that he or she would perform if the asset were purchased. Thus, for the lease to be "cheaper" than owning, the lessor must be able to perform these functions of ownership at a lower cost than the lessee could perform them.

FIGURE 18-3. Comparison of Purchasing with a Simple Financial Lease Agreement

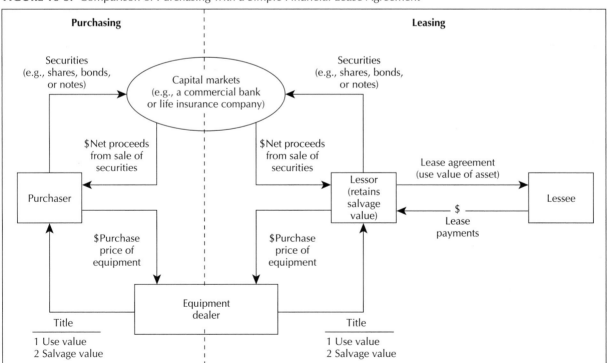

[15]The contributions of Paul F. Anderson in the preparation of this discussion are gratefully acknowledged.

Flexibility and Convenience

A variety of potential benefits are often included under the rubric of flexibility and convenience. It is argued, for example, that leasing provides the firm with flexibility because it allows for piecemeal financing of relatively small asset acquisitions. Debt financing of such acquisitions can be costly and difficult to arrange. Leases, on the other hand, may be arranged more quickly and with less documentation.

Another flexibility argument notes that leasing may allow a division or subsidiary manager to acquire equipment without the approval of the corporate capital-budgeting committee. Depending upon the firm, the manager may be able to avoid the time-consuming process of preparing and presenting a formal acquisition proposal.

A third flexibility advantage relates to the fact that some lease payment schedules may be structured to coincide with the revenues generated by the asset, or they may be timed to match seasonal fluctuations in a given industry. Thus, the firm is able to synchronize its lease payments with its cash cycle—an option rarely available with debt financing.

Arguments for the greater convenience of leasing take many forms. It is sometimes stated that leasing simplifies bookkeeping for tax purposes because it eliminates the need to prepare time-consuming depreciation tables and subsidiary fixed asset schedules. It is also pointed out that the fixed-payment nature of lease rentals allows more accurate forecasting of cash needs. Finally, leasing allows the firm to avoid the "problems" and "headaches" associated with ownership. Executives often note that leasing "keeps the company out of the real estate business." Implicit in this argument is the assumption that the firm's human and material resources may be more profitably allocated to its primary line of business and that it is better to allow the lessor to deal with the obligations associated with ownership.

It is difficult to generalize about the validity of the various arguments for greater flexibility and convenience in leasing. Some companies, under specific conditions, may find leasing advantageous for some of the reasons listed above. In practice, the tradeoffs are likely to be different for every firm. The relevant issue is often that of shifting functions. By leasing a piece of capital equipment, the firm may effectively shift bookkeeping, disposal of used equipment, and other functions to the lessor. The lessee will benefit in these situations if the lessor is able to perform the functions at a lower cost than the lessee and is willing to pass on the savings in a lower lease rate.

The arguments that follow should be viewed in a similar vein. The lessee must estimate how much this greater flexibility and convenience is worth. In many cases, the benefits enjoyed by the firm are not worth the cost. Compounding the problem is the fact that it is often difficult for a lessee firm to quantify such cost-benefit tradeoffs.

Lack of Restrictions

Another suggested advantage relates to the lack of restrictions associated with a lease. Unlike term loan agreements or bond indentures, lease contracts generally do not contain protective covenant restrictions. Furthermore, in calculating financial ratios under existing covenants, it is sometimes possible to exclude lease payments from the firm's debt commitments. Once again, the extent to which lack of restrictions benefits a lessee will depend on the price it must pay. If a lessor views its security position to be superior to that of a lender, it may not require a higher return on the lease to compensate for the lack of restrictions on the lessee. On the other hand, if the prospective lessee is viewed as a marginal credit risk, a higher rate may be charged.

Avoiding the Risk of Obsolescence

Similar reasoning applies to another popular argument for leasing. This argument states that a lease is advantageous because it allows the firm to avoid the risk that the equipment will become obsolete. In actuality, the risk of obsolescence is passed on to the lessee in any financial lease. Since the original cost of the asset is fully amortized over the basic lease term, all of the risk is borne by the lessee. Only in a cancellable operating lease is it sometimes possible to avoid the risk of obsolescence.

A related argument in favour of leasing states that a lessor will generally provide the firm with better and more reliable service in order to maintain the resale value of the asset. The extent to which this is true depends on the lessor's own cost-benefit tradeoff. If the lessor is a manufacturing or a leasing company that specializes in a particular type of equipment, it may be profitable to maintain the equipment's resale value by ensuring that it is properly repaired and maintained. Because of their technical and marketing expertise, these types of lessors may be able to operate successfully in the secondary market for the equipment. On the other hand, bank lessors or independent financial leasing companies would probably find it too expensive to follow this approach.

Conservation of Working Capital

One of the oldest and most widely used arguments in favour of leasing is the assertion that a lease conserves the firm's working capital. Indeed, many managers within the leasing industry consider this to be the number one advantage of leasing.[16] The conservation argument runs as follows: Since a lease does not require an immediate outflow of cash to cover the full purchase price of the asset, funds are retained in the business.

It is clear that a lease does require a lower initial outlay than a cash purchase. However, the cash outlay associated with the purchase option can be reduced or eliminated by borrowing the down payment from another source. This argument leads us directly into the next purported advantage of lease financing.

100 Percent Financing

Another alleged benefit of leasing is embodied in the argument that a lease provides the firm with 100 percent financing. It is pointed out that the borrow-and-buy alternative generally involves a down payment, whereas leasing does not. Given that investors and creditors are reasonably intelligent, however, it is sensible to conclude that they consider similar amounts of lease and debt financing to add equivalent amounts of risk to the firm. Thus, a firm uses up less of its capacity to raise non-equity funds with debt than with leasing. In theory, it could issue a second debt instrument to make up the difference—that is, the down payment.

Tax Savings

The extent to which leasing provides an economic advantage must be weighed against the variables discussed in the *NAL* equation (18-4). For

---

[16]For example, see L. Rochwarger, "The Flexible World of Leasing," *Fortune*, 39 (November 1974), pp. 56-59.

example, a firm which purchases an asset inherits the tax shields from depreciation during the asset's useful life. These deductions cannot be claimed by the lessee firm when leasing the asset. As a result, leasing can offer an economic advantage to the firm only if the tax deductions from the leasing payments are greater than the tax deductions from the capital cost allowances if the asset was purchased.

Ease of Obtaining Credit

Another alleged advantage of leasing is that firms with poor credit ratings are able to obtain assets through leases when they are unable to finance the acquisitions with debt capital. The obvious counterargument is that the firm will certainly face a high lease rate in order to compensate the lessor for bearing the risk of default.

Why Do Firms Lease?

A number of researchers have asked firms why they use financial leases as opposed to purchasing. For example, in a study by Ferrara, Thies, and Dirsmith[17] the following factors were found to affect the leasing decision:

Factor	Rank	Percent of Respondents
Implied interest rate	1	52
Threat of obsolescence	2	37
Income taxes	3	33
Maintain flexibility	4	12
Conserve working capital	5	12
Less restrictive financing	6	6
Off balance sheet finance	7	7

Interestingly, the factor most often mentioned was the implied cost of financing. That is, 52 percent of the lessees considered the cost of lease financing to be an important factor in determining their decision to use lease financing. This factor was followed by concern over the risk of obsolescence followed by tax considerations. In light of the theoretical significance given to tax considerations in the theoretical literature on lease financing, it is interesting to note that only 33 percent of the respondents felt that tax considerations were a factor in their decision to lease.

Ferrara, Thies, and Dirsmith also provide evidence concerning the motives underlying a firm's decision to utilize lease financing and its financial characteristics.[18] Specifically, they observed that smaller and financially

---

[17]W. L. Ferrara, J. B. Thies, and M. W. Dersmith, "The Lease-Purchase Decision," National Association of Accountants, 1980. Cited in "Leasing—A Review of the Empirical Studies," *Managerial Finance*, 15, 1&2 (1989), pp. 13–20.

[18]Anderson and Bird also investigated the reasons why lessees lease. They utilized a survey in which the respondents were asked to indicate both the extent to which they agreed or disagreed with the advantages attributed to leasing and the extent to which a particular advantage was important to their lease decisions. One of the purported advantages to leasing was the following: "All things considered, leasing is less expensive than debt as a means of acquiring equipment." The respondents accorded the lowest agreement rating to this statement (that is, they disagreed that this was true), yet they ranked this same statement third in overall importance in terms of their decision to lease. The authors interpret this finding as evidence that lessees believe that it is important that the cost of leasing be less than the cost of debt financing, but they do not expect to find this to be so in practice.

weaker firms tended to justify the use of lease financing based upon qualitative benefits. These included flexibility, the conservation of working capital, financing restrictions, off balance sheet financing, and transference of the risk of obsolescence. On the other hand, larger and financially stronger firms tended to base their leasing decisions on more quantitative considerations. That is, this latter group tended to utilize more formal comparisons of the cost of leasing versus other forms of intermediate financing.

SUMMARY

Intermediate credit, or simply term credit is any source of financing with a final maturity greater than one year but less than ten. The two major sources of term credit are term loans and financial leases.

Term loans are available from commercial banks, life insurance companies, and pension funds. Although the specifics of each agreement vary, they share a common set of general characteristics. These include

1. A final maturity of one to ten years
2. A requirement of some form of collateral
3. A body of "restrictive covenants" designed to protect the security interests of the lender
4. A loan amortization schedule whereby periodic loan payments, comprised of both principal and interest components, are made over the life of the loan

There are three basic types of lease arrangements:

1. Direct lease
2. Sale and leaseback
3. Leveraged lease

The lease agreement can further be classified as a financial or operating lease; we focused on the financial or capital lease. The Accounting Committee of the CICA requires the inclusion of all financial or capital leases in the lessee firm's balance sheet; whereas, the financial information from operating lease must be included in the financial notes of the balance sheet of the lessee.

The lease versus purchase decision is a hybrid capital-budgeting problem wherein the analyst must consider both the investment and financing aspects of the decision. Many and varied factors are often claimed as "advantages" of leasing as opposed to the use of the firm's usual debt-equity financing mix. Many of the arguments have been found to be at least partially fallacious. However, a complete lease-purchase analysis using a model similar to the one discussed here should provide a rational basis for examining the true advantages of lease financing.

STUDY QUESTIONS

18-1. What characteristics distinguish intermediate-term debt from other forms of debt instruments?

18-2. List and discuss the major types of restrictions generally found in the covenants of term loan agreements.

18-3. Define each of the following:

    a. Direct leasing

    b. Sale and leaseback arrangement

    c. Leveraged leasing

    d. Operating lease

18-4. How are financial leases handled in the financial statements of the lessee firm?

18-5. List and discuss each of the potential benefits from lease financing.

SELF-TEST PROBLEMS

ST-1. (*Analyzing a Term Loan*) Calculate the annual installment payment and the principal and interest components of a five-year loan carrying a 10 percent rate of interest. The loan amount is $50,000.

ST-2. (*Analyzing an Installment Loan*) The S. P. Sargent Sales Company is contemplating the purchase of a new machine. The total cost of the machine is $120,000 and the firm plans to make a $20,000 cash down payment. The firm's bank has offered to finance the remaining $100,000 at a rate of 14 percent. The bank has offered two possible loan repayment plans. Plan A involves equal annual installments payable at the end of each of the next five years. Plan B requires five equal annual payments plus a balloon payment of $20,000 at the end of year 5.

    a. Calculate the annual payment on the loan in plan A.

    b. Calculate the principal and interest components of the plan A installment loan.

    c. Calculate the annual installments for plan B where the loan carries a 14 percent rate.

ST-3. (*Lease Versus Purchase Analysis*) Jensen Trucking, Inc., is considering the possibility of leasing a $100,000 truck-servicing facility. This newly developed piece of equipment facilitates the cleaning and servicing of diesel tractors used on long-haul runs. The firm has evaluated the possible purchase of the equipment and found it to have an $8,000 net present value. However, an equipment leasing company has approached Jensen with an offer to lease the equipment for an annual rental charge of $30,457.85 payable at the beginning of each of the next four years. In addition, should Jensen lease the equipment it would receive insurance and maintenance valued at $4,000 per year (assume that this amount would be payable at the beginning of each year if purchased separately from the lease agreement). Additional information pertaining to the lease and purchase alternatives is found in the following table:

Acquisition price	$100,000
Useful life (used in analysis)	4 years
Salvage value (estimated)	$0
CCA rate	30%
Borrowing rate	12%
Combined corporate tax rate	45%
Weighted cost of capital (based on a target debt/total asset ratio of 30%)	16%
Accounting method of depreciation	Straight-line
Tax method of depreciation	Declining balance

The firm expects that the asset will be the only one in the asset class when it is salvaged after 4 years.

a. Calculate the net advantage of leasing (NAL) the equipment.

b. Should Jensen lease the equipment?

STUDY PROBLEMS (SET A)

18-1A. (*Installment Payments*) Compute the annual payments for an installment loan carrying an 18 percent rate of interest, a five-year maturity, and a face amount of $100,000.

18-2A. (*Principal and Interest Components of an Installment Loan*) Compute the annual principal and interest components of the loan in Problem 18-1A.

18-3A. (*Cost of an Intermediate-Term Loan*) The J. B. Marcum Company needs $250,000 to finance a new minicomputer. The computer sales firm has offered to finance the purchase with a $50,000 down payment followed by five annual installments of $59,663.11 each. Alternatively, the firm's bank has offered to lend the firm $250,000 to be repaid in five annual installments based on an annual rate of interest of 16 percent. Finally, the firm has arranged to finance the needed $250,000 through a loan from an insurance company requiring a lump-sum payment of $385,080, in five years.

    a. What is the effective annual rate of interest on the loan from the computer sales firm?

    b. What will the annual payments on the bank loan be?

    c. What is the annual rate of interest for the insurance company term loan?

    d. Based upon cost considerations only, which source of financing should Marcum select?

18-4A. (*Cost of Intermediate-Term Credit*) Charter Electronics is planning to purchase a $400,000 burglar alarm system for its Alberta plant. Charter's bank has offered to lend the firm the full $400,000. The note would be paid in one payment at the end of four years and would require payment of interest at a rate of 14 percent compounded annually. The manufacturer of the alarm system has offered to finance the $400,000 purchase with an installment loan. The loan would require four annual installments of $140,106 each. Which method of financing should Charter select?

18-5A. (*Lease Versus Purchase Analysis*) Early in the spring of 1987 the Jonesboro Steel Corporation (JSC) decided to purchase a small computer. The computer is designed to handle the inventory, payroll, shipping, and general clerical functions for small manufacturers like JSC. The firm estimates that the computer will cost $60,000 to purchase and will last four years, at which time it can be salvaged for $10,000. The firm's combined tax rate is 45 percent, and its weighted cost of capital for projects of this type is estimated to be 12 percent. Over the next four years the management of JSC feels the computer will reduce operating expenses by $42,000 a year (accounting depreciation expenses included). For accounting purposes, the firm utilizes straight-line depreciation. However, the firm plans to depreciate the asset at a CCA rate of 30 percent using the declining balance method for tax purposes. This machine is expected to be the only asset in the asset class after its four years of use.

    JSC is also considering the possibility of leasing the computer. The computer sales firm has offered JSC a four-year lease contract with payments at the beginning of each year of $18,000. In addition, if JSC leases the computer, the lessor will absorb insurance and maintenance expenses valued at $2,000 per year. Thus, JSC will save $2,000 at the beginning of each year it leases the asset (on a before-tax basis).

    a. Evaluate the net present value of the computer purchase. Should the computer be acquired via purchase? [*Hint:* Refer to Tables 18-3 and 18-4.]

    b. If JSC uses a 40 percent target debt to total assets ratio, evaluate the net present value advantage of leasing. JSC can borrow at a rate of 8 percent with annual installments paid over the next four years. [*Hint:* Recall that the interest tax shelter lost through leasing is based upon a loan equal to the full purchase price of the asset or $60,000.]

c. Should JSC lease the asset?

18-6A. (*Lease Versus Purchase Analysis*) S. S. Johnson Enterprises (SSJE) is evaluating the acquisition of a heavy-duty forklift with 20,000- to 24,000-pound lift capacity. SSJE can purchase the forklift through the use of its normal financing mix (30 percent debt and 70 percent common equity) or lease it. Pertinent details follow:

Acquisition price of the forklift	$20,000
Useful life	4 years
Salvage value (estimated)	$4,000
CCA rate	30%
Annual after depreciation cash savings from the forklift	$11,000
Rate of interest on a 4-year installment loan	10%
Combined corporate tax rate	45%
Annual leasing payments at beginning of the year (4-year lease)	$6,000
Annual operating expenses at the beginning of the year included in the lease	$1,000
Weighted cost of capital	12%
Accounting method of depreciation	Straight-line
Tax method of depreciation	Declining balance

a. Evaluate whether the forklift acquisition is justified through purchase.

b. Should SSJE lease the asset?

18-7A. (*Installment Loan Payment*) Calculate the annual installment payments for the following loans:

a. A $100,000 loan carrying a 15 percent annual rate of interest and requiring 10 annual payments.

b. A $100,000 loan carrying a 15 percent annual rate of interest with quarterly payments over the next five years. [*Hint:* Refer to Chapter 4 for a discussion of semiannual compounding and discounting.]

c. A $100,000 loan requiring annual installments for each of the next five years at a 15 percent rate of interest. However, the annual installments are based on a 30-year loan period. In year 5 the balance of the loan is due in a single (balloon) payment. [*Hint:* Calculate the installment payments using n = 30 years. Next use the procedure given in Table 18-1 to determine the remaining balance of the loan at the end of the fifth year.]

STUDY PROBLEMS (SET B)

18-1B. (*Installment Payments*) Compute the annual payments for an installment loan carrying a 16 percent rate of interest, a seven-year maturity, and a face amount of $100,000.

18-2B. (*Principal and Interest Components of an Installment Loan*) Compute the annual principal and interest components of the loan in Problem 18-1B.

18-3B. (*Cost of an Intermediate Loan*) Azteca Freight Forwarding Company needs $300,000 to finance the construction of several prefabricated metal warehouses. The firm that produces the warehouses has offered to finance the purchase with a $50,000 down payment followed by five annual installments of $69,000 each. Alternatively, Azteca's bank has offered to lend the firm $300,000 to be repaid in five annual installments based on an annual rate of interest of 16 percent. Finally, the firm could finance the needed $300,000 through a loan from an insurance company requiring a lump-sum payment of $425,000 in five years.

a. What is the effective annual rate of interest on the loan from the warehouse producer?

b. What will the annual payments on the bank loan be?

c. What is the annual rate of interest for the insurance company term loan?

d. Based upon cost considerations only, which source of financing should Azteca select?

18-4B. (*Cost of Intermediate-Term Credit*) Powder Meadows, a western ski resort, is planning to purchase a $500,000 ski lift. Powder Meadows' bank has offered to lend it the full $500,000. The note would be paid in one payment at the end of four years and would require payment of interest at a rate of 14 percent compounded annually. The manufacturer of the ski lift has offered to finance the $500,000 purchase with an installment loan. The loan would require four annual installments of $175,000 each. Which method of financing should Powder Meadows select?

18-5B. (*Lease Versus Purchase Analysis*) Early in the spring of 1989 Lubin Landscaping, Inc., decided to purchase a truck-mounted lawn fertilizer tank and spray unit. The truck would replace its hand-held fertilizer tanks, providing substantial reductions in labour expense. The firm estimates that the truck will cost $65,000 to purchase and will last four years, at which time it can be salvaged for $8,000. The firm's combined tax rate is 45 percent, and its weighted cost of capital for projects of this type is estimated to be 14 percent. Over the next four years the management of Lubin feels the truck will reduce operating expenses by $45,250 a year (accounting depreciation included). For accounting purposes, the firm utilizes straight-line depreciation. However, the firm plans to depreciate the asset at a CCA rate of 30 percent using the declining balance method for tax purposes. This machine is expected to be the only asset in the asset class after its four years of use.

Lubin is also considering the possibility of leasing the truck. The truck sales firm has offered Lubin a 4-year lease contract with payments at the beginning of the year of $20,000. In addition, if Lubin leases the truck, the lessor will absorb insurance and maintenance expenses valued at $2,250 per year. Thus, Lubin will save $2,250 at the beginning of each year if it leases the asset (on a before-tax basis).

a. Evaluate the net present value of the truck purchase. Should the truck be acquired via purchase? [*Hint:* Refer to Tables 18-3 and 18-4.]

b. If Lubin uses a 40 percent target debt to total assets ratio, evaluate the net present value advantage of leasing. Lubin can borrow at a rate of 10 percent with annual installments paid over the next four years. [*Hint:* Recall that the interest tax shelter lost through leasing is based upon a loan equal to the full purchase price of the asset or $65,000.]

c. Should Lubin lease the asset?

18-6B. (*Lease Versus Purchase Analysis*) Music Live, Inc., a carnival-operating firm, is considering the acquisition of a new German-made carousel, with a passenger capacity of 30. Music Live can purchase the carousel through the use of its normal financing mix (30 percent debt and 70 percent common equity) or lease it. Pertinent details follow:

Acquisition price of the carousel	$25,000
Useful life	4 years
Salvage value (estimated)	$5,000
CCA rate	30%
Annual after depreciation cash savings from the carousel	$13,250
Rate of interest on a 4-year installment loan	11%
Combined corporate tax rate	45%
Annual leasing payments at beginning of the year (4-year lease)	$7,000

Annual operating expenses at the beginning of the year included in the lease	$1,250
Weighted cost of capital	13%
Accounting method of depreciation	Straight-line
Tax method of depreciation	Declining balance

The firm expects that the asset will be the only one in the asset class when it is salvaged after 4 years.

a. Evaluate whether the carousel acquisition is justified through purchase.

b. Should Music Live lease the asset?

18-7B. (*Installment Loan Payment*) Calculate the annual installment payments for the following loans:

a. A $125,000 loan carrying a 13 percent annual rate of interest and requiring 12 annual payments.

b. A $125,000 loan carrying a 13 percent annual rate of interest with quarterly payments over the next six years. [*Hint:* Refer to Chapter 4 for a discussion of semiannual compounding and discounting.]

c. A $125,000 loan requiring annual installments for each of the next five years at a 13 percent rate of interest. However, the annual installments are based on a 30-year loan period. In year 5 the balance of the loan is due in a single (balloon) payment. [*Hint:* Calculate the installment payments using $n = 30$ years. Next use the procedure given in Table 18-1 to determine the remaining balance of the loan at the end of the fifth year.]

SELF-TEST SOLUTIONS

SS-1.

Time	Payment	Principal	Interest	Remaining Balance
0				$50,000.00
1	$13,189.83	$8,189.83	$5,000.00	41,810.17
2	13,189.83	9,008.81	4,181.02	32,801.36
3	13,189.83	9,909.69	3,280.14	22,891.67
4	13,189.83	10,900.66	2,289.17	11,991.01
5	13,189.83	11,990.73	1,199.10	0.28

SS-2. a.

$$\text{Payment} = \$100,000 \div \sum_{t=1}^{5} \frac{1}{(1.14)^t} = \$29,128.35$$

b.

Time	Payment	Principal	Interest	Remaining Balance
0	—	—	—	$100,000
1	$29,128.35	$15,128.35	$14,000.00	84,871
2	29,128.35	17,246.32	11,882.03	67,625
3	29,128.35	19,660.80	9,467.55	47,964
4	29,128.35	22,413.32	6,715.03	25,551
5	29,128.35	25,551.18	3,577.17	.03 [a]

[a]Rounding error

c. Since the plan B loan includes a $20,000 balloon payment, the five annual installments have a present value of only

$$\$89,613 = \$100,000 - \frac{\$20,000}{(1.14)^5}$$

Therefore, the annual installments can be calculated as follows:

$$\text{Payment} = \$89,613 \div \sum_{t=1}^{5} \frac{1}{(1.14)^t} = \$26,102.79$$

ST-3. a. $NAL = -\$3815$.

b. The NAL is negative, indicating that a purchase would offer cost savings over a lease and therefore a purchase should be used.

Year	After-tax Operating Expenses Paid by Lessor	After-tax Rental Expense	Tax Shelter on Loan Interest	Tax Shelter on Deprecia-tion[d]	Total	Discount Factor at 4 Percent	Present Value
t	$O_t(1 - T)$ −	$R_t(1 - T)$ −	$I_t(T)$ −	$CCA_t(T)$	= SUM ×	DF	= PV
0	$2,200	$16,752	0	0	−$14,552	1.000	−$14,552
1	2,200	16,752	6,600	6,750	−27,902	.938	−26,174
2	2,200	16,752	5,395	11,475	−31,422	.880	−27,651
3	2,200	16,752	4,013	8,033	−26,598	.826	−21,957
4	0	0	2,429	5,623	−8,052	.774	−6,235
						Total	−$96,569
			Terminal loss				−7,246
			Plus: Initial outlay				100,000
			NAL(−$96,570 − $7246 + 100,000)				−$3,815

[a]$4,000 (1 − 0.45) = $2,200. For simplicity we assume that the tax shields on expenses paid at the beginning of the year are realized immediately.

[b]$16,752 = $30,458 (1 − 0.45)

[c]Based upon a $100,000 loan with four end-of-year installments and a 12 percent rate of interest. The loan payments equal $32,923.

[d]The machine is depreciated at a CCA rate of 30 percent using a declining balance method. The following schedule shows the tax shields over four years:

Schedule of Tax Shields

Year	UCC(beg)	CCA	Tax Shields	UCC(end)
1	50000	15000	6750	85000
2	85000	25500	11475	59500
3	59500	17850	8033	41650
4	41650	12495	5623	29155

SELECTED REFERENCES

Anderson, Paul F., and John D. Martin. "Lease vs. Purchase Decisions: A Survey of Current Practice," *Financial Management* (Spring 1977), 41–47.

Ang, J., and P. Peterson. "The Leasing Puzzle," *Journal of Finance*, 39 (September 1984), 1055–1065.

Blose, Laurence E., and John D. Martin. "Federal Government Leasing," *Public Budgeting and Finance*, 9 (Summer 1989), 66–75.

Bower, Richard S. "Issues in Lease Financing," *Financial Management*, 2 (Winter 1973), 25–34.

Bower, Richard S., and George S. Oldfield, Jr. "Of Lessees, Lessors, and Discount Rates and Whether Pigs Have Wings," *Journal of Business Research*, 9 (March 1981), 29–38.

Braud, Steven L. "Leasing—A Review of the Empirical Studies," *Managerial Finance*, 15 (112) (1989), 13–20.

Cason, R. L. "Leasing, Asset Lives and Uncertainty: A Practitioner's Comments," *Financial Management*, 16 (Summer 1987), 13–16.

Clark, T. M. "The Leverage of Leasing—An International Perspective," *Managerial Finance*, 15 (112) (1989), 44–47.

Cooper, Kerry, and Robert H. Strawser. "Evaluation of Capital Investment Projects Involving Asset Leases," *Financial Management*, 4 (Spring 1975), 44–49.

Copeland, T., and J. F. Weston. "A Note on the Evaluation of Cancellable Operating Leases," *Financial Management*, 11 (Summer 1982), 60–67.

Crawford, Peggy J., Charles P. Harper, and John J. McConnell. "Further Evidence on the Terms of Financial Leases," *Financial Management*, 10 (Autumn 1981), 7–14.

Doenges, R. Conrad. "The Cost of Leasing," *Engineering Economist*, 17 (Fall 1971), 31–44.

Drury, Colin. "Evaluating the Lease or Purchase Decision," *Managerial Finance*, 15 (112) (1989), 26–38.

Fabozzi, F., and U. Yaari. "Valuation of Safe Harbor Tax Benefit Transfer Leases," *Journal of Finance*, 38 (May 1983), 595–606.

Grimlund, R., and R. Capettini. "A Note on the Evaluation of Leveraged Leases and Other Investments," *Financial Management*, 11 (Summer 1982), 68–72.

Hodges, Stewart D. "Variable Rate Leases," *Managerial Finance*, 15 (112) (1989), 39–43.

Idol, Charles R. "A Note on Specifying Debt Displacement and Tax Shield Borrowing Opportunities in Financial Lease Valuation Models," *Financial Management*, 9 (Summer 1980), 24–29.

Johnson, Robert W., and Wilbur G. Lewellen. "Analysis of the Lease-or-Buy Decision," *Journal of Finance*, 27 (September 1972), 815–823.

Martin, John D. "Leasing," in *The Handbook of Corporate Finance*. ed. Edward Altman. New York: Wiley, 1986.

Martin, John D., Paul F. Anderson, and Chester L. Allen. "A Pragmatic Approach to the Estimation Problems Encountered in Lease Purchase Analyses," in *Risk, Capital Costs, and Project Financing Decisions*. eds. Frans G. J. Derkinderen and Roy L. Crum. Boston: Martinus Nijhoff Publishing, 1981.

McConnell, J. J., and J. S. Schallheim. "Valuation of Asset Leasing Contracts," *Journal of Financial Economics*, 12 (August 1983), 237–261.

Mukherjee, T. K. "A Survey of Corporate Leasing Analysis," *Financial Management*, 20 (Autumn 1991), 96–107.

Reed, E. W., R. V. Cotter, E. K. Gill, and R. K. Smith. *Commercial Banking*. 3rd ed. Englewood Cliffs, NJ: Prentice-Hall, 1984.

Schall, L. D. "Analytic Issues in Lease Versus Purchase Decisions," *Financial Management*, 16 (Summer 1987), 17–20.

Schall, L. D. "The Lease-or-Buy and Asset Acquisition Decisions," *Journal of Finance*, 29 (September 1974), 1203–14.

Smith, B. "Accelerated Debt Repayment in Leveraged Leases," *Financial Management*, 11 (Summer 1982), 73–80.

Smith, C. W., and L. M. Wakeman. "Determinants of Corporate Leasing Policy," *Journal of Finance*, 40 (3) (July 1985), 896–908.

Weingartner, H. M. "Leasing, Asset Lives and Uncertainty: Guides to Decision Making," *Financial Management*, 16 (Summer 1987), 5–12.

CHAPTER 19

Long-Term Debt, Preferred Shares, and Common Shares

- Bonds or Long-Term Debt

- Preferred Shares

- Common Shares

In this chapter we will concern ourselves with the three major sources of long-term and permanent funds for the firm: long-term debt, preferred shares, and common shares. In Chapters 4 and 9 we discussed the valuation and theory behind the use of long-term sources of funds. In this chapter we will devote our attention to the terminology and basic features common to these securities; we will focus on their similarities and differences, as well as their advantages and disadvantages, as sources of financing to the firm.

BONDS OR LONG-TERM DEBT

A **bond** is any long-term (ten years or more) promissory note issued by the firm. In examining bonds we will first outline bond terminology and features, then examine types of bonds (both secured and unsecured), methods of retiring debt, bond refunding, and advantages and disadvantages of financing with long-term debt.

Basic Bond Terminology and Characteristics

Par Value

The **par value** or the face value of a bond is the amount that is returned to the bondholder at maturity. In general, most corporate bonds are issued in denominations of $1,000, although there are some exceptions to this rule. When bond prices are quoted by either financial managers or in the financial press, prices are generally expressed as a percentage of the bond's par value. For example, a Noranda Mines bond that pays $105 per year interest, and matures in 1999, was recently quoted in *The Financial Post* as selling for 99.75. That does not mean you can buy the bond for $99.75. It does mean that this bond is selling for 99.75 percent of its par value, which happens to be $1,000. Hence, the market price of this bond is actually $997.50. At maturity in 1999, the bondholder will receive the $1,000.

Coupon Interest Rate

The **coupon interest rate** on a bond indicates what percentage of the par value of the bond will be paid out annually in the form of interest. Thus, regardless of what happens to the price of a bond with an 8 percent coupon interest rate and a $1,000 par value, it will pay out $80 annually in interest until maturity.

Maturity

The maturity of a bond indicates the length of time until the bond issuer returns the par value to the bondholder and terminates the bond.

Indenture

An **indenture** is the legal agreement between the firm issuing the bonds and the bond trustee who represents the bondholders.[1] The indenture provides the specific terms of the loan agreement, including a description of the bonds, the rights of the bondholders, the rights of the issuing firm, and the responsibilities of the trustees. This legal document may run 100 pages or more in length, with the majority of it devoted to defining protective provisions for the bondholder. The bond trustee, usually a banking institution or trust company, is then assigned the task of overseeing the relationship between the bondholder and the issuing firm, protecting the bondholder, and seeing that the terms of the indenture are carried out.

Typically, the restrictive provisions included in the indenture attempt to protect the bondholder's financial position relative to that of other outstanding securities. Common provisions involve (1) restrictions on the sale of accounts receivable, (2) constraints on the issuance of common shares dividends, (3) restrictions on the purchase or sale of fixed assets, and (4) constraints on additional borrowing. Restrictions on the sale of accounts receivable are specified because such sales would benefit the firm's short-run liquidity position at the expense of its future liquidity position. Constraints on common share dividends generally means limiting their distribution when working capital falls below a specified level, or simply limiting the maximum dividend payout to 50 or 60 percent of earnings under any circumstance. Fixed-asset restrictions generally require lender permission before the liquidation of any fixed asset or prohibit the use of any existing fixed asset as collateral on new loans. Constraints on additional borrowing are usually in the form of restrictions or limitations on the amount and type of additional long-term debt that can be issued. All these restrictions have one thing in common: they attempt to prohibit action that would improve the status of other securities at the expense of bonds and to protect the status of bonds from being weakened by any managerial action.

Current Yield

The **current yield** on a bond refers to the ratio of the annual interest payment to the bond's market price. If, for example, we are examining a bond

---

[1]The indenture agreement is also referred to as a *trust deed*.

with an 8 percent coupon interest rate, a par value of $1,000, and a market price of $700, it would have a current yield of

$$\text{current yield} = \frac{\text{annual interest payments}}{\text{market price of the bond}} \tag{19-1}$$

$$= \frac{.08 \times \$1000}{\$700} = \frac{\$80}{\$700} = 11.4 \text{ percent}$$

Yield to Maturity

The **yield to maturity** refers to the bond's internal rate of return. It incorporates into the analysis both the annual interest payments and capital gains or losses. Mathematically, the yield to maturity is the discount rate that equates the present value of the interest and principal payments with the current market price of the bond.[2]

Bond Ratings

Both the Canadian Bond Rating Service and the Dominion Bond Rating Service provide ratings on bonds issued in Canada, whereas Moody's, and Standard and Poor's, provide ratings on bonds issued in North America. These ratings involve a judgment about the future risk potential of the bond.[3] Although they deal with expectations, several historical factors seem to play a significant role in their determination.[4] Bond ratings are favourably affected by (1) a low utilization of financial leverage, (2) profitable operations, (3) a low variability in past earnings, (4) large firm size, and (5) little use of subordinated debt. In turn, the rating a bond receives affects the rate of return demanded on the bond by the investors. The poorer the bond rating, the higher the rate of return demanded in the capital markets. An example and description of these ratings is given in Table 19-1. Thus, for the financial manager, bond ratings are extremely important. They provide an indicator of default risk that in turn affects the rate of return that must be paid on borrowed funds. Bennett Stewart of Stern Stewart Management Services provides some perspective on just how bond ratings are actually determined in the next Basic Financial Management in Practice feature, "Bennett Stewart on Bond Ratings."

Determinants of the Cost of Long-Term Debt

In Chapter 3 we defined the investor's required rate of return. We now focus on the factors that determine the required rate of return that investors demand from debt financing. The total cost of debt that the firm will pay depends primarily upon five factors: (1) the size of the issue, (2) the issue's maturity, (3) the issue's riskiness or rating, (4) the restrictive requirements of the issue, and (5) the current riskless interest rate. To a large extent the administrative costs of issuing debt are fixed, and they will decrease in percentage terms as the size of the issue increases. In effect, economies of scale

---

[2]See Chapter 4 for an illustrative example.

[3]Bond ratings are extremely important in that a firm's bond rating tells much about (a) the cost of funds and (b) the firm's access to the debt markets.

[4]See Thomas F. Pogue and Robert M. Soldofsky, "What's in a Bond Rating?" *Journal of Financial and Quantitative Analysis*, 4 (June 1969), pp. 201–228; and George E. Pinches and Kent A. Mingo, "A Multivariate Analysis of Industrial Bond Ratings," *Journal of Finance*, 28 (March 1973), pp. 1–18.

TABLE 19-1
Bond Ratings Used by the Canadian Bond Rating Service

A++

This category encompasses bonds of outstanding quality. They possess the highest degree of protection of principal and interest. Companies with debt rated A++ are generally large national and/or multi-national corporations whose products or services are essential to the Canadian economy.

These companies are the acknowledged leaders in their respective industries and have clearly demonstrated their ability to best withstand adverse economic or trade conditions either national or international in scope. Characteristically these companies have had a long and creditable history of superior debt protection, in which the quality of their assets and earnings has been constantly maintained or improved, with strong evidence that this will continue.

A+

Bonds rated A+ are very similar in characteristics to those rated A++ and can also be considered superior in quality. These companies have demonstrated a long and satisfactory history of growth with above average protection of principal and interest on their debt securities.

These bonds are generally rated lower in quality because the margin of asset or earning protection may not be as large or as stable as those rated A++. In both these categories the nature and quality of the asset and earnings coverages are more important than the numerical values of the ratios.

A

Bonds rated A are considered to be good quality securities and to have favourable long-term investment characteristics. The main feature which distinguishes them from their higher rated securities is that these companies are more susceptible to adverse trade or economic conditions. The protection is consequently lower than for the categories of A++ and A+.

In all cases the A rated companies have maintained a history of adequate asset and earning protection. There may be certain elements that may impair this protection sometime in the future. Our confidence that the current overall financial position will be maintained or improved is slightly lower than for the above rated securities.

B++

Issues rated B++ are classified as medium or average grade credits and are considered to be investment grade. These companies are generally more susceptible than any of the higher rated companies to swings in economic or trade conditions which would cause a deterioration in protection should the company enter a period of poor operating conditions.

There may be factors present either from within or without the company which may adversely affect the long-term level of protection of the debt. These companies bear closer scrutiny but in all cases both interest and principal are adequately protected at the present time.

B+

Bonds which are rated B+ are considered to be lower medium grade securities and have limited long-term protective investment characteristics. Asset and earning coverage may be modest or unstable.

A significant deterioration in interest and principal protection may occur during the periods of adverse economic or trade conditions. During periods of normal or improving economic conditions, asset and earning protection are adequate; however, the company's ability to continually improve its financial position and level of debt protection is at present limited.

B

Securities rated B lack most qualities necessary for long-term fixed income investment. Companies in this category have a general history of volatile operating conditions during which time the assurance that principal and interest protection will be maintained at an adequate level has been in doubt. Current coverages may be below industry standards and there is little assurance that debt protection will significantly improve.

C

Securities in this category are clearly speculative. The companies are generally junior in many respects and there is little assurance that the adequate coverage of principal and interest can be maintained uninterruptedly over a period of time.

D

Bonds in this category are in default of some provisions in their trust deed and the companies may or may not be in the process of liquidation.

Source: Canadian Bond Rating Service, "An Introduction to The CBRS Method of Rating Securities," Montreal, 1985, pp. 14–15.

BASIC FINANCIAL MANAGEMENT IN PRACTICE

Bennett Stewart on Bond Ratings

It is useful to classify financial risk in terms of bond ratings since these provide a framework for analyzing the risks important to all creditors. Furthermore, relating the financial posture adopted to a particular bond rating facilitates a determination of the availability and cost of funds in both the private and public debt markets.

When selecting a particular bond rating and financial posture to pursue, management is really choosing a desired level of financing flexibility. We define financing flexibility to be the degree to which a company's financing options are kept open for raising funds while keeping the equity holders of the company within an acceptable risk level in any economic climate. A company with too low a level of financing flexibility could be forced to raise common equity at an inopportune time to meet a need for funds.

Financial planners must decide what bond rating is right for their company. There is really no one correct bond rating for any particular company. The choice will depend on the levels of financing flexibility and financial risk the company feels comfortable with. We only say that a company should not seek a financial risk level that would endanger management's financing flexibility and give rise to an undue risk of insolvency. In our opinion, companies with ratings of less than Baa/BBB [Moody's or Standard and Poor's Bond Rating] on their long-term senior debt run this risk.

While countless factors affect companies' debt capacity, we have found five which together are most important in explaining bond ratings. Stern Stewart has developed a bond rating simulation framework which focuses on these five factors. Such a framework can aid the long-range financial planning process by showing the projected effect of a company's operating performance and alternative financing strategies on its credit standing.

Briefly, the technique, which is based on a statistical concept known as "discriminant analysis," involves identifying the key quantifiable characteristics that play a major role in determining the financial strength of a company. Each of these characteristics is assigned a "weight" based on its relative importance, and then a weighted "score" of financial strength is calculated. The score is then put on the Bond Rating Score Range to determine the estimated rating (AAA, AA, etc.).

A description of the factors and an interpretation of the significance of each in determining financial strength is presented below.

1. **Size:** Company size, as measured by total assets, is the single most important factor. It acts as a proxy for the company's ease of access to capital markets, a proven track record, continuity and depth of management, control over markets, and diversification of activities by product line and geography. In general, the larger the company, the higher the bond score.

2. **Risk-Adjusted Return:** The risk-adjusted rate of return measures both the level and stability of the economic earnings of a company. The level of earnings is important because it provides a good indication of the profitability of a company. And, for any given leverage implied, the higher a company's return on total capital, the more likely it will be able to pay interest expense out of earnings. The stability of earnings is also important to creditors because they do not participate in the capital gain rewards accorded equity investors. Consequently, creditors wish to avoid the earnings fluctuations caused by economic cycles.

   The risk-adjusted return, which is computed by subtracting one standard deviation from the five year average rate of return on total capital (assets), provides an indication of the minimum rate of return a company may be expected to earn approximately 83 percent of the time. To calculate the return on total capital each year, we divide NOPAT (Net Operating Profits After Tax) by total capital employed. Higher risk-adjusted returns strengthen a company's bond score.

3. **Long-term Debt-to-Capital (Assets) Ratio:** The three-year average of a company's long-term debt-to-capital ratio is a measure of the financial risk of a company. This measure averaged over a three-year period is a better measure of

Continued on page 799

Continued from page 798

permanent leverage policy than the debt-to-capital ratio in any one year; hence, it is a better measure of the expected future financial risk of a company. The higher the long-term debt-to-capital ratio, the weaker the bond score will tend to be.

4. **Pension-Adjusted Liabilities-to-Net-Worth Ratio:** Pension-adjusted liabilities to net worth is calculated as total liabilities plus the lesser of 50 percent of unfunded pension liabilities or 30 percent of net worth, divided by net worth. This is a good measure of asset protection in the event of bankruptcy, since pension-adjusted liabilities include the off-balance sheet liability of unfunded pension liabilities. This liability is senior to almost all other liabilities and can be substantial. It therefore seems reasonable that

the higher this ratio is, the lower the bond score will be.

5. **Investments and Advances to Unconsolidated Subsidiaries-to-Capital Ratio:** Calculated as a percentage of total capital, this measure indicates the proportion of capital of a company that is already supporting debt. The equity in unconsolidated subsidiaries supports debt on its own books and cannot be relied upon to support parent debt as well. Higher ratios of investments and advances to unconsolidated subsidiaries-to-capital will pull down the bond score, all else constant.

Source: Bennett Stewart, "Commentary: A Framework for Setting Required Rates of Return by Line of Business," in *Six Roundtable Discussions of Corporate Finance with Joel Stern*, ed., Donald H. Chew, Jr. (New York: Quorum Books, 1986).

---

are associated with the issuance of debt. The issue's maturity also affects the cost of debt. Borrowers prefer to borrow for long periods in order to lock in interest rates and avoid the problem of frequent refinancing, while lenders would rather not tie up their money for long periods. In order to bring about equilibrium between supply and demand for funds, long-term debt generally carries a higher interest rate than short-term debt. This tends to encourage some borrowers to borrow for shorter periods and some investors to lend for longer periods.

Investors also desire additional return for taking on added risk. Thus, the less risky the bond or the higher the bond rating, the lower will be the interest rate. We can see this by looking at the movement of bond yields for different ratings from 1985 to 1992, as shown in Figure 19-1.[5]

The restrictive requirements and rights of both issuer and holder also affect the interest rate paid on the bond. The more the bondholder requires in the way of protection and rights, the lower the rate of return earned will be.[6] On the other hand, the more rights the issuer demands—for example, the right to repurchase the debt at a predetermined price (called a *call provision* and discussed later in detail)—the higher will be the rate that the issuer will have to offer in order to convince investors to purchase the bond.

Finally, the current riskless interest rate plays a major role in determining

---

[5]Bond prices seem to be particularly vulnerable to price downswings during takeovers and management buyouts. These price downswings occur in cases in which a company takes on large amounts of debt in order to accomplish leveraged buyouts. This was the case for RJR Nabisco bonds which fell 10 percent when the leveraged buyout was proposed.

[6]Bondholders are extremely concerned about the possibility of the firm taking on additional debt, particularly associated with management buyouts or restructuring. As a result, many bondholders are pushing for companies to issue new bonds with covenants that limit losses in the event of future restructuring. An example of such a feature is a poison put which allows the bondholder to sell the bonds back to the company at face value if a restructuring lowers their rating to less than investment grade.

BASIC FINANCIAL MANAGEMENT IN PRACTICE

The Bond Market in the 1990's: The Revolution Will Roll On

With the advent of the 1990's, the bond revolution has now entered its second decade, with five major trends shaping the bond market and fixed income management in the 1990's. These trends will impact institutional investors, investment dealers and borrowers alike.

Trend #1: Globalization of the Securities Market

"Globalization" has ceased to be a buzzword. It is a stark reality that affects all capital market participants. To date, it has had its greatest impact on financing patterns. Governments and corporations are now able to raise funds in their choice markets and currencies, through a choice of domestic or international dealers. These alternatives have allowed borrowers to raise funds more cheaply, while customizing debt issues to meet their requirements. At the end of 1989, over 38% of the outstanding issues of Canadian provinces, municipalities and corporations were denominated in other currencies. The Euro-Canadian market had grown to 15.6% of the domestic market, with outstandings increasing ninefold between 1986 and 1990.

Globalization has benefited borrowers, but has had little direct impact on pension fund lenders. The 10% limit on foreign holdings has effectively prevented Canadian bond managers from utilizing the global market, especially while the bulk of foreign content is directed to equities. Canadian bond managers have watched with envy as foreign investors switch back and forth between liquid U.S. Treasuries and our Canadian domestic market. In North America and offshore, they purchase issues that offer the best expected returns, while our domestic pension fund managers search for Deutschmarks or U.S. dollar bonds that qualify as Canadian property.

Thus the proposed changes in the foreign content legislation for pension plans has been greeted with as much enthusiasm by bond managers as by equity managers and fund sponsors. The outcome will be increased flexibility for fixed income managers and greater potential returns for their clients.

Trend #2: More Foreign Participation in Canadian Bond Market

Globalization of markets has occurred at the same time as huge demands were placed on the Canadian market by deficit financing. The natural outcome has been greater participation in our domestic market by non-Canadian investors. Non-residents held $48 billion, or 36%, of publicly owned Government of Canada marketable bonds in 1989. Only ten years earlier, non-resident holdings amounted to only $5.4 billion, or 15% of the total.

The capital flows controlled by foreign investors can now overwhelm Canadian economic considerations for significant periods of time. This forces Canadian bond managers to monitor international conditions as well as domestic fundamentals. In fact, most 8:30 a.m. conversations with dealers typically start by discussing "what happened overnight in Tokyo and London."

Trend #3: Financing Methods Are Changing

In 1980, Government of Canada issues were underwritten by the Bank of Canada and distributed by Canadian dealers. Provincial issuers had lead managers and large syndicates. Corporate bonds were issued by prospectus, using banking groups to under-

the cost of debt. In fact, corporate bond rates move in the same direction as does the riskless rate of interest. The determination of the riskless interest rate is generally deferred to courses on money and banking, and financial institutions. We note here that one of the major factors affecting the riskless rate of interest is the anticipated rate of inflation.

Claims on Assets and Income

In the case of insolvency, claims of debt are honoured prior to those of both common shares and preferred shares. However, different types of debt may write the risk. These methods have all but disappeared under the combination of increased competition among dealers, globalization and the speed of execution now required in markets.

Approximately 65% of Government of Canada bonds are now distributed through auctions. The "bought deal" accounts for 80% of provincial and corporate issues. Again, the winner in this change has been the borrower, generally at the expense of the investment dealers.

For the bond manager, this era of dealer competition and fast-paced new issues has meant staying ready and alert. Properly priced new issues are sold out in a matter of minutes. Unfortunately, there are as many overpriced issues as properly priced ones to tempt the innocent.

Trend #4: The Growth of the "Quant"

In 1980, Martin Liebowitz of Salomon Brothers had just begun to popularize concepts such as immunization and dedication. Stripped coupons were about to appear. A few dealers offered bond analysis systems that subtracted two yields to find a spread, and bond traders couldn't spell duration, much less define it. In short, quantitative techniques were dirty words and not used in portfolio management. Players with quantitative skills and an interest in bond markets resided in the back room where their efforts focused on writing articles to convince a largely reluctant audience.

This situation changed quickly and dramatically. On the dealer side, the driving forces were a combination of market volatility and increased competition. Market volatility needed carefully orchestrated hedging strategies. Increased competition, including the loss of "old style" business, needed new products to fill the void. Futures, options, warrants, mortgage backed securities and swaps are the result of these forces.

Investment managers were also responding to competitive factors. Quantitative approaches could add extra value to boost relative performance. Moreover, clients were becoming increasingly aware of these new techniques and products. Business retention often depended on the ability to offer a quantitative approach or, at least, discuss its relative merits with key pension fund clients.

Trend #5: The Growth of the Consultant

Years ago, actuaries were concerned with only the liability side of the pension equation. Performance measurement services did only what the name implied. These roles were extended to the lucrative field of manager searches some time ago. When the confusion caused by rapid changes in investment alternatives and practices is added to the requirement of recent legislation, consultants saw an opportunity to create a whole new array of billable services. These typically include an analysis of both the asset side of the pension equation, determining an asset mix, and selecting investment managers to execute the overall strategy.

This could be a risky business for the consultant if investment managers fail to deliver good performance. To sidestep this business risk, the existence of efficient capital markets is recognized, and managers are compared as much by risk and approach, as they are by historical or projected returns. In other words, "philosophy" and "style" are now buzzwords of investment manager marketing. This trend has provided growth and profitability for the consulting community.

Source: Adapted from: Don Webster and Maureen Stapleton, "The Bond Market In The 1990's: The Revolution Will Roll On," *Canadian Investment Review* (Fall 1990), pp. 49–53.

also have a hierarchy among themselves as to the order of their claim on assets.

Bonds also have a claim on income that is prior to those of both common shares and preferred shares. If interest on bonds (other than income bonds, to be discussed later) is not paid, the bond trustees can classify the firm insolvent and force it into bankruptcy. Thus, the bondholder's claim on income is more likely to be honoured than that of common and preferred shareholders, whose dividends are paid at the discretion of the firm's management.

FIGURE 19-1. Bond Yield Averages from 1985 to 1992

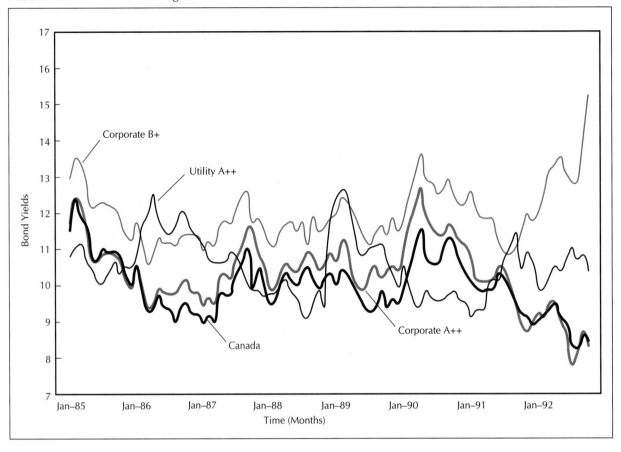

Types of Bonds

Debentures

The term **debentures** applies to any unsecured long-term debt. Because these bonds are unsecured, the earning ability of the issuing corporation is of great concern to the bondholder. Debentures are also viewed as being riskier than secured bonds and as a result must provide investors with a higher yield than secured bonds provide. Often the issuing firm attempts to provide some protection to the holder through the prohibition of any additional encumbrance of assets. This prohibits the future issuance of secured long-term debt that would further tie up the firm's assets and leave the bondholders less protected. A major advantage of issuing debentures is that a firm is not required to provide property as security. This allows the firm to issue debt and still preserve some future borrowing power.

Subordinated Debentures

Many firms have more than one issue of debentures outstanding. In this case a hierarchy may be specified, in which some debentures are given subordinated standing in the case of insolvency. The claims of the **subordinated debentures** are honoured only after the claims of secured debt and unsubordinated debentures have been satisfied.

Income Bonds

An **income bond** requires interest payments only if earned, and failure to meet these interest payments cannot lead to bankruptcy. In this sense income bonds are more like preferred shares (which are discussed in a later section) than bonds. They are generally issued during the reorganization of a firm facing financial difficulties. The maturity of income bonds is usually much longer than that of other bonds in order to relieve pressure associated with the repayment of principal. While interest payments may be passed, unpaid interest is generally allowed to accumulate for some period of time and must be paid prior to the payment of any common share dividends. This cumulative interest feature provides the bondholder with some security.

Mortgage Bonds

A **mortgage bond** is a bond secured by a lien on real property. Typically, the value of the real property is greater than that of the mortgage bonds issued. This provides the mortgage bondholders with a margin of safety in the event that the market value of the secured property declines. In the case of foreclosure, the trustees have the power to sell the secured property and use the proceeds to pay the bondholders. In the event that the proceeds from this sale do not cover the bonds, the bondholders become general creditors, similar to debenture bondholders, for the unpaid portion of the debt.

Equipment Trust Certificates

An **equipment trust certificate** is an example of a financial instrument which uses equipment as security.[7] This type of financing is a cross between lease financing and debt financing. Equipment trust financing is used primarily by railroads and some airlines and oil companies to finance the purchase of rolling stock or airplanes. This type of debt has a fairly short maturity, ranging from 1 to 17 years. The short maturity occurs because of the nature of the collateral, which is subject to substantial wear and tends to deteriorate rapidly. Under this financing method, the railroad or issuing firm first orders the railroad cars or equipment. When the equipment is received, the title is transferred to a trustee. The manufacturer is then paid in full by the trustee, which obtains funds primarily through the issuance of equipment trust certificates. These trust certificates have minimal risk because they are secured by the equipment being purchased, and this is generally quite standardized.

Floating Rate or Variable Rate Bonds

Floating rate or **variable rate bonds** are appealing to issuers and investors during periods of unstable interest rates. Banks and trust companies issue floating rate bonds to eliminate some of the risk and variability in earnings that accompany interest rate swings. To the investor, it eliminates major swings in the market value of the debt that would otherwise have occurred if interest rates had changed.

---

[7]In general, real property includes fixed assets such as land, buildings, and equipment. However, collateral trust bonds are secured by common shares and/or bonds, which are held by a trustee who has the power to liquidate them in the event of default. The indenture will normally contain a clause that the market value must be at least 20 to 50 percent greater than the value of the bonds so as to ensure ample coverage.

As an example, in October 1990 the Royal Bank of Canada issued U.S. $350 million (or CDN $408,345,000) of floating rate debentures due in July 2005. The interest rate on these debentures is subject to semi-annual adjustments of 6.25 basis points above the one month London Interbank Offered rate. However, the Royal Bank guarantees a minimum rate of 5 percent during the first 5 years. The London Interbank Offered Rate, or LIBOR as it is often called, is the rate that most creditworthy international banks charge each other for large loans and is often used as a benchmark to which variable rate loans are pegged. Thus, if the LIBOR was 6.00 percent, the Royal Bank debentures would pay 6.0625 percent and if the LIBOR rose to 6.50% percent at the time of the quarterly adjustment, the Royal Bank debentures would be adjusted to pay 6.5625 percent.

While every floating rate bond is a bit different, these bonds generally possess common characteristics:

1. After an initial period of 3 to 60 months during which a minimum interest rate is guaranteed, the coupon is allowed to float. Then weekly, monthly, quarterly, or semi-annually, the coupon rate changes to a new level, usually 0.5 to 3.0 percent above the preceding week's average treasury bill rate or the LIBOR.

2. The bondholder generally has the option of redeeming the bond at par value every 6 months.

3. The issuer is generally, although not always, a bank or a trust company whose revenues are subject to swings with interest rate fluctuations.

There are, of course, exceptions and variations in the concept of floating rate bonds. For example, the Toronto Dominion Bank raised U.S. $150 million in financing through a variation on the floating-rate debenture called the *collared, subordinated floating rate note*. The coupon rate equals the six-month LIBOR less .125 percent but, the bank is required to pay holders a minimum rate of five percent and a maximum rate of ten percent over the next ten years. In effect, the Toronto Dominion Bank has capped its interest payments between five and ten percent over ten years. In the North American market, there are other innovative examples of variations of this type of feature. For example, bonds issued by Petro-Lewis, a Texas oil firm, and Sunshine Mining Company, a silver-mining firm. In 1980 Petro-Lewis issued bonds in which the interest rate was tied to the price of crude oil from West Texas. If the oil price increased more than ten percent, the bond's interest rate would also increase. The Sunshine Mining Company debt was issued in February 1983 and carried a coupon interest rate of eight percent, with the principal being tied to the price of silver. The common feature of all the variable rate bonds is that an attempt is made to counter uncertainty by allowing the interest rate (or in the case of the Sunshine Mining Bonds, the principal) to float. In this way a decline in cash inflows to the firm should be offset by a decline in interest payments. Table 19-2 gives several examples of variations of floating rate bonds.

Junk Bonds

Junk or **low-rated bonds** are bonds rated by Standard and Poor's Bond Rating Service as BB or below. Originally, the term was used to describe bonds issued by "fallen angels"; that is, firms with sound financial histories that were facing severe financial problems and suffering from poor credit ratings. The most likely participants in the junk bond market are new firms that do not have an established record of performance. Prior to the mid-seventies

TABLE 19-2
Floating Rate (or Floating
Principal) Bonds

Issuer	Maturity (Year)	Initial Interest Rate	Terms of Adjustment
National Bank of Canada	2087	6-month LIBOR plus 0.125%	Adjusted quarterly to 20 basis points (0.20%) above the 6-month LIBOR
National bank of Canada	2083	30-day Bankers' Acceptances Rate plus 0.5%	Adjusted quarterly to 50 basis points (0.5%) above the 30-day Bankers' Acceptance Rate.
Bank of Montreal	1998	London Eurodollar Deposit Rate plus 0.05%. Minimum Rate 6.05%	Adjusted quarterly to 5 basis points (0.05%) above the London Eurodollar Rate.
Bank of Montreal	2089	Canadian 90-day Bankers' Acceptance Rate	Adjusted quarterly to 40 basis points (0.4%) above the Canadian 90-day Bankers' Acceptance Rate.
Sunshine Mining Co.	1995 or whenever redemption value exceeds $2000 for a period of 30 consecutive days.	8.00%	Interest rate is fixed; however, the redemption value at maturity is equal to the greater of $1000 or the market price of 50 ounces of silver.

these new firms simply did not have access to the capital markets because of the reluctance of investors to accept speculative grade bonds. However, this trend changed during the eighties because of the shortage of capital which was needed to finance corporate takeovers, such as the financing of Campeau's acquisition of Federated Department Stores Inc.

The size of the junk bond market in Canada reached about $3 billion in 1990 but was about 100 times smaller than that of the United States.[8] The Canadian junk bond market was smaller because of restrictive covenants which protected the bondholder's investment and the greater due diligence required by institutional investors. Furthermore, the Canadian junk bond market was driven by the needs of the Canadian institutional investors and not by those of the issuers. For example, Canadian institutional investors required the coupons of the junk bonds issued to Sceptre Resources Ltd. to carry an interest rate that was 6.5 percent more than the equivalent Government of Canada bond (A++ grade) rate. Nevertheless, many new firms without established performance records used this financing alternative to secure debt financing through a public offering, rather than being forced to rely on commercial bank loans.

Perspective in Finance

The cost advantages that North American firms have been able to achieve in the Eurobond market are very difficult to explain given the fact that the financial markets are relatively well integrated. In integrated markets the flow of capital between countries should keep interest rates approximately equal in different countries.

Eurobonds

Eurobonds are bonds, issued in a country different from the one in whose currency the bond is denominated. For example, a Eurobond may be issued

[8]Susan Gittins, "Junk Bonds: Handle With Care," *The Financial Post* (April 11, 1990), p. 25.

BASIC FINANCIAL MANAGEMENT IN PRACTICE

Kevin J. Perry and Robert A. Taggart, Jr., on the Role of Junk Bonds in Corporate Financial Policy

When should a corporation consider issuing junk bonds? Stewart Myers' "pecking order" theory provides a useful starting point.[9] Myers notes that a firm's managers typically know more about its true value than other capital market participants. If the managers act in the interests of their existing shareholders, they will thus try to issue securities at times when they know them to be overvalued. Recognizing this incentive, however, market participants will then interpret securities issues as a sign that they are overvalued. That in turn reduces the amounts they are willing to pay for the securities.

This problem of unequal information gives rise to a pecking order of sources of funds. Internally generated funds are unaffected by the problem, since their use entails no new securities issues. The closer a company's debt securities are to being riskless, the less severe is this problem as well. This is because the value of riskless securities will be unaffected by revisions in the estimated value of the company's assets. Riskier securities such as equity, however, will clearly be affected by investors' perceptions of firm

value. Since the mere fact of their issuance is likely to lead to downward revisions in their value, managers will be reluctant to issue these securities.

The pecking order, then, implies the following rules for financial policy: (1) Use internal funds first, until these have been exhausted; (2) to the extent that external funds must be relied upon, issue debt first, the less risky the better; (3) issue common shares only as a last resort, after all debt capacity has been exhausted.

Junk bonds occupy an intermediate position in this pecking order. They are more susceptible to the investor information problem than investment grade debt, but less so than common shares. For a firm that needs large amounts of external financing for its current investment plan, junk bonds can allow the firm to fully use its available debt capacity and thus avoid an equity issue.

Source: Kevin J. Perry and Robert A. Taggart, Jr., "The Growing Role of Junk Bonds," *Journal of Applied Corporate Finance*, 1 (Spring 1988), pp. 37–45.

in France by a Canadian company and will pay interest and principal to the lender in Canadian dollars. The Eurobond market actually has its roots in the 1950s and 1960s as the U.S. dollar became increasingly popular because of its role as the primary international reserve. The characteristics of Eurobonds differ from those issued in the Canadian bond market. For example, Eurobonds have coupon interest payments which are issued on an annual basis, Eurobonds are issued on a bearer basis. Eurobonds have a term-to-maturity of approximately 10–12 years and Eurobonds do not have to be registered with any Security Commission in Canada. The primary attraction to borrowers, aside from favourable rates,[10] in the Eurobond market is the relative lack of regulation, less rigorous disclosure requirements, and the speed with which they can be issued.

The use of Eurobonds by Canadian firms to raise funds has fluctuated dramatically. Their use is dictated by both interest rates and the amount of available capital in the European markets.

---

[9]See "The Capital Structure Puzzle," *Journal of Finance*, 39 (June 1984), pp. 575–592. Reprinted in *Midland Corporate Finance Journal*, 3 (Fall 1985), pp. 6–18.

[10]Two empirical studies have documented the savings. They are D. S. Kidwell, M. W. Marr, and G. R. Thompson, "Eurodollar Bonds: Alternative Financing for U.S. Companies," *Financial Management* (Winter 1985), 18–27. A correction to the above study appears in Financial Management (Spring 1986), 78–79; and M. W. Marr and J. Trimble, "Domestic versus Euromarket Bond Sale: A Persistent Borrowing Cost Advantage," University of Tennessee, Department of Finance Working Paper, 1988.

Zero Coupon or Stripped Bonds

Zero coupon or **stripped bonds** offer an investor no coupon interest payments over the maturity of the bond. As a result, an investor buys the zero coupon or stripped bond at a discount and receives one large payment at the bond's term-to-maturity. For example in 1987, the Government of Canada issued $150 million of zero coupon bonds, called Canada Zeros, which provided a yield-to-maturity of 8.98% when the bonds expired in the year 2001. These bonds were sold at a 70.8% discount from their par value. In other words, investors who purchased these bonds for $292 and who hold them until they mature in the year 2001 will receive an 8.98% yield-to-maturity, with all of this yield coming from appreciation of the bond. To solve for the yield-to-maturity (YTM) on a Canada Zero, one assumes semi-annual compounding:

$$B_0 = \frac{1000}{\left[1+\left(\dfrac{YTM}{2}\right)\right]^{2n}}$$

$$1 + \left(\frac{YTM}{2}\right) = \left(\frac{1000}{292}\right)^{1/28}$$

$$YTM = 8.98\%$$

On the other hand, the Government of Canada has no cash outflows until the bonds mature. However, at that time the Government of Canada will have to pay back $150 million even though it only received $43.8 million when the bonds were first issued.

Zero coupon or stripped bonds first appeared on the Canadian bond market in 1982. Most of the bonds occurred as a result of investment dealers stripping the interest coupons from high-quality government bond issues, such as Government of Canada bonds, and selling both the interest component and the principal component separately. However, in 1991 Bell Canada became the first company in Canada to issue stripped corporate bonds. These bonds were the product of the investment dealer stripping the interest coupons from a corporate bond issue. Both components were then sold separately using receipts: a receipt was sold for the stripped bond or residual and a receipt was sold for the interest coupons. In 1992, Laidlaw Inc. issued $170 million of stripped corporate bonds using a private placement. This issue was sold at a premium of 3% to its par value, offered a coupon rate of 12.08% and matures in the year 2032. The debt offering was issued in the form of receipts: receipts were issued for the principal payment or residual and 2 classes of receipts were issued for the interest coupons. In other words, the first class of receipts was issued for the interest coupons over the first five years and the second class of receipts was issued for interest coupons over the term of the bond.

As with any form of financing, there are both advantages and disadvantages of issuing zero coupon or stripped bonds. The disadvantages are: first, when zero coupon bonds mature the issuing institution will face an extremely large nondeductible cash outflow, much greater than the cash inflow it experienced when the bonds were first issued. Second, discount bonds are not callable and can only be retired at maturity. Thus, if interest rates fell, the issuing institution could not benefit. The advantages of zero coupon or stripped bonds are: first, that annual cash outflows associated with interest payments do not occur with zero coupon bonds; and second, discount bonds have strong investor demand with the price of the bond being bid up causing the yield to fall. As a result, the issuing institution can issue zero coupon or stripped bonds at a lower yield than the traditional coupon bonds. Finally, the issuing institution is able to deduct the annual amortization of the discount on the principal as an interest expense. Zero coupon or stripped bonds offer an advantage to investors who place these investments in registered retirement savings plans (RRSP), since interest income is sheltered from both federal and provincial taxes during high-income earning years.

Retiring Debt

Because bonds have a maturity date, their retirement is a crucial matter. Bonds can be retired at maturity, at which time the bondholder receives the par value of the bond, or they can be retired prior to maturity. Early redemption is generally accomplished through the use of a call provision or a sinking fund.

The Use of the Call Provision

A **call provision** entitles the corporation to repurchase or "call" the bonds from their holders at stated prices over specified periods. This feature provides the firm with the flexibility to recall its debt and replace it with lower-cost debt if interest rates fall. The terms of the call provision are provided in the indenture and generally state the call price above the bond's par value. The difference between the call price and the par value is referred to as the **call premium**. The size of this premium changes over time, becoming smaller as the date of call approaches the bond's scheduled maturity. It is also common to prohibit calling the bond during its first years. Obviously, a call provision works to the disadvantage of the bondholder, who for this reason is generally compensated by a higher rate of return on the bond.

The Use of the Sinking Fund Provision

A bond covenant may have a provision for a **sinking fund** which requires the periodic repayment of debt, thus reducing the total amount of debt outstanding.[11] When a sinking fund is set up, the firm makes annual payments to the trustee, who can then purchase the bonds in the capital markets or use the call provision. The advantage is that the annual retirement of debt through a sinking fund reduces the amount needed to retire the remaining debt at maturity. Otherwise the firm would face a major payment at maturity. If the firm were experiencing temporary financial problems when the debt matured, both the repayment of the principal and the firm's future could be jeopardized. The use of a sinking fund and its periodic retirement of debt eliminates this potential danger.

Perspective in Finance

The bond-refunding decision is actually nothing more than a capital-budgeting decision. While a casual glance at the calculations may appear intimidating, all that the financial manager really does is determine the present value of the annual net cash benefits from the refund and subtract out the initial outlay.

---

[11]Serial Bonds are sinking fund bonds that must be redeemed at par. They are more valuable than the pure sinking bonds since they cannot be repurchased in the marketplace by the borrower.

Bond Refunding

The **bond-refunding** decision—that is, whether or not to call an entire issue of bonds—is similar to the capital-budgeting decision. The present value of the stream of benefits from the refunding decision is compared with the present value of its costs. If the benefits outweigh the costs, the refunding is done.

The costs of refunding a bond issue include flotation costs, the cost of recalling the old issue and any interest expenses occurring during the bond overlap period. An overlap period normally occurs because firms wish to obtain the funds from the new issue before calling the old bonds. During this overlap period, there is a risk of a rise in interest rates or a drying up of funds in the capital markets. Thus, the cost associated with the additional interest payments can be viewed as the cost of eliminating this risk. The call premium is treated as an expense that occurs during the year of refunding. Revenue Canada requires that tax benefits from flotation costs be amortized over the lifetime of the new bond issue. This regulation is applied to bonds issued after 1987. As a result, the present value of all tax shields from flotation costs must be subtracted from the flotation cost to determine the appropriate cost level. The benefits of refunding bonds include any savings from interest expenses and any return from the investment of funds during the overlap period. The interest savings are achieved by replacing older, higher cost debt with less expensive debt as interest rates drop.

While the calculations associated with a bond-refunding decision appear to be quite complex, remember that we are determining the net present value of this decision. The major difference between the refunding decision and capital budgeting, as presented in Chapter 6, is that the discount rate used in refunding is the after-tax cost of borrowing on the new bonds rather than the firm's cost of capital. The after-tax cost of borrowing reflects the firm's default risk, that is the risk of the firm defaulting on interest or principal payments. All other costs or benefits associated with bond refunding, are known with certainty and do not present the firm with any additional risk. The following example illustrates these calculations.[12]

EXAMPLE

Suppose that interest rates have just fallen and that a firm in the 45 percent tax bracket has a $50 million, 9 percent debenture issue outstanding with 20 years remaining to maturity. These old debentures contain a call provision and can be called at $104 (that is, $104 for each $100 of par). The old debenture issue can be replaced with a $50 million issue of 8 percent 20-year bonds. The firm will incur $400,000 in flotation costs for the new issue. The overlap period during which both issues will be outstanding is expected to be one month. Finally, the firm expects a nominal return of 7.50 percent compounded monthly on investments of one month. Assume that the old bonds were issued before 1987 such that tax shields from flotation costs were expensed in the year of issue.

---

[12]The subject of the appropriate discount rate to be used in discounting the benefits of a bond refund back to present has received considerable attention. See, for example, Thomas H. Mayor and Kenneth G. McCoin, "The Rate of Discounting in Bond Refunding," *Financial Management*, 3 (Autumn 1974), 54–58; and Aharon R. Ofer and Robert A. Taggart, Jr., "Bond Refunding: A Clarifying Analysis," *Journal of Finance*, 32 (March 1977), pp. 21–30. Ofer and Taggart show that the relevant discount rate is the after-tax cost of the refunding bonds when new bonds are used to replace the existing bonds.

The procedure for arriving at a decision involves first determining the cash flows from the project's costs and benefits. The discount factor for bond refunding is the after-tax cost of debt for the new bonds (8.0% × (1 − .45)) which in this case is 4.4%. All the cash flows are discounted back to the present, and the net present value of the refunding decision is determined. Table 19-3 shows these calculations. In this example the net present value of the refunding decision is $1,292,103. Since the NPV is positive, the refunding project should be accepted. ■

A typical complication in the analysis of the bond-refunding decision involves a difference in the maturities of the new and old bonds. The old bonds, which have been outstanding for some length of time, may have a shorter maturity than the proposed new bonds that are intended to replace them. Actually, this complication is quite easy to accommodate. The only alteration in the analysis is that only the net benefits up to the maturity of the old bonds are considered; after the old bonds terminate, the analysis terminates.

Advantages and Disadvantages

The corporate financing decision is complicated by the various tradeoffs among alternative financial instruments. In order to better understand the role of long-term debt in this decision process, we will examine its advantages and disadvantages.

Advantages to the Firm

1. Long-term debt is generally less expensive than other forms of financing because (a) investors view debt as a relatively safe investment alternative and demand a lower rate of return, and (b) interest expenses are tax-deductible.
2. Bondholders do not participate in extraordinary profits; the payments are limited to interest.
3. Bondholders do not have voting rights.
4. Flotation costs on bonds are generally lower than those on common shares.

Disadvantages to the Firm

1. Debt (other than income bonds) results in interest payments that, if not met, can force the firm into bankruptcy.
2. Debt (other than income bonds) produces fixed charges, increasing the firm's financial leverage. Although this may not be a disadvantage to all firms, it certainly is for some firms with unstable earnings streams.
3. Debt must be repaid at maturity and thus at some point involves a major cash outflow.
4. The typically restrictive nature of indenture covenants may limit the firm's future financial flexibility.

PREFERRED SHARES

Preferred shares are often referred to as hybrid securities because they have many characteristics of both common shares and bonds. Preferred

TABLE 19-3
Calculations Illustrating the
Bond-Refunding Decision

Step 1:

Calculate the costs.

(a) Determine the cost of the call premium: $\left(\dfrac{\$50,000,000}{\$1,000}\right) \times \$40 = \$2,000,000$

(b) Determine the flotation costs:

Annual flotation costs $= \dfrac{\$400,000}{20} = \$20,000$

Annual tax shield $= (\$20,000) \times (.45) = \$9,000$ per year

$$
\begin{aligned}
\text{Present value of all tax shields} &= \$9,000 \times (PVIFA_{4.4\%,\,20}) \\
&= \$9,000 \times (13.1214) \\
&= \$118,093
\end{aligned}
$$

$$
\begin{aligned}
\text{Net flotation costs} &= \text{flotation costs} - \text{Present value of all tax shields} \\
&= \$400,000 - \$118,093 \\
&= \$281,907
\end{aligned}
$$

(c) Determine overlap interest costs:

$$
\begin{aligned}
\text{After-tax interest rate of old debenture issue} &= 9\% \times (1 - .45) \\
&= 4.95\%
\end{aligned}
$$

$$
\begin{aligned}
\text{Interest cost} &= 0.0495 \times \left(\dfrac{1}{12}\right) \times (\$50,000,000) \\
&= \$206,250
\end{aligned}
$$

(d) Determine total costs:

$$
\begin{aligned}
\text{Total costs} &= \text{Call premium} + \text{Net flotation costs} + \text{Overlap interest costs} \\
&= \$2,000,000 + \$281,907 + \$206,250 \\
&= \$2,488,157
\end{aligned}
$$

Step 2:

Calculate the cash benefit from eliminating the old bonds through refunding.

(a) Determine present value of the interest savings:

$$
\begin{aligned}
\text{Present value of interest savings} &= (\$50,000,000) \times (0.09 - 0.08) \times (1 - 0.45) \times (PVIFA_{4.4\%,\,20}) \\
&= (\$275,000) \times (13.1214) \\
&= \$3,608,385
\end{aligned}
$$

(b) Determine the investment benefits during overlap period:

$$
\begin{aligned}
\text{Investment benefits} &= (\$50,000,000) \times (0.00625)^{a} \times (1 - 0.45) \\
&= \$171,875
\end{aligned}
$$

(c) Determine total benefits:

$$
\begin{aligned}
\text{Total benefits} &= \$3,608,385 + \$171,875 \\
&= \$3,780,260
\end{aligned}
$$

Step 3:

Calculate the refunding decision's net present value.

(a) Present value of the benefits (from Step 2) $3,780,260

(b) Less present value of the costs (from Step 1)   2,488,157

(c) Equals net present value $1,292,103

[a] *Monthly compounding;* $\left[1 + \left(\dfrac{.075}{12}\right)\right]^{1} - 1 = 0.625\%$

shares are similar to common shares in that they have no fixed maturity date, the nonpayment of dividends does not bring on bankruptcy, and dividends are not deductible for tax purposes. On the other hand, preferred shares are similar to bonds in that dividends are limited in amount.

The size of the dividend is generally fixed either as a dollar amount or as a percentage of the par value. For example, the Royal Bank of Canada has issued $1.88 preferred shares, while the Maritime Telegraph and Telephone (MTT) company has some 7.00 percent preferred shares outstanding. The par value on the MTT preferred shares is $10, hence each share pays $7.00\% \times \$10$, or $0.70 in dividends annually. Since these dividends are fixed, preferred shareholders do not share in the residual earnings of the firm but are limited to their stated annual dividend.

In examining preferred shares we will first discuss several features common to almost all preferred shares. Next we will investigate less frequently included features and take a brief look at methods of retiring preferred shares. We will close by examining its advantages and disadvantages.

Features of Preferred Shares

Although each issue of preferred shares is unique, several characteristics are common to almost all issues. These traits include the ability to issue multiple classes of preferred shares, the claim on assets and income, and the cumulative and protective features.

Multiple Classes

If a company desires, it can issue more than one series or class of preferred shares, and each class can have different characteristics. In fact, it is quite common for firms that issue preferred shares to issue more than one series. For example, the Royal Bank of Canada has seven different issues of preferred shares outstanding, while MTT has six different issues of preferred shares outstanding. These issues can be further differentiated by the fact that some are convertible into common shares while others are not, and they have varying priority status with respect to assets in the event of bankruptcy.

Floating Rate

In the early 1980s, another new financing alternative was developed in order to provide investors with some protection against wide swings in principal that occur when interest rates fluctuate up or down. This financing vehicle is called **floating rate preferred shares**. With floating rate preferred, quarterly dividends fluctuate with interest rates under a formula that ties the dividend payment to (1) a chartered bank's prime rate, (2) the Bank of Canada rate, or (3) the rate of bankers acceptances. For example, Canadian Imperial Bank of Commerce class A preferred shares, series 5, have a floating and adjustable cumulative dividends which are determined by applying one quarter of 69 percent of the average of the prime rate of the bank in effect on each day during the period. While floating rate preferred shares allow dividends to be tied to the interest rates, it also provides a maximum and a minimum level to which they can climb or fall called the **dividend rate band**. The purpose of allowing the dividend rate to fluctuate on these preferred shares, is to minimize the fluctuation in the principal of the preferred shares. In times of high and fluctuating interest rates, this is a very appealing feature indeed.

In the North American market, there have been other examples of setting the dividend rate. For example, auction rate preferred shares began to appear in the United States in the late 1980s and early 1990s. Auction rate preferred shares are actually variable rate preferred shares in which the dividend rate is set by an auction process. In the case of auction rate preferred, the dividend rate is set every 49 days. At each auction, buyers and sellers place bids for shares, specifying the yield they are willing to accept for the next seven-week period. The yield is then set at the lowest level necessary to match buyers and sellers. As a result, the yield offered on auction rate preferred shares accurately reflects current interest rates, while keeping the market price of these securities at par.

Convertibility

Many of the preferred shares that are issued today are **convertible** at the discretion of the holder into a predetermined number of common shares. In fact, today about one-third of all preferred shares issued have a convertibility feature. The convertibility feature is, of course, desirable and thus reduces the cost of the preferred shares to the issuer. For example, the preferred share series G of the Royal Bank of Canada is convertible to the bank's common shares only after October 31, 1999. The characteristics common to convertible preferred shares will be discussed in detail in Chapter 20.

Claim on Assets and Income

Preferred shareholders have priority over common shareholders with respect to claims on assets in the case of bankruptcy. The preferred shareholder's claim is honoured after that of bonds and before that of common shareholders. Multiple issues of preferred shares differ according to the priority of their claim. Preferred shareholders also have priority over common shareholders with respect to their claim on income. As a result, a firm must pay dividends to its preferred shareholders before it can distribute other dividends. In terms of risk, preferred shares are safer than common shares because preferred shareholders have priority with respect to their claim on assets and income. However, preferred shares are riskier than long-term debt because preferred shareholders' claim on assets or income comes after those of bonds.

Cumulative Feature

Most preferred shares carry a **cumulative feature** that requires all unpaid dividends in the past to be paid before any new dividends are declared. The purpose of this feature is to provide some degree of protection for the preferred shareholder. Without a cumulative feature a firm could treat both preferred shareholders and common shareholders equally with respect to their priority of receiving a dividend. However, the cumulative feature ensures that unpaid dividends to preferred shareholders be paid before any dividends are distributed to common shareholders.

Protective Provisions

In addition to cumulative features, protective provisions are common to preferred shares. These protective provisions generally allow for voting rights in the event of nonpayment of dividends, or they restrict the payment of dividends if sinking-fund payments are not met or if the firm is in financial difficulty. In effect, the protective features included with preferred shares are similar to the restrictive provisions included with long-term debt.

To examine typical protective provisions, let us look at the preferred shares of the Royal Bank of Canada. The different issues of their preferred shares have a protective provision that provides preferred shareholders with voting rights whenever eight quarterly dividends are in arrears. At that point the preferred shareholders are given the power to elect a majority of the board of directors. The Reynolds Metals company is also another example of a company which precludes the payment of dividends during any period in which the preferred shares sinking fund is in default. These provisions are desirable because they provide protection beyond that provided for by the cumulative provision and thereby reduce the shareholders' risk. In addition, these types of features reduce the cost of preferred shares to the issuing firm.

Participation

Although participating features are infrequent in preferred shares, their inclusion can greatly affect their desirability and cost. The participation feature allows the preferred shareholder to participate in earnings beyond the payment of the stated dividend. This is usually done in accordance with some set formula. For example, MacMillan Bloedel Ltd. has class B participating preferred shares which include the right of dividend only if revenues are received from oil and gas interests. These privately held shares provide the feature of participating in dividends distributed to the common shareholders. Although a participating feature is certainly desirable from the point of view of the investor, it is infrequently included in preferred shares.

PIK Preferred

One by-product of the levered buyout boom of the late 1980s was the creation of pay-in-kind or PIK preferred shares. With PIK preferred, investors receive no dividends initially; they receive more preferred shares, which in turn pay dividends on even more preferred shares. After five or six years the issuing company can replace the payment-in-kind with cash dividends. Needless to say, the issuing firm has to offer hefty dividends, generally ranging from 12 percent to 18 percent, to entice investors to purchase PIK preferred.

Retirement of Preferred Shares

Although preferred shares do not have a set maturity associated with them, issuing firms generally provide for some method of retirement. The retirement of preferred shares enables a firm to take advantage of falling interest rates.

The Use of Call Provisions

Most preferred shares have some type of call provision associated with it. The call feature on preferred shares usually involves an initial premium above the par value or issuing price of the preferred of approximately 10 percent. Then, over time, the call premium generally falls. For example, Quaker Oats in 1976 issued $9.56 cumulative preferred shares with no par value for $100 per share. This issue was not callable until 1980 and then was callable at $109.56. After that the call price gradually drops to $100 in the year 2000, as shown in Table 19-4.

By setting the initial call price above the initial issue price and allowing it to decline slowly over time, the firm protects the investor from an early call that carries no premium. A call provision also allows the issuing firm to plan the retirement of its preferred shares at predetermined prices.

Date		Call Price
Date of issue	until 7/19/80	Not callable
7/20/80	until 7/19/85	$109.56
7/20/85	until 7/19/90	107.17
7/20/90	until 7/19/95	104.78
7/20/95	until 7/19/00	102.39
After 7/19/00		100.00

TABLE 19-4
Call Provision of Quaker Oats $9.56 Cumulative Preferred Shares

The Use of a Sinking Fund Provision

A **sinking fund** provision requires the firm periodically to set aside an amount of money for the retirement of its preferred shares. This money is then used to purchase the preferred shares in the open market or through the use of the call provision, whichever method is cheaper. Although preferred shares do not have a maturity date associated with them, the use of a call provision in addition to a sinking fund can effectively create a maturity date. For example, the Quaker Oats issue we just examined has associated with it an annual sinking fund, operating between the years 1981 and 2005, which requires the annual elimination of a minimum of 20,000 shares and a maximum of 40,000. The minimum payments are designed so that the entire issue will be retired by the year 2005. If any sinking-fund payments are made above the minimum amount, the issue will be retired prior to 2005. The issue of Quaker Oats preferred shares has a maximum life of 30 years, and the size of the issue outstanding decreases each year after 1981.

Advantages and Disadvantages

Preferred shares are a hybrid of bonds and common shares. As a result, preferred shares offer a firm several advantages and disadvantages when compared with bonds and common shares.

Advantages to the Firm

1. Preferred shares do not have any default risk to the issuer. The nonpayment of dividends does not force the firm into bankruptcy, as does the nonpayment of interest on debt.

2. The dividend payments are generally limited to a stated amount. Thus, preferred shareholders do not participate in excess earnings as do common shareholders.

3. Preferred shareholders generally do not have voting rights except in the case of financial distress. Therefore, the issuance of preferred shares does not create a challenge to the owners of the firm.

4. Although preferred shares do not carry a specified maturity, the inclusion of call features and sinking funds provides the ability to replace the issue if interest rates decline.

Disadvantages to the Firm

1. The cost of financing a project with preferred shares is higher than that of bonds because preferred shares are riskier than bonds and their dividends are not tax deductible.

2. Although preferred dividends can be omitted, their cumulative nature makes dividend payment almost mandatory.

COMMON SHARES

A **common share** is a claim of ownership in a corporation. In effect, bondholders and preferred shareholders can be viewed as creditors, while the common shareholders are the true owners of the firm. Common shares do not have a maturity date, but exist as long as the firm does. In addition, common shares have no upper limit on their dividend payments. Dividend payments must be declared by the firm's board of directors before they are distributed to common shareholders. In the event of bankruptcy the common shareholders, as owners of the corporation, cannot exercise their claims on assets until the claims of the bondholders and preferred shareholders have been satisfied.

In examining common shares, we will look first at several of their features or characteristics. Then we will focus on the process of raising funds through rights offerings. Finally, we will investigate the advantages and disadvantages of financing with common shares.

Features or Characteristics

Common shares are distinguished from other financial instruments by their claim on income and assets, their voting rights, and the limited-liability feature.

Claim on Income

As the owners of the corporation, the common shareholders have the right to the residual income after bondholders and preferred shareholders have been paid. This income may be paid directly to the shareholders in the form of dividends or retained and reinvested by the firm. While it is obvious the shareholder benefits immediately from the distribution of income in the form of dividends, the reinvestment of earnings also benefits the shareholder. Plowing back earnings into the firm results in an increase in the value of the firm, in its earning power, and in its future dividends. This action results in an increase in the value of the shares. In effect, residual income is distributed directly to shareholders in the form of dividends or indirectly in the form of capital gains on their common shares.

The right to residual income is advantageous to the common shareholder because the potential return is limitless. Once the claims of the most senior securities—that is, bonds and preferred shares—have been satisfied, the remaining income flows to the common shareholders in the form of dividends or capital gains. The disadvantage of having a right to residual income occurs if the claims of both bondholders and preferred shareholders on income absorb all of the earnings and common shareholders receive nothing. In years when earnings fall, it is the common shareholder who suffers first.

Claims on Assets

Common shareholders also have a residual claim on assets in the case of liquidation. Only after the claims of debt holders and preferred shareholders have been satisfied do the claims of common shareholders receive attention. Unfortunately, when bankruptcy does occur, the claims of the common shareholders generally go unsatisfied. In effect, this residual claim on assets adds to the risk of common shares.

Voting Rights

The common shareholders are entitled to elect the board of directors and are in general the only security holders given a vote. In corporate Canada, many firms have two or more classes of common shares. One or more of the classes may contain restricted shares.[13] Canadian Tire, Molson and Bombardier are examples of large corporations which have two classes of common shares. This practice is common in Canada because many of these corporations are either family-owned or closely held. In contrast, the practice of issuing two classes of common shares was virtually eliminated in the United States because of the regulations implemented by the Securities and Exchange Commission and the New York Stock Exchange's refusal to list common shares without voting privileges. However, with the merger boom of the eighties dual classes of common shares with different voting rights again emerged, this time as a defensive tactic used to prevent takeovers.

Common shareholders not only have the right to elect the board of directors, they also must approve any change in the corporate charter. A typical charter change might involve the authorization to issue new shares or perhaps a merger proposal.

Voting for directors and charter changes occurs at the corporation's annual meeting. While shareholders may vote in person, the majority generally vote by proxy. A **proxy** gives a designated party the temporary power of attorney to vote for the signee at the corporation's annual meeting. The firm's management generally solicits proxy votes and, if the shareholders are satisfied with its performance, has little problem securing them. However, in times of financial distress or when management takeovers are threatened, proxy fights—battles between rival groups for proxy votes—occur.

While each share carries the same number of votes, the voting procedure is not always the same from company to company. The two procedures commonly used are majority and cumulative voting. Under majority voting, each share allows the shareholder one vote, and each position on the board of directors is voted on separately. Since each member of the board of directors is elected by a simple majority, a majority of shares has the power to elect the entire board of directors.

With cumulative voting, each share allows the shareholder a number of votes equal to the number of directors being elected. The shareholder can then cast all of his or her votes for a single candidate or split them among the various candidates. The advantage of a cumulative voting procedure is that it gives minority shareholders the power to elect a director.

Perspective in Finance

In theory, shareholders pick the corporate board of directors, generally through proxy voting, and the board of directors in turn pick management.

---

[13]The Ontario Securities Act recognizes three types of restricted shares: restricted voting shares, subordinated voting shares, and non-voting shares. For a greater discussion on the types of restricted shares, see: William F. Sharpe, Gordon J. Alexander, and David J Fowler, *Investments*, 1st ed. (Scarborough, Ont.: Prentice-Hall Canada, 1993) pp. 391–92.

INTERNATIONAL FINANCIAL MANAGEMENT

Greg A. Jarrell on Dual-Class Recapitalizations

These plans restructure the equity of a firm into two classes having different voting rights. Although not a recent innovation, dual-class recapitalizations have become much more common and controversial in today's active takeover market. The New York Stock Exchange has recently proposed to abandon its long-standing rule of one share, one vote, to accommodate corporate management's growing demand for dual-class structures and to counter the trend of firms to list over-the-counter to meet this demand.

In addition to the recent surge of interest in existing plans, there have been some innovative wrinkles in new dual-class plans, most notably the length-of-time method first used by American Family Corporation. This method involves a change in voting rights of the same common stock based on the length of time the shares are held. All current outstanding common stock becomes "long-term" on the

recapitalization, with each holder entitled to 10 votes per share. But any share traded or sold after the effective date of the recapitalization becomes a "short-term" share and has only one vote, rising to 10 votes only after it has been held continuously for a substantial period of time (generally, four years). This idea of linking voting power to length of time owned has been borrowed by the drafters of the New York and New Jersey antitakeover laws, which disallow hostile acquirers who do not receive prior approval from target management from doing a second-stage merger or from engaging in a list of controlling actions for at least five years after obtaining control.

Source: Gregg A. Jarrell, "Financial Innovation and Corporate Mergers," in *The Merger Boom*, ed. Lynn E. Browne and Eric S. Rosengren (Boston: Federal Reserve Bank of Boston, 1987).

Unfortunately, in reality the system frequently works the other way around. Simply put, under the proxy system any challenge to management is generally prohibitively costly and doomed to failure. Management selects both the issues and the board of director nominees and then distributes the proxy ballots. In effect, shareholders are offered a slate of nominees selected by management from which to choose. The end result is that management effectively selects the directors who then may have more allegiance to the managers than to the shareholders. This in turn sets up the potential for agency problems in which a divergence of interests between managers and shareholders is allowed to exist, with the board of directors not monitoring the managers on behalf of the shareholders as they should.

Limited Liability

Although the common shareholders are the actual owners of the corporation, their liability in the case of bankruptcy is limited to the amount of their investment. The advantage is that investors who might not otherwise invest their funds in the firm become willing to do so. This limited-liability feature aids the firm in raising funds.

Preemptive Rights

The **preemptive right** entitles the common shareholder to maintain a proportionate share of ownership in the firm. When new shares are issued, common shareholders have the first right of refusal. If a shareholder owns 25 percent of the corporation's shares, then he or she is entitled to purchase 25 percent of the new shares. Certificates issued to the shareholders giving them an option to purchase a stated number of new shares at a specified price during a 2- to 10-week period are called **rights**. These rights can be exercised (generally at a price below the common share's current market price), can be allowed to expire, or can be sold in the open market.

The Rights Offering

We will look first at the dates surrounding a rights offering and then examine the process of raising funds and the value of a right.

Dates Surrounding a Rights Offering

Let us examine the announcement of a rights offering by a hypothetical corporation. On March 1 the firm announces that all "holders of record" as of April 6 will be issued rights, which will expire on May 30 and will be mailed to them on April 25. In this example March 1 is the **announcement date**, April 6 the **holder-of-record date**, and May 30 the **expiration date**. While this seems rather straightforward, it is complicated by the fact that if the shares are sold a day or two before the holder-of-record date, the corporation may not have time to record the transaction and replace the old owner's name with that of the new owner; the rights might then be sent to the wrong person. To deal with this problem an additional date has been created, the ex rights date. The **ex rights date** occurs four trading days prior to the holder-of-record date.

On or after the ex rights date, the shares sell without the rights. Whoever owns the shares on the day prior to the ex rights date receives the rights. Thus, if the holder-of-record date is April 6 and four trading days earlier is April 2, anyone purchasing the shares on or before April 1 will receive the rights, while anyone purchasing the shares on or after April 2 will not. The price of the shares prior to the ex rights date is referred to as the **rights-on price**, while the price on or after the ex rights date is the **ex rights price**. The timing of this process and the terminology are shown in Table 19-5.

Raising Funds Through Rights Offerings

Three questions and theoretical relationships must be dealt with if we are to understand rights offerings. First, how many rights are required to purchase a new share? Second, what is the theoretical value of a right? Finally, what effect do rights offerings have on the value of the common shares outstanding?

Let us continue with the example of our hypothetical corporation and assume it has 600,000 shares outstanding, currently selling for $100 per share. In order to finance new projects, this firm needs to raise an additional $10,500,000 and wishes to do so with a rights offering. Moreover, the subscription price on the new shares is $70 per share. The subscription price is

Shares sell rights on	March 1	—	Announcement date
	April 1	—	The owner of the shares as of this date receives the rights
Shares sell ex rights	April 2	—	Ex rights date } four trading days
	April 6	—	Holder-of-record date
	April 25	—	Mailing date
	May 30	—	Expiration date

TABLE 19-5

Illustration of the Timing of a Rights Offering

$30. After the shares went ex rights, the market price was $40. What was the price of the B. Fuller common shares just prior to the rights offering? [*Hint:* Set Equation (19-6) equal to Equation (19-12) and solve for P_{on}.]

STUDY PROBLEMS (SET B)

19-1B. (*Bankruptcy Distribution*) The Finky Corporation is facing bankruptcy. The market value of its mortgaged assets is $40 million and of all other assets $35 million. Finky currently has outstanding $45 million in mortgaged bonds, $15 million in subordinated debentures, $20 million in preferred shares, and $35 million in common shares. If the corporation goes bankrupt, how will the distribution be made?

19-2B. (*Refunding Decision*) The Hook'ems Corporation currently has outstanding a 20-year $12 million bond issue with a 9.5 percent interest rate callable at $103. Because of a decline in interest rates, Hook'ems would be able to refund the issue with a $12 million issue of 8 percent 20-year bonds. The flotation costs for refunding the issue are $250,000. The overlap period during which both issues would be expected to be outstanding is one month. The firm expects a nominal return of 7.50 percent compounded monthly. Assume that the old bonds were issued before 1987 such that tax shields from flotation costs were expensed in the year of issue. The firm has a combined corporate tax rate of 45%.

19-3B. (*Refunding Decision*) Three years ago the Boulder Corporation issued a 30-year $45 million bond issue with a 6.75 percent interest rate callable at $108. During the past three years interest rates have fallen, allowing the Wittman Corporation to replace this bond issue with a 27-year $50 million bond issue with a coupon rate of 6 percent. Flotation costs will drain an additional $350,000. The overlap period during which both issues are expected to be outstanding is one month. The firm expects a nominal return of 5.50 percent compounded monthly. Assume that the old bonds were issued before 1987 such that tax shields from flotation costs were expensed in the year of issue. The firm has a combined corporate tax rate of 45%.

19-4B. (*Junk Bond Indenture Research Project*) As a research project obtain several junk bonds and A+ rated bonds indentures. These can be obtained directly from the corporation issuing the bonds or perhaps through a local stockbroker. Examine the restrictive covenants—do you notice a difference in the restrictive nature of the restrictions on junk versus "normal" bonds? Why do you think this is so?

19-5B. (*Rights Offering*) The Good Gravy Corporation is considering raising $15 million through a rights offering. It has one million common shares outstanding, currently selling for $86 per share. The subscription price on the new shares will be $60 per share.

a. How many shares must be sold to raise the desired funds?

b. How many rights are necessary to purchase one share?

c. What is the value of one right?

19-6B. (*Rights Offering*) The Utlonghorns Corporation, a film company responsible for the hit movie "Revenge of the Nightmare Police Academy the Thirteenth Part VI," is considering a rights offering to raise $75 million to finance new projects. It currently has 1.5 million common shares outstanding, selling for $35 per share. The subscription price on the new shares would be $25 per share.

a. How many shares must be sold to raise the desired funds?

b. How many rights are necessary to purchase one share?

c. What is the value of one right?

19-7B. (*Rights Offerings*) The Gold Castle Corporation is in the process of selling common shares through a rights offering. Prior to the rights offering, the firm had 600,000 common shares outstanding. Through the rights offering, it plans on issuing an additional 100,000 shares at a subscription price of $37. After the shares went ex rights, the market price was $42. What was the price of the Gold Castle common shares just prior to the rights offering? [*Hint:* Set Equation (19-6) equal to Equation (19-12) and solve for P_{on}.]

SELF-TEST SOLUTION

SS-1. a.
$$\text{new shares to be sold} = \frac{\text{desired funds to be raised}}{\text{subscription price}}$$

$$= \frac{\$30,000,000}{\$40}$$

$$= 750,000 \text{ shares}$$

b.
$$\begin{array}{l}\text{number of rights}\\ \text{necessary to purchase}\\ \text{one share}\end{array} = \frac{\text{original number of shares outstanding}}{\text{new shares to be sold}}$$

$$= \frac{3,000,000}{750,000}$$

$$= 4 \text{ rights}$$

c.
$$\text{value of one right} = \frac{P_{on} - S}{N + 1}$$

$$= \frac{\$60 - \$40}{4 + 1}$$

$$= \frac{\$20}{5}$$

$$= \$4$$

SELECTED REFERENCES

Agmon, T., A. R. Ofer, and A. Tamir. "Variable Rate Debt Instruments and Corporate Debt Policy," *Journal of Finance*, 36 (March 1981), 113–126.

Alderson, Michael J., Keith C. Brown, and Scott L. Lummer. "Dutch Auction Rate Preferred Stock," *Financial Management*, 16 (Summer 1987), 68–73.

Allen, David S., Robert E. Lamy, and G. Rodney Thompson. "The Shelf Registration of Debt and Self Selection Bias," *Journal of Finance*, 45 (1990), 275–88.

Altman, Edward I. "Setting the Record Straight on Junk Bonds: A Review of the Research on Default Rates and Returns," *Journal of Applied Corporate Finance*, 3 (1990), 82–95.

Ang, James S. "The Two Faces of Bond Refunding," *Journal of Finance*, 30 (June 1975), 869–874.

Bhagat, Sanjai, James A. Brickley, and Ronald C. Lease. "The Authorization of Additional Common Stock: An Empirical Investigation," *Financial Management*, 15 (Autumn 1986), 45–53.

Bierman, Harold, Jr., and Amir Barnea. "Expected Short-Term Interest Rates in Bond Refunding," *Financial Management*, 3 (Spring 1974), 75–79.

Bildersee, John S. "Some Aspects of the Performance of Non-Convertible Preferred Stocks," *Journal of Finance*, 28 (December 1973), 1187–1202.

Billingsley, Randall S., Robert E. Lamy, and David M. Smith. "Units of Debt with Warrants: Evidence of the 'Penalty-Free' Issuance of an Equity-Like Security," *Journal of Financial Research*, 13 (1990), 187–200.

Block, Stanley, and Marjorie Stanley. "The Financial Characteristics and Price Movement Patterns of Companies Approaching the Unseasoned Securities Market in the Late 1970's," *Financial Management*, 9 (Winter 1980), 30–36.

Bodie, Zvi, and Robert A. Taggart, Jr. "Future Investment Opportunities and the Value of the Call Provision on a Bond," *Journal of Finance*, 33 (September 1978), 1187–1200.

Bowlin, Oswald D. "The Refunding Decision: Another Special Case in Capital Budgeting," *Journal of Finance*, 21 (March 1966), 55–68.

Brennan, Michael J., and Eduardo S. Schwartz. "Savings Bonds, Retractable Bonds and Callable Bonds," *Journal of Financial Economics*, 5 (1977), 66–88.

Brown, Keith and Donald J. Smith. "Forward Swaps, Swap Options, and the Management of Callable Bonds," *Journal of Applied Corporate Finance*, 2 (1990), 59–71.

Caks, John. "Corporate Debt Decisions: A New Analytical Framework," *Journal of Finance*, 33 (December 1978), 1297–1315.

Chang, Rosita P., Peter E. Koveos, and S. Ghon Rhee. "Financial Planning for International Long-Term Financing," *Advances in Financial Planning and Forecasting*, 5, Part I (1990), 33–58.

Cornell, Bradford, and Alan C. Shapiro. "Financing Corporate Growth," *Journal of Applied Corporate Finance*, 1 (Summer 1988), 6–22.

Duvall, Richard M., and Douglas V. Austin. "Predicting the Results of Proxy Contests," *Journal of Finance*, 20 (September 1965), 467–471.

Eibott, Peter. "Trends in the Value of Individual Stockholdings," *Journal of Business*, 47 (July 1974), 339–348.

Elsaid, Hussein H. "The Function of Preferred Stock in the Corporate Financial Plan," *Financial Analysts Journal* (July–August 1969), 112–117.

Emery, Douglas R. "Overlapping Interest in Bond Refunding: A Re-consideration," *Financial Management*, 17 (Summer 1978), 19–20.

Fisher, Donald E., and Glenn A. Wilt, Jr. "Nonconvertible Preferred Stock as a Financing Instrument, 1950–1965," *Journal of Finance*, 23 (September 1968), 611–624.

Halford, Frank A. "Income Bonds," *Financial Analysts Journal*, 20 (January–February 1964), 73–79.

Hansen, Robert S., and Claire E. Crutchley. "Corporate Earnings and Financing: An Empirical Analysis," *Journal of Business*, 63 (1990), 347–71.

Hansen, Robert S., Beverly R. Fuller, and Vahan Janjigian. "The Over-Allotment Option and Equity Financing Flotation Costs: An Empirical Investigation," *Financial Management*, 16 (Summer 1987), 24–32.

Hansen, Robert S., and John M. Pinkerton. "Direct Equity Financing: A Resolution of a Paradox," *Journal of Finance*, 37 (June 1982), 651–665.

Harris, Robert S. "The Refunding of Discounted Debt: An Adjusted Present Value Analysis," *Financial Management*, 9 (Winter 1980), 7–12.

Hatch, James E. and Michael J. Robinson. *Investment Management in Canada*, 2nd ed. Scarborough, Ont.: Prentice-Hall Canada, 1989.

Heinkel, Robert and Josef Zechner. "The Role of Debt and Preferred Stock as a Solution to Adverse Investment Incentives," *Journal of Financial and Quantitative Analysis*, 25 (1990), 1–24.

Houston, Arthur L., Jr., and Carol Olson Houston. "Financing with Preferred Stock," *Financial Management*, 19 (1990), 42–54.

Jarrell, Greg A. "Financial Innovation and Corporate Mergers," in *The Merger Boom*. ed. Lynn E. Browne and Eric S. Rosengren. Boston: Federal Reserve Bank of Boston, 1987.

Jen, Frank C., and James E. Wert. "The Deferred Call Provision and Corporate Bond Yields," *Journal of Financial and Quantitative Analysis*, 3 (June 1968), 157–169.

Johnson, Rodney, and Richard Klein. "Corporate Motives in Repurchases of Discounted Bonds," *Financial Management*, 3 (Autumn 1974), 44–49.

Kalotay, A. J. "On the Advanced Refunding of Discounted Debt," *Financial Management*, 7 (Summer 1978), 14–18.

Kao, Chihwa, and Chunchi Wu. "Sinking Funds and the Agency Costs of Corporate Debt," *Financial Review*, 25 (1990), 95–114.

Keane, S. M. "The Significance of Issue Price in Rights Issues," *Journal of Business Finance*, 4 (September 1972), 40–45.

Kolodny, Richard. "The Refunding Decision in Near Perfect Markets," *Journal of Finance*, 29 (December 1974), 1467–1478.

Laber, Gene. "Repurchases of Bonds through Tender Offers: Implications for Shareholder Wealth," *Financial Management*, 7 (Summer 1978), 7–13.

Logue, Dennis E., and Richard J. Rogalski. "Does It Pay to Shop for Your Bond Underwriter?" *Harvard Business Review*, 57 (July–August 1979), 111–117.

Marr, Wayne, and John Trimble. "The Persistent Borrowing Advantage of Eurodollar Bonds: A Plausible Explanation," *Journal of Applied Corporate Finance*, 1 (Spring 1988), 65–70.

Marshall, William J., and Jess B. Yawitz. "Optimal Terms of the Call Provision on a Corporate Bond," *Journal of Financial Research*, 2 (Fall 1980), 203–211.

Mayor, Thomas H., and Kenneth G. McCoin. "The Rate of Discount in Bond Refunding," *Financial Management*, 3 (Autumn 1974), 54–58.

McConnell, John J., and Gary G. Schlarbaum. "Returns, Risks, and Pricing of Income Bonds, 1956–76," *Journal of Business*, 54 (January 1981), 33–57.

McEnally, Richard W., and Michael L. Rice. "Hedging Possibilities in the Flotation of Debt Securities," *Financial Management*, 8 (Winter 1979), 12–18.

Ofer, Aharon R., and Robert A. Taggart, Jr. "Bond Refunding: A Clarifying Analysis," *Journal of Finance*, 32 (March 1977), 21–30.

Perry, Kevin J., and Robert A. Taggart, Jr. "The Growing Role of Junk Bonds," *Journal of Applied Corporate Finance*, 1 (Spring 1988), 37–45.

Pinches, George E., and Kent A. Mingo. "The Role of Subordination and Industrial Bond Ratings," *Journal of Finance*, 30 (March 1975), 201–206.

Riener, Kenneth D. "Financial Structure Effects on Bond Refunding," *Financial Management*, 9 (Summer 1980), 18–23.

Sharpe, William F., Gordon J. Alexander and David J. Fowler. *Investments*, 1st Canadian ed. Scarborough, Ont: Prentice Hall Canada, 1993.

Sibley, A. M. "Some Evidence on the Cash Flow Effects of Bond Refunding," *Financial Management*, 3 (Autumn 1974), 50–53.

Smith, Clifford W., Jr., and Jerold B. Warner. "On Financial Contracting: An Analysis of Bond Covenants," *Journal of Financial Economics*, 7 (June 1979), 117–161.

Stevenson, Richard A. "Retirement of Non-Callable Preferred Stock," *Journal of Finance*, 25 (December 1970), 1143–1152.

Van Horne, James C. "Called Bonds: How Does the Investor Fare?" *Journal of Portfolio Management*, 6 (Summer 1980), 58–61.

Wansley, James W., Fayez, A. Elayan and Brian A. Maris. "Preferred Stock Returns, CreditWatch, and Preferred Stock Rating Changes," *Financial Review*, 25 (1990), 265–86.

Weinstein, Mark I. "The Seasoning Process of New Corporate Bond Issues," *Journal of Finance*, 33 (December 1978), 1343–1354.

White, R. W., and P. A. Lusztig. "The Price Effects of Rights Offerings," *Journal of Financial and Quantitative Analysis*, 15 (March 1980), 25–40.

Wigmore, Barrie A. "The Decline in Credit Quality of New-Issue Junk Bonds," *Financial Analysts Journal*, 46 (1990), 53–62.

Winger, Bernard J., Carl R. Chen, John D. Martin, J. William Petty, and Steven C. Hayden. "Adjustable Rate Preferred Stock," *Financial Management*, 15 (Spring 1986), 48–57.

Wingler, Tony R. and G. Donald Jud. "Premium Debt Tenders: Analysis and Evidence," *Financial Management*, 19 (1990), 58–67.

Winn, Willis J., and Arleigh Hess, Jr. "The Value of the Call Privilege," *Journal of Finance*, 14 (May 1959), 182–195.

CHAPTER 20

Convertibles, Warrants, Options, and Futures

- Convertible Securities

- Warrants

- Futures

- Options

- The Use of Options and Futures by Financial Managers

In earlier chapters we concerned ourselves with methods of raising long-term funds through the use of common shares, preferred shares, and short- and long-term debt. In this chapter we will examine how convertibles and warrants can be used to increase the attractiveness of these securities. We have grouped convertibles and warrants together in our discussion because both can be exchanged at the owner's discretion for a specified number of common shares. In investigating each financing alternative we look first at its specific characteristics and purpose; then we focus on any special considerations that should be examined before it is issued. Finally, we examine two additional financial instruments that are similar to warrants and convertibles but are not created by the firm: options and futures. Much of our interest in options and futures stems from our ability to use these instruments to eliminate risks associated with the fluctuations of interest rate, exchange rate, and commodity prices.

CONVERTIBLE SECURITIES

A **convertible security** is either a preferred share or a debt issue which can be exchanged for a specified number of common shares at the will of the owner. It provides the stable income associated with preferred shares and bonds in addition to the possibility of capital gains associated with common shares. This combining of features has led convertibles to be called *hybrid* securities.

When the convertible is initially issued, the firm receives the proceeds from the sale, less flotation costs. This is the only time the firm receives any proceeds from issuing convertibles. The firm then treats this convertible as if it were normal preferred shares or debentures, paying dividends or interest regularly. If the security owner wishes to exchange the convertible for common shares, he or she may do so at any time according to the terms specified at the time of issue.[1] The desire to convert generally follows an increase in the price of the common shares. Once the convertible owner trades the convertibles in for common shares, the owner can never trade the shares back for convertibles. From then on the owner is treated as any other common shareholder and receives only cash dividends.

Characteristics and Features of Convertibles

Conversion Ratio

The number of common shares for which the convertible security can be exchanged is set out when the convertible is initially issued. On some convertible issues this **conversion ratio** is stated directly. For example, the convertible may state that it is exchangeable for 15 common shares. Some convertibles give only a **conversion price**, stating, for example, that the security is convertible at $39 per share.[2] This tells us that for every $39 of par value of the convertible security one common share will be received.

$$\text{conversion ratio} = \frac{\text{par value of convertible security}}{\text{conversion price}} \qquad (20\text{-}1)$$

In 1988 Cambridge Shopping Centres, a Canadian real estate developer, issued $110 million of convertible debentures that mature in 2003. These convertibles have a $1,000 par value, a $8\frac{1}{2}$ percent coupon interest rate, and a conversion ratio of 36.9. Thus, the conversion price—the price at which the conversion to shares occurs—is $1000/36.9 = $27.10. The security owner has the choice of holding the $8\frac{1}{2}$ percent convertible debenture or trading it in for 36.9 common shares of Cambridge Shopping Centres.

Conversion Value

The **conversion value** of a convertible security is the total market value of the common shares for which the convertible security can be exchanged. This can be calculated as follows:

$$\begin{matrix}\text{conversion}\\\text{value}\end{matrix} = \begin{pmatrix}\text{conversion}\\\text{ratio}\end{pmatrix} \times \begin{pmatrix}\text{market value per}\\\text{common share}\end{pmatrix} \qquad (20\text{-}2)$$

As an example, Cambridge Shopping Centres' common shares were selling in the third quarter of 1992 for $28 per share and the conversion value for the Cambridge Shopping Centres' convertible would be (36.9)($28.00) = $1033.20. Under these conditions, the market value of the common shares for which the convertible could be exchanged would be $1033.20. Thus, regardless of what this convertible debenture was selling for, it could be converted into $1033.20 worth of common shares.

---

[1]The convertibility feature is essentially a form of a call option on the firm's shares. The option has value.

[2]Note that the conversion price is similar to the idea of an exercise price of an option, and as the share price increases, the convertibility feature increases in value.

TABLE 20-1
Summary of Convertible
Terminology

Conversion ratio: the number of shares for which the convertible security can be exchanged.

$$\text{Conversion ratio} = \frac{\text{par value of convertible security}}{\text{conversion price}} \qquad (20\text{-}1)$$

Conversion value: the total market value of the common shares for which the convertible can be exchanged.

$$\text{Conversion value} = \text{conversion ratio} \times \text{market value per common share} \qquad (20\text{-}2)$$

Security value: the price the convertible security would sell for in the absence of its conversion feature.

Conversion period: the time period during which the convertible can be exchanged for common shares.

Conversion parity price: the price the investor is in effect paying for the common shares.

$$\text{Conversion parity price} = \frac{\text{market price of convertible security}}{\text{conversion ratio}} \qquad (20\text{-}4)$$

Conversion premium: the difference between the convertible's market price and the higher of its security value and its conversion value.

$$\begin{array}{c}\text{Conversion}\\\text{premium}\end{array} = \begin{pmatrix}\text{market price of}\\\text{the convertible}\end{pmatrix} - \begin{pmatrix}\text{higher of the security value}\\\text{and conversion value}\end{pmatrix} \qquad (20\text{-}5)$$

Reasons Given for Issuing Convertibles

There are several reasons that financial managers tend to give for choosing to issue convertibles rather than straight debt, preferred shares, or common shares. These reasons include "sweetening" the long-term debt issue to make it more attractive, delayed equity financing, financing corporate mergers, and the lack of a relationship between the interest rate and the issuing firm's risk level.

Sweetening Long-Term Debt

Before World War II the major reason for adding a convertible feature to preferred shares or debt was to make the security attractive enough to ensure a market for it. At that time convertibles were primarily limited to firms of lower credit standings that would have had a difficult time issuing straight debt or preferred shares. For these firms, adding a convertible feature would increase the attractiveness of the issue and thereby guarantee its success. Since World War II firms of higher credit standing have also entered the convertible market and issued convertibles for other reasons, whereas weaker firms have continued to use convertibles as sweeteners.

Delayed Equity Financing

A company may want to delay issuing of common shares for the following reasons: (1) management feels the current share price is temporarily depressed or (2) management is worried that issuing additional common shares will temporarily drive the firm's earnings per share down and result in a lower share price. As a result, management may resort to issuing convertible securities. Management's hope is that, after a short period of time, the common share price will rise and investors will trade their convertibles in for common shares. For example, if the price of Cambridge Shopping Centres common shares increased and investors subsequently exchanged their convertibles for common shares, they would have in effect purchased the common shares for the conversion parity price, $30.35. That is, for every share of Cambridge Shopping Centres exchanged for convertibles, investors originally received $30.35. Since Cambridge Shopping Centres has set its conversion parity price above the share's market price, the firm will have to give up fewer common shares when the securities are converted than if it raised funds via a common share offering originally. In effect, equity financing is provided only if the market value of the common shares increases. If it does not, financing remains in the form of lower-cost debt or preferred shares.

Although this may be an explanation financial managers commonly give to explain their use of convertible debt, it should be noted that it would be just as appropriate, in rationalizing why convertibles are issued, to look at what the firm's alternatives would have been if the share price increased and straight debt had been chosen. In that case the firm might have been better off as it could then replace the short-term debt with shares that may be selling well in excess of the conversion price.

Financing Corporate Mergers

If the shareholders of an acquired company take cash or debt in exchange for their common shares, they incur an immediate tax liability on any capital gains on their investment. If, however, the exchange is made for common, preferred, or convertible preferred shares, the tax liability is postponed, since the transaction is regarded as a tax-free exchange. Thus, many mergers are financed with common or convertible preferred shares.

Convertible preferred shares frequently provide the most attractive terms possible for the exchange. Holders of shares in the company being acquired can be offered the stable income and limited risk of preferred shares, plus the chance for capital gains afforded by the convertible feature. The issuing company also benefits from the use of convertible preferred shares rather than common shares in that less dilution of earnings occurs. The reason is that investors would have demanded additional common shares if the exchange had been made for straight common shares.

The Convertible's Interest Rate Indifference to the Issuing Firm's Risk Level

While higher risk and uncertainty bring on higher interest costs in straight debt, this is not necessarily the case with convertibles. If we think about a convertible as a package of straight debt and a convertible feature allowing the holder to purchase common shares at a set price, an increase in risk and uncertainty will cause the cost of the straight-debt portion of the convertible to increase. However, the convertibility feature benefits from this increase in risk and uncertainty and the increase in share price volatility that follows. In effect the conversion feature only has value if the share price increases; otherwise it has zero value. The more risk and share price volatility, the greater the likelihood that the conversion feature will be of value at some point before the expiration date. As a result, the additional risk and uncertainty increase the value of the conversion feature of the convertible. Thus, the negative effect of an increase in risk and uncertainty on the straight-debt portion of a convertible is partially offset by the positive effect on the conversion feature. The result of all this is that the interest rate associated with convertible debt is, to an extent, indifferent to the risk level of the issuing firm. The Basic Financial Management in Practice feature "Michael J. Brennan and Eduardo S. Schwartz on the Case for Convertibles" speaks to this issue.

BASIC FINANCIAL MANAGEMENT IN PRACTICE

Michael J. Brennan and Eduardo S. Schwartz on the Case for Convertibles

The institutional explanation of convertibles is that certain financial institutions are restricted as to the amount of common shares they can hold, and that convertibles provide a means by which such institutions can increase their equity position. There may be an element of truth in this. But the further suggestion that such institutions bid up the price of convertibles so that companies can reduce their financing costs by appealing to this restricted segment of the market is unlikely to be true.

A more reasonable account of capital market behavior would show that firms in aggregate supply enough convertibles to satisfy the demand of this segment of the market, so that there are no "scarcity rents"—or, in this case, major cost reductions—to be had. After all, chocolate manufacturers do not expect to make more money on sugarless chocolate because diabetics are prohibited from consuming the regular kind. By the same logic, this preference for convertibles by some institutions should not provide any significant cost reduction to companies issuing them.

A more convincing rationale for convertibles—one that has received a good deal of support in the academic finance community—centers on the effect of changes in risk on the value of securities. Recall that, as a general rule, the higher the risk associated with a company's operations (and the

greater the market's uncertainty about that risk), the higher the interest cost that a company will be forced to pay. At least, on its straight debt. In the case of convertibles, however, higher risk may not mean a correspondingly greater burden of financing costs for the issuing company. That is, the use of convertibles may effectively shelter companies of high and indeterminate risk from prohibitively high costs of straight debt capital.

To see why this is true, note that a convertible is roughly equivalent to a package of straight debt and warrants. [Note: a warrant, which we talk about next in this chapter, is an option to purchase a fixed number of common shares at a predetermined price.] Instead of issuing a $1,000 bond which is convertible into 21.74 shares at a conversion price of $46, a corporation could issue a package of one $1,000 straight bond and 21.74 warrants with an exercise price of $46; and the consequences would be almost identical. Such bond-warrant combinations are indeed a quite popular alternative to convertible bonds.

How, then, would warrants in combination with a debt offering affect investors' perception of the risks involved in holding such securities? Although there are exceptions to this rule, companies with higher operating and financial risk tend to have more volatile share prices. As noted earlier,

Perspective in Finance

Given what you have learned so far about convertibles, it makes sense that convertibles tend to be issued most frequently by smaller firms with lower bond ratings, high growth rates, and more than average leverage. In addition, convertibles tend to be subordinated and unsecured.

Other Factors to Be Considered

Overhanging Issue

An **overhanging issue** occurs if the firm cannot force conversion because the common shares have not increased sufficiently to justify it. The overhanging issue's major disadvantage to the firm is that it limits financing flexibility. Not only does it make additional financing with convertible securities practically impossible, but it may also make long-term debt unacceptable to investors if the firm has been relying on a successful conversion to bring its companies with higher risk, and, hence, greater price volatility pay higher rates for straight debt. And increases in the market's perception of a company's risk will cause a reduction in the value of its straight bonds.

The effect of increased risk and volatility on a warrant, however, is the opposite. Remember that the holder of a warrant profits from increases in the share price above the exercise price, but is protected against declines below the exercise price. That is, there is an "asymmetry" in the return to the warrant which increases as the spread of possible future share prices widens. In other words, as the risk and price volatility of the company increases, the value of the warrant increases. For instance, a warrant on the shares of an electronics company will be worth considerably more than a warrant (with the same conditions) on a utility's shares.

In the case of a convertible security, then, the effect of an increase in risk on the cost of a straight debt offering is offset, to an extent by its effect on the value of the warrant. As a result, the value of an appropriately designed convertible security (or its equivalent package of straight debt and warrants) will be largely unaffected by the risk of the issuing firm.

Practically, this means that two companies at different points along the risk spectrum, facing very different costs of straight debt, could issue convertibles with nearly identical maturities, conversion premiums and coupon rates. Such a case is illustrated [at the right]. Note that while the terms of the convertible debt sold by the medium- and high-risk companies are almost identical, the proportions of the convertible's value which are accounted for by the straight debt element and by the conversion feature will be quite different. For the higher-risk company, less of the convertible's value will be accounted for by the straight debt component, and correspondingly more by the conversion or warrant element.

Coupon Rates Required on New Issues of Straight and Convertible Debt

	Company Risk	
	Medium	High
Convertible Debt	11%	11.25%
Straight Debt	14%	16%

We are not suggesting, in this example, that convertibles offer higher-risk companies a "free-lunch."[3] We are arguing, however, that the inclusion of warrants in a debt package provides a kind of financing "synergy" which allows companies with high and uncertain risk to raise capital on more advantageous terms.

Source: Michael J. Brennan and Eduardo S. Schwartz, "The Case for Convertibles," *Chase Financial Quarterly*, 1 (Spring 1982), pp. 27–46, reprinted in *Journal of Applied Corporate Finance*, 1 (Summer 1988), pp. 55–64.

financial structure back to normal. If this is the case, the conversion has been thwarted by an insufficient increase in the common share price; the only available alternative may be a common shares offering. However, this too may be unacceptable or at least undesirable to the firm's management if it feels the common share price is temporarily depressed.

---

[3]This example is not meant to suggest that because the terms of the two convertible issues are nearly identical, the cost of the convertible is identical for the two companies. Remember that convertible debt is a hybrid security, partly straight debt and partly [a call option on the company's] equity. The opportunity cost of a convertible debt issue should thus be thought of as a weighted average of the company's cost of debt and equity capital. For the higher-risk company in this example, the fact that it has both a higher cost of straight debt and a higher implicit cost of equity suggests that its convertible will have a higher implicit cost. But, more important, the fact that a much greater portion of the value of its convertible rests in the warrant or equity component means that the convertible holder has been promised a more substantial equity stake in the higher-risk company; this, of course, translates into a higher opportunity cost of capital.

Forced Conversion

Although investors have full legal control over the exercise of a convertible security, the firm can often force their investors to convert by calling the convertible or establishing step-up conversion prices. If, for example, the conversion value of a security exceeds its call price, the firm need only call the security to force any rational investor to convert.[4] A second way of inducing conversion is to provide for increasingly larger conversion prices and thus lower conversion ratios over the years. A convertible debenture with a $1,000 par value could have a conversion price of $50 per share for the first five years and $60 per share after that. Suppose the price of the common shares had increased to $100 per share after five years—an investor would have the choice of converting the security into 20 common shares worth $2,000 or not converting and watching the conversion value of the security drop to $1,666.67 as the conversion price is increased to $60 per share. In most cases a step-up conversion price provides enough incentive to induce conversion as long as the conversion value is greater than the security value of the convertible.

Valuation of a Convertible

The valuation of a convertible depends primarily upon two factors: the value of the straight debenture or preferred shares and the value of the security if it were converted into common shares. Complicating the valuation is the fact that investors are in general willing to pay a premium for the conversion privilege, which allows them to hedge against the future. If the price of the common shares should rise, the investor would participate in capital gains; if it should decline, the convertible security will fall only to its value as a straight debenture or preferred shares.

In examining the Cambridge Shopping Centres convertible debenture we found that if it were selling as a straight debenture, its price would be $819.59. Thus, regardless of what happens to the company's common shares, the lowest the value of the convertible can drop to is $819.59. The conversion value, on the other hand is, $1033.20. Thus, this convertible is worth more as common shares than if it were straight debt. However, the real question is: Why are investors willing to pay a conversion premium of 8.4 percent over its security or conversion value for this Cambridge Shopping Centres debenture? Quite simply because investors are willing to pay for the chance for capital gains without the large risk of loss.

Figure 20-1 illustrates the relationship between the value of the convertible and the price of its common shares. The bond value of the convertible serves as a floor for the value of the investment: When the conversion value reaches the convertible's security value (point A), the value of the convertible becomes dependent upon its conversion value. In effect the convertible security is valued as a bond when the price of the common shares is low and as a common share when the price of the common shares increases. Of course, if the firm is doing poorly and in financial distress, both the common share price and the security value will suffer. In the worst-case scenario in which a firm's total value falls to zero, the firm's common shares and debt would have no value. Although the minimum price of the convertible is

[4]The call provision adds negative value to the bond issue. The firm is granted an option by the bondholders.

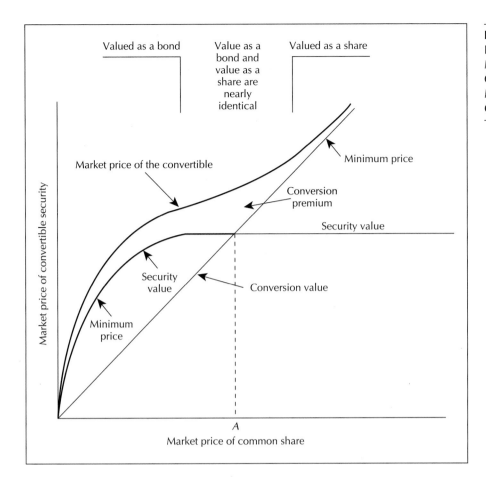

FIGURE 20-1
Relationship Between the
Market Price of the
Common Shares and the
Market Price of the
Convertible Security

determined by the higher of either the straight bond or preferred share price or the conversion value, investors also pay a premium for the conversion option. Again, this premium results because convertible securities offer investors stable income from the debentures or the preferred shares, and thus less risk of price decline due to adverse share conditions, while retaining capital gains prospects from share price gains. In effect, downside share price variability is hedged away, and upside variability is not.

Perspective in Finance

As you look at the convertibles, warrants, options, and futures markets, keep in mind the fact that these markets are continuously evolving. For example, recently a variation of the convertible debenture called an exchangeable debenture has gained popularity. An exchangeable debenture is similar to a convertible debenture except that it can be exchanged at the option of the holder for the common shares of another company. For example, in 1992 Canadian Pacific Limited placed a $105 million issue of unsecured equity exchangeable debentures maturing in 1995. These debentures are identical to convertibles except that they can be exchanged for common shares of United Dominion Industries. The point here is that in this chapter we are only describing several basic securities of which there are unlimited variations in the financial markets.

BASIC FINANCIAL MANAGEMENT IN PRACTICE

The following article describes some of the trends in corporate financing that has occurred in the early nineties.

There have been two big trends on the corporate finance scene in the early nineties. In 1991, investors wanted a little protection for the new issues they were buying, so issuers sold unit offerings, with each unit consisting of a common share plus half a share purchase warrant. A full warrant entitled the holder to purchase a common share at a premium to the issue price. In 1992, the fad was issues being done on an instalment receipt basis. On those deals, investors paid part of the purchase price when the deal closed and the rest later on. For most deals, there were two instalments; occasionally there were three. Instalments were popular on both secondary offerings (where a controlling shareholder was selling a stake) and on new offerings. British Petroleum, RTZ, LASMO PLC, Occidental Petroleum, British Gas and Interprovincial Pipe Line all used this structure for secondary issues, while Suncor used instalments for its new offering when it was effectively privatized.

New Twist on Convertible Debentures

Over 1992, raising equity using, "instalment receipts" has become the norm for large deals. That structure—where an investor pays part of the purchase price of the shares at the time the deal is done and the balance later—offers advantages to all parties.

Buyers like instalment receipts because they only put up 50% of the overall purchase price, but receive a full dividend—effectively doubling their first-year dividend return. Issuers like them because the structure makes possible a bigger deal than could otherwise be done.

Now, thanks to the creative talents of Dennis Dewan, a corporate finance professional at Midland Walwyn Capital Inc., the concept has been extended to convertible debentures. The breakthrough deal is the sale by Brascan Ltd. of $250 million worth of convertible debentures.

The instalment receipt feature is the key innovation of this issue. Brascan will receive the proceeds in two equal instalments—half when the deal closes in October and the rest in one year's time. Receiving the second instalment in a year means the overall amount Brascan will receive in today's terms has to be discounted to reflect the time value of money. Depending on the discount rate used, the gross proceeds to Brascan are probably worth about $19.50 in October terms.

Source: Adapted from: Barry Critchley, "Referendum a Block to New Stock Issues," *The Financial Post* (October 12, 1992) p. 19; and "New Twist on Convertible Debentures," *The Financial Post* (September 21, 1992), p. 26.

WARRANTS

A **warrant** provides the investor with an option to purchase a fixed number of common shares at a predetermined price during a specified time period. Warrants have been used in the past primarily by weaker firms as "sweetener" attachments to bonds or preferred shares to improve their marketability. In 1988, Hollinger Inc. issued warrants with adjustable rate convertible subordinated debentures. Each warrant entitles the holder to purchase one common share for $20 from October 1, 1993 to September 30, 1998. Investment dealers have also used warrants to enable companies to raise capital in the financial markets by combining common shares with warrants to form a "unit." Again, the purpose of a warrant is essentially the same as when they are issued in conjunction with debt or preferred shares; that is, to improve the reception in the market of the new offering or make a tender offer too attractive to turn down.

Although warrants are similar to convertibles in that both provide investors with a chance to participate in capital gains, the mechanics of the two instruments differ greatly. From the standpoint of the issuing firm there are two major differences. First, when convertibles are exchanged for common shares, debt is eliminated and fixed finance charges are reduced; whereas, an exchange of warrants for common shares does not reduce the fixed finance charges. Second, when convertibles are exchanged there is no cash inflow into the firm—the exchange is one type of security for another. But with warrants, since they are options to buy shares at a set price, a cash flow accompanies the exchange.[5]

Characteristics and Features of Warrants

Exercise Price

The **exercise price** represents the price at which the warrant allows its holder to purchase the firm's common shares. The investor trades a warrant plus the exercise price for common shares. Typically, when warrants are issued the exercise price is set above the current market price of the shares. Thus, if the share price does not rise above the exercise price, the warrant will never be converted. In addition there is also a step-up exercise price—that is, a warrant with which the exercise price changes over time.

Expiration Date

Although some warrants are issued with no expiration date, most warrants are set to expire after a number of years. In issuing warrants as opposed to convertibles, the firm gives up some control over when the warrants will be exercised. An issuing company can force conversion of a convertible debenture issue by calling the issue or using step-up conversion prices, whereas with warrants only the approach of the expiration date or the use of step-up exercise prices can encourage conversion.

Detachability

Most warrants are said to be detachable in that they can be sold separately from the security to which they were originally attached. Thus, if an investor purchases a primary issuance of a corporate bond with a warrant attached, he or she has the option of selling the bond alone, selling the warrant alone, or selling the combination intact. Nondetachable warrants cannot be sold separately from the security to which they were originally attached. Such a warrant can be separated from the senior security only by being exercised.

Exercise Ratio

The **exercise ratio** states the number of shares that can be obtained at the exercise price with one warrant. If the exercise ratio on a warrant were 1.5, one warrant would entitle its owner to purchase 1.5 shares of common shares at its exercise price.

Reasons for Issuing Warrants

Sweetening Debt

Warrants attached to debt offerings provide a feature whereby investors can participate in capital gains while holding debt. The firm can thereby increase

---

[5]Warrants are essentially call options. The major differences are that warrants are issued by firms and so there is a limited supply and they have a much longer maturity (two years or more rather than nine months).

the demand for the issue, increase the proceeds, and lower the interest costs. The attachment of warrants to long-term debt provides a potential equity stake to the debt holder. As a result, a warrant increases the marketability and demand for the company's debt.

Additional Cash Inflow

If warrants are added to sweeten a debt offering, the firm will receive an eventual cash inflow when and if the warrants are exercised; a conversion feature would not provide this additional inflow.

Other Factors to Be Considered

Preservation of Debt

When warrants are exercised, the debt or security to which they were originally attached remains in existence. The process of exercising a warrant by an investor provides an additional cash inflow to the company, but this process does not eliminate the original security. In contrast, the process of exercising convertible debt causes no cash flow to occur, but the original security is eliminated. Thus, the decision between convertible and warrant financing becomes a tradeoff between the elimination of debt versus the receipt of additional cash inflows.

Dilution and Flexibility

Since present accounting standards provide that earnings per share be stated as if all the warrants outstanding had been exercised, warrants have the effect of reducing the firm's reported earnings per share. This potential dilution of earnings per share may reduce the firm's financing flexibility. Because of previously issued warrants, the issuance of additional common shares may be hindered or even prohibited. The market's reluctance to accept further equity offerings may be due not only to the potential earnings per share dilution effect of the outstanding warrants, but also to a feeling that only weaker firms have to resort to warrant financing to sweeten their senior security offerings.

Valuation of a Warrant

Since the warrant is an option to purchase a specified number of shares at a specified price for a given length of time, the market value of the warrant will be primarily a function of the common share price. To understand the valuation of warrants we must define two additional terms, the minimum price and the premium. Let us look at the Hollinger warrant that was issued in 1988 with an expiration date of September 30, 1998, an exercise ratio of 1.00, and an exercise price of $20 through the expiration date. This means that any time until expiration on September 30, 1992, an investor with one warrant can purchase one common share of Hollinger at $20 regardless of the market price of those shares. In 1992 these Hollinger warrants were selling at $2.70 and the Hollinger shares were selling for $12.75 per share.

MINIMUM PRICE ■ The **minimum price** of a warrant is determined as follows:

$$\text{minimum price} = \begin{pmatrix} \text{market price of} \\ \text{common shares} \end{pmatrix} - \begin{pmatrix} \text{exercise} \\ \text{price} \end{pmatrix} \times \begin{pmatrix} \text{exercise} \\ \text{ratio} \end{pmatrix} \quad (20\text{-}7)$$

In the Hollinger example the exercise price is greater than the price of the common shares ($20 as opposed to $12.75). In this case the minimum price of the warrant is considered to be zero, because things simply do not sell for negative prices [($12.75 − $20) × 1.00 = –$7.25]. For example, if the price of the Hollinger common shares increased to $26 per share, the minimum price on the warrant would become ($26 − $20) × 1.00 = $6. This would tell us that this warrant could not fall below a price of $6.00, because if it did, investors could realize immediate trading profits by purchasing the warrants and converting them along with the $20 exercise price into common shares until the price of the warrant was pushed up to the minimum price. This process of simultaneously buying and selling equivalent assets for different prices is called *arbitrage*.

PREMIUM ■ The **premium** is the amount above the minimum price for which the warrant sells:

premium = (market price of warrant) − (minimum price of warrant)   (20-8)

In the case of the Hollinger warrant the premium is $2.70 − $0 = $2.70. Investors are paying a premium of $2.70 above the minimum price for the warrant. The potential downside of this investment to the investor is the warrant's market price which represents 21.1 percent of the common share's price. The potential return is large given that value of the warrant increases as the price of the common share increases.

The relationships among the warrant price, the minimum price, and the premium are illustrated graphically in Figure 20-2. Point A represents the exercise price on the warrant. Once the price of the shares is above the exercise price, the warrant's minimum price takes on positive (or nonzero) values.

A hypothetical numerical example based upon Figure 20-2 is provided in Table 20-2. Looking at the graphic representation of the warrant and the example, we find that the warrant premium tends to drop off as the ratio of the share price to the exercise price climbs. Why? As the share price climbs, the warrant loses its leverage ability. Looking at the numerical example, assume an investor purchased $1,000 worth of warrants and $1,000 worth of common shares when the common share price was $40 and the warrant

FIGURE 20-2
Valuation of Warrants

TABLE 20-2
Hypothetical Warrant
Example

Share Price, SP	Exercise Price, EP	Exercise Ratio, ER	Minimum Price: (SP – EP) × ER = MP	Hypothetical Warrant Price, WP	Premium, WP – MP	Share Price/ Exercise Price Ratio, SP/EP
$ 30	$40	1	$ 0	$ 5	$ 5	75 %
40	40	1	0	10	10	100
50	40	1	10	16	6	125
60	40	1	20	25	5	150
70	40	1	30	34	4	175
80	40	1	40	43	3	200
90	40	1	50	52	2	225
100	40	1	60	62	2	250
110	40	1	70	71	1	275
120	40	1	80	81	1	300
130	40	1	90	90	0	325

price was $10; then the price of the shares went up 50 percent to $60 per share, which caused the price of the warrant to go up 150 percent to $25 per share. This leverage feature—the fact that the value of the warrant increases and declines by larger percentages than the value of the underlying shares and thus a small investment has large possible returns—encourages investors to purchase warrants. However, as the share price increases, the leverage ability of the warrant declines. For example, assume that an investor purchases $1,000 worth of common shares selling at $110 per share and $1,000 worth of warrants selling for $71 per share. If the share price went up to $130, the investment in shares would have returned 18 percent and the warrant price would have increased to $90 for a return of 27 percent. In the first example when the share price increased from $40 to $60 per share, the warrant resulted in profits three times greater than on the common shares. In the second example the warrant provided profits only about one and one-half times larger than the common shares. Thus, the warrant premium tends to drop off as the ratio of the share price to the exercise price climbs and the leverage ability of the warrant declines.

Although the share price/exercise price ratio is one of the most important factors in determining the size of the premium, several other factors also affect it. One such factor is the time left until the warrant expiration date. As the warrant's expiration date approaches, the size of the premium begins to shrink, approaching zero. A second factor is investors' expectations concerning the capital gains potential of the shares. If investors expect that the price of the underlying common share will increase, the premium paid for the warrant will also increase because of the relation between the price of the shares and the price of the warrant. Finally, the degree of price volatility on the underlying common shares affects the size of the warrant premium. The more volatile the common share price, the higher the warrant premium. As price volatility increases, so does the probability of and potential size of profits.

FUTURES

Both warrant and convertible debentures are financial instruments which are created by the firm. We now look at two additional financial instruments that are similar to warrants and convertibles but are not created by the firm: futures and options. Despite the fact that these instruments are not issued by the firm, it is important for us to be familiar with them for two reasons. First, these instruments can be used to reduce the risks associated with interest and exchange rate and commodity price fluctuations. Second, as you will see in future finance courses, an understanding of the pricing of options is extremely valuable because many different financial assets can be viewed as options. In fact, warrants, convertible bonds, risky bonds, common shares, and the abandonment decision can all be thought of as types of options.

Perspective in Finance

Although there are many uses for futures and options, our interest focuses on how financial managers use these financial instruments to reduce risk. Keeping this in mind, you will see how they can be used to effectively offset future movements in the price of commodities or interest rates. Options are used to eliminate the effect of unfavourable price movements, and futures are used to eliminate the effect of both favourable and unfavourable price movements.

Commodity and financial futures are perhaps the fastest-growing and in many respects most exciting new financial instrument today. Financial managers who only a few years ago would not have considered venturing into the futures market are now actively using this market to eliminate risk. As the number of participants in this market has grown, so has the number of items on which future contracts are offered, ranging from the old standbys like wheat, oats, and flaxseed to the newer ones like bankers' acceptances and the TSE 35 Index.

A **futures contract** is a contract to buy or sell a stated commodity (such as wheat and oats) or financial claim (such as Government of Canada bonds) at a specified price at some future specified time. It is important to note here that this is a contract that requires its holder to buy or sell the asset, regardless of what happens to its value during the interim. The importance of a futures contract is that it can be used by financial managers to lock in the price of a commodity or an interest rate and thereby eliminate one source of risk. For example, if a corporation is planning on issuing debt in the near future and is concerned about a possible rise in interest rates between now and when the debt would be issued, it might sell a Government of Canada bond contract with the same face value as the proposed debt offering and a delivery date the same as when the debt offering is to occur. Alternatively, Ralston-Purina or Quaker Oats can lock in the future price of corn or oats with the use of a futures contract. As a result, any costs associated with any possible rise in interest rates or commodity prices would be completely offset by the profits made by writing the futures interest rate contract. In effect, futures contracts allow the financial manager to lock in future interest and exchange rates or prices for a number of agricultural commodities like wheat, oats, and barley.

As the use of futures contracts becomes more common in the financial management of the firm, it is important for the financial manager to be familiar with the operation and terminology associated with these financial instruments.

An Introduction to the Futures Markets

The origins of the futures market go back into history to medieval times. In Canada, the origin of the first futures exchange can be traced to the

Winnipeg Grain and Produce Exchange which was formed by local grain merchants and farmers in 1887 and is now known as the Winnipeg Commodity Exchange. Several futures markets were initiated in the United States during the nineteenth century, but it was not until the establishment of the Chicago Board of Trade (CBT) in 1848 that the futures markets were provided with their roots. As we will see, while these markets have been in operation for years, it was not until the early 1970s, when the futures markets expanded from agricultural commodities to financial futures, that financial managers began to regularly venture into this market.

To develop an understanding for futures markets, let us examine several features that distinguish futures contracts from simple forward contracts. To begin with, a forward contract is any contract for delivery of an asset in the future. A futures contract is a specialized form of a forward contract distinguished by (1) an organized exchange, (2) a standardized contract with limited price changes and margin requirements, (3) a clearinghouse in each futures market, and (4) daily resettlement of contracts.

The Organized Exchange

The trading of futures in Canada occurs on the following exchanges: the Winnipeg Commodity Exchange, the Toronto Futures Exchange, and the Montreal Futures Exchange. In the United States, there are over 10 different futures exchanges in operation. In North America, the Chicago Board of Trade is the oldest and largest of the futures exchanges. The importance of having organized exchanges associated with the futures market is that they provide a central trading place. If there were no central trading place, then there would be no potential to generate the depth of trading necessary to support a secondary market, and in a very circular way the existence of a secondary market encourages more traders to enter the market and in turn provides additional liquidity.

An organized exchange also encourages confidence in the futures market by allowing for the effective regulation of trading. The various exchanges set and enforce rules and collect and disseminate information on trading activity and the commodities being traded. Together, the liquidity generated by having a central trading place, effective regulation, and the flow of information through the organized exchanges has effectively fostered their development.

Standardized Contracts

A strong secondary market is developed in any security if there are a large number of identical securities—or in this case, futures contracts—outstanding. In effect, standardization of contracts leads to more frequent trades on that contract, leading to greater liquidity in the secondary market for that contract, which in turn draws more traders into the market. It is for this reason that futures contracts are highly standardized and very specific with respect to the description of the goods to be delivered and the time and place of delivery. Let's look at a Winnipeg Commodity Exchange canola contract. This contract calls for the delivery of 20 metric tonnes of No. 1 Canada grade canola to Vancouver at $309.40 per tonne. In addition, these contracts are written to come due in November, January, March, June and September. Through this standardization of contracts, trading has built up in enough identical contracts to allow for the development of a strong and highly liquid secondary market.

To encourage investors to participate in the futures market, daily price limits are set on all futures contracts. Without these limits, there would be more price volatility on most futures contracts than many investors would be willing to accept. These daily price limits are set to protect investors, maintain order on the futures exchanges, and encourage the level of trading volume necessary to develop a strong secondary market. For example, the Winnipeg Commodity Exchange imposes a $10.00 per tonne ($200 per contract) price movement limit above and below the previous day's settlement price of canola contracts. This limit protects against runaway price movements. These daily price limits do not halt trading once the limit has been reached, but they do provide a boundary within which trading must occur. The price of a canola contract may rise 10 dollars very early in the trading day—"up the limit" in futures jargon. This will not stop trading; it only means that no trade can take place above that level. As a result, any dramatic shifts in the market price of a futures contract must take place over a number of days, with the price of the contract going "up the limit" each day.

Futures Clearinghouse

The main purpose of the futures clearinghouse is to guarantee that all trades will be honoured. This is done by having the clearinghouse interpose itself as the buyer to every seller and the seller to every buyer. Because of this substitution of parties, it is not necessary for the original seller (or buyer) to find the original buyer (or seller) when he or she decides to clear his or her position. As a result, all an individual has to do is make an equal and opposite transaction that will provide a net zero position with the clearinghouse and cancel out that individual's obligation. The Winnipeg Commodity Clearing Ltd. acts as the clearinghouse for the Winnipeg Commodity Exchange.

The trading of futures contracts occur between an individual and the clearinghouse. This type of clearing mechanism ensures that buyers and sellers will realize their market gains. There are other important benefits of a clearinghouse, including providing a mechanism for the delivery of commodities and the settlement of disputed trades, but these benefits also serve to encourage trading in the futures markets and thereby create a highly liquid secondary market.

Daily Resettlement of Contracts

Another safeguard of the futures market is a margin requirement. Although margin requirements on futures resemble margin requirements on shares in that there is an initial margin and a maintenance margin that comes into play when the value of the contract declines, similarities between futures and shares margins end there.

Before we explore margin requirements on futures it would be helpful to develop an understanding of the meaning of a margin on futures. The concept of a margin on futures contracts has a meaning that is totally different from its usage in reference to common shares. The margin on common shares refers to the amount of equity the investor has invested in the shares. With a futures contract, no equity has been invested, since nothing has been bought. In fact, the only consequences of signing a futures contract are the obligation of the two parties to participate in a future transaction and the definition of the terms of that transaction. This is an important thought: There is no actual buying or selling taking place with a futures contract; it is merely an agreement to buy or sell some commodity in the future. As a result, the term *futures margin* refers to "good faith" money the purchaser puts down to ensure that the contract will be carried out.

The initial margin required for commodities (deposited by both buyer and seller) is much lower than the margin required for common shares, generally amounting to only 3 to 10 percent of the value of the contract. For example, if December oats contracts on the Winnipeg Commodity Exchange were selling at $111.00 per metric tonne, then one contract for 5,000 metric tonnes would be selling for $111.00 × 20 = $2220.00. The initial margin on oats is $100 per contract, which represents only about 4.5 percent of the contract price. Needless to say, the leverage associated with futures trading is tremendous—both on the up and down sides. Small changes in the price of the underlying commodity result in very large changes in the value of the futures contract, since very little has to be put down to "own" a contract. Moreover, for many futures contracts, if the financial manager can satisfy the broker that he or she is not engaged in trading as a speculator, but as a hedger, the manager can qualify for reduced initial margins. Because of the low level of the initial margin, there is also a maintenance or variation margin requirement that forces the investor or financial manager to replenish the margin account to a level specified by the exchange after any market loss.

One additional point related to margins deserves mention. The initial margin requirement can be fulfilled by supplying cash, irrevocable letters of credit, Canadian treasury bills, and U.S. treasury bills held in Canadian banks. The advantage of using treasury bills as margin is that the investor earns money on them, whereas brokerage firms do not pay interest on funds in commodity cash accounts. Moreover, if the financial manager is going to carry treasury bills anyway, he or she can just deposit the treasury bills with the broker and purchase the futures contracts with no additional cash outlay.

Suppose you are a manager for Ralston-Purina and are in charge of purchasing raw materials—in particular, oats. For example, a December futures contract for the delivery of oats has a price of $111.00 per metric tonne. The company requires oats for the processing of its product in December. As a manager, you feel that this is an exceptional price and that oats will probably be selling for more than that in December. Thus, you wish to lock in this price, and to do this you purchase one contract for 20 metric tonnes at $111.00 per metric tonne. Upon purchasing the December oats contract the only cash you would have to put up would be the initial margin of $100. Let's further assume that the price of oats futures then falls to a level of $110.00 per metric tonne the day after you make your purchase. In effect, you have incurred a loss of $1 per metric tonne on 20 metric tonnes, for a total loss on your investment of $20.

At this point the concept of daily resettlement comes into play. What this means is that all futures positions are brought to the market at the end of each trading day and all gains and losses, in this case a loss, are then settled. You have lost $20, which is then subtracted from your margin account, lowering it to $80 ($100 initially less the $20 loss). Since your margin account has fallen below the maintenance margin on oats, which is $100, you would have to replenish your account back to its initial level of $100. If on the following day the price of December oats contracts increased $1.50 per metric tonne, you would have made $1.50 per metric tonne on 20 metric tonnes, for a total profit of $30. This brings your margin account up from $100 to $130, which is $30 above the initial margin of $100. You can withdraw this $30 from your margin account.

Obviously, the purpose of margin requirements is to provide some measure of safety for futures traders, and despite the very small level of margin requirements imposed, they do a reasonable job. They are set in accordance with the historical price volatility of the underlying commodity in such a way that it is extremely unlikely that a trader will ever lose more than is in his or her margin account in any one day.

Commodity Futures

As mentioned previously, the futures market is well developed in North America and extends beyond agricultural commodities to commodity types, such as metals, wood products, fibers, livestock, and petroleum. A few examples of these commodities include lumber, orange juice, cotton, gold, platinum, silver, cattle, hogs, pork bellies, crude oil, heating oil, unleaded gasoline and natural gas. For the financial manager these markets provide a means of offsetting the risks associated with future price changes. Here the financial manager is securing a future price for a good that is currently in production, or securing a future price for some commodity that must be purchased in the future. In either case, the manager is using the futures market to eliminate the effects of future price changes on the future purchase or sale of some commodity.

Financial Futures

In Canada, financial futures come in the forms of Government of Canada bonds, bankers acceptances, and the TSE 35 Index. However, in the United States financial futures come in a number of different forms, including treasury bills, notes and bonds, municipal bonds, certificates of deposit, Eurodollars, foreign currencies, and stock indexes. Financial futures first appeared in North America in 1972 in the form of futures on gold and foreign currency. In Canada, the Winnipeg Commodity Exchange began trading financial futures in 1981 but withdrew their facilities in 1985. However, Toronto Futures Exchange trades financial futures on the TSE 35 Index and the Montreal Futures Exchange trade financial futures on Government of Canada bonds and bankers acceptances. Our discussion of financial futures will be divided into three sections: (1) interest rate futures, (2) foreign exchange futures, and (3) stock index futures.

INTEREST RATE FUTURES ■ Currently, Government of Canada bond futures contracts are the most popular futures contract traded in the Canadian futures market. This type of popularity is also seen in the U.S. futures market; the Treasury bond futures are the most popular of all futures contracts in terms of contracts issued. The fact that these interest rate futures contracts are risk-free, long-term bonds with a maturity of at least 15 years has been the deciding factor in making them the most popular of the interest rate futures.

For the financial manager, interest rate futures provide an excellent means for eliminating the risks associated with interest rate fluctuations. As we learned earlier, there is an inverse relationship between bond prices in the secondary market and yields—that is, when interest rates fall bond prices rise, and when interest rates rise bond prices fall. If you think back to the chapter on valuation, you will recall that this inverse relationship between bond prices and yield is a result of the fact that when bonds are issued, their coupon rate is fixed. For the Government of Canada bond futures contract the bond's coupon interest rate is fixed at 9.00%. However, once the bond is issued it must compete in the market with other financial instruments. Since new bonds are issued to yield the current interest rates, yields on old bonds must adjust to remain competitive with the newer issues. Thus, when interest rates rise, the price of an older bond with a lower coupon interest rate must decline to increase the yield on the old bond, making it competitive with the return on newly issued bonds.

Interest rate futures offer investors a very inexpensive way of eliminating the risks associated with interest rate fluctuations. For example, banks, pension funds, and insurance companies all make considerable use of the interest rate futures market to avoid paper losses that might otherwise occur when interest rates unexpectedly increase. Corporations also use interest rate futures to lock in interest rates when they are planning to issue debt. If interest rates rise before the corporation has the opportunity to issue the new debt, the profits on the Government of Canada bond futures contracts they have sold will offset the increased costs associated with the proposed debt offering. Several possible uses for bond futures are given in Table 20-3.

FOREIGN CURRENCY FUTURES ■ Of all the financial futures, foreign currency futures have been around the longest, first appearing in 1972. In North America, the Chicago Mercantile Exchange operates the largest market for foreign currency futures. This type of future works in the same way as other futures, but in this case the commodity is Canadian dollars, German marks, British pounds, or some other foreign currency. As we will see, the similarities between these futures and the others we have examined are great. Not only do foreign currency futures work in the same way as other futures, but they also are used by financial managers for the same basic reasons—to hedge away risks, in this case the risk of currency rate. One of the major participants in the foreign currency futures market is the exporter who will receive foreign currency when its exported goods are finally received and who uses this market to lock in a certain exchange rate. As a result, the

TABLE 20-3
How Features of Bond
Futures Are Used

Protect Portfolio Value and Return: Pension funds, banks, corporations, insurance companies and individual investors can use bond futures as a hedge against losses incurred on fixed-income portfolios when interest rates rise and prices decline. Careful timing in the placement of a hedge can protect the holding period return of a portfolio containing notes and other related instruments. Futures offer flexibility to money managers by allowing them to adapt to a changing market.

Protect Issuance Costs: Corporations that plan to issue intermediate-term debt can control their interest cost by selling bond futures and offsetting the position when the issue comes to market. By hedging, the issuer can take advantage of today's lower rates, thus lessening the cost of raising capital.

Transfer Risk: Underwriters of corporate issues can sell futures to transfer the risk between the time they buy the debt securities until the time they are sold to dealers and investors.

Hedge Participation in Government Auctions: Primary government securities dealers can use the new contract to hedge participation in auctions. Bond futures allow government securities dealers to remain competitive and offer a better price to their customers.

Lock in a Favorable Rate of Return: Portfolio managers can hedge the reinvestment rate of coupon income. If interest rates decline, the reinvestment rate will diminish for note holders. Buying futures today as a substitute for later investments allows the investor to hedge a drop in rates. If rates fall, the decreased return on reinvestment will be offset by a gain in the futures position. If rates rise, the loss on the futures position will be offset by a higher return on investment.

Source: *Ten Year Treasury Futures* (Chicago: Chicago Board of Trade, 1983).

exporter is unaffected by any exchange rate fluctuations that might occur before receiving payment. Foreign currency futures are also used to hedge away possible fluctuations in the value of earnings of foreign subsidiaries.

In the eighties and nineties fluctuations in exchange rates became common. With foreign currency futures a financial manager could eliminate the effects—good or bad—of exchange rate fluctuation with a relatively small investment. The extremely high degree of leverage that was available coupled with the dramatic fluctuations in foreign exchange rates in the 1980s encouraged many financial managers to consider entering the currency rate futures market. One example of a dramatic price movement came as the British pound dropped to a value of just over U.S. $1.07 in early 1985. To get a feel for the degree of leverage experienced in the foreign currency futures market and the large profits and losses that can occur in this market let's look at Figure 20-3, which examines profits and losses resulting from buying and selling British pound futures.

Figure 20-3 illustrates an example of how fortunes can be made or lost by those investing in foreign currency futures. Some firms no doubt save themselves enormous losses by hedging away exchange rate risk, while others benefit by the dramatic swing in the exchange rate. Over just five trading days, the value of an investment in British pound futures went up almost threefold, while the return on the initial margin investment for those selling British pounds dropped almost threefold. Needless to say, the foreign currency futures market is a very risky market, characterized by extreme leverage both on the up and down side and periodic major movements in the underlying values of the foreign exchange currencies. To the financial manager, this market provides a perfect mechanism for eliminating the effect of exchange rate fluctuations.

FIGURE 20-3
Profits and Losses on British Pound Futures in March 1985

STOCK INDEX FUTURES ■ Stock indexes have been around for many years but it has only been recently that financial managers and investors have had the opportunity to trade them directly. In North America, the Kansas City Board of Trade began trading listed stock index futures in 1982. Their index was based on the Value Line Index. It was not until 1984 that the Toronto Futures Exchange began trading the TSE 300 futures contract based on the TSE 300 Composite Index. In 1987 the Toronto Futures Exchange launched the Toronto 35 Index and various derivative products designed to meet the needs of professional fund managers and private investors. The creation of the Toronto 35 Index futures contract enables traders to hedge a portfolio of shares more effectively since the shares of this index are among the largest listed on the TSE and are all actively traded. As a result, both the popularity of the Toronto 35 Index and ease that traders can replicate the Toronto 35 Index, caused the TSE 300 futures contract to be delisted in 1987.

At this point, after looking at other futures contracts, the workings of stock index futures should be clear. They work basically the same way, with one major exception: Stock index futures contracts allow only for cash settlement. There is no delivery, since what is being traded is the future price of the index, not the underlying shares in the index. Currently there are several stock index futures available, with futures on the S&P 500 index clearly dominating in terms of volume. Table 20-4 shows the characteristics of the TSE 35 Index futures contract.

The Toronto 35 Index futures contract is based on shares which have been chosen because they are some of Canada's larger publicly listed corporations and are among the most heavily traded issues on the TSE. The Toronto 35 Index is a modified market value weighted index. A limit of 10 percent has been placed on the weighting on any one share, such that no one company or industry dominates the index. The contract size or value of each contract is $500 times the Toronto 35 Index, which put it at about $97,000 in early 1992.

After the 1987 crash a system of shock absorber limits and circuit breakers were introduced to most index futures markets. These serve the same purpose as do daily price limits, but are not as strict. For example, the New York Futures Exchange has 10-minute, 30-minute, one- and two-hour trading halts that result from wide swings in the stock market. The purpose

TABLE 20-4
Characteristics of TSE 35 Index Futures Contract

Feature	Toronto Futures Exchange
Location	Toronto
Underlying market index	The Toronto 35 Index. This is a modified market value weighted index of 35 stocks from the Toronto Stock Exchange.
Contract size	Five hundred times the Toronto 35 Index
Minimum price change	Tick size is 0.02 points. This represents a change of $10 per tick.
Margins	Hedge $5000 Speculative $9000
Delivery concept	Cash settlement. Actual value of the Toronto 35 Index determines the payment. Final settlement is on the second day following the last trading day of the expiring month.

Source: The Toronto Stock Exchange. "Toronto 35 Index: A Measure of Opportunity" (The Toronto Stock Exchange, Toronto, Ont., 1992).

of these programmed trading halts is to allow investors to rationally appraise the market during periods of large price swings.

To the financial manager, the great popularity of these financial new-comers lies in their ability to reduce or eliminate systematic risk. When we talked about the variability or risk associated with common share returns we said that there were two types of risk: systematic and unsystematic risk. Unsystematic risk accounts for a large portion of the variability of an individual security's returns and is largely eliminated in large portfolios through random diversification. Thus, portfolio managers are more concerned with systematic or market risk which accounts for the variability of returns from a portfolio of securities. The variability of returns in a portfolio of securities is described by the portfolio's beta. Prior to the introduction of stock index futures, a portfolio or pension fund manager was forced to adjust the portfolio's beta if he or she anticipated a change in the direction of the market. Stock index futures allow the portfolio or pension fund manager to eliminate or mute the effects of swings in the market without the large transactions costs that would be associated with the trading needed to modify the portfolio's beta. Although stock index futures eliminate the unwanted effects of market downswings, these types of futures also eliminate the effects of market upswings. In other words, they allow the portfolio or pension fund manager to eliminate as much of the effect of the market as he or she wishes from the portfolio.

OPTIONS

An option contract gives its owner the right to buy or sell a fixed number of shares at a specified price over a limited time period. The trading of listed call options in North America was initiated by the Chicago Board Options Exchange (CBOE) in 1973. In Canada, the Montreal Exchange began trading listed call options in 1975. Several months later, the Toronto Stock Exchange also began listing options. However, in 1977 both of these exchanges agreed to form a corporation, called the Trans Canada Options Inc., which would list and clear stock options on exchanges across Canada.

Obviously, there is too much going on in the options markets not to pay attention to them. Financial managers are just beginning to turn to them as an effective way of eliminating risk for a small price. As we will see, they are fascinating, but they are also confusing—with countless variations and a language of their own. Moreover, their use is not limited to speculators; options are also used by the most conservative financial managers to eliminate unwanted risk.[6] In this section we will discuss the fundamentals of options, their terminology, and how they are used by financial managers.

---

[6]Although options have been around since the time of Aristotle, the first extensive use of options occurred in Holland in the 1700s. In Holland the early options were associated with tulip bulbs, which had become very popular and were viewed by many as a speculative investment at the time. Tulip growers would buy put options from tulip dealers and thereby reduce their exposure to downward price fluctuations. Other growers would write call options and sell them to dealers, who would in turn sell bulbs for future delivery based upon the calls. Unfortunately, the market was totally unregulated and as tulipmania took hold of Holland in the mid-1700s and the price of tulip bulbs skyrocketed and then crashed in 1763, this market also crashed with many put writers either unwilling or unable to honour their commitments.

The Fundamentals of Options

Although the market for options seems to have a language of its own, there are only two basic types of options: a put and a call. Everything else involves some variation. A **call option** gives its owner the right to purchase a given number of common shares or some other asset at a specified price over a given period. This right is essentially the same as a "rain check" or a guaranteed price. As the buyer, you have the option to buy something, in this case common shares. In effect a call option gives you the right to buy, but it is not a promise to buy. Thus, if the price of the underlying common shares or asset goes up, a call buyer makes money. A **put option**, on the other hand, gives its owner the right to sell a given number of common shares or some other asset at a specified price over a given time period. A put buyer is betting that the price of the underlying common shares or asset will drop. Since these are just options to buy or sell shares or some other asset, they do not represent an ownership position in the underlying corporation, as do common shares. In fact, there is no direct relationship between the underlying corporation and the option. An option is merely a contract between two investors.

Since there is no underlying security, a buyer of an option can be viewed as betting against the seller or writer of the option. For this reason the options markets are often referred to as a zero sum game. If someone makes money, then someone must lose money; if profits and losses were added up, the total for all options would equal zero. If commissions are considered, the total becomes negative, and we have a "negative sum" game. As we will see, the options markets are quite complicated and risky. Some experts refer to them as legalized institutions for transferring wealth from the unsophisticated to the sophisticated. Just as with the call option, a put option gives the buyer the right to sell the common shares at a set price, but it is not a promise to sell.

The Terminology of Options

In order to continue with our discussion, it is necessary to define several terms that are unique to options.

THE CONTRACT ■ An option is a contract that allows the buyer to either buy in the case of a call, or sell in the case of a put, the underlying shares or asset at a predetermined price. No asset changes hands, but the price is set for a future transaction which will take place only if and when the option buyer wants it to. In this section we will refer to the process of selling puts and calls as *writing*. The sale of options is often referred to as *shorting* or *taking a short position* in those options and buying an option is referred to as *taking a long position*.

THE EXERCISE OR STRIKING PRICE ■ This is the price at which the shares or asset may be purchased from the writer in the case of a call or sold to the writer in the case of a put.

OPTION PREMIUM ■ The option premium is merely the price of the option. It is generally stated in terms of dollars per share rather than per option contract, which covers 100 shares. Thus, if a call option premium is $2, then an option contract would cost $200 and allow the purchase of 100 shares at the exercise price.

Perspective in Finance

An option premium represents the cost of the option to the buyer. In contrast this premium represents the option writer's payoff regardless of whether or not this option is ever exercised. Furthermore, the option premium does not represent a down payment on the shares' exercise price since the terms of the option do not change when the option premium is paid.

EXPIRATION DATE ■ This is the date on which the option contract expires. An American option is one that can be exercised any time up to the expiration date. A European option can be exercised only on the expiration date.

COVERED AND NAKED OPTIONS ■ If a call writer owns the underlying shares or asset on which he or she writes a call, the writer is said to have written a "covered" call. However, a writer who writes a call on shares or assets that he or she does not own she is said to have written a "naked" call. The consequence of writing a naked call is that the call writer must deliver shares or assets to the buyer if the naked call is exercised.

OPEN INTEREST ■ The term *open interest* refers to the number of option contracts in existence at a point in time. The importance of this concept comes from the fact that open interest provides the investor with some indication of the amount of liquidity associated with that particular option.

IN-, OUT-OF, AND AT-THE-MONEY ■ A call (put) is said to be out-of-the-money if the underlying shares are selling below (above) the exercise price of the option. Alternatively, a call (put) is said to be in-the-money if the underlying shares are selling above (below) the exercise price of the option. If the option is selling at the exercise price, it is said to be selling at-the-money. For example, if Northern Telecom's common shares were selling for $45 per share, a call on Northern Telecom with an exercise price of $42 would be in-the-money, while a call on Northern Telecom with an exercise price of $48 would be out-of-the-money.

INTRINSIC AND TIME (OR SPECULATIVE) VALUE ■ The term *intrinsic value* refers to the minimum value of the option—that is, the amount by which the shares are in-the-money. Thus, for a call the intrinsic value is the amount by which the share price exceeds the exercise price. If the call is out-of-the-money—that is, the exercise price is above the share price—then its intrinsic value is zero. Intrinsic values can never be negative. For a put, the intrinsic value is again the minimum value the put can sell for, which is the exercise price less the share price. For example, the intrinsic value on a Northern Telecom April 42.50 put when Northern Telecom's common shares were selling for $38.50 per share would be $4. If the put was selling for anything less than $4, investors would buy puts and sell the shares until all profits from this strategy were exhausted. Arbitrage is the process of buying and selling similar assets for different prices. This process keeps the price of options at or above their intrinsic value. If an option is selling for its intrinsic value, it is said to be selling at *parity*.

The time value or speculative value of an option is the amount by which the option premium exceeds the intrinsic value of the option. The time value represents the amount above the intrinsic value of an option that an investor is willing to pay to participate in capital gains from investing in the option. At expiration, the time value of the option falls to zero and the option sells for its intrinsic value, since the chance for future capital gains has been exhausted. These relationships are as follows:

$$\text{call intrinsic value} = \text{share price} - \text{exercise price}$$

$$\text{put intrinsic value} = \text{exercise price} - \text{share price}$$

$$\text{call time value} = \text{call premium} - (\text{share price} - \text{exercise price})$$

$$\text{put time value} = \text{put premium} - (\text{exercise price} - \text{share price})$$

EXAMPLE

Perhaps the easiest way to gain an understanding of the pricing of options is to look at them graphically. Figure 20-4 presents a profit and loss graph for the purchase of a call for $2.30 on Northern Telecom's shares with an exercise price of $42.50. This type of option is defined as a Northern Telecom April 42.50 call. In Figure 20-4, and all other profit and loss graphs, the vertical axis represents the profits or losses realized on the option's expiration date, and the horizontal axis represents the share price on the expiration date. Remember that, because we are viewing the value of the option at expiration, the option has no time value and therefore sells for exactly its intrinsic value. To keep the discussion simple, we also ignore any transaction costs.

For the Northern Telecom April 42.50 call shown in Figure 20-4, the

FIGURE 20-4. Investor's Profit/Loss Graph for Northern Telecom 42.50 Call

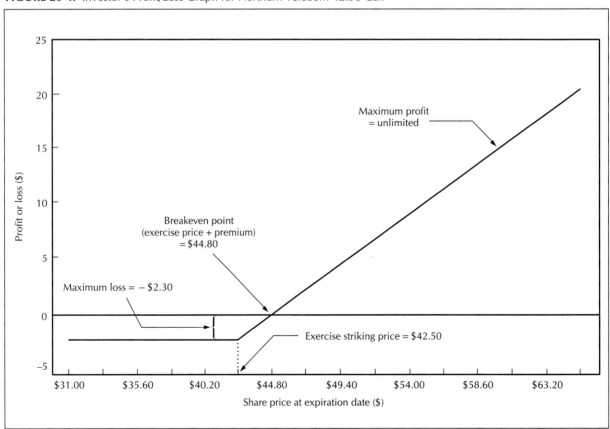

call will be worthless at expiration if the value of the shares is less than the exercise or striking price. An individual would not exercise a call option to purchase Northern Telecom shares for $42.50 per share if the individual could buy the same Northern Telecom shares from a broker at a price less than $42.50. An option would be worthless at expiration if the share price is below the exercise price. In this case, the most an investor can lose is the option premium, that is, how much the individual paid for the option which is in this case $2.30. This amount represents all of the investment but only a fraction of the share price. Once the share price climbs above the exercise price, the call option takes on a positive value and increases in a linear one-to-one basis as the share price increases. Once the price of the Northern Telecom shares increases to $44.80 per share, the investor recovers the initial investment of $2.30, the premium paid for the option.

To the call writer, the profit and loss graph is the mirror image of the call buyer's graph. As we noted earlier, the option market is a zero sum game in which one individual gains at the expense of another. Figure 20-5 shows the profits and losses at expiration associated with writing a call option. Once again we examine the profits and losses at expiration, that is point in time when an option has no time value. The maximum profit earned by the call writer is the premium paid by the buyer of the call; whereas, the call writer's maximum loss is unlimited.

Figure 20-6 illustrates the profits and losses from the purchase of a Northern Telecom April 42.50 put that is bought for $1.30. As the price of

FIGURE 20-5. Writer's Profit/Loss Graph for Northern Telecom 42.50 Call

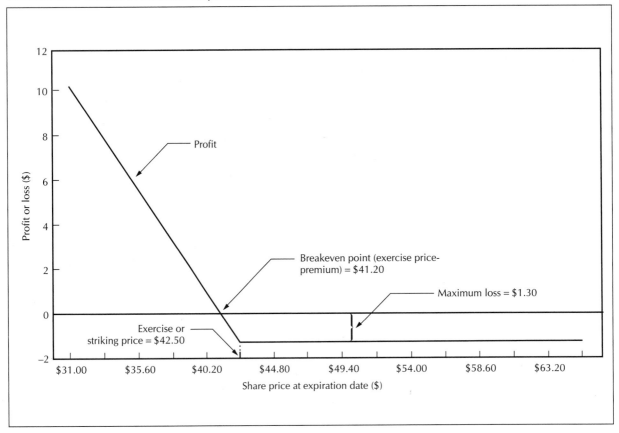

Northern Telecom's shares decreases below $42.50, the value of the put increases. In other words, the put takes on value only if Northern Telecom's shares drop below the exercise price of $42.50 per share. The buyer of the put recovers the initial investment of $1.30, the premium of the option, if Northern Telecom's shares drop to $41.20 per share. The most this investor can loose is the premium, which is small in dollar value relative to the potential gains. The maximum gain associated with the purchase of a put is limited only by the fact that the lowest price a share can fall to is zero.

Figure 20-7 illustrates the profits and losses graph for a writer of a put. This graph is the mirror image of the graph of profits and losses of the buyer of a put. The maximum profit a put writer can earn is the premium for which the put was sold. The potential losses for the put writer are limited only by the fact that the share price cannot fall below zero.

Finally, we demonstrate one of numerous strategies which is available to an investor who wants to speculate while minimizing potential losses of an investment. In this case the investor buys one Northern Telecom April 42.50 call and one Northern Telecom April 42.50 put. Figure 20-8 illustrates the profits and losses at expiration if an investor buys the Northern Telecom April 42.50 call at a premium of $2.30 and the Northern Telecom April 42.50 put at $1.30. An investor who creates this type of position expects the share price of Northern Telecom to fluctuate dramatically in either direction from the exercise price of $42.50. Furthermore, if the investor's expectations of

FIGURE 20-7. Writer's Profit/Loss Graph for Northern Telecom 42.50 Put

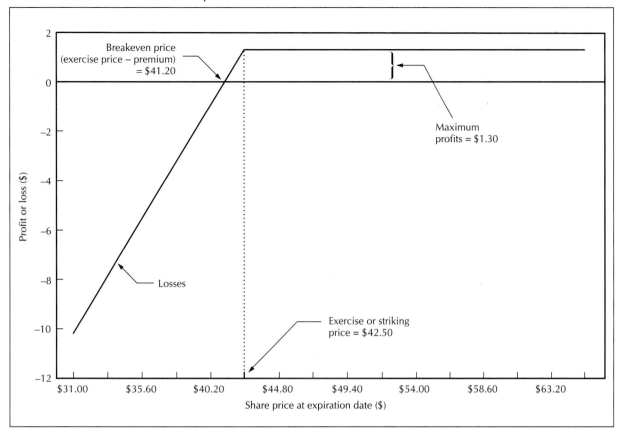

fluctuations in Northern Telecom's share price are not fulfilled, the investor's maximum loss is the cost of buying the two options. Hence, the investor has hedged the investment from important losses if the share price fluctuation does not occur and has speculated on a dramatic fluctuation of the share price if it moves in either direction. Note that the investor does not know with certainty in which direction the share price will move. This type of strategy would be suitable in a situation in which a court decision is expected but the verdict may go in favour of or against a firm, causing the firm's share price to fluctuate in either direction. ■

All of our graphs have shown the intrinsic value of the option at the expiration date. When we re-examine these relationships before the expiration date, we find that options have a value greater than the intrinsic value, that is additional value that can be attributed to the life of the option. In other words, investors are willing to pay more than the intrinsic value for the option because of the uncertainty of the future share price.

Perspective in Finance

The greatest amount you as an investor can lose by purchasing a put or call option is the premium or what you paid for it. Although, this may seem rather small relative to the price of the shares, it is still 100% of your investment.

FIGURE 20-8. Investor's Profit/Loss Graph for Northern Telecom 42.50 Call and 42.50 Put

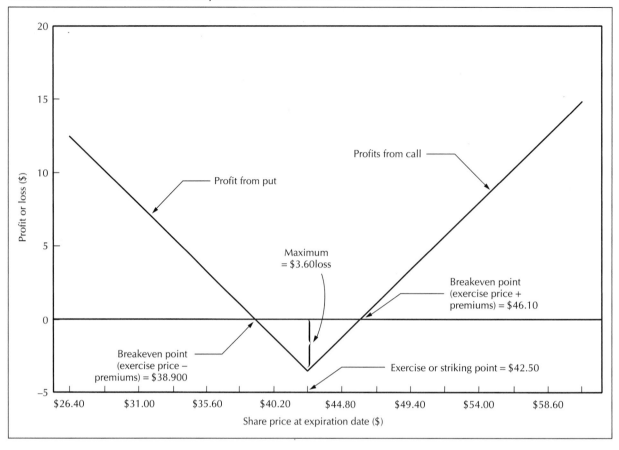

Characteristics of Options

As we examine options from the point of view of the financial manager, we will see that they have some attractive features that help to explain their popularity. There are three reasons for the popularity of options:

1. **Leverage.** Calls allow the financial manager the chance for unlimited capital gains with a very small investment. Since a call is only an option to buy, the most a financial manager can lose is what was invested, which is usually a very small percentage of what it would cost to buy the shares themselves, while the potential for gain is unlimited. As we will see, when a financial manager owns a call, he or she controls or benefits directly from any price increases in the shares. The idea of magnifying the potential return is an example of leverage. It is similar to the concept of leverage in physics, where a small amount of force can lift a heavy load. Here a small investment is doing the work of a much larger investment. Unfortunately, leverage is a double-edged sword: Small price increases can produce a large percentage profit, but small price decreases can produce large percentage losses. With an option, the maximum loss is limited to the amount invested.

2. **Financial insurance.** For the financial manager, this is the most attractive feature of options. A put can be looked on as an insurance policy, with the premium paid for the put being the cost of the policy.

The transactions costs associated with exercising the put can then be looked upon as the deductible. When a put with an exercise price equal to the current share price is purchased, it insures the holder against any declines in the share price over the life of the put. Through the use of a put, a pension fund manager can reduce the risk exposure in a portfolio with little in cost and little change to the portfolio. One dissimilarity between a put and an insurance policy is that with a put an investor does not need to own the asset, in this case the shares, before buying the insurance. A call, since it has limited potential losses associated with it, can also be viewed as an investment insurance policy. With a call option, the investor's potential losses are limited to the price of the call, which is quite a bit below the price of the shares themselves.

3. **Investment alternative expansion.** From the viewpoint of the investor, the use of puts, calls, and combinations of them can materially increase the set of possible investment alternatives available.

Financial managers who use options understand the concept of leverage and the concept of financial insurance. It is these two factors combined that allow for an expansion of the available investment alternatives. Remember, both puts and calls are merely options to buy or sell the shares at a specified price. The worst that can happen is that the options become worthless and the financial manager loses the investment.

Options Exchanges

Before a central marketplace for puts and call options existed, the specifics of each option were negotiated directly between the writer and the buyer of the option. Very seldom did any two options look alike. Generally, every option written had a different expiration date and a different exercise price. As a result, there was little in the way of a secondary market for these individualized options, and the writers and buyers generally had to hold their position until expiration or until the options were exercised.

An important initiative in developing an option market in Canada was the creation of the Trans Canada Options Inc. which lists all of the option trading that takes place on the Montreal, Toronto and Vancouver exchanges. The growth of the option market in Canada can be attributed to the following developments:

1. **Standardization of the option contracts.** Today, the expiration dates for all options are standardized. As a result, there is only one day per month on which a listed option on any shares can expire. The number of shares that a call allows its owner to purchase and a put allows its owner to sell has also been standardized to 100 shares per option contract. In addition, the striking prices have been standardized, generally at five-point intervals, so that there are more identical options. Through this standardization, the number of different option contracts on each stock is severely limited. The result is that more options are identical and the secondary market is made more liquid.

2. **Creation of a regulated central marketplace.** Trans Canada Options Inc., provides a listing of all option trading that occurs on the Montreal, Toronto, and Vancouver exchanges. Each exchange provides a central location for continuous trading on the options listed on their exchange. In 1983, these exchanges agreed to allocate the option listings such that no option is listed more than once in Canada. In addition, these

exchanges have agreed to adhere to strong surveillance and disclosure requirements.

3. **Creation of the options clearinghouse corporation.** The Trans Canada Options Inc. bears full responsibility for honouring all options issued on option exchanges across Canada. In effect, all options held by individuals have been written by the Trans Canada Option Inc. and alternatively all options written by individuals are held by the Trans Canada Option Inc. The purpose of creating a buffer between individual buyers and sellers of options is to provide investors with confidence in the market, in addition to facilitating the clearing and settlement of options. Because of the importance of the Trans Canada Option Inc., let us look for a moment at its operation.

When an options transaction is agreed upon, the seller writes an option contract to the Trans Canada Option Inc., which in turn writes an identical option contract to the buyer. If the buyer later wants to exercise the option, he or she gives the Trans Canada Option Inc. the exercise price associated with the option, which in turn provides the buyer with shares. To get the shares to cover the option, the Trans Canada Option Inc. simultaneously exercises a call option it has on these shares. Because of the operation of the Trans Canada Option Inc. and the strong secondary market created by the stock option exchanges in Canada, options are not exercised very frequently, but are generally sold. Rather than exercise an option, an investor or financial manager usually just sells the option to another investor, and realizes the profits in that manner. Writers of options clear their position by buying an option identical to the one they wrote. As a result the writer has two identical contracts on both sides of the market with the Trans Canada Option Inc. These positions then cancel each other out.

4. **Trading was made certificateless.** Instead of issuing certificates, the Trans Canada Option Inc. maintains a continuous record of traders' positions. In addition to making the clearing of positions (the cancelling out of an option writer's obligation when an identical option is purchased) easier, it has also allowed for an up-to-date record of existing options to be maintained.

5. **Creation of a liquid secondary market with dramatically decreased transactions costs.** There has also been a self-fulfilling generation of volume adding to the liquidity of the secondary market. That is, the innovations created a liquid secondary market for options, and this liquid secondary market attracted more investors into the options market, which in turn created even more liquidity in the secondary market.

Recent Innovations in the Options Market

Recently, new variations of the traditional option have appeared: the long-term equity anticipated securities (LEAPS), the stock index option, the interest rate option, the foreign currency option, and the Canada Government bond futures option.

LONG-TERM EQUITY ANTICIPATED SECURITIES ■ LEAPS are long-term options which can expire in 2 years or less. These instruments are advantageous to investors because they sell for less than the price of the underlying common share which provides a greater opportunity for leverage and diversification of the investor's portfolio. For example, the Trans Canada Options Inc. lists LEAPS on the common shares of the National Bank which expire in 1995 and have an exercise price of $7.00.

STOCK INDEX OPTIONS ■ In Canada, the options on stock indexes were first traded on the Toronto Stock Exchange in 1984. The first stock index option was based on TSE 300 Composite Index. However, in 1987 the Toronto Stock Exchange introduced stock index options on the Toronto 35 Index and phased out the stock index options based on the TSE 300 Composite Index. In North America, there are a variety of different index options, which are based upon stock market indexes or industry indexes such as a computer industry index. However, the broader stock market indexes have carried the bulk of the popularity of index options. Stock index options have proved to be extremely popular in Canada. In fact, the Toronto 35 Index was the most active option contract traded in 1991, accounting for more than 20 percent of trading volume of Canadian options.

The reason for this popularity is quite simple. These options allow portfolio managers and other investors holding broad portfolios cheaply and effectively to eliminate or adjust the market risk of their portfolios. When we talked about systematic and unsystematic risk, we noted that in a large and well-diversified portfolio unsystematic risk was effectively diversified away, leaving only systematic risk. Thus, the return on a large and well-diversified portfolio was a result of the portfolio's beta and the movement of the market. As a result, since the movements of the market cannot be controlled, portfolio managers periodically attempt to adjust the beta of the portfolio when they feel a change in the market's direction is at hand. Index options allow them to make this change without the massive transaction costs that would otherwise be incurred.

In general, stock index options are used in exactly the same way traditional options are used; that is, for leverage and for investment insurance. However, because of the unusual nature of the "underlying shares," these concepts take on a different meaning. In the case of leverage, the portfolio manager is speculating that the market will head either up or down and is able to cash in on any market volatility with a relatively small investment. The following example demonstrates how an investor can use this type of option and take advantage of broad market movements.

EXAMPLE

An investor decides to buy a January call on the Toronto 35 Index with an exercise price of 170. As shown in Figure 20-9 the investor pays 2.75 or $275.00 with the Toronto 35 Index priced at 169.27. Ten days later when the index closed at 178.14, the stock index option is worth 9.375, or $937.50. On the other hand, an investor who purchased a put for 3.25, or $325, would have had the value of the investment drop to $25. All this dramatic price movement was the result of only a 5.24 percent change in the underlying index. ■

In the case of the investment insurance motive for holding index options, the manager is really using them to eliminate the effects of a possible downward movement in the market. For example, a portfolio manager who wants to insure the portfolio against a downturn in the market might purchase a put on the Toronto 35 Index. Thus, if the market declines, the put will appreciate in value, hopefully offsetting the loss in the investor's portfolio.

FIGURE 20-9
January 170 Option on the
Toronto 35 Index

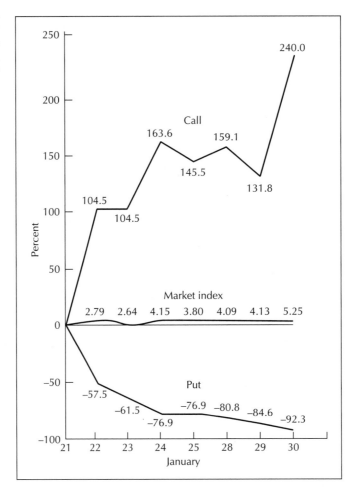

In effect, index options can be used in the same way as the more traditional options. The only difference is that here the profits or losses depend upon what happens to the value of the index, rather than to one share.

OPTIONS ON CANADA BOND FUTURES ■ Options on Canada bond futures work the same way as any other option. The only difference between them and other bond options is that they involve the acquisition of a futures position rather than the delivery of actual bonds. To the creative financial manager, they provide a flexible tool to insure against adverse changes in interest rates while retaining the opportunity to benefit from any favourable interest rate movement that might occur. While a futures contract establishes an obligation for both parties to buy and sell at a specified price, an option only establishes a right. It is therefore exercised only when it is to the option holder's advantage to do so. In effect, a call option on a futures contract does not establish a price obligation, but rather a maximum purchase price. Conversely, a put option on a futures contract is used to establish a minimum selling price. The buyer of an option on a futures contract can achieve immunization against any unfavourable price movements; whereas, the buyer of a futures contract can achieve immunization against any price movements regardless of whether they are favourable or unfavourable.

In their short history, options on Canada bond futures have proved to be extremely popular. Their popularity can be traced to several important advantages they possess:

1. **Efficient price determination of the underlying instrument.** The Canada bond futures contract is well traded on the Montreal Exchange. As a result, there is a continuous stream of market-determined price information concerning these contracts. Conversely, price information on most other types of bonds is unreliable because of the substantial time intervals between trades and the wide gap between existing bid and ask prices.

2. **Unlimited deliverable supply.** Because the clearing corporation can create as many futures contracts as are needed, the process of exercising an option is made extremely simple. When an option on a futures contract is exercised, the buyer simply assumes a futures position at the exercise price of the option. Since the clearing corporation can create as many futures contracts as are needed, the market price of these contracts is not affected by the exercise of the options on them. Conversely, if an option holder on an actual bond were to exercise his or her option, he or she would have to take delivery of the underlying bond. Since the supply of any particular bond is limited, this might create serious price pressure on that bond, provided the bond does not enjoy sufficient liquidity. Thus, because of the unlimited deliverable supply of futures contracts, the exercise of options on futures does not affect the price of those futures.

3. **Greater flexibility in the event of exercise.** If the option proves to be profitable, the buyer or writer can settle the transaction in cash by offsetting the futures position acquired by exercise, or do nothing temporarily and assume the futures position and make or take delivery of the actual bonds when the futures contract comes due.

4. **Extremely liquid market.** Because of the other advantages of options on Canada bond futures, a great number of these options have been created and are traded daily. As a result of the large volume, options on Canada bond futures have developed a very liquid and active secondary market, which has encouraged other traders to enter this market.

Financial institutions seem to be major participants in the options on Canada bond futures market, although there are many potential users of financial futures. They use futures options to alter the risk-return structure of their investment portfolios and actually reduce their exposure to downside risk. A common strategy is to purchase put options and thereby eliminate the possibility of large losses while retaining the possibility of large gains. There is a cost associated with this strategy, since the option premium must be paid regardless of whether or not the option is exercised. An additional return is also generated by those who write call options against a bond portfolio. With this strategy, the premium increases the overall return if bond yields remain stable or rise; however, a maximum return is also established for the portfolio, since it is this tail of the distribution that is sold with the option.

Other examples of how options can be used on financial instruments in North America include interest rate options and foreign exchange options. Interest rate options on 30-year Treasury bonds are also traded on the Chicago Board Options Exchange. Although the trading appeal of interest rate options is somewhat limited, they do open some very interesting doors to the financial manager. In terms of the insurance and leverage traits, they allow the financial manager to insure against the effects of future changes in interest rates. We know that as interest rates rise the market value of outstanding bonds falls; thus, through the purchase of an interest rate put, the market value of a portfolio manager's bonds can be protected. Alternatively, a financial manager who is about to raise new capital through a debt offering and who is worried about a possible rise in interest rates before the offering takes place may purchase an interest rate put. This would have the effect of locking in current interest rates as the maximum level that the firm would have to pay.

Foreign currency options are the same as the other options we have examined except the underlying asset is the British pound, the Japanese yen, or some other foreign currency. While foreign currency options are limited to the Philadelphia Exchange, there is a considerable amount of interest in them largely due to the wide fluctuations foreign currency has had in recent years relative to the American dollar. In terms of the insurance and leverage traits, these options allow multinational firms to guard against fluctuations in foreign currencies that might adversely affect their operations. The leverage trait allows investors to speculate in possible future foreign currency fluctuations with a minimum amount of exposure to possible losses.

THE USE OF OPTIONS AND FUTURES BY FINANCIAL MANAGERS

The use of options and financial futures by financial managers is in the early stages. In a survey of the Fortune 500, 19.2 percent of firms that responded reported that they used either futures or options in the conduct of their financial affairs.[7] There also seemed to be some relationship between the size of the firm and the utilization rate. For example, among large firms (over $1 billion in assets), 23.7 percent used interest rate futures. However, among smaller firms, only 5.36 percent did.

Of the various options and futures available, by far the most popular were treasury bill futures and Eurodollar futures. This is shown in Table 20-5. Of those firms that did not use financial futures and options, the rea-

TABLE 20-5 Financial Futures and Options Most Frequently Used		

Security	Category	Number of Firms Utilizing the Instrument
Treasury bill	Future	16
Eurodollar	Future	14
Certificate of deposit	Future	7
Treasury bond	Future	4
Treasury bill	Option	4
Treasury bond	Option	4
Treasury note	Future	2
Treasury note	Option	1
GNMA[a]	Future	1
	Total	53

[a] GNMA represents Government National Mortgage Association securities.
Source: Stanley B. Block and Timothy J. Gallagher, "The Use of Interest Rate Futures and Options by Corporate Financial Managers," *Financial Management*, 15 (Autumn 1986), pp. 73–78.

[7]See Stanley B. Block and Timothy J. Gallagher, "The Use of Interest Rate Futures and Options by Corporate Financial Managers," *Financial Management*, 15 (Autumn 1986), pp. 73–78.

sons most commonly cited were the resistance of top management and lack of knowledge on the part of the financial manager. It would seem that these two reasons for not using futures and options go together. It would also seem that as the advantages of using financial futures and options to hedge away interest rate and exchange rate risk become more widely understood, their use will become more common.

SUMMARY

Convertible securities are preferred shares or debentures that can be exchanged for a specified number of common shares. Corporations issue convertible securities to sweeten debt for marketing purposes, to delay equity financing, and to provide a source of temporarily inexpensive funds during expansions. Conversely, a corporation that issues convertible securities incurs the risk of an overhanging issue which reduces the flexibility of the firm to change its financial structure. The valuation of convertible securities is a function of both its value as a straight bond and its value if converted into common shares. Since the convertible provides the security of debt with the capital gains potential of common shares, it generally sells for a premium above the higher of its bond or conversion value.

A warrant is an option to purchase a fixed number of common shares at a predetermined price during a specified period. Although warrants are generally issued in association with debt, most warrants are detachable in that they can be bought and sold separately from the debt to which they were originally attached. They are generally issued as a sweetener to debt in order to make it more marketable and lower the interest costs. In addition, unlike convertibles, warrants provide for an additional cash inflow when they are exercised. Conversely, the exercise of convertibles results in the elimination of debt, while the exercise of warrants does not. Thus, there is a tradeoff—additional cash inflow versus elimination of debt—involved in the warrants versus convertibles decision. Since a warrant is an option to purchase a specified number of shares during a given period, its market value is primarily a function of the price of the common shares. Warrants generally sell above their minimum price, the size of the premium is determined by the degree of leverage they provide, the time left to expiration, investors' expectations as to the future movement of the share price, and the share's price volatility.

A futures contract is a contract to buy or sell a stated commodity (such as soybeans or corn) or financial claim (such as Government of Canada bonds) at a specified price at some future specified time. This is a contract that requires its holder to buy or sell the asset regardless of what happens to its value during the interim. The importance of a futures contract is that it can be used by financial managers to lock in the price of a commodity or an interest rate and thereby eliminate one source of risk. A futures contract is a specialized form of a forward contract distinguished by (1) an organized exchange, (2) a standardized contract with limited price changes and margin requirements, (3) a clearinghouse in each futures market, and (4) daily resettlement of contracts.

A call option gives its owner the right to purchase a given number of shares at a specified price over a given time period. Thus, if the price of the underlying common shares goes up, a call buyer makes money. A put, conversely, gives its owner the right to sell a given number of common shares at a specified price over a given time period. Thus, a put buyer is betting that the price of the underlying common shares will drop. Since options provide the right to buy or sell shares, they do not represent an ownership position in the underlying corporation, as do common shares.

STUDY QUESTIONS

20-1. Define the following terms:
   a. Conversion ratio
   b. Conversion value
   c. Conversion parity price
   d. Conversion premium

20-2. What are some reasons commonly given for issuing convertible securities?

20-3. Why does a convertible debenture sell at a premium above its value as a bond or common shares?

20-4. Convertible debentures are said to provide the capital gains potential of common shares and the security of bonds. Explain this statement both verbally and graphically. What happens to the graph when interest rates rise? When they fall?

20-5. Convertible debentures generally carry lower coupon interest rates than do nonconvertible bonds. If this is so, does it mean that the cost of capital on convertible debentures is lower than on nonconvertible? Why or why not?

20-6. Since convertible securities allow for the conversion price to be set above the current common share price, is it true that the firm is actually issuing its common shares at a price above the current market price?

20-7. In light of our discussion of the common shareholders' preemptive right in Chapter 19, explain why convertibles are often sold on a rights basis.

20-8. Although only the holder of a convertible has the right to convert the security, firms are often able to force conversion. Comment on this statement.

20-9. Explain the difference between a convertible security and a warrant.

20-10. How do firms force the exercising of warrants?

20-11. Explain the valuation of warrants both verbally and graphically.

20-12. What factors affect the size of the warrant premium? How?

20-13. What is the difference between a commodity future and financial future? Give an example of a commodity future and a financial future.

20-14. Describe a situation in which a financial manager might use a commodity future. Assume that during the period following the transaction the price of that commodity went up. Describe what happened. Now assume that the price of that commodity went down. Now what happened?

20-15. Describe a situation in which a financial manager might use an interest rate future. Assume that during the period following the transaction the interest rates went up. Describe what happened. Now assume that interest rates went down following the transaction. Now what happened?

20-16. Define a call option.

20-17. Define a put option.

20-18. Compare the two strategies for buying a call and writing a put. What are the differences between the two?

20-19. Draw a profit or loss graph (similar to Figure 20-4) for the buyer of a call contract with an exercise price of $65 for which a $9 premium is paid. Identify the breakeven point, maximum profits, and maximum losses. Now draw the profit or loss graph assuming an exercise price of $70 and a $6 premium.

20-20. Draw a profit or loss graph (similar to Figure 20-5) for the writer of a call contract with an exercise price of $65 for which a $9 premium is paid. Identify the breakeven point, maximum profits, and maximum losses. Now draw the profit or loss graph assuming an exercise price of $70 and a $6 premium.

20-21. Draw a profit or loss graph (similar to Figure 20-6) for the buyer of a put contract with an exercise price of $45 for which a $5 premium is paid. Identify the breakeven point, maximum profits, and maximum losses.

20-22. Draw a profit or loss graph (similar to Figure 20-7) for the writer of a put contract with an exercise price of $45 for which a $5 premium is paid. Identify the breakeven point, maximum profits, and maximum losses.

20-23. What is an option on a futures contract? Give an example of one.

SELF-TEST PROBLEMS

ST-1. (*Convertible Terminology*) Winky's Cow Paste, Inc., issued $10 million of $1,000 par value, 10 percent semiannual convertible debentures that mature in 20 years. The conversion price on these convertibles is $16.75 per share. The common shares were selling for $14.75 per share on a given date shortly after these convertibles were issued. These convertibles have a B+ rating, and straight B+ debentures were yielding 14 percent on that date. The market price of the convertible was $970 on that date. Determine the following:

    a. Conversion ratio

    b. Conversion value

    c. Security value

    d. Conversion parity price

    e. Conversion premium in absolute dollars

    f. Conversion premium in percentage

ST-2. (*Warrant Terminology*) Petro-Tech, Inc., currently has some warrants outstanding that allow the holder to purchase, with one warrant, one common share at $18.275. If the common shares were selling at $25 per share and the warrants were selling for $9.50, what would be the

    a. Minimum price?

    b. Warrant premium?

STUDY PROBLEMS (SET A)

20-1A. (*Convertible Terminology*) The Andy Fields Corporation issued some $1,000 par value, 6 percent convertible debentures that mature in 20 years. The conversion price on these convertibles is $40 per share. The price of the common shares is now $27.25 per share. These convertibles have a B+ rating, and straight B+ debentures are now yielding 9 percent. The market price of the convertible is now $840.25. Determine the following (assume bond interest payments are made annually):

    a. Conversion ratio

    b. Conversion value

    c. Security value

    d. Conversion parity price

    e. Conversion premium in absolute dollars

    f. Conversion premium in percentage

20-2A. (*Convertible Terminology*) The L. Padis, Jr., Corporation has an issue of 5 percent convertible preferred shares outstanding. The conversion price on these securities is $27 per share until 9/30/99. The price of the common shares is now $13.25 per share. The preferred shares are selling for $17.75. The par value of the preferred shares is $25 per share. Similar quality preferred shares without the conversion feature are currently yielding 8 percent. Determine the following:

   a. Conversion ratio

   b. Conversion value

   c. Conversion premium (in both absolute dollars and percentages)

20-3A. (*Warrant Terminology*) The T. Kitchel Corporation has a warrant that allows the purchase of one common share at $30. The warrant is currently selling at $4 and the common shares are priced at $25 per share. Determine the minimum price and the premium of the warrant.

20-4A. (*Warrant Terminology*) Cobra Airlines has some warrants outstanding that allow the purchase of common shares at the rate of one warrant for each common share at $11.71.

   a. Given that the warrants were selling for $3 each and the common shares were selling for $10 per share, determine the minimum price and warrant premium as of that date.

   b. Given that the warrants were selling for $9.75 each, and the common shares were selling for $16.375 per share, determine the minimum price and warrant premium as of that date.

20-5A. (*Warrant Terminology*) International Corporation has some warrants outstanding that allow the purchase of common shares at the price of $22.94 per share. These warrants are somewhat unusual in that one warrant allows for the purchase of 3.1827 common shares at the exercise price of $22.94 per share. Given that the warrants were selling for $6.25 each, and the common shares were selling for $7.25 per share, determine the minimum price and the warrant premium as of that date.

20-6A. (*Warrants and Their Leverage Effect*) A month ago you purchased 100 Bolster Corporation warrants at $3 each. When you made your purchase, the market price of Bolster's common shares was $40 per share. The exercise price on the warrants is $40 per share while the exercise ratio is 1.0. Today, the market price of Bolster's common shares has jumped up to $45 per share, while the market price of Bolster's warrants has climbed to $7.50 each. Calculate the total dollar gain that you would have received if you had invested the same dollar amount in common shares versus warrants. What is this in terms of return on investment?

STUDY PROBLEMS (SET B)

20-1B. (*Convertible Terminology*) The P. Mauney Corporation issued some $1,000 par value, 7 percent convertible debentures that mature in 20 years. The conversion price on these convertibles is $45 per share. The price of the common shares is now $26 per share. These convertibles have a B+ rating, and straight B+ debentures are now yielding 9 percent. The market price of the convertible is now $840.25. Determine the following (assume bond interest payments are made annually):

   a. Conversion ratio

   b. Conversion value

   c. Security value

   d. Conversion parity price

   e. Conversion premium in absolute dollars

   f. Conversion premium in percentage

20-2B. (*Convertible Terminology*) The Ecotosleptics Corporation has an issue of 6 percent convertible preferred shares outstanding. The conversion price on these securities is $28 per share until 9/30/99. The price of the common shares is now $14 per share. The preferred shares are selling for $20.00. The par value of the preferred shares is $25 per share. Similar quality preferred shares without the conversion feature is currently yielding 8 percent. Determine the following:

    a. Conversion ratio

    b. Conversion value

    c. Conversion premium (in both absolute dollars and percentages)

20-3B. (*Warrant Terminology*) The Megacorndoodles Corporation has a warrant that allows the purchase of one common share at $32 per share. The warrant is currently selling at $5 and the common shares are priced at $24 per share. Determine the minimum price and the premium of the warrant.

20-4B. (*Warrant Terminology*) Taco Fever has some warrants outstanding that allow the purchase of common shares at the rate of one warrant for each common share at $11.75.

    a. Given that the warrants were selling for $4 each and the common shares were selling for $9 per share, determine the minimum price and warrant premium as of that date.

    b. Given that the warrants were selling for $7 each, and the common shares were selling for $15.375 per share, determine the minimum price and warrant premium as of that date.

20-5B. (*Warrant Terminology*) Fla'vo'phone Corporation has some warrants outstanding that allow the purchase of common shares at the price of $22.94 per share. These warrants are somewhat unusual in that one warrant allows for the purchase of 4.257 common shares at the exercise price of $22.94 per share.

    a. Given that the warrants were selling for $6.75 each, and the common shares were selling for $8 per share, determine the minimum price and the warrant premium as of that date.

20-6B. (*Warrants and Their Leverage Effect*) A month ago you purchased 100 Annie Kay's Corporation warrants at $2.75 each. When you made your purchase, the market price of Annie Kay's common shares was $35 per share. The exercise price on the warrants is $35 per share while the exercise ratio is 1.0. Today, the market price of Annie Kay's common shares has jumped up to $40 per share, while the market price of Annie Kay's warrants has climbed to $6.75 each. Calculate the total dollar gain that you would have received if you had invested the same dollar amount in common shares versus warrants. What is this in terms of return on investment?

SELF-TEST SOLUTIONS

SS-1. a.

$$\text{conversion ratio} = \frac{\text{par value of convertible security}}{\text{conversion price}}$$

$$= \frac{\$1000}{\$16.75}$$

$$= 59.70 \text{ shares}$$

b.

$$\text{conversion value} = (\text{conversion ratio}) \times \left(\begin{array}{c}\text{market value}\\\text{per common share}\end{array}\right)$$

$$= 59.70 \text{ shares} \times \$14.75/\text{share}$$

$$= \$880.58$$

c.

$$\text{security value} = \sum_{t=1}^{40} \frac{\$50}{(1 + .07)^t} + \frac{\$1000}{(1 + .07)^{40}}$$

$$= \$50(13.332) + \$1000(.067)$$

$$= \$666.60 + \$67$$

$$= \$733.60$$

[*Note:* Since this debenture pays interest semiannually, $t = 20$ years $\times$ 2 $= 40$ and $i = 14\%/2 = 7\%$ in the calculations.]

d.

$$\text{conversion parity price} = \frac{\text{market price of convertible security}}{\text{conversion ratio}}$$

$$= \frac{\$970.00}{59.70}$$

$$= \$16.25$$

e.

$$\begin{array}{c}\text{conversion premium} \\ \text{in absolute dollars}\end{array} = \left(\begin{array}{c}\text{market price of} \\ \text{the convertible}\end{array}\right) - \left(\begin{array}{c}\text{higher of the bond value} \\ \text{and conversion value}\end{array}\right)$$

$$= \$970.00 - \$880.58$$

$$= \$89.42$$

f.

$$\begin{array}{c}\text{conversion premium} \\ \text{in absolute dollars}\end{array} = \frac{\left(\begin{array}{c}\text{market price of} \\ \text{the convertible}\end{array}\right) - \left(\begin{array}{c}\text{higher of the bond value} \\ \text{and conversion value}\end{array}\right)}{\left(\begin{array}{c}\text{higher of the bond value} \\ \text{and conversion value}\end{array}\right)}$$

$$= \frac{\$970.00 - \$880.58}{\$880.58}$$

$$= 10.15\%$$

SS-2. **a.**

$$\text{minimum price} = \left(\begin{array}{c}\text{market price of} \\ \text{common shares}\end{array} - \begin{array}{c}\text{exercise} \\ \text{price}\end{array}\right) \times \left(\begin{array}{c}\text{exercise} \\ \text{ratio}\end{array}\right)$$

$$= (\$25.00 - \$18.275) \times (1.0)$$

$$= \$6.725$$

b.

$$\text{warrant premium} = \left(\begin{array}{c}\text{market price} \\ \text{of warrant}\end{array}\right) - \left(\begin{array}{c}\text{minimum price} \\ \text{of warrant}\end{array}\right)$$

$$= \$9.50 - \$6.725$$

$$= \$2.775$$

SELECTED REFERENCES

Alexander, Gordon J., and David B. Kuhnau. "Market Timing Strategies in Convertible Debt Financing," *Journal of Finance*, 34 (March 1979), 143–155.

Alexander, Gordon J., and Robert D. Stover. "The Effect of Forced Conversion on Common Stock Prices," *Financial Management*, 9 (Spring 1980), 39–45.

Alexander, Gordon J., and Robert D. Stover. "Pricing in the New Issue Convertible Debt Market," *Financial Management*, 6 (Fall 1977), 35–39.

Bacon, Peter W., and Edward L. Winn, Jr. "The Impact of Forced Conversion on Stock Prices," *Journal of Finance*, 24 (December 1969), 871–874.

Baumol, William J., Burton G. Malkiel, and Richard E. Quandt. "The Valuation of Convertible Securities," *Quarterly Journal of Economics*, 80 (February 1966), 48–59.

Billingsley, Randall S. and Don M. Chance. "Options Market Efficiency and the Box Spread Strategy," *Financial Review*, 20 (1985), 287–301.

Billingsley, Randall S. and Don M. Chance. "The Pricing and Performance of Stock Index Futures Spreads," *Journal of Futures Markets*, 8 (1988), 303–10.

Billingsley, Randall S., Robert E. Lamy, and David M. Smith. "Units of Debt Warrants: Evidence of the 'Penalty-Free' Issuance of an Equity-Like Security," *Journal of Financial Research*, 13 (1990), 187–200.

Billingsley, Randall S., Robert E. Lamy, and G. Rodney Thompson. "Valuation of Primary Issue Convertible Bonds," *Journal of Financial Research*, 9 (1986), 251–259.

Black, Fisher. "Fact and Fantasy in the Use of Options," *Financial Analysts Journal* (July–August 1975), 61–72.

Black, Fisher. "The Pricing of Commodity Contracts," *Journal of Financial Economics*, 3 (January–March 1976), 167–79.

Black, Fisher, Emanuel Derman and William Troy. "A One Factor Model of Interest Rates and Its Application to Treasury Bond Options," *Financial Analysts Journal*, 46 (1990), 33–39.

Black, Fisher, and M. Scholes. "The Pricing of Options and Corporate Liabilities," *Journal of Political Economy*, 81 (May–June 1973), 637–654.

Black, Fisher, and M. Scholes. "The Valuation of Option Contracts and a Test of Market Efficiency," *The Journal of Finance* (May 1972), 399–418.

Block, Stanley B., and Timothy J. Gallagher. "The Use of Interest Rate Futures and Options by Corporate Financial Managers," *Financial Management*, 15 (Autumn 1986), 73–78.

Brennan, Michael J., and Eduardo S. Schwartz. "Analyzing Convertible Bonds," *Journal of Financial and Quantitative Analysis*, 15 (November 1980), 907–929.

Brennan, Michael J., and Eduardo S. Schwartz. "The Case for Convertibles," *Journal of Applied Corporate Finance*, 1 (Spring 1988), 55–64.

Brigham, Eugene F. "An Analysis of Convertible Debentures: Theory and Some Empirical Evidence," *Journal of Finance*, 21 (March 1966), 35–54.

Chance, Don M. "Boundary Condition Tests of Bid and Ask Prices of Index Call Options," *Journal of Financial Research*, 11 (1988), 21–32.

Chance, Don M. "Option Volume and Stock Market Performance," *Journal of Portfolio Management*, 16 (1990), 42–51.

Chance, Don M. *An Introduction to Options and Futures*, 2nd. ed. Chicago, IL: Dryden Press, 1991.

Chen, A. H. Y. "A Model of Warrant Pricing in a Dynamic Market," *Journal of Finance*, 25 (December 1970), 1041–1059.

Cheung, C. Sherman, Clarence C. Y. Kwan and Patrick C. Y. Yip. "The Hedging Effectiveness of Options and Futures: A Mean-Gini Approach," *Journal of Futures Markets*, 10 (1990), 61–74.

Constantinides, George M. "Warrant Exercise and Bond Conversion in Competitive Markets," *Journal of Financial Economics*, 13 (September 1984), 371–397.

Courtadon, George. "The Pricing of Options on Default-Free Bonds," *Journal of Financial and Quantitative Analysis*, 17 (March 1982), 75–100.

Cowan, Arnold R., Nandkumar Nayar, and Ajai K. Singh. "Stock Returns Before and After Calls of Convertible Bonds," *Journal of Financial and Quantitative Analysis*, 25 (1990), 549–54.

Dann, Larry Y., and Wayne H. Mikkelson. "Convertible Debt Issuance, Capital Structure Change, and Financing-Related Information: Some New Evidence," *Journal of Financial Economics*, 13 (June 1984), 157–187.

Emanuel, David C. "Warrant Valuation and Exercise Strategy," *Journal of Financial Economics*, 12 (August 1983), 211–235.

Fabozzi, Frank J. and Gregory M. Kipnis (eds.). *Stock Index Futures*, Homewood, IL: Dow Jones-Irwin, 1984.

Fishe, Raymond P. H., Lawrence G. Goldberg, Thomas F. Gosnell, and Sujata Sinha. "Margin Requirements in Futures Markets: Their Relationship to Price Volatility," *Journal of Futures Markets*, 10 (1990), 541–54.

Followill, Richard A. and Billy P. Helms. "Put-Call Futures Parity and Arbitrage Opportunity in the Market for Options on Gold Futures Contracts," *Journal of Futures Markets*, 10 (1990), 339–52.

Fooladi, Iraj, and Gordon S. Roberts. "On Preferred Stock," *Journal of Financial Research*, 9 (Winter 1986), 319–324.

Frank, Werner G., and Charles O. Kroncke. "Classifying Conversions of Convertible Debentures over Four Years," *Financial Management*, 3 (Summer 1974), 33–42.

French, Kenneth R. "Pricing Financial Futures Contracts: An Introduction," *Journal of Applied Corporate Finance*, 1 (Winter 1989), 59–66.

Galai, Dan, and Mier I. Schneller. "Pricing of Warrants and the Value of the Firm," *Journal of Finance*, 33 (December 1978), 1333–1342.

Green, Richard C. "Investment Incentives, Debt and Warrants," *Journal of Financial Economics*, 13 (March 1984), 115–136.

Harris, Milton, and Arthur Raviv. "A Sequential Signaling Model of Convertible Debt Policy," *Journal of Finance*, 40 (December 1985), 1263–1281.

Hayes, Samuel L., III, and Henry B. Reiling. "Sophisticated Financing Tool: The Warrant," *Harvard Business Review*, 47 (January–February 1969), 137–150.

Hein, Scott E., Christopher K. Ma and S. Scott MacDonald. "Testing Unbiasedness in Futures Markets: A Clarification," *Journal of Futures Markets*, 10 (1990), 555–62.

Janjigian, Vahan. "The Leverage Changing Consequences of Convertible Debt Financing," *Financial Management*, 16 (Autumn 1987), 15–21.

Jennings, Edwards H. "An Estimate of Convertible Bond Premiums," *Journal of Financial and Quantitative Analysis*, 9 (January 1974), 33–56.

Jordan, James V. and George Emir Morgan. "Default Risk in Futures Markets: The Customer-Broker Relationship," *Journal of Finance*, 45 (1990), 909–34.

Kaufman, Perry J. *Handbook of Futures Markets*. New York: Wiley-Interscience, 1984.

Kidwell, David S., M. Wayne Marr, and G. Rodney Thompson. "Eurodollar Bonds: Alternative Financing for U.S. Companies," *Financial Management*, 14 (Winter 1985), 18–27.

Kolb, Robert W. *Understanding Futures Markets*, Glenview, IL: Scott, Foresman, 1985.

Lauterbach, Beni and Paul Schultz. "Pricing Warrants: An Empirical Study of the Black-Scholes Model and Its Alternatives," *Journal of Finance*, 45 (1990), 1181–1209.

Leonard, David C. and Michael E. Solt. "On Using the Black-Scholes Model of Value Warrants," *Journal of Financial Research*, 13 (1990), 81–92.

Lewellen, Wilbur G., and George A. Racette. "Convertible Debt Financing," *Journal of Financial and Quantitative Analysis*, 7 (December 1973), 777–792.

Long, Michael S. and Stephan E. Sefcik. "Participation Financing: A Comparison of the Characteristics of Convertible Debt and Straight Bonds Issued in Conjunction with Warrants," *Financial Management*, 19 (1990), 23–24.

Loosigian, Allan M. *Foreign Exchange Futures*. Homewood, IL: Dow Jones-Irwin, 1981.

Loosigian, Allan M. *Interest Rate Futures*. Homewood, IL: Dow Jones-Irwin, 1980.

MacBeth, James D., and Larry J. Merville. "Tests of the Black-Scholes and Cox Call Option Valuation Models," *Journal of Finance* (May 1980), 285–300.

Marr, M. Wayne, and G. Rodney Thompson. "The Pricing of New Convertible Bond Issues," *Financial Management*, 13 (Summer 1984), 31–37.

Martell, Terrence F., and Ruben C. Trevino. "The Intraday Behavior of Commodity Futures Prices," *Journal of Futures Markets*, 10 (1990), 661–72.

Pinches, George E. "Financing with Convertible Preferred Stocks, 1960–1967," *Journal of Finance*, 25 (March 1970), 53–64.

Rothstein, Nancy H. (ed.) *The Handbook of Financial Futures*. New York: McGraw-Hill, 1984.

Rubinstein, Mark, and John C. Cox. *Option Markets*. Englewood Cliffs, NJ: Prentice-Hall, 1982.

Rush, David F., and Ronald W. Melicher. "An Empirical Examination of Factors Which Influence Warrant Prices," *Journal of Finance*, 29 (December 1974), 1449–1466.

Samuelson, Paul A. "Rational Theory of Warrant Pricing," *Industrial Management Review*, 6 (Spring, 1965), 13–31.

Schwartz, Eduardo S. "The Valuation of Warrants: Implementing a New Approach," *Journal of Financial Economics*, 4 (January 1977), 79–93.

Shelton, John P. "The Relation of the Price of a Warrant to the Price of Its Associated Stock," *Financial Analysts Journal*, 23 (May–June and July–August 1967), 88–99 and 143–151.

Smith, C., Jr. "Option Pricing: A Review," *Journal of Financial Economics* (January–March 1976), 1–51.

Smith, C., Jr., and J. B. Warner. "On Financial Contracting: An Analysis of Bond Covenants," *Journal of Financial Economics* (June 1979), 117–161.

Soldofsky, Robert M. "Yield-Risk Performance of Convertible Securities," *Financial Analysts Journal*, 39 (March-April 1971), 61–65.

Sterk, W. "Comparative Performance of the Black-Scholes and the Roll-Geske-Whaley Option Pricing Models," *Journal of Financial and Quantitative Analysis* (September 1983), 345–354.

Sterk, W. "Tests of Two Models for Valuing Call Options on Stocks with Dividends," *Journal of Finance*, 37 (December 1982), 1229–37.

Stoll, Hans R. "The Relationship Between Put and Call Option Prices," *Journal of Finance* (December 1969), 802–824.

Stoll, Hans R. and Robert E. Whaley. "The Dynamics of Stock Index and Stock Index Futures Returns," *Journal of Financial and Quantitative Analyses*, 25 (1990), 441–68.

Strong, Robert A. *Speculative Markets: Options, Futures, and Hard Assets*. Chicago, IL: Longman Financial Services Publishing, 1989.

Van Horne, James C. "Warrant Valuation in Relation to Volatility and Opportunity Costs," *Industrial Management Review*, 10 (Spring 1969), 19–32.

Weil, Roman L., Jr., Joel E. Segall, and David Green, Jr. "Premiums on Convertible Bonds," *Journal of Finance*, 23 (June 1968), 445–463.

Whaley, R. "On the Valuation of American Call Options on Stocks with Known Dividends," *Journal of Financial Economics*, 9 (June 1981), 207–211.

Whaley, R. "Valuation of American Call Options on Dividend-Paying Stocks: Empirical Tests," *Journal of Financial Economics*, 10 (March 1982), 29–58.

PART SEVEN

Special Topics in Financial Management

CHAPTER 21

Corporate Restructuring: Combinations and Divestitures

- Mergers and Acquisitions
- Why Mergers Might Create Wealth
- Determining a Firm's Value
- Financing and Corporate Restructuring
- Tender Offer
- Resisting the Merger
- Divestitures

Corporate restructuring during the eighties has dramatically affected the perceptions most of us have business and finance—not to mention the significant change in the number and structure of firms that existed only a few years ago. The decade of the eighties was well known even to the most casual observer as the period of the **hostile takeover**, meaning that managers of the acquired firm resisted being taken over by investors who might be less than friendly to the current management. These years were also characterized by the use of large amounts of leverage in acquiring other companies. This type of acquisition is known as a **leveraged buyout** (LBO). Managers also used large amounts of borrowed funds to buy the firms they managed. This type of acquisition is now known as the **management buyout** (MBO). In short, the mergers and acquisitions of the last decade created a great amount of interest and represents an area of study in finance. In examining mergers and acquisitions, we have five objectives:

1. Understand why mergers create value;

2. Identify and explain the basic factors that determine the value of an acquisition target;

3. Examine the techniques used in financing an acquisition;

4. Explain the use of tender offers in acquiring a new business;

5. Study the methods managements use to resist an undesired suitor wanting to acquire their firm.

MERGERS AND ACQUISITIONS[1]

In Canada, there are different methods that a manager can use to undertake a merger. For example, a **statutory amalgamation** occurs if two firms merge together to form a new legal entity with one business charter. Another example of a merger is a business combination in which one firm acquires another firm, but both firms maintain their own legal identities. Each of these methods of merger has different legal and tax implications. Although the terms *merger* and *acquisition* have different legal implications, we will use them interchangeably to represent a combination of two or more businesses into a single operational entity.

Company growth through the merging of two firms has been a part of the North American economic scene for many years. For example, during the 1920s a surge of combinations developed; big businesses, such as IBM and General Foods expanded into new products and/or market extensions, creating vertically integrated companies. The decade of the sixties was another period of merger activity. This period is known as the conglomerate age because firms in different industries were combined into one corporate entity, called a **conglomerate**.[2]

The creation of a conglomerate was thought to be an efficient way of monitoring individual businesses by subjecting them to regular quantitative evaluations by the central office. The conglomerate allowed funds to be reallocated from slow growing subsidiaries that generated cash, such as insurance and finance, to fast growing, high technology businesses that required investment funds.

With hindsight we now see that conglomerate acquisitions have for the most part proven unsuccessful. The evidence suggests that buyers often paid too much to acquire the businesses and that mergers were frequently followed by a decline in earnings. Perhaps the most important reason may have been a disregard for the principle that specialization increases productivity. Many important business decisions were made by managers who had limited information and who divided their attention and resources between multiple businesses. Furthermore, conglomerates developed large and expensive central offices for the purpose of monitoring their various businesses. This type of monitoring by the conglomerate's central office proved to be less effective

---

[1]Many of the comments in this section come from an article by Andrei Shleifer and Robert W. Vishny, "The Takeover Wave of the 1980s," *Journal of Applied Corporate Finance* (Fall 1991), pp. 49–56, and from J. Fred Weston, Kwang S. Chung, and Susan Hoag, *Mergers, Restructuring, and Corporate Control*, Englewood Cliffs, NJ: Prentice-Hall, Inc., 1990.

[2]The following reasons provide some insight as to why firms diversify through mergers and acquisitions: (1) the world can be seen as a portfolio, where all that matters is expected return and volatility of returns; (2) undervalued companies can be restructured to capture the "true value" of the firm; and (3) mergers and acquisitions are ways to transfer skills or share activities between two companies. The first two reasons imply that we have superior ability in finding undervalued securities. The third reason simply suggests that we can take advantage of technical skills or lower costs as a result of a merger or acquisition. This last reason has the greatest chance of success.

than the market discipline to which stand-alone businesses are generally subjected. Since the subsidiaries of conglomerates are insulated from market forces, they can afford to lose money and be subsidized by other divisions. As a result, these subsidiaries are not as competitive and do not raise as much external capital as the stand-alone firms.

Because of the merger wave, the eighties have been called the decade of the deal. The eighties provided favourable equity markets and the availability of large amounts of debt financing, amounts previously not thought possible. As a consequence, there occurred a strong demand for expansion through acquisition. Several of the largest mergers that occurred in North America during the eighties had Canadian players: for example, Campeau Corp.'s takeover of Federated Department Stores Inc. for $6.64 billion; Campeau's $4.9 billion purchase of Allied Stores; and Conoco Canada acquiring Dome Petroleum for $4.8 billion.

Many of the mergers and acquisitions during the eighties consisted of acquiring a conglomerate, breaking it up into its individual business units, and selling off the units to large corporations in the same businesses. A number of the firms created in this process were temporary organizations intended to last as was required to divest the pieces of the acquired firm to other corporations. Any remaining business units were then offered to the public, especially when the business unit's value had been enhanced by improvements in the firm's operations.

The decade of the deal came to an end in the late 1980s, largely because the huge amounts of debt financing used to fund many of the acquisitions dried up. Furthermore, the recession of the early nineties caused liquidity crises to occur in some major firms.

Mergers and acquisitions during the eighties represented a return to more specialized and focused firms as compared to the earlier years of diversification. Most acquisitions during the latter years involved companies buying other firms in their own lines of business. Most often, firms were taken over and their various business lines were sold off to different buyers in the same line of business. To a significant extent, hostile takeovers and leveraged buyouts that attracted so much public attention facilitated this process of deconglomeration. Some of the most common objections to takeovers, such as a reduction of competition and cutbacks in employment, investment and R&D, are not supported by data.[3]

Perspective in Finance

Mergers and acquisitions are usually justified by management on the grounds that merging diversifies the firm, thus reducing risk. However, it may be that the shareholder can diversify personally with more ease and less expense by buying shares in the two companies. There must be other reasons for the merger.

WHY MERGERS MIGHT CREATE WEALTH

Clearly, for a merger to create wealth it would have to provide shareholders with something they could not get by merely holding the individual shares of

[3]See, for example, Amar Bhide, "The Causes and Consequences of Hostile Takeovers," *Journal of Applied Corporate Finance* (Summer 1989), pp. 36–59.

BASIC FINANCIAL MANAGEMENT IN PRACTICE

Corporate Restructuring: The New Thinking

The fundamental assumptions about how businesses should be organized have changed significantly from what they were several years ago. Financial market behavior, economic logic and plain common sense suggest that focusing on a single business, or on a very small number of genuinely linked businesses, is the only way to build the value of a company in the long term. The tempting, even seductive, aphorisms of the past—diversify to reduce risk; diversify for higher growth; manage a balanced portfolio of businesses—are about as useful on today's corporate battlefield as is horse cavalry in a modern tank war. Sadly, these old assumptions are still cherished by some corporate managers today.

The Financial Rules of the Game

The financial markets, however, have imposed their own set of rules on corporate management. Two key points highlight the difference between the old and new thinking:

(1) Managements cannot create value by doing what shareholders can do for themselves. Unless there are real economic and business connections that lead to sustainable improvements in operating performance, managements do nothing by making acquisitions that investors cannot do for themselves by making a telephone call to a broker. Investors can diversify their risks by investing at the market price. They do not want corporate managements to do it for them by paying acquisition premiums of 50–100% above the going rate.

This sounds straightforward enough, but it actually strikes at the heart of many, if not most, of the reasons given for corporate acquisitions in the US and UK. Many managements seem to operate under the illusion that they should act as a substitute for the capital markets, making resource-allocation decisions that take them well beyond the activities in which they enjoy true operating advantages.

Few topics have been subjected to as much measurement and analysis as corporate diversification, and there is a large body of evidence that points to one conclusion: Unless an acquired business gains a sustainable operating advantage from becoming part of another company, no value for the acquiror's shareholders will be created by the acquisition. The fact that two businesses operate in adjacent or apparently similar areas of activity is not enough to justify the acquisition of one by the other.

In fact, much of the restructuring we have seen over the past several years has been the unwinding of grandiose schemes devised by those self-deluding managements that have confused their own role with that of the financial markets. The markets are now exhibiting a healthy impatience with such fantasies.

(2) Shareholders will unlock values suppressed by management. If investors notice that a particular company's strategy is causing it to trade at a discount to its true value, the defenses installed by managements will not, in the long run, stop the investors from getting their way. Investors can be misled, and they frequently misprice securities; however, years of bitter experience and their increasing sophistication have made investors far less willing to accept management rationales for diversifying acquisitions. They are much more likely to seek ways to evade the various barriers erected by managements to protect their empires.

Furthermore, size is no longer a barrier. Some corporate managements acquire businesses as part of a defensive strategy, believing that bigger is, if not better, at least tougher to knock over. However, unless such acquisitions achieve sustainable operating advantages for the company, they only put off the evil day. Indeed, all such acquisitions really do is increase the size of the discount in absolute dollars and make the acquiring company even more attractive to well-financed or imaginative predators.

The New Business Environment

The changes in the ground rules mentioned above show that if companies do not restructure themselves, the financial markets will do it for them. Even without the prodding from the financial markets, however, there are compelling business reasons for companies to restructure:

(1) Competition. In a fiercely competitive environment, a broad span of businesses is a luxury that is less and less affordable. Indeed, today's managers are seeing a heightened sense of competitor performance. Absolute measures of success mean much less. Whatever the subject—whether product cost or quality, the rate of innovation, quality of service, or almost any other dimension of business—it is all relative to the competition.

Continued on page 880

Continued from page 879

(2) Flexibility. The quick and the dead. Rapidity of response is becoming crucial to corporate survival and success. Technological developments in information, production and distribution systems and an increased consumer demand for variety are causing major shifts in the pattern of business activity. As a result, diversified firms are in for a tough time. It is hard to jump in several directions at once.

(3) Excessive corporate overhead. Too much value is absorbed by unnecessary corporate expense. Such expense is often worse than unnecessary; it can be positively damaging. In order to justify their existence, corporate headquarters frequently embark upon acquisition programs that create no value for their shareholders. After all, acquisitions are exciting, dramatic and glamorous.

For example, the financial statements of one major diversified corporation reveal an item called "corporate expense" that totals slightly under $200 million. Compare this amount to the company's net income, which (after various adjustments for extraordinary items) totals about $1.3 billion. While adjusted net income has grown at slightly under 15% per annum over the past few years, corporate expense has been growing at the staggering rate of just under 50% per annum over the same period. Adjusting the corporate expense to an aftertax figure and applying the company's price/earnings ratio to the net expense produces a cost of over $1.4 billion. Even assuming that some of the expense is necessary, there is clearly a lot of value being wasted by excessive overhead.

The Role of Finance

Under these new ground rules, the CFO must play a more active role in planning the direction of the company. However, good finance is not a substitute for good strategy and operations. The CFO's role is overlapping more and more with those of the CEO and COO because of the growing interconnectedness of finance, strategy and operations. Unless this interconnectedness is acknowledged and encouraged, the best finance function in the world will not be able to make up for poor strategy or inferior performance.

Therefore, the CFO needs to be centrally involved in strategy formulation, not just to ensure that the strategy is financially sound, but to bring a financial market perspective and ensure that strategic plans translate directly into shareholder value. He also needs to be more closely involved in operations, if only to ensure that the operators are fully aware of the financial dimension of operating decisions and make certain that the real causes of poor financial performance are addressed and remedied.

Source: Simon Duffy, "Corporate Restructuring: The New Thinking," *Business International Money* (January 9, 1989), pp. 1–3.

the two firms.[4] Such a requirement is the key to the creation of wealth under the capital asset pricing model. Restating the question: What benefits are there to shareholders from holding the shares of a new, single firm that has been created through a merger as opposed to holding shares in the two individual firms prior to their merger? Let's consider some of these benefits.

Tax Benefits

For a business combination which maintains the legal identities of the two firms, Revenue Canada requires that each firm report their earned income and file a corporate tax return. The acquisition of control by an acquiring firm causes the acquired firm to loose its right to carry forward any net capital losses, property losses or non-capital losses. An exception to this rule occurs if the business generating the non-capital losses is continued with a reasonable expectation of profit by the acquiring firm. Under these circumstances, the acquired firm may carry forward its non-capital losses and

[4]Michael C. Jensen, "The Takeover Controversy: Analysis and Evidence," *Midland Corporate Finance Journal*, 4 (2) (Summer 1986), 6–32.

investment tax credits to reduce future taxable income that is generated by the acquired business.[5]

In a statutory amalgamation the new firm can also benefit from tax losses. In general, net capital losses that could not be utilized by the predecessor firms can now take on value for the new firm. However, non-capital losses and investment tax credits can only be utilized on taxable income from the business which generated these non-capital losses and investment tax credits. Again the business generating these non-capital losses and investment tax credits must be continued and have a reasonable expectation of profit. Depreciable capital property is transferred from predecessor corporations at their original costs. Hence, the new firm will continue to benefit from tax shields which result from the depreciation of assets.[6]

Reduction of Agency Costs

As we know, the agency problem can occur if management and the ownership in the firm are separated. To compensate for the agency problem, shareholders and bondholders impose a premium on funds supplied to the firm to compensate them for any inefficiency in management. A merger, particularly when it results in a holding company or conglomerate organizational form, may reduce the significance of this problem, because top management is created to monitor the management of the individual companies making up the conglomerate. As a result, management of the individual companies can be effectively monitored without any forced public announcement of proprietary information, such as new product information that might aid competitors. If investors recognize this reduction in the agency problem as material, they may provide funds to the firm at a reduced cost, no longer charging as large an "agency problem premium."

Alternatively, it can be argued that the creation of a conglomerate might result in increased agency costs. Shareholders of conglomerates may feel they have less control over the firm's managers as a result of the additional layers of management between them and the decision makers. Moreover, the resultant expenditures necessary to monitor conglomerates, because of their multi-industry nature, may give further rise to agency cost.

Free Cash Flow Problem: A Specific Case of the Agency Problem

The "free cash flow" problem was first identified by Michael Jensen in 1986. Free cash flow refers to the operating cash flow in excess of what is necessary to fund all profitable investments available to the firm; that is, to fund all projects with a positive net present value. As we know from our discussion of shareholder-wealth maximization, this free cash flow should be paid out to shareholders; otherwise it would be invested in projects returning less than the required rate of return, in effect less than shareholders could earn elsewhere.

Unfortunately, managers may not wish to pass these funds to the shareholders, because they may feel that their power would be reduced. Moreover, if they return these surplus funds they may be forced to go outside for

[5]Canadian Limited. "Acquisition of Control," In: *Canadian Income Tax Act with Regulations*, 61st ed. (CCH Canadian Limited, Don Mills: Ont., 1991) Section 111(5).
[6]Ibid., Section 111(4).

financing if more profitable investment opportunities are identified at a later date. Certainly, what we are describing here is a form of the agency problem. However, we need to see these actions in the context of the corporate management culture rather than as an attempt by the managers to maintain their own position. In other words, as economic conditions change, managers who have successfully managed firms over the years of growing markets may have difficulty in adjusting their financial strategies to conditions in which not all cash flows can be invested at the required rate of return. Jensen argues that this was the case in the oil and gas industry in the late 1970s and resulted in much of the merger activity that took place in those markets during that period.[7] A merger can create wealth by allowing the new management to pay this free cash flow out to the shareholders, thus allowing them to earn a higher return on this excess than would have been earned by the firm.

Economies of Scale

Wealth can also be created in a merger through economies of scale. For example, administrative expenses including accounting, data processing, or simply top-management costs, may fall as a percentage of total sales as a result of sharing these resources.

The sharing of resources can also lead to an increase in the firm's productivity. For example, if two firms sharing the same distribution channels merge, distributors carrying one product may now be willing to carry the other, thereby increasing the sales outlets for the products. In effect, wealth would be created by the merger of the two firms and shareholders should benefit.

Unused Debt Potential

Some firms simply do not exhaust their debt capacity. If a firm with unused debt potential is acquired, the new management can then increase debt financing, and reap the tax benefits associated with the increased debt.

Complementarity in Financial Slack

The merger of cash-rich bidders and cash-poor targets may create wealth for the shareholders of the merged firm. For example, the merged firm would choose positive NPV projects which the cash-poor firm would have passed up. Thus, while these cash-poor firms are selling at a firm price, the discounted value of their future cash flow is below their potential price. In effect, a merger allows positive NPV projects to be accepted that would have been rejected if the merger had not taken place.

Removal of Ineffective Management

Any time a merger can result in the replacement of inefficient operations, whether in production or management, shareholders wealth is created. If a firm with ineffective management can be acquired, it may be possible to replace the current management with a more efficient management team,

[7]Michael C. Jensen, "The Takeover Controversy: Analysis and Evidence," *Midland Corporate Finance Journal*, 4(2) (Summer 1986), pp. 6–32.

and thereby create wealth.[8] Such is the case for firms that have grown from solely production into production and distribution companies or R&D firms that have expanded into productions and distribution; the managers simply may not know enough about the new aspects of the firm to manage it effectively.

Increased Market Power

The merger of two firms can result in an increase in the market power of the two firms. While this can result in increased wealth, it may also be illegal. In Canada, the Competition Act (Bill C-91) which was enacted in 1986, makes any merger or proposed merger illegal if it prevents or lessens, or is likely to prevent or lessen competition substantially. As a result, the Competition Tribunal has been given the powers to dissolve any merger that causes a reduction of competition. The Competition Tribunal is a body composed of judges from the Trial Division of the Federal Court and lay experts. The judges are responsible for determining questions of law, while the lay experts provide expertise on complex economic and financial issues.

Reduction in Bankruptcy Costs

There is no question that firm diversification, when the earnings from the two firms are less than perfectly positively correlated, can reduce the chance of bankruptcy. The question is whether or not there is any wealth created by such an activity. Quite obviously, in the real world there is a cost associated with bankruptcy. First, if a firm fails, its assets in general cannot be sold for their true economic value. Moreover, the amount of money actually available for distribution to shareholders is further reduced by selling costs and legal fees that must be paid. Finally, the opportunity cost associated with the delays related to the legal process further reduces the funds available to the shareholder. Therefore, since costs are associated with bankruptcy, reduction of the chance of bankruptcy has a very real value to it.

The risk of bankruptcy also entails indirect costs associated with changes in the firm's debt capacity and the cost of debt. As the firm's cash flow patterns stabilize, the risk of default will decline, giving the firm an increased debt capacity and possibly reducing the cost of the debt. Because interest payments are tax deductible, whereas dividends are not, debt financing is less expensive than equity financing. Thus, monetary benefits are associated with an increased debt capacity. These indirect costs of bankruptcy also spread out into other areas of the firm, affecting things like production and the quality and efficiency of management. Firms with higher probabilities of bankruptcy may have a more difficult time recruiting and retaining quality managers and employees because jobs with that firm are viewed as less secure. The lack of appropriate expertise causes firms to be less productive. In addition, firms with higher probabilities of bankruptcy may have a more difficult time marketing their product because of customer concern over future availability of the product. In short, there are real costs to bankruptcy. If a merger reduces this possibility of bankruptcy, it creates some wealth.

---

[8]Mergers may overcome the resistance to change within an organization because new management may negotiate more favourable contract concessions with unions than existing management had been unable to acquire.

"Chop-Shop" Approach—Buying Below Replacement Cost

The "chop-shop" approach, which will be discussed more fully later, suggests that the individual parts of a firm are worth more than the current value of the firm as a whole. In the 1980s, many corporate raiders were driven by the fact that it was less expensive to purchase assets through an acquisition than it was to obtain those assets in any other way. This was particularly true of both conglomerates and oil companies. For conglomerates, corporate raiders found that they often sold for less than the sum of the market value of their parts. Much of the merger and acquisition activity associated with oil companies was driven by the fact that it was cheaper to acquire new oil reserves by purchasing a rival oil company than it was through exploration. If assets are mispriced, as this approach seems to suggest, then identifying those assets and revealing this information about the undervalued assets to investors may result in the creation of wealth.[9]

It should be noted that the free cash flow theory could explain this creation of wealth as easily as a mispricing theory. In particular, the oil industry was characterized in the late 1970s and early 1980s by overexploration and drilling activity in the face of reduced consumption while oil price increases created large cash flows. During this time period, managers attempted to increase reserves to protect them from possible future market fluctuations. In effect, the free cash flow problem appeared to exist in the oil industry. As mergers and restructuring raged through the oil industry, wealth was created. Again, this creation of wealth did not necessarily come about through any correction of mispricing. It may have been the elimination of wasted expenditures that created the wealth.

BASIC FINANCIAL MANAGEMENT IN PRACTICE

The '90s Way to Tackle the Recession

Restructuring is one of those words that doesn't ring so much as thud with the heft of purpose and deliberation. To have a structure you need a blueprint. To restructure, you need a revised blueprint. The emphasis is on design, on doing things differently, instead of just trying to do the same old things more cheaply. If there's a reason why companies choose to describe their activities as restructuring rather than cost cutting, this is probably it. In a time of increasingly testy and assertive shareholders, the word implies that management has a game plan and has thought through the contingencies. For this reason, today's corporate reorganizations more often involve a redesign of the entire company and its activities than they do paring and elimination.

Companies practise all kinds of restructuring, but most such exercises can be characterized as either calm or desperate. The calm, thoughtful approach usually involves a cash-rich company with a good balance sheet that embarks on a lengthy

Continued on page 885

---

[9] Restructuring may be beneficial to shareholders for at least two reasons: first, restructuring may provide the means for transferring business assets to a higher-valued use or to a more efficient user. For example, restructuring of oil and gas firms in the early 1980s helped prompt needed retrenchment in the industry which would have eventually occurred. Second, restructuring may permit improvements in management accountability and a strengthening of incentives for managers to act in the best interest of the firm's shareholders.

Continued from page 884

strategic planning process. It's a total rethink that involves all managers, analyzes markets, identifies strengths and weaknesses and decides what businesses the company should be in and the best ways to compete in them. This is textbook restructuring, with management doing precisely the job it is supposed to: looking out for the long-term health of the company. The makeovers of Alcan Aluminium Ltd. and Imperial Oil Ltd. a few years ago were good examples.

Then there is gun-to-head restructuring—the kind that companies such as Magna International Inc. and Campeau Corp. were forced to do. Atonement for past sins comes so much later in the cycle for these companies that they have no choice but to restructure. The CEOs of these unfortunate companies usually have less freedom of action than before. In many cases, there are new financial masters—such as unpaid creditors—calling the shots. These companies ignore the danger signals until the last moment and restructure as a final alternative to receivership. The two different types involve entirely different processes.

"If you're smart, you restructure yourself before someone does it for you," says Joe Wright, director with Burns Fry Ltd. "Darwin lives in business just as he lives in the jungle, and restructuring is an essential part of the process of renewal".

Canada Malting, the Canadian division of Canadian Malting Co. Ltd., recently completed a corporate makeover begun under its own initiative in 1985. The early warning signals in this case were declining earnings on flattening sales. The company had six plants across Canada and major export markets across South America. It also had a balance sheet with underutilized assets and lots of potential. There was plenty of cash, strong cash flow and little debt, all of which could have been working much harder for the shareholders.

Using outside facilitators, Jonathan Bamberger, the company's vice president of Finance, began a three-month strategic planning exercise that had senior managers analyze the strengths and weaknesses of the company and where it stood in the markets. "The conclusion we came to," says Bamberger, "was that there was overcapacity in the world malting industry and that we were part of it. So we closed our three least productive plants, laid off 120 employees and withdrew from low-margin export markets in Central and South America where it was getting increasingly difficult to get paid."

The company then launched the proactive half of its plan—going after growth markets.

Bamberger and his management team decided that their main customers, breweries, were getting bigger and fewer as the industry became more international. They also reasoned that it was increasingly important for international breweries to maintain product quality and consistency from country to country. To do this they would favour bigger suppliers such as Canada Malting, provided they could come up with the goods. The company expanded production in its more modern facilities and marketed itself as international supplier of high-quality products.

Canada Malting's balance sheet shows the results, and few accountants would now describe its assets as underutilized. In the year of the strategic planning session, 1985, revenues for the malting operation were declining $155 million with $4 million in net earnings. In 1989, revenues topped $200 million, earnings were $16 million and both trendlines angle nicely upward. Where the company's major export market was a tottering Latin America then, it is a dynamic, beer-thirsty Japan now. Bamberger's reward was to become vice-president of the international company and general manager of the Canadian company.

This is textbook restructuring—using the luxury of time and solvency to craft a plan and get things right on the first try. The gun-to-head syndrome affords few such luxuries. Here, the company restructures in a brief window before receivership that usually requires new money for new partners and concessions from existing shareholders and creditors. Allan Crosbie, managing partner of merchant bankers Crosbie & Co. Inc., specializes in restructuring troubled companies and often takes a temporary stake in them. He says, "Companies seldom restructure and get it right the first time. It usually takes about three attempts because the first rarely goes far enough."

More often than not, the main problem is the management group that got the company group into hot water in the first place. Although the first, modest restructuring usually places limits on management's power—especially spending—the group still holds sway in the face of divided shareholders and creditors. Crosbie says the management typically downplays the severity of the company's situation, lacks the fortitude to deal with it, and assumes that the same ground rules apply for it as for sound companies. In today's financial environment, nothing could be further from the truth.

Source: Adapted from: Randall Litchfield, The '90s Way To Tackle The Recession," *Canadian Business* (November 1990), pp. 80–84.

DETERMINING A FIRM'S VALUE

One of the first problems in analyzing a potential merger involves placing a value on the acquired firm. This task is not easy. The value of a firm depends not only upon its cash flow generation capabilities, but also upon the operating and financial characteristics of the acquiring firm. As a result, no single dollar value exists for a company. Instead, a range of values is determined that would be economically justifiable to the prospective acquirer. The final price within this range is then negotiated by the two managements.

To determine an acceptable price for a corporation, a number of factors are carefully evaluated. We know that the objective of the acquiring firm is the maximization of shareholders' wealth (share price). However, quantifying the relevant variables for this purpose is difficult at best. For instance, the primary reason for a merger might be to acquire managerial talent, or to complement a strong sales staff with an excellent production department. This potential synergistic effect is difficult to measure using the historical data of the companies involved. Even so, several quantitative variables are frequently used in an effort to estimate a firm's value. These factors include (1) book value, (2) appraisal value, (3) market price of the firm's common shares, and (4) expected cash flows.

Book Value

The **book value** of a firm's net worth is the balance sheet amount of the assets less its outstanding liabilities, or in other words, the owners' equity. For example, if a firm's historical cost less accumulated depreciation is $10 million and the firm's debt totals $4 million, the aggregate book value is $6 million. Furthermore, if 100,000 common shares are outstanding, the book value per share is $60 ($6 million/100,000 shares).

Book value does not measure the true market value of a company's net worth because it is based on the historical cost of the firm's assets. Seldom do such costs bear a relationship to the value of the organization or its ability to produce earnings.

Although the book value of an enterprise is clearly not the most important factor, it should not be overlooked. It can be used as a starting point to be compared with other analyses. Also, a study of the firm's working capital is particularly important to acquisitions involving a business consisting primarily of liquid assets such as financial institutions. Furthermore, in industries where the ability to generate earnings requires large investments in such items as steel, cement, and petroleum, the book value could be a critical factor, especially where plant and equipment are relatively new.

Appraisal Value

An **appraisal value** of a company may be acquired from an independent appraisal firm. The techniques used by appraisers vary widely; however, this value is often closely tied to replacement cost. This method of analysis is not adequate by itself, since the value of individual assets may have little relation to the firm's overall ability to generate earnings, and thus the going-concern value of the firm. However, the appraised value of an enterprise may be beneficial when used in conjunction with other valuation methods. Also, the appraised value may be an important factor in special situations, such as in financial companies, natural resource enterprises, or organizations that have been operating at a loss.[10]

The use of appraisal values does yield several additional advantages. The value determined by independent appraisers may permit the reduction of accounting goodwill by increasing the recognized worth of specific assets. Goodwill results when the purchase price of a firm exceeds the value of the individual assets. Consider a company having a book value of $60,000 that is purchased for $100,000 (the $40,000 difference is goodwill). The $60,000 book value consists of $20,000 in working capital and $40,000 in fixed assets. However, an appraisal might suggest that the current values of these assets are $25,000 and $55,000, respectively. The $15,000 increase ($55,000 − $40,000) in fixed assets permits the acquiring firm to record a larger depreciation expense than would otherwise be possible, thereby reducing taxes.

A second reason for an appraisal is to provide a test of the reasonableness of results obtained through methods based upon the going-concern concept. Third, the appraiser may uncover strengths and weaknesses that otherwise might not be recognized, such as in the valuation of patents, secret processes, and partially completed R&D expenditures.

Thus, the appraisal procedure is generally worthwhile if performed with additional evaluation processes. In specific instances, it may be an important instrument for valuing a corporation.

Stock Market Value

The **stock market value**, as expressed by stock market quotations, is another approach to estimate the net worth of a business. If the stock is listed on a major securities exchange, such as the Toronto Stock Exchange, and is widely traded, an approximate value can be established on the basis of the market value. The justification is based upon the fact that the market quotations indicate the consensus of investors as to a firm's cash flow potential and the corresponding risk.

The market-value approach is the one most frequently used in valuing large corporations. However, this value can change abruptly. Analytical factors compete with purely speculative influences and are subject to people's sentiments and personal decisions. Thus,

> [T]he market is not a weighing machine, on which the value of each issue is recorded by an exact and impersonal mechanism, in accordance with the specific qualities. Rather, should we say that the market is a voting machine, whereon countless individuals register choices which are the product partly of reason and partly of emotion.[11]

In short, the market-value approach is probably the one most widely used for determining the worth of a firm; a 10 to 20 percent premium above the market price is often required as an inducement for the current owners to sell their shares.[12] Even so, executives who place their entire reliance upon this method are subject to an inherent danger of market psychology.

---

[10]The assets of a financial company and a natural resources firm largely consist of securities and natural reserves, respectively. The value of these individual assets has a direct bearing on the firm's earning capacity. Also, a company operating at a loss may only be worth its liquidation value, which would approximate the appraisal value.

[11]Benjamin Graham, David L. Dodd, and Sidney Cottle, *Security Analysis*, 4th ed. (New York: McGraw-Hill, 1962), p. 42.

[12] The price paid for a firm in an acquisition may exceed the current market price for the following reasons: (1) the increased efficiencies provided by the combination; (2) an inducement for owners to sell the company; (3) the benefits provided from being able to control the acquired company; and (4) the possible tax advantages to the buyer.

The "Chop-Shop" Value

The **"chop-shop"** approach to valuation was first proposed by Dean Lebaron and Lawrence Speidell of Batterymarch Financial Management. Specifically, it attempts to identify multi-industry companies that are undervalued and would be worth more if separated into their parts. This approach conceptualizes the practice of attempting to buy assets below their replacement cost.

Any time we confront a technique that suggests that stocks may be inefficiently priced, we must be a bit skeptical. In the case of multi-industry firms, the inefficiency in pricing may be brought on by the high cost of obtaining information. Alternatively, these firms may be worth more if split up because of agency problems. Shareholders of multi-industry companies may feel they have less control of the firm's managers, since additional layers of management may have developed within multi-industry firms. These agency costs may take the form of increased expenditures necessary to monitor the managers, costs associated with organizational change and opportunity costs associated with poor decisions made as a result of the manager acting in his or her own best interests rather than the best interest of the shareholders.

The "chop-shop" approach attempts to value companies by their various business segments. As it is implemented by Batterymarch, it first attempts to find "pure-play" companies—that is, companies in a single industry—from which it computes average "valuation ratios." The ratios frequently used compare total capitalization (debt plus equity) to total sales, to assets, and to income. In effect, these ratios represent the average value of a dollar of sales, a dollar of assets, and a dollar of income for a particular industry based upon the average of all pure companies in that industry. Assuming that these ratios hold for the various business segments of a multi-industry firm, the firm can then be valued by its parts.

For the chop-shop valuation technique to be feasible, we must naturally have information about the various business segments within the firm. This requirement is fulfilled, at least in part, by the reporting rules set forth by the Accounting Standards Committee of the CICA. This standard (*CICA Handbook*, 1700.07) requires that firms disclose financial statements which segment their total operations, first by industry and second by geographic area. Of course, we know that not all firms in the same industry are in fact the same—some simply have more potential growth or earnings ability than others. This methodology should be viewed cautiously since financial managers are reluctant to release information which competitors can use for their benefit.

The "chop-shop" approach is actually a three-step process:

1. Identify the firm's various business segments and calculate the average capitalization ratios for firms in those industries.

2. Calculate a "theoretical" market value based upon each of the average capitalization ratios.

3. Average the "theoretical" market values to determine the "chop-shop" value of the firm.

EXAMPLE

To illustrate the chop-shop approach, consider Cavos, Inc., with common shares currently trading at a total market price of $13 million. For Cavos, the accounting data set forth four business segments: industrial specialties, basic chemicals, consumer specialties, and basic plastics. Data for these four segments are as follows:

Business Segment	Segment Sales ($000)	Segment Assets ($000)	Segment Income ($000)
Industrial specialties	$2,765	$2,206	$186
Basic chemicals	5,237	4,762	165
Consumer specialties	2,029	1,645	226
Basic plastics	1,506	1,079	60
Total	$11,537	$9,692	$637

The three steps for valuing Cavos would be

Step 1: We first identify "pure" companies, those being firms that operate solely in one of the above industries; we then calculate the average capitalization ratios for those firms. This could easily be done using a computer database, such as the TSE/Western Database for TSE 300 Index returns, which provides detailed financial information on most publicly traded firms. Assume the average capitalization ratios for the four business segments that Cavos is active in have been determined and are as shown in Table 21-1.

Step 2: Once we have calculated the average market capitalization ratios for the various market segments, we need only multiply Cavos' segment values (that is, segment sales, segment assets, and segment income) times the capitalization ratios to determine the theoretical market values. This is done in Table 21-2.

Step 3: Finally, the theoretical values must be averaged to calculate the "chop-shop" value of the firm. The average of the three theoretical values in Table 21-2 is $18,913,000, computed as follows:

$$\frac{\text{value based on sales} + \text{value based on assets} + \text{value based on income}}{3}$$

or

$$\frac{(\$23,518,500 + \$21,087,700 + \$12,132,800)}{3}$$

$$= \$18,913,000$$

Hence, Cavos, Inc., is selling for significantly less than its "chop-shop" value, $13 million compared to $18.9 million.

The major limitation of a valuation model, such as the "chop-shop" approach, is that it is not derived from any theoretical basis. What it does is assume that average industry capitalization relationships—in this case, ratios of capitalization to sales, assets, and operating income—hold for all firms or conglomerate subsidiaries in that particular industry. Of course, this is frequently not the case. It is easy to identify specific companies that

Business Segment	Capitalization Sales	Capitalization Assets	Capitalization Operating Income
Industrial specialties	0.61	1.07	21.49
Basic chemicals	2.29	2.43	17.45
Consumer specialties	3.58	2.92	19.26
Basic plastics	1.71	2.18	15.06

TABLE 21-1
Average Capitalization Ratios for Industries in Which Cavos, Inc., Is Active

Value Based on Market Capitalization/Sales

Business Segment	(A) Market Capitalization Sales	(B) Segment Sales	(A) × (B) Theoretical Market Value
Industrial specialties	0.61	$2,765	$ 1,686.7
Basic chemicals	2.29	5,237	11,992.7
Consumer specialties	3.58	2,029	7,263.8
Basic plastics	1.71	1,506	2,575.3
Total			$23,518.5

Value Based on Market Capitalization/Assets

Business Segment	(A) Market Capitalization Assets	(B) Segment Assets	(A) × (B) Theoretical Market Value
Industrial specialties	1.07	$2,206	$ 2,360.4
Basic chemicals	2.43	4,762	11,571.7
Consumer specialties	2.92	1,645	4,803.4
Basic plastics	2.18	1,079	2,352.2
Total			$21,087.7

Value Based on Market Capitalization/Income

Business Segment	(A) Market Capitalization Income	(B) Segment Income	(A) × (B) Theoretical Market Value
Industrial specialties	21.49	$186	$ 3,997.1
Basic chemicals	17.45	165	2,879.3
Consumer specialties	19.26	226	4,352.8
Basic plastics	15.06	60	903.6
Total			$12,132.8

simply produce superior products and whose future earnings growth is, as a result, brighter. These companies, because of their expected future growth, should have their sales, assets, and operating income valued higher. This only makes sense, because as we know the valuation of any asset is based upon the market's expectations.

The "chop-shop" valuation approach reflects the idea that the replacement value of a firm's assets may exceed the value placed upon the firm as a whole in the market. This approach attempts to value the multi-industry firm by its parts. Moreover, as we will see as we explore the cash flow approach to valuation, there simply is no way to estimate the value of a takeover candidate with complete confidence. Thus, this method may provide the decision maker with additional information. ■

The Cash Flow Value

Our last look at valuation models should be familiar to us, given our prior work in finding the present value of cash flows, as we did in our studies in capital budgeting. Using the cash flow approach to merger valuation requires that we estimate the incremental net cash flows available to the bidding firm as a result of the merger or acquisition. The present value of these cash flows represents the maximum amount that should be paid for the target firm. If initial outlay is subtracted out, we determine the net present value from the merger. This approach is similar to that of the capital-budgeting problem, but the approach differs in the estimation of the initial outlay.

Finding the present value of the cash flows for a merger involves a five-step process:

1. Estimate the incremental cash flows available from the target firm. This estimation of incremental after-tax cash flows includes all synergistic cash flows (including those to both the bidding and target firms) created as a result of the acquisition. It should also be noted that interest expenses are not included in these cash flows, as they are accounted for in the required rate of return.

2. Estimate the risk-adjusted discount rate associated with cash flows from the target firm. The target firm's, not the bidding firm's, required rate of return is appropriate here. If there is any anticipated change in financing associated with the target firm as a result of the acquisition, this change should be taken into account.

3. Calculate the present value of the incremental cash flows from the target firm.

4. Estimate the initial outlay associated with the acquisition. The initial outlay is defined here as the market value of all securities and cash paid out plus the market value of all debt liabilities assumed.

5. Calculate the net present value of the acquisition by subtracting the initial outlay from the present value of the incremental cash flows from the target firm.

Financial managers have difficulty in accurately estimating the synergistic gains which are obtained from the merger of two firms. This type of estimation also increases the uncertainty of the incremental cash flows after-tax. For example, it is very difficult to estimate the gains that might be expected from any reduction in bankruptcy costs, increased market power, or reduction in agency costs that might occur. Still, it is imperative to estimate these gains if we are to place a value on the target firm. Once the required rate of return is determined, the present value of the incremental cash flows from acquiring the target firm can then be calculated.

The final step then becomes the calculation of the initial outlay associated with the acquisition.

EXAMPLE

Let's look at the example of Tabbypaw Pie, Inc., which is being considered as a possible takeover target by ALF Inc. Currently Tabbypaw Pie uses 30 percent debt in its capital structure, but ALF plans on increasing the debt ratio to 40 percent (we will assume that only debt and equity are used) once the acquisition is completed. The after-tax cost of debt capital for Tabbypaw Pie is estimated to be 7 percent, and we will assume that this rate does not change as Tabbypaw's capital structure changes. The cost of equity after the acquisition is expected to be 20.8 percent. The current market value of Tabbypaw's debt outstanding is $110 million, all of which will be assumed by ALF. Also, let's assume that ALF intends to pay $260 million in cash and common shares for all of Tabbypaw Pie's shares in addition to assuming all of Tabbypaw's debt. Currently, the market price of Tabbypaw Pie's common shares is $210 million.

Step 1: Estimate the incremental cash flows from the target firm, including the synergistic flows, such as any possible flows from the firm's use of tax credits. One of the firm's financial analysts has estimated that the firm will be eligible to use the following accounting depreciation expenses and tax shields:

Year	1994	1995	1996	1997	1998 and thereafter
Accounting Depreciation	$39	$40	$41	$42	$43
Tax Shields	60	42	29	21	7

The estimation for Tabbypaw's cash flows after-tax is provided in Table 21-3. Here we are assuming that any cash flows after 1998 will be constant at $85 million. Also, we subtract any funds that must be reinvested in the firm in the form of capital expenditures that are required to support the firm's increasing profits.

Step 2: Determine an appropriate risk-adjusted discount rate for evaluating Tabbypaw. Here we will use the weighted cost of capital (WCC) for Tabbypaw as our discount rate, where the weighted cost of capital is calculated as

$$WCC = W_d K_d + W_c K_c$$

where W_d, W_c = the percentage of funds provided by debt and common, respectively

K_d, K_c = the cost of debt and common, respectively

For Tabbypaw,

$$WCC = (.40)(.07) + (.60)(.208) = .1528, \text{ or } 15.28\%$$

Step 3: Next we must calculate the present value of the incremental cash flows expected from the target firm, as given in Table 21-3. Assuming

TABLE 21-3
Estimated Incremental Cash Flows from Tabbypaw Pie, Inc. ($ millions)

	1994	1995	1996	1997	1998 and Thereafter
Incremental operating revenues	$496	$536	$606	$670	$731
Incremental operating expenses (including accounting depreciation)	421	455	517	577	632
+ Accounting Depreciation	39	40	41	42	43
Net Operating Revenue before Taxes	114	121	130	135	142
Taxes (@45%)	51	54	59	61	64
Net Operating Income	63	67	72	74	78
Tax Shields	60	42	29	21	7
Net after-tax cash flow	$123	$108	$101	$ 95	$ 85

that cash flows do not change after 1998, but continue at the 1998 level in perpetuity, and discounting these cash flows at the 15.28 percent, we get

$$\left(\begin{array}{c}\text{present value}\\ \text{of all}\\ \text{cash flows}\end{array}\right) = \left(\begin{array}{c}\text{present value}\\ \text{of 1994--1997}\\ \text{cash flows}\end{array}\right) + \left(\begin{array}{c}\text{present value of cash}\\ \text{flows of 1998}\\ \text{and thereafter}\end{array}\right)$$

where the present value of cash flows for the first four years of 1994 through 1997 would be $307.408 million, determined as follows:

$$PV(\text{cash flows 1994--1997}) = \frac{\$123}{(1.1528)^1} + \frac{\$108}{(1.1528)^2} + \frac{\$101}{(1.1528)^3} + \frac{\$95}{(1.1528)^4}$$

and the present value of the $85 million cash flow stream,[13] beginning in 1998 is computed to be $314.978

$$PV(\text{cash flows 1998, thereafter}) = \frac{\left(\dfrac{\$85}{.1528}\right)}{(1.1528)^4} = \$314.978$$

Thus, the present value of the cash inflows associated with the acquisition of Tabbypaw Pie by ALF is $622.386 million, or $622,386,000; that is, the sum of $307,408,000 and $314,978,000.

Step 4: Next, we estimate the initial outlay associated with the acquisition. As already noted, the initial outlay is defined as the market value of all securities and cash paid out plus the market value of all debt liabilities assumed. In this case, the market value of the debt obligations is $110 million. This amount, along with the acquisition price of $260 million, comprise the initial outlay of $370 million used to calculate the acquisition's initial outlay.

Step 5: Finally, the net present value of the acquisition is calculated by subtracting the initial outlay (calculated in step 4) from the present value of the incremental cash flows from the target firm (calculated in step 3):

$$\text{NPV acquisition} = \text{PV inflows} - \text{initial outlay}$$

$$= \$622,386,000 - \$370,000,000$$

$$= \$252,386,000$$

Thus, this acquisition should be undertaken since it has a positive net present value. In fact, ALF could pay up to $622,386 million for Tabbypaw Pie. ∎

---

[13] Remember that we find the present value of an infinite stream of cash flows, where the amount is constant in each year, as follows:

$$\text{value} = \frac{\text{annual cash flow}}{\text{required rate of return}}$$

Since the cash flows do not begin until the fifth year, our equation is finding the value at the end of the fourth year; thus, we must discount the value back four years.

FINANCING AND CORPORATE RESTRUCTURING[14]

Significant changes have occurred in the financing practices of North American firms, in part due to corporate restructuring. The outstanding debt of many companies increased as they borrowed heavily to finance restructuring activity. As part of this restructuring, three popular types of heavily leveraged transactions have developed: the management buyout (MBO), the leveraged buyout (LBO), and the leveraged employee stock ownership plan (leveraged ESOP). These three financing approaches are briefly described below:[15]

MBOs

An MBO occurs if a group of investors form a shell corporation to acquire the target firm or buys the target firm directly. The distinguishing features of an MBO are: (1) the group of investors includes members of the management of the target company; (2) following the acquisition the newly formed company goes private (that is, common shares are delisted from the stock exchanges); and (3) the acquisition is financed primarily by debt, so the resulting firm is much more highly leveraged than most publicly traded companies.

LBOs

An LBO is a more general type of restructuring approach that can be distinguished from an MBO by the following characteristics: (1) the new owners do not necessarily have to include members of the original management team, and (2) the firm is not necessarily taken private following the acquisition. The majority of LBOs are MBOs, and the term LBO is generally used to describe high leverage acquisitions and restructurings.

Leveraged ESOPs

In a leveraged ESOP the rank-and-file employees participate with management in the purchase of stock in their corporation. A purchase agreement sets out the conditions for using a loan to purchase the firm's shares. The loan is repaid from the employee's retirement account. The employer corporation typically guarantees the loan. Generally, the shares are held under an escrow agreement until the participating employee retires or terminates employment. Provincial governments within Canada provide tax credits for share purchases by the employees. For example, in British Columbia there is a lifetime limit on the tax credit of $10,000 per employee. Similar tax incentives exist in other provinces such as Ontario, Quebec, Saskatchewan, and Manitoba.

---

[14]The ideas in this section come largely from Raymond Rupert, "The Acquirers Within: When Employees Buy the Company," *Mergers and Acquisitions in Canada* (March 1992), pp. 1–11, and Leland Crabbe, Margaret Pickering, and Stephen Prowse, "Recent Developments in Corporate Finance," *Federal Reserve Bulletin* (August 1990), pp. 595–603.

[15]Taken from John D. Martin and John W. Kensinger, *Exploring the Controversy Over Corporate Restructuring*, Morristown, N.J.: Financial Executive Institute Research Foundation, 1990, p. 46.

BASIC FINANCIAL MANAGEMENT IN PRACTICE

Leveraged Buyouts: How Everyone Can Win

There are many different forms of corporate acquisition. Some employ more financial leverage than others and those that use more are called 'leveraged buyouts' or LBOs. There is no standardized definition of an LBO for two reasons. The degree and type of leverage can vary greatly from LBO to LBO. More importantly, the philosophy, corporate direction and strategic motivation among acquirers varies greatly.

No doubt, leveraging a company by way of an acquisition, recapitalization or otherwise, has a significant impact on its present and future business activities. It results in a financial overhead burden which can, depending on the company and its management, become either a restrictive or a positive and motivational force. Some argue that leverage is dysfunctional and does not result in any value creation. Others argue that there are material benefits and value creation opportunities in a well structured LBO acquired at the right price.

An LBO, combined with the stock ownership, can provide the catalyst to refocus management's operating efforts in a way that cannot be achieved otherwise. There is no longer room for complacency. The business must now be managed with great intensity. Opportunities for enhancing cash flow and profitability must continually be examined. And this must be done without jeopardizing the value and strategic development opportunities of the business.

The Ideal LBO Candidate

Before you can structure an LBO, you first have to identify LBO targets. The ideal LBO candidate has most of these eleven characteristics:

1. An experienced and strong management team;
2. A history of consistent and proven profitability;
3. Maintainable profit margins;
4. Strong and predictable cash flows;
5. Intrinsic financial strength;
6. Quality assets, both hard as well as those of a less tangible proprietary nature;
7. A distinctive market position with well known brand or productive names;
8. Competitive distinction through low cost producer advantage, information technology or differentiation;
9. Growth potential within the business as well as by acquisition;
10. Low technological risk to products or services;
11. Non-cyclical, non-commodity or non-regulated business.

Once acquired, the LBO must be subjected to a specific structural discipline if all LBO stakeholders are to be winners.

Management Must Have Ownership Interest

We noted earlier that acquirers all have their own philosophies and strategic directions. Some are going to be more successful than others. Onex, for example, is a diversified company that uses the leverage buyout technique as a way to enhance returns for its shareholders. It believes that the management of the operating companies must have a material financial interest in their business.

Ownership by management increases the focus on value creation. It ensures that management is properly motivated and rewarded through their performance and successful achievement of operating and financial targets. Management stands to accumulate substantial wealth through an increase in the value of their shares. Ownership establishes a direct linkage between success of the LBO and wealth creation for the management and all other shareholders.

Controlling Expenses and Managing Working Capital

Overhead costs and operating expenses are an important source of potential savings. It is amazing how these costs tend to increase over the years and often compromise non-essential and difficult to justify items. Elimination of these costs result in a leaner and more effective organization. Payment for performance in cost reductions is a good way to reinforce management's thrust and focus. This ensures that goals are communicated to all levels of management and is particularly effective in motivating those who do not have stock ownership in the company. This establishes a direct relationship between effective performance and financial returns.

An explicitly defined financial framework establishes financial covenants and investor return objectives. These covenants and objectives in turn focus on the management team on a more efficient utilization of working capital. This means managing

Continued on page 896

Continued from page 895

the business in a way that maximizes cash flow. However, great skill is required to do so without impairing the strength of the business or negating the opportunities for further growth and development. To achieve this, improved inventory and receivable turnover as well as negotiated/extended payment terms from suppliers has yielded with commensurate savings in interest costs.

Better Focus on Capital Expenditures

Capital expenditures often consume great amounts of cash without producing the requisite or targeted rates of return. Subsidiary companies of large multi-national corporations especially tend to spend money whenever they can order to obtain their share of group resources. But when such a subsidiary moves to a stand-alone basis, a more judi-

cious consumption of capital is a *sine qua non*. A disciplined approach to improved cash management and debt reduction discourages undesirable or unnecessary capital expenditures.

Achieving an acceptable return on investment becomes an imperative when the alternative is, on a zero risk basis, to use the cash to pay down debt and to reduce interest costs. This serves to encourage better maintenance programs which are an effective way to avoid or at least defer replacement capital expenditures. This enables capital rationing to be focused on new equipment that can better achieve efficiencies and cost reductions, thereby leading to value creation and competitive differentiation.

Source: Adapted from: Tony Melman, "Leveraged Buyouts: How Everyone Can Win," *Canadian Investment Review* (Spring 1990), pp. 67–69.

Junk Bonds

Junk Bonds have been closely linked to large and at times unsuccessful mergers of the 1980s. Due in part to conservatism of financial managers in Canada the use of these bonds has not been as prevalent in Canada as compared to the use of financial managers in the United States. However, junk bonds have been associated with some of the worst financial disasters in North America during the late 1980s. Examples include the failure of the Campeau retailing empire and the bankruptcy of Drexel, Burrnham, Lambert.

Some critics blame many of the market ills on junk bonds. According to these critics, junk bonds fuelled the merger mania of the 1980s, caused the excessive use of debt, and created instability in financial markets. While these opinions are certainly understandable, the evidence does not support these extreme charges against junk bonds.[16] Junk bonds meet our expectations in terms of risk and expected returns. This type of bond is not inherently different from other securities—they have greater risk, but also greater expected return. Although the market for junk bonds in North America was significant, it was too small to account directly for the growth in corporate debt.

The junk market essentially evaporated at the conclusion of the 1980s. As a consequence of the lack of new financing in the low grade bond market, merger activity in North America declined noticeably in the early 1990s. The decline in merger activity can also be attributed to the more cautious attitude of commercial banks and the weakening in the market for asset sales. Nevertheless, well-structured acquisition proposals, especially those aimed at enhancing a firm's competitive position within its own line of business, are still well received by financial managers of the 1990s.

[16]These ideas come from Sean Beckett, "The Truth About Junk Bonds," *Federal Reserve Bank of Kansas City Economic Review* (July/August 1990), pp. 45–54.

TENDER OFFER

As an alternative approach in purchasing another firm, the acquiring corporation may consider using a tender offer. A tender offer involves a bid by an interested party for controlling interest in another corporation. The prospective purchaser approaches the shareholders of the firm, rather than the management, to encourage them to sell their shares, typically at a premium over the current market price. For instance, in late January of 1988 Campeau Corporation offered $47 for each share of Federated Department Stores Inc., a general retailer based in Cincinnati. The Federated stock sold for $35.87 on the New York Stock Exchange the preceding Friday. This bid represented a premium of 31 percent to Federated shareholders. Several days later, Federated rejected Campeau's offer indicating that it was grossly inadequate since market forces had pushed the share price to the 60 dollar range. In early April of 1988, Campeau Corporation accomplished the takeover of Federated Department Stores Inc., with a tender offer of $73.50 for each of the 90.4 million fully diluted shares outstanding, a value of $6.64 billion.

Since the tender offer is a direct appeal to the shareholders, prior approval is not required by the management of the target firm. However, the acquiring firm may choose to approach the management of the target firm. If the two managements are unsuccessful in negotiating the terms, a tender offer may then be attempted. Alternatively, a firm's management interested in acquiring control of a second corporation may try a surprise takeover without contacting the management of the latter company. The American, T. Boone Pickens, is a prime example of corporate raider who used the tender offer in his efforts to acquire such firms as Cities Service and Gulf.

RESISTING THE MERGER

In response to "unfriendly" merger attempts, especially tender offers, the management of the firm under attack will frequently strike back. A number of defense tactics are used to counter tender offers. These defensive maneuvers include white knights, shark repellents, poison pills, and golden parachutes. Let us examine these more closely.

A **white knight** is a company that comes to the rescue of a corporation that is being targeted for a takeover. For example, when Campeau Corporation made a tender offer for Federated Department Stores Inc., Federated's management opposed the Campeau attempt. To prevent the takeover, Federated's management encouraged R. H. Macy and Co. Inc., a large U.S. retailer, to make a tender offer of cash and stock, in a friendly takeover bid.

Shark repellents are used to discourage unfriendly takeovers. As an example, a firm may revise its bylaws to stagger the terms of directors so that only a few come up for election in any one year. A firm making a tender offer would have to wait at least two years before gaining a majority of board members. Other tactics used to discourage unfriendly takeovers include the introduction of a super majority voting amendment and a fair price amendment. The former amendment requires that any takeover or change to the board of directors be approved by the super majority of preferred and common share voters. The latter amendment requires the introduction of a fair price for tender offers. In certain cases a tender offer may make a bid for the shares at two different prices or tiers. The fair price amendment would disallow a second tier that is lower than the first tier.[17]

Halpern has observed that most of these tactics known as shark repellents are not as common in Canada as compared to the United States.[18] The following reasons were given for this observation: most takeover bids would have to be negotiated with the majority shareholder since most Canadian companies are closely held and the provincial securities regulations in certain provinces preclude two-tier tender offers.

In Canada a tactic that was used to defend a firm from hostile takeovers in the late eighties was the **poison pill**. Inco Ltd. was the first company in Canada to introduce the poison pill in 1988. The purpose of the poison pill is to discourage an unfriendly party trying to acquire the firm and to give the board of directors time to follow other alternatives to maximize shareholder value. For instance, management might devise a plan whereby all the firm's debt becomes due, if the management is removed. Another example of a management plan that can be used is the **golden parachute**, which stipulates that the acquiring company must pay the executives of the acquired firm a substantial sum of money to "let them down easy" as new management is brought into the company. Advocates of the poison pill indicate that the poison pill is in the best interest of the shareholder since it ensures a better deal for the shareholder. The following article summarizes the arguments of Professor MacIntosh, a law professor at the University of Toronto, against the use of the poison pill.

The disadvantages of the unfriendly takeover are readily apparent from the preceding examples. If the target firm's management attempts to block it, the costs of executing the offer may increase significantly. Also, the purchasing company may fail to acquire a sufficient number of shares to meet the objective of controlling the firm. On the other hand, if the offer is not strongly contested, it may possibly be less expensive than the normal route for acquiring a company, in that it permits control by purchasing a smaller portion of the firm. Also, the tender offer has proven somewhat less susceptible to judicial inquiries regarding the fairness of the purchase price, since each shareholder individually decides the fairness of the price.

DIVESTITURES

While the mergers-and-acquisition phenomenon has been a major influence in restructuring the corporate sector, **divestitures**, or what we might call "reverse mergers," may have become an equally important factor. In fact, preliminary research to date would suggest that we may be witnessing a "new era" in the making—one where the public corporation is becoming a more efficient vehicle for increasing and maintaining shareholder wealth.[19]

---

[17]Paul Halpern, "Poison Pills: Whose Interests Do They Serve?," *Canadian Investment Review* (Spring 1990), pp. 57–66.

[18]Ibid.

[19]See G. Alexander, P. Benson, and J. Kampmeyer, "Investigating the Valuation Effects of Voluntary Corporate Sell-offs," *Journal of Finance*, 39 (1984), pp. 503–517; and D. Hearth, "Voluntary Divestitures and Value," *Financial Management* (1984).

BASIC FINANCIAL MANAGEMENT IN PRACTICE

Poison Pills Always Bad News, Professor Says

MacIntosh believes takeovers have two benefits. They bring shareholders a premium in excess of the market price of their shares. The threat of a takeover encourages management efficiency.

Poison pills discourage takeovers because they give too much power to management, which almost always has an interest in stopping a change on control. He said, "Officers of a corporation often lose their job after a takeover so they have an interest in resisting any bid. Officers, especially the CEO, have great influence over the board of directors, so good bids may be resisted."

MacIntosh doesn't attribute such resistance to bad faith by managers: "It's just human nature to fight some hostile force threatening to seize your company," he said.

In 1989 MacIntosh published an investigation of the effects of poison pills in the U.S. "I found that adopting a poison pill caused share prices to go down."

Toronto securities lawyer Philip Anisman has just published a report examining the 19 pills which have been adopted in Canada and he came to the same conclusion, MacIntosh said.

"Even if we consider a case where there is good, well-intentioned management, and the pill is in the interests of the shareholders of the target company, the availability of poison pills is not in the interests of society as a whole," MacIntosh said.

He believes poison pills remove management from the discipline of the market. "The possibility of takeovers keeps management on its toes," he said.

If poison pills give management too much control and they cause a drop in share prices, why do shareholders vote to ratify them?

Two phenomena, the "collective action problem" and co-opting of institutional investors contribute to the adoption of unfavourable measures, according to MacIntosh.

The collective action problem occurs when small investors feel it is not worth their while to study complicated procedures and try to weigh the merits of management proposals. Consequently, they tend just to go along with the proposal.

Institutional investors, on the other hand, have a strong incentive to side with management if they do business with the company. "Institutional investors were co-opted into voting approval for the Inco shareholders' rights plan, even though it was against their interest as shareholders," said MacIntosh.

Poison pills can be improved, if they are giving a short life. "If their horizon were limited so that they had to be voted in every five years, management would be more accountable."

He concedes that good management may feel more secure with pills in place, and that may allow for long-term planning. "But it is impossible for shareholders to determine when a plan will be in their interest. Even if there is good management now, that may change, and once a pill is in place there may be no getting rid of inefficient officers. It is still better to avoid the pill."

Despite his reservations, MacIntosh would not support an outright ban on poison pill provisions. "This is a tough question, but I am a noninterventionist" he said. "I still believe in a free market. Shareholder approval mechanisms can be corrupted but, in the end, we must have faith in investors' ability to protect their own interests."

Source: Adapted from James Carlisle, "Poison Pills Always Bad News, Professor Says," *Financial Post* (February 15), 1990, p. 15.

Chew calls it the "new math," when he writes that a new kind of arithmetic has come into play. Whereas corporate management once seemed to behave as if $2 + 2$ were equal to 5, especially during the conglomerate heyday of the '60s, the wave of reverse mergers seems based on the counter proposition that $5 - 1$ is 5. And the market's consistently positive response to such deals seems to be providing broad confirmation of the "new math."[20]

---

[20]Joel M. Stern, and Donald H. Chew, Jr. (eds.), *The Revolution in Corporate Finance* (New York: Basis Blackwell, 1986), p. 416.

INTERNATIONAL FINANCIAL MANAGEMENT

KKR Learns ABCs of LBOs, 1977

Kohlberg Kravis Roberts & Co. on April 7, 1977, used mostly bank loans to buy a small truck-suspension maker, thus launching the leveraged buy-out's modern era.

Such buy-outs by a few investors using loans date back to obscure transactions in the late 1940s, but KKR gave them prominence in the late 1970s. And new twists: Buy a public company with bank loans and high-interest junk bonds; sell off parts of it to reduce the debt; and then resell the company to the public or to another firm. LBO makers gain whopping profits from the later sale, plus fees along the way.

KKR, formed by three former Bear Stearns partners in May 1976 with $120,000 in capital, set up in spartan Manhattan offices and became by far the No. 1 LBO firm of the 200 or so firms in the hot field in the mid-1980s.

In that first $25.6 million KKR buy-out of A.J. Industries in 1977, KKR partners invested only $1.7 million; they sold it in 1985 for $75 million. KKR has since done more than 30 LBOs.

Within seven years KKR—especially aided since 1981 by big state employee pension plan investors—was buying companies totalling more than $1 billion in size. And early this year it bought RJR Nabisco for a record takeover tag of $25 billion, picking up $75 million in fees.

KKR's managing partners became wealthy. Henry Kravis pledged $10 million in 1987 to the Metropolitan Museum of Art to complete the Henry R. Kravis Wing by 1990. As to criticism that LBOs only line their makers' pockets, Kravis, in a Fortune interview, said: "Greed really turns me off. To me, money means security."

Recently, LBOs have been tested by the weakness in junk bonds, the souring of some debt-plagued LBOs and the failure of banks to provide the financing for UAL's planned LBO. But LBOs have bounced back before; so experts aren't predicting their end.

Source: "KKR Learns ABCs of LBOs, 1977," *Wall Street Journal* (November 6, 1989), B1.

A successful divestiture allows the firm's assets to be used more efficiently, and therefore to be assigned a higher value by the market forces. It essentially eliminates a division or subsidiary that does not fit strategically with the rest of the company; that is, it removes an operation that does not contribute to the company's basic purposes.

The different types of divestitures may be summarized as follows:

1. **Sell-off.** A sell-off is the sale of a subsidiary, division, or product line by one company to another. For example, Joseph E. Seagram & Sons sold seven of its product lines to American Brands Inc., for $372.5 million in 1991.

2. **Spin-off.** A spin-off involves the separation of a subsidiary from its parent, with no change in the equity ownership. The management of the parent company gives up operating control of the subsidiary, but the shareholders retain the same percentage ownership in both firms. New shares representing ownership in the diverted assets are issued to the original shareholders on a pro-rata basis. For example, in 1993 John Labatt Ltd. announced that it would spin-off its dairy operations, Ault Foods Ltd. in Canada to form a stand-alone company.[21]

---

[21] S. Feschuk, "Labatt Switches Dairy Plans" (*The Globe and Mail*, Toronto, Ont., March 13, 1993) p. B5.

3. **Liquidation.** A liquidation in this context is not a decision to shut down or abandon an asset. Rather, the assets are sold to another company, and the proceeds are distributed to the shareholders.

4. **Going private.** Going private results when a company whose shares are traded publicly is purchased by a small group of investors, and the shares are no longer bought and sold on a public exchange. The ownership of the company is transferred from a diverse group of outside shareholders to a small group of private investors, usually including the firm's management.

5. **Leveraged buyout.** The leveraged buyout is a special case of going private. The existing shareholders sell their shares to a small group of investors. The purchasers of the shares use the firm's unused debt capacity to borrow the funds to pay for the shares. Thus, the new investors acquire the firm with little, if any, personal investment. However, the firm's debt ratio may increase by as much as tenfold.

SUMMARY

Business combinations historically have represented a major influence in the growth of firms within the North America. This avenue for growth has been particularly important during selected periods, such as the latter part of the 1980s.

The assertion that merger activity creates wealth for the shareholder cannot be maintained with certainty. Only if the merger provides something that the investor cannot do on his or her own can a merger or acquisition be of financial benefit. There may in fact be certain benefits that accrue to the shareholders, but we must be careful to take a position that can be justified.

Valuing a Firm

Determining the worth of a firm is a difficult task. In addition to projecting the firm's future profitability, which is a cornerstone in valuation, the acquirer must consider the effects of joining two businesses into a single operation. What may represent a "good investment" may not be a good merger.

In estimating a firm's worth the following factors are frequently considered: (1) the firm's book value; (2) the firm's appraisal value; (3) the stock market value of a firm's common shares; (4) the firm's "chop-shop" value; and (5) the present value of future free cash flows.

Financing the Merger

Financial innovation frequently has come in conjunction with corporate restructuring; the most notable examples include MBOs, LBOs, and leveraged ESOPs. These concepts are not new, but the extent of their application has increased significantly. In more recent years, we have seen a marked increase in the use of debt. Before the takeovers of the 1980s, managers endeavoured to maintain a targeted capital structure. In the 1980s, the use of an LBO sometimes meant that an acquired firm's debt might be increased tenfold; the intent was not to maintain that high level of debt, but rather to bring it down to a more acceptable level as soon as possible. In the 1990s, the failure of some large firms to meet their large debt obligations brought on by mergers, has caused the use of equity to be the favoured way to finance a merger.

Tender Offers

Normally, the invested purchaser approaches the management of the firm to be acquired. Alternatively, the purchasing firm can directly approach the shareholders of the firm under consideration. This bid for ownership, called a tender offer, has been used with increasing frequency. This approach may be cheaper, but often managers of the target firm attempt to block it.

Divestitures

A divestiture represents a variety of ways to eliminate a portion of the firm's assets. It has become an important vehicle in restructuring the corporation into a more efficient operation.

STUDY QUESTIONS

21-1. What is the difference between a statutory amalgamation and a business combination?

21-2. Why might merger activities create wealth?

21-3. Why is book value alone not a significant measure of the worth of a company?

21-4. What advantages are provided by the use of an appraisal value in valuing a firm?

21-5. What is the concept of the "chop-shop" valuation procedure?

21-6. Compare the net-present-value approach used in valuing a merger with the same approach in capital budgeting.

21-7. What are the advantages of using convertible securities as a method of financing mergers?

21-8. Describe an MBO, an LBO, and a leveraged ESOP.

21-9. What are the prerequisites for an earn-out plan to be effective?

21-10. Under the base-period earn-out, the amount of future payments depends on what factors?

21-11. What are the disadvantages of the tender offer?

21-12. Explain the different types of divestitures.

SELF-TEST PROBLEMS

ST-1. Using the chop-shop approach, assign a value for the Calvert Corporation, where its common shares are currently trading at a total market price of $5 million. For Calvert, the accounting data set forth two business segments: auto sales and auto specialties. Data for the firm's three segments are as follows:

Business Segment	Segment Sales ($000)	Segment Assets ($000)	Segment Income ($000)
Auto sales	$3,000	$1,000	$150
Auto specialties	2,500	3,000	500
Total	$5,500	$4,000	$650

Industry data for "pure-play" firms have been compiled and are summarized as follows:

Business Segment	Capitalization Sales	Capitalization Assets	Capitalization Operating Income
Auto sales	1.40	3.20	18.00
Auto specialties	.80	.90	8.00

STUDY PROBLEMS (SET A)

21-1A. (*Chop-Shop Valuation*) Using the chop-shop approach, assign a value for Dabney, Inc., whose common shares are currently trading at a total market price of $10 million. For Dabney, the accounting data sets forth three business segments: consumer wholesaling, specialty services, and retirement centres. Data for the firm's three segments are as follows:

Business Segment	Segment Sales ($000)	Segment Assets ($000)	Segment Income ($000)
Consumer wholesaling	$2000	$1500	$175
Specialty services	1000	500	100
Retirement centers	3500	4000	600
Total	$6500	$6000	$875

Industry data for "pure-play" firms have been compiled and are summarized as follows:

Business Segment	Capitalization Sales	Capitalization Assets	Capitalization Operating Income
Consumer wholesaling	0.80	.70	12.00
Specialty services	1.20	1.00	6.00
Retirement centres	1.20	.70	7.00

21-2A. (*Chop-Shop Valuation*) Using the chop-shop approach, assign a value for Aramus Inc., whose common shares are currently trading at a total market price of $20 million. For Aramus the accounting data set forth three business segments: consumer wholesaling, specialty services, and retirement centres. Data for the firm's three segments are as follows:

Business Segment	Segment Sales ($000)	Segment Assets ($000)	Segment Income ($000)
Consumer wholesaling	$ 3500	$ 1000	$ 350
Specialty services	2000	1500	250
Retirement centers	6500	8500	1200
Total	$12000	$11000	$1800

Industry data for "pure-play" firms have been compiled and are summarized as follows:

Business Segment	Capitalization Sales	Capitalization Assets	Capitalization Operating Income
Consumer wholesaling	1.00	.80	8.00
Specialty services	0.90	.80	10.00
Retirement centres	1.20	1.00	7.00

21-3A. (*Free Cash Flow Valuation*) The Argo Corporation is viewed as a possible takeover target by Hilary, Inc. Currently, Argo uses 20 percent debt in its capital structure, but Hilary plans to increase the debt ratio to 30 percent if the acquisition is consummated. The after-tax cost of debt capital for Argo is estimated to be 8 percent, which holds constant. The cost of equity after the acquisition is expected to be 18 percent. The current market value of Argo's debt outstanding is $40 million, all of which will be assumed by Hilary. Hilary intends to pay $250 million in cash and common shares for all of Argo's shares in addition to assuming all of Argo's debt. Currently, the market price of Argo's common shares is $200 million. Selected items from Argo's financial data are as follows:

	1994	1995	1996	1997	Thereafter
Net sales	$200	$225	$240	$250	$275
Administrative and selling expenses	15	20	27	28	30
Depreciation	10	15	17	20	24
Capital expenditures	12	13	15	17	20

In addition, the cost of goods sold runs 60 percent of sales and the marginal tax rate is 45 percent. For tax purposes, the tax shields are $30, $21, $15, $10, $4 for the years 1994, 1995, 1996, 1997, and thereafter, respectively. Compute the net present value of the acquisition.

21-4A. (*Free Cash Flow Valuation*) The Whatever Corporation is viewed as a possible takeover target by Big Boy, Inc. Currently, Whatever uses 25 percent debt in its capital structure, but Big Boy plans to increase the debt ratio to 40 percent if the acquisition is consummated. The after-tax cost of debt capital for Whatever is estimated to be 10 percent, which holds constant. The cost of equity after the acquisition is expected to be 20 percent. The current market value of Whatever's debt outstanding is $30 million, all of which will be assumed by Big Boy. Big Boy intends to pay $150 million in cash and common shares for all of Whatever's shares in addition to assuming all of Whatever's debt. Currently, the market price of Whatever's common shares is $200 million. Selected items from Whatever's financial data are as follows:

	1994	1995	1996	1997	Thereafter
Net sales	$300	$330	$375	$400	$425
Administrative and selling expenses	40	50	58	62	65
Depreciation	25	30	35	38	40
Capital expenditures	30	37	45	48	50

In addition, the cost of goods sold runs 60 percent of sales and the marginal tax rate is 45 percent. For tax purposes, the tax shields are $51, $36, $25, $18, $6 for the years 1994, 1995, 1996, 1997, and thereafter, respectively. Compute the net present value of the acquisition.

STUDY PROBLEMS (SET B)

21-1B. (*Chop-Shop Valuation*) Using the chop-shop approach, assign a value for Cornutt, Inc., whose common shares are currently trading at a total market price of $8 million. For Cornutt, the accounting data set forth three business segments: consumer wholesaling, specialty services, and retirement centres. Data for the firm's three segments are as follows:

Business Segment	Segment Sales ($000)	Segment Assets ($000)	Segment Income ($000)
Consumer wholesaling	$1500	$ 750	$100
Specialty services	800	700	150
Retirement centers	2000	3000	600
Total	$4300	$4450	$850

Industry data for "pure-play" firms have been compiled and are summarized as follows:

Business Segment	Capitalization Sales	Capitalization Assets	Capitalization Operating Income
Consumer wholesaling	0.75	.60	10.00
Specialty services	1.10	.90	7.00
Retirement centres	1.00	.60	6.00

21-2B. (*Chop-Shop Valuation*) Using the chop-shop approach, assign a value for Wrongway Inc., whose common shares are currently trading at a total market price of $10 million. For Wrongway the accounting data sets forth three business segments: consumer wholesaling, specialty services, and retirement centres. Data for the firm's three segments are as follows:

Business Segment	Segment Sales ($000)	Segment Assets ($000)	Segment Income ($000)
Consumer wholesaling	$2200	$ 600	$200
Specialty services	1000	700	150
Retirement centers	3500	5000	500
Total	$6700	$6300	$850

Industry data for "pure-play" firms have been compiled and are summarized as follows:

Business Segment	Capitalization Sales	Capitalization Assets	Capitalization Operating Income
Consumer wholesaling	0.80	1.00	8.00
Specialty services	1.20	.90	10.00
Retirement centres	1.20	1.10	12.00

21-3B. (*Free Cash Flow Valuation*) The Brown Corporation is viewed as a possible takeover target by Cicron, Inc. Currently, Brown uses 20 percent debt in its capital structure, but Cicron plans to increase the debt ratio to 25 percent if the acquisition is consummated. The after-tax cost of debt capital for Brown is estimated to be 8 percent, which should not change. The cost of equity after the acquisition is expected to be 22 percent. The current market value of Brown's debt outstanding is $75 million, all of which will be assumed by Cicron. Cicron intends to pay $225 million in cash and common shares for all of Brown's shares in addition to assuming all of Brown's debt. Currently, the market price of Brown's common shares is $200 million. Selected items from Brown's financial data are as follows:

	1994	1995	1996	1997	Thereafter
Net sales	$260	$265	$280	$290	$300
Administrative and selling expenses	25	25	25	30	30
Depreciation	15	17	18	23	30
Capital expenditures	22	18	18	20	22

In addition, the cost of goods sold runs 60 percent of sales and the marginal tax rate is 45 percent. For tax purposes, the tax shields are $32, $22, $16, $11, $4 for the years 1994, 1995, 1996, 1997, and thereafter, respectively. Compute the net present value of the acquisition.

21-4B. (*Free Cash Flow Valuation*) The Little Corporation is viewed as a possible takeover target by Big, Inc. Currently, Little uses 20 percent debt in its capital structure, but Big plans to increase the debt ratio to 50 percent if the acquisition is consummated. The after-tax cost of debt capital for Little is estimated to be 15 percent, which holds constant. The cost of equity after the acquisition is expected to be 25 percent. The current market value of Little's debt outstanding is $12 million, all of which will be assumed by Big. Big intends to pay $15 million in cash and common shares for all of Little's shares in addition to assuming all of Little's debt. Currently, the market price of Little's common shares is $35 million. Selected items from Little's financial data are as follows:

	1994	1995	1996	1997	Thereafter
Net sales	$200	$220	$245	$275	$300
Administrative and selling expenses	30	35	38	40	45
Depreciation	18	20	22	25	30
Capital expenditures	20	22	25	28	30

In addition, the cost of goods sold runs 70 percent of sales and the marginal tax rate is 45 percent. For tax purposes, the tax shields are $32, $22, $16, $11, $4 for the years 1994, 1995, 1996, 1997, and thereafter, respectively. Compute the net present value of the acquisition.

SELF-TEST SOLUTIONS

SS-1. a.

	Capital-to-Sales	Segment Sales	Theoretical Values
Auto sales	1.40	$3000	$4200
Auto specialties	0.80	2500	2000
			$6200

	Capital-to-Assets	Segment Assets	Theoretical Values
Auto sales	3.20	$1000	$3200
Auto specialties	0.90	3000	2700
			$5900

	Capital-to-Income	Segment Income	Theoretical Values
Auto sales	18.00	$150	$2700
Auto specialties	8.00	500	4000
			$6700

Theoretical value based on:	
Sales	$6200
Assets	5900
Income	6700
Average value	$6267

SELECTED REFERENCES

Alexander, G., P. Benson, and J. Kampmeyer. "Investigating the Valuation Effects of Voluntary Corporate Sell-offs," *Journal of Finance*, 39 (1984), 503–517.

Altman, Edward I. "Setting the Record Straight on Junk Bonds: A Review of the Research on Default Rates and Returns," *Journal of Applied Corporate Finance* (Summer 1990), 82–95.

Asquith, P. "Merger Bids, Uncertainty, and Stockholder Returns," *Journal of Financial Economics*, 11 (April 1983).

Bhide, Amar. "Reversing Corporate Diversification," *Journal of Applied Corporate Finance*, (Summer 1990), 70–81.

Bradley, M. "Interfirm Tender Offers and the Market for Corporate Control," *Journal of Business* (October 1980), 345–376.

Brown, David T. and Michael D. Ryngaert. "The Mode of Acquisition in Takeovers: Taxes and Asymmetric Information," *The Journal of Finance* (June 1991), 653–70.

Choi, Dosoung, and George C. Philippatos. "An Examination of Merger Synergism," *Journal of Financial Research*, 6 (Fall 1983), 239–256.

DeAngelo, H., L. DeAngelo, and E. Rice. "Going Private: Minority Freezeouts and Stockholder Wealth," *Journal of Law Economics* (October 1984).

Fridson, Martin S. "What Went Wrong with Highly Leveraged Deals? (Or, All Variety of Agency Costs)," *Journal of Applied Corporate Finance* (Fall 1991), 57–67.

Giliberto, S. Michael and Nikhil P. Varaiya. "The Winner's Curse and Bidder Competition in Acquisitions: Evidence from Failed Bank Auctions," *The Journal of Finance* (March 1989), 59–76.

Hearth, D., and J. Zaima. "Voluntary Divestitures and Value," *Financial Management*, 13 (Spring 1984), 10–16.

Hite, G., and J. Owers. "Sale Divestitures: Implications for Buyers and Sellers," unpublished manuscript, Southern Methodist University, Dallas, TX, 1984.

Jarrell, Gregg A. and Annette B. Poulsen. "The Returns to Acquiring Firms in Tender Offers: Evidence from Failed Bank Auctions," *The Journal of Finance* (March 1989), 59–76.

Joehnk, Michael D., and James F. Nielsen. "The Effects of Conglomerate Merger Activity on Systematic Risk," *Journal of Financial and Quantitative Analysis*, 9 (March 1974), 215–227.

Kohlberg Kravis Roberts and Co. (with Deloitte Haskins and Sells). "Leveraged Buyouts," *Journal of Applied Corporate Finance*, 2(1) (Spring 1989), 64–70.

Little, W. Brian, and Steven B. Klinsky. "How Leveraged Buyouts Can Really Work: A Look at Three Cases," *Journal of Applied Corporate Finance*, 2(1) (Spring 1989), 71–75.

Loderer, Claudio and Kenneth Martin. "Corporate Acquisitions by Listed Firms: The Experience of a Comprehensive Sample," *Journal of Financial Management* (Winter 1990), 17–33.

Mohan, Nancy and Carl R. Chen. " A Review of the RJR-Nabisco Buyout," *Journal of Applied Corporate Finance* (Summer 1990), 102–108.

Ryngaert, Michael D. "Firm Valuation Takeover Defenses, and the Delaware Supreme Court," *Journal of Financial Management* (Autumn 1989), 20–28.

Schipper, K., and A. Smith. "Effects of Recontracting on Shareholder Wealth: The Case of Voluntary Spin-offs," *Journal of Financial Economics*, 12 (1983), 437–467.

Shleifer, Andrei. "The Takeover Wave of the 1980s," *Journal of Applied Corporate Finance* (Fall 1991), 49–56.

Thompson, Steve, Mike Wright, and Ken Robbie. "Management Buyouts, Debt, and Efficiency: Some Evidence From the U.K.," *Journal of Applied Corporate Finance*, 2(1) (Spring 1989), 76–86.

Wansley, James W., William R. Lane and Salil Sarkar. "Managements' View on Share Repurchase and Tender Offer Premiums," *Journal of Financial Management* (Autumn 1989), 97–110.

Wansley, James W., William R. Lane, and Ho C. Yang. "Abnormal Returns to Acquired Firms by Type of Acquisition and Method of Payment," *Financial Management*, 12 (Autumn 1983), 16–22.

Wansley, James W., Rodney L. Roenfeldt, and Philip L. Cooley. "Abnormal Returns from Merger Profiles," *Journal of Financial and Quantitative Analysis*, 18 (June 1983), 149–162.

Wright, Mike, Ken Robbie, and Steve Thompson. "Corporate Restructuring, Buy-Outs, and Managerial Equity: The European Dimension," *Journal of Applied Corporate Finance* (Winter 1991), 46–58.

CHAPTER 22

Failure and Reorganization

- What Failure Is

- Frequent Causes of Failure

- Symptoms of Bankruptcy

- Voluntary Remedies to Insolvency

- Reorganization

- Liquidation

Decline and embarrassment—hardly topics we like to discuss, especially when we are personally involved. We prefer to address growth and success. In ancient Greece, people frequently blamed their failures on the whims of the gods. In our own age, failure is for many a crushing disgrace, which probably contributes to our tendency to avoid the subject or to hold on to a bad idea beyond the point of rationality. Despite our aversion to the subject, we can learn from failure. The learning process may help us avoid losses and insolvency. More than likely, a financial manager will eventually be called upon to work with a customer who is having severe financial problems. So managers must be aware of the issues associated with failure in business.

In this chapter, we have the following objectives:

1. Explain the general terms of business failure;

2. Identify frequent causes of company failures;

3. Identify the financial characteristics that generally develop within a firm facing possible bankruptcy;

4. Explain the procedural aspects for reorganizing or liquidating a business.

WHAT FAILURE IS

The term *failure* is used in a variety of contexts. **Economic failure** suggests that the company's costs exceed its revenues. Stated differently, the internal rates of return on investments are less than the firm's cost of capital. **Insolvency** also is frequently used to specify serious financial problems. A firm is technically insolvent when it can no longer honour its financial obligations. Although the book value of assets may exceed total liabilities, indicating a positive net worth, the company simply does not have sufficient liquidity to pay its debts. This condition may be temporary or irreversible. Another term used is *insolvency in bankruptcy*. Here the company's liabilities are actually greater than the fair valuation of its assets, which means a negative net worth. Regardless of the liquidity of its assets, the company is completely and unquestionably unable to meet maturing obligations. This situation generally indicates that liquidation rather than a reorganization of the firm is necessary.

FREQUENT CAUSES OF FAILURE

During the period 1987 to 1992, the number of business bankruptcies in Canada has increased steadily from 7,371 in 1987 to 13,851 in 1992.[1] The value of liabilities declared by the debtors during this period tripled; the value of liabilities declared in 1987 was $1,557,561,000 as compared to $5,564,681,000 declared in 1992. Although causes of business failure vary from firm to firm, we can identify several common ones.

These causes render the firm vulnerable to several mistakes. First, management may be negligent in developing effective accounting systems. Second, the company may be unresponsive to change—unable to adjust to a general recession and unfavourable industry developments. Third, management may be inclined to undertake an investment that is disproportionately large relative to firm size. If the project fails, the probability of insolvency is greatly increased. Finally, management may come to rely so heavily on debt financing that even a minor problem can place the firm in a dangerous position.

In an attempt to determine the reasons for business failure, Dun & Bradstreet, Inc., has surveyed a sample of a large number of companies that have experienced failure.[2] The reasons given for these business casualties are shown in Table 22-1. Clearly, the primary causes relate to economic factors beyond management's control and financial problems, such as excessive use of debt or insufficient capital.

Although the probability is much less, large corporations are subject to failure. In fact, the failure statistics do not include large corporations that for all practical purposes failed but were either merged into another company or received governmental assistance. For example, the collapse of Central Guaranty Trust Co. was avoided only by a merger with Toronto Dominion Bank and a bail-out by Canada Deposit Insurance Corp., a federal government corporation. Thus, while small companies have a much greater chance of failure relative to large corporations, the issue is real for both.

SYMPTOMS OF BANKRUPTCY

As a company enters the final stages prior to failure, a pattern may develop in terms of a changing financial profile. Although bankruptcy or insolvency

---

[1] Canadian Economic Observer, "Business Bankruptcies and Liabilities," Statistics Canada, Catalogue No. 11-210, 1991/1992.

[2] *The 1990 Dun & Bradstreet Business Failure Record* (New York: Dun & Bradstreet, Inc., 1991), p. 18.

TABLE 22-1
Causes of Business Failures
in 1990

	Manufacturers	Wholesalers	Retailers	Construction	All-firm Total
Neglect	1.9%	2.0%	2.0%	1.9%	1.6%
Disaster	.6	.6	.6	.4	.4
Fraud	.6	.5	.4	.2	.3
Economic factors	67.7	70.7	71.2	72.8	71.7
Lack of experience	18.4	17.1	20.1	19.4	20.3
Sales problems	10.4	10.2	13.0	11.9	11.1
Expense problems	6.4	5.6	5.8	6.0	8.1
Customer problems	.8	.7	.3	.8	.4
Excessive assets	.2	.2	.3	.2	.2
Capital problems	.6	.5	.7	.6	.5
Total[a]	100.0%	100.0%	100.0%	100.0%	100.0%

[a]Since some failures are attributable to a combination of causes, the totals may exceed 100 percent.
Source: *The 1990 Dun & Bradstreet Business Failure Record* (New York: Dun & Bradstreet Inc., 1991), p. 19.

cannot be predicted with certainty, several financial ratios have proven to be useful indicators of impending disaster. A study by Altman[3] developed a statistical model that found the financial ratios best predicting bankruptcy.[4] Based upon Altman's sample of bankrupt firms, the study yielded an equation that used five ratios to predict bankruptcy:

$$\text{bankruptcy score} = 1.2X_1 + 1.4X_2 + 3.3X_3 + .6X_4 + .999X_5$$

where X_1 = (net working capital/total assets)

X_2 = (retained earnings/total assets)

X_3 = (earnings before interest and taxes/total assets)

X_4 = (total market value of stock/book value of total debt)

X_5 = (sales/total assets)

With this equation, the criterion for separating firms with a strong likelihood of bankruptcy from those that probably will not fail should be as follows. If the score exceeds 2.99, no concern for bankruptcy should exist. On the other hand, a score less than 1.81 suggests that the firm is a likely candidate for failure. Values between 1.81 and 2.99 are difficult to classify. However, although a firm in this "gray area" can easily be misclassified in terms of the final outcome, the best way to set up a dividing line is to predict that a company will fail if its score is less than 2.675. Alternatively, a score exceeding

---

[3]Edward I. Altman, *Corporate Bankruptcy in America* (Lexington, MA: Heath Lexington Books, 1971).

[4]Altman and Lavallee (1980) predicted the probability bankruptcy for a sample of Canadian firms (See, E. Altman and M. Lavallee, "Un Modèle Discriminant de Prédiction des Faillites au Canada," *Finance*, 1 (1980), pp. 74–81). Using the zeta technique, they developed the following equation:
$$Z = -1.61 + 0.23X_1 + 0.62X_2 + 0.89X_3 + 0.66X_4 + 0.50X_5$$
where,
X_1 = Sales/Total assets; X_2 = Net profit/Total assets; X_3 = Current ratio; X_4 = Net profit/Total debt; X_5 = Growth rate of equity − growth rate of total assets.

2.675 may be used as an indicator that success is more likely than failure. These guidelines are shown in Table 22-2.

We may conclude that a potentially failing corporation begins to invest less in current assets (X_1). Since X_2 is a cumulative indicator of profitability relative to time, the findings suggest that younger companies have a greater chance of bankruptcy. Variable X_3 reflects the firm's general earnings power. Deterioration in this factor was shown to be the best single indicator that bankruptcy may be forthcoming. Variable X_4 depicts the firm's financial leverage position. Finally, X_5, the asset turnover ratio, measures management's ability to generate sales from the firm's assets.

Although the financial information flowing from a firm helps us identify problems, the predictions we make with it certainly are not perfect. Owing to factors unique to the firm, as well as to the tendency for managements of problem firms to do some "window dressing" of the financial statements, the ratios will not always effectively identify corporations that face bankruptcy within the near future. Even so, they will help us assess the likelihood of bankruptcy.[5]

Financial distress is a general term that describes the financial condition of a firm which does not have sufficient liquidity to pay its debts; the condition may be either temporary or irreversible. If a company finds itself in financial distress, management must answer some very important questions as to the severity of the condition. If the condition of financial distress is evaluated not to be severe, management may choose to renegotiate its financial obligations by extending the duration of the payment period or by reducing interest payments. This type of situation is typical of smaller firms that are economically viable and still have the confidence of their creditors.

In a severe condition of financial distress, a firm can no longer meet its financial obligations on a regular basis, even though the book value of the firm's assets may exceed total liabilities. However, the severity of the financial condition requires management to make an objective analysis of the firm's financial health. For example, management must answer this question: Is the firm worth more dead or alive? A decision to continue operating has to be based upon the costs of reorganizing the firm as opposed to the benefits of liquidating the business.

If the condition of financial distress is severe, the secured creditors may place the firm in receivership.[6] The process requires the secured creditor to give a 10-day notice to the insolvent firm. After the 10-day notice has expired, the secured creditor can appoint a receiver in order to pursue the

Bankruptcy Score		
Less than 1.81	**Between 1.81 and 2.99**	**Greater than 2.99**
Probability of failure is high	Probability of failure is difficult to determine	Probability of failure is remote
Predict failure	Less than 2.675—predict failure Greater than 2.675—predict success	Predict success

TABLE 22-2
Altman's Bankruptcy Criterion

---

[5]Firm will purposely undertake transactions just prior to publishing financial reports in order do some "window dressing."

[6]Christina S. R. Drummond, "Receivership, Liquidation and Dissolution," In: *Canada Business Corporations Act—An Accountant's Review of the Highlights* (3rd ed., Toronto, Butterworths, 1987).

insolvent firm for payments on the debt. Generally, the provisions of a security-backed debt contract require that an appointed receiver or receiver-manager be appointed to act in the interest of the secured creditors if the firm cannot meet or is in default of its secured debt payments.[7] The extent of the receiver's involvement with the firm activities can range from ensuring that payments on debt are recovered in full to the managing of firm's activities with the object of liquidating the firm's assets.[8] In some cases, the firm's activities can be continued by reorganizing the financial structure through the issue of new securities, replacing existing management and liquidating certain assets. In other cases, the receiver will begin liquidation of the firm assets to recover the debt payments of the secured creditors. However, we should note that the declaration of bankruptcy by the courts takes precedence over receivership, and such a declaration may ensure a more equitable distribution of the firm's assets to all of its creditors. Furthermore, recent amendments to the Bankruptcy and Insolvency Act provide the debtor with a stay from both secured and unsecured creditors in order to formulate a reorganization plan.

Figure 22-1 shows that if a firm is experiencing technical insolvency, management must either modify the operating and financial conditions or terminate the firm's life. If the decision is made to alter the company in the hopes of revitalizing its operations, either voluntary agreements with the investors or a formal court-arranged reorganization must be used. If, on the other hand, the difficulties are believed to be insurmountable, a liquidation will take place, either by assignment of the assets to an independent party for liquidation or by formal bankruptcy proceedings.

FIGURE 22-1
Reorganization Versus Liquidation

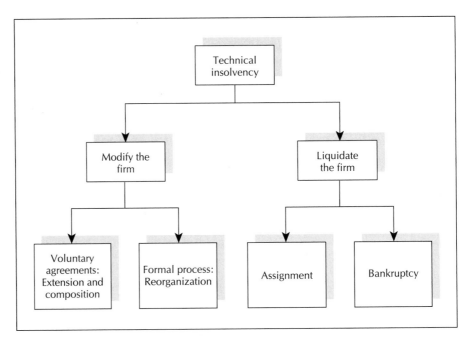

---

[7]As of November 30, 1992, both receivers and secured creditors must comply with Part XI of the Bankruptcy and Insolvency Act.

[8]Under the Act's provisions, receivers are protected from any loss or damage occurring during the administration of the receivership. However, the receiver must act in compliance with the provisions of the act. For a more detailed discussion of the rules for receivers, see Marcel Gauvreau and David Stewart, "New Rules For Receivers," *CGA Magazine*, (November 1992), pp. 31–33.

VOLUNTARY REMEDIES TO INSOLVENCY

If a thorough analysis of the firm's financial condition suggests that the company's going-concern value is greater than its liquidation value, management may attempt to arrange for a financial restructuring of the firm through an informal arrangement with the firm creditors. This type of arrangement may allow the firm an extension of time to pay the debts, or even reduce the amount ultimately to be paid.

Prerequisites[9]

An informal arrangement avoids the formal procedures and the legal costs of a court settlement. However, any creditor who refuses to participate may legally prohibit the arrangement for the remaining creditors. If a bankruptcy case reaches the courts, a smaller settlement may result; thus, unanimous agreement by the creditors is the key to the success of an informal arrangement. Whether a reasonable chance exists for the creditors to finalize such a plan is based upon (1) the debtor's proven honesty and integrity, (2) the firm's potential for recovery, and (3) the economic prospects for the industry.

Procedure

In most cases, the debtor confers with the creditors to explain the firm's financial condition and to request that they consider developing a plan that restructures the firm. An informal arrangement is a contract between creditors and debtors. As a result, the terms of the agreement must abide by the rules of contract law. To be effective the arrangement should involve the minimum number of creditors whose claims are large enough to make the business financially viable after the restructuring. Creditors who decline to accept the arrangement must be paid in full or according to the priority of their claim. Furthermore, the contract is not binding on creditors if their agreement was obtained through misrepresentation, non-disclosure, or other improper means. Typically, this informal arrangement may be classified as an extension, a composition, or some combination thereof.

Extension

Although an **extension** requires that the debtor pay the amount owed in full, the period over which payments are made is extended. For instance, the arrangement may stipulate that all new purchases are to be made on a cash basis, and the outstanding balance from prior purchases is to be paid over an extended period. Also, the contract may place the existing debt in subordination to new liabilities during the extension period. Clearly, the creditors must have confidence in the company's management and in the economic conditions affecting the firm; otherwise they would not agree to such concessions.

Although the creditors' basis for an extension does depend upon their trust in the present management, several control mechanisms may be used during this period of uncertainty. For example, the plan may prohibit any dividend payments to the shareholders until the firm is financially sound

---

[9]E. Bruce Leonard, *Guide to Commercial Insolvency in Canada* (Toronto, Butterworths, 1988).

again. In fact, the shareholders may have to place their shares in escrow with the creditors' committee. Also, the arrangement may require that the firm's assets be assigned to the creditors' committee for the duration of the extension period. Finally, a requirement may be incorporated into the contract stipulating that a member of the creditors' committee countersign cheques.

Composition

A **composition** permits the debtor to pay less than the full balance owed the creditors. In other words, the creditors receive a pro-rated share of their claims. The amount received represents final settlement of the indebtedness. The creditors agree to a partial payment because the only remaining option is bankruptcy proceedings, the costs of which can quickly deplete the firm's resources. Negotiations between debtor and creditors hinge on the savings that may be expected by avoiding the legal costs associated with bankruptcy. Also, the debtor avoids the stigma attached to bankruptcy.

Evaluation of Voluntary Remedies

The primary advantages of an arrangement relate to the minimization of costs and the informality of the process. A significant amount of legal, investigative, and administrative expenses may be avoided, resulting in a higher return to the creditors. Also, the bargaining process is greatly simplified, and a more congenial atmosphere typically prevails than in the bankruptcy courts.

One of the difficulties of an arrangement is that a creditor may refuse to participate. To encourage participation and cooperation of the firm's creditors, a composition generally allows for the payment in full of small claims. For instance, the terms of the contract may state that all creditors are to receive $50 plus a pro-rated share of the remaining claim. This provision eliminates the small claims. However, it means that the larger creditors partially underwrite the amounts payable to small creditors.

Another disadvantage, particularly for the extension, is that the debtor maintains control of the business. If the underlying problems confronting the business are not corrected, the company's assets may continue to erode in value, which clearly works to the detriment of the creditors. However, as already explained, controls may be initiated to minimize any potential losses due to continued inefficient management.

REORGANIZATION

If a voluntary remedy, such as an extension or composition, is not workable, a company can declare voluntarily or be forced involuntarily by its creditors into bankruptcy. As a part of this process, the firm is either reorganized or liquidated. In Canada, a reorganization of a company can occur either through the Bankruptcy and Insolvency Act (Bill C-22) or through the Companies' Creditors Arrangement Act. Both of these acts have as their objective to revitalize the firm by changing its operating procedures and the capital structure. However, the Companies' Creditors Arrangement Act provides for the reorganization of financially troubled companies under the Bankruptcy Court, but without disruption caused by the activities of trustees working under the Bankruptcy Insolvency Act.

Reorganization Through the Bankruptcy Act

A reorganization can be accomplished through the use of a proposal. The provisions of the proposal have been set out in the Bankruptcy and Insolvency Act. The proposal represents a compromise between the debtor and the firm's creditors. If the proposal is accepted, it is legally binding on all creditors who participated in its development. In effect, a proposal enables a financially unsound business which is viable, the opportunity to save the business and provide creditors with a return greater than that expected from a liquidation.

New legislation enacted by the Bankruptcy and Insolvency Act (Bill C-22) gives the debtor the right to be heard and more time to develop a reorganization proposal before assets can be seized by secured creditors. In effect, the debtor[10] can file a notice of intention to file a proposal with the Official Receiver, which gives the debtor an automatic 30-day stay against both secured and unsecured creditors. The debtor is also permitted to apply for extensions of 45 days up to a maximum of five months after the initial 30-day stay in order to develop a definitive proposal for reorganization. In addition, the law enables the debtor to revoke leases with landlords and set the maximum rental payable at six months if the lease is broken. However, throughout this period the debtor must provide detailed cash-flow statements to the court.

The procedure of a proposal requires that a trustee be appointed to represent the debtor during the proceedings. The responsibility of the trustee is to report on the proposal to both the creditors and the court. The proposal requires that creditors be defined according to classes. A class of creditors is defined on the basis of nature of debt, priority of claim, and commonality of interest.[11] A simple majority of creditors with 66.7 percent in dollar value of the proven claims must be obtained for the proposal to be binding on class of creditors. The trustee must then apply for the approval of the Bankruptcy Court. The Bankruptcy Court will examine the terms of the proposal to see if they are reasonable and are in the best interests of the creditors. If accepted by the Bankruptcy Court, the proposal is binding on all creditors with claims proven under the Bankruptcy and Insolvency Act.

The Reorganization Decision

In the reorganization process, the trustee has to establish the going-concern value for the debtor's business after the reorganization. This procedure requires an estimation of the company's future earnings. With this projection in hand, a capitalization rate (or equivalently a price/earnings ratio) for a similar but prosperous firm is determined. When this rate is applied to the earnings, a going-concern value may be approximated. For example, assume that a corporation may reasonably expect to make $1 million in annual earnings after the reorganization. If the price/earnings multiple for a comparable firm is 8, the going-concern value is $8 million ($1 million earnings × 8 price/earnings ratio).

---

[10]The term *debtor* in this context means insolvent persons, bankrupts, trustee in bankruptcy, and liquidator or receiver under security under the Bankruptcy and Insolvency Act.

[11]For a more detailed discussion on the 1992 amendments to the Bankruptcy and Insolvency Act, see Stephen H. Barnes "What Do You Propose?" *CGA Magazine*, (November 1992), pp. 34–37.

After a going-concern value has been estimated, the trustee devises a proposal, including a way of restructuring the firm's capital to meet the criteria of fairness and feasibility. In developing this proposal, the trustee evaluates what changes are necessary to place the company in a more profitable posture. Also, in revamping the capital structure, concern is given to the firm's ability to cover the financial fixed charges: interest, principal repayments, and preferred dividends.

If the facts indicate that a reorganization is fair and feasible to the respective creditors and the shareholders, new securities are issued to reflect the revised capital structure. The principal guideline in this procedure has generally been the **rule of absolute priority**, which simply indicates that the company must completely honour senior claims on assets before settling junior claims. However, plans are frequently based on a blend of absolute and relative priorities, where a junior claim receives partial payment even though a senior claim has not been paid in its entirety. Such a compromise is at times necessary in order to satisfy small creditors who might otherwise vote against the proposal.

EXAMPLE

To illustrate the priorities that might be used in a reorganization plan, consider the Paine Corporation, which is currently undergoing a reorganization. Table 22-3 presents the firm's balance sheet. The creditors have filed a petition for reorganization. The court has named a trustee, who is developing a possible plan of organization. Based upon the trustee's evaluation, an internal reorganization is considered to be both fair and feasible to the existing investors. The trustee has projected the company's earnings, and by using an

TABLE 22-3
Paine Corporation
Balance Sheet

Assets	
Current assets	$ 2,000,000
Net plant and equipment	15,500,000
Other assets	1,000,000
Total assets	$18,500,000

Liabilities and Equity	
Current liabilities	
Accounts payable	$ 1,000,000
Notes payable	3,000,000
Total current liabilities	$ 4,000,000
Long-term liabilities	
Mortgage bonds (8% due in 2001)	$ 4,000,000
Subordinated debentures (9% due in 2001)[a]	8,000,000
Total long-term liabilities	$12,000,000
Total liabilities	$16,000,000
Equity	
Common shares	500,000
Capital surplus	14,000,000
Retained earnings	(12,000,000)
Total equity	$2,500,000
Total liabilities and equity	$18,500,000

[a]Subordinated to the mortgage bonds

Creditors	Amount of Claim	50 Percent of Claim	New Claim After Subordination
Accounts payable	$ 1,000,000	$ 500,000	$ 500,000
Notes payable	3,000,000	1,500,000	1,500,000
Mortgage bonds	4,000,000	2,000,000	4,000,000
Subordinated debentures[a]	8,000,000	4,000,000	2,000,000
	$16,000,000	$8,000,000	$8,000,000

New Securities Issued in the Reorganization

Old Security	New Securities	
Accounts payable	Accounts payable	$ 250,000
	Common shares	250,000
Notes payable	Preferred shares	750,000
	Common shares	750,000
Mortgage bonds	Mortgage bonds (8%)	2,000,000
	Subordinated debentures (9½%)	1,000,000
	Preferred shares (10%)	1,000,000
Subordinated debentures	Common shares	2,000,000
		$8,000,000

[a]Subordinated to the mortgage bonds

TABLE 22-4
Paine Corporation
Reorganization Plan

appropriate price/earnings multiple has estimated the firm's going-concern value to be $8 million, as compared with a $6 million liquidation value (the approximate amount that would be received if the business were terminated and the assets sold individually).

Table 22-4 presents the proposed plan for reorganizing the company. The first portion of the table specifies the amounts of the distribution to be made to each group of creditors. Since the going-concern value is $8 million, only 50 percent of the $16 million in debt can be honoured. As a result, the common shareholders will not be entitled to any of the distribution. Also, the subordinated debentures are not to participate in the reorganization until the mortgage bondholders have been repaid in full. Consequently, the $4 million in securities that would have been distributed to the owners of the debentures has to be reduced by $2 million. The final distribution, after recognizing the subordination, is shown in the last column of Table 22-4.

The lower section of Table 22-4 reflects the trustee's proposed changes in the firm's capital structure. The objective is to reduce the financial leverage to a point commensurate with the company's ability to cover the fixed financial charges from earnings. For example, the original accounts payable balance is reduced to $500,000, with the creditors entitled to a short-term claim of $250,000 and $250,000 in new common shares. The final capital structure, if the trustee's plan is adopted, is provided in Table 22-5. ∎

Accounts payable	$ 250,000
Mortgage bonds (8%)	2,000,000
Subordinated debentures (9½%)	1,000,000
Preferred shares (10%)	1,750,000
Common shares	3,000,000
	$8,000,000

TABLE 22-5
Paine Corporation
Liabilities and Equity
After Reorganization

Reorganization through the Companies' Creditors Arrangement Act

The Companies' Creditors Arrangement Act (CCAA) was originated to facilitate the financial reorganization of larger companies which have outstanding issues of secured and unsecured debt. Prior to 1992, the CCAA provided provisions for a debtor to deal with claims of secured creditors, whereas the Bankruptcy and Insolvency Act does not have these types of provisions. However, amendments to the Bankruptcy and Insolvency Act now enable debtors to deal with the claims of secured creditors. As a result of these amendments, both large and small firms are able to deal with their secured creditors under both acts. Both acts differ significantly in their approach to developing a framework for bankruptcy proceedings. The Bankruptcy and Insolvency Act provides detailed and specific provisions for proposals, whereas the CCAA requires that procedures be developed through a series of court orders. This lack of framework in the CCAA favours large corporations which have the legal resources to develop the required procedures in court.

The CCAA enables management of the debtor company to develop a plan of arrangement which deals with making the payments required under the new capital structure and paying any deferred obligations as they mature. Again, the court may prohibit legal suits by both secured and unsecured creditors before a definitive plan of arrangement is filed with the courts. The plan for arrangement generally includes all creditors. Since all creditors do not have the same priority in claim, the CCAA allows creditors to be classified according to the nature of their claims. However, the Act does not provide any direction as how to classify creditors' claims. A fair and feasible compromise must be obtained between the debtor and creditors since the debtor's plan of arrangement must be approved by 50 percent of the creditors who have at least 75 percent of the dollar value of the creditors voting on the plan. The court provides final approval of the plan of arrangement which is binding on all participating creditors.

The reorganization of Olympia and York Development Ltd. (O&Y) is an example of a company that used the CCAA to file for protection from its creditors. The Canadian court action protects O&Y from claims on $8.4 billion in secured loans and about $200 million in unsecured bills. As a consequence of filing for creditor protection, the privately held O&Y had to release their financial statements which disclosed details of specific debts, cash flow levels and even staff salaries.

In March of 1992, O&Y publicly admitted to a liquidity crisis which was caused by a depressed North American real estate industry. O&Y filed for creditor protection under the CCAA on May 14, 1992. Over the next eight months, the company produced several debt-restructuring proposals, but these proposals were rejected by secured creditors. In late October of 1992, a proposal was made public which outlined a plan to restructure the real estate empire's massive debt. The major points of this restructuring plan were:[12]

- The Reichmanns would give up 90 percent of the privately owned O&Y if unsecured creditors were not fully repaid within five years. In the interim, O&Y would pay no interest on unsecured creditors' claims and these claims would be exchanged for company bonds.

[12]*The Gazette*, Montreal, "Reichmanns Would Give Up 90 per cent of Olympia & York," October 29, 1992. pp. E1–E2; and Dan Westell, "Reichmanns Release Details of O&Y Restructuring Plan," *The Globe and Mail*, November 11, 1992, p. B2.

- Three of O&Y's major properties in Toronto would be placed under the control of a joint venture owned 20 percent by O&Y Properties and 80 percent owned by the Bank on Nova Scotia, the Canadian Imperial Bank of Commerce, the National Bank, and the Royal Bank. In exchange for this concession, the proposal required interest rates on outstanding bank loans, conversion of $131 million in loans to capital and a new credit line to attract tenants.

- The spinning off of the company into three: a Canadian real estate holding company which holds the main Canadian buildings; a U.S. real estate and investment company holding U.S. real estate properties; and a residual Canadian company holding investments and some real estate.

The reorganization plan was dependent on O&Y retaining its investment in Gulf Canada Resources Ltd. and Abitibi-Price Inc., and on office rental rates rising about 33 percent over the period 1992 to 1998. This reorganization plan was the basis for developing a final reorganization plan on which both secured creditors and unsecured creditors voted in late January, 1993. Eight classes of secured creditors voted to turn down the reorganization plan and won their right to foreclose on their collateral which included a $475 million mortgage on O&Y's flagship First Canadian Place in Toronto. However, the plan was structured such that only the unsecured creditors class could veto the reorganization. Rejection of the proposal by this class of unsecured creditors would have meant liquidation of the firm's assets through the Bankruptcy and Insolvency Act. On January 26, 1993, the unsecured creditors voted to accept the reorganization plan. The Reichmanns ended up owning 100 percent of a new company, called O&Y Properties, which would manage the former real estate assets under the control of secured creditors.[13]

LIQUIDATION

If the likelihood is small that reorganization of an insolvent firm will result in a profitable business, the firm should be liquidated. In this situation the liquidation value exceeds the going-concern value, and it is to the investor's advantage to terminate the business by liquidating its assets. Continuing the operation at this point generally results only in further losses. A firm's management can voluntarily declare bankruptcy by filing for an assignment in bankruptcy or the firm can be forced involuntarily into bankruptcy by creditors filing a petition. The objective of either procedure is to distribute any proceeds from the liquidation to the creditors.

Liquidation by Assignment

If an **assignment** is used to liquidate the business, the final settlement is done privately with a minimum amount of court involvement. The debtor transfers the title of the firm's assets to a third party, who has been appointed by the Official Receiver. This individual, known as a **trustee**, administers

---

[13]Canadian Press. "O&Y Merger to Proceed" (The *Globe and Mail*, January 27, 1993) p. B11; and Margaret Philip, "O&Y Plan Comes to Crunch" (*The Globe and Mail*, January 26, 1993) pp. B1, B2.

the liquidation process and sees that an appropriate distribution is made of the proceeds. Under an assignment, the debtor is not automatically discharged of the remaining balance due a creditor. When the liquidation funds are distributed to the creditors, a notation on the cheques should be made indicating that endorsement of the cheque represents the creditor's acceptance of the money as full settlement of the claim. However, even then a creditor can refuse to accept the payment, considering that his or her interests would be better served by a court-administered liquidation. Owing to the possible nonacceptance of the assignment by one or more creditors, the debtor may attempt to reach a prior agreement with the creditors that the assignment will represent a complete settlement of claims.

An assignment has several advantages over a formal bankruptcy procedure. The assignment is usually quicker, is less expensive, and requires less legal formality. The trustee can take quicker action to avoid further depletion in the value of inventories and equipment and typically is more familiar with the debtor's business, which should improve the final results. However, the assignment does not legally discharge the debtor from the responsibility of unpaid balances, and the creditor is not protected against fraud; consequently, formal bankruptcy proceedings may be preferred by either the debtor or creditors.

Liquidation by Bankruptcy

The Liquidation Process

A bankruptcy case is initiated by filing a petition with the Bankruptcy Court. A petition may be filed by the firm's management (voluntary) or by its creditors (involuntary). To initiate an involuntary reorganization, the creditors must show that the debtor has debts outstanding of at least $1000 and has committed an act of bankruptcy within the six months preceding the date of the petition. The Bankruptcy and Insolvency Act contains several provisions defining what constitutes an act of bankruptcy. Examples of these provisions include: the debtor giving notice to suspend payment of debts, the debtor failing to meet maturing obligations, or the debtor committing an act of fraud towards a creditor.

After the filing and approval of the bankruptcy petition by the Official Receiver, the Bankruptcy Court will issue a receiving order which formally declares the firm bankrupt and authorizes liquidation of the company's assets. The court will also appoint an interim receiver, who serves as temporary caretaker of the company's assets, until a trustee can be appointed by the creditors. The interim receiver then requests from the debtor a list of assets and liabilities.

A meeting of the creditors is called by the interim receiver. At the meeting, the creditors will be required to appoint a trustee and a board of inspectors. This board of inspectors will represent the creditors throughout the bankruptcy proceedings by providing advice to the trustee on behalf of the creditors. In addition, both the financial position of the debtor company and a list of its assets and liabilities will be disclosed at the meeting. The debtor may be questioned for additional information relevant to the proceedings.

The trustee initiates plans to liquidate the company's assets. As a part of this conversion process, individuals owing money to the debtor are contacted in an effort to collect these outstanding balances. Appraisers are selected to determine a value for the property, and these values are used as guidelines in liquidating assets. After all assets have been converted into cash through private sales or public auctions, all expenses incurred in the bankruptcy process are paid. The remaining cash is distributed on a pro rata basis to the creditors according to the rule of absolute priority.

Priority of Claims

Following the rule of absolute priority, claims are honoured in the following order:

1. Secured creditors, with the proceeds from the sale of the specific property going first to these creditors. If any portion of the claim remains unpaid, the balance is treated as an unsecured loan.

2. Expenses incurred in administering the bankrupt estate.

3. Expenses incurred after the bankruptcy petition has been filed but prior to a trustee being appointed.

4. Salaries and commissions not exceeding $2,000 per employee that were earned within the three months preceding the bankruptcy petition.

5. Federal Government's statutory payroll deductions.[14]

6. Unsecured creditors.

7. Preferred shares.

8. Common shares.

When the distribution of the proceeds is completed the trustee provides a final accounting to the creditors and files a final report to the Superintendent of bankruptcy. If all claims are satisfied in full and the company is not to be dissolved, the trustee may apply to the court on behalf of the debtor's company for a discharge from bankruptcy. Once the discharge is granted, the directors and officers of the corporate entity regain the right to sign legal documents and their powers to perform their business functions. However, if the claims of the creditors are not satisfied in full, the company will remain in the state of bankruptcy until it ceases to exist under the Canada Business Corporation Act.

An example will illustrate the order of payments from a liquidation. The Poverty Stricken Corporation has been judged bankrupt; its balance sheet is shown in Table 22-6. Although the historical cost of the assets was $100 million, the trustee in bankruptcy was able to realize only $44 million from their sale. In addition, costs of $8 million were incurred in administering the bankruptcy.

The order of settling the claims is listed in Table 22-7. As the table shows, the first mortgage bondholders are entitled to receive the net proceeds resulting from the sale of specific property identified in the lien (an office building). We are assuming that the sale price of this property is $10 million, which leaves an unpaid balance of $4 million to be treated as an unsecured claim. Next, the administrative costs associated with filing and executing the bankruptcy petition, the employees' salaries, and the tax liabilities are to be paid.

After all payments have been made for prior claims, $22,400,000 is available for general unsecured creditors, whose claims total $56 million; dividing

---

[14]Under the 1992 amendments of the Act, the claims of the Crown have been designated unsecured claims rather than preference claims. The exception to these claims is the statutory payroll deductions which have priority to all other creditors.

TABLE 22-6
Poverty Stricken Corporation
Balance Sheet ($000)

Assets		
Current assets		$ 20,000
Net plant and equipment		80,000
Total assets		$100,000

Liabilities		
Current liabilities		
Accounts payable	$22,000	
Accrued wages[a]	3,600	
Notes payable	20,000	
Total current liabilities		$45,600
Long-term liabilities		
First mortgage bonds[b]	$14,000	
Subordinated debentures[c]	10,000	
Total long-term liabilities		$24,000
Total liabilities		$ 69,600
Equity		
Preferred shares	$ 4,000	
Common shares	$26,400	
Total equity		$ 30,400
Total liabilities and equity		$100,000

[a]No single claim exceeds $2,000.
[b]These bonds have a first lien on an office building.
[c]Subordinated to the notes payable.

TABLE 22-7
Poverty Stricken Corporation
Priority of Claims ($000)

Distribution of Proceeds		
Liquidation value of assets		$44,000
Priority of claims:		
1. First-mortgage receipts from the sale of an office building	$10,000	
2. Administrative expenses	8,000	
3. Salaries due employees	3,600	
Total prior claims		21,600
Amount available for settling claims of general creditors		$22,400

22.4 by 56, we find that the claimants are entitled to 40 percent of the original loan. This percentage is computed from the amount available for general creditors, $22,400,000, relative to the total claims of $56 million. However, an adjustment must be made to recognize the subordination of the debentures to the notes payable. In essence, the owners of debentures must relinquish their right to any money until the notes payable have been settled in full. In this situation, $12 million of the note balance remains unpaid. As a consequence, the $4 million originally shown to be received by the debentures must be paid to the investors owning the notes payable. The actual distributions to the unsecured creditors are shown in the last column of Table 22-8.

General Claims	Claim	40% of Claims	Adjustment for Subordination
Accounts payable	$22,000,000	$ 8,800,000	$ 8,800,000
Notes payable	20,000,000	8,000,000	12,000,000
Remaining portion of first mortgage bond	4,000,000	1,600,000	1,600,000
Subordinated debenture	10,000,000	4,000,000	–0–
Totals	$56,000,000	$22,400,000	$22,400,000

TABLE 22-8
Poverty Stricken Corporation
Claims of General Creditors

SUMMARY

Facing financial adversity is never easy, but managers need to be aware of the implications and consequences of financial trouble. This information may prove useful if reorganization or liquidation is on the horizon for the firm or if similar action becomes necessary for one of the firm's customers.

Business failure is principally the result of financial problems, economic factors beyond management's control, or a deficiency in management structure, such as imbalance of skills. The symptoms of insolvency are often readily identifiable in the firm's financial statements. A company in financial trouble can generally be identified by a decrease in both its investment of liquid assets and its profitability. Also, the use of financial leverage increases significantly. Finally, management's efficient use of assets, as depicted by the asset turnover ratio, may deteriorate.

When a business becomes technically insolvent, one of two decisions must be made. The firm has to be reorganized or liquidated. In either case, the process may be relatively informal or closely controlled by the court. In the reorganization of a firm, voluntary agreements may be arranged, taking the form of either an extension or a composition. If, however, these plans are not acceptable to the creditors, a court-administered reorganization may be necessary. If the company's liquidation value is thought to exceed its going-concern value, the firm should be dissolved.

In the process of liquidation a firm's assets may be assigned to a trustee who sells them and distributes the funds according to the rule of absolute priority. Such an assignment aims to avoid the more costly court-ordered bankruptcy filing. Yet, if the debtor or creditors consider formal bankruptcy proceedings preferable, voluntary or involuntary bankruptcy may be requested. If the debtor is judged to be bankrupt, a referee is selected to liquidate the firm's assets and distribute the proceeds in accordance with the rule of absolute priority.

STUDY QUESTIONS

22-1. Explain the following terms: economic failure, technical insolvency, and insolvency in bankruptcy.

22-2. What are the most frequent causes of business failure?

22-3. To what potential mistakes is a firm vulnerable if it is experiencing any of the deficiencies cited in Question 22-2?

22-4. What are the prerequisites to a successful voluntary remedy?

22-5. What procedure is usually followed in arranging a voluntary agreement?

22-6. Compare an extension with a composition.

22-7. What are the advantages and disadvantages of voluntary remedies?

22-8. Explain the process of liquidation by assignment.

SELF-TEST PROBLEMS

ST-1. (*Predicting Bankruptcy*) You are studying five companies and have decided to use Altman's model to predict the probability of bankruptcy for each. The data needed are given below. What are the bankruptcy scores for these companies and how are they interpreted?

	Variables				
Company	X_1	X_2	X_3	X_4	X_5
A	15%	20%	35%	335%	1.60×
B	25	45	40	175	1.95×
C	20	25	15	125	.75×
D	15	12	10	110	.55×
E	40	35	30	175	1.50×

ST-2. (*Reorganization*) Brogham, Inc., is filing for bankruptcy. The trustee has estimated the firm's liquidation value to be $1,260,000. Given the liabilities and equity from the balance sheet, compute the distributions of proceeds.

Brogham, Inc.

Liabilities and equity	
Current liabilities	
Accounts payable	$ 120,000
Notes payable	300,000
Total current liabilities	$ 420,000
Long-term liabilities	
Long-term notes payable	$ 420,000
Subordinated debentures[a]	1,260,000
Total long-term liabilities	$1,680,000
Total liabilities	$2,100,000
Equity	
Common shares	$ 500,000
Capital surplus	2,000,000
Total equity	$2,500,000
Total liabilities and equity	$4,600,000

[a]Subordinated to the long-term notes payable.

ST-3. (*Distribution of Proceeds in Bankruptcy*) Pioneer Enterprises is bankrupt and being liquidated. The liabilities and equity portion of its balance sheet are given below. The book value of the assets was $60 million, but the realized value when liquidated was only $31.58 million, of which $7.55 million was from the sale of the firm's office building. Administrative expenses associated with the liquidation were $7.2 million. Determine the distribution of the proceeds.

Pioneer Enterprises Liabilities and Equities		
Current debt		
Accounts payable	$ 6,500,000	
Accrued wages[a]	2,250,000	
Notes payable	15,000,000	
Total current debt		$23,750,000
Long-term debt		
Bonds[b]	$14,000,000	
Subordinated debentures[c]	8,500,000	
Total long-term debt		22,500,000
Equity		
Preferred shares	$ 2,850,000	
Common shares	$10,900,000	
Total equity		13,750,000
Total debt and equity		$60,000,000

[a]No single claim exceeds $2,000.
[b]Have first lien on the office building.
[c]Subordinated to the mortgage bonds.

STUDY PROBLEMS (SET A)

22-1A. (*Predicting Bankruptcy*) You are considering investing in the securities of three companies. Using the Altman model and the information given below, compute the bankruptcy score for each company. Which companies would you invest in?

	Company		
	A	B	C
Sales	$1,500,000	$ 800,000	$3,000,000
Total assets	4,000,000	1,000,000	4,500,000
Net working capital	1,100,000	650,000	2,000,000
Earnings before interest and taxes	1,000,000	500,000	1,000,000
Retained earnings	800,000	350,000	1,500,000
Stock market value	1,250,000	500,000	2,200,000
Debt book value	750,000	100,000	1,250,000

22-2A. (*Reorganization*) The trustee for the reorganization of Warner Corporation has established the going-concern value at $7.5 million. The creditors and the amounts owed are given below. As part of the reorganization plan, the accounts payable are to be settled by renewal of $500,000 of the accounts, with a due date of six months. Any remaining amount to be received by these claimants is to be realized in the form of long-term notes payable. The current owners of the firm's notes are to be paid in preferred shares. The mortgage bondholders will receive half of their adjusted claim under the reorganization in the form of newly issued bonds, with the remainder being common shares. The investors owning the subordinated debentures are to receive common shares in settlement of their claim. What will Warner's liabilities and equity be after reorganization?

Warner Corporation	
Creditors	Amount of Claims
Accounts payable	$ 2,000,000
Notes payable	1,000,000
Mortgage bonds	4,000,000
Subordinated debentures[a]	3,000,000
	$10,000,000

[a]Subordinated to the mortgage bonds.

22-3A. (*Reorganization*) Pepertyme, Inc., has filed for voluntary reorganization. The firm's liabilities are shown below. The firm has an estimated going-concern value of $1,825,000 and a liquidation value of $1,400,000. What will Pepertyme's liabilities and equity be after reorganization if the following rules are applied?

a. Accounts payable are to receive 50 percent of their claim in accounts payable due in 30 days and 50 percent in 90-day notes payable.

b. Notes payable are to receive 50 percent of their claim in short-term notes payable and 50 percent in long-term notes payable.

c. Mortgage bondholders will receive half of their claim in new bonds and half in common shares.

d. Subordinated debentures will receive their claim as 50 percent preferred shares and 50 percent common shares.

Pepertyme, Inc.	
Creditors	Claims
Accounts payable	$ 650,000
Short-term notes payable	500,000
Mortgage bonds	1,000,000
Subordinated debentures[a]	1,500,000
	$3,650,000

[a]Subordinated to the mortgage bonds

22-4A. (*Distribution of Proceeds in Bankruptcy*) Loggins Industries has filed a bankruptcy petition and is in the process of being liquidated. Its liabilities and equity are shown below. The book value of the assets is $80 million, but the liquidation value is $42 million. Administrative expenses of the liquidation procedures were $2 million. What is the distribution of proceeds?

Loggins Industries Liabilities and Equities		
Current debt		
Accounts payable	$10,000,000	
Accrued wages[a]	5,000,000	
Notes payable	17,000,000	
Total current debt		$32,000,000
Long-term debt		
Bonds	$25,000,000	
Subordinated debentures[b]	18,000,000	
Total long-term debt		43,000,000
Equity		
Preferred shares	$ 1,000,000	
Common shares	4,000,000	

Total equity	5,000,000
Total debt and equity	$80,000,000

[a]No single claim exceeds $2,000.
[b]Subordinated to notes payable.

22-5A. (*Distribution of Proceeds in Bankruptcy*) Heinburner, Inc., a local manufacturing concern, is bankrupt and is being liquidated. The book value of the assets is $1.5 million. When the firm was liquidated, $1.25 million was realized. Administrative costs for the liquidation were $150,000. Determine the distribution of proceeds.

Heinburner Inc., Liabilities and Equities

Current debt		
Accounts payable	$200,000	
Accrued wages[a]	150,000	
Notes payable	350,000	
Total current debt		$ 700,000
Long-term debt		$ 300,000
Equity		
Preferred shares	$100,000	
Common shares	400,000	
Total equity		500,000
Total debt and equity		$1,500,000

[a]No single claim exceeds $2,000.

22-6A. (*Predicting Bankruptcy*) You are considering investing in the securities of three companies. Using the Altman model and the information given below, compute the bankruptcy score for each company. Which companies would you invest in?

	Company		
	A	**B**	**C**
Sales	$2,000,000	$ 6,000,000	$3,500,000
Total assets	3,000,000	13,000,000	5,000,000
Net working capital	1,400,000	4,500,000	2,200,000
Earnings before interest and taxes	1,500,000	3,000,000	2,500,000
Retained earnings	1,000,000	2,500,000	1,800,000
Stock market value	1,600,000	5,000,000	2,800,000
Debt book value	900,000	3,200,000	1,500,000

22-7A. (*Reorganization*) Juarez, Inc., has filed for voluntary reorganization. The firm's liabilities are shown below. The firm has an estimated going-concern value of $8,400,000 and a liquidation value of $6,500,000. What will Juarez's liabilities and equity be after reorganization if the following rules are applied?

a. Accounts payable are to receive 33 percent of their claim in accounts payable due in 30 days and the remainder in long-term notes payable.

b. Notes payable are to receive 50 percent of their claim in short-term notes payable and 50 percent in preferred shares.

c. Mortgage bondholders will receive half of their claim in new bonds and half in common shares.

d. Subordinated debentures will receive common shares in settlement of their claim.

Juarez, Inc.

Creditors	Claims
Accounts payable	$ 3,000,000
Short-term notes payable	2,000,000
Mortgage bonds	2,000,000
Subordinated debentures[a]	5,000,000
	$12,000,000

[a]Subordinated to the mortgage bonds

22-8A. (*Distribution of Proceeds in Bankruptcy*) Sanchez Firefighting Inc. has filed a bankruptcy petition and is in the process of being liquidated. Its liabilities and equity are shown below. The book value of the assets is $3.75 million, but the liquidation value totals only $3,125,000. Administrative expenses of the liquidation process totalled $375,000. What is the distribution of proceeds?

Sanchez Firefighting Inc. Liabilities and Equities

Current debt		
Accounts payable	$550,000	
Accrued wages[a]	300,000	
Notes payable	950,000	
Total current debt		$1,800,000
Long-term debt		$ 700,000
Equity		
Preferred shares	$500,000	
Common shares	700,000	
Total equity		1,200,000
Total debt and equity		$3,700,000

[a]No single claim exceeds $2,000.

STUDY PROBLEMS (SET B)

22-1B. (*Predicting Bankruptcy*) You are considering investing in the securities of three companies. Using the Altman model and the information given below, compute the bankruptcy score for each company. Which companies would you invest in?

	Company		
	A	B	C
Sales	$1,550,000	$ 900,000	$2,750,000
Total assets	4,000,000	1,000,000	4,500,000
Net working capital	1,100,000	650,000	2,000,000
Earnings before interest and taxes	975,000	500,000	1,000,000
Retained earnings	800,000	350,000	1,500,000
Stock market value	1,150,000	550,000	2,000,000
Debt book value	750,000	100,000	1,300,000

22-2B. (*Reorganization*) The trustee for the reorganization of Hester Corporation has established the going-concern value at $7 million. The creditors and the amounts owed are given below. As part of the reorganization plan, the accounts payable are to be settled by renewal of $500,000 of the accounts, with a due date of six months. Any remaining amount to be received by these claimants is to be realized in the form of long-term notes payable. The current owners of the firm's notes are to be paid in preferred shares. The mortgage bondholders will receive half of their adjusted claim under the reorganization in the form of newly issued bonds, with the remainder being common shares. The investors owning the subordinated debentures are to receive common shares in settlement of their claim. What will Hester's liabilities and equity be after reorganization?

Hester Corporation	
Creditors	**Amount of Claims**
Accounts payable	$ 2,250,000
Notes payable	1,000,000
Mortgage bonds	3,750,000
Subordinated debentures[a]	3,250,000
	$10,250,000

[a]Subordinated to the mortgage bonds.

22-3B. (*Reorganization*) Topher, Inc., has filed for voluntary reorganization. The firm's liabilities are shown below. The firm has an estimated going-concern value of $1,900,000 and a liquidation value of $1,500,000. What will Topher's liabilities and equity be after reorganization if the following rules are applied?

a. Accounts payable are to receive 50 percent of their claim in accounts payable due in 30 days and 50 percent in 90-day notes payable.

b. Notes payable are to receive 50 percent of their claim in short-term notes payable and 50 percent in long-term notes payable.

c. Mortgage bondholders will receive half of their claim in new bonds and half in common shares.

d. Subordinated debentures will receive their claim as 50 percent preferred shares and 50 percent common shares.

Topher, Inc.	
Creditors	**Claims**
Accounts payable	$ 575,000
Short-term notes payable	520,000
Mortgage bonds	1,250,000
Subordinated debentures[a]	1,500,000
	$3,845,000

[a]Subordinated to the mortgage bonds

22-4B. (*Distribution of Proceeds in Bankruptcy*) Grigsby Industries has filed a bankruptcy petition and is in the process of being liquidated. Its liabilities and equity are shown below. The book value of the assets is $84 million, but the liquidation value is $43 million. Administrative expenses of the liquidation procedures were $2 million. What is the distribution of proceeds?

Grigsby Industries Liabilities and Equities		
Current debt		
Accounts payable	$12,000,000	
Accrued wages[a]	5,000,000	
Notes payable	17,000,000	
Total current debt		$34,000,000

Long-term debt		
Bonds	$25,000,000	
Subordinated debentures[b]	20,000,000	
Total long-term debt		45,000,000
Equity		
Preferred shares	$ 1,000,000	
Common shares	4,000,000	
Total equity		5,000,000
Total debt and equity		$84,000,000

[a]No single claim exceeds $2,000.
[b]Subordinated to notes payable.

22-5B. (*Distribution of Proceeds in Bankruptcy*) Scoggins, Inc., a local manu-facturing concern, is bankrupt and is being liquidated. The book value of the assets is $1.5 million. When the firm was liquidated, $1.25 million was realized. Administrative costs for the liquidation were $150,000. Determine the distribution of proceeds.

Scoggins Inc., Liabilities and Equities		
Current debt		
Accounts payable	$190,000	
Accrued wages[a]	152,000	
Notes payable	350,000	
Total current debt		$ 692,000
Long-term debt		$ 250,000
Equity		
Preferred shares	$100,000	
Common shares	500,000	
Total equity		600,000
Total debt and equity		$1,542,000

[a]No single claim exceeds $2,000.

22-6B. (*Predicting Bankruptcy*) You are considering investing in the securities of three companies. Using the Altman model and the information given below, compute the bankruptcy score for each company. Which companies would you invest in?

	Company		
	A	**B**	**C**
Sales	$3,000,000	$2,000,000	$3,200,000
Total assets	4,000,000	4,500,000	5,500,000
Net working capital	2,500,000	1,800,000	2,000,000
Earnings before interest and taxes	2,000,000	900,000	1,800,000
Retained earnings	1,800,000	800,000	1,400,000
Stock market value	2,300,000	1,700,000	2,900,000
Debt book value	1,400,000	1,100,000	1,300,000

22-7B. (*Reorganization*) Insuba, Inc., has filed for voluntary reorganization. The firm's liabilities are shown below. The firm has an estimated going-concern value of $3,800,000 and a liquidation value of $3,200,000. What will Insuba's liabilities and equity be after reorganization if the following rules are applied?

a. Accounts payable are to receive 67 percent of their claim in accounts payable due in 30 days and the remainder in long-term notes payable.

b. Notes payable are to receive 40 percent of their claim in short-term notes payable and 60 percent in preferred shares.

c. Mortgage bondholders will receive 40 percent of their claim in new bonds and 60 percent in common shares.

d. Subordinated debentures will receive common shares in settlement of their claim.

Insuba, Inc.	
Creditors	**Claims**
Accounts payable	$1,200,000
Short-term notes payable	1,000,000
Mortgage bonds	1,000,000
Subordinated debentures[a]	2,500,000
	$5,700,000

[a]Subordinated to the mortgage bonds

22-8B. (*Distribution of Proceeds in Bankruptcy*) Trans Canada Boot Inc. has filed a bankruptcy petition and is in the process of being liquidated. Its liabilities and equity are shown below. The book value of the assets is $8.4 million, but the liquidation value totals only $7.85 million. Administrative expenses of the liquidation process totalled $900,000. What is the distribution of proceeds?

Trans Canada Boot Inc.		
Current debt		
Accounts payable	$2,450,000	
Accrued wages[a]	620,000	
Notes payable	3,150,000	
Total current debt		$ 6,220,000
Long-term debt		$ 450,000
Equity		
Preferred shares	$1,200,000	
Common shares	2,800,000	
Total equity		4,000,000
Total debt and equity		$10,670,000

[a]No single claim exceeds $2,000.

SELF-TEST SOLUTIONS

SS-1. Bankruptcy score $= 1.2X_1 + 1.4X_2 + 3.3X_3 + 0.6X_4 + 0.999X_5$

where, $X_1 =$ (net working capital/total assets)

$X_2 =$ (retained earnings/total assets)

$X_3 =$ (earnings before interest and taxes/total assets)

$X_4 =$ (market value of stock/book value of debt)

$X_5 =$ (sales/total assets)

Company A
$1.2(.15) + 1.4(.20) + 3.3(.35) + 0.6(3.35) + 0.999(1.60) = 5.22$

Company B

$$1.2(.25) + 1.4(.45) + 3.3(.40) + 0.6(1.75) + 0.999(1.95) = 5.25$$

Company C

$$1.2(.20) + 1.4(.25) + 3.3(.15) + 0.6(1.25) + 0.999(0.75) = 2.58$$

Company D

$$1.2(.15) + 1.4(.12) + 3.3(.10) + 0.6(1.10) + 0.999(0.55) = 1.88$$

Company E

$$1.2(.40) + 1.4(.35) + 3.3(.30) + 0.6(1.75) + 0.999(1.50) = 4.51$$

Interpretation of results:

Score < 1.81 —Likely candidate for failure

Score > 2.99 —No concern of bankruptcy

1.81 < Score < 2.675 —Probability of failure greater than success

2.675 < Score < 2.99 —Probability of success greater than failure

The probability of failure is greater than that of success for companies C and D. Companies A, B, and E need not be concerned with bankruptcy.

SS-2.

Brogham, Inc., Reorganization Plan

Creditors	Amount	60% of Claim	Claim After Subordination
Accounts payable	$ 120,000	$ 72,000	$ 72,000
Notes payable	300,000	180,000	180,000
Mortgage bonds	420,000	252,000	420,000
Subordinated debentures	1,260,000	756,000	588,000
	$2,100,000	$1,260,000	$1,260,000

$$\text{Percentage of claim} = \frac{\text{going-concern value}}{\text{total liabilities}}$$

$$= \frac{\$1,260,000}{\$2,100,000}$$

$$= 60\%$$

SS-3.

Pioneer Enterprises

Distribution of Proceeds

Liquidation value of assets		$31,580,000
Priority of claims		
1. Administrative expenses	$7,200,000	
2. Wages payable	2,250,000	
3. First mortgage receipts from building sale	7,550,000	
Total prior claims		17,000,000
Amount available to general creditors		$14,580,000

Claims of General Creditors

Creditors	Amount	40% of Claim	Claim After Subordination
Accounts payable	$ 6,500,000	$ 2,600,000	$ 2,600,000
Notes payable	15,000,000	6,000,000	6,000,000
Remainder of first mortgage bonds	6,450,000	2,580,000	5,980,000

Subordinated debentures	8,500,000	3,400,000	–0–
	$36,450,000	$14,580,000	$14,580,000

$$\text{Percentage of claims} = \frac{\text{amount available to general creditors}}{\text{amount of claims}}$$

$$= \frac{\$14,580,000}{\$36,450,000}$$

$$= 40\%$$

SELECTED REFERENCES

Altman, Edward I. "Corporate Bankruptcy Potential, Stockholder Returns and Share Valuation," *Journal of Finance*, 24 (December 1969), 887–900.

Altman, Edward I. *Corporate Financial Distress*. New York: John Wiley, 1983.

Altman, Edward I. "A Further Empirical Investigation of the Bankruptcy Cost Question," *Journal of Finance*, 39 (September 1984),1067–89.

Altman, Edward I., and Menachem Brenner. "Financial Ratios, Discriminant Analysis and the Prediction of Corporate Bankruptcy," *Journal of Finance*, 23 (September 1968), 589–609.

Ang, James S., Jess H. Chua, and John J. McConnell. "The Administrative Costs of Corporate Bankruptcy: A Note," *Journal of Finance*, 37 (March 1982), 219–226.

Argenti, John. *Corporate Collapse: The Causes and Symptoms*, New York: Wiley, 1976.

Chen, Kung H., and Thomas A. Shimerda. "An Empirical Analysis of Useful Financial Ratios," *Financial Management*, 10 (Spring 1981), 51–60.

Clark, Truman A., and Mark I. Weinstein. "The Behavior of the Common Stock of Bankrupt Firms," *Journal of Finance*, 38 (May 1983), 489–504.

Edmister, Robert O. "An Empirical Test of Financial Ratio Analysis for Small Business Failure Prediction," *Journal of Financial and Quantitative Analysis*, 7 (March 1972), 1477–1493.

Gilson, Stuart C. "Managing Default: Some Evidence on How Firms Choose Between Workouts and Bankruptcy," *Journal of Applied Corporate Finance* (Summer 1991), 62–70.

Gombola, Michael J., Mark E. Haskins, J. Edward Ketz, and David D. Williams. "Cash Flow in Bankruptcy Prediction," *Financial Management*, 16 (Winter 1987), 55–65.

Kalaba, Robert E., Terence C. Langetieg, Nima Rasakhoo, and Mark I. Weinstein. "Estimation of Implicit Bankruptcy Costs," *Journal of Finance*, 39 (July 1984), 629–642.

Morse, Dale, and Wayne Shaw. "Investing in Bankrupt Firms," *Journal of Finance*, 43 (December 1988), 1193–1206.

Paroush, Jacob. "The Domino Effect and the Supervision of the Banking System," *Journal of Finance*, 43 (December 1988), 1207–1218.

Rohman, Mark C. "Financing Chapter 11 Companies in the 1990s," *Journal of Applied Corporate Finance* (Summer 1990), 96–101.

Scott, James. "The Probability of Bankruptcy," *Journal of Banking and Finance*, 5 (September 1981), 317–344.

Weiss, Lawrence A. "The Bankruptcy Code and Violations of Absolute Priority," *Journal of Applied Corporate Finance* (Summer 1991), 71–78.

White, Michelle J. "Bankruptcy Costs and the New Bankruptcy Code," *Journal of Finance*, 38 (May 1983), 477–488.

Wruck, Karen H. "What Really Went Wrong at Revco," *Journal of Applied Corporate Finance* (Summer 1991), 79–92.

- Globalization of Product and Financial Markets
- Exchange Rates
- Exchange Rates and Arbitrage
- The Interest Parity Theory
- Purchasing Power Parity
- Exposure to Exchange Rate Risk
- Multinational Working-Capital Management
- International Financing and Capital Structure Decisions
- Direct Foreign Investment

Both the integration of product and financial markets on an international scale and the presence of a firm's operations in more than one country, require us to examine how financial managers operate in an international environment. Moreover, the "purely domestic" firm is now subject to and influenced by both international events and global economic forces. Thus, managers of all companies must be sensitive to the international aspects of business finance.

Firms can operate internationally in various ways. In the simplest instance, a firm exports to (or imports from) a single foreign country. Other export or import firms operate in many countries simultaneously. For example, banks conduct business in many countries, lending in some currencies and borrowing in others. Many manufacturing companies set up production facilities in foreign countries to sell abroad or to import their output back to the home country.

Some companies have more elaborate international operations. A Japanese automobile company may have a plant in Japan for manufacturing engines, another plant in the U.S. for drive trains, a third in Asia for other components, and an assembly plant in Canada. The final product, the automobile, may be destined for all markets in North America. This is an example of a **multinational corporation (MNC)**.

The basic problems facing international companies differ from those facing domestic companies. Examples of additional complexities of conducting international business would include the following:

1. **Multiple currencies.** Revenues may be denominated in one currency, costs in another, assets in a third, liabilities in a fourth, and share price in a fifth. Thus, maximization of the wealth of the owners must consider changing currency values.

2. **Differing legal and political environments.** International variations exist in tax laws, depreciation allowances, and other accounting prac-

934

tices, as well as in government regulation and control of business activity. Repatriation of profits may be a problem in certain countries.[1]

3. **Differing economic and capital markets.** The extent of government regulation and control of the economy and capital markets may differ greatly across nations. For example, the ability of a foreign company to raise different types and amounts of capital may be restricted.

4. **Internal control challenge.** It may be difficult to organize, evaluate, and control different divisions of a company when they are separated geographically and when they operate in different environments.

Perspective in Finance

This chapter will highlight multiple currencies as the major dimension of international finance that firms must consider. Effective strategies for the reduction of foreign exchange risk will be discussed. Working-capital management and capital-structure decisions in the international context will also be covered. For the international firm, direct foreign investment is a capital-budgeting decision—with some additional complexities.

GLOBALIZATION OF PRODUCT AND FINANCIAL MARKETS

World trade has grown much faster over the last few decades than world aggregate output. Global exports and imports were about one-fifth of global aggregate output in 1962. This figure had increased to about one-fourth by 1972, to more than one-third by 1982, and it continues to increase. However, Figure 23-1 illustrates that the proportion of both exports and imports has averaged about one-fourth of Canadian GDP during the period 1970 to 1992. The value of world exports has grown from $U.S. 129 billion in 1962 to $U.S. 3.3 trillion in 1990. This remarkable increase in international trade is reflected in the increased openness of almost all national economies to international influences. In fact, the value of exports of goods and services in Canada has increased from $7,939 million in 1962 to $182,200 million in 1992.

Some industries are even more dependent on the international economy. As an example, the electronic consumer products and automobile industries are now widely considered global industries. There has also been a rise in the global level of international portfolio and direct investment. As an example, both direct and portfolio investment in Canada have been increasing faster than Canadian investment overseas. **Direct investment** occurs when the MNC has control over the investment, such as when it builds an off-shore manufacturing facility. **Portfolio investment** involves financial assets with maturities greater than one year, such as the purchase of foreign shares and bonds. Both portfolio and direct foreign investments in Canada now exceed such Canadian investments overseas.

A major reason for long-run overseas investments of Canadian companies is the high rates of return obtainable from investments in other coun-

---

[1]Repatriation of profits refers to the withdrawal of profits of foreign operations to the home country of the MNC.

FIGURE 23-1
Canadian Trade as a Share
of Canadian GDP

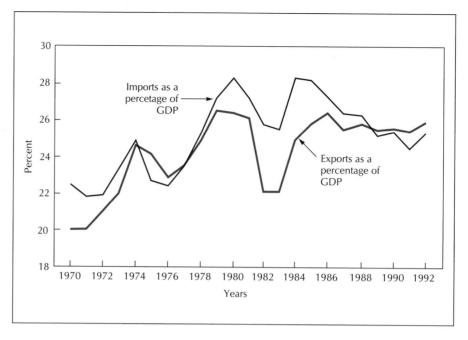

tries. The amount of Canadian direct foreign investments (DFI) abroad is large and growing. A large number of Canadian corporations are now highly dependent upon their overseas investments. Significant amounts of the total assets, sales, and profits of Canadian MNCs are attributable to foreign investments and their foreign operations. Direct foreign investments are not limited to Canadian firms. Many European and Japanese firms have operations abroad, too. During the last decade these firms have been increasing their sales and setting up production facilities in Canada and abroad.

Capital flows between countries for international financial investment purposes have also been increasing. Many firms, investment companies, and individuals invest in the capital markets of foreign countries. The motivation is twofold: to obtain returns higher than those obtainable in the domestic capital markets and to reduce portfolio risk through international diversification. The increase in world trade and investment activity is reflected in the recent globalization of financial markets. The Eurodollar market is larger than any domestic financial market. Companies are increasingly turning to this market for funds. Even companies and public entities that have no overseas presence are beginning to rely on this market for financing.

In addition, most national financial markets are becoming more integrated with global markets because of the rapid increase in the volume of interest rate and currency swaps. Because of the widespread availability of these types of swaps, the currency denomination and the source country of financing for many globally integrated companies are dictated by accessibility and relative cost considerations regardless of the amount of currency needed by the firm.

The foreign exchange markets have also grown rapidly, and the weekly trading volume in these globally integrated markets, between $3 and $5 trillion, exceeds the annual trading volume on the world's securities markets. Even a purely domestic firm that buys all its inputs and sells all its output in its home country is not immune to foreign competition, nor can it totally ignore the workings of the international financial markets.

EXCHANGE RATES

Recent History of Exchange Rates

Between 1949 and 1970 the exchange rates between the major currencies were fixed. However, the Government of Canada pursued both a floating rate policy and a fixed rate policy during the period 1949 to 1972. All countries were required to set a specific parity rate for their currency vis-à-vis the U.S. dollar.[2] For example, consider the German currency, the Deutsche mark (DM). In 1949 the parity rate was set at 4.0 DM to $1. The actual exchange rate prevailing on any day was allowed to lie within a narrow band around the parity rate. The DM was allowed to fluctuate between 4.04 and 3.96 per U.S. dollar. A country could effect a major adjustment in the exchange rate by changing its parity rate with respect to the U.S. dollar. When the currency was made cheaper with respect to the U.S. dollar, this adjustment was called a *devaluation*. A *revaluation* resulted when a currency became more expensive with respect to the dollar. In 1969 the DM parity rate was adjusted to 3.66 per U.S. dollar. This adjustment was a revaluation of the DM parity by 9.3 percent. The new bands around the parity were 3.7010 and 3.6188 DM per U.S. dollar.

Since 1973 a floating-rate international currency system has been operating. For most currencies, there are no parity rates and no bands within which the currencies fluctuate.[3] Most major currencies, including the Canadian dollar, fluctuate freely, depending upon their values as perceived by the traders in foreign exchange markets.[4] The country's relative economic strengths, its level of exports and imports, the level of monetary activity, and the deficits or surpluses in its balance of payments (BOP) are all important factors in the determination of exchange rates.[5] Short-term, day-to-day fluctuations in exchange rates are caused by changing supply and demand conditions in the foreign exchange market.

The Foreign Exchange Market

The foreign exchange market provides a mechanism for the transfer of purchasing power from one currency to another. This market is not a physical entity like the Toronto Stock Exchange; it is a network of telephone and cable connections among banks, foreign exchange dealers, and brokers.[6] The market operates simultaneously at three levels. At the first level, customers buy and sell foreign exchange through their banks. At the second level, banks

---

[2]From 1870 until World War I, the world economic system operated under a gold standard. All settlements between countries had to be met in gold. Thus, a country that ran a trade deficit would lose gold reserves. The system of fixed rates was established by the Bretton Woods Conference in July 1944. Under this system all currencies were pegged to the dollar and the dollar was pegged to gold.

[3]The system of floating rates is referred to as the "floating-rate regime."

[4]In practice, the floating rate policy may be misleading since the Government of Canada actively supports the Canadian dollar by selling and buying its foreign money reserves.

[5]The balance of payments reflects the difference between the imports and the exports of goods (the trade balance) and services (capital inflows and outflows are tabulated under services).

[6]The foreign exchange market is an over-the-counter market.

buy and sell foreign exchange from other banks in the same commercial centre. At the last level, banks buy and sell foreign exchange from banks in commercial centres in other countries. Some important commercial centres for foreign exchange trading are New York, London, Zurich, Frankfurt, Hong Kong, Singapore, Tokyo, and Montreal.

An example will illustrate this multilevel trading. A manufacturer in Ontario may buy foreign exchange (pounds) from the Royal Bank for payment to a British supplier against some purchase made. The Royal Bank may buy the pounds from another bank in New York or from a bank in London.

Since this market provides transactions in a continuous manner for a very large volume of sales and purchases, the exchange market is efficient. In other words, it is difficult to make a profit by shopping around from one bank to another. Minute differences in the quotes from different banks are quickly eliminated by arbitrageurs. In fact, the arbitrage mechanism ensures that quotes to different buyers in London and New York are likely to be the same.

Two major types of transactions are carried out in the foreign exchange markets: *spot* and *forward transactions*.

Spot Exchange Rates

A typical spot transaction involves a Canadian firm buying foreign currency from its bank and paying for it in Canadian dollars. The price of foreign currency in terms of the domestic currency is the exchange rate. Another type of a spot transaction occurs if a Canadian firm receives foreign currency from abroad. The firm typically would sell the foreign currency to its bank for Canadian dollars. These are both **spot transactions**, because one currency is exchanged for another currency today. The actual exchange rate quotes are expressed in several different ways, as discussed below.

Direct and Indirect Quotes

In the spot exchange market the quoted exchange rate is typically called a **direct quote**. A direct quote indicates the number of units of the home currency required to buy one unit of the foreign currency. That is, in Montreal the typical exchange-rate quote indicates the number of Canadian dollars needed to buy one unit of a foreign currency: dollars per pound, dollars per mark, and so on. The spot rates in Table 23-1 are the direct exchange quotes taken from the *Globe and Mail* on July 24, 1992. In order to buy one U.S. dollar on July 23, 1992, 1.1883 Canadian dollars were needed. In order to buy one pound and one mark, 2.2744 dollars and 1.2484 dollars were needed, respectively. The quotes in the spot market in Frankfurt are given in terms of marks and those in London in terms of pounds.

An **indirect quote** indicates the number of units of foreign currency that can be bought for one unit of the home currency. This reads as U.S. dollars per dollar, pounds per dollar, and so on. Some indirect quotes are given in the Table 23-1.

In summary, a direct quote is the dollar/foreign currency rate, and an indirect quote is the foreign currency/dollar rate. Therefore, an indirect quote is the reciprocal of a direct quote and vice versa. The following example illustrates the computation of an indirect quote from a given direct quote.

EXAMPLE

Compute the indirect quotes from the direct quotes of spot rates for U.S. dollars, pounds, and marks given of Table 23-1. The direct quotes are: U.S. dol-

(1) Country	(2) Contract	(3) Direct Quote (Canadian $ Equivalent)	(4) Indirect Quote (Currency per Canadian $)
U.S. (dollar)	Spot	1.1883	.8415
	1-month forward	1.1906	.8399
	6-month forward	1.1984	.8344
	12-month forward	1.2055	.8295
Britain (pound)			
	Spot	2.2744	.4396
	1-month forward	2.2658	.4413
	6-month forward	2.2197	.4505
	12-month forward	2.1717	.4604
Germany (mark)			
	Spot	1.2484	.8010
	1-month forward	1.2528	.7982
	6-month forward	1.2770	.7831
	12-month forward	1.3031	.7674

Adapted from the *Globe and Mail*, Friday July 24, 1992.

lar, 1.1883; pound, 2.2744; and the mark, 1.2484. The related indirect quotes are computed as follows:

$$\text{indirect quote} = \frac{1}{\text{direct quote}}$$

Thus
U.S. Dollars:

$$\frac{1}{1.1883(\$/\text{U.S. dollar})} = .8415(\text{U.S. dollar}/\$)$$

Pounds:

$$\frac{1}{2.2744\ (\$/£)} = .4396\ (£/\$)$$

Marks:

$$\frac{1}{1.2484\ (\$/\text{DM})} = .8010\ (\text{DM}/\$) \blacksquare$$

Notice that the above direct quotes and indirect quotes are identical to those shown in Table 23-1.

Direct and indirect quotes are useful in conducting international transactions as the following examples show.

EXAMPLE

A Canadian business must pay 1,000 marks to a German firm on July 23, 1992. How many dollars would have been required for this transaction?

$$1.2484\ (\$/\text{mark}) \times 1000\ (\text{marks}) = \$1{,}248.40 \blacksquare$$

EXAMPLE

A Canadian business must pay $2,000 to a British resident on July 23, 1992. How many pounds did the British resident receive?

$$0.4396\ (£/\$) \times 2000\ (\$) = £\ 879.2 \blacksquare$$

EXCHANGE RATES AND ARBITRAGE

The foreign exchange quotes in two different countries must be in line with each other. For example, the direct quote for Canadian dollars in London is given in dollars/pound. Since the foreign exchange markets are efficient, the direct quotes for the Canadian dollar in London, on July 23, 1992, must be very close to the indirect rate of .4396 pound/dollar prevailing in Montreal on that date.

If the exchange-rate quotations between the London and Montreal spot exchange markets were out of line, then an enterprising trader could make a profit by buying in the market where the currency was cheaper and selling it in a market where the currency is more expensive. Such a buy-and-sell strategy would involve a zero net investment of funds for a very short time, and no risk bearing would provide a sure profit. Such a person is called an **arbitrageur**, and the process of buying and selling in more than one market to make a riskless profit is called **arbitrage**. Spot exchange markets are efficient in the sense that arbitrage opportunities do not persist for any length of time. That is, the exchange rates between two different markets are quickly brought in line, aided by the arbitrage process. Simple arbitrage eliminates exchange rate differentials across the market for a single currency, as in the above example for the Montreal and London quotes. Triangular arbitrage does the same across the markets for all currencies. Covered interest arbitrage eliminates differentials across currency and interest rate markets.

Suppose that London quotes .4500 £/$ instead of .4396 £/$. If you simultaneously bought a pound in Montreal for .4396 £/$ and sold a pound in London for .4500 £/$ you would have done the following: taken a zero net investment position since you bought one pound and sold one pound, locked in a sure profit of .0104 £/$ no matter which way the pound subsequently moves, and set in motion the forces that will eliminate the different quotes in Montreal and London. As others in the marketplace learn of your transaction, they will attempt to make the same transaction. The increased demand to buy pounds in Montreal will lead to a higher quote there and the increased supply of pounds will lead to a lower quote in London. The workings of the market will produce a new spot rate that lies between .4396 £/$ and .4500 £/$ and is the same in Montreal and in London.

Asked and Bid Rates

In the spot exchange market two types of rates are quoted: the asked and the bid rates. The *asked rate* is the rate the bank or the foreign exchange trader "asks" the customer to pay in home currency for foreign currency when the bank is selling and the customer is buying. The asked rate is also known as the *selling rate* or the *offer rate*. The *bid rate* is the rate at which the bank buys the foreign currency from the customer by paying in home currency. The bid rate is also known as the buying rate. Note that Table 23-1 contains only the selling, offer, or asked rates, and not the buying rate.

The bank sells a unit of foreign currency for more than it pays for it. Therefore, the direct asked quote ($/foreign currency) is greater than the direct bid quote. The difference is known as the *bid-asked spread*. Thus, the indirect asked quote must be less than the indirect bid quote. For example, assume the direct asked and bid quotes are 1.2 and 1.15, respectively. The indirect asked quote will be $1/1.2 = .8333$. The indirect bid quote will be

1/1.15 = .8696. The indirect bid is greater than the indirect asked quote.

When there is a large volume of transactions and the trading is continuous, the spread between the asked and the bid rates can be as small as 0.5 percent for major currencies. The spread is much higher for infrequently traded currencies than for frequently traded currencies. The spread exists to compensate the banks for holding the risky foreign currency and for providing the service of converting currencies.[7]

Cross Rates

A **cross rate** is the exchange rate for a currency derived from the exchange rates of two other currencies. The following example illustrates how this works.

The dollar/pound and the mark/dollar rates are given in Table 23-1. From this information, we could determine the mark/pound and pound/mark exchange rates.

We see that

$$\left(\frac{\$}{£}\right) \times \left(\frac{DM}{\$}\right) = \left(\frac{DM}{£}\right)$$

or

$$2.2744 \times .8010 = 1.8217 \left(\frac{DM}{£}\right)$$

Thus, the pound/mark exchange rate is

$$\frac{1}{1.8217} = .5489 \left(\frac{£}{DM}\right) \blacksquare$$

Cross-rate computations make it possible to use quotations in Montreal to compute the exchange rate between pounds, marks, and francs. Arbitrage conditions hold in cross rates, too. For example, the pound exchange rate in Frankfurt (the direct quote or the DM/£) must be 1.8217. The mark exchange rate in London must be .5489 £/DM. If the rates prevailing in Frankfurt and London were different from the computed cross rates, using quotes from Montreal, a trader could use three different markets and lock in arbitrage profits through this process. The arbitrage condition for the cross rates is called *triangular arbitrage*.

Forward Exchange Rates

A forward exchange contract requires delivery, at a specified future date, of one currency for a specified amount of another currency. The exchange rate for the future transaction is agreed upon today; the actual payment of one currency and the receipt of another currency take place at the future date. For example, a 1-month contract on the 1st of March is good for delivery on the 1st of April. Note that the forward rate is not the same as the spot rate that will prevail in the future. The actual spot rate that will prevail is not known today; only the forward rate is known. The actual spot rate will

---

[7]The spread can also be seen as the bank's compensation for bearing exchange rate risk as well as holding both long and short positions simultaneously.

depend upon the market conditions at that time; it may be more or less than today's forward rate. **Exchange rate risk** is the risk that tomorrow's exchange rate will differ from today's rate.

As indicated earlier, it is extremely unlikely that the future spot rate will be exactly the same as the forward rate quoted today. Assume that you are going to receive a payment denominated in pounds from a British customer in 1 month. If you wait for 1 month and exchange the pounds at the spot rate, you will receive a dollar amount reflecting the exchange rate 1 month hence (that is, the future spot rate). As of today, you have no way of knowing the exact dollar value or your exact future dollar receipts. Consequently, you cannot make precise plans about the use of these dollars. If, on the other hand, you buy a forward contract, then you know the exact dollar value of your future receipts, and you can make precise plans concerning their use. Therefore, the forward contract can reduce your uncertainty about the future. This reduction of uncertainty or risk reduction is the major advantage of using the forward market.

Forward contracts are usually quoted for periods of 1, 3, 6, and 12 months. A contract for any intermediate date can be obtained, usually with the payment of a small premium. Contracts for periods greater than one year can be costly.

Forward rates, like spot rates, are quoted in both direct and indirect form. The direct quotes for the 1-month, 6-month, and 12-month forward contracts on U.S. dollars, pounds, and marks are given in Table 23-1. The indirect quotes for forward contracts are reciprocals of the direct quotes. The indirect quotes are indicated in Table 23-1. The direct quotes are the dollar/foreign currency rate, and the indirect quotes are the foreign currency/dollar rate similar to the spot exchange quotes.

The 1-month forward quote for pounds is $2.2658 per pound. This means that if one purchases the contract for forward pounds on July 23, 1992, the bank will deliver a pound against the payment of $2.2658 on August 24, 1992. The bank is contractually bound to deliver the pound at this price, and the buyer of the contract is legally obligated to buy it at this price on August 24, 1992. Therefore, this is the price the customer must pay regardless of the actual spot rate prevailing on August 24, 1992. If the spot price of the pound is less than $2.2658, then the customer pays more than the spot price. If the spot price is greater than $2.2658, then the customer pays less than the spot price.

The forward rate is often quoted at a **premium** or **discount** from the existing spot rate. For example, the 1-month pound forward rate may be quoted at a .0086 discount (2.2744 spot rate − 2.2658 forward rate). If the forward contract is selling for fewer dollars than the spot—that is, a smaller direct quote—the forward contract is said to be selling at a discount. This example implies that the dollar is expected to be strengthened against the pound. In other words, the market expects that in the future fewer dollars will be required to buy a pound. Conversely, the pound is expected to be worth fewer dollars in the future. When the forward contract sells for more dollars than the spot—a larger direct quote—the forward rate is said to be at a premium from the spot rate. Notice in Table 23-1 that the forward contracts are selling at a premium over the spot for U.S. dollars and marks and at a discount for pounds. This premium or discount is also called the *forward-spot differential*.

The relationship may be written as

$$F - S = p \text{ (or } d)$$

(23-1)

where
F = the forward rate, direct quote

S = the spot rate, direct quote

p = the premium, when F is greater than S

d = the discount, when S is greater than F

The premium or discount can also be expressed as an annual percent rate, computed as follows:

$$\frac{(F - S)}{S} \times \frac{12}{n} \times 100 = P \text{ (or } D) \qquad (23\text{-}2)$$

where
F, S = the forward and spot rates defined earlier

n = the number of months of the forward contract

P = the annualized percentage premium on forward, if $F > S$

D = the annualized percentage discount on forward, if $S > F$

EXAMPLE

Compute the percent-per-annum premium on the 1-month forward pound.

Step 1: Identify F, S, and n.

$$F = 2.2658, S = 2.2744, n = 1 \text{ month}$$

Step 2: Since S is greater than F, we compute D via Equation (23-2).

$$D = \frac{(2.2744 - 2.2658)}{2.2744} \times \frac{12 \text{ months}}{1 \text{ month}} \times 100 = 4.537\%$$

The percent-per-annum discount on the 1-month pound is 4.537 percent.

The percent-per-annum premiums or discounts on the 1-month and 6-month U.S. dollar, pound, and mark contracts are computed similarly. The results are given in Table 23-2. ∎

Examples of Exchange Rate Risk

The concept of exchange rate risk applies to all types of international businesses. The measurement of these risks, and the type of risk, may differ among businesses. Let us see how exchange risk affects international trade contracts, international portfolio investments, and direct foreign investments.

Exchange Rate Risk in International Trade Contracts

The idea of exchange risk in trade contracts is illustrated in the following situations.

CASE I ∎ A Canadian automobile distributor agrees to buy a car from the manufacturer in Oshawa. The distributor agrees to pay $9,500 upon delivery of the car, which is expected to be one month from today. The car is deliv-

	1-month	*6-month*
Pound	(4.537)%	(4.810)%
U.S. Dollar	2.323	1.700
Mark	4.229	4.662

TABLE 23-2
Percent-per-Annum
Premium (Discount)

943

ered one month from today and the distributor pays $9,500. Notice that, from the day this contract was written until the day the car was delivered, the buyer knew the exact dollar amount of the liability. There was, in other words, no uncertainty about the value of the contract.

CASE II ■ A Canadian automobile distributor enters into a contract with a British supplier to buy a car from the United Kingdom for 5,000 pounds. The amount is payable on the delivery of the car, one month from today. From Figure 23-2, we see the range of spot rates that we believe can occur on the date the contract is consummated. One month from today, the Canadian importer will pay some amount in the range of $11,260 (5000£ × 2.252$/£) to $11,759 (5000£ × 2.359$/£) for the car. Today, the Canadian firm is not certain what its future dollar outflow will be one month hence. That is, the dollar value of the contract is uncertain.

These two examples help illustrate the idea of foreign exchange risk in international trade contracts. In the domestic trade contract the exact dollar amount of the future dollar payment is known today with certainty. In the case of the international trade contract, it is written in the foreign currency—the exact dollar amount of the contract is not known. The variability of the exchange rate induces variability in the future cash flow.

Exchange rate risk exists when the contract is written in terms of the foreign currency or denominated in foreign currency. There is no direct exchange risk if the international trade contract is written in terms of the domestic currency. If the contract in Case II was written in dollars, the Canadian importer would face no direct exchange risk. With the contract written in dollars, the British exporter would bear all the exchange risk because the British exporter's future pound receipts would be uncertain. That is, the British exporter would receive payment in dollars, which would have to be converted into pounds at an unknown (as of today) pound-dollar exchange rate. In international trade contracts of the type discussed here, at least one of the two parties to the contract always bears the exchange risk.

FIGURE 23-2
A Subjective Probability Distribution of the Pound Exchange Rate, 6 Months in the Future

Rules	Example		
	UK	Germany	
Inflation:	10%	vs. 6%	
Exchange:	£0.40/DM		
Interest:	13.3% vs. 9.18%		
Forward:	£0.4151/DM		
Future spot:	£0.4151/DM		

UFR: unbiased forecast of spot rate = forward rate
IFE: international Fisher effect

Certain types of international trade contracts are denominated in a third currency, different from either the importer's or the exporter's domestic currency. In Case II the contract might have been denominated in, say, the Deutsche mark. With a mark contract, both importer and exporter would be subject to exchange rate risk.

Exchange risk is not limited to the two-party trade contracts, this type of risk also exists in foreign portfolio investments and direct foreign investments.

Exchange Risk in Foreign Portfolio Investments

Let us look at an example of exchange risk in the context of portfolio investments. A Canadian investor buys a German security. The exact return on the investment in the security is unknown. Thus, the security is a risky investment. The investment return in the holding period of, say, three months stated in marks could be anything from –2 to +8 percent. In addition, the mark-dollar exchange rate may depreciate by 4 percent or appreciate by 6 percent in the three-month period during which the investment is held. The return to the Canadian investor, in dollars, will therefore be in the range of –6 to +14 percent.[8] Notice that the return to a German investor, in marks, is in the range of –2 to +8 percent. Clearly, for the Canadian investor, the exchange factor induces a greater variability in the dollar rate of return. Hence, the exchange rate fluctuations may increase the riskiness of the investments.

Exchange Risk in Direct Foreign Investment

The exchange risk of a direct foreign investment (DFI) is more complicated. In a DFI the parent company invests in assets denominated in a foreign currency. That is, the balance sheet and the income statement of the subsidiary are written in terms of the foreign currency. The parent company receives the repatriated profit stream in dollars. Thus, the exchange risk concept applies to fluctuations in the dollar value of the assets located abroad as well as to the fluctuations in the home-currency-denominated profit stream. Exchange risk not only affects immediate profits, but also affects the future profit stream as well.

Corporations which engage in multinational operations are exposed to greater risk due to fluctuating exchange rates, but are compensated for by a greater expected return than available in their domestic market.

Relevant Measures of Exchange Risk

The relevant measures of exchange risk differ for different types of businesses. Exchange risk represents the variability in expected returns caused by exchange rate fluctuations. Again, total exchange risk can be separated into diversifiable exchange risk and non-diversifiable risk. For example, a Canadian trader who does not trade on international markets frequently faces total exchange risk. Because this trader is not well diversified in

---

[8]Example: Assume the spot exchange rate is .50 dollars per mark. In three months the exchange rate would be $.50 \times (1 - .04) = .48$ to $.50 \times (1 + .06) = .53$. A $50 investment today is equivalent to a 100-mark investment. The 100-mark investment would return 98 to 108 marks in three months. The return, in the worst case, is 98 marks $\times .48 = \$47.04$. The return, in the best case, is 108 marks $\times .53 = \$57.24$. The holding-period return, on the $50 investment, will be between –6 percent ($47.04 − $50)/$50) and +14 percent ($57.24 − $50)/$50).

trading on international markets, total exchange risk is equal to the total variability in expected returns due to exchange rate fluctuations. For an export-import firm that does continual business in a number of countries, the relevant risk measure is non-diversifiable risk of exchange rate fluctuations. The diversification argument also applies to a multinational corporation that has plants and operations in numerous countries. For corporations with very large investments in a single foreign country, the total variability of the exchange rate is the appropriate measure of exchange risk.

THE INTEREST PARITY THEORY

All the forward rates given in Table 23-1 entail a premium or a discount relative to current spot rates. However, these forward premiums and discounts differ between currencies and maturities (see Table 23-2). These differences depend solely on the difference in the level of interest rates between the two countries, called the *interest rate differential*. The value of the premium or discount can be theoretically computed from the **interest-rate parity theory** (IRPT). This theory states that (except for the effects of small transactions costs) the forward premium or discount should be equal and opposite in sign to the difference in the interest rates of securities that have the same maturity.

Specifically, the premium or discount on the percent-per-annum basis should be equal to the following:[9]

$$P \text{ (or } D) = \left(-\frac{I^f - I^d}{1 + I^f} \right) = \left(\frac{I^d - I^f}{1 + I^f} \right) \tag{23-3a}$$

where P (or D) = the percent-per-annum premium (or discount) on the forward rate

              I^f = the annualized interest rate on a foreign instrument having the same maturity as the forward contract

              I^d = the annualized interest rate on a domestic instrument having the same maturity as the forward contract

Note that in order to compute the forward premium on, say, a 6-month forward U.S. dollar contract, we need to have the 6-month Treasury bill rate in Canada and its counterpart in the United States, both expressed as annual rates.

The IRPT states that the P (or D) calculated by the use of Equation (23-3a) should be the same as the P (or D) calculated by using Equation (23-2), except for small variations due to political and commercial risks and transactions costs. When the interest rates are relatively low, Equation (23-3a) can be approximated by:

$$P \text{ (or } D) \cong -(I^f - I^d) = (I^d - I^f) \tag{23-3b}$$

[9]Note that equation implies an equilibrium condition that eliminates any arbitrage opportunities and says nothing about expected future exchange rates. In reality, the equilibrium condition may not hold true at every particular point in time.

Notice in Table 23-2 that the 6-month forward U.S. dollar is selling at a premium of approximately 1.700 percent. The IRPT says that the 6-month interest rate in the United States must be approximately 1.700 percent (annualized) less than the 6-month Treasury bill rate in Canada, as indicated by Equation (23-3a).

Covered Interest Arbitrage

The rationale for the interest rate parity theory is provided by the covered interest arbitrage argument. This argument states that if the premiums (or discounts) in forward rates are not exactly equal to the interest rate differential, then arbitrage or riskless profits can be made.[10] The arbitrage mechanics involved here are substantially more complicated than the "simple" and "triangular" arbitrage discussed earlier. The covered interest arbitrage argument is best explained by the following examples.

EXAMPLE

The U.S. dollar spot and 6-month forward rates are $1.1883 and $1.1906, respectively, on July 23, 1992. The 6-month Canada T-bill rate on July 23, 1992, expressed as an annual rate was approximately 5.25 percent. Assume now that the rate on 6-month American instruments on July 23, 1992, was 3.24 percent, annualized. Given these data, does a riskless profit (or arbitrage) opportunity exist?

Step 1: Compute the forward premium using Equation (23-2).

$$P = 1.700 \text{ percent}$$

Step 2: Compute the interest rate differential by Equation (23-3).

$$P = \frac{(0.0521 - 0.0324)}{(1 + 0.0324)} = 0.01908 = 1.908\%$$

The premiums computed by the use of the two equations are not identical. The IRPT is violated. Profit opportunities exist.[11]

Since profit opportunities exist, what can the arbitrageur do to make a profit? A Canadian arbitrageur can take the following steps.

On July 23, 1992:

Step 1: Borrow 1 million U.S. dollars for 6 months from the United States money markets at a 3.24 percent annual rate of interest. For 6 months the interest is 1.62 percent.[12] On January 24, 1993, the arbitrageur will need to repay 1 million U.S. dollars × 1.0162 = 1,016,200 U.S. dollars.

Step 2: Exchange the borrowed U.S. dollars into dollars at the spot exchange rate of $1.1883 per U.S. dollar on July 23, 1992. The arbitrageur receives 1 million U.S. dollars × $1.1883 = $1,188,300.

Step 3: Invest the dollars in the Canadian money market for 6 months at 5.25 percent annual rate. For 6 months the rate is 2.6255 percent. Receive, on January 24, 1993, $1,188,300 × 1.026255 = $1,219,499.

---

[10]Interest rate differential is approximately equal to the right-hand side of Equation (23-3b).

[11]Note that the interest rate differential was greater than the forward premium and it was better to hold Canadian dollars. If the interest rate differential was less, then one would hold the foreign currency.

[12]The 6-month rate, as an approximation, is equal to the annual rate × 6/12.

Step 4: Enter into a 6-month forward contract to buy 1,016,200 U.S. dollars on January 24, 1993. On January 24, 1993, the arbitrageur will need to pay 1,016,200 × 1.1984 = \$1,217,814 to receive the 1,016,200 U.S. dollars needed to repay the loan principal and interest on the 1 million U.S. dollar loan taken in Step 1.

On January 24, 1993, the arbitrage position is closed out as follows:
    Step 1: Receive \$1,219,499 from the Canadian money market investment (\$1,188,300 invested plus \$31,199 interest at a monthly rate of 2.6255 percent).
    Step 2: Pay \$1,217,814 to the bank to obtain 1,016,200 U.S. dollars at a 1.1984 exchange rate.
    Step 3: Pay 1,016,200 U.S. dollars toward the principal and interest on the 1 million U.S. dollar loan. ■

On January 24, 1993, the Canadian arbitrageur's net position is no liability and no assets. However, a net profit has been made of \$1,685 (\$1,219,499 − \$1,217,814). None of the arbitrageur's own funds were invested, there was no risk (since the arbitrageur knew payments and receipts exactly on July 24, 1992), yet the arbitrageur made a net profit of \$1,685. This arbitrage was accomplished by simultaneously borrowing in one market, investing in another money market, and covering the exchange position in the forward exchange market. The entire process is known as covered interest arbitrage.

    Note that the arbitrage profit was possible because the forward premium was not equal to the interest rate differential. Under such circumstances, arbitrageurs enter the market, increase the demand for the forward foreign currency, and drive up the price of the forward contract. The equilibrium price of the forward contract again obeys the interest parity theory.

EXAMPLE

Assume that the interest rates indicated in the previous example are the actual rates prevailing in Canada and the United States. What should be the "correct" price of the forward contract, consistent with the interest rates in the two countries?
    Step 1: Compute the premium using Equation (23-3a).

$$P = \frac{(0.0521 - 0.0324)}{(1 + 0.0324)} = 0.01908 = 1.908\%$$

    Step 2: Using this premium in Equation (23-2), compute the forward rate, *F*.

$$\frac{(F - 1.1883)}{1.1883} \times \frac{12 \text{ months}}{1 \text{ month}} \times 100 = 1.908\%$$

$$F = 1.19019\% ■$$

The example illustrates the technique for computing the correct price of the forward contract. If the quote is less than the computed price, the forward contract is *undervalued*. If the quote is greater than the computed price, the forward contract is *overvalued*. In our example, the forward contract is undervalued.

    The forward markets are *efficient* in the sense that the quotes in the market represent the "correct" price of the contract. The markets' efficiency also implies that no profit can be made by computing the prices at every instant and buying the forward contract when they appear undervalued. Some minor deviations from the computed correct price may exist for short periods. These deviations, however, are such that after the transactions costs involved in the four separate arbitrage steps have been recognized, no net profit can be made. Numerous empirical studies attest to the efficiency of the forward markets.

In the previous example the correct price of the forward U.S. dollar was computed under the assumption that the 6-month interest rate in the United States was 3.24 percent. All the other data for the examples were obtained from the actual market quotes in Montreal. We now ask, given the data on spot rate, forward rate, and the Canadian treasury bill rate, can we compute the interest rate for the 6-month United States instrument? The answer is given in the next example.

The spot rate and forward rate for the U.S. dollar are 1.1883 and 1.1984, respectively. The 6-month Canadian T-bill rate is 5.25 percent annualized. What is the 6-month American rate?

Step 1: Compute the premium using Equation (23-2). From previous computations,

$$P = 1.700\%$$

Step 2: Using Equations (23-3a), solve for the unknown foreign interest rate.

$$0.01700 = \frac{(0.0525 - I^f)}{(1 + I^f)}$$

$$I^f = .0349, \text{ or } 3.49\%$$

Thus, the actual 6-month rate in the United States on July 23, 1992, must have been 3.49 percent annualized. ∎

PURCHASING POWER PARITY

Long-run changes in exchange rates are influenced by international differences in inflation rates and the purchasing power of each nation's currency. Exchange rates of countries with high rates of inflation will tend to decline. According to the purchasing power parity (PPP) theory, exchange rates will tend to adjust in such a way that each currency will have the same purchasing power (especially in terms of internationally traded goods). Thus, if the United Kingdom experiences a 10 percent rate of inflation in a year that Germany experiences only a 6 percent rate, the U.K. currency (the pound) will be expected to decline in value approximately by 4 percent ($10\% - 6\%$) against the German currency (the mark). More accurately, according to the PPP

$$S_{t+1} = S_t \frac{(1 + P_d)}{(1 + P_f)^n}$$

$$\cong S_t (1 + P_d - P_f)^n$$

where S_t = the direct exchange rate (units of domestic currency per unit of the foreign currency) at time t

$$P_f = \text{the foreign inflation rate}$$

$$P_d = \text{the domestic inflation rate}$$

$$n = \text{number of time periods}$$

Thus, if the beginning value of the mark was 0.40, with a 6 percent inflation rate in Germany and a 10 percent inflation rate in the U.K., according to the PPP, the expected value of the mark at the end of that year will be 0.40 × [1.10/1.06], or 0.4151.

The Law of One Price

Underlying the PPP relationship is the Law of One Price. This law is actually a proposition that in competitive markets where there are no transportation costs or barriers of trade, the same good sold in different countries sells for the same price if all the different prices are expressed in terms of the same currency. The idea is that the worth, in terms of marginal utility, of a good does not depend on where it is bought or sold. Since inflation will erode the purchasing power of any currency, its exchange rate must adhere to the PPP relationship if the Law of One Price is to hold over time. The following example illustrates the workings of this proposition.

EXAMPLE

Given the information above, assume that today a widget costs DM 100.00 in Germany and £40.00 in the U.K. At the current exchange rate the Law of One Price appears to be holding since Germans can buy widgets for DM 100.00 (× £0.40/DM = £40) and the British can buy German widgets for £40 (× DM/£.40 = DM 100). It is possible to determine how the exchange rate must change for the Law of One Price holds in relative form—for example, over the next year. We might expect that the exchange rate will change to reflect the decline in each currency's domestic purchasing power caused by next year's inflation. Today we know:

$$\text{DM } 100 = 1 \text{ widget} = £40.00$$

At this point, Germans would be indifferent between buying German widgets or U.K. widgets. Given that inflation in the U.K. is expected to be 10%, one U.K. widget can be expected to cost £44.00 = (£40.00)(1 + .10). At the current exchange rate, in one year U.K. widgets would cost Germans DM 110.00:

$$\text{DM } 110.00 = 1 \text{ widget} = £44.00$$

$$= £44.00 \times \left(\frac{\text{DM}}{.40}\right)$$

We will ignore the effects of German inflation for the moment. Germans would not buy U.K. widgets for DM 110.00 in one year; they would buy German widgets for DM 100.00. Thus at the current exchange rate, PPP would not hold. Germans might, however, be willing to continue spending DM 100.00 one year from now for U.K. widgets. This could happen only if the DM were to strengthen against the pound. The new exchange rate implied by U.K. inflation is:

$$\text{DM } 100.00 = 1 \text{ widget} = £44.00$$

$$\left(\frac{£}{DM}\right) = \frac{£44.00}{100.00 \ DM} = \frac{£.44}{DM}$$

or:

$$\left(\frac{£}{DM}\right) = £0.40 \times (1 + P_{U.K.}) = £0.40 \times 1.10$$

Note that the terms of trade are important—Germans want the same amount of goods for the same number of DM before and after the U.K. inflation. After the U.K. inflation, the DM buys more pounds at the new exchange rate. In addition, the British will also be paying £40.00 per widget in today's pounds—all U.K. goods will cost 10 percent more next year because of inflation. In other words, widgets will cost more in nominal terms next year in the U.K., but the real cost of widgets will be unchanged.

Now we will consider German inflation. If Since DM's purchasing power is also expected to decline over the next year, Germans would be willing to pay DM 106.00 ($= $ DM $100.00 \times (1 + P_{DM})$) for an U.K. widget in one year since this is what they would have to pay for a German widget at that time. The new exchange rate becomes the same as the PPP estimate calculated above:

$$DM \ 106.00 = 1 \ widget = £44.00$$

$$\left(\frac{£}{DM}\right) = \frac{£44.00}{DM \ 106.00} = \frac{£.4151}{DM}$$

or:

$$\left(\frac{£}{DM}\right) = (£0.40) \frac{(1 + P_{U.K.})}{(1 + P_{DM})} = \frac{£0.4151}{DM} \ \blacksquare$$

International Fisher Effect

According to the Fisher effect, interest (I) rates reflect the expected inflation rate (P) and a real rate of return (I_r). In other words

$$1 + I = (1 + P)(1 + I_r)$$

and

$$I = P + I_r + PI_r$$

While there is mixed empirical support for the Fisher effect internationally, it is widely commented that for the major industrial countries, I_r is about 3 percent, when a long-term period is considered. In such a case, with the previous assumption regarding inflation rates, interest rates in the U.K. and Germany would be $(1 + 0.10) (1 + 0.03) - 1$ or 13.3 percent and $(1 + 0.06)$ $(1 + 0.03) - 1$ or 9.18 percent, respectively.

In addition, according to the IRPT, the expected premium for the mark forward rate should be $(0.133 - 0.0918)/1.0918$ or 3.774 percent (rounded off). Starting with a mark value of 0.40 gives us a one-year forward rate of £0.40 × (1.03774) = £0.4151. As you may notice, this one-year forward rate is exactly the same as the PPP expected spot rate one year from today. In other words, if the real rate (I_r) is the same in both Germany and the U.K. and expectations regarding inflation rates hold true, today's one-year forward rate is likely to be the same as the future spot rate one year from now. Thus, it is contended that in efficient markets, with rational expectations, the forward rate is an unbiased (not necessarily accurate) forecast of the future spot rate. These relationships between inflation and interest rates, and spot and forward rates are depicted in Figure 23-3.

FIGURE 23-3
Efficient Foreign Exchange
Market Relationships

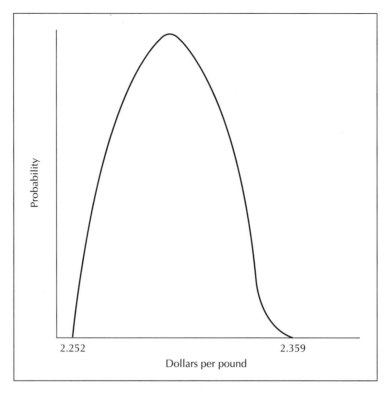

The actual future spot rate, as of today, is a random variable. In Figure 23-2 we indicated a possible hypothetical distribution of the pound spot rate on January 24, 1993. This distribution is what we, on July 23, 1992, subjectively believe the future spot rate to be. Notice in Figure 23-2 that the exchange rate may be as low as 2.252 dollars or as high as 2.359 dollars per pound with different probabilities.

Yet given the available information, we have done our best to accurately forecast the future spot exchange rate. Such forecasts are useful in eliminating exchange risk for near-term international transactions, called *hedging*. However, there is no easy way to hedge long-term cash flows for international operations. The problem is that the terms of trade can also change; exchange rate changes can go beyond PPP-induced changes, leading to real exchange rate changes. Currency gains and losses from nominal exchange rate changes will generally be offset over time by differences in relative rates of inflation between two countries if PPP holds and there are no real exchange rate changes.

EXPOSURE TO EXCHANGE RATE RISK

An asset which is denominated in or valued in terms of foreign currency cash flows will lose value if that foreign currency declines in value. It can be said that such an asset is exposed to exchange rate risk. However, this possible decline in asset value may be offset by the decline in value of any liability that is also denominated or valued in terms of that foreign currency. Thus, a firm would normally be interested in its net exposed position (exposed assets – exposed liabilities) for each period in each currency.

While expected changes in exchange rates can often be included in the cost-benefit analysis relating to such transactions, in most cases there is an unexpected component in exchange rate changes and often the cost-benefit analysis for such transactions does not fully capture even the expected change in the exchange rate. For example, price increases for the foreign operations of many MNCs often have to be less than those necessary to fully offset exchange rate changes due to the competitive pressures generated by local businesses.

A company can follow one of three policies with regard to the management of its foreign currency exposure. In the two simplest policies, the firm covers all exposed positions or covers no exposed positions. A firm may cover all exposed foreign currency positions if it considers the generally small but positive difference between the average cost of cover and the average expected loss due to exchange rate changes to be less important than the need to maintain stability in the dollar value of its foreign currency cash flows. Such a policy is usually suitable for small firms with limited expertise and/or little business in foreign currencies. If the firm covers no foreign currency exposure, it generally expects foreign exchange losses and gains to offset each other, with the net balance representing one of the costs of doing business. Such a policy may be particularly suitable for large, well-diversified companies. Other companies would have to consider adopting the third policy of using various hedging or covering alternatives for most but not all of their currency exposure.

The three measures of foreign exposure are: translation exposure, transaction exposure, and economic exposure. Translation exposure arises because the foreign operations of MNCs have accounting statements denominated in the local currency of the country in which the operation is located. For Canadian MNCs, the reporting currency for its consolidated financial statements is the Canadian dollar, so assets, liabilities, revenues, and expenses of the foreign operations must be translated into dollars. International transactions often require a payment to be made or received in a foreign currency in the future, so these transactions are exposed to exchange rate risk. Economic exposure exists over the long-term since the value of future cash flows in the reporting currency from foreign operations are exposed to exchange rate risk. Indeed, the whole stream of future cash flows is exposed. The three measures of exposure are now examined more closely.

Translation Exposure

Foreign currency assets and liabilities are considered exposed if their foreign currency value for accounting purposes is to be translated into the parent company currency. The currency rate used for translation of monetary assets is the current exchange rate—the exchange rate in effect on the balance sheet date. Other assets and liabilities and equity amounts that are generally translated at the historic exchange rate—the rate in effect when these items were first recognized in the company's accounts—are not considered to be exposed. The rate (current or historic) used to translate various accounts depends on the translation procedure used.

While transaction exposure can result in exchange rate change-related losses and gains that are realized and have an impact on both reported and taxable income, translation exposure results in exchange rate losses and gains that are reflected in the company's accounting books, but that are unrealized and have little or no impact on taxable income. Thus, if financial markets are efficient and managerial goals are consistent with owner wealth maximization (agency and signalling costs are negligible), a firm should not have to waste real resources hedging against possible paper losses caused by translation exposure. However, if there are significant agency or information costs or if markets are not efficient (that is, if translation losses and gains raise information costs for investors, or if they endanger the firm's ability to satisfy debt or other covenants, or if the evaluation of the firm's managers depends on translated accounting data), a firm may indeed find it economical to hedge against translation losses or gains.

Transactions Exposure

Accounts receivable, accounts payable, and fixed priced sales or purchase contracts are examples of foreign currency transactions whose monetary value was fixed at a time different from the time when these transactions are actually completed. *Transactions exposure* is a term that describes net contracted foreign currency transactions for which the settlement amounts are subject to changing exchange rates over a period too short to allow for compensating changes in prices fully. A company normally must set up an additional reporting system to track transactions exposure, since a number of these amounts are not recognized in the accounting books of a firm.

Exchange risk may be neutralized or hedged by a change in the asset and liability position in the foreign currency. An exposed asset position, such as an account receivable, can be hedged or covered by creating a liability of the same amount and maturity denominated in the foreign currency. The liability used for hedging could be a forward contract to sell the foreign currency. An exposed liability position, such as an account payable, can be covered by acquiring assets of the same amount and maturity in the foreign currency. The asset could be a forward contract to buy the foreign currency. The objective is to have a zero net asset position in the foreign currency.[13] This eliminates exchange risk, since the loss (gain) in the liability (asset) is exactly offset by the gain (loss) in the value of the asset (liability) when the foreign currency appreciates (depreciates). Two popular forms of hedge are the money-market hedge and the exchange-market or forward-market hedge. In both types of hedge the amount and the duration of the asset (liability) positions are matched. The next two sections demonstrate how IRP assures that each hedge provides the same cover.

Money-Market Hedge

In a money-market hedge, the exposed position in a foreign currency is offset by borrowing or lending in the money market. Consider the case of the Canadian firm with a net liability position of 3,000 pounds. The firm knows the exact amount of its pound liability in 1 month, but it does not know the liability in dollars. Assume that the 1-month money-market rates in both Canada and United Kingdom are, respectively, 1 percent for lending and 1.5 percent for borrowing. The Canadian business can take the following steps:

Step 1: Calculate the present value of the foreign currency liability (3,000 pounds) that is due in 1 month. Use the money-market rate applicable for the foreign country (1 percent in the United Kingdom). The present value of 3,000 pounds is 2,970.30 pounds, computed as follows: 3000/(1 + .01).

---

[13]Note that the hedge will work well only to the extent that both the assets and liabilities move together.

Step 2: Exchange dollars on today's spot market to obtain the 2,970.30 pounds. The dollar amount needed today is $6,755.65 (2970.30 × $2.2744).

Step 3: Invest 2,970.30 pounds in a United Kingdom one-month money-market instrument. This investment will compound to exactly 3,000 pounds in one month. The future liability of 3,000 pounds is covered by the 2,970.30 pounds investment.[14]

Note: If the Canadian business does not own this amount today, it can borrow it from the Canadian money market at the going rate of 1.5 percent. In one month the Canadian business will need to repay $6,856.98 [$6755.65 × (1 + .015)].

Assuming that the Canadian business borrows the money, its management may base its calculations on the knowledge that the British goods, upon delivery in one month, will cost it $6,856.98. The British business will receive 3,000 pounds. The Canadian business need not wait for the future spot exchange rate to be revealed. On today's date, the future dollar payment of the contract is known with certainty. This certainty helps the Canadian business in making its pricing and financing decisions.

The mechanics of the money-market hedge indicate that the Canadian firm, on today's date, knows the exact dollar amount of its future liability. Thus, the exchange risk is entirely eliminated. Many businesses hedge in the money market. The firm creates a liability by borrowing in one market, lending or investing in the other money market, and using the spot exchange market on today's date. The mechanics of covering a net asset position in the foreign currency are the exact reverse of the mechanics of covering the liability position. With a net asset position in pounds: Borrow in the United Kingdom money market in pounds, convert to dollars on the spot exchange market, invest in the Canadian money market. The cost of hedging in the money market is the cost of doing business in three different markets. Information about the three markets is needed, and analytical calculations of the type indicated here must be made.

Many small and infrequent traders find the cost of the money-market hedge prohibitive, owing especially to the need for information about the market. These traders use the exchange or the forward-market hedge, which has very similar hedging benefits.

The Forward-Market Hedge

The forward market provides a second possible hedging mechanism. It works as follows: A net asset (liability) position is covered by a liability (asset) in the forward market. Consider again the case of the Canadian firm with a liability of 3,000 pounds that must be paid in one month. The firm may take the following steps to cover its liability position.

Step 1: Buy a forward contract today to purchase 3,000 pounds in one month. The 1-month forward rate is, say, $2.2658 per pound.

Step 2: On the thirtieth day pay the banker $6,797.40 (3000 × $2.2658) and collect 3,000 pounds. Pay these pounds to the British supplier.

By the use of the forward contract the Canadian business knows the exact worth of the future payment in dollars ($6,797.40). The exchange risk in pounds is totally eliminated by the net asset position in the forward pounds. In the case of a net asset exposure, the steps open to the Canadian

---

[14]Observe that 2970.30 pounds × (1 + .01) = 3000 pounds.

firm are the exact opposite: Sell the pounds forward, and on the future day receive and deliver the pounds to collect the agreed-upon dollar amount.[15]

The use of the forward market as a hedge against exchange risk is simple and direct. This type of position requires that the liability or asset position be matched against an offsetting position in the forward market. For example, a firm directs its banker to buy or sell a foreign currency on a future date, and the banker gives forward quote.

The forward hedge and the money-market hedge give an identical future dollar payment (or receipt) if the forward contracts are priced according to the interest rate parity theory. The alert student may have noticed that the dollar payments in the money-market hedge and the forward-market hedge examples were, respectively, $6,856.98 and $6,797.40. Recall from our previous discussions that in efficient markets, the forward contracts do indeed conform to the IRPT. However, the numbers in our example are not identical because the forward rate used in the forward hedge is not exactly equal to the interest rates in the money-market hedge.

Currency Future and Option Contracts

The forward-market hedge is not adequate for some types of exposure. If the foreign currency asset or liability position occurs on a date for which forward quotes are not available, the forward hedge cannot be accomplished. In certain cases the forward hedge may cost more than the money-market hedge. In these cases a corporation with a large amount of exposure may prefer the money-market hedge. In addition to forward and money-market hedges, a company can also hedge its exposure by buying (or selling) some relatively new instruments—foreign currency futures contracts and foreign currency options. While futures contracts are similar to forward contracts in that they provide fixed prices for the required delivery of foreign currency at maturity, options permit fixed (strike) price foreign currency transactions anytime prior to maturity. Futures contracts and options differ from forward contracts in that, unlike forward contracts, which are customized with regard to amount and maturity date, futures and options are traded in standard amounts with standard maturity dates. In addition, while forward contracts are written by banks, futures and options are traded on organized exchanges, and individual traders deal with the exchange-based clearing organization rather than with each other. The purchase of futures requires the fulfillment of margin requirements (about 5 to 10 percent of the face amount), while the purchase of forward contracts requires only good credit standing with a bank. The purchase of options requires an immediate outlay that reflects a premium above the strike price and an outlay equal to the strike price when and if the option is exercised.

Economic Exposure

This is the extent to which the economic value of a company can decline because of exchange rate changes. This decline in value may be caused by a rate-change-induced decline in the level of expected cash flows and/or by an increase in the riskiness of these cash flows. Thus, economic exposure refers to the overall impact of exchange rate changes on the value of the firm and

[15]The use of forward contracts provides the firm with flexibility since this type of contract is tailor made to the needs of the firm. However, the firm will incur higher transaction costs.

therefore includes not only the strategic impact of changes in competitive relationships between alternative foreign locations that arise from exchange rate changes, but also the economic impact of transactions exposure and the economic impact, if any, of translation exposure.

Economic exposure to exchange rate changes depends on the competitive structure of the markets for a firm's inputs and its outputs and how these markets are influenced by changes in exchange rates. This influence, in turn, would depend on a number of economic factors, including price elasticities of the products, the degree of competition from foreign markets and direct (through prices) and indirect (through incomes) impact of exchange rate changes on these markets. Assessing the economic exposure faced by a particular firm thus depends on the ability to understand and model the structure of the markets for its major inputs (purchases) and outputs (sales).

A company need not engage in any cross-border business activity in order to be exposed to losses due to exchange rate changes, because product and financial markets in most countries are related and influenced to a large extent by the same global forces. The output of a company engaged in business activity only within one country may be competing with imported products, or it may be competing for its inputs with other domestic and foreign purchasers. The degree of competition in these markets may change with changes in exchange rates. For example, a Canadian chemical company that did no cross-border business nevertheless found that its profit margins depended directly on the Canadian dollar–Japanese yen exchange rate. The company used coal as an input in its production process, and the Canadian price of coal was heavily influenced by the extent to which the Japanese bought Canadian coal, which in turn depended on the yen-dollar exchange rate.

While translation exposure need not be managed, it might be useful for a firm to manage its transaction and economic exposures since they affect firm value directly. In most companies, transaction exposure is generally tracked and managed by the office of the corporate treasurer. Economic exposure is difficult to define in operating terms, and very few companies manage it actively. In most companies, economic exposure is generally considered part of the strategic planning process, rather than as a treasurer's or finance function.

BASIC FINANCIAL MANAGEMENT IN PRACTICE

A corporate treasurer must have access to international financial markets to manage the firm's transaction and economic exposure. Examples of financial institutions which provide access to international markets include the International Banking Centres, the International Financial Offices and the International Financial Centres. The following article discusses the objectives these financial institutions.

Around the World in 80 Ways
International Financial Centres (IFC), International Financial Offices (IFO), and International Banking

Centres (IBC) are all businesses that specialize in international financial transactions, and get tax breaks for doing so. The differences are in eligible transactions and in the tax laws that govern them. IFCs, the creation of the Quebec government, operate only in that province. IFOs are the BC equivalent. IBCs, under the federal Income Tax Act, can operate in Vancouver and Montreal and get federal as well as provincial tax breaks.

In addition to the political and economic factors coming into play in Montreal and Vancouver

Continued on page 958

Continued from page 957

(the only two Canadian cities in which international financial institutions are eligible for tax relief), the governments involved had five objectives in creating these institutions:

1. To increase the number and size of international financial transactions carried out in Canada, as opposed to New York, London or elsewhere.

2. To attract specialists in international financial markets to Canada and consequently to develop Canadian expertise in those areas.

3. To make foreign capital more accessible for the different governments involved, as well as for Canadian companies and individuals.

4. To give Canada a higher profile on international financial markets.

5. To diversify Canadian financial activity, by developing poles in the west (Vancouver) and the east (Montreal).

Why were Montreal and Vancouver chosen to host these enterprises? Because they are major centres with established stock exchanges. It may also have been an effort by the three governments to decentralize stock trading and financial activities. Others suggest that Montreal is the Canadian doorway to European markets, and Vancouver the gateway to Asia.

These institutions can help companies wishing to obtain financing for projects abroad. For example, an IFC can help a Canadian company that has just obtained a contract to build a turnkey plant in Australia to finance the project from down under, in Australian dollars. They can also help clients reduce their vulnerability to exchange fluctuations, diversify their portfolios, learn to play the exchange market, or obtain capital more easily and at more affordable rates. Even small investors can think of acquiring foreign debt securities or shares in deutsche marks, yen or other foreign currencies.

There are many other commercial services that IFCs, IBCs, and IFOs can now offer, including the issue of letters of credit for foreign companies, purchases and sales of foreign currencies, forward exchange contracts, and loans in other currencies. They are generally specialized in those fields, and can even offer competitive rates and conditions.

Any company financing a major project may want to investigate the advantages of using foreign capital. Having access to experts in Canada who can evaluate such projects, and are familiar with the other country's economy and political and financial situation, can make locating these new sources of capital much easier.

All that having been said, IFCs, IBCs and IFOs must nevertheless meet various criteria before their transactions are eligible for tax breaks. For a transaction to be "international," and hence eligible for these institutions, it must either be conducted with a nonresident or involve a security issued on foreign markets, regardless of the other party to the transaction. The security may have been issued by a Canadian body (government, company, or individual), provided that it can be traded on a market outside Canada.

For example, a Canadian resident purchases shares of Société Générale, a French bank whose shares are listed on the Paris stock market; a Japanese resident purchases Bell Canada shares; a Canadian company building a plant in Australia wishes to have its projects financed in Australian dollars; a Canadian manufacturer sells goods to Italians and enters into a forward exchange contract to sell Italian lira that it will receive two months later.

The federal government has considerably limited the eligible transactions of IBCs, however—as compared with provincially governed IFCs and IFOs—because of lobbying from Toronto. For an IBC to be exempt from income tax, for example, its total eligible deposits must represent at least 96% of its eligible loans, for each working day. If this condition is not met, the amount eligible for exemption will be determined on a pro rata basis. Because the daily matching of daily deposits and loans is a fairly laborious exercise, the condition complicates the centre's operations and can cut substantially into its profitability.

In 1989, IFCs, and IFOs had a tax rate of only 29%, the lowest in North America, because of their exemption from provincial income tax. It is surprising, then, that so few companies have requested certification as international centres. From a taxation point of view, Montreal and Vancouver are the most profitable North American cities in which to conduct certain international transactions—such as loans to or deposits by nonresidents when the IFC or IFO is also an IBC. In that case, the net revenue from the transaction is tax-free in Canada. In fact, Montreal and Vancouver can be considered true tax-free zones for international financial transactions.

Source: Excerpts from: Michel Drouin and Evelyn Paquin, "Around the World in 80 Ways," *CA Magazine* (October, 1991), pp. 28–34.

MULTINATIONAL WORKING-CAPITAL MANAGEMENT

The basic principles of working-capital management for a multinational corporation are similar to those for a domestic firm. However, tax and exchange rate factors are additional considerations for the multinational corporation (MNC). For an MNC with subsidiaries in many countries, the optimal decisions in management of working capital are made by considering the company as a whole. The global or centralized financial decision for an MNC is superior to the set of independent optimal decisions for the subsidiaries. This is the control problem of the MNC. If the individual subsidiaries make decisions that are best for them individually, the consolidation of such decisions may not be best for the MNC as a whole. In order to effect global management, sophisticated computerized models—incorporating a large number of variables for each subsidiary—are solved to provide the best overall decision for the MNC.

Before considering the components of working-capital management, we examine two techniques that are useful in the management of a wide variety of working-capital components.

Leading and Lagging

Two important risk-reduction techniques for many working-capital problems are called leading and lagging. Often, forward- and money-market hedges are not available to eliminate exchange risk. Under such circumstances, leading and lagging may be used to reduce exchange risk.

Recall that a net asset (long) position is not desirable in a weak or potentially depreciating currency. If a firm has a net asset position in such a currency, it should expedite the disposal of the asset. The firm should get rid of the asset earlier than it otherwise would have, or **lead**, and convert the funds into assets in a relatively stronger currency. By the same reasoning, the firm should **lag** or delay the collection against a net asset position in a strong currency. If the firm has a net liability (short) position in the weak currency, then it should delay the payment against the liability, or lag, until the currency depreciates. In the case of an appreciating or strong foreign currency and a net liability position, the firm should lead the payments— that is, reduce the liabilities earlier than it would otherwise have.

These principles are useful in the management of working capital of an MNC. However, management cannot eliminate the foreign exchange risk. If exchange rates change continuously, managers find it impossible to determine by what amount or at what time the currency will depreciate or appreciate. As a result, the risk of exchange rate changes cannot be eliminated. Nevertheless, the reduction of risk, or the increase in the amount of gain from exchange rate changes, via the lead and lag is useful for cash management, accounts receivable management, and short-term liability management.

Cash Management and Positioning of Funds

Positioning of funds takes on an added importance in the international context. Funds may be transferred from a subsidiary of the MNC in country A to another subsidiary in country B such that the foreign exchange exposure and the tax liability of the MNC as a whole are minimized. It bears repeating that, owing to the global strategy of the MNC, the tax liability of the subsidiary in country A may be greater than it would otherwise have been, but the overall tax payment for all units of the MNC is minimized.

The transfer of funds among subsidiaries and the parent company is done by royalties, fees, and transfer pricing. A transfer price is the price a subsidiary or a parent company charges other companies that are part of the MNC for its goods or services. A parent that wishes to transfer funds from a subsidiary in a depreciating-currency country may charge a higher price on the goods and services sold to this subsidiary by the parent or by subsidiaries from strong-currency countries.

Centralized cash management of all the affiliates at the global level, achieved with the help of computer models, reduces both the overall cost of holding cash and the foreign exchange exposure of the MNC as a whole with respect to cash. The excess cash balance of one subsidiary is transferred to a cash-deficit subsidiary in the guise of a loan. The optimal holdings of cash in different currencies are calculated in a manner similar to the optimal portfolio problem discussed in Appendix 14A in Chapter 14.

INTERNATIONAL FINANCING AND CAPITAL STRUCTURE DECISIONS

A multinational corporation has access to many more financing sources than a domestic firm. It can tap not only the financing sources in its home country that are available to its domestic counterparts, but also sources in the foreign countries in which it operates. Host countries often provide access to low-cost subsidized financing in order to attract foreign investment. In addition, the MNC may enjoy preferential credit standards because of its size and investor preference for its home currency. In addition, an MNC may be able to access capital markets in countries which it does not operate but which may have large, well-functioning capital markets. Finally, an MNC can also access external currency markets: either the Eurodollar, Eurocurrency, or Asian dollar markets. These external markets are unregulated, and because of their lower spread, can offer very attractive rates for financing and for investments. With the increasing availability of interest rate and currency swaps, a firm can raise funds in the lowest-cost maturities and currencies and swap them into funds with the maturity and currency denomination it requires. MNCs have a more continuous access to external finance and a lower cost of capital as compared to a domestic company for the following reasons: the MNCs have the ability to tap a larger number of financial markets and the MNCs are able to avoid the problems or limitations of any one financial market.

Access to national financial markets is regulated by governments. For example, in Canada, access to capital markets is governed by both federal and provincial regulations. Access to Japanese capital markets is governed by regulations issued by the Ministry of Finance. Some countries have extensive regulations; other countries have relatively open markets. These regulations may differ depending on the legal residency terms of the company raising funds. A company that cannot use its local subsidiary to raise funds in a given market will be treated as foreign. In order to increase their visibility in a foreign capital market, a number of MNCs are now listing their equities on the stock exchanges of many of these countries.

The external currency markets are predominantly centred in Europe. In fact, most external currency markets can be characterized as Eurodollar markets. We define the Eurodollar (Euro-Canadian dollar) as a U.S. dollar deposit (Canadian dollar deposit) made with a European bank. The Eurodollar market is an international market which consists of an active short-term money market and an intermediate-term capital market with maturities ranging up to 15 years and averaging about 7 to 9 years. The intermediate-term market consists of the Eurobond and the Syndicated Eurocredit markets. Eurobonds are usually issued as unregistered bearer bonds and generally tend to have higher flotation costs but lower coupon rates compared to similar bonds issued in Canada. A Syndicated Eurocredit loan is simply a large term loan that involves contributions by a number of lending banks. Most large Canadian banks are active in the external currency markets.

In arriving at its capital-structure decisions, an MNC has to consider a number of factors. First, the capital structure of its local affiliates is influenced by local norms regarding capital structure in that industry and in that country. Local norms for companies in the same industry can differ considerably from country to country. Second, the local affiliate capital structure must also reflect corporate attitudes toward exchange rate and political risk in that country, which would normally lead to higher levels of local debt and other local capital. Third, local affiliate capital structure must reflect home country requirements with regard to the company's consolidated capital structure. Finally, the optimal MNC capital structure should reflect its wider access to financial markets, its ability to diversify economic and political risks, and its other advantages over domestic companies.

DIRECT FOREIGN INVESTMENT

The MNC makes direct foreign investments abroad in the form of plants and equipment. The decision process for this type of investment is very similar to the capital-budgeting decision in the domestic context—with some additional twists. Most real-world capital-budgeting decisions are made with uncertain future outcomes. Recall that a capital-budgeting decision has three major components: the estimation of the future cash flows (including the initial cost of the proposed investment), the estimation of the risk in these cash flows, and the choice of the proper discount rate. We will assume that the net-present-value criterion is appropriate as we examine (1) the risks associated with direct foreign investment and (2) factors to be considered in making the investment decision that may be unique to the international scene.

Risks in Direct Foreign Investments

Risks in domestic capital budgeting arise from two sources: business risk and financial risk. The international capital-budgeting problem has these risks as well as political risk and exchange risk.

Business Risk and Financial Risk

International business risk is due to the response of business to economic conditions in the foreign country. Thus, the Canadian MNC needs to be aware of the business climate in both Canada and the foreign country. Additional business risk is due to competition from other MNCs, local businesses, and imported goods. Financial risk refers to the risks introduced in the profit stream by the firm's financial structure. The financial risks of foreign operations are not very different from those of domestic operations.

Political Risk

Political or sovereignty risk arises because the foreign subsidiary conducts its business in a political system different from that of the home country. Many foreign governments, especially those in the Third World, are less stable than the Canadian government. A change in a country's political setup frequently brings a change in policies with respect to businesses, and especially with respect to foreign businesses. An extreme change in policy might involve nationalization or even outright expropriation of certain businesses. These are the political risks of conducting business abroad. A business with no investment in plants and equipment is less susceptible to these risks. Some examples of political risk are listed below:

1. Expropriation of plants and equipment without compensation

2. Expropriation with minimal compensation that is below actual market value

3. Nonconvertibility of the subsidiary's foreign earnings into the parent's currency—the problem of blocked funds

4. Substantial changes in the laws governing taxation

5. Governmental controls in the foreign country regarding the sale price of the products, wages, and compensation to personnel, hiring of personnel, making of transfer payments to the parent, and local borrowing

6. Some governments require certain amounts of local equity participation in the business. Some require that the majority of the equity participation belong to their country.

All these controls and governmental actions introduce risks in the cash flows of the investment to the parent company. These risks must be considered before the foreign investment decision. An MNC may decide against investing in countries with risks of types 1 and 2. Other risks can be borne—provided that the returns from the foreign investments are high enough to compensate for them. Insurance against some types of political risks may be purchased from private insurance companies. It should be noted that while an MNC cannot protect itself against all foreign political risks, political risks are also present in domestic business.

Exchange Risk

The exposure of the fixed assets is best measured by the effects of the exchange rate changes on the firm's future earnings stream: that being economic exposure rather than translation exposure. For instance, changes in the exchange rate may adversely affect sales by making competing imported goods cheaper. Changes in the cost of goods sold may result if some components are imported and their price in the foreign currency changes because of exchange rate fluctuations. The thrust of these examples is that the effect of exchange rate changes on income statement items should be properly measured to evaluate exchange risk. Finally, exchange risk affects the dollar-denominated profit stream of the parent company, whether or not it affects the foreign-currency profits.

International Capital Budgeting

Capital budgeting for international operations involves more extensive analysis than does capital budgeting for domestic operations. As in a domestic company, an MNC must develop estimates of the investment needed and the net cash flow generated by a proposed foreign capital investment. It must also assess the riskiness of these cash flows. Finally, it must summarize the cash flow and risk analysis information into a measure of desirability for the project, such as the net present value. The company can then compare the proposed investment with other possibilities and make a decision.

While this basic outline of steps necessary to evaluate a specific long-term foreign investment is not much different from that followed for evaluating a domestic capital investment, the cross-border nature of the foreign investment may require the consideration of a number of additional factors, such as the impact of currency and political risks on project value. Here we discuss some of the issues that may have to be considered in international capital budgeting.

For example, should the proposed capital investment be evaluated from the viewpoint of the local firm or from the viewpoint of the parent? The objective of maximizing shareholder wealth would indicate that the parent company perspective be used. However, the parent company may have supplied only part or none of the initial investment for the project. When using the parent company perspective, the project should be evaluated in terms of the parent's currency with the parent company's net initial investment and its net receipt of cash flows from the project discounted at a rate appropriate for the risks of the project cash flows with the inflation rate in the parent's currency. However, cash flows to the parent depend not just on the performance of the project, but also on how the local cash flows are managed. For example, because of tax considerations, it may not be optimal to remit all project cash flows to the parent only to have to send some or all of them back to be reinvested in the original foreign affiliate. In addition, value added by a project to a foreign affiliate will normally be reflected in the value of the parent company.

Thus, it may be better, even for shareholder wealth maximization, to evaluate a foreign capital proposal from the perspective of its local affiliate, using the total investment for the project and all of its cash flows discounted at a rate that reflects the local inflation rate and the riskiness of the project. In practice, most MNCs use at least the local perspective to evaluate a foreign project, while some supplement the local perspective with present value analysis from the parent's perspective. In such a case, the foreign affiliate perspective is the primary basis for a decision, while the parent perspective is used to ensure that the structure of the investment and the disposition of the cash flows are consistent with corporate objectives.

It is important that cash flow projections be realistic and reflect local conditions regarding competition, inflation, price controls, and other government regulations. When taking the local currency perspective, the discount rate should also reflect a realistic assessment of the expected local inflation rate. This may be especially difficult, given that capital markets in many foreign countries are often not free or efficient and interest rates do not reflect market expectations. Project cash flows should also reflect the advantages of using subsidized financing that may have been used to finance the project. When using the parent currency perspective, the discount rate should reflect the expected inflation rate in the parent currency, and foreign currency cash flows should be converted to parent currency cash flows using projected exchange rates. These projections are often based on the assumption that purchasing power parity holds during the life of the project. In such a case, it may be possible to take initial-year cash flows and assume that increases because of local inflation will be offset exactly by purchasing power parity related declines in the exchange rate. However, if significant deviations from purchasing power parity are expected, such a simplifying assumption would be inappropriate. In addition, high inflation rates may be accompanied by government price controls. A company may face a lag between allowed price increases and inflation, or may be accompanied by other economic and political instabilities. In such cases, simply assuming that purchasing power parity will hold may be insufficient, and additional analysis to reflect these factors should be undertaken.

In the domestic case, an NPV less than zero leads to rejection of a project. In the international context, an NPV less than zero leads to rejection of the direct foreign investment; however, the MNC then has other options open to it.

If the foreign sales volume is expected to be low, the MNC may consider setting up a sales office in the foreign country. The product may be exported to the foreign country from production facilities in the home country or from some other foreign subsidiary. An NPV calculation may now be employed. The acceptance of this scheme is ensured, since no direct capital investment is needed. If the estimated sales levels are high enough that the establishment of a plant in the foreign country appears profitable, owing to the potential savings in the transportation costs, yet the NPV of the direct foreign investment (DFI) is negative, the MNC may consider licensing or an affiliate arrangement with a local company. The MNC provides the technology, and the interested domestic firm finances and sets up the plant. The MNC does not bear the risks of a DFI, but receives a royalty payment from the sales of the affiliate company instead.

SUMMARY

The growth of the global economy, the increase in the number of multinational companies and the increase in foreign trade underscore the importance of the study of international finance.

Exchange rate mechanics were discussed in the context of the prevailing floating rates. Under this system, exchange rates between currencies vary in an apparently random fashion in accordance with the supply and demand conditions in the exchange market. Important economic factors affecting the level of exchange rates include the relative economic strengths of the countries involved, the balance-of-payments mechanism, and the countries' monetary policies. The asked and the bid rates are terms which describe the selling and buying rates of currencies. The direct quote is the units of home currency per unit of foreign currency, while the indirect quote is the reciprocal of the direct quote. Cross-rate computations reflect the exchange rate between two foreign currencies. Finally, simple arbitrage for indirect quote and triangular arbitrage for cross rates were shown to hold. The efficiency of spot exchange markets implies that no arbitrage (riskless) profits can be made by buying and selling currencies in different markets.

The forward-exchange market provides a valuable service by quoting rates for the delivery of foreign currencies in the future. The foreign currency is said to sell at a premium (discount) forward from the spot rate when the forward rate is greater (less) than the spot rate, in direct quotation. The computation of the percent-per-annum deviation of the forward from the spot rate was used to demonstrate the interest rate parity theory (IRPT), which states that the forward contract sells at a discount or premium from the spot rates, owing solely to interest rate differential between the two countries. The IRPT was shown to hold by means of the covered interest arbitrage argument. In addition, the influences of purchasing power parity (PPP) and the international Fisher effect (IFE) in determining the exchange rate were discussed. In rational and efficient markets, forward rates are unbiased forecasts of future spot rates that are consistent with the PPP.

Exchange risk exists because the exact spot rate that prevails on a future date is not known with certainty today. The concept of exchange risk is applicable to a wide variety of businesses, including export-import firms and firms involved in making direct foreign investments or international investments in securities. Exchange exposure is a measure of exchange risk. There are different ways of measuring the foreign exposure, including the net asset (net liability) measurement. Different strategies are open to businesses to counter the exposure to this risk, including the money-market hedge, the forward-market hedge, futures contracts, and options. Each involves different costs.

In discussing working-capital management in an international environment we found leading and lagging techniques useful in minimizing exchange risks and increasing profitability. In addition, funds positioning is a useful tool for reducing exchange risk exposure. The MNC may have a lower cost of capital because it has access to a larger set of financial markets than a domestic company. In addition to the home, host, and third country financial markets, the MNC can tap the rapidly growing external currency markets. In making capital-structure decisions, the MNC must consider political and exchange risks and host and home country capital-structure norms.

The complexities encountered in the direct foreign investment decision include the usual sources of risk—business and financial—and additional risks associated with fluctuating exchange rates and political factors. Political risk is due to differences in political climates, institutions, and processes between the home country and abroad. Under these conditions the estimation of future cash flows and the choice of the proper discount rates are more complicated than for the domestic investment situation. Rejection of a DFI proposal may lead either to the setting up of a sales office abroad or to an affiliate arrangement with a foreign company.

STUDY QUESTIONS

23-1. What additional factors are encountered in international as compared with domestic financial management? Discuss each briefly.

23-2. What different types of businesses operate in the international environment? Why are the techniques and strategies available to these firms different?

23-3. What is meant by *arbitrage profits*?

23-4. What are the markets and mechanics involved in generating (a) simple arbitrage profits, (b) triangular arbitrage profits, (c) covered interest arbitrage profits?

23-5. How do the purchasing power parity, interest rate parity, and the Fisher effect explain the relationships between the current spot rate, the future spot rate, and the forward rate?

23-6. What is meant by (a) exchange risk, (b) political risk?

23-7. How can exchange risk be measured?

23-8. What are the differences between transaction, translation, and economic exposures? Should all of them ideally be reduced to zero?

23-9. What steps can a firm take to reduce exchange risk? Indicate at least two different techniques.

23-10. How are the forward-market and the money-market hedges affected? What are the major differences between these two types of hedges?

23-11. Compare and contrast the use of forward contracts, futures contracts, and options to reduce foreign exchange exposure. When is each instrument most appropriate?

23-12. Indicate two working-capital management techniques that are useful for international businesses to reduce exchange risk and potentially increase profits.

23-13. How do the financing sources available to an MNC differ from those available to a domestic firm? What do these differences mean for the company's cost of capital?

23-14. What risks are associated with direct foreign investment? How do these risks differ from those encountered in domestic investment?

23-15. How is the direct foreign investment decision made? What are the inputs to this decision process? Are the inputs more complicated than those to the domestic investment problem? If so, why?

23-16. A corporation desires to enter a particular foreign market. The DFI analysis indicates that a direct investment in the plant in the foreign country is not profitable. What other course of action can the company take to enter the foreign market? What are the important considerations?

23-17. What are the reasons for the acceptance of a sales office or licensing arrangement when the DFI itself is not profitable?

SELF-TEST PROBLEMS

The data for self-test Problems ST-1 and ST-2 are given in the following table:

Selling Quotes for the German Mark in Montreal		
Country	*Contract*	*$/DM*
Germany—mark	Spot	0.8502
	1-month forward	0.8466
	6-month forward	0.8292

ST-1. You own $10,000. The dollar rate on the German mark is 1.1835. The German mark rate is given in the table above. Are arbitrage profits possible? Set up an arbitrage scheme with your capital. What is the gain (loss) in dollars?

ST-2. If the interest rates on the 1-month instruments in Canada and Germany are 6 and 8 percent (annualized), respectively, what is the correct price of the 1-month forward mark?

STUDY PROBLEMS (SET A)

The data for Study Problems 23-1A through 23-10A are given in the following table:

Selling Quotes for Foreign Currencies in Montreal		
Country	**Contract**	**$/Foreign Currency**
U.S.—dollar	Spot	1.1963
	1-month	1.1977
	6-month	1.2038
Japan—yen	Spot	0.009706
	1-month	0.009711
	6-month	0.009760
Switzerland—franc	Spot	0.9498
	1-month	0.9475
	6-month	0.9359

23-1A. A Canadian business needs to pay (a) 10,000 American dollars, (b) 2 million yen, and (c) 50,000 Swiss francs to businesses abroad. What are the dollar payments to the respective countries?

23-2A. A Canadian business pays $10,000, $15,000, and $20,000 to suppliers in, respectively, Japan, Switzerland, and the U.S. How much, in local currencies, do the suppliers receive?

23-3A. Compute the indirect quote for the spot and forward American dollar, yen, and Swiss franc contracts.

23-4A. The spreads on the contracts as a percent of the asked rates are 2 percent for yen, 3 percent for American dollars, and 5 percent for Swiss francs. Show, in a table similar to the one above, the bid rates for the different spot and forward rates.

23-5A. You own $10,000. The dollar rate in Tokyo is 106.0454. The yen rate in Montreal is given in the table above. Are arbitrage profits possible? Set up an arbitrage scheme with your capital. What is the gain (loss) in dollars?

23-6A. Compute the American dollar/yen and the yen/Swiss franc spot rate from the data in the table above.

23-7A. Compute the simple premium (discount) on the 1-month and 6-month yen, Swiss franc, and the American dollar quotes. Tabulate the percent-per-annum deviations as in Table 23-2.

23-8A. Assume that the interest rate on the Canadian 1-month T-bill is 5 percent (annualized). The corresponding American rate is 3 percent. The spot and the forward rates are shown in the table above. Can a Canadian trader make arbitrage profits? If the trader had $100,000 to invest, indicate the steps he or she would take. What would be the net profit? (Ignore transactions and other costs.)

23-9A. If the interest rates on the 1-month instruments in Canada and Japan are 5 and 2 percent (annualized), respectively, what is the correct price of the 1-month forward yen? Use the spot rate from the table.

23-10A. The 1-month T-bill rate in Canada is 5 percent annualized. Using the 1-month forward quotes, compute the 30-day interest rates in the U.S., Switzerland, and Japan.

STUDY PROBLEM (SET B)

The data for Study Problems 23-1B through 23-10B are given in the following table:

Selling Quotes for Foreign Currencies in Montreal		
Country	**Contract**	**$/Foreign Currency**
U.S.—dollar	Spot	1.2024
	1-month	1.2046
	6-month	1.2130
Japan—yen	Spot	0.009642
	1-month	0.009652
	6-month	0.009706
Switzerland—franc	Spot	0.8861
	1-month	0.8836
	6-month	0.8710

23-1B. A Canadian business needs to pay (a) 15,000 American dollars, (b) 1.5 million yen, and (c) 55,000 Swiss francs to businesses abroad. What are the dollar payments to the respective countries?

23-2B. A Canadian business pays $20,000, $5,000, and $15,000 to suppliers in, respectively, Japan, Switzerland, and the U.S. How much, in local currencies, do the suppliers receive?

23-3B. Compute the indirect quote for the spot and forward American dollar, yen, and Swiss franc contracts.

23-4B. The spreads on the contracts as a percent of the asked rates are 4 percent for yen, 3 percent for American dollars, and 6 percent for Swiss francs. Show, in a table similar to the one above, the bid rates for the different spot and forward rates.

23-5B. You own $10,000. The dollar rate in Tokyo is 106.3649. The yen rate in Montreal is given in the table above. Are arbitrage profits possible? Set up an arbitrage scheme with your capital. What is the gain (loss) in dollars?

23-6B. Compute the American dollar/yen and the yen/Swiss franc spot rate from the data in the table above.

23-7B. Compute the simple premium (discount) on the 1-month and 6-month yen, Swiss franc, and American dollar quotes. Tabulate the percent-per-annum deviations as in Table 23-2.

23-8B. Assume that the interest rate on the Canadian 1-month T-bill is 7 percent (annualized). The corresponding American rate is 4 percent. The spot and the forward rates are shown in the table above. Can a Canadian trader make arbitrage profits? If the trader had $100,000 to invest, indicate the steps he or she would take. What would be the net profit? (Ignore transactions and other costs.)

23-9B. If the interest rates on the 1-month instruments in Canada and Japan are 6 and 3 percent (annualized), respectively, what is the correct price of the 1-month forward yen? Use the spot rate from the table.

23-10B. The 1-month T-bill rate in Canada is 6 percent annualized. Using the 1-month forward quotes, compute the 1-month interest rates in the U.S., Switzerland, and Japan.

SELF-TEST SOLUTIONS

SS-1. The German rate is 1.1835 DM/$1, while the (indirect) Montreal rate is

$$\frac{1}{0.8502} = 1.1762 \; \frac{DM}{\$}$$

Assuming no transaction costs, the rates between Germany and Montreal are out of line. Thus, arbitrage profits are possible.

Step 1: Since the mark is cheaper in Germany, buy $10,000 worth of marks in Germany. The number of marks purchased would be

$$\$10,000 \times 1.1835 = 11,835 \text{ DM}$$

Step 2: Simultaneously sell the marks in Montreal at the prevailing rate. The amount received upon the sale of the marks would be:

$$11,835 \text{ DM} \times \frac{\$.8502}{\text{DM}} = \$10,062.12$$

net gain is $10,062.12 - \$10,000 = \$62.12$

SS-2. *Step 1:* Compute the percent-per-annum premium on the forward rate using Equation (23-3a):

$$D = \frac{I^f - I^d}{1 + I^f} \tag{23-3a}$$

where I^d = the annualized interest rate on a domestic instrument having the same maturity as the forward contract

I^f = the annualized interest rate on a foreign instrument having the same maturity as the forward contract

Thus,

$$D = \frac{0.08 - 0.06}{1.08} = \frac{0.02}{1.08} = 0.01852 = 1.852\%$$

Step 2: Using this premium in Equation (23-2), compute the forward rate F:

$$\frac{(S - F)}{S} \times \frac{12 \text{ months}}{1 \text{ month}} \times 100 = D \tag{23-2}$$

where F = the forward rate, direct quote

S = the spot rate, direct quote

n = the number of months of the forward contract

D = the annualized percent discount

$$\frac{(0.8502 - F)}{0.8502} \times \frac{12 \text{ months}}{1 \text{ month}} \times 100 = 1.852\%$$

$$\frac{(1020.24 - 1200F)}{0.8502} = 1.852\%$$

$$1020.24 - 1200F = 1.57444$$

$$F = 0.8489$$

Thus the correct price of the forward rate is 0.8489.

SELECTED REFERENCES

Adler, Michael, and Bernard Dumas. "International Portfolio Choice and Corporate Finance: A Synthesis," *Journal of Finance*, 38 (June 1983), 925–984.

Aggarwal, Raj. "Distribution of Exchange Rates and Risk Premia," *Decision Sciences*, 21 (Summer 1990).

Aggarwal, Raj. "International Differences in Capital Structure Norms," *Management International Review*, 21 (1981), 75–88.

Aggarwal, Raj, and Cheng-Few Lee (eds.). *Advances in International Financial Planning and Forecasting.* Greenwich, CT: JAI Press, 1990.

Aggarwal, Raj, and Luc Soenen. "Cash and Foreign Exchange Management: Theory and Practice," *Journal of Business Finance and Accounting*, 16 (Winter 1989), 599–619.

Aggarwal, Raj, and Luc Soenen. "Managing Persistent Real

Changes in Exchanges Rates," *Columbia Journal of World Business*, 24 (Fall 1989).

Beidleman, Carl (ed.). *The Handbook of International Investing.* Chicago: Probus, 1987.

Caves, Richard. *Multinational Enterprises and Economic Analysis.* Cambridge, Eng.: Cambridge University Press, 1982.

Choi, Fred D. S., and Gerhardt Mueller. *An Introduction to Multinational Accounting.* Englewood Cliffs, NJ: Prentice-Hall, 1984.

Eiteman, David K., and Arthur I. Stonehill. *Multinational Business Finance.* Reading, MA: Addison-Wesley, 1989.

Folks, William R., and Raj Aggarwal. *International Dimensions of Financial Management.* Boston: Kent Publishing Company, 1988.

Goodman, Lauri S. "Pricing of Syndicated Eurocurrency Credits," *Federal Reserve Bank of New York Quarterly Review* (Summer 1980), 39–49.

Grabbe, J. Orlin. *International Financial Markets.* New York: Elsevier, 1986.

Hodder, James E. "Evaluation of Manufacturing Investments: A Comparison of U.S. and Japanese Practices," *Financial Management*, 15 (Winter 1986), 17–24.

Kelly, Marie W. *Foreign Investment Practices of U.S. Multinational Corporations.* Ann Arbor, MI: UMI Research Press, 1981.

Kobrin, Steven J. *Environmental Assessment in the International Firm.* Berkeley: University of California Press, 1982.

Levich, Richard M. *The International Money Market: An Assessment of Forecasting Techniques and Market Efficiency.* Greenwich, CT: JAI Press, 1979.

Owens, E. A. *International Aspects of U.S. Income Taxation.* Cambridge, MA: Harvard Law School, 1980.

Shapiro, Alan C. *Multinational Financial Management.* Boston: Allyn and Bacon, 1988.

Stern, Joel M., and Donald H. Chew (eds.). *New Developments in International Finance.* Cambridge, MA: Basil Blackwell, 1988.

CHAPTER 24

Financial Management: Small and Mid-Sized Business Perspective

- What Is a Small Business?
- Small Versus Large: Is There a Difference?
- Cash Management in the Small Firm
- Capital Budgeting in the Small Firm
- Financing the Small Firm
- Going Public

Small companies have been a major driving force of the Canadian economy, creating most of the new jobs and technological innovation. Approximately 2.1 million net new jobs were added by small businesses during the past decade.[1] Practically every innovation in the computer industry since the development of the mainframe has been started or commercialized by companies financed by venture capitalists. Examples include the microprocessor, the personal computer, the minicomputer, workstations, the supercomputer, and most of the accompanying software. Large North American corporations have lost their leadership in key industries ranging from consumer electronics to steel. Management flexibility has become more important than the long-touted economies of scale in research, production, and marketing. For example, some of the smaller steel makers can produce a ton of steel with about one-third of the labour used by their larger competitors. In computing, the smaller firms can develop a new computer three to five times faster than can the "giants." Even management guru Peter Drucker, who often used General Motors as an example of a successful large corporation, now believes that large companies have essentially outlived their usefulness, noting that most of the recent growth and innovation in North American business has come from mid-sized companies that employ 200 to 4,000 people. Drucker states that, "A penalty of size is that you try to do everything, and no one can do everything well."[2]

While "small is beautiful," in the eyes of many, there are some skeptics. Some would argue that small firms will not be able to withstand the increas-

---

[1]Small businesses with fewer than 50 employees created 81 percent of all the new jobs in Canada between 1979 and 1989. See, Industry, Science and Technology Canada, Small Business in Canada 1991 From Best Practice to Competitiveness, Minister of Supply and Services, Catalogue No. C28-1/2-199E.

[2]Peter Drucker quoted by John A. Byrne, "Is Your Company Too Big?" *Business Week* (March 27, 1989), 84–94.

ing global competition. The large corporation, combined with government support, is thought to be the key to long-term competitiveness. For example, small businesses are limited with respect to resources and cannot commit money to a project that requires five years to complete. Some undertakings inherently necessitate size and staying power. While we might not take issue with such a proposition, the corporate restructuring that is pervasive in the North American economy is largely an effort to reduce the many layers of middle management that have developed in the large corporations and to encourage managers to "think small."[3] Canada Packers is an example of a large food processing company which has restructured to try to take advantage of smallness by encouraging their divisions to act as stand-alone businesses.

The debate about size will long be with us, but the fact remains that small firms are a major part of the economy and deserve some of our attention as we study finance. This chapter examines financial management from the perspective of small and mid-sized firms. We will first define small and mid-sized businesses and then identify their financial attributes. Next, we will consider the importance of cash management for small and mid-sized firms. Finally, we will identify financing sources available to the small and mid-sized firms, including the process of entering the public capital markets.

WHAT IS A SMALL BUSINESS?

Many definitions of "small business" have been offered; however, the definition and size restrictions used by Industry, Science, and Technology Canada (ISTC) are probably the most widely used.[4] ISTC defines a small business as any firm with fewer than 50 paid employees and annual revenues less than $5 million. The exception to this definition is the manufacturing sector whereby a small business is any firm with fewer than 100 paid employees. A mid-size firm is defined as a firm with greater than 100 paid employees and fewer than 500 paid employees.

In this chapter it is not necessary to define a small business in the precise manner indicated by the ISTC. In general, we will define a small business as one that is growth-oriented and does not have easy access to the capital and money markets.

SMALL VERSUS LARGE: IS THERE A DIFFERENCE?

Walker and Petty have studied the financial differences between large and small firms, as measured by various financial ratios.[5] To compare these two

---

[3]This introduction comes from John Byrne, "Is Your Company Too Big?" *Business Week* (March 27, 1989), pp. 84–94.

[4]Industry, Science and Technology Canada, Small Business in Canada 1991 From Best Practice to Competitiveness, Minister of Supply and Services, Catalogue No. C28-1/2-199E.

[5]Ernest W. Walker and J. William Petty II, "Financial Differences between Large and Small Firms," *Financial Management* (Winter 1978), pp. 61–68.

groups, financial data were gathered for a sample of growth manufacturing firms with sales not exceeding $5 million. The small-firm sample consisted of businesses that had filed prospectuses with American securities regulatory bodies in an effort to "go public." Thus, Walker and Petty were looking at operations involving successful closely held companies that were trying to tap the public equity markets. Similar data for a sample of large companies in the same industries were also compiled. The results are compared in Table 24-1.

In examining Table 24-1 we see that there clearly are some differences between small and large firms. The most prominent difference is the disparity in dividend policies. For example, dividends as a percent of earnings are approximately 3 percent and 40 percent for small and large firms, respectively. The low dividend payout ratio, which is generally thought to be typical of small firms,[6] is seen to be characteristic even of small firms entering the public markets. In fact, 74 percent of the small firms made no distribution in the form of cash dividends in the year preceding the offering. Thus, the incentive, as well as the opportunity, for small firms to pay dividends in anticipation of a favourable impact upon the common shares when entering the marketplace is in no way apparent. The investors purchasing such securities must have believed that these securities represented shares in "growth companies." They were evidently willing to rely almost solely on the capital gains potential from their investment.

The second major difference between small and large firms is liquidity. Large firms have more liquidity, as reflected by the current ratio. The differ-

	Average Values	
	Small Firms	Large Firms
Liquidity indicators		
Current ratio	2.00×	2.77×
Accounts receivable turnover	7.04×	6.40×
Inventory turnover	8.47×	5.31×
Current liabilities/total debt	83.70%	62.99%
Profitability indicators		
Operating profit margin	10.91%	9.20%
Accounts receivable turnover	7.04×	6.40×
Inventory turnover	8.47×	5.31×
Fixed assets turnover	9.40×	3.50×
Financing indicators		
Debt/total assets	49.00%	38.05%
Current liabilities/total debt	83.70%	62.99%
Fixed charges coverage	33.16×	22.47×
Business risk indicator		
Variability of operating income	21.94%	7.71%
Dividend policy indicator		
Dividend/earnings	2.91%	40.52%

Source: Ernest W. Walker and J. William Petty II, "Financial Differences Between Large and Small Firms," *Financial Management* (Winter 1978), pp. 61–68.

TABLE 24-1
Financial Data for Small and Large Companies

---

[6]Lower dividend payout may be the result of more variability in future earnings as indicated by the variability of the operating income as seen in Table 24-1. Lintner's findings on dividend policy support this observation.

ence would seem to be the result of two factors. First, small firms retain smaller amounts of accounts receivable and inventory, as reflected by higher accounts receivable and inventory turnovers. Second, small firms rely more heavily on current liabilities, as shown by the current liabilities/total debt ratio. Thus, small firms typically maintained less liquidity.

The apparent difference in liquidity between the large and small firms lends further support to the belief that a working-capital shortage is a problem for small firms. The difference could be the result of at least two factors. First, the small firm's limited access to the capital markets may impose the need for more economy in the use of working capital. Second, the management style of the "entrepreneur" could have a bearing upon the working-capital decisions within the small firm. If the managers of small firms are willing to assume greater risk, as experience would suggest, their attitude may well be reflected in the small firm's liquidity position.

Business risk and financial risk also help distinguish between small and large firms. Business risk, as measured by the variability of earnings before interest and taxes, is greater for small firms. The inability to diversify across investments, as well as geographically, increases the small firm's volatility of profits. Also, the small firm's capital structure is more debt-oriented, with an even greater tendency for using short-term credit. This heavy use of debt is usually perceived as one of the basic characteristics of managing a small firm.

Unquestionably there are differences in the financial management of small and large businesses. Based upon the Walker-Petty study, these differences may be summarized as follows:

1. Small firms are less liquid than their larger counterparts, where short-term cash flow patterns become critical to the success of the small business.

2. Small companies have more volatile profits and cash flows over time, owing to the greater business and financial risk experienced by smaller entities.

3. Small firms use relatively large amounts of debt in the financing of the business, which may be the consequence of entrepreneurs' greater propensity to assume risk. However, it is more likely that the issue relates to the small company's inaccessibility to the public capital markets, especially the equity markets.

4. The inaccessibility of the small corporation to the capital markets means the value of the firm is more difficult to determine. Also, the absence of market data for the firm's securities makes determining the cost of capital a difficult, if not impossible, job.

Table 24-1 demonstrates some differences between the large and small firm in terms of their financial data. There are some underlying reasons for these differences. It has been said that "a small company is not just a little big business," the issue is more than a matter of the number of zeros.[7] In other words, there are reasons why traditional financial analysis may not tell the story at times. The following reasons can be cited:

1. The owner may not always be a value maximizer. There may be other

---

[7]See J. A. Welsh, and J. F. White, "A Small Business Is Not a Little Big Business," *Harvard Business Review* (July–August 1981), pp. 18–32 and Richard Levin and Virginia Travis, "Small Company Finance: What the Books Don't Say," *Havard Business Review* (November–December 1987), pp. 30–35.

personal goals that are of equal, if not greater importance. Personal life styles which are realized through the company may distort the economic content of the financial statements, such as a firm owning a house on a lake. If the small firm is an extension of the owner, it becomes difficult to separate the firm from the owner in a financial context without causing distortions. For example, in making an investment decision, the need to create autonomy outside the firm may be as important as the investment's net present value.

2. For the small company, the goal of survival may supersede ideal financial practices, due largely to the small firm's limited access to the public capital markets, and banker's insistence on looking to the owner's personal guarantees in addition to the firm's financial position.

3. Traditional definitions of debt and equity, as we have studied them, may not apply. For instance, loans to the owners may in reality be a form of equity, if the firm is unable to repay the loan. In fact, the owner's personal preference for financial risk may be more important than minimizing the firm's cost of capital when determining the desired level of debt.

The implications of these differences are truly significant to the small owner. In making financial decisions, the owner should seek to maximize the total value of both corporate and individual wealth, subject to personal life style preferences. Second, small business owners should make every effort to maintain flexibility when dealing with bankers and other providers of capital. Finally, the owner should always prepare a cash budget along with the income statement, and contingency planning should be a constant.

CASH MANAGEMENT IN THE SMALL FIRM

The nature and importance of cash management were described in Chapter 14. Although it is important that a "mature" firm be cognizant of its cash requirements, it is even more important for a firm encountering change and for a firm that is undercapitalized, both of which are frequently characteristic of small businesses. For instance, an undercapitalized enterprise results in a working-capital shortage such that the turnover of working capital from the point of investing in raw materials to the final collection of receivables continues to plague the management of the company. In such an atmosphere, the executive is compelled to keep close tabs on the company's cash flow.

The second factor associated with many small businesses that should encourage the implementation of careful cash management is the growth element. The ownership of a small business facing an expansion has to be more cognizant of the cash inflows and the necessary outflows. Contrary to the belief of many small business owners, growth is not synonymous with financial prosperity. A growth firm is especially susceptible to financing difficulties, and thus requires a closer watch on funds flows. The belief that cash flows in a business equal profits plus depreciation gives the impression that a profitable business will not experience cash flow difficulties, which is wrong and misleading when applied to a growth firm.

A third instance in which the small firm may find cash planning essential is in approaching parties who represent potential sources of financing. The financing for the small business usually comes from the banker. In requesting a bank loan that entails a substantial amount, the cash plan becomes an important tool in two ways. First, the small business owner-manager is more familiar with the realities of the loan request, especially in having a better understanding of how the loan is to be repaid. This issue is generally a key concern to the banker. Second, and of equal importance, is the opportunity for the small business owner to establish credibility with the banker if, when requesting the loan, he or she can explicitly set forth detailed projected cash flows.[8]

Despite the importance of careful cash management for the small firm, large firms typically make more extensive use of cash plans. Most managers of small firms believe they do not have the time to spend on forecasting. Besides, they view themselves as being close enough to the events so that they are able to plan adequately in an informal fashion, without having to prepare a written budget. Such an argument may be true of a few business owners; however, for most of them time has a way of making financial details hazy. As a result, the benefit of past experience is not nearly so critical. An understanding of the cash flow cycle, as well as the process for implementing a forecast, is particularly relevant for the small firm.

CAPITAL BUDGETING IN THE SMALL FIRM

We have examined capital-budgeting techniques in Chapters 6 and 7, which described the discounted cash flow (DCF) techniques in valuing capital projects. Now we will consider (1) how the managers-owners of small firms actually evaluate capital investments and (2) how ought they to do so, given the nature of the small firm.

Capital-Budgeting Practices of Small Firms

In 1963, Robert Soldofsky surveyed the owners of a large number of small firms, about how they went about analyzing capital-budgeting projects.[9] The response would not be encouraging to a finance professor, with 50 percent of the respondents saying they use the payback technique; and even worse, 40 percent of the firms used no formal analysis at all. In defense of DCF techniques, we would quickly note that these findings are extremely dated, going back almost 30 years. Even the large firms, for the most part, would not have been using discounted cash flow techniques to any great extent so long ago; so we need to find a more recent study.

In 1983, L. R. Runyon again surveyed over 200 small companies with their net worth between $500,000 and $1 million.[10] In probing into their approaches for evaluating the merits of proposed capital investments, he learned that only 14 percent of the firms used any form of a discounted cash

---

[8]With increased risk and the limited access to the financial markets, the liquidity position of a small firm contributes further to the importance of a open relationship between a small firm and its bank.

[9]Robert M. Soldofsky, "Capital Budgeting Practices in Small Manufacturing Companies," in *Studies in the Factor Markets for Small Business Firms*, ed. Dudley G. Luckett (Washington, DC: Small Business Administration, 1964).

[10]L. R. Runyon, "Capital Expenditure Decision Making in Small Firms," *Journal of Business Research* (September 1983), pp. 389–97.

flow technique; 70 percent indicated they used no DCF approach at all; and 9 percent used no formal analysis of any form. Surprisingly, we may judge that time has had little impact on the investment decision-making process within small firms. While we may be encouraged that the practice of not relying on any formal analysis has declined significantly, little use is made of any market-value rules afforded by present-value analysis.

Why are the findings of the above studies so dismal? Why has there been so little change in 20 years? Have small-firm decision makers not been exposed to modern financial theory? Maybe, but we believe that the issue is bigger than training. Since Runyon was dealing with the "smaller of the smalls," with their net worth not exceeding $1 million, there probably are a significant number who have not been exposed to financial theory. However, the cause for such limited use of DCF tools probably rests more with the nature of the small firm itself. We would argue that several more important reasons exist, among them the following:

1. The firm's activities and owner's personal goals are inseparable. As a consequence, nonfinancial variables may play a significant part in their decisions. For instance, the desire to be viewed as a respected part of the community may be more important to the owner than the present value of a decision.

2. The frequent undercapitalization and liquidity problems of the small firm impact directly on the decision-making process within the small firm, where survival becomes the top priority.

3. The greater uncertainty of cash flows within the small firm makes long-term forecasts and planning unappealing, and even viewed as a waste of time. The owner simply has no confidence in his or her ability to reasonably predict cash flows beyond two or three years. Thus, calculating the cash flows for the entire life of a project is viewed as an effort in futility.

4. Since the value of a closely held firm is not as observable as a publicly held firm, where the market value of the firm's securities are actively traded in the marketplace, the owner of the small firm may consider the market value rule of maximizing net present values as irrelevant. In this environment, estimating the firm's cost of capital is also difficult. If computing the large firm's cost of capital is difficult at best, the measurement for the small firm becomes virtually impossible.

5. The smaller size of projects of a small firm may make net-present-value computations not feasible in practice. Much of the time and costs required to analyze a capital investment are fixed; thus, the small firm incurs a diseconomy of scale in evaluation costs.

6. Management talent within a small firm is a scarce resource. Also, the training of the owner-managers is frequently of a technical nature, as opposed to a business or finance orientation. The perspective of these owners is influenced greatly by their backgrounds.

The foregoing characteristics of the small firm, and equally important the owners, have a significant impact on the decision-making process within the small firm, whether or not we agree with the logic. The result is a short-term mind set, somewhat by necessity and partly by choice. Nevertheless, given the nature of the environment, what could we recommend to the owner-managers of the small firm? What process can owner-managers use to make investment decisions for the firm?

A Better Way of Capital Budgeting for the Small Firm

Management of a large firm can sometimes become more concerned with its own priorities than serving the owners' best interests. This type of agency problem must be considered if we are to understand the financial nature of the firm. Owners cannot ignore potential conflicts if they develop within a large firm. In the case of the small firm, we have owner-managers which are one and the same. The decision to be wealth satisficers rather than wealth maximizers cannot be criticized. If the owners are maximizing their utility, which includes more than financial considerations, who is to say they are wrong? What finance can do, however, is address the potential need of the small firm to consider liquidity on an equal footing with value maximization, as well as the problem of estimating cash flows in the long-term future. Furthermore, we may at least partially resolve the difficulty in measuring the firm's cost of capital.

The Need for Liquidity

While not an ideal answer, a case may be developed for the small firm to use a discounted payback period in evaluating a proposed investment.[11] The payback method was shown in Chapter 6 to have limitations when applied to investment proposals. However, this method does give us an indication of how long our funds are tied up in an investment. This type of indication gives us some measure of liquidity, which may be vitally important for the small firm. Also, while we had faulted the payback approach for ignoring cash flows beyond the payback period, such a limitation may have less significance for the small firm, since the cash flows are more uncertain over the long run.

EXAMPLE

To illustrate the use of the discounted payback period, we have estimated the cash flows for a project for the first five years of its life. The project is expected to cost $50,000, and the owners have a required rate of return of 15 percent. The expected cash flows for the first five years are as follows:

Years	Expected Cash Flows	Present Value of Expected Cash Flows
1	$12,000	$10,435
2	14,000	10,586
3	17,000	11,178
4	20,000	11,435
5	20,000	9,944
	Total present value	$53,578

The payback period for the investment would be 3.35 years ($43,000 received in three years and the remaining $7,000 recouped in .35 years, i.e., $7,000/$20,000). However, when we recognize the owner's required rate of return of 15 percent, we find the present value of the first five years' expected

[11]See Richard Wacht, "Capital Investment Analysis for the Small Firm," Working Paper (February 1988).

cash flows to be $53,578. Using these present values, we see that the owners recoup their investment in 4.64 years ($43,634 of the investment received in four years and the remaining $6,366 in .64 year, i.e., $6366/$9944). By comparing projects in this manner, we give consideration both to the present value criterion and the liquidity of the project. ■

Measuring the Cost of Capital: A Direct Approach

The methodology used in Chapter 5 for measuring the cost of capital cannot be applied to a small firm. We simply do not have access to market data for the small firm as we do for the large corporation whose shares are traded on the Toronto Stock Exchange. Thus, we must resort to some alternative method.

As noted in Chapter 5, the cost of capital is an opportunity-cost concept. Shareholders should receive from their investment in the firm an amount at least equal to the rate of return available in the capital markets, given the level of risk. We use the market data of the firm's securities to estimate these opportunity costs. However, no such information is available for most small companies. We therefore need to modify our approach.

We will assume that the small business is either family-owned or closely held. Since the shares of this firm are not publicly traded, we cannot use this type of data to estimate the owner's opportunity costs of investing in the next best project. However, the marketplace will give a well-informed owner a competitive rate of return which can be used as a proxy for the owner's required rate of return. We would then suggest using the "residual NPV approach," which compares the cash flows going to the shareholders to their required rate of return, rather than using a weighted cost of capital for all investors.

The Residual Net Present Value

The residual net present value is a slight modification of the conventional weighted cost-of-capital approach. Rather than computing the present value of the expected cash flows going to all investors discounted at the weighted cost of capital, we estimate the cash that will flow to the owners after all debt and preferred shareholders have been paid their returns. We then discount these flows at the owners' required rate of return. As a financial advisor to the small firm, we recommend the following method:

1. Determine a target position for the firm's debt-equity ratio.

2. Compute the residual after-tax cash flows available to the owners of the company, net of interest expense, debt principal repayment, and preferred dividend payments. In Chapters 6 and 7, we used after-tax operating cash flows (cash flows available to all investors of the firm, that is, debt, preferred shares, and common shares) in our net-present-value calculations. However, with the weighted cost of capital, our discount rate recognized the required rates of return for all these investors as well.

3. Have the owners of the company decide what is a fair rate of return for the project, given its level of business risk. This rate may be somewhat subjective; however, an appropriate rate can be determined by recognizing alternative uses of the funds and by allowing for any personal factors that affect the owners' total utility from operating the business.

4. Calculate the present value of the residual cash flows going to the owners and determine the project's discounted payback period. Use these

results to evaluate the proposed investment against other investments under consideration or investments that have been recently accepted.[12]

Assume the Arganes Corporation is contemplating an investment that costs $55,000. The project would have an expected life of about 15 years; however, the uncertainty of these cash flows makes management uncomfortable at projecting the flows beyond six years. The firm has a 40 percent target debt ratio; the interest rate on the debt is expected to be 10 percent; and the principal on the debt is to be repaid by reducing the balance by 10 percent at the end of each year. The asset will be depreciated on a straight-line basis over 10 years for accounting purposes. However, for tax purposes the asset will be depreciated using the declining balance method at a CCA rate of 30 percent. The asset class is expected to remain open and the asset is not expected to have a salvage value (SV = $0) after its useful life of 15 years. The firm's tax rate is 22 percent. The residual cash flows which accrue to the owners in each year are computed in Table 24-2.

In the case of the small business, we are interested cash flows accruing to the owners of the firm. These cash flows accrue to the owners only after interest payments and debt principal are paid. This condition requires that we adjust for the tax benefits from interest payments by adding the interest

TABLE 24-2. Arganes Corporation Project Analysis

	Years					
	1	2	3	4	5	6
Operating revenue	$40,000	$48,000	$52,000	$52,000	$55,000	$55,000
Operating expenses (including accounting expenses)	−25,500	−30,500	−32,500	−32,500	−33,500	−33,500
Accounting depreciation	5,500	5,500	5,500	5,500	5,500	5,500
Operating income (EBIT)	20,000	23,000	25,000	25,000	27,000	27,000
Taxes (@22%)	−4,400	−5,060	−5,500	−5,500	−5,940	−5,940
Net operating income	15,600	17,940	19,500	19,500	2,1060	21,060
Interest tax shields[a]	484	436	392	353	318	286
Depreciation tax shields[a]	1,815	3,086	2,160	1,512	1,058	741
Cash before debt payment	17,899	21,462	22,052	21,365	2,2436	22,087
Debt payment	−2,200	−2,200	−2,200	−2,200	−2,200	−2,200
Cash flow to owners	$15,699	$19,262	$19,852	$19,165	$20,236	$19,887
Present value	$13,651	$14,565	$13,053	$10,958	$10,061	$ 8,598
Cumulative present value	$13,651	$28,216	$41,269	$52,227	$62,288	

[a]Schedule for Depreciation and Interest Tax Shields

Year	UCC (Beg)	CCA	CCA (T)	UCC (End)	Loan Balance (Beg)	I	I (T)	Loan Balance (End)
1	$27,500	$ 8,250	$1,815	$46,750	$22,000	$2,200	$484	$19,800
2	46,750	14,025	3,086	32,725	19,800	1,980	436	17,820
3	32,725	9,818	2,160	22,907	17,820	1,782	392	16,038
4	22,907	6,872	1,512	16,035	16,038	1,604	353	14,434
5	16,035	4,811	1,058	11,224	14,434	1,443	318	12,991
6	11,224	3,367	741	7,857	12,991	1,299	286	11,692

[12]If the project payback period is shorter than the expected life of the investment, we may be assured that the project will have a positive net present value.

tax shields to net operating income. This type of adjustment is similar to that of adding the depreciation tax shields to net operating income. Finally, the payments which decrease debt principal are subtracted from the operating cash flows after tax. The residual cash flows accrue to the owners of the firm and should be discounted at the owner's required rate of return (15%) to obtain their present value. The last row of Table 24-2 shows the present value of these residual cash flows.

From the present values of the annual cash flows in Table 24-2, we can determine the discounted payback period as follows:

discounted payback period = (4 years of cash flows with present value of $52,227)

+ .276 years to receive remaining cash flow of $2,773 or $2,773/10,061

= 4.276 years

Thus, in 4.276 years, the owners may expect to recoup their original investment, while earning their required rate of return of 15 percent. The decision to accept or reject the project would come only after comparing it with other alternative uses of the funds, and the impact of the project on key nonfinancial variables that only the owners can know, based upon their preferences. ■

We will now direct our attention to the valuation of the small firm, which has been a matter of great interest to all involved in the management of the small firm.

FINANCING THE SMALL FIRM

In studying how a small firm is financed, we will first describe the financing stages a firm experiences during its business life. We will then look at a special group of investors called "venture capitalists" that may be particularly significant for a small growth business, but not for a large business. Next, we will examine the different sources of financing in an effort to identify the

---

BASIC FINANCIAL MANAGEMENT IN PRACTICE

Factors for Small Business Survival

Money helps: 84 percent survival rate for businesses with initial investment of $50,000 or more; 74 percent survival rate for businesses with initial investment of $20,000 or less.

Bigger is better: 82 percent survival rate for companies starting with six or more employees; 71 percent survival rate for companies starting with fewer than two employees.

Work hard, but don't overwork: 80 percent success rate for owners who work between 60 and 69 hours per week; 75 percent success rate for owners who work more than 69 hours per week.

Source: "Factors for Small Business Survival: Profiles of Success," an American Express Study of New Business as reported in *The Dallas Morning News* (October 11, 1989), p. D1.

more important ones for the small firm. Naturally, the conventional sources of short-term and long-term debt and common shares apply to all firms, small and large. However, the desirability and the availability of these various funds for the small firm may be different from those for the large firm. Finally, the decision to "go public" may be a serious consideration for a successful growth firm that has expanded beyond the financing capabilities of its owners. The advantages and disadvantages of issuing shares to the public are discussed in the concluding section of the chapter.

Stages of Financing

As shown in Figure 24-1, the business firm goes through three primary financing stages in the earlier segment of its business life cycle. Phase one, the initial investment, consists of the owner's personal capital and the credit provided by the chartered banker, and a host of miscellaneous sources. Examples of miscellaneous sources in this phase would include (1) friends and relatives, (2) leasing companies, and (3) trusts, credit unions, caisses populaires, and commercial finance companies.

FIGURE 24-1
Business Financing Stages

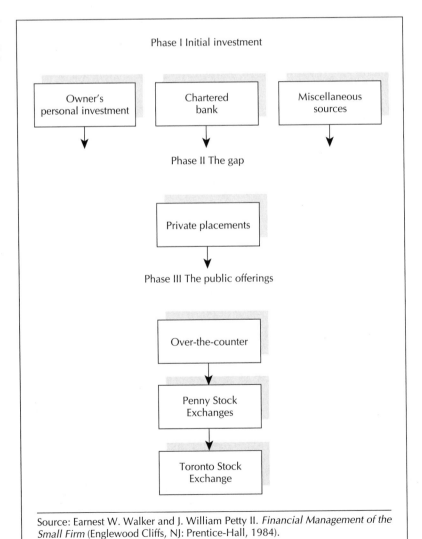

Source: Earnest W. Walker and J. William Petty II. *Financial Management of the Small Firm* (Englewood Cliffs, NJ: Prentice-Hall, 1984).

Phase two of a young firm's financial existence may be referred to as *the gap*. During this period the firm has grown to the level beyond which the owners have the capability to finance all investments; however, the firm is not large enough to justify a public offering. At this point it must sell securities to private individuals or groups. As shown in Figure 24-2 a number of sources for private placements exist and may be directly placed to come through an investment dealer. For instance, financial institutions (banks and trusts or credit unions), investor groups, and venture capitalists may be approached either directly or through an investment dealer acting as a liaison.[13] Large corporations may provide financing for a small firm but are generally approached directly. Furthermore, the kind of financing available from these respective sources varies, with financial institutions providing primarily debt financing and large corporations providing equity financing. Between the two extremes, a mixture of debt and equity capital would be available.

The final stage of development for the small firm in terms of financing sources is the raising of funds in the public markets. As explained in Chapter 17, a firm's shares are first traded publicly over-the-counter, then on to one of the major Canadian exchanges such as the Vancouver Stock Exchange or the Toronto Stock Exchange.

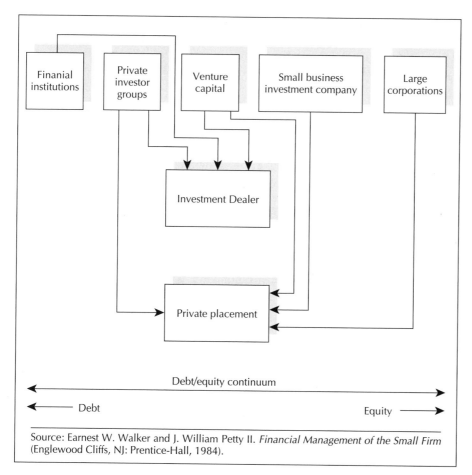

FIGURE 24-2
Sources of Private Placements

Source: Earnest W. Walker and J. William Petty II. *Financial Management of the Small Firm* (Englewood Cliffs, NJ: Prentice-Hall, 1984).

---

[13]The term *venture capitalist* is used to describe professional investors interested in investing in high-risk firms with potentially large returns. A more detailed explanation is provided in the next section.

Before looking at specific sources of financing, we will discuss the nature of venture capital.

Venture Capital and the Small Firm

The venture capitalist has increasingly become a source of financing for small businesses. A definition of venture capital investing is difficult, in that venture capitalists have a broad range of interests and activities. Most venture capitalists, however, would fall somewhere along the following spectrum of investment interests:

1. Providing capital for any high-risk financial venture;

2. Providing seed capital for a start-up situation;

3. Investing in a firm that is unable to raise capital from conventional sources;

4. Investing in large, publicly traded corporations where risk is significant.[14]

Which definition is most descriptive depends in part on the eye of the beholder. For instance, some venture capitalists believe that providing seed money is too risky. Others, however, believe that such start-up capital is the primary intent of their investments. Thus, generalities become difficult, but three underlying attributes normally prevail with venture capital investing. First, the investor is usually "locked in" to the firm for some duration of time, without an opportunity to sell shares quickly in response to a change in the firm's position, either favourable or unfavourable. Second, the venture capitalist normally represents the first equity financing from an "independent" party, as opposed to a friend or relative. However, additional financing from the venture capitalist may be required at a later date. Finally, venture capital investors have divergent interests. An investment having no appeal to one venture capital group might be of extreme interest to another group. For this reason, the management of a firm seeking funds should be aware of the compatibility of interests of the firm and the venture capitalist being approached.

If a financing package comprised of debt financing is presented to a venture capitalist, two major issues are involved. First, the venture capitalist may insist upon protective covenants if the financial condition of the firm deteriorates or does not materialize as anticipated. These covenants, similar to the protective restrictions of a bank loan, are particularly common in start-up situations, with effective control of the organization being more easily lost through default on these long-term covenants than through the loss of majority ownership of the equity shares.

Second, the venture capitalist considers the tradeoff between the interest rate and the conversion privilege. The use of debt by venture capital investors generally involves a convertibility feature or bonds with warrants attached. By attaching either warrants or a conversion privilege, a significant reduction in interest charges usually results. For a small growth business a reduction in interest payments is not only desirable but essential, since most small businesses may have difficulty meeting the interest requirements associated with straight debt. The following excerpt profiles the venture capital industry.

[14]See Patrick R. Liles, "Venture Capital: What It Is and How to Raise It," *New Business Ventures and the Entrepreneur* (Homewood, IL: Richard D. Irwin, 1974), p. 461.

BASIC FINANCIAL MANAGEMENT IN PRACTICE

Venture Capital

Financial institutions now offer many competitive services, and the traditional boundaries among them are becoming blurred. Three elements differentiate venture capital from other sources of financing: the investment involves equity or equity like participation; the investment is long-term; and investors are actively involved in the companies they finance.

Venture capital firms provide long-term financing by supporting businesses through a broad range of transactions. These transactions range from seed investment for the development of new products to the acquisition of established firms. The venture capitalist generally assumes greater risks than other agents in the financial system, and venture capital firms fill critical roles in the economy by taking equity positions in companies where there are insufficient assets to use as collateral for loans. For new or rapidly growing firms with relatively few assets, venture capital firms may be the only source of financing available. Venture capital firms make a commitment for a longer time frame than some other financial institutions and are usually prepared to provide subsequent financing to companies already in their portfolios.

Frequently, in contrast to other sources of financing, venture capital firms offer strategic management support for the companies in which they invest. These efforts to ensure the realization of the company's potential growth are often referred to as the value-added brought to the transaction by the venture capitalist and may include advising the firm through representation on the board of directors or assisting the personnel of the firm in order to strengthen the management team. If the portfolio company prospers, the venture capitalist can "exit" positively from the investment in a number of ways: generally the equity stake is sold as part of a public offering of shares, purchased by another firm or repurchased by the portfolio firm.

When viewed in an international context, Canadian venture capital firms are notably smaller than foreign counterparts. The average capital base of the Canadian firms is equal to approximately two-thirds of the average for American firms and one-third that of the British firms. Canadian venture capital firms average four professionals each, although some companies have a staff of 20.

Four subgroups comprise the Canadian professional venture capital industry: independent firms, venture affiliates or subsidiaries of Canadian corporations, Crown-related venture groups and "hybrids" having a mixture of government and private sector support.

The past number of years has seen a significant change in the sources of funds for the professional venture capital industry. As a result of federal initiatives to stimulate institutional investment activity and the higher profile that venture investing thus received, pension funds tremendously increased their funding of independent venture firms, and they became the dominant financiers of these firms. Corporations, insurance companies and individual still invested in venture capital firms, but their overall significance was lessened.

This shift in the source of funds for venture firms brought about a refocusing of types of investments. Venture investing was new to pension fund managers during the mid-1980s. To allay their concerns about risk, venture portfolios were often structured to focus more on established firms and away from investments in newer, high-risk company start-ups. This move was reflected in the surge of buyouts of established firms. Such deals involve relatively low risk and are often larger and more profitable than the average venture placement.

Independent venture capital funds usually have a fixed lifetime. Those that have matured recently or are maturing in the early 1990s have so far performed below investor expectations in general, as a result of abnormally high investment losses and high transaction costs in the mid 1980s.[15] The lower returns have resulted in a notable slowdown in the flow of money from major institutional investors to new Canadian venture capital funds, as evidenced by the absence of growth in the industry's capital during 1990. However, the general impact of this slowdown over the medium term may not be great. The flow of resources to venture capital funds tends to be cyclical. A troubling aspect of the situation is that a large proportion of the industry's funds available for investment are concentrated in firms that focus on Quebec and Alberta, thus creating liquidity concerns in other parts of the country.

Source: Adapted from: "Industry Profile, 1990–1991, Venture Capital" (Communications Branch, Industry, Science and Technology Canada, 1991).

---

[15]A. G. Fells, "Venture Capital: A Five-Year Update," (Toronto: SB Capital Corporation Ltd. 1988), p. 8.

Debt as a Source of Financing

Assuming that the business owners have depleted all available equity funds or want to take advantage of what they hope will be favourable financial leverage, management will no doubt search for debt financing. Potential sources of such financing for a small firm include (1) chartered banks, (2) governmental assistance programs, and (3) insurance companies.

Chartered Banks

The commercial bank is the leading source of borrowed funds available to the small business. The loans available through the bank are primarily of two types: short-term and mortgage loans. However, the short-term instruments, although "formally" being defined as short-term, provide considerable long-term financing for the small business entity. And although statistics indicate that the bank is principally a provider of short-term capital, such figures can be misleading.[16] For instance, a loan with a maturity of 90 or 180 days, although being "classified" as short-term, provides long-term financing through regular renewals as the indebtedness approaches the due date. Turning the debt over frequently is a technique by which the owners of a small firm convert short-term financing to an equivalent long-term status. This approach carries one distinct disadvantage in that the firm's financing is at the discretion of the banker each time the debt matures, which may cause some anxiety for the small business owner. The second and more formal source of long-term financing is the mortgage loan. These obligations relate to a specific purchase of real estate that is used as collateral in securing the financing arrangement.

In relying on the bank as a source of funds, the small business owner should develop a relationship with the banker prior to the actual need for funds. Ideally, the interaction should be on a professional and a personal basis. As part of the relationship, the business owner should be completely open with the banker. Only in this way can the banker be of maximum effectiveness in providing services. Also, in maintaining an association with the banker, the owner should continue to examine the benefits being received. He or she should be aware of the services being provided by competitive banks, as well as the costs related to these services.

The affiliation with a banker is not purely a function of the interest rate being charged, but involves a number of factors. The mere fact that a bank is charging a slightly higher interest rate does not necessarily justify changing banks. A long-term relationship is important, especially if monetary conditions are tight or if the firm temporarily encounters adversity. Finally, an inquiry should be made as to the banker's expertise and the bank's capabilities in terms of loan size. The firm's owner should seek a bank having particular expertise in the firm's type of operation. That is, not only is the accessibility of capital important, but a source of counselling may be of substantial benefit. In selecting a bank, the size of the bank should also be considered. If large sums of money will be required, a small bank may not have the capability to service such loans. On the other hand, if the credit requirements are not so extensive, it may be quite beneficial to use a small bank where the owner of the firm has access to key bank officers.

[16]In general, banks provide short-term financing by extending open lines of credit; however, banks do provide longer-term financing from three to five years via revolving lines of credit.

Governmental Sources of Assistance[17]

The federal government provides assistance in the startup and the improvement of small and mid-size businesses through governmental bodies such as Industry, Science, and Technology Canada (ISTC), the Federal Business Development Bank (FBDB), and the Canadian International Development Agency (CIDA). ISTC has been created with a mandate to improve the competitiveness of Canadian industry. With respect to the small business area, ISTC has the responsibility to "develop and implement national policies to foster entrepreneurship and the startup, growth and expansion of small business." ISTC has implemented several programs to provide business intelligence, technology, and financial assistance. After the Small Business Loans Act was passed in 1961, all chartered banks and other financial institutions were authorized to make business improvements loans to assist in the startup and the financing of fixed assets needs. The Federal Business Development Bank is a crown corporation which has a mandate to promote the creation and development of business in Canada. The FBDB provides assistance to owners of small businesses through management and financial services. For example, the corporation's financial services include loans, working capital loans and loan guarantees for the expansion, acquisition of fixed assets and the purchase of existing businesses. The Canadian International Developmental Agency has a mandate to administer Canada's development assistance to developing countries which includes the Canadian private sector's involvement in these countries. CIDA's assistance includes financial assistance that supports long-term business relationships with developing countries through joint ventures and licensing arrangements. The agency will also finance and provide professional advice on conducting preliminary and detailed studies of capital projects to potential clients in developing countries.

Insurance Companies

The executive of the small firm may find that an insurance company is a source of financing. As a financial intermediary, an insurance company has large sums of money available for investments. Only a small portion of such funds is available for the small firm, but to the extent that such funds may be used, the extension of credit generally comes in the form of a mortgage loan. Hence, a life insurance company may be a potential long-term source of financing for a small firm planning the construction of a real estate investment, such as a plant or an office. In examining the request for a loan, the insurance company looks closely at the type of building being constructed, with a preference for a facility having potential multiple uses. As to the size of loans, most insurance companies are interested in making loans in large amounts; however, loans for as little as $10,000 have been granted. In general, mortgage loans extend over a 10- to 20-year period, with the amount of the mortgage being limited to approximately 70 percent of the appraised value of the property.

In addition to the mortgage loan, the insurance company may issue credit on an unsecured long-term basis to the borrower who has an excellent credit rating. Such loans, if granted, generally extend for periods of 10 years with an interest rate exceeding that of the bank by 1 to 2 percent.

---

[17]Industry, Science and Technology Canada, Small Business in Canada 1991 From Best Practice to Competitiveness, Minister of Supply and Services, Catalogue No. C28-1/2-199E.

Common Shares as a Source of Financing

In examining common shares as a source of financing for the small firm, three areas are of primary concern: (1) the problems a small firm may encounter in issuing common shares, (2) the forms of common shares used

---

BASIC FINANCIAL MANAGEMENT IN PRACTICE

Investing in Mid-Sized Firms: Unique Problems, Unique Opportunities

Mid-sized firms are critically important in market oriented economies with an increasing orientation towards knowledge and service industries, and where manufacturing industries are experiencing extensive restructuring. This is because it is in the mid-sized firm sector of such economies that entrepreneurship, innovation, human and financial resources and market base reach a joint critical mass. In a Canadian context, it is in the mid-sized firm sector especially where we must hold our own under the North American Free Trade Arrangement and in a liberalized world trading environment generally.

A striking feature of our mid-sized firms is the extensive use of debt in their capital structures. The use of debt as described by the debt/equity ratio can have a range over 150 percent for Canadian-controlled mid-sized firms, double that of mid-sized foreign-controlled firms and large Canadian-controlled firms. The Canadian Chamber of Commerce investment study FOCUS 2000 comments: "While Canada has one of the most sophisticated capital markets in the world for debt, its ability to provide equity is not well developed." Indeed, Canada's bankers and mezzanine financiers do an excellent job getting debt money to mid-sized firms.

The Shape of Things to Come: A Growing Private Placements Market

Besides the volatility of equity markets and LBO-related factors, there are other factors pointing to a growing private placement market at the expense of the public markets. From an institutional perspective, private placements are simple, easily negotiated because only a small a group of professional investors is involved. More and more frequently, direct placements will be done without the use of an investment dealer, eliminating the intermediary fee. Also, with private placements the company does not have to deal with the securities commissions, does not have to worry about public statements, and is only answerable to a board which consists of friendly institutions or their representatives. These consid-

erations have a great deal to commend to investors and to large and small investees alike.

The disadvantages, of course, are an absence of liquidity and the fact that there is no measurement of success in the public market. Also, a quick exit through the public markets if the company gets into trouble is no longer available. In the new world, exits are going to be outright sales of companies through private transactions, recapitalizations where companies acquire an enhancing debt raising capacity over a period and raise money by way of debt to pay out the original equity holders, or redemptions or buyouts by formula which give institutional investors a negotiated yield over a defined investment period. These kinds of solutions will likely flourish and grow.

Private Placements and Canadian Mid-Sized Companies

Today most investments in mid-sized companies are done through intermediaries such as venture capitalists, leveraged buy-out funds, or mezzanine finance pools. The reason is that many mid-sized companies which raise money need nursing. Institutional investors such as pension funds have thus far been ill-equipped to do this. But there are so many pools of funds out there that entrepreneurs are increasingly using intermediaries to make the right match-up with the right capital pool.

Between the fees charged by capital pool managers and by the matchmakers, the cost of putting out the money to the entrepreneur has been rising, reducing investor returns. In the U.S. this has caused large institutional investors such as Prudential to eliminate all intermediaries and take the requisite skills in-house. It is only a matter of time before large Canadian institutions begin to do the same thing on a large scale.

Source: Adapted from: Gordon R. Sharwood, "Investing In Mid-sized Firms: Unique Problems, Unique Opportunities," *Canadian Investment Review* (Spring 1990), pp. 27–30.

by small firms, and (3) a review of specific sources of common equity that may be available to small firms.

Problems of Common Shares for the Small Firm

Chapter 19 discussed the basic characteristics of common shares, along with their advantages and disadvantages as a source of financing. The following problems involving common shares are unique to the small firm:

1. Because of the lack of marketability of most securities of small firms, particularly common shares, it may be necessary to price the common share so that it will yield a significantly higher return than that of a similar firm having a ready market for its shares. Naturally, the result is an increased cost of common capital.

2. The flotation cost of selling a small issue, particularly in the public markets, becomes almost prohibitive for the small firm. For instance, such expenses may approach 25 percent of the issue size.

3. Issuing common shares to external investors permits a potential dilution of control for existing shareholders. Although such a loss may only be psychological, most small owners are averse to placing themselves in a position that even slightly compromises their control over the firm.

Forms of Common Shares

Common shares can be classified in terms of the shareholders' claim on income, claim on assets, and voting rights. Typically, Class A shares have a higher claim on dividend income and assets but less extensive voting power, even to the point of voting being nonexistent. In contrast, Class B common shares have a lesser claim on income and assets but greater voting power. This classification mechanism permits the owners to maintain greater control or be able to attract outside investors by providing greater income and protection upon liquidation. In the same context, "founders' shares" have been used by small business. These shares are similar to a Class B shares except that the owners of the shares maintain the sole voting rights but generally have no right to dividends for a specified number of years. The objective of the founders' shares is to permit the organizers of a company to maintain complete control of the company during the early years of the operation, often with a minimal investment.

Beyond relatives and friends, the owner of the small business must look to venture capitalists for common share financing. Specific sources are described below.

Sources of Common Equity for the Small Firm

PUBLICLY OWNED VENTURE CAPITAL INVESTMENT COMPANIES ■ These organizations are publicly owned by a broad base of investors, including companies listed on the Toronto Stock Exchange.

PRIVATE VENTURE CAPITAL INVESTORS ■ The private venture capital investor is primarily concerned with the development of small enterprises needing long-term capital for growth, companies for sale due to the death or retirement of the owner, or firms requiring professional management. These private companies operate under a high degree of flexibility and therefore may be interested in long-term capital appreciation, in which funds are frequently invested in participation with others to enable the small private venture com-

BASIC FINANCIAL MANAGEMENT IN PRACTICE

Factors Affecting the Initial Public Offering Subscription Price

Information would seem a critical Initial Public Offering (IPO) pricing determinant. We review the theoretical and empirical relevance of three categories of information. These are the direct accounting disclosures contained in the offering prospectus, the quality and fee structure of the auditors that attest to the validity of disclosed financial data and the underwriters that manage the disclosure of information to investors, and the "signals" about expected future performance that are conveyed to outsiders in the offering prospectus.

Direct Disclosures About Past Performance and Operations

For seasoned firms, the value of historical accounting information is believed to lie primarily in the areas of monitoring and in the confirmation of prior expectations. It contains only limited information which is useful for predictive purposes. In contrast, potential investors in IPOs had no need to monitor or to form expectations regarding management performance prior to the offering. Anyway, very little information is publicly available, since the investment community does not normally gather information about firms which are privately held.

Hence, investors may rely on accounting information relating to past performance, since the new equity issue involves acquiring claims on firm assets and establishing a relationship with the firm's management team. Historical financial data may provide outside investors with measures of the firms' success in initiating and managing operations. A high profit margin on existing operations may also alleviate concerns over the historical level of managerial shirking and/or perquisite consumption.

In U.S. studies of IPOs, sales and earnings from existing operations were found to significant in explaining initial firm value. In a recent Canadian study, however, no significant relationship between initial firm value and either historical sales revenue or the profit margin of existing operations was detected. The magnitude of assets in place proved to be the only direct accounting disclosure that was relevant to the valuation process. That is, after controlling for other information available to investors, firms with more assets in place prior to the offering are valued more highly. This finding may indicate that the lack of information problem is more severe for small firms undertaking initial offerings, implying a size-related bias in the capital acquisition process.

The Quality and Fee Structures of Auditors and Underwriters

Direct disclosures in the offering prospectus are intermediated by the issuing firm's auditors and

---

Size Constraint

As would be expected, the management of the small enterprise has to be concerned with the question: "Is the firm large enough to go public?" The size criterion generally involves two aspects: (1) the level of earnings and (2) the size of the issue. With regard to the size of the issue (earnings capacity is addressed in a later section), not only may a small issue in terms of dollars be infeasible because of high costs, but a related factor, the number of shares, also has to be considered. Formulating a general guideline, however, is difficult, with the minimal size depending on the philosophy of the investment dealer. Regardless of the number of shares being quoted by an individual dealer, an important standard is the potential for developing an active market.[20] Specifically, without a reasonable number of shares outstanding for active trading, the investment dealer has difficulty justifying involvement in the financing.

---

[20] Small company shares which trade publicly at prices less than a dollar per share are called "penny stocks." The centre of trading activity for penny stocks in Canada is the Vancouver Stock Exchange.

underwriters. The quality of the information intermediaries can be described in terms of the amount and accuracy of the information supplied to investors. The higher the quality of the information provider, the more accurately can capital suppliers estimate a firm's future cash flows. Outsiders place greater confidence in disclosures verified by prestigious intermediaries, since they are expected to disclose favourable information only for high quality investment projects. An owner with more favourable projects is believed to select higher-quality investment dealers and auditors, and the higher the quality, the higher the price at which the new issue can be sold. Entrepreneurs with less favourable information are not expected to select high quality intermediation services, since they would incur the added cost and risk but cannot expect to receive as large a marginal benefit by doing so.

Consistent with this view is the observation that many firms switch from local to national auditors when going public. This raises two empirical questions. First, whether the reputation of information provided enters into the fee structure for their service and second, whether initial firm value is related to the selected quality of information intermediaries after controlling for other variables. In fact, higher quality auditors and underwriters have been shown to charge higher fees, after controlling for measures of marginal cost of performing information intermediation services. That is, they are able to charge a fee for their reputation capital. Further, as expected, initial firm value has been shown to be higher for those issuing firms that employ the services of prestigious intermediaries.

Signals of Expected Future Performance by the Owners

There is a general assumption that entrepreneurs have better information than outsiders about the expected value of their projects, but there are moral hazard problems associated with the direct disclosure of this information. Indirect disclosure may be achieved through the observable and promised financial actions of inside owners. Three such disclosures are the percentage of ownership insiders retain in the firm, the proposed use of issue proceeds and the promised future dividend policy.

Initial firm value should be a positive function of the fraction of equity in the firm retained by the entrepreneurs. Since entrepreneurs are risk averse and must hold imperfectly diversified personal investment portfolios, it is only in their interest to invest a large fraction of their wealth in ventures they view very favourably. Thus, an insiders' willingness to invest serves as a signal of investment market's assessment of the offer price. If the offer price is below the value at which the shares trade immediately after issuance, then the initial returns to IPOs investors are positive and the issue is said to be "underpriced."

Source: An excerpt from: Wendy Rotenberg, "Pricing Initial Public Equity Offerings: Who Wins, Who Loses And Why?," *Canadian Investment Review* (Spring 1990), pp. 17–24.

Marketability

A second item of concern to investment dealers is the creation of a substantial market. All else being constant, they prefer to develop a market sufficiently large to provide the investor additional liquidity in terms of the ability to buy and sell securities as needed. To investment dealers, the depth and liquidity of the market are crucial. Without the possibility of developing such a market, investment dealers are usually not interested.

Established Earnings Record

Management of a firm entertaining the thought of going public must be aware that the size, quality, and trend of earnings are of utmost importance in public financing. The size and quality of earnings must also be considered, with the quality being a function of the stability and the source of earnings. Finally, the trend of earnings is related to the likelihood that a long-term upward trend from the current source of income will continue to exist. The earnings trend must be "significant," must have grown at a steady rate during the most recent years, and must be expected to continue into the future.

The Management Team

The investigation into a company preparing for public financing includes an analysis of the basic quality and philosophy of top management. In examining the quality of management, the factors to consider include experience, integrity, and depth of the corporate leadership. While no one of these three factors can be emphasized at the expense of the others, depth of management is often a difficult problem for the small business. A family-owned company typically relies on the capabilities of the second generation. Thus, the second generation has to be able and willing to continue the operation, or management personnel external to the family must be available within the organization.

Growth Potential

Although "growth" and public markets are not necessarily mutually exclusive, the owners of an enterprise interested in making a public offering should be aware of the uphill battle to be fought if growth is not evident. When competing for funds, an organization having negligible growth potential can anticipate serious difficulties in attracting the public investor. Hence, steady growth patterns expected to continue into the future are a strong factor in the company's favour when entering the public market. In addition, the continued growth of the firm's operation requires that careful attention be given to the public disclosure requirements. For instance, accounting information being reported to the public is costly requiring increased supervision and monitoring by accountants and managers.

Products and Services

The reputation and image of an entity's products or services should also be considered. Concisely stated, the sound reputation of an organization's products or services is an essential ingredient for a successful public offering.

SUMMARY

In this chapter, we examined the differences between the financing of large corporations and the financing of small and mid-sized businesses. We observed that small and mid-sized businesses will (1) tend to rely more heavily on the retention of earnings as a way to build equity, (2) have less liquidity, (3) use greater amounts of debt, and (4) experience more business risk. We then considered the implications of these differences with respect cash management, capital budgeting and sources of financing.

As small and mid-sized firms mature over time, the owner-manager may want to raise funds in the public equity markets. The prerequisites for going public include: size, marketability, earnings record, management, growth potential, and the product or services. Going public remains a major business decision for most owners of small firms.

STUDY QUESTIONS

24-1. Describe the financial difference between a small and a large firm.

24-2. Why is cash management important for the small firm?

24-3. What factors unique to the small firm must be considered in analyzing capital investments?

24-4. Explain the stages of financing that a firm may experience during its growth.

24-5. What are the prerequisites for a firm to go public?

SELECTED REFERENCES

Aggarwal, Reena and Pietra Rivoli. "Fads in the Initial Public Offering Market?" *Journal of Financial Management* (Winter 1990), 45–54.

Ang, James S. "Small Business Uniqueness and the Theory of Financial Management," *Journal of Small Business Finance* (Spring 1991), 1–14.

Beedles, William L. "Size, Liquidity, and the Cost of Equity," *Journal of Small Business Finance* (Spring 1991), 29–44.

Bamberger, I. "Portfolio Analysis for the Small Firm," *Long-Range Planning* (December 1982), 49–57.

Barry, Christopher, Chris J. Muscarella, John W. Peavy III and Michael R. Vetsuypens. "The Role of Venture Capital in the Creation of Public Companies," *Journal of Financial Economics* (October 1990), 448–71.

Boardman, Calvin M., John W., Bartley, and Richard L. Ratliff. "Small Business Growth Characteristics," *American Journal of Small Business*, 5 (Winter 1981), 33–43.

Bygrave, William D. "The Entrepreneurship Paradigm: I. A Philosophical Look at Its Research Methodologies," *Entrepreneurship: Theory and Practice* (Fall 1989), 7–26.

Case, Daniel H. III. "An Overview of Venture Capital," in Richard D. Harroch, ed. *Start-up Companies*. Law Journal Seminars Press, 1985.

Churchill, W. C., and V. L. Lewis. "The Five Stages of Small Business Growth," *Harvard Business Review* (November-December 1983), 30ff.

Cooper, Arnold C., William C. Dunkelberg, and Carolyn Y. Woo. "Survival and Failure: A Longitudinal Study," *Frontiers of Entrepreneurship Research* (1988), 225–237.

Cornell, Bradford and Alan Shapiro. "Financing Corporate Growth," *Journal of Applied Corporate Finance* (Summer 1988), 6–22.

Crandall, Arthur L. "A Practical Approach to Valuing a Closely Held Business," *The Practical Accountant* (March 1985), 79–90.

DeThomas, A. R. "Valuing the Ownership Interest in the Privately-Held Small Firm," *American Journal of Small Business* (Winter 1985), 50–59.

Finegan, Patrick T. "Maximizing Share Value at the Private Company," *Journal of Applied Corporate Finance* (Spring 1991), 30–45.

Florida, R. L. and M. Kenney. "Venture Capital-Financed Innovation and Technological Changes in the U.S.," *Research Policy*, 17 (no. 3) (1988), 119–37.

Freear, John and William E. Wetzel, Jr. "The Informal Venture Capital Market in the Year 2000," presented at the State of the Art Entrepreneurship Conference, The Frank Hawkins Kenan Institute of Private Enterprise, The University of North Carolina, Chapel Hill, October 1990.

Gatewood, Elizabeth J., Lee Ogden, and Frank S. Hoy. "Incubator Center Evolution—The Next Five to Ten Years," *Frontiers of Entrepreneurship Research* (1986), 526–544.

Glassman, Cynthia A., and Peter L. Struck. *Survey of Commercial Bank Lending to Small Business*. Washington, DC: Interagency Task Force on Small Business Finance, January 1982.

Golder, Stanley C. "Structuring and Pricing the Financing," in Stanley A. Pratt and Jane K. Morris, ed. *Guide to Venture Capital*. Wellesley Hills, MA: Venture Economics, 1986.

Gorman, Michael, and William A. Sahlman. "What Do Venture Capitalists Do?" *Frontiers of Entrepreneurship Research* (1986), 414–436.

Goslin, L. N., and B. Barge. "Entrepreneurial Qualities Considered in Venture Capital Support," *Frontiers of Entrepreneurship Research* (1986), 366–379.

Gupta, M. C. "The Effect of Size, Growth, and Industry on the Financial Structure of Manufacturing Companies," *Journal of Finance* (June 1969), 517–529.

Higgins, R. C. "How Much Growth Can a Firm Afford?" *Financial Management* (Fall 1977), 7–16.

Hornaday, John A., and Neil C. Churchill. "Current Trends in Entrepreneurial Research," *Frontiers of Entrepreneurship Research* (1987), 1–21.

Levin, Richard and Virginia Travis. "Small Company Finance: What Do Venture Capitalists Do?" *Frontiers of Entrepreneurship Research* (1986), 414–436.

MacMillan, Ian C., Robin Siegel, and P. N. Subba Narashimha. "Criteria Used by Venture Capitalists to Evaluate New Venture Proposals," *Journal of Business Venturing*, 1 (1985), 119–128.

MacMillan, Ian C., and P. N. Subba Narashimha. "Characteristics Distinguishing Funded from Unfunded Business Plans Evaluated By Venture Capitalists," *Frontiers of Entrepreneurship Research* (1986), 404–413.

McConnell, John J., and R. Richardson Petit. *Application of the Modern Theory of Finance to Small Business Firms*. Washington, DC: Interagency Task Force on Small Business Finance, October 1980.

Ritter, Jay. "The Long-Run Performance of Initial Public Offerings," *The Journal of Finance* (March 1991), 3–28.

Sahlman, William. "Aspects of Financial Contracting in Venture Capital," *Journal of Applied Corporate Finance* (Summer 1988), 23–36.

Sahlman, William. "The Structure and Governance of Venture-Capital Organizations," *Journal of Financial Economics* (October 1990), 473–521.

Sandburg, William R., David M. Schweiger, and Charles W. Hofer. "Determining Venture Capitalists' Decision Criteria: The Use of Verbal Protocols," *Frontiers of Entrepreneurship Research* (1987), 392–407.

Shannon, Pratt P. *Valuing Small Businesses and Professional Practices*. Homewood, IL: Dow Jones-Irwin, 1986.

The State of Small Business: *A Report of the President*. Transmitted to the Congress, March 1988.

Stevenson, Howard H., Daniel F. Muzyka, and Jeffrey A. Timmons. "Venture Capital in a New Era: A Simulation of the Impact of Changes in Investment Patterns," *Frontiers of Entrepreneurship Research* (1986), 380–403.

Stoll, Hans R. Small Firms' Access to Public Equity Financing. Washington, DC: *Interagency Task Force on Small Business Finance*, December 1981.

Tyebjee, Tyzoon T., and Albert V. Bruno. "Venture Capital: Investor and Investee Perspectives," *Technovation*, 2 (1984), 185–208.

Walker, Ernest W., and J. William Petty II. "Financial Differences between Large and Small Firms," *Financial Management* (Winter 1978), 61–68.

Welsh, J. A., and J. F. White. "A Small Business Is Not a Little Big Business," *Harvard Business Review* (July–August 1981), 1ff.

Wetzel, William E., Jr. "The Informal Venture Capital Market: Aspects of Scale and Market Efficiency," *Frontiers of Entrepreneurship Research* (1987), 412–428.

APPENDICES

APPENDIX A: Compound Sum of $1 FV

n	1%	2%	3%	4%	5%	6%	7%	8%	9%	10%
1	1.010	1.020	1.030	1.040	1.050	1.060	1.070	1.080	1.090	1.100
2	1.020	1.040	1.061	1.082	1.102	1.124	1.145	1.166	1.188	1.210
3	1.030	1.061	1.093	1.125	1.158	1.191	1.225	1.260	1.295	1.331
4	1.041	1.082	1.126	1.170	1.216	1.262	1.311	1.360	1.412	1.464
5	1.051	1.104	1.159	1.217	1.276	1.338	1.403	1.469	1.539	1.611
6	1.062	1.126	1.194	1.265	1.340	1.419	1.501	1.587	1.677	1.772
7	1.072	1.149	1.230	1.316	1.407	1.504	1.606	1.714	1.828	1.949
8	1.083	1.172	1.267	1.369	1.477	1.594	1.718	1.851	1.993	2.144
9	1.094	1.195	1.305	1.423	1.551	1.689	1.838	1.999	2.172	2.358
10	1.105	1.219	1.344	1.480	1.629	1.791	1.967	2.159	2.367	2.594
11	1.116	1.243	1.384	1.539	1.710	1.898	2.105	2.332	2.580	2.853
12	1.127	1.268	1.426	1.601	1.796	2.012	2.252	2.518	2.813	3.138
13	1.138	1.294	1.469	1.665	1.886	2.133	2.410	2.720	3.066	3.452
14	1.149	1.319	1.513	1.732	1.980	2.261	2.579	2.937	3.342	3.797
15	1.161	1.346	1.558	1.801	2.079	2.397	2.759	3.172	3.642	4.177
16	1.173	1.373	1.605	1.873	2.183	2.540	2.952	3.426	3.970	4.595
17	1.184	1.400	1.653	1.948	2.292	2.693	3.159	3.700	4.328	5.054
18	1.196	1.428	1.702	2.026	2.407	2.854	3.380	3.996	4.717	5.560
19	1.208	1.457	1.753	2.107	2.527	3.026	3.616	4.316	5.142	6.116
20	1.220	1.486	1.806	2.191	2.653	3.207	3.870	4.661	5.604	6.727
21	1.232	1.516	1.860	2.279	2.786	3.399	4.140	5.034	6.109	7.400
22	1.245	1.546	1.916	2.370	2.925	3.603	4.430	5.436	6.658	8.140
23	1.257	1.577	1.974	2.465	3.071	3.820	4.740	5.871	7.258	8.954
24	1.270	1.608	2.033	2.563	3.225	4.049	5.072	6.341	7.911	9.850
25	1.282	1.641	2.094	2.666	3.386	4.292	5.427	6.848	8.623	10.834
30	1.348	1.811	2.427	3.243	4.322	5.743	7.612	10.062	13.267	17.449
40	1.489	2.208	3.262	4.801	7.040	10.285	14.974	21.724	31.408	45.258
50	1.645	2.691	4.384	7.106	11.467	18.419	29.456	46.900	74.354	117.386

n	11%	12%	13%	14%	15%	16%	17%	18%	19%	20%
1	1.110	1.120	1.130	1.140	1.150	1.160	1.170	1.180	1.190	1.200
2	1.232	1.254	1.277	1.300	1.322	1.346	1.369	1.392	1.416	1.440
3	1.368	1.405	1.443	1.482	1.521	1.561	1.602	1.643	1.685	1.728
4	1.518	1.574	1.630	1.689	1.749	1.811	1.874	1.939	2.005	2.074
5	1.685	1.762	1.842	1.925	2.011	2.100	2.192	2.288	2.386	2.488
6	1.870	1.974	2.082	2.195	2.313	2.436	2.565	2.700	2.840	2.986
7	2.076	2.211	2.353	2.502	2.660	2.826	3.001	3.185	3.379	3.583
8	2.305	2.476	2.658	2.853	3.059	3.278	3.511	3.759	4.021	4.300
9	2.558	2.773	3.004	3.252	3.518	3.803	4.108	4.435	4.785	5.160
10	2.839	3.106	3.395	3.707	4.046	4.411	4.807	5.234	5.695	6.192
11	3.152	3.479	3.836	4.226	4.652	5.117	5.624	6.176	6.777	7.430
12	3.498	3.896	4.334	4.818	5.350	5.936	6.580	7.288	8.064	8.916
13	3.883	4.363	4.898	5.492	6.153	6.886	7.699	8.599	9.596	10.699
14	4.310	4.887	5.535	6.261	7.076	7.987	9.007	10.147	11.420	12.839
15	4.785	5.474	6.254	7.138	8.137	9.265	10.539	11.974	13.589	15.407
16	5.311	6.130	7.067	8.137	9.358	10.748	12.330	14.129	16.171	18.488
17	5.895	6.866	7.986	9.276	10.761	12.468	14.426	16.672	19.244	22.186
18	6.543	7.690	9.024	10.575	12.375	14.462	16.879	19.673	22.900	26.623
19	7.263	8.613	10.197	12.055	14.232	16.776	19.748	23.214	27.251	31.948
20	8.062	9.646	11.523	13.743	16.366	19.461	23.105	27.393	32.429	38.337
21	8.949	10.804	13.021	15.667	18.821	22.574	27.033	32.323	38.591	46.005
22	9.933	12.100	14.713	17.861	21.644	26.186	31.629	38.141	45.923	55.205
23	11.026	13.552	16.626	20.361	24.891	30.376	37.005	45.007	54.648	66.247
24	12.239	15.178	18.788	23.212	28.625	35.236	43.296	53.108	65.031	79.496
25	13.585	17.000	21.230	26.461	32.918	40.874	50.656	62.667	77.387	95.395
30	22.892	29.960	39.115	50.949	66.210	85.849	111.061	143.367	184.672	237.373
40	64.999	93.049	132.776	188.876	267.856	378.715	533.846	750.353	1051.642	1469.740
50	184.559	288.996	450.711	700.197	1083.619	1670.669	2566.080	3927.189	5988.730	9100.191

APPENDIX A: Compound Sum of $1 *(continued)*

n	21%	22%	23%	24%	25%	26%	27%	28%	29%	30%
1	1.210	1.220	1.230	1.240	1.250	1.260	1.270	1.280	1.290	1.300
2	1.464	1.488	1.513	1.538	1.562	1.588	1.613	1.638	1.664	1.690
3	1.772	1.816	1.861	1.907	1.953	2.000	2.048	2.097	2.147	2.197
4	2.144	2.215	2.289	2.364	2.441	2.520	2.601	2.684	2.769	2.856
5	2.594	2.703	2.815	2.932	3.052	3.176	3.304	3.436	3.572	3.713
6	3.138	3.297	3.463	3.635	3.815	4.001	4.196	4.398	4.608	4.827
7	3.797	4.023	4.259	4.508	4.768	5.042	5.329	5.629	5.945	6.275
8	4.595	4.908	5.239	5.589	5.960	6.353	6.767	7.206	7.669	8.157
9	5.560	5.987	6.444	6.931	7.451	8.004	8.595	9.223	9.893	10.604
10	6.727	7.305	7.926	8.594	9.313	10.086	10.915	11.806	12.761	13.786
11	8.140	8.912	9.749	10.657	11.642	12.708	13.862	15.112	16.462	17.921
12	9.850	10.872	11.991	13.215	14.552	16.012	17.605	19.343	21.236	23.298
13	11.918	13.264	14.749	16.386	18.190	20.175	22.359	24.759	27.395	30.287
14	14.421	16.182	18.141	20.319	22.737	25.420	28.395	31.691	35.339	39.373
15	17.449	19.742	22.314	25.195	28.422	32.030	36.062	40.565	45.587	51.185
16	21.113	24.085	27.446	31.242	35.527	40.357	45.799	51.923	58.808	66.541
17	25.547	29.384	33.758	38.740	44.409	50.850	58.165	66.461	75.862	86.503
18	30.912	35.848	41.523	48.038	55.511	64.071	73.869	85.070	97.862	112.454
19	37.404	43.735	51.073	59.567	69.389	80.730	93.813	108.890	126.242	146.190
20	45.258	53.357	62.820	73.863	86.736	101.720	119.143	139.379	162.852	190.047
21	54.762	65.095	77.268	91.591	108.420	128.167	151.312	178.405	210.079	247.061
22	66.262	79.416	95.040	113.572	135.525	161.490	192.165	228.358	271.002	321.178
23	80.178	96.887	116.899	140.829	169.407	203.477	244.050	292.298	349.592	417.531
24	97.015	118.203	143.786	174.628	211.758	256.381	309.943	374.141	450.974	542.791
25	117.388	144.207	176.857	216.539	264.698	323.040	393.628	478.901	581.756	705.627
30	304.471	389.748	497.904	634.810	807.793	1025.904	1300.477	1645.488	2078.208	2619.936
40	2048.309	2846.941	3946.340	5455.797	7523.156	10346.879	14195.051	19426.418	26520.723	36117.754
50	13779.844	20795.680	31278.301	46889.207	70064.812	104354.562	154942.687	229345.875	338440.000	497910.125

n	31%	32%	33%	34%	35%	36%	37%	38%	39%	40%
1	1.310	1.320	1.330	1.340	1.350	1.360	1.370	1.380	1.390	1.400
2	1.716	1.742	1.769	1.796	1.822	1.850	1.877	1.904	1.932	1.960
3	2.248	2.300	2.353	2.406	2.460	2.515	2.571	2.628	2.686	2.744
4	2.945	3.036	3.129	3.224	3.321	3.421	3.523	3.627	3.733	3.842
5	3.858	4.007	4.162	4.320	4.484	4.653	4.826	5.005	5.189	5.378
6	5.054	5.290	5.535	5.789	6.053	6.328	6.612	6.907	7.213	7.530
7	6.621	6.983	7.361	7.758	8.172	8.605	9.058	9.531	10.025	10.541
8	8.673	9.217	9.791	10.395	11.032	11.703	12.410	13.153	13.935	14.758
9	11.362	12.166	13.022	13.930	14.894	15.917	17.001	18.151	19.370	20.661
10	14.884	16.060	17.319	18.666	20.106	21.646	23.292	25.049	26.924	28.925
11	19.498	21.199	23.034	25.012	27.144	29.439	31.910	34.567	37.425	40.495
12	25.542	27.982	30.635	33.516	36.644	40.037	43.716	47.703	52.020	56.694
13	33.460	36.937	40.745	44.912	49.469	54.451	59.892	65.830	72.308	79.371
14	43.832	49.756	54.190	60.181	66.784	74.053	82.051	90.845	100.509	111.19
15	57.420	64.358	72.073	80.643	90.158	100.712	112.410	125.366	139.707	155.567
16	75.220	84.953	95.857	108.061	121.713	136.968	154.002	173.005	194.192	217.793
17	98.539	112.138	127.490	144.802	164.312	186.277	210.983	238.747	269.927	304.911
18	129.086	148.022	169.561	194.035	221.822	253.337	289.046	329.471	375.198	426.875
19	169.102	195.389	225.517	260.006	299.459	344.537	395.993	454.669	521.525	597.625
20	221.523	257.913	299.937	348.408	404.270	468.571	542.511	627.443	724.919	836.674
21	290.196	340.446	398.916	466.867	545.764	637.256	743.240	865.871	1007.637	1171.343
22	380.156	449.388	530.558	625.601	736.781	865.668	1018.238	1194.900	1400.615	1639.878
23	498.004	593.192	705.642	838.305	994.653	1178.668	1394.986	1648.961	1946.854	2295.829
24	652.385	783.013	938.504	1123.328	1342.781	1602.988	1911.129	2275.564	2706.125	3214.158
25	854.623	1033.577	1248.210	1505.258	1812.754	2180.063	2618.245	3140.275	3761.511	4499.816
30	3297.081	4142.008	5194.516	6503.285	8128.426	10142.914	12636.086	15716.703	19517.969	24201.043
40	49072.621	66519.313	89962.188	121388.437	163433.875	219558.625	294317.937	393684.687	525508.312	700022.688

APPENDIX B: Present Value of $1 PV

n	1%	2%	3%	4%	5%	6%	7%	8%	9%	10%
1	.990	.980	.971	.962	.952	.943	.935	.926	.917	.909
2	.980	.961	.943	.925	.907	.890	.873	.857	.842	.826
3	.971	.942	.915	.889	.864	.840	.816	.794	.772	.751
4	.961	.924	.888	.855	.823	.792	.763	.735	.708	.683
5	.951	.906	.863	.822	.784	.747	.713	.681	.650	.621
6	.942	.888	.837	.790	.746	.705	.666	.630	.596	.564
7	.933	.871	.813	.760	.711	.665	.623	.583	.547	.513
8	.923	.853	.789	.731	.677	.627	.582	.540	.502	.467
9	.914	.837	.766	.703	.645	.592	.544	.500	.460	.424
10	.905	.820	.744	.676	.614	.558	.508	.463	.422	.386
11	.896	.804	.722	.650	.585	.527	.475	.429	.388	.350
12	.887	.789	.701	.625	.557	.497	.444	.397	.356	.319
13	.879	.773	.681	.601	.530	.469	.415	.368	.326	.290
14	.870	.758	.661	.577	.505	.442	.388	.340	.299	.263
15	.861	.743	.642	.555	.481	.417	.362	.315	.275	.239
16	.853	.728	.623	.534	.458	.394	.339	.292	.252	.218
17	.844	.714	.605	.513	.436	.371	.317	.270	.231	.198
18	.836	.700	.587	.494	.416	.350	.296	.250	.212	.180
19	.828	.686	.570	.475	.396	.331	.277	.232	.194	.164
20	.820	.673	.554	.456	.377	.312	.258	.215	.178	.149
21	.811	.660	.538	.439	.359	.294	.242	.199	.164	.135
22	.803	.647	.522	.422	.342	.278	.226	.184	.150	.123
23	.795	.634	.507	.406	.326	.262	.211	.170	.138	.112
24	.788	.622	.492	.390	.310	.247	.197	.158	.126	.102
25	.780	.610	.478	.375	.295	.233	.184	.146	.116	.092
30	.742	.552	.412	.308	.231	.174	.131	.099	.075	.057
40	.672	.453	.307	.208	.142	.097	.067	.046	.032	022
50	.608	.372	.228	.141	.087	.054	.034	.021	.013	.009

n	11%	12%	13%	14%	15%	16%	17%	18%	19%	20%
1	.901	.893	.885	.877	.870	.862	.855	.847	.840	.833
2	.812	.797	.783	.769	.756	.743	.731	.718	.706	.694
3	.731	.712	.693	.675	.658	.641	.624	.609	.593	.579
4	.659	.636	.613	.592	.572	.552	.534	.516	.499	.482
5	.593	.567	.543	.519	.497	.476	.456	.437	.419	.402
6	.535	.507	.480	.456	.432	.410	.390	.370	.352	.335
7	.482	.452	.425	.400	.376	.354	.333	.314	.296	.279
8	.434	.404	.376	.351	.327	.305	.285	.266	.249	.233
9	.391	.361	.333	.308	.284	.263	.243	.225	.209	.194
10	.352	.322	.295	.270	.247	.227	.208	.191	.176	.162
11	.317	.287	.261	.237	.215	.195	.178	.162	.148	.135
12	.286	.257	.231	.208	.187	.168	.152	.137	.124	.112
13	.258	.229	.204	.182	.163	.145	.130	.116	.104	.093
14	.232	.205	.181	.160	.141	.125	.111	.099	.088	.078
15	.209	.183	.160	.140	.123	.108	.095	.084	.074	.065
16	.188	.163	.141	.123	.107	.093	.081	.071	.062	.054
17	.170	.146	.125	.108	.093	.080	.069	.060	.052	.045
18	.153	.130	.111	.095	.081	.069	.059	.051	.044	.038
19	.138	.116	.098	.083	.070	.060	.051	.043	.037	.031
20	.124	.104	.087	.073	.061	.051	.043	.037	.031	.026
21	.112	.093	.077	.064	.053	.044	.037	.031	.026	.022
22	.101	.083	.068	.056	.046	.038	.032	.026	.022	.018
23	.091	.074	.060	.049	.040	.033	.027	.022	.018	.015
24	.082	.066	.053	.043	.035	.028	.023	.019	.015	.013
25	.074	.059	.047	.038	.030	.024	.020	.016	.013	.010
30	.044	.033	.026	.020	.015	.012	.009	.007	.005	.004
40	.015	.011	.008	.005	.004	.003	.002	.001	.001	.001
50	.005	.003	.002	.001	.001	.001	.000	.000	.000	.000

APPENDIX B: Present Value of $1 *(continued)*

n	21%	22%	23%	24%	25%	26%	27%	28%	29%	30%
1	.826	.820	.813	.806	.800	.794	.787	.781	.775	.769
2	.683	.672	.661	.650	.640	.630	.620	.610	.601	.592
3	.564	.551	.537	.524	.512	.500	.488	.477	.466	.455
4	.467	.451	.437	.423	.410	.397	.384	.373	.361	.350
5	.386	.370	.355	.341	.328	.315	.303	.291	.280	.269
6	.319	.303	.289	.275	.262	.250	.238	.227	.217	.207
7	.263	.249	.235	.222	.210	.198	.188	.178	.168	.159
8	.218	.204	.191	.179	.168	.157	.148	.139	.130	.123
9	.180	.167	.155	.144	.134	.125	.116	.108	.101	.094
10	.149	.137	.126	.116	.107	.099	.092	.085	.078	.073
11	.123	.112	.103	.094	.086	.079	.072	.066	.061	.056
12	.102	.092	.083	.076	.069	.062	.057	.052	.047	.043
13	.084	.075	.068	.061	.055	.050	.045	.040	.037	.033
14	.069	.062	.055	.049	.044	.039	.035	.032	.028	.025
15	.057	.051	.045	.040	.035	.031	.028	.025	.022	.020
16	.047	.042	.036	.032	.028	.025	.022	.019	.017	.015
17	.039	.034	.030	.026	.023	.020	.017	.015	.013	.012
18	.032	.028	.024	.021	.018	.016	.014	.012	.010	.009
19	.027	.023	.020	.017	.014	.012	.011	.009	.008	.007
20	.022	.019	.016	.014	.012	.010	.008	.007	.006	.005
21	.018	.015	.013	.011	.009	.008	.007	.006	.005	.004
22	.015	.013	.011	.009	.007	.006	.005	.004	.004	.003
23	.012	.010	.009	.007	.006	.005	.004	.003	.003	.002
24	.010	.008	.007	.006	.005	.004	.003	.003	.002	.002
25	.009	.007	.006	.005	.004	.003	.003	.002	.002	.001
30	.003	.003	.002	.002	.001	.001	.001	.001	.000	.000
40	.000	.000	.000	.000	.000	.000	.000	.000	.000	.000
50	.000	.000	.000	.000	.000	.000	.000	.000	.000	.000

n	31%	32%	33%	34%	35%	36%	37%	38%	39%	40%
1	.763	.758	.752	.746	.741	.735	.730	.725	.719	.714
2	.583	.574	.565	.557	.549	.541	.533	.525	.518	.510
3	.445	.435	.425	.416	.406	.398	.389	.381	.372	.364
4	.340	.329	.320	.310	.301	.292	.284	.276	.268	.260
5	.259	.250	.240	.231	.223	.215	.207	.200	.193	.186
6	.198	.189	.181	.173	.165	.158	.151	.145	.139	.133
7	.151	.143	.136	.129	.122	.116	.110	.105	.100	.095
8	.115	.108	.102	.096	.091	.085	.081	.076	.072	.068
9	.088	.082	.077	.072	.067	.063	.059	.055	.052	.048
10	.067	.062	.058	.054	.050	.046	.043	.040	.037	.035
11	.051	.047	.043	.040	.037	.034	.031	.029	.027	.025
12	.039	.036	.033	.030	.027	.025	.023	.021	.019	.018
13	.030	.027	.025	.022	.020	.018	.017	.015	.014	.013
14	.023	.021	.018	.017	.015	.014	.012	.011	.010	.009
15	.017	.016	.014	.012	.011	.010	.009	.008	.007	.006
16	.013	.012	.010	.009	.008	.007	.006	.006	.005	.005
17	.010	.009	.008	.007	.006	.005	.005	.004	.004	.003
18	.008	.007	.006	.005	.005	.004	.003	.003	.003	.002
19	.006	.005	.004	.004	.003	.003	.003	.002	.002	.002
20	.005	.004	.003	.003	.002	.002	.002	.002	.001	.001
21	.003	.003	.003	.002	.002	.002	.001	.001	.001	.001
22	.003	.002	.002	.002	.001	.001	.001	.001	.001	.001
23	.002	.002	.001	.001	.001	.001	.001	.001	.001	.000
24	.002	.001	.001	.001	.001	.001	.001	.001	.000	.000
25	.001	.001	.001	.001	.001	.000	.000	.000	.000	.000
30	.000	.000	.000	.000	.000	.000	.000	.000	.000	.000
40	.000	.000	.000	.000	.000	.000	.000	.000	.000	.000

APPENDIX C: Sum of an Annuity of $1 for n Periods FV

n	1%	2%	3%	4%	5%	6%	7%	8%	9%	10%
1	1.000	1.000	1.000	1.000	1.000	1.000	1.000	1.000	1.000	1.000
2	2.010	2.020	2.030	2.040	2.050	2.060	2.070	2.080	2.090	2.100
3	3.030	3.060	3.091	3.122	3.152	3.184	3.215	3.246	3.278	3.310
4	4.060	4.122	4.184	4.246	4.310	4.375	4.440	4.506	4.573	4.641
5	5.101	5.204	5.309	5.416	5.526	5.637	5.751	5.867	5.985	6.105
6	6.152	6.308	6.468	6.633	6.802	6.975	7.153	7.336	7.523	7.716
7	7.214	7.434	7.662	7.898	8.142	8.394	8.654	8.923	9.200	9.487
8	8.286	8.583	8.892	9.214	9.549	9.897	10.260	10.637	11.028	11.436
9	9.368	9.755	10.159	10.583	11.027	11.491	11.978	12.488	13.021	13.579
10	10.462	10.950	11.464	12.006	12.578	13.181	13.816	14.487	15.193	15.937
11	11.567	12.169	12.808	13.486	14.207	14.972	15.784	16.645	17.560	18.531
12	12.682	13.412	14.192	15.026	15.917	16.870	17.888	18.977	20.141	21.384
13	13.809	14.680	15.618	16.627	17.713	18.882	20.141	21.495	22.953	24.523
14	14.947	15.974	17.086	18.292	19.598	21.015	22.550	24.215	26.019	27.975
15	16.097	17.293	18.599	20.023	21.578	23.276	25.129	27.152	29.361	31.772
16	17.258	18.639	20.157	21.824	23.657	25.672	27.888	30.324	33.003	35.949
17	18.430	20.012	21.761	23.697	25.840	28.213	30.840	33.750	36.973	40.544
18	19.614	21.412	23.414	25.645	28.132	30.905	33.999	37.450	41.301	45.599
19	20.811	22.840	25.117	27.671	30.539	33.760	37.379	41.446	46.018	51.158
20	22.019	24.297	26.870	29.778	33.066	36.785	40.995	45.762	51.159	57.274
21	23.239	25.783	28.676	31.969	35.719	39.992	44.865	50.422	56.764	64.002
22	24.471	27.299	30.536	34.248	38.505	43.392	49.005	55.456	62.872	71.402
23	25.716	28.845	32.452	36.618	41.430	46.995	53.435	60.893	69.531	79.542
24	26.973	30.421	34.426	39.082	44.501	50.815	58.176	66.764	76.789	88.496
25	28.243	32.030	36.459	41.645	47.726	54.864	63.248	73.105	84.699	98.346
30	34.784	40.567	47.575	56.084	66.438	79.057	94.459	113.282	136.305	164.491
40	48.885	60.401	75.400	95.024	120.797	154.758	199.630	295.052	337.872	442.580
50	64.461	84.577	112.794	152.664	209.341	290.325	406.516	573.756	815.051	1163.865

n	11%	12%	13%	14%	15%	16%	17%	18%	19%	20%
1	1.000	1.000	1.000	1.000	1.000	1.000	1.000	1.000	1.000	1.000
2	2.110	2.120	2.130	2.140	2.150	2.160	2.170	2.180	2.190	2.200
3	3.342	3.374	3.407	3.440	3.472	3.506	3.539	3.572	3.606	3.640
4	4.710	4.779	4.850	4.921	4.993	5.066	5.141	5.215	5.291	5.368
5	6.228	6.353	6.480	6.610	6.742	6.877	7.014	7.154	7.297	7.442
6	7.913	8.115	8.323	8.535	8.754	8.977	9.207	9.442	9.683	9.930
7	9.783	10.089	10.405	10.730	11.067	11.414	11.772	12.141	12.523	12.916
8	11.859	12.300	12.757	13.233	13.727	14.240	14.773	15.327	15.902	16.499
9	14.164	14.776	15.416	16.085	16.786	17.518	18.285	19.086	19.923	20.799
10	16.722	17.549	18.420	19.337	20.304	21.321	22.393	23.521	24.709	25.959
11	19.561	20.655	21.814	23.044	24.349	25.733	27.200	28.755	30.403	32.150
12	22.713	24.133	25.650	27.271	29.001	30.850	32.824	34.931	37.180	39.580
13	26.211	28.029	29.984	32.088	34.352	36.786	39.404	42.218	45.244	48.496
14	30.095	32.392	34.882	37.581	40.504	43.672	47.102	50.818	54.841	59.196
15	34.405	37.280	40.417	43.842	47.580	51.659	56.109	60.965	66.260	72.035
16	39.190	42.753	46.671	50.980	55.717	60.925	66.648	72.938	79.850	87.442
17	44.500	48.883	53.738	59.117	65.075	71.673	78.978	87.067	96.021	105.930
18	50.396	55.749	61.724	68.393	75.836	84.140	93.404	103.739	115.265	128.116
19	56.939	63.439	70.748	78.968	88.211	98.603	110.283	123.412	138.165	154.739
20	64.202	72.052	80.946	91.024	102.443	115.379	130.031	146.626	165.417	186.687
21	72.264	81.698	92.468	104.767	118.809	134.840	153.136	174.019	197.846	225.024
22	81.213	92.502	105.489	120.434	137.630	157.414	180.169	206.342	236.436	271.028
23	91.147	104.602	120.203	138.295	159.274	183.600	211.798	244.483	282.359	326.234
24	102.173	118.154	136.829	158.656	184.166	213.976	248.803	289.490	337.007	392.480
25	114.412	133.333	155.616	181.867	212.790	249.212	292.099	342.598	402.038	471.976
30	199.018	241.330	293.192	356.778	434.738	530.306	647.423	790.932	966.698	1181.865
40	581.812	767.080	1013.667	1341.979	1779.048	2360.724	3134.412	4163.094	5529.711	7343.715
50	1668.723	2399.975	3459.344	4994.301	7217.488	10435.449	15088.805	21812.273	31514.492	45496.094

n	21%	22%	23%	24%	25%	26%	27%	28%	29%	30%
1	1.000	1.000	1.000	1.000	1.000	1.000	1.000	1.000	1.000	1.000
2	2.210	2.220	2.230	2.240	2.250	2.260	2.270	2.280	2.290	2.300
3	3.674	3.708	3.743	3.778	3.813	3.848	3.883	3.918	3.954	3.990
4	5.446	5.524	5.604	5.684	5.766	5.848	5.931	6.016	6.101	6.187
5	7.589	7.740	7.893	8.048	8.207	8.368	8.533	8.700	8.870	9.043
6	10.183	10.442	10.708	10.980	11.259	11.544	11.837	12.136	12.442	12.756
7	13.321	13.740	14.171	14.615	15.073	15.546	16.032	16.534	17.051	17.583
8	17.119	17.762	18.430	19.123	19.842	20.588	21.361	22.163	22.995	23.858
9	21.714	22.670	23.669	24.712	25.802	26.940	28.129	29.369	30.664	32.015
10	27.274	28.657	20.113	31.643	33.253	34.945	36.723	38.592	40.556	42.619
11	34.001	35.962	38.039	40.238	42.566	45.030	47.639	50.398	53.318	56.405
12	42.141	44.873	47.787	50.895	54.208	57.738	61.501	65.510	69.780	74.326
13	51.991	55.745	59.778	64.109	68.760	73.750	79.106	84.853	91.016	97.624
14	63.909	69.009	74.528	80.496	86.949	93.925	101.465	109.611	118.411	127.912
15	78.330	85.191	92.669	100.815	109.687	119.346	129.860	141.302	153.750	167.285
16	95.779	104.933	114.983	126.010	138.109	151.375	165.922	181.867	199.337	218.470
17	116.892	129.019	142.428	157.252	173.636	191.733	211.721	233.790	258.145	285.011
18	142.439	158.403	176.187	195.993	218.045	242.583	269.885	300.250	334.006	371.514
19	173.351	194.251	217.710	244.031	273.556	306.654	343.754	385.321	431.868	483.968
20	210.755	237.986	268.783	303.598	342.945	387.384	437.568	494.210	558.110	630.157
21	256.013	291.343	331.603	377.461	429.681	489.104	556.710	633.589	720.962	820.204
22	310.775	356.438	408.871	469.052	538.101	617.270	708.022	811.993	931.040	1067.265
23	377.038	435.854	503.911	582.624	673.626	778.760	900.187	1040.351	1202.042	1388.443
24	457.215	532.741	620.810	723.453	843.032	982.237	1144.237	1332.649	1551.634	1805.975
25	554.230	650.944	764.596	898.082	1054.791	1238.617	1454.180	1706.790	2002.608	2348.765
30	1445.111	1767.044	2160.459	2640.881	3227.172	3941.953	4812.891	5873.172	7162.785	8729.805
40	9749.141	12936.141	17153.691	22728.367	30088.621	39791.957	52570.707	69376.562	91447.375	120389.375

n	31%	32%	33%	34%	35%	36%	37%	38%	39%	40%
1	1.000	1.000	1.000	1.000	1.000	1.000	1.000	1.000	1.000	1.000
2	2.310	2.320	2.330	2.340	2.350	2.360	2.370	2.380	2.390	2.400
3	4.026	4.062	4.099	4.136	4.172	4.210	4.247	4.284	4.322	4.360
4	6.274	6.362	6.452	6.542	6.633	6.725	6.818	6.912	7.008	7.104
5	9.219	9.398	9.581	9.766	9.954	10.146	10.341	10.539	10.741	10.946
6	13.077	13.406	13.742	14.086	14.438	14.799	15.167	15.544	15.930	16.324
7	18.131	18.696	19.277	19.876	20.492	21.126	21.779	22.451	23.142	23.853
8	24.752	25.678	26.638	27.633	28.664	29.732	30.837	31.982	33.167	34.395
9	33.425	34.895	36.429	38.028	39.696	41.435	43.247	45.135	47.103	49.152
10	44.786	47.062	49.451	51.958	54.590	57.351	60.248	63.287	66.473	69.813
11	59.670	63.121	66.769	70.624	74.696	78.998	83.540	88.335	93.397	98.739
12	79.167	84.320	89.803	95.636	101.840	108.437	115.450	122.903	130.822	139.234
13	104.709	112.302	120.438	129.152	138.484	148.474	159.166	170.606	182.842	195.928
14	138.169	149.239	161.183	174.063	187.953	202.925	219.058	236.435	255.151	275.299
15	182.001	197.996	215.373	234.245	254.737	276.978	301.109	327.281	355.659	386.418
16	239.421	262.354	287.446	314.888	344.895	377.690	413.520	452.647	495.366	541.985
17	314.642	347.307	383.303	422.949	466.608	514.658	567.521	625.652	689.558	759.778
18	413.180	459.445	510.792	567.751	630.920	700.935	778.504	864.399	959.485	1064.689
19	542.266	607.467	680.354	761.786	852.741	954.271	1067.551	1193.870	1334.683	1491.563
20	711.368	802.856	905.870	1021.792	1152.200	1298.809	1463.544	1648.539	1856.208	2089.188
21	932.891	1060.769	1205.807	1370.201	1556.470	1767.380	2006.055	2275.982	2581.128	2925.862
22	1223.087	1401.215	1604.724	1837.068	2102.234	2404.636	2749.294	3141.852	3588.765	4097.203
23	1603.243	1850.603	2135.282	2462.669	2839.014	3271.304	3767.532	4336.750	4989.379	5737.078
24	2101.247	2443.795	2840.924	3300.974	3833.667	4449.969	5162.516	5985.711	6936.230	8032.906
25	2753.631	3226.808	3779.428	4424.301	5176.445	6052.957	7073.645	8261.273	9642.352	11247.062
30	10632.543	12940.672	15737.945	19124.434	23221.258	28172.016	34148.906	41357.227	50043.625	60500.207

APPENDIX D: Present Value of an Annuity of $1 for *n* Periods PV

n	1%	2%	3%	4%	5%	6%	7%	8%	9%	10%
1	.990	.980	.971	.962	.952	.943	.935	.926	.917	.909
2	1.970	1.942	1.913	1.886	1.859	1.833	1.808	1.783	1.759	1.736
3	2.941	2.884	2.829	2.775	2.723	2.673	2.624	2.577	2.531	2.487
4	3.902	3.808	3.717	3.630	3.546	3.465	3.387	3.312	3.240	3.170
5	4.853	4.713	4.580	4.452	4.329	4.212	4.100	3.993	3.890	3.791
6	5.795	5.601	5.417	5.242	5.076	4.917	4.767	4.623	4.486	4.355
7	6.728	6.472	6.230	6.002	5.786	5.582	5.389	5.206	5.033	4.868
8	7.652	7.326	7.020	6.733	6.463	6.210	5.971	5.747	5.535	5.335
9	8.566	8.162	7.786	7.435	7.108	6.802	6.515	6.247	5.995	5.759
10	9.471	8.983	8.530	8.111	7.722	7.360	7.024	6.710	6.418	6.145
11	10.368	9.787	9.253	8.760	8.306	7.887	7.499	7.139	6.805	6.495
12	11.255	10.575	9.954	9.385	8.863	8.384	7.943	7.536	7.161	6.814
13	12.134	11.348	10.635	9.986	9.394	8.853	8.358	7.904	7.487	7.103
14	13.004	12.106	11.296	10.563	9.899	9.295	8.746	8.244	7.786	7.367
15	13.865	12.849	11.938	11.118	10.380	9.712	9.108	8.560	8.061	7.606
16	14.718	13.578	12.561	11.652	10.838	10.106	9.447	8.851	8.313	7.824
17	15.562	14.292	13.166	12.166	11.274	10.477	9.763	9.122	8.544	8.022
18	16.398	14.992	13.754	12.659	11.690	10.828	10.059	9.372	8.756	8.201
19	17.226	15.679	14.324	13.134	12.085	11.158	10.336	9.604	8.950	8.365
20	18.046	16.352	14.878	13.590	12.462	11.470	10.594	9.818	9.129	8.514
21	18.857	17.011	15.415	14.029	12.821	11.764	10.836	10.017	9.292	8.649
22	19.661	17.658	15.937	14.451	13.163	12.042	11.061	10.201	9.442	8.772
23	20.456	18.292	16.444	14.857	13.489	12.303	11.272	10.371	9.580	8.883
24	21.244	18.914	16.936	15.247	13.799	12.550	11.469	10.529	9.707	8.985
25	22.023	19.524	17.413	15.622	14.094	12.783	11.654	10.675	9.823	9.077
30	25.808	22.397	19.601	17.292	15.373	13.765	12.409	11.258	10.274	9.427
40	32.835	27.356	23.115	19.793	17.159	15.046	13.332	11.925	10.757	9.779
50	39.197	31.424	25.730	21.482	18.256	15.762	13.801	12.234	10.962	9.915

n	11%	12%	13%	14%	15%	16%	17%	18%	19%	20%
1	.901	.893	.885	.877	.870	.862	.855	.847	.840	.833
2	1.713	1.690	1.668	1.647	1.626	1.605	1.585	1.566	1.547	1.528
3	2.444	2.402	2.361	2.322	2.283	2.246	2.210	2.174	2.140	2.106
4	3.102	3.037	2.974	2.914	2.855	2.798	2.743	2.690	2.639	2.589
5	3.696	3.605	3.517	3.433	3.352	3.274	3.199	3.127	3.058	2.991
6	4.231	4.111	3.998	3.889	3.784	3.685	3.589	3.498	3.410	3.326
7	4.712	4.564	4.423	4.288	4.160	4.039	3.922	3.812	3.706	3.605
8	5.146	4.968	4.799	4.639	4.487	4.344	4.207	4.078	3.954	3.837
9	5.537	5.328	5.132	4.946	4.772	4.607	4.451	4.303	4.163	4.031
10	5.889	5.650	5.426	5.216	5.019	4.833	4.659	4.494	4.339	4.192
11	6.207	5.938	5.687	5.453	5.234	5.029	4.836	4.656	4.487	4.327
12	6.492	6.194	5.918	5.660	5.421	5.197	4.988	4.793	4.611	4.439
13	6.750	6.424	6.122	5.842	5.583	5.342	5.118	4.910	4.715	4.533
14	6.982	6.628	6.303	6.002	5.724	5.468	5.229	5.008	4.802	4.611
15	7.191	6.811	6.462	6.142	5.847	5.575	5.324	5.092	4.876	4.675
16	7.379	6.974	6.604	6.265	5.954	5.669	5.405	5.162	4.938	4.730
17	7.549	7.120	6.729	6.373	6.047	5.749	5.475	5.222	4.990	4.775
18	7.702	7.250	6.840	6.467	6.128	5.818	5.534	5.273	5.033	4.812
19	7.839	7.366	6.938	6.550	6.198	5.877	5.585	5.316	5.070	4.843
20	7.963	7.469	7.025	6.623	6.259	5.929	5.628	5.353	5.101	4.870
21	8.075	7.562	7.102	6.687	6.312	5.973	5.665	5.384	5.127	4.891
22	8.176	7.645	7.170	6.743	6.359	6.011	5.696	5.410	5.149	4.909
23	8.266	7.718	7.230	6.792	6.399	6.044	5.723	5.432	5.167	4.925
24	8.348	7.784	7.283	6.835	6.434	6.073	5.747	5.451	5.182	4.937
25	8.442	7.843	7.330	6.873	6.464	6.097	5.766	5.467	5.195	4.948
30	8.694	8.055	7.496	7.003	6.566	6.177	5.829	5.517	5.235	4.979
40	8.951	8.244	7.634	7.105	6.642	6.233	5.871	5.548	5.258	4.997
50	9.042	8.305	7.675	7.133	6.661	6.246	5.880	5.554	5.262	4.999

APPENDIX D: Present Value of an Annuity of $1 for *n* Periods *(continued)*

n	21%	22%	23%	24%	25%	26%	27%	28%	29%	30%
1	.826	.820	.813	.806	.800	.794	.787	.781	.775	.769
2	1.509	1.492	1.474	1.457	1.440	1.424	1.407	1.392	1.376	1.361
3	2.074	2.042	2.011	1.981	1.952	1.923	1.896	1.868	1.842	1.816
4	2.540	2.494	2.448	2.404	2.362	2.320	2.280	2.241	2.203	2.166
5	2.926	2.864	2.803	2.745	2.689	2.635	2.583	2.532	2.483	2.436
6	3.245	3.167	3.092	3.020	2.951	2.885	2.821	2.759	2.700	2.643
7	3.508	3.416	3.327	3.242	3.161	3.083	3.009	2.937	2.868	2.802
8	3.726	3.619	3.518	3.421	3.329	3.241	3.156	3.076	2.999	2.925
9	3.905	3.786	3.673	3.566	3.463	3.366	3.273	3.184	3.100	3.019
10	4.054	3.923	3.799	3.682	3.570	3.465	3.364	3.269	3.178	3.092
11	4.177	4.035	3.902	3.776	3.656	3.544	3.437	3.335	3.239	3.147
12	4.278	4.127	3.985	3.851	3.725	3.606	3.493	3.387	3.286	3.190
13	4.362	4.203	4.053	3.912	3.780	3.656	3.538	3.427	3.322	3.223
14	4.432	4.265	4.108	3.962	3.824	3.695	3.573	3.459	3.351	3.249
15	4.489	4.315	4.153	4.001	3.859	3.726	3.601	3.483	3.373	3.268
16	4.536	4.357	4.189	4.033	3.887	3.751	3.623	3.503	3.390	3.283
17	4.576	4.391	4.219	4.059	3.910	3.771	3.640	3.518	3.403	3.295
18	4.608	4.419	4.243	4.080	3.928	3.786	3.654	3.529	3.413	3.304
19	4.635	4.442	4.263	4.097	3.942	3.799	3.664	3.539	3.421	3.311
20	4.657	4.460	4.279	4.110	3.954	3.808	3.673	3.546	3.427	3.316
21	4.675	4.476	4.292	4.121	3.963	3.816	3.679	3.551	3.432	3.320
22	4.690	4.488	4.302	4.130	3.970	3.822	3.684	3.556	3.436	3.323
23	4.703	4.499	4.311	4.137	3.976	3.827	3.689	3.559	3.438	3.325
24	4.713	4.507	4.318	4.143	3.981	3.831	3.692	3.562	3.441	3.327
25	4.721	4.514	4.323	4.147	3.985	3.834	3.694	3.564	3.442	3.329
30	4.746	4.534	4.339	4.160	3.995	3.842	3.701	3.569	3.447	3.332
40	4.760	4.544	4.347	4.166	3.999	3.846	3.703	3.571	3.448	3.333
50	4.762	4.545	4.348	4.167	4.000	3.846	3.704	3.571	3.448	3.333

n	31%	32%	33%	34%	35%	36%	37%	38%	39%	40%
1	.763	.758	.752	.746	.741	.735	.730	.725	.719	.714
2	1.346	1.331	1.317	1.303	1.289	1.276	1.263	1.250	1.237	1.224
3	1.791	1.766	1.742	1.719	1.696	1.673	1.652	1.630	1.609	1.589
4	2.130	2.096	2.062	2.029	1.997	1.966	1.935	1.906	1.877	1.849
5	2.390	2.345	2.302	2.260	2.220	2.181	2.143	2.106	2.070	2.035
6	2.588	2.534	2.483	2.433	2.385	2.339	2.294	2.251	2.209	2.168
7	2.739	2.677	2.619	2.562	2.508	2.455	2.404	2.355	2.308	2.263
8	2.854	2.786	2.721	2.658	2.598	2.540	2.485	2.432	2.380	2.331
9	2.942	2.868	2.798	2.730	2.665	2.603	2.544	2.487	2.432	2.379
10	3.009	2.930	2.855	2.784	2.715	2.649	2.587	2.527	2.469	2.414
11	3.060	2.978	2.899	2.824	2.752	2.683	2.618	2.555	2.496	2.438
12	3.100	3.013	2.931	2.853	2.779	2.708	2.641	2.576	2.515	2.456
13	3.129	3.040	2.956	2.876	2.799	2.727	2.658	2.592	2.529	2.469
14	3.152	3.061	2.974	2.892	2.814	2.740	2.670	2.603	2.539	2.477
15	3.170	3.076	2.988	2.905	2.825	2.750	2.679	2.611	2.546	2.484
16	3.183	3.088	2.999	2.914	2.834	2.757	2.685	2.616	2.551	2.489
17	3.193	3.097	3.007	2.921	2.840	2.763	2.690	2.621	2.555	2.492
18	3.201	3.104	3.012	2.926	2.844	2.767	2.693	2.624	2.557	2.494
19	3.207	3.109	3.017	2.930	2.848	2.770	2.696	2.626	2.559	2.496
20	3.211	3.113	3.020	2.933	2.850	2.772	2.698	2.627	2.561	2.497
21	3.215	3.116	3.023	2.935	2.852	2.773	2.699	2.629	2.562	2.498
22	3.217	3.118	3.025	2.936	2.853	2.775	2.700	2.629	2.562	2.498
23	3.219	3.120	3.026	2.938	2.854	2.775	2.701	2.630	2.563	2.499
24	3.221	3.121	3.027	2.939	2.855	2.776	2.701	2.630	2.563	2.499
25	3.222	3.122	3.028	2.939	2.856	2.776	2.702	2.631	2.563	2.499
30	3.225	2.124	3.030	2.941	2.857	2.777	2.702	2.631	2.564	2.500
40	3.226	3.125	3.030	2.941	2.857	2.778	2.703	2.632	2.564	2.500
50	3.226	3.125	3.030	2.941	2.857	2.778	2.703	2.632	2.564	2.500

APPENDIX E: Using a Calculator
(a tutorial on the Texas Instruments BAII Plus)

As you prepare for a career in business, the ability to use a financial calculator is essential, whether you are in the finance division or the marketing department. In most positions, it will be assumed that you can use a calculator in making computations that at one time were simply not possible without extensive time and effort. The following examples let us see what is possible, but they represent only a beginning into the benefits of the use of the calculator in finance.

With just a little time and effort, you will be surprised at how much you can do with the calculator, such as calculating a stock's beta, or determining the value of a bond on a specific day given the exact date of maturity, or finding net present values and internal rates of return, or calculating the standard deviation. The list is almost endless.

In demonstrating how calculators may make our work easier, we must first decide which calculator to use. The options are numerous, and largely depend on personal preference. Nevertheless, we have chosen to demonstrate the Texas Instruments BAII Plus.

We will limit our discussion to the following issues:

   I. Introductory Comments

  II. A Good Starting Point

 III. Calculating Table Values for:

     A. Appendix A (Compound sum of $1)

     B. Appendix B (Present value of $1)

     C. Appendix C (Sum of an annuity of $1 for *n* periods)

     D. Appendix D (Present value of an annuity of $1 for *n* periods)

 IV. Calculating Present Values

  V. Calculating Future Values

 VI. Calculating the Number of Payments or Receipts

 VII. Calculating the Payment Amount

VIII. Calculating the Interest Rate

 IX. Bond Valuation

     A. Computing the value of a bond

     B. Calculating the yield to maturity on a bond

  X. Computing the Net Present Value and Internal Rate of Return

     A. Where future cash flows are equal amounts in each period (annuity)

     B. Where future cash flows are unequal amounts in each period

 XI. Calculating Alpha and Beta of the Regression Equation

I. INTRODUCTORY COMMENTS

In the examples that follow, you are told (1) which keystrokes to use, (2) the resulting appearance of the calculator display, and (3) a supporting explanation.

The keystrokes column tells you which keys to press. Keys shown in a box are dedicated keys on the keyboard. For example, $\boxed{+}$ adds two numbers. To use a function printed in white lettering above a key, always press the $\boxed{2nd}$ key first, then the function key. For example, $\boxed{2nd}$ $\boxed{e^x}$ calculates the exponential function.

The display shows entries and results with up to 10 digits. The display indicators provide information about the status of the calculator and tell you what keys are available at different times.

II. A GOOD STARTING POINT

Purpose: Before each new calculation, clear the variables, and if need be, change the number of digits displayed.

Example: You want to display four numbers to the right of the decimal.

Keystrokes	Display	Explanation
2nd FORMAT 4 ENTER		Sets display to show four numbers to the right of the decimal.
2nd QUIT	0.0000	Clears display.

III. CALCULATING TABLE VALUES FOR:

A. The compound sum of $1 (Appendix A)

Purpose: Compute the table values for Appendix A, the future value of $1.

Method: Solve for the future value of $1: $FV_n = \$1(1 + i)^n$

Example: What is the table value for the compound sum of a $1 for 5 years at a 12 percent annual interest rate?

Keystrokes	Display	Explanation
2nd QUIT		Return to standard calculator mode.
2nd P/Y 1 ENTER	P/Y = 1.0000	Sets 1 payment per year.
CE/C CE/C 2nd CLR TVM	0.0000	Clears TVM variables.
1 +/− PV	PV = -1.0000	Stores initial $1 as a negative present value.
5 N	N = 5.0000	Stores number of periods.
12 I/Y	I/Y = 12.0000	Stores interest rate.
CPT FV	FV = 1.7623	Table value.

B. The present value of $1 (Appendix B)

Purpose: Compute the table values for Appendix B, the present value of $1.

Method: Solve for the present value of $1: $PV = \dfrac{\$1}{(1 + i)^n}$

Example: What is the table value for the present value of a $1 for 8 years at a 10 percent annual interest rate?

Keystrokes	Display	Explanation
CE/C CE/C 2nd CLR TVM	0.0000	Clears TVM variables.
1 +/− FV	FV = -1.0000	Stores future amount as negative value.
8 N	N = 8.0000	Stores number of periods.
10 I/Y	I/Y = 10.0000	Stores interest rate.
CPT PV	PV = 0.4665	Table value.

C. The sum of an annuity of $1 for n periods (Appendix C)

Purpose: Compute the table values for Appendix C, the sum of an annuity of $1.

Method: Solve for the future value of an annuity of $1: $FV_n = \$1 \sum_{t=1}^{n} (1 + i)^t$,

which may also be solved as $FV_n = \dfrac{(1 + i)^n - 1}{i}$

Example: What is the table value for the compound sum of an annuity of $1 for 6 years at a 14 percent annual interest rate?

Keystrokes	Display	Explanation
CE/C CE/C 2nd CLR TVM	0.0000	Clears TVM variables.
1 +/− PMT	PMT = -1.0000	Stores annual payment (annuity) as a negative number.
6 N	N = 6.0000	Stores number of periods.
14 I/Y	I/Y = 14.0000	Stores interest rate.
CPT FV	FV = 8.5355	Table value.

D. The present value of an annuity of $1 for n periods (Appendix D)

Purpose: Compute the table values for Appendix D, the present value of an annuity of $1.

Method: Solve for the present value of an annuity of $1: $PV_n = \sum_{t=1}^{n} \dfrac{1}{(1 + i)^t}$,

which may also be solved as $PV = \dfrac{1 - [1/(1 + i)^n]}{i}$

Example: What is the table value for the present value of an annuity of $1 for 12 years at a 9 percent annual interest rate?

Keystrokes	Display	Explanation
CE/C CE/C 2nd CLR TVM	0.0000	Clears TVM variables.
1 +/− PMT	PMT = 1.0000	Stores annual payment (annuity) as a negative number.
12 N	N = 12.0000	Stores number of periods.
9 I/Y	I/Y = 9.0000	Stores interest rate.
CPT PV	PV = 7.1607	Table value.

IV. CALCULATING PRESENT VALUES

Purpose: Be able to compute the present value of a future cash flow stream (CF_t) involving equal amounts plus an additional amount to be received at the end of the period (FV_n).

Method: Solve for the present value of: $PV_n = \sum_{t=1}^{n} \dfrac{\$CF_t}{(1+i)^t} + \dfrac{\$FV_n}{(1+i)^n}$

Example: You are considering the purchase of a franchise of quick-oil-change locations, which you believe will provide an annual cash flow of $50,000. At the end of ten years, you believe that you will be able to sell the franchise for an estimated $900,000. Calculate the maximum amount you should pay for the franchise (present value) in order to realize at least an 18 percent annual yield.

Keystrokes	Display	Explanation
CE/C CE/C 2nd CLR TVM	0.0000	Clears TVM variables.
10 N	N = 10.0000	Stores n, the holding period.
18 I/Y	I/Y = 18.0000	Stores i, the required rate of return.
50,000 PMT	PMT = 50,000	Stores PMT, the annual cash flow to be received.
900,000 FV	FV = 900,000	Stores FV, the cash flow to be received at the end of the project.
CPT PV	PV = -396,662.3350	The present value, given a required rate of return of 18 percent. (Note: The present value is displayed with a minus sign since it represents cash paid out.)

V. CALCULATING FUTURE VALUES (COMPOUND SUM)

Purpose: Compute the future value of expected cash flows (CF_t) involving equal amounts each year.

Method: Solve for the compound sum value of: $FV_n = \$CF_t \sum_{t=1}^{n} (1 + i)^t$

Example: If you deposit $300 a month (at the beginning of each month) into a new account that pays 6.25% annual interest compounded monthly, how much will you have in the account after 5 years?

Keystrokes	Display	Explanation
CE/C CE/C 2nd CLR TVM	 0.0000	Clears TVM variables.
2nd P/Y 12 ENTER 2nd BGN 2nd SET CE/C	 P/Y = 12.0000 END BGN 0.0000	Sets 12 payments per year; begin mode (BGN) assumes cash flows are at the beginning of each month.
60 N	N = 60.0000	Stores n, the number of months for the investment.
6.25 I/Y	I/Y = 6.2500	Calculates and stores i, the monthly interest rate (6.25% ÷ 12 months).
300 +/− PMT	PMT = -300.0000	Stores PMT, the monthly amount invested (with a minus sign for cash paid out).
CPT FV	FV = 21,175.7615	The future value after 5 years.

VI. CALCULATING THE NUMBER OF PAYMENTS OR RECEIPTS

Purpose: Compute the number of payments for a given future value.

Method: Solve for n in the equation: $FV_n = \$CF_t \sum_{t=1}^{n} (1 + i)^t$

Example: If you wish to retire with $500,000 saved, and can only afford payments of $500 each month, how long will you have to contribute toward your retirement if you can earn a 10% return on your contributions?

Keystrokes	Display	Explanation
CE/C CE/C 2nd CLR TVM	 0.0000	Clears TVM variables.

Keystrokes	Display	Explanation
2nd P/Y 12 ENTER 2nd BGN 2nd SET CE/C	P/Y = 12.0000 END BGN 0.0000	Sets 12 payments per year; begin mode (BIG) assumes cash flows are at the beginning of each month.
10 I/Y	I/Y = 10.0000	Stores i, the interest rate.
500 +/− PMT	PMT = −500.0000	Stores PMT, the monthly amount invested (with a minus sign for cash paid out).
500,000 FV	FV = 500,000.0000	The value we want to achieve.
CPT N	N = 268.2539	Number of months (since we considered monthly payments) required to achieve our goal.

VII. CALCULATING THE PAYMENT AMOUNT

Purpose: Compute the amount of equal payments needed to achieve a given future value in a known period of time.

Method: Solve for CF in the equation: $FV_n = \$CF_t \sum_{t=1}^{n}(1 + i)^t$

Example: Suppose your retirement needs were $750,000. If you are currently 25 years old and plan to retire at age 65, how much will you have to contribute each month for retirement if you can earn 12.5% on your savings?

Keystrokes	Display	Explanation
CE/C CE/C 2nd CLR TVM	0.0000	Clears TVM variables.
2nd P/Y 12 ENTER 2nd BGN 2nd SET CE/C	P/Y = 12.0000 END BGN 0.0000	Sets 12 payments per year; begin mode (BGN) assumes cash flows are at the beginning of each month.
12.5 I/Y	I/Y = 12.5000	Stores i, the interest rate.
480 N	N = 480.0000	Stores N, the number of periods until we stop contributing (40 years × 12 months/year = 480 months).
750,000 FV	FV = 750,000.0000	The value we want to achieve.
CPT PMT	PMT = −53.8347	Monthly contribution required to achieve our ultimate goal (shown as negative since it represents cash paid out).

VIII. CALCULATE THE INTEREST RATE

Purpose: Compute the nominal annual interest rate of investments made in future periods.

Method: Solve for i in the equation: $FV_n = \$1(1 + i)^n$

Example: If you invest $300 at the end of each month for six years (72 months) for a promised $30,000 return at the end, what interest rate are you earning on your investment?

Keystrokes	Display	Explanation
CE/C CE/C 2nd CLR TVM	 0.0000	Clears TVM variables.
2nd P/Y 12 ENTER 2nd BGN 2nd SET CE/C	 P/Y = 12.0000 BGN END 0.0000	Sets 12 payments per year; end mode (END) assumes cash flows are at the end of each month.
72 N	N = 72.0000	Stores n, the number of deposits (investments).
300 +/− PMT	PMT = −300.0000	Stores PMT, the monthly amount invested (with a minus sign for cash paid out).
30,000 FV	FV = 30,000.0000	Stores the future value to be received in 6 years.
CPT I/Y	I/Y = 10.5892	The annual interest rate earned on the investment.

IX. BOND VALUATION

A. Computing the value of a bond

Purpose: Calculate the value of a bond.

Method: Assuming the maturity value, M, (also face or par value) of a bond is $1,000 and interest, I_t, is paid semiannually for n years, solve for the value that the bond should sell for, V_b, given the investor's required rate of return, R_b; that is,

$$V_b = \sum_{t=1}^{2n} \frac{\$I_t/2}{(1 + R_b/2)^t} + \frac{\$M}{(1 + R_b/2)^{2n}}$$

Example: Assume the current date is January 1, 1993, and that you want to know the value of a bond that matures in 10 years and has a coupon rate of 9 percent (4.5% semiannually). Your required rate of return is 12 percent.

Keystrokes	Display	Explanation
CE/C CE/C 2nd CLR TVM	 0.0000	Clears TVM variables.

2nd P/Y		Sets 2 payments per year; end mode (END) assumes
2 ENTER	P/Y = 12.0000	cash flows are at the end of each 6-month period.
2nd BGN	BGN	
2nd SET	END	
CE/C	0.0000	
20 N	N = 20.0000	Stores the number of semiannual periods (10 years × 2).
12 I/Y	I/Y = 12.0000	Stores annual rate of return.
45 PMT	PMT = 45.0000	Stores the semiannual interest payments.
1,000 FV	FV = 1,000.0000	Stores the bond's maturity or par value.
CPT PV	PV = –827.9512	Value of the bond, expressed as a negative number.

Solution using the bond feature

CE/C CE/C		Clears bond variables.
2nd		
BOND		
2nd	SDT = 12-31-1990	
CLR WORK		
0.0193	SDT = 1-01-1993	Stores settlement (current) date (day, month, year).
ENTER		
↓ 9 ENTER	CDN = 9.0000	Stores coupon interest rate.
01.0103	RDT = 1-01-2003	Stores maturity date (day, month, year).
ENTER		
↓	RV = 100.0000	Stores redemption value.
↓ 2nd SET	360	Stores 30/360 day count.
↓ 2nd SET	2/Y	Stores 2 coupon payments per year.
↓ 12 ENTER	VLD = 12.0000	Stores investor's required rate of return.
↓ CPT	PRICE = 82.7951	Value of bond as a % of par value; i.e., value of bond is $827.95.

B. Computing the yield to maturity

Purpose: Calculate the yield to maturity on a bond, given its current market value.

Method: Assuming the maturity value, M, (also face or par value) of a bond is $1,000 and interest, I_t, is paid semiannually for n years, and the bond is selling for V_b, solve for the yield to maturity (YTM); that is,

$$V_b = \sum_{t=1}^{2n} \frac{\$I_t/2}{(1 + YTM/2)^t} + \frac{\$M}{(1 + YTM/2)^{2n}}$$

Example: Assume the current date is January 1, 1994, and that you want to know your yield to maturity on a bond that matures in 8 years and has a coupon rate of 12 percent (6% semiannually). The bond is selling for $1,100.

Keystrokes	Display	Explanation
CE/C CE/C 2nd CLR TVM	 0.0000	Clears TVM variables.
2nd P/Y 2 ENTER CE/C CE/C	P/Y = 2.0000 0.0000	Sets 2 payments per year.
16 N	N = 16.0000	Stores the number of semiannual periods (8 years × 2).
1,100 +/− PV	PV = −1,100.0000	Value of the bond, expressed as a negative number.
60 PMT	PMT = 60.0000	Stores the semiannual interest payments.
1,000 FV	FV = 1,000.0000	Stores the bond's maturity or par value.
CPT I/Y	I/Y = 10.1451	The yield to maturity, expressed on an annual basis.

Solution using the bond feature

Keystrokes	Display	Explanation
CE/C CE/C 2nd BOND 2nd CLR WORK	 STD = 12-31-1990	Clears bond variables.
01.0194 ENTER	STD = 1-01-1994	Stores settlement (current) date (day, month, year).
↓ 12 ENTER	CPN = 12.0000	Stores coupon interest rate.
↓ 01.0102 ENTER	RDT = 1-01-2002	Stores maturity date (day, month, year).
↓	RV = 100.0000	Stores redemption value.
↓ 2nd SET	360	Stores 30/360 day count.
↓ 2nd SET	2/Y	Stores 2 coupon payments per year.
↓	YLD = 0.0000	Pass over yield.
↓ 110 ENTER	PRI = 110.0000	Stores bond value as a percentage of par value.
↑ CPT	YLD% = 10.1451	Bond's yield to maturity.

X. COMPUTING THE NET PRESENT VALUE AND INTERNAL RATE OF RETURN

Purpose: Determine the net present value (NPV) and the internal rate of return (IRR) for a capital investment where the cash flows are equal amounts in each of the future periods.

Method: Solve for the NPV of the project, given the investment outlay (*IO*), the project's future cash flows (CF_t), the life of the project (n), and the firm's required rate of return or cost of capital (K), using the following equation:

$$NPV = \sum_{t=1}^{n} \frac{\$CF_t}{(1 + K)^t} - IO$$

Then solve for the discount rate that results in a zero net present value, which is the internal rate of return.

A. Where future cash flows are equal amounts in each period (annuity)

Example: The firm is considering a capital project that would cost $80,000. The firm's cost of capital is 12 percent. The project life is 10 years, during which time the firm expects to receive $15,000 per year.

Keystrokes	Display	Explanation
CE/C CE/C 2nd CLR TVM	 0.0000	Clears TVM variables.
2nd P/Y 1 ENTER 2nd BGN 2nd SET CE/C	 P/Y = 1.0000 BGN END 0.0000	Sets 1 payment per year; end mode (END) assumes cash flows are at the end of each year.
15,000 PMT	PMT = 15,000.0000	Stores the annual cash flows of $15,000.
10 N	N = 10.0000	Stores the life of the project.
12 I/Y	I/Y = 12.0000	Stores the cost of capital.
CPT PV	PV = –84,753.3454	Calculates present value.
+ 80,000 = +/–	 4,753.3454	Calculates net present value by adding back the initial investment and changing signs.
80,000 +/– PV CPT I/Y	 I/Y = 13.4344	Calculates the IRR.

B. Where future cash flows are unequal amounts in each period

Example: The firm is considering a capital project that would cost $110,000. The firm's cost of capital is 15 percent. The project life is 5 years, with the following expected cash flows: –25,000, 50,000, 60,000, 60,000, and 70,000. In addition, you expect to receive $30,000 in the last year from the salvage value of the equipment.

Keystrokes	Display	Explanation
CF 2nd CLR WORK	CF_0 = 0.0000 CF_0 = 0.0000	Clears all variables of worksheet.

110,000 [+/−] [ENTER]	CF_0 = −110,000.0000	Stores CF_0, the initial investment (with a minus sign for a negative cash flow).
[↓] 25,000 [+/−] [ENTER]	CØ1 = -25,000.0000	Stores CØ1, the first year's cash flow (with a minus sign for a negative cash flow).
[↓]	FØ1 = 1.0000	Stores the number of years CØ1 is repeated (in this case, one year only).
[↓] 50,000 [ENTER]	CØ2 = 50,000.0000	Stores CØ2
[↓]	FØ2 = 1.0000	Stores the number of years CØ2 is repeated.
[↓] 60,000 [ENTER]	CØ3 = 60,000.0000	Stores CØ3.
[↓]	FØ3 = 1.0000	Stores the number of years CØ3 is repeated.
[↓] 60,000 [ENTER]	CØ4 = 60,000.0000	Stores CØ4.
[↓]	FØ4 = 1.0000	Stores the number of years CØ4 is repeated.
[↓] 100,000 [ENTER]	CØ5 = 100,000.0000	Stores CØ5, $70,000, plus expected salvage value of $30,000.
[↓]	FØ5 = 1.0000	Stores the number of years CØ4 is repeated.
[NPV]	I = 0.0000	Ends storage of individual cash flows and NPV. Function is activated.
15 [ENTER]	I = 15.0000	Stores interest rate.
[↓] [CPT]	NPV = 29,541.8951	Calculates the project's NPV at the stated interest rate.
[IRR] [CPT]	IRR = 22.0633	Calculates the project's IRR.

XI. CALCULATING ALPHA AND BETA FOR A REGRESSION EQUATION

Purpose: Calculate alpha and beta of the regression equation using monthly holding-period returns of Coca-Cola and TSE 300 index.

Method: Regress the monthly holding-period returns of Coca-Cola (dependent variable) on the monthly holding-period returns of the TSE 300 Index (independent variable).

Example: We will use Coca-Cola's returns for the 12 months ending November 1991. These returns, along with the corresponding returns for the TSE 300 Index are shown below.

Month and Year	Coca-Cola Monthly Returns	TSE 300 Index Returns
December 1990	0.54%	3.36
January 1991	4.84	0.49

February 1991	7.44	5.79
March 1991	3.58	0.96
April 1991	-2.76	-0.77
May 1991	8.53	2.23
June 1991	-4.80	-2.26
July 1991	10.32	2.13
August 1991	9.36	-0.61
September 1991	-1.90	-3.70
October 1991	3.29	3.78
November 1991	4.13	-1.91

Keystrokes	Display	Explanation
ENTER DATA		
2nd DATA	X01 (old contents)	Select Data-Entry Portion of Statistics Worksheet
2nd CLR WORK	X01 = 0.00	Clear Worksheet
3.36 ENTER	X01 = 3.36	Enter X01
↓ 0.54 ENTER	Y01 = 0.54	Enter Y01
↓ 0.49 ENTER	X02 = 0.49	Enter X02
↓ 4.84 ENTER	Y02 = 4.84	Enter Y02
↓ 5.79 ENTER	X03 = 5.79	Enter X03
↓ 7.44 ENTER	Y03 = 7.44	Enter Y03
↓ 0.96 ENTER	X04 = 0.96	Enter X04
↓ 3.58 ENTER	Y04 = 3.58	Enter Y04
↓ 0.77 +/− ENTER	X05 = −0.77	Enter X05
↓ 2.76 +/− ENTER	Y05 = −2.76	Enter Y05
↓ 2.23 ENTER	X06 = 2.23	Enter X06
↓ 8.53 ENTER	Y06 = 8.53	Enter Y06
↓ 2.26 +/− ENTER	X07 = −2.26	Enter X07
↓ 4.80 +/− ENTER	Y07 = −4.80	Enter Y07
↓ 2.13 ENTER	X08 = 2.13	Enter X08
↓ 10.32 ENTER	Y08 = 10.32	Enter Y08
↓ 0.61 +/− ENTER	X09 = −0.61	Enter X09
↓ 9.36 ENTER	Y09 = 9.36	Enter Y09
↓ 3.70 +/− ENTER	X10 = −3.70	Enter X10
↓ 1.90 +/− ENTER	Y10 = −1.90	Enter Y10

↓ 3.78 ENTER	X11 = 3.78	Enter X11
↓ 3.29 ENTER	Y11 = 3.29	Enter Y11
↓ 1.91 +/− ENTER	X12 = −1.91	Enter X12
↓ 4.13 ENTER	Y12 = 4.13	Enter Y12
2nd STAT	LIN	Call statistics program—linear regression
↓	n = 12.00	Sample size = 12
↓	$\bar{x}$ = 0.79	Mean of x = 0.79
↓	Sx = 2.79	Sample standard deviation of X = 2.79
↓	σx = 2.67	Population standard deviation of Y = 2.67
↓	$\bar{y}$ = 3.55	Mean of Y = 3.55
↓	Sy = 4.95	Sample standard deviation of Y = 4.95
↓	σy = 4.74	Population standard deviation of Y = 4.74
↓	a = 2.84	Y intercept = 2.84
↓	b = 0.897	Slope = 0.897
↓	r = 0.506	Correlation coefficient = 0.506
↓ 2 ENTER	x^1 = 2.00	New X1 = 2.00
↓ CPT	y^1 = 4.633	Predicted Y1 = 4.633

APPENDIX F: Solutions for Selected End-of-Chapter Problems

To provide check figures, this appendix supplies intermediate answers and final solutions for a select set of end-of-chapter problems. Usually, we have provided the solutions to odd-numbered problems; however, there are exceptions. Note that some of the problems may have more than one correct solution and that differences in answers also may result from rounding errors. Finally, not all solutions are readily expressed as brief answers.

CHAPTER 2 THE FINANCIAL ENVIRONMENT

2-1A. Nominal rate = 11.28%
Inflation premium = 7.28%

2-3A. Nominal rate = 8.15%
Inflation premium = 3.15%

2A-1A. Net Income = $292,050
Tax Income = $518,750

2A-3A. Net Income = $220,000
Taxable income = $350,000
Total Taxes Payable = $142,940

2A-5A. Net Income = ($5,500)
Taxable income = ($25,000)

2A-7A. Net Income = $89,100
Taxable income = $160,000

2A-9A. Taxable Income = $370,000
Combined corporate tax rate = 43.84%

CHAPTER 3 RISK AND RATES OF RETURN

3-1A. $\overline{X}$ = 9.1%; σ = 3.06%

3-3A. Security A: $\overline{X}$ = 16.7%; σ = 10.12%
Security B: $\overline{X}$ = 9.2%; σ = 3.57%

3-5A. About 0.50

3-7A. 10.56%

3-9A.

Time	Asman Return
2	20.0%
3	–8.3
4	18.2

3-11A. **a.** Expected Return = 15.8%
b. Beta = 0.95

3B-1. Alpha 1.31%
Beta 0.72
Arka:
Average return: 12.25%
Standard deviation: 5.32%
TSE 300:
Average return: 15.25%
Standard deviation: 7.37%

3C-1. Estimated risk-free rate: 6.2%

Market Premiums for Factors

1	2	3	4
–185.5%	144.5%	12.4%	–274.4%

Stock A return: 6.2% – 185.5%(–0.070) + 144.5%(–0.020) + 12.4%(0.010) – 274.4%(0.003) = 15.60%

Stock B return: 6.2% – 185.5%(–0.070) + 144.5%(0.030) + 12.4%(0.005) – 274.4%(0.010) = 20.84%

Stock C return: 6.2% – 185.5%(–0.070) + 144.5%(–0.010) + 12.4%(0.006) – 274.4%(0.009) = 15.34%

CHAPTER 4 VALUATION OF FINANCIAL ASSETS

4-1A. **a.** $12,970
c. $3,019.40

4-2A. **a.** n = 15 years

4-3A. **b.** 5%
c. 9%

4-4A. **b.** PV_0 = $235.20

4-5A. **a.** $6,289
c. $302.89

4-6A. **c.** $1,562.96

4-7A. **a.** FV_1 = $10,600
FV_5 = $13,380
FV_{15} = $23,970

4-9A. **a.** $6,690
b. Semiannual: $6,720
Bimonthly: $6,740

4-11A. Year 1: 18,000 books
Year 2: 21,600 books
Year 3: 25,920 books

4-13A. $262.79

4-15A. 8%

4-17A. $658; $197.85

4-19A. **a.** $29,910
b. $13,371
c. $26,700

4-21A. **b.** $8,333.33

4-22A. $824.36

4-26A. $6,509

4-28A. 22%

4-29A. $6,934.81

4-32A. **a.** $1,989.73

4-35A. $752.52

4-37A. $1,058.34; $1,057.23

4-39A. 4.63%

4-41A. $51.50

4-43A. $24.50

4-45A. $39.96

4-47A. 9.65%

4-49A. **a.** 7.06%

      b. $847.48

4-51A. **a.** 14.07%

      b. $57.02

4A-1. **a.** $V_b = $863.78

      b. V_b @ 15% = $707.63; V_b @ 8% = $1,171.19

      d. V_b @ 12% = $927.90; V_b @ 8% = $1,079.85

CHAPTER 5   COST OF CAPITAL

5-1A. **a.** $K_d = 5.54\%$

      b. $K_p = 8.77\%$

      c. $K_c = 15.14\%$

      d. $K_{nc} = 15.57\%$

      e. $K_d = 6.72\%$

5-3A. $K_{nc} = 12.06\%$

5-5A. $K_d = 4.94\%$

5-7A. $K_p = 14.29\%$

5-9A. **a.** $1,320.52

      b. $1,181.87

      c. 424

      d. $K_d = 6.12\%$

5-11A. $K_c = 17.43\%$
       $K_{nc} = 18.10\%$

5-13A. WCC = 15.06%

5-15A. $K_d = 5.32\%$; $K_{nc} = 13.84\%$; $K_p = 8.83\%$
       WCC = 9.85% (when issuing new shares)

5-17A. $Breaks in Weighted Marginal Cost Curve
       Debt $750,000
       Preferred shares $625,000; $1,250,000
       Common shares $1,000,000

Weighted cost of capital	
$0–$625,000	10.88%
$625,001–$750,000	10.96%
$750,001–$1,000,000	11.56%

5-19A. Cost of debt 4.48%; 5.04%; 5.88%
       Cost of preferred shares 10.63%; 11.33%
       Cost of common shares 13.16%; 13.90%; 14.20%

$0–$250,000	10.30%
$250,000–$500,000	10.75%
$500,001–$625,000	10.93%

5-21A. Required rate
       A: 16.30%
       B: 14.35%

CHAPTER 6   CAPITAL BUDGETING

6-1A.

Project	*A*	*B*
AROR	63.9%	62.5%

6-3A. **a.** IRR = 7%

      b. IRR = 17%

6-5A. **a.** NPV = $56,777

      b. PI = 1.71

      c. 47.2%

6-7A. **a.** NPV = $68,663

      b. PI = 1.035

      c. 10.17%

6-9A. $IRR_A = 23.3\%$
       $IRR_B = 7.9\%$
       $IRR_C = 15.89\%$

CHAPTER 7   CAPITAL BUDGETING UNDER UNCERTAINTY

7-1A. **a.**

Taxes on Capital Gain	*Taxes on Recaptured Depreciation (Terminal Loss)*		*Total Taxes*
@$35,000	$1,687.50	$7,877	$9,565
@$25,000	0	5,627	$5,627
@$15,000	0	1,127	$1,127
@$12,000	0	(222)	($222)

7-3A. **a.** NPV= –$36,975

      b. 0.82

      c. 1.8%

7-5A. **a.** 162,334

      b. 1.35

      c. 21.35%

7-7A. **a.** Initial outlay = $35,000

      b. PV (Project's net savings after taxes) = $34,542

c. Terminal cash flow = $15,238

e. NPV=$10,853

f. 1.79

g. 31.97%

7-9A. a. NPV = $10,795.54

b. 1.79

c. 31.92%

7-11A. a. Payback A = 1.589
Payback B = 3.019

b. NPV_A = $8,743
NPV_B = $11,615

c. IRR_A = 40%
IRR_B = 30%

e. EAA_A = $3,830
EAA_B = $2,098

7-13A a. NPV_A = $136.30
NPV_B = $454

b. PI_A = 1.2726
PI_B = 1.0908

c. IRR_A = 40%
IRR_B = 20%

7-14A. b. NPV_A = $53,212.50
NPV_B = $58,265

7-16A. NPV = –$330

7-18A. NPV_A = $9,813.25

7-19A. IRR= 13.8%

7-23A. NPV(Steel Mills) = $20,628;NPV(Honeybilt) = $5,295

CHAPTER 8   ANALYSIS AND IMPACT OF LEVERAGE

8-1A. a. Jake's EBIT = $154,067.40
Sarasota = 480,000
Jefferson = 28,970

b. Jake's = 8,232
Sarasota = 1,789
Jefferson = 8,310

c. Jake's = 1.78
Sarasota = 2.77
Jefferson = 4.09

d. Jefferson Wholesale would suffer the largest decline in profitability.

8-3A. a. 6,296 pairs of shoes

b. $534,591.19

c. At 7,000, EBIT = $19,000
At 9,000, EBIT = $73,000
At 15,000, EBIT = $235,000

d. 9.95 times; 3.33 times; 1.72 times

8-4A. a. 9,000 units

b. $1,620,000

8-6A. a. $77,840.91

b. 6407 units;$172,979.8

8-8A. 1.94 times

8-10A. a. 10,000 units

b. $1,800,000

8-12A. a. F = $191,807.20

b. 15,984 units;S*= $319,678.7

8-18A. a. 5,000 units

b. $125,000

c. –$10,000;$10,000;$30,000

8-20A. 5 times

8-22. A. 1,400,000 units

8-24A. a. 3 times

b. 1.25 times

c. 3.75 times

d. $8 million

8-26A. b. 35%

c. $84,000

CHAPTER 9   PLANNING THE FIRM'S FINANCING MIX

9-1A. a. EBIT = $2,000,000

b.

	Plan A	Plan B
Net Income	$1,000,000	$700,000

d. Plan B.

9-3A. a. $240,000

b.

Plan A	Plan B
$187,200	$93,600

9-5A. a. $450,000

9-6A. a. EBIT = $640,000

b.

	Plan A	Plan B
Net Income	$320,000	$160,000

c. Plan B

9-8A. a. EBIT = $300,000

b.

Plan A	Plan B
$234,000	$156,000

9-10A. a. Plan A

b. 10.42

9-12A. **a.** Firm B
b. Firm C

9-14A. **a.** V = 20,000,00
b. K_c = 25%; K_0=25%
c. Kc = 25.89%; DPS = $5.18; 3.58%; 3.58%; 25.04%

9-16A. **a.** Plan A vs. Plan B = $9,000
Plan A vs. Plan C = $18,000

CHAPTER 10   DIVIDEND POLICY AND INTERNAL FINANCING

10-1A. 95,238 shares

10-3A. Equity financing needed = $384,000
Dividend = $16,000

10-5A. Price for Plan A or Plan B = $31.76

10-7A. **a.** Shares before split = 122,500
b. Net gain = $24,500

10-8A. **a.** Year 1 = $.70; Year 3 = $.93
b. $.90
c. Year 1 = $.50; Year 3 = $.68

10-9A. **a.** $52.00
b. 9,615 shares

10-11A. Equity financing needed = $360,000;
Dividend = $90,000

CHAPTER 11   EVALUATING FINANCIAL PERFORMANCE

11-1A. $500,000.00

11-3A. **a.** Return on total assets = 10%
b. Sales growth = 20%
c. Return on equity = 17.1%

11-5A.

	Beginning	End
Current Ratio	6×	4×
ACP	137 days	107 days
Fixes Asset T/O	1×	1.04×
Net Profit Margin	10%	12.4%

11-7A.

Cash flow from	
Operations	$87,000
Investing	($142,500)
Financing	63,000

11-9A. **a.** 25%; 2.25×; 11.11%
b. 19.5%
c. 14.5%

CHAPTER 12   FINANCIAL FORECASTING, PLANNING, AND BUDGETING

12-1A. Total assets = $1.8 million

12-3A. Total assets = $2 million
Long-term debt = $.4 million

12-5A.

	July	August	September
Net Monthly Change	$(10,600)	(600)	7,800
Cumulative Borrowing	10,600	11,306	3,619

12-7A. **a.** Acounts receivable = $22,222
b. Accounts receivable = $31,111

12-11A. **a.** Average collection Period = 40 days
b. Reduction in accounts receivable = $100,000

12-13A.

	Jan	Feb	March
Net Monthly Change	$38,300	($900)	($91,500)
Cumulative Borrowing	0	0	52,100

CHAPTER 13   INTRODUCTION TO WORKING-CAPITAL MANAGEMENT

13-1A. **a.** Return on equity = 19.48%
b. Return on equity = 14.05%

13-3A. Net operating income = $195,666
Net income = $101,200

CHAPTER 14   CASH AND MARKETABLE SECURITIES MANAGEMENT

14-1A. **a.** Yes; the company will save $160,199 annually

14-3A. **a.** Yes; the firm will generate $35,288 net annual savings

14-4A. **b.** 15%

14-5A. **a.** $2,625,000
b. $241,500

14-6A. Yes; annual savings = $211,000

14-8A. 0.5322 days

14-10A. **b.** 12%

14-12A. Net annual savings = $3,375

14-14A. 0.4106 days

14-16A. $10,667

14-18A. $14,247

14-25A. **a.** $912.44

b. $87.56

c. $17.59

14A-1A. a. $158,698

    b. $856.96

    c. 5.95 days

    d. $79,349

CHAPTER 15 ACCOUNTS RECEIVABLE AND INVENTORY MANAGEMENT

15-1A. a. 44.32%

    b. 44.59%

15-3A. a. $90,000

    b. $53,333

15-5A. $58,202

15-7A. a. 775 units

15-9A. a. 816 units

    b. $61,237

15-11A. a. 35.2 orders per year

CHAPTER 16 SHORT-TERM FINANCING

16-1A. EAC = 14.52%

16-3A. a. EAC = 44.59%

    b. EAC = 109.84%

    c. EAC = 44.86%

    d. EAR = 17.81%

16-7A. a. EAC = 11.09%

16-9A. EAC = 17.67%

16-11A. Pledging: EAR = 16.99%
             Inventory loan: EAR = 14.53%

16-13A. EAR = 12.96%

CHAPTER 18 TERM LOANS AND LEASES

18-1A. a. $31,977.78

18-3A. a. 15%

    b. $76,352.35

    c. 9.02%

18-5A. a. NPV(P) = $6,781.87; NPV(L)= –$2,621

18-7A. a. $19,925.20

    c. $15,229.97

CHAPTER 19 LONG-TERM DEBT, PREFERRED SHARES, AND COMMON SHARES

19-3A. Yes, NPV = $571,569

19-5A. a. 200,000 shares

    b. 5 rights

c. V_r = $4

19-6A. a. 1,000,000 shares

    b. 2 rights

    c. $5

CHAPTER 20 CONVERTIBLES, WARRANTS, OPTIONS, AND FUTURES

20-1A. a. 25 shares

    b. $681.25

20-2A. a. 0.92593

    b. $12.27

20-3A. a. 0

    b. $4

20-4A. a. minimum price = $1.71
       warrant premium = $1.29

    b. Minimum price = $4.67
       Warrant price = $5.08

CHAPTER 21 CORPORATE RESTRUCTURING: COMBINATIONS AND DIVESTITURES

21-1A. Average theoretical value: $6,083

21-3A. NPV = –$57.78

CHAPTER 22 FAILURE AND REORGANIZATION

22-1A. Bankruptcy score for company A = 2.810
       Bankruptcy score for company B = 6.719
       Bankruptcy score for company C = 3.455

22-3A.

Corporate Structure After Reorganization	
Accounts Payable	$162,500
Short-term Notes Payable	287,500
Long-term Note Payable	125,000
Mortgage Bonds	500,000
Preferred Shares	125,000
Common Shares	625,000

22-5A.

	Claim	Claim after Subordination
Accounts Payable	$200,000	$200,000
Notes Payable	350,000	350,000
Debt	300,000	300,000
Preferred shares	100,000	100,000
Subordinated debentures	0	0
Final distribution to common shareholders = $0		

22-7A.

Corporate Structure After Reorganization

Accounts Payable	$693,000
Short-term Notes Payable	700,000
Long-term Note Payable	1,407,000
Mortgage Bonds	1,000,000
Preferred Shares	700,000
Common Shares	3,900,000

CHAPTER 23 INTERNATIONAL BUSINESS FINANCE

23-1A. **a.** $11,963

b. $19,412

c. $47,490

23-3A. U.S.: 0.8359; 0.8349; 0.8307
Japan: 103.0291; 102.976; 102.459
Switzerland: 1.0529; 1.0554; 1.0685

23-5A. Net gain = $292.77

23-7A. U.S.: 1.404%; 1.254%
Japan: 0.618%; 1.113%
Switzerland: (2.906%); (2.932%)

23-9A. 0.00973

Accounting Rate of Return (AROR). A capital-budgeting criterion that relates the returns generated by the project, as measured by average accounting profits after tax, to the average dollar size of the investment required.

Accrual Basis of Accounting. A method of accounting whereby income is recorded when earned whether or not the money has been received at that time, and expenses are recorded when incurred, whether or not any money has actually been paid out.

Acid Test Ratio. (Current assets – inventories – prepaid expenses) ÷ current liabilities. This ratio is a more stringent measure of liquidity than the current ratio in that it subtracts inventories (the least liquid current asset) from current assets.

Acquisition. A combination of two or more businesses into a single operational entity.

Agency Costs. The costs, such as a reduced share price, associated with potential conflict between managers and investors when these two groups are not the same.

Amortized Loans. Loans that are paid off in equal periodic payments.

Analytical Income Statement. A modified income statement which shows the effects of the firm's total variable costs and total fixed costs on earnings before interest and taxes (EBIT).

Announcement Date. The date a firm announces when "holders of record" will be issued rights, when they will be mailed, and when they will expire.

Annuity. A series of equal dollar payments for a specified number of years.

Anticipatory Buying. Buying in anticipation of a price increase in order to secure the goods at a lower cost.

Appraisal Value. The value of a company as stated by an independent appraisal firm.

Arbitrage. The process of buying and selling in more than one market in order to make a riskless profit.

Arbitrage-Pricing Model. A theory that relates share returns and risk. The theory maintains that security returns vary from their expected amounts when there are unanticipated changes in basic economic forces. Such forces would include unexpected changes in industrial production, inflation rates, term structure of interest rates, and the difference between interest rates of high-and-low risk bonds.

Arbitrageur. A person involved in the process of buying and selling in more than one market to make a riskless profit.

Arrangement. A reorganizational plan involving a petition to the court requesting that the firm be required to make only partial or a delayed payment to its creditors.

Arrearage. An overdue payment, generally referring to omitted preferred share dividends.

Assignee. See **Trustee**.

Assignment. A method of liquidating a business that has been declared insolvent. To minimize court involvement (and therefore costs), a third party receives title for the firm's assets and is responsible for the disposal of the assets and distribution of the proceeds. Creditors have the right to refuse such a settlement, and if they so choose, to force the debtor into a court-administered liquidation.

Authorized Share Capital. A term used to indicate the total number of shares the firm can issue and is specified in the articles of incorporation.

Automated Depository Transfer System. A system that moves funds from local bank accounts to concentration accounts electronically. This eliminates the mail float from the local banks to the concentration banks.

Average Collection Period. Accounts receivable/(annual credit sales/365). A ratio that expresses how rapidly the firm is collecting its credit accounts.

Average Tax Rate. The rate calculated by dividing the total tax liability by the entity's taxable income.

Balance Sheet. A basic accounting statement that represents the financial position of a firm on a given date.

Balance Sheet Leverage Ratios. Financial ratios used to measure the extent of a firm's use of borrowed funds calculated using information found in the firm's balance sheet.

Bankers' Acceptances. A draft (order to pay) drawn on a specific bank by a seller of goods in order to obtain payment for goods that have been shipped (sold) to a customer. The customer maintains an account with that specific bank.

Bank Wire. A wire service used and supported by the banks in Canada for the transfer of funds.

Benefit/Cost Ratio. See **Profitability Index**.

Beta. The relationship between an investment's returns and the market returns. This is a measure of the investment's non-diversifiable risk.

Bird-in-the-Hand Dividend Theory. The belief that dividend income has a higher value to the investor than does capital gains income, since dividends are more certain than capital gains.

Bond. A long-term (ten-year or more) promissory note issued by the borrower, promising to pay the owner of the security a predetermined and fixed amount of interest each year.

Bond Par Value. The face value appearing on the bond, which is to be returned to the bondholder at maturity.

Bond-Refunding Decision. Choice of whether or not to call an entire issue of bonds.

Book Value. The depreciated value of a company's assets (original cost less accumulated depreciation) less the outstanding liabilities.

Book-Value Weights. The percentage of financing provided by different capital sources as measured by their book values from the company's balance sheet.

Bought Deal. Distribution method of reselling securities bought from the issuing firm.

Break-Even Analysis. An analytical technique used to determine the quantity of output or sales that results in a zero level of earnings before interest and taxes (EBIT). Relationships among the firm's cost structure, volume of output, and EBIT are studied.

Budget. A forecast of future events.

Business Organizations. Legal organizations, such as proprietorships, partnerships, and corporations.

Business Risk. The relative dispersion or variability in the firm's expected earnings before interest and taxes (EBIT). The nature of the firm's operations causes its business risk. This type of risk is affected by the firm's cost structure, product demand characteristics, and intra-industry competitive position. In capital-structure theory, business risk is distinguished from financial risk. See **Financial Risk**.

Call Option. A call option gives its owner the right to purchase a given number of shares or some other asset at a specified price over a given time period.

Call Premium. The difference between the call price and the security's par value.

Call Provision. A provision that entitles the corporation to repurchase its bonds or preferred shares from their holders at stated prices over specified periods.

Capital Asset. All property used in conducting a business other than assets held primarily for sale in the ordinary course of business or depreciable and real property used in conducting a business.

Capital Asset Pricing Model. An equation stating that the expected rate of return on a project is a function of (1) the risk-free rate, (2) the investment's systematic risk, and (3) the expected risk premium in the market.

Capital Budgeting. The decision-making process with respect to investment in fixed assets. Specifically it involves measuring the incremental cash flows associated with investment proposals and evaluating those proposed investments.

Capital Cost. The sum of the purchase cost of the asset and any incremental cost associated with the installation, engineering, training, or administration of the purchase.

Capital Cost Allowance. The amount of depreciation (write-off) claimed by a taxpayer for tax purposes on an asset.

Capital Cost Allowance System. A system that permits a taxpayer to deduct a portion of the depreciable property's capital cost as an expense.

Capital Gain. For tax purposes, a capital gain is determined from the difference between the proceeds of the sale or exchange and the capital cost of the asset.

Capital Loss. For tax purposes, a capital loss is determined from the difference between the capital cost and the proceeds from the sale or exchange of a non-depreciable asset.

Capital Market. All institutions and procedures that facilitate transactions in long-term financial instruments.

Capital Rationing. The placing of a limit by the firm on the dollar size of the capital budget.

Capital Structure. The mix of long-term sources of funds used by the firm. This is also called the firm's *capitalization*.

The relative total (percentage) of each type of fund is emphasized.

Cash. Currency and coin on hand in petty cash drawers, in cash registers, or in chequing accounts.

Cash Breakdown Analysis. Another version of break-even analysis that includes only the cash costs of production within the cost components. This means noncash expenses, like depreciation, are omitted in the analysis.

Cash Breakeven Analysis. A version of the basic cost-volume-profit analysis whereby non-cash expenses are not included in determining the company's fixed or variable costs.

Cash Budget. A detailed plan of future cash flows. This budget is composed of four elements: cash receipts, cash disbursements, net change in cash for the period, and new financing needed.

Cash Flow Cycle Diagram. Diagram depicting a firm's operations as a large pump that pushes cash through various reservoirs, such as inventories and accounts receivable, and dispenses cash for taxes, interest, principal payments on debt, and cash dividends to the shareholders.

Cash Flow Process. The process of cash generation and disposition in a typical business setting.

Certainty Equivalents. The amount of cash a person would require with certainty to make him or her indifferent between this certain sum and a particular risky or uncertain sum.

Certificate of Deposit. A non-marketable receipt for funds that have been deposited with a bank for a fixed time period. The corporate CD is issued at par in blocks of $100,000 and the owner receives the full amount deposited plus the earned interest.

Characteristic Line. The line of "best fit" through a series of returns for a firm's shares relative to the market returns. The slope of the line, frequently called beta, represents the average movement of the firm's share returns in response to a movement in the market's returns.

Chattel Mortgage Agreement. A loan agreement in which the lender can increase his security interest by having specific items of inventory identified in the loan agreement. The borrower retains title to the inventory but cannot sell the items without the lender's consent.

Chop-Shop Value. A valuation approach that values a firm based on its various business segments. It is an attempt to identify multi-industry companies that are undervalued and would be worth more if separated into their parts.

Clientele Effect. The belief that individuals and institutions that need current income will invest in companies that have high dividend payouts. Other investors prefer to avoid taxes by holding securities that offer only small dividend income, but large capital gains. Thus, we have a "clientele" of investors.

Coefficient of Variation. The relative dispersion of a probability distribution.

Commercial Paper. Short-term unsecured promissory notes sold by large businesses in order to raise cash. Unlike most other money market instruments, commercial paper has no developed secondary market.

Common Share. A claim of ownership in a corporation. Common shares have no maturity date, but exist as long as the firm does.

Common Size Financial Statements. Financial statements that have been converted to a percent of either sales in the case of the income statement or total assets in the case of the balance sheet. The information within the common size statements is standardized and consequently can be used to compare firms of very different sizes.

Company-Unique Risk. See **Unsystematic Risk**.

Compensating Balance. A balance of a given amount that the firm maintains in its demand deposit account. It may be required by either a formal or informal agreement with the firm's commercial bank. Such balances are usually required by the bank (1) on the unused portion of a loan commitment, (2) on the unpaid portion of an outstanding loan, or (3) in exchange for certain services provided by the bank, such as cheque-clearing or credit information. These balances raise the effective rate of interest paid on borrowed funds.

Composition. A voluntary remedy to insolvency in which the creditors receive a portion of the amounts originally owed to them. This may be preferable to forcing bankruptcy due to the high costs of bankruptcy courts and the possibility that the insolvent firm's resources may be further depleted by the bankruptcy proceedings.

Compounding. The process of determining the future value of a payment or series of payments when applying the concept of compound interest.

Compound Interest. The situation in which interest paid on the investment during the first period is added to the principal and, during the second period, interest is earned on the original principal plus the interest earned during the first period.

Concentration Bank. A bank where the firm maintains a major disbursing account.

Conditional Outcomes. The cash flows that occur if an event (outcome) takes place.

Conditional Probability. The probability associated with an event (outcome) taking place.

Conglomerate. A multifaceted corporation involved in a variety of products and services.

Constant Dividend Payout Ratio. A dividend payment policy in which the percentage of earnings paid out in dividends is held constant. The dollar amount fluctuates from year to year as profits vary.

Contractual Interest Rate. The interest rate to be paid on a bond expressed as a percent of par value.

Contributed Surplus. A surplus paid-in by shareholders which includes premiums on shares issued, any portion of the proceeds of issue of shares without par value not allocated to share capital, gain on forfeited shares, proceeds arising from donated shares, credits resulting from redemption or conversion of shares at less than the amount set up as share capital, and any other contribution by shareholders in excess of amounts allocated to share capital.

Contribution Margin. The difference between a product's selling price and its unit variable costs. It is usually measured on a per unit basis.

Conversion Parity Price. The price for which the investor in effect purchases the company's common shares when purchasing a convertible security. Mathematically it is the market price of the convertible security divided by the conversion ratio.

Conversion Period. Time period during which convertible securities may be exchanged.

Conversion Premium. The difference between a convertible's market price and the higher of its security value and its conversion value.

Conversion Price. See **Conversion Parity Price**.

Conversion Ratio. The number of common shares for which a convertible security can be exchanged.

Conversion Value. The total market value of the common shares for which a convertible security can be exchanged.

Convertibles. Preferred shares or debentures that can be exchanged for a specified number of common shares at the will of the owner.

Corporate Bylaws. Regulations that govern the internal affairs of the corporation, designating such items as the time and place of the shareholders' meetings, voting rights, the election process for selecting members of the board of directors, the procedures for issuing and transferring share certificates, and the policies relating to the corporate records.

Corporation. An entity that *legally* functions separate and apart from its owners.

Cost Budgets. Budgets prepared for every major expense category of the firm, such as production cost, selling cost, administrative cost, financing cost, and research and development cost.

Cost of Capital. The rate that must be earned in order to satisfy the required rate of return of the firm's investors. It may also be defined as the rate of return on investments at which the price of the firm's common shares will remain unchanged. The cost of capital is based on the opportunity cost of funds as determined in the capital markets.

Cost of Capital–Capital Structure Argument. Controversy as to whether a firm can affect its overall cost of funds by varying the mixture of financing sources used.

Cost of Common Shares. The rate of return the firm must earn in order for the common shareholders to receive their required rate of return. The rate is based on the opportunity cost of funds for the common shareholders in the capital markets.

Cost of Debt. The rate that has to be received from an investment in order to achieve the required rate of return for the creditors. The cost is based on the debtholders' opportunity cost of debt in the capital markets.

Cost of Preferred Shares. The rate of return that must be earned on the preferred shareholders' investment to satisfy their required rate of return. The cost is based on the preferred shareholders' opportunity cost of preferred shares in the capital markets.

Cost-Volume-Profit Analysis. Another way of referring to ordinary break-even analysis.

Coupon Interest Rate. The interest to be paid annually on a bond as a percent of par value, which is specified in the contractual agreement.

Coverage Ratios. A group of ratios that measure a firm's ability to meet its recurring fixed charge obligations, such as interest on long-term debt, lease payments, and/or preferred share dividends.

Credit Scoring. The numerical evaluation of credit applicants where the score is evaluated relative to a predetermined standard.

Cross Rates. The indirect computation of the exchange rate of one currency from the exchange rates of two other currencies.

Cumulative Feature. A requirement that all past unpaid preferred share dividends can be paid before any common share dividends are declared.

Current Assets. All assets that a firm expects to convert into cash within a year, including cash, marketable securities, accounts receivable, and inventories.

Current Ratio. Current assets/current liabilities. A ratio that indicates a firm's degree of liquidity by comparing its current assets to its current liabilities.

Date of Record. Date at which the share transfer books are to be closed for determining the investor to receive the next dividend payment. See **Ex-Dividend Date**.

Debenture. Any unsecured long-term debt.

Debt Capacity. The maximum proportion of debt that the firm can include in its capital structure and still maintain its lowest weighted cost of capital.

Debt Ratio. Total liabilities/total assets. A ratio that measures the extent to which a firm has been financed with debt.

Declaration Date. The date upon which a dividend is formally declared by the board of directors.

Default Risk. The uncertainty of expected returns from a security attributable to possible changes in the financial capacity of the security issuer to make future payments to the security owner. Treasury bills are considered to be default-free. Default risk is also referred to as "financial risk" in the context of marketable securities management.

Degree of Combined Leverage. The percentage change in earnings per share caused by a percentage change in sales. It is the product of the degree of operating leverage and the degree of financial leverage.

Delivery-Time Stock. Inventory needed between the order date and the receipt of inventory ordered.

Depository Transfer Cheques. A means for moving funds from local bank accounts to concentration accounts. The depository transfer cheque itself is an unsigned, nonnegotiable instrument. It is payable only to the bank of deposit for credit to the firm's specific account.

Depreciation. The means by which an asset's value is expensed over its useful life for accounting purposes.

Direct Costs. See **Variable Costs**.

Direct Investment. See **Foreign Direct Investment**.

Direct Quotes. The exchange rate that indicates the number of units of the home currency required to buy one unit of foreign currency.

Disbursing Float. Funds available in the company's bank account until its payment cheque has cleared through the banking system.

Discount Bond. A bond that sells at a discount below par value.

Discounting. The inverse of compounding. This process is used to determine the present value of a cash flow.

Discount Rate. The interest rate used in the discounting process.

Diversifiable Risk. See **Unsystematic Risk**.

Divestitures. The removal of a division or subsidiary from the company. Typically, the part of the firm being separated is viewed as not contributing to the company's basic purposes.

Dividend Payout Ratio. The amount of dividends relative to the company's net income or earnings per share.

Dividend Rate Band. Range between the maximum and minimum levels to which preferred share dividends can climb or fall.

Dividend Yield. The dividend per share divided by the price of the security.

Double-Declining Balance Depreciation. A method for computing declining balance depreciation expense in which the constant percentage is equal to 2/N, where N represents the depreciable life of the asset.

Dunning Letters. Past-due letters sent out to delinquent accounts.

Duration. A measure of responsiveness of the bond price to a change in interest rates.

EBIT. Common financial notation for **earnings before interest and taxes**.

EBIT-EPS Indifference Point. The level of earnings before interest and taxes (EBIT) that will equate earnings per share (EPS) between two different financing plans.

Economic Failure. Situation in which the company's costs exceed its revenues. Stated differently, the internal rates of return on investments are less than the firm's cost of capital.

Effective Annual Cost. The compounded interest rate which is expressed on an annual basis.

Efficiency Ratio. A financial ratio which provides a basis for assessing how effectively the firm is using its resources to generate sales.

Efficient Market. A market in which the values of all assets and securities at any instant in time fully reflect all available information.

EPS. Typical financial notation for **earnings per** (common) **share**.

Equipment Trust Certificate. A financial instrument which uses equipment as security.

Equivalent Annual Annuity (EAA). An annuity cash flow that yields the same present value as the project's NPV. It is calculated by dividing the project's NPV. It is calculated by dividing the project's NPV by the appropriate PVIFA$_{1\%, n \, yr}$

Eurodollar Loan. A loan that is denominated in U.S. dollars which is borrowed from the banking market (e.g., Canadian affiliate bank) in Europe. The advantages of using this type of financing include a reduced level of regulation and lower interest costs as compared to North American financial markets.

Exchange Risk. The variability in future cash flows caused by variations in the exchange rates.

Ex-Dividend Date. The date upon which stock brokerage companies have uniformly decided to terminate the right of ownership to the dividend, which is four days prior to the record date.

Exercise Price. The price at which a warrant allows its holder to purchase the firm's common shares.

Exercise Ratio. The number of shares that can be obtained at the exercise price with one warrant.

Expected Rate of Return. The arithmetic mean or average of all possible outcomes where those outcomes are weighted by the probability that each will occur.

Explicit Cost of Capital. The real cost of any source of capital.

Ex-Rights Date. The date on or after which the shares sell without rights.

Extension. An arrangement requiring that the debtor pay the amount owed in full, but providing an extension in time.

External Common Equity. A new issue of common shares.

Factor. A firm that acquires the receivables of other firms. A commercial finance company that engages solely in the factoring of receivables is known as an old-line factor.

Factoring of Accounts Receivable. The outright sale of a firm's accounts to another party (the factor) without recourse. The factor, in turn, bears the risk of collection.

Fair Value. The present value of an asset's expected future cash flows.

Field Warehouse Financing Agreement. A security agreement in which inventories are used as collateral, physically separated from the firm's other inventories, and placed under the control of a third-party field warehousing firm.

Financial Analysis. The assessment of a firm's financial condition or well being. Its objectives are to determine the firm's financial strengths and to identify its weaknesses. The primary tool of financial analysis is the financial ratio.

Financial Assets. Claims for future payment by one economic unit upon another.

Financial Intermediaries. Major financial institutions, such as commercial banks, trust companies, caisses populaires, credit unions, life insurance companies, and mutual funds, that assist the transfer of savings from economic units with excess savings to those with a shortage of savings.

Financial Lease. A noncancellable contractual commitment on the part of the firm leasing the asset (the lessee) to make a series of payments to the firm that actually owns the asset (the lessor) for the use of the asset.

Financial Leverage. The use of securities bearing a fixed (limited) rate of return to finance a portion of the firm's assets. Financial leverage can arise from the use of either debt or preferred share financing. The use of financial leverage exposes the firm to **financial risk.**

Financial Markets. Institutions and procedures that facilitate transactions in all types of financial claims (securities).

Financial Risk. The added variability in earnings available to the firm's common shareholders, and the added chance of insolvency caused by the use of securities bearing a limited rate of return in the firm's financial structure. The use of financial leverage gives rise to financial risk.

Financial Structure Design. The activity of seeking the proper mixture of a firm's short-term, long-term, and permanent financing components to minimize the cost of raising a given amount of funds.

Financial Structure. The mix of *all* funds sources that appear on the right-hand side of the balance sheet.

Firm-Specific Risk. See **Unsystematic Risk**.

Fixed Asset Turnover. Sales/fixed assets. A ratio indicating how effectively a firm is using its fixed assets to generate sales.

Fixed Costs. Charges that do **not** vary in total amount as sales volume or the quantity of output changes over some relevant range of output.

Floating Rate Preferred Shares. Preferred shares whose dividends are tied to the prevailing interest rate level at the time of distribution.

Flotation Costs. The underwriter's spread and issuing costs associated with the issuance and marketing of new securities.

Foreign Direct Investment. Physical assets, such as plant and equipment, acquired outside a corporation's home country but operated and controlled by that corporation.

Formal Control. Control vested in the shareholders having the majority of the voting common shares.

Forward Exchange Contract. A contract which requires delivery of one currency at a specified future date for a specified amount of another currency.

Free Cash Flow Value. The value of a firm based on the cash flows available for distributing to any investors, both debt and equity. The free cash flows equal operating cash flows less any incremental investments made to support a firm's future growth. The value of these flows is equal to their present value.

Functional Control. Control executed by the corporate officers in conducting the daily operations.

Futures Contract. A futures contract is a contract to buy or sell a stated commodity (such as soybeans or corn) or financial claim (such as Government of Canada bonds) at a specified price at some future, specified time.

Future Value. The value in future dollars of today's payment compounded to the future at the required rate of return.

General Partnership. A partnership in which all partners are fully liable for the indebtedness incurred by the partnership.

Golden Parachute. A target management's attempt to

ensure its own future in the event of an acquisition; stipulations regarding severance pay, extension of benefits, and other "extras" to be provided to outgoing management by the acquirer.

Gross Income. The firm's dollar sales from its product or services less the cost of producing or acquiring the product or service.

Gross Profit Margin. Gross profit/net sales. A ratio denoting the gross profit of the firm as a percentage of net sales.

Hedge. A means to neutralize exchange risk on an exposed asset position, whereby a liability of the same amount and maturity is created in a foreign currency.

Hedging Concept. See **Hedging Principle.**

Hedging Principle. A working capital management policy which states that the cash flow generating characteristics of a firm's investments should be matched with the cash flow requirements of the firm's sources of financing. Very simply, short-lived assets should be financed with short-term sources of financing while long-lived assets should be financed with long-term sources of financing.

Holder-of-Record Date. The date when rights are officially issued to shareholders.

Holding-Period Return. The return an investor would receive from holding a security for a designated period of time. For example, a monthly holding-period return would be the return for holding a security during a particular month.

Hostile Takeover. A merger or acquisition in which management resists the group initiating the transaction.

Hurdle Rate. The required rate of return used in capital budgeting.

Implicit Cost of Debt. The change in the cost of common equity brought on by using financial leverage.

Income Bond. A bond that requires interest payments only if earned. Failure to meet these interest payments will not result in bankruptcy.

Income Statement. A basic accounting statement that measures the results of a firm's operations over a specified period, commonly one year. Also known as the profit and loss statement. The bottom line of the income statement shows the firm's profit or loss for the period.

Increasing-Stream Hypothesis of Dividend Policy. A smoothing of the dividend stream in order to minimize the effect of company reversals. Corporate managers make every effort to avoid a dividend cut, attempting instead to develop a gradually increasing dividend series over the long-term future.

Incremental Cash Flows. The cash flows that result from the acceptance of a capital-budgeting project.

Indenture. The legal agreement between the firm issuing the bonds and the bond trustee who represents the bondholders, providing the specific terms of the loan agreement.

Indirect Costs. See **Fixed Costs.**

Indirect Quote. The exchange rate that expresses the required number of units of foreign currency to buy one unit of home currency.

Information Asymmetry. The difference in accessibility to information between managers and investors, which may result in a lower share price than would be true if we had conditions of certainty.

Insolvency. The inability to meet interest payments or to repay debt at maturity.

Interest-Rate Parity Theory. States that (except for the effect of small transaction costs) the forward premium or discount should be equal and opposite in size to the difference in the national interest rates for securities of the same maturity.

Interest-Rate Risk. The uncertainty that envelops the expected returns from a security caused by changes in interest rates. Price changes induced by interest-rate changes are greater for long-term than for short-term financial instruments.

Internal Common Equity. Profits retained within the business for investment purposes.

Internal Growth. A firm's growth rate in earnings resulting from reinvesting company profits rather than distributing the earnings in the form of dividends. The growth rate is a function of the amount retained and the return earned on the retained funds.

Internal Rate of Return (IRR). A capital-budgeting technique that reflects the rate of return a project earns. Mathematically it is the discount rate that equates the present value of the inflows with the present value of the outflows.

Intrinsic Value. The present value of the investment's expected future cash flows, discounted at the investor's required rate of return.

Inventory Loans. Loans secured by inventories. Examples include floating or blanket lien agreements, chattel mortgage agreements, field warehouse receipt loans, and terminal warehouse receipt loans.

Inventory Management. The managerial functions required to monitor the balance between the costs and benefits associated with the investment in inventory. These functions also include the control of assets that are produced to be sold in the normal course of a firm's operations.

Inventory Turnover Ratio. Cost of goods sold/inventory. A ratio that measures the number of times a firm's inventories are sold and replaced during the year. This ratio reflects the relative liquidity of inventories.

Investment Dealer. A financial specialist who underwrites and distributes new securities and advises corporate clients about raising new funds.

Investor's Required Rate of Return. The minimum rate of return necessary to attract an investor to purchase or hold a security.

Joint Probability. The product of probabilities associated with two or more successive events (outcomes) taking place.

Junk Bonds. Any bond rated B+ or below.

Just-in-Time Inventory Control. A production and management system in which inventory is cut down to a minimum through adjustments to the time and physical distance between the various production operations. Under this system the firm keeps a minimum level of inventory on hand relying upon suppliers to furnish parts "just-in-time" for them to be assembled.

Lead and Lag Strategies. Techniques used to reduce exchange risk where the firm maximizes its asset position in the stronger currency and its liability position in the weaker currency.

Lease. A contract requiring payments by the user (lessee) to its owner (lessor) for the use of an asset. In accordance with disclosure requirements of the *CICA Handbook*, the gross amount of assets under capital leases and related accumulated amortization should be disclosed. However for operating leases, only the future minimum lease payments, in the aggregate and for each of the five succeeding years, is required for disclosure purposes.

Least-Squares Regression. A procedure for "fitting" a line through a scatter of observed data points in a way that minimizes the sum of the squared deviations of the points from the fitted line.

Leveraged Buyout. A corporate restructuring where the existing shareholders sell their shares to a small group of investors. The purchasers of the shares use the firm's unused debt capacity to borrow the funds to pay for the shares.

Leveraged Leasing. A leasing arrangement in which the lessor will generally supply equity funds of 20 to 30 percent of the purchase price and borrow the remainder from a third-party lender.

Leverage Ratio. A liquidity ratio that provides a basis to determine how a firm has financed its assets and whether the firm can afford the level of fixed charges associated with its use of non-owner-supplied funds.

Limited Partnership. A partnership in which one or more of the partners has limited liability, restricted to the amount of capital he or she invests in the partnership.

Line of Credit. Generally an informal agreement or understanding between the borrower and the bank as to the maximum amount of credit the bank will provide the borrower at any one time. Under this type of agreement there is no "legal" commitment on the part of the bank to provide the stated credit. See **Revolving Credit Agreement.**

Liquidation by Assignment. A proceeding in which the debtor transfers title of the firm's assets to a third party, who has been appointed either by the creditors or by the court. This individual, known as a trustee, administers the liquidation process and sees that an appropriate distribution is made of the proceeds.

Liquidation Value. The dollar sum that could be realized if an asset were sold independently of the going concern.

Liquidity. A firm's ability to pay its bills on time. Liquidity is related to the ease and quickness with which a firm can convert its noncash assets into cash, as well as the size of the firm's investment in noncash assets vis-à-vis its short-term liabilities.

Liquidity Preference Theory. The shape of the term structure of interest rates is determined by an investor's additional required interest rate in compensation of additional risks.

Liquidity Premium. The additional required interest rate return needed to compensate for the risk of changing future interest rates.

Liquidity Ratios. Financial ratios used to assess the ability of a firm to pay its bills on time. Examples of liquidity ratios include the current ratio and the acid test ratio.

Loan Amortization Schedule. A breakdown of the interest and principle payments on an amortized loan.

Long-Term Debt to Total Capitalization Ratio. A leverage ratio indicating the extent to which a firm has used long-term debt in its permanent financing.

Long-Term Residual Dividend Policy. A dividend plan by which the residual capital is distributed smoothly to the investors over the planning period.

Mail Float. Funds tied up during the time that elapses from the moment a customer mails a remittance cheque until the firm begins to process it.

Management Buyout. The purchase of a firm by its managers, using large amounts of borrowed funds.

Marginal Cost of Capital. The cost of capital that represents the weighted cost of each additional dollar of financing from all sources, debt, preferred shares, and common shares.

Marginal Tax Rate. The tax rate that would be applied to the next dollar of income.

Market Equilibrium. The situation in which expected returns equal required returns.

Market-Related Risk. See **Systematic Risk.**

Market Risk. See **Systematic Risk.**

Market Segmentation Theory. The shape of the term structure of interest rates implies that the rate of interest for a particular maturity is determined solely by demand and supply for a given maturity. This demand is independent of the demand and supply for securities having different maturities.

Market Value. The value observed in the market place, where buyers and sellers negotiate a mutually acceptable price for the asset.

Market-Value Weights. The percentage of financing provided by different capital sources, measured by the current market prices of the firm's bonds and preferred and common shares.

Matching Principle. Principle of accounting in which expenses are matched with revenues.

Marketable Securities. Security investments that the firm can quickly convert into cash balances.

Maturity Date. The date upon which a borrower is to repay a loan.

Merger. A combination of two or more businesses into a single operational entity.

Minimum Price of a Warrant. (Market price of common shares – exercise price) × exercise ratio.

Money Market. All institutions and procedures that facilitate transactions in short-term instruments issued by borrowers with very high credit ratings.

Money Market Mutual Funds. Investment companies that

purchase a diversified array of short-term, high-grade (money market) debt instruments.

Monitoring Costs. A form of agency costs. Typically these costs arise when bond investors take steps to ensure that protective covenants in the bond indenture are adhered to by management.

Mortgage Bonds. Bonds secured by a lien on real property.

Multinational Corporation. A corporation with holdings and/or operations in more than one country.

Mutually Exclusive Projects. A set of projects that perform essentially the same task, so that acceptance of one will necessarily mean rejection of the others.

Negotiable Certificates of Deposit. Marketable receipts for funds deposited in a bank for a fixed period. The deposited funds earn a fixed rate of interest. More commonly, these are called CDs.

Net Income. A figure representing the firm's profit or loss for the period. It also represents the earnings available to the firm's common *and* preferred shareholders.

Net Income Approach to Valuation. A method used to measure a firm's value whereby the marketplace capitalizes (discounts) the firm's expected net income stream. The firm's capital structure has an impact on the total market volume.

Net Income Available to Common Equity. Net income after interest taxes and preferred dividends.

Net Lease. Agreement in which the lessee firm assumes the risk and burden of ownership over the term of the lease.

Net-Net Lease. Agreement which requires that the lessee meet all the requirements of a net lease as well as return the asset, still with a pre-established value, to the lessor at the end of the lease term.

Net Operating Income Approach to Valuation. A method used to measure a firm's value whereby the marketplace capitalizes (discounts) the firm's expected net operating income stream. The capital structure of the firm has no impact on total market value.

Net Operating Loss Carryback and Carryforward. A tax provision that permits the taxpayer first to apply the loss against the profits in the three prior years (carryback). If the loss has not been completely absorbed by the profits in these three years, it may be applied to taxable profits in each of the seven following years (carryforward).

Net Present Value (NPV). A capital-budgeting concept defined as the present value of the project's annual net cash flows after tax less the project's initial outlay.

Net Profit Margin. Net income/sales. A ratio that measures the net income of the firm as a percent of sales.

Net Working Capital. The difference between the firm's current assets and its current liabilities.

Non-Diversifiable Risk. See **Systematic Risk**.

Nominal Interest Rate. The interest rate paid on debt securities without an adjustment for any loss in purchasing power.

Normal Probability Distribution. A special class of bell-shaped distributions with symmetrically decreasing density, where the curve approaches but never reaches the X-axis.

Old Line Factor. A commercial finance company that engages solely in the factoring of receivables.

Operating Income Return on Investment. The ratio of net operating income divided by total assets.

Operating Lease. A contractual commitment on the part of the firm leasing the asset (the lessee) to make a series of payments to the firm that actually owns the asset (the lessor) for use of the asset. An operating lease differs from a financial lease in that it can be cancelled at any time after proper notice has been given to the lessor.

Operating Leverage. The responsiveness to sales changes of the firm's earnings before interest and taxes. This responsiveness arises from the firm's use of fixed operating costs.

Operating Profit Margin. Net operating income/sales. A firm's earnings before interest and taxes. This ratio serves as an overall measure of operating effectiveness.

Opportunity Cost of Funds. The next best rate of return available to the investor for a given level of risk.

Opportunity Set. The return-risk relationship available for an investor interested in the purchase or sale of securities.

Optimal Capital Structure. The capital structure that minimizes the firm's weighted cost of capital (maximizes the common share price) for raising a given amount of funds.

Optimal Range of Financial Leverage. The range of various capital structure combinations that yield the lowest overall cost of capital for the firm.

Option Contract. An option contract gives its owner the right to buy or sell a fixed number of shares at a specified price over a limited time period.

Organized Security Exchanges. Formal organizations involved in the trading of securities. Such exchanges are tangible entities that conduct auction markets in listed securities.

Overhanging Issue. Occurs when a firm cannot force conversion because the price of common shares has not increased sufficiently to justify it.

Over-the-Counter Markets. All security markets *except* the organized exchanges. The money market is an over-the-counter market. Most corporate bonds also are traded in this market.

Partnership. An association of two or more individuals joining together as co-owners to operate a business for profit.

Par Value. On the face of a bond, the stated amount that the firm is to repay upon the maturity date.

Payable-Through Draft. A legal instrument that has the physical appearance of an ordinary cheque but is not drawn on a bank. A payable-through draft is drawn on and paid by the issuing firm. The bank serves as a collection point and passes the draft on to the firm.

Payback Period. A capital-budgeting criterion defined as the number of years required to recover the initial cash investment.

Payment Date. The date on which the company mails a dividend cheque to each investor.

Percent of Sales Method. A method of financial forecasting that involves estimating the level of an expense, asset, or liability for a future period as a percent of the sales forecast.

Perfect Markets. Hypothetical markets under the assumptions that (1) information is readily available to all investors at no cost, (2) there are no transaction costs, (3) investment opportunities are readily accessible to all prospective investors, and (4) financial distress and bankruptcy costs are nonexistent.

Permanent Investment. An investment that the firm expects to hold longer than one year. The firm makes permanent investments in fixed and current assets. Contrast with **Temporary Investments**.

Perpetuity. An annuity with an infinite life.

Physical Budgets. Budgets for unit sales, personnel or manpower, unit production, inventories, and physical facilities. These budgets are used as the basis for generating cost and profit budgets.

Pledging Accounts Receivable. A loan the firm obtains from a commercial bank or a finance company using its accounts receivable as collateral.

Poison Pill. A tactic used by the target of a hostile takeover; an unfavourable event, such as immediate repayment of all outstanding debt, triggered by an unfriendly party's acquisition of significant share holdings.

Portfolio Beta. The relationship between a portfolio's returns and the market returns. It is a measure of the portfolio's nondiversifiable risk.

Portfolio Diversification Effect. The fact that variations of the returns from a portfolio or combination of assets may be less than the sum of the variation of the individual assets making up the portfolio.

Portfolio Investment. An investment whereby financial assets are added to a corporation's portfolio of assets (for example, when a multinational company which invests in foreign securities).

Preauthorized Cheque (PAC). A cheque that resembles the ordinary cheque but does not contain or require the signature of the person on whose account it is being drawn. A PAC is created only with the individual's legal authorization. The PAC system is advantageous when the firm regularly receives a large volume of payments of a fixed amount from the same customer over a long period.

Preemptive Right. The right entitling the common shareholder to maintain his or her proportionate share of ownership in the firm.

Preferred Share. A security which is similar to a common share in that it has no fixed maturity date, the nonpayment of dividends does not bring on bankruptcy, and its dividends are not deductible to individual investors for tax purposes. The preferred shareholder's claim to income precedes the common shareholder's claim, but follows the bondholder's claim.

Preliminary Prospectus. A document outlining the important features of a new issue, which may be distributed to potential investors. The preliminary prospectus contains no selling price information or offering date.

Present Value. The value in today's dollars of a future payment discounted back to present at the required rate of return.

Present Value of Dividend Growth (PVDG). The net present value of any dividend growth resulting from the reinvestment of future earnings.

Price/Earnings Ratio (P/E). The price the market places on $1 of a firm's earnings. For example, if a firm has an earnings per share of $2, and a share price of $30, its price/earnings ratio is 15 ($30 ÷ $2).

Price Pegging. Buying orders placed by an underwriting syndicate manager for the security being marketed by his selling group. The objective is to stabilize the market price of the new issue.

Primary Markets. Financial markets in which securities are offered for the first time to potential investors.

Principle of Self-Liquidating Debt. See the **Hedging Principle**.

Private Placement. Case where a corporation gives a limited number of investors the opportunity to purchase securities.

Privileged Subscription. A new issue marketed to a definite and select group of investors.

Probability Tree. A schematic representation of a problem in which all possible outcomes are graphically displayed.

Processing Float. Funds tied up during the time required for the firm to process remittance cheques before they can be deposited in the bank.

Profitability Ratio. A financial ratio that can be used to determine how much of each sales dollar a firm's management was able to convert into profits and how much profit the firm earned on each dollar of assets under its control.

Profit and Loss Statement. See **Income Statement**.

Profit Budget. A budget of forecasted profits based on information gleaned from the cost and sales budgets.

Profit Margins. Financial ratios (sometimes simply referred to as margins) that reflect the level of firm profits relative to sales. Examples include the gross profit margin (gross profit divided by sales), operating profit margin (operating earnings divided by sales), and the net profit margin (net profit divided by sales).

Profitability Index (PI). A capital budgeting criterion defined as the ratio of the present value of the future net cash flows to the initial outlay.

Pro Forma Financial Statement. A statement which depicts the end result of forecasting a period's operations.

Pro Forma Income Statement. A statement of planned profit or loss for a future period.

Prospectus. A condensed version of the full registration statement filed with the Securities Commission that describes a new security issue.

Proxy. A means of voting in which a designated party is provided with the temporary power of attorney to vote for the signee at the corporation's annual meeting.

Public Offering. Case where a corporation gives both individual and institutional investors the opportunity to purchase securities.

Purchasing Power Parity. In the long run, exchange rates adjust so that the purchasing power of each currency tends to remain the same and, thus, exchange rate changes tend to reflect international differences in inflation rates. Countries with high rates of inflation tend to experience declines in the value of their currency.

Put Option. A put option gives its owners the right to sell a given number of common shares or some other asset at a specified price over a given time period.

Ratio Analysis. A method of making meaningful comparisons between a firm's financial data at different points in time with that of other firms. For example, examination of the average collection period, the ratio of receivables to assets, the ratio of credit sales to receivables, and the amount of bad debts relative to sales over time.

Raw Materials Inventory. Basic materials purchased from other firms to be used in a firm's production operations.

Real Assets. Tangible assets like houses, equipment, and inventories; real assets are distinguished from financial assets.

Real Interest Rate. The nominal rate of interest less any loss in purchasing power of the dollar during the time of the investment.

Red Herring. Finance jargon for a preliminary prospectus, which outlines the important features of a new issue without specifying the selling price and offering date.

Refunding. See **Bond-Refunding Decision**.

Registration Statement. A lengthy document filed with the Securities Commission containing pertinent facts about a firm planning to sell new securities.

Remote Disbursing. A cash management service specifically designed to extend disbursing float.

Reorganization. A procedure, administered by the courts, that attempts to revitalize a firm by changing its operating procedures and capital structure.

Repurchase Agreements. Legal contracts that involve the sale of short-term securities by a borrower to a lender of funds. The borrower commits to repurchase the securities at a later date at the contract price plus a stated interest charge.

Required Rate of Return. The minimum rate of return necessary to attract an investor to purchase or hold a security. It is also the discount rate that equates the present value of the cash flows with the value of the security.

Residual Dividend Theory. A theory asserting that the dividends to be paid should equal the equity capital *left over* after the financing of profitable investments.

Restrictive Covenants. Provisions in the loan agreement that place restrictions on the borrower and make the loan immediately payable and due when violated. These restrictive covenants are designed to maintain the borrower's financial condition on a par with that which existed at the time the loan was made.

Return on Common Equity. Net income available to the common shareholders/common equity. A ratio relating earned income to the common shareholder's investment.

Return on Equity Ratio. A profitability ratio which measures the rate of return earned on the shareholder's investment.

Return on Total Assets. Net income/total assets. This ratio determines the yield on the firm's assets by relating net income to total assets.

Return-Risk Line. A specification of the appropriate required rates of return for investments having different amounts of risk.

Revenue Realization Principle. Method of accounting which assures that revenue is recognized in the period in which it is earned.

Revolving Credit Agreement. An understanding between the borrower and the bank as to the amount of credit the bank will be legally obligated to provide the borrower. See **Line of Credit**.

Right. A certificate issued to common shareholders giving them an option to purchase a stated number of new shares at a specified price during a two- to ten-week period.

Risk. The possible variation associated with the expected return measured by the standard deviation or coefficient of variation.

Risk-Adjusted Discount Rate. A method for incorporating the project's level of risk into the capital budgeting process, in which the discount rate is adjusted upward to compensate for higher-than-normal risk or downward to compensate for lower-than-normal risk.

Riskless Rate of Return. The rate of return on risk-free investments, such as the interest rate on short-term Government of Canada securities.

Risk Premium. The additional return expected for assuming risk.

Risk-Return Tradeoff. A framework used by managers for decision-making in which return is examined in terms of risk. For example, the risk-return tradeoff involved from investing in current assets is one of added liquidity (reduced risk) versus reduced profitability (reduced return).

Rule of Absolute Priority. Rule that the company must completely honour senior claims on assets before settling junior claims.

Sale and Leaseback Arrangement. An arrangement arising when a firm sells land, buildings, or equipment that it already owns and simultaneously enters into an agreement to lease the property back for a specified period, under specific terms.

Sales Forecast. The key ingredient in a firm's planning process which reflects (1) any past trend in sales that is expected to carry through into the new year and (2) the influence of any events that might materially affect that trend.

Salvage Value. The value of an asset or investment project at the end of its usable life.

Scatter Diagram Method. A method of financial forecasting that involves visually "fitting" a line through a scatter of points so that the distance of points about the line is minimized.

Scenario Analysis. Simulation analysis that focuses on an examination of the range of possible outcomes.

Secondary Market. Transactions in currently outstanding securities. This is distinguished from the new issues or primary market.

Secured Credit. Sources of credit that require security in the form of pledged assets. In the event the borrower defaults in payment of principal or interest the lender can seize the pledged assets and sell them to settle the debt.

Security Market Line. The return line that reflects the attitudes of investors regarding the minimal acceptable return for a given level of systematic risk.

Security Value. The price a convertible security would sell for in the absence of its conversion feature.

Sell-Off. The sale of a subsidiary, division, or product line by one company to another.

Selling Group. A collection of securities dealers that participates in the distribution of new issues to final investors. A selling group agreement links these dealers to the underwriting syndicate.

Semifixed Costs. See **Semivariable Costs.**

Semivariable Costs. Charges that behave as variable costs over certain ranges of output and as fixed costs over other ranges of output.

Share Capital. All outstanding common and preferred shares.

Share Repurchase. The repurchase of common shares by the issuing firm for any of a variety of reasons resulting in a reduction of shares outstanding.

Shark Repellents. Any of a variety of legalistic means used to counteract a tender offer by the firm under attack.

Simulation. The process of imitating the performance of an investment project through repeated evaluations, usually using a computer. In the general case, experimentation upon a mathematical model that has been designed to capture the critical realities of the decision-making situation.

Sinking Fund. A required annual payment that allows for the periodic retirement of debt.

Size Disparity Problem. Ranking problem which occurs when mutually exclusive projects of unequal size are examined.

Skewed Distribution. A distribution that has a longer "tail" to the right or left.

Sole Proprietorship. A business owned by a single individual.

Spin-Off. The separation of a subsidiary from its parent, with no change in the equity ownership. The management of the parent company gives up operating control over the subsidiary, but the shareholders maintain their same percentage ownership in both firms. New shares representing ownership in the averted company are issued to the original shareholders on a pro-rata basis.

Spontaneous Financing. The trade credit and other accounts payable that arise "spontaneously" in the firm's day-to-day operations.

Spot Transaction. A transaction made immediately in the market place at the market price.

Stable Dollar Dividend per Share. A dividend policy that maintains a relatively stable dollar dividend per share over time.

Standard Deviation. A statistical measure of the spread of a probability distribution calculated by squaring the difference between each outcome and its expected value, weighting each value by its probability, summing over all possible outcomes, and taking the square root of this sum.

Statement of Changes in Financial Position. A basic accounting statement which identifies the firm's sources and uses of cash flows over a period of time.

Statutory Amalgamation. A type of merger in which two firms join together to form one legal entity.

Stock Dividend. A distribution of shares issued on a pro-rata basis to current shareholders.

Stock Market Value. See **Market Value**.

Stock of Cash. The cash a firm keeps on hand so that bills can be paid without collection of accounts.

Stock Split. A transaction that increases the number of shares outstanding in proportion to the number of shares currently owned by shareholders.

Straight-Line Depreciation. A method for computing depreciation expenses in which the cost of the asset is divided by the asset's useful life.

Stretching on Trade Credit. Failing to pay within the prescribed credit period. For example, under credit terms of 2/10, net 30, a firm would be stretching its trade credit if it failed to pay by the 30th day and paid on the 60th day.

Stripped Bonds. See **Zero Coupon Bonds**.

Subordinated Debentures. Debentures which are given subordinated standing in the case of insolvency. The claims of the subordinated debentures are honoured only after the claims of secured debt and unsubordinated debentures have been satisfied.

Subscription Price. The price for which the security may be purchased in a rights offering.

Synergistic Effect. An often-used reason for mergers; the benefit derived from the combination of the acquirer's operations (or financing capabilities) with the target's. Also referred to as "the sum of the parts equalling more than the whole."

Target Debt Ratio. A desired proportion of long-term debt in the firm's capital structure. Alternatively, it may be the desired proportion of total debt in the firm's financial structure.

Taxable Income. Gross income from all sources, except for allowable exclusions, less any tax deductible expenses.

Tax Liability. The amount owed the federal, provincial, or municipal taxing authorities.

Technical Insolvency. Situation in which the firm can no longer honour its financial obligations. Although its assets may exceed its total liabilities, thereby indicating a positive net worth, the company simply does not have sufficient liquidity to pay its debts.

Temporary Financing. Financing (other than spontaneous sources) that will be repaid within a period of one year or less. Included among these sources of short-term debt are secured and unsecured bank loans, commercial paper, loans secured by accounts receivable, and loans secured by inventories.

Temporary Investments. These investments are comprised of the firm's investment in current assets that will be liquidated and not replaced within a period of one year or less. Examples include seasonal expansions in inventories and accounts receivable.

Tender Offer. A bid by an interested party, usually a corporation, for controlling interest in another corporation.

Terminal Warehouse Agreement. A security agreement in which the inventories pledged as collateral are transported to a public warehouse that is physically removed from the borrower's premises. This is the safest (and a costly) form of financing secured by inventory.

Term Loans. Loans that have maturities of one to ten years and are repaid in periodic installments over the life of the loan. Term loans are usually secured by a chattel mortgage on equipment or a mortgage on real property.

Terms of Sale. Terms identifying the possible discount for early payment, the discount period, and the total credit period.

Term Structure of Interest Rates. The relationship between interest rates and the term to maturity, where the risk of default is held constant.

Time Disparity Problem. Ranking problem that results from the differing re-investment assumptions made by the net present value and internal rate of return decision criteria.

Times Interest Earned Ratio. Earnings before interest and taxes (EBIT)/interest expense. A ratio that measures the firm's ability to meet its interest payments from its annual operating earnings.

Total Asset Turnover. Sales/total tangible assets. An overall measure of the relation between the firm's tangible assets and the sales they generate.

Trade Credit. Credit made available by a firm's suppliers in conjunction with the acquisition of materials. Trade credit appears on the balance sheet as accounts payable.

Transaction Loan. A loan where the proceeds are designated for a specific purpose—for example, a bank loan used to finance the acquisition of a piece of equipment.

Transit Float. Funds tied up during the time necessary for a deposited cheque to clear through the commercial banking system and become usable funds to the company.

Treasury Bills. Direct debt obligations of the Canadian government sold on a regular basis by the Bank of Canada.

Trend Analysis. An analysis of a firm's financial ratios over time.

Trustee. The third party responsible for disposal of the debtor firm's assets and distribution of the proceeds to the creditors in an assignment.

Type of Customer. Variable in determining credit-worthiness.

Unbiased Expectations Theory. The shape of the term structure of interest rates is determined by an investor's expectations about future interest rates.

Uncommitted Earnings per Share. Earnings per share *minus* sinking-fund payments per share.

Undepreciated Capital Cost. The capital cost of the asset net of any capital cost allowances claimed by the firm. The UCC of an asset class is the sum of the UCCs for each depreciable asset in the class.

Underwriting. The purchase and subsequent resale of a new security issue. The risk of selling the new issue at a satisfactory (profitable) price is assumed by the investment dealer.

Underwriting Syndicate. A temporary association of investment dealers formed to purchase a new security issue and quickly resell it at a profit. Formation of the syndicate spreads the risk of loss among several investment dealers, thereby minimizing the risk exposure of any single underwriter.

Undiversifiable Risk. The portion of the variation in investment returns that cannot be eliminated through investor diversification.

Unique Risk. See **Unsystematic Risk.**

Unlisted Securities. Securities that are not traded on an organized security exchange.

Unsecured Credit. All sources of credit that have as their security only the lender's faith in the borrower's ability to repay the funds when due.

Unsystematic Risk. The portion of the variation in investment returns that can be eliminated through investor diversification. These variations result from factors that are unique to the particular firm.

Value of a Bond. The present value of the interest payments, I_t in period t, plus the present value of the redemption or par value of the indebtedness, M, at the maturity date.

Value of a Security. The present value of all future cash inflows expected to be received by the investor owning the security.

Variable Costs. Charges that vary in total as output changes. Variable costs are fixed per unit of output.

Venture Capitalists. Investors interested in supplying capital to particularly high-risk situations, such as start-ups or firms denied conventional financing.

Voluntary Remedy. A voluntary reorganization that is acceptable to the creditors.

Warrant. An option to purchase a fixed number of common shares at a predetermined price during a specified time period.

Weighted Cost of Capital. A composite of the individual costs of financing incurred by each capital source. A firm's weighted cost of capital is a function of (1) the individual costs of capital, (2) the capital structure mix, and (3) the level of financing necessary to make the investment.

Weighted Marginal Cost of Capital. The weighted cost for each additional dollar of financing. The marginal cost of capital represents the appropriate criterion for making investment decisions.

"What If?" Analysis. Analysis which involves determining how the distribution of possible net present values or internal rates of return for a particular project is affected by a change in one particular input variable. Also known as **Sensitivity Analysis**.

White Knight. A defensive tactic to a tender offer whereby an able company comes to the rescue of the firm targeted for takeover.

Working Capital. A concept traditionally defined as a firm's investment in current assets. Net working capital refers to the difference between current assets and current liabilities.

Work in Process Inventory. Partially finished goods requiring additional work before they become finished goods.

Yield to Maturity. The rate of return the investor will earn if the bond is held to maturity.

Zero Balance Accounts. A cash management tool that permits centralized control over cash outflow while maintaining divisional disbursing authority. Objectives include: (1) Achieve better control over cash payments; (2) reduce excess cash balances held in regional banks for disbursing purposes; and (3) increase disbursing float.

Zero Coupon Bonds. Bonds which offer an investor no coupon interest payments over the maturity of the bond.

INDEX

SUBJECT INDEX

CORPORATE NAME INDEX

A

Compound Sum of $1: $(1 + I)^n$ *[handwritten: FUTURE VALUE]*

Period	1%	2%	3%	4%	5%	6%	7%	8%	9%	10%	12%	14%	15%	16%	18%	20%	24%	28%	32%	36%
1	1.0100	1.0200	1.0300	1.0400	1.0500	1.0600	1.0700	1.0800	1.0900	1.1000	1.1200	1.1400	1.1500	1.1600	1.1800	1.2000	1.2400	1.2800	1.3200	1.3600
2	1.0201	1.0404	1.0609	1.0816	1.1025	1.1236	1.1449	1.1664	1.1881	1.2100	1.2544	1.2996	1.3225	1.3456	1.3924	1.4400	1.5376	1.6384	1.7424	1.8496
3	1.0303	1.0612	1.0927	1.1249	1.1576	1.1910	1.2250	1.2597	1.2950	1.3310	1.4049	1.4815	1.5209	1.5609	1.6430	1.7280	1.9066	2.0972	2.3000	2.5155
4	1.0406	1.0824	1.1255	1.1699	1.2155	1.2625	1.3108	1.3605	1.4116	1.4641	1.5735	1.6890	1.7490	1.8106	1.9388	2.0736	2.3642	2.6844	3.0360	3.4210
5	1.0510	1.1041	1.1593	1.2167	1.2763	1.3382	1.4026	1.4693	1.5386	1.6105	1.7623	1.9254	2.0114	2.1003	2.2878	2.4883	2.9316	3.4360	4.0075	4.6526
6	1.0615	1.1262	1.1941	1.2653	1.3401	1.4185	1.5007	1.5869	1.6771	1.7716	1.9738	2.1950	2.3131	2.4364	2.6996	2.9860	3.6352	4.3980	5.2899	6.3275
7	1.0721	1.1487	1.2299	1.3159	1.4071	1.5036	1.6058	1.7138	1.8280	1.9487	2.2107	2.5023	2.6600	2.8262	3.1855	3.5832	4.5077	5.6295	6.9826	8.6054
8	1.0829	1.1717	1.2668	1.3686	1.4775	1.5938	1.7182	1.8509	1.9926	2.1436	2.4760	2.8526	3.0590	3.2784	3.7589	4.2998	5.5895	7.2058	9.2170	11.703
9	1.0937	1.1951	1.3048	1.4233	1.5513	1.6895	1.8385	1.9990	2.1719	2.3579	2.7731	3.2519	3.5179	3.8030	4.4355	5.1598	6.9310	9.2234	12.166	15.916
10	1.1046	1.2190	1.3439	1.4802	1.6289	1.7908	1.9672	2.1589	2.3674	2.5937	3.1058	3.7072	4.0456	4.4114	5.2338	6.1917	8.5944	11.805	16.059	21.646
11	1.1157	1.2434	1.3842	1.5395	1.7103	1.8983	2.1049	2.3316	2.5804	2.8531	3.4785	4.2262	4.6524	5.1173	6.1759	7.4301	10.657	15.111	21.198	29.439
12	1.1268	1.2682	1.4258	1.6010	1.7959	2.0122	2.2522	2.5182	2.8127	3.1384	3.8960	4.8179	5.3502	5.9360	7.2876	8.9161	13.214	19.342	27.982	40.037
13	1.1381	1.2936	1.4685	1.6651	1.8856	2.1329	2.4098	2.7196	3.0658	3.4523	4.3635	5.4924	6.1528	6.8858	8.5994	10.699	16.386	24.758	36.937	54.451
14	1.1495	1.3195	1.5126	1.7317	1.9799	2.2609	2.5785	2.9372	3.3417	3.7975	4.8871	6.2613	7.0757	7.9875	10.147	12.839	20.319	31.691	48.756	74.053
15	1.1610	1.3459	1.5580	1.8009	2.0789	2.3966	2.7590	3.1722	3.6425	4.1772	5.4736	7.1379	8.1371	9.2655	11.973	15.407	25.195	40.564	64.358	100.71
16	1.1726	1.3728	1.6047	1.8730	2.1829	2.5404	2.9522	3.4259	3.9703	4.5950	6.1304	8.1372	9.3576	10.748	14.129	18.488	31.242	51.923	84.953	136.96
17	1.1843	1.4002	1.6528	1.9479	2.2920	2.6928	3.1588	3.7000	4.3276	5.0545	6.8660	9.2765	10.761	12.467	16.672	22.186	38.740	66.461	112.13	186.27
18	1.1961	1.4282	1.7024	2.0258	2.4066	2.8543	3.3799	3.9960	4.7171	5.5599	7.6900	10.575	12.375	14.462	19.673	26.623	48.038	85.070	148.02	253.33
19	1.2081	1.4568	1.7535	2.1068	2.5270	3.0256	3.6165	4.3157	5.1417	6.1159	8.6128	12.055	14.231	16.776	23.214	31.948	59.567	108.89	195.39	344.53
20	1.2202	1.4859	1.8061	2.1911	2.6533	3.2071	3.8697	4.6610	5.6044	6.7275	9.6463	13.743	16.366	19.460	27.393	38.337	73.864	139.37	257.91	468.57
21	1.2324	1.5157	1.8603	2.2788	2.7860	3.3996	4.1406	5.0338	6.1088	7.4002	10.803	15.667	18.821	22.574	32.323	46.005	91.591	178.40	340.44	637.26
22	1.2447	1.5460	1.9161	2.3699	2.9253	3.6035	4.4304	5.4365	6.6586	8.1403	12.100	17.861	21.644	26.186	38.142	55.206	113.57	228.35	449.39	866.67
23	1.2572	1.5769	1.9736	2.4647	3.0715	3.8197	4.7405	5.8715	7.2579	8.9543	13.552	20.361	24.891	30.376	45.007	66.247	140.83	292.30	593.19	1178.6
24	1.2697	1.6084	2.0328	2.5633	3.2251	4.0489	5.0724	6.3412	7.9111	9.8497	15.178	23.212	28.625	35.236	53.108	79.496	174.63	374.14	783.02	1602.9
25	1.2824	1.6406	2.0938	2.6658	3.3864	4.2919	5.4274	6.8485	8.6231	10.834	17.000	26.461	32.918	40.874	62.668	95.396	216.54	478.90	1033.5	2180.0
26	1.2953	1.6734	2.1566	2.7725	3.5557	4.5494	5.8074	7.3964	9.3992	11.918	19.040	30.166	37.856	47.414	73.948	114.47	268.51	612.99	1364.3	2964.9
27	1.3082	1.7069	2.2213	2.8834	3.7335	4.8223	6.2139	7.9881	10.245	13.110	21.324	34.389	43.535	55.000	87.259	137.37	332.95	784.63	1800.9	4032.2
28	1.3213	1.7410	2.2879	2.9987	3.9201	5.1117	6.6488	8.6271	11.167	14.421	23.883	39.204	50.065	63.800	102.96	164.84	412.86	1004.3	2377.2	5483.8
29	1.3345	1.7758	2.3566	3.1187	4.1161	5.4184	7.1143	9.3173	12.172	15.863	26.749	44.693	57.575	74.008	121.50	197.81	511.95	1285.5	3137.9	7458.0
30	1.3478	1.8114	2.4273	3.2434	4.3219	5.7435	7.6123	10.062	13.267	17.449	29.959	50.950	66.211	85.849	143.37	237.37	634.81	1645.5	4142.0	10143.
40	1.4889	2.2080	3.2620	4.8010	7.0400	10.285	14.974	21.724	31.409	45.259	93.050	188.88	267.86	378.72	750.37	1469.7	5455.9	19426.	66520.	*
50	1.6446	2.6916	4.3839	7.1067	11.467	18.420	29.457	46.901	74.357	117.39	289.00	700.23	1083.6	1670.7	3927.3	9100.4	46890.	*	*	*
60	1.8167	3.2810	5.8916	10.519	18.679	32.987	57.946	101.25	176.03	304.48	897.59	2595.9	4383.9	7370.1	20555.	56347.	*	*	*	*

*FVIF > 99,999.

B

Present Value of $1: $\dfrac{\$1}{(1 + I)_n}$ *[handwritten: OF A SINGLE FUTURE VA]*

Period	1%	3%	5%	6%	7%	8%	9%	10%	11%	12%	13%	14%	15%	16%	17%	18%	19%	20%	24%	28%
1	.9901	.9709	.9524	.9434	.9346	.9259	.9174	.9091	.9009	.8929	.8850	.8772	.8696	.8621	.8547	.8475	.8403	.8333	.8065	.7813
2	.9803	.9426	.9070	.8900	.8734	.8573	.8417	.8264	.8116	.7972	.7831	.7695	.7561	.7432	.7305	.7182	.7062	.6944	.6504	.6104
3	.9706	.9151	.8638	.8396	.8163	.7938	.7722	.7513	.7312	.7118	.6930	.6750	.6575	.6407	.6244	.6086	.5934	.5787	.5245	.4768
4	.9610	.8885	.8227	.7921	.7629	.7350	.7084	.6830	.6587	.6355	.6133	.5921	.5718	.5523	.5336	.5158	.4987	.4823	.4230	.3725
5	.9515	.8626	.7835	.7473	.7130	.6806	.6499	.6209	.5934	.5674	.5428	.5194	.4972	.4761	.4561	.4371	.4190	.4019	.3411	.2910
6	.9420	.8375	.7462	.7050	.6663	.6302	.5963	.5645	.5346	.5066	.4803	.4556	.4323	.4104	.3898	.3704	.3521	.3349	.2751	.2274
7	.9327	.8131	.7107	.6651	.6227	.5835	.5470	.5132	.4817	.4523	.4251	.3996	.3759	.3538	.3332	.3139	.2959	.2791	.2218	.1776
8	.9235	.7894	.6768	.6274	.5820	.5403	.5019	.4665	.4339	.4039	.3762	.3506	.3269	.3050	.2848	.2660	.2487	.2326	.1789	.1388
9	.9143	.7664	.6446	.5919	.5439	.5002	.4604	.4241	.3909	.3606	.3329	.3075	.2843	.2630	.2434	.2255	.2090	.1938	.1443	.1084
10	.9053	.7441	.6139	.5584	.5083	.4632	.4224	.3855	.3522	.3220	.2946	.2697	.2472	.2267	.2080	.1911	.1756	.1615	.1164	.0847
11	.8963	.7224	.5847	.5268	.4751	.4289	.3875	.3505	.3173	.2875	.2607	.2366	.2149	.1954	.1778	.1619	.1476	.1346	.0938	.0662
12	.8874	.7014	.5568	.4970	.4440	.3971	.3555	.3186	.2858	.2567	.2307	.2076	.1869	.1685	.1520	.1372	.1240	.1122	.0757	.0517
13	.8787	.6810	.5303	.4688	.4150	.3677	.3262	.2897	.2575	.2292	.2042	.1821	.1625	.1452	.1299	.1163	.1042	.0935	.0610	.0404
14	.8700	.6611	.5051	.4423	.3878	.3405	.2992	.2633	.2320	.2046	.1807	.1597	.1413	.1252	.1110	.0985	.0876	.0779	.0492	.0316
15	.8613	.6419	.4810	.4173	.3624	.3152	.2745	.2394	.2090	.1827	.1599	.1401	.1229	.1079	.0949	.0835	.0736	.0649	.0397	.0247
16	.8528	.6232	.4581	.3936	.3387	.2919	.2519	.2176	.1883	.1631	.1415	.1229	.1069	.0930	.0811	.0708	.0618	.0541	.0320	.0193
17	.8444	.6050	.4363	.3714	.3166	.2703	.2311	.1978	.1696	.1456	.1252	.1078	.0929	.0802	.0693	.0600	.0520	.0451	.0258	.0150
18	.8360	.5874	.4155	.3503	.2959	.2502	.2120	.1799	.1528	.1300	.1108	.0946	.0808	.0691	.0592	.0508	.0437	.0376	.0208	.0118
19	.8277	.5703	.3957	.3305	.2765	.2317	.1945	.1635	.1377	.1161	.0981	.0829	.0703	.0596	.0506	.0431	.0367	.0313	.0168	.0092
20	.8195	.5537	.3769	.3118	.2584	.2145	.1784	.1486	.1240	.1037	.0868	.0728	.0611	.0514	.0433	.0365	.0308	.0261	.0135	.0072
25	.7798	.4776	.2953	.2330	.1842	.1460	.1160	.0923	.0736	.0588	.0471	.0378	.0304	.0245	.0197	.0160	.0129	.0105	.0046	.0021
30	.7419	.4120	.2314	.1741	.1314	.0994	.0754	.0573	.0437	.0334	.0256	.0196	.0151	.0116	.0090	.0070	.0054	.0042	.0016	.0006
40	.6717	.3066	.1420	.0972	.0668	.0460	.0318	.0221	.0154	.0107	.0075	.0053	.0037	.0026	.0019	.0013	.0010	.0007	.0002	.0001
50	.6080	.2281	.0872	.0543	.0339	.0213	.0134	.0085	.0054	.0035	.0022	.0014	.0009	.0006	.0004	.0003	.0002	.0001	*	*
60	.5504	.1697	.0535	.0303	.0173	.0099	.0057	.0033	.0019	.0011	.0007	.0004	.0002	.0001	.0001	*	.0000	*	*	*

*The factor is zero to four decimal places.